Adobe®

Photoshop® CS2

Comprehensive Concepts and Techniques

Gary B. Shelly
Thomas J. Cashman
Joy L. Starks

THOMSON
COURSE TECHNOLOGY™

THOMSON COURSE TECHNOLOGY
25 THOMSON PLACE
BOSTON, MA 02210

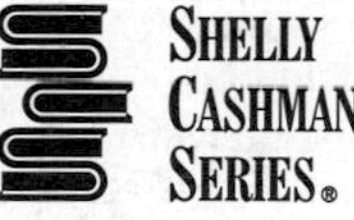

Australia • Canada • Denmark • Japan • Mexico • New Zealand • Philippines • Puerto Rico • Singapore
South Africa • Spain • United Kingdom • United States

THOMSON
COURSE TECHNOLOGY

Adobe® Photoshop® CS2 Comprehensive Concepts and Techniques

Gary B. Shelly
Thomas J. Cashman
Joy L. Starks

Contributing Author:
Karla M Whitney

Executive Editor:
Alexandra Arnold

Marketing Manager:
Joy Stark-Vancs

Senior Product Managers:
Karen Stevens, Reed Curry

Product Manager:
Heather Hawkins

Developmental Editor:
Mali Jones

Associate Product Manager:
Klenda Martinez

Editorial Assistant:
Jon Farnham

Print Buyers:
Julio Esperas, Justin Palmeiro

Production Editor:
Marissa Falco

Copy Editor:
Nancy Lamm

Proofreader:
John Bosco

QA Manuscript Reviewers:
Chris Scriver, John Freitas, Peter S. Stefanis, Susan Whalen

Cover Artist:
John Still

Composition:
GEX Publishing Services

Printed in the United States of America

1 2 3 4 5 6 7 8 9 10
BM 10 09 08 07

For more information, contact
Thomson Course Technology
25 Thomson Place
Boston, Massachusetts 02210

Or find us on the World Wide Web at:
www.course.com

ISBN 13: 978-1-4188-5941-1
ISBN 10: 1-4188-5941-9

ADOBE

Photoshop CS2

Comprehensive Concepts and Techniques

Contents

Special Feature 1

An Introduction to the Fundamentals of Graphic Design

Project Four

Drawing and Painting with Color

Project Five

Enhancing and Repairing Photos

Project Six

Creating Color Channels and Actions

Special Feature 2

Designing Basic Layouts Using Color and Typography

Project Seven

Applying Filters and Patterns

Project Eight

Working with Vector Graphics

Project Nine

Using Web Tools

Special Feature 3

Graphic Design From Concept to Finished Product

Appendix A

Changing Screen Resolution and Editing Preferences

Appendix B

Using the Adobe Help Center

Appendix C

Using Adobe Bridge

Preface

The Shelly Cashman Series® offers the finest textbooks in computer education. We are proud of the fact that our textbook series has been the most widely used books in education. *Adobe® Photoshop® CS2: Comprehensive Concepts and Techniques* continues with the innovation, quality, and reliability that you have come to expect from the Shelly Cashman Series.

Adobe Photoshop CS2 is the standard in image editing software. Some of the ways that Adobe Photoshop CS2 enhances the work experience for users: timesaving file handling with Adobe Bridge®; multiple layer control; customizable workspaces and menus; spot healing brush; and one-click red-eye reduction.

In this *Adobe Photoshop CS2* book, you will find an educationally sound and easy-to-follow pedagogy that combines a step-by-step approach with corresponding screens. All projects and exercises in this book are designed to introduce students to working with Adobe Photoshop CS2. The Other Ways and More About features provide greater knowledge of Adobe Photoshop CS2. The Learn It Online page presents a wealth of additional exercises to ensure your students have all the reinforcement they need. The project material is developed carefully to ensure that students will see the importance of learning Adobe Photoshop CS2 for future coursework.

Objectives of This Textbook

Adobe Photoshop CS2: Comprehensive Concepts and Techniques is intended for a course that offers an in-depth presentation of Photoshop and image editing. No previous experience with Adobe Photoshop CS2 is assumed, and no mathematics beyond the high school freshman level is required. The objectives of this book are:

- To teach the fundamentals and more advanced features of Adobe Photoshop CS2
- To expose students to image editing and graphic design fundamentals
- To develop an exercise-oriented approach that allows learning by doing
- To encourage independent study and help those who are working alone
- To show how to use effective graphics in both business and personal situations
- To assist students in designing successful graphical documents from scratch and from components

The Shelly Cashman Approach

Features of the Shelly Cashman Series *Adobe Photoshop CS2* books include:

- **Project Orientation** Each project in the book presents a practical problem and complete solution using an easy-to-understand approach.
- **Step-by-Step, Screen-by-Screen Instructions** Each of the tasks required to complete a project is identified throughout the project. Full-color screens with callouts accompany the steps.
- **Thoroughly Tested Projects** Unparalleled quality is ensured because every screen in the book is produced by the author only after performing a step, and then each project must pass Thomson Course Technology's award-winning Quality Assurance program.
- **Other Ways Boxes and Quick Reference** The Other Ways boxes displayed at the end of many of the step-by-step sequences specify the other ways to do the task completed in the steps. Thus, the steps and the Other Ways box make a comprehensive reference unit. The Quick Reference at the back of the book provides a quick reference to common mouse, menu, palette, and keyboard shortcuts.
- **More About Feature** These marginal annotations provide background information and tips that complement the topics covered, adding depth and perspective to the learning process.
- **Integration of the World Wide Web** The World Wide Web is integrated into the Photoshop CS2 learning experience by (1) More About annotations that send students to Web sites for up-to-date information and alternative approaches to tasks; and (2) the Learn It Online page at the end of each project, which has project reinforcement exercises, learning games, and other types of student activities.

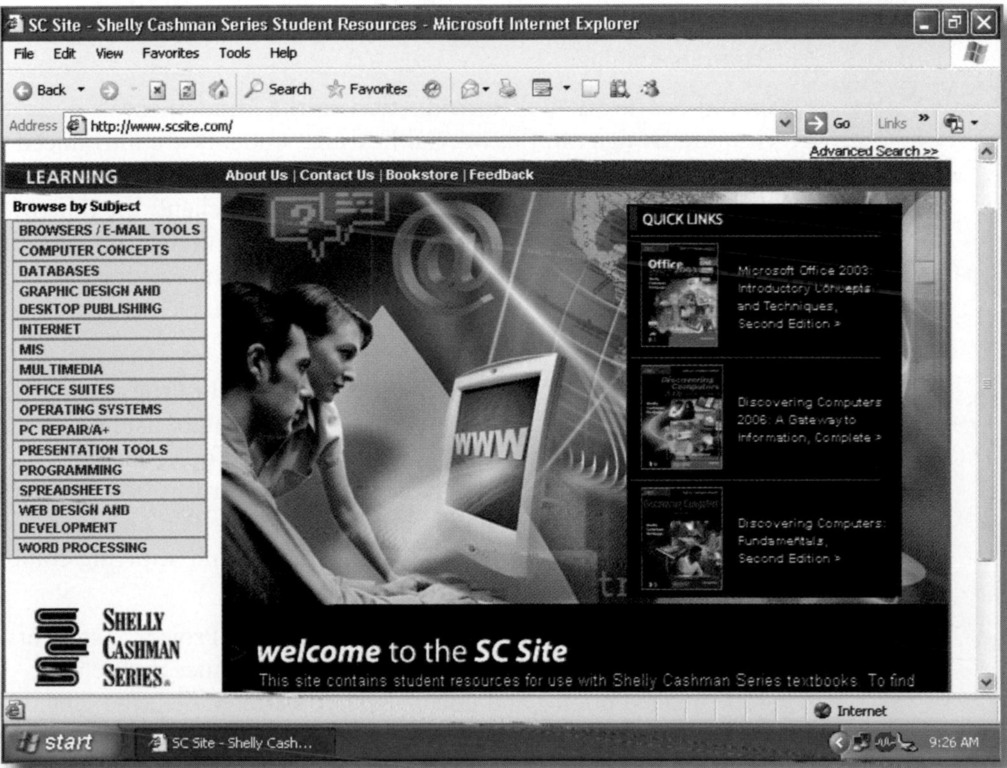

Organization of This Textbook

Adobe Photoshop CS2: Comprehensive Concepts and Techniques provides detailed instruction on how to use Adobe Photoshop CS2. The material is divided into nine projects, three special features, three appendices, and a quick reference summary.

Project 1 – Editing a Photoshop Image In Project 1 students are introduced to the Photoshop environment. Students learn how to identify parts of the Photoshop window, how to customize Photoshop, and how to open a photo. Topics include starting and quitting Photoshop; explanation of file types; cropping and resizing a photo; using the navigator palette and Zoom tool; creating a blending border; printing a photo; and saving a photo for print and the web; viewing files in Adobe Bridge; and an overview of Adobe Help Center.

Project 2 – Using Selection Tools In Project 2 students learn how to explain the terms perspective, layout, and storyboard, and describe selection tools. Topics include opening a file, selecting objects, and saving a file; using the marquee tools; moving selections; making transformation edits; viewing states in the History palette; employing the lasso tools; adding and subtracting from selections; creating ruler guides; selecting objects using the Magic Wand tool; and creating new keyboard shortcuts.

Project 3 – Using Layers In Project 3 students learn how to create a layer and use the Layers palette. Topics include saving a file in PSD format; selecting, naming, coloring, hiding, and viewing layers; creating a new layer from another image or selection; setting layer properties; resizing a layer; erasing portions of layers and images; using the Erase, Magic Eraser, and Background Eraser tools; creating layer masks; making level adjustments and opacity changes; creating a later style and adding a render filter; using the Clone Stamp tool; and flattening a composite image.

Special Feature 1 – An Introduction to the Fundamentals of Graphic Design In this Special Feature, students are introduced to how graphic design is defined and three important considerations for all graphic designers; concepts of the client, the design of an idea, and the process. Topics include planning and developing a project; and understanding different types of images, learning about universal, visual and conceptual elements and techniques; and design systems.

Project 4 – Drawing and Painting with Color In Project 4, students will create a composite image from scratch, using gradients, color, brushes, shapes, and graphics. Topics include applying gradients; using the Color Picker and Brush Preset picker; choosing brushes; using the shape tools; using the Pen and Line tools; choosing color with the Eyedropper tool; and applying color via brush strokes and the Paint Bucket.

Project 5 – Enhancing and Repairing Photos In Project 5, students will learn photo restoration techniques as they enhance and repair several damaged photos and documents. Topics include using digital cameras and scanners for the best original production; repairing documents with aging damage, color damage, light damage, physical tears, and blemishes; sharpening and fading images; using the healing brushes, and the Dodge, Burn, Patch and Red Eye tools; correcting angle and perspective distortions; and using text elements.

Project 6 – Creating Color Channels and Actions Project 6 provides students with the skills and knowledge to use channels effectively for color separations and selections. It then explains how to create user-defined actions. Topics include color separations, alpha channels, snapshots, states, the action commands, color conversions, the Channel Mixer, decorative text and shapes, and prepress activities. The project explores resampling and interpolation methods associated with resizing graphical documents.

Special Feature 2 – Designing Basic Layouts Using Color and Typography In this Special Feature, students identify the components of a graphic design layout including background, foreground, color, type, and visual hierarchy. Topics include reproducing graphic designs using one-, two- or four-color printing processes, color selection for Web design, identifying characteristics of letterforms, and determining appropriate typographic choices for graphic design layouts.

Project 7 – Applying Filters and Patterns In Project 7 students will learn about the many filters in Photoshop as they create a magazine cover from scratch. They will use the Filter gallery to apply Artistic, Blur, Stylize, and Distort filters with strokes and masks of color. Topics also include creating and using new patterns, the proper use of lighting effects, and the purpose of knockouts, trapping, text overlays, leading, and special effects.

Project 8 – Working with Vector Graphics Project 8 provides students the opportunity to create and work with vector graphics in the creation of a piece of clip art. Students will learn more about shape layers, paths, and filling pixels. Topics include the categories and legal use of clip art, transparent backgrounds, layer groups, locking layers, the Pen and Freeform Pen tools, manipulating anchor points, reshaping, the magnetic pen, creating impact lines, color overlays, shadows, and reflections, notes and audio annotation, and the Export Transparent Image Wizard.

Project 9 – Using Web Tools In Project 9 students will learn about Web photo galleries and Animation as they create an e-portfolio. Topics include collecting products and photos, creating a gallery, planning a Web site, using a storyboard, using Web-safe colors, inserting hyperlinks and navigation bars, creating slices, moving back and forth between Photoshop and ImageReady, creating rollovers, using the Animation palette, creating frame layers, tweening, and working interactively with Web pages.

Special Feature 3 – Graphic Design from Concept to Finished Product In this Special Feature, students will learn about the anatomy of a graphic design, the seven stages of development of a graphic design for print and Web, and the iterative design process. Topics include developing navigation maps, identifying project specifications, analyzing and critiquing work, and organizing budgets, schedules, and contracts.

Appendices The book includes three appendices. Appendix A covers changing screen resolution and editing preferences; Appendix B presents the Adobe Help Center; and Appendix C illustrates how to use Adobe Bridge.

Quick Reference In Photoshop, you can accomplish a task in a number of ways, such as using the mouse, menu, palette, and keyboard. The Quick Reference provides a quick reference to common shortcuts.

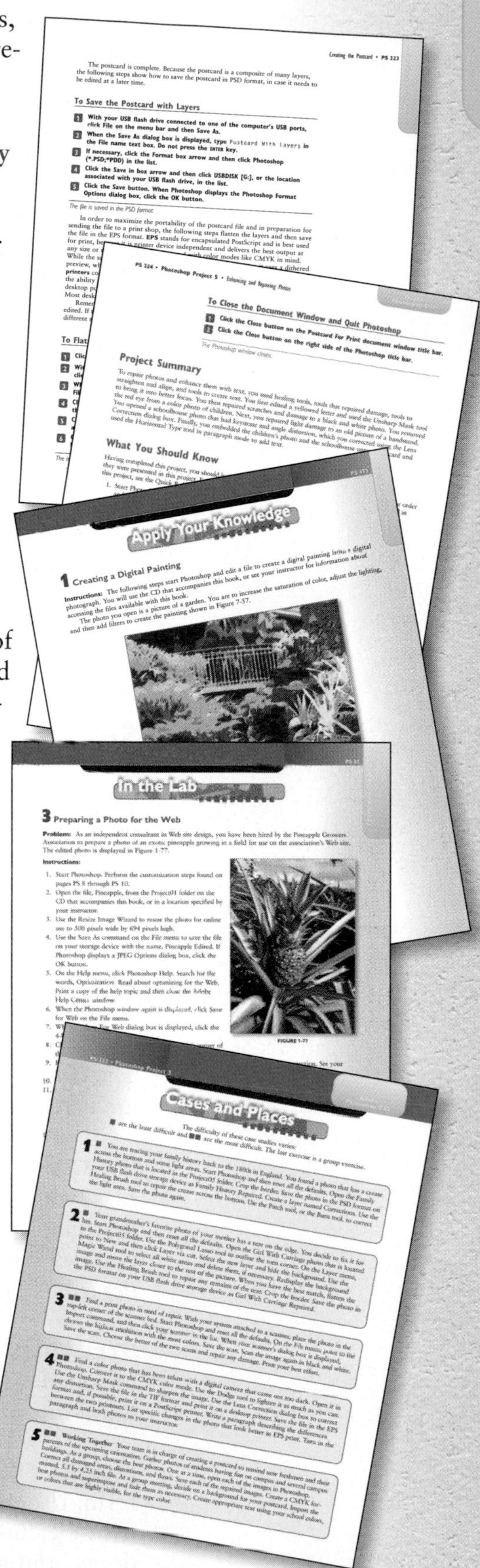

End-of-Project Student Activities

A notable strength of the Shelly Cashman Series *Adobe Photoshop CS2* books is the extensive student activities at the end of each project. Well-structured student activities can make the difference between students merely participating in a class and students retaining the information they learn. The activities in the Shelly Cashman Series *Adobe Photoshop CS2* books include the following:

- **What You Should Know** A listing of the tasks completed within a project together with the pages on which the step-by-step, screen-by-screen explanations appear.
- **Learn It Online** Every project features a Learn It Online page comprising ten exercises. These exercises include True/False, Multiple Choice, and Short Answer reinforcement questions, Flash Cards, Practice Test, Learning Games, Tips and Tricks, Expanding Your Horizons, and Search Sleuth.
- **Apply Your Knowledge** This exercise usually requires students to open and manipulate a file that is provided in the Data Files for Students. The Data Files for Students are available on the CD-ROM that ships with this textbook, or can be downloaded from the Web by following the instructions on the inside back cover.
- **In the Lab** Three in-depth assignments per project require students to utilize the project concepts and techniques to create additional Photoshop documents.
- **Cases and Places** Five unique real-world case-study situations, including one small-group activity.

Shelly Cashman Series Instructor Resources

The Shelly Cashman Series is dedicated to providing you with all of the tools you need to make your class a success. Information on all supplementary materials is available through your Thomson Course Technology representative or by calling one of the following telephone numbers: Colleges, Universities, Continuing Education Departments, and Post-Secondary Vocational Schools: 800-648-7450; Career Colleges, Business, Industry, Government, Trade, Retailer, Wholesaler, Library, and Resellers: 800-477-3692; K-12, Secondary Vocational Schools, Adult Education, and School Districts: 800-824-5179.

The Instructor Resources for this textbook include both teaching and testing aids. The contents of each item on the Instructor Resources CD-ROM (ISBN 1-4188-5942-7) are described below.

INSTRUCTOR'S MANUAL The Instructor's Manual is made up of Microsoft Word files, which include detailed lesson plans with page number references, lecture notes, teaching tips, classroom activities, discussion topics, projects to assign, and transparency references. The transparencies are available through the Figure Files described below.

SYLLABUS Sample syllabi, which can be customized easily to a course, are included. The syllabi cover policies, class and lab assignments and exams, and procedural information.

FIGURE FILES Illustrations for every figure in the textbook are available in electronic form. Use this ancillary to present a slide show in lecture or to print transparencies for use in lecture with an overhead projector. If you have a personal computer and LCD device, this ancillary can be an effective tool for presenting lectures.

POWERPOINT PRESENTATIONS PowerPoint Presentations is a multimedia lecture presentation system that provides slides for each project. Presentations are based on project objectives. Use this presentation system to present well-organized lectures that are both interesting and knowledge based. PowerPoint Presentations provides consistent coverage at schools that use multiple lecturers.

SOLUTIONS TO EXERCISES Solutions are included for the end-of-project exercises, as well as the Project Reinforcement exercises.

TEST BANK & TEST ENGINE The ExamView test bank includes 110 questions for every project (25 multiple-choice, 50 true/false, and 35 completion) with page number references, and when appropriate, figure references. A version of the test bank you can print also is included. The test bank comes with a copy of the test engine, ExamView, the ultimate tool for your objective-based testing needs. ExamView is a state-of-the-art test builder that is easy to use. ExamView enables you to create paper-, LAN-, or Web-based tests from test banks designed specifically for your Course Technology textbook. Utilize the ultra-efficient QuickTest Wizard to create tests in less than five minutes by taking advantage of Course Technology's question banks, or customize your own exams from scratch.

DATA FILES FOR STUDENTS All the files that are required by students to complete the exercises are included on the Instructor Resources CD-ROM and on a student CD-ROM that ships with the student book. You can also distribute the files on the Instructor Resources CD-ROM to your students over a network, or you can have them follow the instructions on the inside back cover of this book to obtain a copy of the Data Files for Students.

ADDITIONAL ACTIVITIES FOR STUDENTS These additional activities consist of Project Reinforcement Exercises, which are true/false, multiple choice, and short answer questions that help students gain confidence in the material learned.

Online Content

Thomson Course Technology offers textbook-based content for Blackboard and WebCT.

BLACKBOARD AND WEBCT As the leading provider of IT content for the Blackboard and WebCT platforms, Thomson Course Technology delivers rich content that enhances your textbook to give your students a unique learning experience. Thomson Course Technology has partnered with WebCT and Blackboard to deliver our market-leading content through these state-of-the-art online learning platforms.

Adobe Photoshop CS2 Trial Download

A copy of the Photoshop CS2 trial version can be downloaded from the Adobe Web site (www.adobe.com). You will need to register on Adobe's site to access Trial Downloads. Point to Downloads in the top navigation bar, click Trial Downloads, and then follow the on-screen instructions. Thomson Course Technology and Adobe provide no product support for this trial edition.

The minimum system requirements for the trial edition is an Intel® Xeon™, Xeon Dual, Intel Centrino™, or Pentium® III or 4 processor; Microsoft® Windows® 2000 with Service Pack 4, or Windows XP with Service Pack 1 or 2; 320MB of RAM (384MB recommended); 650MB of available hard-disk space; 1,024 × 768 monitor resolution with 16-bit video card; and a CD-ROM drive.

To the Student... Getting the Most Out of Your Book

Welcome to *Adobe Photoshop CS2: Comprehensive Concepts and Techniques*. You can save yourself a lot of time and gain a better understanding of Adobe Photoshop CS2 if you spend a few minutes reviewing the figures and callouts in this section.

1 Project Orientation

The project orientation lets you see firsthand how image editing challenges are approached from start to finish using Photoshop CS2. Each project begins by presenting a practical image editing challenge and then shows the image that will be created to address the challenge. The remainder of the project steps through creating the image.

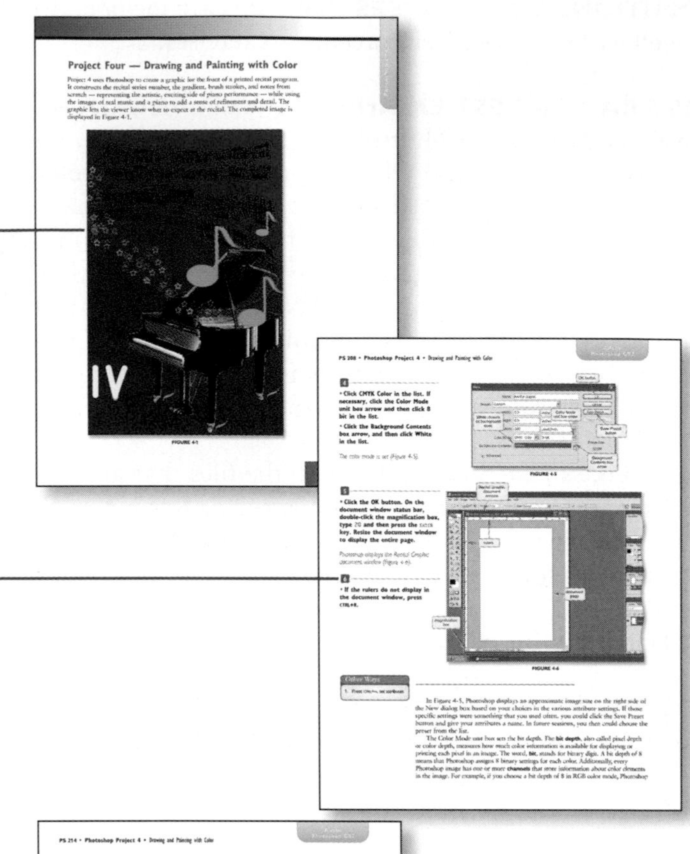

2 Consistent Step-By-Step, Screen-By-Screen Presentation

Project solutions are built using a step-by-step, screen-by-screen approach. This pedagogy allows you to build the solution on a computer as you read through the project. Generally, each step is followed by an italic explanation that indicates the result of the step.

3 More Than Just Step-By-Step

More About annotations in the margins of the book and substantive text in the paragraphs provide background information, image editing techniques, and tips that complement the topics covered, adding depth and perspective. When you finish with this book, you will be ready to use Photoshop CS2 to create sophisticated images on your own.

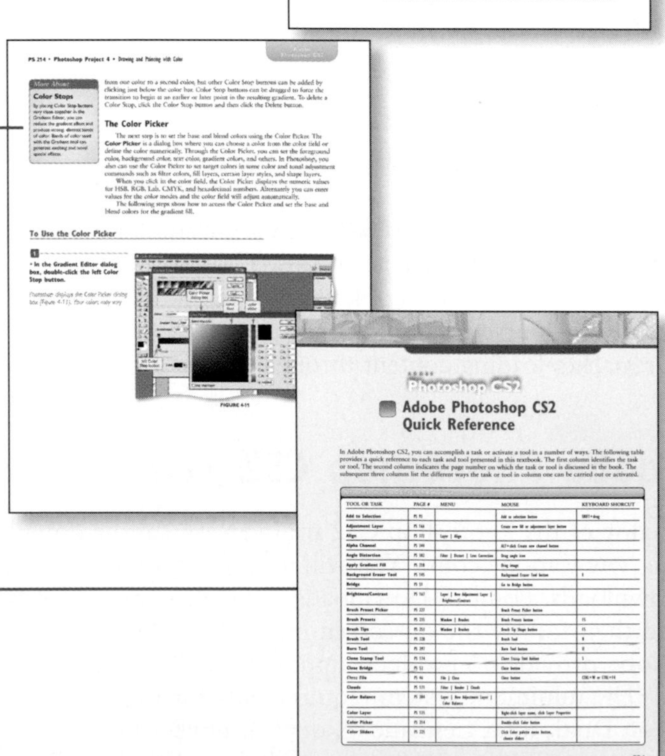

4 Photoshop CS2 Quick Reference

The Quick Reference provides a listing of common mouse, menu, palette, and keyboard shortcuts to use with Photoshop CS2.

5 Refer to the Special Features for Graphic Design Guidelines

In any image editing project, including the exercises at the end of each project, you should use a systematic methodology to create images that adhere to principles good graphic design. The Special Features provide you with the fundamental building blocks of good graphic design.

6 Review

After you successfully step through a project, a section titled What You Should Know summarizes the project tasks with which you should be familiar. Terms you should know for test purposes are bold in the text.

7 Reinforcement and Extension

The Learn It Online page at the end of each project offers reinforcement in the form of review questions, learning games, and practice tests. Also included are Web-based exercises that require you to extend your learning beyond the book.

8 Laboratory Exercises

If you really want to learn how to edit images using Photoshop CS2, then you must design and implement solutions on your own. Every project concludes with several carefully developed laboratory assignments that increase in complexity. In addition, the Cases and Places exercises at the end of each project are unique real-world situations, including one small-group activity.

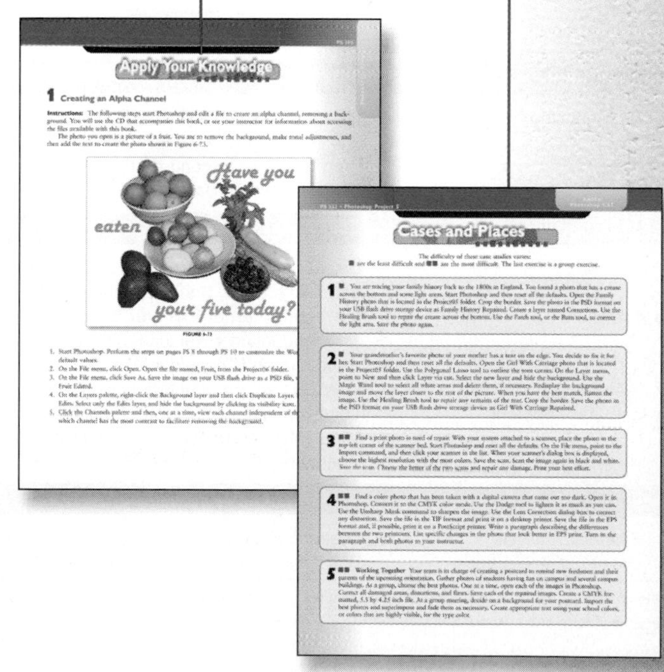

Shelly Cashman Series – Traditionally Bound Textbooks

The Shelly Cashman Series presents the following computer subjects in a variety of traditionally bound textbooks. For more information, see your Course Technology representative or call 1-800-648-7450. For Shelly Cashman Series information, visit Shelly Cashman Online at **scseries.com**

COMPUTER CONCEPTS	
Computer Concepts	Discovering Computers 2007: A Gateway to Information, Complete Discovering Computers 2007: A Gateway to Information, Introductory Discovering Computers 2007: A Gateway to Information, Brief Discovering Computers: Fundamentals, Third Edition Teachers Discovering Computers: Integrating Technology in the Classroom, Fourth Edition Essential Introduction to Computers, Sixth Edition (40-page)
WINDOWS APPLICATIONS	
Office Suites	Microsoft Office 2003: Essential Concepts and Techniques, Second Edition (5 projects) Microsoft Office 2003: Brief Concepts and Techniques, Second Edition (9 projects) Microsoft Office 2003: Introductory Concepts and Techniques, Second Edition (15 projects) Microsoft Office 2003: Introductory Concepts and Techniques, Premium Edition (15 Projects) Microsoft Office 2003: Advanced Concepts and Techniques (12 projects) Microsoft Office 2003: Post Advanced Concepts and Techniques (11 projects) Microsoft Office XP: Essential Concepts and Techniques (5 projects) Microsoft Office XP: Brief Concepts and Techniques (9 projects) Microsoft Office XP: Introductory Concepts and Techniques, Windows XP Edition (15 projects) Microsoft Office XP: Introductory Concepts and Techniques, Enhanced Edition (15 projects) Microsoft Office XP: Advanced Concepts and Techniques (11 projects) Microsoft Office XP: Post Advanced Concepts and Techniques (11 projects) Teachers Discovering and Integrating Microsoft Office: Essential Concepts and Techniques, Second Edition
E-mail Tools	Microsoft Outlook 2002: Essential Concepts and Techniques • Microsoft Office Outlook 2003: Introductory Concepts and Techniques
Microsoft Windows	Microsoft Windows XP: Comprehensive Concepts and Techniques, Service Pack 2 Edition[2] Microsoft Windows XP: Brief Concepts and Techniques Microsoft Windows 2000: Comprehensive Concepts and Techniques[2] Microsoft Windows 2000: Brief Concepts and Techniques
Notebook Organizer	Microsoft Office OneNote 2003: Introductory Concepts and Techniques
Word Processing	Microsoft Office Word 2003: Comprehensive Concepts and Techniques, CourseCard Edition[2] • Microsoft Word 2002: Comprehensive Concepts and Techniques[2]
Spreadsheets	Microsoft Office Excel 2003: Comprehensive Concepts and Techniques, CourseCard Edition[2] • Microsoft Excel 2002: Comprehensive Concepts and Techniques[2]
Databases	Microsoft Office Access 2003: Comprehensive Concepts and Techniques, CourseCard Edition[2] • Microsoft Access 2002: Comprehensive Concepts and Techniques[2]
Presentation Tools	Microsoft Office PowerPoint 2003: Comprehensive Concepts and Techniques, CourseCard Edition[2] • Microsoft PowerPoint 2002: ComprehensiveConcepts and Techniques[2] • Microsoft Producer 2003: Essential Concepts and Techniques
Desktop Publishing	Microsoft Office Publisher 2003: Comprehensive Concepts and Techniques[2] • Microsoft Publisher 2002: Comprehensive Concepts and Techniques[1]
Graphic Design	Adobe Photoshop CS2: Comprehensive Concepts and Techniques[2]
PROGRAMMING	
Programming	Microsoft Visual Basic .NET: Comprehensive Concepts and Techniques[2] • Microsoft Visual Basic 6: Complete Concepts and Techniques[1] • Java Programming: Comprehensive Concepts and Techniques, Third Edition[2] • Structured COBOL Programming, Second Edition • Understanding and Troubleshooting Your PC • Programming Fundamentals Using Microsoft Visual Basic .NET
INTERNET	
Concepts	Discovering the Internet: Brief Concepts and Techniques, Second Edition • Discovering the Internet: Complete Concepts and Techniques, Second Edition
Browsers	Microsoft Internet Explorer 6: Introductory Concepts and Techniques, Windows XP Edition • Microsoft Internet Explorer 5: An Introduction • Netscape Navigator 6: An Introduction • Introduction to the World Wide Web • Mozilla Firefox: Introductory Concepts and Techniques
Web Design and Development	Web Design: Introductory Concepts and Techniques, Second Edition • HTML: Comprehensive Concepts and Techniques, Third Edition[2] • Microsoft Office FrontPage 2003: Comprehensive Concepts and Techniques, CourseCard Edition[2] • Microsoft FrontPage 2002: Comprehensive Concepts and Techniques[2] • Macromedia Dreamweaver 8: Comprehensive Concepts and Techniques[2]
MIS	
Systems Analysis	Systems Analysis and Design, Sixth Edition
Data Communications	Business Data Communications: Introductory Concepts and Techniques, Fourth Edition

[1]Also available as an Introductory Edition, which is a shortened version of the complete book, [2]Also available as an Introductory Edition and as a Complete Edition, which are shortened versions of the comprehensive book.

ADOBE

Photoshop CS2

Adobe PHOTOSHOP CS2

ADOBE

Photoshop CS2

Editing a Photoshop Image

PROJECT

1

CASE PERSPECTIVE

Ralph Hooton plans to open a parasailing attraction for island tourists. The new company, Up, Up & Away, will be located in the bustling harbor among cruise ship docks, and piers for sports fishing. He already has secured his business licenses, boats, sails, and financing.

Parasailing, also known as parascending, is a recreational activity where one or two people are towed behind a speedboat while attached to a parachute. As the boat accelerates, the wind causes the parachute to rise several hundred feet above the water. The parasailer needs no previous experience and has only to sit back and enjoy the view. Ralph's planned route will follow the coastline allowing the parasailer to see the most interesting parts of the island.

Ralph wants to advertise his parasailing business on the Up, Up & Away Web site and also with printed display-stand cards, known as rack cards. Rack cards typically measure 4 × 9 inches and are printed on both sides. Ralph knows of your interest in Adobe Photoshop and has asked you to begin work on a rack card by editing one of his many photographs. He would like the photograph to be more dramatic by eliminating much of the background sky, by focusing on the parasailers, and by adding a defining border. Ralph wants to use the eye-catching photograph in the upper portion on the front of the rack card, which he then will duplicate professionally on glossy card stock and distribute to local hotels and travel agencies.

As you discuss the project, you remind Ralph that the photograph used for print publications cannot always be in the same format as the one he might post on his Web site. You promise to investigate Photoshop's Web features.

As you read through this project, you will learn how to use Photoshop to load, edit, save, and print a photograph that displays a border. You also will save the image for use on the Web.

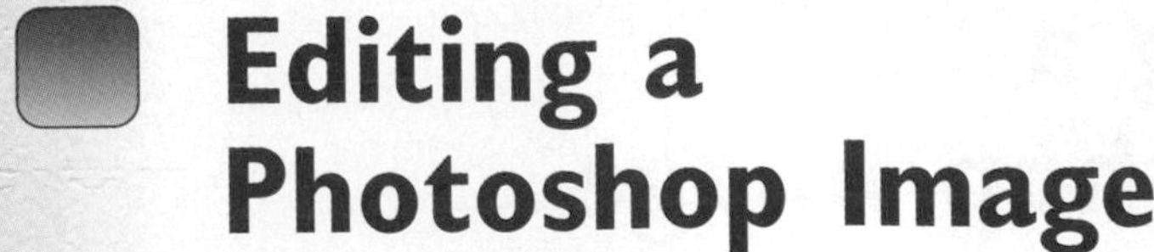

Editing a Photoshop Image

PROJECT

Objectives

You will have mastered the material in this project when you can:

- Start Photoshop and customize the Photoshop window
- Open a Photo
- Identify parts of the Photoshop window
- Explain file types
- Save a photo for both print and the Web
- Edit the photo using the Navigator palette and the Zoom Tool
- Crop and resize a photo
- Create a blended border
- Print a photo
- View files in Adobe Bridge
- Use Adobe Help Center
- Close a photo and quit Photoshop

What is Photoshop CS2?

Photoshop CS2 is a popular, image editing software produced by Adobe Systems Incorporated. Image editing software refers to computer programs that allow you to create and modify **digital images**, or pictures in electronic form. One type of digital image is a digital **photograph** or **photo**, originally produced on light-sensitive film but now commonly captured and stored as a digitized array inside a camera. The photo then is converted into a print, a slide, or, if necessary, a digital file. Other types of digital images include scanned images or electronic forms of original artwork created from scratch. Digital images are used in graphic applications, advertising, publishing, and on the Web. Image editing software, such as Photoshop, can be used for basic adjustments such as rotating, cropping, or resizing, as well as more advanced manipulations, such as airbrushing, retouching, removing red-eye, changing the contrast of an image, balancing, or combining elements of different images. Because Photoshop allows you to save multilayered, composite images and then return later to extract parts of those images, it works well for repurposing a wide variety of graphic-related files.

Photoshop CS2 is part of the Adobe Creative Suite, but often it is used independently as a stand-alone application. Photoshop CS2 is available for both the PC and Macintosh computer systems. The projects in this book are described using the PC platform running the Windows XP operating system.

Project One — Editing a Photoshop Image

To illustrate the features of Photoshop CS2, this book presents a series of projects that use Photoshop to edit photos similar to those you will encounter in academic and business environments, as well as photos for personal use. Project 1 uses Photoshop to enhance a photograph of parasailers to be used as an advertising piece for a parasailing business. The original photo is displayed in Figure 1-1a. The edited photo is displayed in Figure 1-1b

(a) original photo

(b) edited photo

FIGURE 1-1

The enhancements will emphasize the sail and parasailers by focusing on the main object and positioning it to make the layout appear more visually dynamic. A rounded border will blend with the clouds in the photo. A light border color will enhance the image of the sail. Finally, the photo will be resized to fit in the upper portion of the 4 × 9 inch rack card and then optimized for the Web.

Starting and Customizing Photoshop

To start Photoshop, Windows must be running. The steps on the next page show how to start Photoshop, or ask your instructor how to start Photoshop for your system.

To Start Photoshop

1

- **Click the Start button on the Windows taskbar, point to All Programs on the Start menu, point to Adobe Photoshop CS2 on the All Programs submenu.**

Windows displays the commands on the Start menu above the Start button and displays the All Programs submenu (Figure 1-2).

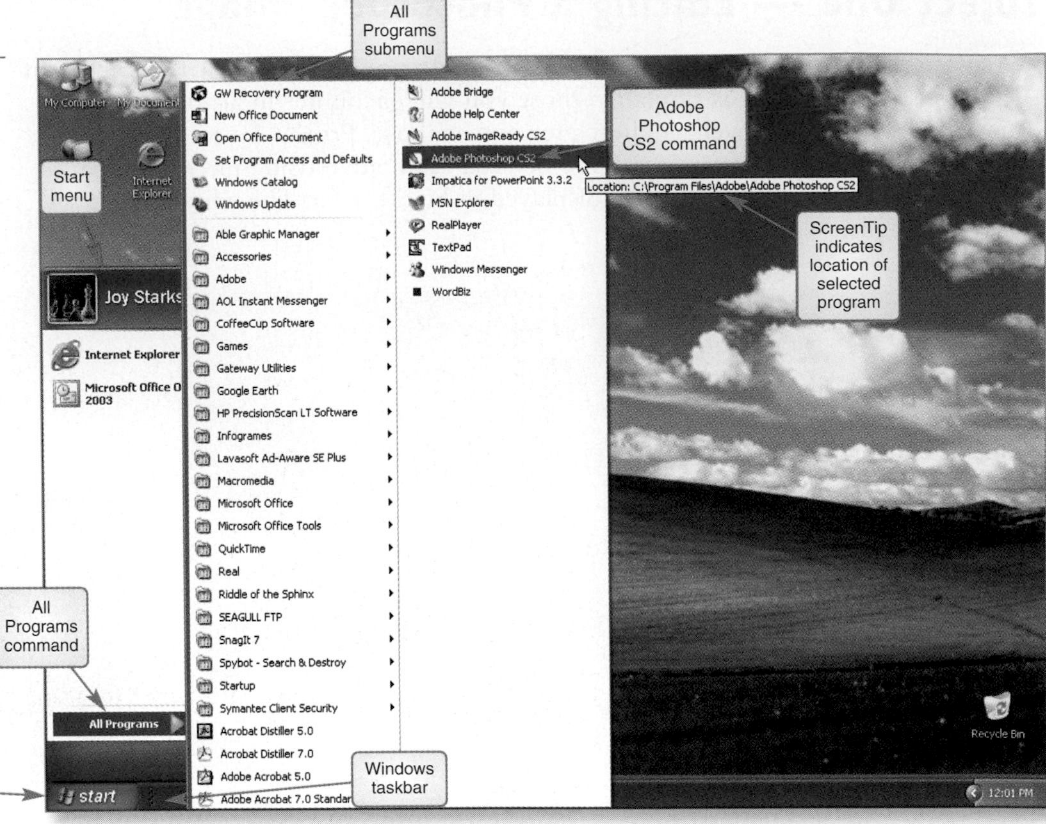

FIGURE 1-2

2

- **Click Adobe Photoshop CS2.**

Photoshop starts. While the program loads, Photoshop displays information about the version, owner, and creators. After a few moments, Photoshop may display the Welcome Screen window as shown in Figure 1-3. If you do not wish to display the Welcome screen in the future, click to remove the check in the Show this dialog at startup check box.

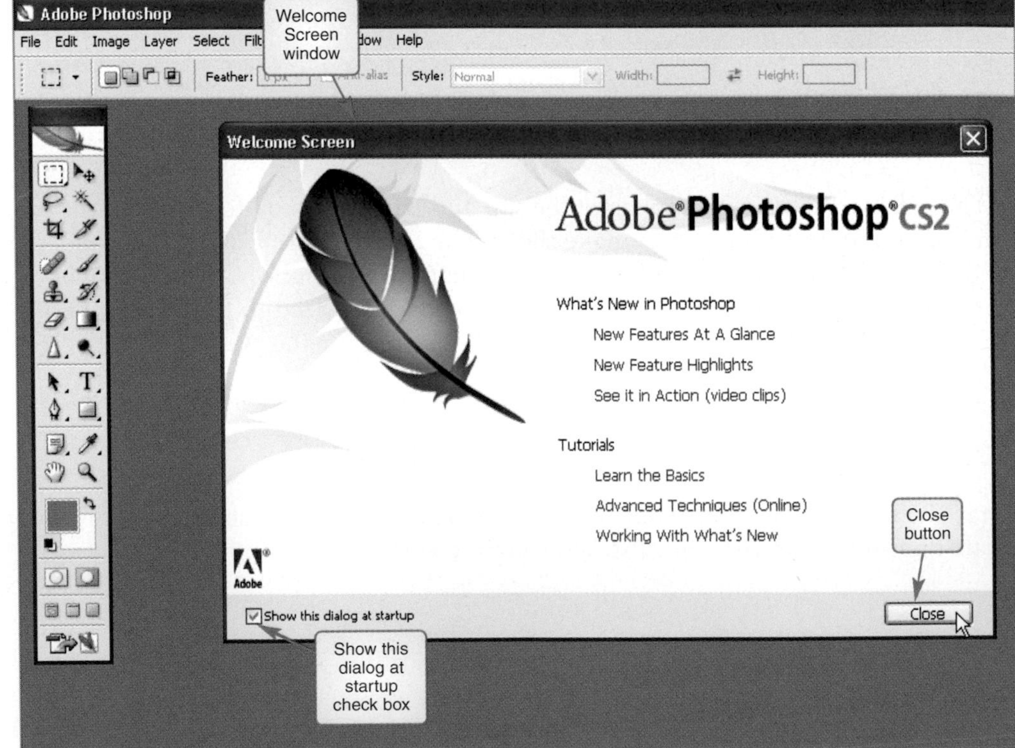

FIGURE 1-3

3

- **If Photoshop displays the Welcome Screen window, click the Close button in the Welcome Screen window.**
- **If the Adobe Photoshop window is not maximized, double-click its title bar to maximize it.**

The Adobe Photoshop window is displayed (Figure 1-4). The Windows taskbar displays the Adobe Photoshop button indicating that Photoshop is running.

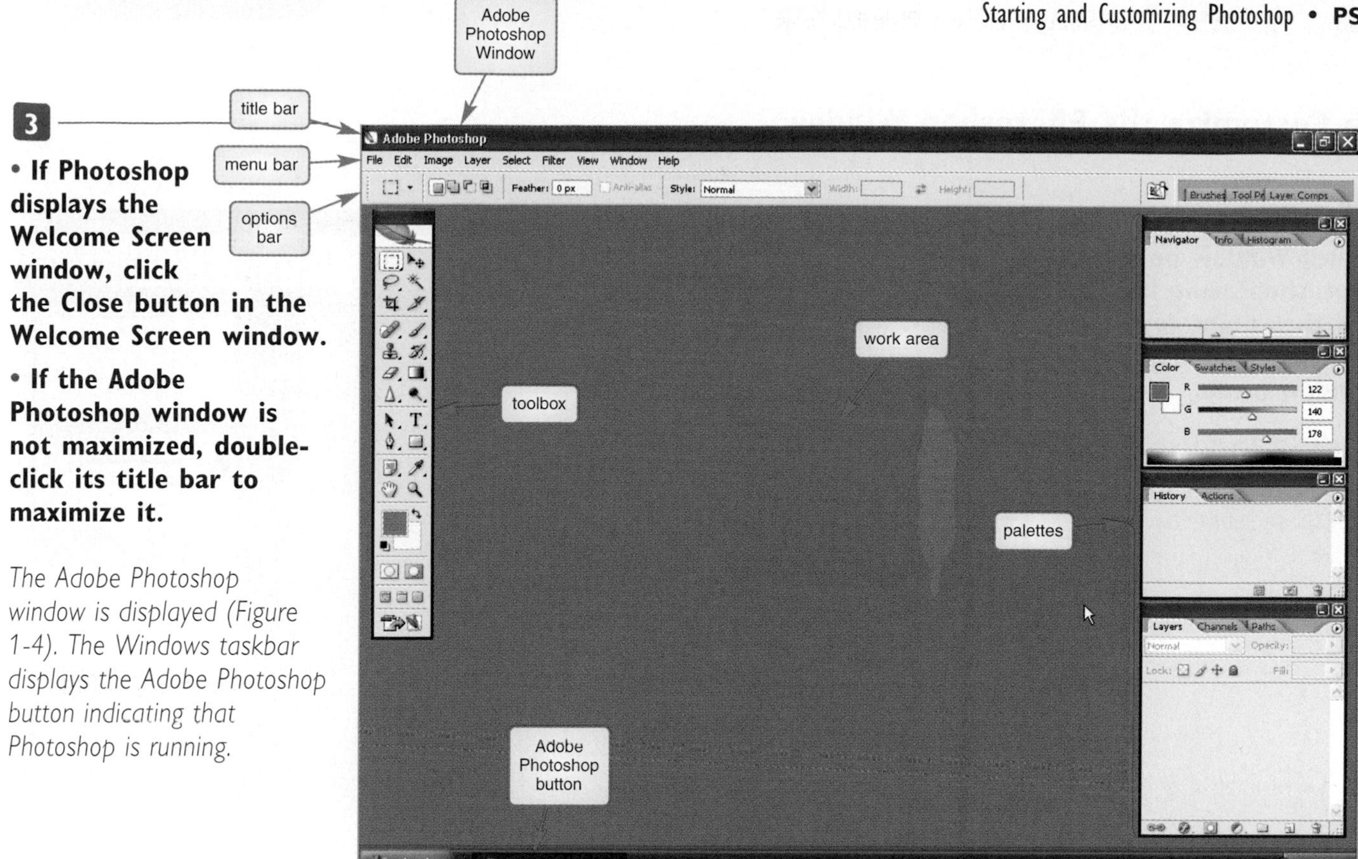

FIGURE 1-4

Other Ways

1. Double-click Photoshop icon

The screen in Figure 1-4 shows how the Photoshop window looks the first time you start Photoshop after installation on most computers. Photoshop does not open a blank or default photo automatically; rather, it displays a menu bar and a toolbar, called the options bar, across the top of the screen with a gray work area below the options bar. A toolbox is displayed on the left, and palettes on the right. The grey work area, the options bar, the toolbox and palettes are referred to collectively as the **Workspace**. As you work in Photoshop, the palettes, the selected tool, and the options bar settings may change. Therefore, if you want your screen to match the figures in this book, you should reset the palettes, the toolbox, and the options bar settings. You also may need to change your computer's resolution to 1024 × 768. For more information about how to change the resolution on your computer, and other advanced Photoshop settings, read Appendix A.

The steps on the next page illustrate how to reset the palettes, reset the selected tool, and all tool settings.

To Customize the Photoshop Window

1

- **Click Window on the Photoshop menu bar, and then point to Workspace on the Window menu.**

Photoshop displays the Window menu and the Workspace submenu (Figure 1-5).

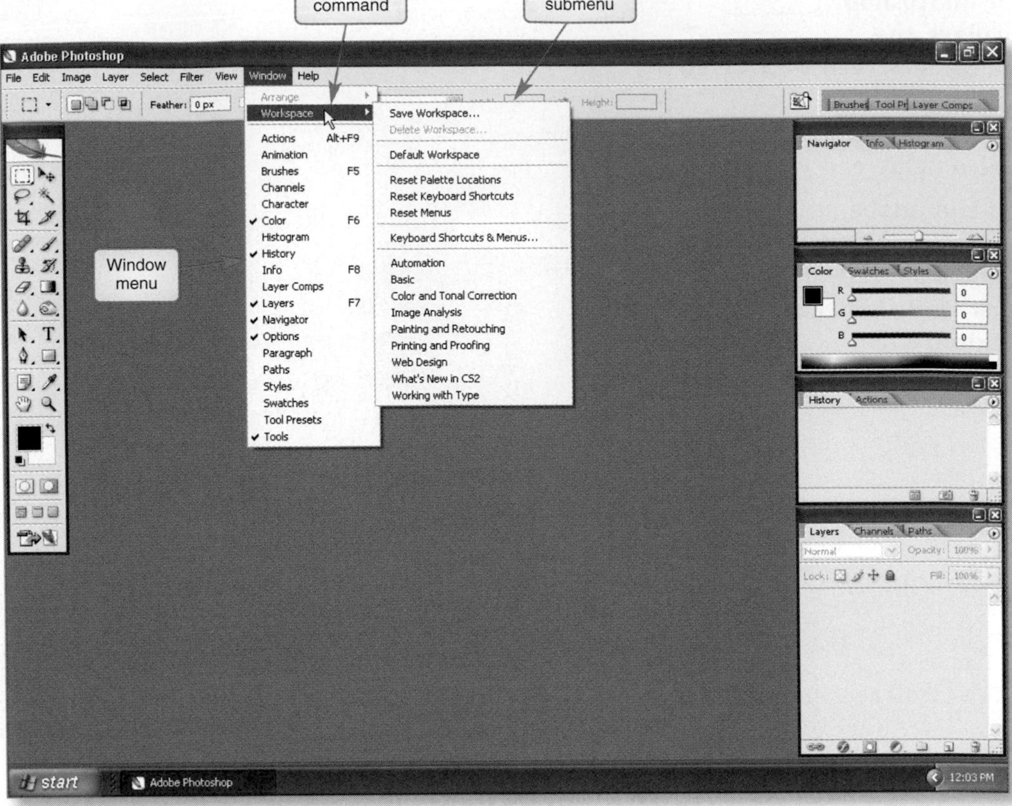

FIGURE 1-5

2

- **Click Default Workspace.**

After a few moments, Photoshop resets the placement of the palettes and toolbox (Figure 1-6). If Photoshop is a new installation on your system, you may notice few changes in the window.

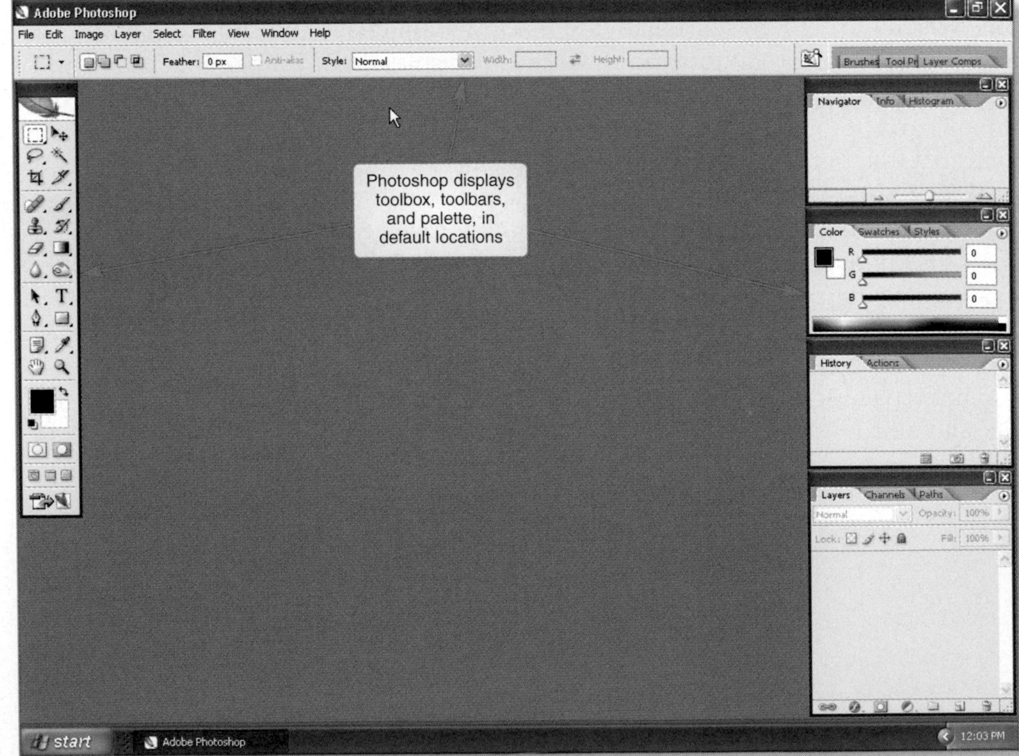

FIGURE 1-6

3

• **Right-click the top-left tool in the toolbox.**

Photoshop displays a list of tools on the context menu (Figure 1-7). Your tool button may display a different icon.

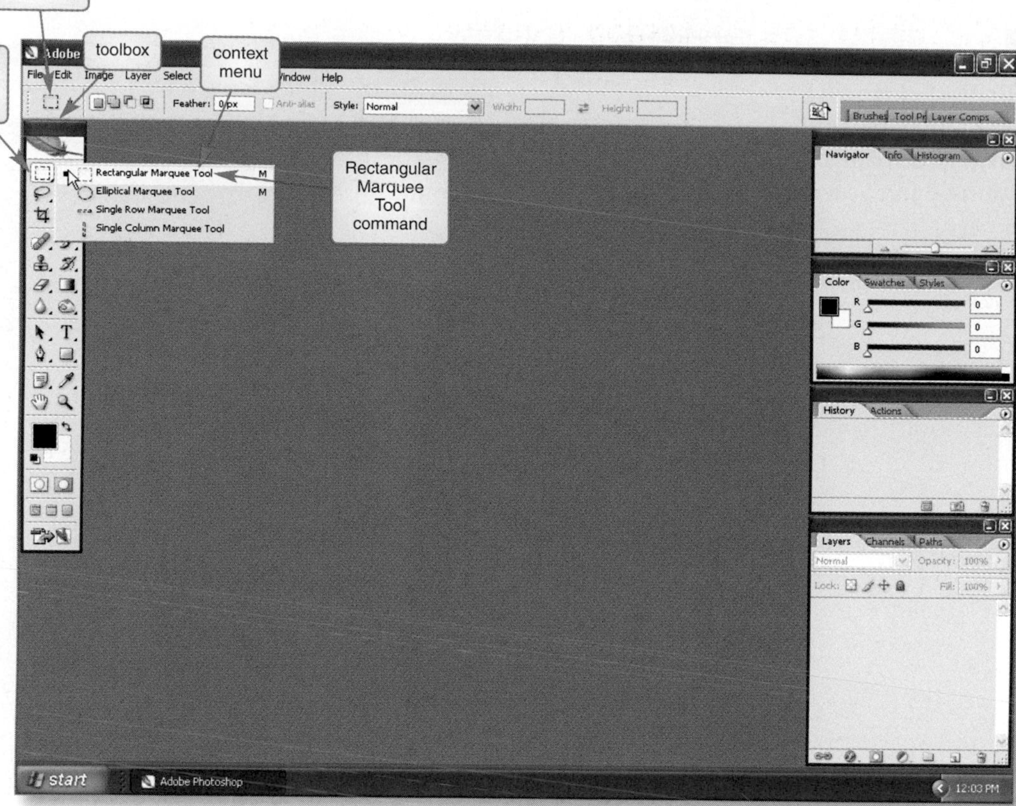

FIGURE 1-7

4

• **If necessary, click the Rectangular Marquee Tool to select it.**

Photoshop displays the Rectangular Marquee Tool (M) in the toolbox and on the options bar (Figure 1-8). Your screen may not reflect any change if the Rectangular Marquee Tool (M) already was selected.

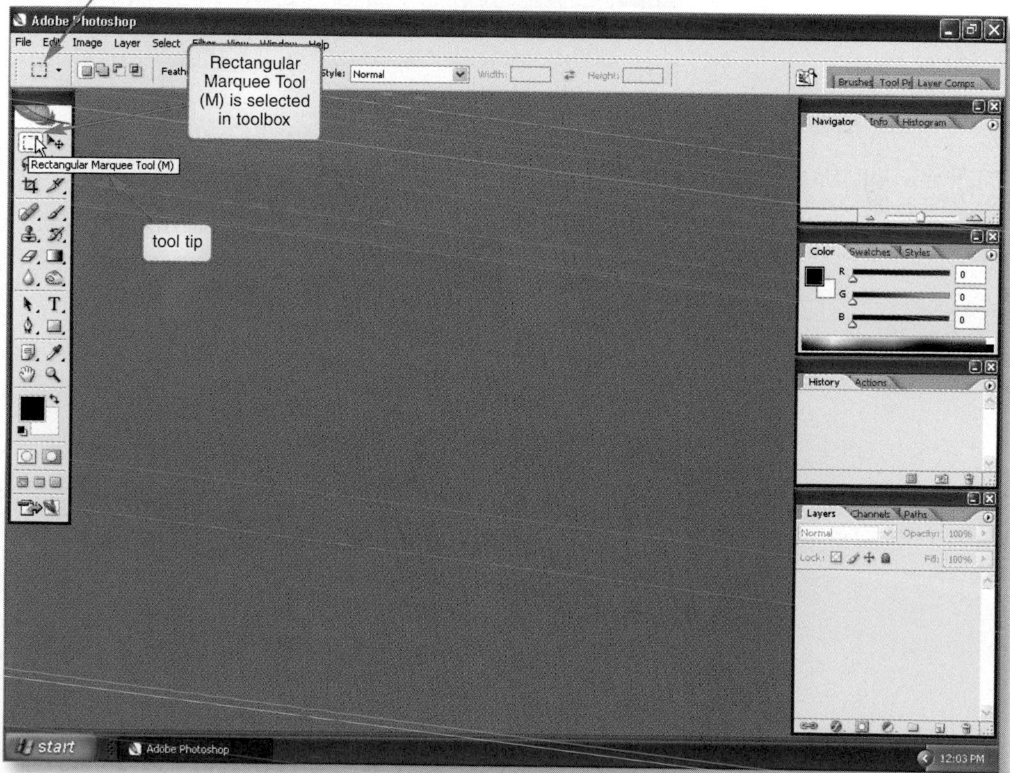

FIGURE 1-8

5

• **Right-click the Rectangular Marquee Tool (M) button on the options bar.**

Photoshop displays the context menu (Figure 1-9).

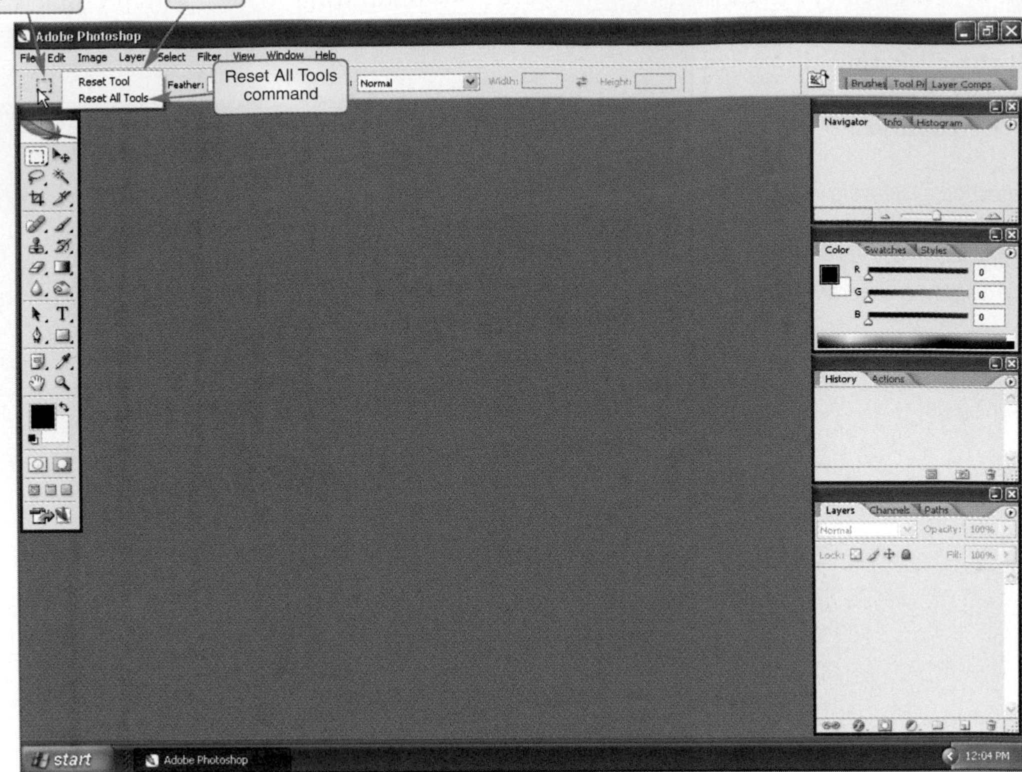

FIGURE 1-9

• **Click Reset All Tools.**

Photoshop displays a dialog box (Figure 1-10).

7

• **Click the OK button.**

The tools on the options bar, and other tool settings that are not currently visible, are reset to their default settings. On a new installation of Photoshop, you may not see any changes.

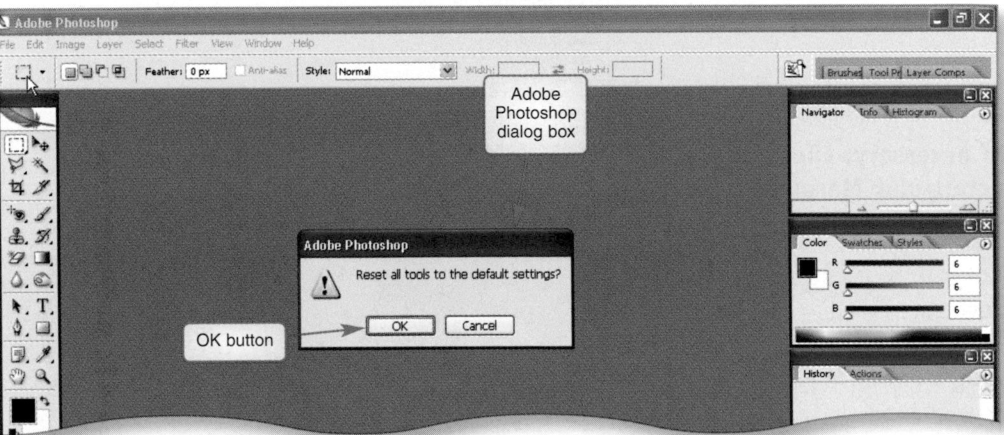

FIGURE 1-10

As an alternative to Step 3 on the previous page, you can click a tool in the toolbox and hold down the mouse button. In a few seconds, the tool's context menu will display. Whether you right-click, or click and hold to display the menu, depends on your personal preference.

When you point to many objects in the Photoshop window, such as a tool or button, Photoshop displays a tool tip. A **tool tip** is a short on-screen note associated with the object to which you are pointing. An example of a tool tip is shown in Figure 1-8. Some tool tips in Photoshop contain links leading to additional information about the tool. When you right-click some objects in the Photoshop window, Photoshop displays a context menu. A **context menu**, or **shortcut menu**, displays commands relevant to the active tool, selection, or palette.

Because of a default preferences setting, each time you start Photoshop, the Photoshop window is displayed the same way it was the last time you used Photoshop. If the palettes are relocated, then they will display in their new locations the next time you start Photoshop. Similarly, if values on the options bar are changed or a different tool is selected, they will remain changed the next time you start Photoshop. If you wish to return the screen to its default settings, follow the previous steps each time you start Photoshop. Appendix A discusses how to change more of these default settings.

As you work through the projects, editing and creating photos, you will find that the options bar is **context sensitive**, which means it changes as you select different tools. You will learn the palettes and the palette tabs as you use them.

More About

Photos Online

Many Web sites offer royalty free stock photos. Visit the Shelly Cashman More About Web site for a list of links to pages where you can search for free photos.

Opening a Photo

To open a photo in Photoshop it must be stored as a digital file on your computer system or an external storage device. To **open** a photo, you bring a copy of the file from the storage location to the screen where you can **edit** or make changes to the photo. The changes do not become permanent, however, until you **save** or store them on a storage device. The photos used in this book are stored on a CD located in the back of the book. Your instructor may designate a different location for the photos.

The following steps illustrate how to open the file, Parasailing, from a CD located in drive E.

To Open a Photo

1

- **Insert the CD that accompanies this book into your CD drive. After a few seconds, if Windows displays a dialog box, click its Close button.**
- **With the Photoshop window open, click File on the menu bar.**

Photoshop displays the File menu (Figure 1-11).

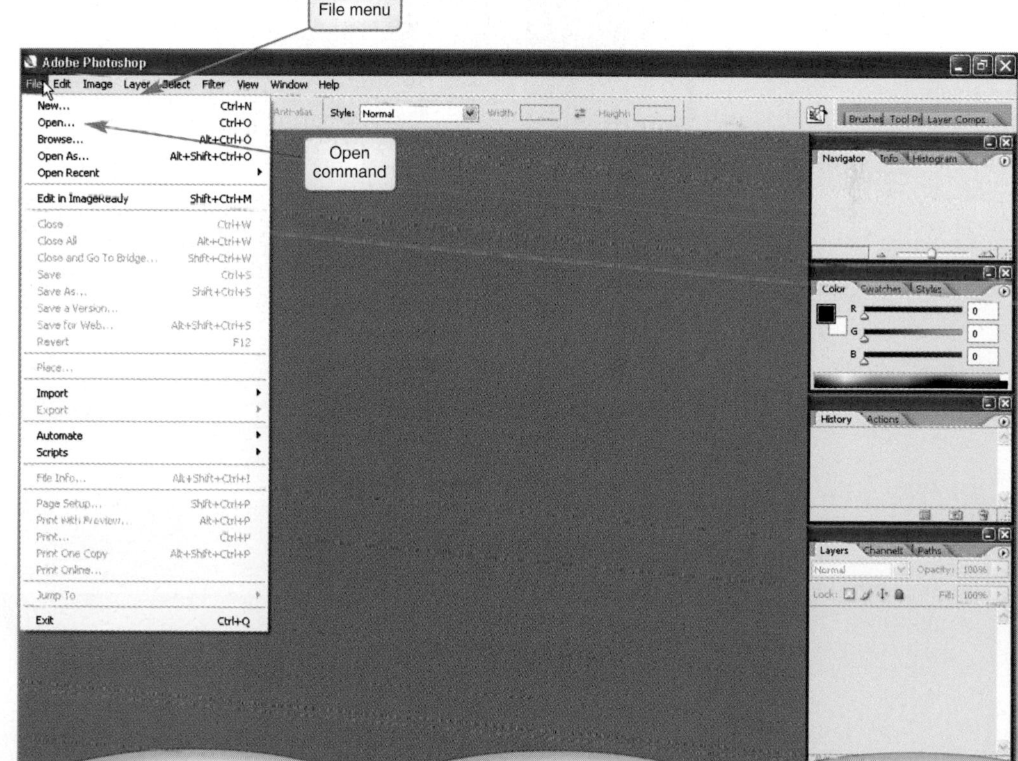

FIGURE 1-11

2

• Click Open. When the Open dialog box is displayed, click the Look in box arrow.

Photoshop displays the Open dialog box (Figure 1-12). A list of the available storage locations is displayed. Your list may differ depending on your system configuration.

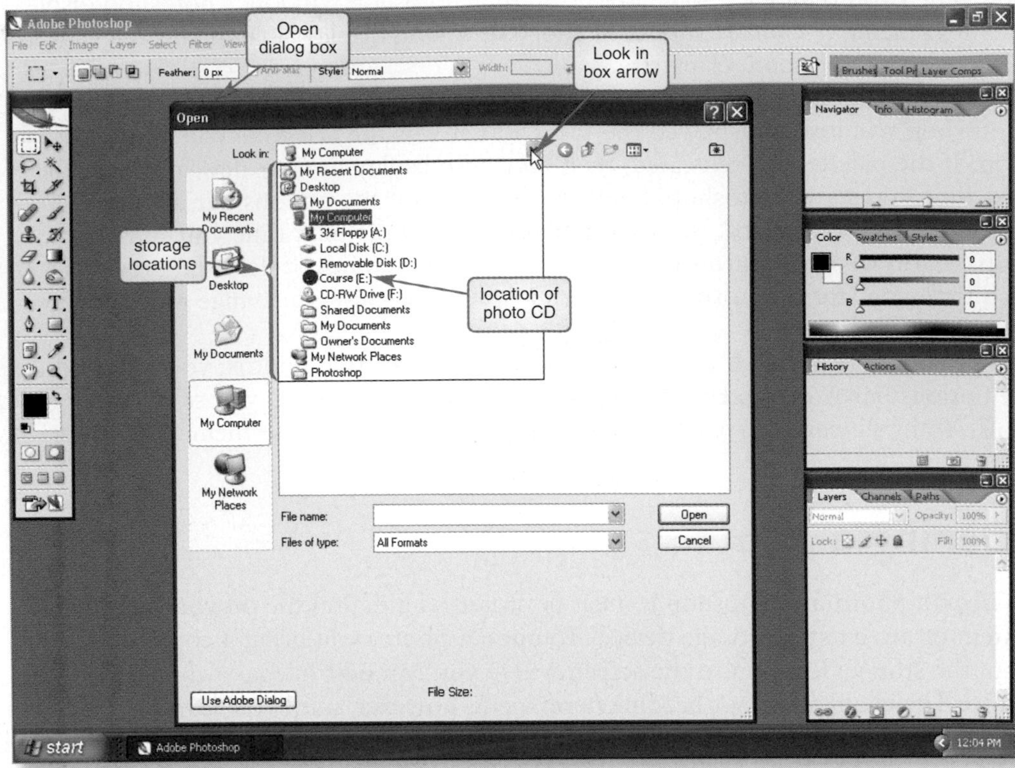

FIGURE 1-12

3

• Click drive E or the drive associated with your CD.

The folders located on the CD are displayed in the dialog box (Figure 1-13).

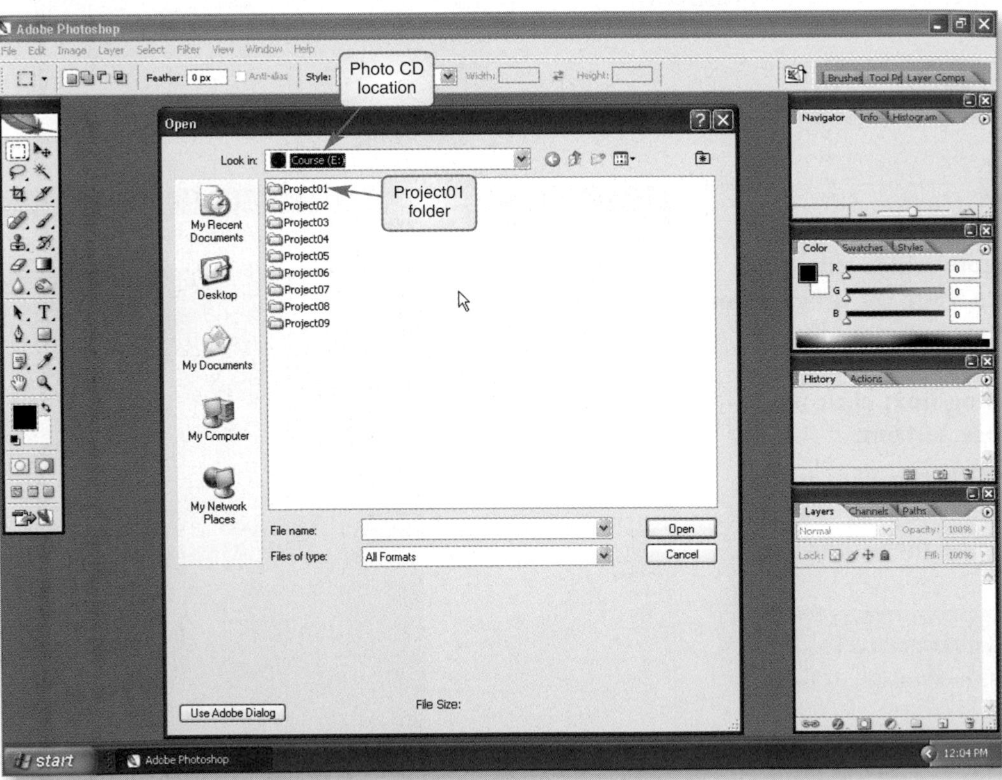

FIGURE 1-13

4

• **Double-click the Project01 folder and then click the file, Parasailing, to select it.**

The files located in the Project01 folder are displayed (Figure 1-14). Photoshop displays a preview in the Open dialog box.

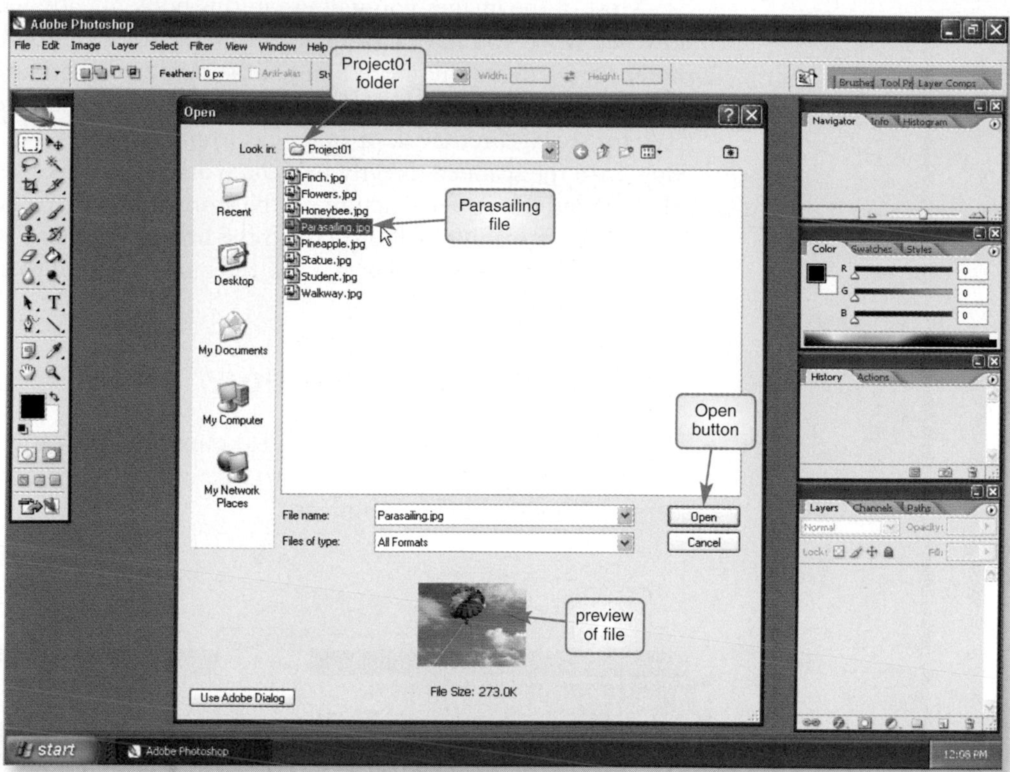

FIGURE 1-14

5

• **Click the Open button.**

Photoshop opens the file, Parasailing, from the CD in drive E. The photo is displayed in the Photoshop window (Figure 1-15).

FIGURE 1-15

Other Ways

1. In Windows, right-click file, click Open With, click Adobe Photoshop CS2
2. On options bar, click Go to Bridge button, double-click photo
3. Press CTRL+O, select File, click Open

Most of the images you will use in this book already will be stored in digital format; however, when you have a print copy of a picture that you wish to use in Photoshop, rather than a digital file stored on your system, it sometimes is necessary to scan the picture using a scanner. A **scanner** is a device used to convert an image into a digital form for storage, retrieval, or other electronic purposes. Photoshop allows you to bring a copy from the scanner, directly into the work area. Make sure that your scanner is properly installed. Place your picture on the scanner and then click Import on the File menu. Your system's scanner will display on the Import submenu. Click your scanner. When the scanner dialog box is displayed, click the button related to starting a new scan.

The Photoshop Window

The **Photoshop window** (Figure 1-16) consists of a variety of components to make your work more efficient and photo documents more professional. The following sections discuss these components.

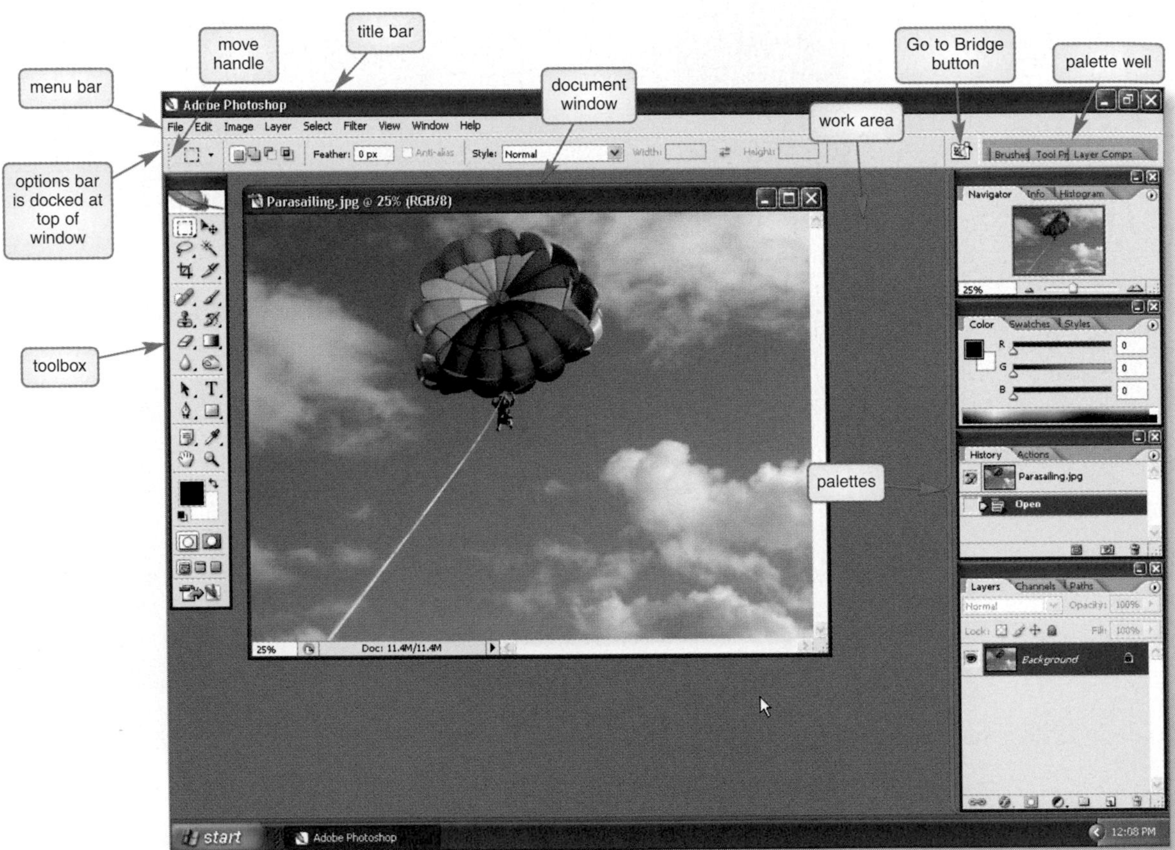

FIGURE 1-16

The Menu Bar and Options Bar

The menu bar and options bar display at the top of the screen just below the title bar (Figure 1-16).

MENU BAR The **menu bar** is a special toolbar that displays the Photoshop menu names. Each **menu** contains a list of commands you can use to perform tasks such as opening, saving, printing, and editing photos. When you point to a menu name on the menu bar, the area of the menu bar containing the name changes to a button. To display a menu, such as the Edit menu, click the Edit menu name on the menu bar. If you point to a command on a menu that has an arrow to its right edge, as shown in Figure 1-17, a **submenu**, or secondary menu, displays another list of commands.

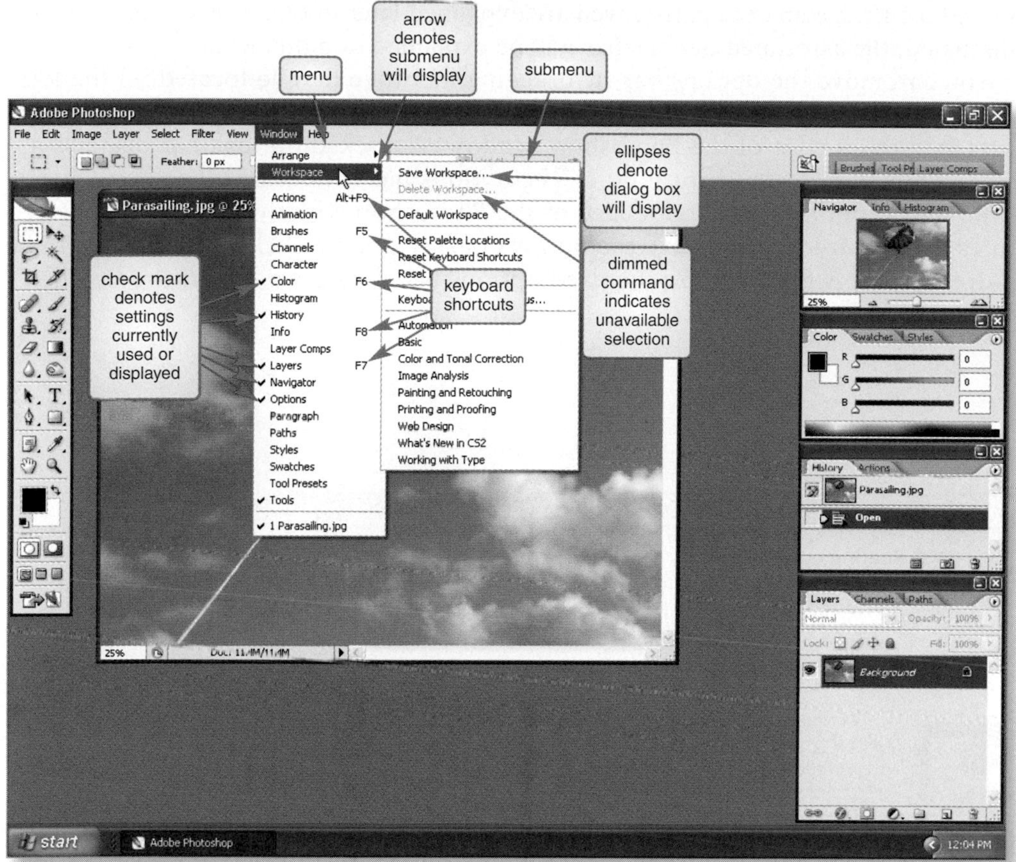

FIGURE 1-17

Menus may display **keyboard shortcuts** that indicate keys you can press on the keyboard to perform the same tasks as clicking a command on the menu. A **check mark** in a Photoshop menu means the setting is currently used or displayed. Three dots, called **ellipses**, follow some menu commands. When a command displaying ellipses is clicked, Photoshop will display a dialog box. Photoshop displays some **dimmed commands** that appear gray, or dimmed, instead of black, which indicates they are not available for the current selection.

When Photoshop first is installed, all of the menu commands display when you click a menu name. To hide seldom used menu commands, you can click Menus on the Edit menu and follow the on-screen instructions. A **hidden command** does not currently display on a menu. If menu commands have been hidden, a Show All Menu Items command will display at the bottom of the menu list. Click the Show All Menu Items command, or press and hold CTRL when you click the menu name, to display all menu commands including hidden ones.

OPTIONS BAR The **options bar** is displayed below the menu bar. It contains buttons and boxes that allow you to perform tasks more quickly than using the menu bar and related menus. Most buttons on the options bar display words or images to help you remember their functions. When you point to a button or box on the options bar, a tool tip is displayed below the mouse pointer. The options bar changes to reflect the tool currently selected in the toolbox. For example, a tool related to text may display a font box on the options bar, whereas a tool related to painting will display a brush button. The selected tool always is displayed as the first button on the options bar. On each tool's options bar is a Go to Bridge button to activate the file browsing and organization tool, Adobe Bridge. On the far right of the options bar is the palette well. Both Adobe Bridge and the palette well are explained later in this project. As each tool is discussed, the associated options bar will be explained in more detail.

You can move the options bar by dragging its **move handle** located on the left of the options bar (Figure 1-16 on page PS 14). The options bar is **docked** when it is attached to an edge of the Photoshop window. A docked options bar displays a move handle with seven vertical dots. The options bar is **floating** when it has been moved and is not attached to an edge of the Photoshop window (Figure 1-18a). You can **minimize** or **maximize** the options bar by double-clicking its move handle (Figure 1-18b). A floating or minimized options bar displays a blue move handle.

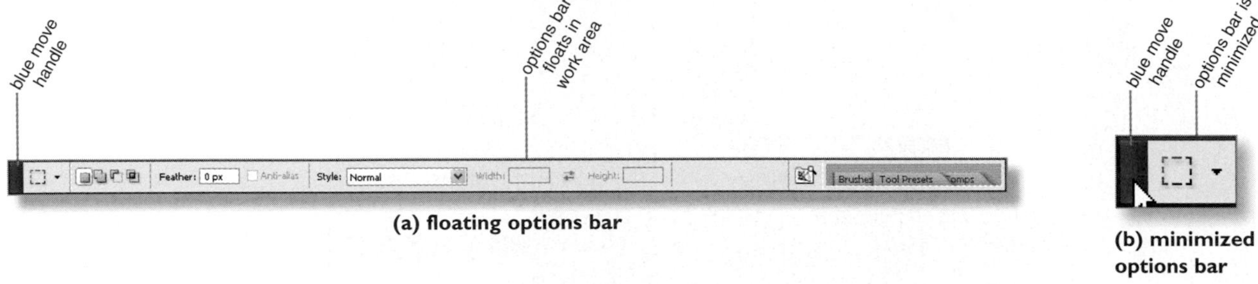

(a) floating options bar

(b) minimized options bar

FIGURE 1-18

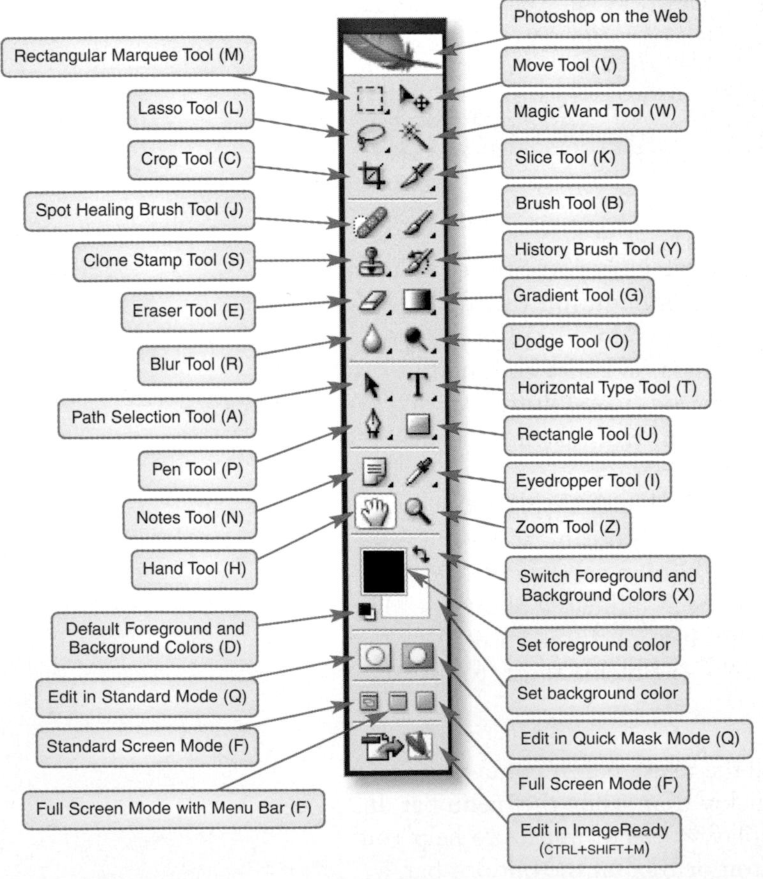

FIGURE 1-19

The Work Area

The Photoshop **work area** or workspace, located below the menu bar and options bar, is arranged to help you focus on creating and editing photos. The toolbox, document window, and palettes display on a gray background (Figure 1-16 on page PS 14).

The Toolbox

On the left side of the work area is the Photoshop **toolbox**. A toolbox is a group of **tools** or buttons, similar in general purpose, organized into a movable palette or pane. In Photoshop the toolbox is floating. You can move the toolbox by dragging its title bar. You also can show or hide the toolbox by clicking Tools on the Window menu. Each tool in the toolbox displays a **tool icon.** When you point to the tool, a tool tip will display the name of the tool including its shortcut key. You can expand some tools to show hidden tools beneath them. Expandable tools display a small triangle in the lower-right corner of the tool icon. Click and hold the tool button or right-click a tool to see or select one of its hidden tools from the context menu. The default tool names are listed in Figure 1-19.

When you click a tool in the toolbox to use it, Photoshop selects the button, changes the options bar as necessary, and changes the mouse pointer to reflect the selected tool. Some tools also open a dialog box.

The toolbox is organized by purpose. At the very top of the toolbox is a button to access Photoshop on the Web at www.adobe.com. Below that, the selection tools display, then the crop and slice tools, followed by retouching, painting, drawing and type, annotation, measuring, and navigation tools. At the bottom of the toolbox is a button to start ImageReady, a graphics editor packaged with Photoshop.

More About

The Workspace

Pressing the TAB key toggles the display of palettes, toolbox, and options bar on and off. To hide or show all palettes except for the toolbox and options bar, press SHIFT+TAB.

The Document Window

The **document window**, also called the **active image area**, displays the active open file. The document window can be resized by dragging the border of the window. The document window contains the title bar, display area, scroll bars, and status bar (Figure 1-20).

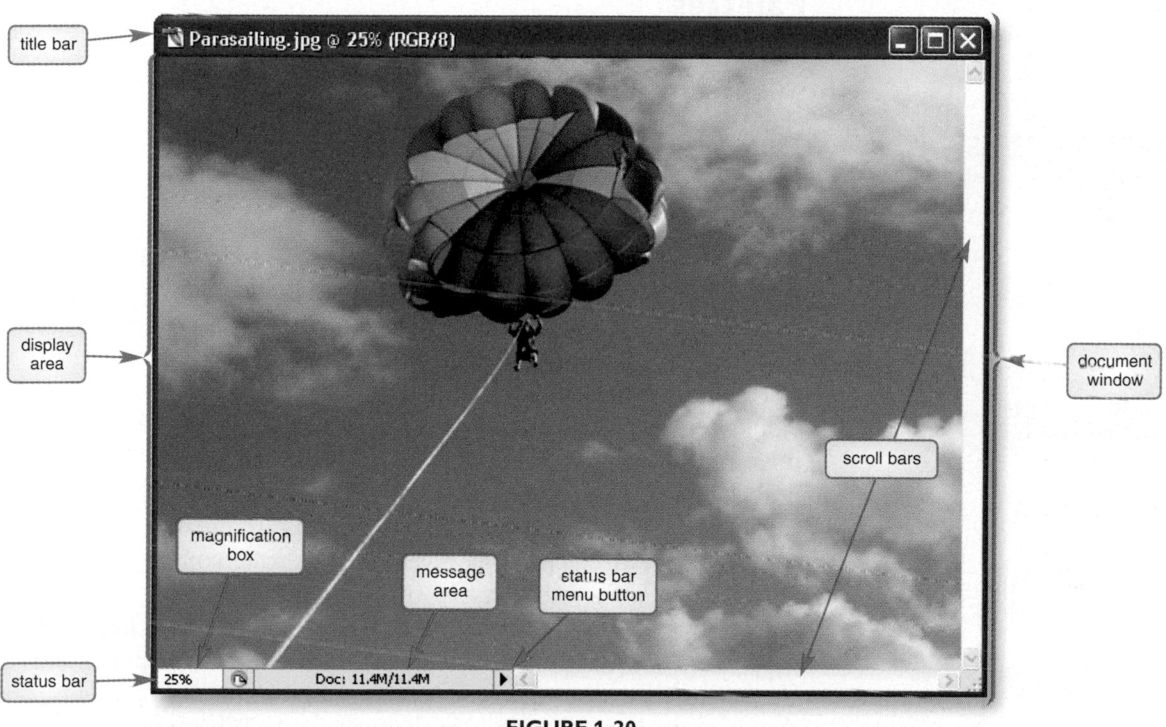

FIGURE 1-20

TITLE BAR The **title bar** of the document window displays the name of the file, the magnification, and the color mode. You can maximize the document window by double-clicking the title bar. When the document window is maximized, the toolbox and palettes display on top of the document window.

DISPLAY AREA The **display area** is the portion of the document window that displays the photo or image. You perform most tool tasks and edit the photo in the display area.

SCROLL BARS **Scroll bars** display on the right side and bottom of the document window. When the photo is bigger than the document window, the scroll bars become active and display scroll arrows and scroll boxes to move the image up, down, left, and right.

STATUS BAR Across the bottom of the document window, Photoshop displays the **status bar**. The status bar contains a magnification box. **Magnification** refers to the percentage of enlargement or reduction on the screen. For example, 50% magnification in the box means the entire photo is displayed at 50 percent of its original size. Magnification does not change the size of the photo physically; it merely displays it on the screen at a different size. You can type a new percentage in the magnification box to zoom to a different view of the photo.

Next to the magnification box is the **message area**. Messages may display information about the file size, the current tool, or the document dimensions. On the right side of the status bar is the **status bar menu button**, that when clicked, displays a status bar menu. You use the status bar menu to change the message area or change to other versions of the document.

Your installation of Photoshop may display rulers at the top and left of the document window. You will learn about rulers later in this project.

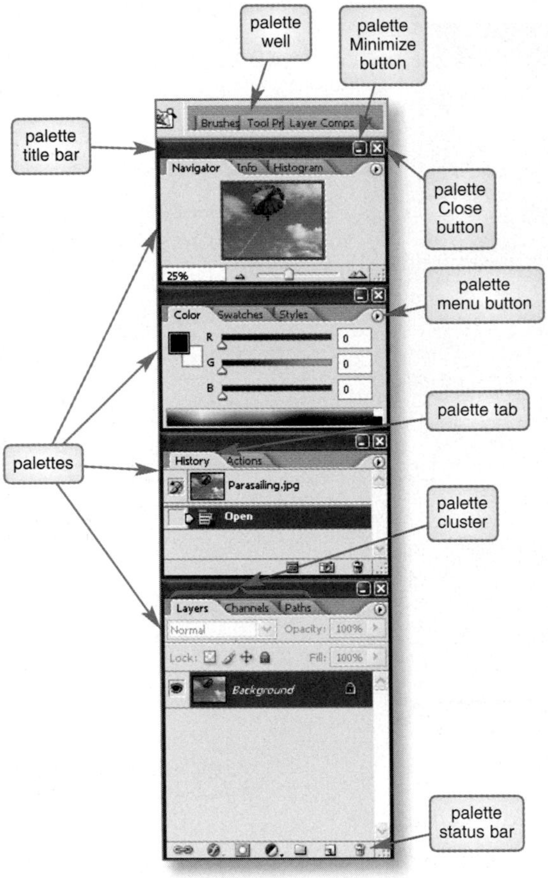

Palettes

A **palette**, named for the board that provides a flat surface on which artists mix paints, is a collection of graphically displayed choices and commands, such as those involving colors, brushes, actions, or layers. In Photoshop, some palettes display by default as stacked tabs in small windows on the right side of the workspace. These small windows have a title bar that contains a Minimize button, a Close button, and a menu button (Figure 1-21). Palettes may have one or more **tabs** or pages of choices. A palette may display buttons, boxes, sliders, scroll bars, drop-down lists, or status bars. Palettes help you modify or monitor your photos.

You can arrange and reposition the available palettes either individually or in groups. Palettes float in the work area. You can move them individually by dragging their tabs, or as a stacked group by dragging their title bars. Additionally, Photoshop allows you to drag each palette tab away from an existing group to create a separate window for that palette. The reverse also is true; you can **cluster** individual palettes into groups of your preference.

Palettes that are not being used may be placed or docked in the **palette well,** a storage location on the right side of the options bar. You can click palettes in the palette well to display their contents, or they may be dragged to float in the work area. When you close a palette by clicking the Close button, it no longer is displayed. You can redisplay the palette by clicking the palette name on the Window menu. On the upper-right side of each palette is a palette menu button. Palette status bars display additional information and buttons.

Photoshop comes with 17 palettes as described in Table 1-1.

FIGURE 1-21

Table 1-1 Photoshop Palettes

PALETTE NAME	PURPOSE	DEFAULT DISPLAY LOCATION
Actions	to record, play, edit, and delete individual actions	third palette in the work area
Animation	to create a sequence of images, or frames, that is displayed over time	does not initially display
Brushes	to select preset brushes and design custom brushes	in the palette well
Channels	to create and manage channels	fourth palette in the work area
Character	to provide options for formatting characters	does not initially display
Color	to display the color values for the current foreground and background colors	second palette in the work area
Histogram	to view tonal and color information about an image	first palette in the work area
History	to jump to any recent state of the image created during the current working session	third palette in the work area
Info	to display color values and document status information	first palette in the work area
Layer Comps	to display multiple compositions of a page layout	in the palette well
Layers	to show and hide layers, create new layers, and work with groups of layers	fourth palette in the work area
Navigator	to change quickly the view of your artwork using a thumbnail display and to change the magnification	first palette in the work area
Paragraph	to change the formatting of columns and paragraphs	does not initially display
Paths	to list the name and a thumbnail image of each saved path, the current work path, and the current vector mask	fourth palette in the work area
Styles	to view and select preset styles	second palette in the work area
Swatches	to store colors that you need to use often	second palette in the work area
Tool Presets	to save and reuse tool settings	in the palette well

As each palette is introduced, its function and characteristics will be explained.

File Types

A **file type** refers to the internal characteristics of digital files; it designates the operational or structural characteristics of a file. Each digital file, graphic or otherwise, is stored with specific kinds of formatting related to how the file is displayed on the screen, how it prints, and the software it uses to do so. Computer systems use the file type to help users open the file with the appropriate software. File types are distinguished by a special file extension. **File extensions**, in most computer systems, are identified by a three- or four-letter specification after the file name. For example, Parasailing.jpg refers to a file named Parasailing with the extension and file type JPG. A period separates the file name and its extension. When you are exploring files on your system, you may see the file extensions as part of the file name or you may see a column of information about file types.

More About

Palettes

To collapse a palette group to display titles only, double-click the palette's tab, or click the Minimize button. You can open the palette menu even when the palette is collapsed.

More About

File Extensions

The default setting for file extensions in Photoshop is to use a three-letter extension, all in lowercase letters. If you wish to change that as you save a file, in the File name text box, type the file name, period, and extension within quotation marks.

Graphic files are created and stored using many different file types and extensions. The type of file sometimes is determined by the creating hardware or software. Other times, when the user has a choice in applying file types, it commonly is decided by the intended purpose of the graphic file, such as whether or not the file is to be used on the Web, the file size, or the desired color mode. **Color modes**, or **color models**, use a numerical method to determine how to display and print colors. You may have heard of the RGB color model that creates its colors based on combinations of red, green, and blue. You will learn more about color models in a later project.

A few common graphic file types are listed in Table 1-2.

Table 1-2 Graphic File Types

FILE EXTENSION	FILE TYPE	DESCRIPTION
BMP	Bitmap	BMP is a standard Windows image format used on DOS and Windows-compatible computers. BMP format supports many different color modes.
EPS	Encapsulated PostScript	EPS files can contain both bitmap and vector graphics. They are supported by almost all graphics, illustration, and page-layout programs. EPS format can be used to transfer PostScript artwork between applications. While editing of EPS files is limited, Photoshop allows users to save any photo as an EPS file for use in other programs.
GIF	Graphics Interchange Format	GIF commonly is used to display graphics and images on Web pages. It is a compressed format designed to minimize file size and electronic transfer time.
JPEG OR JPG	Joint Photographic Experts Group	JPG files commonly are used to display photographs on Web pages. JPEG format supports many different color modes. JPEG retains all color information in an RGB image, unlike GIF format. JPEG compresses file size by selectively discarding data. Most digital cameras produce JPG files.
PDF	Portable Document	PDF is a flexible file format based on the PostScript imaging model that is cross-platform and cross-application. PDF files accurately display and preserve fonts, page layouts, and graphics. PDF files can contain electronic document search and navigation features such as hyperlinks. While editing of PDF files is limited, Photoshop allows users to save any photo as a PDF file for use in other programs.
PSD	Photoshop Document	PSD format is the default file format in Photoshop and the only format that supports all Photoshop features. Other Adobe applications can import PSD files directly and preserve many Photoshop features due to the tight integration between Adobe products.
RAW	Photoshop Raw	RAW format is a flexible file format used for transferring images between applications and computer platforms. There are no pixel or file size restrictions in this format. Documents saved in the Photoshop Raw format cannot contain layers.
TIFF OR TIF	Tagged Image File Format	TIFF is a flexible bitmap image format supported by almost all paint, image-editing, and page-layout applications. This format often is used for files that are to be exchanged between applications or computer platforms. Most desktop scanners can produce TIFF images.

To preserve the most features such as layers, effects, masks, and styles, Photoshop encourages the use of its own format, **PSD**, which stands for Photoshop Document format. Similarly to most file formats, PSD supports files up to 2 gigabytes (GB) in size. As you complete the projects in this book, you will examine file types more closely.

Table 1-3 displays information about the parasailing photo. It was created by a digital camera and is stored as a JPG file. **JPG**, or **JPEG**, stands for Joint Photographic Experts Group, a standard format used by photo hardware devices that supports many different color modes, and one that can be used on the Web.

Table 1-3 Parasailing Photo Characteristics

FILE NAME	PARASAILING
File Type	JPG
Document Size	7.68 × 5.76 inches
Color Mode	RGB
Resolution	300 pixels/inch
File Size	274 KB

Saving a Photo

As you make changes to a file in Photoshop, the computer stores it in memory. If you turn off the computer or if you lose electrical power, the document in memory is lost. If you plan to use the photo later, you must save it on a storage device such as a USB flash drive, or hard disk. The following steps illustrate how to save a file on a USB flash drive using the Save As command on the File menu.

You will save the photo with a new file name and in a new location. Even though you have yet to edit the photo, it is a good practice to save the file on your personal storage device early in the process. You will name the file Parasailing Edited. The following steps illustrate how to save a photo.

To Save a Photo

1

- **With your USB flash drive connected to one of the computer's USB ports, click File on the menu bar.**

Photoshop displays the File menu (Figure 1-22).

FIGURE 1-22

2

• **Click Save As. When the Save As dialog box is displayed, type** `Parasailing Edited` **in the File name text box. Do not press the ENTER key after typing the file name.**

The file name Parasailing Edited is displayed in the File name text box (Figure 1-23).

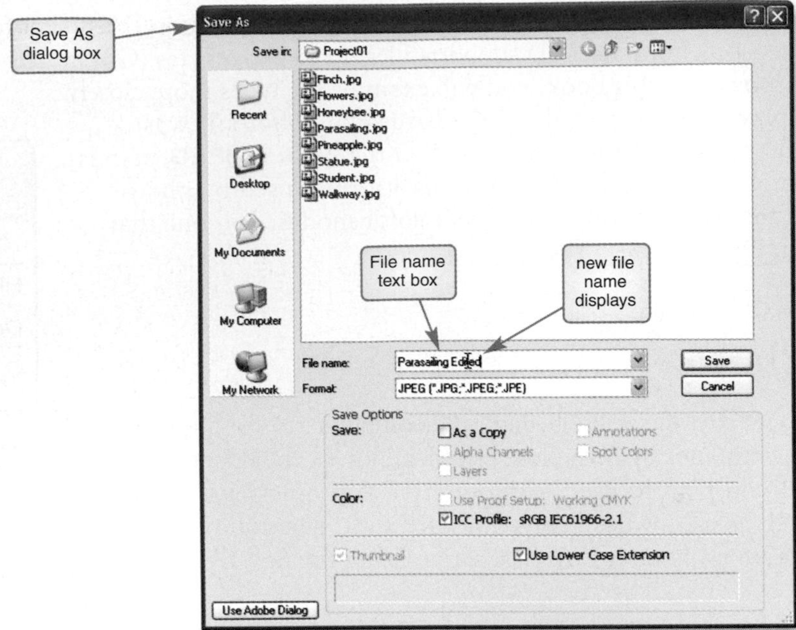

FIGURE 1-23

3

• **Click the Save in box arrow and then click USBDISK [G:], or the location associated with your USB flash drive, in the list.**

Photoshop displays the folders and files on drive G (Figure 1-24). Your list may vary.

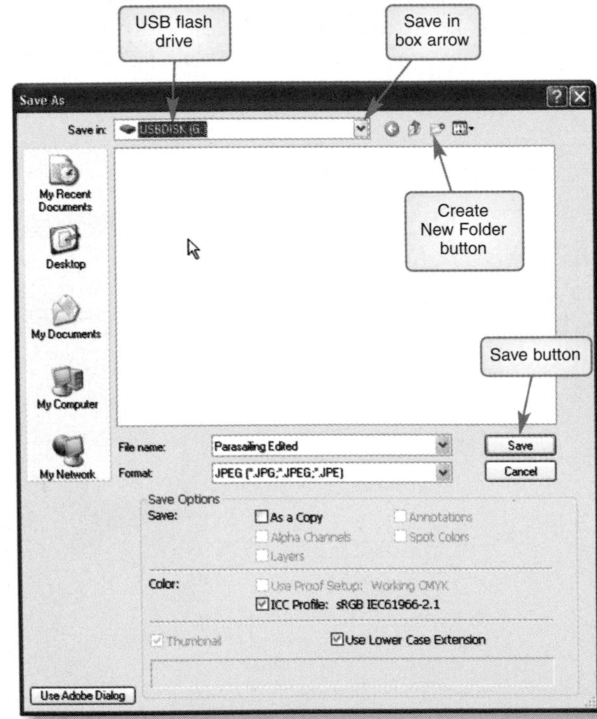

FIGURE 1-24

4

• **Click the Save button in the Save As dialog box. If Photoshop displays a JPEG Options dialog box, click its OK button.**

Photoshop saves the file on the USB flash drive with the file name Parasailing Edited and displays the new name on the document window title bar (Figure 1-25). Although the photo is saved on a storage device, it also remains in main memory and is displayed on the screen.

FIGURE 1-25

You may wish to create a folder for each project in this book. If so, click the Create New Folder button in the Save As dialog box (Figure 1-24). When the new folder is displayed, type a project name such as Project01. Double-click the new folder to open it and then click the Save button in the Save As dialog box.

Editing the Photo

Editing, or making corrections and changes to photos, involves a wide variety of tasks such as changing the focus of interest, recoloring portions of the photo, correcting defects, and changing the file type for specific purposes. Table 1-4 on the next page suggests typical categories and types of edits you might perform on photos; there are many others. These edits commonly overlap, and, when performed in combination, they may create new editing varieties. You will learn more about edits as you work through the projects in this book.

Table 1-4 Photo Edits

CATEGORY	TYPES OF EDITS
Resize and Focus	cropping, shrinking, enlarging, slicing, changing the aspect, rotating, leveling, mirroring, collinearity editing
Enhancements and Layering	filters, layers, clones, borders, artwork, text, animation, painting, morphing, ordering, styles, masks, cut aways, selections, depth perception, anti-aliasing, move, warp, shapes, rasterizing
Color	correction, contrast, blending, modes and systems, separations, resolution, screening, levels, ruling, trapping, matching, black and white
Correction	sharpening, red eye, tears, correcting distortion, retouching, reducing noise
File Type	camera raw, print, Web, animated images

Editing always should be performed with design principles in mind. From a design point of view, the parasailing photo would serve the customer better if more emphasis were placed on the parasailers. If you want to emphasize a single object on a fairly solid background, it is important to bring that object closer and trim extraneous space around the object. When movement or motion needs to be portrayed, it is common for designers to place a central object slightly toward one edge of the photo, whereas static photos such as a headshot for a yearbook could display centered. Adding a border or decorative frame around a photo sometimes can be an effective way to highlight or make the photo stand out on the page. Using a border color that complements one of the colors already in the photo, creates a strong, visually connected image.

Editing the parasailing photo to emphasize, to create motion, and to highlight will involve three parts. First, you will zoom in and crop the photo to remove excessive background. Next, you will add a border, smooth its edges, and fill it with color. Finally, you will resize the photo to fit the intended use and size requirements.

More About

Zooming

There are many ways to zoom. You can use the Zoom tool in the toolbox. You can type a magnification in the status bar of the document window or Navigator palette. You can click the Zoom In or Zoom Out button on the Zoom options bar or in the Navigator palette. Or, you can use the shortcut keys CTRL+ and CTRL–. Which way you zoom depends on your personal preference and whether or not you wish to change the current tool while editing.

Zooming

In order to make careful edits in a photo, you sometimes need to change the magnification or **zoom** to a certain portion of the photo. Zooming allows you to focus on certain parts of the photo, such as a specific person in a crowd scene or details in a complicated picture. Magnification is measured by a percentage that is displayed on the document window title bar. A magnification of 100 percent means the photo is displayed in its actual size. Zooming in enlarges the magnification and percentage of the photo; zooming out reduces the magnification.

The **Zoom Tool (Z)** button displays a magnifying glass icon in the Photoshop toolbox. When you use the Zoom tool each click magnifies the image to the next preset percentage and centers the display at the point you click. Right-clicking with the Zoom tool in the photo allows you to choose to zoom in or zoom out on a shortcut menu.

The following steps illustrate how to use the Zoom Tool (Z) button in the toolbox to zoom in on the parasail for careful editing later in the project.

To Use the Zoom Tool (Z)

1

• **Click the Zoom Tool (Z) button in the toolbox. Point to the center of the parasail.**

The mouse pointer changes to a magnifying glass with a plus sign in it (Figure 1-26). The options bar displays choices associated with zooming. Notice the current magnification is 25%.

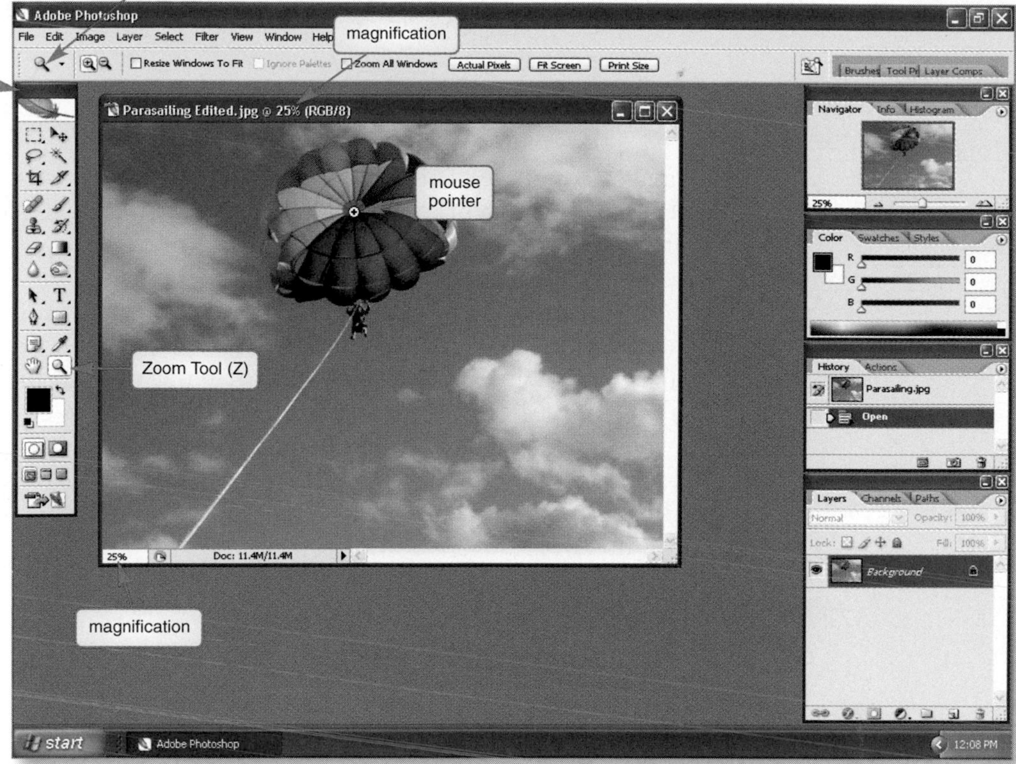

FIGURE 1-26

2

• **Click the parasail.**

The magnification increases to 33.33% (Figure 1-27).

FIGURE 1-27

Other Ways

1. On View menu, click Zoom In
2. On the document window status bar, type percentage in magnification box
3. Press CTRL++

On the options bar, you can cause the Zoom tool to reduce the magnification by clicking the Zoom Out button. In the case of Zoom Out, the mouse pointer displays a magnifying glass with a subtraction sign. Other options include fitting the photo on the screen, displaying the actual pixels, and displaying the photo at its print size.

The Navigator Palette

Another convenient way to zoom and move around the photo is to use the Navigator palette. The **Navigator palette** (Figure 1-28) is used to change the view of your artwork using a thumbnail display. The colored box in the Navigator palette is called the **proxy view area** or **view box**, which outlines the currently viewable area in the window. Dragging the proxy view area changes the portion of the picture that is displayed in the document window. When you click the **palette menu button**, Photoshop displays a menu with choices specific to that palette. In Figure 1-28, the Navigator palette menu displays choices to dock the palette to the menu well and to change the outline color of the proxy view area. In the lower portion of the Navigator palette, you can type in the desired magnification, or you can use the slider or buttons to increase or decrease the magnification. To move the palette, drag its title bar. To change the size of the palette, drag its border.

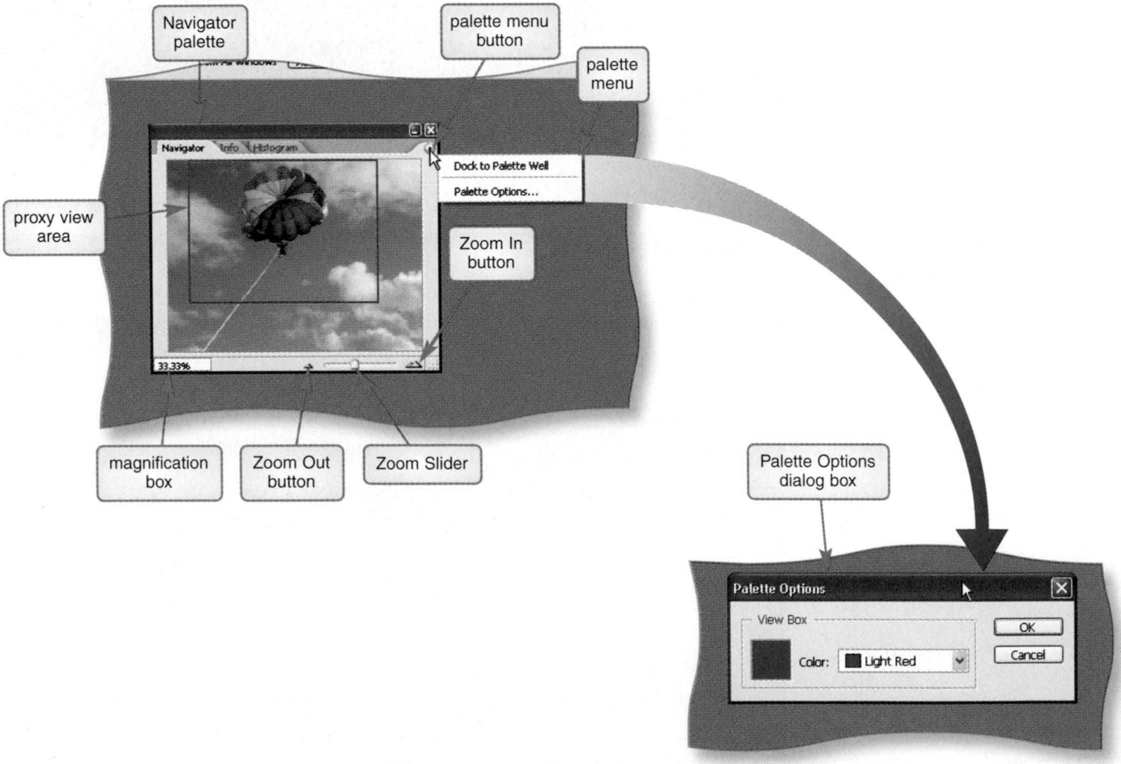

FIGURE 1-28

The following step uses the Navigator palette to position the view in the document window.

To Use the Navigator Palette

1

- **Drag the proxy view area to the top and left.**

The document window displays the reposition (Figure 1-29). When the mouse pointer is positioned over the proxy view area, it displays a hand.

FIGURE 1-29

Other Ways

1. Use scroll bars in document window

When you are using a different tool in the toolbox, such as a text or brush editing tool, it is easier to use the Navigator palette to zoom and move around in the photo. That way, you do not have to change to the Zoom tool, perform the zoom, and then change back to your editing tool.

The Hand tool also can be used to move around in the photo, if the photo has been magnified to be larger than the document window. To use the Hand tool, click the Hand Tool (H) button in the toolbox (Figure 1-29) and then drag in the display area of the document window.

Viewing Rulers

In order to make careful edits in a photo, sometimes it is necessary to use precise measurements, in addition to zooming and navigating. In these cases, changing the Photoshop document window, in order to view the rulers is important. **Rulers** display on the top and left sides of the document window. Rulers help you position images or elements precisely. As you move your mouse over a photo, markers in the ruler display the mouse pointer's position.

The steps on the next page describe how to view the rulers.

To View Rulers

1

- **Click View on the menu bar.**

Photoshop displays the View menu (Figure 1-30).

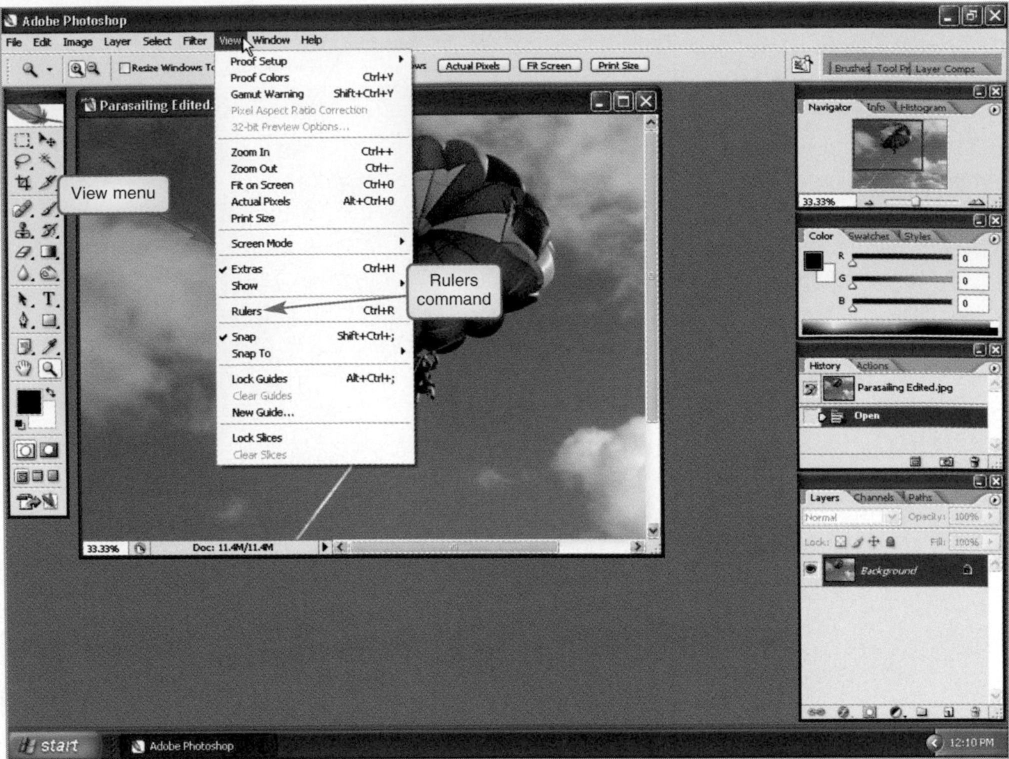

FIGURE 1-30

2

- **Click Rulers.**

Photoshop displays the rulers on the top and left of the document window (Figure 1-31).

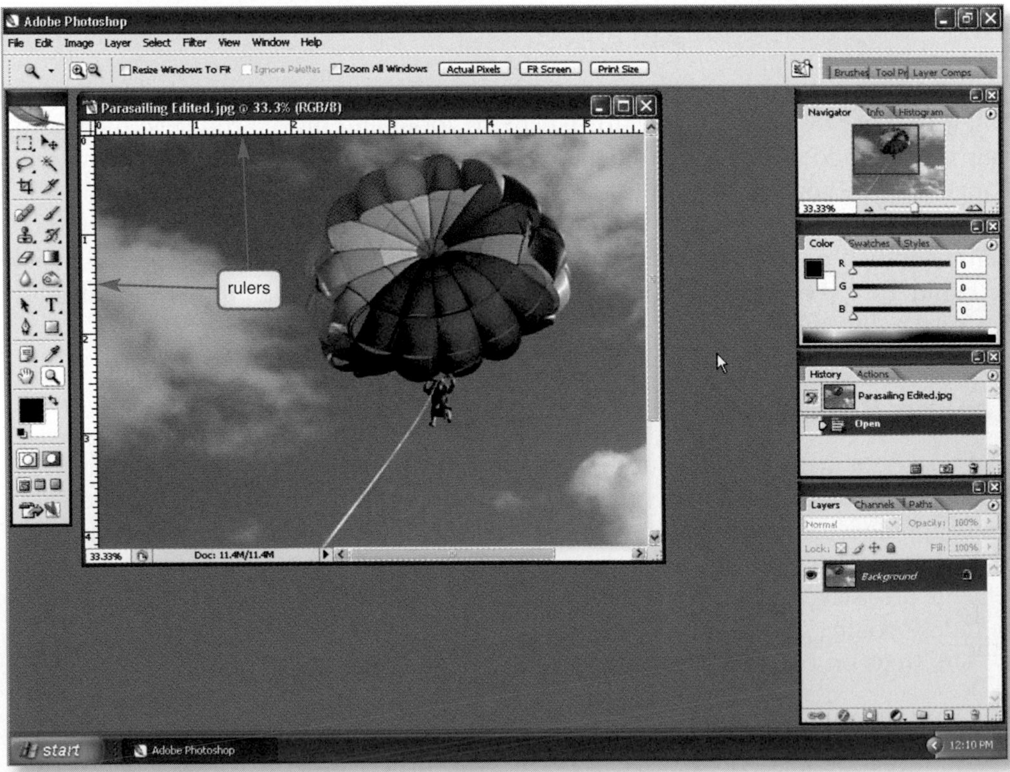

FIGURE 1-31

Other Ways

1. Press CTRL+R

Rulers display inches by default, but you can right-click a ruler to change the measurement to pixels, centimeters, or other measurements. You can drag the mouse from a ruler to any position in the photo to display a **ruler guide**, or green line, which helps you straighten or align objects by providing a visual cue. Ruler guides do not print.

Cropping

The next step in editing the parasailing photo is to **crop** or trim away some of the blue sky so the photo focuses on the parasail and the parasailers. Photographers try to compose and capture images full-frame, which means the object of interest fills the dimensions of the photo. When that is not possible, photographers and graphic artists crop the image either to create an illusion of full-frame, to fit unusual shapes in layouts, or to make the image more dramatic. From a design point of view, sometimes it is necessary to crop a photo to straighten an image, remove distracting elements, or enlarge small portions. The goal of most cropping is to make the most important feature in the original photo stand out. Cropping sometimes is used to convert a digital photo's proportions to those typical for traditional photos.

Many photographers and graphic artists use the **rule of thirds** when placing the focus of interest. Imagine that the scene is divided into thirds both vertically and horizontally. The intersections of these imaginary lines suggest four positions for placing the focus of interest (Figure 1-32). The position you select depends on the subject and how you would like that subject to be presented. For instance, there may be a shadow, path, or line of sight you wish to include; or, in the case of moving objects, you generally should leave space in front of them into which they can move.

More About

Cropping

To evaluate an image for cropping, make a printout. Then cut two "L" shapes from a piece of paper or cardboard, large enough to cover the image you are evaluating. By arranging the L's in various configurations, a size and shape rectangle can be formed to isolate a portion of the image. When you decide how you want to crop, draw straight lines on the printout to use as a guide when cropping in Photoshop.

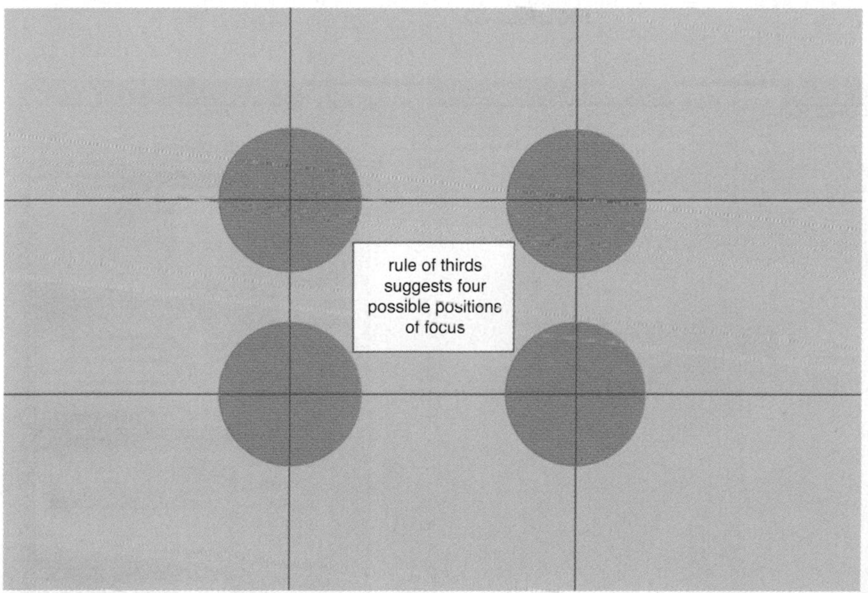

FIGURE 1-32

The steps on the next page demonstrate cropping the photo to place the parasail to the right and slightly above center while still leaving some blue sky on all edges. Using the rule of thirds, the middle of the sail will be centered in the upper-right to emphasize the sail and to indicate motion.

To Crop a Photo

1

- **Click the Crop Tool (C) button in the toolbox.**

The Crop Tool (C) button is selected indicating the active editing tool (Figure 1-33).

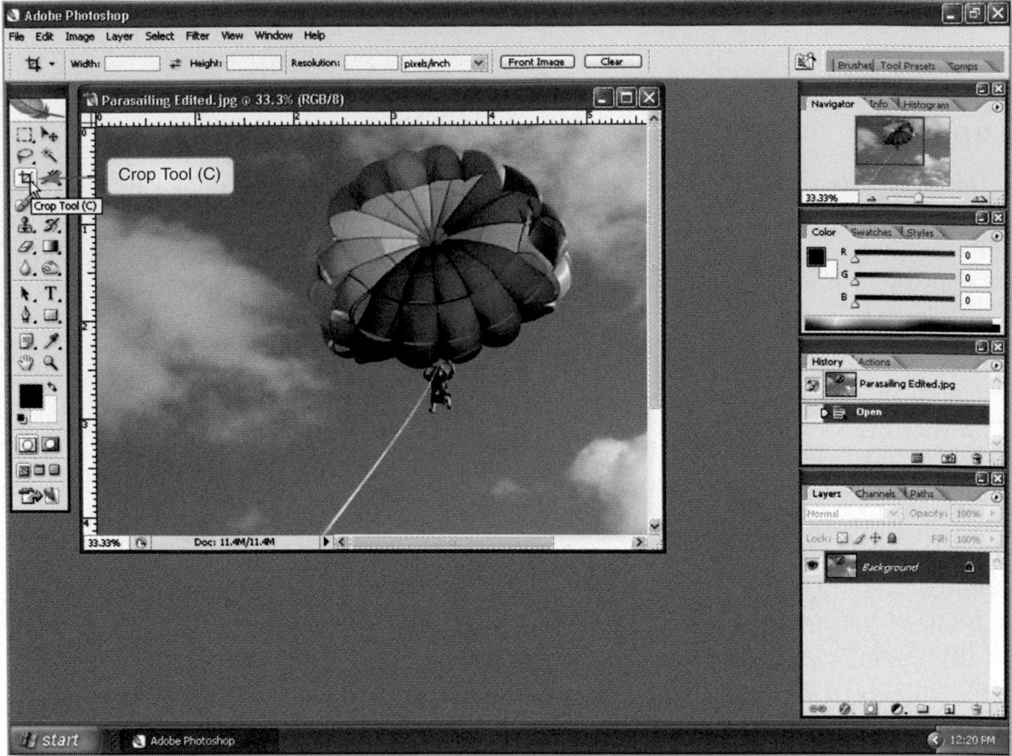

FIGURE 1-33

2

- **Using the rulers as guides, drag a rectangle beginning at the top of the photo, approximately 1 inch from the left edge. Continue dragging right to approximately 5⅛ inches on the horizontal ruler, and down to approximately 3¼ inches on the vertical ruler. Do not release the mouse button.**

Photoshop displays the cropping selection. The mouse pointer changes to a cropping symbol when using the Crop tool (Figure 1-34).

FIGURE 1-34

3

• **Release the mouse button.**

Photoshop displays the area to crop darker than the selection (Figure 1-35). The selection indicator sometimes is called a marquee or marching ants.

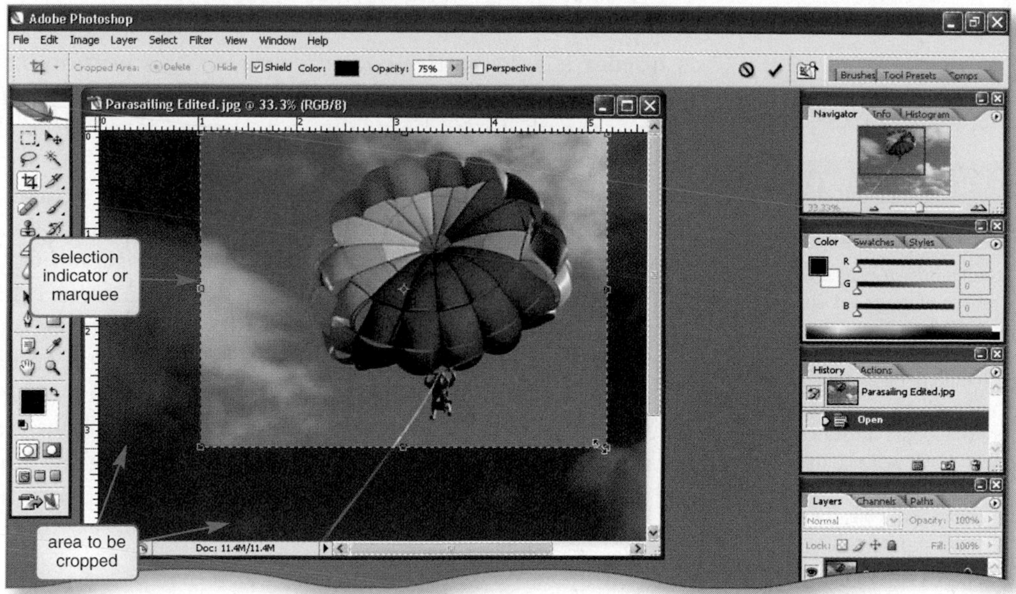

FIGURE 1-35

4

• **Press the ENTER key.**

Photoshop crops the photo (Figure 1-36).

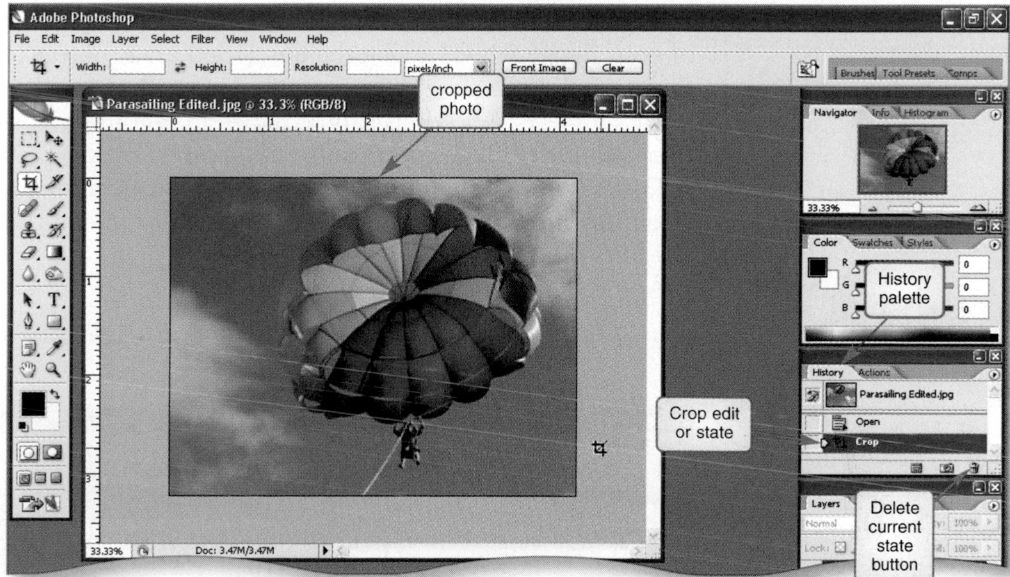

FIGURE 1-36

If you make a mistake while dragging the cropping area and want to start over, you can press the ESC key which cancels the selection.

If you already have performed the crop and change your mind, you have several choices. You can click the **Undo command** on the Edit menu, or you can press CTRL+Z to undo the last edit. Additionally, Photoshop keeps track of all your edits in the **History palette** (Figure 1-36). Each edit or **state** of the photo is recorded sequentially in the History palette. If you want to step back through the edits or go back to a particular state, such as the previous crop, the History palette has a **Delete current state button** that displays a trash can as its icon. If you wish to use it, click the desired state, and then click the Delete current state button. A dialog box will confirm your decision to delete.

Other Ways

1. To crop, right-click cropping selection, click Crop
2. Use Rectangular Marquee tool to select image, on Image menu, click Crop
3. To select Crop tool, press C

Creating a Blended Border

A **border** is a decorative edge on a photo or a portion of a photo. Photoshop provides several ways to create a border, ranging from simple color transformations around the edge of the photo, and predefined decorated layers, to styled photo frames. A border helps define the edge of the photo especially when the photo may be placed on colored paper or on a Web page with a background texture. A border visually separates the photo from the rest of the page. Rounded borders soften the images in a photo. Square borders are more formal. Decorative borders on a static photo can add interest and amusement, but can easily detract from the focus on a busier photo. Blended borders are not a solid fill; they blend a fill color from the outer edge toward the middle. A border that complements the photo in style, color, and juxtaposition is best.

To add a border to the parasailing photo, you first will select pixels along the edge of the image. A **pixel** is an individual dot of light that is the basic unit used to create digital images. After you select pixels along the edges, you then will smooth the corners. Finally, you will blend the color white into the border pixels creating an appropriate frame for the photo.

More About

Resolutions

Resolution refers to the number of pixels per linear inch. Graphic images can be created at a variety of resolutions, depending upon their purpose. Graphics for print purposes usually contain more pixels per inch than graphics intended for the Web. For example, the graphics in this book are 300 pixels per inch. However, images designed for use on the Web always are limited by the resolution of the computer screen. Most computer system monitors have resolutions that vary from 72 to 96 pixels per inch.

Making Selections

Specifying or isolating an area of your photo for editing is called making a **selection**. By selecting specific areas, you can edit and apply special effects to portions of your image while leaving the unselected areas untouched. Selections can be simple shapes such as rectangles or ovals, or unusually shaped areas of a photo outlining specific objects. Selections can be the entire photo or as small a portion as one pixel. Photoshop has many commands to help users make selections. In the case of the parasailing photo, the region you wish to edit by adding a border is the entire photo. The following steps show how to use the Select menu to select all of the photo.

To Select All

1

- **Click Select on the menu bar (Figure 1-37).**

FIGURE 1-37

2

• **Click All on the Select menu.**

Photoshop displays the selection (Figure 1-38).

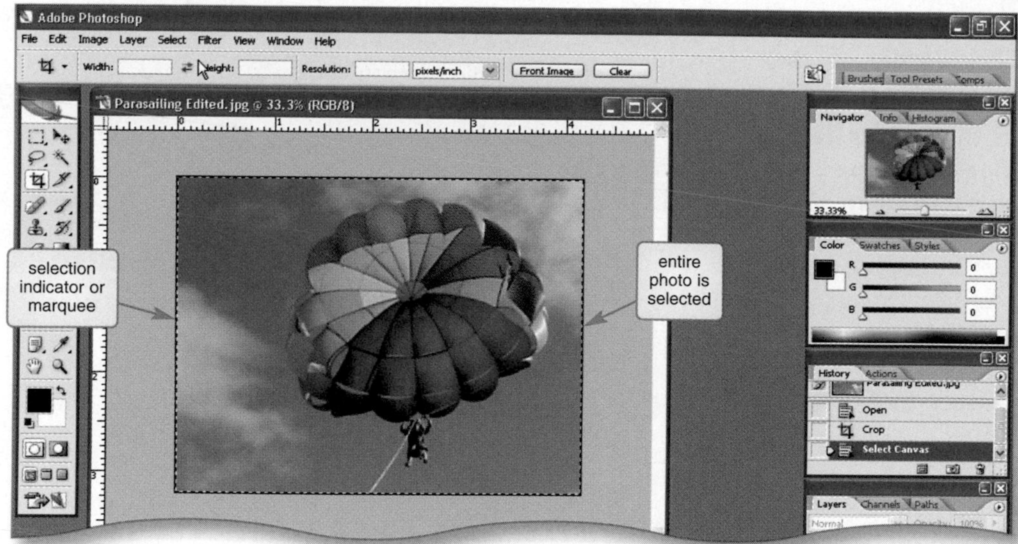

FIGURE 1-38

Other Ways

1. To select all, press CTRL+A
2. To select areas, use selection tools

When you select all, Photoshop displays the photo with a selection around all four edges. The selection tools in the toolbox also can help you make selections in the photo. The Rectangular Marquee, Lasso, and Magic Wand tools will be discussed in Project 2.

Modifying the Border

Selections can be outlined in Photoshop with simple lines or wider borders. When modifying a border, you must identify how many pixels wide the border should be as described in the following steps.

To Modify a Border

1

• **Click Select on the menu bar, and then point to Modify.**

Photoshop displays the Modify submenu (Figure 1-39).

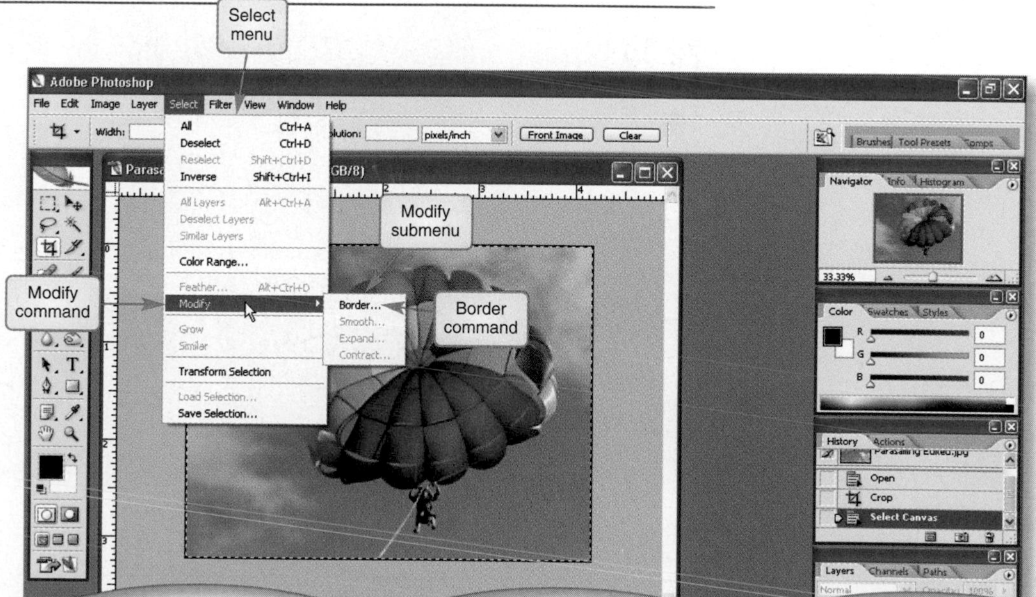

FIGURE 1-39

2

- **Click Border on the Modify submenu.**
- **In the Border Selection dialog box, type** 100 **in the Width box.**

Photoshop displays the Border Selection dialog box (Figure 1-40). Entering 100 pixels will cause the selection to create a border around the edge of the photo.

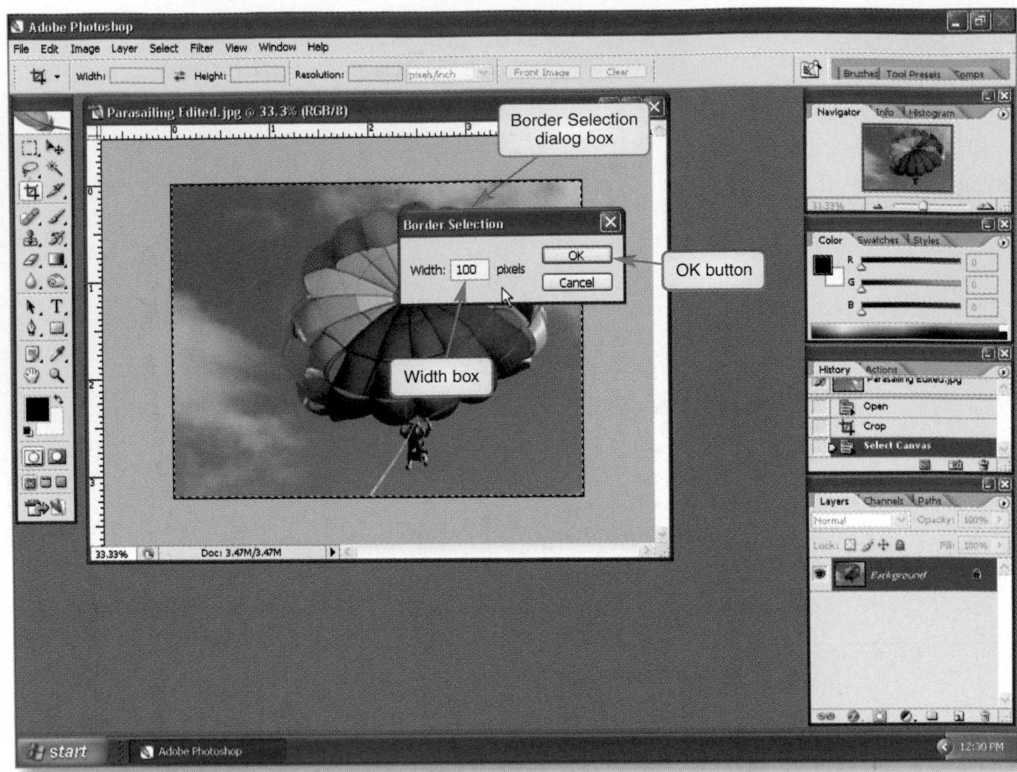

FIGURE 1-40

3

- **Click the OK button in the Border Selection dialog box.**

The selection now contains 100 pixels on each edge (Figure 1-41).

FIGURE 1-41

Smoothing the Border

Smoothing the border adjusts the radius of the pixels at the inner corners of the border and adds them to the selection, resulting in a rounded, rectangular border selection. The following steps illustrate how to smooth the border.

To Smooth the Border

1

- **Click Select on the menu bar, and then point to Modify.**

Photoshop again displays the Modify submenu (Figure 1-42).

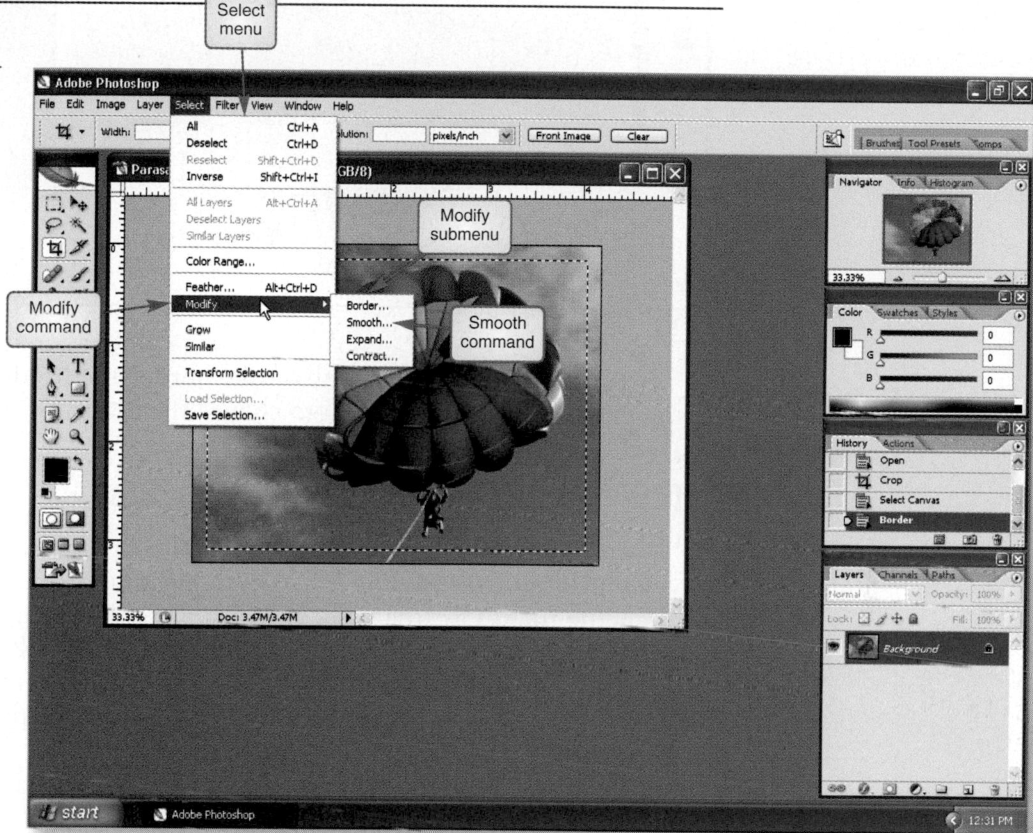

FIGURE 1-42

2

- **Click Smooth on the Modify submenu.**
- **In the Smooth Selection dialog box, type** 50 **in the Sample Radius box.**

Photoshop displays the Smooth Selection dialog box (Figure 1-43). The Sample Radius box accepts a pixel unit of measure.

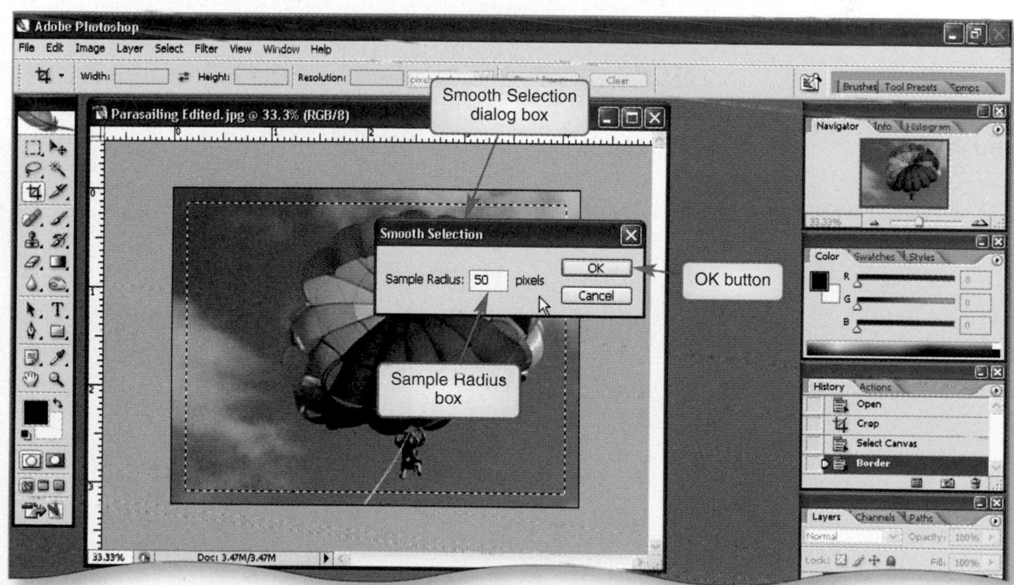

FIGURE 1-43

3

• **Click the OK button in the Smooth dialog box.**

Photoshop adjusts the corners of the selection (Figure 1-44). You may see a progress bar while Photoshop smoothes the corners and selects the border area.

FIGURE 1-44

If you wish to expand or contract the border, the Modify submenu (Figure 1-42 on the previous page) allows you to change the border as little as one pixel at a time.

Filling a Selection

When you **fill** a selection, you **blend** a color or a pattern into the selection area. Photoshop allows you to choose a color, a blending mode, and a percentage of opacity. **Blending modes** are the ways in which pixels in the image are affected by a color. Examples of blending modes include normal, lighten, darken, and other color manipulations. **Opacity** refers to the level at which you can see through the color to reveal the paper or layer beneath it. For example, 1% opacity appears nearly transparent, whereas 100% opacity appears completely opaque.

The following steps fill the border selection with white using a Normal blending mode.

To Fill a Selection

1

• **Click Edit on the menu bar.**

Photoshop displays the Edit menu (Figure 1-45).

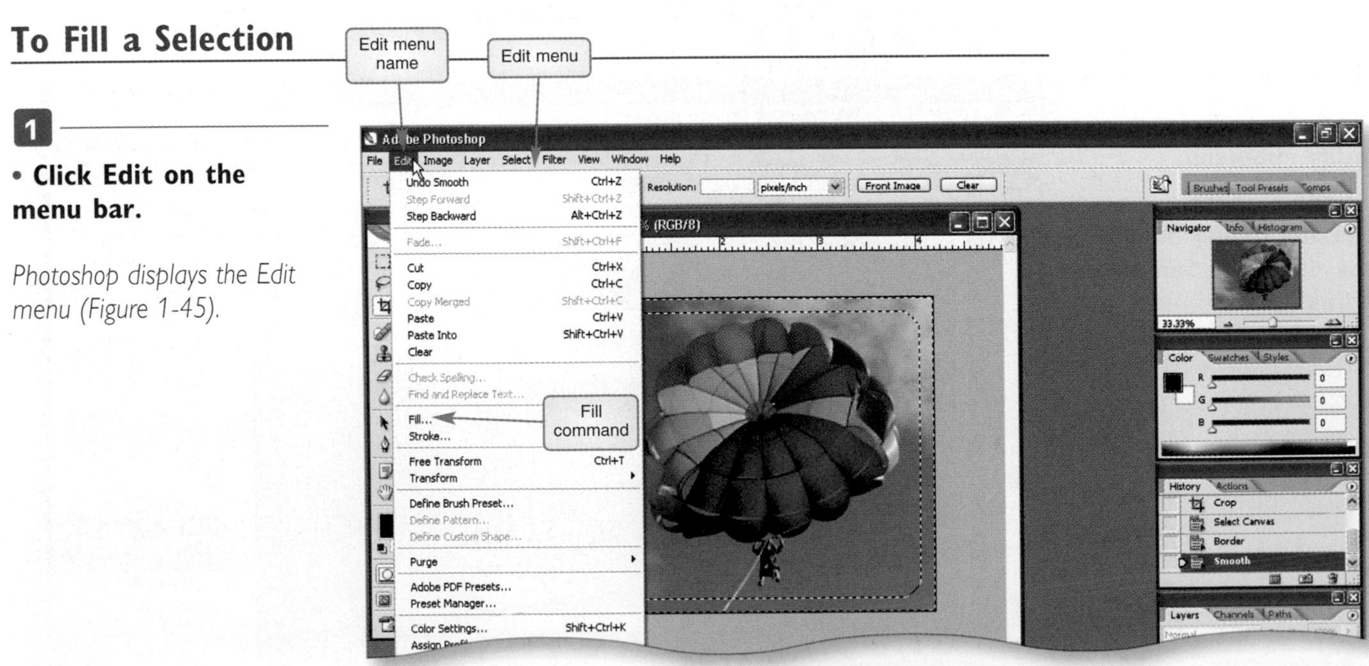

FIGURE 1-45

2

- **Click Fill on the Edit menu.**
- **Click the Use box arrow in the Fill dialog box.**

Photoshop displays the Fill dialog box (Figure 1-46). The Use box allows you to choose colors or patterns to fill the border selection.

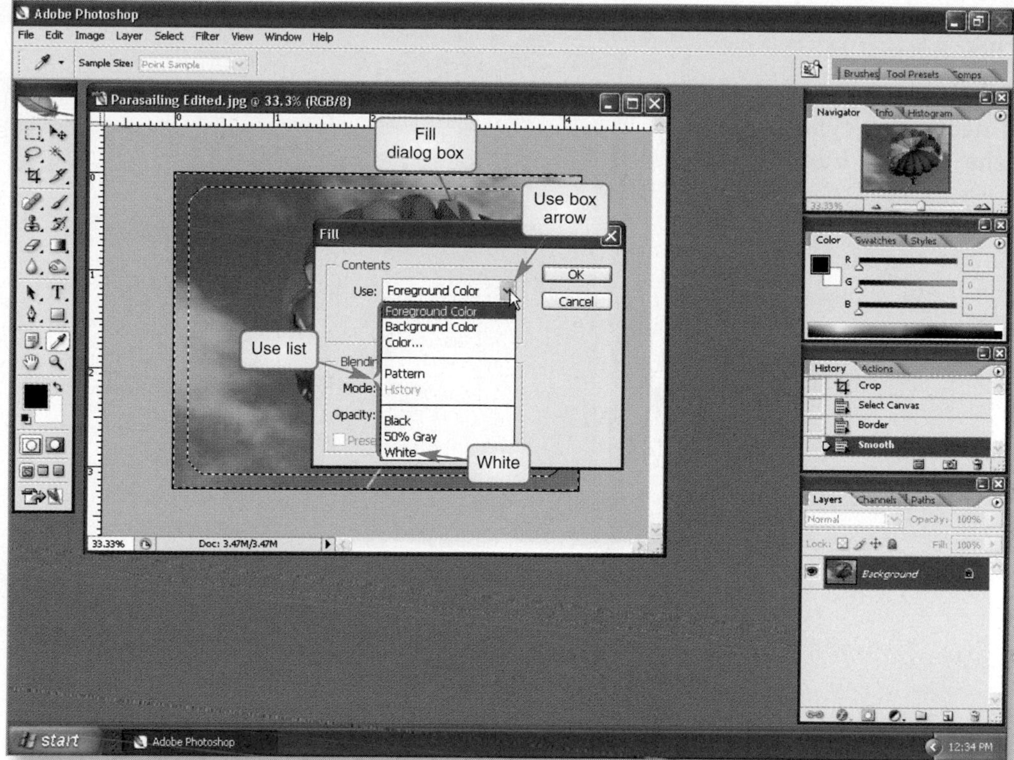

FIGURE 1-46

3

- **Click White in the Use box list.**
- **Click the Mode box arrow.**

The Mode box allows you to choose a blending mode (Figure 1-47).

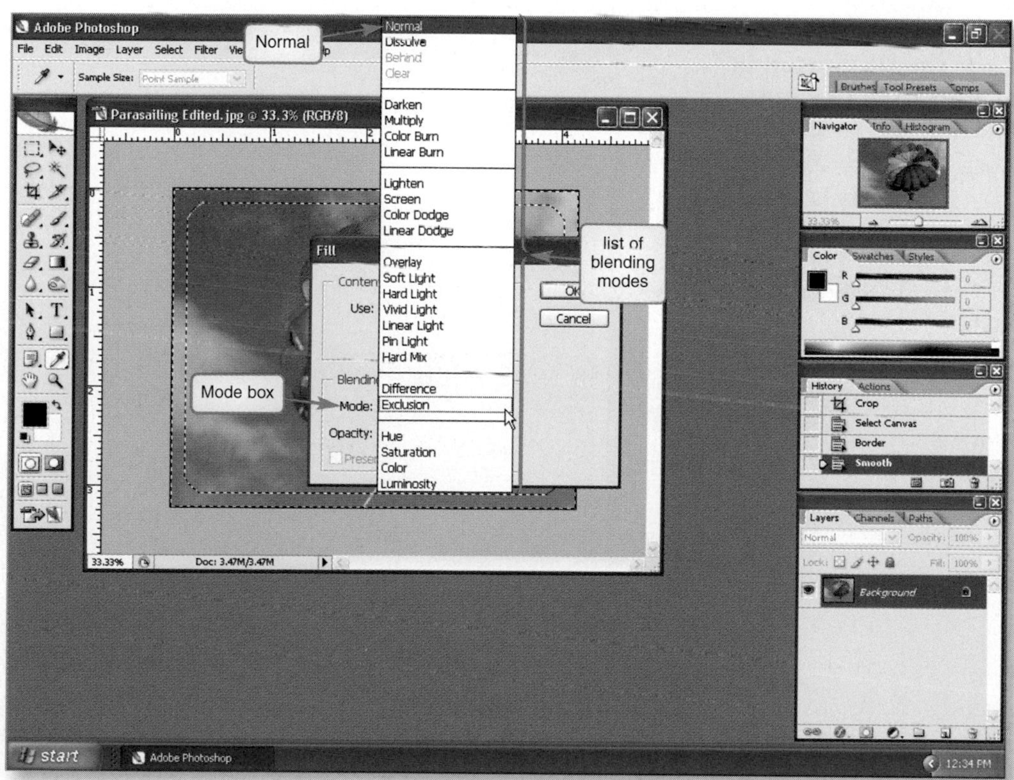

FIGURE 1-47

4

- **Click Normal in the list.**
- **If necessary, type** 100% **in the Opacity box.**

Photoshop will use a white color with a normal blend (Figure 1-48).

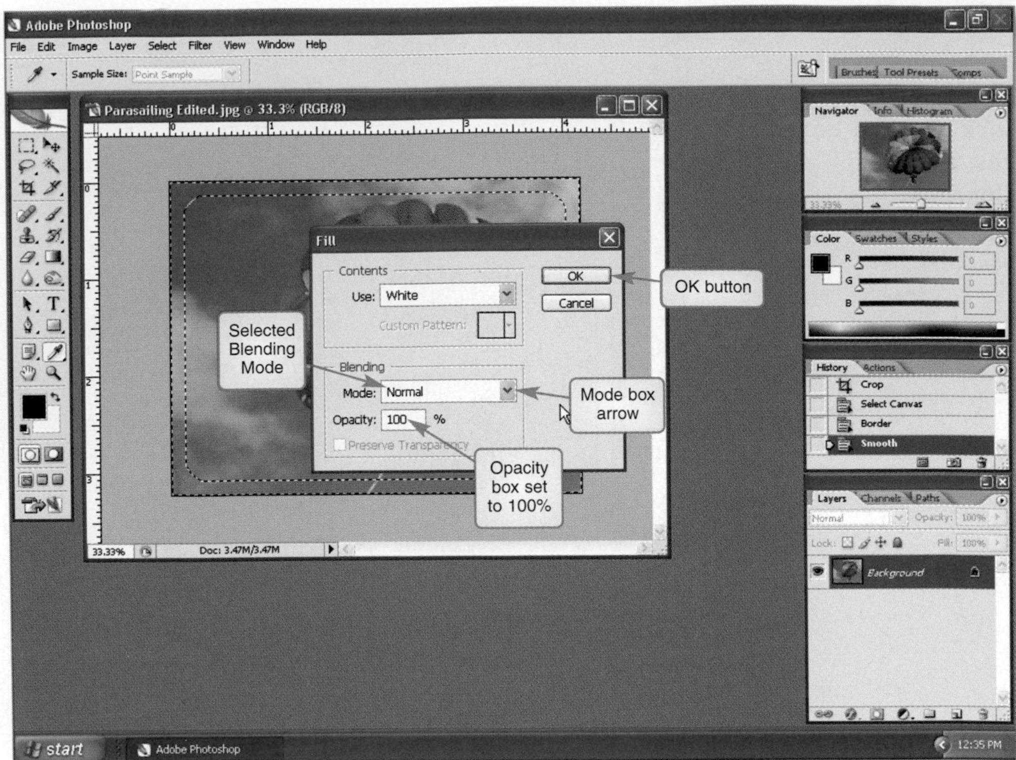

FIGURE 1-48

5

- **Click the OK button in the Fill dialog box.**

A white, blended border with smooth corners is displayed around the photo (Figure 1-49).

FIGURE 1-49

Other Ways

1. To display the Fill dialog box, press SHIFT+F5

Deselecting

When you are done editing a selection, you should remove the selection indicator so it no longer is displayed. To **deselect** a previous selection, click the document window away from the selection as described in the following step.

To Deselect

1

• **Click anywhere in the document window to remove the selection.**

The selection indicator no longer is displayed (Figure 1-50).

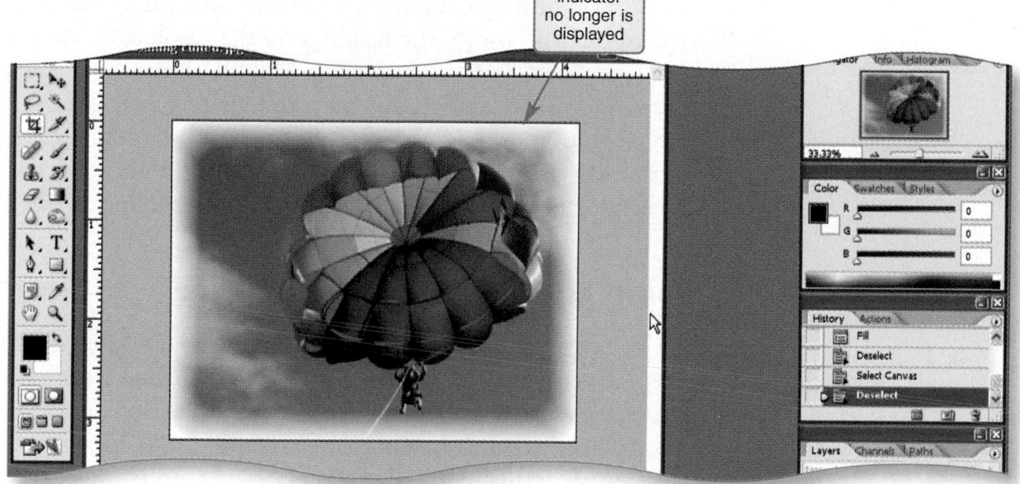

FIGURE 1-50

Other Ways

1. On Select menu, click Deselect
2. Press CTRL+D

Saving a Photo with the Same File Name

Because you have made many edits to the photo, it is a good idea to save the photo again. When you saved the document the first time, you assigned a file name to it (Parasailing Edited). When you use the following procedure, Photoshop automatically assigns the same file name to the photo and it is stored in the same location.

To Save a Photo with the Same File Name

1 **Click File on the menu bar.**

2 **Click Save on the File menu. If Photoshop displays a JPEG Options dialog box, click the OK button.**

Photoshop saves the photo on a USB flash drive using the currently assigned file name, Parasailing Edited.

Changing Image Sizes

Sometimes it is necessary to resize an image to fit within certain space limitations. **Resize** means to scale or change the dimensions of the photo. Zooming in or dragging a corner of the document window to change the size is not the same as actually changing the dimensions of the photo. Resizing in a page layout program, such as Publisher or InDesign, merely stretches the pixels. In Photoshop, resizing means adding or subtracting the number of pixels.

Photoshop uses a mathematical process called **interpolation**, or **resampling**, when it changes the number of pixels. The program interpolates or calculates how to add new pixels to the photo to match those already there. Photoshop samples the pixels and reproduces them to determine where and how to enlarge or reduce the photo.

When you resize a photo, you must take many things into consideration, such as the type of file, the width, the height, and the resolution. **Resolution** refers to the number of pixels per inch, printed on a page. Not all photos lend themselves to resizing. Some file types lose quality and sharpness when resized. Fine details cannot be interpolated from low resolution photos. Resizing works best for small changes where exact dimensions are critical. If possible, it usually is better to take a photo at the highest feasible resolution or rescan the image at a higher resolution rather than resizing it later.

Using the Resize Image Wizard

In those cases where it is impossible to create the photo at the proper size, an interactive wizard in Photoshop helps you scale your photos for print or online media. A **wizard** asks you several basic questions and then, based on your responses, uses various tools to prepare and format a photo for you. The **Resize Image Wizard** asks you whether your photo will be printed or displayed online, the desired size of the photo, and the desired quality. Because the photo will be printed on a rack card of a specific size, you will use the Resize Image Wizard to prepare the photo for printing 4 inches wide. The wizard will ask for a halftone screen value measured in lines per inch (LPI). **Halftone screens** consist of dots that control how much ink is deposited at a specific location. Finally, the wizard will ask for a quality measurement. The Resize Image Wizard creates a new, resized photo in a separate document window. The next steps describe how to use the Resize Image Wizard to create a custom-sized photo for printing.

To Use the Resize Image Wizard

1

- **Click Help on the menu bar.**

Photoshop displays the Help menu (Figure 1-51).

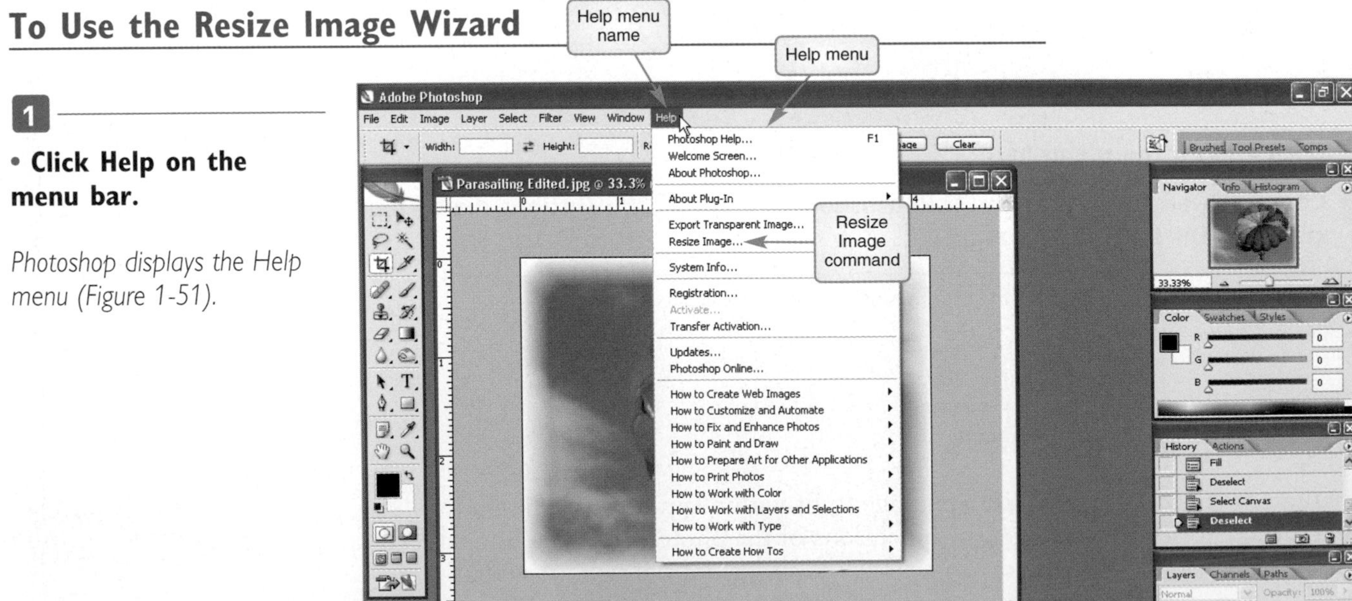

FIGURE 1-51

2

• **Click Resize Image. When the Resize Image Wizard window is displayed, if necessary, click the Print option button.**

The first window of the Resize Image Wizard is displayed (Figure 1-52). The wizard is asking whether the photo will be printed or published online.

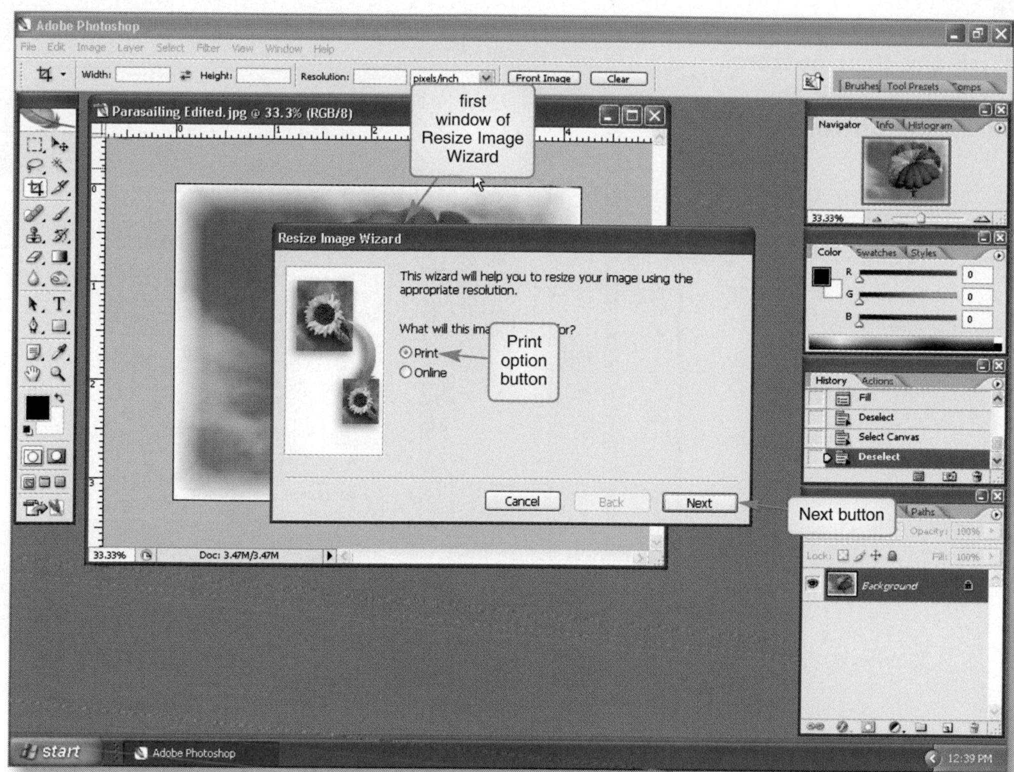

FIGURE 1-52

3

• **Click the Next button. Double-click the value in the Width box and then type** 4 **to replace the previous value.**

The second window of the Resize Image Wizard is displayed (Figure 1-53). The wizard is asking for a specific size. When you enter the width, the height automatically is adjusted to maintain the proportions of the photo. Your exact height may differ slightly depending on how closely you cropped the original photo.

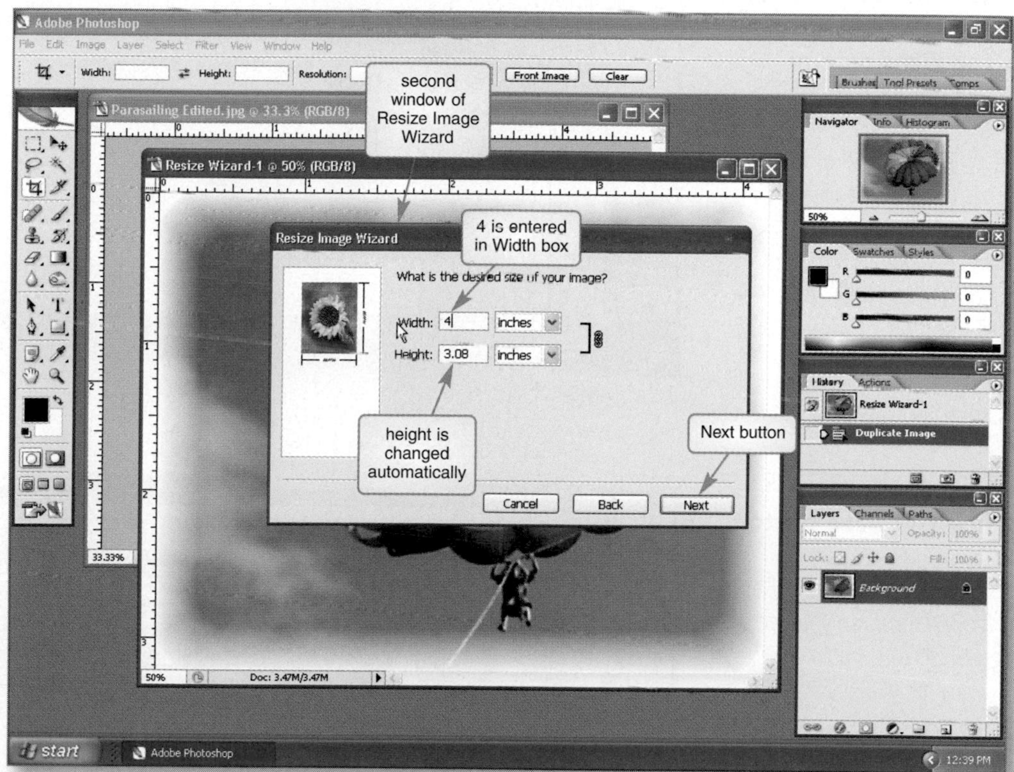

FIGURE 1-53

4

• **Click the Next button. If necessary, click the 150 option button.**

The third window of the Resize Image Wizard is displayed (Figure 1-54). The wizard is asking for a value for halftone screen printing (LPI). When clicked, each value displays a description of its use.

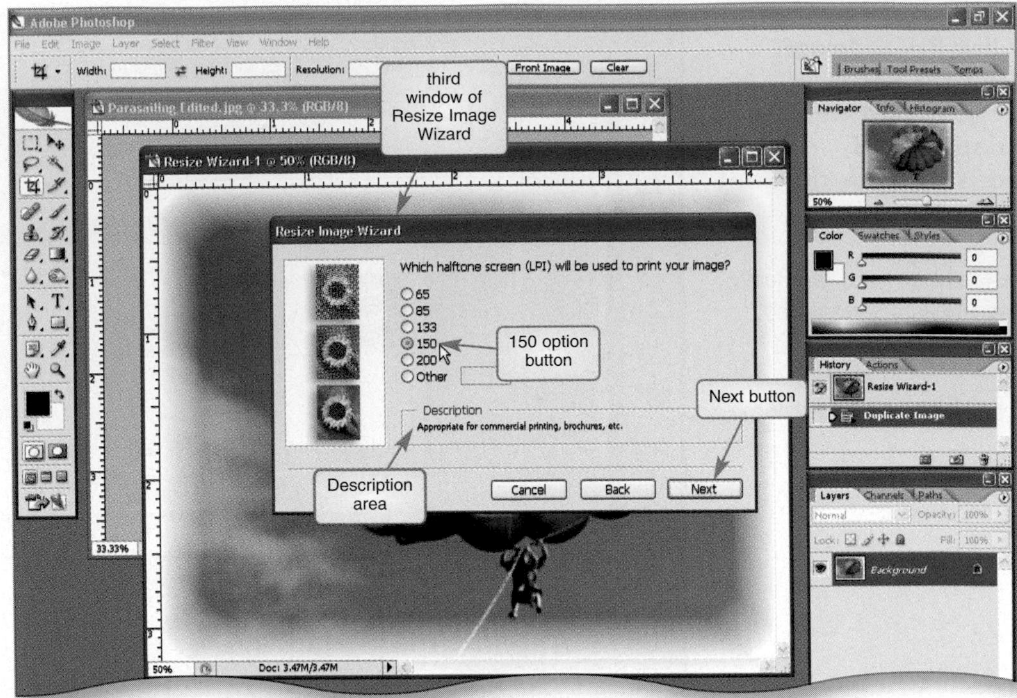

FIGURE 1-54

5

• **Click the Next button. Drag the slider triangle to the right side of the scale.**

The fourth window of the Resize Image Wizard is displayed (Figure 1-55). The wizard is asking about the quality of the photo. A higher quality setting creates a larger file size.

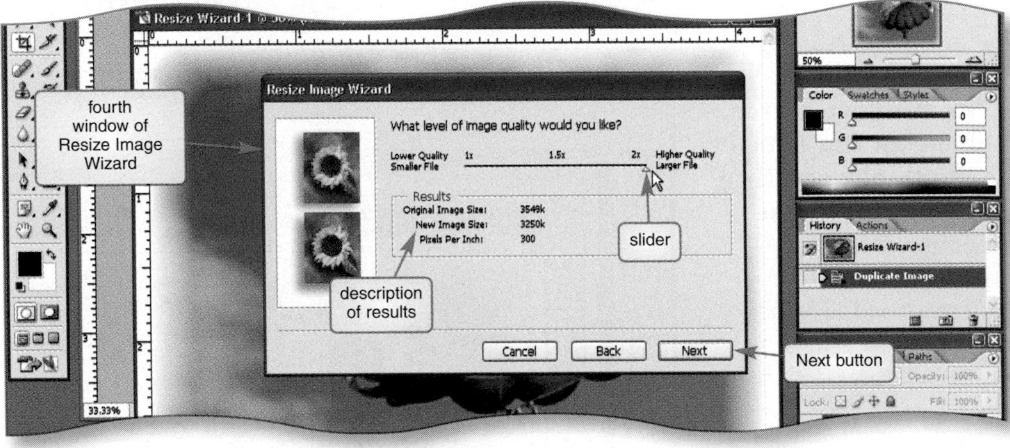

FIGURE 1-55

6

• **Click the Next button.**

The final window of the Resize Image Wizard is displayed (Figure 1-56).

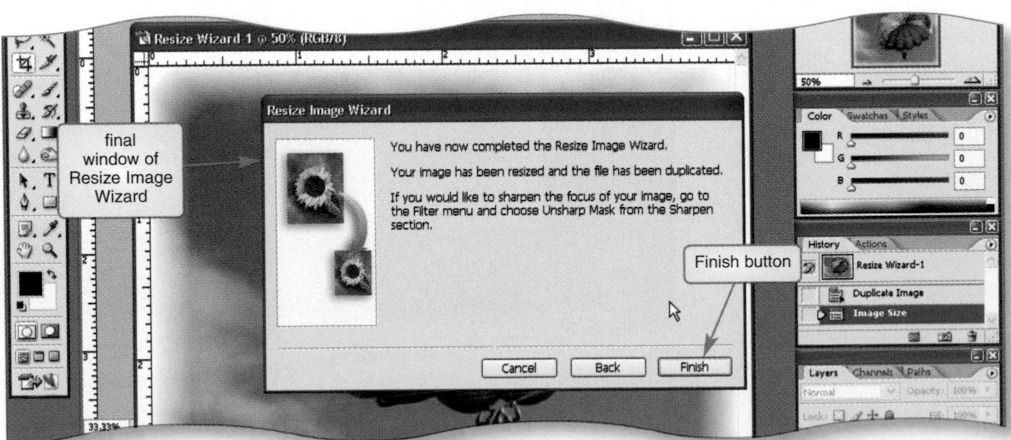

FIGURE 1-56

7

- **Click the Finish button.**

The resized image is displayed in a new window (Figure 1-57).

FIGURE 1-57

Other Ways

1. On Image menu, click Resize, enter width and height

If you choose to resize the image for online publication, the Resize Image Wizard will ask for the width and height in pixels.

When multiple document windows are displayed in the Photoshop work area, the photo in front, with the darker blue title bar, is the **active document window** (Figure 1-57). All edits are performed in the active document window.

The photo now can be printed, saved, taken to a professional print shop, or sent online to a printing service. In this project, you will print the resized photo, save it, and then close it — returning to the original photo to prepare a Web version.

Printing a Photo

The next step is to print a copy of the resized photo. A printed version of the photo is called a hard copy or printout. The steps on the next page show how to print the photo created in this project.

To Print a Photo

1

- **Ready the printer according to the printer instructions.**
- **Click File on the menu bar.**

Photoshop's Print command is available on the menu or by using a shortcut key (Figure 1-58). There is no Print button on the option bar.

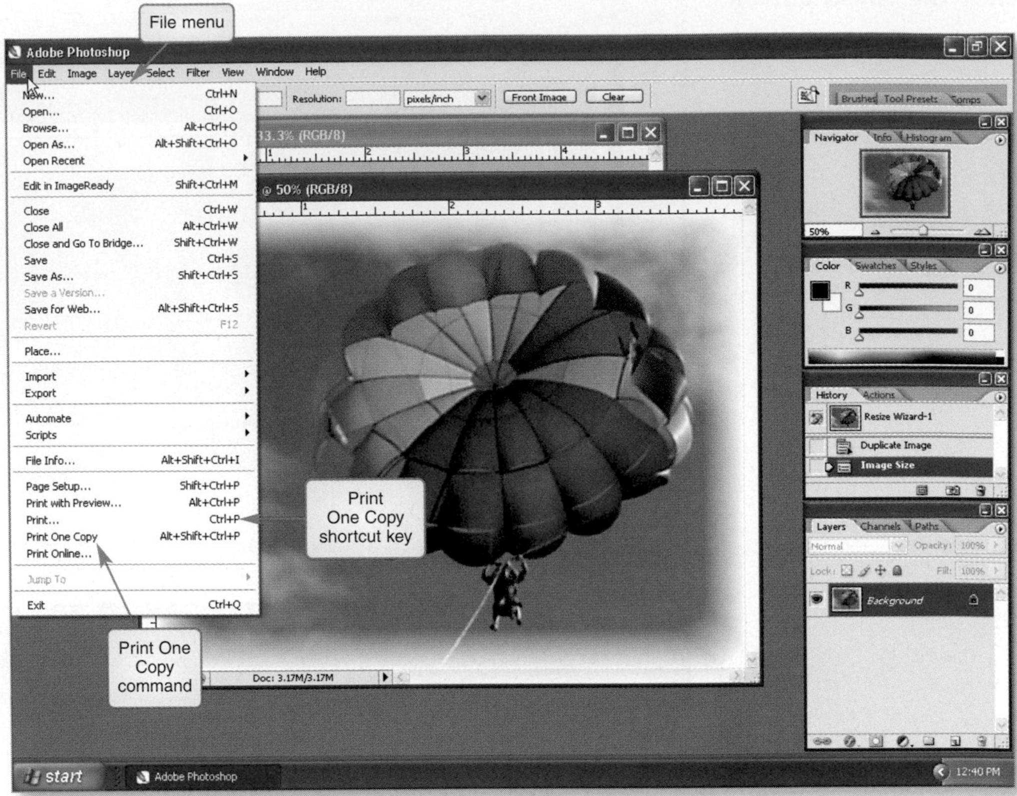

FIGURE 1-58

2

- **Click Print One Copy on the File menu.**

The mouse pointer briefly changes to an hourglass shape as Photoshop prepares to print the photo. While the photo is printing, a printer icon is displayed in the notification area on the Window taskbar as shown in Figure 1-59.

FIGURE 1-59

Other Ways

1. To print one copy, press ALT+SHIFT+CTRL+P
2. To display the Print dialog box, press CTRL+P

When you use the Print One Copy command to print a document, Photoshop prints the photo automatically using preset options. You then may distribute the printout or keep it as a permanent record of the photo.

If you wanted to print multiple copies of the document, display the Print dialog box by clicking File on the menu bar, clicking Print and entering the number of copies you want to print. In addition to the number of copies, the Print dialog box has several printing options. The Page Setup and Print With Preview commands also display options specific to your printer, printer drivers, and operating system with color management options. Print Online allows you to send your print file directly to an online service, if it is available, that will do the printing for you.

Saving the Resized Photo

Many graphic designers will save multiple copies of the same photo with various edits. Because this photo has been resized and optimized for printing, you need to save it with a different name as described in the following steps.

To Save the Resized Photo

1

- **With the Resize Wizard 1 document window active, click File on the menu bar and then click Save As.**

2

- **When Photoshop displays the Save As dialog box, type** `Parasailing for Print` **in the File name box.**
- **If necessary, click the Look in box arrow and then click USBDISK (G:), or the location of your USB flash drive and appropriate folder in the list.**

The photo will save on the USB flash drive (Figure 1-60).

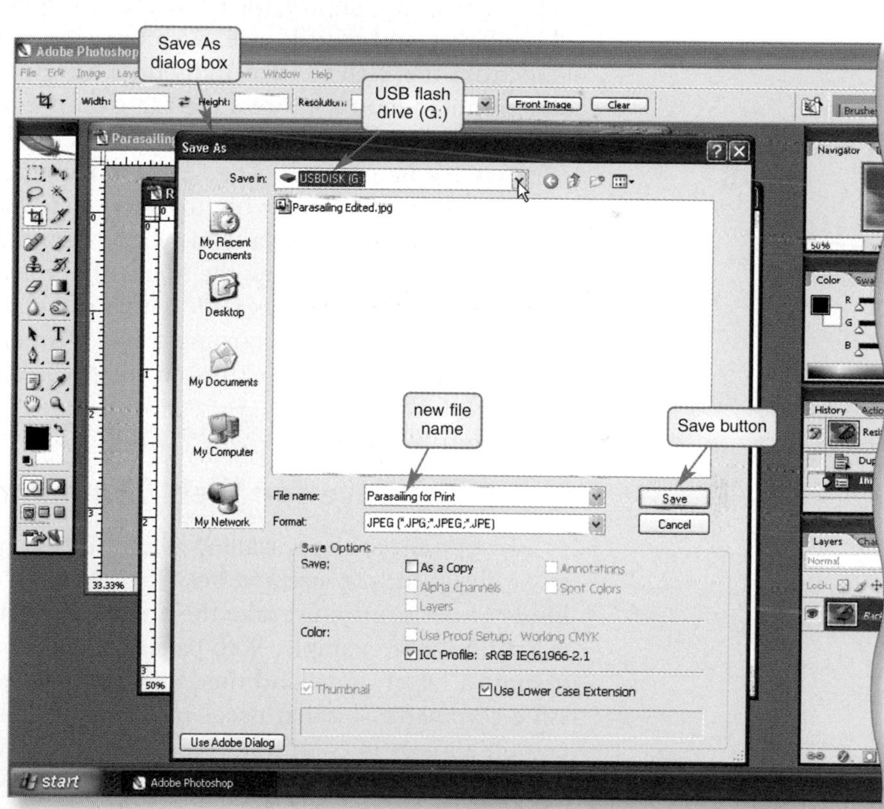

FIGURE 1-60

3

- **Click the Save button.**
- **If Photoshop displays a JPEG Options dialog box, click the OK button without making any further changes.**

The file is saved in the same location with the name Parasailing for Print.

Other Ways

1. Press SHIFT+CTRL+S

Closing a Photo

When you are finished editing a photo, you should close it. Closing a photo helps save system resources. You can close a photo after you have saved it and continue working in Photoshop. Or if something goes wrong, you may want to close the photo entirely and start over.

To Close a Photo

1. **With the Parasailing for Print document window selected, click the Close button in the document window.**
2. **If Photoshop displays a dialog box, click the No button to ignore the changes since the last time you saved the photo.**

Photoshop closes the Parasailing for Print document window.

Other Ways

1. On File menu, click Close
2. Press CTRL+W

Saving a Photo for the Web

When preparing photos for the Web, you often need to compromise between display quality and the file size. Web users do not want to wait while large photos load from the Web to their individual computer systems. Photoshop provides several commands to compress the file size of an image while optimizing its online display quality. **Optimization** is the process of changing the photo to make it most effective for its purpose. The Save for Web command allows you to preview optimized images in different file formats, and with different file attributes, for precise optimization. You simultaneously can view multiple versions of a photo and modify settings as you preview the image. Photoshop allows you to save the photo in a variety of formats such as **GIF**, which is a compressed graphic format designed to minimize file size and electronic transfer time, or as an **HTML** (Hypertext Markup Language) file, which contains all the necessary information to display your photo in a Web browser.

Using the Save for Web Command

To optimize the parasailing photo for use on the Web, you need to make decisions about the file size and how long it might take to load on a Web page. These kinds of decisions must take the audience and the nature of the Web page into consideration. For example, Web pages geared for college campuses probably could assume a faster download time than those who target a wide range of home users. An e-commerce site that needs high-quality photography to sell its product will make certain choices in color and resolution. The hardware and software of Web users also is taken into consideration. For instance, if a Web photo contains more colors than the user's monitor can display, most browsers will **dither**, or approximate, the colors that it cannot display by blending colors that it can. Many other appearance settings play a role in the quality of Web graphics, some of which are subjective in nature. As you become more experienced in Photoshop, you will learn how to make choices about color, texture, and layers, which also play a role in Web pages.

The followings steps describe using the Save for Web command to display previews for four possible Web formats, to choose a connection speed, and to save the photo as a GIF.

To Save for Web

1

- **With the Parasailing Edited photo selected in the work area, click File on the menu bar.**

Photoshop displays the File menu (Figure 1-61).

FIGURE 1-61

2

- **Click Save for Web.**
- **When Photoshop displays the Save For Web dialog box, if necessary, click the 4-Up tab.**
- **Click the Zoom level box arrow.**

Photoshop displays 4 previews — the original photo and three others converted to different resolutions to optimize download times on the Web (Figure 1-62). The Zoom level list displays many magnifications at which to display the previews.

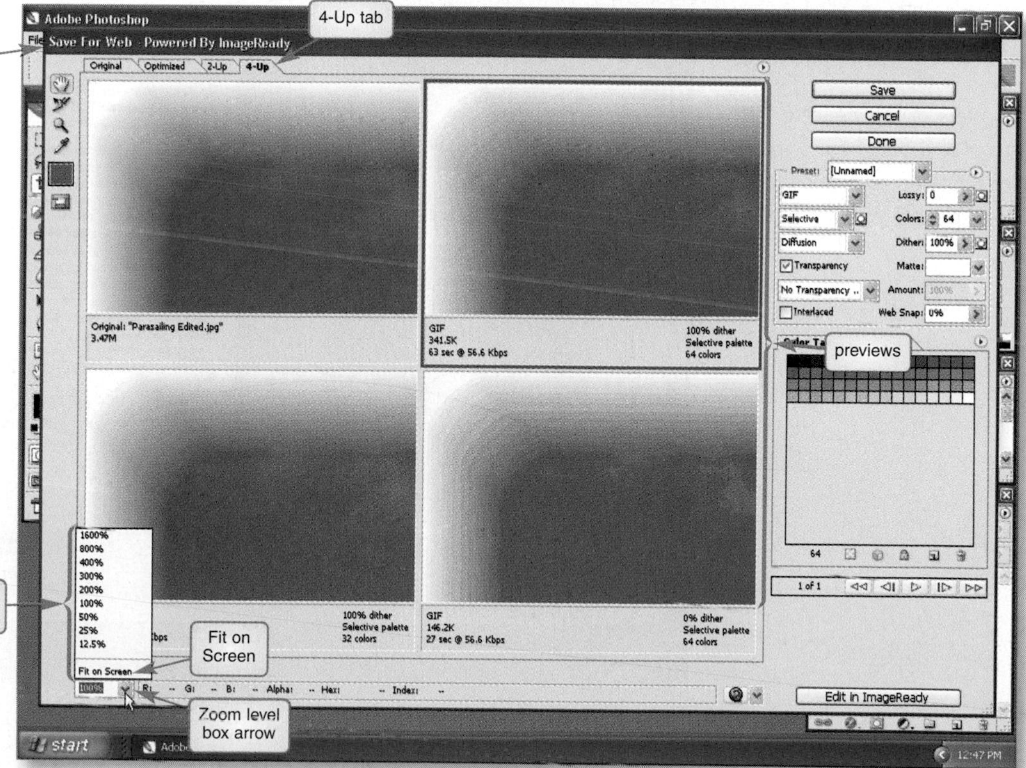

FIGURE 1-62

3

- **Click Fit on Screen in the list.**
- **Click the upper-right preview.**
- **Click the Colors box arrow.**

The previews now display the entire photo (Figure 1-63). Your display may differ. The Colors list displays the number of colors to use for the Web version of the photo. The default file type is GIF.

FIGURE 1-63

4

- **Click 256 in the list.**
- **Right-click the upper-right preview.**

The colors of the preview change and the shortcut menu displays different connection speeds (Figure 1-64). Your list may differ.

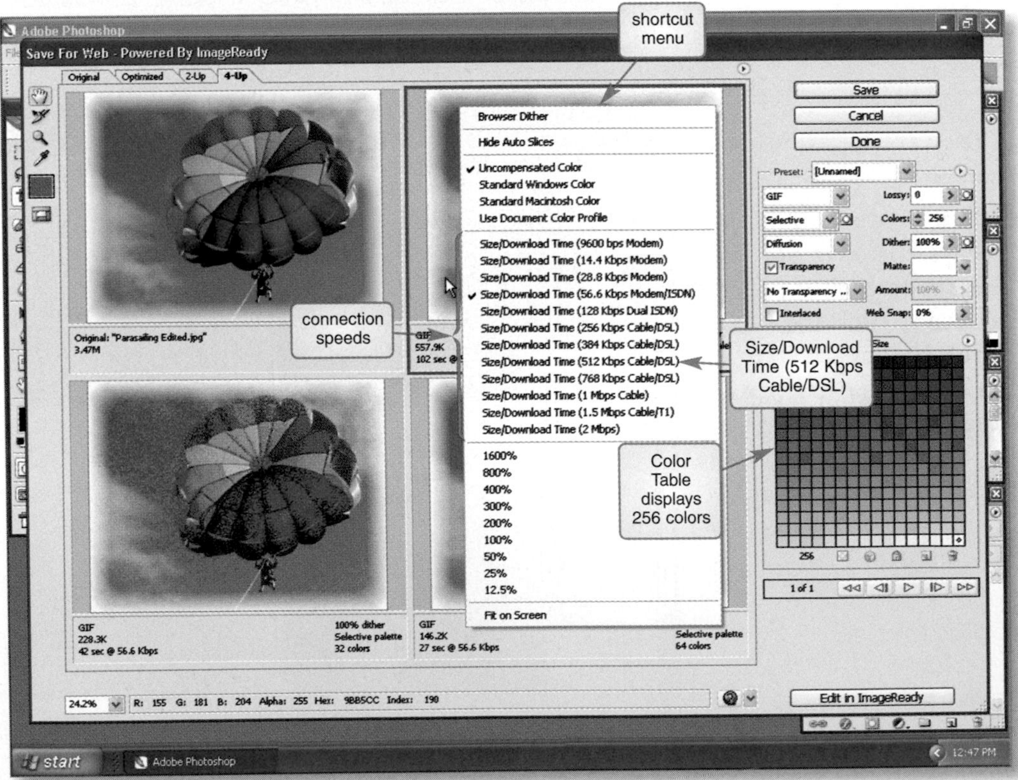

FIGURE 1-64

5

- **Click Size/Download Time (512 Kbsp Cable/DSL) in the list.**
- **Click the Image Size tab on the right in the Save for Web settings.**
- **Double-click the Width box and type** `500` **to replace the width value.**
- **Click the Apply button.**

At 512 kilobytes per second, with a size of 500 x 375 pixels, the upper-right preview will load on the Web in 12 seconds (Figure 1-65). Your load time may differ. The selected preview displays with a blue box. The height automatically adjusts proportionally when you enter a width.

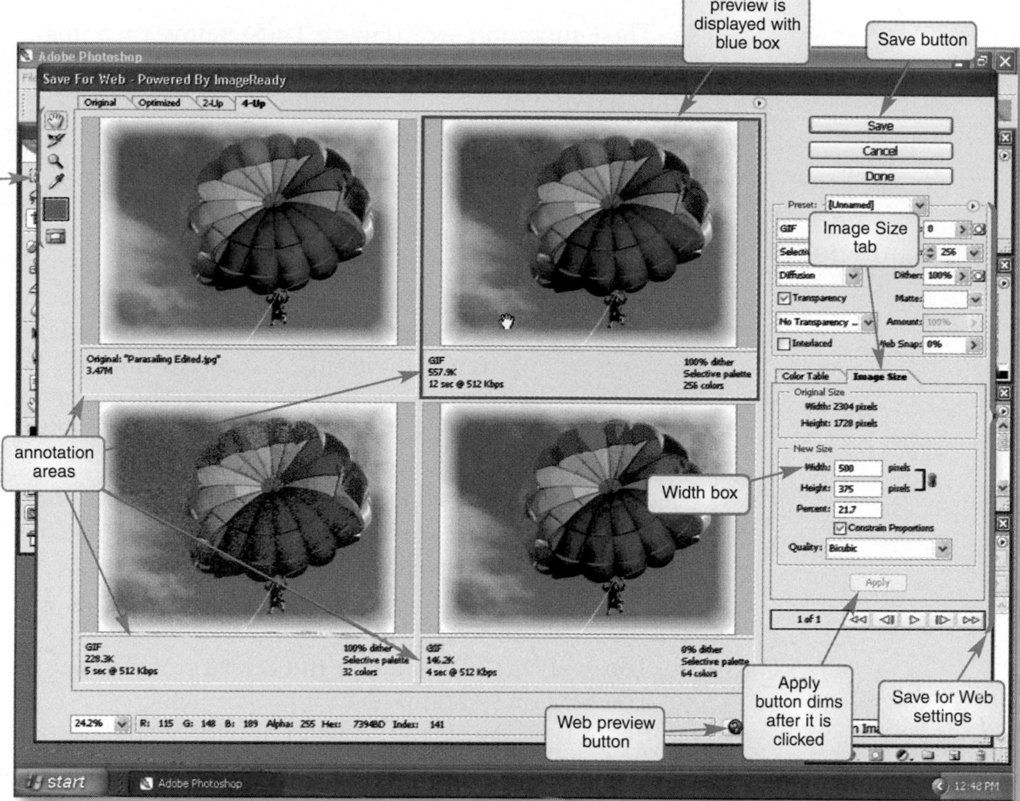

FIGURE 1-65

6

- **Click the Save button.**
- **When the Save Optimized As dialog box is displayed, type** `Parasailing-for-Web` **in the File name box.**
- **If necessary, click the Look in box arrow and then click USBDISK (G:), or the location of your USB flash drive and appropriate folder in the list.**

Photoshop displays the Save Optimized As dialog box (Figure 1-66). Notice that the words in the default file name are hyphenated as is standard for Web graphics.

7

Click the Save button.

The file saves in the specified location. Unlike the resized image, the Web photo does not display in the Photoshop window.

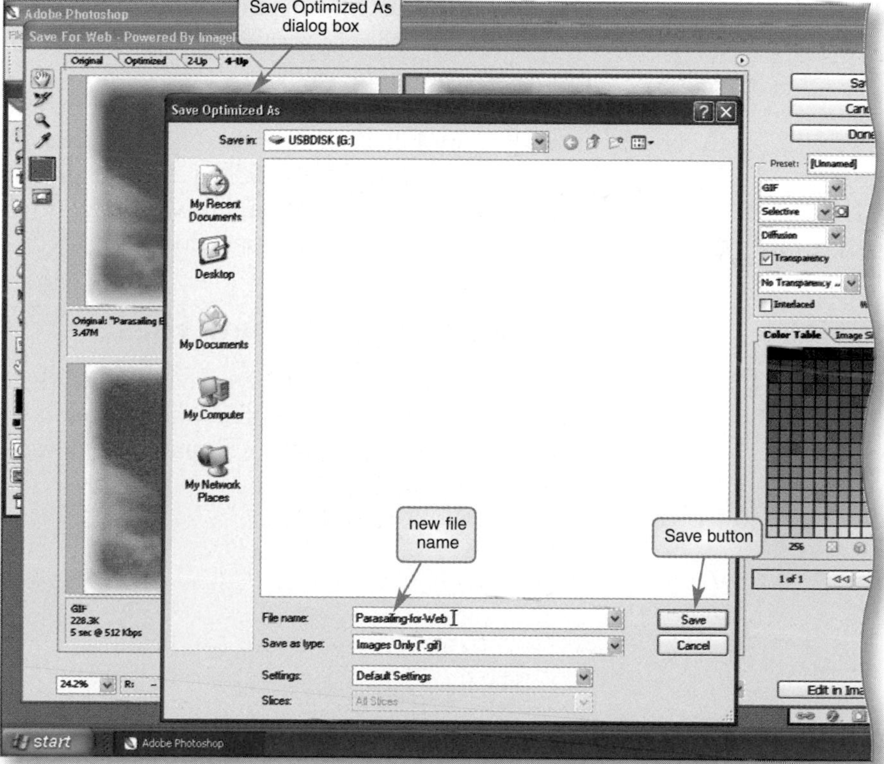

FIGURE 1-66

The annotation area (Figure 1-65) below each image in the Save For Web dialog box provides optimization information such as the size of the optimized file, and the estimated download time using the selected modem speed.

On the left side of the Save For Web dialog box, Photoshop provides several tools to move, zoom, select colors, and slice a portion of the selected preview.

Along the bottom of the Save For Web dialog box are zoom levels, color indicators, and a Web preview button.

If you choose a preview other than the original located on the upper-left, the Save For Web dialog box displays options in the Preset area on the right. The Preset area lets you make changes to the selected preview such as the file type, the number of colors, transparency, dithering, and photo finishes. Fine-tuning theses kinds of optimization settings allows you to balance the image quality and file size.

Below the Preset area are two tabs. The Color Table tab displays the Color Table Panel. Based on the choices you made in the Preset area, the colors used in the selected preview can be locked, deleted, set to transparent, or adjusted for standard Web palettes. The Image Size tab allows you to make changes to the size of the image similar to those changes you made using the Resize Image Wizard. Changing the image size affects all four previews. The settings are not permanent until you click the Save button.

You will learn more about the Preset area and the Color Table tab in Project 4.

The resulting optimized Web photo then can be referenced in HTML code or inserted into a page layout generated with Web development software. The photo must be uploaded to a file server along with the Web page or code.

Adobe Bridge

Adobe **Bridge** is a file exploration tool similar to Windows Explorer. New to Photoshop CS2, Bridge replaces previous file browsing techniques and can be used with any of the software programs in the suite. Using Bridge, you can locate, drag, organize, browse, and standardize color settings across your content for use in print, on the Web, and even on mobile devices. A useful Bridge tool allows you to attach or assign keywords, or **metadata**, used for searching and categorizing photos. Metadata is divided into three categories: file information, image usage, and image creation data. The Bridge interface is explained in detail in Appendix C.

Using Bridge to View Files

So far in this project, you have saved the original parasailing photo, the edited photo, a version for printing, and a version for the Web. The following steps show how to view those files in Thumbnails view.

To Use Bridge to View Files

1

- **Click the Go to Bridge button on the options bar.**
- **When the Desktop - Adobe Bridge window is displayed, click the Location box arrow.**

Adobe Bridge opens in a new window (Figure 1-67). Your location and displayed files may differ.

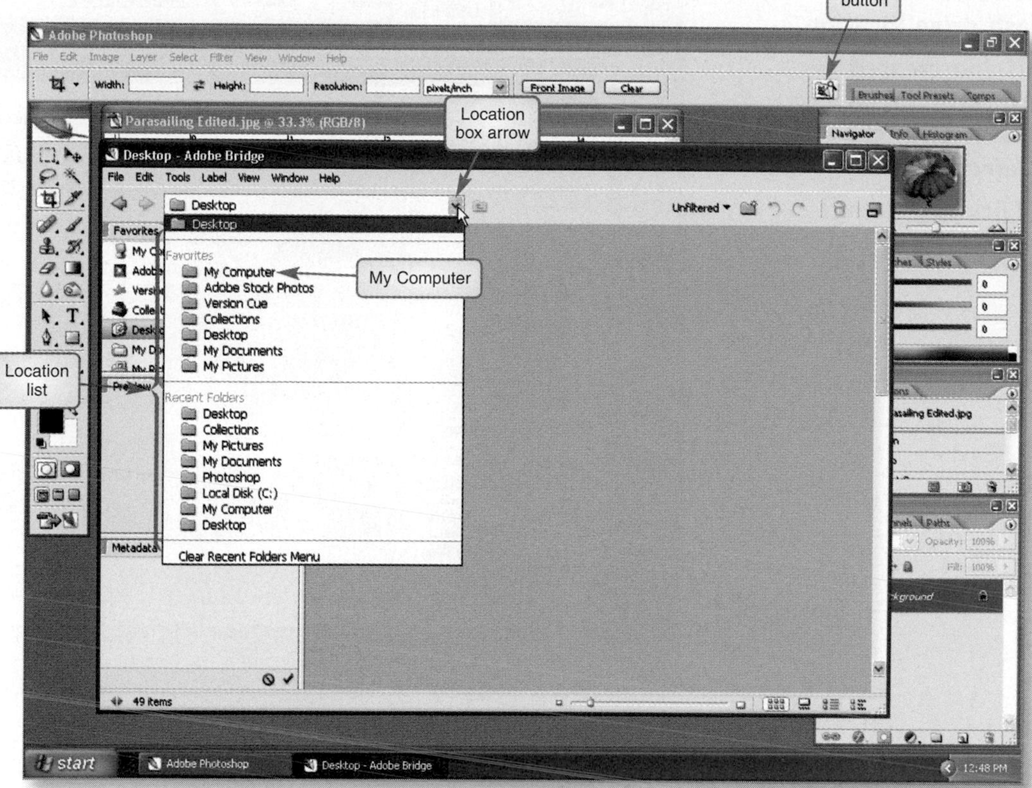

FIGURE 1-67

2

- **Click My Computer in the List.**
- **If necessary, click the Thumbnails view on the Adobe Bridge status bar.**

The storage locations on your system are displayed in Thumbnails view (Figure 1-68).

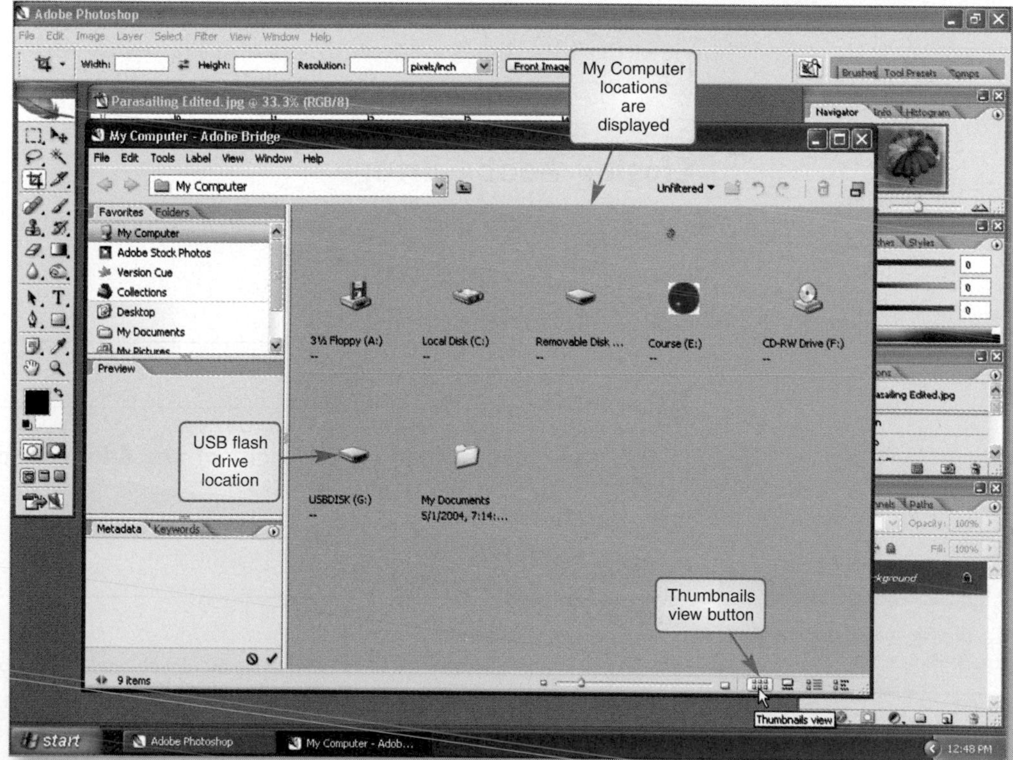

FIGURE 1-68

3

- **Double-click your USB flash drive location.**
- **If you created a Project01 folder, double-click the Project01 folder.**
- **Click the Details view button.**

The files you have saved in the project are displayed in Details view (Figure 1-69).

FIGURE 1-69

Other Ways

1. Click Start button, point to All Programs, click Adobe Bridge

You can use Bridge to organize your photos into folders, set keywords for future searching, or simply to open a file by double-clicking the thumbnail. In Thumbnails view, the files that are currently open in Photoshop display a small, round icon in the lower-right corner of the thumbnail. Bridge is like a database for your photos.

Closing Adobe Bridge

The next step illustrates how to close Adobe Bridge.

To Close Bridge

1

- **Click the Close button on the right of the Adobe Bridge title bar (Figure 1-69).**

Adobe Bridge closes and returns you to Photoshop.

Other Ways

1. On File menu, click Exit
2. Press CTRL+Q

If you are working with multiple photos, or organizing your photos, it may be more convenient to use the Bridge tool to open files. In other cases, use the Open command on the Photoshop File menu if you only want to open a single photo for editing.

Adobe Help Center

At anytime while you are using Photoshop you can get answers to questions through the **Adobe Help Center**. You activate the Adobe Help Center either by clicking Help on the menu bar, by pressing F1, or by choosing Adobe Help Center on your system's Start menu. The Help menu includes commands to display more information about your copy of Photoshop as well as a list of how-to guides for common tasks. Once inside the Adobe Help Center, a wealth of assistance is available including tutorials with detailed instructions accompanied by illustrations.

Used properly, this form of online assistance can increase your productivity and reduce your frustration by minimizing the time you spend learning how to use Photoshop.

The following section shows how to obtain answers to your questions in the Adobe Help Center by using the Type in a word or phrase box. Additional information about using the Adobe Help Center is available in Appendix B.

Using the Type in a Word or Phrase Box

The Type in a word or phrase box, located on the right side of the Adobe Help Center menu bar (Figure 1-71), allows you to type words or phrases about which you want additional information and help, such as cropping or printing images. When you click the Search button, Photoshop responds by displaying a list of topics related to the word or phrase you typed. The following steps show how to use the **Type in a word or phrase box** to obtain information about the toolbox.

To Use the Type in a Word or Phrase Box

1

• **Click Help on the menu bar.**

Photoshop displays the Help menu (Figure 1-70). When clicked, the Photoshop Help command will open the Adobe Help Center in a new window, as will the various How to commands.

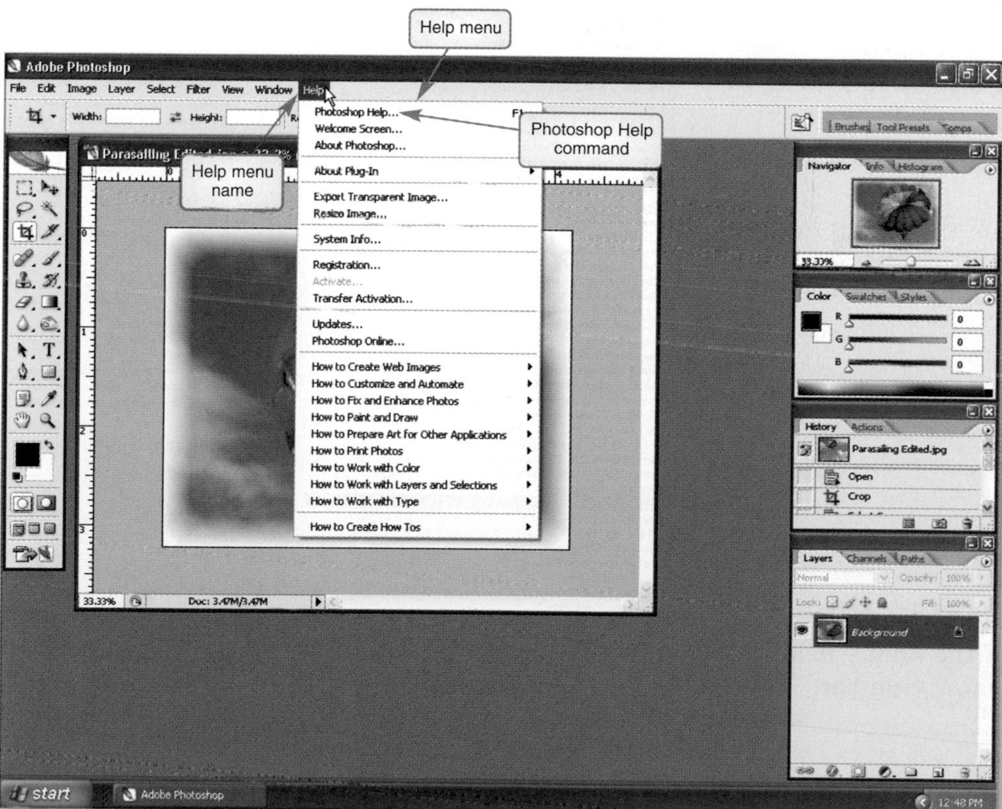

FIGURE 1-70

2

- **Click Photoshop Help.**
- **When the Adobe Help Center window is displayed, double-click its title bar to maximize the window.**
- **Click the Type in a word or phrase box on the right side of the menu bar and then type** `toolbox` **(Figure 1-71).**

The Adobe Help Center window is displayed. Because the Adobe Help Center was activated from Photoshop, Adobe Photoshop CS2 is displayed in the Help for box. The pane on the left displays tabs to navigate by contents (topics), index, or previously stored bookmarks. For more information on the tabs, see Appendix B.

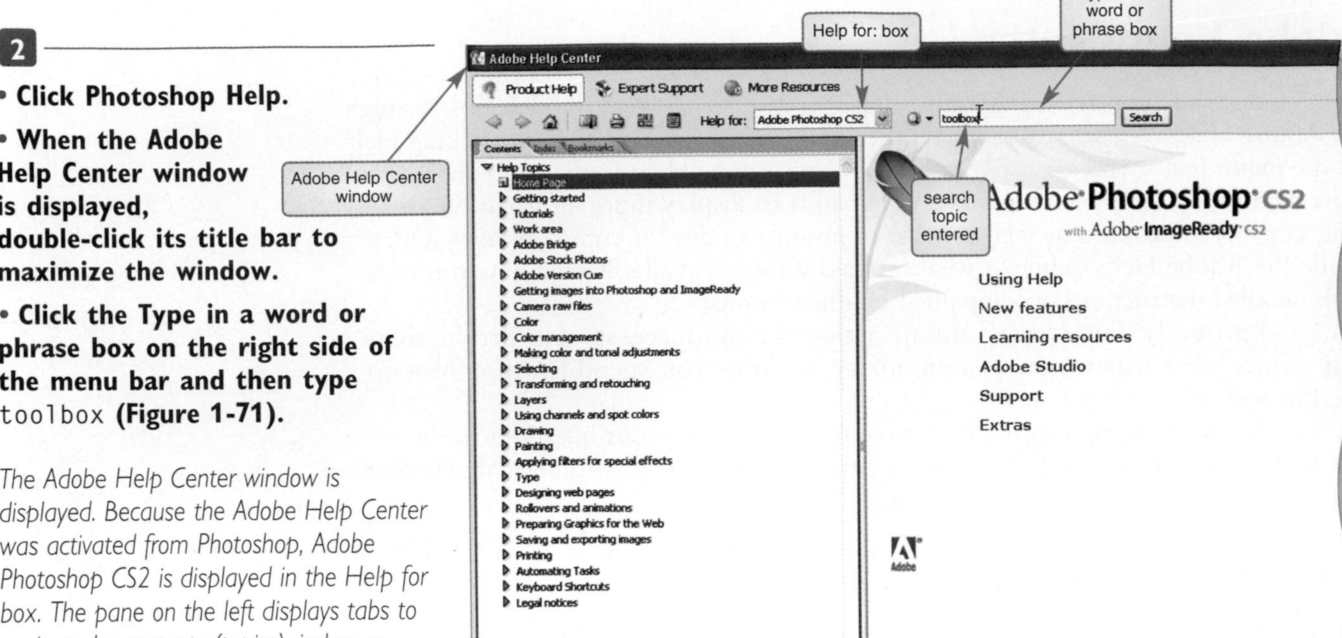

FIGURE 1-71

3

- **Press the ENTER key.**
- **When Photoshop displays the Search Results for pane, scroll to display the topic, To use a tool.**
- **Click To use a tool.**

Photoshop displays the Search Results for task pane with a list of topics related to the word, toolbox (Figure 1-72). When the To use a tool link is clicked, Photoshop displays information about the topic in the main window.

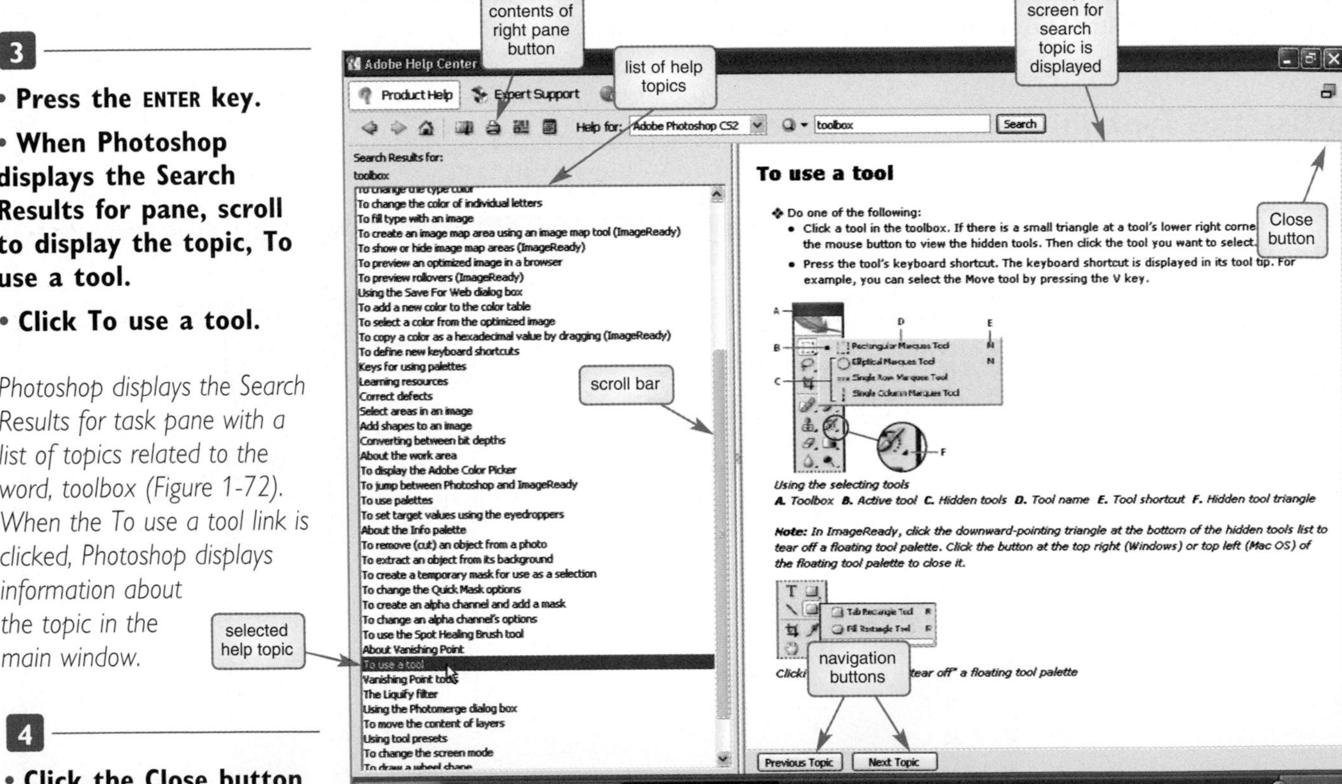

FIGURE 1-72

4

- **Click the Close button on the Adobe Help Center title bar.**

The Adobe Help Center window closes and the Adobe Photoshop window again is active.

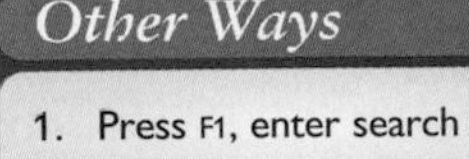

1. Press F1, enter search topic

Use the buttons in the upper-left corner of the Adobe Help Center window (Figure 1-72) to navigate through the Help system, change the display, set bookmarks, or print the contents of the window. To navigate the help topics in order, use the Previous Topic and Next Topic buttons at the bottom of the main window.

Quitting Photoshop

After you create, save, and print the photo, Project 1 is complete. The following steps show how to quit Photoshop and return control to Windows.

To Quit Photoshop

1

- **Point to the Close button on the right side of the Photoshop title bar (Figure 1-73).**

2

- **Click the Close button.**
- **If Photoshop displays a dialog box asking you to save changes, click the No button.**

The Photoshop window closes.

FIGURE 1-73

Other Ways

1. On File menu, click Exit
2. Press CTRL+Q

When you quit Photoshop, a dialog box may display asking if you want to save the changes. This occurs if you make changes to the photo since the last save. Clicking the Yes button in the dialog box saves the changes; clicking the No button ignores the changes; and clicking the Cancel button returns to the photo. If you did not make any changes since you saved the photo, this dialog box usually is not displayed.

Project Summary

In editing the parasailing photo in this project, you gained a broad knowledge of Photoshop. First, you were introduced to starting Photoshop. You learned about the Photoshop window. You learned how to open a photo and zoom in. You learned about design issues related to the placement of points of interest. You then learned how to crop a photo to eliminate extraneous background. After you added a border, you resized the image for printing.

Once you saved the photo, you learned how to print it. You used the Save for Web command to optimize and save a Web version. You learned how to use Adobe Bridge to view files, and the Adobe Help Center to research specific help topics. Finally, you learned how to quit Photoshop.

What You Should Know

Having completed this project, you should be able to perform the tasks below. The tasks are listed in the same order they were presented in this project. For a list of the buttons, menus, toolbars, and other commands introduced in this project, see the Quick Reference Summary at the back of this book and refer to the Page Number column.

1. Start Photoshop (PS 6)
2. Customize the Photoshop Window (PS 8)
3. Open a Photo (PS 11)
4. Save a Photo (PS 21)
5. Use the Zoom Tool (PS 25)
6. Use the Navigator Palette (PS 27)
7. View Rulers (PS 28)
8. Crop a Photo (PS 30)
9. Select All (PS 32)
10. Modify a Border (PS 33)
11. Smooth the Border (PS 35)
12. Fill a Selection (PS 36)
13. Deselect (PS 39)
14. Save a Photo with the Same File Name (PS 39)
15. Use the Resize Image Wizard (PS 40)
16. Print a Photo (PS 44)
17. Save the Resized Photo (PS 45)
18. Close a Photo (PS 46)
19. Save for Web (PS 47)
20. Use Bridge to View Files (PS 51)
21. Close Bridge (PS 52)
22. Use the Type in a Word or Phrase Box (PS 53)
23. Quit Photoshop (PS 55)

Learn It Online

Instructions: To complete the Learn It Online exercises, start your browser, click the Address bar, and then enter the Web address `scsite.com/photoshop/learn`. When the Photoshop CS2 Learn It Online page is displayed, follow the instructions in the exercises below. Each exercise has instructions for printing your results, either for your own records or for submission to your instructor.

1 Project Reinforcement TF, MC, and SA

Below Photoshop Project 1, click the Project Reinforcement link. Print the quiz by clicking Print on the File menu for each page. Answer each question.

2 Flash Cards

Below Photoshop Project 1, click the Flash Cards link and read the instructions. Type 20 (or a number specified by your instructor) in the Number of playing cards text box, type your name in the Enter your Name text box, and then click the Flip Card button. When the flash card is displayed, read the question and then click the ANSWER box arrow to select an answer. Flip through Flash Cards. If your score is 15 (75%) correct or greater, click Print on the File menu to print your results. If your score is less than 15 (75%) correct, then redo this exercise by clicking the Replay button.

3 Practice Test

Below Photoshop Project 1, click the Practice Test link. Answer each question, enter your first and last name at the bottom of the page, and then click the Grade Test button. When the graded practice test is displayed on your screen, click Print on the File menu to print a hard copy. Continue to take practice tests until you score 80% or better.

4 Who Wants To Be a Computer Genius?

Below Photoshop Project 1, click the Computer Genius link. Read the instructions, enter your first and last name at the bottom of the page, and then click the PLAY button. When your score is displayed, click the PRINT RESULTS link to print a hard copy.

5 Wheel of Terms

Below Photoshop Project 1, click the Wheel of Terms link. Read the instructions, and then enter your first and last name and your school name. Click the PLAY button. When your score is displayed, right-click the score and then click Print on the shortcut menu to print a hard copy.

6 Crossword Puzzle Challenge

Below Photoshop Project 1, click the Crossword Puzzle Challenge link. Read the instructions, and then enter your first and last name. Click the SUBMIT button. Work the crossword puzzle. When you are finished, click the Submit button. When the crossword puzzle is redisplayed, click the Print Puzzle button to print a hard copy.

7 Tips and Tricks

Below Photoshop Project 1, click the Tips and Tricks link. Click a topic that pertains to Project 1. Right-click the information and then click Print on the shortcut menu. Construct a brief example of what the information relates to in Photoshop to confirm you understand how to use the tip or trick.

8 Expanding Your Horizons

Below Photoshop Project 1, click the Expanding Your Horizons link. Click a topic that pertains to Project 1. Print the information. Construct a brief example of what the information relates to in Photoshop to confirm you understand the contents of the article.

9 Search Sleuth

Below Photoshop Project 1, click the Search Sleuth link. To search for a term that pertains to this project, select a term below the Project 1 title and then use the Google search engine at google.com (or any major search engine) to display and print two Web pages that present information on the term.

10 Photoshop Online Training

Below Photoshop Project 1, click the Photoshop Online Training link. When your browser displays the Web page, click one of the Photoshop tutorials that covers one or more of the objectives listed at the beginning of the project on page PS 4. Print the first page of the tutorial before stepping through it.

Apply Your Knowledge

1 Editing and Printing a Photo

Instructions: The following steps start Photoshop, reset the display toolbox and tool settings, and then open a photo. The photo required for this project can be found on the CD that accompanies this book in the Project01 folder, or in a location specified by your instructor.

The photo you open is a picture of Black-Eyed Susan flowers with a honeybee. You are to edit the photo to focus on the honeybee and save it so it looks like Figure 1-74. You will prepare both a print and Web version of the photo.

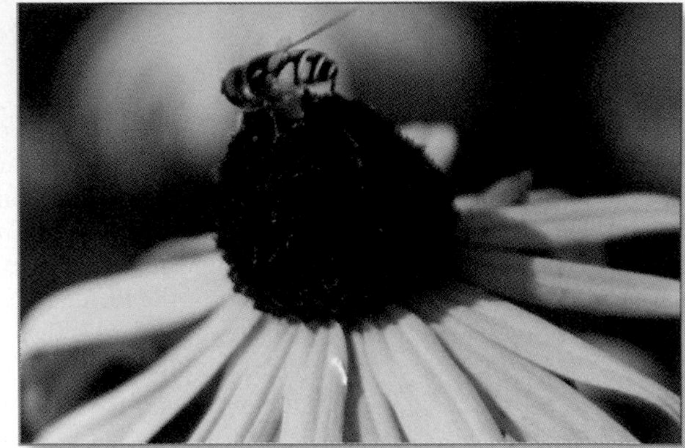

FIGURE 1-74

1. Start Photoshop. Click Workspace on the Window menu and then click Default Workspace.
2. In the toolbox, right-click the top-left tool and then click Rectangular Marquee Tool in the list.
3. On the options bar, right-click the Rectangular Marquee Tool (M) button and then click Reset All Tools. When the Reset All Tools dialog box is displayed, click the OK button.
4. Using the Open command on the File menu, open the file, Honeybee.
5. On the File menu, click Save As. When the Save As dialog box displays, type the file name `Honeybee Edited`. Do not press the ENTER key. Click the Look in box arrow and choose your USB flash drive from the list. Click the Save button. If Photoshop displays a JPEG Options dialog box, click the OK button.
6. Click the Zoom Tool (Z) button in the Photoshop toolbox. When the Adobe Bridge window is displayed, click the flower with the honeybee until the magnification is 150 percent.
7. In the Navigator palette, drag the proxy view area to display the honeybee in the upper-right third of the photo.
8. Click the Crop Tool (C) button in the Photoshop toolbox. Drag an area to crop, where the focus will be on the honeybee and the flower it sits on. Include as few of the other flowers as possible.
9. Press the ENTER key to complete the crop.
10. Save the file again, by clicking Save on the File menu. If Photoshop displays a JPEG Options dialog box, click the OK button.
11. Click the Go to Bridge button on the options bar. When the Adobe Bridge window is displayed, click the box arrow in the Bridge toolbar and then click My Computer in the list.
12. When the list of locations is displayed, double-click your USB flash drive location.
13. At the bottom of the window, using the buttons on the right of the Bridge status bar, view the photos on your flash drive in both Thumbnails view and Details view.
14. Close the Adobe Bridge window to return to the Adobe Photoshop window.
15. Press the F1 key to access the Adobe Help Center. When the Adobe Help Center window is displayed, click the Type in a word or phrase box and then type `desktop printing`. Click the Search button.
16. When Photoshop displays the help topics on desktop printing, click three different topics, one at a time. Read each one. Choose one of the help topics to print, and then click the Print contents of the right pane button (Figure 1-72 on page PS 54) on the Adobe Help Center toolbar.
17. Close the Adobe Help Center window. When Photoshop again displays the Honeybee Edited photo, click Print One Copy on the File menu.
18. Turn in the hard copies of the photo and the help topic to your instructor.
19. Quit Photoshop.

In the Lab

1 Using Precise Measurements to Crop and Resize a Photo

Problem: As a member of your high school reunion committee, it is your task to assemble the class photo directory. You are to edit the photo of a high school picture and prepare it for print in the reunion directory. The photo needs to fit in a space 1.75 inches high and 1.33 inches wide. Each photo needs to have approximately the same amount of space above the headshot — .25 inches. The edited photo is displayed in Figure 1-75.

FIGURE 1-75

Instructions:

1. Start Photoshop. Perform the customization steps found on pages PS 8 through PS 10.
2. Open the file, Student, from the Project01 folder on the CD that accompanies this book, or in a location specified by your instructor.
3. Use the Save As command on the File menu to save the file on your storage device with the name, Student Edited. If Photoshop displays a JPEG Options dialog box, click the OK button.
4. Use the Navigator palette to zoom the photo to 50 percent magnification, if necessary.
5. If the rulers do not display, press CTRL+R to view the rulers.
6. Drag from the horizontal ruler down into the photo until the green ruler guide touches the top of the student's head. Obtain the vertical measurement of the top of the student's head by measuring where the line touches the vertical ruler. Drag a second ruler guide to a position .25 inches above the first one. If you make a mistake while dragging a ruler guide, click Undo New Guide on the Edit menu.
7. Select the Crop tool. Drag from the left margin at the upper green line, down and to the right to include all the lower portion of the photo. *Hint:* If your selection is not perfect, press the ESC key and redo Step 6 above.
8. Press the ENTER key. If your crop does not seem correct, click the Undo command on the Edit menu and repeat steps 6 and 7.
9. Once your photo has .25 inches of space above the student's head, save the photo again.
10. Click the Resize Image command on the Help menu and choose the following settings as each window of the wizard is displayed:
    a. Choose to use the image for print.
    b. Type 1.75 for the height of the photo.
    c. Select 200 halftone screen (LPI).
    d. Drag the image quality slider all the way to the right to select the highest quality.
    e. Click the Finish button.
11. Save the resized file with a new file name, Student for Print. If a JPEG Options dialog box is displayed, click the OK button.
12. Use the Print One Copy command on the File menu to print a copy of the photo.
13. Close both document windows.
14. Quit Photoshop.
15. Send the photo as an e-mail attachment to your instructor, or follow your instructor's directions for submitting the lab assignment.

In the Lab

2 Creating a Border

Problem: The owner of Birdhouses Incorporated is preparing a booklet to ship along with the custom ordered birdhouses he creates for his clientele. He would like you to take one of the pictures he has taken of an oriole atop a tree and create a bordered photo of just the oriole. The blended border should be black with a normal blend and 30 pixels wide to match the other bird photos in the booklet.

The edited photo is displayed in Figure 1-76.

Instructions:

1. Start Photoshop. Perform the customization steps found on pages PS 8 through PS 10.
2. Open the file, Finch, from the Project01 folder on the CD that accompanies this book, or in a location specified by your instructor.
3. Use the Save As command on the File menu to save the file on your storage device with the name, Finch Edited. If a JPEG Options dialog box is displayed, click the OK button.
4. Click the Zoom Tool (Z) button in the toolbox. Click the bird to center it in the display. Zoom in as necessary so you can make precise edits.
5. Crop the picture with approximately .75 inches on all four sides of the bird. Use the ruler to help you determine how much room to leave around the bird.
6. Save the photo again.
7. Press CTRL+A to select all of the photo.
8. To create the border, do the following:
   a. On the Select menu, point to Modify, and then click Border.
   b. When the Border Selection dialog box is displayed, type 30 in the Width Box. Click OK.
   c. Press SHIFT+F5 to access the Fill command.
   d. When the Fill dialog box is displayed, click the Use box arrow and then click Black in the list.
   e. Click the Mode box arrow and then click Normal in the list.
   f. Type 100 in the Opacity box. Click OK.
9. Save the photo again.
10. Use the Print One Copy command on the File menu to print a copy of the photo.
11. Close the document window.
12. Quit Photoshop.
13. Send the photo as an e-mail attachment to your instructor, or follow your instructor's directions for submitting the lab assignment.

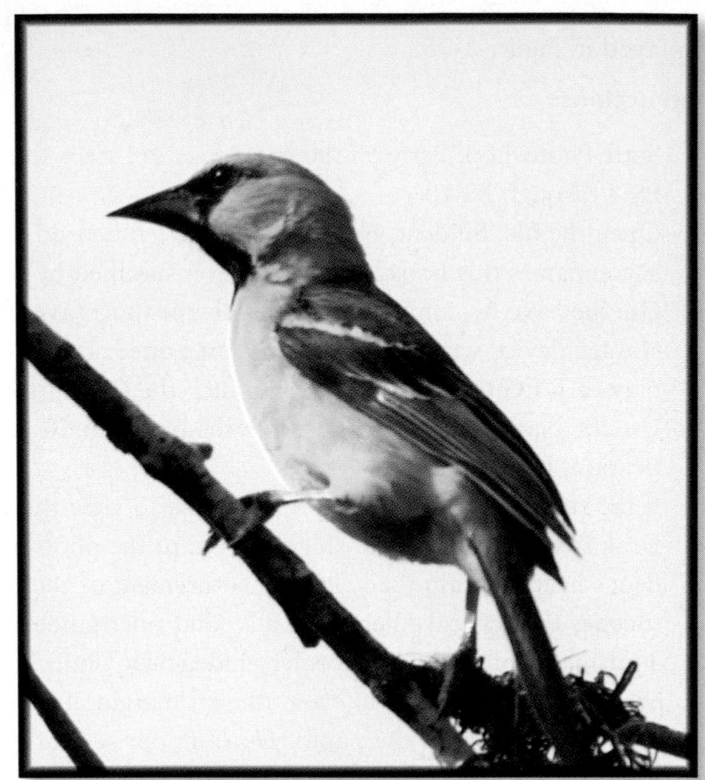

FIGURE 1-76

In the Lab

3 Preparing a Photo for the Web

Problem: As an independent consultant in Web site design, you have been hired by the Pineapple Growers Association to prepare a photo of an exotic pineapple growing in a field for use on the association's Web site. The edited photo is displayed in Figure 1-77.

Instructions:

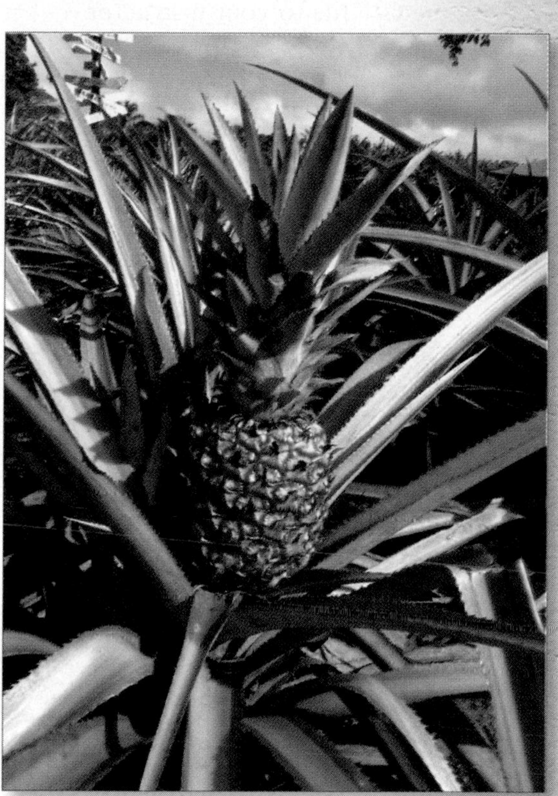

FIGURE 1-77

1. Start Photoshop. Perform the customization steps found on pages PS 8 through PS 10.
2. Open the file, Pineapple, from the Project01 folder on the CD that accompanies this book, or in a location specified by your instructor.
3. Use the Resize Image Wizard to resize the photo for online use to 500 pixels wide by 694 pixels high.
4. Use the Save As command on the File menu to save the file on your storage device with the name, Pineapple Edited. If Photoshop displays a JPEG Options dialog box, click the OK button.
5. On the Help menu, click Photoshop Help. Search for the words, Optimization. Read about optimizing for the Web. Print a copy of the help topic and then close the Adobe Help Center window.
6. When the Photoshop window again is displayed, click Save for Web on the File menu.
7. When the Save For Web dialog box is displayed, click the 4-Up tab.
8. Click the Zoom Level box arrow in the lower-left corner of the dialog box and then click Fit on Screen.
9. Right-click any of the previews and choose the connection speed of your Internet connection. See your instructor if you are not sure of your connection speed.
10. Click the preview that looks the best on the screen.
11. Make the following changes to the Save for Web settings at the right side of the Save For Web dialog box. Some of the settings already may be set correctly. If you are unsure of a setting, point to the setting to display its tool tip.
    a. Click the Color reduction algorithm box arrow, and then click Selective in the list.
    b. Click the Specify the dither algorithm box arrow, and then click Noise in the list.
    c. Click the Maximum number of colors in the Color Table box arrow, and then click 256 in the list.
12. For extra credit, create a Web page by doing the following lettered steps. Otherwise skip to Step 13.
    a. Click the Preview in Default Browser button in the lower-right corner on the Save For Web status bar.
    b. The Web preview will open a browser window. In the lower portion of the window, the browser will display the HTML code necessary to display the picture as a Web page. Drag the code to select it. Press CTRL+C to copy it.
    c. Open a text editor program such as Notepad or TextPad and press CTRL+V to paste the code into the editing window. Save the file as Pineapple.html in the same folder as your photo. Close the text editor.
    d. Click the Close button in the browser window.

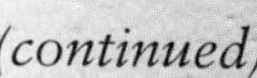

(continued)

Preparing a Photo for the Web *(continued)*

13. Click the Save button in the Save For Web dialog box. When the Save Optimized As dialog box is displayed, type Pineapple-for-Web in the Name box, and then click the Save button.
14. Close the document window and quit Photoshop.
15. Send the GIF file to your instructor.
16. If you did the extra credit, view your HTML file as a Web page. See your instructor for instructions on uploading the GIF and HTML files to a server or other ways to submit your assignment.

Cases and Places

The difficulty of these case studies varies:
■ are the least difficult and ■■ are the most difficult. The last exercise is a group exercise.

1 ■ Your cousin Steve has dropped by to tell you about his recent vacation. While you look at his photos, Steve admits he is not the best photographer. He asks you if you can enhance one of his photos on the computer. After starting Photoshop, you select the photo, Park Statue, from the Project01 folder on the CD that accompanies this book. Save the photo on your USB flash drive storage device as Park Statue Edited. Crop the photo to remove the excess sky and add a black border of approximately 100 pixels. Save the photo again and print a copy for your instructor.

2 ■ You are an intern with the Chamber of Commerce. In cooperation with the town, the old historic district has been revitalized. The Chamber of Commerce wants to publish a brochure about the old historic district with high-quality photos to help attract tourism. The photo submitted by the Chamber of Commerce is named Walkway and is located in the Project01 folder on the CD that accompanies this book. Crop the photo at both the bottom and right to focus attention on the many store fronts. Keep the old-fashioned light fixture and the oval wall plaque in the photo.

3 ■■ Use a scanner to scan a favorite photo. Using the scanner's software, save the photo in the highest possible resolution, using the most color settings. Bring the picture into Photoshop and save it on your storage device. Crop it to remove extra background images. Use the rule of thirds to focus on the main point of interest. Resize the photo to fit your favorite frame. Add a blended border if it will not detract from the images in the photo. Send the edited photo via e-mail to a friend or use it in a page layout program to create a greeting card.

4 ■■ Look through magazines or newspapers for color photos that might be cropped. If possible, cut out three photos and mark them with cropping lines. Write a short paragraph for each one describing why you think the photo could benefit from cropping. If the cropped photo needs to be resized, give the exact dimensions. List at least two uses for the photo, other than the one in which it was displayed. Attach the photos to the descriptions and submit them to your instructor.

5 ■■ **Working Together** Your school would like to display a picture of the main building or student center on the Web site's home page. Your team has been assigned to take the photo and optimize it for the Web. Using a digital camera or camera phone, each team member should take a picture of the building from various angles. As a team, open each digital file and choose one or two that best incorporate the styles and suggestions in this project. Choose a border that highlights the color and dynamic of the photo. Resize the photo to less than 500 x 500 pixels. As a group, make decisions in the Save For Web dialog box on the 4-Up tab as to which optimization would best suit the school's needs. Show the final products to another person or group in your class for suggestions. Submit the best one to your instructor.

ADOBE
Photoshop CS2

Using Selection Tools

PROJECT

2

CASE PERSPECTIVE

Kevin Bernard leads the graphic design team at Achievement Advertising Agency, a medium-sized firm that caters to small business accounts. As an aggressive and versatile firm, they believe in the fundamentals of communication strategies and have developed a reputation for effective, on-target marketing. The agency's marketing strategy is to maximize exposure and response to the client's products and needs.

Kevin has hired you as a graphic design intern with the company. Your first assignment is to work on a gift shop catalog the ad agency is producing. The gift shop owner has submitted an illustration with candles and candies for the catalog. When complete, the gift shop catalog will consist of 48 pages with full color photos, illustrations, and descriptions of the various gifts sold by the company. One full page of the catalog measures 8 × 11 inches. This illustration, ultimately to be used with text describing the product, is to fill one-half of the page, approximately 8 × 5½ inches. The catalog will be mailed to a large population in time for the holiday season. Kevin has asked you to create a visually pleasing layout of these candles and candies, as a single image, which will appear in the catalog next to the description and pricing.

The copy editors will write the text description and price list around your finished image. With your basic knowledge of Photoshop, you decide to explore the selection tools to copy, transform, clone, and move the objects into an attractive display. Kevin suggests you try to straighten the tall candle in your final layout.

As you read through this project, you will learn how to use the marquee tools, the lasso tools, the Magic Wand tool, and the Move tools in Photoshop to make selections and rearrange objects in a photo. You also will apply transformations to selected objects.

Using Selection Tools

PROJECT

Objectives

You will have mastered the material in this project when you can:

- Explain the terms perspective, layout, and storyboard
- Describe selection tools
- Open a file, select objects in a photo, and save a file
- Use the marquee tools
- Move a selection
- Make transformation edits
- View states in the History palette
- Employ the lasso tools
- Add and subtract from selections
- Create ruler guides
- Select objects using the Magic Wand tool
- Create new keyboard shortcuts

Introduction

In Project 1, you learned about the Photoshop interface as well as navigation and zooming techniques. You cropped and resized a photo, added a border, and saved the photo for both Web and print media. You learned about online Help, along with opening, saving, and printing photos. This project continues to emphasize those topics and presents some new ones.

Recall that specifying or isolating an area of your photo for editing is called making a selection. By selecting specific areas, you can edit and apply special effects to portions of your image while leaving the unselected areas untouched. The new topics covered in this project include the marquee tools to select rectangular or elliptical areas, the lasso tools to choose freeform segments or shapes, and the Magic Wand tool to select consistently colored areas. Finally, you will learn how to use transformation tools and cut, copy, paste, drag, and drop those selections.

Project Two — Managing Selections

Project 2 illustrates the creation of an advertising piece used in a gift catalog. You will begin with the image in Figure 2-1a that shows candles and candies that are for sale by the owner of the gift shop. You then will manipulate the image by selecting, editing, and moving the objects to produce a more attractive layout, creating Figure 2-1b that will display in the gift catalog.

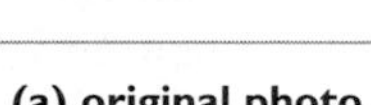

(a) original photo

(b) edited photo

FIGURE 2-1

Figure 2-2 illustrates the design decisions made to create the final advertising piece. An attractive layout using multiple objects is a good marketing strategy, visually and subconsciously encouraging the viewer to purchase more than one item. **Layout** refers to placing visual elements into a pleasing and readable arrangement, suggestive of how the product or products might look in a buyer's home. Advertising or product designers try to determine how the target consumer will use the product and group objects accordingly.

From a design point of view, creating a visual diagonal line between the tall candles, along with the rule of thirds, creates perspective. **Perspective** is the technique photographers, designers, and artists use to create the illusion of three dimensions on a flat or two-dimensional surface. Perspective is a means of fooling the eye by making it appear as if there is depth or receding space in the image. Adjusting the sizes and juxtaposing the objects, creates asymmetrical balance and visual tension between the featured products. The diagonal alignment of the tall candles leads the viewer to the background, as does the placement of candy in front of the short candle.

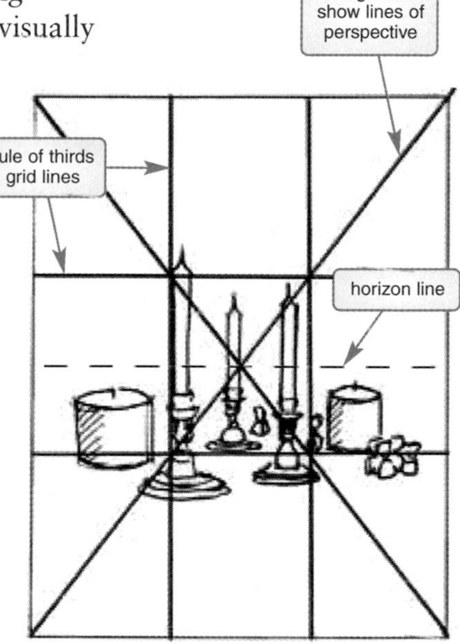

FIGURE 2-2

The horizon line in perspective drawing is a virtual horizontal line across the picture. The placement of the horizon line determines from where the viewer seems to be looking, such as from a high place, or from close to the ground. In the candle scene, the horizon line runs across the center of the drawing. The viewer is high enough to see the top of the short candles.

Using white space, or non-image area, is effective in directing the viewer to see what is important. The products, grouped this way, are in a sense framed by the white space.

This product layout, using the rule of thirds grids, also helps other members of the design team when it is time to make decisions about type placement. The group of products can be shifted up or down, as one image, to accommodate the layout and text including the font sizes, placement, title, description, and price information. The rule of thirds offers a useful means to make effective layouts for image and text.

Designing a preliminary layout sketch, similar to Figure 2-2, to help you make choices about placement, size, perspective, and spacing is referred to as creating a **storyboard**, **thumbnail**, or **rough**.

Starting and Customizing Photoshop

To start and customize Photoshop, Windows must be running. If you are stepping through this project on a computer and you want your screen to match the figures in this book, then you should change your computer's resolution to 1024 × 768 and reset the tools and palettes. For more information about how to change the resolution on your computer, and other advanced Photoshop settings, read Appendix A.

The following steps describe how to start Photoshop and customize the Photoshop window. You may need to ask your instructor how to start Photoshop for your system.

To Start Photoshop

1. **Click the Start button on the Windows taskbar, point to All Programs on the Start menu, and then click Adobe Photoshop CS2 on the All Programs submenu.**
2. **After a few moments, if Photoshop displays a Welcome screen, click the Close button on the Welcome Screen.**
3. **If the Adobe Photoshop window is not maximized, double-click its title bar to maximize it.**
4. **Click Window on the Photoshop menu bar, point to Workspace on the Window menu, and then click Default Workspace on the Workspace submenu.**
5. **Right-click the top-left button in the toolbox and then click Rectangular Marquee Tool on the context menu.**
6. **Right-click the Rectangular Marquee Tool (M) button on the options bar and then click Reset All Tools. When Photoshop displays a confirmation dialog box, click the OK button.**

Photoshop starts and, after a few moments, displays the toolbox and palettes in the work area (shown in Figure 2-3). Photoshop resets the tools, palettes, and options.

Opening a File

To open a file in Photoshop it must be stored as a digital file on your computer system. The photos and images used in this book are stored on a CD located in the back of the book. Your instructor may designate a different location for the photos.

The following steps illustrate how to open the file, Candles, from a CD located in drive E.

To Open a File

1. **Insert the CD that accompanies this book into your CD drive. After a few seconds, if Windows displays a dialog box, click its Close button.**
2. **With the Photoshop Window open, click File on the menu bar and then click Open.**
3. **When the Open dialog box is displayed, click the Look in box arrow, and then click drive E or the drive associated with your CD.**
4. **Double-click the Project02 folder and then click the file, Candles, to select it.**
5. **Click the Open button.**

6 **When Photoshop displays the image in the document window, if the magnification is not 25% as shown on the title bar, double-click the magnification box on the document window status bar, type** 25**, and then press the** ENTER **key.**

Photoshop opens the file, Candles, from the CD in drive E. The image is displayed in the document window at 25% magnification (Figure 2-3).

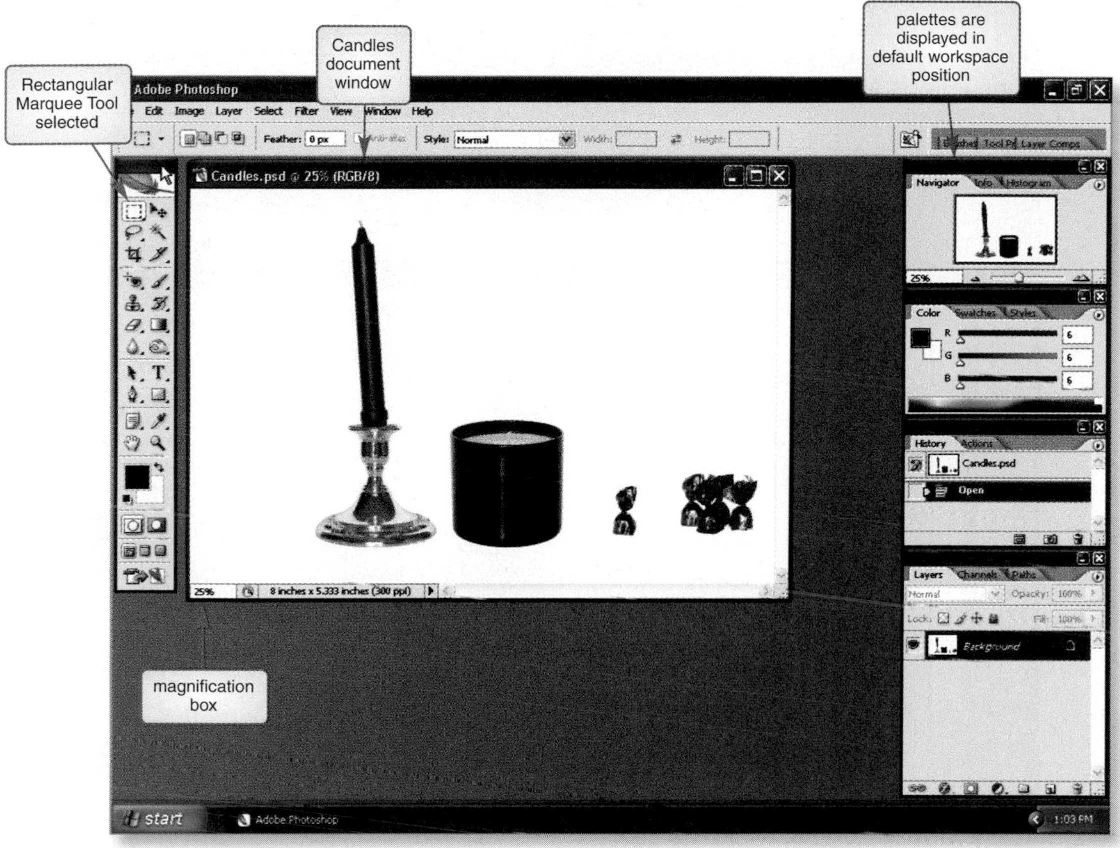

FIGURE 2-3

Table 2-1 displays information about the Candles photo. It was created as a Photoshop document and is stored as a PSD file. **Photoshop Document format** (**PSD**) is the default file format and the only format that supports all of the Photoshop features. Like most file formats, PSD can support files up to 2 GB in size. Adobe applications can directly import PSD files and preserve many Photoshop features, as can most page layout applications.

Table 2-1 Candles Image Characteristics

File Name	Candles
File Type	PSD
Image Dimensions	8 × 5.333 inches
Color Mode	RGB
Resolution	300 pixels/inch
File Size	1, 574 KB

Saving a File

Even though you have yet to edit the photo, it is a good practice to save the file on your personal storage device early in the process. The next step is to save the photo with the name, Candles Edited, as the steps on the next page illustrate.

To Save a Photo

1. **With your USB flash drive connected to one of the computer's USB ports, click File on the menu bar and then click Save As.**
2. **When the Save As dialog box is displayed, type** `Candles Edited` **in the File name text box. Do not press the ENTER key after typing the file name.**
3. **Click the Save in box arrow and then click USBDISK [G:], or the location associated with your USB flash drive, in the list.**

The Save As dialog box is displayed (Figure 2-4). Other files on your storage device may not be listed because the Save As dialog box is displaying only PSD files.

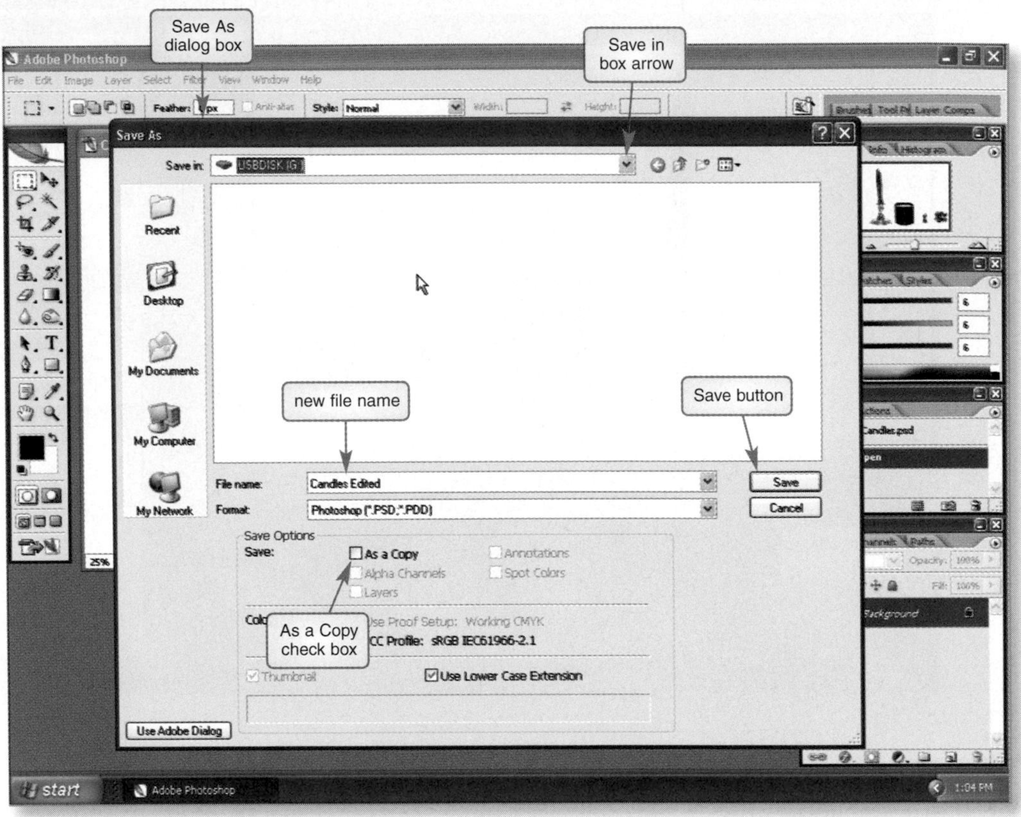

FIGURE 2-4

4. **Click the Save button in the Save As dialog box.**

Photoshop saves the file on the USB flash drive with the file name, Candles Edited, and displays the new name on the document window title bar. Although the image is saved on a storage device, it also remains in main memory and is displayed on the screen.

> *More About*
>
> **More About Saving**
>
> Working off your USB drive is convenient if you are in a public lab. At home, it is recommended that you work off your hard drive, in a folder such as My Documents, as a hard drive is more reliable and faster when saving files.

The Save As dialog box (Figure 2-4) also contains the **As a Copy check box.** When checked, Photoshop automatically appends the word, Copy, to the file name, thus allowing you to save a second copy of the file in the same location. A copy file has the same attributes and can be edited in the same manner as the original file. Making multiple copies of an original file also is useful if you want to make and save several different versions of a layout.

In the following sections, you will learn about the various selection tools available in Photoshop, including the marquee tools, the lasso tools, and the Magic Wand tool, as you make changes to the Candles Edited file.

The Marquee Tools

The **marquee tools** let you draw a marquee that selects a portion of the document window. A **marquee** is a selection that displays with a flashing or pulsating selection border sometimes described as marching ants. Marquees are useful when the part of an image or photo that you wish to select fits into rectangular or elliptical shapes. Photoshop has four marquee tools (Figure 2-5) that display in a context menu when you click the tool and hold down the mouse button, or right-click the tool. You can select any of the marquee tools from this context menu.

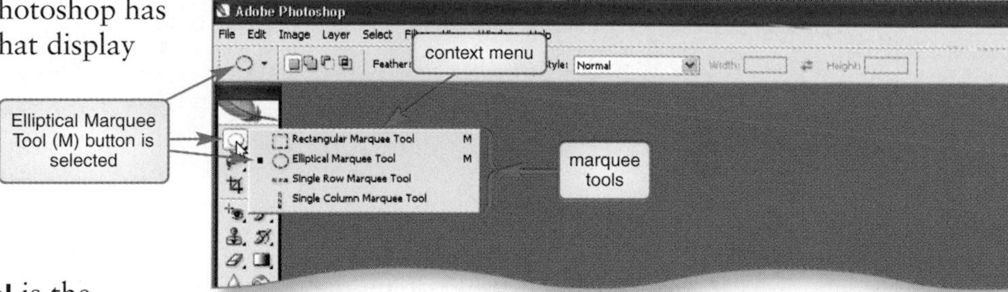

FIGURE 2-5

The **Rectangle Marquee tool** is the default marquee tool that selects a rectangular or square portion of the image or photo. The **Elliptical Marquee tool** allows you to select an ellipsis, oval, or circular area.

Dragging with the Rectangular or Elliptical Marquee tools creates a marquee drawn from a corner. If you press the SHIFT key while dragging a marquee, Photoshop **constrains** the proportions of the shape creating a perfect square or circle. If you press the ALT key while drawing a selection, the marquee is created from the center. Pressing SHIFT+ALT starts from the center and constrains the proportions.

The **Single Row Marquee tool** allows you to select a single row of pixels. The **Single Column Marquee tool** allows you to select a single column of pixels. You must choose the row and column marquees from the context menu — there is no keyboard shortcut. A single click in the document window creates the selection. Because a single row or column of pixels is so small, it is easier to use these two marquee tools at higher magnifications.

Table 2-2 describes the four marquee tools.

More About

Marquee Tools Selection

If you are using a different tool, and want to activate the marquee tools, you can click the Rectangular Marquee Tool (M) button in the toolbox or press the M key on the keyboard to select the marquee tool. Once the marquee tool is selected, pressing SHIFT+M toggles between the Rectangular and Elliptical Marquee tools.

Table 2-2 The Marquee Tools

TOOL	PURPOSE	SHORTCUT	BUTTON
Rectangular Marquee	selects a rectangular or square portion of the document window	M SHIFT+M toggles to Elliptical Marquee	
Elliptical Marquee	selects an elliptical or oval portion of the document window	M SHIFT+M toggles to Rectangular Marquee	
Single Row Marquee	selects a single row of pixels in the document window	(none)	
Single Column Marquee	selects a single column of pixels in the document window	(none)	

The Marquee Options Bar

The options bar associated with each of the marquee tools displays many buttons and settings to draw effective marquees (Figure 2-6 on the next page). The options bar displays the chosen marquee on the left followed by the Tool Preset picker. The **Tool Preset picker** allows you to save and reuse toolbar settings. You will learn how to save toolbar settings in a later project.

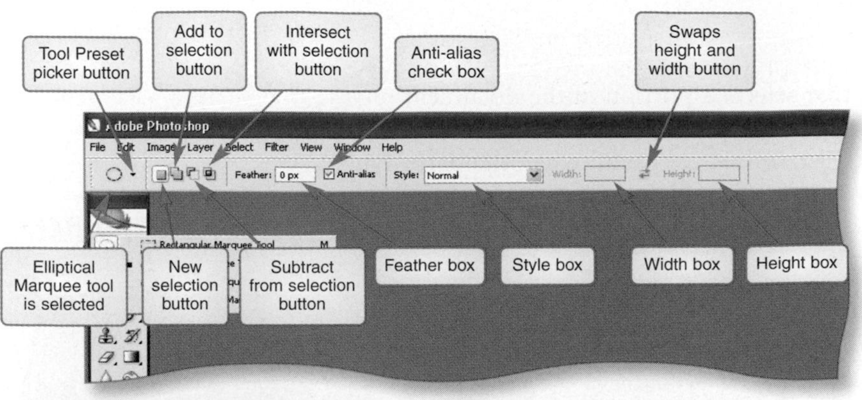

FIGURE 2-6

The options bar associated with each of the marquee tools displays four buttons to adjust the selection (Figure 2-6). The **New selection button** allows you to draw a new marquee.

The **Add to selection button** allows you to draw an adjacent rectangle or ellipsis to expand the selection. The Add to selection button is useful for selecting the extra corners of an L-shaped object or for shapes that do not fit within a single rectangle or ellipsis. To activate the Add to selection button, you can click it on the options bar or hold down the SHIFT key while dragging a second selection. When adding to a selection, the mouse pointer changes to a crosshair with a plus sign.

The **Subtract from selection button** allows you to deselect or remove a portion of an existing selection. The new rectangle or ellipsis is removed from the original selection. It is useful for removing block portions of the background around oddly-shaped images or for deselecting ornamentation in an object. To activate the Subtract from selection button, you can click it on the options bar, or hold down the ALT key while dragging. When subtracting from a selection, the mouse pointer changes to a crosshair with a minus sign.

The **Intersect with selection button** allows you to draw a second rectangle or ellipsis across a portion of the previously selected area, resulting in a selection border only around the area in which the two selections intersect. When creating an intersection, the mouse pointer changes to a crosshair with an x.

Once an area has been selected, there are options for further manipulating the selected area. Right-clicking a selection provides access to many other useful commands such as deselecting, or selecting the **inverse**, which means selecting everything in the image except the previous selection. Right-clicking a selection also enables you to create layers, apply color fills and strokes, and make other changes to a selection, which you will learn about in future projects.

To the right of the selection buttons, the options bar displays a Feather box. **Feathering** softens the edges of the selection for blending into backgrounds. The width of the feather is measured in pixels. When using the Elliptical Marquee tool, you can further specify blending by selecting the **Anti-alias check box** to adjust the blocklike, staircase look of rounded corners. Figure 2-7 shows a rectangle with no feathering and one with 5 pixels of feathering. Figure 2-7 also shows an ellipsis with no anti-aliasing and one created with a check mark in the Anti-alias check box.

When using the Rectangle Marquee tool or the Elliptical Marquee tool, you can click the **Style box arrow** to choose how the size of the marquee selection is determined. A **Normal** style sets the selection marquee proportions by dragging. A **Fixed Aspect Ratio** sets a height-to-width ratio using decimal values. For example,

More About

The Tool Preset Picker

The Tool Preset Picker button displays on most options bars. When you click the button, Photoshop displays a list of settings used during the current Photoshop session, or previously saved options bar settings. The list makes it easier to save and reuse tool settings. You can load, edit, and create libraries of tool presets in conjunction with the Tool Presets palette. To choose a tool preset, click the Tool Preset picker in the options bar, and then select a preset from the pop up palette.

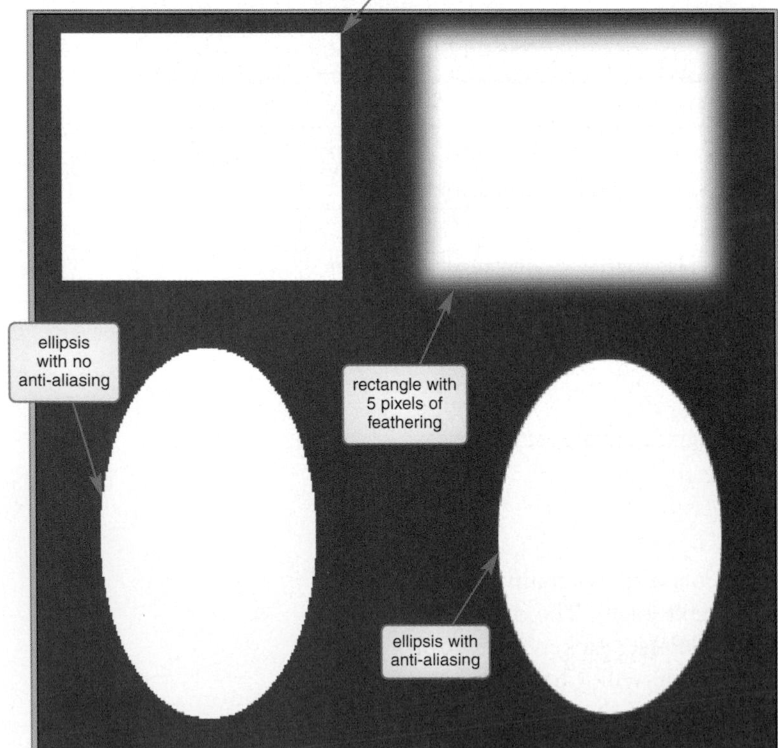

FIGURE 2-7

to draw a marquee twice as wide as it is high, type 2 for the width and 1 for the height. A **Fixed Size** allows you to specify exact pixel values for the marquee's height and width.

> *More About*
>
> **Anti-aliasing**
>
> Anti-aliasing is available for the Lasso tool, the Polygonal Lasso tool, the Magnetic Lasso tool, the Elliptical Marquee tool, and the Magic Wand tool. You must specify this option before using these tools. Once a selection is made, you cannot add anti-aliasing.

Using the Rectangular Marquee Tool

The following step illustrates how to select the short candle in the Candles Edited image, using the Rectangular Marquee tool.

To Use the Rectangular Marquee Tool

1

- **Right-click the Rectangular Marquee Tool (M) button in the toolbox and then click Rectangular Marquee Tool. If necessary, on the options bar, click the New selection button.**
- **In the photo, use the mouse to draw a rectangle as close as possible around the short candle.**

The selection border, or marquee, pulsates around the short candle (Figure 2-8). The mouse pointer displays an arrow with a selection rectangle.

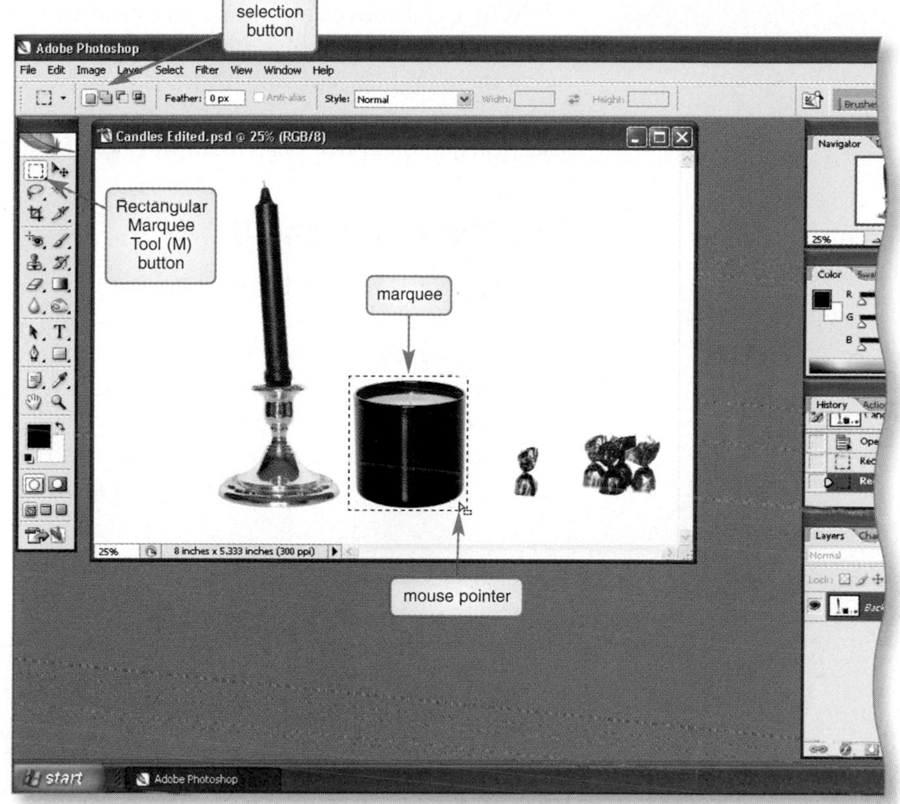

FIGURE 2-8

If you make a mistake or change your mind when drawing a marquee, you can do one of three things. 1) If you want to start over, you can click somewhere else in the document window to deselect the marquee; then, simply draw a new marquee. 2) If you have already drawn the marquee, but wish to move or reposition it, you can drag the selection to the new location. 3) If you want to reposition while you are creating the marquee, do not release the mouse button. Press and hold the SPACEBAR, drag the marquee to the new location, and then release the SPACEBAR. At that point, you can continue dragging to finish drawing the marquee.

When dragging selections, most designers begin at the upper-left corner and drag down and to the right. Photoshop will create a marquee from any corner, however.

If you were to drag a newly defined marquee, the image inside the marquee would not move. Dragging a marquee only moves the selection border to outline a new portion of the image. To move the selection border and its contents, you use the Move tool.

The Move Tool

The **Move Tool** in the Photoshop toolbox is used to move or make other changes to selections. Activating the Move tool by clicking the Move Tool (V) button or pressing the V key on the keyboard allows you to move the selection border and its contents by dragging them in the document window. When you first begin to drag with the Move tool, the mouse pointer changes to an arrow with scissors indicating a cut from the original position. To move the selection in a straight line, press and hold the SHIFT key before dragging. If you press and hold the ALT key before dragging, you **duplicate** or move only a copy of the selected area, effectively copying and pasting the selection. While moving a copy, the mouse pointer changes to a black arrow with a white arrow behind it.

When you move selections, you need to be careful about overlapping images. As you will learn in Project 3, Photoshop layers or overlaps portions of images when you move them. While that sometimes is preferred when creating collages or composite images, it is undesirable if an important object is obscured. Close tracing while creating selections, and careful placement of moved selections, will prevent unwanted layering.

The Move Options Bar

The Move options bar displays tools to help define the scope of the move (Figure 2-9). As you learn about layers later in this book, you will use the **Auto Select Layer check box** to move only the topmost layer. The **Auto Select Groups check box** selects layer groupings. When selected, the **Show Transform Controls check box** causes Photoshop to display sizing handles on the selection border and adds a center reference point indicator to the selection. The align and distribute buttons help position selections when more than one layer is selected.

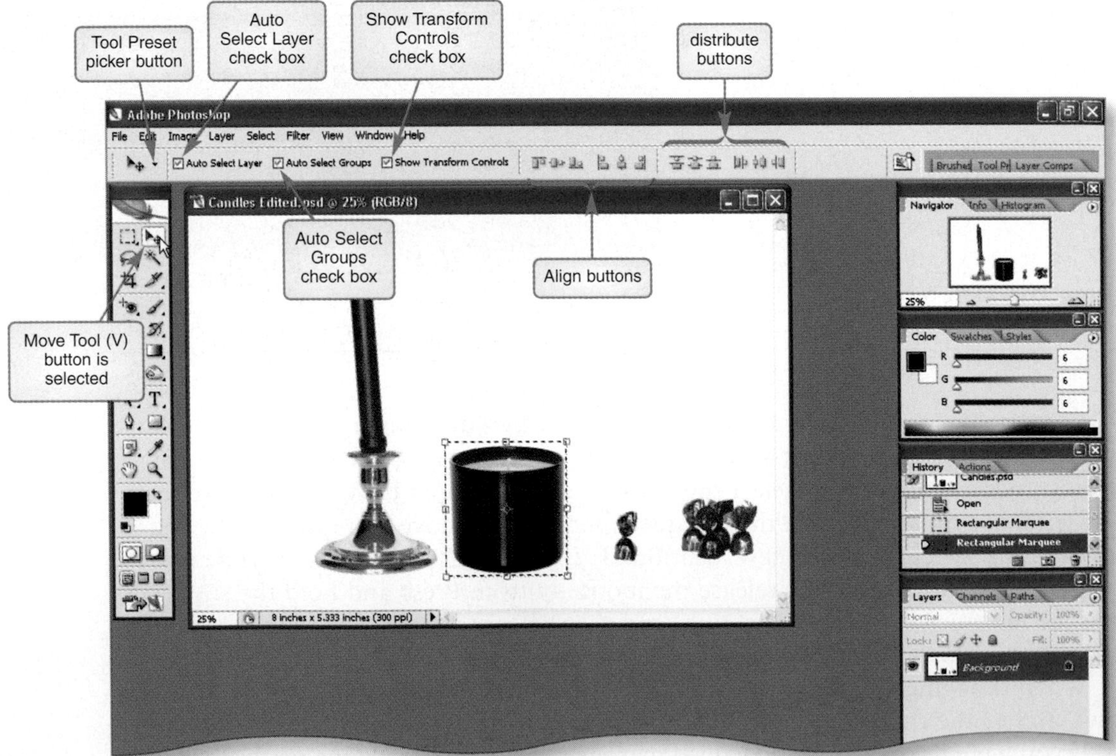

FIGURE 2-9

Using the Move Tool

The next step in preparing the layout for the catalog involves rearranging the components of the original image. Using the Move tool, the short candle is moved to the left of the tall candle and slightly higher in the image. Then a copy of the candle is moved to a location above the single piece of candy. The following steps show how to use the Move tool.

To Use the Move Tool

1

• **With the short candle still selected, click the Move Tool (V) button in the toolbox. If necessary, on the options bar, click the Auto Select Layer check box so it does not display a check mark. If necessary, click the Show Transform Controls check box so it does not display its check mark.**

The Move Tool (V) button is selected (Figure 2-10).

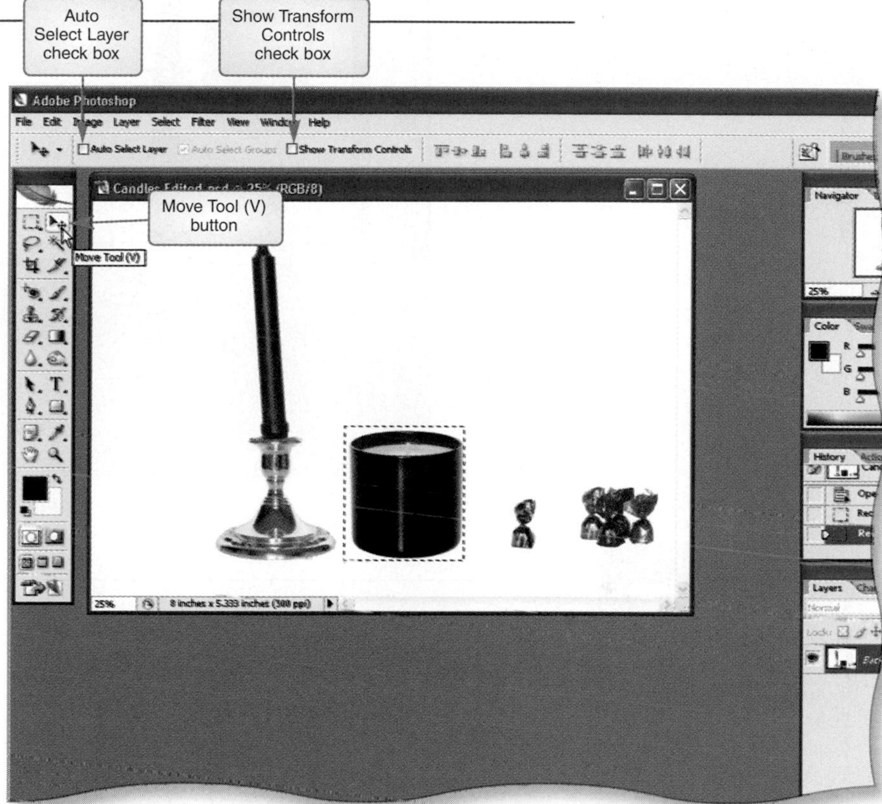

FIGURE 2-10

2

• **Drag the candle to a position left of the tall candle and slightly higher. Do not allow the moved selection to overlap any portion of the tall candle.**

Photoshop moves the selection and displays the short candle to the left of the tall candle (Figure 2-11).

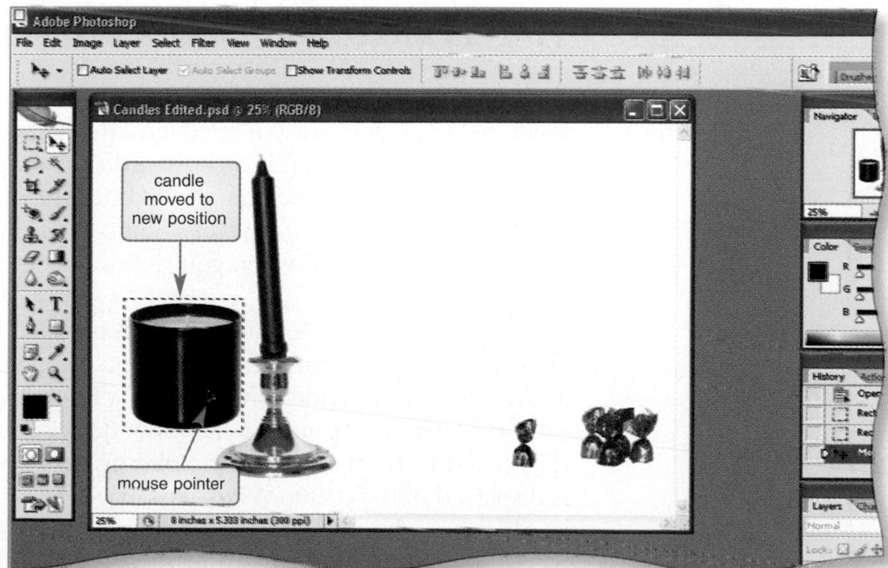

FIGURE 2-11

3

• With the short candle still selected, press and hold the ALT key and then drag the selection to a location above the candy.

Photoshop copies the selection to the new location (Figure 2-12).

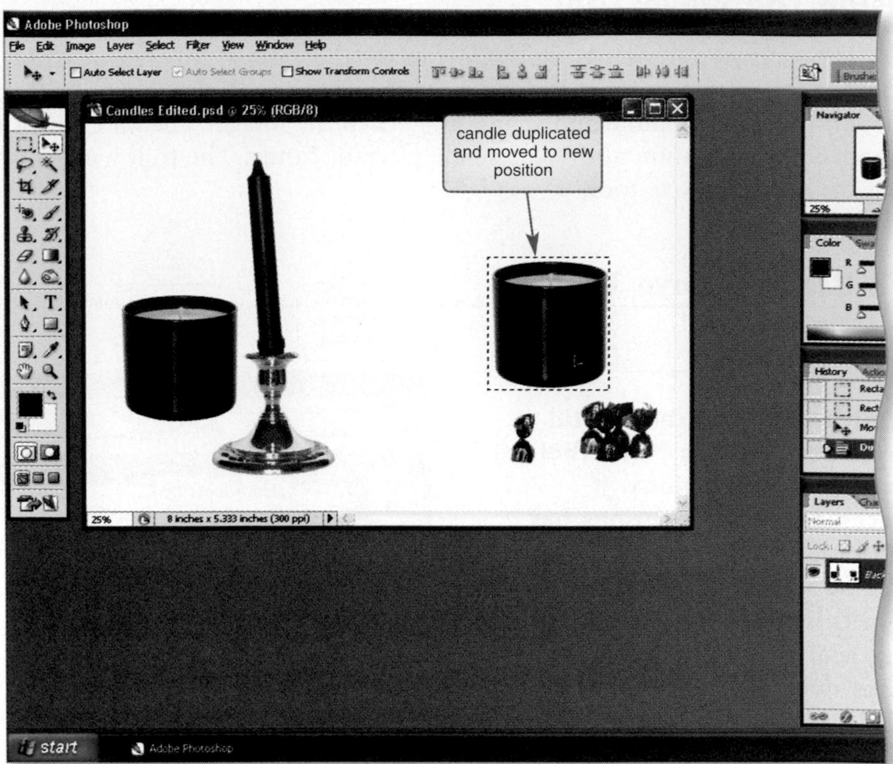

FIGURE 2-12

Other Ways

1. To duplicate, on Edit menu click Copy, click Paste, drag copy to new location
2. To move, press V key, drag selection
3. To duplicate, press CTRL+C, press CTRL+V, drag copy to new location
4. To duplicate, press F3 key, press F4 key, drag copy to new location

Just as you do in other applications, you can use the Cut, Copy, and Paste commands from the Edit menu or shortcut keys to make changes to selections. Unless you predefine a selection area by dragging a marquee, the Paste command pastes to the center of the document window.

The copy of the short candle now will be resized using a transformation command as described in the next section.

The Transformation Commands

In Photoshop, the word, **transform**, is used to make physical changes to a selection. To choose a transformation command, click the Edit menu, point to Transform, and then click the desired transformation. Or, you can click Transform Selection on the shortcut menu that is displayed when you right-click the selection.

When you choose a transformation or when you click the Show Transform Controls check box on the Move options bar, Photoshop displays a **bounding box** or border with six sizing handles around the selection (Figure 2-13). A small **reference point** or fixed pivot point is displayed in the center of the selection.

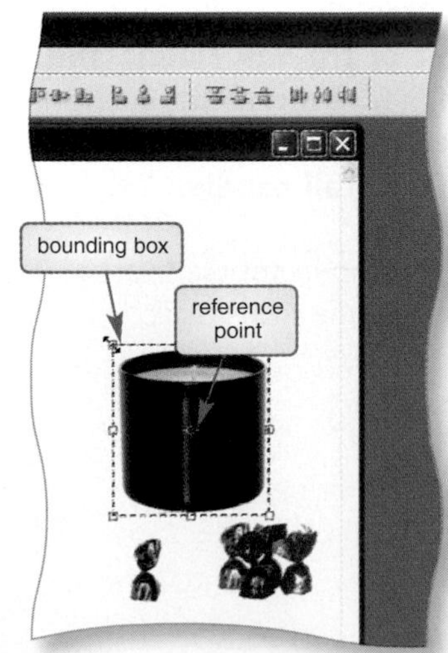

FIGURE 2-13

If you click a sizing handle or the reference point of the bounding box, you enter transformation mode. In **transformation mode**, the Transform options bar

(Figure 2-14 on the next page) is displayed and the associated shortcut menu displays the transformation commands. In transformation mode, the bounding box displays a solid line on the top and left, and a pulsating line on the bottom and right.

Table 2-3 lists the types of transformations you can perform on a selection, the techniques used to perform the transformation, and the result of the transformation. If you choose **Free Transform,** you must use the mouse techniques to perform the transformation.

Table 2-3 Transformation Commands

CHOOSE A TRANSFORMATION FROM THE MENU	USING THE MOUSE (FREE TRANSFORM)	USING THE OPTIONS BAR	RESULT
Scale	Drag a sizing handle on the bounding box; SHIFT+drag to scale proportionately.	To scale numerically, enter percentages in the Width and Height boxes, shown as W and H, on the options bar. Click the Link icon to maintain the aspect ratio.	Selection is displayed at a different size.
Rotate Rotate 180° Rotate 90° CW Rotate 90° CCW	Move the mouse pointer outside the bounding box border. It becomes a curved, two-headed arrow. Drag in the direction you wish to rotate. SHIFT+drag to constrain the rotation to 15° increments.	In the Rotate box, type a positive number for clockwise rotation or a negative number for counter-clockwise rotation.	Selection is rotated or revolved around a reference point.
Skew	Drag a side of the bounding box. ALT+drag to skew both vertically and horizontally.	To skew numerically, enter decimal values in the horizontal skew and vertical skew boxes on the options bar.	Selection is slanted or tilted, either vertically or horizontally.
Distort	Drag a corner sizing handle to stretch the bounding box.	Enter new numbers in the location, size, rotation, and skew boxes.	Selection is larger on one edge of the selection than the others.
Perspective	Drag a corner sizing handle to apply perspective to the bounding box.	Enter new numbers in the size, rotation, and skew boxes.	A portion of the selection appears closer on one edge than the others.
Warp	When the warp mesh is displayed, drag any line or point.	Click the Custom box arrow. Click a custom warp.	Selection is displayed reshaped with bulge, arch, wrapped corner, or twist.
Flip	Flipping is available only on the menu.	Flipping is available only on the menu.	Selection is displayed upside down or rotated 90 degrees.

After you are finished making transformations, you **commit changes** or apply the transformations by pressing the ENTER key or by clicking the Commit transform (Return) button on the Transform options bar. If you change your mind and do not wish to make the transformation, selecting another tool will cause a dialog box to display. Click the Don't Apply button in the dialog box.

The Transform Options Bar

To display the Transform options bar, create a selection and then press CTRL+T. Photoshop displays a Transform options bar (Figure 2-14a) or a warp options bar (Figure 2-14b) that contain boxes and buttons to help you with your transformation.

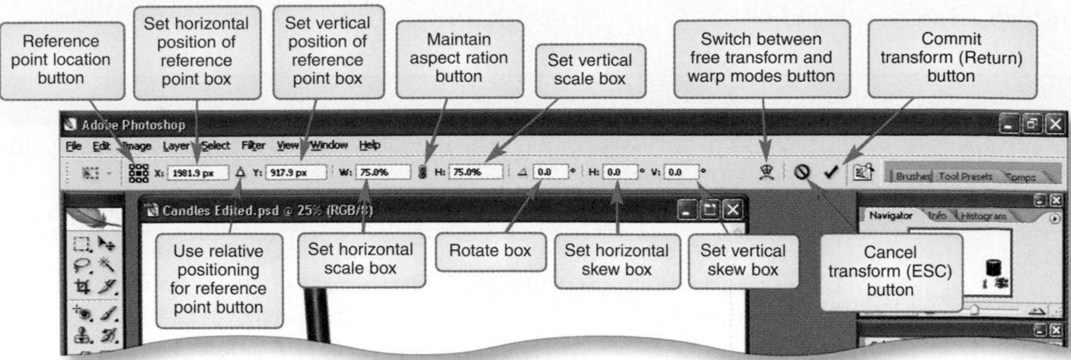

(a) Transform Options Bar

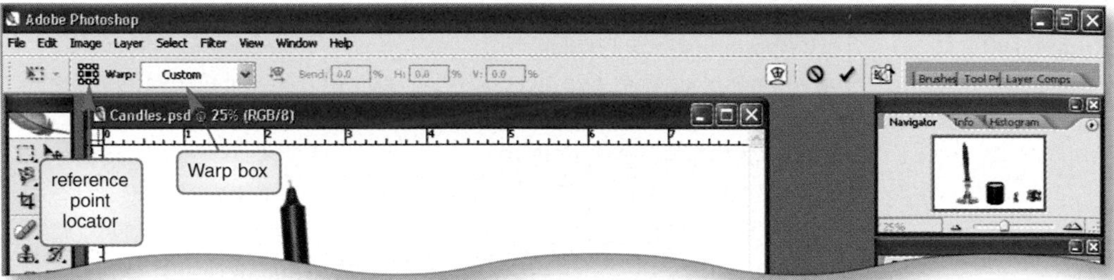

(b) Warp Options Bar

FIGURE 2-14

On the left side of the Transform options bar, Photoshop displays the **Reference point location button**. Each of the nine squares on the button corresponds to a point on the bounding box. Any transformations applied to the selection will be made in relation to the selected reference point. The middle square is selected by default. To select a different reference point, click a different square on the Reference point location button. The other boxes on the Transform options bar display information about the selected square's location in the document.

The X and Y boxes allow you to enter a horizontal and vertical location for the selected reference point, thus altering the location of the selection in the document. The new location is based on the actual pixel measurements entered. When you click the **Use relative positioning for reference point button** in between the X and Y boxes, the movement of the selection is relative to the current location of the selected reference point.

The W and H boxes allow you to scale the width and height of the selection. When you click the **Maintain aspect ratio button** between the W and H boxes, the aspect ratio of the selection is maintained.

To the right of the scale boxes is a Rotate box. Entering a positive number rotates the selection clockwise; a negative number rotates the selection counter-clockwise.

The H and V boxes, to the right of the Rotate box, set the horizontal and vertical skews of the selection, measured in degrees. A positive number skews the selection to the right; a negative number skews to the left.

A unique feature is the ability to drag the labels left of the text boxes. For example, if you drag the H, Y, W, or other labels, the values in the text boxes change. Dragging to the right increases the value; dragging to the left decreases the value. When you point to any of the labels on the Transform options bar, the mouse pointer changes to a hand with a double-headed arrow indicating its ability to drag.

On the far right of the Transform options bar are three special buttons. The first one switches between the Transform options bar and the Warp options bar. The second button cancels the transformation. The third button commits the transformation. After transforming a selection, you must cancel or commit the transformation before Photoshop will let you perform another action.

Scaling a Selection

As described in Table 2-3, when you scale a selection, you resize it by changing its width, height, or both. The following steps illustrate how to use the Show Transform Controls check box to display the bounding box. Then, to reduce the size of the candle proportionally, the steps show how to freely transform by SHIFT+dragging a corner sizing handle.

To Scale a Selection

1

- **With the Move Tool (V) button still selected, click the Show Transform Controls check box on the options bar.**
- **Point to the upper-left sizing handle of the selection border.**

The mouse pointer changes to a two-headed arrow when positioned over a sizing handle (Figure 2-15).

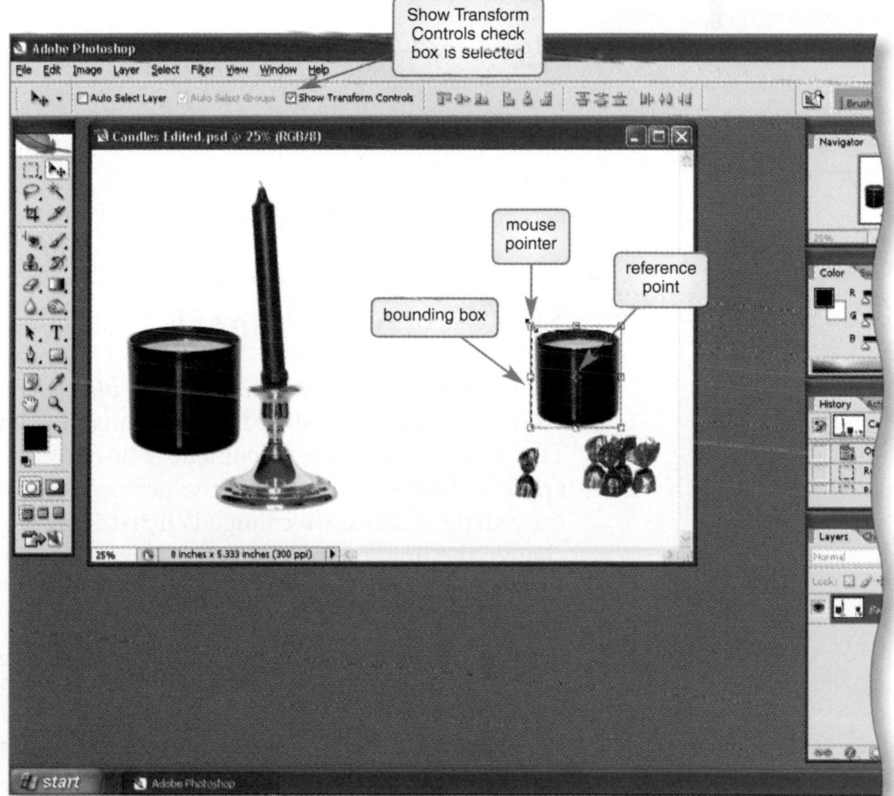

FIGURE 2-15

2

• **SHIFT+drag the upper-left sizing handle toward the center of the candle until it is resized to approximately 75% of its original size.**

The candle is resized. The W: and H: boxes on the options bar display 75% (Figure 2-16).

• **Press the ENTER key to commit the change.**

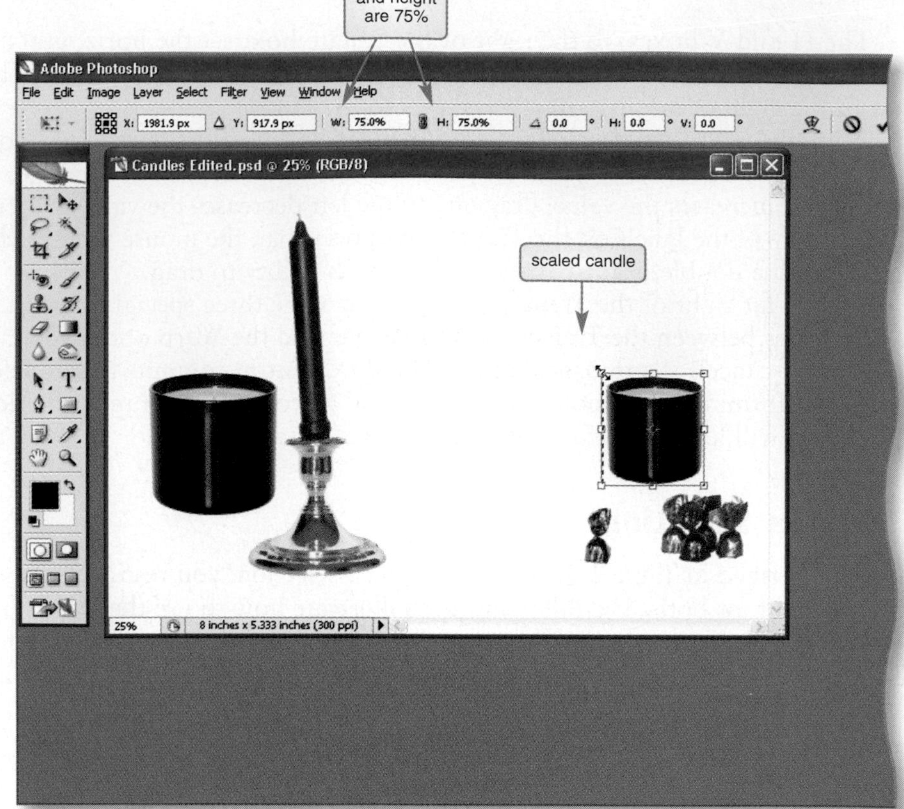

FIGURE 2-16

> *Other Ways*
>
> 1. On Transform options bar, enter new width and height, press ENTER key

Photoshop allows you to apply some transformations to entire images or photos, rather than just selections. For example, you can change the size of the photo or rotate the image using the Image menu. You then can enter dimensions or rotation percentages on the submenu and subsequent dialog boxes.

The History Palette

The **History palette**, usually located in the third palette down on the right of the Photoshop window, records each change or new state of the file you are working on. The initial state of the document is displayed at the top of the palette. Each time you apply a change to an image, the new **state** of that image is added to the bottom of the palette. Each state change is listed with the name of the tool or command used to change the image. For example, when you performed the scale transformation on the short candle, the words, Free Transform, were displayed as a step in the history of the file (Figure 2-17). The step just above the Free Transform in the History palette denotes the duplication of the candle when you dragged a new copy to its current location.

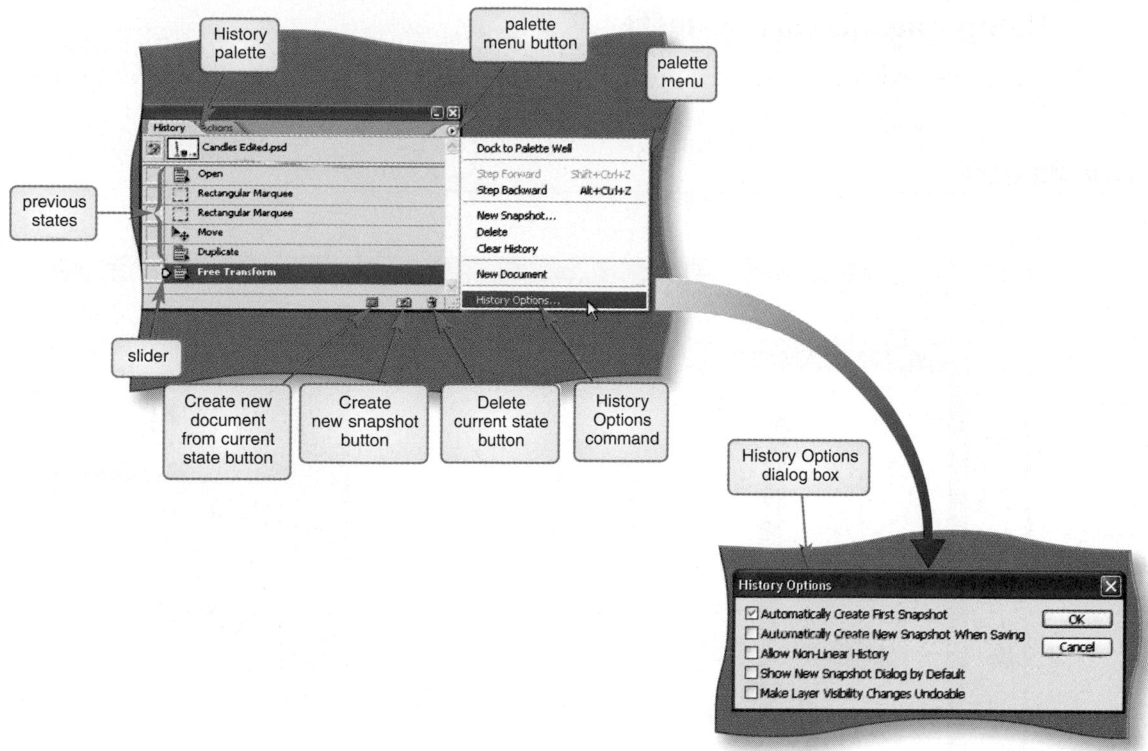

FIGURE 2-17

The History palette is used in several different ways. When you select one of the states, the image reverts to how it looked when that change first was applied. You can view the state temporarily, or start working again from that point. Selecting a state and then changing the image eliminates all the states in the History palette that came after it. If you select a state and change the image by accident, you can use the Undo command on the Edit menu to restore the eliminated states. By default, deleting a state deletes that state and those that came after it. If you select the Allow Non-Linear History box in the History Options dialog box, deleting a state deletes only that state.

You can use the History palette to jump to any recent state of the image created during the current working session. Either click the state, or drag the slider to the state you wish to view. Alternately, you also can give a state a new name called a **snapshot**. Naming a snapshot makes it easy to identify. Snapshots are stored at the top of the history palette and make it easy to compare effects. For example you can take a snapshot before and after a series of transformations. Then, by clicking between the two snapshots in the History palette you can see the total effect or choose the before snapshot and start over. Snapshots are not saved with the image — closing an image deletes its snapshots. To create a snapshot, right-click the step and then click New Snapshot on the shortcut menu, or click the Create new snapshot button on the History palette status bar.

Not all steps are recorded in the history palette. For instance, changes to palettes, color settings, actions, and preferences, are not reflected in the History palette, because they are not changes to a particular image.

By default, the History palette lists the previous 20 states. You can change the number of remembered states by changing a preference setting (see Appendix A). Older states are automatically deleted to free more memory for Photoshop. Once you close and reopen the document, all states and snapshots from the last working session are cleared from the palette.

Using the History Palette

The following steps show how to use the History palette to view a previous state.

To Use the History Palette

1

• **In the History palette, click the Move state above the Free Transform and Duplicate states. Do not click anywhere else.**

The document window displays the candle before you created a second copy (Figure 2-18).

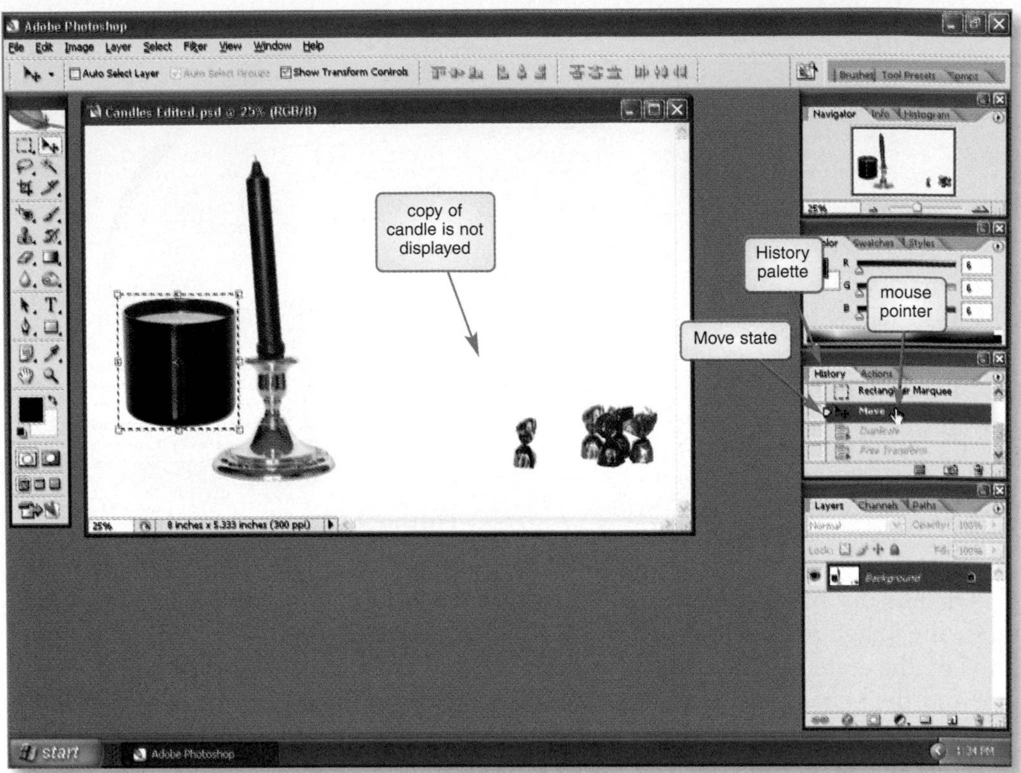

FIGURE 2-18

2

• **In the History palette, click the Free Transform state at the bottom of the list.**

The document window again displays the second candle, scaled to 75% (Figure 2-19).

FIGURE 2-19

Like the Navigator palette that you learned about in Project 1, the History palette also has a palette menu where you can clear all states, change the history settings, or dock the palette (Figure 2-17 on page PS 81). To display the palette menu, click the History palette menu button. To move the palette, drag its title bar. To change the size of the palette, drag its border. Buttons on the History palette status bar allow you to create a new document, a new snapshot, or delete the selected state.

The Lasso Tools

The lasso tools are used to draw a freehand selection border around objects, which provides more flexibility than the marquee tools with their standardized shapes. There are three kinds of lasso tools. The first is the default **Lasso tool** that allows you to create a selection by using the mouse to drag around any object in the document window. You select the Lasso Tool (L) button in the toolbox. You then begin to drag around the desired area. When you release the mouse, Photoshop connects the selection border to the point where you began dragging, finishing the loop. The Lasso tool is useful for a quick, rough selection.

The **Polygonal Lasso tool** is chosen from the Lasso tool context menu. It is similar to the Lasso tool in that it draws irregular shapes in the image; however, the Polygonal Lasso tool uses straight line segments. To use the Polygonal Lasso tool, choose the tool, click in the document window, release the mouse button, and then move the mouse in straight lines, clicking each time you turn a corner. When you get back to the beginning of the polygon, double-click to complete the selection.

The **Magnetic Lasso tool** also can be chosen from the context menu. You then click close to the edge of the object you wish to select. The Magnetic Lasso tool tries to find the edge of the object by looking for the closest color change and attaches the selection to the pixel on the edge of the color change. As you move the mouse, the Magnetic Lasso tool follows that change with a magnetic attraction. The magnetic lasso displays **fastening points** on the edge of the object. You can click points as you drag to force a change in direction or adjust the magnetic attraction. When you get all the way around the object, you click at the connection point to complete the loop, or double-click to have Photoshop connect the loop for you. Because the magnetic lasso looks for changes in color to define the edges of an object, it may not be very effective for making selections on images with a busy background or images with low contrast.

Table 2-4 describes the three lasso tools.

More About

Lasso Tool Selection

If you are using a different tool, and want to activate the Lasso tool, you can click the Lasso Tool (L) button in the toolbox or press the L key on the keyboard to select the Lasso tool. Once the Lasso tool is selected, pressing SHIFT+L cycles through the three lasso tools.

Table 2-4 The Lasso Tools

TOOL	PURPOSE	SHORTCUT	BUTTON
Lasso	To draw freeform segments of a selection border	L SHIFT+L toggles through all three lasso tools	
Polygonal Lasso	To draw straight-edged segments of a selection border	L SHIFT+L toggles through all three lasso tools	
Magnetic Lasso	To draw a selection border that snaps to the edges of defined areas in the image	L SHIFT+L toggles through all three lasso tools	

The Lasso Options Bar

Each of the lasso tools displays an options bar similar to the Marquee options bar, with buttons to add to, subtract from, and intersect with the selection, as well as the ability to feather the border. The Magnetic Lasso options bar (Figure 2-20) also includes an Anti-alias check box to smooth the borders of a selection. Unique to the Magnetic Lasso options bar, however, is a text box to enter the **edge contrast** or sensitivity of color that Photoshop will consider in making the path selection. A higher value detects only edges that contrast sharply with their surroundings; a lower value detects lower-contrast edges. The Width box causes the Magnetic Lasso tool to detect edges only within the specified distance from the mouse pointer. A **Frequency** box allows you to specify the rate at which the lasso sets fastening points. A higher value anchors the selection border in place more quickly. A **Use tablet pressure to change pen width button** on the right is used to change the pen width when using graphic drawing tablets instead of a mouse.

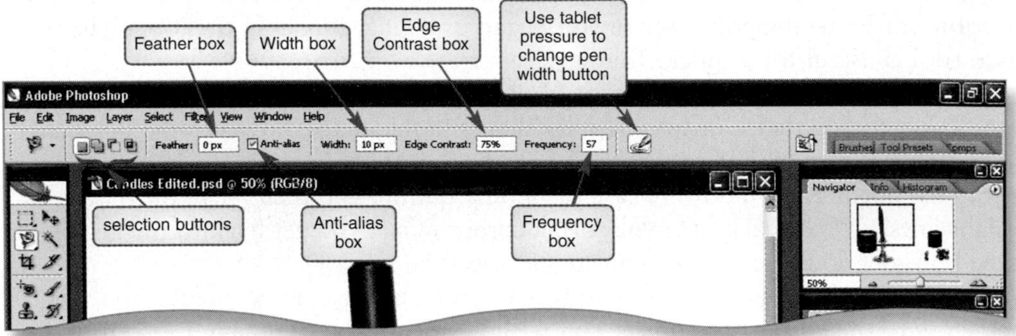

FIGURE 2-20

Using the Magnetic Lasso Tool

You will use the Magnetic Lasso tool to select the tall candle on top of the candle holder. You then will rotate and move the candle to straighten it. As you work with the Magnetic Lasso tool, remember that you can undo errors by clicking Undo on the Edit menu, and undo state changes by clicking the Delete button on the History palette status bar. Clicking as you turn corners with the Magnetic Lasso tool helps set the fastening points.

The following steps illustrate how to zoom to 50% magnification and resize the document window to facilitate selecting the candle.

To Zoom and Resize the Document Window

1. **On the Navigator palette status bar, click the Zoom In button twice to display the document window at 50%.**
2. **Drag the lower-right corner of the document window to enlarge the display area.**
3. **Scroll the document window to display the entire tall candle.**

The magnification increases, making the candle appear larger (Figure 2-21).

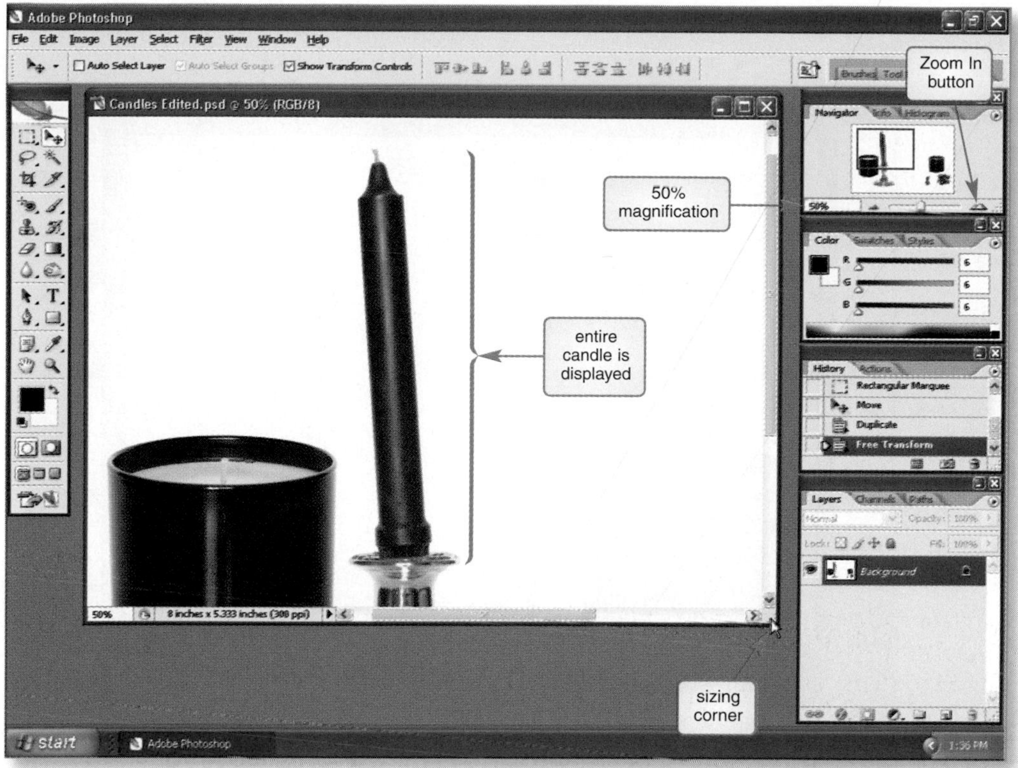

FIGURE 2-21

With the magnification increased, it now is easier to use the magnetic lasso to select the candle on top of the candle holder. In the following steps, the Magnetic Lasso Tool (L) button is selected and then the edge contrast is changed to 75 to detect only edges that contrast sharply with their surroundings, increasing the magnetism of the edge of the red candle on a white background.

As you use the Magnetic Lasso tool, if you make a mistake and want to start over, double-click to complete the lasso and then press CTRL+Z, click Undo on the Edit menu, or delete the state in the History palette. The following steps show how to use the Magnetic Lasso tool.

To Use the Magnetic Lasso Tool

1

- **Right-click the Lasso Tool (L) button in the toolbox.**

The context menu is displayed (Figure 2-22).

FIGURE 2-22

2

- **Click Magnetic Lasso Tool.**
- **If necessary, on the options bar, click the New selection button. Double-click the Edge Contrast box and type** 75 **to replace the value.**
- **Move the mouse pointer close to the edge of the tall candle.**

The mouse pointer changes to a magnetic lasso (Figure 2-23). The end of the lasso's rope is the actual location when clicked.

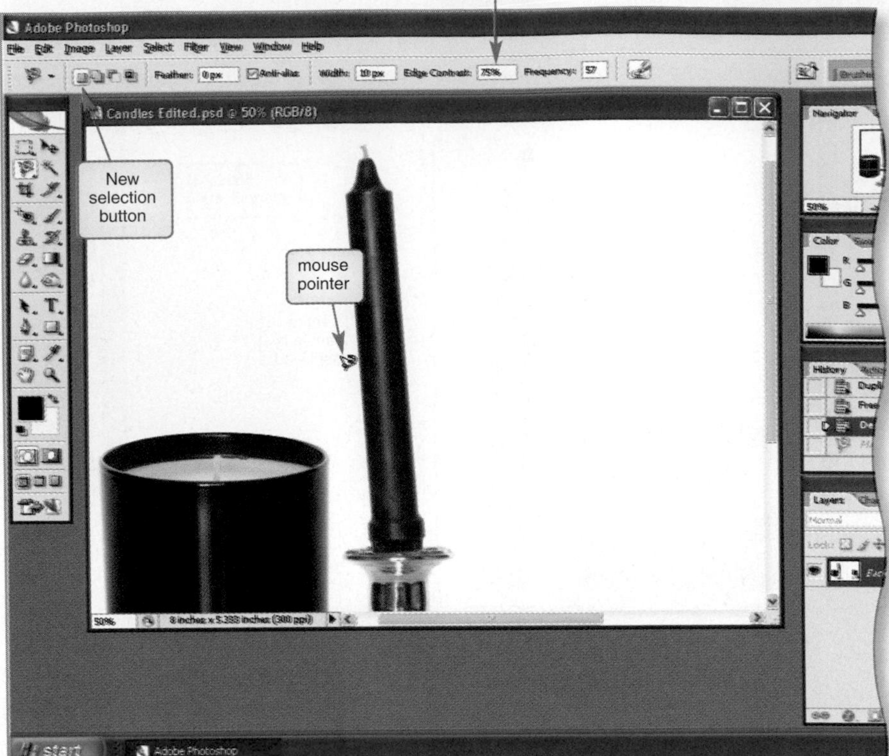

FIGURE 2-23

3

- **Click the white space close to the left edge of the candle.**
- **Release the mouse button.**

A gray fastening point is displayed (Figure 2-24).

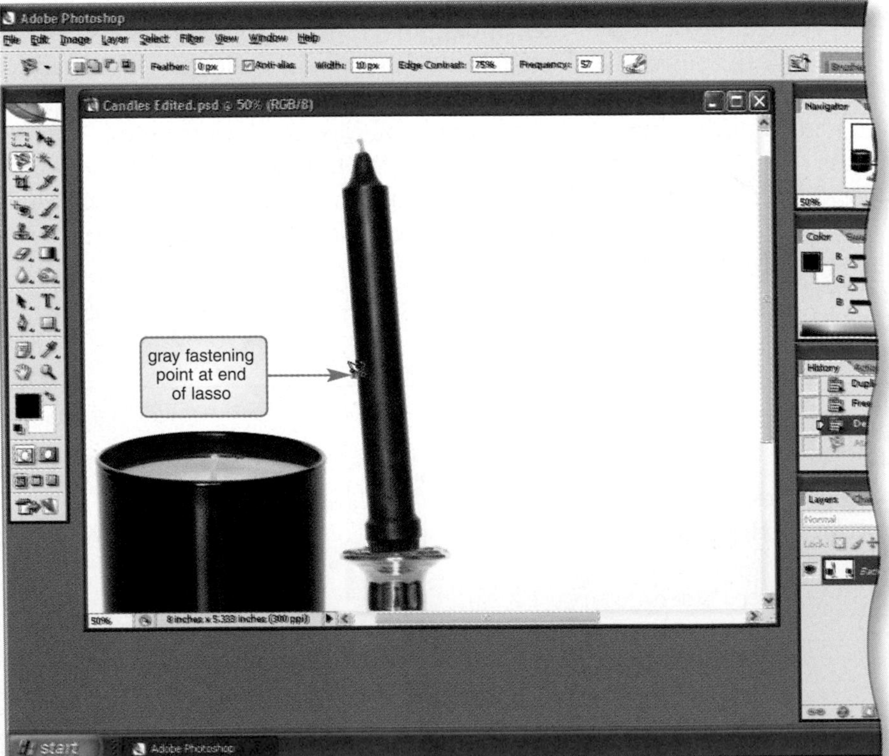

FIGURE 2-24

4

• Move the mouse up, staying close to the edge of the candle.

As you move the mouse, the fastening points move to the edge of the candle's red color on the white background (Figure 2-25).

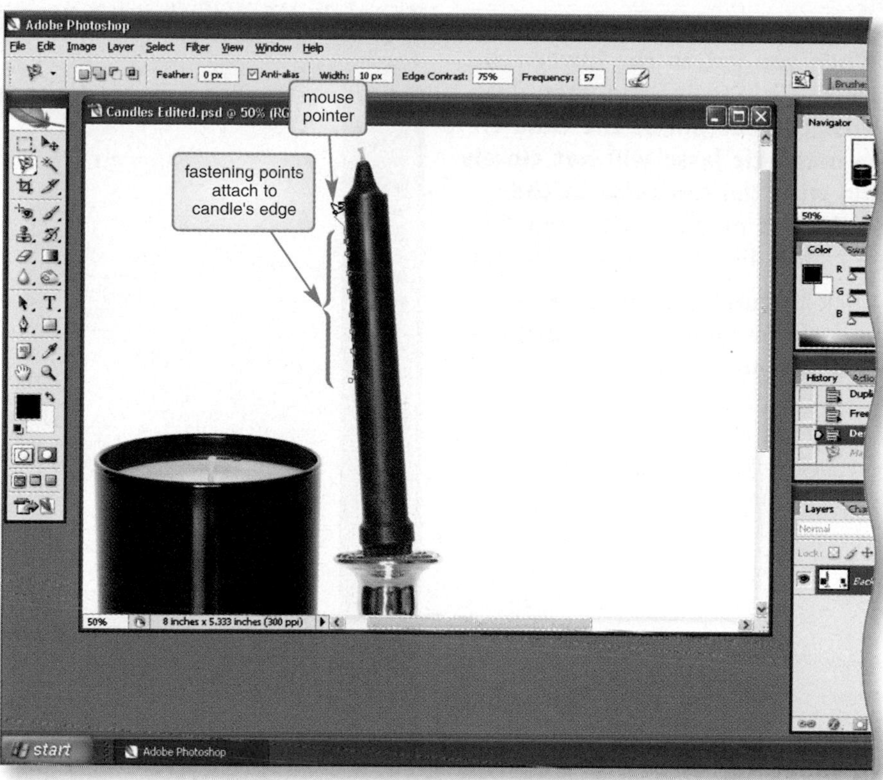

FIGURE 2-25

5

• Continue moving the mouse slowly to the top of the candle. Stay close to the edge of the candle and click whenever you want to change direction, for example when the candle tapers toward the wick. As you encounter corners in the candle, click the white space slightly away from the candle, so the lasso includes the entire corner.

• When you get to the top of the wick, click before moving to the right.

• Click again to turn the corner and come down the right side of the candle.

The fastening points adhere to the edge of the candle and the wick (Figure 2-26). Your selection may be slightly different. Do not worry if you have included some extra white space around the candle or wick.

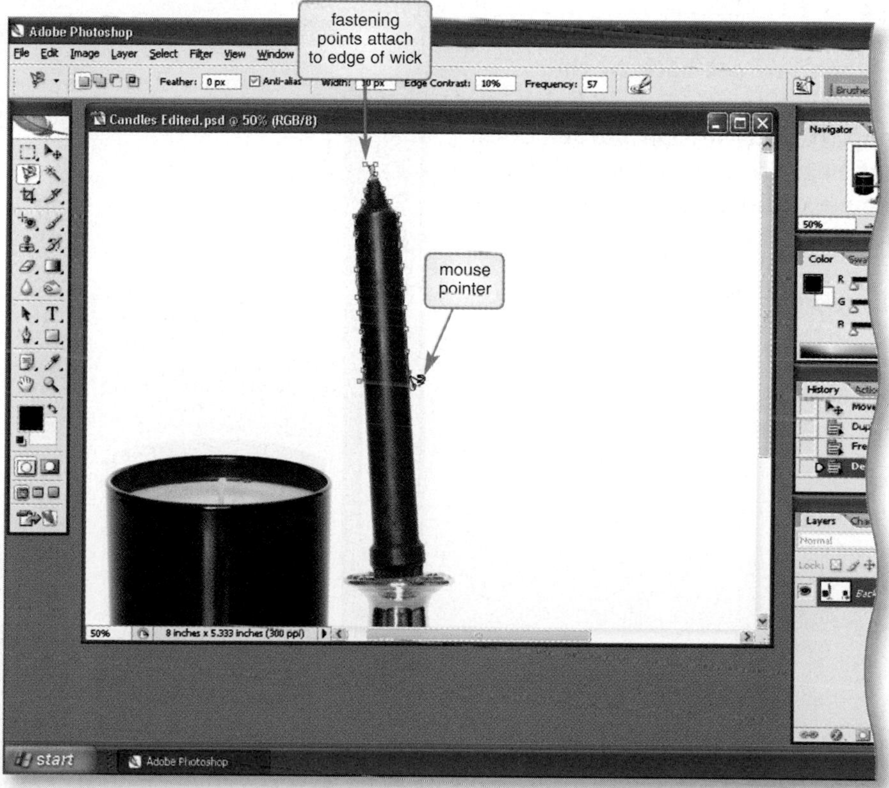

FIGURE 2-26

6

- **When you get to the lower-right corner, click again, and then drag across the bottom of the candle. The magnetic lasso will not closely align with the red color in the candle, but may include some of the candle holder in the selection.**
- **Click to turn the corner and move the mouse up toward the beginning point.**

The magnetic lasso includes some of the candle holder in the selection (Figure 2-27).

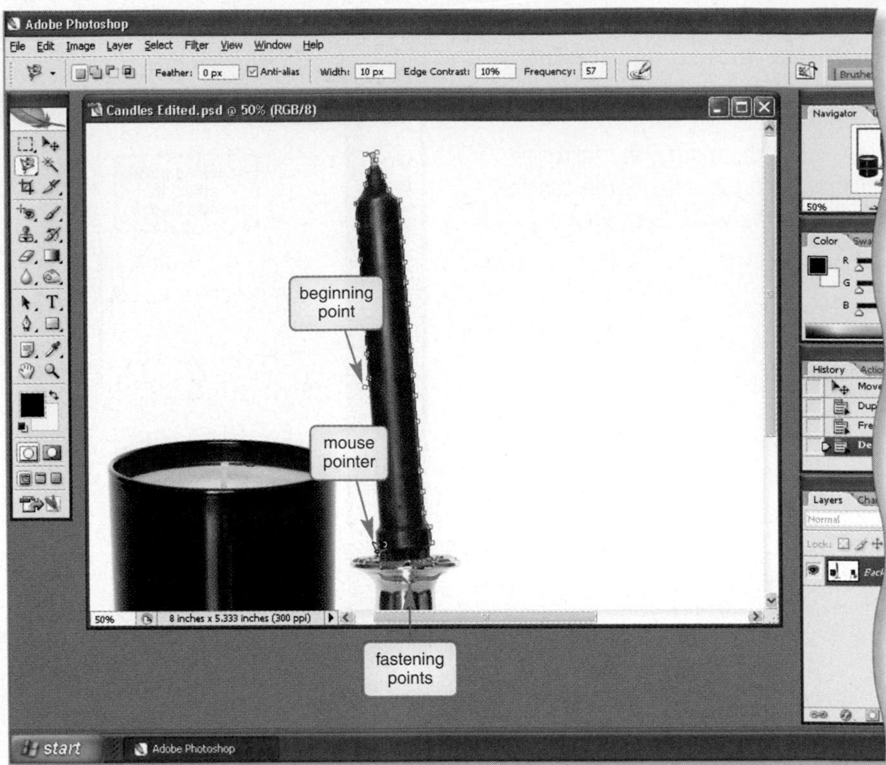

FIGURE 2-27

7

- **When you get back to the beginning point, click to finish the loop. If the selection border does not begin to pulsate, move the mouse closer to the beginning point and click again.**

The selection border flashes or pulsates around the candle (Figure 2-28).

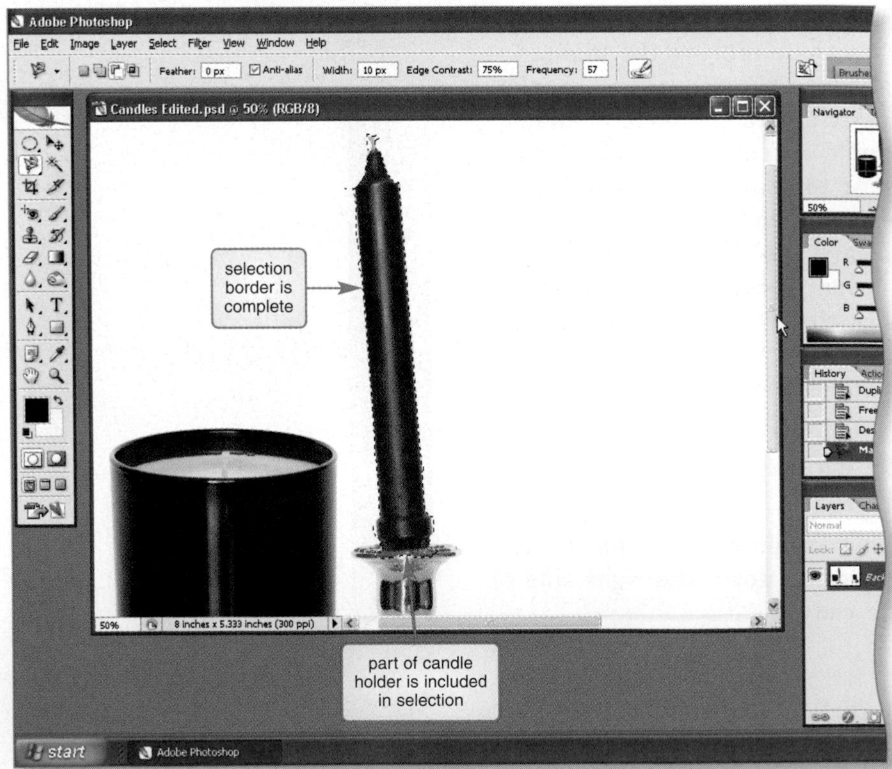

FIGURE 2-28

Other Ways

1. Press SHIFT+L twice, click image, move mouse

Subtracting from the Selection using the Polygonal Lasso Tool

The following steps show how to select the Polygonal Lasso tool and then use it to subtract the candle holder from the selection. You also may use the tool to subtract other portions of the image you may have selected inadvertently.

To Select the Polygonal Lasso Tool

1

- **Right-click the Magnetic Lasso Tool (L) button in the toolbox.**

The context menu is displayed (Figure 2-29).

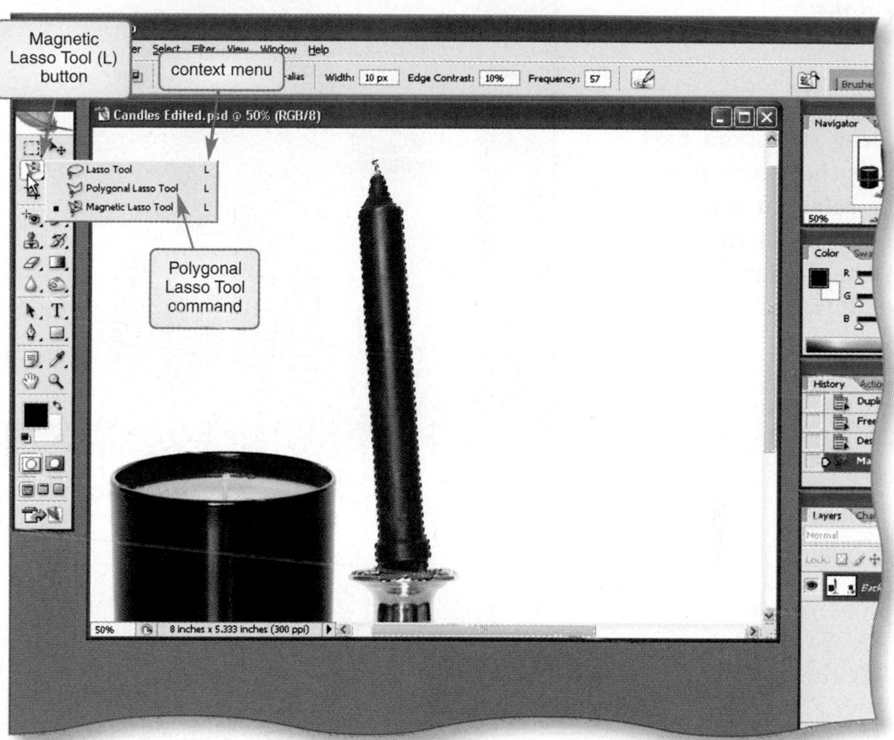

FIGURE 2-29

2

- **Click Polygonal Lasso Tool in the list.**

The tool button icon changes to reflect the polygonal lasso (Figure 2-30).

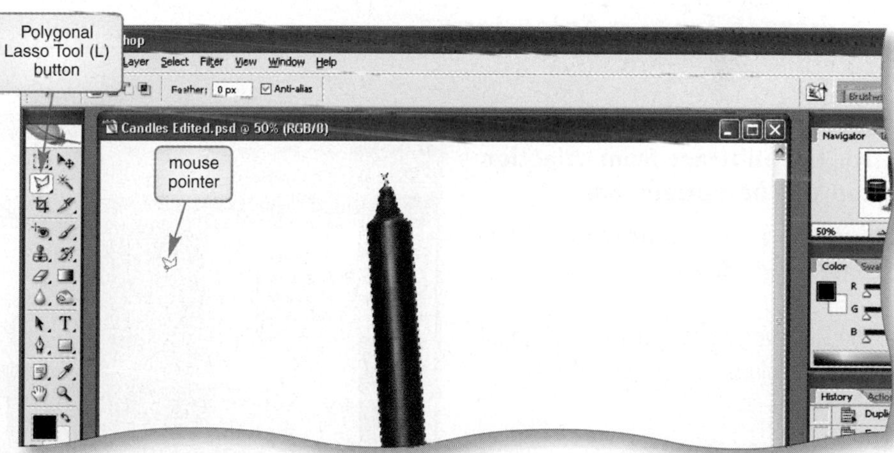

FIGURE 2-30

Other Ways

1. From Magnetic Lasso tool, press SHIFT+L twice

When subtracting from small portions of the document window, it often is necessary to zoom the magnification greater than 100% and then scroll the document window as shown in the steps on the next page.

To Zoom and Reposition the Document Window

1

- **On the Navigator palette status bar, click the Zoom In button several times to display the document window at 200%.**

2

- **Drag the scroll bars until the lower part of the selected area is displayed in the center of the document window.**

The selection border is displayed around the candle and a portion of the candle holder (Figure 2-31).

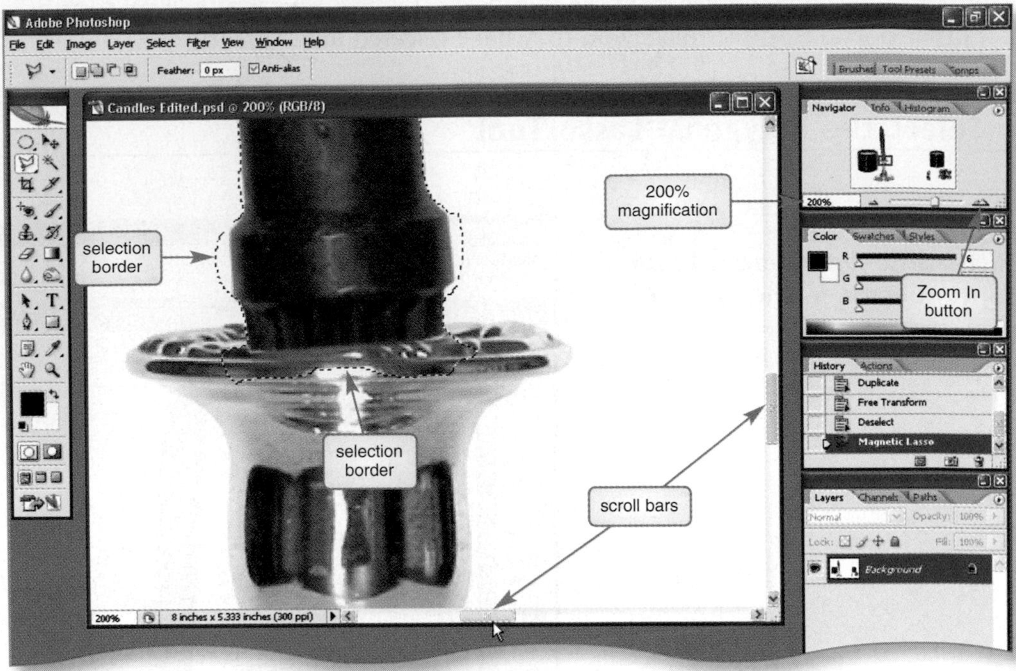

FIGURE 2-31

In the next section, you will use the Subtract from selection button and the Polygonal Lasso tool to subtract from the selection so only the candle is selected as the following steps illustrate. While you are drawing the selection, if you make a mistake, double-click to finish the selection and then click Undo on the Edit menu.

To Subtract from a Selection

1

- **Click the Subtract from selection button on the options bar.**
- **Move the mouse pointer into the document window.**

The mouse pointer changes to a polygonal lasso with a minus sign (Figure 2-32).

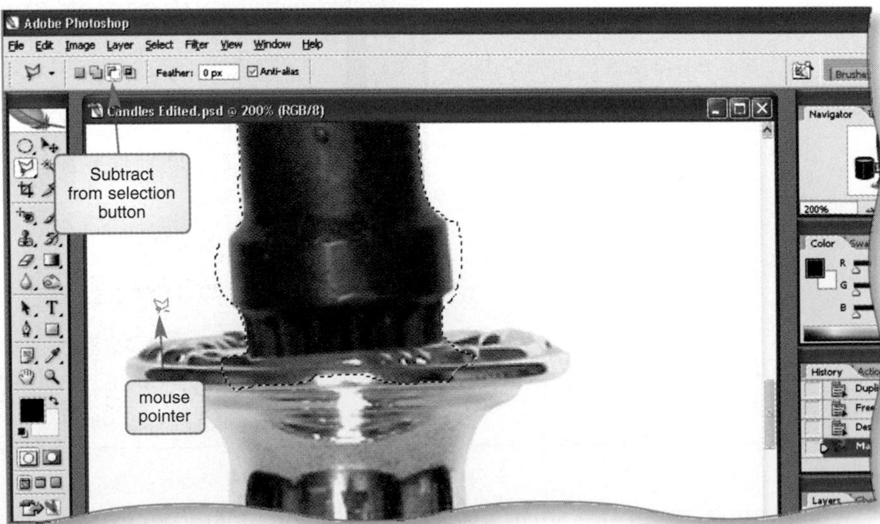

FIGURE 2-32

2

- **Click to the left of the candle holder level with the bottom of the candle.**

The beginning point of the lasso selection is set (Figure 2-33).

FIGURE 2-33

3

- **Move the mouse across the selection border, along the bottom of the candle, clicking at any curve you see in the bottom of the candle.**
- **Move the mouse pointer to the right side of the candle holder and then click.**

The lasso tool draws a line across the bottom of the candle (Figure 2-34).

FIGURE 2-34

4

- **Move the mouse down, staying outside the selection border.**
- **When you are completely below the selection border, click and then move left.**
- **When you get to the lower-left corner of the selection, click and then move up toward the beginning point.**

The lasso tool draws a box around the portion of the selection containing the candle holder across the bottom of the candle (Figure 2-35).

FIGURE 2-35

5

- **Position the mouse as closely as possible to the beginning point fastener and then click.**

The polygonal lasso selection is subtracted from the previous selection (Figure 2-36).

6

- **If you have other portions of the selection that do not include the candle itself, repeat Steps 2 through 5 to subtract them.**

FIGURE 2-36

Other Ways

1. To subtract from selection, ALT+drag

If you make errors using the Polygonal Lasso tool, and want to go back to the original selection, in the History palette, scroll if necessary to display the state labeled Magnetic Lasso. Click the state and begin again.

If you notice a corner or edge of the candle not included in the selection, click the Add to selection button on the options bar and then draw a lasso encompassing the corner or edge.

Rotating a Selection

Finally, you will use the Move tool to straighten the candle. Recall that the Move tool can be used to make several kinds of transformations other than simple moves. The following steps illustrate how to rotate the candle to a straighter position on the candle holder. The arrow keys are used to **nudge**, or move, the selection in small increments.

To Rotate a Selection

1

- **Click the Zoom Out button in the Navigator palette until the magnification is 33.33%.**
- **Click the Move Tool (V) button in the toolbox.**
- **If necessary, click the Show Transform Controls box to select it.**
- **Move the mouse pointer to a location slightly above and to the right of the selection, until the mouse pointer displays a rotation icon.**

Photoshop displays the bounding box, and the mouse pointer displays a rotation icon (Figure 2-37).

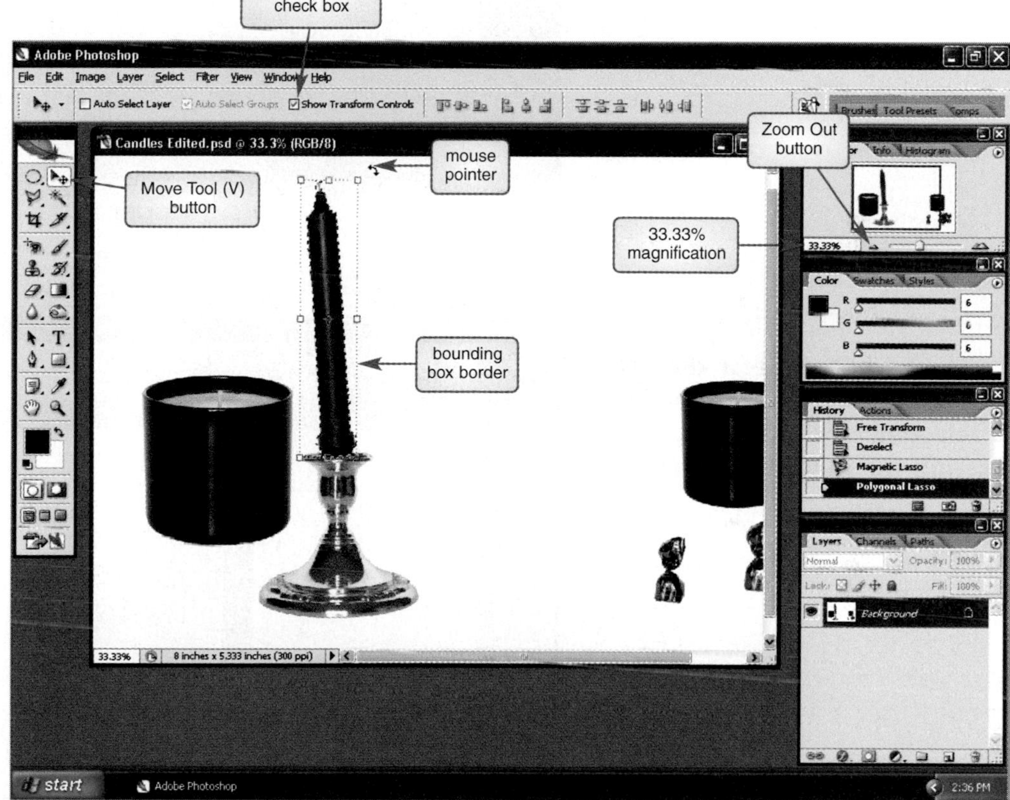

FIGURE 2-37

2

• **Drag down slightly to straighten the candle.**

Photoshop moves the selection clockwise (Figure 2-38).

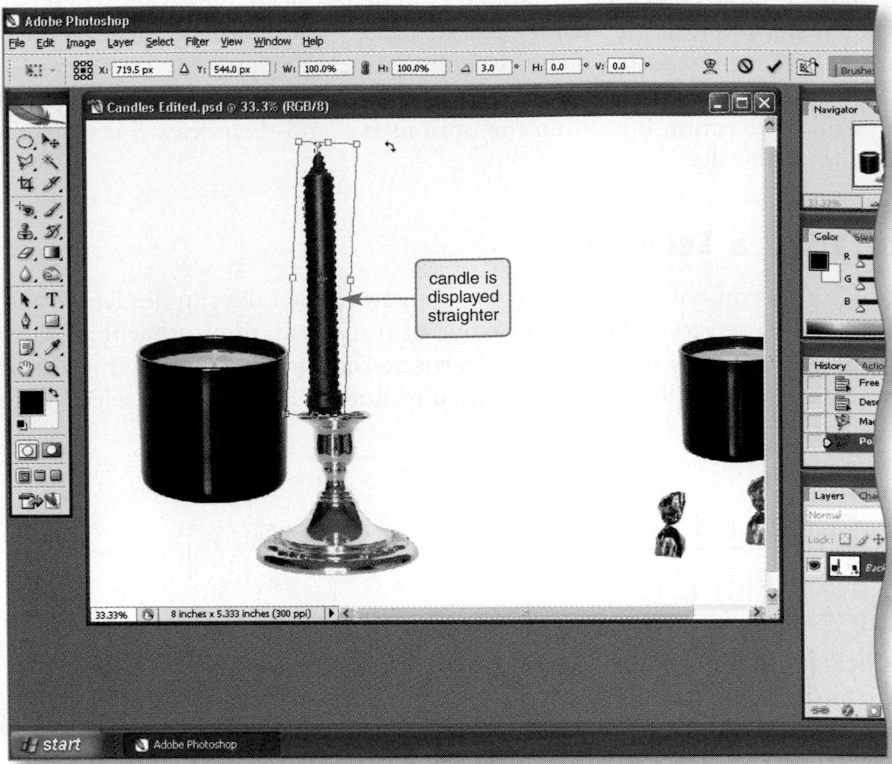

FIGURE 2-38

3

• **On the keyboard, press the RIGHT ARROW key several times to nudge the selection to the right, centering the candle over the candle holder.**

Photoshop moves the selection to the right (Figure 2-39).

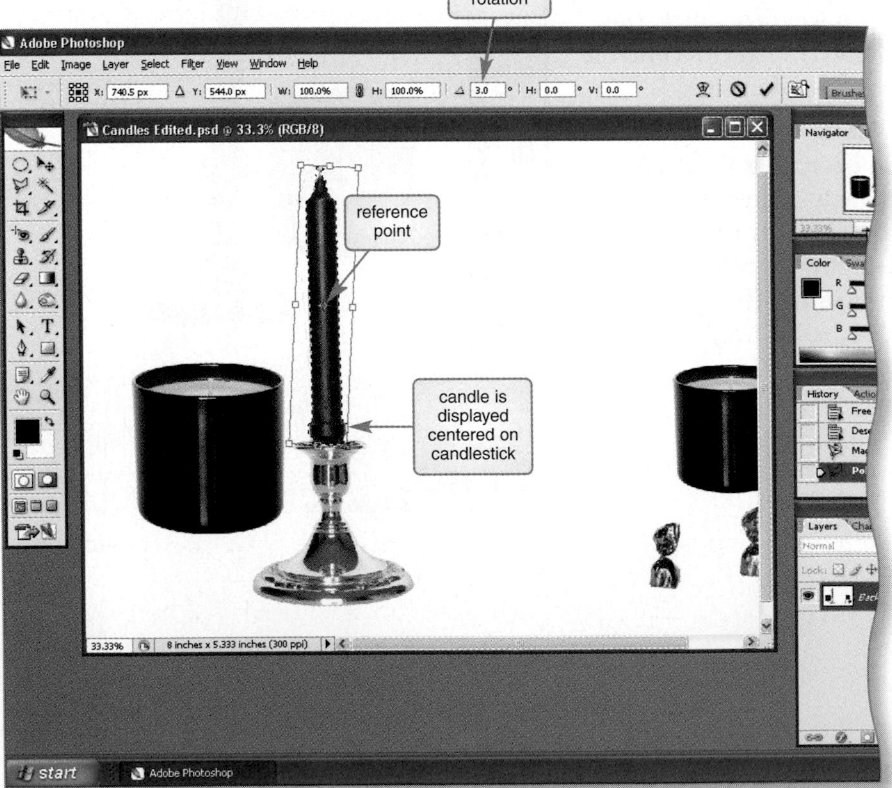

FIGURE 2-39

4

- **Press the ENTER key to commit the changes.**
- **Click Select on the menu bar and then click Deselect on the Select menu.**

Photoshop deselects the candle (Figure 2-40).

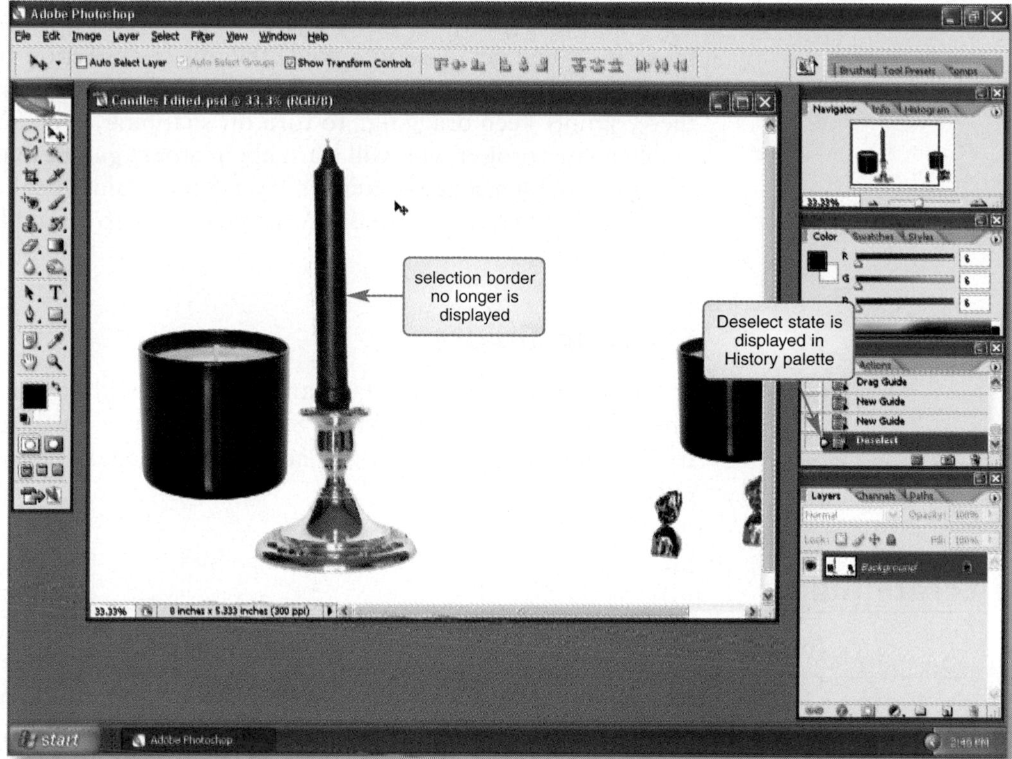

FIGURE 2-40

Other Ways

1. To rotate, on options bar enter degree rotation in Rotate box
2. To nudge, on options bar enter new horizontal or vertical placement value
3. To deselect, press CTRL+D

The reference point, the small circle at the center of a selection, serves as the pivot point during rotation (Figure 2-39). The default placement is in the center of the selection. If you drag the reference point to another location, any rotation performed on the selection will pivot around that new location.

Now that the candle is straight, it is time to use the lasso tools to select the candle and its holder, make two copies, and then move and resize them. To help position the candles, you first will learn about creating guides.

Creating Guides

A **guide** is a nonprinting ruler line that graphic designers use to align objects or mark key measurements. To create a guide, you turn on the ruler display and then drag from the horizontal ruler at the top of the document window or from the vertical ruler at the left side of the document window. When you release the mouse, a light, blue-green line is displayed across the image.

Photoshop also has a **grid** of lines that can be displayed over the top of the image. To display the grid, click Show on the View menu and then click Grid. The grid is useful for laying out elements symmetrically. The grid can display as nonprinting lines or as dots. Guides and grids help position images or elements precisely.

More About

Guides and Grids

You can change the color or style of guides and grids. On the Edit menu, point to Preferences, and then click Guides, Grids, & Slices.

The term **snapping** refers to the ability of objects to attach, or automatically align with, a grid or guide. For example, if you select an object in your image and begin to move it, as you get close to a guide the object's selection border will attach itself to the guide. It is not a permanent magnetic hold. If you do not wish to leave the object there, simply keep dragging. To turn off snapping, click Snap on the View menu.

In a later project, you will learn about **smart guides** that are displayed automatically when you draw a shape or move a layer. Smart guides further help align shapes, slices, selections, and layers. Appendix A describes how to set guides and grid preferences using the Edit menu.

Creating Guides

To copy and place the tall candles, guides will be placed in the image to create nine areas. Figure 2-2 on page PS 67 uses the rule of thirds to draw the reader's eye to the important aspects of this advertising image. The following steps show how to create guides.

To Create Guides

1

- **If the rulers do not display in the document window, click Rulers on the View menu.**
- **Click the horizontal ruler at the top of the document window and then drag down into the image.**
- **Do not release the mouse button.**

A ruler guide is displayed across the image (Figure 2-41).

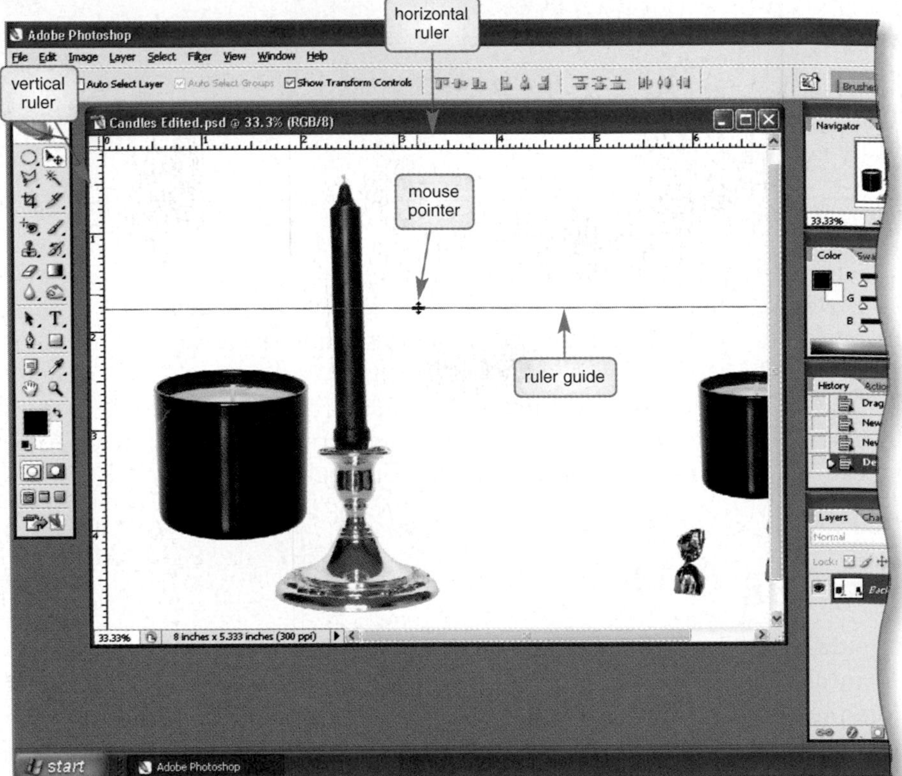

FIGURE 2-41

2

- **Drag until the ruler guide is approximately even with the 1¾ inch mark on the vertical ruler.**
- **Release the mouse button.**
- **If Photoshop does not display the guide, click View on the menu bar, point to Show, and then click Guides on the Show submenu.**

Photoshop displays a light, blue-green horizontal ruler guide at 1¾ inches (Figure 2-42).

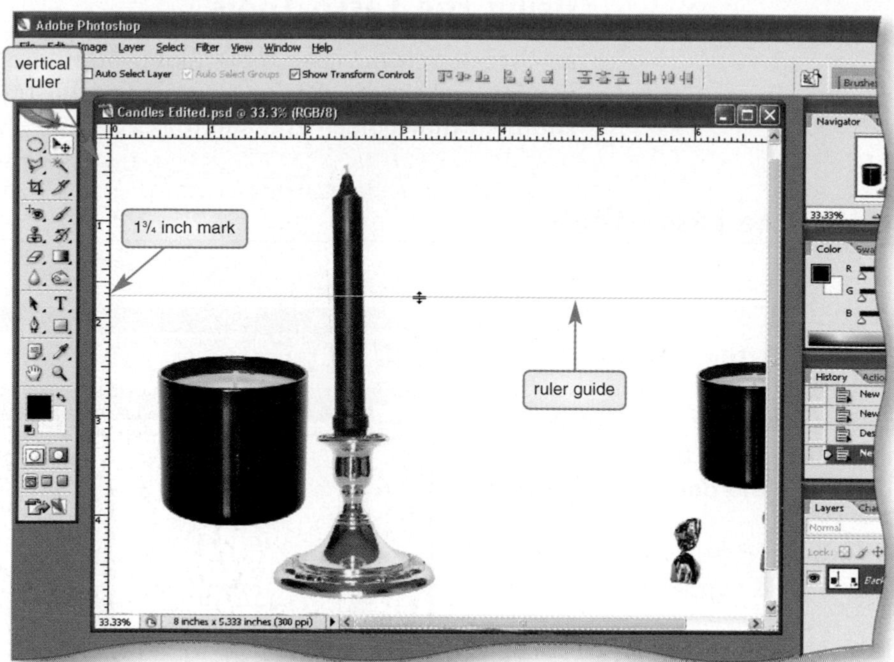

FIGURE 2-42

3

- **Using the same technique, drag another guide from the horizontal ruler and release the mouse button at 3½ inches as measured on the vertical ruler.**
- **Drag from the vertical ruler to create guides at 2⅝ inches and 5¼ inches as measured on the horizontal ruler.**

Photoshop displays ruler guides splitting the image into thirds both vertically and horizontally (Figure 2-43).

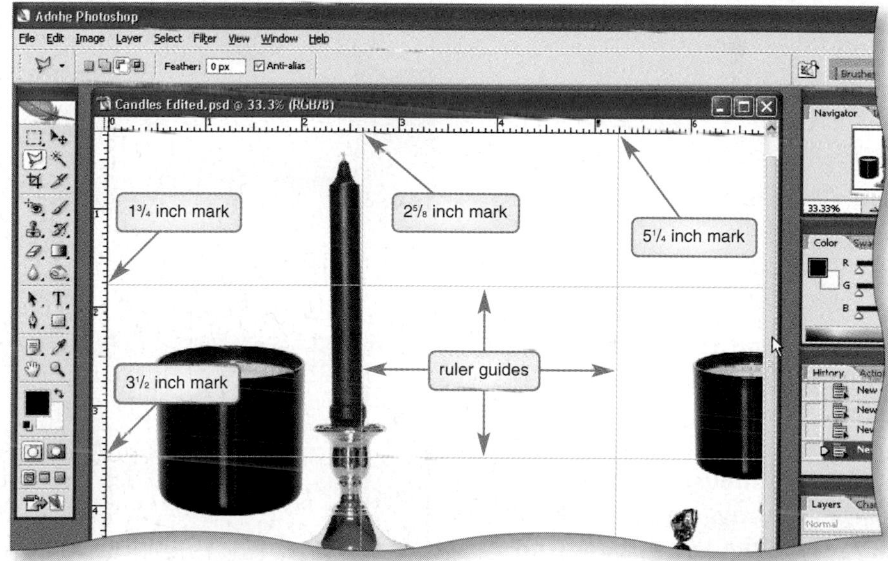

FIGURE 2-43

Other Ways

1. To display or turn off guides, press CTRL+;
2. To create guide, on View menu click New Guide

To move a guide, drag it. To remove a guide, drag it back to the ruler. To clear all guides, click Clear Guides on the View menu. To turn the display of the guides on and off, you can point to Show on the View menu and then click Guides on the Show submenu. Pressing CTRL+; also toggles the guides on and off. To lock the guides in place, click Lock Guides on the View menu.

Now that the guides are in place, the steps on the next page describe how to use the lasso tools to select the large candle in order to create copies.

Using the Lasso Tools

Recall that the lasso tools allow you to drag around any object in the document window to select it. The following steps illustrate how to draw around the tall candle and the candleholder freehand to select it.

To Use the Lasso Tools

1

• **Right-click the Polygonal Lasso Tool (L) button in the toolbox and then click Lasso Tool in the list. Move the mouse pointer to the document window.**

The Lasso tool is displayed on the button and as the mouse pointer (Figure 2-44).

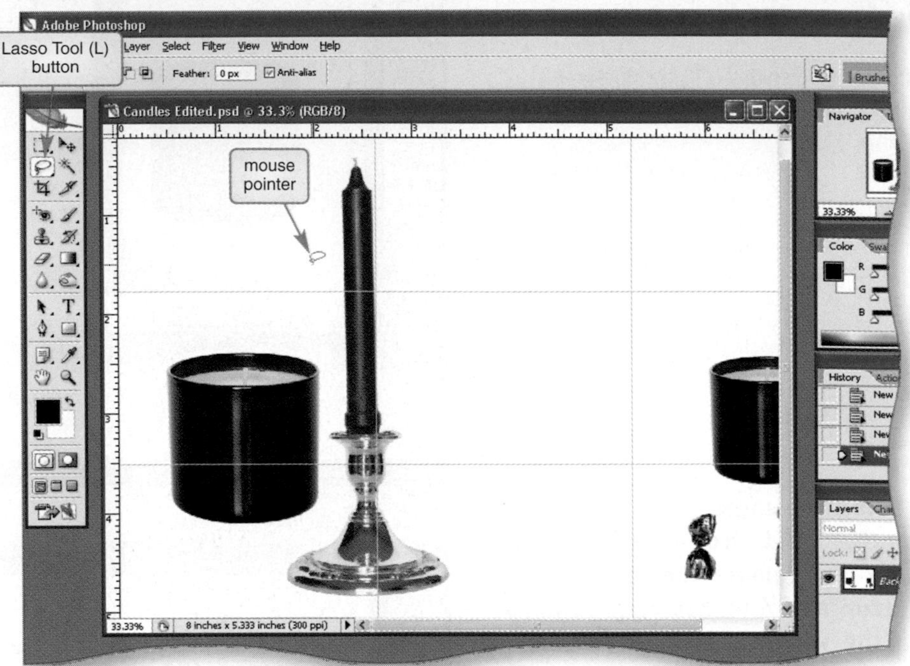

FIGURE 2-44

2

• **Drag around the candle and the candle holder. Be careful not to include any other object in the image. If you make a mistake, release the mouse, press CTRL+D and begin dragging again. When you get all the way around the image, release the mouse button close to the beginning of the lasso.**

Photoshop displays the selection border around the candle (Figure 2-45)

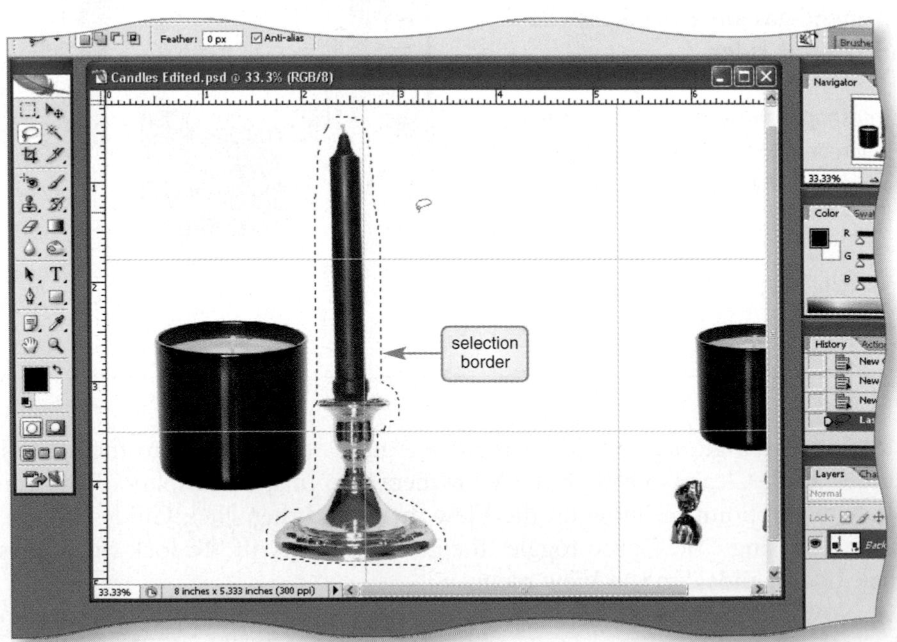

FIGURE 2-45

Other Ways

1. Press SHIFT+L until Lasso tool is active

The following steps show how to duplicate the candle by pressing the ALT key while dragging. The candle then is scaled proportionately.

To Duplicate and Scale the Candle

1

- **With the candle and candle holder selected, click the Move Tool (V) button in the toolbox.**
- **ALT+drag the selection to the right and slightly up, to a location near the rightmost vertical ruler guide. The candle will overlap the candy.**

A second copy of the candle is displayed with bounding box borders (Figure 2-46).

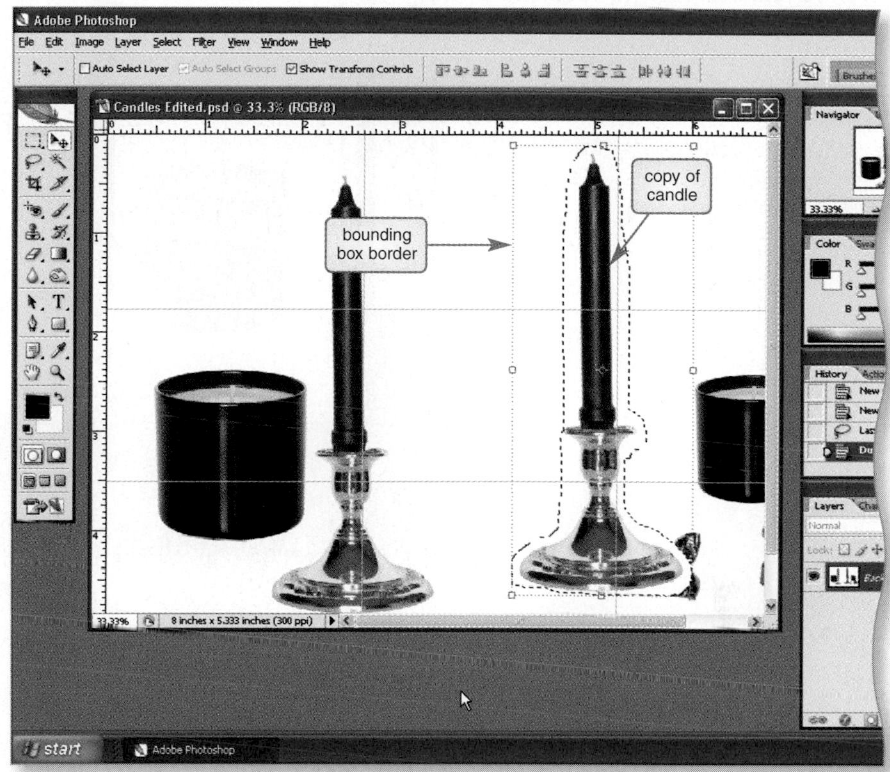

FIGURE 2-46

2

- **SHIFT+drag the lower-left sizing handle toward the middle of the candle, until the bounding box no longer overlaps the candy.**

Photoshop scales the selection (Figure 2-47). Recall that shift-dragging maintains the height to width ratio.

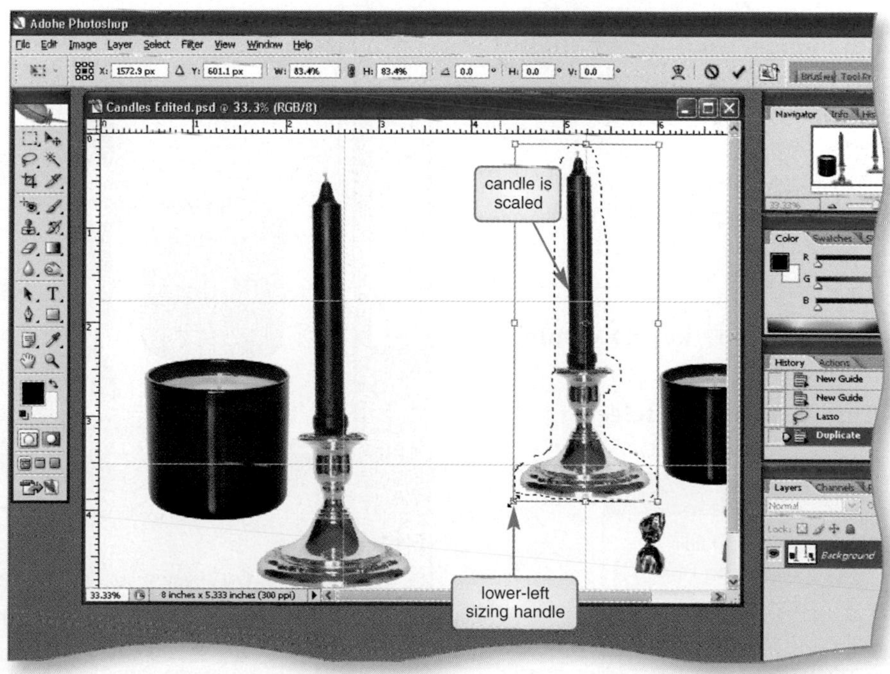

FIGURE 2-47

3

- **Press the ENTER key to commit the transformation.**
- **ALT+drag the selection down and to the left to create another copy. The third candle will be located just right of center.**

A third candle is displayed (Figure 2-48).

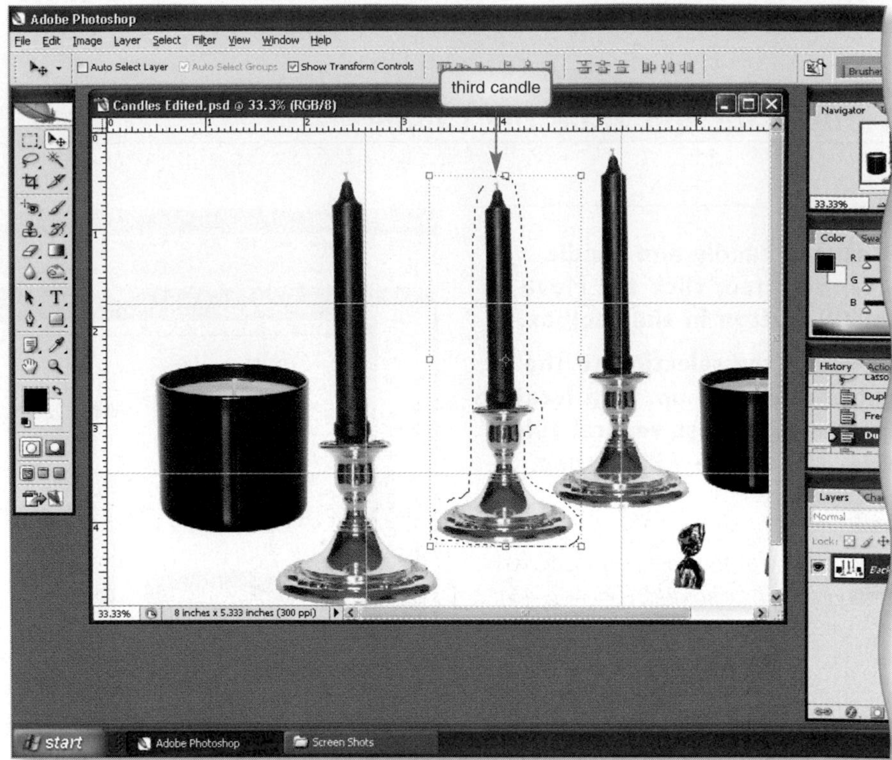

FIGURE 2-48

4

- **SHIFT+drag the lower-left sizing handle toward the middle of the candle, until it is displayed approximately 75% as small as it was before. The bottom of the candle holder will be approximately even with the lower horizontal ruler guide.**

Photoshop scales the selection (Figure 2-49). The options bar displays 75%.

5

- **Press the ENTER key to commit the changes.**
- **Press CTRL+D to deselect.**

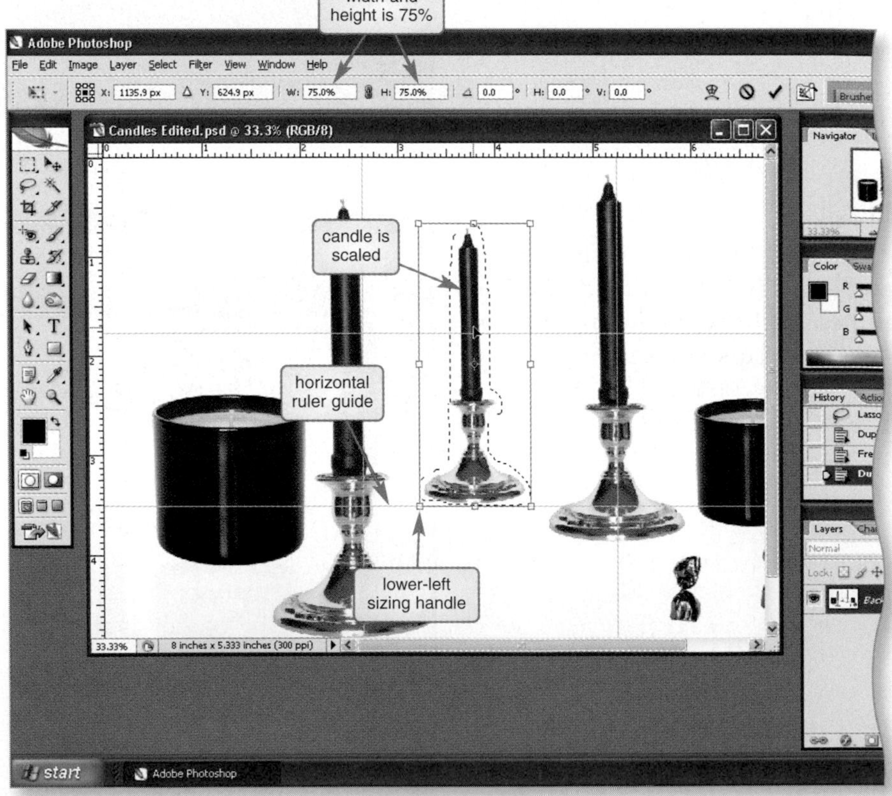

FIGURE 2-49

Other Ways

1. To duplicate, on Edit menu click Copy, Paste
2. To duplicate, press CTRL+C, press CTRL+V
3. To resize, on options bar enter height and width values

The next steps show how to move and copy the single piece of candy.

To Move and Duplicate the Single Piece of Candy

1. **Click the Lasso Tool (L) button in the toolbox. Scroll and zoom as necessary to display the single piece of candy.**
2. **Draw around the single piece of candy to create a selection border with only a small amount of white space.**
3. **Click the Move Tool (V) button in the toolbox.**
4. **Drag the candy to a location between the middle and right tall candles.**
5. **ALT+drag a copy to a location between the rightmost tall candle and the short candle as shown in Figure 2-50.**

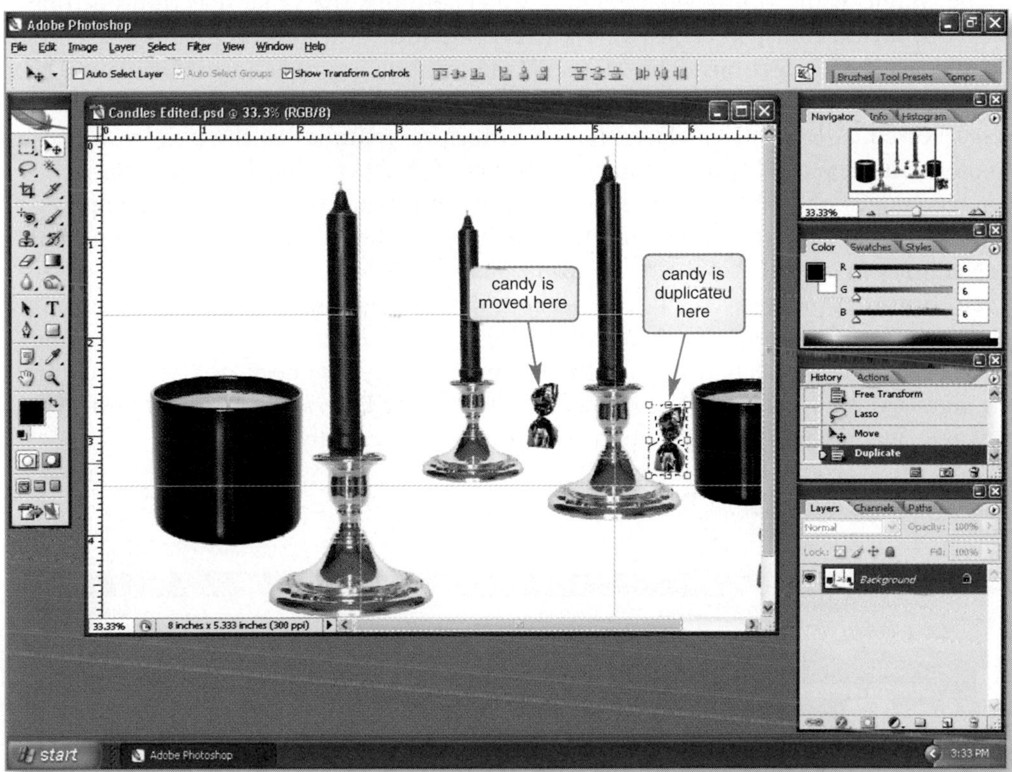

FIGURE 2-50

The history palette will list a Duplicate state when the ALT key is used to copy a selection. The word, Paste, will display when the Copy and Paste commands are used from the keyboard or menu. The Copy command alone does not affect how the image looks, it merely sends a copy to the system clipboard, therefore it is not saved as a state.

The Magic Wand Tool

Another selection tool useful in situations where you want to select an entire object is the Magic Wand tool. Some objects, like a flower with many curves and corners, would be difficult to trace with the lasso tools. The **Magic Wand tool** lets you select a consistently colored area without having to trace its outline. To use the Magic

Wand tool, you click the Magic Wand Tool (W) button in the toolbox or press the W key on the keyboard. When you use the Magic Wand tool and click in the image, Photoshop selects every pixel that contains the same or similar colors as the location you clicked. The default setting is to select contiguous pixels only; but Photoshop allows you to change that setting in order to select all pixels of the same color. You also can set the color range or tolerance, and specify a smoothed edge.

The Magic Wand tool especially is effective for solid colored objects. When used in conjunction with the Subtract from selection button, the Magic Wand tool can remove background colors in land-locked openings to create a selection that appears three dimensional and floating when moved around. When used in conjunction with the Select inverse command, the Magic Wand tool is useful for selecting only the objects on a solid background.

The Magic Wand Options Bar

The Magic Wand options bar (Figure 2-51) contains the same selection buttons as other selection tools, to create a new selection, add to or subtract from a selection, and intersect with selections. The Magic Wand options bar also has a **Tolerance** box that allows you to enter a value that determines the similarity or difference of the pixels selected. A low value selects the few colors very similar to the pixel you click. A higher value selects a broader range of colors. The Anti-alias check box smoothes the jagged edges of a selection by softening the color transition between edge pixels and background pixels. While anti-aliasing is useful when cutting, copying, and pasting selections to create composite images, it may leave behind a trace shadow when the selection is cut or moved. When checked, the **Contiguous** check box selects only adjacent areas using the same colors. Otherwise, all pixels in the entire image using the same colors are selected. Finally, the **Sample All Layers** check box selects colors using data from all visible layers. You will learn about layers in Project 3. Otherwise, the Magic Wand tool selects colors from the active layer only.

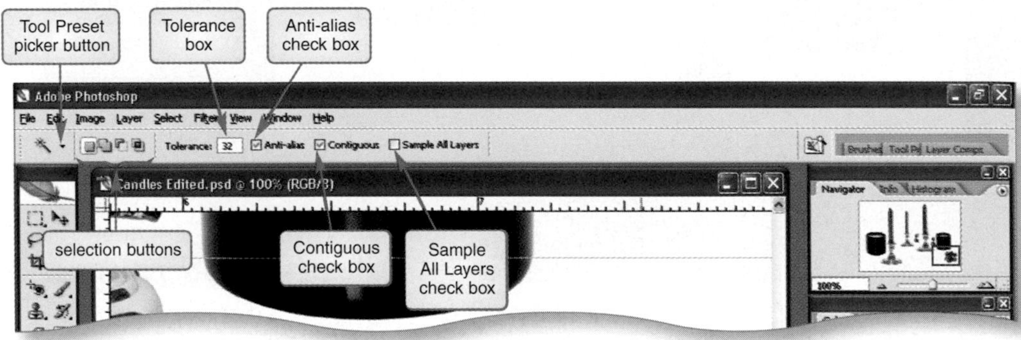

FIGURE 2-51

Using the Magic Wand Tool

You will use the Magic Wand tool to eliminate background around and in between the pieces of candy that are grouped together. First you will use the Rectangular Marquee tool to select the candies; then, you will remove the white background with the Magic Wand tool as the following steps illustrate

To Select the Candies with the Rectangular Marquee Tool

1 **Use the Navigator palette to zoom to 100% and then scroll to display the group of candies. If a previous selection still is displayed, press CTL+D to remove it.**

2 **Click the Rectangular Marquee Tool (M) button in the toolbox.**

3 **Draw a rectangle around the group of candies leaving a small amount of white space on all four sides.**

The selection border pulsates around the candy (Figure 2-52).

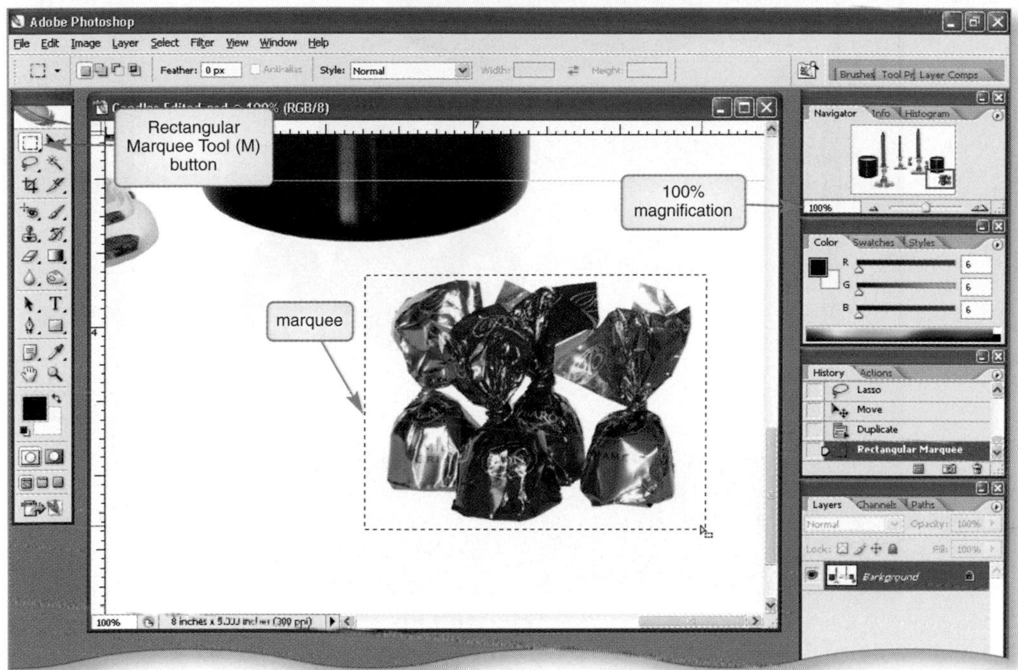

FIGURE 2-52

As you use the Magic Wand tool, remember that if you make a mistake while selecting, you can cancel the previous step by clicking Undo on the Edit menu or go back several steps by clicking a previous state in the History palette.

To Use the Magic Wand Tool

1

- **With the rectangular area around the candies still selected, click the Magic Wand Tool (W) button in the toolbox.**
- **Move the mouse pointer into the document window.**

Photoshop changes the mouse pointer to a magic wand (Figure 2-53).

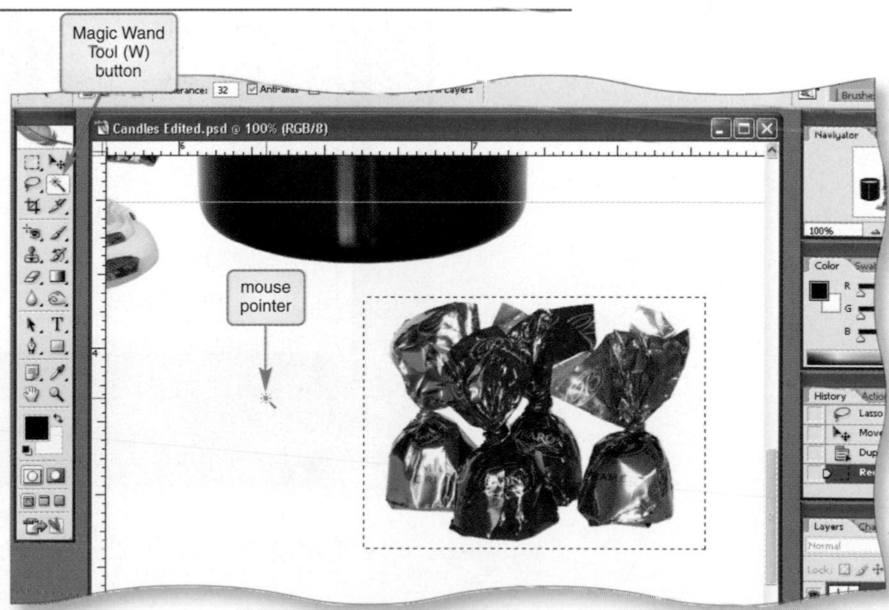

FIGURE 2-53

2

- **Click the Subtract from selection button on the Magic Wand options bar.**
- **Click the Anti-alias check box so it does not display a check mark.**

The options bar displays the new settings (Figure 2-54).

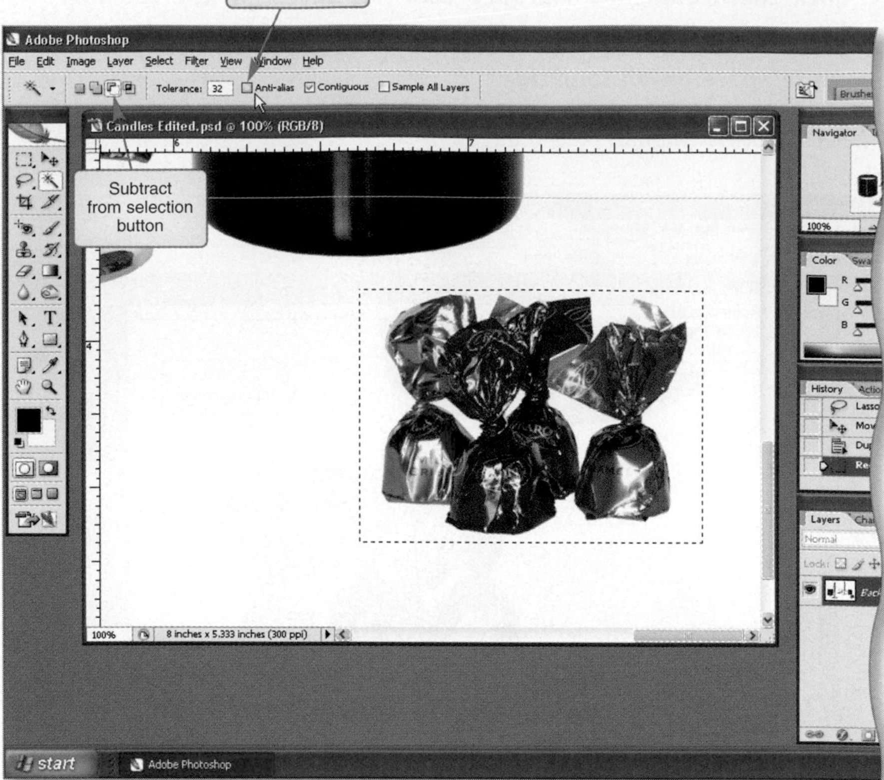

FIGURE 2-54

3

- **Using the tip of the Magic Wand mouse pointer, click each of the white spaces between the candies.**

Photoshop removes the white space from the selection. The pulsating border is displayed around the inner edges of the candy (Figure 2-55).

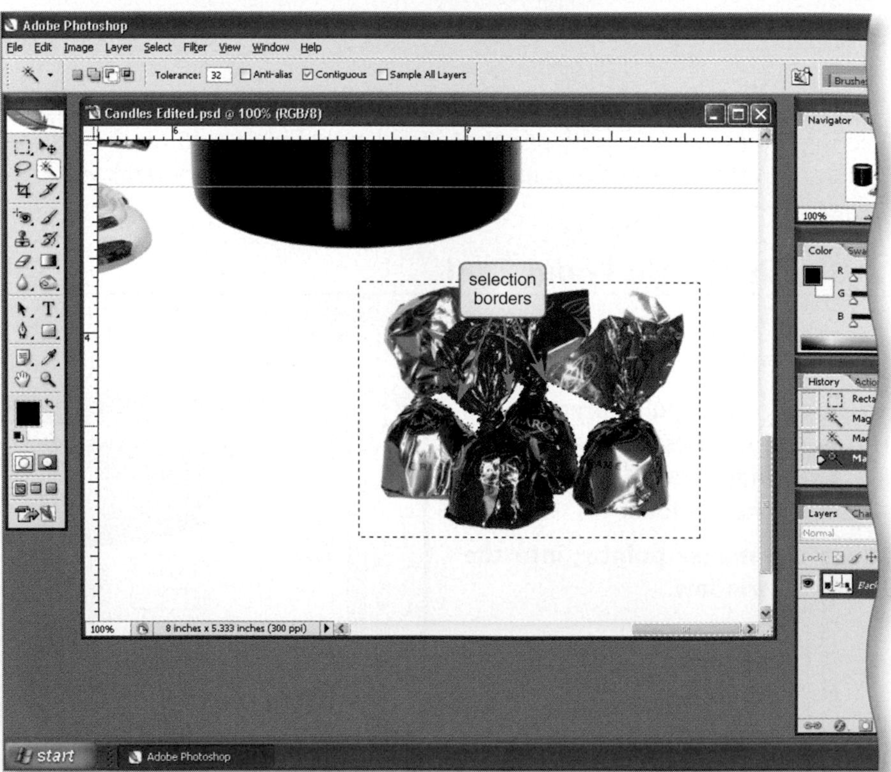

FIGURE 2-55

4

• **Click the white area around the candy but still inside the selection border.**

Photoshop removes the white space around the outside of the candies (Figure 2-56). Now the candies only are selected — without any white background around or between the images.

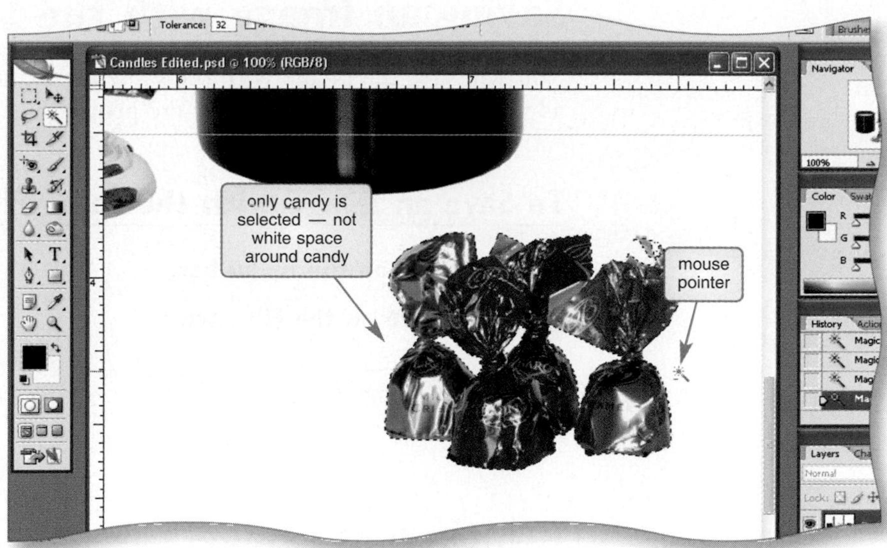

FIGURE 2-56

Other Ways

1. Press W key, then click image

The next step is to move the candies in front of the short candle and then deselect them as shown in the following steps.

To Move the Candies and Deselect

1 **On the Navigator palette, click the Zoom Out button until the magnification is 25%.**

2 **Click the Move Tool (V) button in the toolbox.**

3 **Drag the candies to a location on the lower-right corner of the short candle, as shown in Figure 2-57.**

4 **Press CTRL+D to deselect the candies.**

The candies display in front of the candle. Part of the candle's color can be seen between the pieces of candy.

Other Ways

1. To deselect, press CTRL+D
2. To move, press V key, then drag selection

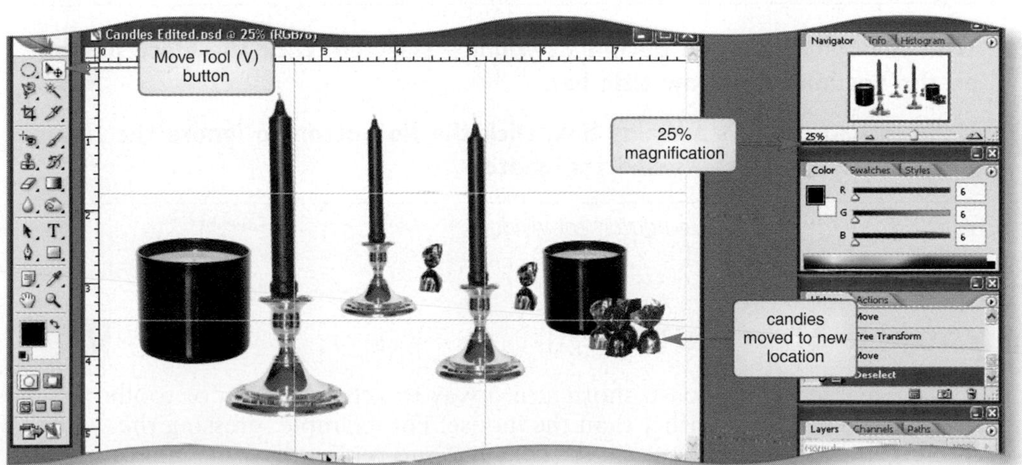

FIGURE 2-57

Saving an Image with the Same File Name

You will save the image with the same file name, Candles Edited, to the same location as you used at the beginning of the project.

To Save an Image with the Same File Name

1. **Click File on the menu bar.**
2. **Click Save on the File menu.**

Photoshop saves the image on a USB flash drive using the currently assigned file name, Candles Edited.

Printing an Image

The final step is to print a hard copy of the advertising image. The following steps show how to print the photo created in this project.

To Print an Image

1. **Ready the printer according to the printer instructions.**
2. **Click File on the menu bar. Click Print One Copy on the File menu.**
3. **When the printer stops printing the photo, retrieve the printout, which should look like Figure 2-1b on page PS 67.**

Other Ways

1. To print one copy, press ALT+SHIFT+CTRL+P
2. To display the Print dialog box, press CTRL+P

Closing a Photo

Recall that when you are finished editing a photo, you should close it. Closing a photo helps save system resources. You can close a photo after you have saved it and continue working in Photoshop, as the following steps illustrate.

To Close a Photo

1. **With the Candles Edited document window selected, click the Close button on the document window title bar.**
2. **If Photoshop displays a dialog box, click the No button to ignore the changes since the last time you saved the photo.**

Photoshop closes the Candles Edited document window.

Other Ways

1. On File menu, click Close
2. Press CTRL+W

Keyboard Shortcuts

As you have learned, a keyboard shortcut is a way to activate menu or toolbox commands using the keyboard rather than the mouse. For example, pressing the W key on the keyboard immediately selects the Magic Wand tool without having to move your mouse away from working in the image. Shortcuts with two keystrokes are common as well, such as the use of CTRL+A to select an entire image. Shortcuts are useful when you do not want to take the time to traverse the menu system, or when you are making precise edits and selections with the mouse and do not want to go back to the toolbox or palette to change tools. A Quick Reference Summary describing Photoshop's keyboard shortcuts is included in the back of the book.

While many keyboard shortcuts already exist in Photoshop, there may be times when additional shortcuts would be useful. For instance, the Single Row and Single Column Marquee tools have no shortcut key. If those are tools that you use frequently, a keyboard shortcut might be helpful. Photoshop allows users to create, customize, and save keyboard shortcuts in one of three areas: menus, palettes, and tools. When you create keyboard shortcuts, you can add them to Photoshop's default settings, save them in a personalized set for retrieval in future editing sessions, or delete them from your system.

Creating a Keyboard Shortcut

To create a new keyboard shortcut, Photoshop provides a dialog box interface accessible from the Edit menu. Using that dialog box, you can choose one of the three shortcut areas and then choose a shortcut key or combination of keys. Photoshop immediately warns you if you have chosen a keyboard shortcut used somewhere else in the program.

In the following steps, you will learn how to create a shortcut for the Default Workspace command. While that command is accessible via the Window menu and the Workspace submenu, a one keystroke shortcut would save time when you need to restore the workspace palettes and toolbox to their original locations.

To Create a New Keyboard Shortcut

1

- **Click Edit on the menu bar and then point to Keyboard Shortcuts.**

Photoshop displays the Edit menu (Figure 2-58).

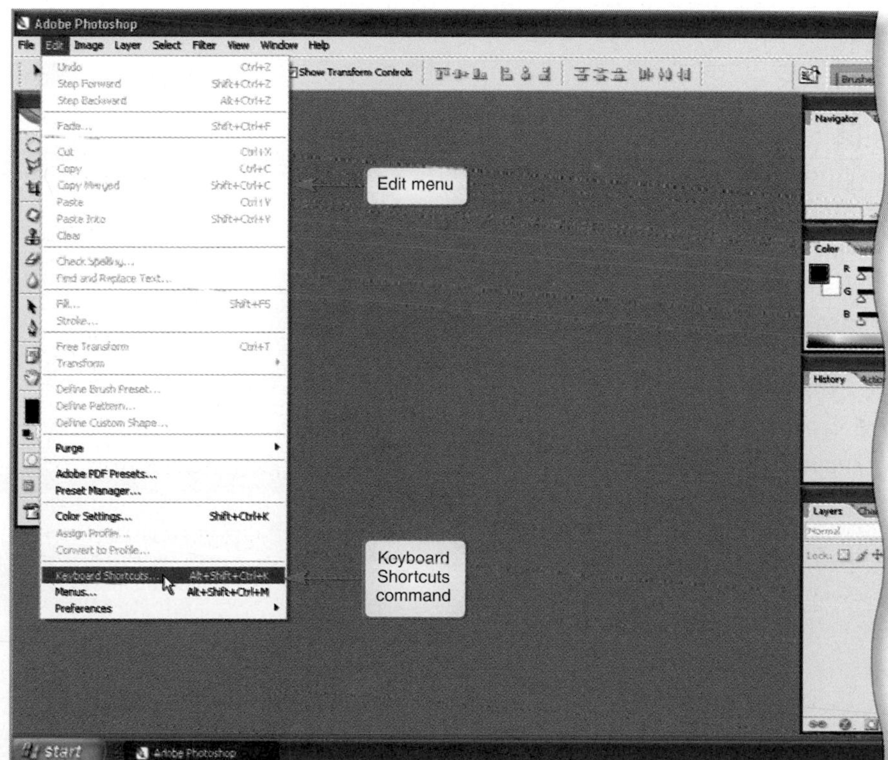

FIGURE 2-58

2

• **Click Keyboard Shortcuts.**

• **When the Keyboard Shortcuts and Menus dialog box is displayed, if necessary, click the Keyboard Shortcuts tab.**

• **If the Set box does not display Photoshop Defaults, click the Set box arrow and then click Photoshop Defaults in the list.**

• **If the Shortcuts For box does not display Application Menus, click the Shortcuts For box arrow and then click Application Menus in the list.**

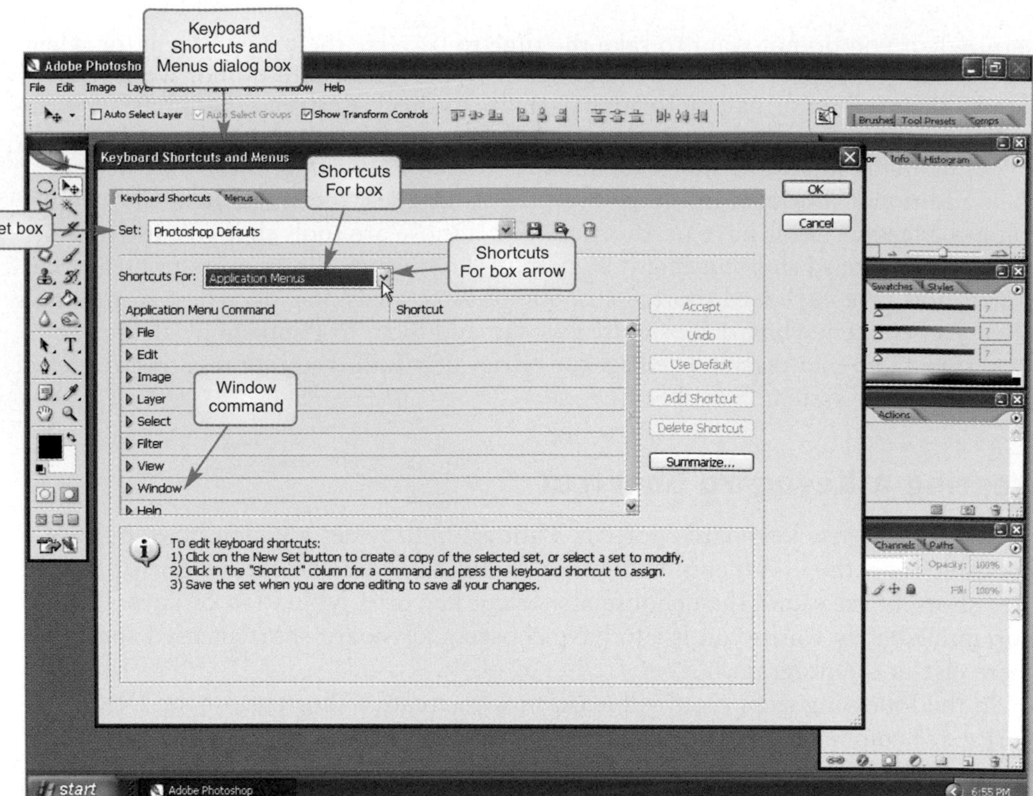

FIGURE 2-59

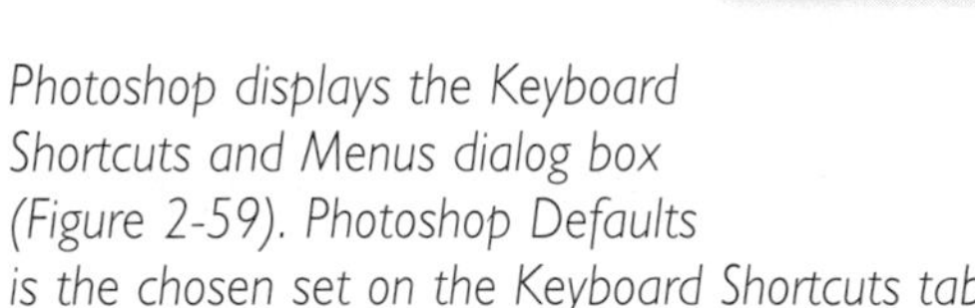

Photoshop displays the Keyboard Shortcuts and Menus dialog box (Figure 2-59). Photoshop Defaults is the chosen set on the Keyboard Shortcuts tab.

3

• **Double-click the Window command in the Application Menu Command list.**

• **Scroll down to display Workspace> under the Windows menu and Default Workspace under the Workspace submenu.**

• **Click Default Workspace.**

Photoshop displays a blank text box next to Default Workspace (Figure 2-60).

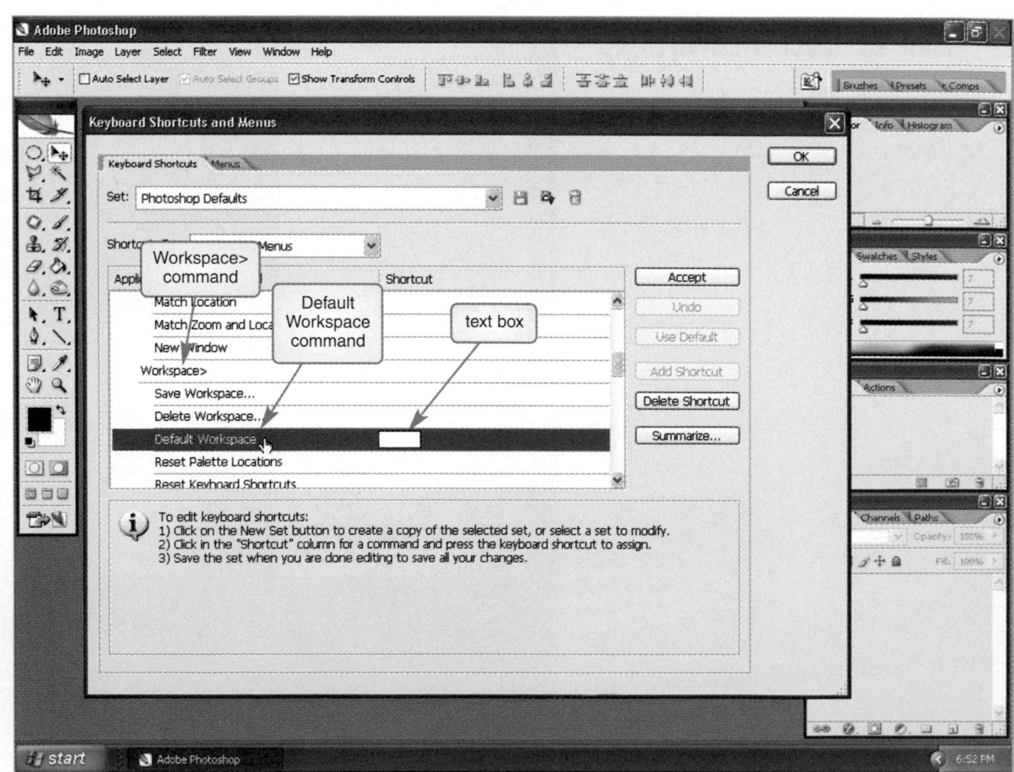

FIGURE 2-60

4

• **Press the F12 key.**

Photoshop warns you that F12 is being used as a shortcut for a different command (Figure 2-61).

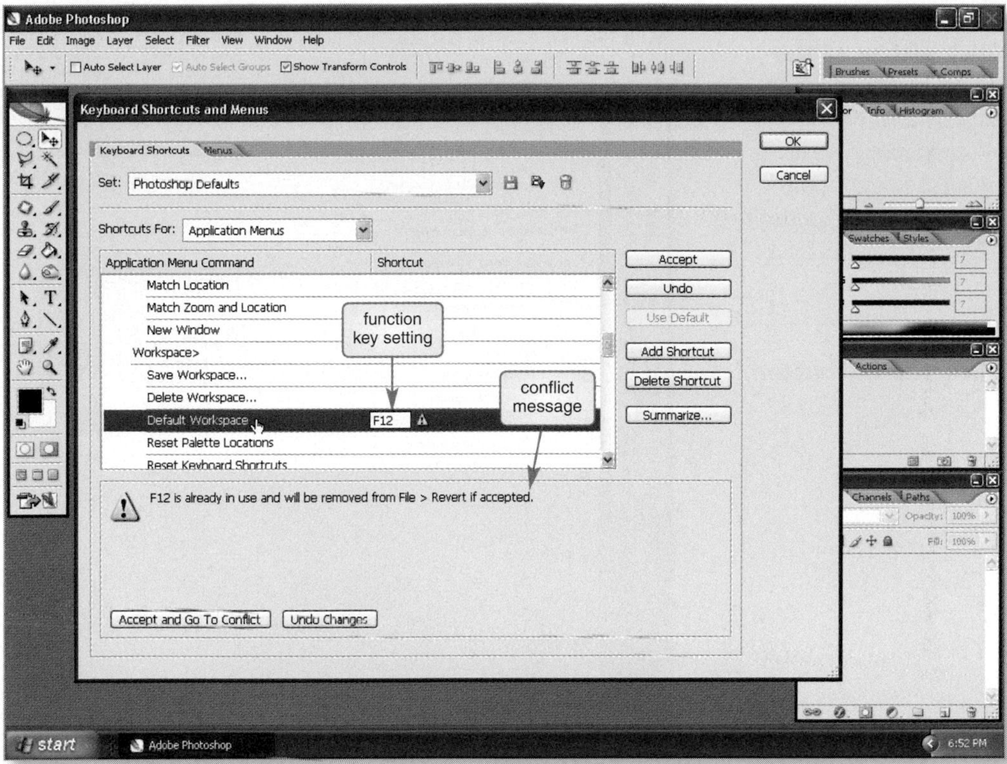

FIGURE 2-61

5

• **Press the F11 key.**

Photoshop displays a message indicating the F11 key is available to use (Figure 2-62).

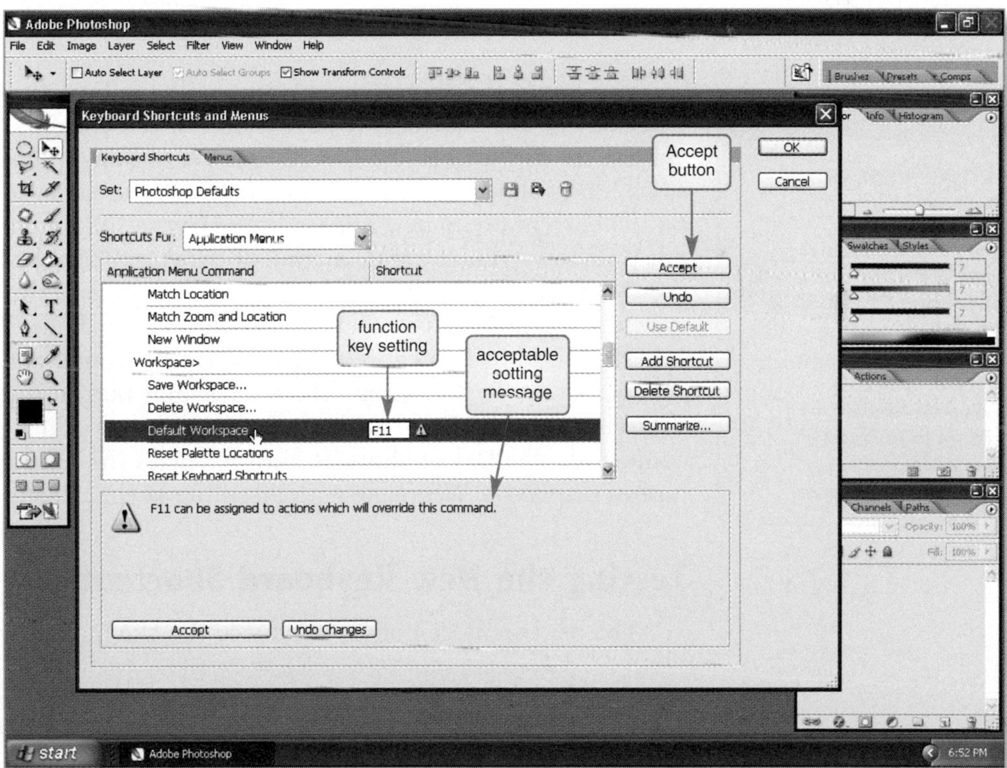

FIGURE 2-62

• **Click either of the Accept buttons.**

Photoshop displays the shortcut, and the word, modified, has been added in the Set box (Figure 2-63).

• **Click the OK button.**

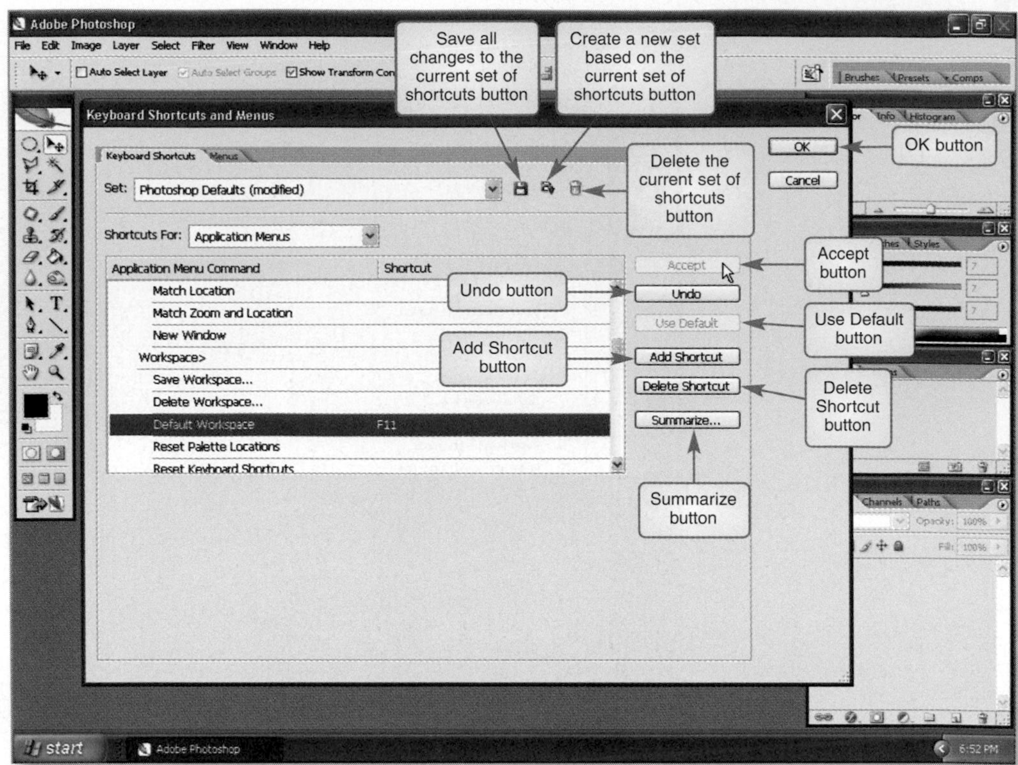

FIGURE 2-63

> *More About*
>
> **The Presets Folder**
>
> The Presets folder stores many of the tool settings and preferences for Photoshop. To view the contents of the Presets folder, on most systems, open a My Computer window and browse to C:\Program Files\Adobe\Adobe Photoshop CS2\Presets

The Keyboard Shortcuts and Menus dialog box displays three buttons to use when saving the shortcuts (Figure 2-63). When clicked, the Save all changes to the current set of shortcuts button allows you to name the set for retrieval in future sessions. Photoshop stores the set in a file with the extension .kys in the Presets folder on the current computer. The Create a new set based on the current set of shortcuts button allows you to create a copy of the current keyboard shortcut settings. Finally, the Delete the current set of shortcuts button deletes the set. If you do not save the new keyboard shortcuts, they last for the current Photoshop session only.

The Undo button cancels the most recent setting and after it is clicked the button changes to the Redo button. The Use Default button restores a deleted Photoshop shortcut. The Add Shortcut button allows you to add a second shortcut to the same command. The Delete Shortcut button deletes the selected shortcut. The Summarize button displays a Web page with all of the keyboard shortcuts in the set.

Testing the New Keyboard Shortcut

The next steps demonstrate how to test the new keyboard shortcut.

To Test the New Keyboard Shortcut

1

- **Drag the Navigator palette title bar toward the center of the document window.**
- **Drag the toolbox handle toward the center of the document window (Figure 2-64).**

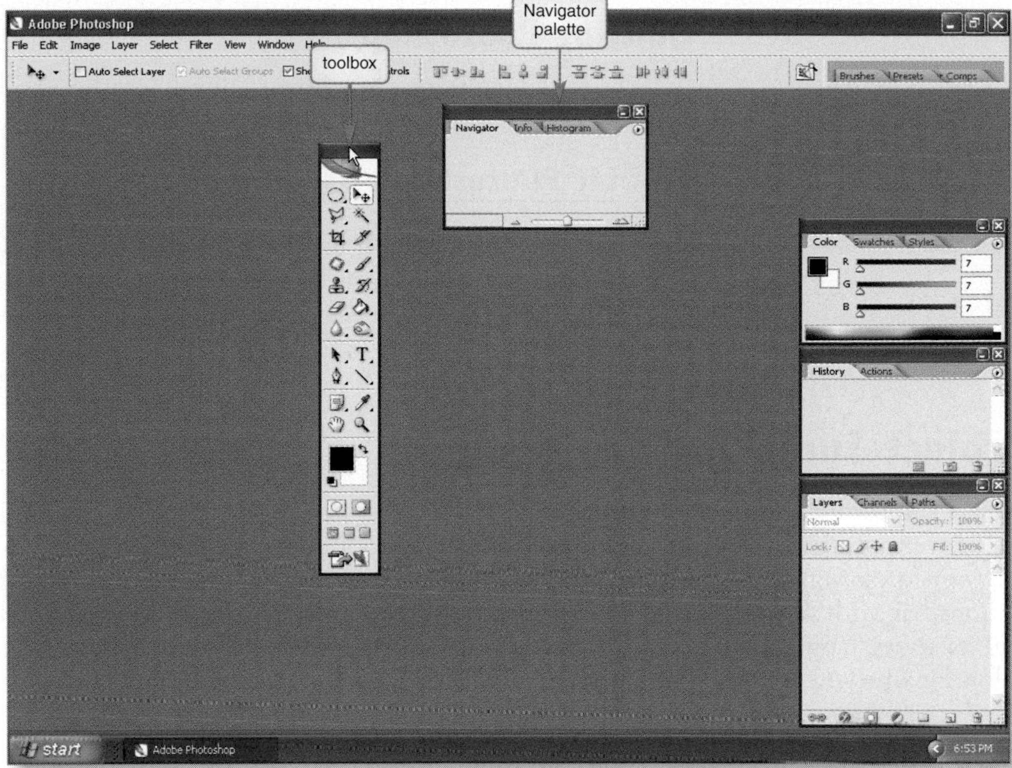

FIGURE 2-64

2

- **Press the F11 key. Do not press the ENTER key.**

Photoshop restores the Navigator palette and the toolbox to their original locations (Figure 2-65).

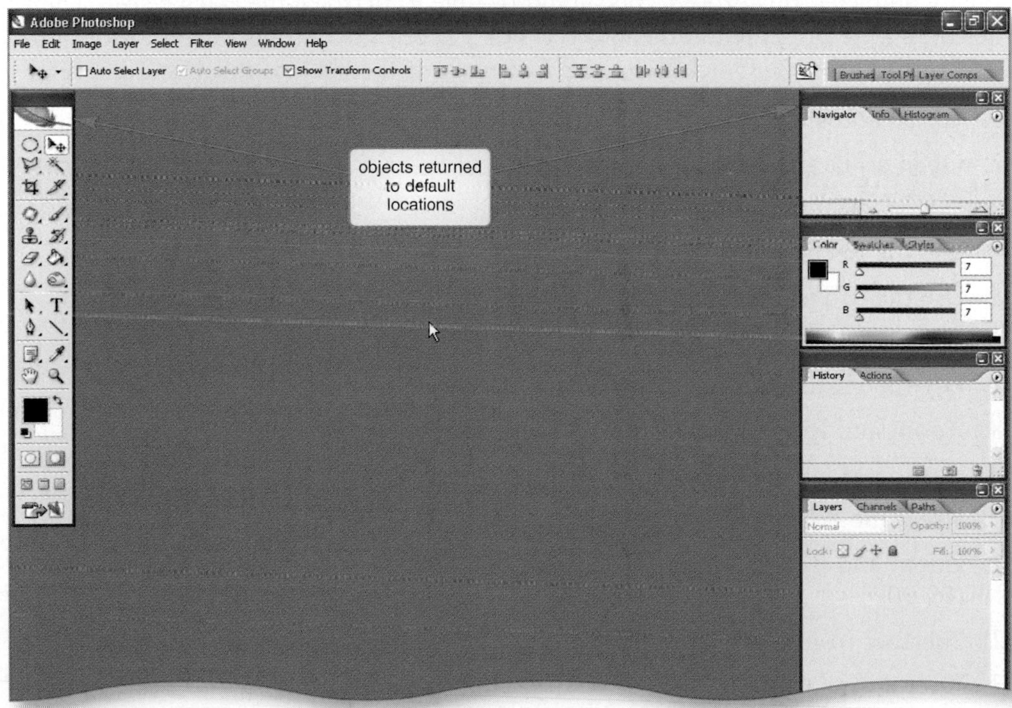

FIGURE 2-65

Keyboard shortcuts assigned to menu commands will display on the right of the command in the menu system.

Quitting Photoshop

The following steps show how to quit Photoshop and return control to Windows.

To Quit Photoshop

1 Click the Close button on the right side of the title bar. If Photoshop displays a dialog box asking you to save changes, click the No button.

The Photoshop window closes.

Project Summary

Project 2 introduced you to several new selection tools. You learned how to use the Rectangular Marquee tool, the Move tool, the lasso tools, and the Magic Wand tool. Once you drew a selection, you then learned many of the transformation commands including scaling and rotating. Each of the tools and commands had its own options bar with settings to control how the tool or command worked. You learned about the History palette and its states. You used the Magic Wand tool to subtract from selected portions of the image with the same color. Finally, you learned how to create and test a new keyboard shortcut.

What You Should Know

Having completed this project you should be able to perform the tasks below. The tasks are listed in the same order they were presented in this project. For a list of the buttons, menus, tools, and other commands introduced in this project, see the Quick Reference Summary at the back of this book and refer to the Page Number column.

1. Start Photoshop (PS 68)
2. Open a File (PS 68)
3. Save a Photo (PS 70)
4. Use the Rectangular Marquee Tool (PS 73)
5. Use the Move Tool (PS 75)
6. Scale a Selection (PS 79)
7. Use the History Palette (PS 82)
8. Zoom and Resize the Document Window (PS 84)
9. Use the Magnetic Lasso Tool (PS 85)
10. Select the Polygonal Lasso Tool (PS 89)
11. Zoom and Reposition the Document Window (PS 90)
12. Subtract from a Selection (PS 90)
13. Rotate a Selection (PS 93)
14. Create Guides (PS 96)
15. Use the Lasso Tools (PS 98)
16. Duplicate and Scale the Candle (PS 99)
17. Move and Duplicate the Single Piece of Candy (PS 101)
18. Select the Candies with the Rectangular Marquee Tool (PS 102)
19. Use the Magic Wand Tool (PS 103)
20. Move the Candies and Deselect (PS 105)
21. Save an Image with the Same File Name (PS 106)
22. Print an Image (PS 106)
23. Close a Photo (PS 106)
24. Create a New Keyboard Shortcut (PS 107)
25. Test the New Keyboard Shortcut (PS 111)
26. Quit Photoshop (PS 112)

Learn It Online

Instructions: To complete the Learn It Online exercises, start your browser, click the Address bar, and then enter the Web address `scsite.com/photoshop/learn`. When the Photoshop CS2 Learn It Online page is displayed, follow the instructions in the exercises below. Each exercise has instructions for printing your results, either for your own records or for submission to your instructor.

1 Project Reinforcement TF, MC, and SA

Below Photoshop Project 2, click the Project Reinforcement link. Print the quiz by clicking Print on the File menu for each page. Answer each question.

2 Flash Cards

Below Photoshop Project 2, click the Flash Cards link and read the instructions. Type 20 (or a number specified by your instructor) in the Number of playing cards text box, type your name in the Enter your Name text box, and then click the Flip Card button. When the flash card is displayed, read the question and then click the ANSWER box arrow to select an answer. Flip through Flash Cards. If your score is 15 (75%) correct or greater, click Print on the File menu to print your results. If your score is less than 15 (75%) correct, then redo this exercise by clicking the Replay button.

3 Practice Test

Below Photoshop Project 2, click the Practice Test link. Answer each question, enter your first and last name at the bottom of the page, and then click the Grade Test button. When the graded practice test is displayed on your screen, click Print on the File menu to print a hard copy. Continue to take practice tests until you score 80% or better.

4 Who Wants To Be a Computer Genius?

Below Photoshop Project 2, click the Computer Genius link. Read the instructions, enter your first and last name at the bottom of the page, and then click the PLAY button. When your score is displayed, click the PRINT RESULTS link to print a hard copy.

5 Wheel of Terms

Below Photoshop Project 2, click the Wheel of Terms link. Read the instructions, and then enter your first and last name and your school name. Click the PLAY button. When your score is displayed, right-click the score and then click Print on the shortcut menu to print a hard copy.

6 Crossword Puzzle Challenge

Below Photoshop Project 2, click the Crossword Puzzle Challenge link. Read the instructions, and then enter your first and last name. Click the SUBMIT button. Work the crossword puzzle. When you are finished, click the Submit button. When the crossword puzzle is redisplayed, click the Print Puzzle button to print a hard copy.

7 Tips and Tricks

Below Photoshop Project 2, click the Tips and Tricks link. Click a topic that pertains to Project 2. Right-click the information and then click Print on the shortcut menu. Construct a brief example of what the information relates to in Photoshop to confirm you understand how to use the tip or trick.

8 Expanding Your Horizons

Below Photoshop Project 2, click the Expanding Your Horizons link. Click a topic that pertains to Project 2. Print the information. Construct a brief example of what the information relates to in Photoshop to confirm you understand the contents of the article.

9 Search Sleuth

Below Photoshop Project 2, click the Search Sleuth link. To search for a term that pertains to this project, select a term below the Project 2 title and then use the Google search engine at google.com (or any major search engine) to display and print two Web pages that present information on the term.

10 Photoshop Online Training

Below Photoshop Project 2, click the Photoshop Online Training link. When your browser displays the Web page, click one of the Photoshop tutorials that covers one or more of the objectives listed at the beginning of the project on page PS 66. Print the first page of the tutorial before stepping through it.

Apply Your Knowledge

1 Transforming Selections

Problem: Your older sister teaches grade school and is planning a science unit on outer space. To elicit enthusiasm among her students, she is planning a bulletin board with the theme, "Blast off with Science!" She knows you have been studying Photoshop and has found a picture that she wants you to edit. She hopes you can add a sense of motion to the photo. You decide to angle the rocket ship, apply perspective, and warp the trail of flames.

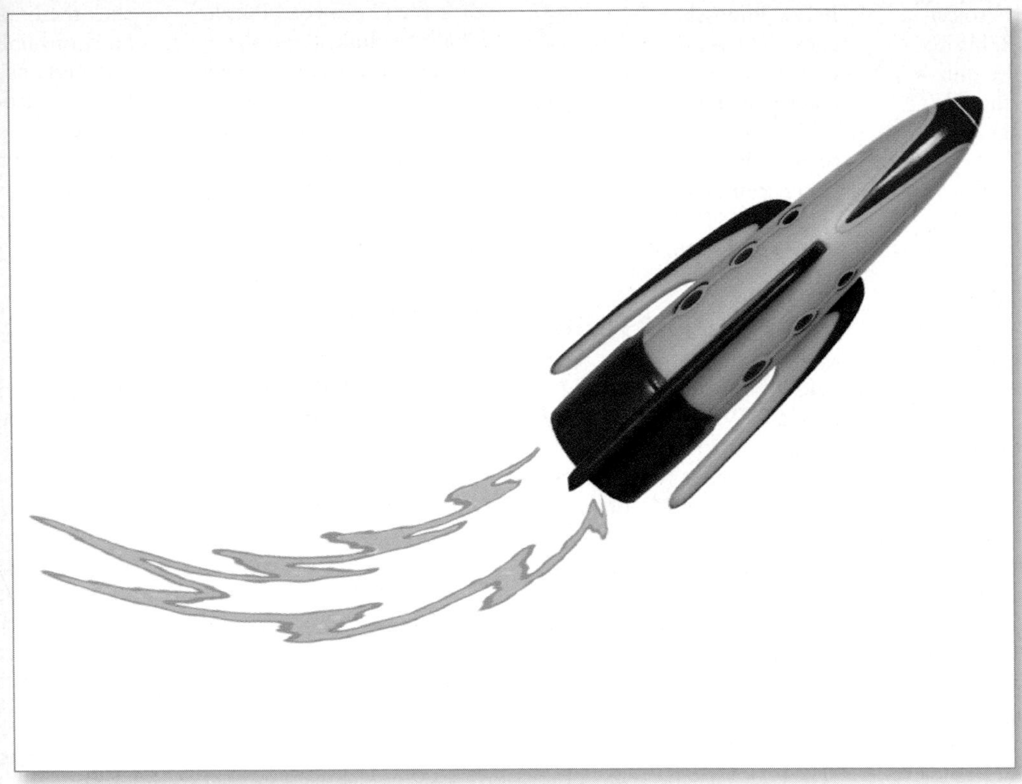

FIGURE 2-66

Instructions: Start Photoshop and set the workspace and tools to default settings. Open the Toy Rocket file from the Project02 student data files, located either on the CD that came with this book, or in a location specified by your instructor. The purpose of this exercise is to apply a series of transformations to add a sense of motion to a photograph. The edited photo is displayed in Figure 2-66.

1. Use the Save As command on the File menu to save the file on your storage device with the name, Toy Rocket Edited. If Photoshop displays a JPEG Options dialog box, click the OK button.
2. Zoom in to approximately 150% and enlarge the document window to focus on the rocket ship.
3. Use the Magnetic Lasso tool to draw carefully around the rocket ship only. Do not include the trail of flames. Use the Polygonal Lasso tool to add or subtract from the selection as necessary to include only the rocket ship.
4. Zoom out to 100% and then click the Move Tool (V) button.

Apply Your Knowledge

5. To rotate the rocket ship:
   a. When Photoshop displays the bounding box, point to a location outside the upper-right corner of the rocket ship. The mouse pointer will change to the rotate icon.
   b. Drag down or clockwise until the rocket ship displays at approximately a 50 degree angle. *Hint*: Use the Rotate box on the options bar to view the angle as you drag.
6. To add perspective to the rocket ship:
   a. Right-click the selection and then click Perspective on the shortcut menu.
   b. Locate the upper-right sizing handle in relation to the rocket ship. Drag the sizing handle toward the nose of the rocket. Recall that perspective is different than a slant created by skewing. It makes part of the image look farther away.
   c. Press the ENTER key to commit the transformation.
7. Use the Rectangular Marquee tool to select the trail of flames.
8. To rotate and scale the trail of flames:
   a. Press CTRL+T to freely transform the marquee. Photoshop displays the bounding box.
   b. Rotate the selection clockwise 50 degrees as you did with the rocket ship.
   c. Right-click the selection and then click Scale on the shortcut menu.
   d. Locate the top-center sizing handle in relation to the trail of flames. Drag the sizing handle to scale the selection vertically to approximately 250% as shown in the H: box on the options bar.
   e. Press the ENTER key to commit the transformation.
9. To move and warp the trail of flames:
   a. Drag the selection to a position behind the rocket ship.
   b. Press CTRL+T to freely transform.
   c. Right-click the selection and then click Warp on the shortcut menu.
   d. When the Warp options bar is displayed, click the Custom box arrow and then click Arc. The selection will display a grid with one sizing handle.
   e. Drag the sizing handle down until the trail of flames curves as shown in Figure 2-66. Reposition the trail of flames as necessary.
   f. Press the ENTER key to commit the transformation.
10. Deselect the trail of flames.
11. Use the Resize Image Wizard that you learned about in Project 1 to enlarge the image to a high quality print, 11 inches wide. Save the image with the name, Toy Rocket for Print. If Photoshop displays a JPEG Options dialog box, click the OK button.
12. Print the image in landscape mode.
13. Close the document window.
14. Quit Photoshop.

1 Using the Keyboard with the Magic Wand

Problem: As e-cards gain popularity, the need for good graphics also has increased. A small e-commerce site has hired you as its photo specialist to assist with images and photos used in the greeting cards provided online. Your first assignment is to provide a clean image for a card whose greeting will read, "Happy birthday! My how you've grown!" A photographer has submitted a photo of a giraffe, but the layout artist wants the giraffe to face the other way to fit in with the greeting he has designed. He also needs the background sky removed. You decide to practice using the function keys to perform most of the editing tasks. The edited photo displays in Figure 2-67. (*Hint*: In future chapters, you will learn how to feather and smooth edges for a more natural appearance. For the purposes of this assignment, be as careful as you can when removing portions of the background sky.)

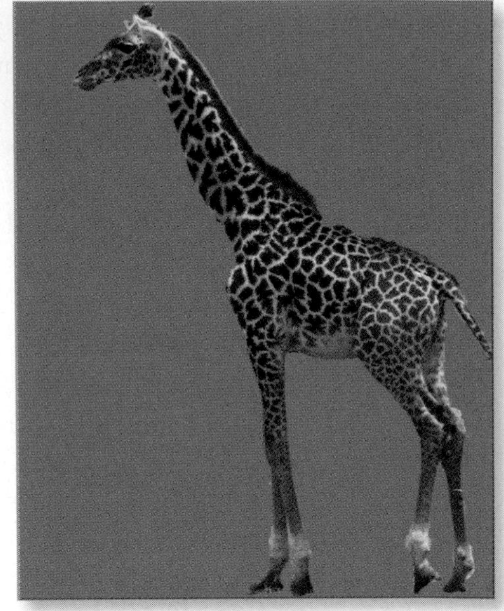

FIGURE 2-67

Instructions:

1. Start Photoshop. Set the default workspace and reset all tools.
2. Press CTRL+O to open the Giraffe file from the Project02 folder on the CD that accompanies this book, or from a location specified by your instructor.
3. Press SHIFT+CTRL+S to use the Save As command to save the file on your storage device with the name, Giraffe Edited. If Photoshop displays a JPEG Options dialog box, click the OK button.
4. If the photo does not display at 100% magnification, press CTRL++ or CTRL+- to zoom in or out as necessary.
5. If necessary, resize the document window to display the entire photo.
6. Press the W key to choose the Magic Wand Tool (W) button in the toolbox.
7. Click the area of blue sky to the left of the giraffe.
8. SHIFT+CLICK the area of blue sky to the right of the giraffe.
9. Click any other portions of the sky that are not already selected.
10. Press CTRL+X to delete the selected areas.
11. Press CTRL+D to remove any selection border, if necessary.
12. If some area of blue still is displayed, repeat Steps 8 through 11. If you make an error or some areas are deleted by mistake, click the first state in the History palette and begin again with Step 6.
13. On the Magic Wand options bar, double-click the Tolerance box and type 0 to replace the value. Click the Anti-alias check box so it does not display its check mark. Click the Sample All Layers check box so it displays its check mark.
14. With the Add to selection button still selected, use the Magic Wand tool to select all the white areas of the photo.
15. Press SHIFT+CTRL+I to select the inverse. The giraffe now should be selected.
16. Press CTRL+T to freely transform the giraffe selection. Right-click the selection and then click Flip Horizontal on the shortcut menu.
17. Press the ENTER key to commit the transformations.
18. Press CTRL+D to deselect, if necessary.
19. Press CTRL+S to save the file with the same name.
20. Press ALT+SHIFT+CTRL+P to use the Print One Copy command on the File menu to print a copy of the photo.

In the Lab

21. Close the document window by pressing CTRL+W.
22. Quit Photoshop by pressing CTRL+Q.
23. Send the photo as an e-mail attachment to your instructor, or follow your instructor's directions for submitting the lab assignment.

2 Skew, Perspective, and Warp

Problem: Hobby Express, a store that specializes in model trains and remote control toys wants a new logo. They would like to illustrate the concept of a train engine that looks like it is racing to the store. The picture will display on their letterhead, business cards, and advertising pieces. They would like a digital file so they can use the logo for other graphic purposes. The edited photo is shown in Figure 2-68.

FIGURE 2-68

Instructions:

1. Start Photoshop. Set the default workspace and reset all tools.
2. Open the file, Engine, from the CD that accompanies this book, or from a location specified by your instructor.
3. Use the Save As command to save the file on your storage device with the name Engine Edited. When Photoshop displays a JPEG Options dialog box, type 8 in the Quality box, and then click the OK button.
4. Click the Magic Wand Tool (W) button in the toolbox and deselect the Contiguous check box on the options bar. Select all of the blue background.
5. To add the green grass in the lower-right corner of the photo to the selection, on the Magic Wand options bar, click the Add to selection button. Type 50 in the Tolerance box, click the Contiguous check box so it displays its check mark, and then click the grass.
6. Press the DELETE key to delete the selected areas.
7. On the Select menu, click Inverse.

(continued)

Skew, Perspective, and Warp *(continued)*

8. On the Edit menu, point to Transform, and then click Warp. When Photoshop displays the warp grid, locate the upper-left warp point that displays as a gray circle on the grid. Drag the warp point to the right until the smokestack bends slightly.
9. Right-click the selection and then click Skew on the shortcut menu. Drag the upper-left sizing handle to the left.
10. Experiment with the Perspective and Distort commands to make the engine look as if it were moving. The front of the engine should appear closer than the rear. The smokestack should curve backward to simulate motion. Apply any transformations.
11. Save the photo again and print a copy for your instructor.

3 Creating Shortcuts, Saving Sets, and Viewing the Shortcut Summary

Problem: You have decided that many times, while you are working with tools in Photoshop, it would be beneficial to reset the options bar settings back to their defaults as you change tools. You decided to create a new keyboard shortcut to reset all tools, rather than having to move the mouse to the options bar, right-click, and then choose to reset all tools. Additionally, you take a lot of photos with your digital camera and routinely resize them — a shortcut key to activate the Resize Image Wizard would be very helpful. Because other family members work on your computer system, you would like to save the new shortcuts in a separate set for your personal use. You also would like to see a complete listing of the Photoshop shortcuts for your system.

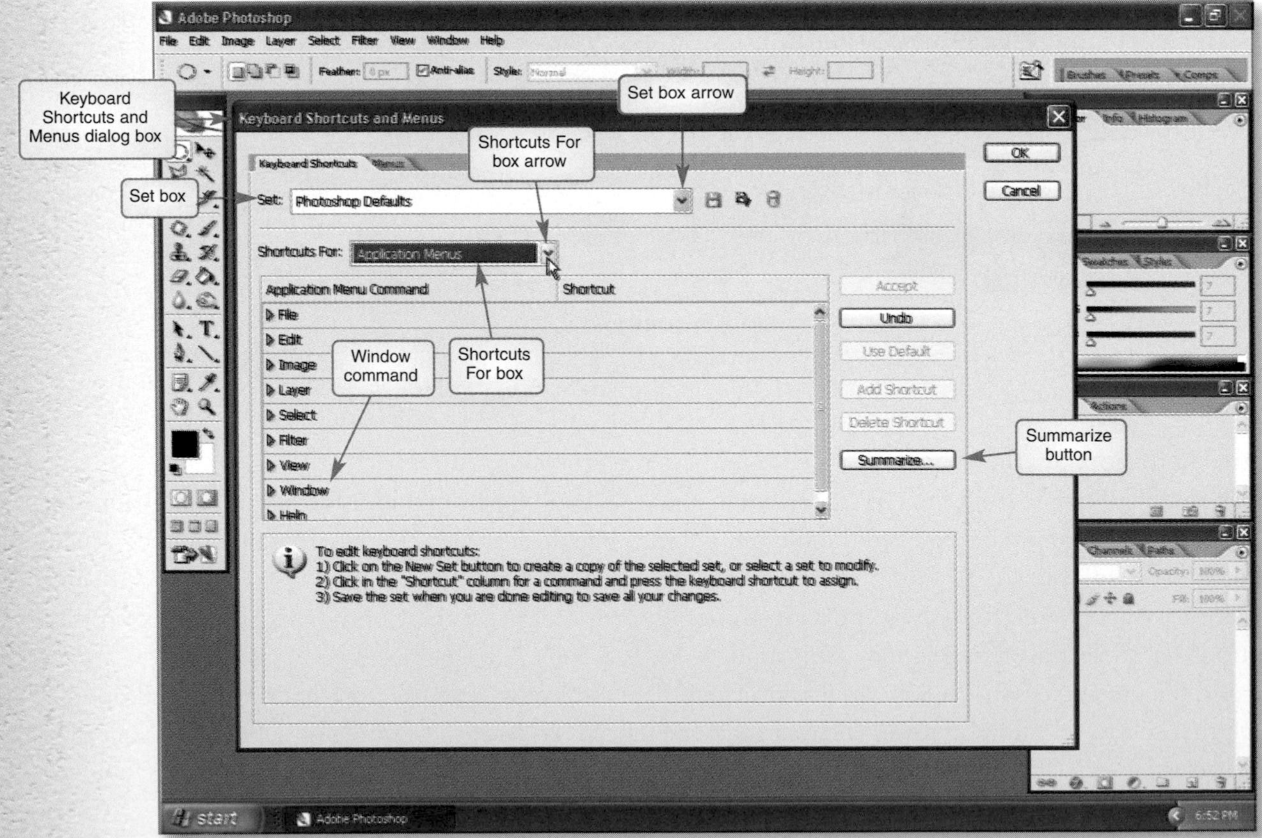

FIGURE 2-69

In the Lab

Instructions:

1. Start Photoshop. Set the default workspace and reset all tools.
2. On the Edit menu, click Keyboard Shortcuts.
3. When the Keyboard Shortcuts and Menus dialog box is displayed (Figure 2-69), if necessary click the Keyboard Shortcuts tab. If necessary, click the Set box arrow and then click Photoshop Defaults in the list.
4. Click the Shortcuts For box arrow and then click Palette Menus in the list.
5. Double-click Tool Presets in the list.
6. Click Reset All Tools in the list and then press the F10 key to choose it as the shortcut.
7. Click either Accept button.
8. Click the Shortcuts For box arrow and choose Application Menus in the list.
9. Double-click the Help command.
10. Click the Resize Image command.
11. Press CTRL+/ to create a shortcut for the Resize Image command.
12. Click either Accept button.
13. Click the Create a new set based on the current set of shortcuts button. When the Save dialog box is displayed, type your name in the File name box. Click the Save button.
14. When the Keyboard Shortcuts and Menus dialog box again is displayed, click the Summarize button. When the Save dialog box is displayed, type `My Shortcut Summary` in the File name box. Click the Save in box arrow and choose your USB flash drive location. Click the Save button.
15. The Shortcut Summary should open automatically in your browser. If it does not, use a My Computer window or an Explore window to navigate to your USB flash drive. Double-click the My Shortcut Summary HTML file. When the summary displays, print the page and turn it in to your instructor.
16. Close the browser. Click the OK button to close the Keyboard Shortcuts and Menus dialog box. Quit Photoshop.

Cases and Places

The difficulty of these case studies varies:
■ are the least difficult and ■■ are the most difficult. The last exercise is a group exercise.

1 ■ The city of Springfield has an annual hot air balloon festival. They are sending out a brochure to attract balloon enthusiasts from all across the state. The photo submitted by the festival organizers is named, Balloon, and is located in the Project02 folder on the CD that accompanies this book. Using the rule of thirds and taking into consideration the layout and perspective, begin by using paper and pencil to sketch several quick roughs that include more than one balloon. Start Photoshop and use the techniques you learned in Projects 1 and 2 to create several more balloons on the background. You can use the Magnetic Lasso tool to select the balloons or the Magic Wand tool to select the sky and then select the inverse. Save the file with the name, Balloon Edited, on your USB flash drive storage device.

2 ■ Your local bank is starting an initiative to encourage children to open a savings account using their loose change. The bank would like a before and after picture showing how money can grow with interest. A file named Coins is located on the CD that accompanies this book. Start Photoshop and use the Elliptical Marquee tool to select each coin and duplicate it several times to fill the image with coins. Rotate and layer some of the coins to make it look more interesting. Save the photo with the name, Coins Edited on your USB flash drive storage device.

3 ■■ Use your digital camera to take a picture of a small object in your home, such as a can of soup or a piece of fruit. Transfer the picture to your computer system and open it with Photoshop. Duplicate the object several times and perform a different transformation technique on each copy, such as scale, rotate, skew, warp, distort, and perspective. Save the photo and send a copy to your instructor as an attachment to an e-mail.

4 ■■ Look through magazines or newspapers for color photos with distinctive transformations such as perspective, skew, or warp. If possible, cut out three photos. Write a short paragraph for each example describing how you think the image was generated. List the tool, the transformation, and the potential problems associated with duplicating the process. List the idea being conveyed by the photo and describe a second possible conceptual application for the photo. Attach the photos to the descriptions and submit them to your instructor. If directed by your instructor to do so, recreate the image.

5 ■■ **Working Together** Your group has been assigned to create a group photo from individual photos. Using a digital camera or camera phone, take a picture of each team member from the shoulders up. Using Photoshop, open each digital file and select only the team member's head and shoulder area. Invert the selection and press the DELETE key to eliminate the background. Save each file. Choose the picture with the most white space around the team member's picture to be the master photo. In each of the other photos, use the Magnetic Lasso tool to select the individual. Copy the selection and then paste it into the master photo creating a group picture. Scale and move the selections as necessary to make the picture look good. Try to match the proportions for a realistic composition, or exaggerate proportions for more humorous results. Experiment with overlapping shoulder areas. Use the History palette to return to previous states when errors are made. Submit the final result to your teacher.

ADOBE Photoshop CS2

Using Layers

PROJECT 3

CASE PERSPECTIVE

You are a freelance graphic designer whose work has caught the eye of Javier Caserne, general manager of Essentials Landscaping Company. Mr. Caserne's market is midsized homeowners, usually those with new construction, who want to create outdoor landscapes that fit both their style and price range. Essentials Landscaping Company specializes in a tiered approach, adding landscaping components in small sets, as the home owner desires, to improve the grounds in either a practical or aesthetic way.

In order to provide a more realistic view of the finished product to his clients, Mr. Caserne has been using two-dimensional layout sketches and pictures of other homes with similar designs. While that offers a homeowner one vision of what is possible, Mr. Caserne would like an even more realistic and personal approach. He has taken a picture of a client's home and wants you to insert the softscape objects such as lawn, bushes, and trees, and also hardscape, inanimate objects such as a statuary into the photo. Mr. Caserne wants to show his clients what their home will look like five or more years from now as the plants and trees mature.

You decide to investigate Photoshop's layering capabilities to create a composite image from several photographs of landscaping components provided by Mr. Caserne. The Clone Stamp tool will help you apply the image of sod into the corners with precision. You will use the Layers palette combined with Photoshop's color and contrast adjustments to insert flowers, bushes, and trees to give the house a lived-in look. The Move tool will help you position layers in the composite image. Using one of the Photoshop filters, you will create a cloud-filled sky to make the house appear in a summer-like setting. Duplicating a layer, the lion statuary will give the drive a formal elegance and improve the curb appeal. Mr. Caserne's potential client will want to hire the firm right away!

Using Layers

PROJECT 3

Objectives

You will have mastered the material in this project when you can:

- Save a file in PSD format
- Create a layer via cut and use the Layers palette
- Select, name, color, hide, and view layers
- Create a new layer from another image or selection
- Set layer properties
- Resize a layer
- Erase portions of layers and images
- Use the Eraser, Magic Eraser, and Background Eraser tools
- Create layer masks
- Make level adjustments and opacity changes
- Create a layer style and add a render filter
- Use the Clone Stamp tool
- Flatten a composite image

Introduction

Whether it is adding a new person into a photograph, combining artistic effects from different genres, or creating 3-D animation, the concept of layers in Photoshop allows you to work on one element of an image without disturbing the others. A **layer** is an image superimposed or separated from other parts of the document. You may think of layers as sheets of clear film stacked one on top of the other. You can see through **transparent** areas of a layer to the layers below. The nontransparent or **opaque** areas of a layer are solid and eclipse lower layers. You can change the composition of an image by changing the order and attributes of layers. In addition, special features such as adjustment layers, layer masks, fill layers, and layer styles let you create sophisticated effects.

Another tool that graphic designers use when they want to recreate a portion of another photo is the Clone Stamp tool. As you will learn in this project, the Clone Stamp tool takes a sample of an image, and then applies, as you draw, an exact copy of that image to your document.

Graphic designers use layer and clones along with other tools in Photoshop to create **composite** images that combine or merge multiple images and drawings to create a new image, also referred to as a montage. Composite images illustrate the power of Photoshop and are used to prepare documents for businesses, advertising, marketing, and media artwork. Composite images such as navigation bars can be created in Photoshop and used on the Web along with layered buttons, graphics, and background images.

Project Three — Using Layers

Project 3 uses Photoshop to create a composite image from several photographs by using layers. Specifically, it begins with a photo of a recently constructed house, and creates a composite image by inserting layers of flowers, bushes, trees, a statuary, and sod. The process is illustrated in Figure 3-1.

FIGURE 3-1

The enhancements will show how the home will look after some time with appropriate landscaping. Sod will replace the dirt; bushes and trees will be planted. The photo will be edited to display a bright summer day with clouds in the sky. Finally, statuary will be added to give the house maximum curb appeal.

Starting and Customizing Photoshop

If you are stepping through this project on a computer and you want your screen to match the figures in this book, you should change your computer's resolution to 1024 × 768 and reset the tools and palettes. For more information about how to change the resolution on your computer, and other advanced Photoshop settings, read Appendix A.

The following steps describe how to start Photoshop and customize the Photoshop window. You may need to ask your instructor how to start Photoshop for your system.

To Start Photoshop and Reset the Palettes, Toolbox, and Options Bar

1. **Start Photoshop as described on pages PS 6 and PS 7.**
2. **Choose the Default Workspace as described on page PS 8.**
3. **Select the Rectangular Marquee tool and then reset all tools as described on pages PS 9 and PS 10.**

Photoshop starts and then resets the tools, palettes, and options.

Opening a File

To open a file in Photoshop it must be stored as a digital file on your computer system. The photos and images used in this book are stored on a CD located in the back of the book. Your instructor may designate a different location for the photos.

The next steps show how to open the file, House, from a CD located in drive E.

To Open a File

1. **Insert the CD that accompanies this book into your CD drive. After a few seconds, if Windows displays a dialog box, click its Close button.**
2. **Click Open on the Photoshop File menu and then navigate to the Project03 folder. Double-click the file named, House.**
3. **When Photoshop displays the image in the document window, if the magnification is not 25 percent as shown on the title bar, double-click the magnification box on the document window status bar, type** 25**, and then press the ENTER key.**
4. **Drag the window to the lower center portion of the work area.**
5. **If the rulers do not display, press CTRL+R.**
6. **Click the status bar menu button, point to Show, and then click Document Dimensions.**

Photoshop opens the file, House, and displays it in the document window at 25 percent magnification (Figure 3-2).

FIGURE 3-2

Table 3-1 displays information about the House photo. It is a photo saved as a JPG file. In the next steps you will convert the image to a PSD file.

Table 3-1 House Image Characteristics	
File Name	House
File Type	JPG
Image dimensions	8 x 6 inches
Color Mode	CMYK
Resolution	300 pixels/inch
File Size	870 KB

The PSD Format

The **Photoshop Document Format** (**PSD**) is the default file format in Photoshop and the only format that supports all Photoshop features. When working with composite objects, to maintain the integrity of each element and to provide maximum flexibility in future editing, it is a good idea to save the file in PSD format. Many Photoshop users save files in multiple formats. For example, a Web version of an image might be saved as a GIF or JPG, the print version as a TIFF or EPS, and the composite file as a PSD. The PSD format maximizes file compatibility and provides a more portable file that can be read by other applications, including previous versions of Photoshop. It also maintains the appearance of blended layers. See Appendix A for instructions on setting Photoshop preferences regarding file formats and saving with different extensions.

Saving a File in the PSD Format

Because you plan to add multiple objects to the house image, you will save it in the PSD format. To save files in a different format, you use the Save As command on the File menu as the steps on the next page illustrate. In the Save As dialog box, the Format box provides a list of available file formats from which you can choose PSD.

To Save a File in the PSD format

1 **With your USB flash drive connected to one of the computer's USB ports, click File on the menu bar and then click Save As.**

2 **When the Save As dialog box is displayed, type** `House Edited` **in the File name text box. Do not press the ENTER key after typing the file name.**

3 **Click the Format box arrow and then click Photoshop (*.PSD, *.PDD) in the list.**

4 **Click the Save in box arrow and then click USBDISK [G:], or the location associated with your USB flash drive, in the list.**

5 **Click the Save button in the Save As dialog box.**

The Save As dialog box displays the file name, format, and location settings (Figure 3-3). Your list of files may differ.

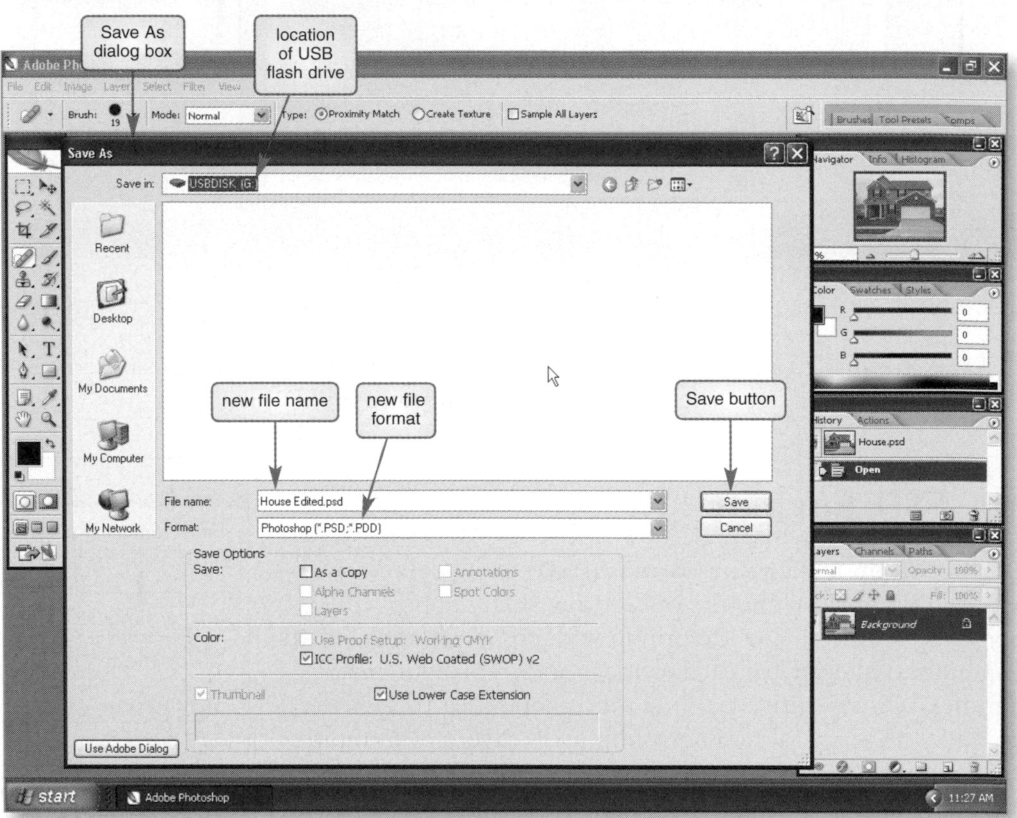

FIGURE 3-3

Photoshop saves the file on the USB flash drive with the file name, House Edited, in the PSD format, and displays the new name on the document window title bar. As you work through the rest of this project, save your file often. That way, if the power goes out, or your system locks, you will have a current copy.

> *More About*
>
> **Photoshop File Formats**
>
> PSD format is the default file format in Photoshop and the only format that supports all Photoshop features. Other Adobe applications can import PSD files directly and preserve many Photoshop features due to the tight integration between Adobe products. The PDD, or portable document format, is used by other Adobe applications such as PhotoDeluxe and Photoshop Elements.

Layers

Creating layers is one of the most powerful tools in Photoshop. A layer is a section within a Photoshop document that you can manipulate independent from the rest of the document. Layers can be stacked one on top of the other, resembling sheets of clear film, to form a composite image.

Layers can be created, copied, deleted, displayed, hidden, merged, locked, grouped, repositioned, and flattened. Layers can be images, patterns, text, shapes, colors, or filters. You can use layers to apply special effects, correct or colorize pictures, repair damaged photos, or import text elements. In previous projects you worked with images in a single layer called the **background**. In this project you will create, name, and manipulate multiple layers.

There are several ways to create a layer. You can:

- Isolate a portion of the image and then cut or make a layer copy
- Create a new layer by copying from a different image
- Duplicate a layer that already exists
- Create a new, blank layer on which you can draw or create text

When you add a layer to an image, a new layer is created above, or on top of, the currently selected layer creating a **stacking order**. By default, layers are named and numbered sequentially. The stacking order of layers in an image can be rearranged to change the appearance of the image. The final appearance of an edited Photoshop document is a view of the layer stack from the top down. These layer manipulations are performed using the Layers palette, which you will learn about later in this project.

Creating a Layer via Cut

In the House Edited photo, you will create a new layer that includes only the sky. You will use the Magic Wand tool to select the sky and then use the Layer via Cut command to isolate the sky from the rest of the photo, creating a new layer. To ensure your layers match the figures in this book, you will use the keyboard shortcut by pressing the D key on your keyboard to activate the default color scheme of black and white.

To Create a Layer via Cut

1

- **With the House Edited image displaying in the document window, press the D key.**
- **In the toolbox, click the Magic Wand tool. If necessary, on the options bar, type** 32 **in the Tolerance box and then click the Contiguous check box so it is selected.**
- **In the photo, click the sky.**

The sky displays a selection border (Figure 3-4).

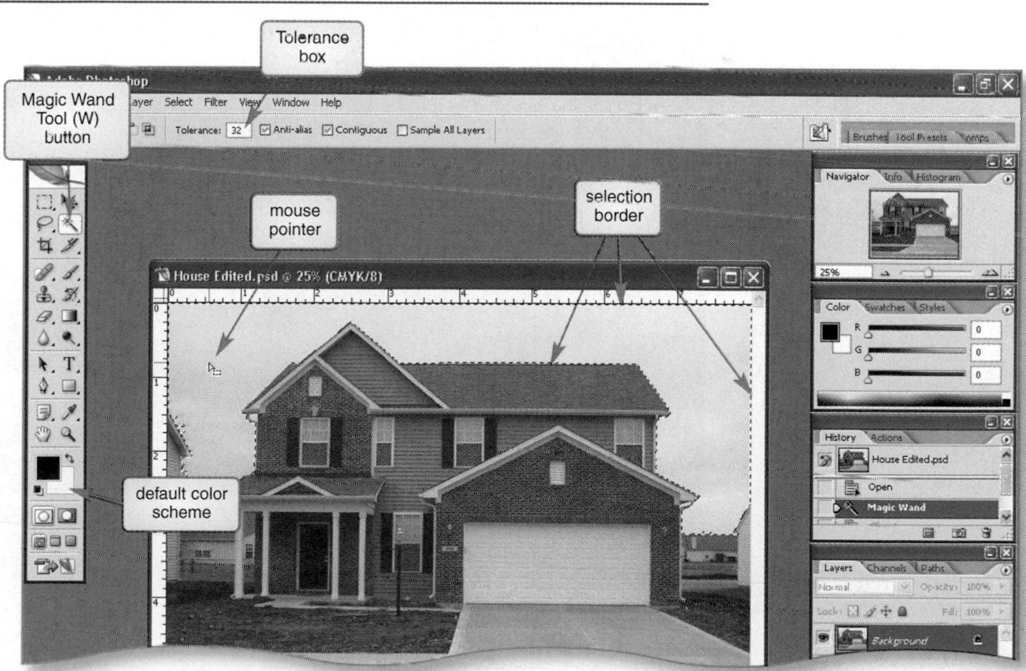

FIGURE 3-4

2

• **Right-click the sky.**

Photoshop displays the Selection shortcut menu (Figure 3-5).

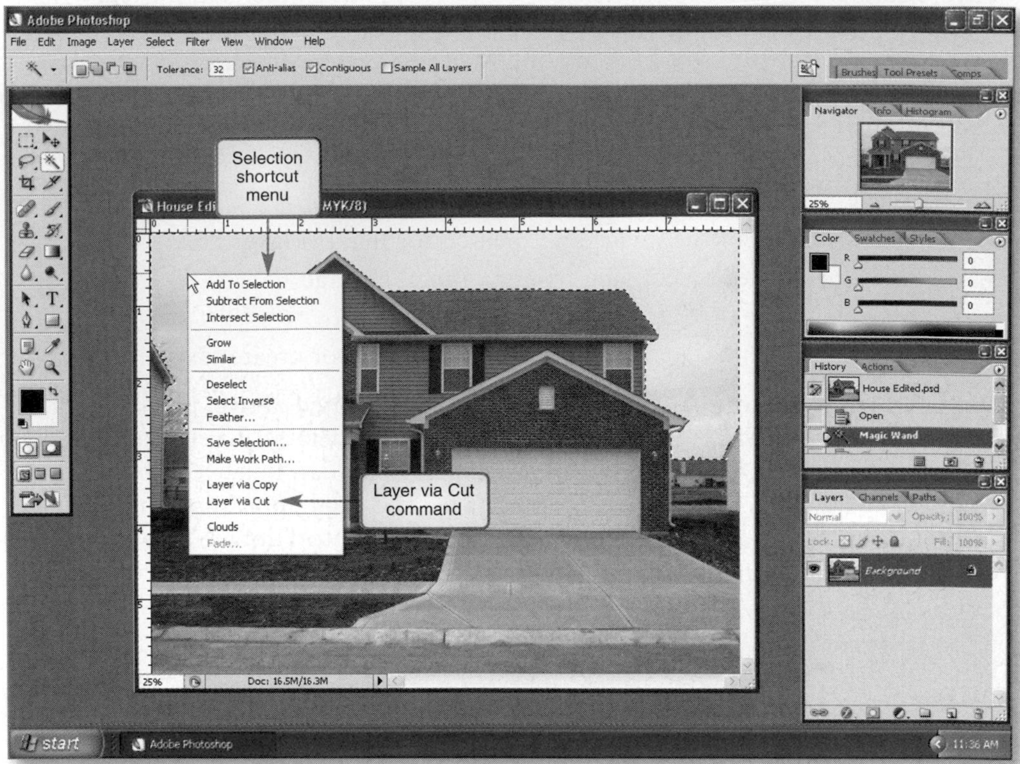

FIGURE 3-5

3

• **Click the Layer via Cut command on the shortcut menu.**

The Layers palette displays a new layer above the Background layer (Figure 3-6).

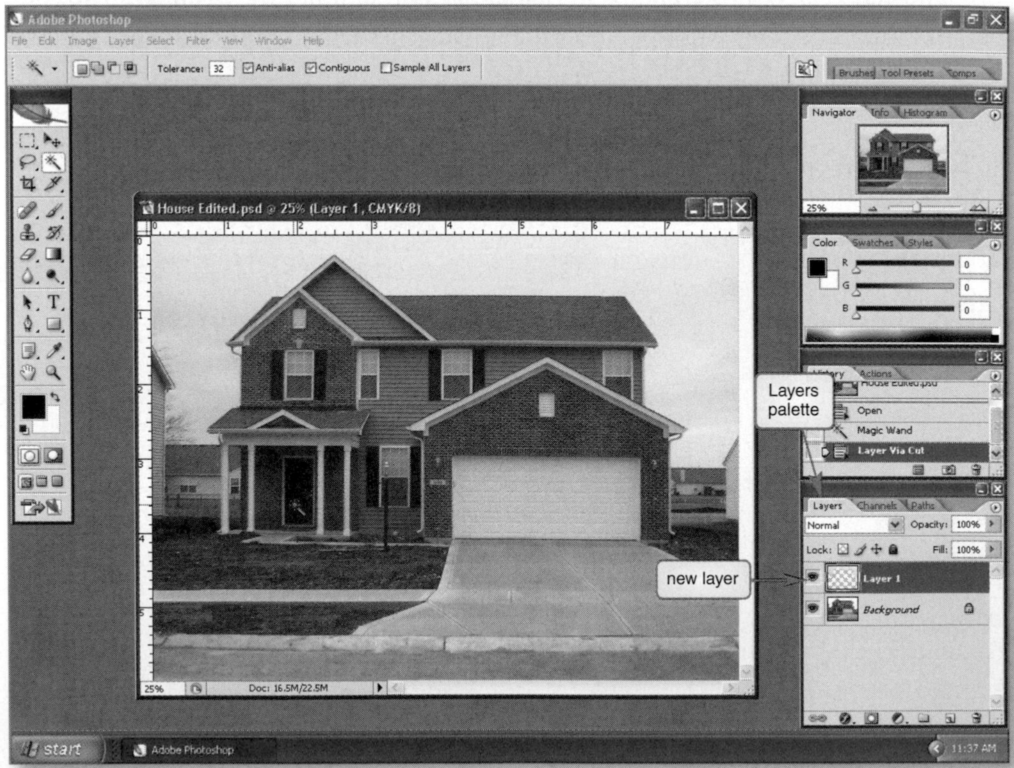

FIGURE 3-6

Other Ways

1. Create selection, press SHIFT+CTRL+J
2. On Layer menu, point to New, click Layer via Cut

The Layer via Cut command is different from the Layer via Copy command in that it removes the selection from the background. Future edits to the background, such as changing the color or lighting will not affect the cut layer.

Now that you have a background layer and a second layer of the sky, you can use the Layers palette to customize and manipulate the layers.

The Layers Palette

The **Layers palette**, usually located in the lowest level of palettes on the right of the Photoshop window, lists all layers, groups, and layer effects in an image (Figure 3-7). Each time you insert a layer in an image, the new layer is added to the top of the palette. The default display of a layer in the Layers palette includes a visibility icon, a thumbnail of the layer, and the layer's name. To the right of the layer's name a locking icon may display.

The Layers palette is used in several different ways. You can use the palette to show and hide layers, create new layers, and work with groups of layers. You can access additional commands and attributes by clicking the Layers palette menu button or by right-clicking a layer. The Layers palette defines how layers interact. As you use the buttons and boxes in the Layers palette, each will be explained.

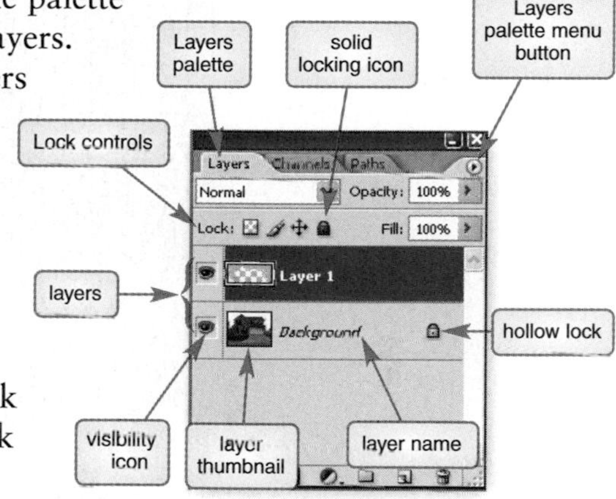

FIGURE 3-7

Photoshop allows you to **lock layers** in several ways. The first button to the right of the word, Lock, in the Layers palette, Lock transparent pixels, confines editing to the opaque portions of the layer. The second button, Lock image pixels, prevents modification of the layer's pixels using any of the painting tools. The third button, Lock position, prevents the layer from being moved. The fourth button, Lock all, enables all of the other three ways of locking every layer.

When a layer is locked, a lock icon appears to the right of the name in the Layers palette. A fully locked layer displays a solid lock; a partially locked layer displays a hollow lock.

The Background layer is partially locked by default — it displays a hollow lock (Figure 3-7). While Photoshop allows background editing, as you have done in previous chapters, the Background layer cannot be moved, nor can its transparency be changed. In other words, the Background layer fills the document window and there is no layer behind the background. If you want to convert the Background layer into a fully editable layer, double-click the layer in the Layers palette, and then when the New Layer dialog box is displayed, click the OK button.

Changing the Palette Options

The **Palette Options** command, accessible from the Layers palette menu, allows you to change the view and size of the thumbnail related to each layer. A **thumbnail** is a small visual display of the layer in the Layers palette. Clicking Palette Options displays a dialog box in which you can choose small, medium, large, or no thumbnails. In addition, you can specify thumbnail contents by choosing the Layer Bounds option that causes the Layers palette to display only the layer, restricting the thumbnail to the object's pixels on the layer.

The steps on the next page show how to display a medium-sized thumbnail of each layer with the Layer Bounds option.

To Change Palette Options

1

- **Click the Layers palette menu button.**

Photoshop displays the palette menu (Figure 3-8).

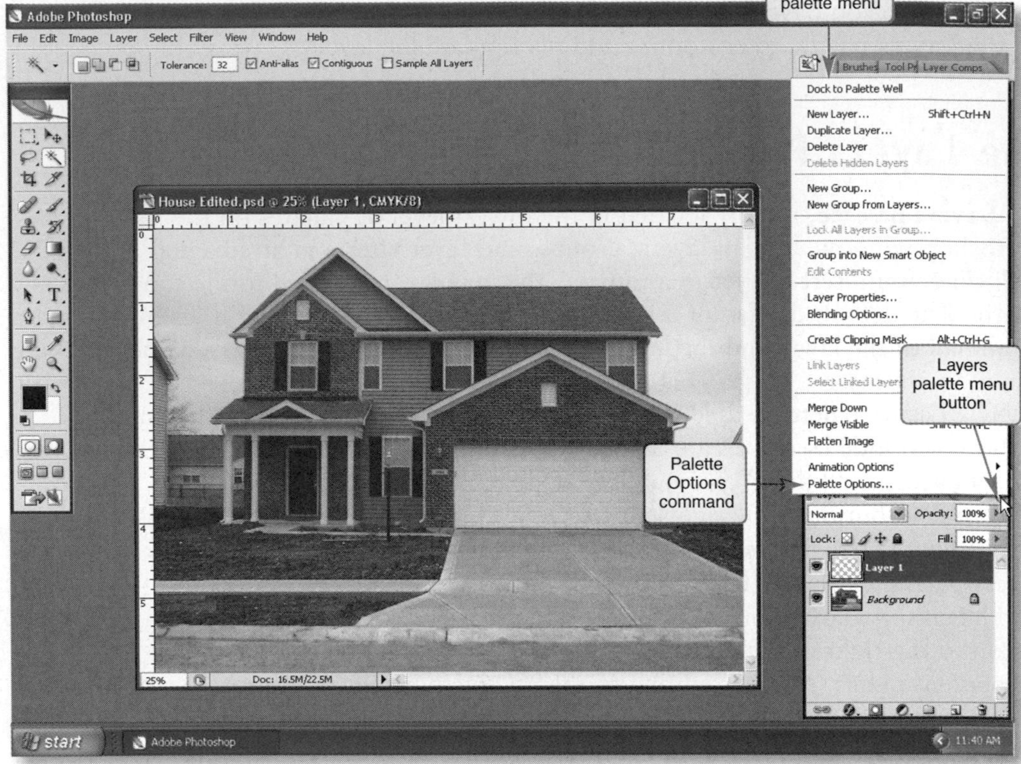

FIGURE 3-8

2

- **Click Palette Options on the menu.**
- **When the Layers Palette Options dialog box is displayed, click the medium thumbnail and Layer Bounds.**

The Layers Palette Options dialog box displays settings to change the look and feel of the Layers palette (Figure 3-9).

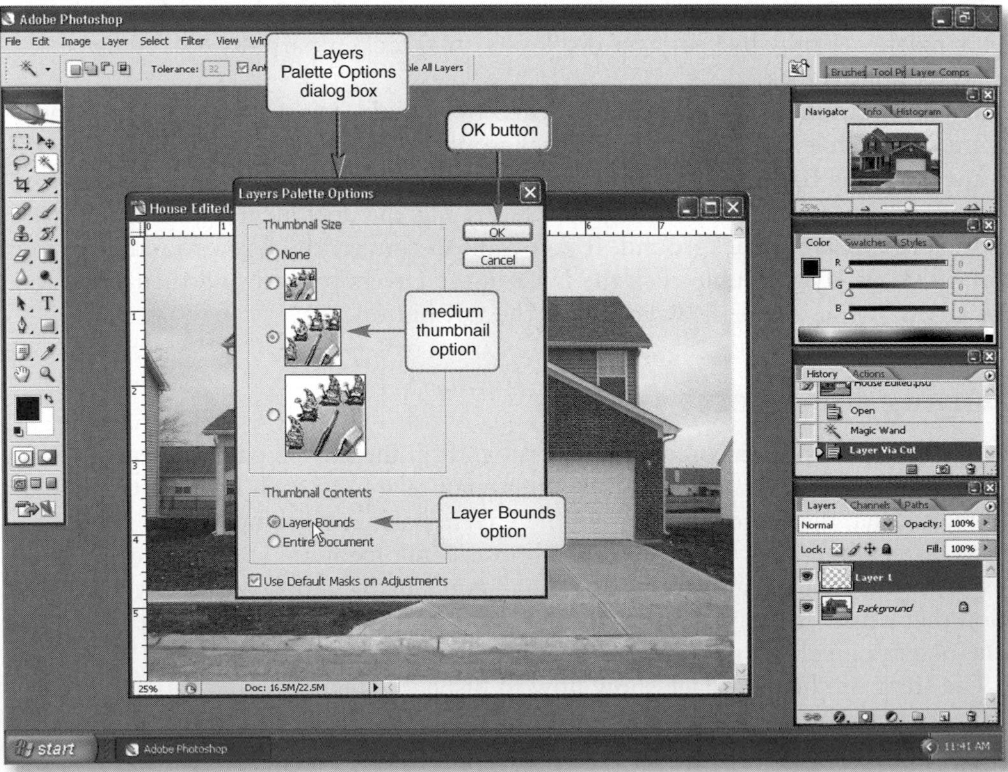

FIGURE 3-9

3

• **Click the OK button.**

The Layers palette now displays small pictures of each layer independent of the background (Figure 3-10).

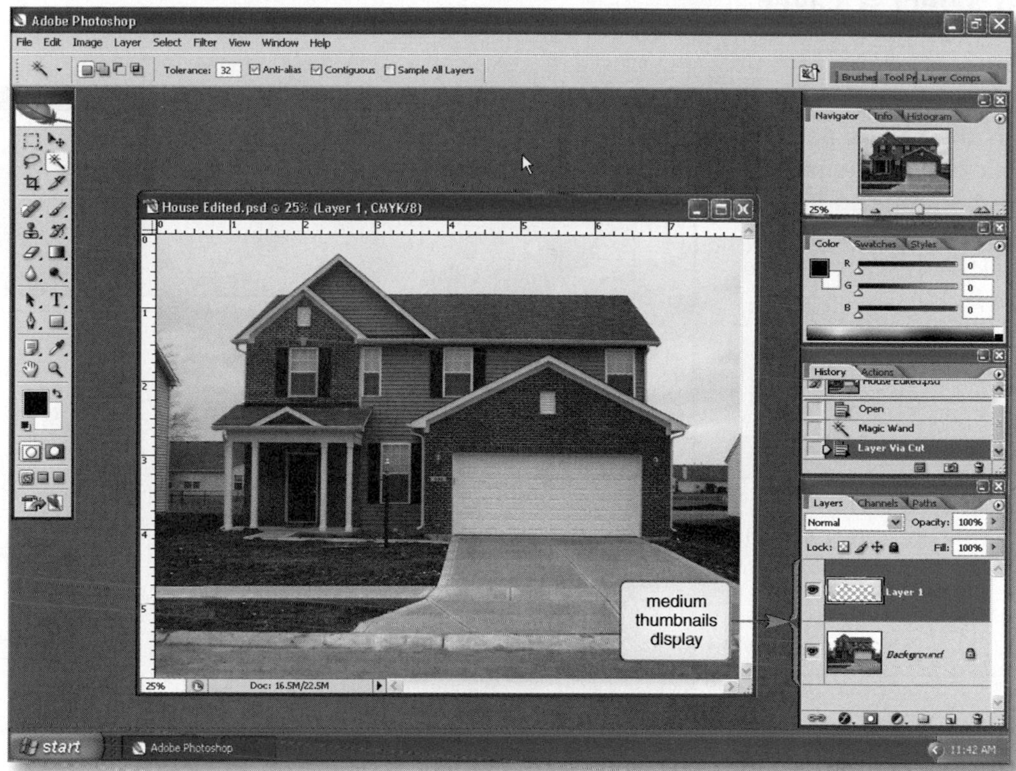

FIGURE 3-10

Other Ways

1. In Layers palette, right-click thumbnail, choose thumbnail size

Displaying thumbnails of each layer allows you to see easily what the layer looks like and helps you to be more efficient when editing a layer. To improve performance and save monitor space, however, some Photoshop users choose not to display thumbnails.

Selecting Layers

When you click a layer in the Layers palette, it becomes the active, editable portion of the image. The selected layer also is referred to as the **active layer** in the Layers palette. To select or activate a layer, you click the layer name or the thumbnail in the Layers palette as the steps on the next page show. While a layer is active, you cannot edit other portions of the image.

To Select a Layer

• In the Layers palette, click the thumbnail of the background layer.

The layer is displayed with a blue background indicating that it is the active layer (Figure 3-11).

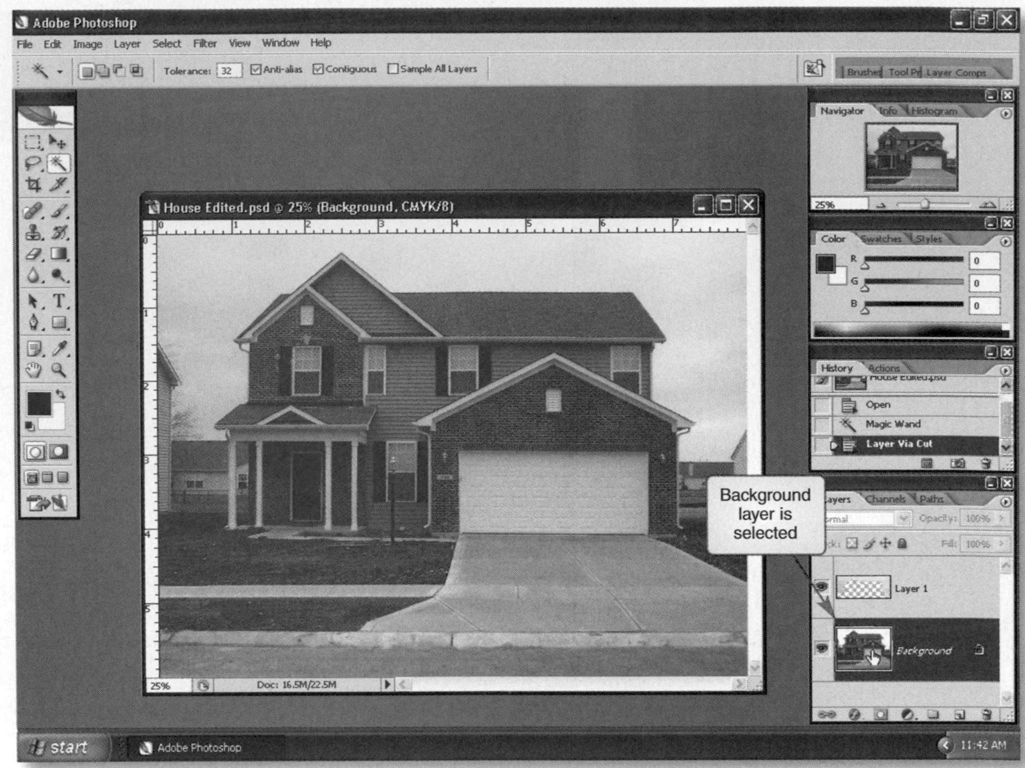

FIGURE 3-11

Other Ways

1. To select top layer, press ALT+.
2. To select bottom layer, press ALT+,
3. To select next layer, press ALT+] or ALT+[

More About

Selecting

Creating a selection in the document window should not be confused with selecting the layer. A selection, displayed by a marquee, refers to encompassing pixels in order to edit them. Selecting a layer is done in the Layers palette and allows you to work with only that layer in the document window. In other words, you can create a selection that is all or part of a selected layer.

More About

The Layers Palette Shortcut Menus

The Layers palette displays many ways to work with layers. For example, right-clicking the layer name displays a different shortcut menu from the one you see when right-clicking the thumbnail. Double-clicking the layer name allows you to rename the layer; double-clicking the thumbnail opens the Layer Style dialog box.

To select all layers, click All Layers on the Select menu, or press ALT+CTRL+A.

Naming Layers

It is a good practice to give each layer a unique name so you can identify it more easily. When you name a layer, the name displays in the Layers palette. The name of the active layer also displays on the title bar of the document window. Photoshop allows you to give each layer its own color identification as well. To name and color a layer, right-click the layer and click Layer Properties to display the Layer Properties dialog box as the following steps illustrate.

To Name and Color a Layer

1

- **In the Layers palette, right-click the layer name Layer 1.**

Photoshop displays the layer shortcut menu (Figure 3-12).

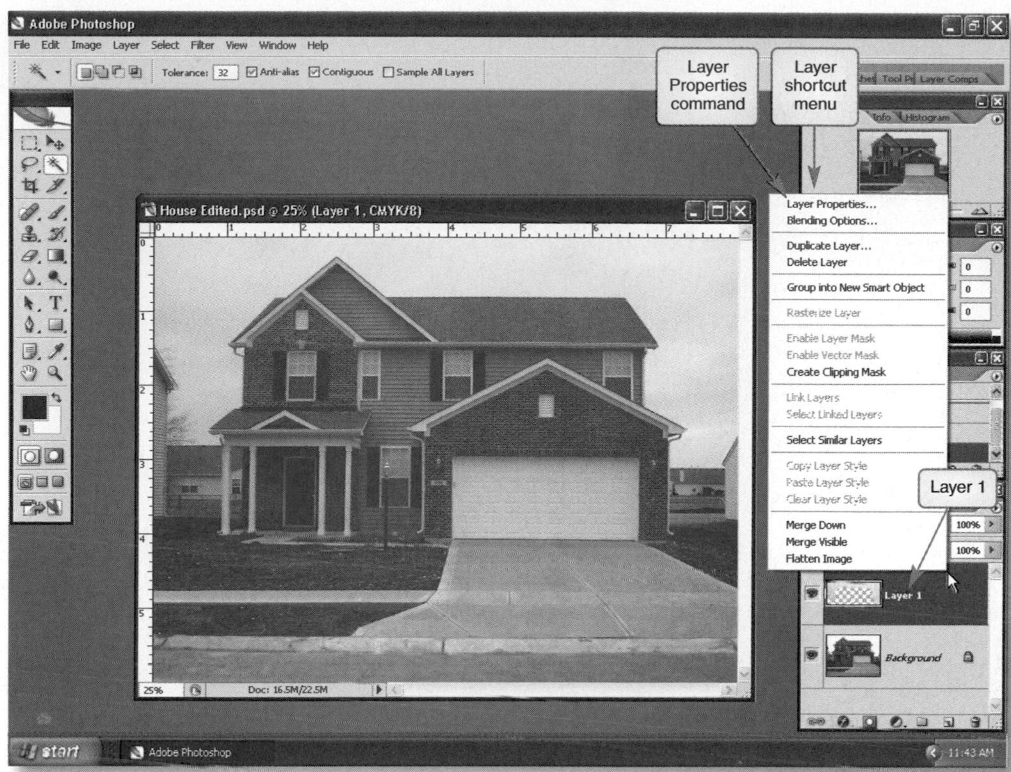

FIGURE 3-12

2

- **Click the Layer Properties command.**
- **When the Layer Properties dialog box is displayed, type** `sky` **in the Name box.**
- **Click the Color box arrow and then click Blue in the list.**

Photoshop displays the Layer Properties dialog box (Figure 3-13).

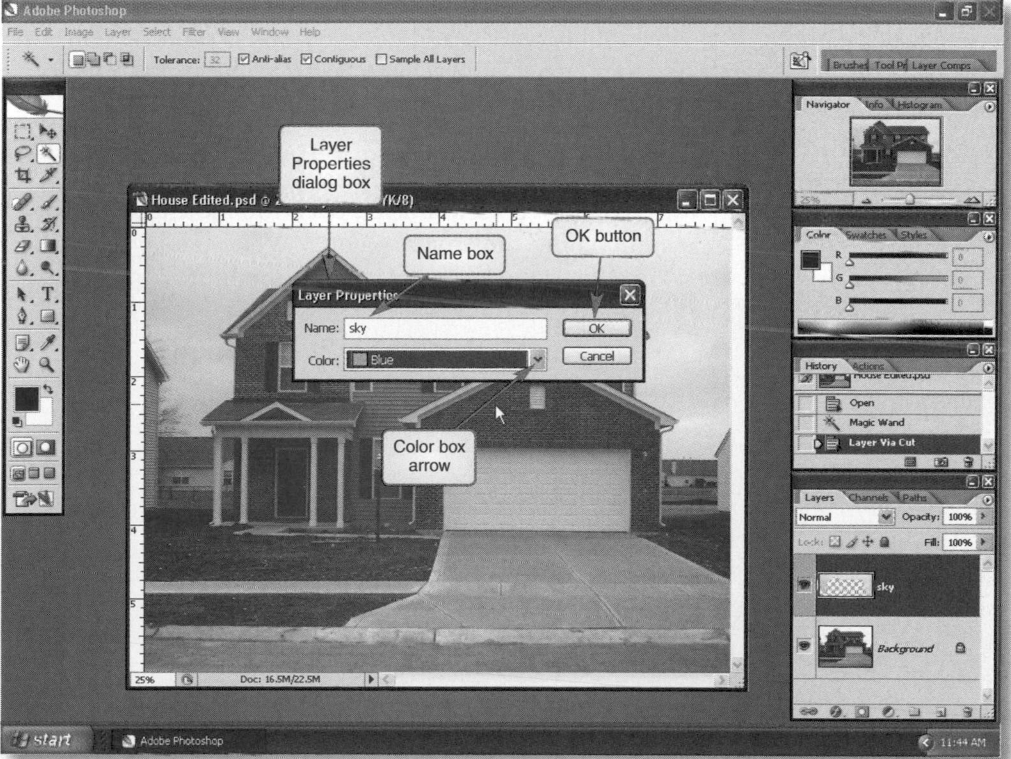

FIGURE 3-13

• **Click the OK button.**

The layer is renamed and the color blue displays to the left of the sky layer in the Layers palette. (Figure 3-14).

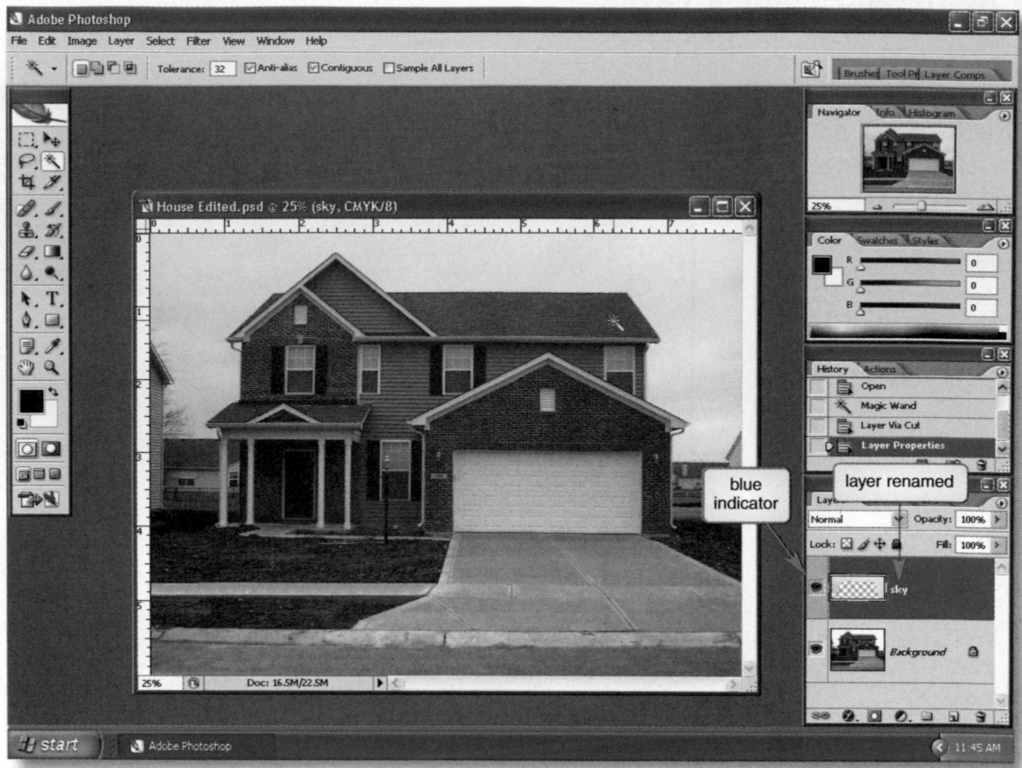

FIGURE 3-14

Other Ways

1. On Layer menu, click Layer Properties, enter new name, click OK
2. In Layers palette, ALT+double-click thumbnail, enter new name, click OK
3. In Layers palette, double-click layer name, type new name, press ENTER

More About

Creating Layer Groups

Layer groups help you manage and organize layers in a logical manner. To create a layer group, click the New Group button in the Layers palette. A new layer will appear with a folder icon. You then can drag layers into the folder or use the Layers palette menu to insert a new layer. You can apply attributes and masks to the entire group.

Photoshop reserves seven colors for color coding layers: red, orange, yellow, green, blue, violet, and gray. If you have more than seven layers, you can group layers that have similar characteristics with one color.

Hiding and Viewing Layers

To hide or view a layer, click the Indicates layer visibility button to the left of the thumbnail in the Layers palette. When the layer is visible, the button displays an eye icon. When the layer is invisible, the button is blank.

To Hide and View a Layer

1

- **Click the Indicates layer visibility button to the left of the sky layer.**

The sky layer is invisible in the document window (Figure 3-15).

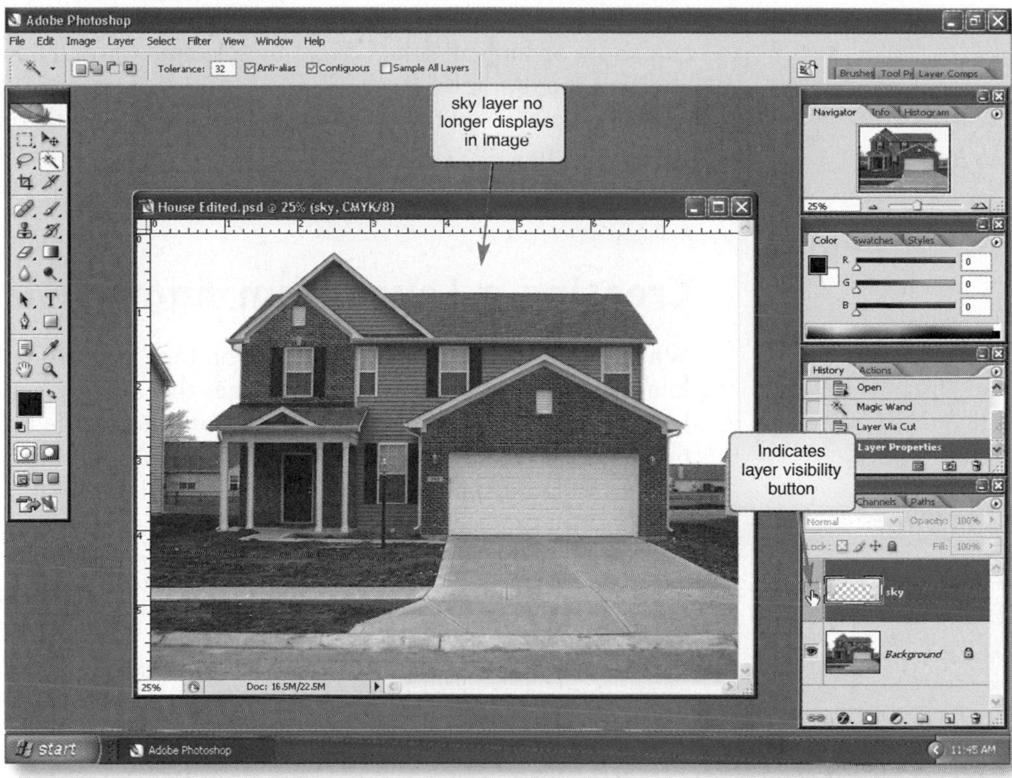

FIGURE 3-15

2

- **Click the Indicates layer visibility button again.**

The sky layer is visible and the Layers palette again displays the eye icon (Figure 3-16).

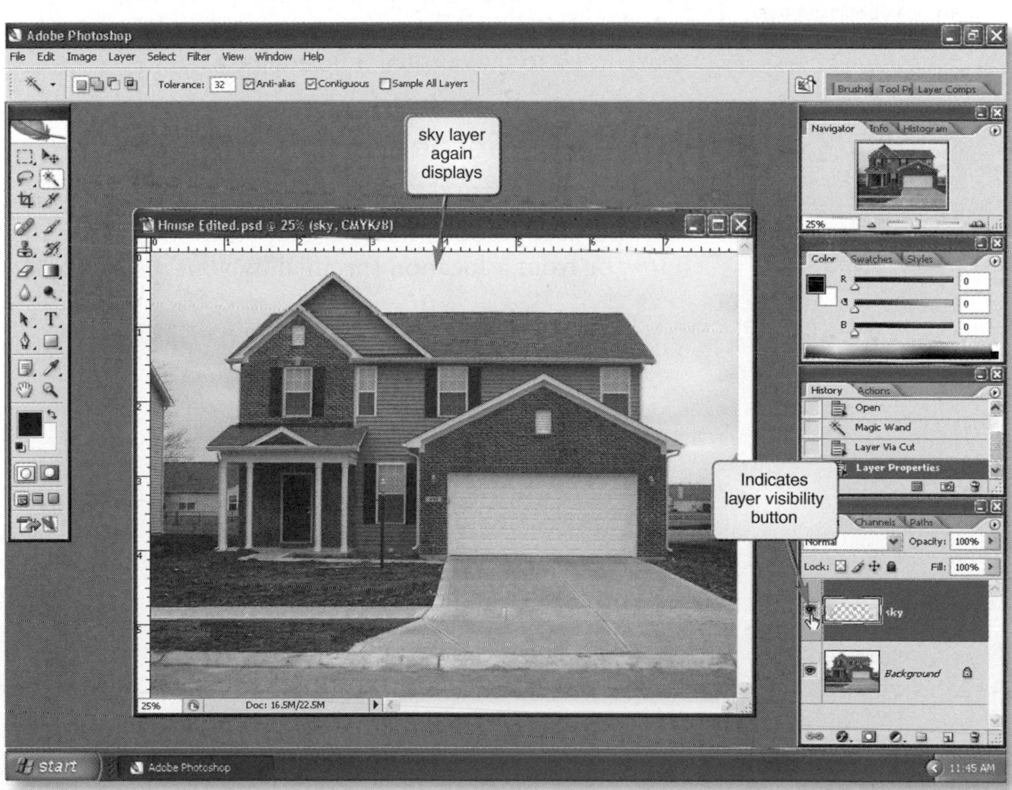

FIGURE 3-16

Other Ways

1. Right-click visibility icon, click Hide this layer or Show this layer
2. On Layer menu, click Hide Layers or Show Layers

Sometimes, if you have multiple layers, you may wish to view only one layer. In that case, rather than turning off all of the other layers one by one, you can press ALT+click on the visibility icon for the layer you wish to view. All other layers will be hidden. Pressing ALT+click again restores the previous visibility settings. You also can show or hide all other layers by selecting Show/Hide all other layers from the shortcut menu.

To hide or view several contiguous layers, drag through the eye column.

To delete a layer permanently, right-click the layer name and then click Delete Layer on the shortcut menu, or activate the layer and press the DELETE key.

Creating a Layer from Another Image

When you create composite images, you may want to create layers from other images. It is important to choose images that closely match or complement color, lighting, size, and perspective if you want your image to look natural. While adjustments can be made, it is easier to start with as close a match as possible. One of the keys to successful image compositions is finding the best source material with similar lighting situations and tonal qualities.

Many sources for components exist for composite images. For example, you can use your own digital photos, scanned images, images from royalty free Web sites, or you can draw your own images. If you use a photo or image from the Web, make sure you have legal rights to use the image. Legal rights include permission from the photographer or artist to use the image, or purchasing these rights, via a contract, through an online store.

The basic process of creating a new layer from another image involves opening a second image, selecting the area you wish to use, and then moving it to the original photo in a drag-and-drop or cut-and-paste fashion. Once the layer exists in the original photo, some editing may need to take place to remove portions of the layer, to resize it, or to make tonal adjustments.

More About

Adobe Stock Images

Photoshop offers the option to download low-resolution, complementary versions of many images. You can work with the complementary images until you make your final decision, at which point you can purchase and download a high-resolution image.

Opening a Second Image

In order to add a landscaped flower bed as a layer to the House Edited image, you will need to open the PSD file, Flowerbed, from the CD that accompanies this book, or from a location specified by your instructor.

To Open a Second Image

1

- **On the File menu, click Open.**
- **When the Open dialog box is displayed, if necessary, click the Look in box arrow, and then navigate to the Project03 folder on the CD that accompanies this book, or a location specified by your instructor.**
- **If necessary, double-click the Project03 folder.**
- **Click the file named, Flowerbed.**

The Project03 folder is displayed in the Open dialog box (Figure 3-17). Your list of files may differ.

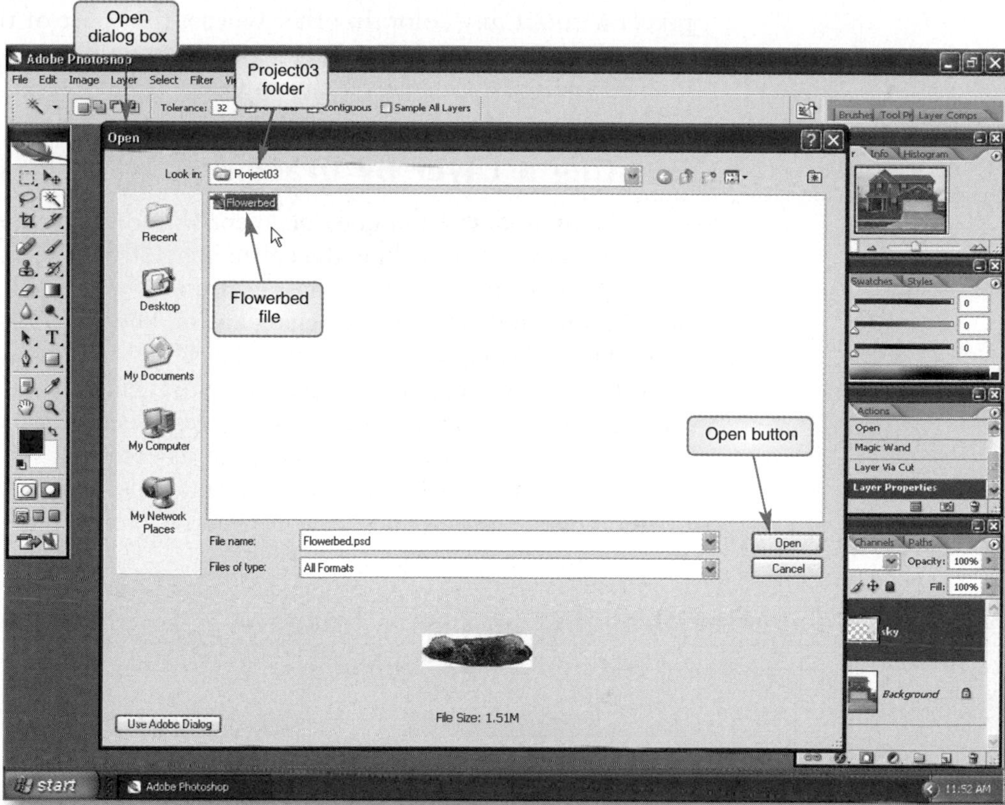

FIGURE 3-17

2

- **Click the Open button.**
- **When the Flowerbed window opens, drag its title bar to a position in the work area slightly above the House Edited title bar, if necessary.**
- **If necessary, type** 25 **in the magnification box at the bottom of the Flowerbed window and then press the ENTER key.**

Photoshop displays the second document window (Figure 3-18).

FIGURE 3-18

Other Ways

1. Press CTRL+O, select file, click Open
2. Click Go to Bridge button, navigate to location of file, double-click file

The gray and white checkerboard effect in the Flowerbed file (Figure 3-18) represents portions of the document window that are transparent, or containing pixels without any color. In other words, that part of the document window is blank. Because document windows are rectangular in nature, a nonrectangular image usually will display some transparent parts.

Creating a Layer by Dragging an Entire Image

When you drag from one document window to the other, Photoshop creates a layer. If you want to include the entire image from the source window, click the Move Tool (V) button and then drag from any location in the source window to the destination window. When dragging layers, Photoshop users adjust their document windows to display in various ways depending upon personal preference. You may want to resize the document window by dragging a border or move the document window by dragging the title bar so you can see both images more clearly.

The flowerbed image will be used in its entirety as a landscaping feature in the front yard to the left of the driveway. You will move the image from the source window, Flowerbed, to the destination window, House Edited.

To Create a Layer by Dragging an Entire Image

1

- **If necessary, click the Flowerbed window title bar to make it the active document window.**
- **Click the Move Tool (V) button in the toolbox.**
- **Point to the center of the image.**

The mouse pointer displays the move icon (Figure 3-19).

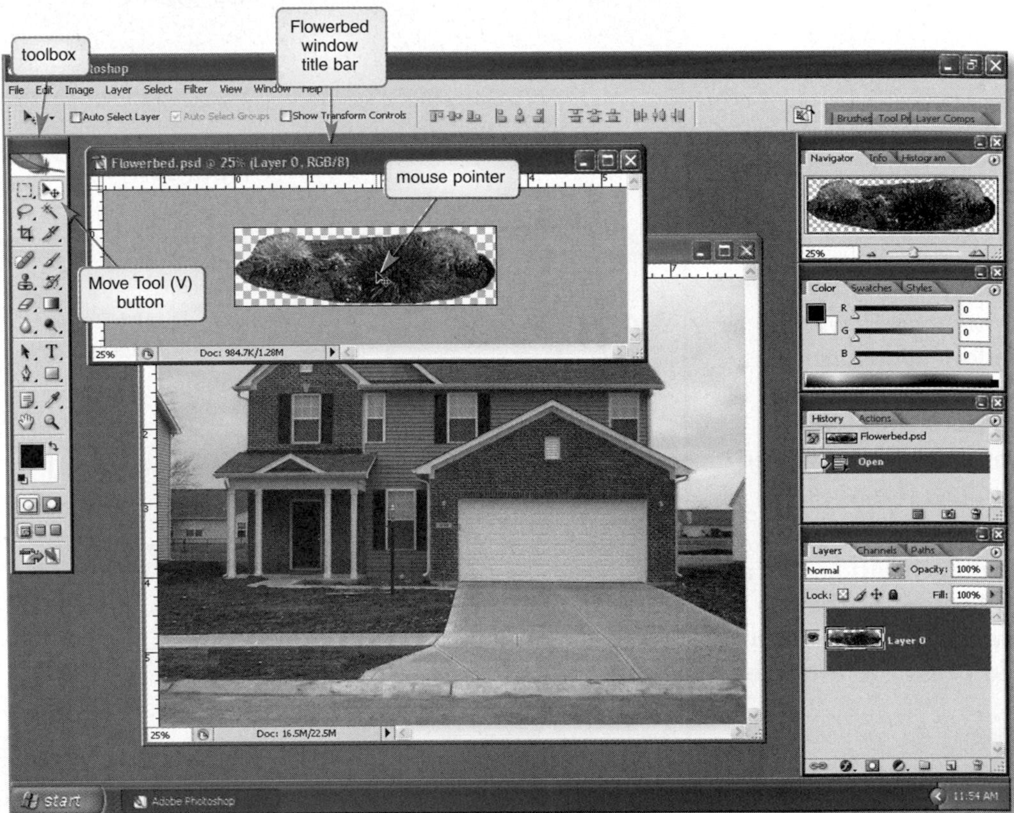

FIGURE 3-19

2

• **Drag the flowerbed image into the House Edited window and drop it to the left of the driveway.**

The superimposed flowerbed is displayed in the House Edited window, and a layer is created at the top of the Layers palette (Figure 3-20).

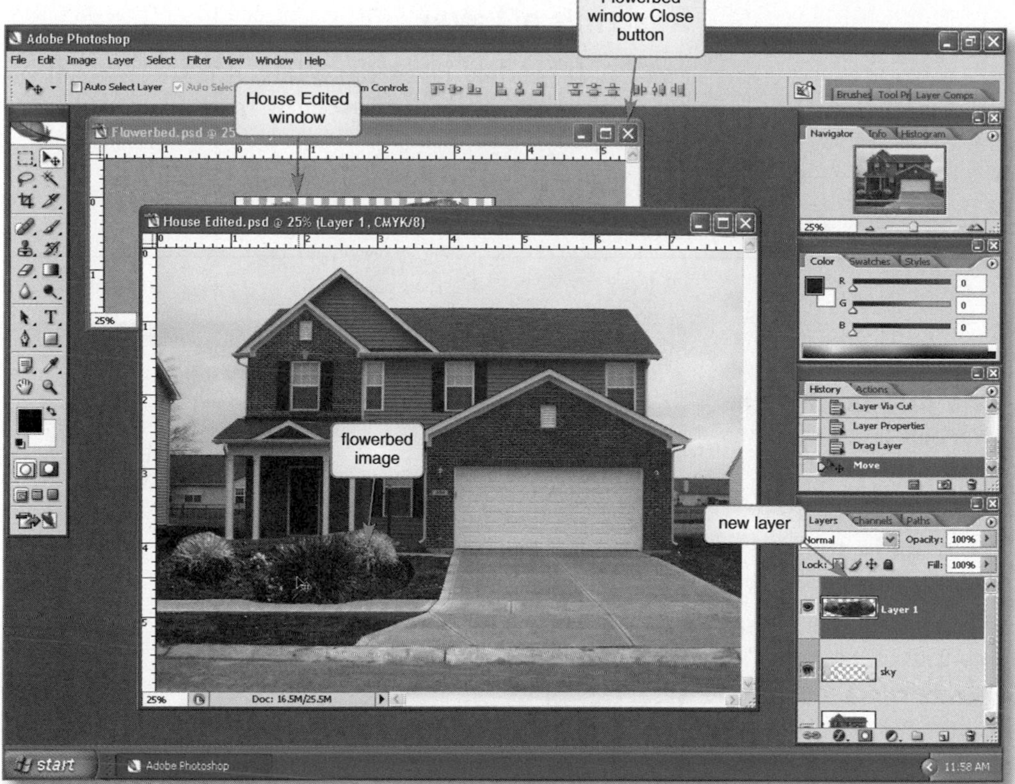

FIGURE 3-20

Other Ways

1. To select all, press CTRL+A, drag image
2. To select Move tool, press V key, drag image

The original or source image remains unchanged. Dragging between document windows is an automatic duplication rather than a true move. The following step shows how to close the Flowerbed window.

To Close the Flowerbed Window

1 **Click the Close button in the Flowerbed window. If Photoshop asks if you want to save changes to the document, click the No button.**

The window closes and the House Edited window becomes active.

The new layer is displayed in the Layers palette above the layer of the sky. The following steps illustrate how to set the layer properties.

To Set the Flowerbed Layer Properties

1 **Right-click Layer 1 in the Layers palette. Click Layer Properties on the shortcut menu.**

2 **Type** `flowerbed` **in the Name box. Click the Color box arrow and then click Green.**

3 **Click the OK button.**

The flowerbed layer displays a green indicator in the Layers palette as shown in Figure 3-21 on the next page. The History palette displays the step.

Resizing a Layer

The flowerbed layer is too large for the amount of yard in front of the house. The following steps illustrate how to resize a layer. The process is the same as resizing any selection.

To Resize a Layer

1

- **If necessary, in the Layers palette, click the flowerbed layer to activate it.**
- **Click the Move Tool (V) button in the toolbox.**
- **If necessary, click the Show Transforms Controls check box on the options bar to select it.**

Photoshop displays the layer with a bounding box (Figure 3-21).

FIGURE 3-21

2

- **SHIFT+drag the lower-right sizing handle toward the center of the layer until the layer is approximately the size of the front porch of the house.**

The resized layer is displayed (Figure 3-22). Recall that SHIFT+drag maintains the width to height ratio when resizing selections.

3

- **Press the ENTER key to apply the transformation.**

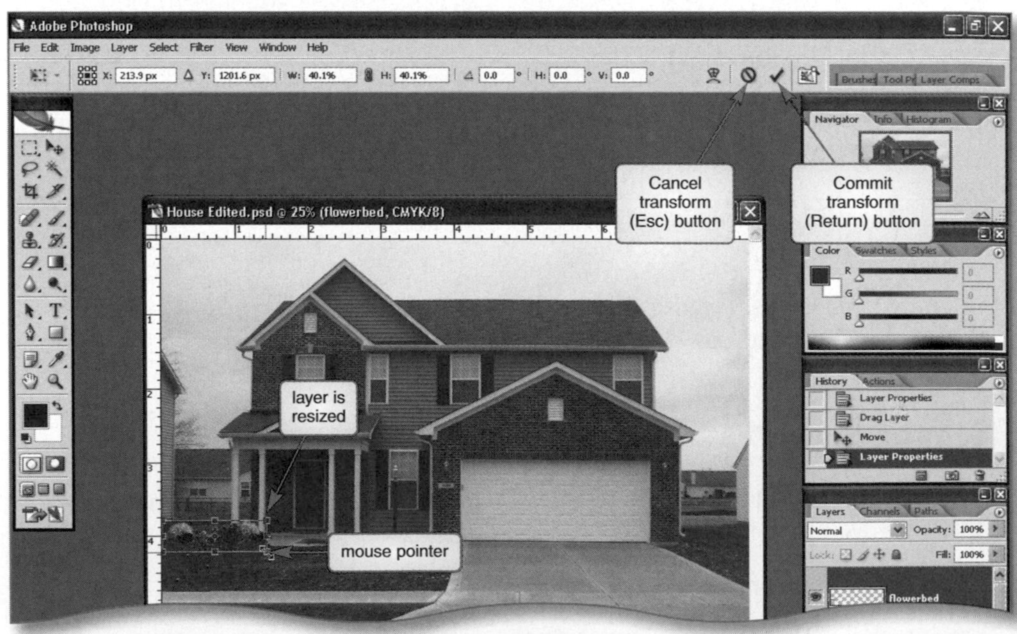

FIGURE 3-22

Applying or committing a transformation tells Photoshop that you are finished resizing. You cannot choose another tool until you apply the transformation. To cancel the transformation, click the Cancel transform (Esc) button on the options bar (Figure 3-22) or press the ESC key.

The next step shows how the layer is moved.

To Move the Flowerbed Layer

1 With the layer selected, drag the layer so its horizontal center is approximately even with the left column on the porch and its vertical center is between the house and the street. Do not drag the center reference point.

The layer is moved (Figure 3-23).

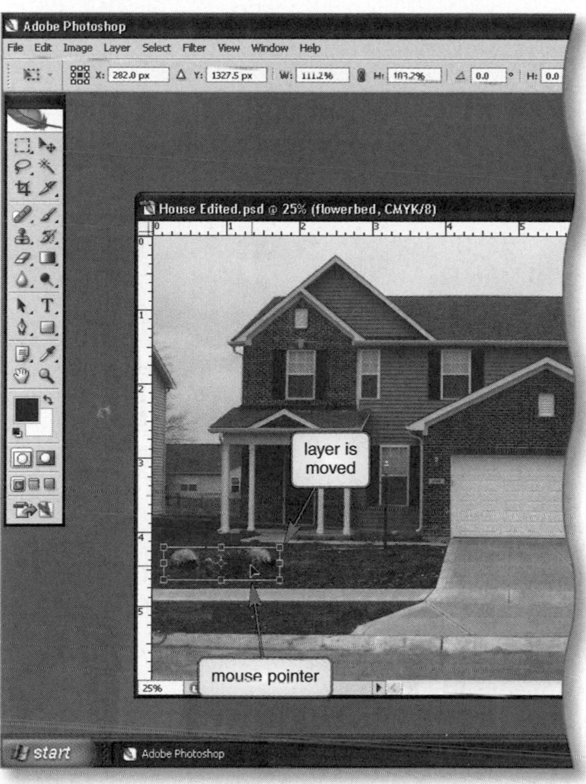

FIGURE 3-23

In the next section, you will create a layer that includes only a selected area from another image. First, the following steps illustrate how to open a file named, Flowers.

To Open the Flowers Image

1 On the File menu, click Open.

2 When the Open dialog box is displayed, click the Look in box arrow, and then navigate to the Project03 folder on the CD that accompanies this book, or a location specified by your instructor.

3 Double-click the Project03 folder.

4 Click the file named, Flowers, and then click the Open button.

5 Change the magnification to 25 percent. Resize the window and scroll as necessary to display the red and pink flowers as shown in Figure 3-24.

Photoshop displays the Flowers window (Figure 3-24).

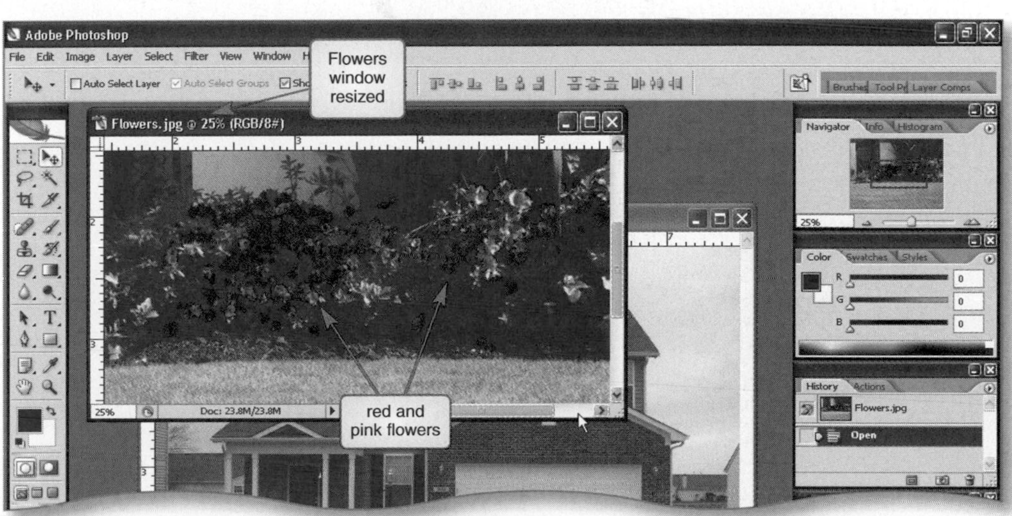

FIGURE 3-24

Creating a Layer by Dragging a Selection

The flowers that will display between the porch and sidewalk are a part of a larger image. Therefore, you will have to select a portion of the image and then drag the selection to create a layer. You will move the selection from the source window, Flowers, to the destination window, House Edited. The following steps illustrate how to create a layer by dragging.

To Create a Layer by Dragging a Selection

1

- **With the Flowers window active, if necessary, right-click the Lasso Tool (L) button and then click Magnetic Lasso on the context menu.**
- **Drag around the light and dark pink flowers including some greenery. Avoid including in the selection the building behind the flowers and the ground below the flowers. Use the Add to selection and Subtract from selection buttons on the options bar, as necessary, to create your selection. If you make a mistake while selecting, press CTRL+D to deselect, then begin again.**

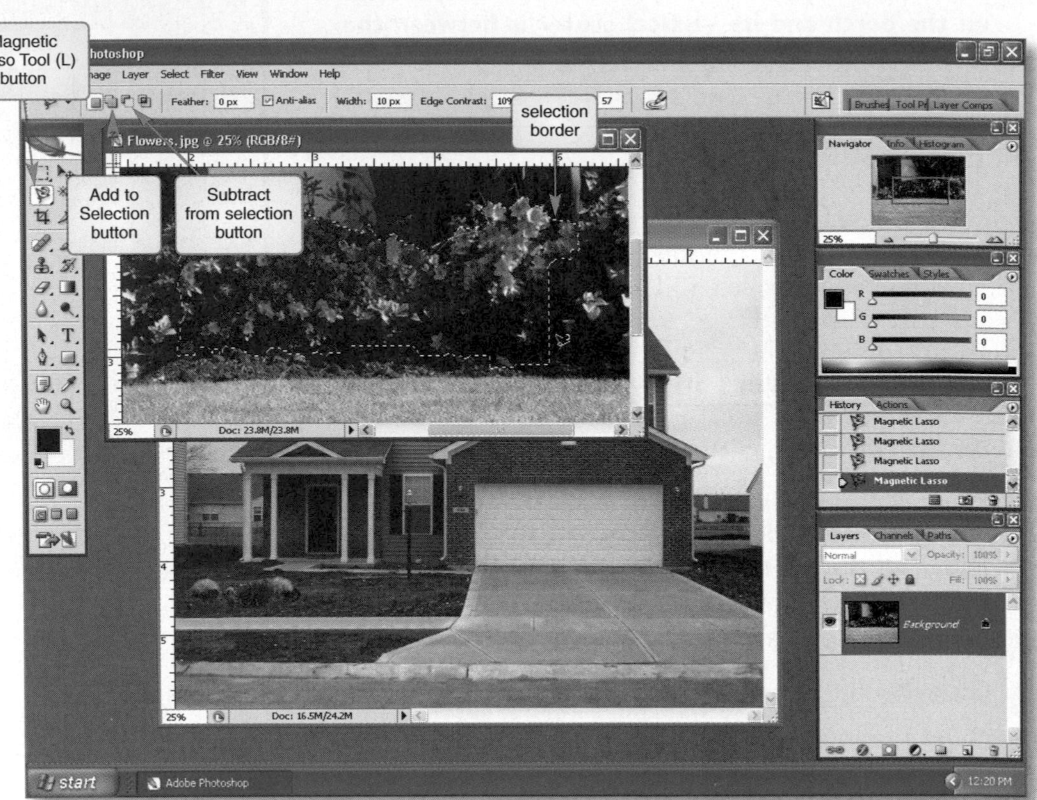

FIGURE 3-25

Photoshop displays the selection border around the flowers (Figure 3-25). Your exact selection does not have to match the one in the figure.

2

• **Click the Move Tool (V) button in the toolbox.**

• **ALT+drag the selection and drop it in the House Edited window. On the options bar, if necessary, click the Show Transforms Control check box to select it.**

The flowers are displayed in the House Edited window with the bounding box (Figure 3-26). Recall that ALT+drag of a selection creates a copy of the selection rather than a cut.

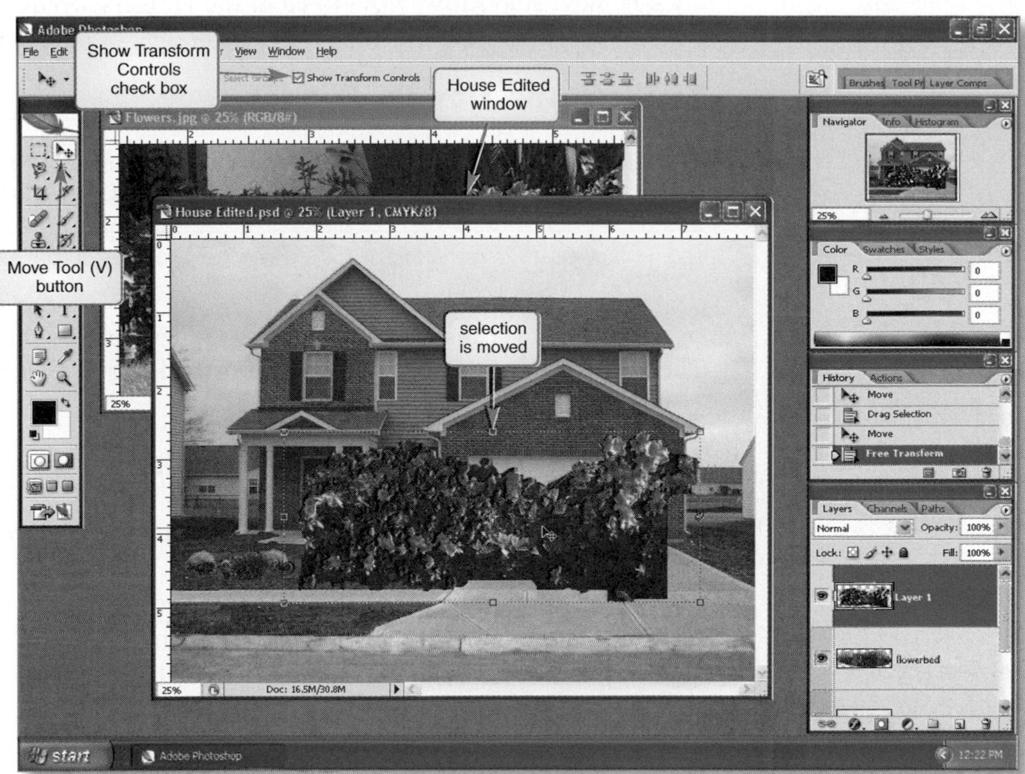

FIGURE 3-26

3

• **SHIFT+drag a corner sizing handle to reduce the size of the flowers to approximately 1.0 by 0.5 inches.**

Drag the selection to the area between the porch and sidewalk as shown in Figure 3-27.

4

• **Press the ENTER key to apply the transformation.**

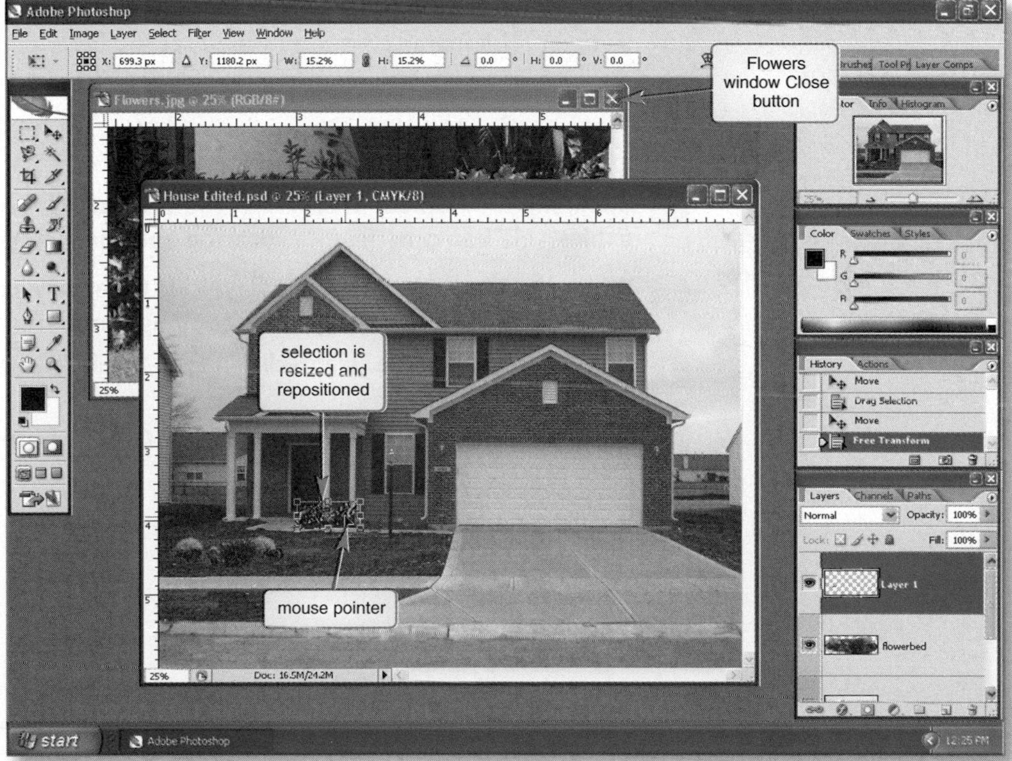

FIGURE 3-27

Other Ways

1. In source window, create selection, on Edit menu, click Copy, in destination window, click Paste

The next step shows how to close the Flowers window.

To Close the Flowers Window

1. **Click the Close button in the Flowers window. If Photoshop displays a dialog box asking if you want to save the changes, click the No button.**

The window closes and the House Edited window becomes active.

The new layer displays in the Layers palette above the layer of the flowerbed. The following steps illustrate how to set the layer properties.

To Set the Flowers Layer Properties

1. **Right-click Layer 1 in the Layers palette. Click Layer Properties on the shortcut menu.**
2. **Type** `flowers` **in the Name box. Click the Color box arrow and then click Red.**
3. **Click the OK button.**

The flowers layer displays a red indicator in the Layers palette as shown in Figure 3-28.

The flowers fit the space but may need some tonal adjustment, which you will learn about later in this project.

In preparation for editing a layer that includes a tree, the followings steps show how to open a file named Tree, and then set the layer properties.

To Create the Tree Layer

1. **Open the file named, Tree, from the Project 03 folder on the CD that accompanies this book, or from a location specified by your instructor.**
2. **When the Tree window is displayed, if necessary press the v key to access the Move tool, and then drag the tree image into the House Edited window.**
3. **In the Layers palette, right-click Layer 1. Click Layer Properties on the shortcut menu.**
4. **Type** `tree` **in the Name box. Click the Color box arrow and then click Gray.**
5. **Click the OK button.**

The tree layer is displayed in the document window and is renamed and colored in the Layers palette (Figure 3-28).

FIGURE 3-28

The Eraser Tools

When creating a composite image, you can limit the selected area of the source image as you did in the flowers layer, but sometimes a layer still has extra color or objects that are not appropriate for the composite image. The image may be oddly shaped that makes selecting a portion tedious; or, there are other images in the background that come along with the selection no matter what you do. In those cases, dragging the image into a layer and then erasing part of that layer gives you more freedom and control in how the layer displays.

Using the Eraser Tools

The **Eraser tool** changes pixels in the image as you drag through them. On most layers, the Eraser tool simply erases the pixels or changes them to transparent. On the background layer, the pixels are changed to white. On a locked layer, the Eraser tool changes the pixels to the background color.

When you right-click the Eraser Tool (E) button in the toolbox, you can choose other eraser tools. The **Magic Eraser tool** is similar to the Eraser tool except it erases all similarly colored pixels with one click. You have the choice of contiguous or noncontiguous pixels.

The **Background Eraser tool** erases the background while maintaining the edges of an object in the foreground, based on a set color that you choose for the background.

On the next page, Table 3-2 describes the eraser tools.

Table 3-2 Eraser Tools

TOOL	PURPOSE	SHORTCUT	BUTTON
Eraser Tool	erases pixels beneath the cursor or brush tip	E SHIFT+E toggles through all three eraser tools	
Background Eraser Tool	erases sample color from center of brush	E SHIFT+E toggles through all three eraser tools	
Magic Eraser Tool	erases all similarly colored pixels	E SHIFT+E toggles through all three eraser tools	

Erasing with the Magic Eraser

The following steps illustrate how to use the Magic Eraser tool to remove the sky around, and in back of, the tree. The Magic Eraser options bar (Figure 3-30) allows you to enter a **tolerance** value to define the range of colors that can be erased. A lower tolerance erases pixels within a range of color values very similar to the pixel you click. A higher tolerance erases pixels within a broader range. You will choose to erase noncontiguous pixels, which means all pixels with similar colors in the selected layer will be erased.

To Erase Using the Magic Eraser

1

- **With the tree layer still selected, right-click the Eraser Tool (E) button in the Photoshop toolbox.**

Photoshop displays the context menu (Figure 3-29).

FIGURE 3-29

2

- **Click Magic Eraser Tool.**
- **On the Magic Eraser options bar, type** 50 **in the Tolerance box. If necessary, click the Anti-Alias check box to select it. If necessary, click the Contiguous check box to deselect it.**
- **Move the mouse to a portion of the tree layer containing sky.**

The mouse pointer changes to a Magic Eraser icon (Figure 3-30). Choosing non-contiguous will select all pixels of similar color.

FIGURE 3-30

3

- **Click the sky.**

Photoshop deletes all of the sky color (Figure 3-31).

4

- **If some sky still remains in your layer, click it.**

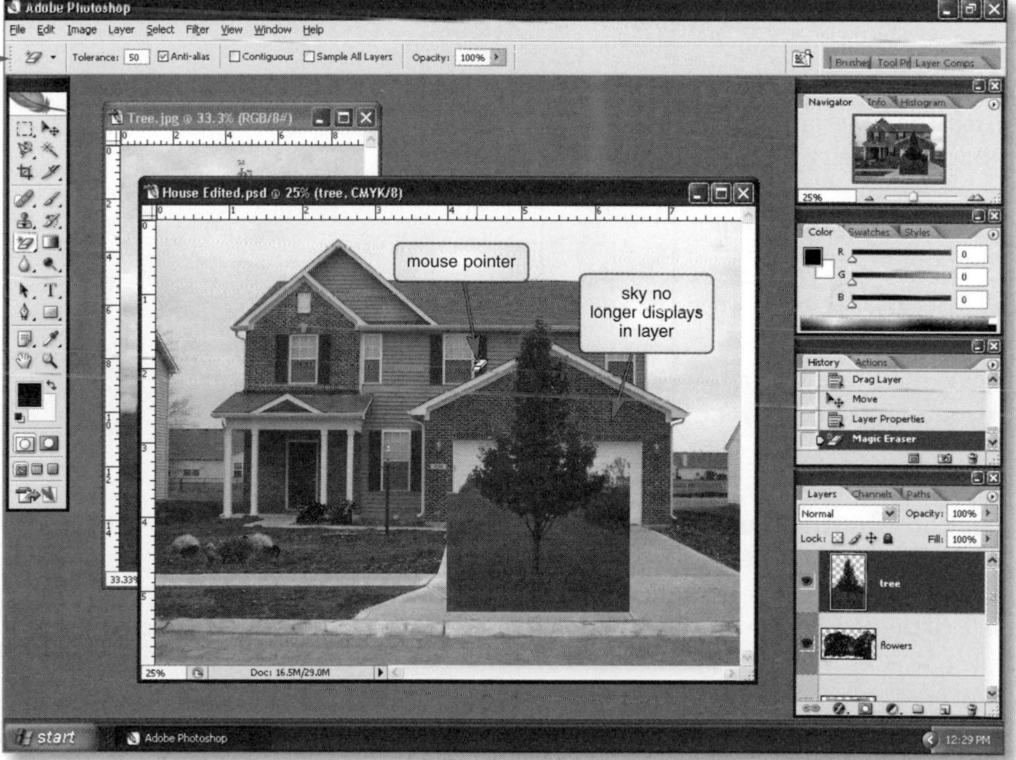

FIGURE 3-31

Other Ways

1. From another eraser tool, press SHIFT+E until Magic Eraser tool is selected, click in document

Recall that the Anti-alias check box creates a smooth edge that can apply to both selecting and erasing. The tolerance setting of 50 affects a fairly broad range in the color spectrum.

Erasing with the Eraser Tool

To erase more of the background in the tree layer, the following steps use the Eraser tool. The Eraser tool options bar (Figure 3-32) displays a Mode box in which you can choose a shape for erasure, an Opacity box to specify the depth of the erasure, and a Flow box to specify how quickly the erasure is performed. In addition, you can specify whether or not the erasure becomes a state in the History palette.

The right-bracket key on your keyboard ( ]) is used to increase the size of the eraser. The left bracket key ([ ) decreases the size of the eraser. Some users find it easier to erase in a layer when only that layer is displayed. If you want to display only the layer, click the visibility icon next to the background and all layers other than the tree layer. When you are finished erasing, click the visibility box again to redisplay the background and other layers. The following steps illustrate how to use the Erase tool.

To Erase Using the Eraser tool

1

- **If necessary, increase the magnification of the document window to view the tree layer more precisely.**
- **With the tree layer still selected, right-click the Eraser Tool (E) button in the Photoshop toolbox.**
- **Click Eraser Tool on the context menu.**
- **Move the mouse to a portion of the tree layer containing grass.**
- **Press the] key several times to resize the brush until the mouser pointer changes from a dot to a small circle.**

Photoshop displays the mouse pointer as a circle (Figure 3-32). Notice the brush size setting changes on the options bar as you click the bracket key.

FIGURE 3-32

2

- **Drag the mouse across a portion of the grass. Do not drag across the tree or its trunk.**

The Eraser tool erases the pixels under the mouse (Figure 3-33).

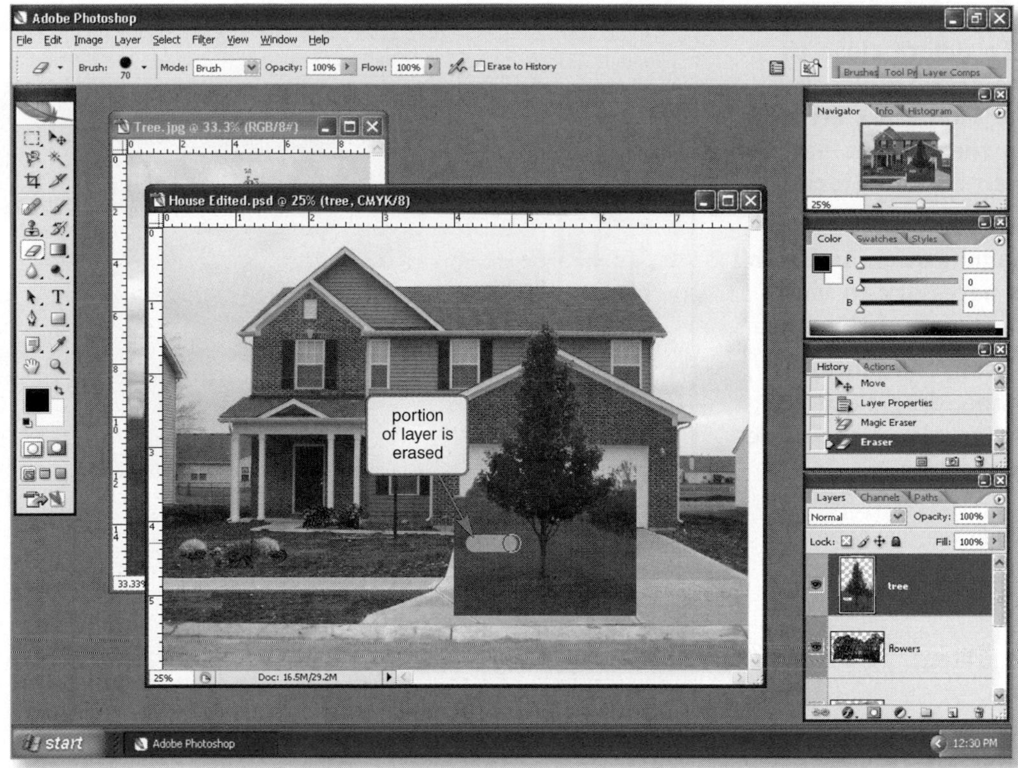

FIGURE 3-33

3

- **Continue dragging, using the [and] keys to change the size of your eraser. Zoom in as necessary, to erase the majority of the grass and background bushes. Do not try to erase the grass showing behind the tree limbs.**

Most of the grass is deleted (Figure 3-34).

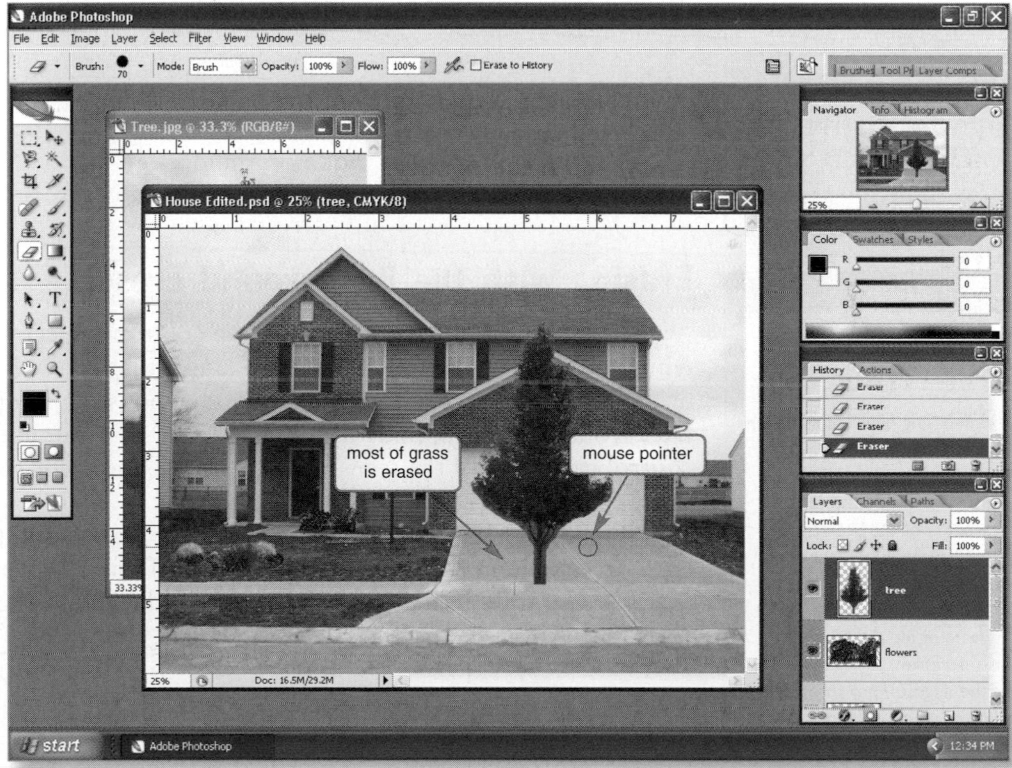

FIGURE 3-34

4

- **To delete close to the tree trunk, click the Mode box arrow on the options bar and then choose Block.**
- **Increase the magnification and scroll as necessary to view the trunk of the tree.**
- **Using the Block shape, drag close to the trunk on each side of the tree.**

The Eraser tool erases the pixels under the mouse (Figure 3-35). Some grass color will remain close to the leaves of the trees.

FIGURE 3-35

5

- **If necessary, change the magnification back to 50 percent by typing** 50 **in the magnification box at the bottom of the document.**

Other Ways

1. From another eraser tool, press SHIFT+E until Eraser tool is selected, click in document

The Block and Pencil mode on the options bar are not resizable like the Brush mode.

More About

The Background Eraser Tool

By specifying different sampling and tolerance options, you can control the range of the transparency and the sharpness of the boundaries. The Background Eraser tool samples the hot spot and deletes that color wherever it appears inside the brush. It also performs color extraction at the edges of any foreground objects, so color halos are not visible if the foreground object is later pasted into another image. The Background Eraser tool overrides the lock transparency setting of a layer.

Erasing with the Background Eraser

The Background Eraser samples the color in the center of the mouse pointer which is called the **hot spot** and then erases that color as you drag, leaving the rest of the layer as foreground. You release the mouse to sample a different color. On the Background Eraser options bar (Figure 3-36) you can use the tolerance setting to control the range of the transparency, sample the color selections, and adjust the sharpness of the boundaries by setting limits.

The following steps show how to use the Background Eraser tool to remove the grass from behind the branches of the tree. If you make a mistake while erasing, click the previous state in the History palette and begin erasing again.

To Erase Using the Background Eraser

1

- **With the tree layer still selected and the magnification at 50 percent, right-click the Eraser Tool (E) button in the Photoshop toolbox.**
- **Click Background Eraser Tool on the context menu.**
- **On the options bar, click the Sampling: Once button. Click the Limits box arrow and then choose Discontiguous. Type** 25 **in the Tolerance box and press the ENTER key. Click the Protect Foreground Color check box to select it.**
- **Move the mouse to the document window and then press the] key several times to increase the size of the eraser. Position the mouse pointer directly over a portion of the grass that still is displayed.**

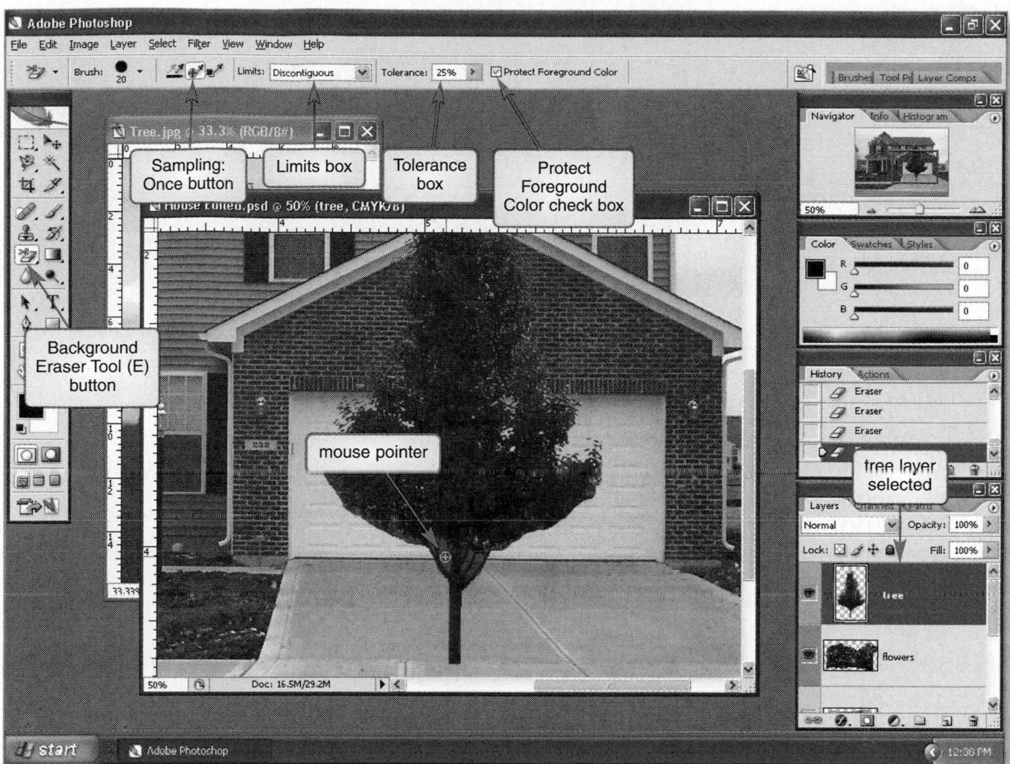

FIGURE 3-36

Photoshop displays the mouse pointer as a circle with a cross in the middle (Figure 3-36).

2

• With the cross directly over green grass, click and hold the mouse button. Slowly drag across the lower limbs of the tree.

Photoshop erases all of the grass in the background (Figure 3-37).

3

• If any parts of the layer still need to be erased to display only the tree, right-click the Eraser Tool (V) button in the toolbox and then click Eraser Tool. Adjust the brush size as necessary with the bracket keys and carefully erase small portions at a time.

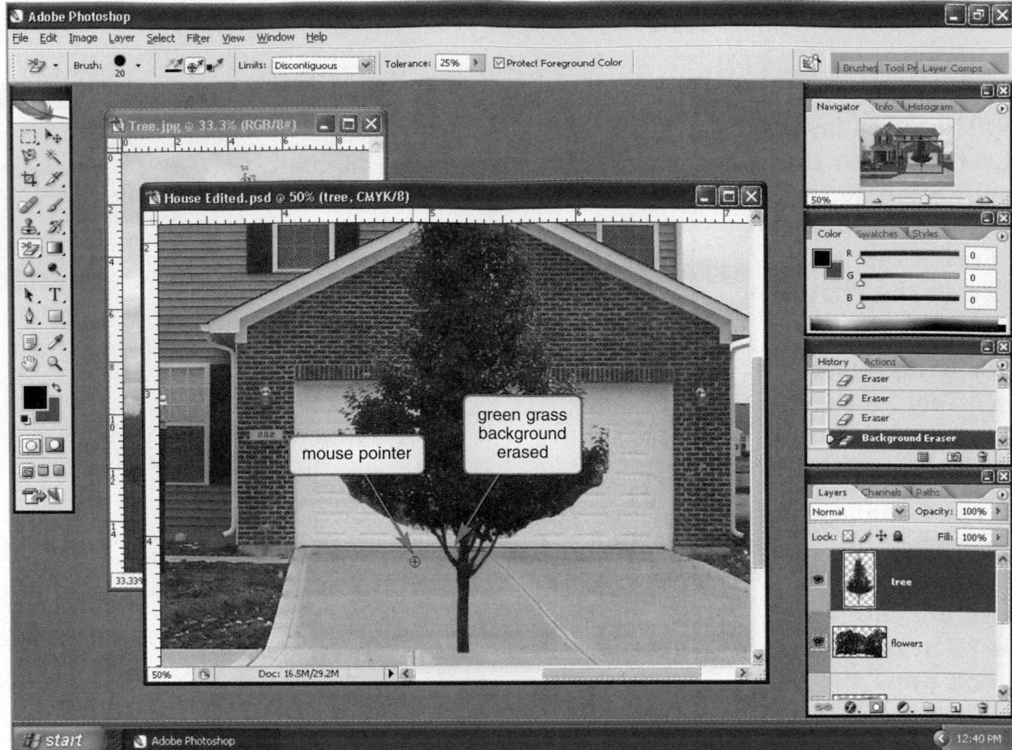

FIGURE 3-37

Other Ways

1. From another eraser tool, press SHIFT+E until Background Eraser tool is selected, click in document

More About

Arranging Layers

If you want to rearrange your layers in order to change their visibility or to better organize them, simply drag the layer up or down in the Layers palette. Release the mouse button when the highlighted line appears where you want to place the layer or group. The topmost layer in the Layers palette displays in front of any other layers in the document window. The Layer menu on the Photoshop menu bar also contains an Arrange submenu to help you organize your layers.

To alternate among the three eraser tools, press SHIFT+E. To access the eraser tools after using a different tool, press the E key.

When using the eraser tools, it is best to erase small portions at once. That way each erasure is a separate state in the History palette. If you make mistakes you can click earlier states in the palette. Small erasures also can be undone. To **undo** an erasure, click Edit on the menu bar and then click Undo Eraser, or press CTRL+Z to undo.

When working with layers, it is important to make sure which layer you are editing by looking at the active layer in the Layers palette. If a layer is partially eclipsed, or overlapped, by another layer do the following. Select the layer in the Layers palette. Click Layer on the menu bar, point to Arrange, and then click one of the options to bring the layer to the front or send it to the back.

The final step in editing the tree layer is to move it to a position in the flowerbed.

To Reposition the Tree Layer

1. **Decrease the magnification to 25 percent.**
2. **With the tree layer selected, press the V key to activate the Move tool.**
3. **Drag the layer to a location left of the front door of the house, so the base of the tree is in the flowerbed (Figure 3-38). Part of the tree will be eclipsed by the left margin.**

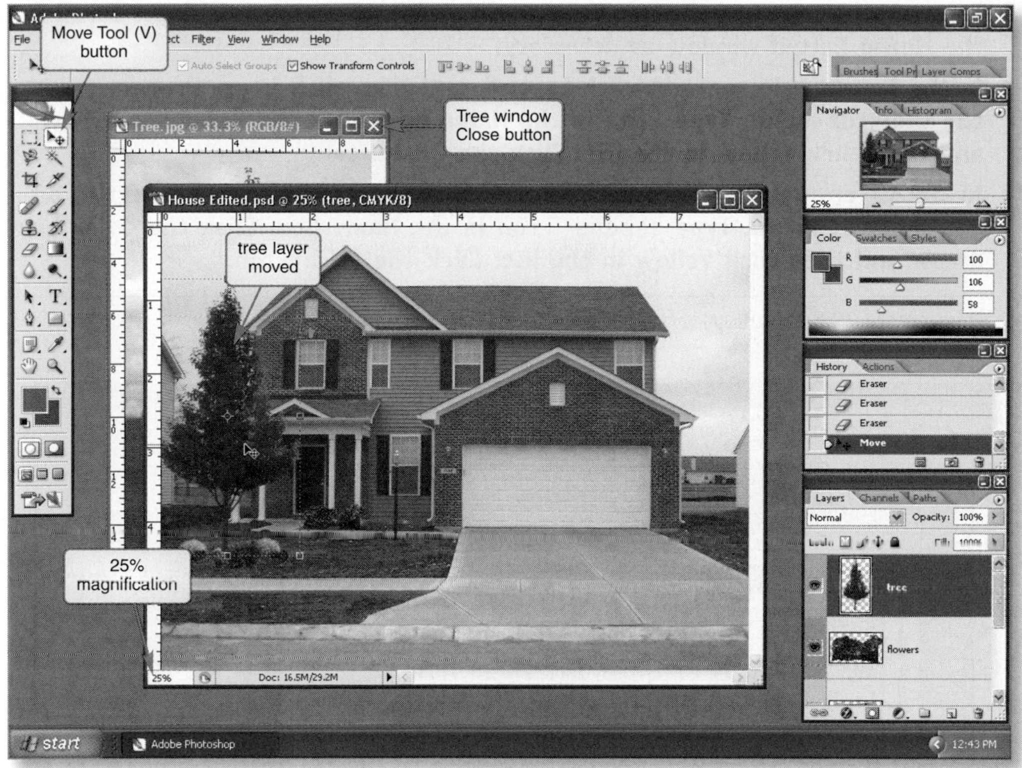

FIGURE 3-38

Because you are finished with the original tree image, it is time to close the Tree window as shown in the following step.

To Close the Tree Window

1 **Click the Close button on the Tree window title bar. If Photoshop displays a dialog box asking if you want to save the changes, click the No button.**

The window closes and the House Edited window becomes active.

The next piece of landscaping is to add a lion statue on each side of the driveway. The two layers are created as the following steps illustrate.

To Insert the Lion Layers

1 **Open the file named, Lion, from the Project03 folder on the CD that accompanies this book, or from a location specified by your instructor.**

2 **When Photoshop displays the Lion window, drag its title bar above the House Edited window title bar.**

3 **Press the w key to activate the Magic Wand tool. Click in the white space. Right-click the selection and then click Select Inverse on the shortcut menu.**

4 **Press the v key to activate the Move tool. If necessary, click the Show Transform Controls check box to deselect it. Drag the selection to the House Edited image and position it on one side of the garage door, close to the house.**

5 **Drag another copy of the lion to the other side of the garage door. Scroll in the House Edited window as necessary.**

6 **In the Layers palette, right-click Layer 1 and then click Layer Properties on the shortcut menu. Type** `lion` **in the Name box. Click the Color box arrow and then click Yellow in the list. Click the OK button.**

7 **In the Layers palette, right-click Layer 2 and then click Layer Properties on the shortcut menu. Type** `second lion` **in the Name box. Click the Color box arrow and then click Yellow in the list. Click the OK button.**

Photoshop creates two more layers (Figure 3-39).

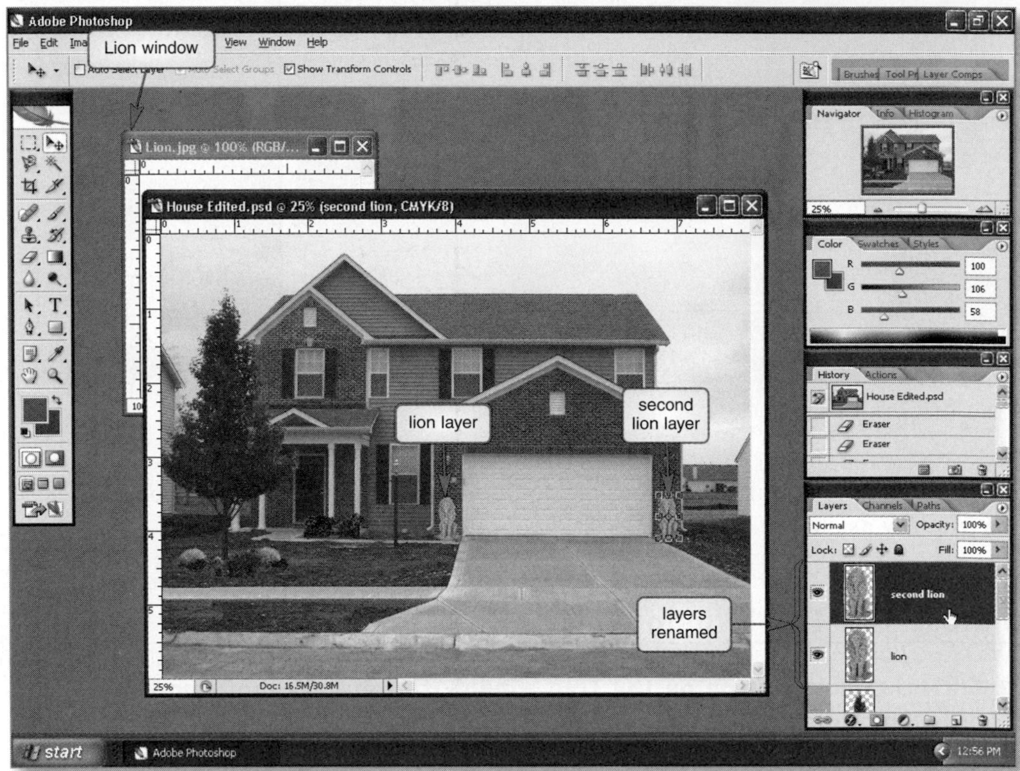

FIGURE 3-39

The next step closes the Lion window.

> *More About*
>
> **Layer Groups**
>
> If you work with large numbers of layers when compositing, you may want to group layers. Layer groups help you organize and manage layers, and reduce clutter in the Layers palette. You can use groups to apply attributes to several layers at a time. To create a layer group, click a layer in the Layers palette and then SHIFT+click additional layers. Press CTRL+G or click the Group Layers command on the Layer menu.

To Close the Lion Window

1 **Click the Close button on the Lion window title bar. If Photoshop displays a dialog box asking if you want to save the changes, click the No button.**

The window closes and the House Edited window becomes active.

Instead of dragging an image twice to create two layers, you can **duplicate a layer**, by right-clicking a layer in the Layers palette, and then click Duplicate Layer on the shortcut menu. Photoshop then allows you to name the new layer and specify to which open document window the layer should be added. A duplicate layer can be used to create an entirely new document in the same manner.

In preparation for editing a layer that includes a bush, the followings steps show how to open the file named, Bush, and set the layer properties.

To Create the Bush Layer

1. **Open the file named, Bush, from the Project03 folder on the CD that accompanies this book, or from a location specified by your instructor.**
2. **When the Bush window is displayed, drag the title bar slightly above the House Edited title bar. Reduce the magnification to 25 percent and reduce the size of the window by dragging the lower-right corner of the window toward the center.**
3. **Press the V key to access the Move tool, and then drag the bush image into the House Edited image.**
4. **Right-click Layer 1 in the Layers palette. Click Layer Properties on the shortcut menu.**
5. **Type** bush **in the Name box. Click the Color box arrow and then click Violet.**
6. **Click the OK button.**

The bush layer is displayed in the House Edited window and is renamed in the Layers palette as shown in Figure 3-40.

FIGURE 3-40

Layer Masks

Another way to edit layers is by creating a mask. A **mask** is used to show or hide portions of a layer or protect areas from edits. A mask does not change the layer as the Eraser tool did; it merely overlays a template to conceal a portion of the layer.

Photoshop provides two types of masks. **Layer masks** are resolution-dependent bitmap images that are created with the painting or selection tools. **Vector masks** are resolution independent and are created with a pen or shape tool. In this project you will create a layer mask.

You can edit a layer mask to add or subtract from the masked region. A layer mask is a **grayscale** image, which means each pixel in the image is represented by a single sample value, or shade of overall luminance, on a scale from black to white. Therefore in the mask, areas you create in black are hidden because the mask is in front of the layer. Areas you create in white are visible. Shades of gray display in various levels of transparency.

Masks have advantages over other kinds of layer editing. If you change your mind or make mistakes, you have not altered the original layer image. With the Eraser tool you would have to delete the layer, open the second image again, recreate the layer, and then begin to edit again. With masks, you simply create a new mask.

A special kind of mask is a **clipping mask** that masks the layers above it. The transparent pixels of the bottom layer mask or clip the content of layers above it, much like a color overlay.

Creating a Layer Mask

To create a layer mask, Photoshop provides an Add layer mask button in the lower part of the Layers palette. When clicked, the button adds a second thumbnail to the layer's description in the palette. By default the mask is **linked** or connected to the selected layer. A link icon displays between the layer thumbnail and the mask thumbnail.

After you add the mask, you will paint with black to identify masked portions of the layer. Pressing the B key on the keyboard will activate the brush to paint in the layer. To paint, simply drag in the layer. The layer added to the House Edited image is a photo of a bush planted in a pot. You will need to mask all of the layer except for the area containing the bush.

The following steps show how, if you make a mistake while creating the mask, you can press the X key on the keyboard to toggle to the default foreground color, white, and paint to unmask the error.

To Create a Layer Mask

1

- **If necessary, press the D key to activate the default color scheme.**
- **With the bush layer selected, click the Add layer mask button in the lower part of the Layers palette.**
- **If necessary, press the X key to exchange the black and white colors in the toolbox, so that black is the foreground color.**

Photoshop adds a layer mask to the selected layer in the palette (Figure 3-41). The link icon links the mask to the layer. The mask is selected.

FIGURE 3-41

2

- **With the mask selected, press the B key to activate the brush.**
- **Move the mouse pointer to the document window and press] to increase the size of the brush's circle, as necessary.**
- **Drag the mouse across a lower portion of the layer.**

The black color masks the layer to reveal the background underneath (Figure 3-42).

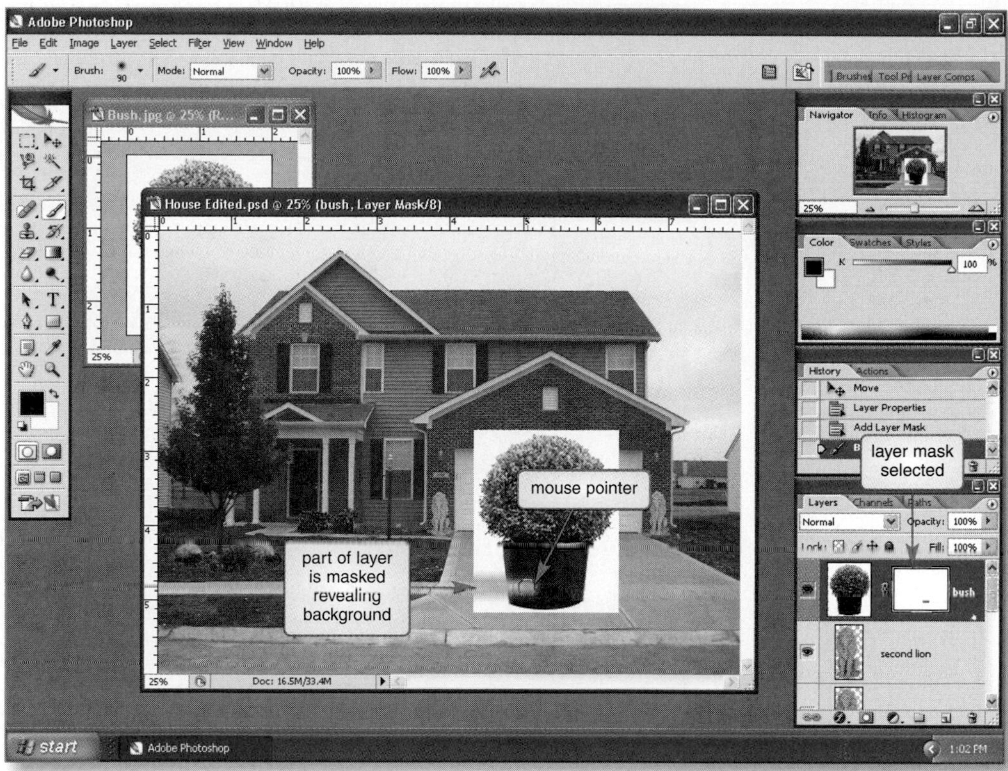

FIGURE 3-42

3

- **Continue dragging through the layer to remove everything except the bush itself. Adjust the size of the brush as necessary using the [and] keys.**

Only the bush is visible (Figure 3-43). The rest of the layer is masked.

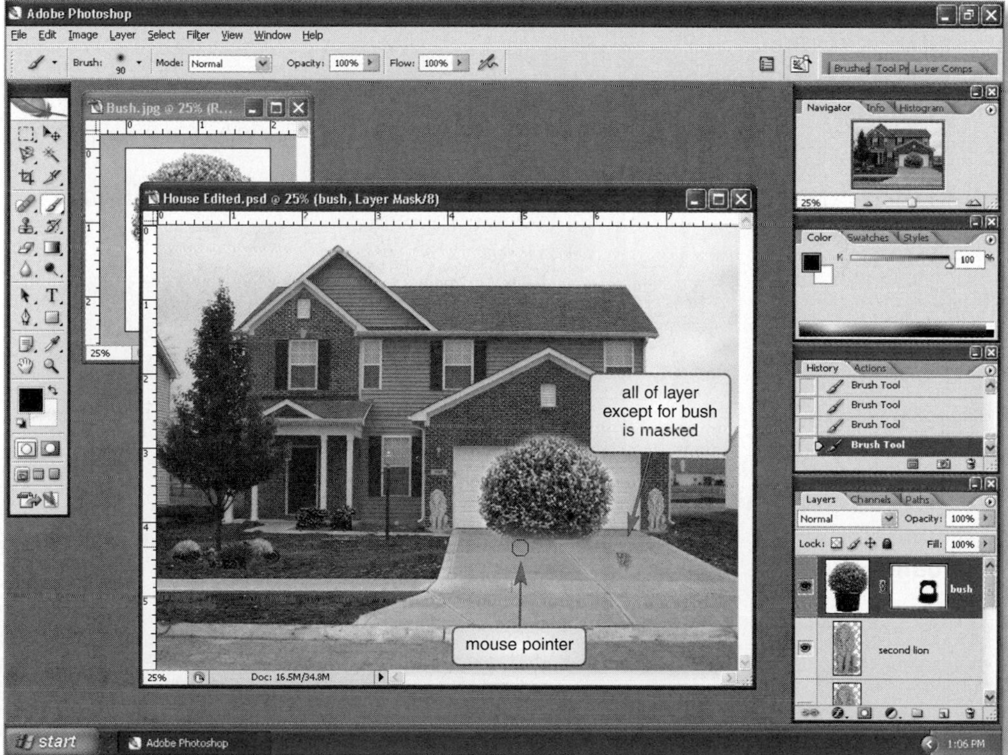

FIGURE 3-43

4

• **Drag across the bush.**

Part of the bush is masked (Figure 3-44).

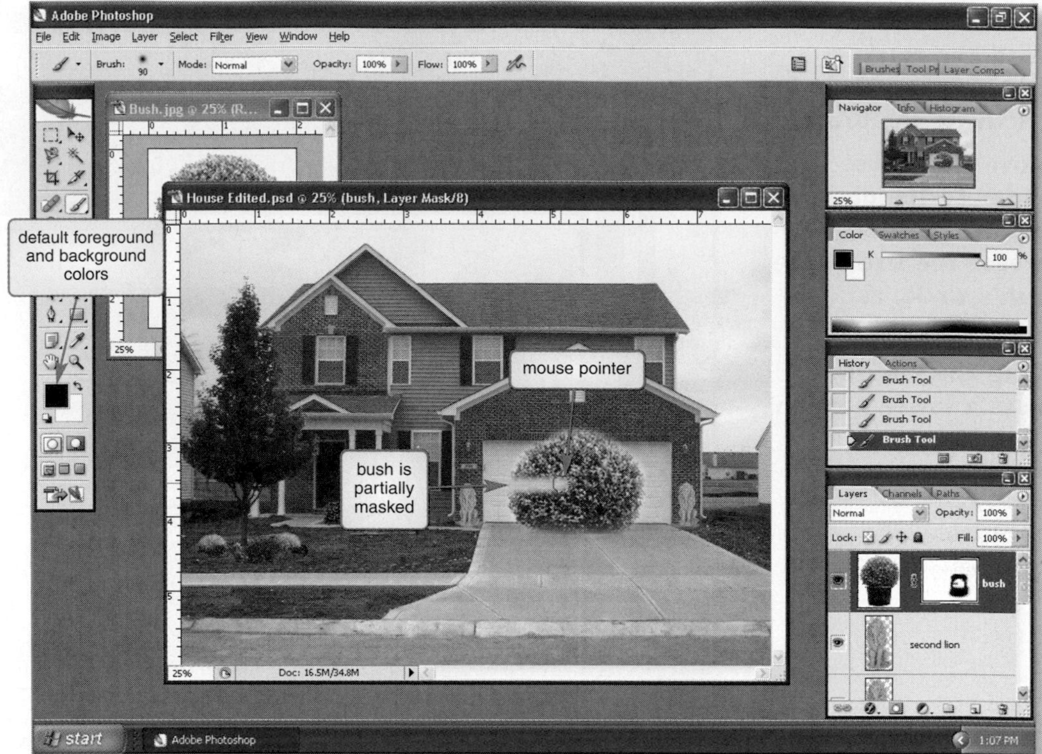

FIGURE 3-44

5

• **Press the X key and then drag across the same portion of the bush.**

The X key toggles the foreground and background colors, effectively painting with white to unmask the error (Figure 3-45).

6

• **Press the X key again to return to the default foreground and background colors.**

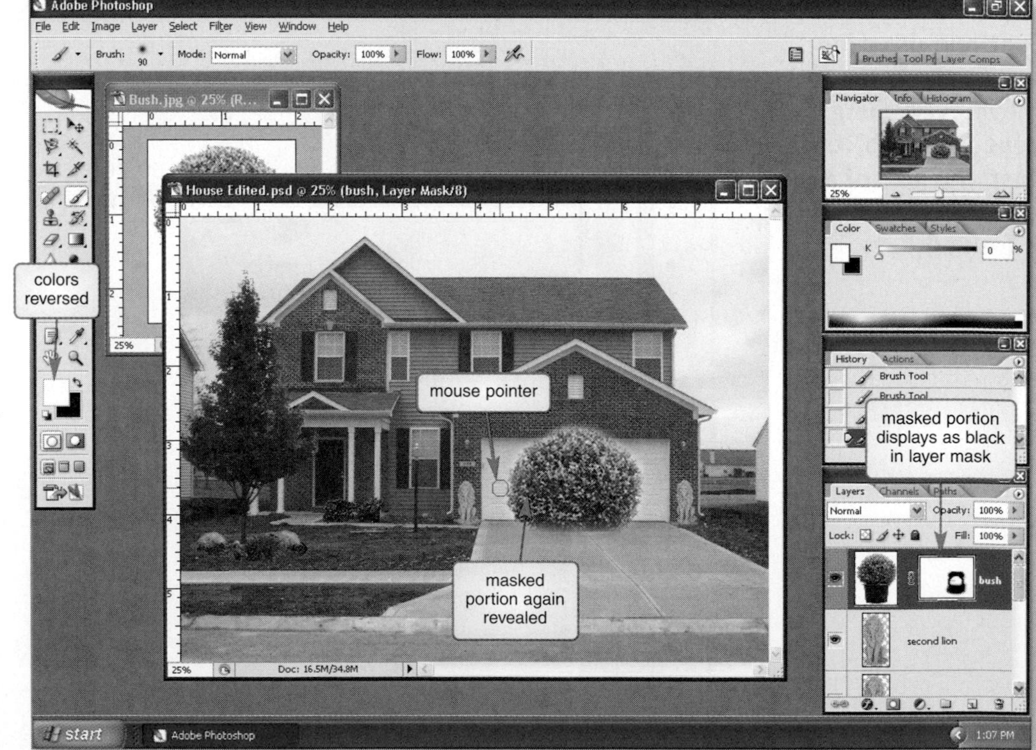

FIGURE 3-45

Other Ways

1. On Layer menu, point to Layer mask, click Reveal All

Once you have created a mask, you may want to perform other manipulations on the mask. For example, if you want to unlink a mask to move it independently of its layer, click the link icon in the Layers palette. To unlink a mask temporarily, SHIFT+click the link icon. If you want to mask the entire layer completely, you can ALT+click the Add layer mask button. In that case, painting with white in the mask would reveal portions of the mask. To make the mask permanent and reduce overall file size, apply the mask using a command on the mask's shortcut menu.

The following steps show how the bush layer is moved to a location between the sidewalk and the house.

To Resize and Move the Bush Layer

1. **With the layer selected, press the V key to activate the Move tool. Click the Show Transforms Control check box to select it.**
2. **SHIFT+drag a corner sizing handle to decrease the size of the layer to approximately 25 percent as displayed in the Transformation options bar scale boxes.**
3. **Press the ENTER key to confirm the transformation.**
4. **Drag the layer to a location between the house and sidewalk as shown in Figure 3-46 on the next page. Do not drag the center reference point.**

Later in this project you will make tonal adjustments to the layer so it better blends into the composite image.

Creating a Layer Mask from a Selection

A **selection layer mask** is a layer mask created by making a selection in the layer. Instead of painting in the layer mask, the selection border dictates the transparent portion of the layer.

The steps on the next page illustrate how to add a second bush to the House Edited image by creating a layer, selecting an area, and then adding a layer mask.

To Create a Selection Mask

1

- **Select the Bush window.**
- **If necessary, press the V key to activate the Move tool.**
- **Drag the image into the House Edited window.**

The new layer is displayed (Figure 3-46).

FIGURE 3-46

2

- **In the toolbox, right-click the Rectangular Marquee Tool (M) button, and then select Elliptical Marquee Tool from the context menu.**
- **Drag an area of the layer to include as much of the bush as possible, but not the pot.**

The bush is selected (Figure 3-47).

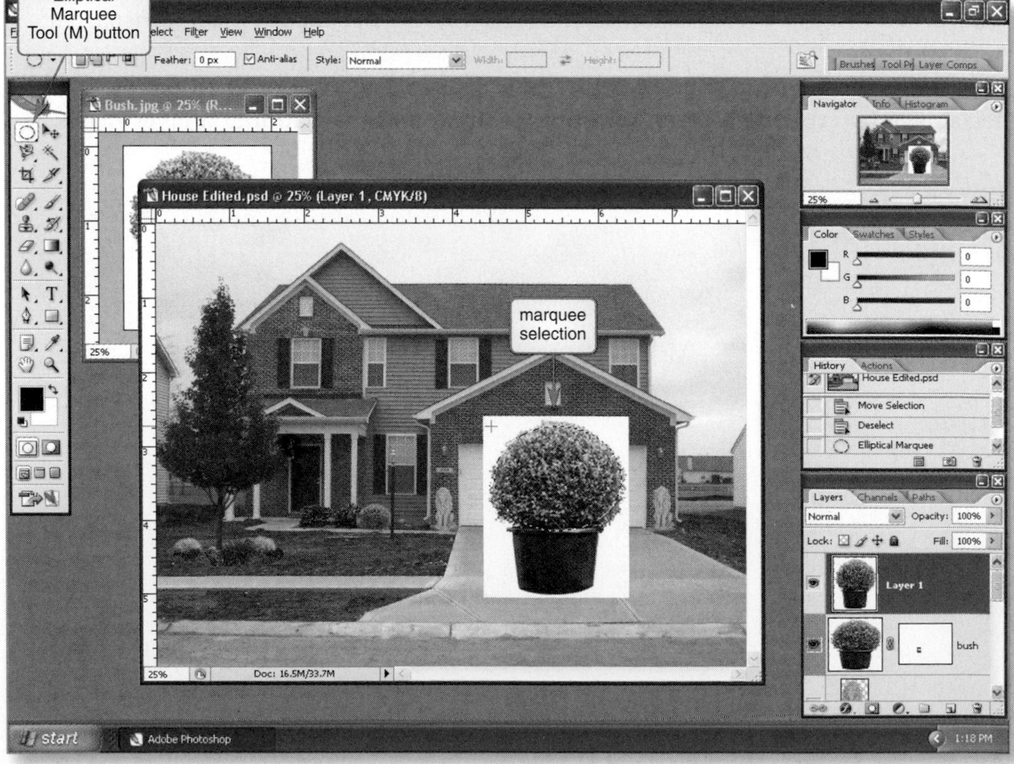

FIGURE 3-47

3

• **In the Layers palette, click the Add layer mask button.**

Only the selected area is visible (Figure 3-48).

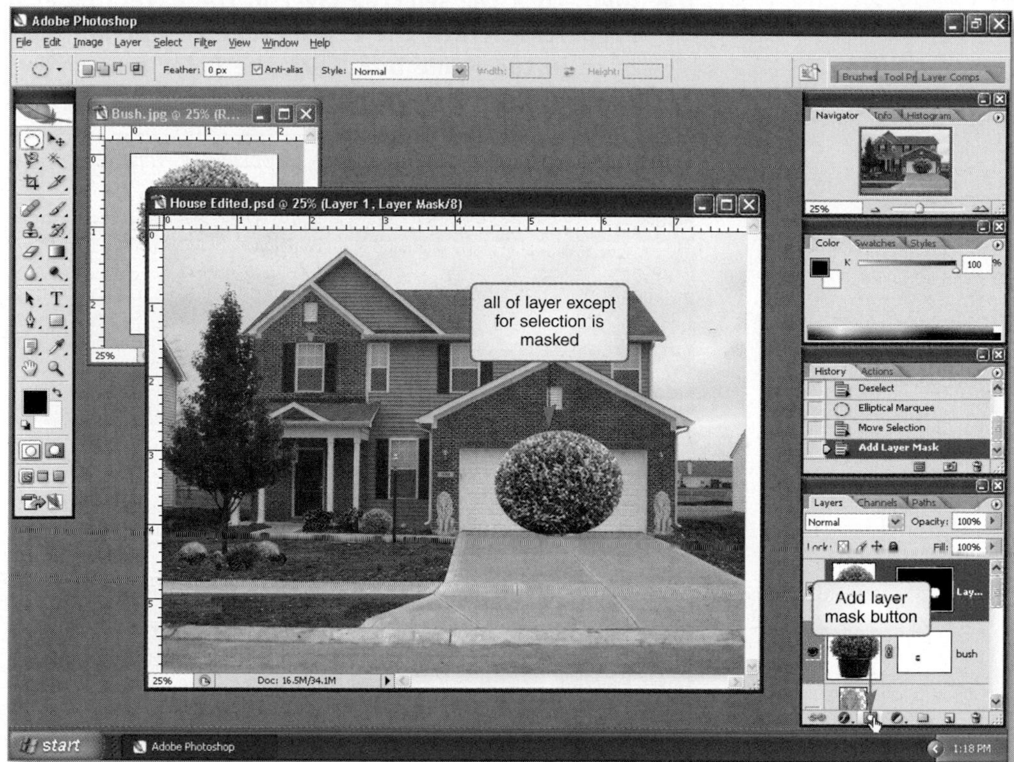

FIGURE 3-48

If you want to change the masked portion of the layer, you can change the visible area by moving the mask around the image. To move the mask, first click the link icon in the Layers palette to unlink the mask from the layer. Select the Move tool in the toolbox. Then, in the document window, click the layer and drag to reposition it. When the mask is correctly positioned, click between the layer and layer mask in the Layers palette to relink the mask and the layer.

To complete the bush layer, it must be resized, repositioned, and named as shown in the following steps.

To Resize, Reposition, and Name the Layer

1. **With the layer selected, press the V key to activate the Move tool. If necessary, click the Show Transforms Control check box to select it.**
2. **SHIFT+drag a corner sizing handle to decrease the size of the layer to approximately 25 percent as displayed in the Transformation options bar scale boxes.**
3. **Press the ENTER key to apply the transformation.**
4. **Drag the layer to a location between the house and sidewalk, on the other size of the lamppost. Do not drag the center reference point.**

5 **Right-click the selected layer in the Layers palette and then click Layer Properties. When the Layer Properties dialog box is displayed, type** `second bush` **in the Name box. Click the Color box arrow and then click Violet in the list. Click the OK button.**

The second bush layer is renamed and repositioned (Figure 3-49).

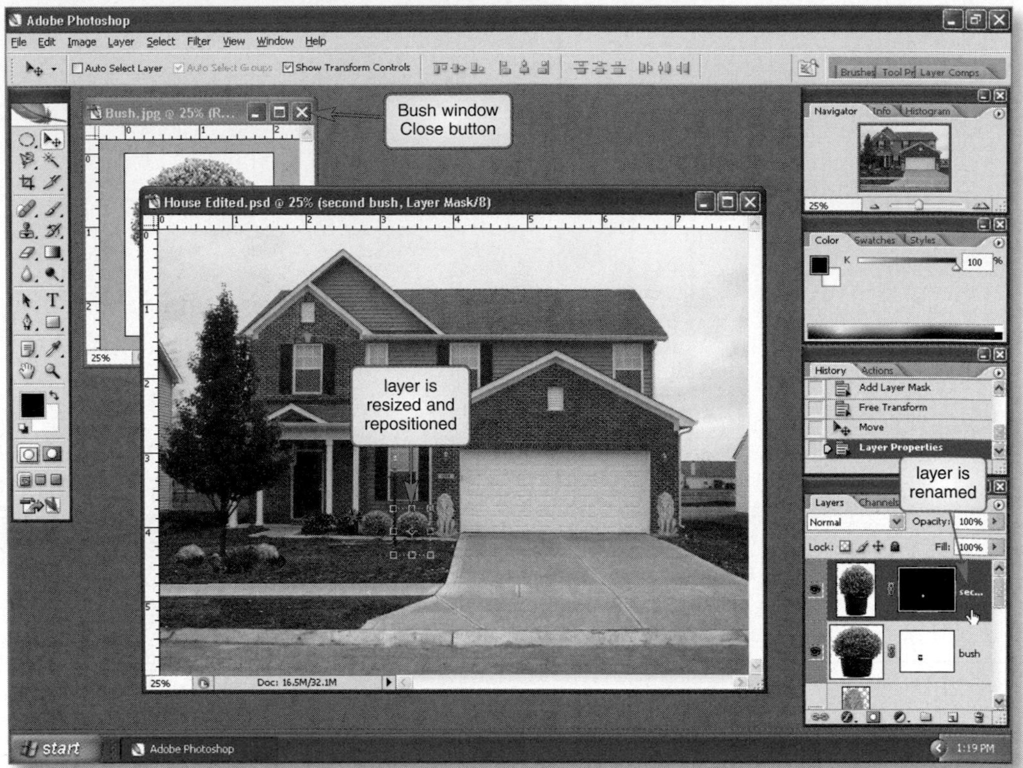

FIGURE 3-49

When you are finished using the Bush window, close it to save resources and memory on your system. The following step closes the window.

To Close the Bush Window

1 **Click the Close button in the Bush window. If Photoshop displays a dialog box asking if you want to save the changes, click the No button.**

The window closes and the House Edited window becomes active.

Fine-Tuning Layers

Sometimes layers need special adjustments in order to fit into their new surroundings in the document window. This fine-tuning usually involves **tonal adjustments** that affect the tonal range of color, lighting, opacity, level, or fill; **style adjustments** such as special effects or blends; or **filter adjustments** that let you apply predetermined pictures, tiles, or patterns.

You can make tonal, style, and filter changes to the pixels of the layer itself, or you can create an adjustment layer or fill layer that is applied over the top without changing the original layer. With the right adjustment, a layer seems to meld into the image and maintains a consistency of appearance for the overall composite image.

Making an Opacity Change to a Layer

In the Layers palette, the **Opacity box** allows you to change the opacity or transparency of a layer. Setting an opacity percentage specifies the level at which you can see through the layer to reveal the image or layer beneath it. You can control exactly how solid the objects on a specific layer appear. For example, if you wanted to display an American flag in an image, superimposed over the top of a memorial or monument, you might change the flag layer's opacity to 50 percent. The monument would be easily visible through the flag.

The next steps show how to lighten the color in the sky layer by lowering the opacity.

To Make an Opacity Change to a Layer

1

- **In the Layers palette, scroll down and then click the sky layer.**
- **Click the Opacity box arrow.**

Photoshop displays a slider to adjust the opacity (Figure 3-50).

FIGURE 3-50

2

• **Drag the Opacity slider to the left until the Opacity box displays 85%.**

The color of the sky lightens (Figure 3-51).

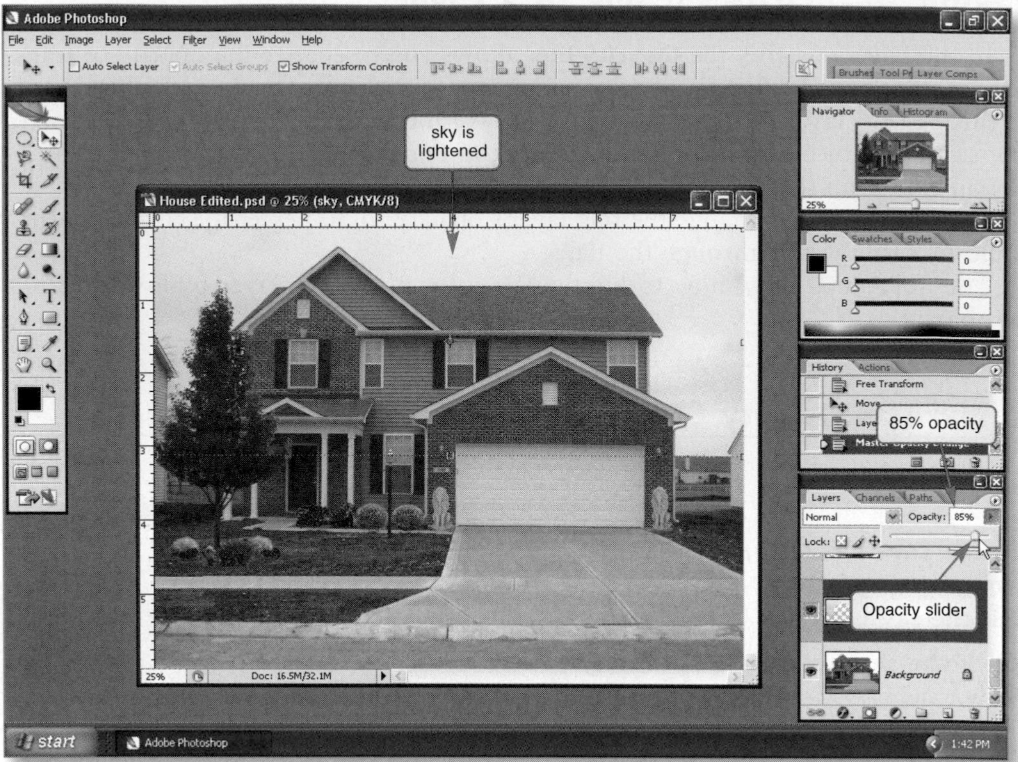

FIGURE 3-51

Beneath the Opacity box is the **Fill box** (Figure 3-52). Changing the fill of a layer is similar to changing its opacity, but editing the Fill percentage changes only the pixels in the layer rather than any layer styles or blending modes. When you click either the Opacity box arrow or the Fill box arrow, a slider displays to adjust the percentage. You also can type a percentage in either box.

Making Level Adjustments

A **level adjustment** is one way to make tonal changes to the shadows and highlights in a layer or to the entire image. In the Levels dialog box, Photoshop displays black, gray, and white sliders to adjust any or all of the three tonal ranges. Experimenting with the gray slider changes the intensity values of the middle range of gray tones without dramatically altering the highlights and shadows.

In the bush layer of the image, you will adjust the gray tones slightly to make the layer match the picture. The following steps illustrate how to make level adjustments in a layer.

To Make a Level Adjustment

1

- **In the Layers palette, scroll up and then click the bush layer thumbnail, not the layer mask.**
- **Increase the magnification to 50 percent and scroll to display the bush in the center of the document window.**
- **Click Image on the menu bar and then point to Adjustments.**

The Adjustments submenu displays many possible adjustments (Figure 3-52).

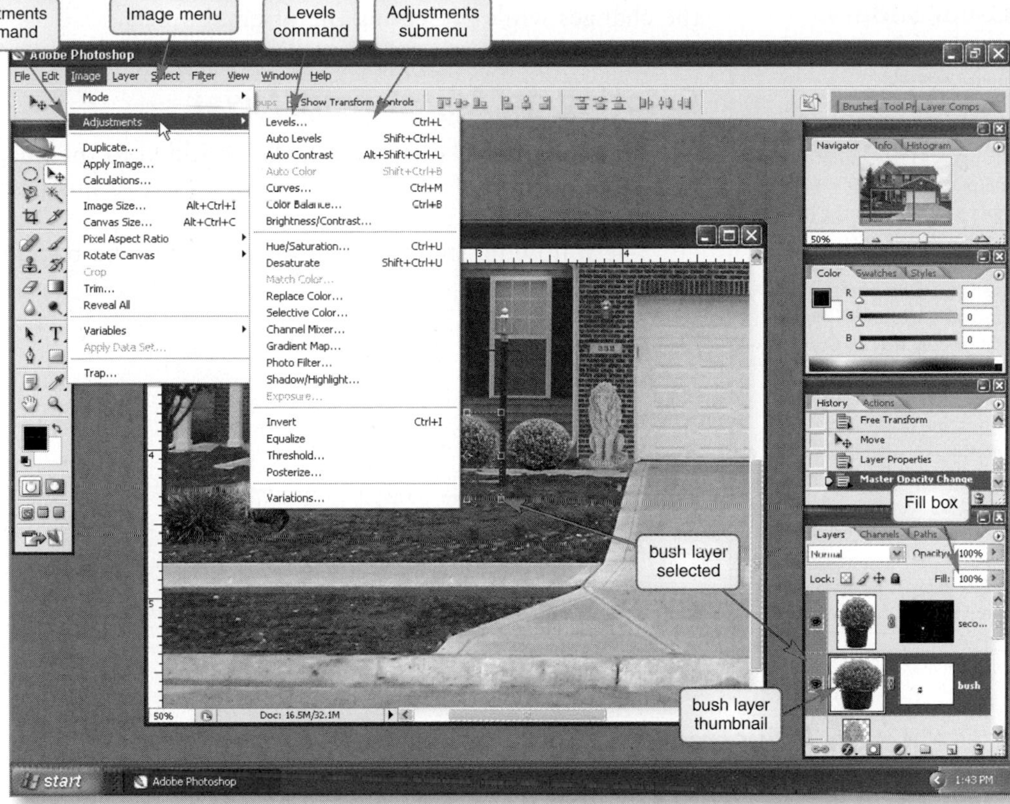

FIGURE 3-52

2

- **Click Levels.**
- **When the Levels dialog box is displayed, in the Input area, drag the gray slider to the right until the middle Input levels box displays .75.**

The gray slider adjusts the midtone colors (Figure 3-53).

3

- **Click the OK button.**
- **Repeat the process for the second bush layer.**

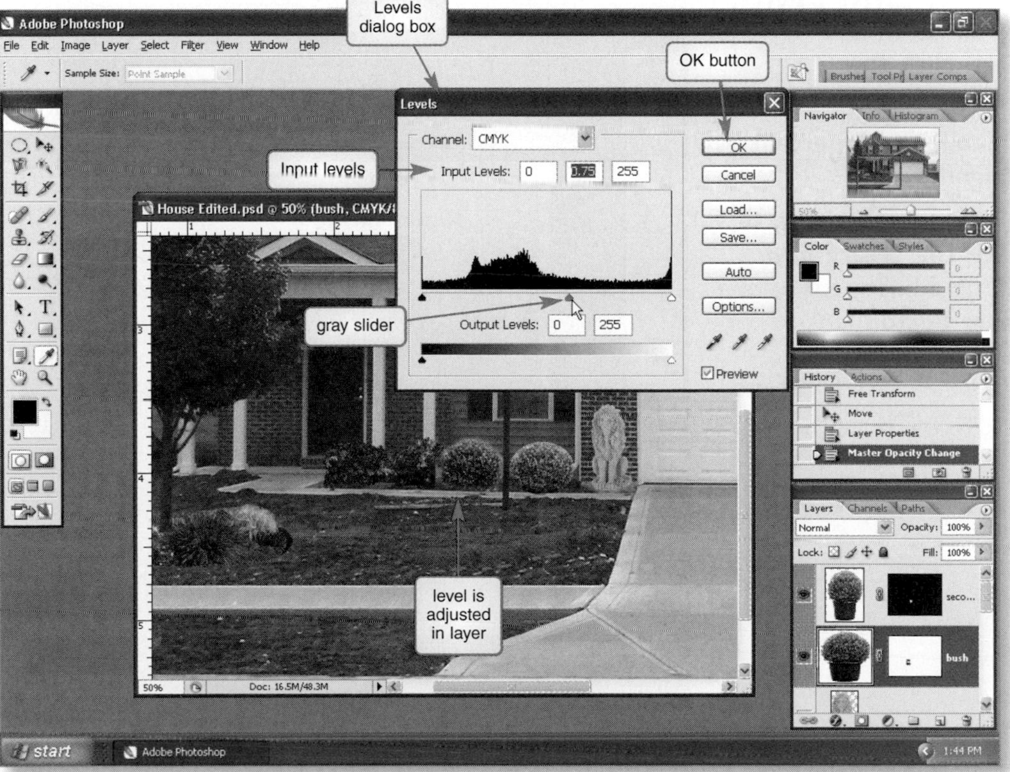

FIGURE 3-53

Other Ways

1. Press CTRL+L

More About

Level Sliders

In the Levels dialog box, the Input Level sliders on each end map the black point (on the left) and white point (on the right) to the settings of the Output sliders. The middle Input slider adjusts the gamma in the image. It moves the midtone and changes the intensity values of the middle range of gray tones without dramatically altering the highlights and shadows. If you move one of the Input Level sliders, the black point, midtone, or white point changes in the Output sliders and all the remaining levels are redistributed. This redistribution increases the tonal range of the image, in effect increasing the overall contrast of the image.

The opacity and level changes in the previous steps were made to the actual pixels in the layer. In the next section, you will learn how to create an extra layer to maintain the changes while preserving the original pixels.

Creating an Adjustment Layer

An **adjustment layer** is a new layer added to the image to affect a tonal change to a large portion of the image. You can create adjustment layers for the entire composite image or just the background.

The following steps show how to lighten the background by creating an adjustment layer.

To Create an Adjustment Layer

1

- **In the Layers palette, scroll down and then click the Background layer.**
- **Zoom to 25 percent magnification.**
- **In the Layers palette, click the Create new fill or adjustment layer button.**

The button menu is displayed (Figure 3-54).

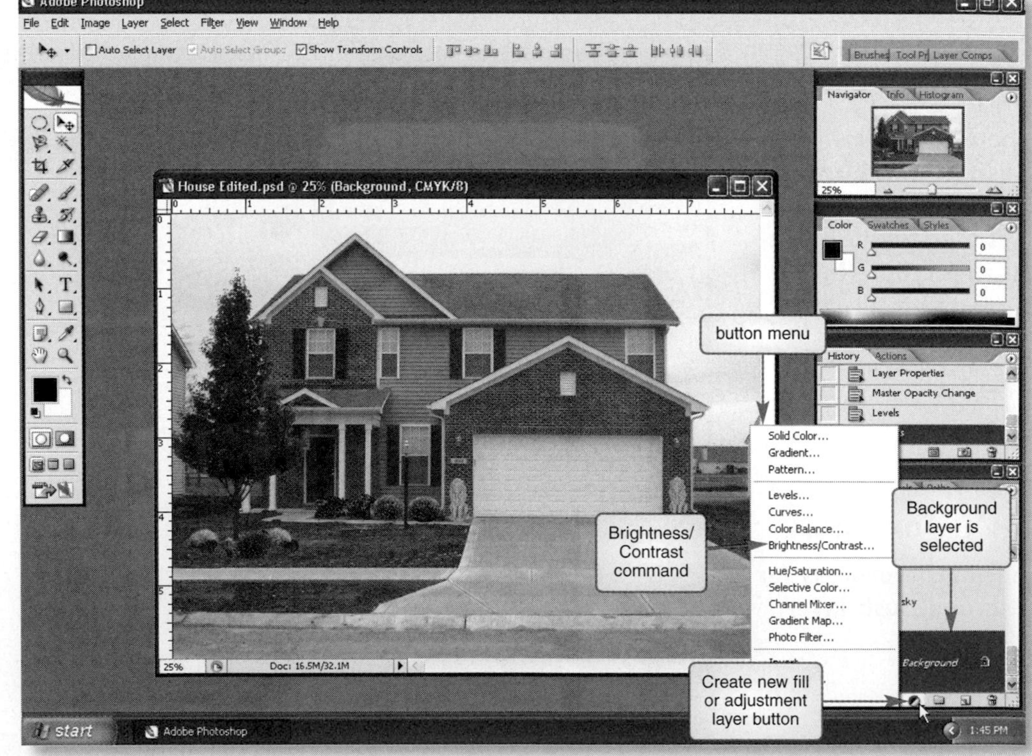

FIGURE 3-54

2

- **Click the Brightness/ Contrast command.**
- **When the Brightness/Contrast dialog box is displayed, drag the Brightness slider to +15 and the Contrast slider to +10.**

The increase in brightness and contrast will create the illusion of a sunnier day in the image (Figure 3-55).

FIGURE 3-55

3

- **Click the OK button.**

The Layers palette displays the new layer (Figure 3-56).

FIGURE 3-56

Other Ways

1. On Layer menu, point to New Adjustment Layer, click Brightness/Contrast, name layer

Adjustment layers have several advantages. They are nondestructive which means you can try different settings and re-edit the adjustment layer at any time. Adjustment layers reduce the amount of damage you do to an image by making direct edits. Adjustment layers also can be copied to other images, which saves time and maintains consistency.

Adding a Layer Style

Similar to a layer adjustment, **a layer style** is applied to a layer rather than changing the layer's actual pixels. Layer styles, or layer effects, include shadows, glows, bevels, overlays, and strokes, among others. A layer can display multiple styles or effects. Table 3-3 describes some of the Layer Style options. The options apply to many different effects.

Table 3-3 Layer Style Options

OPTION	DESCRIPTION
Angle	sets a degree value for the lighting angle at which the effect is applied
Anti-alias	blends the edge pixels of a contour or gloss contour
Blend Mode	determines how a layer style blends with its underlying layers
Color	assigns the color of a shadow, glow, or highlight
Contour	allows you to create rings of transparency such as gradients, fades, beveling and embossing, and sculpting
Distance	specifies the offset distance for a shadow or satin effect
Depth	sets the depth of a bevel or pattern
Global Angle	turns on global lighting for the effect
Gloss Contour	creates a glossy, metallic appearance on a bevel or emboss
Gradient	indicates the gradient of a layer effect
Highlight or Shadow Mode	specifies the blending mode of a bevel or emboss highlight or shadow
Jitter	varies the color and opacity of a gradient
Layer Knocks Out Drop Shadow	controls the drop shadow's visibility in a semitransparent layer
Noise	assigns the number of random elements in the opacity of a glow or shadow
Opacity	sets the opacity or transparency
Pattern	specifies the pattern
Range	controls which portion or range of the glow is targeted for the contour
Size	specifies the amount of blur or the size of the shadow
Soften	blurs the results of shading to reduce unwanted artifacts
Source	specifies the source for an inner glow
Style	specifies the style of a bevel or emboss

When a layer has a style, an *f* icon appears to the right of the layer's name in the Layers palette. You can expand the style in the Layers palette to view all of the applied effects and edit them to change the style.

The following steps show how the Add a layer style button is used to apply a shadow to the lion statue.

To Add a Layer Style

1

- **In the Layers palette, scroll up and then click the lion layer. Adjust the magnification to 100 percent and then scroll to center the lion in the document window.**
- **Click the Add a layer style button.**

The button menu is displayed (Figure 3-57).

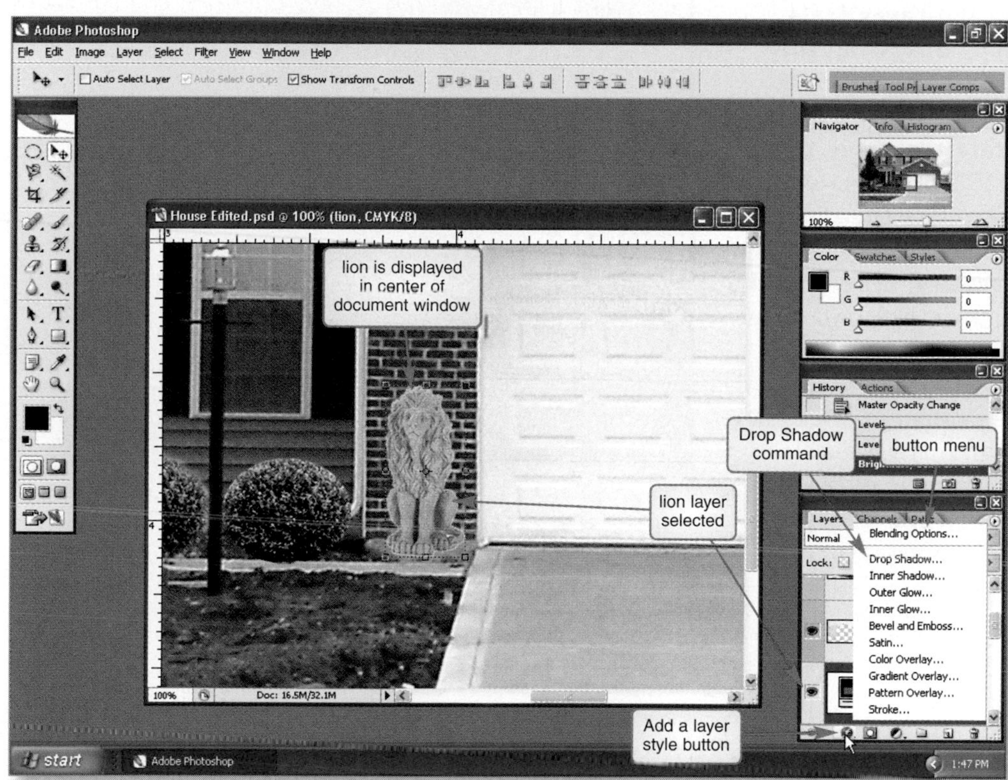

FIGURE 3-57

2

- **Click Drop Shadow.**
- **When Photoshop displays the Layer Style dialog box, drag the dialog box title bar up and to the right so the lion is visible.**
- **In the Layer Style dialog box, drag the Opacity slider to 50. Drag the radius line to rotate the Angle radius to 135 degrees, which will adjust the direction of the shadow. If necessary, type** 5 **in the Distance box and type** 5 **in the Size box.**

The Drop Shadow dialog box displays many different settings to change how, where, and from what distance the shadow is created (Figure 3-58). A shadow now displays to the right of the lion statue.

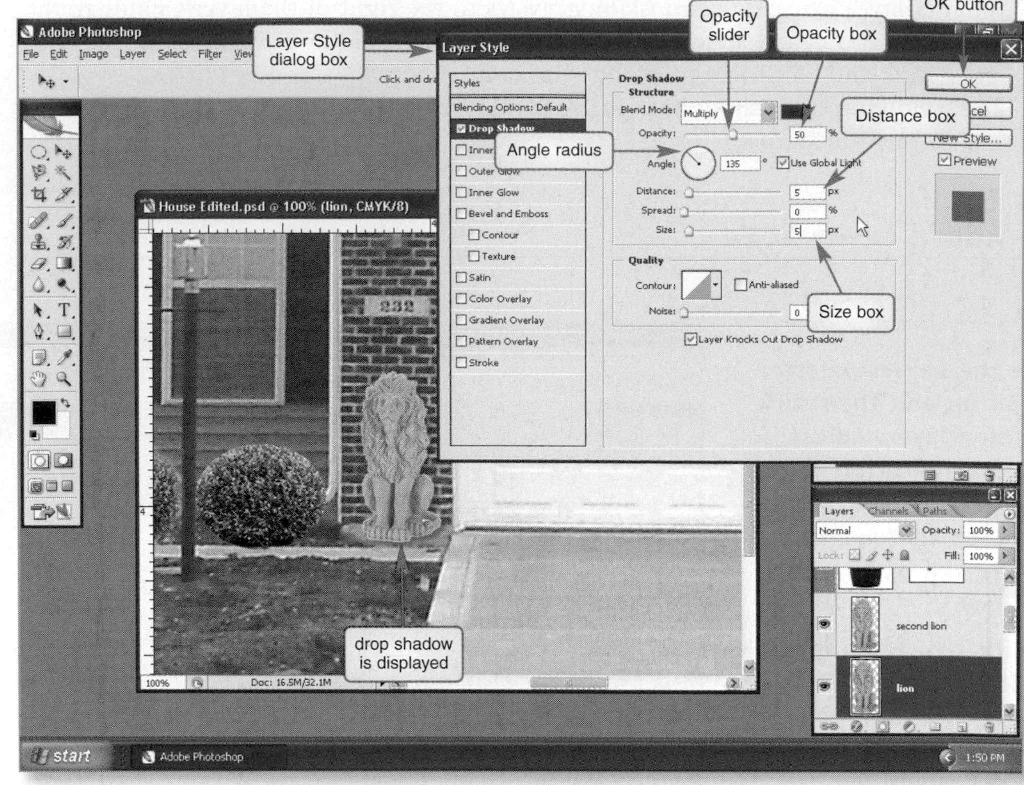

FIGURE 3-58

3

- **Click the OK button.**
- **In the Layers palette, click the Reveals layer effects in the palette button.**

Photoshop displays the added effects in the Layers palette (Figure 3-59).

4

- **Click the button again to hide the layer effects.**

Other Ways

1. On Layer menu, point to Layer Style, click Drop Shadow

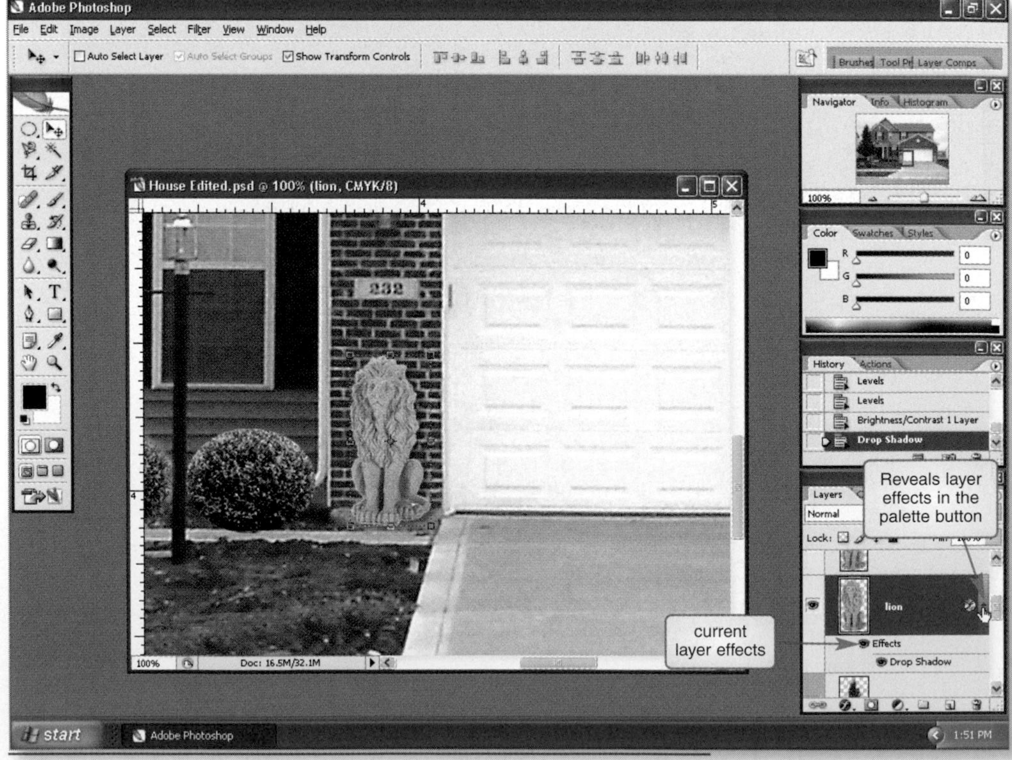

FIGURE 3-59

As you can tell from Figure 3-58, there are a large number of layer styles and settings in Photoshop. As you use them, many of these settings will be explained in future projects.

The next steps illustrate how to copy the layer style to the second lion.

To Copy a Layer Style

1 **In the Layers palette, right-click the lion layer. Do not right-click the thumbnail. When the shortcut menu is displayed, click Copy Layer Style.**

2 **Right-click the second lion layer. When the shortcut menu is displayed, click Paste Layer Style. Decrease the magnification if necessary.**

Both lions now display a small shadow, as if the sun is shining from the top, left of the picture (Figure 3-60).

FIGURE 3-60

Other Ways

1. On Layer menu, click Duplicate Layer

Adding a Render Filter

Photoshop uses many different filters, blends, styles, and color changes to produce special effects. One special effect that will be useful in the House Edited image is that of clouds. Clouds is a **render filter** that purposefully distorts the colors in a layer or mask to simulate clouds in the sky. Among the more than 100 filters that come installed with Photoshop, the render filters help you create cloud patterns, fiber patterns, refraction patterns, and simulated light reflections. Other examples of filters include artistic filters, blurs, textures, and sketches, among others.

On the next page, Table 3-4 displays the render filters included in an initial installation of Photoshop.

Table 3-4 Render Filters

RENDER FILTER	DESCRIPTION
Clouds	Filter produces a cloud pattern using the current foreground and the background colors. To generate a bolder cloud pattern, hold down the ALT key while creating the filter.
Difference Clouds	Filter produces a softer, hazier cloud pattern using the current foreground and the background colors. Applying the filter several times creates marble-like rib and vein patterns.
Fibers	Filter produces a woven fiber pattern using the foreground and background colors. Variance and Strength settings control the color, length, and weave of the fibers.
Lens Flare	Filter produces a glare that simulates refraction caused by shining a bright light into a camera lens.
Lighting Effects	Filter produces a lighting effect based on choices made in style, type, property, and channel. It cannot be used with a mask.

The followings steps show how a render filter is applied to a layer mask on the sky layer, creating more clouds.

To Create a Render Filter

1

- **In the Navigator palette, click the Zoom Out button until the magnification is 25 percent.**
- **In the Layers palette, scroll down and then click the sky layer.**
- **Click the Add layer mask button at the bottom of the Layers palette.**

The mask is selected in the sky layer (Figure 3-61).

FIGURE 3-61

2

- **Press and hold the ALT key. Click and hold Filter on the menu bar. Drag to Render and then drag to Clouds. Do not release the mouse button.**

Photoshop displays the Render submenu (Figure 3-62).

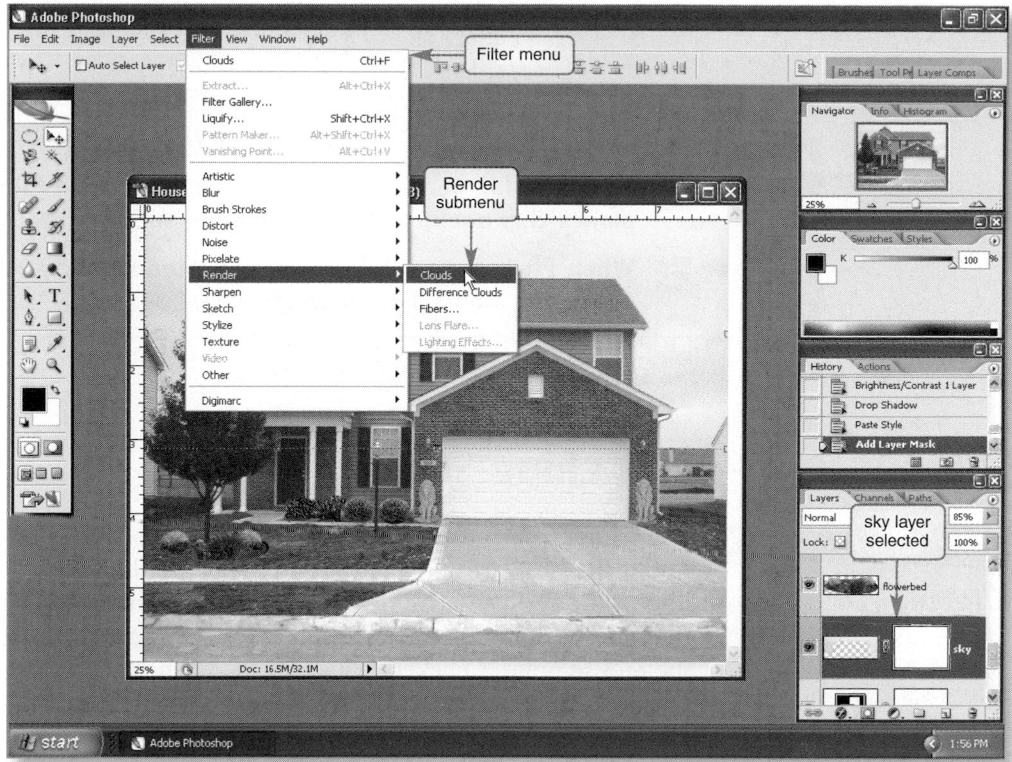

FIGURE 3-62

3

- **Release the mouse button.**

Holding the ALT key creates a bolder cloud pattern (Figure 3-63). Because the cloud pattern randomizes colors, your pattern will differ.

FIGURE 3-63

To finish the composite image of the house and landscaping you will add sod to the yard. The following steps open the Sod file.

To Open the Sod File

1. **Open the file named, Sod, from the Project 03 folder on the CD that accompanies this book, or from a location specified by your instructor.**
2. **When Photoshop displays the Sod window, drag its title bar to a location above the House Edited window.**

Photoshop displays the Sod window as shown in Figure 3-64.

The Clone Stamp Tool

More About

Cloning

The source of the clone will display a small crosshair as you move the mouse pointer. In the destination location, the mouse pointer is a brush circle or tip.

The **Clone Stamp tool** is used to reproduce portions of an image changing the pixels, rather than by creating a layer. After clicking the Clone Stamp Tool (S) button in the Photoshop toolbox, you press and hold ALT while clicking in the portion of the picture that you wish to copy. Photoshop takes a **sample** of the image, remembering where the mouse pointer clicked. You then move the mouse pointer to the position where you wish to create the copy. As you drag with the brush, like you did with the layer mask, the image is applied. Each stroke of the tool paints on more of the sample. The Clone Stamp tool is useful for duplicating an object or removing a defect in an image.

The Clone Stamp options bar (Figure 3-64) displays some of the same settings as you used with layer masks, along with an Aligned check box and Sample All Layers check box. When Aligned is selected, the sample point is not reset if you start dragging in a new location; in other words, the sampling moves to a relative point in the original image. When Aligned is not selected, the sample point begins again as you start a new clone. The default value is to sample only the current layer or background. When Sample All Layers is selected, the clone displays all layers. One restriction when using the Clone Stamp tool from one image to another is that both images have to be in the same color mode such as RGB.

Creating a Clone

In the House Edited image, there is no grass. Using the Clone Stamp tool, you will sample the sod image and then clone it all around the yard in the House Edited image, as shown in the following steps. As you clone the sod, adjust the magnification of the image to view clearly the corners and small areas. If you make a mistake while cloning, click the previous state in the History palette and begin dragging again.

To Create a Clone

1

- **With the Sod window active, right-click the Clone Stamp Tool (S) button in the Photoshop toolbox.**

Photoshop displays the context menu (Figure 3-64).

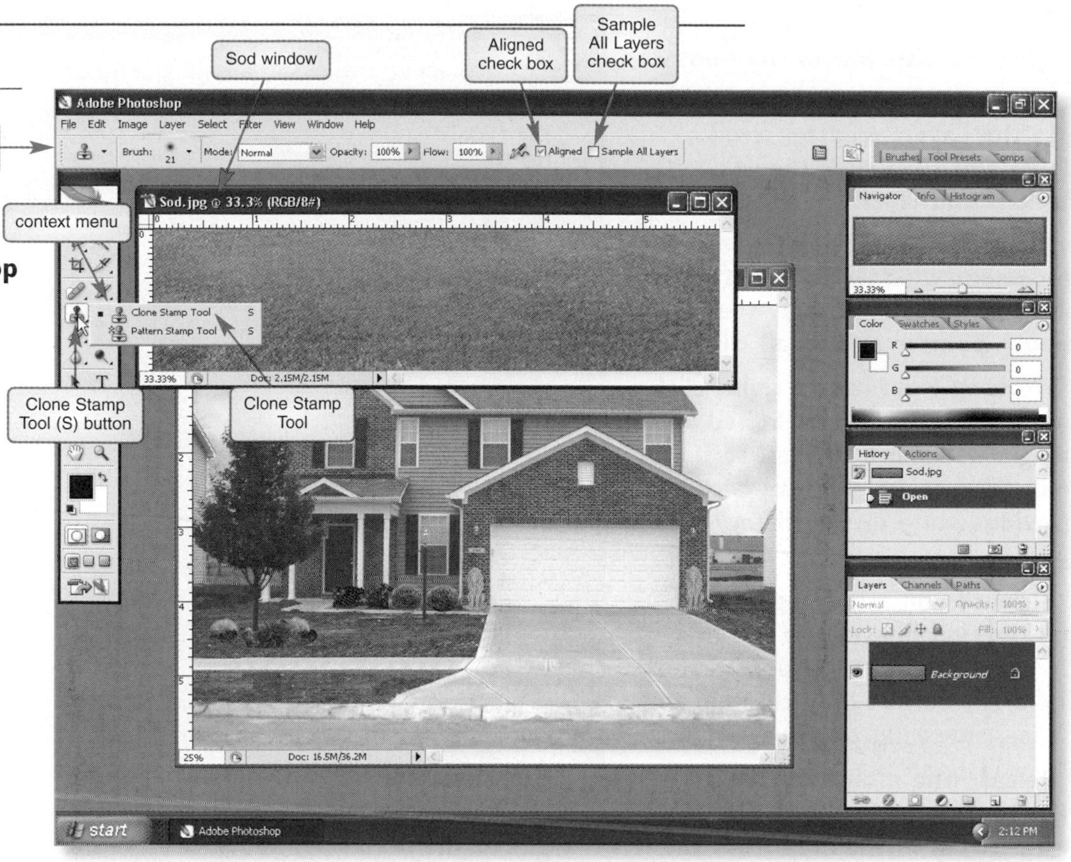

FIGURE 3-64

2

- **Click Clone Stamp Tool.**
- **On the options bar, click the Aligned check box to deselect it.**
- **Move the mouse pointer to the Sod window and ALT+click in the upper-left corner of the sod.**

As you ALT+click, the Clone Stamp tool displays a crosshair mouse pointer (Figure 3-65).

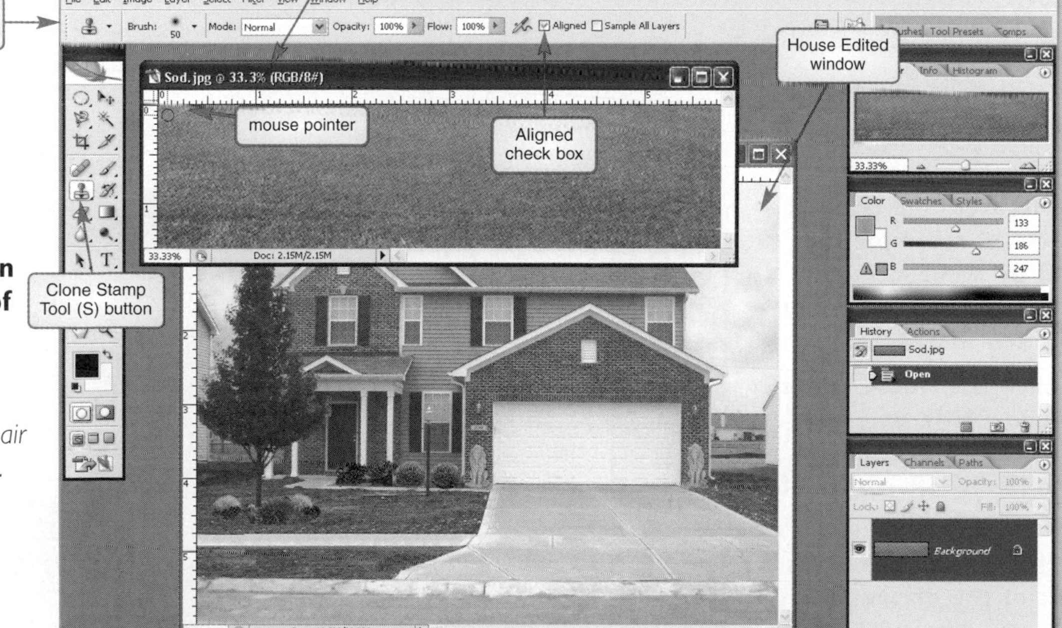

FIGURE 3-65

3

- **Click the title bar of the House Edited window to make it active.**
- **In the Layers palette, scroll down and then click the Background layer.**
- **Move the mouse pointer into the document window and then press the] or [key to display the mouse pointer as a small circle.**
- **Working from left to right, click and drag in the House Edited image. Use short strokes, so if you make a mistake, you can click a previous state in the History palette.**
- **Because you are dragging the background image, you can drag through any of the layers, such as the tree. Do not drag through the house, sidewalk, or driveway.**
- **Release the mouse button as necessary and then click and drag again to fill in the area from the left margin to the driveway, above the flowerbed. Change the magnification as necessary to fill in small areas.**

FIGURE 3-66

Photoshop displays grass (Figure 3-66).

4

- **Click the Sod window title bar, again.**
- **To create a more variegated and realistic pattern, resample the sod by ALT+clicking in the lower-left corner of the sod image.**
- **Click the House Edited window title bar, and then begin dragging in the lower-left corner of the image.**
- **Fill in all of the areas left of the driveway.**

The grass on the left side of the driveway is complete (Figure 3-67).

FIGURE 3-67

5

• Using the techniques in the previous steps, clone as necessary to fill in the grass on the right side of the driveway.

The grass is complete (Figure 3-68).

FIGURE 3-68

Other Ways

1. From another tool, press S key, ALT+click sample, drag clone
2. From Pattern Stamp tool, press SHIFT+S, ALT+click sample, drag clone

On the Clone Stamp Tool (S) context menu (Figure 3-64 on page PS 175), a second kind of stamp, the **Pattern Stamp Tool (S)**, allows you to paint with a pattern chosen from Photoshop's pattern library. A **pattern** is an image that is repeated, or tiled, when you use it to fill a layer or selection. On the Pattern Stamp options bar, a Pattern Picker box arrow displays patterns in a list. You can import additional patterns into the Pattern Picker box.

The next step is to close the Sod window.

To Close the Sod Window

1 **Click the Close button in the Sod window. If Photoshop asks if you want to save changes to the document, click the No button.**

The window closes and the House Edited window becomes active.

Flattening a Composite Image

Flattening composite images reduces the file size by merging all visible layers into the background, discarding hidden layers and applying masks. A flattened file is easier to print, export, and display on the Web. It is a good practice, however, to save the layered version in PSD format in case you want to make further changes to the file. It is very important to remember that once a file is flattened and saved, no changes can be made to individual layers.

First you will save the file in PSD format with the name, House Composite. Then you will flatten the composite image. Finally, you will save the file in TIF format with the name, House Complete.

To Save the Composite Image

1. **With your USB flash drive connected to one of the computer's USB ports, click File on the menu bar and then click Save As.**
2. **When the Save As dialog box is displayed, type** `House Composite` **in the File name text box. Do not press the ENTER key after typing the file name.**
3. **If necessary, click the Format box arrow and then choose Photoshop (*.PSD, *.PDD) in the list.**
4. **If necessary, click the Save in box arrow and then click USBDISK [G:], or the location associated with your USB flash drive, in the list.**
5. **Click the Save button in the Save As dialog box. If Photoshop displays an options dialog box, click the OK button.**

Photoshop saves the file on the USB flash drive with the file name House Composite, in the PSD format, and displays the new name on the document window title bar.

To Flatten a Composite Image

1

• **Click Layer on the menu bar.**

Photoshop displays the Layer menu (Figure 3-69).

FIGURE 3-69

2

• **Click Flatten Image on the Layer menu.**

After a few moments, the image is flattened and a single Background layer displays in the Layers palette (Figure 3-70).

FIGURE 3-70

If you flatten an image and then change your mind, if the file is still open, you can click the previous state in the History palette to restore all of the layers.

If you want to save each layer as a separate file, click File on the menu bar, point to Scripts, and then click Export Layers To Files. This script is useful if you think you may want to use your layers from this document in other composite images.

Saving a File in the TIF Format

TIF or TIFF is a flexible raster image format. A raster image is a digital image represented by a matrix of pixels. TIFF stands for Tagged Image File Format and is a common file format for images acquired from scanners and screen capture programs. Because TIFF files are supported by virtually all paint, image-editing, and page-layout applications, it is a versatile format for cross platform applications.

The steps on the next page save the flattened image as a TIF file.

To Save a File in the TIF Format

1

- **With your USB flash drive connected to one of the computer's USB ports, click File on the menu bar and then click Save As.**
- **When the Save As dialog box is displayed, type** `House Complete` **in the File name text box. Do not press the ENTER key after typing the file name.**
- **Click the Format box arrow and then click TIFF (*.TIF, *TIFF) in the list.**
- **Click the Save in box arrow and then click USBDISK [G:], or the location associated with your USB flash drive, in the list.**

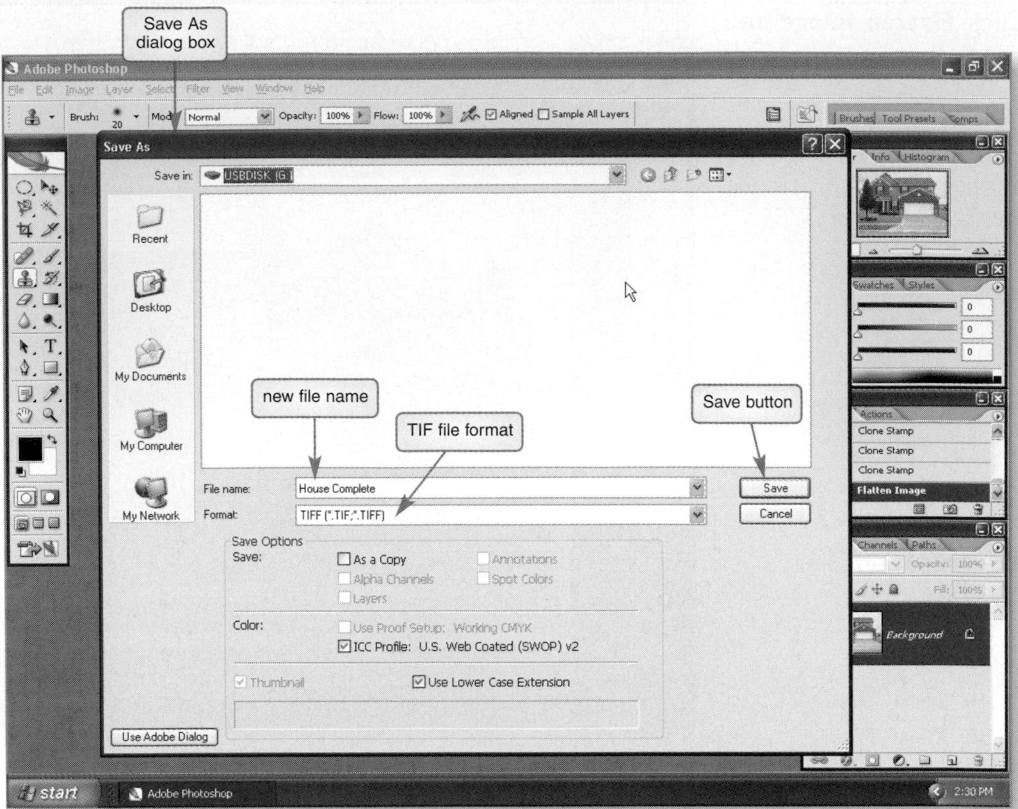

FIGURE 3-71

The Save As dialog box displays the file name, format, and location settings (Figure 3-71).

2

- **Click the Save button in the Save As dialog box.**
- **When Photoshop displays the TIFF Options dialog box, click the OK button.**

The following steps illustrate how to print a copy of the House Complete image.

To Print the House Complete Image

1 **Ready the printer according to the printer instructions.**

2 **Click File on the menu bar and then click Print One Copy on the File menu.**

The image prints on the default printer.

Closing a Photo

The project is complete. The final steps close the document window and quit Photoshop.

To Close the Document Window and Quit Photoshop

1. **With the House Complete window selected, click the Close button in the document window.**
2. **If Photoshop displays a dialog box, click the No button to ignore the changes since the last time you saved the photo.**
3. **Click the Close button on the right side of the Photoshop title bar.**

The Photoshop window closes.

More About

The TIF Options Dialog Box

The TIF Options dialog box displays commands to compress the image. Some compressions techniques are not supported by older versions of applications that handle TIF files. Pixel Order writes the TIF file with the channels data interleaved or organized by plane. Byte Order selects the platform on which the file can be read. Save Image Pyramid preserves multi-resolution information. Save Transparency preserves transparency as an additional alpha channel when the file is opened in another application. Transparency is always preserved when the file is reopened in Photoshop. Layer Compression specifies a method for compressing data for pixels in layers.

Project Summary

In editing the landscape of the house image, you gained a broad knowledge of Photoshop's layering capabilities. First, you were introduced to the PSD format and the concept of layers. You created a layer via cut, a layer from another image, and a layer from a selection, using the Layers palette to set options, select, rename, color, view, and hide layers. Then you used the eraser tools to erase portions of the layer that were not needed in the final composite image.

You learned how to hide portions of layers with layer masks and selection masks. You fine tuned layers with layer adjustments, styles, and render filters. Finally, you used the Clone Stamp tool to recreate grass in the composite image. The file was flattened and saved in the TIF format.

What You Should Know

Having completed this project, you should be able to perform the tasks below. The tasks are listed in the same order they were presented in this project. For a list of the buttons, menus, toolbars, and other commands introduced in this project, see the Quick Reference Summary at the back of this book and refer to the Page Number column.

26. Close the Lion Window (PS 154)
27. Create the Bush Layer (PS 155)
28. Create a Layer Mask (PS 156)
29. Resize and Move the Bush Layer (PS 159)
30. Create a Selection Mask (PS 160)
31. Resize, Reposition, and Name the Layer (PS 161)
32. Close the Bush Window (PS 162)
33. Make an Opacity Change to a Layer (PS 163)
34. Make a Level Adjustment (PS 165)
35. Create an Adjustment Layer (PS 166)
36. Add a Layer Style (PS 169)
37. Copy a Layer Style (PS 171)
38. Create a Render Filter (PS 172)
39. Open the Sod File (PS 174)
40. Create a Clone (PS 175)
41. Close the Sod Window (PS 177)
42. Save the Composite Image (PS 178)
43. Flatten a Composite Image (PS 178)
44. Save a File in the TIF Format (PS 180)
45. Print the House Complete Image (PS 180)
46. Close the Document Window and Quit Photoshop (PS 181)

Learn It Online

Instructions: To complete the Learn It Online exercises, start your browser, click the Address bar, and then enter the Web address `scsite.com/photoshop/learn`. When the Photoshop CS2 Learn It Online page is displayed, follow the instructions in the exercises below. Each exercise has instructions for printing your results, either for your own records or for submission to your instructor.

1 Project Reinforcement TF, MC, and SA

Below Photoshop Project 3, click the Project Reinforcement link. Print the quiz by clicking Print on the File menu for each page. Answer each question.

2 Flash Cards

Below Photoshop Project 3, click the Flash Cards link and read the instructions. Type 20 (or a number specified by your instructor) in the Number of playing cards text box, type your name in the Enter your Name text box, and then click the Flip Card button. When the flash card is displayed, read the question and then click the ANSWER box arrow to select an answer. Flip through Flash Cards. If your score is 15 (75%) correct or greater, click Print on the File menu to print your results. If your score is less than 15 (75%) correct, then redo this exercise by clicking the Replay button.

3 Practice Test

Below Photoshop Project 3, click the Practice Test link. Answer each question, enter your first and last name at the bottom of the page, and then click the Grade Test button. When the graded practice test is displayed on your screen, click Print on the File menu to print a hard copy. Continue to take practice tests until you score 80% or better.

4 Who Wants To Be a Computer Genius?

Below Photoshop Project 3, click the Computer Genius link. Read the instructions, enter your first and last name at the bottom of the page, and then click the PLAY button. When your score is displayed, click the PRINT RESULTS link to print a hard copy.

5 Wheel of Terms

Below Photoshop Project 3, click the Wheel of Terms link. Read the instructions, and then enter your first and last name and your school name. Click the PLAY button. When your score is displayed, right-click the score and then click Print on the shortcut menu to print a hard copy.

6 Crossword Puzzle Challenge

Below Photoshop Project 3, click the Crossword Puzzle Challenge link. Read the instructions, and then enter your first and last name. Click the SUBMIT button. Work the crossword puzzle. When you are finished, click the Submit button. When the crossword puzzle is redisplayed, click the Print Puzzle button to print a hard copy.

7 Tips and Tricks

Below Photoshop Project 3, click the Tips and Tricks link. Click a topic that pertains to Project 3. Right-click the information and then click Print on the shortcut menu. Construct a brief example of what the information relates to in Photoshop to confirm you understand how to use the tip or trick.

8 Expanding Your Horizons

Below Photoshop Project 3, click the Expanding Your Horizons link. Click a topic that pertains to Project 3. Print the information. Construct a brief example of what the information relates to in Photoshop to confirm you understand the contents of the article.

9 Search Sleuth

Below Photoshop Project 3, click the Search Sleuth link. To search for a term that pertains to this project, select a term below the Project 3 title and then use the Google search engine at google.com (or any major search engine) to display and print two Web pages that present information on the term.

10 Photoshop Online Training

Below Photoshop Project 3, click the Photoshop Online Training link. When your browser displays the Web page, click one of the Photoshop tutorials that covers one or more of the objectives listed at the beginning of the project on page PS 122. Print the first page of the tutorial before stepping through it.

Apply Your Knowledge

1 Creating Layers

Instructions: Start Photoshop, and set the workspace and tools to default settings. Open the Beach file from the Project03 folder, located either on the CD that accompanies this book or in a location specified by your instructor. The purpose of this exercise is to create a composite photo by creating layers, and to create both a PSD and TIF version of the final photo. The edited photo is displayed in Figure 3-72.

FIGURE 3-72

1. Use the Save As command to save the image on your USB flash drive as a PSD file, with the file name, Beach Composite.
2. Remove the visitors from the beach:
   a. Press the S key to select the Clone Stamp tool. On the options bar, click Aligned so it does not display a check. ALT+click the sand to the right of the people on the beach. Drag over the people to erase them from the beach.
3. Insert the gull and create a duplicate:
   a. Press CTRL+O and open the gull image from the Project03 folder.
   b. When Photoshop displays the image, use the Magic Wand tool with a tolerance setting of 50 to select the sky around the bird. On the Select menu, click Inverse.
   c. Right-click the selection and then click Grow to increase the selection slightly.
   d. Press the V key to select the Move tool. Drag the gull into the beach scene.
   e. Click the Show Transforms Control check box to select it. SHIFT+drag the gull to resize it. Drag the gull to a position as shown in Figure 3-72.

Apply Your Knowledge

f. Rename the layer, gull, and use a Violet identification color.
g. Right-click the gull layer and then click Duplicate Layer. Name the duplicate layer, second gull. (*Hint*: The second gull will display directly over the top of the first gull.)
h. Press the V key to activate the Move tool and then drag the second gull to a position above the first. If necessary, press CTRL+T to display the bounding box. SHIFT+drag a corner sizing handle to make the second gull smaller, thereby giving the composite image a sense of perspective.
i. Close the Gull window.

4. Next, insert the large umbrella and add a layer mask:
   a. Press CTRL+O and open the large umbrella image from the Project03 folder.
   b. When Photoshop displays the image, press the V key to select the Move tool. Drag from the Large Umbrella window to the beach scene. Position the layer between the trees.
   c. In the Layers palette, click the Add a layer mask button. Press the E key to access the eraser tools and then, if necessary, press SHIFT+E to access the Eraser tool.
   d. Press the D key to select the default colors and then press the B key to activate the brush. Drag to erase any portions of the umbrella that eclipse the trees. (*Hint*: If you make a mistake and erase too much, press the X key to alternate to white and drag over the error.
   e. Rename the layer, umbrella, and use a Blue identification color.
   f. Close the Large Umbrella window.
5. Insert the beach ball and add a Drop Shadow:
   a. Press CTRL+O and open the Beach Ball file from the Project03 folder.
   b. When Photoshop displays the image, press the V key to select the Move tool. Drag from the Beach Ball window to the beach scene.
   c. Press the E key to select the eraser tools and then, if necessary, press SHIFT+E to toggle to the Magic Eraser tool. On the options bar, type `15` in the Tolerance box. Click the Contiguous check box so it displays a check. Click the white portions around the edges of the beach ball.
   d. Drag the beach ball to a position in the lower part of the scene.
   e. In the Layers palette, click the Add a layer style button and then click Drop Shadow. When the Layer Styles dialog box is displayed, type `70` in the Opacity box; drag the Angle radius to 97. Type `8` in the Distance box. Click the OK button.
   f. Rename the layer, ball, and use a Red identification color.
   g. Close the Beach Ball window.
6. Finally, insert the beach pail:
   a. Press CTRL+O and open the Beach Pail file from the Project03 folder.
   b. When Photoshop displays the image, drag a rectangular marquee around the beach pail staying as close to the edges of the pail as possible. Press the V key to select the Move tool. Drag the selection into the beach scene.
   c. Right-click the Magic Eraser Tool (E) button and then click the Eraser Tool. Erase any areas around the pail that should not display in the layer. Do not erase the shadow beneath the bucket.
   d. Rename the layer, pail, and use a Yellow identification color.
   e. Close the Beach Pail window.
7. Save the file again, by pressing CTRL+S. Flatten the image.
8. Press SHIFT+CTRL+S to open the Save As dialog box. Type `Beach Complete` in the Name box. Click the Format box arrow and then click TIF in the list. Click the Save button. If Photoshop displays a dialog box, click the OK button.
9. Turn in a hard copy of the photo to your instructor.
10. Quit Photoshop.

1 Making Level Adjustments Using Masks

Problem: A local tourist company has hired you to create its latest brochure about historic homes. You encounter a photo that is too dark to use in the brochure. You decide to try adjusting the levels to lighten the trees, grass, and bushes in the photo and prepare it for print in the brochure. The edited photo displays in Figure 3-73.

FIGURE 3-73

Instructions:

1. Start Photoshop. Set the default workspace and reset all tools.
2. Open the file, Historic Home, from the Project03 folder on the CD that accompanies this book, or from a location specified by your instructor.
3. Click the Save As command on the File menu. Type `Historic Home Edited` as the file name. Click the Format box arrow and click PSD in the list. Browse to your USB flash drive storage device. Click the Save button. If Photoshop displays a Format Options dialog box, click the OK button.
4. Use the Navigator palette to zoom the photo to 100% magnification, if necessary.
5. In the toolbox, right-click the current lasso tool. Click Lasso Tool (L) on the context menu. Drag with the Lasso tool to draw around the house.
6. Press the W key to activate the Magic Wand tool. On the options bar, click the Add to selection button and then, if necessary, click the Contiguous check box so it displays a check.
7. In the document window, click the Sky.
8. Click Select on the menu bar and then click Inverse to select the inverse of the house and sky which would be the trees, bushes, and grounds.
9. Click Layer on the menu bar, point to New, and then click Layer via Cut.
10. In the Layers palette, rename the layer, grounds.
11. With the layer selected, press CTRL+L to open the Levels dialog box. Drag the white slider to the left until the grounds are lighter and the features easily discerned.
12. In the toolbox, double-click the Set Foreground Color button. When the Color Picker dialog box is displayed, click a light blue color.
13. Press the W key to activate the Magic Wand tool. On the options bar, click the New selection button and then, if necessary, click the Contiguous check box so it displays a check. In the Layers palette, click the Background layer. In the document window, click the sky.
14. Click Filter on the menu bar, point to Render, and then click Clouds.
15. Press CTRL+S to save the photo again.
16. Press SHIFT+CTRL+S to access the Save As dialog box. Choose the TIF format and name the file, Historic Home Complete.
17. Print a copy and turn it in to your instructor.

In the Lab

2 Creating a Composite from Multiple Images

Problem: You are thinking about moving to a new apartment. After visiting the complex, the landlord gave you a floor plan of a corner unit with two bedrooms. You decide to use Photoshop to experiment with different placements of the furniture to create the best layout and maintain the most free space. In a file called Apartment, the floor plan is stored as the background, and sample furniture images as layers. The floor plan is displayed in Figure 3-74.

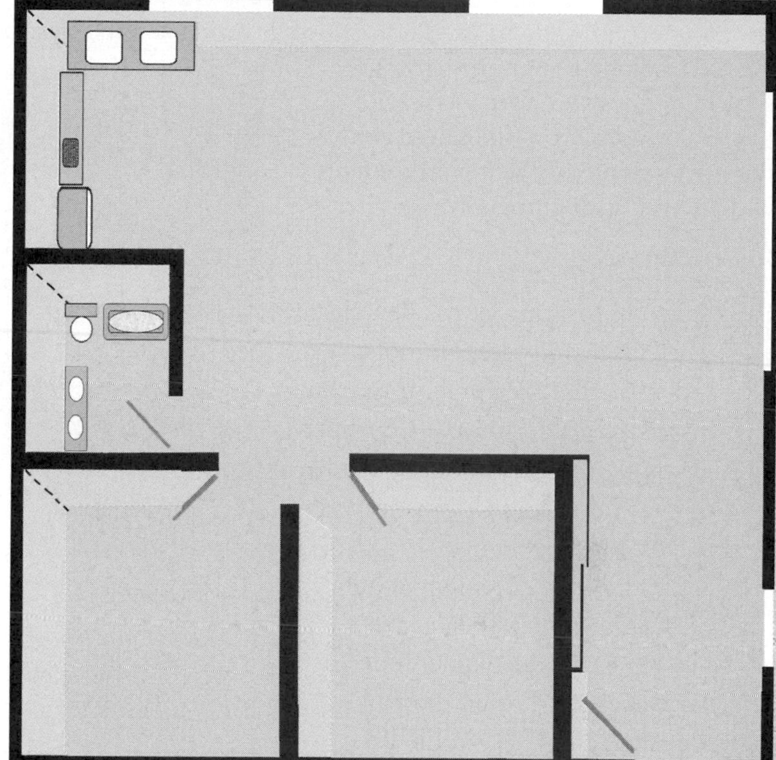

FIGURE 3-74

Instructions:

1. Start Photoshop. Set the default workspace and reset all tools.
2. Open the file, Apartment, from the Project03 folder on the CD that accompanies this book, or from a location specified by your instructor.
3. Click the Save As command on the File menu. Type `Apartment Edited` as the file name. If necessary, click the Format box arrow and then click PSD in the list. Browse to your USB flash drive storage device, if necessary. Click the Save button. If Photoshop displays a Format Options dialog box, click the OK button.
4. One at a time, click each layer in the palette. Look at the layer and rename it with a descriptive name such as chair or desk.
5. Choose a layer to place in the apartment. Click the layer's visibility icon. When Photoshop displays the layer in the document window, click the Move Tool (V) button in the toolbox and drag the layer to an appropriate place. If you need to resize the layer so it better fits the location, select the Show Transform Controls check box and then SHIFT+drag a corner sizing handle. If you need to flip the layer, click Edit on the menu bar, point to Transform, and then click Flip Horizontal.
6. Repeat Step 5 choosing each of the remaining layers.
7. Once you have placed all of the layers, duplicate at least three layers to create more furniture. Resize and flip as necessary.
8. When you are finished, save the changes and then use the Flatten Image command to flatten all of the layers into the background.
9. Save the flattened image as Apartment Complete.
10. For extra credit, take digital pictures of your own furniture. Open the pictures in Photoshop and use the Layer via Copy command to create new layers in the apartment image.

3 Using the Clone Tool and Creating a Layer with Outer Glow

Problem: The marketing agency that you work for has asked you to edit the latest advertisement for Qintara perfume. You decide to use Photoshop's layering capabilities to insert the image of the perfume bottle. You also decide to clone the Q of their logo multiple times to create a stylistic band of color across the advertisement. A sample of the advertisement is displayed in Figure 3-75.

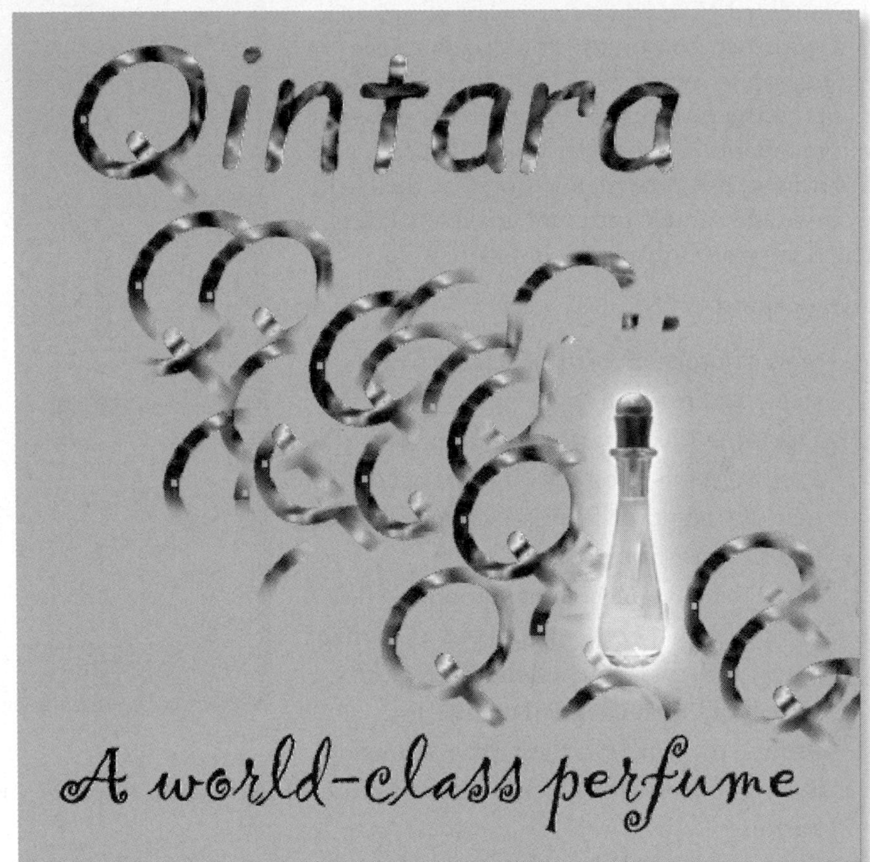

FIGURE 3-75

Instructions:

1. Start Photoshop. Set the default workspace and reset all tools.
2. Open the file, Perfume, from the Project03 folder on the CD that accompanies this book, or from a location specified by your instructor.
3. Click the Save As command on the File menu. Type `Perfume Edited` as the file name. If necessary, click the Format box arrow and then click PSD in the list. Browse to your USB flash drive storage device. Click the Save button. If Photoshop displays a Format Options dialog box, click the OK button.
4. Select the layer named slogan. Move the layer to the lower portion of the image.
5. Open the file, Bottle, from the Project03 folder on the CD that accompanies this book, or from a location specified by your instructor. Select all of the image and then, using the Move tool drag a copy to the Perfume Edited window.
6. In the perfume Edited window, name the new layer, bottle.
7. Use the Add layer mask button to create a layer mask in the bottle layer. Use the Brush tool with black to make the area around the bottle transparent.
8. Use the Add a layer style button in the Layers palette to create an Outer Glow layer style. When the Layer Style dialog box is displayed, type `25` in the Size box.
9. Click the background layer. Click the Clone Stamp tool in the toolbox. ALT-click the top of the letter Q in the logo. Move the mouse down and to the right. Drag to create a clone of the Q.
10. Repeat step 9, creating multiple, overlapped clones of the letter Q as shown in Figure 3-75. Use short strokes. If you make a mistake, click the previous state in the History palette and drag again.
11. When you are satisfied with your clones, flatten the image.
12. Save the file again and submit a copy to your instructor.

Cases and Places

The difficulty of these case studies varies:
■ are the least difficult and ■■ are the most difficult. The last exercise is a group exercise.

1 ■ You have been hired as an intern with a greeting card company. You were given several photos to use in preparing holiday cards. The photo named, Santa Scene, is located in the Project03 folder. You want to use the figure of Santa Claus only, on the front of a card. Save the photo in the PSD format on your USB flash drive storage device as Santa Layered. Create a rectangular marquee selection around the figure. Use the Layer via Cut command and name the new layer, Santa. Hide the background. Create a layer mask, painting with black to display only the figure. Print with the background hidden.

2 ■ Earlier in this project, a suggestion was made to create a flag with 50 percent opacity superimposed over a memorial. Locate a photo of a memorial in your city and a picture of your flag. Obtain permission to use a digital photo or scan the images. Open the photos. Select only the flag and then drag it as a new layer into the memorial photo. Resize the layer to fit across the memorial. Change the opacity to 50 percent. Make other corrections as necessary. Save the composite photo and print a copy.

3 ■■ You are planning a family reunion at a vacation spot and want to create a photo to advertise the event to your family. Use a scanner to scan photos of the vacation spot and photos of your family members. Using the scanner's software, save the photos in the highest possible resolution, using the most color settings. Bring the vacation photo into Photoshop and save it on your storage device. One at a time open each of the family member photos and drag the images into layers on top of the vacation spot photo. Use Layer masks to hide the background in the layers and adjust the levels so the family members fit into the picture. Flatten the photo and save it in the TIF format. Send the edited photo via e-mail to members of your family or to your instructor as directed.

4 ■■ You recently took a photo of a deer at the local forest preserve. To make the picture more interesting you decide to create a layer and clone the deer. Open the photo named, Deer, located in the Project03 folder. Click the Layer command on the menu bar, point to New and then click Layer. Click the background, choose the Clone tool, and take a sample of the middle of the deer. Click the new layer and clone the deer. On the Edit menu, click Free Transform and resize the deer so it appears to be further away. Save the file as Deer Edited on your storage device.

Cases and Places

5 ■■ **Working Together** Graphic layers in advertising and marketing are commonplace. Designers who know how to work effectively with layers are in demand. In preparation for an upcoming job fair, your instructor has asked you to research layers used in advertising. Ask each member of your team to bring in their favorite cereal box. As a group, examine the boxes. Choose 3 boxes that you believe have layered images and/or text. Create a list of each layer in order, from the top layer to the background. List notable characteristics of each layer including items from the Layer styles button menu in the Layers palette (Figure 3-57 on page PS 169) and the Adjustments submenu (Figure 3-52 on page PS 165).

ADOBE Photoshop CS2

An Introduction to the Fundamentals of Graphic Design

Objectives

You will have mastered the material in this special feature when you can:

- Define the term graphic design
- Identify the graphic designer's concerns and considerations
- Understand the planning and development stages of a design idea
- Differentiate between representational, symbolic, and abstract images
- Describe the different visual elements and techniques
- Understand the basics of primary, RGB, and CMYK color
- Use a grid to create a layout
- Explain the terms perspective, layout, and storyboard

Defining Graphic Design

Graphic design is a term generally used to describe the act of arranging words and images to convey a particular, intended message effectively to a specific audience. The graphic designer takes an idea and makes it into something tangible. Graphic design sometimes is referred to as design, graphic arts, visual communication, graphic communication, or visual problem solving. The term, graphic design, also is used to describe an area of study, which can lead to a seemingly infinite number of related professions, including the following:

- printing
- advertising
- interactive design
- publications, including newspapers, magazines, and books
- Web design
- computer information technology
- marketing collateral, which specifically means printed marketing material including brochures, newsletters, annual reports, etc.
- illustration
- animation
- software design
- packaging
- computer-aided design / computer-aided manufacturing (CAD/CAM)
- mechanical engineering technology

Photoshop and other computer software enables you to manipulate and reproduce graphic images for countless varied uses. The best designers have an innate ability at recognizing a well-designed graphic layout. But even if graphic design sensibility does not come naturally to you, you can develop basic skills for consistently producing competent, effective, and well thought out graphic design layouts. Practice, learning from mistakes, and careful analysis of work done by others are ways of increasing your graphic design ability. Knowing the fundamentals of graphic design, and developing a working knowledge of computers and software, is essential.

Graphic Designer's Considerations

Graphic designers deal with *the client, the design of an idea,* and the *process.* To produce competent, comprehensive results, graphic designers must consider three simple facts about graphic design described in Figure SF 1-1.

GRAPHIC DESIGNER'S CONCERNS

1. CLIENT/AUDIENCE/CONSUMER
You are usually making it for someone else.

2. DESIGN OF AN IDEA
Defined by its purpose, it must function as intended.

3. PROCESS
Technical & creative methods are combined to achieve results.

FIGURE SF 1-1

1. *You are usually creating a product for someone else.* It is important to identify and research your **client, audience,** and **topic.** The client is the person or company who hires you. The audience, also referred to as the target consumer, the user, or the end user, are the people who will be seeing and using your design. The topic is the subject matter of your graphic design. For example, if your topic is to design a catalog for a candle and candy company, you need to research the client, in this case the company itself, so you can satisfy the marketing needs of the company's owners. You also need to understand your audience, who in this example are people who will be receiving this catalog.

One of the best tools for preliminary research is listening. Listen to what your client tells you and take notes of their ideas. For example your client may own a sports uniform mail order catalog company. The client explains that the company was established in 1949 and has a reputation for being traditional and reliable. Yet they are concerned with keeping abreast of current trends in sports uniform fashion. They want you to design a new catalog which would appeal to a younger audience. Listening to your client you glean the importance of blending the new with the old by giving the catalog a contemporary look while simultaneously emphasizing the company's longstanding reputation.

Follow that up with market research. For example, if your topic is a shopping catalog, your research would include analyzing and comparing the visual effectiveness of several existing catalogs.

2. *The design is defined by its purpose, it must function as intended.* Once you know what you are creating and for whom, the next step is to come up with the best possible ideas. You must answer the following questions:

- What am I trying to do?
- What is the problem I am trying to solve?
- What is the intended outcome?

For example, you may be asked to design a public service poster for your community advertising "Free Testing". The problem you must solve is how to include the required information about where and when to go for this service while at the same time making a poster which is highly visible and graphically engaging. The goal is to grab the attention of your audience and present them with all the necessary information in readable form. The design should function as intended by making the message you need to convey clear to the audience. Most graphic design concepts and layouts evolve from having a clear vision of the desired outcome of the project.

3. *Technical and creative methods are combined to achieve results.* Graphic designers are the conduit between an idea or concept and the actual finished product. Creative consideration means producing a design based on research, intuition, and skillful application of basic design principles. Technical ability refers to an understanding of computers, printing, and Web processes, and knowing how to use design related software such as Photoshop. Graphic designers, and anyone in related fields, need to possess an understanding of both technical and creative aspects to create and produce a design.

Because design is a complex field with constantly changing technology, no single person can know everything. Success often is achieved by cooperation between people who share their expertise in a given area. Many designers will focus on the conceptualization of a project, then work with a technician who has advanced skills with software to fine-tune the final project. Many Web programmers rely on the expertise of designers to make their Web site competitively marketable.

Professionals involved in graphic design share a basic fundamental body of required knowledge, language, materials, concepts, and tools. No matter what the assignment is, all graphic designers use similar visual techniques and methods to ensure their designs are effective and persuasive.

Planning and Developing a Project

Planning and developing a project includes primarily two critical steps: organizing and documenting materials, and developing an idea.

Organizing and Documenting Materials

Graphic designers develop good organizational skills for documenting a project's development. It is the designer's responsibility to keep track of computer files, backup disks, and hard copy (paper printouts) related to a project.

Label actual folders, computer desktop folders, and disks with the name of the project; keep track of the dates, the software you used, the font (or type style), and types of images. It also is your responsibility to keep track of original versions of the work, art and text documents, and schedules.

Developing an Idea

Once you know what you are designing and for whom, your job is to take the idea and work out some real, visual examples. Usually you have two or three different concepts that you would like to explore with your client. Computer software programs like Photoshop give designers the opportunity to experiment, save, and view or print different versions of ideas.

The graphic designer's vocabulary, also called design **vernacular**, contains many words used to describe the developmental stage of an idea. Although these terms often are used interchangeably, they have specific meaning.

Graphic designers develop individual methods for conceiving and documenting ideas, and coming up with strong concepts. Most designers use their research to brainstorm on paper by drawing a mind map. Mind maps are used to document multiple random

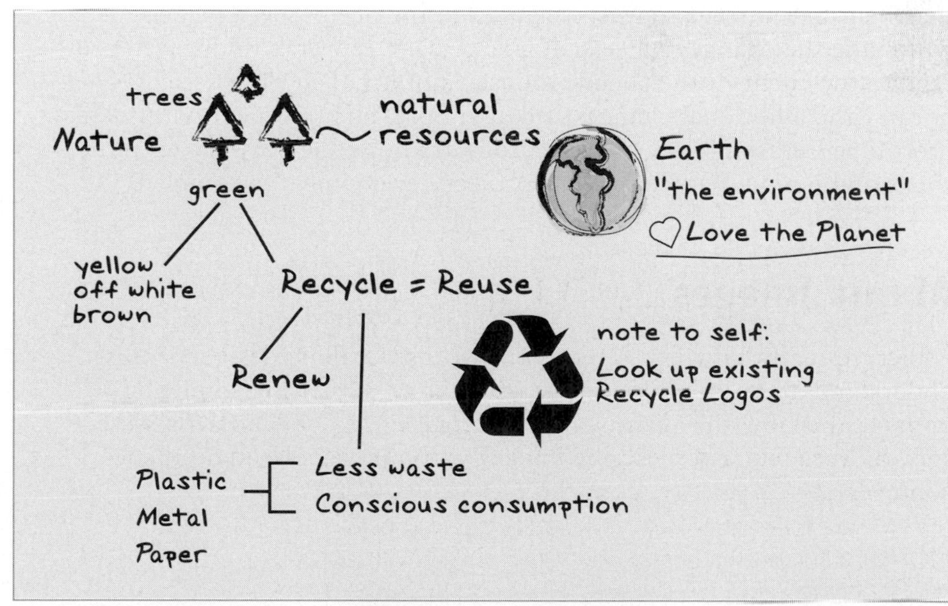

FIGURE SF 1-2 Mind Map

thoughts and related ideas associated with a topic. Figure SF 1-2 is an example of a mind map a designer might sketch to begin a design project such as a poster or brochure about recycling and renewable resources.

Sketches, roughs, and **thumbnails** are quick pencil or pen drawings used to get the idea from your head onto paper. Designers often begin their sketches during the initial meeting with the client.

Dummies and **mock-ups** are roughs made for two-sided or multipage pieces like brochures, books, or magazines. For example, a piece of 8½" × 11" paper could be folded into 3 panels to make a tri-fold brochure dummy. The dummy enables you to see both sides of the brochure.

Comps, or comprehensive layouts, are developed from the best ideas taken from your roughs. They are renderings which look as close as possible to how you imagine the finished project. Comps, dummies, and mock-ups are made by hand or using a computer.

FIGURE SF 1-3 Rough Sketch for a Web site

Storyboards are used for sequential designs, like movies, video, and animation; anything that involves a scene-by-scene plot plan. Storyboards also explain in frames, using drawings or photos, the planned actions of a scene. The rough sketch for a Web site in Figure SF 1-3 may serve as a preliminary draft for a storyboard because it illustrates the planned sequence of pages.

A **prototype** is another word for a mock-up. A graphic designer makes a version, or prototype, of a layout or product. This version of the design is tested on the client or audience to determine how well it functions. The development of a graphic design piece is **iterative**. The word, iterative, means to repeat. From a graphic design point of view, it means the client or audience suggests changes in the prototype. The designer will make the changes suggested, and present a new and improved prototype to the client. If the client proposes more changes, the designer incorporates the additional changes and again presents the client with the next prototype iteration. As many iterations are done as necessary until the client and designer agree that the project development is complete.

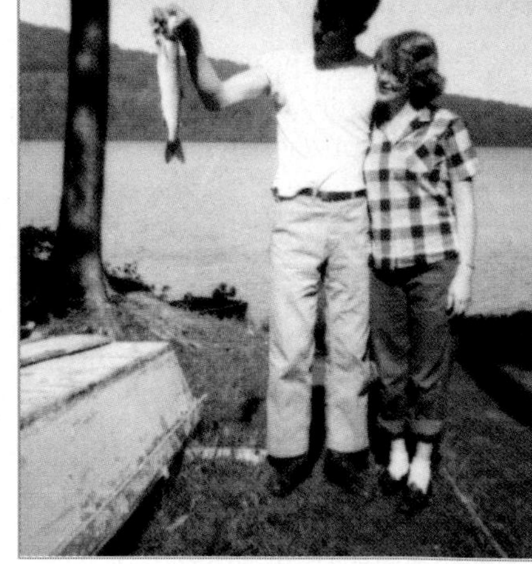

(a)

About Images

A picture really IS worth a thousand words. Graphic designers must understand about the different types of images, their meaning and impact, and how they can be manipulated. Designers and artists use a specific vernacular to describe images within a visual and aesthetic context.

(b) **FIGURE SF 1-4**

Images are classified as being representational, symbolic, or abstract. A **representational image** is the real thing. The image, whether it is a photograph or rendered as an illustration, is realistic (Figure SF 1-4a).

Symbolic images use something graphical to represent a different, nongraphical concept. A letter is a symbol that represents a sound. A red circle with a slash is a common symbol indicating something not permitted (Figure SF 1-4b).

Abstract images are nonrepresentational. No specific implied meaning exists in the visual arrangement of color, shape, or form. Abstract images often convey feeling and emotion that are open to personal interpretation (Figure SF 1-4c).

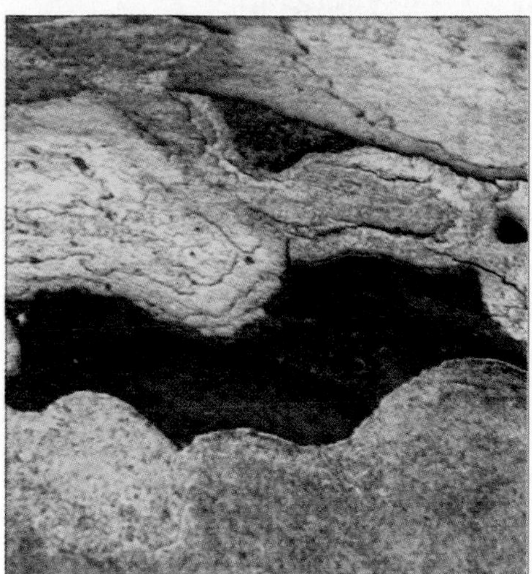

FIGURE SF 1-4(c)

Table SF 1-1 Elements

ELEMENTS	DESCRIPTION
Dot, line, and shape	the most basic elements of which all images are made
Graphic image	the visible object also known as the graphic, the image, or design — including type, symbols, abstract shapes, and pictures
Image area	describes the area of a plane or surface on which images are placed, such as a computer screen or a piece of paper
Nonimage area	describes the area around graphic images, also known as white space
Color	shade or hue of emotion or feeling

Table SF 1-2 Techniques

TECHNIQUES	DESCRIPTION
Composition	the arrangement of elements
Juxtaposition	images placed next to one another
Unity	compositional harmony of diverse elements
Balance	how images relate to the horizontal and vertical centerline of a surface or plane
Simplicity	understated and direct message from a minimum of elements
Contrast	elements placed in opposition to show emphasis
Exaggeration	distorted or overstated from true and real form
Scale	size and proportion of elements in relationship to one another
Perspective	using scale to give the illusion of depth or dimension (3D) on a flat surface
Motion	kinetic, nonstatic quality of elements on a surface
Repetition	same image repeated for visual or conceptual impact
Sequence	changing images shown in logical, narrative order
Transparency	less saturated images or see-through colors
Opacity	solid, dense, nontransparent color or image
Texture	the look and feel of a surface or image

Elements & Techniques

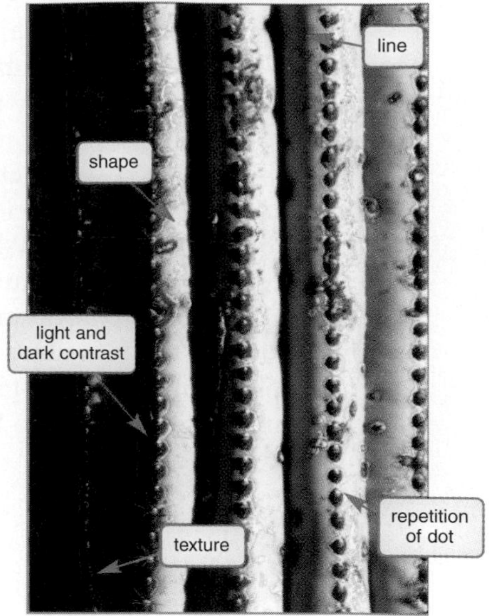

(a)

All designers, artists, and photographers use the same universal, visual, and conceptual **elements** and **techniques**. Elements are manipulated using techniques to create layouts with graphic intent. Table SF 1-1 lists elements and Table SF 1-2 lists techniques commonly used by graphic designers.

Every image, such as a photograph, or graphic design layout contains recognizable elements and techniques. Figure SF 1-5a is a close-up photograph of a cactus. A graphic designer could describe the qualities of this photograph in terms of the basic elements it exhibits. Dot, line, and shape create the form. Light and shadow provide contrast. The natural dots inherent in a cactus create a visual rhythm through repetition. These dots engage the viewer's eye, indicating vertical motion from top to bottom of the page. The overall surface has a textured quality.

Contrast is a commonly applied technique. Contrast can mean a comparison of tones of colors, or images of different sizes. In Figure SF 1-5b the composition made from juxtaposing two photographs emphasizes contrast in light and scale. By placing the close-up of the baby next to the smaller image of the woman, meaning is implied by the contrast of young and old. The composition of these images creates a sense of unity and balance.

Unity, which is the compositional harmony of elements, often depends on the balance of the image or layout. **Balance** can be **symmetrical**, in which the same image is placed in the same position on each side of a center line. With **asymmetrical** balance the image is not identical, but still has a sense of visual unity. Repeating the shell photograph in Figure SF 1-5c demonstrates symmetrical balance. The single shell in Figure SF 1-5d demonstrates asymmetrical balance.

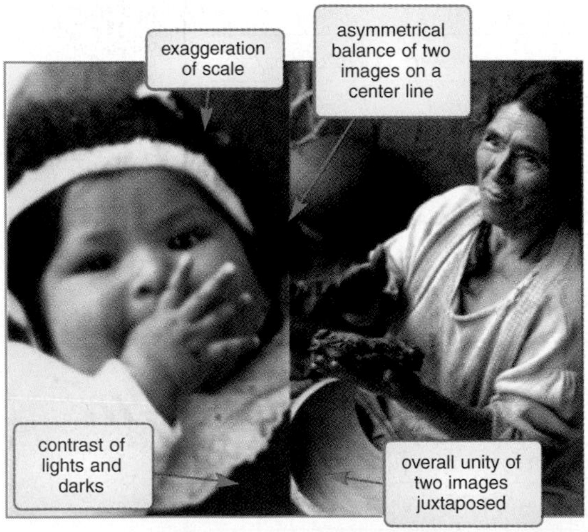

(b)

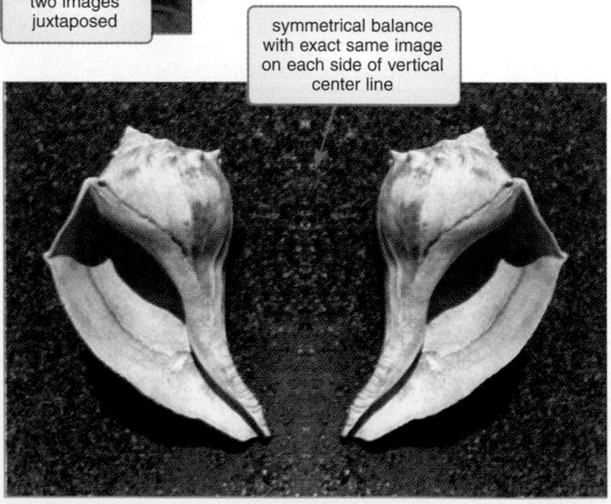

(c)

(d)

FIGURE SF 1-5

Continue to analyze Figure SF 1-5d to identify the other elements and techniques. The shell itself could be considered the image, and the sand could be considered the nonimage area because it is the background. Both the sand and shell have texture. The smooth shell and rough sand create contrast. Simplicity and unity are conveyed through the single image and noncontrasting, soothing colors.

Color

Color is the most powerful design element. It catches attention and leaves a lasting impression. Color can evoke a physiological response from your audience; it can sooth or stimulate. Color used symbolically tells you when to stop, when to go, and when to go slow. Color also is referred to as **hue**.

For an artist mixing paint or pigment to use on paper or canvas, the primary colors are red, yellow, and blue. Combinations of primary colors make secondary colors. A general rule is that warm colors (red, yellow, and orange) advance, and cool colors (blue, green, and violet) recede. Complementary colors face each other on the color model as shown in Figure SF 1-6. For example, yellow and violet are complementary colors. Complementary colors provide good contrast, and when juxtaposed make each other stand out more brightly. **Shades** of a color are created by adding black to the hue; **tints** are created by adding white.

Colors on a TV screen or a computer monitor are visual illusions made from reflected light. All colors you see on a monitor are created from combinations of red, green, and blue, which are referred to as RGB as you see in Figure SF 1-7.

To print on paper, designers and printers use **process colors**, which are always cyan, magenta, yellow, and black, or **CMYK**. As shown in Figure SF 1-8, CMYK are called process colors because they are fundamental to the printing process. Carefully controlled percentages of these colors mixed together create the illusion of all the colors you see in print.

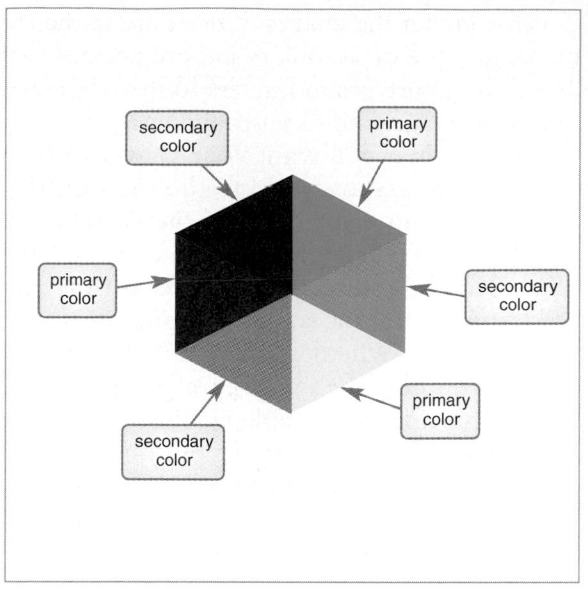

FIGURE SF 1-6

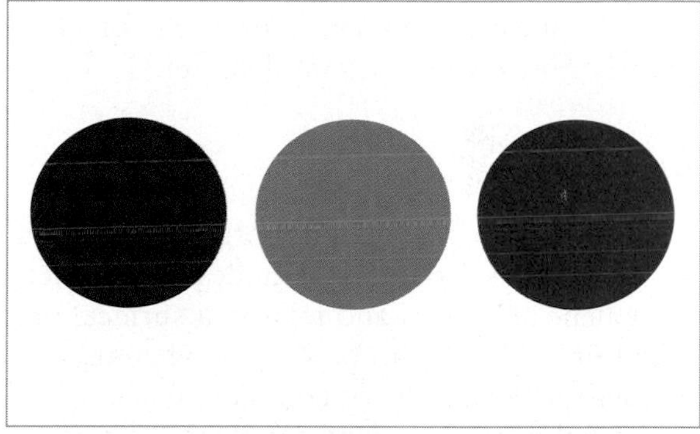

FIGURE SF 1-7

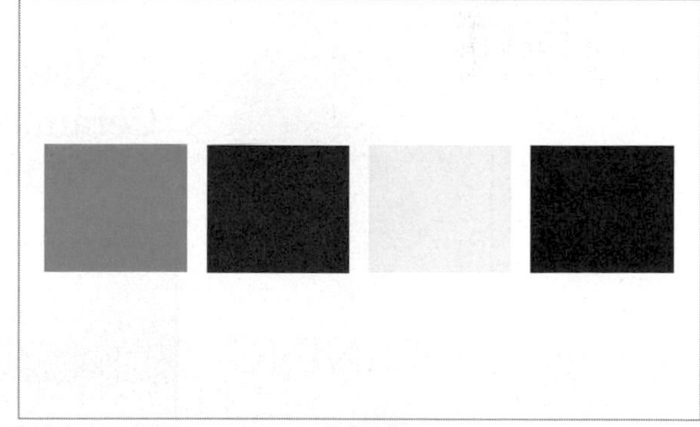

FIGURE SF 1-8

Design Systems

In addition to creativity, inspiration, and intuition, design requires common sense and adherence to a few rules and established systems.

Layout

Layout involves applying design principles within a given space, page, or screen for maximum visual impact. Design layout encompasses the whole process of thoughtfully and skillfully arranging elements and content on a plane or surface. Content is both **visual** — words, images, colors, etc. that you see, and **perceptual** — meanings or ideas that you feel. Layouts include either images or type, also referred to as objects, or a combination of both.

In a layout the images in front are in the foreground. Elements that are of secondary importance are in the background. The term, **figure-ground**, refers to the relationship between an object or image, and its surroundings.

Images that you want your viewer to focus on often are placed slightly above, and to the right of, the actual center line of a layout. This is called the **visual center**. Usually you should avoid placing images too close to the bottom of a page, because it directs the viewer off the page.

Cropping means to cut or resize an image for maximize visual impact. Whether a layout is dynamic or static often depends on how the images are cropped. A **static layout** is very stable and predictable as illustrated in Figure SF 1-9a. This centered layout is static and illustrates unity and simplicity in composition. Notice the objects, which include text and an image, are centered within the layout.

A **dynamic layout** is active and promotes audience participation as illustrated in Figure SF 1-9b. A more dynamic layout makes use of different type, color in the foreground and background, layers of complexity, and repetition of a basic shape to indicate motion. Notice the objects are centered slightly above the horizontal center.

You are invited
to our Beach Party!

Come have a ball!

(a)

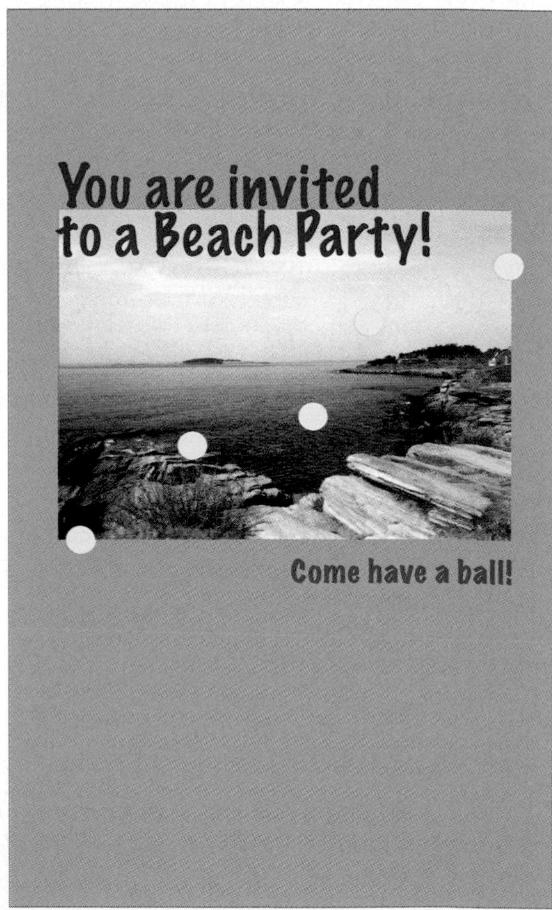

(b)

FIGURE SF 1-9

Grids

Visual elements often are organized according to an underlying grid. Grids are invisible guides used to determine the best placement of images and text on a surface, providing overall visual unity. Grids can be simple, when used for a small advertisement for example, or complex, when used for a multiple paged publication such as a catalog. The most basic grid might

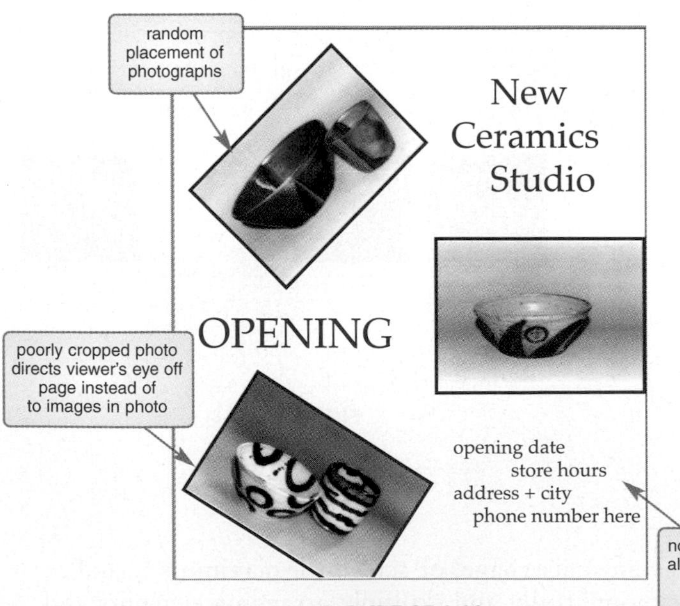

FIGURE SF 1-10a

place margins at the top, bottom, and sides of a piece of paper, using the space within the margins for your layout. A complex grid might might indicate a standard for placement of several photographs and columns of text.

The amount of text, the length of a headline, **information hierarchy**, meaning what is most and least important, the size and number of images you are using are all factors in determining a grid structure.

Figure SF 1-10a is of a layout made without using a grid. The juxtaposition of elements is random. The overall layout lacks unity and balance.

Figure SF 1-10b uses the same images as Figure SF 1-11a, but a simple grid is used to help with placement. The overall composition is unified and balanced.

grid lines are placed equal distance from top and sides of page
OPENING
text lines up with photos making it easy for viewer to read top to bottom and across page, smoothly integrating words and images
New Ceramics Studio
space between photos is equal
opening date
store hours
address + city
phone number here
bottom margin is slightly bigger than top and side margins

FIGURE SF 1-10(b)
Simple grid provides unity and visual structure by organizing the placement of images and text.

Understanding limitations provided by a grid gives you a framework to apply your creative thinking. Grids provide a structure of guides to help with placement, but do not limit your possibilities. You usually can break your own rules to make a layout "look right" by placing an image outside the grid structure. Some layouts, like packaging for 3D objects, might require strict adherence to the grid to prevent losing key images or information on a fold or flap.

Grids are excellent design tools for the following reasons:

- For the layout of a single page project, the grid helps determine the point of visual focus.
- For the layout of a multipage project (Figures SF 1-11), grids provide unity, consistency, rhythm, structure, and balance from page to page.
- Ideas are unlimited. Time is not. For decision making and production, grids save time.

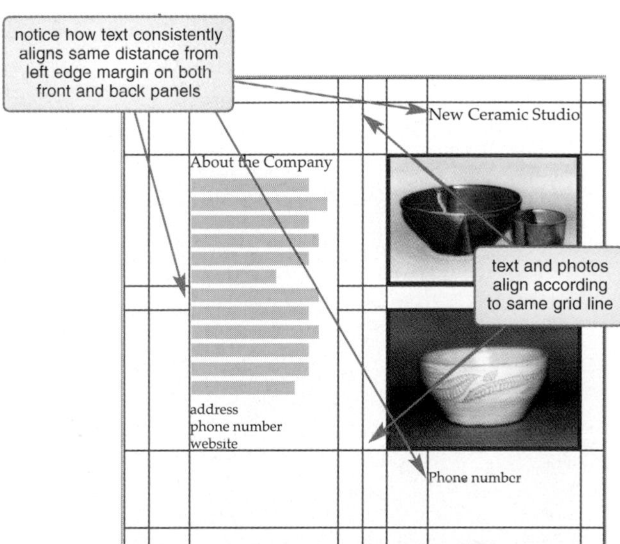

(a) Brochure Front and Back Panels
For this two-sided brochure, a more complex grid provides a structure so the whole piece has continuity and unity from panel to panel and front to back.

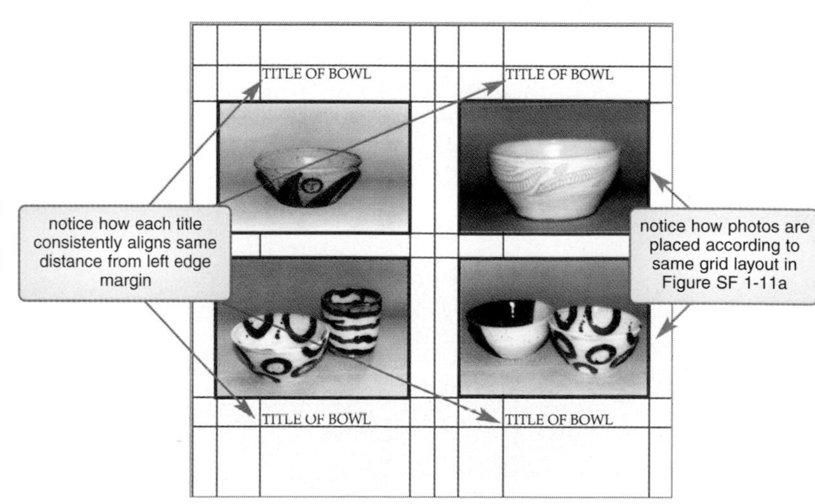

(b) Brochure Inside Panels

FIGURE SF 1-11

Summary

To plan a graphic design project you need to identify the assignment or topic, the client, the audience, and the basic processes used to complete the job. Photoshop and other computer software allows you to manipulate images for different types of graphic design layouts.

Color, a powerful and useful design element, conveys emotion and feeling. Color also has technical considerations depending on what you are designing. Designing for a computer screen makes use of the RGB model, while designing for print uses the CMYK color model.

Understanding the graphic designer's vernacular helps you to describe the way images are used. Using elements such as image and type, and techniques such as composition, unity, and balance, helps you to develop good ideas into successful graphic design layouts. Design layouts are made by arranging images and text on a surface. Grids provide a structure for placing images within a layout. Layouts made using grids often exhibit more visual unity and balance in their overall composition.

Drawing and Painting with Color

PROJECT

4

CASE PERSPECTIVE

Each fall, the School of Music at Halverhout Conservatory sponsors a series of piano recitals where piano performance majors get a chance to perform publicly some of their senior repertoire.

Dr. Walter Cook, head of the piano performance department in the School of Music, contacted your professor in computer graphics technology. Dr. Cook wants a student with some Photoshop experience to design the graphic for the program cover of the winter recital series. Your professor recommended you!

When you met with Dr. Cook, he gave you a sketch of his idea of the program cover. He would like you to use a picture of a baby grand piano and sheet music. He left the selection of the colors and other details up to you, but reminded you that the overall impression should convey a winter theme for an evening concert. You both agreed that the graphic should portray classical music as exciting, thereby dispelling its perceived austerity in order to attract a younger audience.

You decide to explore the painting tools, brushes, colors, and associated palettes in Photoshop as you plan a graphic layout that includes lots of colors and brush styles. Using the Warp command on the sheet music in the background, and adding motion lines at the feet of the piano legs, will add visual movement. Using a brush, you will draw a Roman numeral representing the number of the recital in the series.

As you read through this project, you will learn how to use Photoshop brushes with the Pen and Line tools. You will set foreground and background colors and create shapes. You will use the Eyedropper tool to pick up a color, and the Paint Bucket tool to apply the color. You will learn how to apply gradient color and effects.

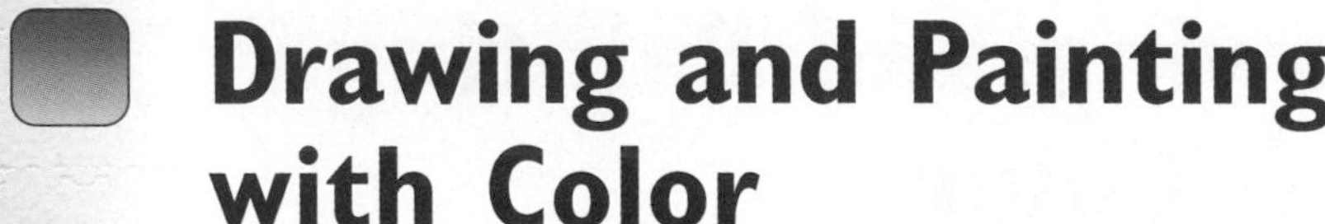

Drawing and Painting with Color

PROJECT

Objectives

You will have mastered the material in this project when you can:

- Create a document from scratch
- Apply gradients using the Gradient tool
- Use the Color Picker
- Display color information in the Info palette
- Paint and draw using Photoshop brushes
- Change the hardness and diameter settings of brushes
- Use the Info, Swatches, Paths, and Brushes palettes
- Differentiate among the shape tools
- Load new brushes
- Use the Brush Preset picker
- Use the Pen, Ellipse, and Line tools
- Edit colors and set color dynamics
- Differentiate between color modes
- Choose colors with the Eyedropper tool
- Apply colors with the Paint Bucket tool

Introduction

In both academic and business environments, you will be called upon to create graphics from scratch using the tools and techniques available in Photoshop. While many sources of graphics, such as clip art and stock photos, are widely available, some are copyrighted, rights-controlled, or expensive to buy. Others have to be edited enough that it might be easier to start from scratch. Still others simply do not fit the particular circumstances for the required project. By creating the graphic from scratch, you solve many of the problems that occur from using ready-made images. If you have good artistic and drawing skills and a graphics tablet, the kinds of graphics you can create are endless.

You also can start from scratch and add images that are real photographs or scans. That way, your image has the best of both worlds — incorporating the texture and lines of drawing with the realism of actual pictures. In Photoshop, working from scratch to create an image or illustration is better when the subject is proposed, conceptual, imaginative, less formal or open to interpretation. Beginning with a digital photo or scan is better when the subject is living, tangible, for sale, or more formal; photography does not risk loss of meaning through interpretation. Whatever style of imagery you choose, you need to know how to use the drawing and painting tools in Photoshop.

Project Four — Drawing and Painting with Color

Project 4 uses Photoshop to create a graphic for the front of a printed recital program. It constructs the recital series number, the gradient, brush strokes, and notes from scratch — representing the artistic, exciting side of piano performance — while using the images of real music and a piano to add a sense of refinement and detail. The graphic lets the viewer know what to expect at the recital. The completed image is displayed in Figure 4-1.

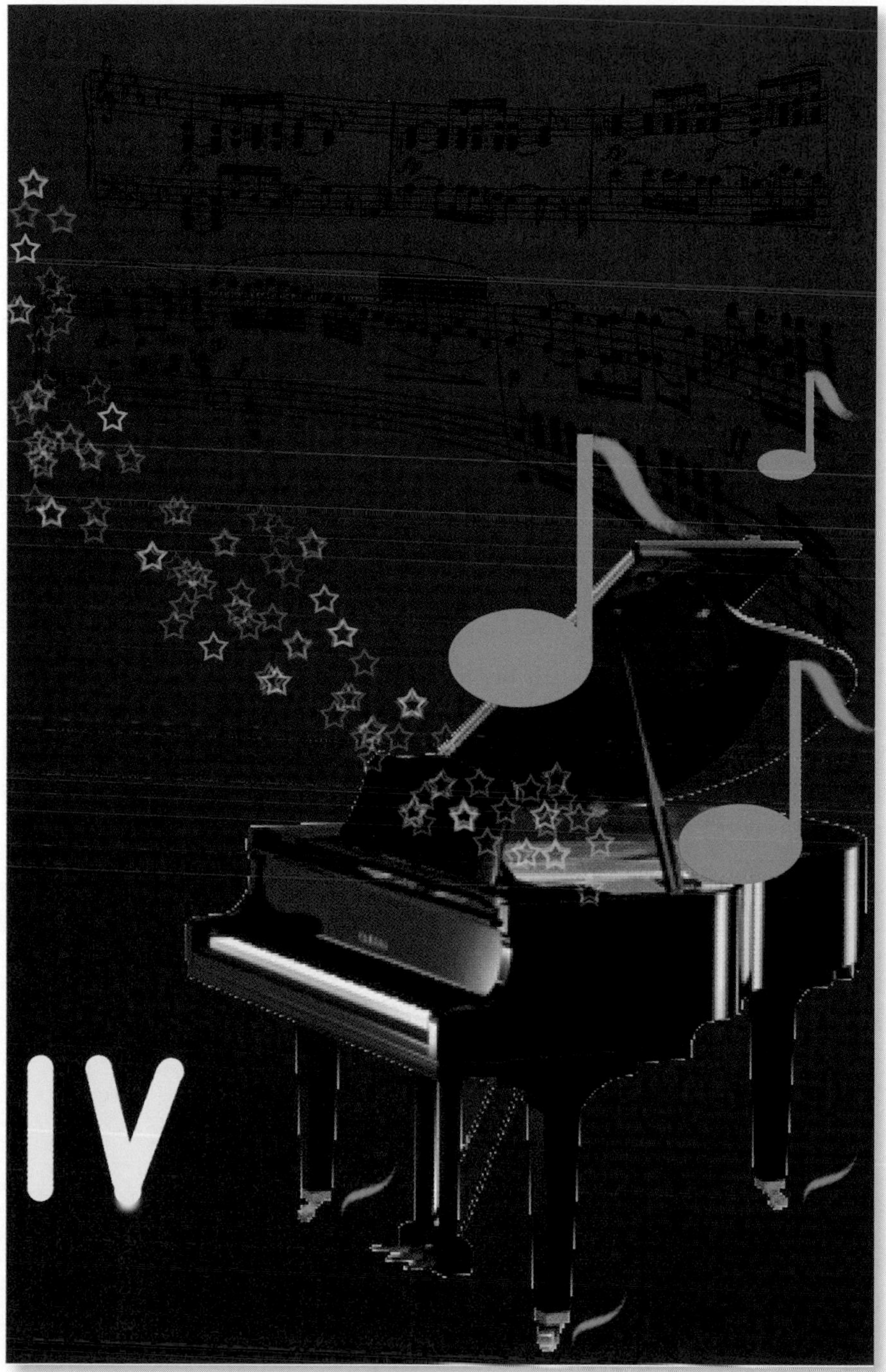

FIGURE 4-1

Starting and Customizing Photoshop

If you are stepping through this project on a computer and you want your screen to match the figures in this book, you should change your computer's resolution to 1024 × 768 and reset the tools and palettes. For more information about how to change the resolution on your computer, and other advanced Photoshop settings, read Appendix A.

The following steps describe how to start Photoshop and customize the Photoshop window. You may need to ask your instructor how to start Photoshop for your system.

To Start Photoshop and Reset the Palettes, Toolbox, and Options Bar

1. **Start Photoshop as described on pages PS 6 and PS 7.**
2. **Choose the Default Workspace as described on page PS 8.**
3. **Select the Rectangular Marquee Tool (M) in the toolbox and then reset all tools as described on pages PS 9 and PS 10.**

Photoshop starts and then resets the tools, palettes, and options.

Resetting the Layers Palette

The following steps show how to reset the Layers palette to make the thumbnails match the figures shown in this book.

To Reset the Layers Palette

1. **Click the Layers palette menu button and then click Palette Options on the list.**
2. **When Photoshop displays the Layers Palette Options dialog box, click the option button corresponding to the smallest of the thumbnail sizes.**
3. **If necessary, click the Layer Bounds option button.**
4. **Click the OK button.**

The Layers palette will display small thumbnails for each layer.

Resetting the Colors

The following step shows how to reset the default colors in the Photoshop window.

To Reset the Colors

1. **If black and white are not shown as the default colors in the toolbox, press the D key on the keyboard. If necessary, press X to invert the colors.**

Black is set as the foreground color; white is set as the background color.

Creating a New File

In this project, you will create a new Photoshop document from scratch. Photoshop allows you to customize the attributes of file name, image size, resolution, color mode, and background when creating a new document image. Alternately, Photoshop provides several groups of attributes that are preset. The new image size can be set in pixels, inches, or centimeters, among others. You can set the width and height independently. When setting the resolution of an image, you specify the number of pixels per inch (ppi), or pixels per centimeter, that are printed on a page.

A **color mode**, or **color method**, determines the number of colors and combinations of colors used to display and print the image. Each color mode uses a numerical method called a **color model**, or **color space**, which describes the color. Photoshop bases its color modes on the color models that commonly are useful when publishing images. Color modes also directly affect the file size of an image. As you will learn in this project, choosing a color mode determines which Photoshop tools and file formats are available.

A **gamut**, or **color gamut**, is the range of colors that can be displayed or printed. The color gamut on your monitor may not be the same as on your printer. For example, the RGB color mode displays a wider range of discernible colors than does CMYK. When you print an RGB image that displays on your monitor, it must be reproduced with CMYK inks on your printer. Because the gamut of color that can be reproduced with ink is smaller than what we see with our eyes, any color that cannot be printed is referred to as **out of gamut**. In Photoshop, you will see an out of gamut warning if you select colors that have to be converted from RGB used in editing, to CMYK used in printing. If you plan to send your image to a professional print shop, be sure to ask about color modes, models, and gamuts before the image is printed.

Table 4-1 describes the common color modes. When choosing a color mode, you must take into consideration many factors including purpose, printing options, file size, number of colors, and layers that may be flattened in later conversions between color modes.

Table 4-1 Color Modes

PHOTOSHOP COLOR MODE	COLOR COMBINATIONS	DESCRIPTION	TYPICAL USE
RGB	red, green, blue	a basic additive color mode used for color video display	monitor, scanners, and digital cameras
CMYK	cyan, magenta, yellow, black	a basic subtractive color mode used for printing	color printing
LAB Color or CIELAB	lightness setting, A-axis colors (magenta to green), B-axis colors (yellow to blue)	a color mode that is independent of the type of device or media, used for display or printing	photo CD images; images where the luminance and color values are edited independently
Grayscale	shades of gray	a color mode where pixels are measured with a brightness value from 0 (black) to 255 (white), or as a percentage from 0% (black) to 100% (white)	images produced using black and white or grayscale scanners, other black and white images

More About

RGB

RGB is considered an additive color mode because its colors are created by adding together different wave lengths of light in various intensities. On a computer monitor, each color is stored in 8 bits of Information; therefore it is sometimes called 24-bit color, or true color. RGB color mode is used typically for images that are reproduced on monitors such as a cathode ray tube (CRT), liquid crystal display (LCD), or gas plasma display (GPD). Other uses for RGB include those created by the colored gels in spotlights or via film recorders. It is ideal for slides, transparencies, and the Web.

More About

CMYK

CMYK is considered a subtractive color mode because its colors are created when light strikes an object or image and the wave lengths are absorbed. Subtractive color modes include all colors produced in printed materials and those composed of dyes and pigments. Also called four-color process, the CMYK color mode is used by most desktop printers and commercial printing. Because there are four colors involved instead of three, CMYK images use 33 percent more file space than RGB images.

More About

Converting between Modes

In Photoshop, you can easily convert from one color mode to another. When you point to Mode on the Image menu, the various color modes can be selected. As you choose a new color mode, Photoshop will inform you of any problems converting the image.

More About

The LAB Color Mode

Three basic parameters make up the LAB color mode. First, the lightness of the color is measured from 0 (indicating black) to 100 (indicating white). The second parameter represents the color's position between magenta and green — negative values indicate green while positive values indicate magenta. Finally, the third parameter indicates a color's position between yellow and blue — negative values indicate blue while positive values indicate yellow.

More About

The Indexed Color Mode

When converting to Indexed color, Photoshop builds a color lookup table (CLUT), which stores and indexes the colors in the image. If a color in the original image does not appear in the table, Photoshop chooses the closest one, or dithers the available colors to simulate the color.

More About

Grayscale

Although a grayscale reproduction on a computer screen can display up to 256 levels of gray, a printing press can reproduce only about 50 levels of gray per ink. For this reason, a grayscale image printed with only black ink can look very coarse compared to the same image printed with two, three, or four inks, with each individual ink reproducing up to 50 levels of gray.

Table 4-1 Color Modes *(continued)*

PHOTOSHOP COLOR MODE	COLOR COMBINATIONS	DESCRIPTION	TYPICAL USE
Bitmap	black or white	a color mode where all pixels are reduced to two colors, black and white, greatly simplifying the color information in the image and reducing its file size	line art, black-and-white logos, illustrations, or black-and-white special effects
Indexed Color	8-bit image files with at most 256 colors	a color mode where the palette of colors is limited in order to reduce file size yet maintain some visual quality	Adobe PDF files, multimedia presentations, and other formats that need, or can use, reduced file sizes
Monotone, Duotone, Tritone, Quadtone	a specific number of inks (1, 2, 3, or 4)	a color mode that uses colored inks to produce blacks, grays, and other colors to increase the tonal range of colors	single color images, tinted grays using black and gray ink, spot color documents using black and a highlight or color, and tricolor or four-color documents like newspapers or brochures
HSB	hue, saturation, and brightness	a color mode where the user indicates a value for hue, saturation, and brightness	used as an alternate to RGB to create specific gradient colors

Photoshop's **color management system** (CMS) translates colors from the color space of one device into a device-independent color space. The process is called **color mapping**, or **gamut mapping**.

Creating a File from Scratch

The recital graphic will be approximately 5.5 × 8.5 inches to accommodate the size of the printed program. A resolution of 300 ppi will be used to maintain a high-quality printed image. The color mode will be CMYK. The background will be white. The background when creating a new document image commonly is set to white, however, Photoshop lets you change to a background color or make it transparent.

The following steps show how to use the New command on the File menu and set the attributes for a new document image.

To Create a File from Scratch

1

- **Click File on the menu bar, and then click New.**
- **When the New dialog box is displayed, type** `Recital Graphic` **in the Name box.**

Photoshop displays the New dialog box (Figure 4-2). Your settings will differ.

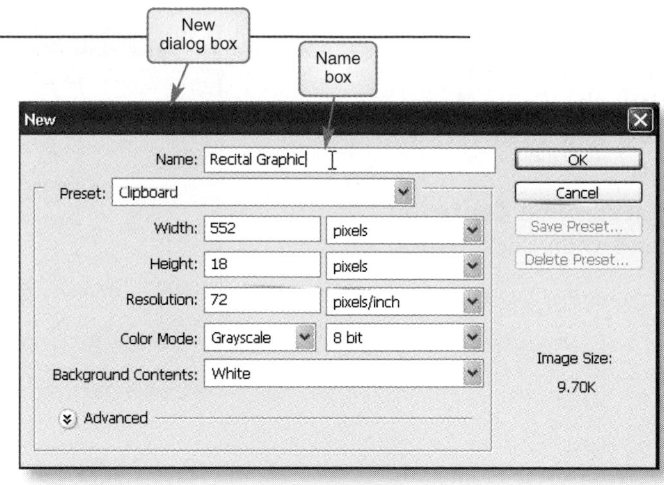

FIGURE 4-2

2

- **Click the Preset box arrow, scroll up in the list, and then click Custom.**
- **Double-click the Width box and then type** `5.5` **as the entry. Click the Width unit box arrow, and then click inches in the list.**
- **Double-click the Height box and then type** `8.5` **as the entry. If necessary, click the Height unit box arrow, and then click inches in the list.**

The width and height are set for the new image (Figure 4-3). Photoshop allows you to choose various scales for new photos, including inches, pixels, centimeters, millimeters, points, and others.

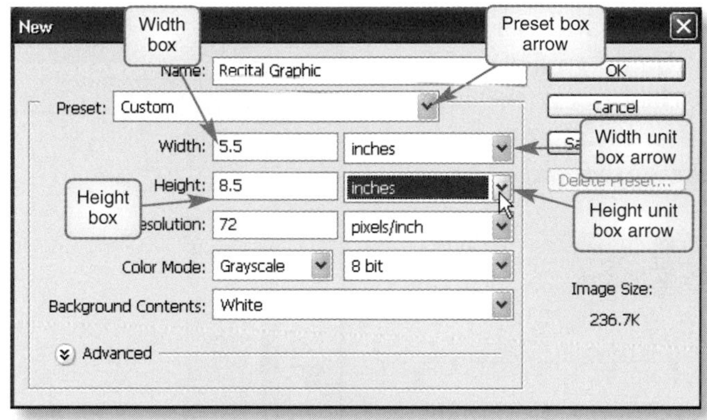

FIGURE 4-3

3

- **Double-click the Resolution box and then type** `300` **as the entry. If necessary, click the Resolution unit box arrow, and then click pixels/inches in the list.**
- **Click the Color Mode box arrow.**

The resolution is set and Photoshop displays the available color modes (Figure 4-4).

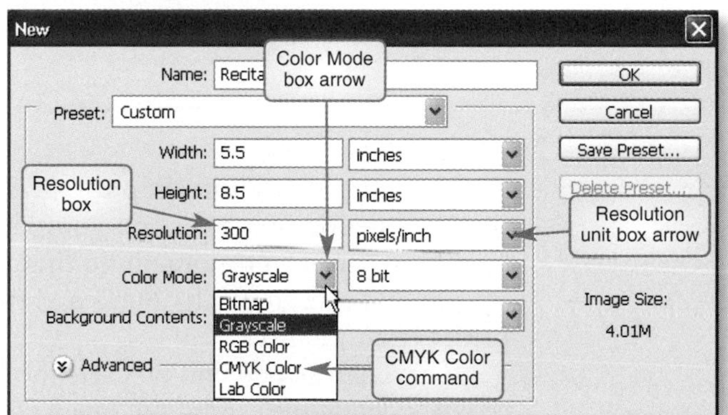

FIGURE 4-4

4

- **Click CMYK Color in the list. If necessary, click the Color Mode unit box arrow and then click 8 bit in the list.**
- **Click the Background Contents box arrow, and then click White in the list.**

The color mode is set (Figure 4-5).

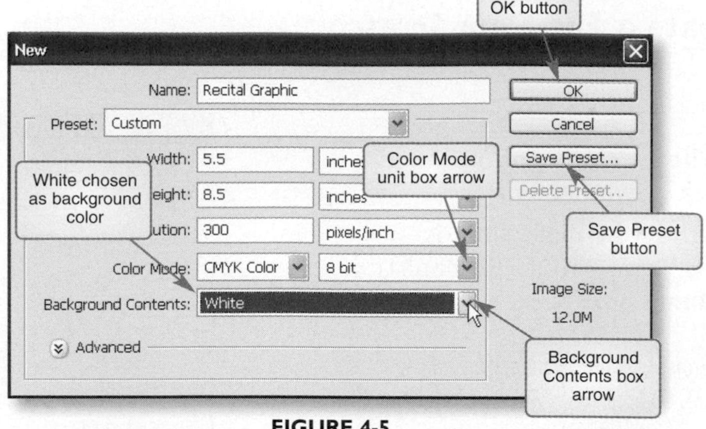

FIGURE 4-5

5

- **Click the OK button. On the document window status bar, double-click the magnification box, type** 20 **and then press the** ENTER **key. Resize the document window to display the entire page.**

Photoshop displays the Recital Graphic document window (Figure 4-6).

6

- **If the rulers do not display in the document window, press CTRL+R.**

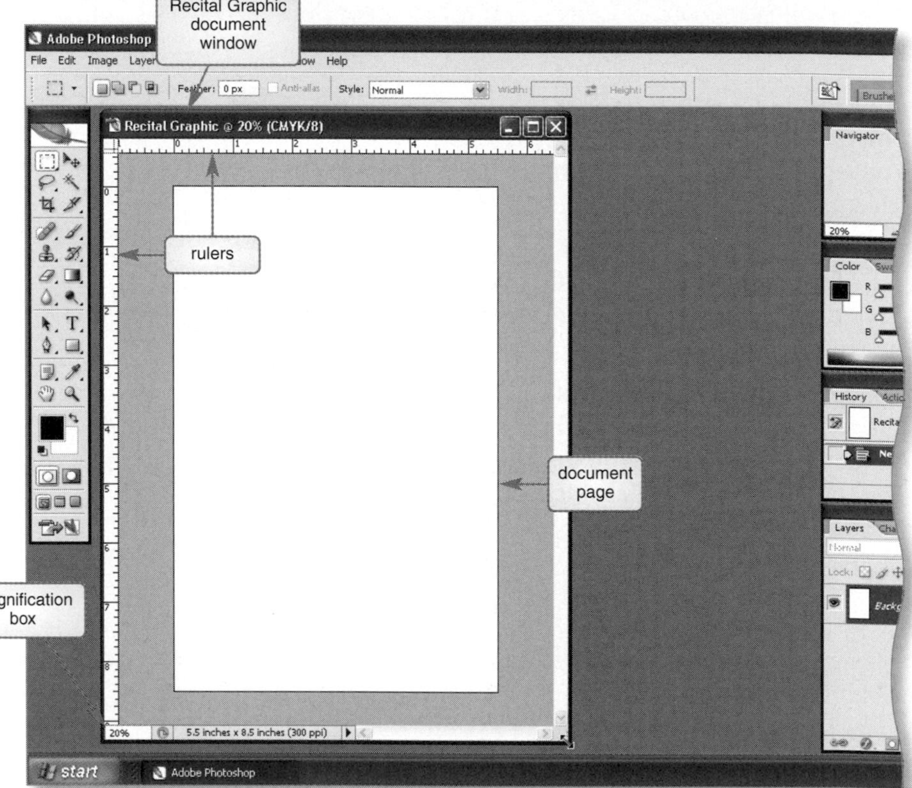

FIGURE 4-6

Other Ways

1. Press CTRL+N, set attributes

In Figure 4-5, Photoshop displays an approximate image size on the right side of the New dialog box based on your choices in the various attribute settings. If those specific settings were something that you used often, you could click the Save Preset button and give your attributes a name. In future sessions, you then could choose the preset from the list.

The Color Mode unit box sets the bit depth. The **bit depth**, also called pixel depth or color depth, measures how much color information is available for displaying or printing each pixel in an image. The word, **bit**, stands for binary digit. A bit depth of 8 means that Photoshop assigns 8 binary settings for each color. Additionally, every Photoshop image has one or more **channels** that store information about color elements in the image. For example, if you choose a bit depth of 8 in RGB color mode, Photoshop would set the channels for red, green, and blue, each using an 8-bit representation. Each channel has 8 binary settings, or 2^8 values, resulting in 256 possible colors per channel. Combining the three channels creates the possibility of more than 16 million different colors. You will learn more about channels in a later project.

More About

Web Colors

The Web typically uses a six-digit hexadecimal number to represent its color mode. Hexadecimal is a numbering system based on groups of 16, using the numbers 0 through 9 and the letters A through F. For example, a hexadecimal representation in RGB mode, reserves the first two digits for the value of red, the second two digits for green, and the final two digits for blue. In that color system, FF0000 is bright red. In decimal numbers, used for color modes other than the Web, three separate numbers are used for each of the 256 available colors per channel. Bright red would be noted as 255, 0, and 0, representing red, green, and blue, respectively.

Saving a File

Even though the file has a name in the document window title bar, it is not saved on a storage device. The next step is to save the file with the name, Recital Graphic, as the following steps illustrate.

To Save the File

1. **With your USB flash drive connected to one of the computer's USB ports, click File on the menu bar and then click Save As.**
2. **Click the Save in box arrow and then click USBDISK [G:], or the location associated with your USB flash drive, in the list.**
3. **If necessary, click the Format box arrow, and then click Photoshop (*.PSD, *.PDD) in the list.**
4. **Click the Save button in the Save As dialog box.**

Photoshop saves the file on the USB flash drive with the file name, Recital Graphic.

Other Ways

1. Press CTRL+SHIFT+S

You should save your work often by pressing CTRL+S, while working through the steps in this project.

Gradients

A **gradient**, or **gradient fill**, is a graphic effect consisting of a smooth blend, change, or transition from one color to another. Typically used as a graduated blend between the foreground and background colors of an image, the direction of the transition can be top to bottom, bottom to top, side to side, or diagonally. Gradients can be applied to the entire image or a selected portion of an image.

A gradient can be used to create depth, add visual interest, or to highlight a portion of an image. Photoshop permits you to choose from preset gradient fills, or to create your own.

Gradients work best with RGB or CMYK colors. The Gradient tool cannot be used with the Bitmap or Index color modes.

The Gradient Options Bar

To create a gradient, you select an area of an image and then click the **Gradient Tool (G) button** in the toolbox. If you right-click the Gradient Tool (G) button, its context menu includes the Gradient tool and the Paint Bucket tool. The **Gradient options bar** (Figure 4-7 on the next page) allows you to set the style, blending mode, and other attributes for the gradient fill. If you do not select a portion of the image, the gradient will be applied to the entire image.

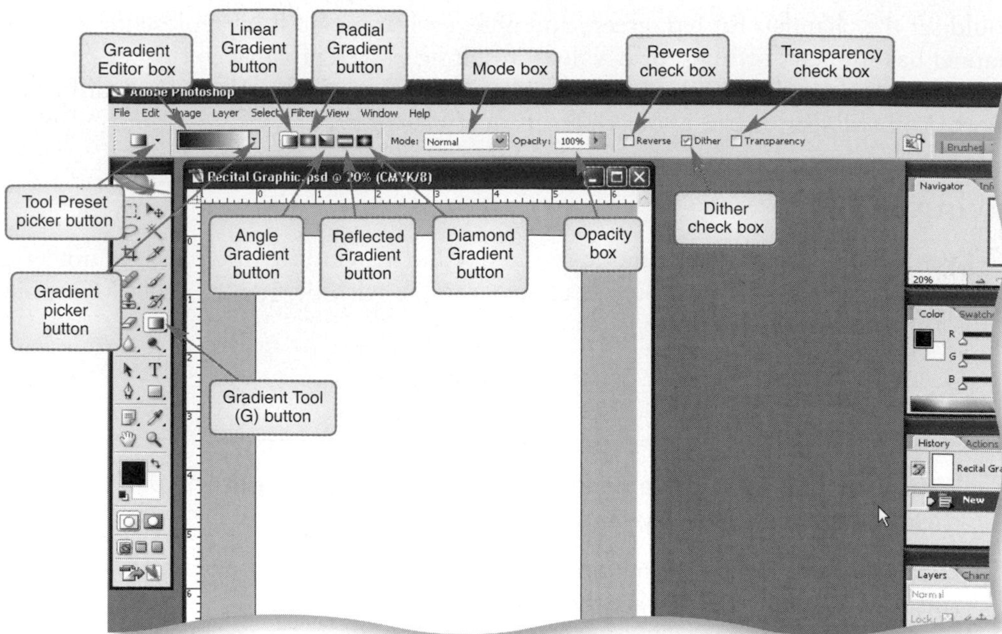

FIGURE 4-7 Gradient options bar

You can click the Gradient Editor box to display the Gradient Editor dialog box, or you can choose a preset gradient by clicking the Gradient picker button.

To the right of the Gradient Editor button are the gradient styles or shades. A **gradient style** is the way the light reflects in the gradient. Table 4-2 displays the five gradient styles.

Table 4-2 Gradient Styles

GRADIENT	STYLE	BUTTON
Linear	shades from the starting point to the ending point in a straight line	
Radial	shades from the starting point to the ending point in a circular pattern	
Angle	shades in a counterclockwise sweep around the starting point	
Reflected	shades using symmetric linear gradients on either side of the starting point	
Diamond	shades from the starting point outward in a diamond pattern — the ending point defines one corner of the diamond	

On the right side of the Gradient options bar, Photoshop includes an Opacity box to set the percentage of opacity, a Reverse checkbox to reverse the order of colors in the gradient fill, a Dither checkbox to create a smoother blend with less banding, and a Transparency checkbox to create a transparency mask for the gradient fill.

Blending Modes

The Mode box arrow displays a list of **blending modes,** which are the ways in which pixels in the image are affected by a color. The default value is Normal, which is sometimes called the **threshold.** Each blending mode creates a different gradient. The combination of these blending modes, with the other settings on the Gradient options bar, creates an almost infinite number of possibilities.

Some of the modes are not available to every color event. For example, the Burn-based blending modes are more appropriate for applying a gradient over another image or layer. Other blending modes result in solid white or black unless the opacity setting is changed. The Light-based blending modes — hard, vivid, and linear — react differently for colors on either side of the 50% gray threshold.

When using blending modes with gradients, the mode controls how the pixels in the image are affected by a painting or editing tool. The **base color** is the original color in the image. The **blend color** is the color being applied with the painting or editing tool. The **result color** is the color resulting from the blend.

Experimenting with the blending modes can give you a better feel for how they work. The Adobe Help Center has example images of each of the blending modes. Table 4-3 describes some of the blending modes

More About

Hard Light and Soft Light Blending Modes

If the blend color (light source) is lighter than 50 percent gray, the image is lightened similar to the dodge blend. If the blend color is darker than 50 percent gray, the image is darkened similar to the burn blend. Painting with pure black or white produces a distinctly darker or lighter area but does not result in pure black or white.

Table 4-3 Blending Modes

BLENDING MODE	DESCRIPTION
Normal	paints each pixel to make it the result color
Dissolve	used in conjunction with opacity to paint each pixel randomly with the result color
Darken	the result color becomes the darker of either the base or blend color — pixels lighter than the blend color are replaced, and pixels darker than the blend color do not change
Multiply	multiplies the base color by the blend color resulting in a darker color
Color Burn	darkens the base color to reflect the blend color by increasing the contrast
Linear Burn	darkens the base color to reflect the blend color by decreasing the brightness
Lighten	the result color becomes the lighter of either the base or blend color — pixels darker than the blend color are replaced, and pixels lighter than the blend color do not change
Screen	multiplies the inverse of the blend and base colors resulting in a lighter color
Color Dodge	brightens the base color to reflect the blend color by decreasing the contrast
Linear Dodge	brightens the base color to reflect the blend color by increasing the brightness
Overlay	preserves the highlights and shadows of the base color, as it is mixed with the blend color to reflect the lightness or darkness of the original color
Soft Light	darkens or lightens the colors depending on the blend color — the effect is similar to shining a diffused spotlight on the image
Hard Light	multiplies or screens the colors depending on the blend color. The effect is similar to shining a harsh spotlight on the image
Vivid Light	burns or dodges the colors by increasing or decreasing the contrast depending on the blend color
Linear Light	burns or dodges the colors by decreasing or increasing the brightness depending on the blend color
Pin Light	replaces the colors depending on the blend color, creating a special effect
Difference	looks at the color information in each channel and subtracts either the blend color from the base color, or the base color from the blend color, depending on which has the greater brightness value; blending with white inverts the base color values; blending with black produces no change
Exclusion	creates an effect similar to, but lower in contrast than, the Difference blending mode
Hue	creates a result color with the luminance and saturation of the base color, and the hue of the blend color
Saturation	creates a result color with the luminance and hue of the base color, and the saturation of the blend color
Color	creates a result color with the luminance of the base color, and the hue and saturation of the blend color
Luminosity	creates a result color with the hue and saturation of the base color, and the luminance of the blend color

Using the Gradient Editor

To create a gradient fill in the Recital Graphic image, you will click the Gradient Tool (G) button in the toolbox and then access the Gradient Editor, setting the gradient type and smoothness. The **Gradient Editor** lets you define a new gradient by modifying a copy of an existing gradient or preset, or by choosing colors to create a new blend.

To Use the Gradient Editor

1

- **Press the G key to access the Gradient tool. If necessary, right-click the Paint Bucket Tool (G) button and then click Gradient Tool in the list.**

The Gradient tool is selected and the Gradient options bar is displayed (Figure 4-8).

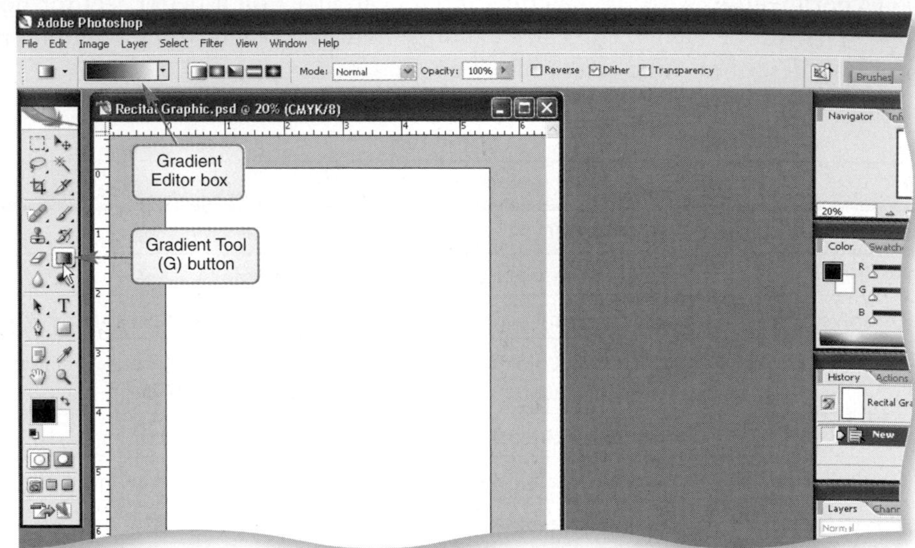

FIGURE 4-8

2

- **On the Gradient options bar, click the Gradient Editor box.**
- **If necessary when the Gradient Editor dialog box opens, click the Gradient Type box arrow and then click Solid in the list. If necessary, type 100 in the Smoothness box.**

Photoshop displays the Gradient Editor dialog box (Figure 4-9). The preset thumbnails on your system may differ. The fill will have a 100 percent smooth transition between colors.

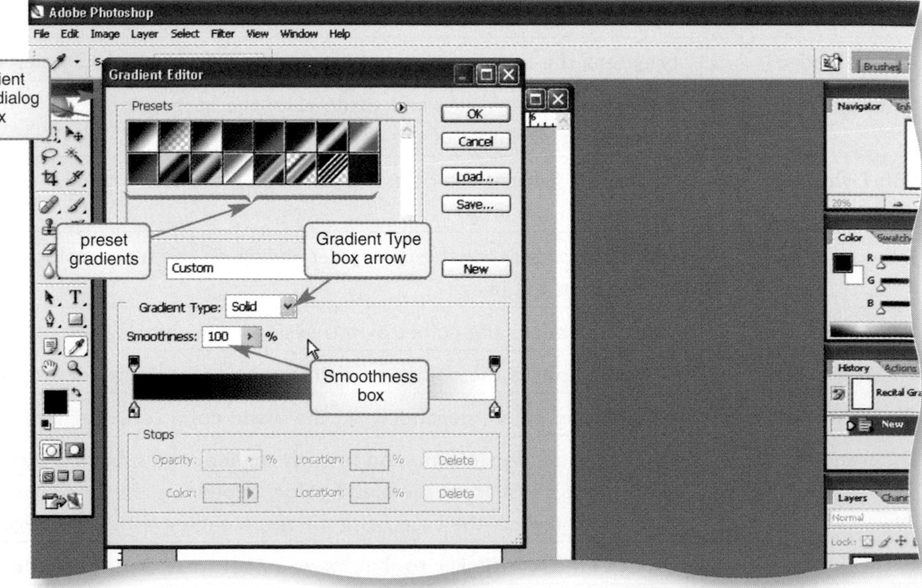

FIGURE 4-9

Other Ways

1. Press SHIFT+G, click Gradient Editor box, choose settings

In the Gradient Editor dialog box, the Presets area contains a menu button. When clicked, the Presets menu button displays choices for thumbnail size and other gradient presets (Figure 4-10). Photoshop has eight sets of gradients that can be used to create a wide variety of special fill effects. When you choose to use one of the additional sets, Photoshop will ask if you want to replace or append the new gradient set. Clicking the Reset Gradients command changes the presets back to the default list.

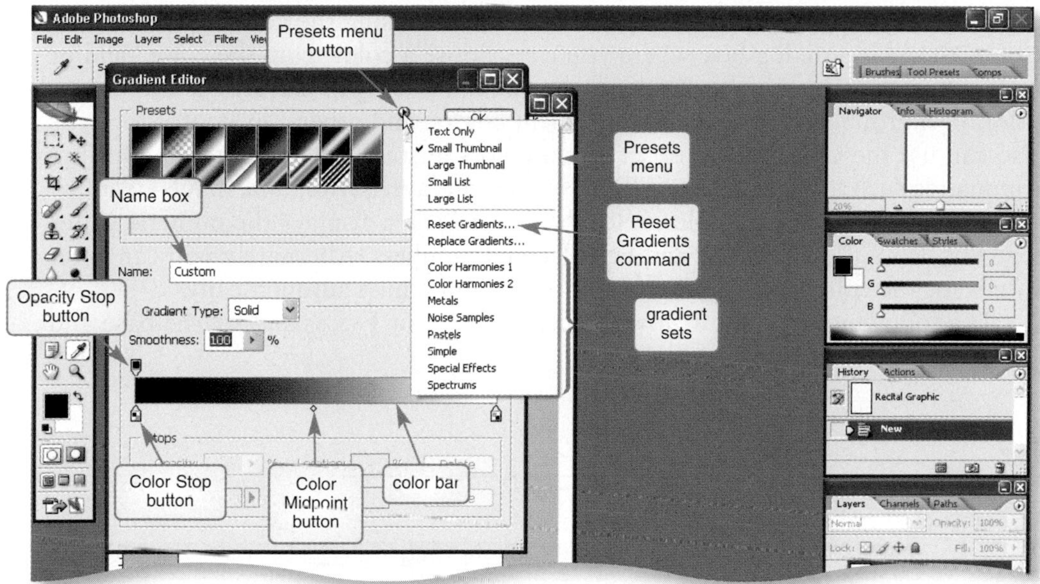

FIGURE 4-10

If the gradient you create is one that you plan to use several times, you can name it in the Name box and then click the Save button to save it as a gradient file within Photoshop. In subsequent sessions, you then can load the saved gradient to use it again.

In addition to the **solid gradient** that creates a solid color spectrum transition through the gradient, you alternately can choose the noise gradient. A **noise gradient** is a gradient that contains randomly distributed colors within the range of colors that you specify.

The **smoothness** setting is a percentage determining the smoothness of the transition between color bands. One hundred percent indicates an equally weighted transition in color pixels. Using lower values, the gradient colors will appear more pixelated, with abrupt transitions in the color bands. This effect is more evident on nonadjacent colors in the color spectrum. When working with a noise gradient, the Smoothness box becomes a Roughness box indicating how vividly the colors transition between one another.

The **color bar** in the Gradient Editor dialog box has stop buttons for opacity above it and for color below it. Once colors are selected, the small diamond below the color bar is the **Midpoint Color button**, the place in the gradient where it displays an even mix of the starting and ending colors. You can drag the diamond to adjust the midpoint location.

Clicking an **Opacity Stop** button allows you to enter a percentage of opacity and a location within the color bar for the opacity to begin. Recall that opacity determines to what degree the color obscures or reveals any layers beneath it. A layer with 1 percent opacity appears nearly transparent, whereas one with 100 percent opacity appears completely opaque.

Clicking a **Color Stop** button accesses the Color Picker as described in the next section. By default, Photoshop displays two Color Stop buttons to produce a gradient

More About

Color Stops

By placing Color Stop buttons very close together in the Gradient Editor, you can reduce the gradient effect and produce strong, distinct bands of color. Bands of color used with the Gradient tool can generate exciting and novel special effects.

from one color to a second color, but other Color Stop buttons can be added by clicking just below the color bar. Color Stop buttons can be dragged to force the transition to begin at an earlier or later point in the resulting gradient. To delete a Color Stop, click the Color Stop button and then click the Delete button.

The Color Picker

The next step is to set the base and blend colors using the Color Picker. The **Color Picker** is a dialog box where you can choose a color from the color field or define the color numerically. Through the Color Picker, you can set the foreground color, background color, text color, gradient colors, and others. In Photoshop, you also can use the Color Picker to set target colors in some color and tonal adjustment commands such as filter colors, fill layers, certain layer styles, and shape layers.

When you click in the color field, the Color Picker displays the numeric values for HSB, RGB, Lab, CMYK, and hexadecimal numbers. Alternately you can enter values for the color modes and the color field will adjust automatically.

The following steps show how to access the Color Picker and set the base and blend colors for the gradient fill.

To Use the Color Picker

1

- **In the Gradient Editor dialog box, double-click the left Color Stop button.**

Photoshop displays the Color Picker dialog box (Figure 4-11). Your colors may vary.

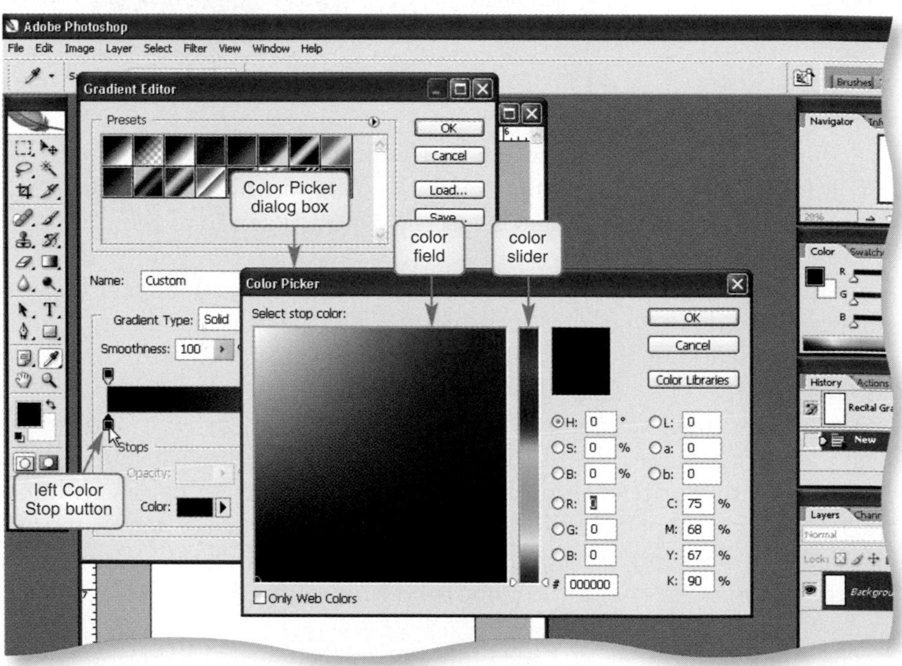

FIGURE 4-11

2

• Click at the top of the color slider and then click in the upper-right portion of the color field, to choose the color red.

The red color numerical values display in the color mode boxes and a small circle is displayed in the color field (Figure 4-12). Your color does not have to match exactly.

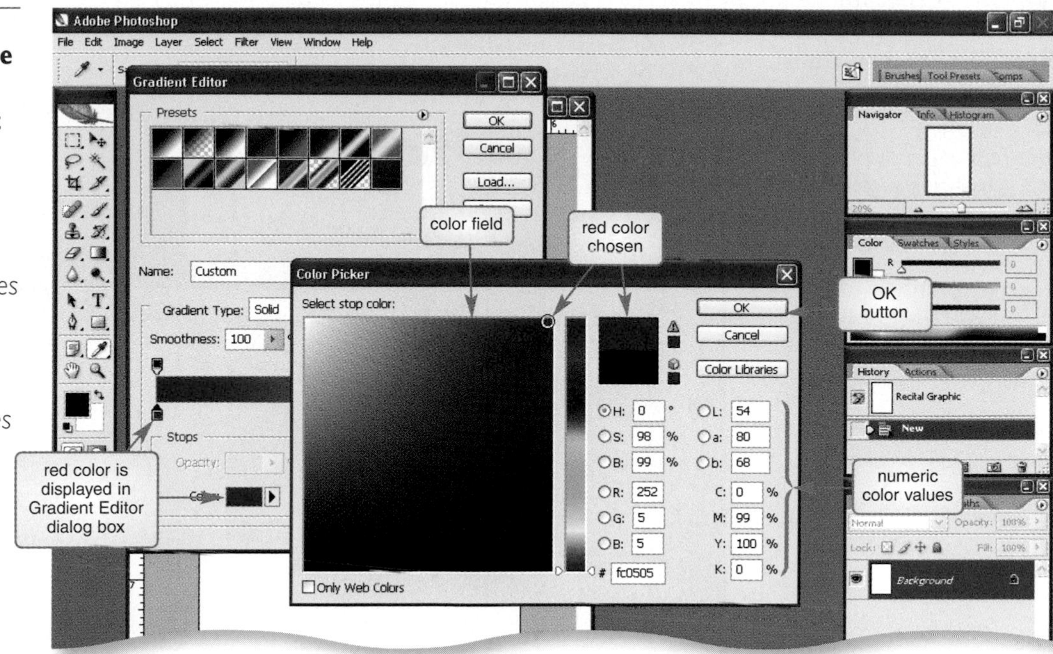

FIGURE 4-12

3

• Click the OK button in the Color Picker dialog box.

The red color displays in the color bar, in the left Color Stop button, and in the Color box (Figure 4-13).

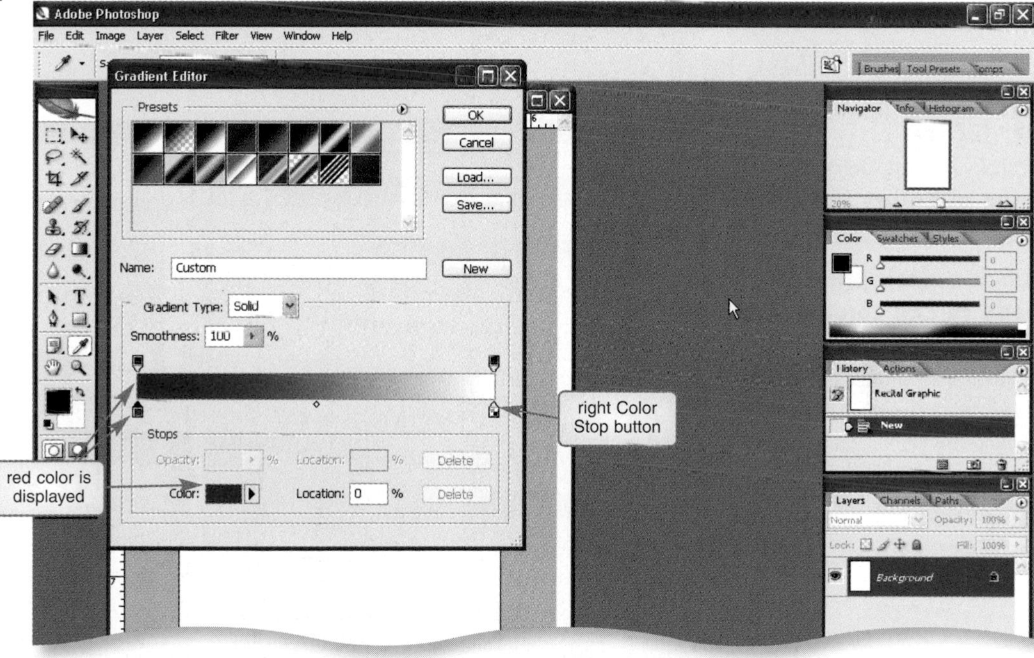

FIGURE 4-13

4

• **Double-click the right Color Stop button.**

Photoshop again displays the Color Picker dialog box (Figure 4-14).

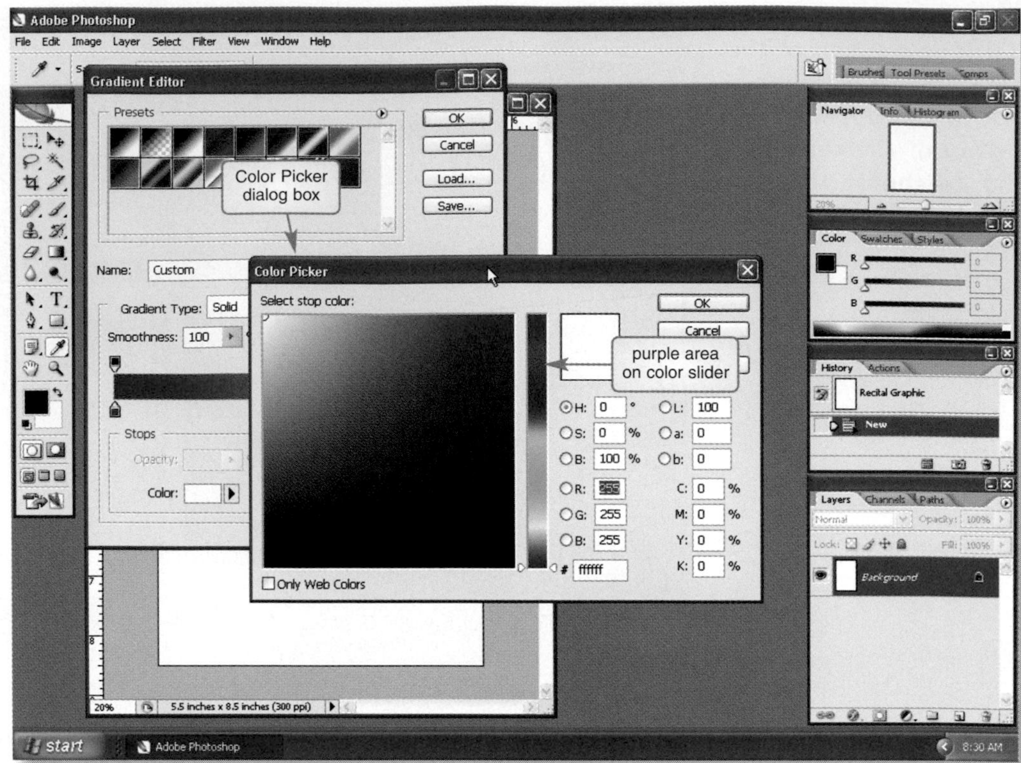

FIGURE 4-14

5

• **Click in the purple range of colors in the color slider.**

• **Click a dark purple shade in the color field.**

The color field changes to display purple colors (Figure 4-15). Locating the purple color may differ slightly depending on your color palette.

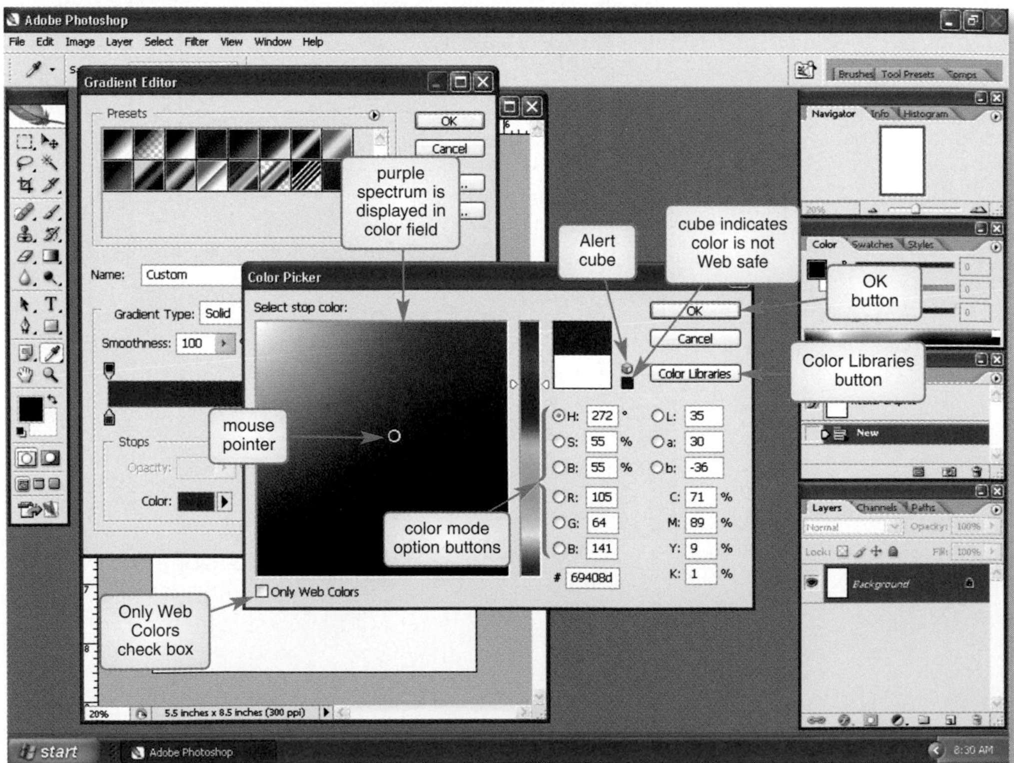

FIGURE 4-15

6

• **Click the OK button in the Color Picker dialog box.**

The color bar displays the gradient (Figure 4-16).

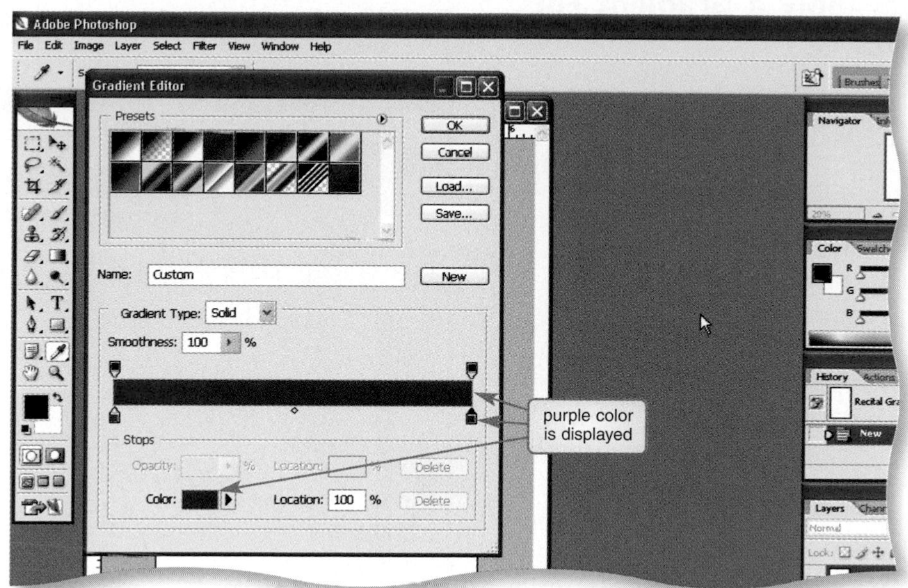

FIGURE 4-16

> **Other Ways**
>
> 1. In Gradient Editor dialog box, click Color box, select color

The Only Web Colors box (Figure 4-15) configures the Color Picker to display only **Web-safe colors** — the 216 colors that display solid, nondithered, and consistently on any computer monitor.

If Photoshop displays an exclamation point inside a triangle in the Color Picker, it means that the chosen color cannot be printed using CMYK inks. A cube displays when the chosen color is not Web safe.

The option buttons next to the color mode values are used to change the color spectrum in the color field and slider.

When you click the Color Libraries button, Photoshop displays a dialog box with other custom color systems, such as **Pantone**, a standard color-matching system used by printers and graphic designers for inks, papers, and other materials. This kind of color matching is performed using actual, printed reference books that provide examples of how each color displays when printed, as opposed to how it appears on the monitor.

Applying the Gradient Fill

In the Recital Graphic image, a gradient will be applied from the upper-right to the lower-left, across the entire image, as shown in the steps on the next page. To apply the gradient, you drag in the image or selected area at the point where you want the base color to begin transitioning into the blend color. The rate of transition is dependent on the settings in the Gradient Editor dialog box with its color stops and midpoint.

To Apply a Gradient Fill

1

- **Click the OK button in the Gradient Editor dialog box.**
- **In the Recital Graphic window, point to the upper-right corner of the image.**

The mouse pointer changes to a small cross (Figure 4-17).

FIGURE 4-17

2

- **Drag down and left to the lower-left corner of the image and then release the mouse button.**

After a few moments, Photoshop displays the gradient (Figure 4-18).

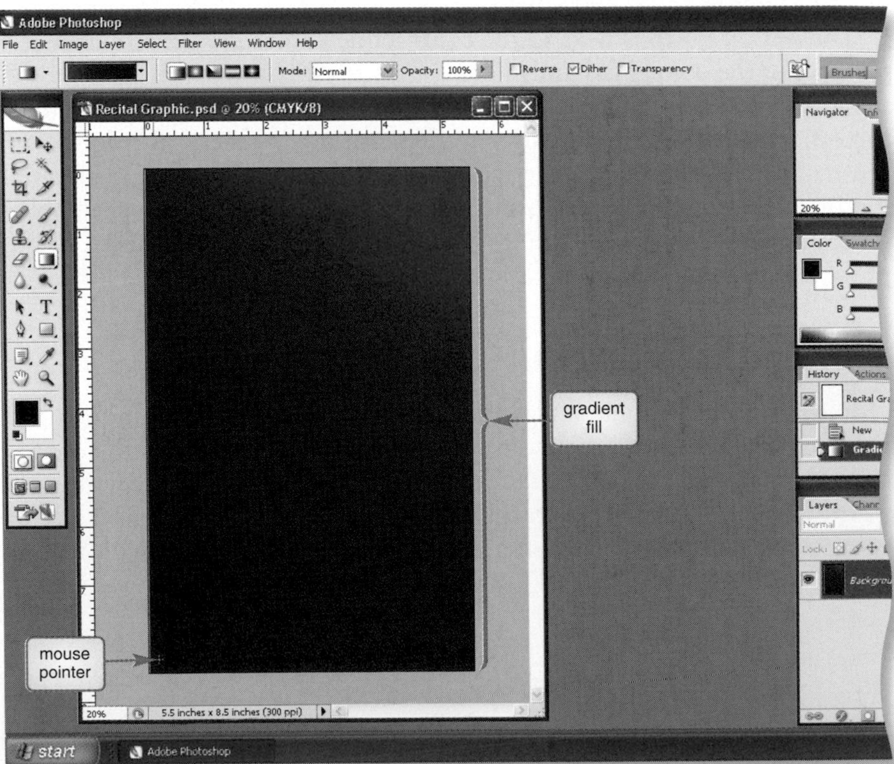

FIGURE 4-18

You can create a gradient at any straight line, angle, or position of an image or selected area. If you start and end in the extreme corners of the frame, the grade is across the entire area. To leave the corners solid and start the grade more toward the center, drag and end closer to the middle of the area. To constrain the line angle to a multiple of 45°, hold down the SHIFT key as you drag.

If you are creating a gradient by using one of the predefined gradient styles, click the Gradient picker button first, select the gradient style, and then drag in the image. When using one of the predefined styles, it is common to drag from the center of the image to one of the corners. Figure 4-19 displays a sample of a radial and a diamond gradient style.

(a) Radial gradient

(b) Diamond gradient

FIGURE 4-19

Now that the background of the Recital Graphic image is complete, the next steps are to add the music and piano graphics.

Creating the Music Graphic

The music graphic is located in a file named, Music, on the CD located in the back of the book. Your instructor may designate a different location for the file. The graphic will become a layer in the Recital Graphic image and then will be warped to add a stylistic flair.

The following steps illustrate how to open the file, Music, from a CD located in drive E.

To Open the Music File

1. **Insert the CD that accompanies this book into your CD drive. After a few seconds, if Windows displays a dialog box, click its Close button.**

2. **In the Photoshop window, click File on the menu bar and then click Open. Navigate to the Project04 folder, and then double-click the file named, Music.**

3 **When Photoshop displays the image in the document window, double-click the magnification box on the document window status bar, type** 20**, and then press the** ENTER **key.**

4 **Drag the window to the lower-right portion of the work area.**

The new window is displayed (Figure 4-20).

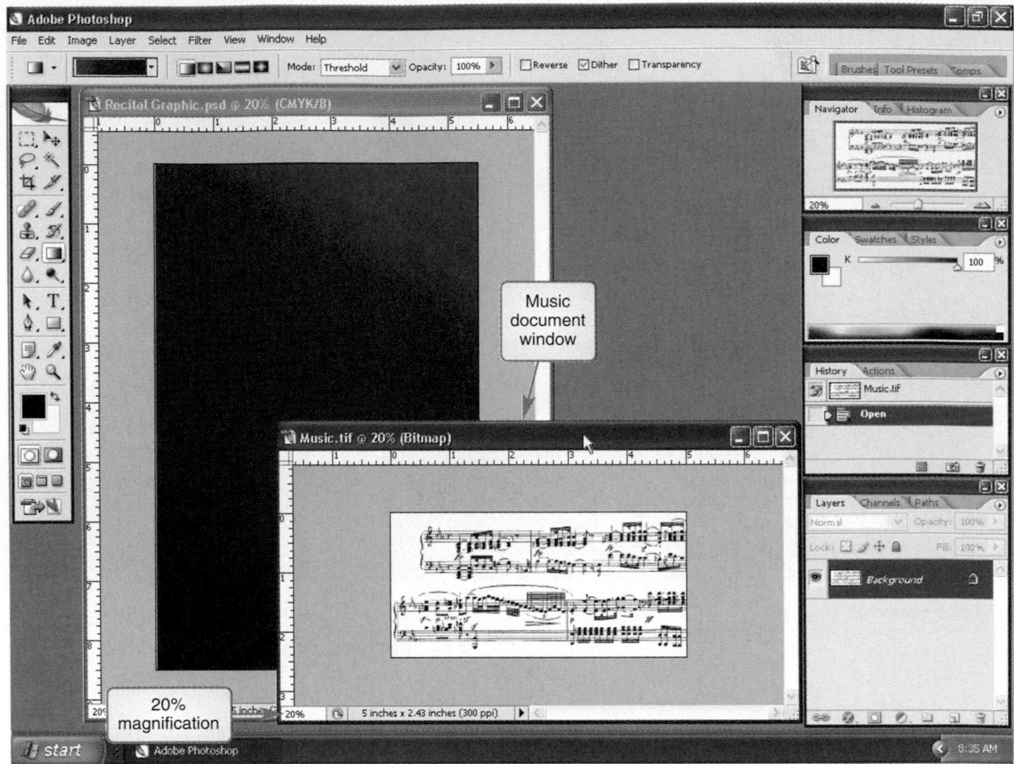

FIGURE 4-20

The next step is to select the music and drag it to the Recital Graphic image to create a layer. The layer will be named music, and the white background will be erased so only the musical notes display in the Recital Graphic image.

To Create a Layer

1 **With the Music window active, press** CTRL+A **to select the entire graphic.**

2 **Click the Move Tool (V) button in the toolbox.**

3 **Drag the selection to the upper portion of the Recital Graphic window.**

4 **Click the Close button on the Music window title bar.**

5 **In the Layers palette, double-click the name, Layer 1, and then type** music **as the name. Press the** ENTER **key to complete the name change.**

6 **Right-click the Eraser tool and then click Magic Eraser Tool on the context menu.**

7 **On the Magic Eraser options bar, if necessary, click the Contiguous check box so it does not display a check mark.**

8 **In the document window, click the white area of the layer.**

The new layer is displayed (Figure 4-21). The music is displayed without the white background.

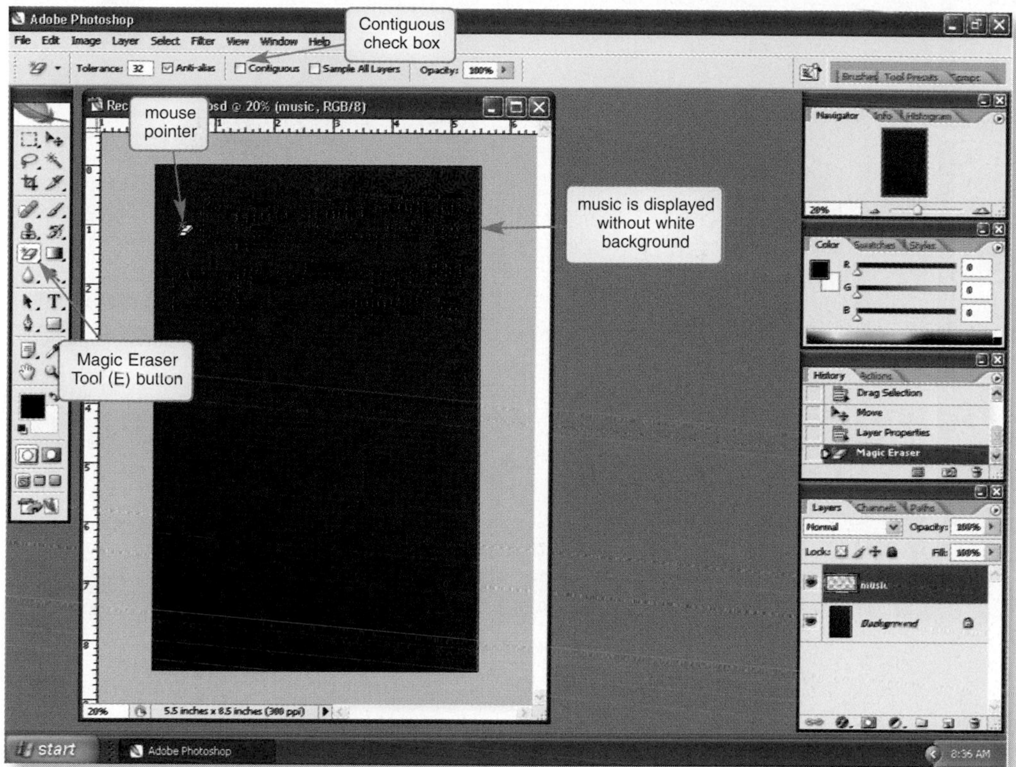

FIGURE 4-21

The following steps show how to warp the layer.

To Warp a Layer

1 **Press CTRL+T to display the transform options bar. On the options bar, click the Switch between free transform and warp modes button.**

2 **When Photoshop displays the warp grid, drag the upper-left sizing handle slightly up and to the left.**

3 **On the top edge of the bounding box, drag the right-center sizing handle slightly down.**

4 **Drag the lower-right sizing handle down to a point approximately halfway down the image, as shown in Figure 4-22.**

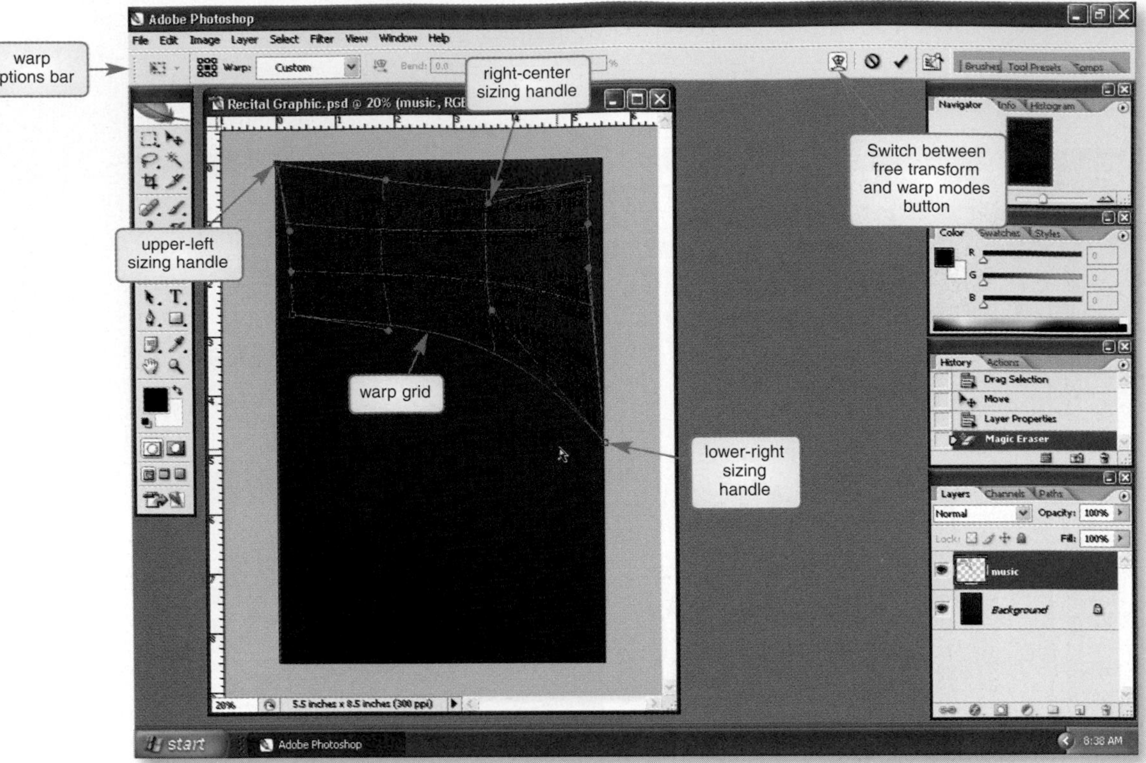

FIGURE 4-22

5 Press the ENTER key to commit the transformation.

Creating the Piano Graphic

The piano graphic is located in a file named, Piano, on the CD located in the back of the book. Your instructor may designate a different location for the file. The graphic will become a layer in the Recital Graphic image.

The following steps illustrate how to open the file, Piano, from a CD located in drive E.

To Open the Piano File

1 Insert the CD that accompanies this book into your CD drive. After a few seconds, if Windows displays a dialog box, click its Close button.

2 In the Photoshop window, click File on the menu bar and then click Open. Navigate to the Project04 folder, and then double-click the file named, Piano.

3 When Photoshop displays the image in the document window, double-click the magnification box on the document window status bar, type 20 **as the entry, and then press the ENTER key.**

4 Drag the window to the upper-right portion of the work area. Resize the Piano document window as necessary.

The new window is displayed (Figure 4-23).

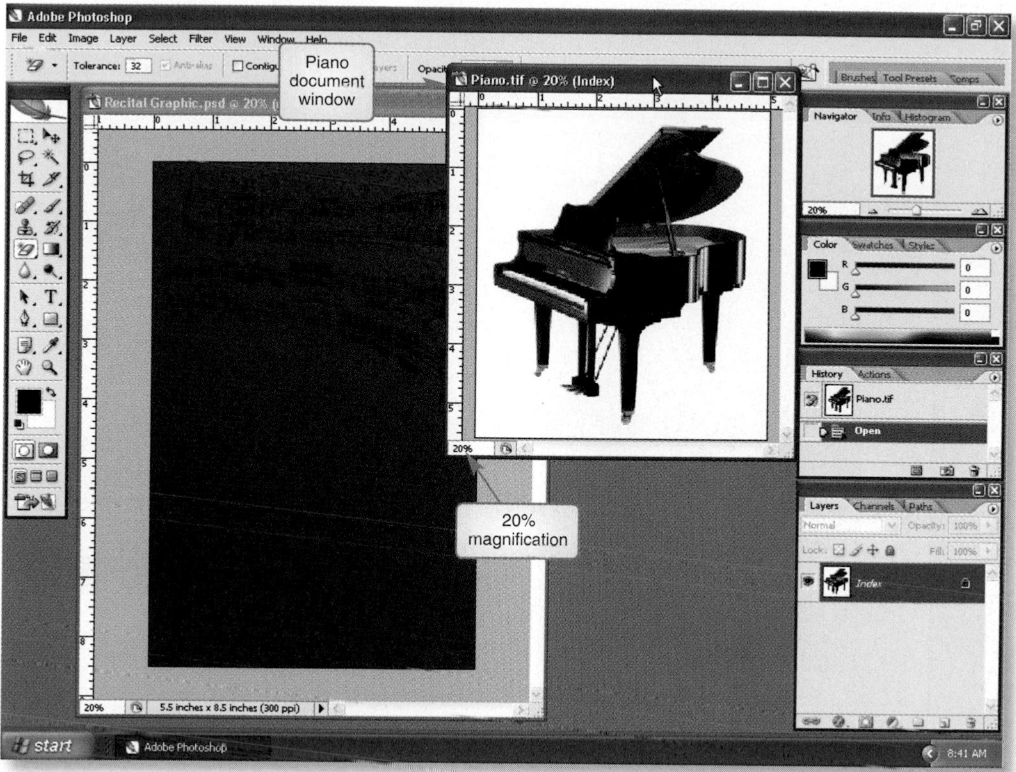

FIGURE 4-23

The next step is to select the piano and drag it to the Recital Graphic image to create a layer. The layer will be named piano, and the white background will be erased so only the piano itself displays in the Recital Graphic.

To Create the Piano Layer

1. **With the Piano window active, press CTRL+A to select the entire graphic.**
2. **Click the Move Tool (V) button in the toolbox.**
3. **Drag the selection to the lower-right portion of the Recital Graphic window. The piano legs should display close to the bottom margin. The body of the piano should display close to the right margin. The piano lid will cover some of the music.**
4. **Click the Close button on the Piano window title bar.**
5. **In the Layers palette, double-click the name, Layer 1, and then type** `piano` **as the name. Press the ENTER key to complete the name change.**
6. **Click the Magic Eraser tool.**
7. **On the Magic Eraser options bar, click the Contiguous check box so it displays a check mark.**
8. **In the document window, click each white area in the layer. Do not click the white keys on the keyboard.**

The new layer is displayed (Figure 4-24). The piano is displayed without the white background.

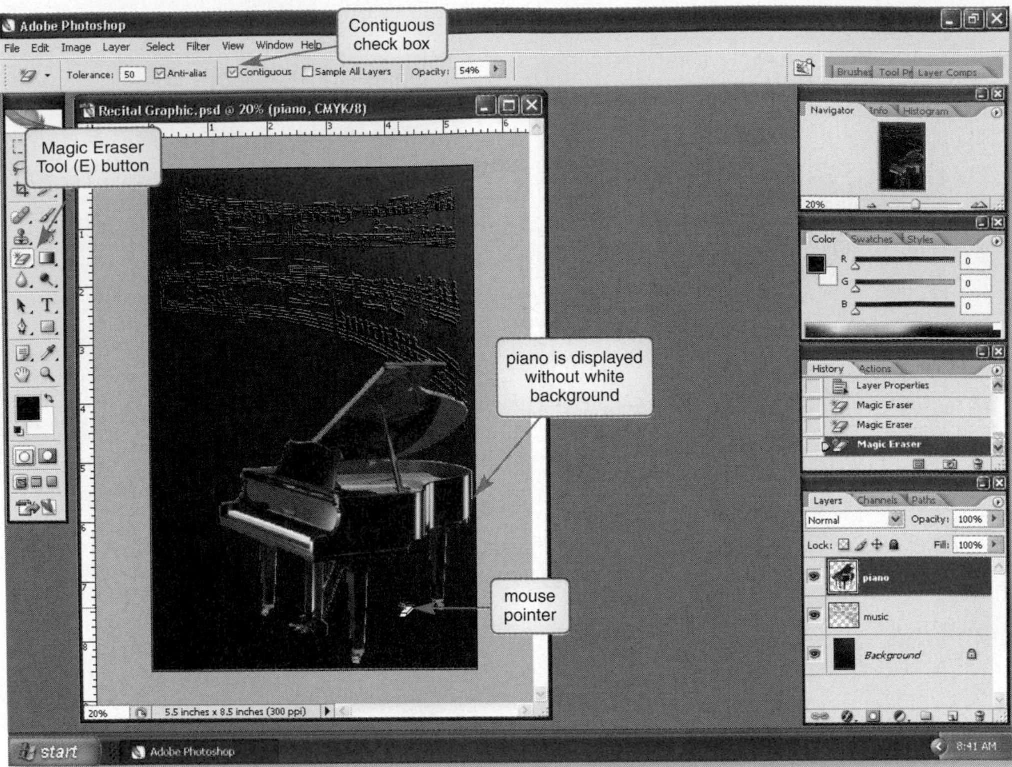

FIGURE 4-24

With the layers complete, it is time to select colors and use some of the pen and brush tools to add graphic effects.

Selecting Colors

Photoshop has many different ways to select or specify colors for use in the document window. You specify colors when you use paint, gradient, or fill tools. Previously in this chapter you used the Color Picker to choose colors. Some other ways include using the Color palette, the Swatches palette, the Eyedropper tool, the Color Sampler tool, and the Info palette.

The Color Palette

A convenient way to select and edit colors is to use the **Color palette** (Figure 4-25), usually docked below the Navigation palette in the workspace.

The Color palette contains icons, sliders, boxes, and a color ramp. The square color icons to the left of the sliders allow you to toggle between foreground and background colors. Using sliders in the Color palette, you can edit the colors using different color modes. Other color modes may be chosen from the palette menu. If you know the color mode values of the desired colors, they can be entered in the associated boxes. Clicking in the color ramp automatically sets the current foreground or background color.

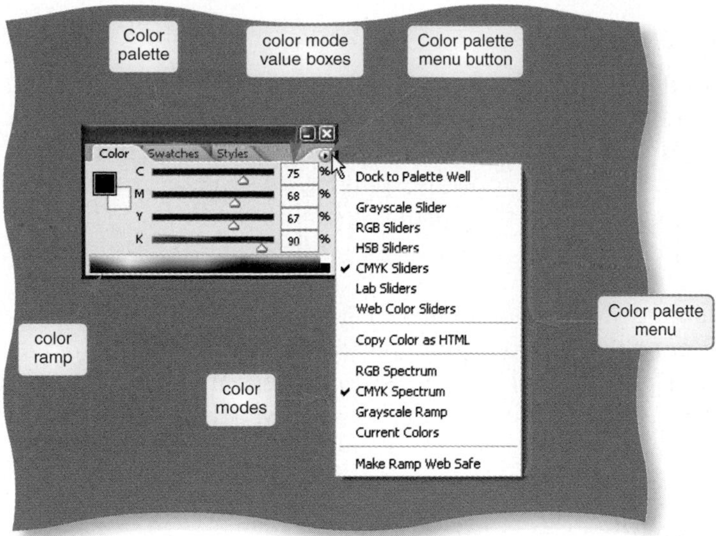

FIGURE 4-25

The following step shows how to select a color by choosing CMYK sliders in the Color palette to enter color values.

To Use the Color Palette

1

- **Click the Color palette menu button and then click CMYK sliders in the list.**
- **In the Color palette, type** 5 **in the C box, type** 0 **in the M box, type** 60 **in the Y, and type** 0 **in the K box.**

The new yellow color is displayed in the foreground square on the Color palette and in the toolbox (Figure 4-26).

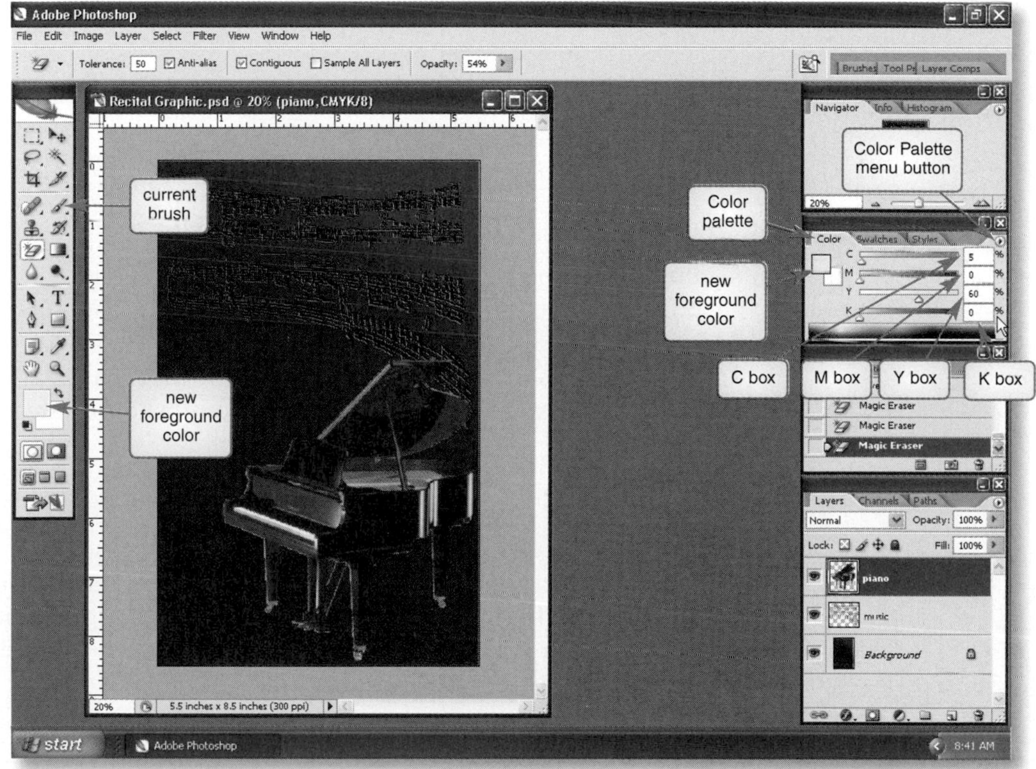

FIGURE 4-26

Painting

The **painting tools** change the color of pixels in an image. As you have seen, the Gradient tool and the Fill command are used to color large areas with color. In the following sections you will learn that the Brush tool, the Pencil tool, and the Pen tool work like traditional drawing tools by applying color with brush strokes. The Blur tool and Smudge tool modify the existing colors in the image. The Paint Bucket tool can apply color to large areas. Almost every tool in Photoshop is affected by color in some way.

By specifying how each tool applies or modifies the color, you can create an endless number of possibilities. You can apply color gradually, with soft or hard edges, with small or large brush strokes, with various brush dynamics and blending properties, as well as by using brushes of different shapes. You even can simulate spraying paint with an airbrush.

The Brush Tool

The **Brush tool** paints the current foreground color on an image with strokes of color as you drag. When you click the Brush Tool (B) button in the toolbox, the **Brush options bar** is displayed (Figure 4-27).

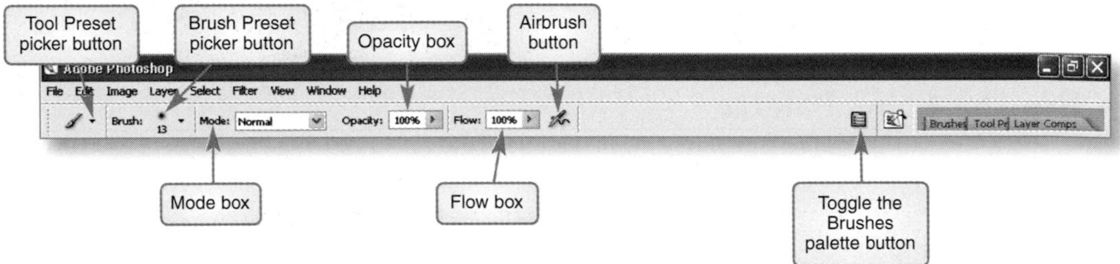

FIGURE 4-27 Brush options bar

When you click the Tool Preset picker button, Photoshop displays a list of recently used brush tip settings. The Brush Presets picker button displays the current set of brush tips and settings such as brush size and hardness. As with other tools, the Mode box arrow displays Brush blending modes when clicked, and the Opacity box allows you to specify the degree of transparency. Entering a value in the Flow box specifies how quickly the paint is applied. A lower number applies paint more slowly. The Airbrush button enables airbrush capabilities. On the right side of the options bar is a button to show/hide the Brushes palette.

Using the Brush Preset Picker

You will use the **Brush Preset picker** to choose a brush stroke with a diameter of 50 pixels to draw the Roman numeral in the graphic. Photoshop uses a percentage value, called **hardness**, to denote how solid the edge of the brush stroke is displayed. The brush stroke for the Roman numeral will have a hardness level of 100 percent. The following step illustrates how to use the Brush Preset picker.

To Use the Brush Preset Picker

1

- **Press the B key to access the brush tools. If necessary, right-click the current brush button and then click Brush Tool in the list.**
- **On the Brush options bar, click the Brush Preset picker button.**
- **Drag the Master Diameter slider to 50.**
- **Drag the Hardness slider to 100.**

The new settings are displayed in the Brush Preset picker (Figure 4-28).

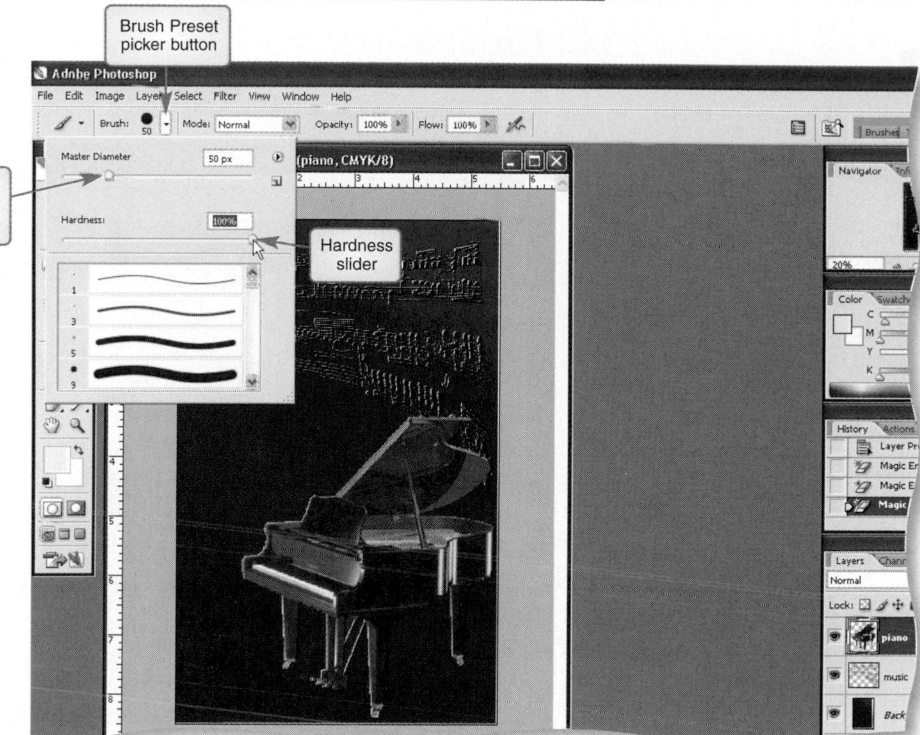

FIGURE 4-28

Once you choose a diameter and hardness setting, and later a brush tip, the Brush Preset picker button displays an icon with a visual representation of the brush (Figure 4-28). As you draw with the Brush tool in the next series of steps, the strokes will display with those settings in the selected foreground color.

Drawing Straight Lines with the Brush Tool

You will use the Brush tool to draw the Roman numeral IV in the lower-left corner of the Recital Graphic image to indicate the fourth concert in the recital series. Pressing the SHIFT key while dragging with a brush, creates straight brush strokes. SHIFT+clicking in the document window connects the brush stroke color from one place to another.

The following steps show how first to drag two ruler guides to help you position the Roman numeral, and then drag to create the brush strokes. Remember that if you make a mistake while creating the brush strokes, you can click Undo on the Edit menu, press CTRL+Z to undo, or click a previous state in the History palette, and then begin again.

To Draw Straight Lines with the Brush Tool

1

- **In the Layers palette, click the Background layer.**
- **In the document window, drag from the horizontal ruler down to the 6.5 inch mark on the vertical ruler.**
- **Drag from the horizontal ruler again, to the 7.5 inch mark on the vertical ruler.**

Two ruler guides are displayed (Figure 4-29).

FIGURE 4-29

2

- **To create the I of the Roman numeral, with the Brush tool still selected, SHIFT+drag close to the left side of the document window, beginning at the upper ruler guide and ending at the lower ruler guide.**

The Brush tool creates a straight, yellow brush stroke (Figure 4-30).

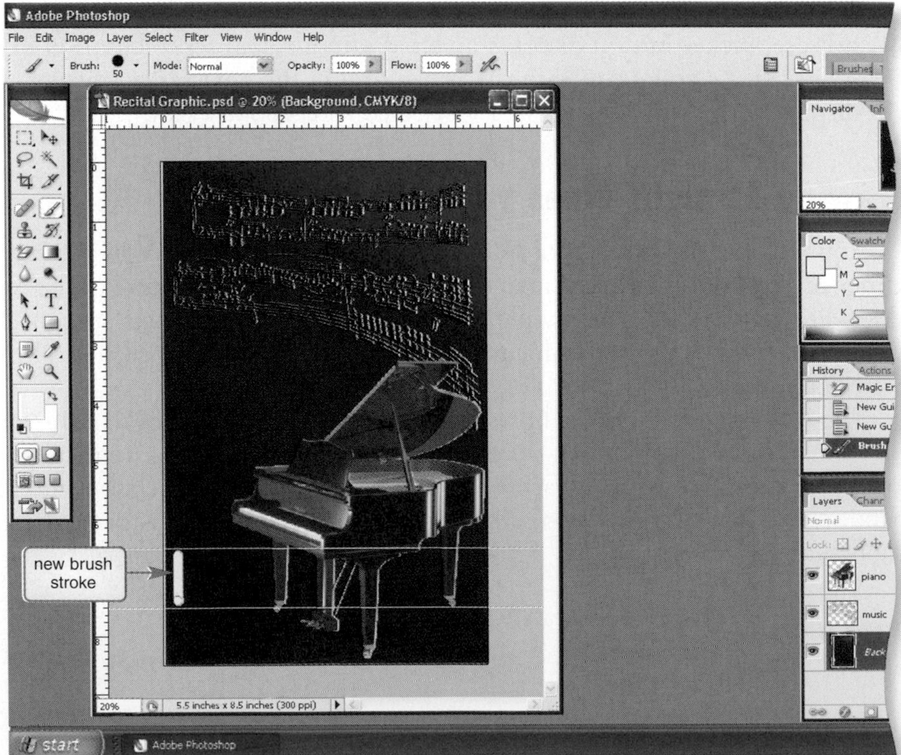

FIGURE 4-30

3

- **To position the upper-left corner of the Roman numeral V, move the mouse close to the upper ruler guide and just to the right of the previous brush stroke.**
- **Click the document window.**

A single circle of color is displayed (Figure 4-31).

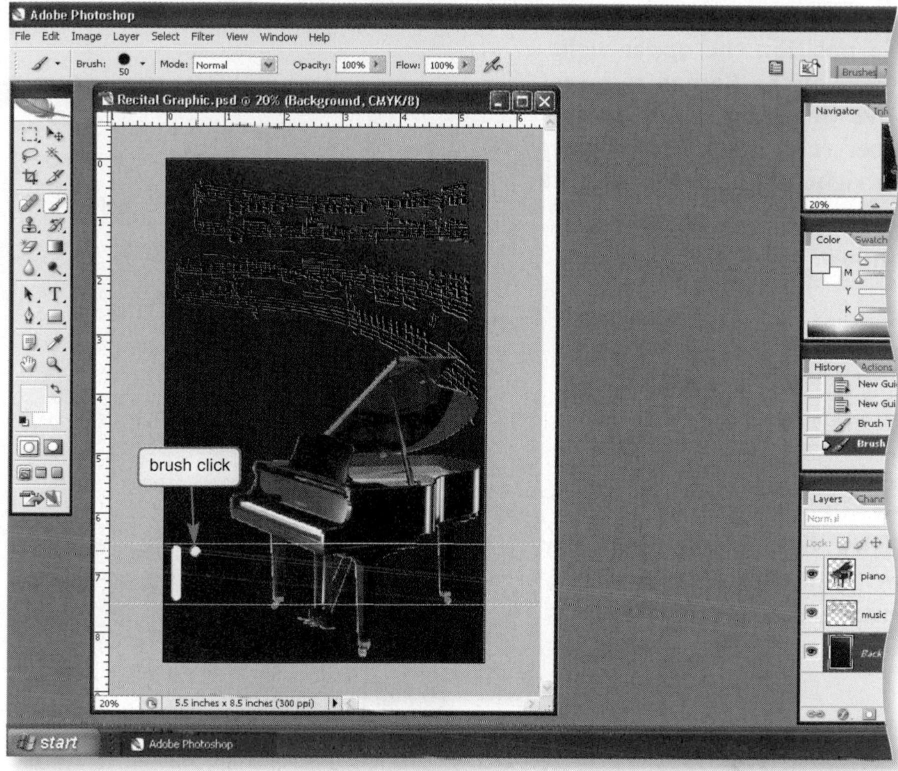

FIGURE 4-31

4

- **To position the bottom of the Roman numeral V, move the mouse down and slightly to the right of the previous click, just above the lower ruler guide.**
- **SHIFT+click the document window.**

Photoshop creates a stroke of color from the location of the previous click to the current location (Figure 4-32). Your stroke does not have to match exactly.

FIGURE 4-32

5

- **To position the upper-right corner of the Roman numeral V, move the mouse close to the upper ruler guide and slightly to the right of the previous click.**
- **SHIFT+click the document window.**

Photoshop creates a stroke of color from the location of the previous click to the current location (Figure 4-33). Your brush strokes do not have to match exactly.

- **Click View on the menu bar, and then click Clear Guides to remove the ruler guides.**

FIGURE 4-33

Dragging, without using the SHIFT key, creates strokes of color that may include corners, curves, and arcs. Graphic designers who create a lot of free-hand brush strokes sometimes use a **graphics tablet**, which is an input device that uses a stylus, or specialized mouse, to draw on a tablet surface. The drawing strokes display on the computer monitor.

Accessed from the Brush tool's context menu, the Pencil and Color Replacement tools are closely related to the Brush tool. The only difference between the Pencil and Brush tools is that the Brush tool paints with an anti-aliased or smooth edge, and the **Pencil tool** draws with an aliased or rough edge. The **Color Replacement tool** replaces specific colors when you paint over a targeted color with a corrective color. The Color Replacement tool does not work with Bitmap or Indexed color modes.

The Eyedropper Tool

The **Eyedropper tool** samples color in a graphic or palette to assign a new foreground or background color. The Eyedropper options bar (Figure 4-34) allows you to change the size of the area that you sample. The Sample Size box arrow contains three choices. The default size, Point Sample, samples the precise color of the pixel you click. The other two samples sizes, 3 by 3 Average and 5 by 5 Average, sample the color of the pixel and its surrounding pixels, calculating an average color value of the area.

Photoshop uses the **foreground color** to paint and fill selections and create text. The **background color** commonly is used with fills and masks. The foreground and background colors also are used by some special effects filters.

Using the Eyedropper Tool

In the Recital Graphic image, you will sample the gold color inside of the piano in preparation for using it to create further graphic effects. The following steps show how to click the Eyedropper Tool (I) button in the toolbox and sample the color. Clicking the color assigns it to the foreground color. Pressing ALT+click assigns the color to the background.

To Select a Color Using the Eyedropper Tool

1

- **Press the I key to access the Eyedropper tool. If necessary, right-click the current color sample tool, and then click Eyedropper Tool in the list.**
- **Move the mouse to a position inside the piano string assembly.**

The mouse pointer becomes an eyedropper (Figure 4-34). Photoshop displays the Eyedropper options bar.

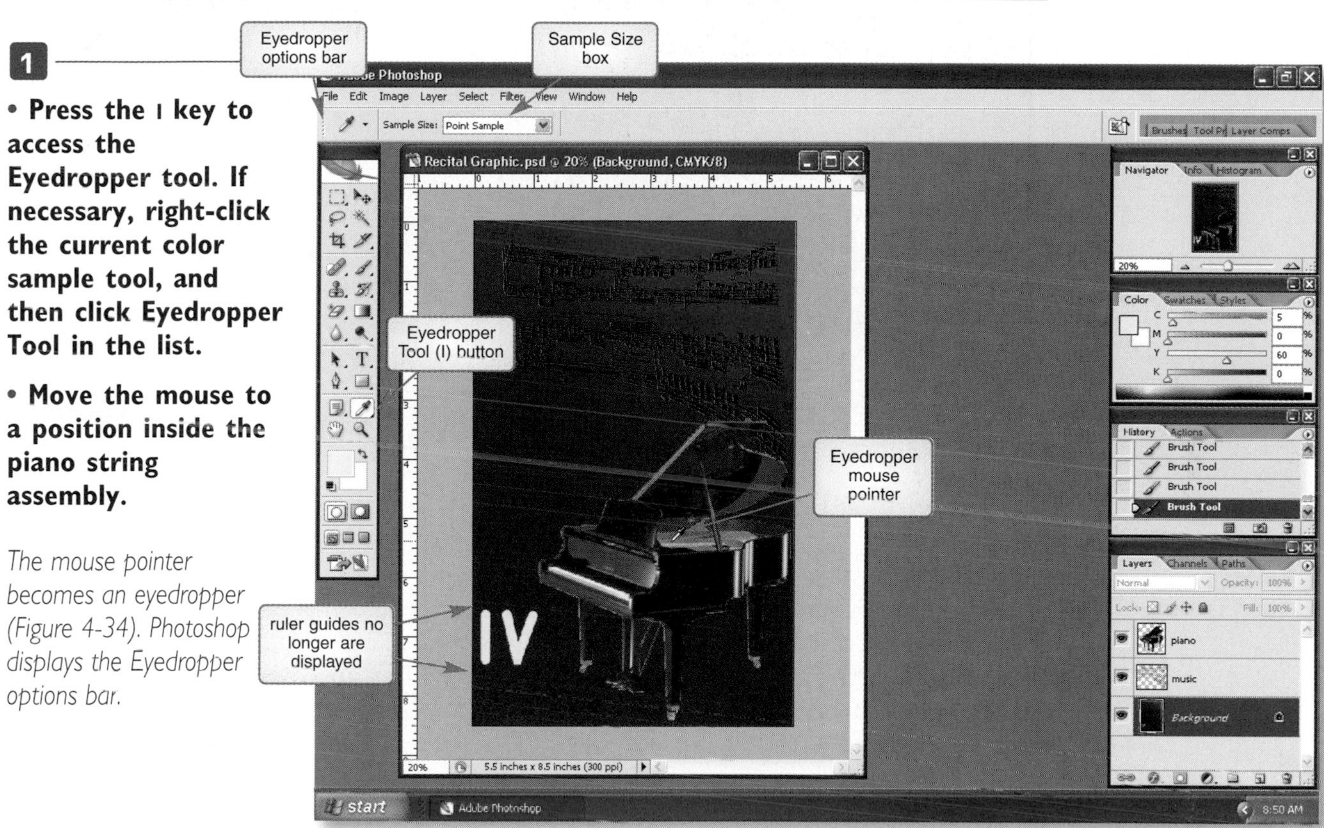

FIGURE 4-34

2

• Position the tip of the eyedropper on a gold color in the string assembly and then click.

The foreground color is changed in the toolbox and in the Color palette (Figure 4-35).

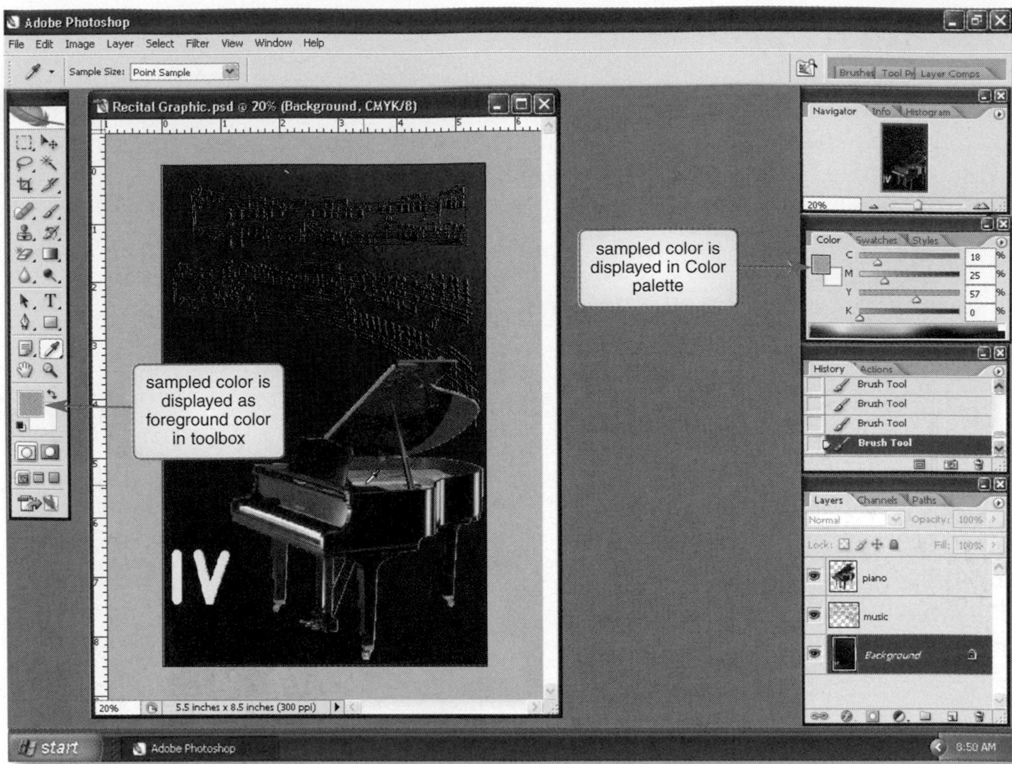

FIGURE 4-35

If you right-click the Eyedropper Tool (I) button, you can choose the Color Sampler Tool (I) button. Clicking with the **Color Sampler tool** will display the color mode values in the Info palette. You can click to select up to four color samples per image. Figure 4-36 shows a color sample from the Recital Graphic image and the values in the Info palette.

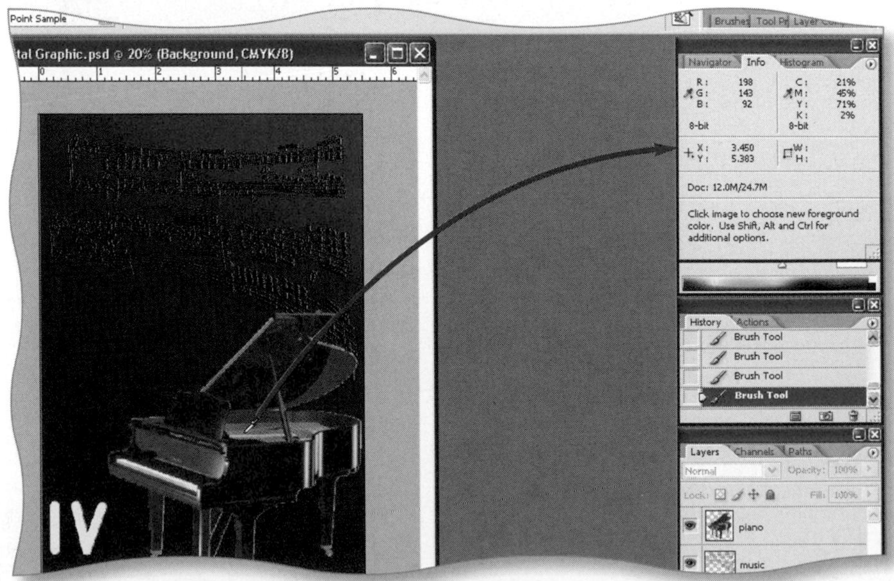

FIGURE 4-36

The Info Palette

The Info palette (Figure 4-36) displays information about the color values beneath the mouse pointer and other useful information depending on the tool that you use. For example, the Info palette can tell you if the color you are using will not print in certain color modes. To view the Info palette, click the tab in the palette well, or press the F8 key on the keyboard.

Table 4-4 displays some of the ways to use the Info palette with various tools, color modes, and commands.

Table 4-4 Info Palette Displays

TOOLS	INFO PALETTE
CMYK color mode	displays an exclamation point next to the CMYK values if the color is out of the printable CMYK color gamut
Color Adjustment dialog box	displays before-and-after color values for the pixels beneath the pointer and beneath color samplers
Color Sampler tool	displays up to four color mode values, and the X and Y coordinates of the mouse pointer position
Crop tool or Zoom tool	displays the width and height of the angle of rotation of the crop marquee
Eyedropper tool	displays information about the color underneath the mouse pointer and its X and Y position
Line tool, Pen tool, or Gradient tool	displays the X and Y coordinates of the starting position, the change in those coordinates, the angle, and the distance as the mouse pointer is moved
Marquee tool	palette displays the X and Y coordinates of the pointer position and the width and height of the marquee
Show Tool Hints option	displays hints for using the tool selected in the toolbox

When you click the Info palette menu button, Photoshop displays a list containing palette options to change the order of color readouts and the unit of measurement.

The next series of steps uses the previously chosen eyedropper color with a brush tip chosen from the Brushes palette to create star shapes coming out of the piano.

The Brushes Palette

The **Brushes palette** (Figure 4-37) contains numerous options for setting brush presets, brush tips, and painting characteristics. When you click the Brushes palette menu button, Photoshop displays a list of available commands, thumbnail sizes, and sets of brushes that can replace or be appended to the current list.

More About

Brushes

Many vendors provide brush packages that can be purchased and used as plug-in files with Photoshop. This opens up the possibility of loading an endless number of specialized brushes to the program. You can purchase brushes that simulate everything from fabric rips to tree limbs. For more information on vendor brush packages, visit the Shelly Cashman Photoshop CS2 Web site.

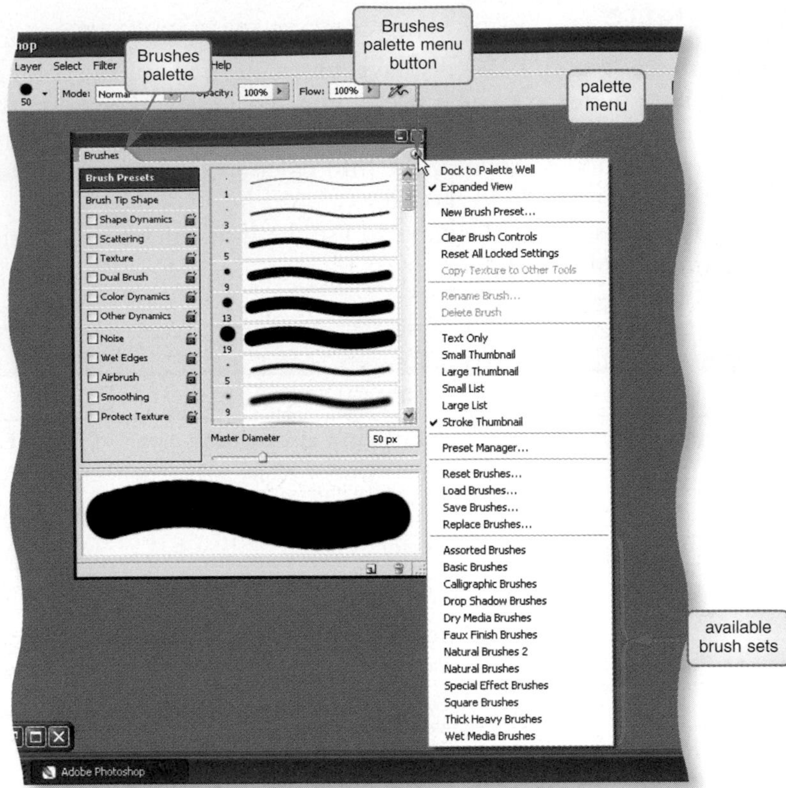

FIGURE 4-37

To customize your brush strokes, you may choose a brush preset and specify the diameter as illustrated in the following steps.

To Use the Brushes Palette

1

- **Press the B key to access the Brush tool. If necessary, right-click the current tool and then click Brush Tool in the list. On the Brush options bar, click the Toggle the Brushes palette button.**

Photoshop displays the Brushes palette (Figure 4-38).

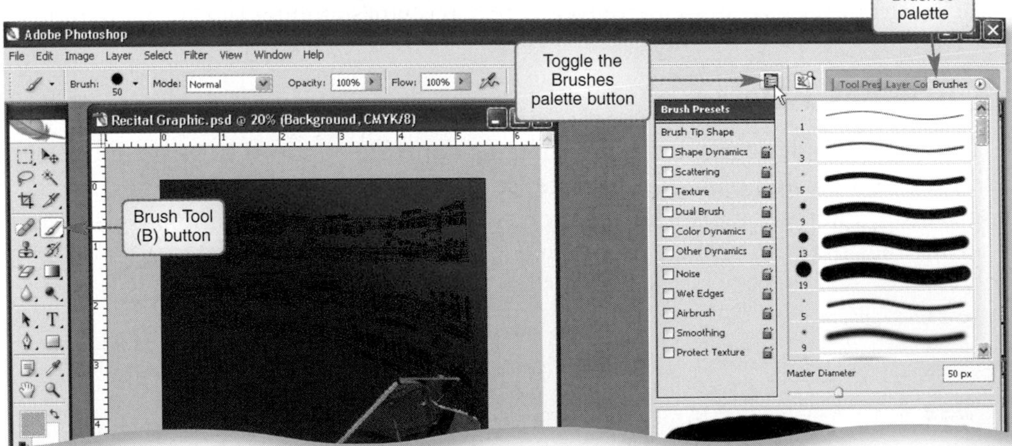

FIGURE 4-38

2

- **If necessary, click the Brush Presets button.**
- **Scroll down in the list and click the Flowing Stars preset.**

The Brushes palette displays a preview of the brush stroke (Figure 4-39).

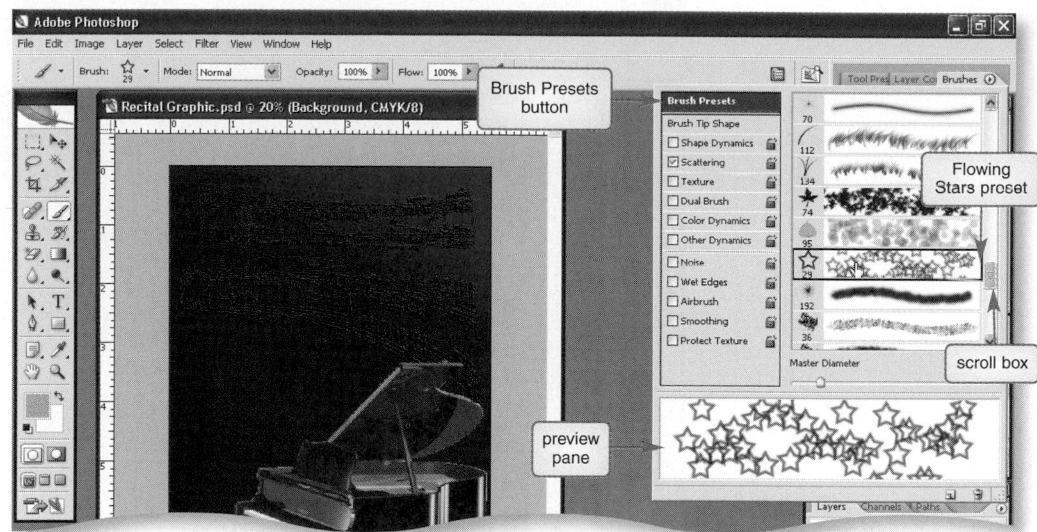

FIGURE 4-39

3

- **Drag the Master Diameter slider to 60.**

The Brush Preset picker button on the options bar displays a visual representation of the brush (Figure 4-40).

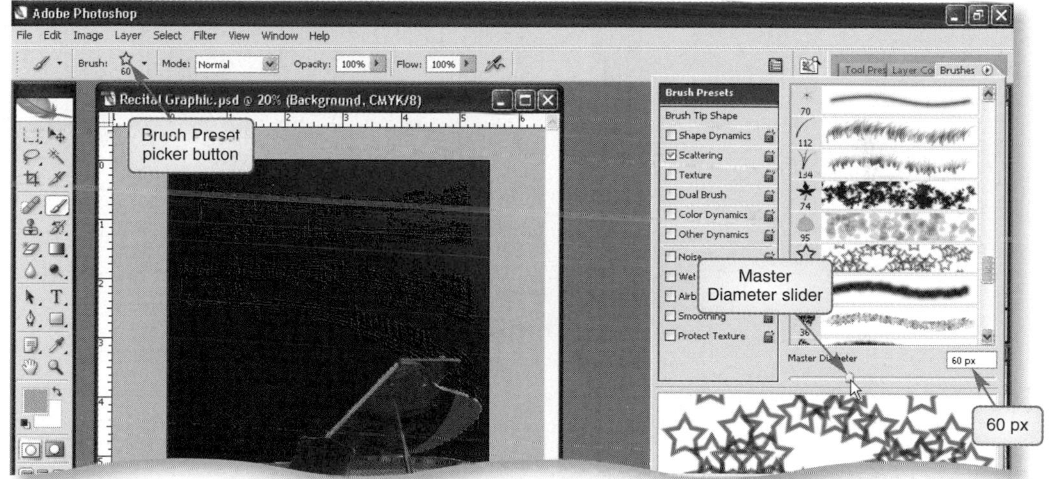

FIGURE 4-40

Other Ways

1. Click Brushes palette tab in palette well, choose settings
2. On Window menu, click Brushes, choose settings
3. Press F5 key, choose settings

You will learn about brush tip shapes and dynamics that allow you to customize your brush strokes later in this project.

After choosing a color and brush preset, the next step draws the stars coming out of the piano. While creating the stars, if you make a mistake, click the previous state in the History palette or press CTRL+Z.

To Use the Brush Tool with a Flowing Star Stroke

1 **In the Layers palette, click the piano layer.**

2 **Using short strokes, drag short curved lines from the inside of the piano, up and over the music stand. Click to make individual stars. Double-click to make some stars brighter.**

3 **Continue the stars up toward the music graphic and the left side of the document window, as shown in Figure 4-41.**

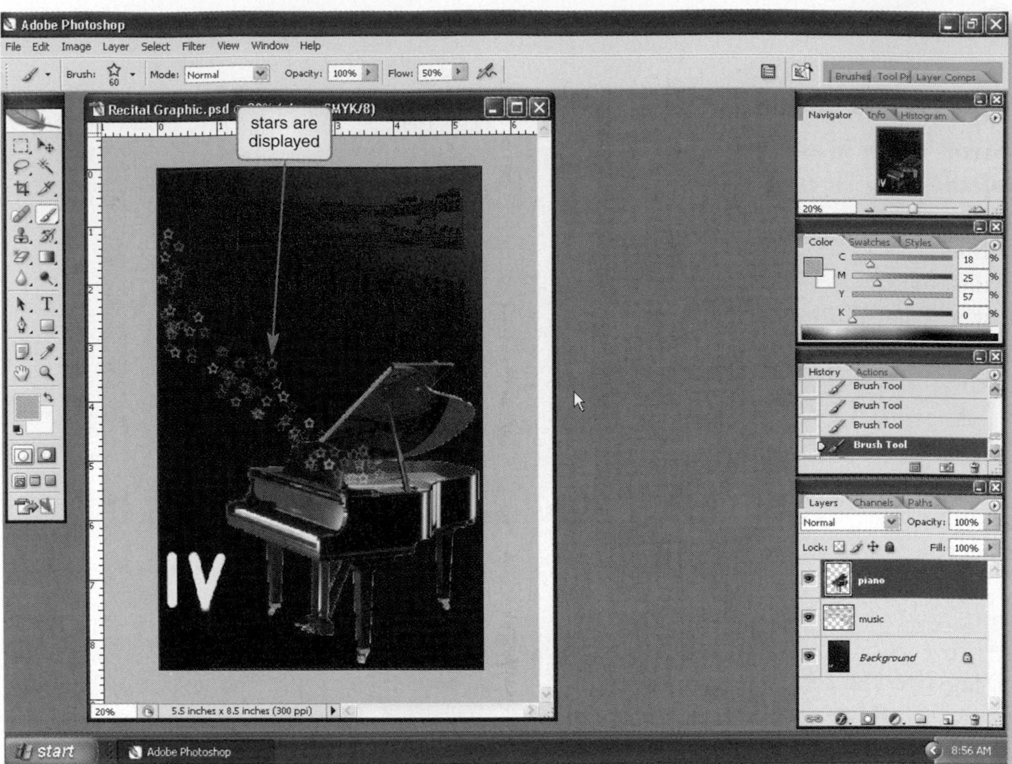

FIGURE 4-41

With the stars complete, it is a good time to save the file again.

To Save Changes to the File

1 **Press CTRL+S.**

> **More About**
>
> **Removing Color Casts**
>
> A color cast is a shade in a photo that should not exist. For example, a photo of green grass should not have a red color cast. You can remove a color cast using the Match Color dialog box. Click the Neutralize check box and then drag the sliders until the preview displays no color cast.

Other Color Commands

Photoshop has many other commands related to color, blending, and tonal adjustments, many of which are available by pointing to Adjustments on the Image menu. For example, the **Auto Color** command adjusts the contrast and color of an image or layer by neutralizing the midtones and clipping the black and white pixels. The **Color Balance** command, displays a dialog box where you can set specific color levels and balance tones. The **Match Color** command matches colors between multiple images, layers, or selections, allowing you to change the luminance, change the color range, or neutralize a color cast. The Match Color command works only in RGB mode. The **Replace Color** command displays a dialog box to change colors by setting the hue, saturation, and lightness of the selected areas. It also allows you to remove fuzziness. In later projects, you will learn more about these commands as you fix and adjust images.

Shapes

One of the more creative uses for Photoshop is creating shapes. A **shape** is a specific figure or form that can be drawn or inserted into an image. A shape is usually a **vector object**, which means it does not lose its crisp appearance if it is resized or reshaped cleanly. A vector shape is made up of lines and curves defined by mathematical vectors or formulas. Photoshop provides six standard shapes, a variety of custom shapes, or the ability to create new shapes using a path. A path is a special kind of vector shape that you will learn about in a later project.

FIGURE 4-42

A shape also can be a **raster object**, which is composed of a fixed number of individual pixels and cannot be resized or reshaped. An advantage of a rasterized shape is that it occupies a smaller file size. A disadvantage is that the object is resolution-dependent because it is bitmapped or pixel-based. The edges of a raster object may not be as smooth as a vector object. A filled selection is an example of a rasterized shape.

Figure 4-42 displays the difference between a vector circle and a raster circle.

To access the **shapes options bar** (Figure 4-43), you click either one of the pen tools or one of the shape tools such as the Rectangle tool or the Ellipse tool.

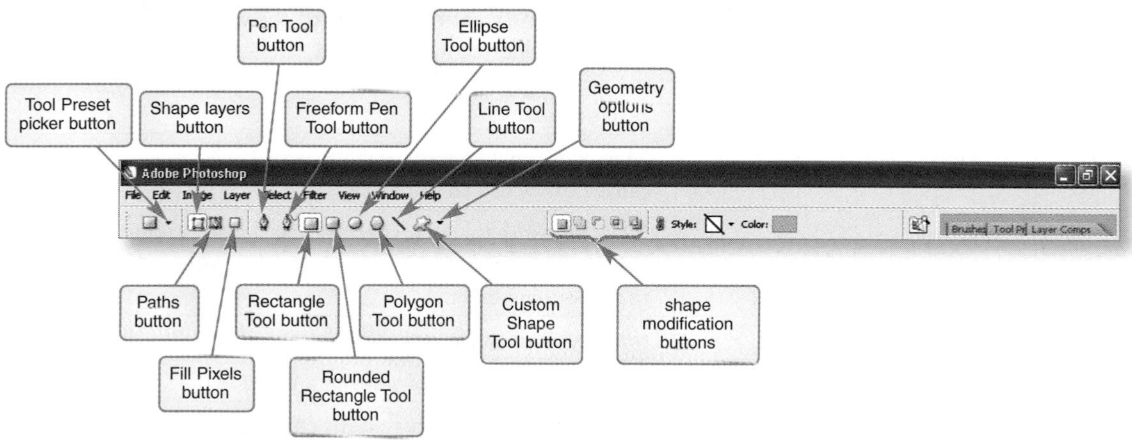

FIGURE 4-43

The Pen tool, the Freeform Pen tool, and each of the six standard shapes on the shapes options bar has special settings available by clicking the Geometry options button. Table 4-5 displays the options, the tool with which they are associated, and a description of their functions.

Table 4-5 Shape Options

OPTIONS	TOOL	DESCRIPTION
Arrowheads, Width, Length, Concavity	Line	adds arrowheads to a line, specifies the proportions of the arrowhead as a percentage of the line width, specifies concavity value defining the amount of curvature on the widest part of the arrowhead
Circle	Ellipse	constrains to a circle
Curve Fit	Freeform Pen	controls how sensitive the final path is to the movement of your mouse or stylus based on a value between 0.5 and 10.0 pixels — a higher value creates a simpler path with fewer anchor points
Define Proportions	Rectangle, Rounded Rectangle, Ellipses, Custom Shape	renders proportional shape based on the values you enter in the W (width) and H (height) boxes
Defined Size	Custom Shape	renders a custom shape based on the size at which it was created
Fixed Size	Rectangle, Rounded Rectangle, Ellipses, Custom Shape	renders a fixed size based on the values you enter in the W (width) and H (height) text boxes
From Center	Rectangle, Rounded Rectangle, Ellipses Custom Shape	renders the shape from the center
Magnetic	Freeform Pen	lets you draw a path that snaps to the edges of defined areas, allowing you to define the range and sensitivity of the snapping behavior, as well as the complexity of the resulting path
Pen Pressure	Freeform Pen	when working with a stylus tablet, an increase in pen pressure causes the width to decrease
Radius	Polygon	for rounded rectangles, specifies the corner radius; for polygons, specifies the distance from the center of a polygon to the outer points
Rubber band	Pen	previews path segments as you draw
Sides	Polygon	specifies the number of sides in a polygon
Smooth Corners or Smooth Indents	Polygon	renders the shape with smooth corners or indents
Snap to Pixels	Rectangle	snaps edges of a rectangle or rounded rectangle to the pixel boundaries
Square	Rectangle, Rounded Rectangle	constrains a rectangle to square
Star	Polygon	creates a star from the specified radius — a 50% setting creates points that are half the total radius of the star; a larger value creates sharper, thinner points; a smaller value creates fuller points
Unconstrained	Rectangle, Rounded Rectangle, Ellipses, Custom Shape	does not constrain shapes

An alternative to using the pen or shape tools is to create a selection with one of the marquee tools and then fill it with color. Filled selections are drawn on the selected layer as raster objects.

Shape Modes

If you decide to use a shape tool in Photoshop, you can draw in one of three different **shape modes**: shape layers, paths, and fill pixels. You choose a mode by clicking the appropriate button on the options bar when you have a shape or pen tool selected (Figure 4-43 on page PS 237).

A **shape layer** is a vector object that occupies its own layer. Because shape layers are easily moved, resized, aligned, and distributed, they are useful for creating Web graphics. In Photoshop, you can choose to draw multiple shapes on a layer. A shape layer consists of a fill layer that defines the shape color and a linked vector mask that defines the shape outline.

A **path**, or work path, is an outline that you can turn into a shape, selection, or fill, and stroke with color. You change the shape of a path by editing its anchor points. A work path is temporary unless you save it. Paths appear in the Paths palette that you will learn about later in this project.

The **Fill Pixels button** paints directly on a layer, as other painting tools do; but it does not create a vector graphic. You paint and work with shapes, just as you do with any raster image. You can fill pixels with any of the shape tools but not with the Pen or Freeform Pen tools.

> *More About*
> **Resizing Shapes**
> If you create a shape and later decide it should be larger or smaller, simply press CTRL+T to display the shape's bounding box. Resize the shape by dragging the sizing handles and then press the ENTER key.

> *More About*
> **The Polygon Shape**
> When you select the Polygon tool, you can decide how many sides it should have. For example, to create a triangle, enter 3 in the Sides box on the options bar. If you click the Geometry options button, you can change the polygon to a star. The number of sides then becomes the number of points on the star.

Creating Shapes

In order to gain experience using the different ways that Photoshop creates shapes, the following sections create the musical notes using shapes in three different ways. Each note will be drawn on its own layer.

- **Elliptical Marquee with Paint Bucket** After creating a new layer, the first note will be drawn using the Swatches palette, the Elliptical Marquee tool, and the Paint Bucket tool.
- **Ellipses Tool with Shape Layer** The second note will be created using the Ellipses Tool in shape layer mode.
- **Pen Tool with Path** The third note will be created using the Pen tool in path mode, and then filling the path with the foreground color.

Finally to draw the stems, you will use the Line tool. The eighth-note flag will be drawn using a brush tip shape from the set of Special Effects Brushes.

The Swatches Palette

The **Swatches palette** stores frequently used colors for use with various Photoshop tools (Figure 4-44). To view the Swatches palette, click the tab in the palette well or click Swatches on the Window menu.

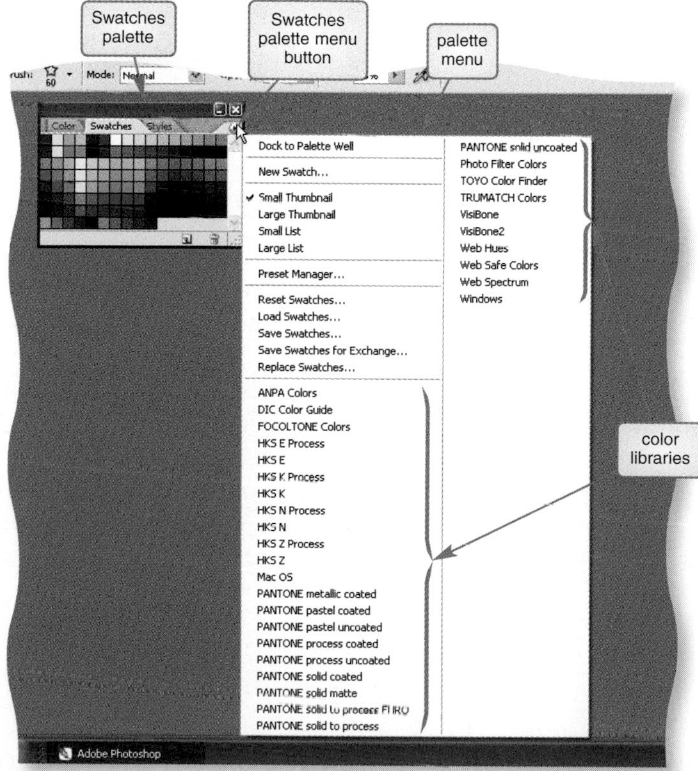

FIGURE 4-44

You can add or delete colors from the Swatches palette or display different libraries of colors such as Pantone. To add a color, select the color and then click the New Swatch button in the lower part of the Swatches palette. Alternately, you can click in the palette itself, after the last color square. Photoshop will give you the option of naming the new color. To delete a color from the palette, drag the color square to the Delete Swatch button in the Swatches palette. To activate a color library, select it from the Swatches palette.

To Select a Color Using the Swatches Palette

1

- **Click the Swatches palette tab in the second set of palettes.**
- **Point to Light Green in the palette.**

The mouse pointer is displayed as an eyedropper (Figure 4-45). Each color displays a tool tip description.

2

- **Click Light Green.**

The foreground color in the toolbox changes to light green, as shown in Figure 4-46.

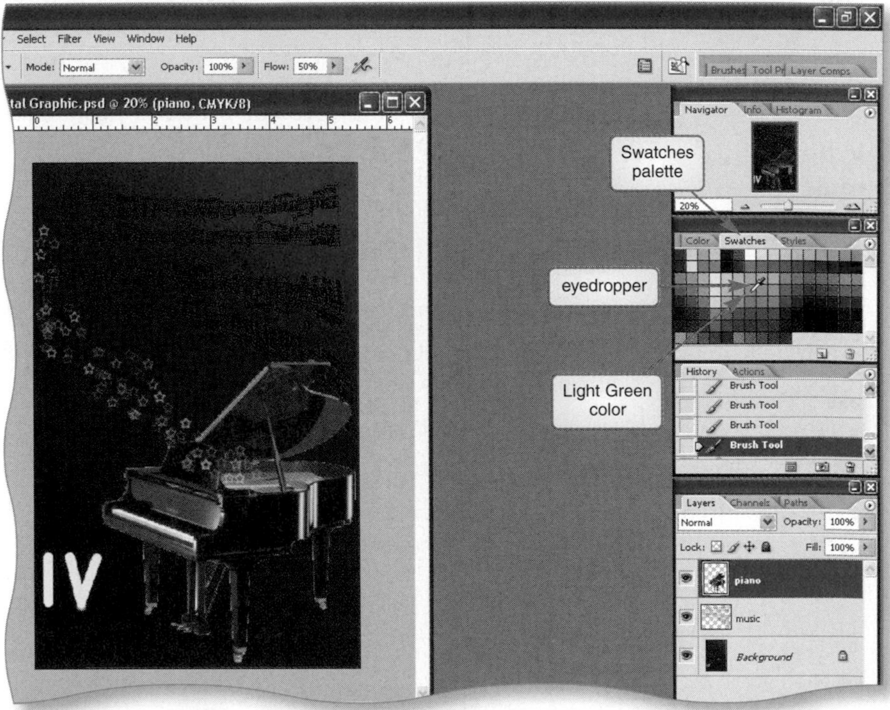

FIGURE 4-45

The Swatches palette commonly is used to make quick choices, as opposed to the Color palette where exact CMYK values can be entered with a wider array of shades and tints. Standard colors are obvious in the Swatches palette and selected with a single click. New colors that you plan to reuse can be added easily. Clicking the color automatically changes the foreground color. If you wish to choose a new background color, press CTRL+click.

The following steps show how to draw the first musical note as a shape using the Elliptical Marquee tool.

To Create a Shape Using the Elliptical Marquee

1

- **Press SHIFT+CTRL+N to create a new layer. When the New Layer dialog box is displayed, type `first note` to rename the layer. Click the OK button.**
- **Press the M key to choose the marquee tools. If necessary, right-click the current marquee tool and then click Elliptical Marquee Tool in the list.**
- **If necessary, on the options bar click the New selection button. If necessary, click the Anti-Alias check box so it displays a check mark.**
- **Move the mouse pointer into the document window slightly to the left of the piano lid, approximately halfway between the bottom and top of the lid.**

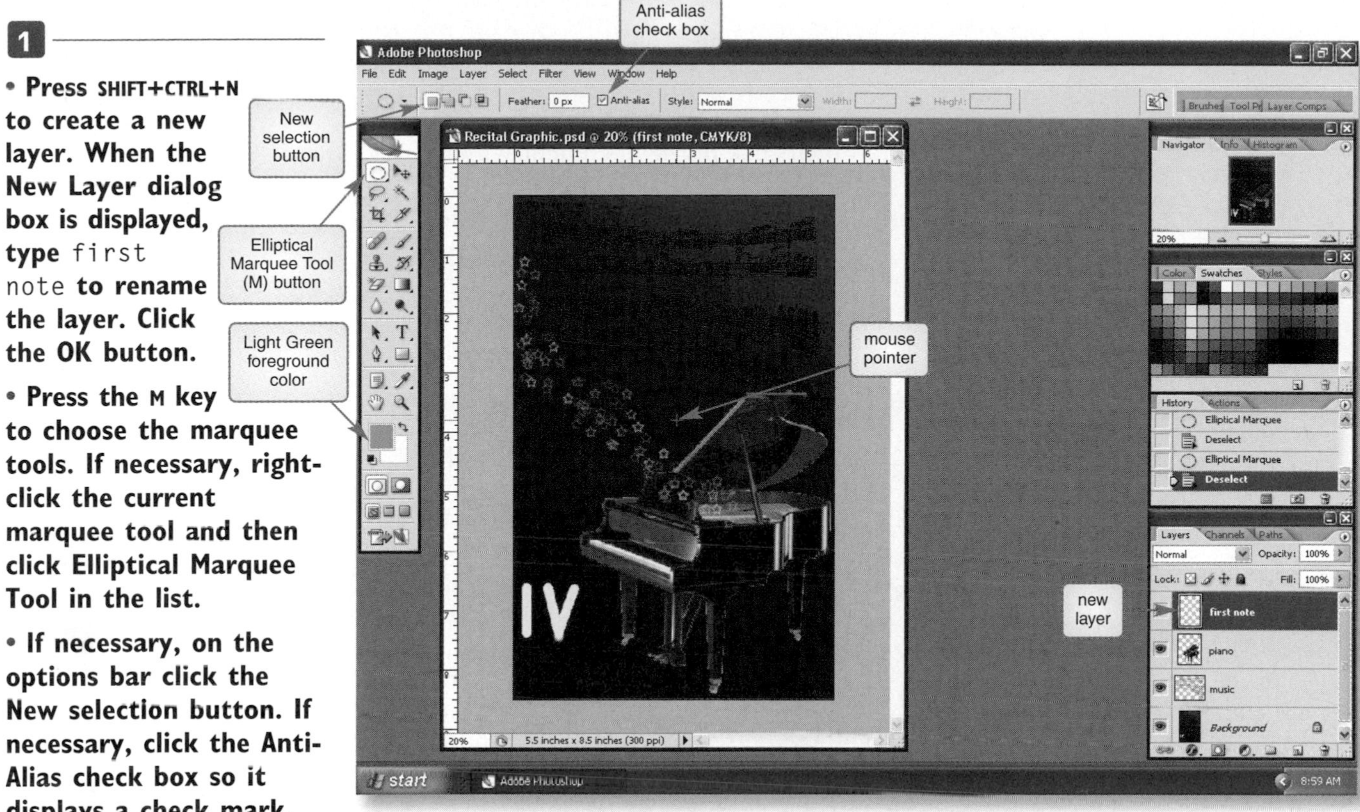

FIGURE 4-46

The Elliptical Marquee tool is chosen and the mouse pointer displays a cross (Figure 4-46). The note will be drawn on the new layer.

2

- **Drag the mouse to draw an elliptical marquee across the edge of the piano lid, approximately 1 inch wide and .5 inches tall.**

Photoshop creates the selection (Figure 4-47). The size of your marquee does not have to match exactly.

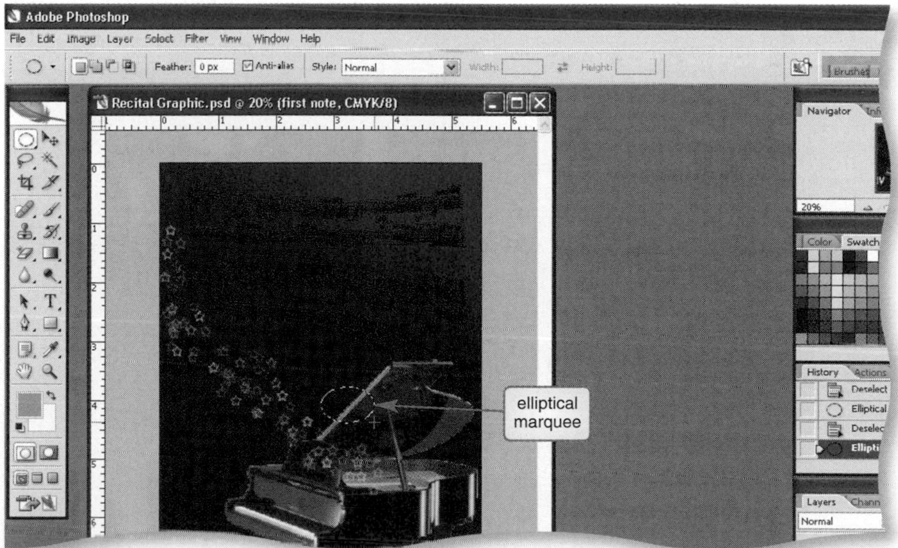

FIGURE 4-47

With the shape created, the following section explains how to use the Paint Bucket tool to fill the selection with color.

The Paint Bucket Tool

The **Paint Bucket tool** fills adjacent, similar pixels with color. To use the Paint Bucket tool you select it in the toolbox and then click in the document window. Recall that the Paint Bucket tool displays on the same context menu as the Gradient tool. The Paint Bucket options bar displays choices to fine-tune the use of the Paint Bucket tool (Figure 4-48).

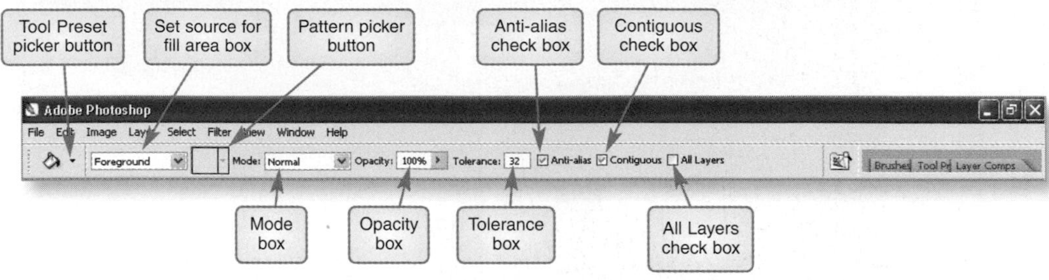

FIGURE 4-48

You can set the source for the fill area or choose from a predefined pattern when filling with the Paint Bucket tool. The Mode, Opacity, and Tolerance boxes work the same way as they did for the Magic Wand and the Eraser tools. Recall that higher tolerance values, fill a wider range of colors. The Contiguous check box allows you to fill all adjacent pixels of the same color within the tolerance.

To Fill Using the Paint Bucket Tool

1

- **Press the G key to access the Gradient or Paint Bucket Tool. Right-click the button and then click Paint Bucket Tool in the list.**
- **Move the mouse pointer into the document window to the selection.**

The mouse pointer changes to a paint bucket and the Paint Bucket options bar is displayed (Figure 4-49).

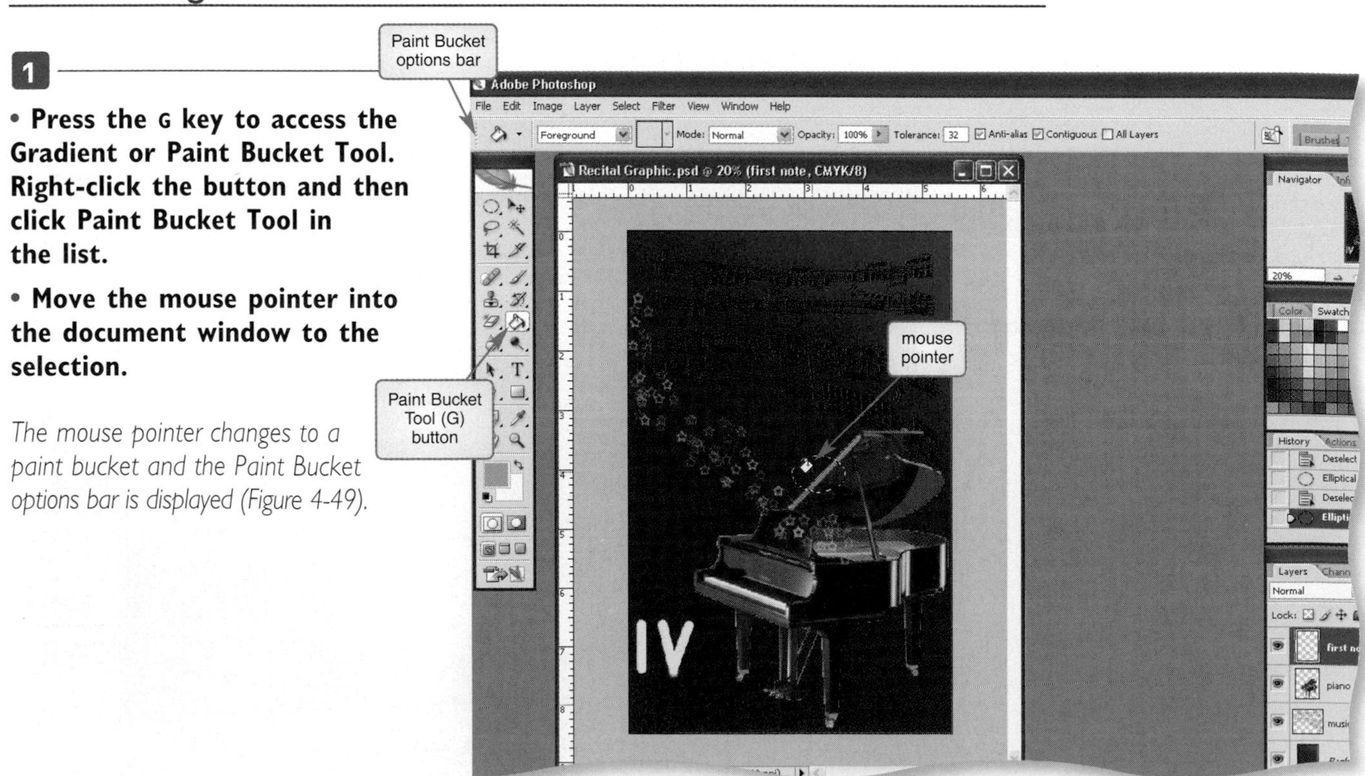

FIGURE 4-49

2

• **Click inside the selection.**

Photoshop colors the selection with the foreground color (Figure 4-50).

3

• **Press CTRL+D to remove the selection marquee.**

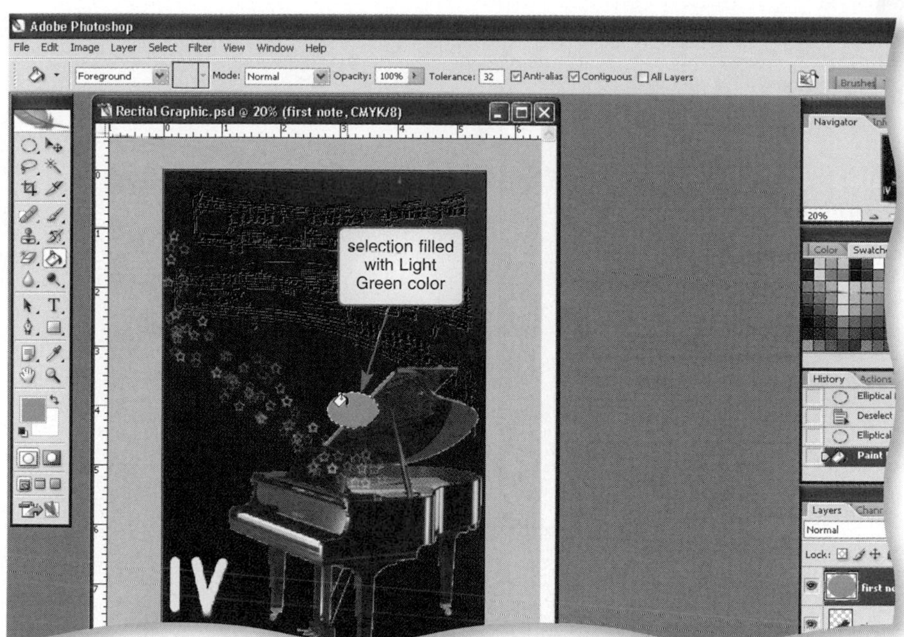

FIGURE 4-50

Using the Ellipse Tool

The second musical note will be created using the Ellipse tool and the shape layer mode. Recall that the shape layer mode will create a new layer in the Layers palette while drawing the selected shape.

To Create a Shape Layer Using the Ellipse Tool

1

• **Press the U key to access the shape tool. If necessary, right-click the current shape tool and then click Ellipse Tool in the list.**

• **On the shape options bar, click the Shape layers button.**

• **Click the Geometry options button.**

Photoshop displays the Ellipse Options box (Figure 4-51).

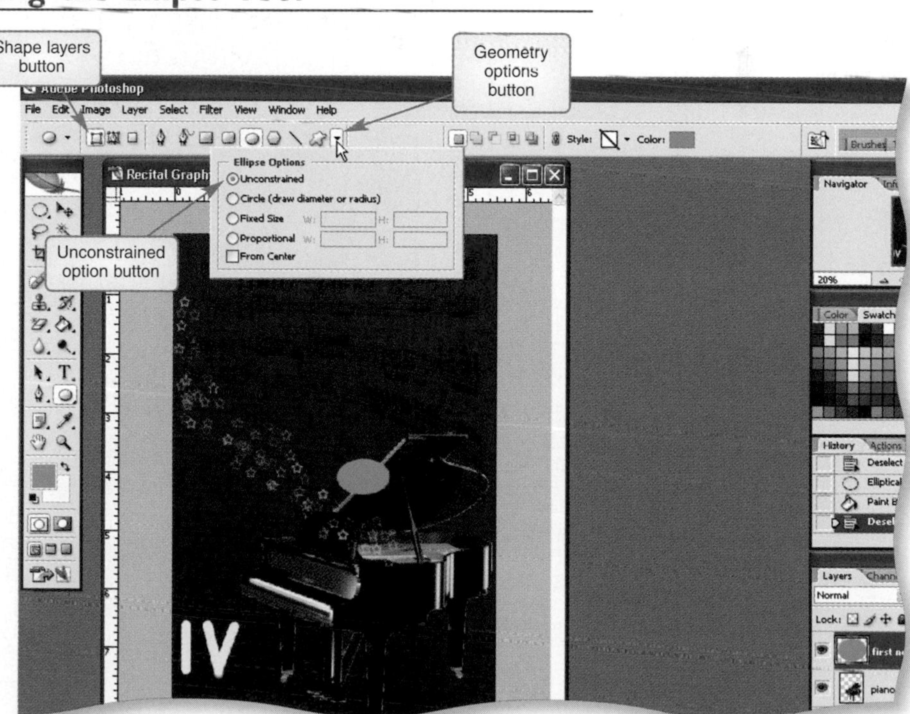

FIGURE 4-51

2

- **If necessary, click Unconstrained.**
- **Move the mouse pointer into the document window to a position inside the piano assembly.**

The mouse pointer changes to a crosshair (Figure 4-52).

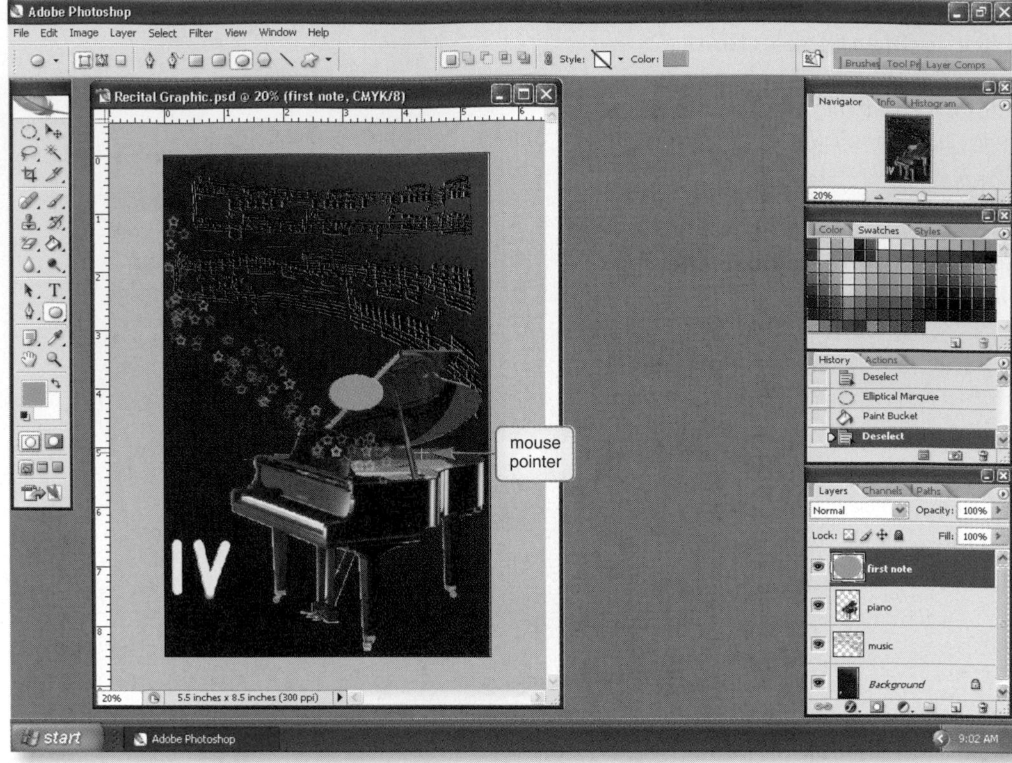

FIGURE 4-52

3

- **Drag to draw an ellipse approximately .75 inches wide and .5 inches tall.**

Photoshop colors the ellipse with the default foreground color (Figure 4-53). A new layer is added to the Layers palette.

4

- **In the Layers palette, double-click the Shape 1 layer name and then type** second note **to rename the layer. Press the** ENTER **key.**

The new layer is renamed.

FIGURE 4-53

Using the Pen Tool and the Paths Palette

The **Pen tool** creates straight lines and smooth curves to draw both lines and shapes. Complex shapes can be created when using the Pen tool in conjunction with other shape tools. The default setting of the Pen tool is to draw a line beginning at a middle point. As you drag, the line becomes longer on both ends.

The Pen tool uses **anchor points** to mark the end points of line segments or points on a curved segment. On curved segments, each selected anchor point displays one or two direction lines, ending in direction points. The positions of lines and points determine the size and shape of a curved segment. Moving the anchor points reshapes the curves. Smooth curves are connected by anchor points called smooth points. Sharply curved paths are connected by corner points.

The line between the end points becomes the path. A path can be closed, with no beginning or end such as a circle, or open with distinct end points such as a line. If you click the Paths button on the shapes option bar, the Pen tool creates a temporary work path. When used with the Shape layers button, the Pen tool creates a vector mask. You will learn more about vector masks in a later project.

Paths display in the document window as lines with anchor points and in the Paths palette. The **Paths palette** (Figure 4-54), usually located in the lowest group of palettes, lists the name and a thumbnail image of each saved path, the current work path, and the current vector mask. Similar to the Layers palette, to select a path, you click the path name in the Paths palette; however, only one path can be selected at a time. The Paths palette menu displays choices to save and delete paths, make new paths, fill or stroke the path, and access palette options.

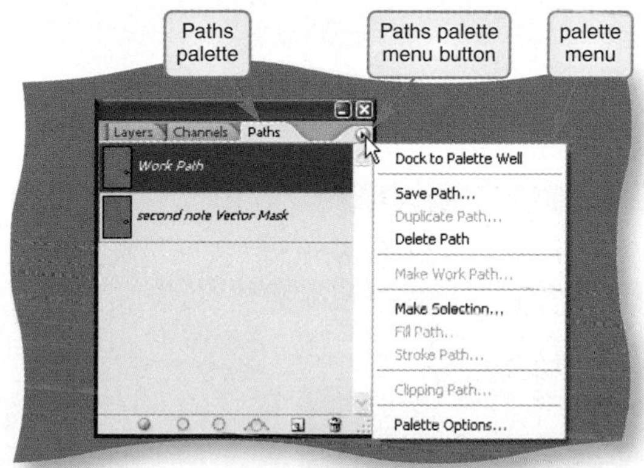

FIGURE 4-54

Anchor points and lines can be manipulated in many ways. For example, if you press the SHIFT key while dragging, Photoshop creates a horizontal or vertical line parallel to the document window's border. Pressing the ALT key while dragging creates a line in one direction rather than both. Drawing a second line creates a curved path between the two center points.

The shape modification buttons on the options bar determine how overlapping path components intersect. The Add to path area (+) button inserts a new area to overlapping path areas. The Subtract from path area (-) button removes the new area from the overlapping path area. The Intersect path areas button restricts the path to the intersection of the new area and the existing area. Finally, the Exclude overlapping path areas excludes the overlap area in a consolidated path.

Creating paths, based on existing images using the Path tool itself, will be explained in a later project.

The following steps show how to create a new layer for the third note and then draw an ellipse using the Pen tool.

To Create a Path Using the Pen Tool

1

- **Press SHIFT+CTRL+N to create a new layer. When the New Layer dialog box is displayed, type** `third note` **to rename the layer. Click the OK button.**

Photoshop displays the new layer (Figure 4-55).

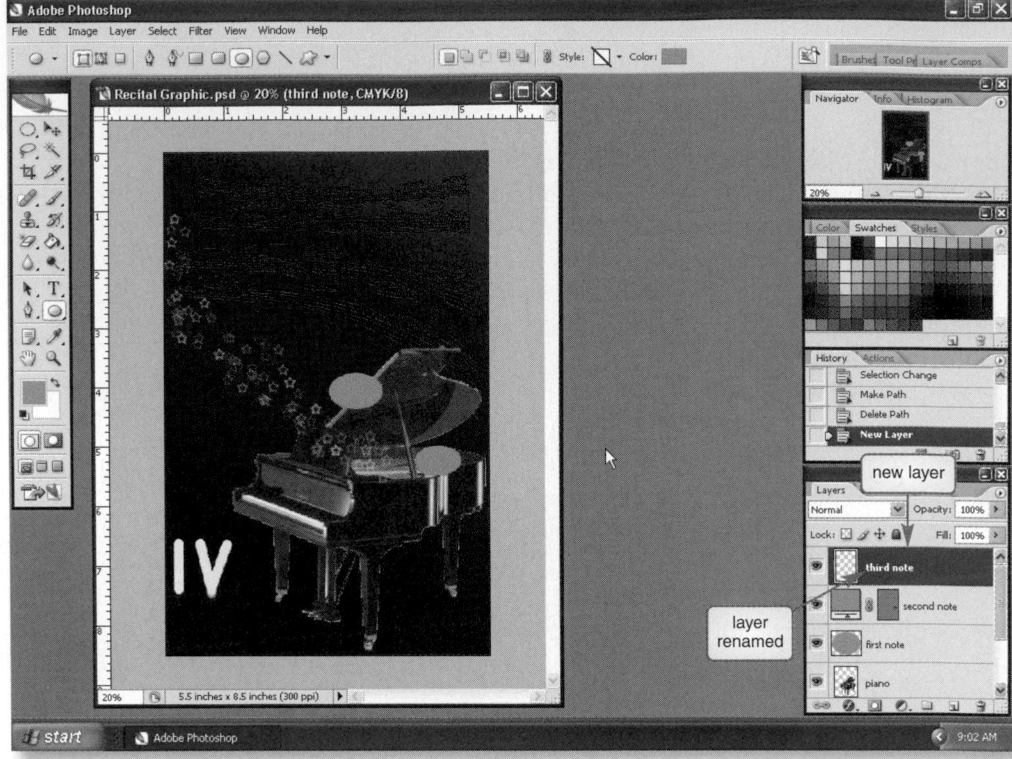

FIGURE 4-55

2

- **Click the Paths palette tab in the fourth set of palettes.**
- **On the shapes option bar, click the Paths button and the Pen Tool button. If necessary, click the Add to path area (+) button.**
- **Zoom to 50% and scroll to display the top of the piano lid.**
- **Move the mouse pointer to the document window at a location approximately 1 inch above the upper-right corner of the piano lid.**

The mouse pointer is displayed as a pen tip with an x (Figure 4-56).

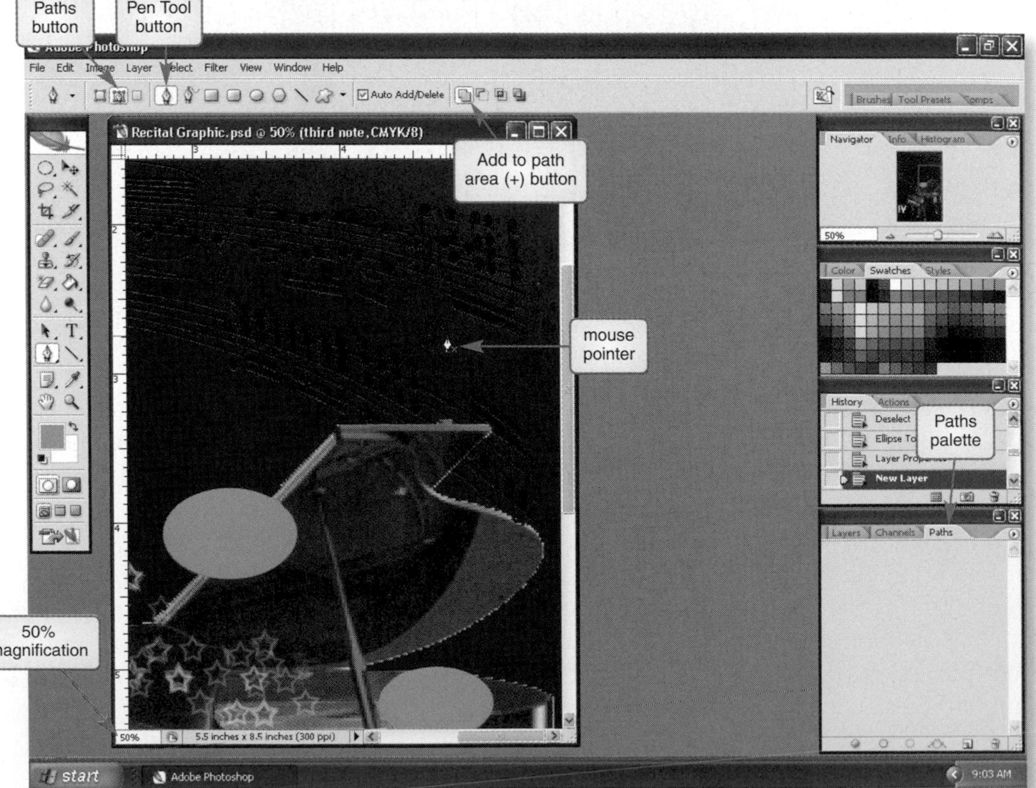

FIGURE 4-56

3

• **SHIFT+drag from left to right to draw a line approximately .5 inches.**

Photoshop displays the line with center and end anchor points (Figure 4-57). A work path also is created in the Paths palette.

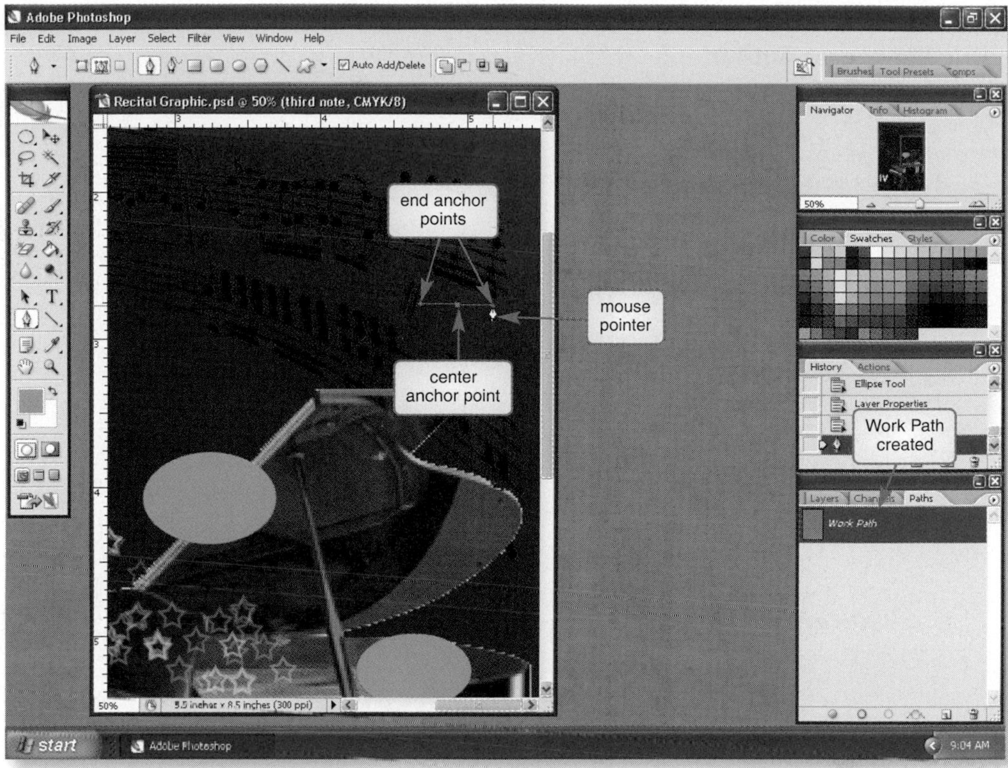

FIGURE 4-57

4

• **Move the mouse pointer to a location approximately .5 inches below the previous line, directly under the center point of the previous line.**

• **To create a second line, SHIFT+drag from right to left to draw a line parallel to the first line and equal in length.**

Photoshop displays the new line and connects the center anchor points with a curved line (Figure 4-58). The original path line now appears shorter.

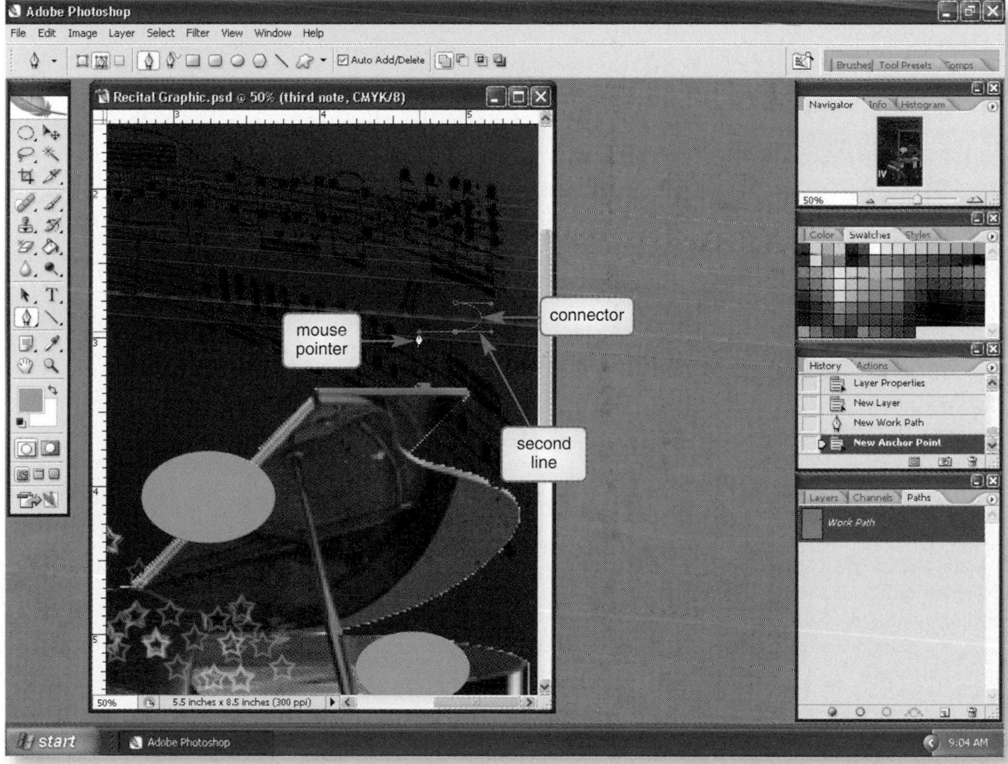

FIGURE 4-58

5

• **Click the center anchor point of the first line.**

Photoshop completes the path (Figure 4-59).

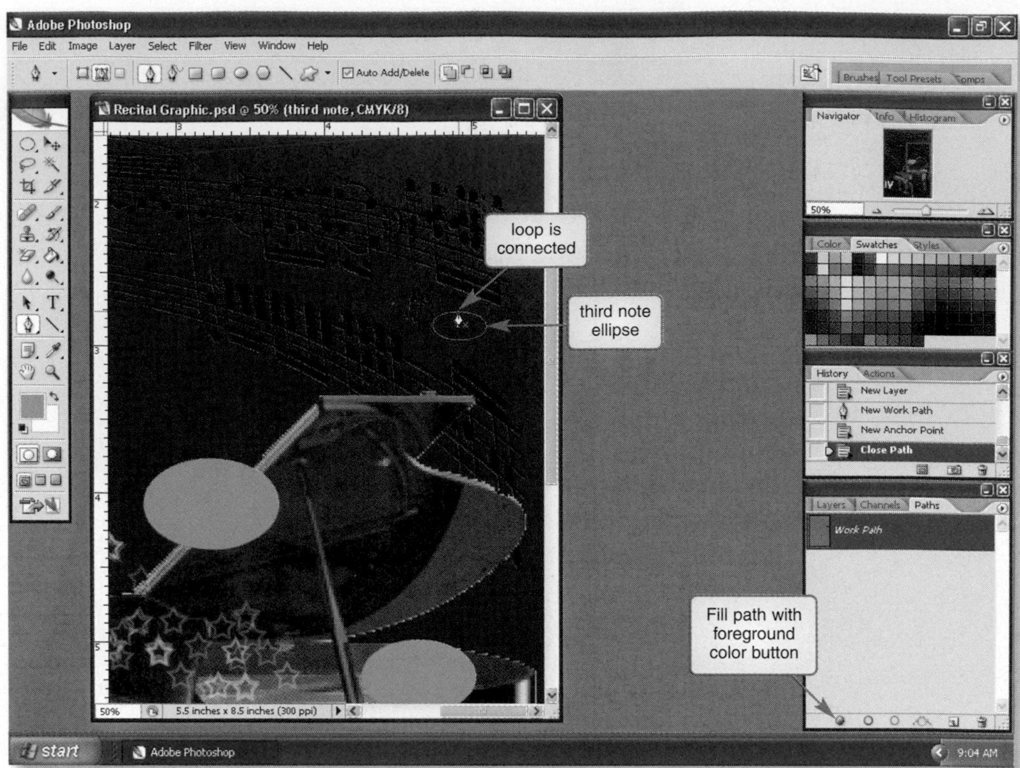

FIGURE 4-59

> ***More About***
>
> **Anchors**
>
> To add a new anchor point without changing the shape of the segment, click anywhere in the path. To add a new anchor point and change the shape of the segment, drag from the path.
> To delete an anchor, select the Delete Anchor Point tool, and then click the anchor.
> To move an anchor, select the path name in the Paths palette, and use the Direct Selection tool to select an anchor point in the path. Drag the point or its handles to a new location.

To end an open path without completing it, you can press CTRL+click at a location away from the path. To close or complete a path, position the pen pointer over the first anchor point — a small loop appears next to the pen tip when positioned correctly. Click to close the path.

When you right-click the Pen tool in the Photoshop toolbox, you can select the Freeform Pen too. The **Freeform Pen tool** lets you draw as you drag, as if you were drawing with a pencil on paper. Less precise than the Pen tool, the Freeform Pen tool sets anchor points automatically as you draw. Once the path is complete, you can adjust the anchor points.

Filling a Path with Color

A path created with the Pen tool does not become an image element until you fill or stroke it using a specified color or pattern. The following step shows how to fill the previously created path with the foreground color.

To Fill a Path with Color

1

- **At the bottom of the Paths palette, click the Fill path with foreground color button.**

Photoshop fills the ellipse (Figure 4-60).

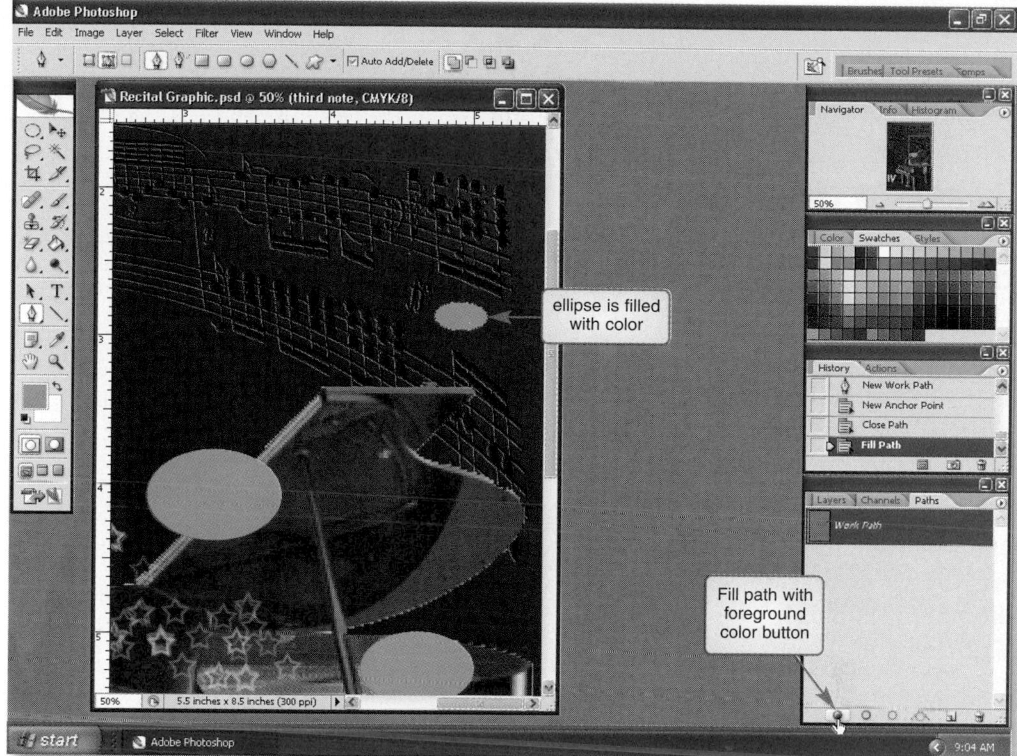

FIGURE 4-60

There can be only one path called the work path with each document image. If you use more paths in your drawing, you should save the work path with a new name and then create the next path.

The Line Tool

The **Line tool** is used to draw lines and arrows in an image. Photoshop allows you to set the weight or thickness of the line, the length of the line, whether or not the ends have arrowheads, and the concavity of the arrowhead, which defines the amount of curvature on the widest part.

The next steps show how to draw a line to act as the stem of the musical notes. You will draw one on each of the three notes.

To Use the Line Tool

1

- **Click the Layers palette tab. Click the first note layer.**
- **On the shape options bar, click Line Tool button.**
- **Click the Fill pixels button and then click the Line tool button.**
- **In the Weight box, type** `30 px` **to specify the line's thickness.**
- **SHIFT+drag from the upper-right side of the first note up, creating a line approximately 1.5 inches long.**

Photoshop displays a line 30 pixels wide using the foreground color (Figure 4-61).

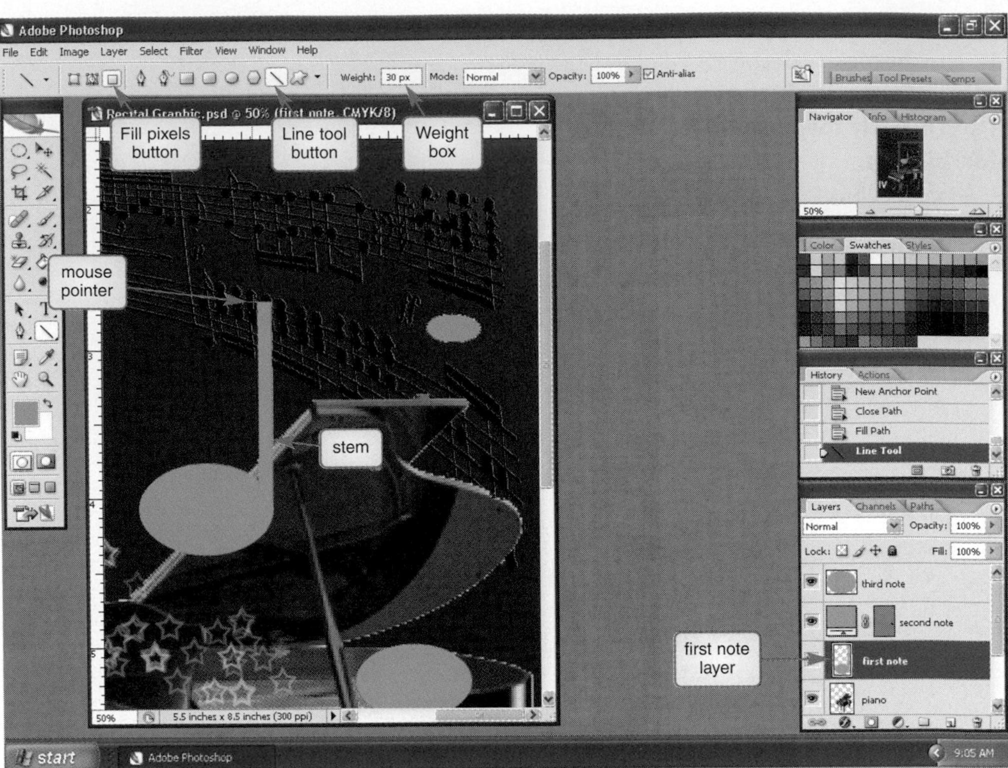

FIGURE 4-61

- **Type** `22 px` **in the Weight box. SHIFT+drag from the upper-right side of the second note up, creating a line approximately 1 inch long.**
- **Type** `15 px` **in the Weight box. SHIFT+drag from the upper-right side of the third note up, creating a line approximately .5 inches long.**

Photoshop displays the stems on the notes (Figure 4-62).

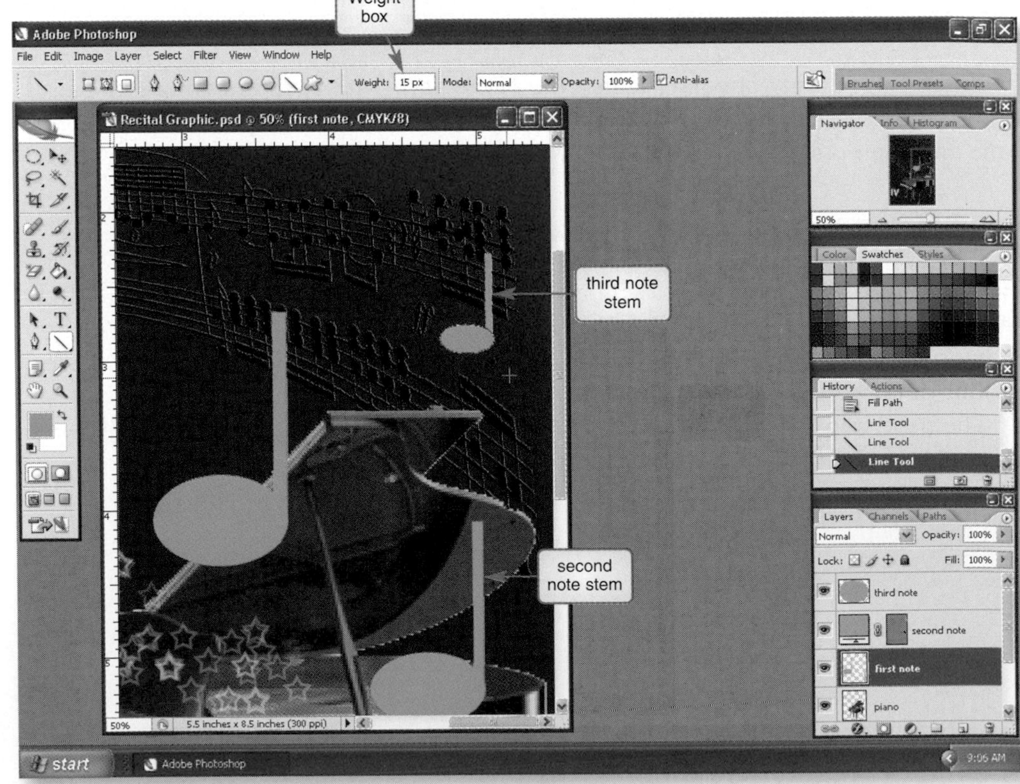

FIGURE 4-62

Finally the eighth-note flags and the motion lines underneath the piano will be drawn using a preset brush tip selected from the set of Special Effects Brushes.

Brush Tip Shapes

A preset brush tip is a brush with a tip that has specific characteristics such as size, shape, and hardness. When you use the Brush tool, the tip creates the shape that paints in the document window. Besides the basic brush tips, Photoshop offers 11 other libraries of brush tips which you can load into your working list. If you change the size, shape, or hardness of a preset brush, the change is temporary; the next time you choose that tip, the brush goes back to its original settings. If you use certain characteristics often, you should save your settings and select the tip from the Tool Preset menu on the options bar.

To access the brush tips, you use the Brushes palette and then click **Brush Tip Shape** (Figure 4-63). You can set the diameter which scales the size of the brush tip. Once changed, the Use Sample Size button is displayed to allow you to reset the brush tip back to its default size.

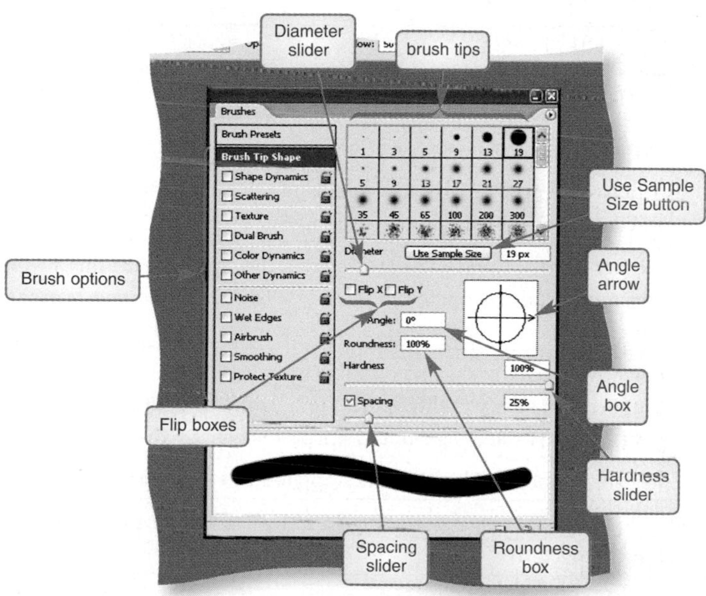

FIGURE 4-63

The flip boxes change the direction of the brush tip on the specified axis. For example, a brush tip that displays a leaf image with the stem down, would display stem up if the Flip X check box was checked. The Angle box allows you to enter degrees of flat rotation. Positive numbers rotate the brush tip counterclockwise; negative numbers rotate the brush tip clockwise. For example, a brush tip of a raindrop with the pointed end straight up would point left if rotated 90 degrees.

The Roundness percentage specifies the ratio between the brush's short and long axes. Adjusting the roundness makes the brush tip appear to rotate on its vertical axis in a 3D fashion. A value of 100% indicates a full view or circular brush tip. A value of 0% indicates a sideways view or linear brush tip. Values in between 0% and 100% represent partial view or elliptical brush tips. For example a star brush tip set at 50% roundness creates a star that is tipped backward from the top.

The Spacing slider controls the distance between the brush marks in a stroke. The lower the percentage, the closer together the brush tips display within the stroke. For example, a snowflake brush tip set at 1% spacing would display a snowflake

More About

The Preset Manager

The Preset Manager helps you manage the libraries of preset brushes, gradients, styles, custom shapes, patterns, and other tools that come with Photoshop. The Preset Manager is used to change the current set of preset items or to create new libraries. While most palette menus have a command to load new presets, The Preset Manager lists them all in one place for easy access. To use the Preset Manager, click Preset Manager on the Edit menu.

connected to an almost solid brush stroke with another snowflake shape at the other end. Higher percentages — up to 1000% — space the brush tips farther apart as you drag. For example, a spacing value of 200% would create snowflakes all across the brush stroke with some space in between each one. When the Spacing box is deselected, the speed of the cursor determines the spacing.

Solid brush tips have a hardness setting that indicates the amount of anti-aliasing for the Brush tool. The higher the percentage, the cleaner the edge appears.

Brush Options

The brush options display as check boxes in the Brushes palette. When you choose an option, settings specific to that dynamic display on the right of the Brushes palette. Table 4-6 displays some of the options not previously mentioned, along with their settings and descriptions.

Table 4-6 Brush Shape Options

OPTION	SETTING	DESCRIPTION
Shape Dynamic	Jitter	specifies how the size, angle, or roundness of brush marks vary in a stroke
	Fade	fades the size of brush marks between the initial diameter and the minimum diameter in the specified number of steps
	Pen Pressure, Pen Tilt, Stylus Wheel, Rotation	available only with graphic tablets — varies the size of brush marks between the initial diameter and the minimum diameter based on the pen pressure, pen tilt, position of the pen thumbwheel, or rotation of the pen
Scattering	Scatter	specifies how brush marks are distributed in a stroke — if Both Axes is selected, brush marks are distributed in a radial direction; if Both Axes is deselected, brush marks are distributed perpendicular to the stroke path
	Count	specifies the number of brush marks applied at each spacing interval
Texture	Invert	used for patterns — inverts the high and low points in the texture based on the tones in the pattern
	Scale	specifies the scale of the pattern
	Depth	specifies how deeply the paint penetrates into the texture
Dual Brush	Mode	sets a blending mode to use when combining brush marks from the primary tip and the dual tip
Color Dynamics	Hue, Saturation, Brightness, Purity	specifies a percentage by which the hue, saturation, or brightness of the paint can vary in a stroke
Other Dynamics	Flow	specifies how the flow of paint varies in a brush stroke
Noise		adds additional randomness to individual brush tips
Wet Edges		causes paint to build up along the edges of the brush stroke, creating a watercolor effect
Airbrush		applies gradual tones to an image, simulating traditional airbrush techniques
Smoothing		produces smoother curves in brush strokes
Protect Texture		applies the same pattern and scale to all brush presets that have a texture

Choosing a Brush Tip and Setting

The following steps show how to load a new set of brushes and append them to the current list. Then a brush tip is chosen, with diameter and angle settings along with the smoothing option, to create the eighth-note flags on the musical notes. The Darken blending mode is chosen in the option bar.

> *More About*
>
> **Dual Brushes**
>
> A dual brush uses two tips to create brush marks. For example, a solid border, circle brush tip used as the primary tip could be dressed up with a secondary feather tip for a customized look of a feathered circle. For the primary tip you set a regular brush tip shape. For the second brush tip click Dual Brushes and choose the desired settings.

To Choose a Brush Tip and Settings

1

- **Press the B key to choose the Brush Tool.**
- **Click the Brushes palette tab. Drag the tab of the palette out of the palette well so it displays, in full, in the Photoshop workspace.**
- **Click the Brushes palette menu button.**

The palette menu is displayed (Figure 4-64).

FIGURE 4-64

2

- **Click Assorted Brushes. When the Adobe Photoshop dialog box is displayed, click the Append button. If necessary, click the Brush Tip Shape button.**
- **Scroll as necessary and click the Ornament 3 41 brush tip.**

Photoshop displays the Brushes palette and the default settings for Ornament 3 41(Figure 4-65). Your settings may differ.

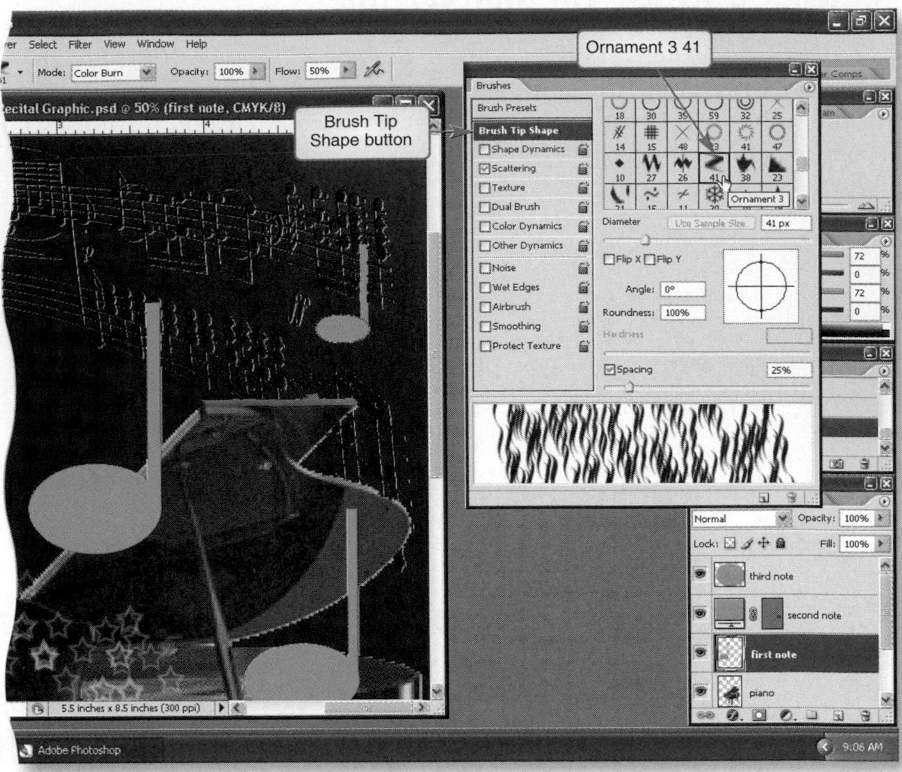

FIGURE 4-65

3

- **Below the tip pane, drag the Diameter slider to 400.**
- **Drag the Angle arrow to approximately 45 degrees.**
- **Type** 75% **in the Roundness box.**
- **Click the Smoothing check box so it displays a check mark, if necessary. Remove all other check marks.**

The new settings are displayed (Figure 4-66).

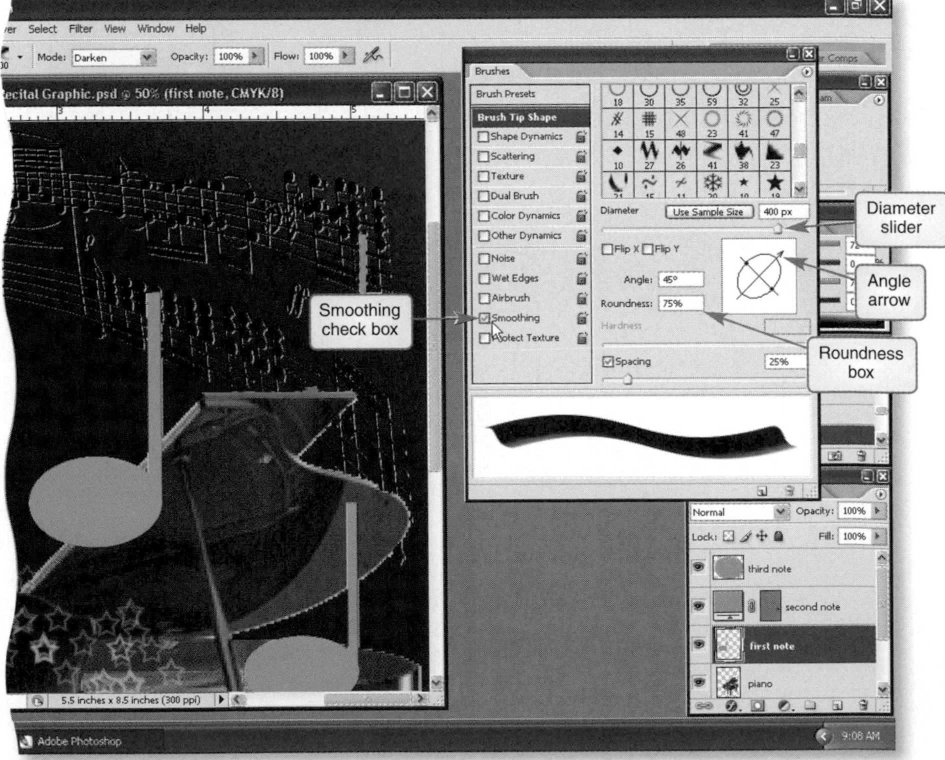

FIGURE 4-66

4

- **On the Brushes option bar, click the Mode box arrow and then click Darken in the list.**
- **With the first note layer selected, in the document window, position the left side of the mouse pointer at the top of the first note's stem.**
- **Click and drag slightly down to create the flag.**

The flag is displayed on the stem (Figure 4-67). If you want your flag to be darker, click more than once.

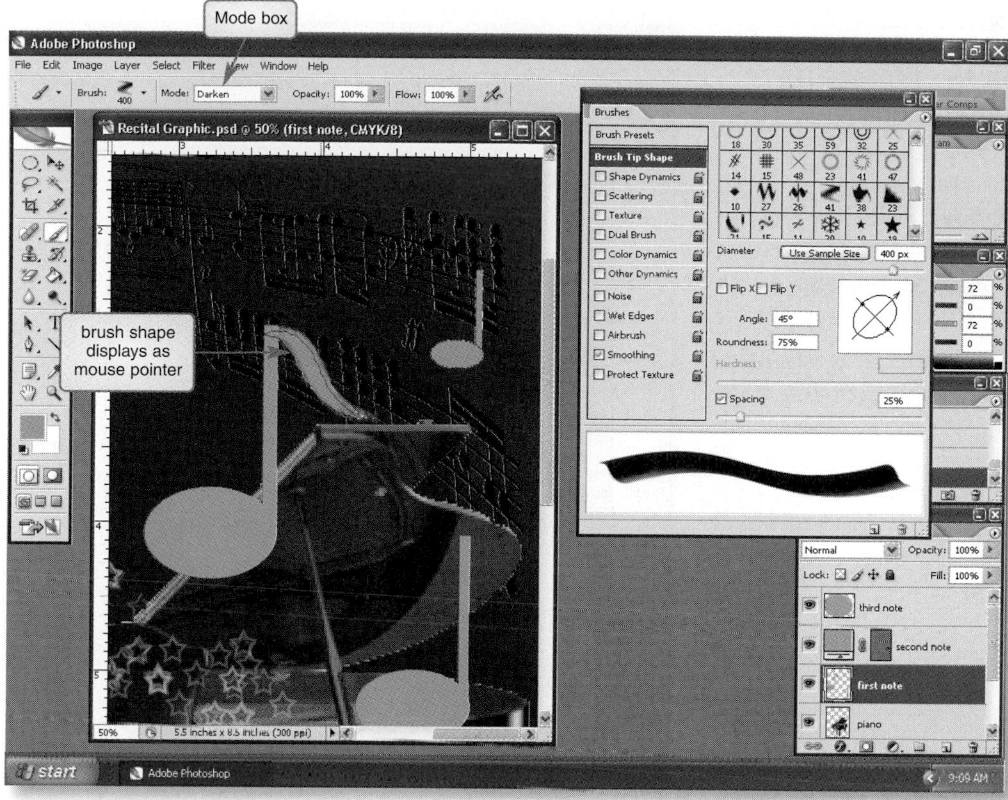

FIGURE 4-67

5

- **In the Brushes palette, drag the Diameter slider to 300.**
- **In the document window, position the left side of the mouse pointer at the top of the second note's stem.**
- **Click and drag slightly down to create the flag.**

The second flag is displayed on the stem (Figure 4-68).

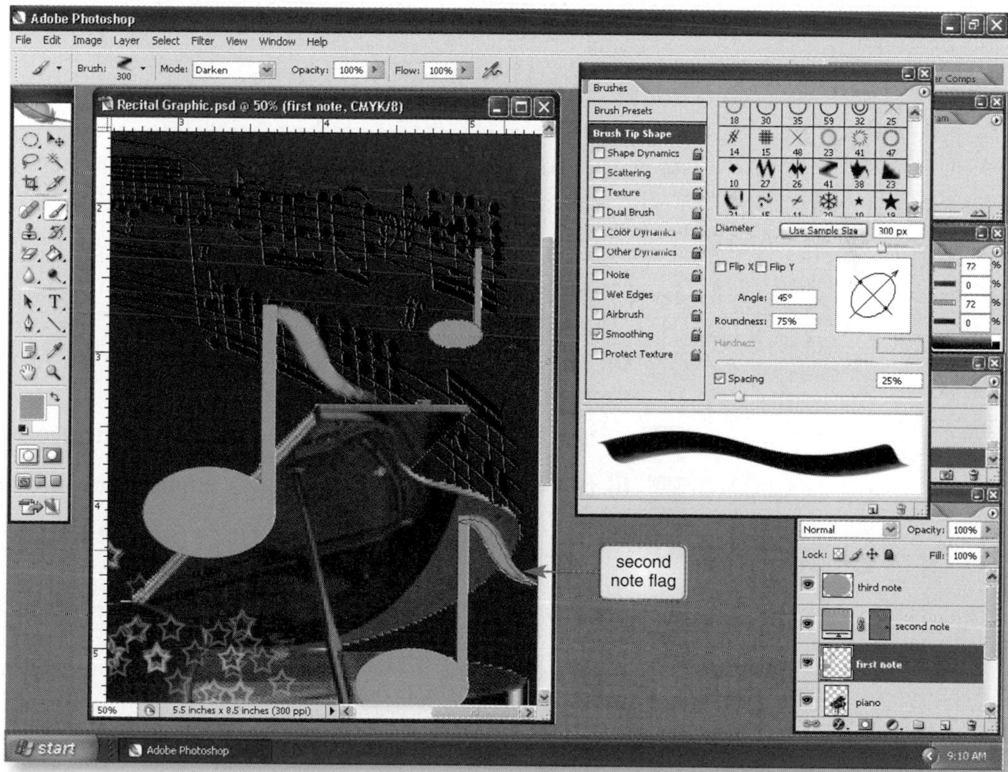

FIGURE 4-68

6

• **In the Brushes palette, drag the Diameter slider to 200.**

• **In the document window, position the left side of the mouse pointer at the top of the third note's stem.**

• **Click and drag slightly down to create the flag.**

The third flag is displayed on the stem (Figure 4-69).

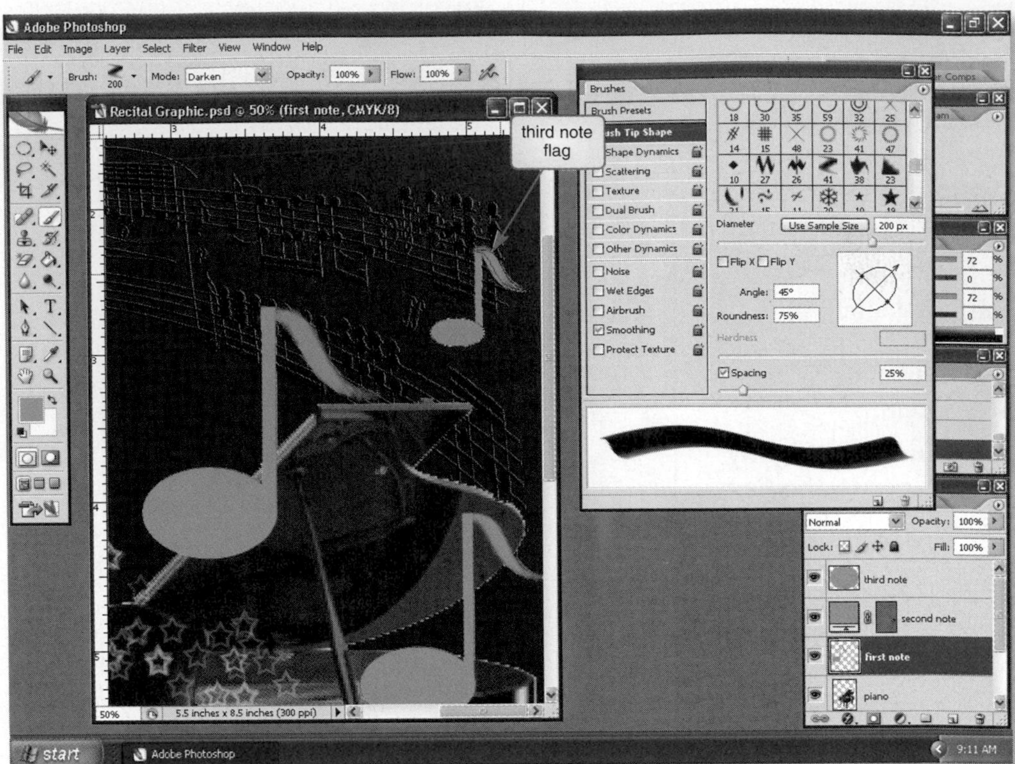

FIGURE 4-69

Creating the Motion Lines

The final step is to create the motion lines at the base of the piano legs. You will set a diameter, angle, and texture with a Color Dodge blending mode. Recall that Color Dodge brightens the base color by decreasing the contrast.

To Create the Motion Lines

1. **On the document window status bar, type** 20 **in the magnification box and then press the ENTER key.**
2. **In the Layers palette, click the Background layer.**
3. **In the Brushes palette, Drag the Angle arrow to 125 degrees.**
4. **On the options bar, click the Mode box arrow and then click Color Dodge in the list.**
5. **Click once at the right of each of the three piano legs.**

The motion lines are displayed (Figure 4-70). Your colors may not match exactly depending on the previous gradient colors.

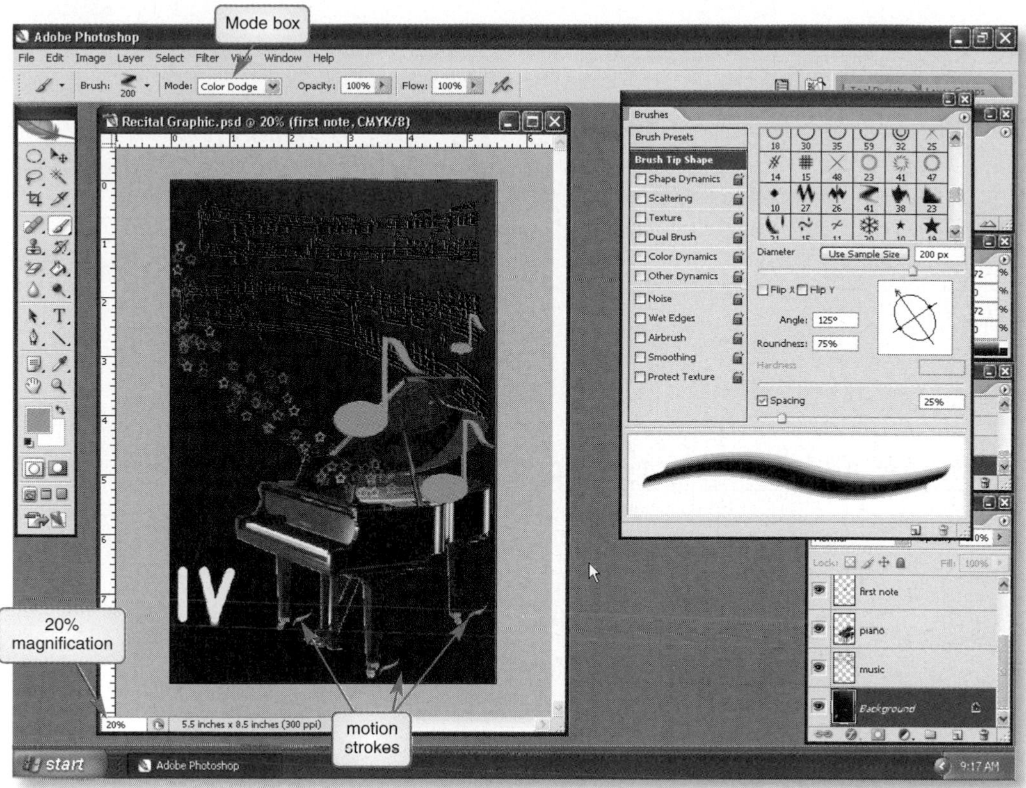

FIGURE 4-70

Because the brush strokes are done, the next step shows how to dock the Brushes palette back in the palette well.

To Dock the Brushes Palette

1. **Click the Brushes palette menu button.**
2. **Click Dock to Palette Well.**

Now that the graphic is complete, before you flatten the image, it is a good idea to save the file again to maintain the layers for future editing, if necessary.

To Save the File before Flattening

1. **Press CTRL+S.**

The following steps illustrate how to flatten the image and save it as a TIF file for printing in the recital program.

To Flatten and Save the File

1. **On the Layer menu, click the Flatten Image command.**
2. **With your USB flash drive connected to one of the computer's USB ports, click File on the menu bar and then click Save As.**

3 **When the Save As dialog box is displayed, if necessary, click the Save in box arrow and then click USBDISK [G:], or the location associated with your USB flash drive, in the list.**

4 **In the Name box, type Recital Graphic Complete. Click the Format box arrow and then click TIFF (*.TIF, *.TIFF) in the list.**

5 **Click the Save button. When Photoshop displays the TIFF Options dialog box, click the OK button.**

The file, Recital Graphic Complete, is saved.

The final step is to close the document window and quit Photoshop.

To Close the Document Window and Quit Photoshop

1 **With the Recital Graphic Complete window selected, click the Close button in the document window.**

2 **Click the Close button on the right side of the Photoshop title bar.**

The Photoshop window closes.

Project Summary

You used many tools and palettes as you created the recital graphic in this project. You started a new file from scratch and used the Gradient tool to add two colors blended together. You added images of music and a piano. You selected a brush and drew the Roman numeral IV, and then selected a different brush to create stars coming out of the piano. As you learned about the many ways to create shapes, you created musical notes with using shape layers, paths, and selections. The Line tool was used to create a stem for each note. The eighth-note flags as well as the motion lines used a special brush tip with dynamic settings. Finally, you docked the Brushes palette, flattened the image, and saved the file.

What You Should Know

Having completed this project, you should be able to perform the tasks below. The tasks are listed in the same order they were presented in this project. For a list of the buttons, menus, toolbars, and other commands introduced in this project, see the Quick Reference Summary at the back of this book and refer to the Page Number column.

1. Start Photoshop and Reset the Palettes, Toolbox, and Options Bar (PS 204)
2. Reset the Layers Palette (PS 204)
3. Reset the Colors (PS 204)
4. Create a File from Scratch (PS 207)
5. Save the File (PS 209)
6. Use the Gradient Editor (PS 212)
7. Use the Color Picker (PS 214)
8. Apply a Gradient Fill (PS 218)
9. Open the Music File (PS 219)
10. Create a Layer (PS 220)
11. Warp a Layer (PS 221)
12. Open the Piano File (PS 222)
13. Create the Piano Layer (PS 223)
14. Use the Color Palette (PS 225)
15. Use the Brush Preset Picker (PS 227)
16. Draw Straight Lines with the Brush Tool (PS 228)
17. Select a Color Using the Eyedropper Tool (PS 231)
18. Use the Brushes Palette (PS 234)
19. Use the Brush Tool with a Flowing Star Stroke (PS 235)
20. Save Changes to the File (PS 236)
21. Select a Color Using the Swatches Palette (PS 240)
22. Create a Shape Using the Elliptical Marquee (PS 241)
23. Fill Using the Paint Bucket Tool (PS 242)
24. Create a Shape Layer Using the Ellipse Tool (PS 243)
25. Create a Path Using the Pen Tool (PS 246)
26. Fill a Path with Color (PS 249)
27. Use the Line Tool (PS 250)
28. Choose a Brush Tip and Settings (PS 253)
29. Create the Motion Lines (PS 256)
30. Dock the Brushes Palette (PS 257)
31. Save the File before Flattening (PS 257)
32. Flatten and Save the File (PS 257)
33. Close the Document Window and Quit Photoshop (PS 258)

Learn It Online

Instructions: To complete the Learn It Online exercises, start your browser, click the Address bar, and then enter the Web address scsite.com/photoshop/learn. When the Photoshop CS2 Learn It Online page is displayed, follow the instructions in the exercises below. Each exercise has instructions for printing your results, either for your own records or for submission to your instructor.

1 Project Reinforcement TF, MC, and SA

Below Photoshop Project 4, click the Project Reinforcement link. Print the quiz by clicking Print on the File menu for each page. Answer each question.

2 Flash Cards

Below Photoshop Project 4, click the Flash Cards link and read the instructions. Type 20 (or a number specified by your instructor) in the Number of playing cards text box, type your name in the Enter your Name text box, and then click the Flip Card button. When the flash card is displayed, read the question and then click the ANSWER box arrow to select an answer. Flip through Flash Cards. If your score is 15 (75%) correct or greater, click Print on the File menu to print your results. If your score is less than 15 (75%) correct, then redo this exercise by clicking the Replay button.

3 Practice Test

Below Photoshop Project 4, click the Practice Test link. Answer each question, enter your first and last name at the bottom of the page, and then click the Grade Test button. When the graded practice test is displayed on your screen, click Print on the File menu to print a hard copy. Continue to take practice tests until you score 80% or better.

4 Who Wants To Be a Computer Genius?

Below Photoshop Project 4, click the Computer Genius link. Read the instructions, enter your first and last name at the bottom of the page, and then click the PLAY button. When your score is displayed, click the PRINT RESULTS link to print a hard copy.

5 Wheel of Terms

Below Photoshop Project 4, click the Wheel of Terms link. Read the instructions, and then enter your first and last name and your school name. Click the PLAY button. When your score is displayed, right-click the score and then click Print on the shortcut menu to print a hard copy.

6 Crossword Puzzle Challenge

Below Photoshop Project 4, click the Crossword Puzzle Challenge link. Read the instructions, and then enter your first and last name. Click the SUBMIT button. Work the crossword puzzle. When you are finished, click the Submit button. When the crossword puzzle is redisplayed, click the Print Puzzle button to print a hard copy.

7 Tips and Tricks

Below Photoshop Project 4, click the Tips and Tricks link. Click a topic that pertains to Project 4. Right-click the information and then click Print on the shortcut menu. Construct a brief example of what the information relates to in Photoshop to confirm you understand how to use the tip or trick.

8 Expanding Your Horizons

Below Photoshop Project 4, click the Expanding Your Horizons link. Click a topic that pertains to Project 4. Print the information. Construct a brief example of what the information relates to in Photoshop to confirm you understand the contents of the article.

9 Search Sleuth

Below Photoshop Project 4, click the Search Sleuth link. To search for a term that pertains to this project, select a term below the Project 4 title and then use the Google search engine at google.com (or any major search engine) to display and print two Web pages that present information on the term.

10 Photoshop Online Training

Below Photoshop Project 4, click the Photoshop Online Training link. When your browser displays the Web page, click one of the Photoshop tutorials that covers one or more of the objectives listed at the beginning of the project on page PS 202. Print the first page of the tutorial before stepping through it.

Apply Your Knowledge

1 Creating a Book Cover

Instructions: Start Photoshop, and set the workspace and tools to default settings. Open the Book Cover file from the Project04 folder, located either on the CD that accompanies this book, or in a location specified by your instructor. The purpose of this exercise is to create a composite photo by adding a gradient and custom shape to create a graphic similar to the one shown in Figure 4-71.

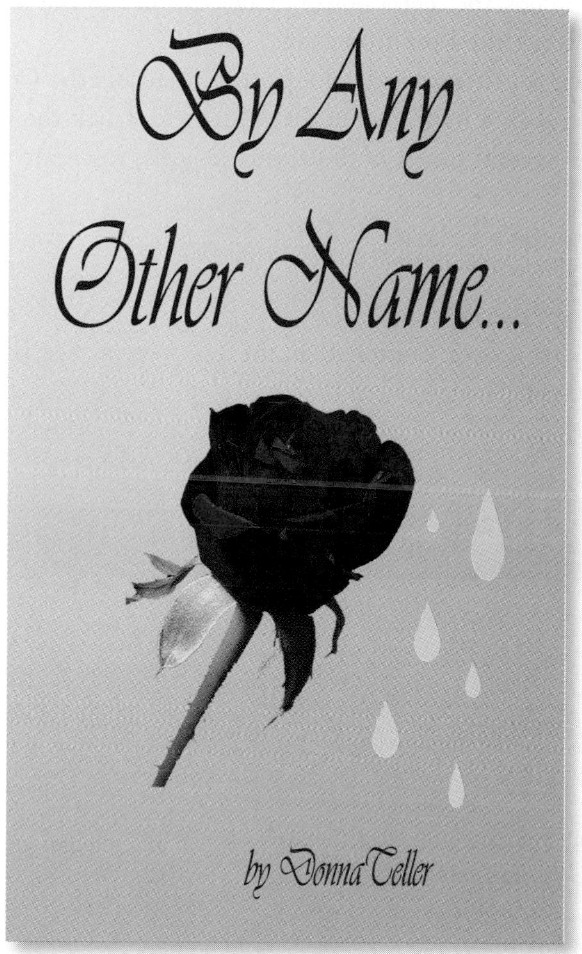

FIGURE 4-71

1. Use the Save As command to save the image on your USB flash drive as a PSD file, with the file name, Book Cover Edited.
2. Click the Layers palette and hide the text layers.
3. Select the Gradient tool. Click the Gradient Editor box. Use the left Color Stop button to set a yellow color. Use the right Color Stop button to set a light orange or peach color. If other Color Stop buttons are displayed, click them and then click the Delete button in the Gradient Editor dialog box. When you are finished, click the OK button.
4. Drag from the upper-left to the lower-right to create the gradient.
5. Open the file named, Rose, from the CD that accompanies this book or from a location specified by your instructor.

(continued)

Apply Your Knowledge

Creating a Book Cover *(continued)*

6. When the Rose document window is displayed, select the entire image. Use the Move tool to drag it into the Book Cover document window.
7. Use the Magic Eraser tool to erase the black background from the Rose layer. Rename the new layer, Rose.
8. In the toolbox, click the current shape tool. In the shape options bar, click the Custom Shape button. Click the Shape box arrow, and then click the menu button. Click Nature in the list. When Photoshop asks, choose to append the shapes. Click the Raindrop shape.
9. In the toolbox, double-click the Set foreground color button to access the Color Picker. Click in the color slider to choose blue, and then click a light blue in the color field. Click the OK button.
10. Drag in the document window several times, with varying lengths, to create the raindrops similar to those shown in Figure 4-71.
11. Click the Visibility icon next to the text layer.
12. Save the file.
13. Click Flatten Image on the Layer menu.
14. Save the file with the name, Book Cover Complete, in the TIF format. See your instructor for instructions on how to turn in this assignment.

1 Creating an Advertisement Using Gradients and Shapes

Problem: A friend of your father's owns a small golf course on the edge of town. He has heard of your study of Photoshop and would like you to create an advertisement for him. He plans to place the color ad in a regional golfing magazine, therefore he wants a high resolution, CMYK file to submit to the publisher. The owner has a file with the appropriate text copy, an image of a golf ball, and an image of a golfer. You need to put it all together, adding a gradient background and inserting a shape. A sample solution is shown in Figure 4-72.

FIGURE 4-72

Instructions:

1. Start Photoshop. Set the default workspace and reset all tools.
2. Press CTRL+O to open a file. Navigate to the Project04 file on the CD that accompanies this book, or to a location specified by your instructor. Open the file named, Golf Outing.
3. Click the Save As command on the File menu. Browse to your USB flash drive storage device. Click the Save button. If Photoshop displays a format Options dialog box, click the OK button.
4. In the Layers palette, click the Visibility icons to hide all text layers. Click the Background layer to select it, if necessary.
5. Press the G key to access the Gradient tool. If the Paint Bucket tool is active, press SHIFT+G to toggle to the Gradient tool.
6. On the Gradient options bar, click the Gradient Editor box. When Photoshop displays the Gradient Editor dialog box, click the Gradient Type box arrow and then click Solid. Double-click the Smoothness box and then type `100`.
7. Below the color bar, double-click the left Color Stop button. When the Color Picker dialog box is displayed, choose a light blue color. Click the OK button.
8. Below the color bar, double-click the right Color Stop button. When the Color Picker dialog box is displayed, choose a light yellow color. Click the OK button.
9. Below the center of the color bar, double-click to create a new Color Stop button. When the Color Picker dialog box is displayed, choose a light orange color. Click the OK button.
10. Drag the orange Color Stop button slightly to the right until the gradient flows smoothly, similar to that shown in Figure 4-72. Adjust any Color Midpoint diamonds as necessary.
11. Click the OK button in the Gradient Editor. Draw a gradient by dragging from the upper-right corner of the page in the document window to the lower-left corner.
12. In the Layers palette, click to display the text layers.
13. Press CTRL+O and then navigate to the file named, Golfer. Open the file.
14. In the Golfer document window, press CTRL+A to select the entire image. Press the V key to activate the Move tool. Drag the image to the Golf Outing document window. Position the golfer as shown in Figure 4-72.
15. Close the Golfer document window. In the Layers palette, rename the new layer, golfer.
16. Press CTRL+O and then navigate to the file named, Golf ball. Open the file.
17. In the Golf ball document window, press CTRL+A to select the entire image. Press the V key to activate the Move tool. Drag the image to the Golf Outing document window. Position the golf ball as shown in Figure 4-72.
18. Increase the magnification as necessary in the Golf Outing document window. Press the E key to access the current Eraser tool. Press SHIFT+E until the Magic Eraser tool is active. Click the blue areas around the golf ball to erase them.
19. Resize the golf ball to make it smaller by pressing CTRL+T to display the bounding box. SHIFT+drag a corner sizing handle and then press the ENTER key.
20. Close the Golf ball document window. In the Layers palette, rename the new layer, golf ball.
21. Press the U key to access the shape tools. On the shape options bar, click the Shape Layers button. Click the Custom Shape Tool button.
22. On the shapes option bar, click the Shape box arrow. When the shapes display, click the menu button and then click Web in the list. When Photoshop asks if you want to replace or append the shapes, click the Append button. When the new shapes are displayed, scroll as necessary and double-click the Time shape.

(continued)

Creating an Advertisement Using Gradients and Shapes *(continued)*

23. On the shapes option bar, click the Color box. When the Color Picker dialog box is displayed, select a Light Gray color. Click the OK button.
24. In the document window, SHIFT+drag to create a clock in the lower-right portion of the image, similar to the one shown in Figure 4-72. A border may appear around the edges of the clock. It will disappear when you flatten the image.
25. On the File menu, click Save.
26. On the Layer menu, click Flatten Image.
27. Press SHIFT+CTRL+S to access the Save As dialog box. In the File name box, type `Golf Outing Complete` as the name. Click the Format box arrow and then choose the TIF format from the list. Click the Save button. When the TIF Options dialog box is displayed, click the OK button.
28. Quit Photoshop. E-mail the file as an attachment to your instructor.

2 Creating a Web Graphic from Scratch

Problem: A planetarium is holding a contest to choose a Web graphic to advertise its new exhibit. The winning promotional piece will represent themes related to the search for life in deep space. The winner of the contest will receive $500 and a family membership to the planetarium. You decide to enter. Using a gradient, a shape, and brush strokes, you create a piece that symbolizes the planets, the sky, motion, searching, and life. A sample image is displayed in Figure 4-73.

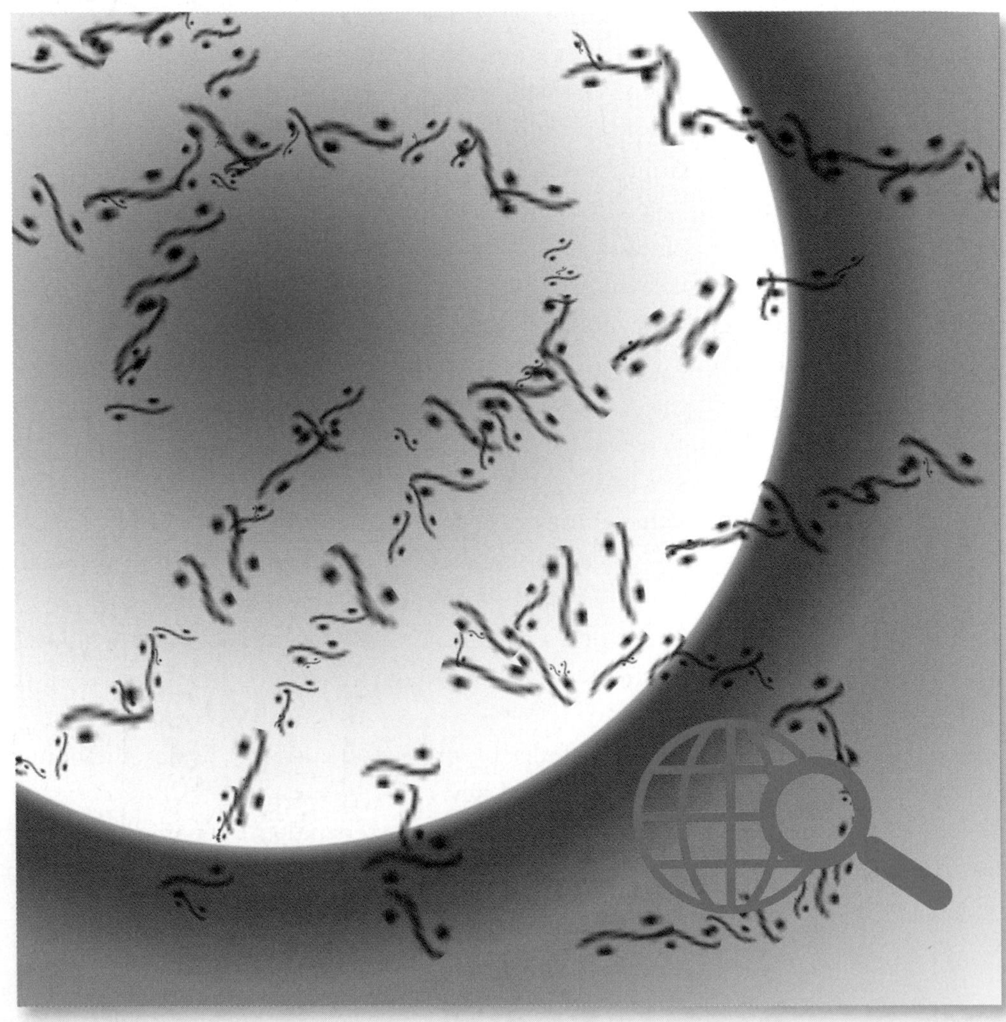

FIGURE 4-73

Instructions:

1. Start Photoshop. Set the default workspace and reset all tools.
2. Click New on the File menu. When the New dialog box is displayed, use the following settings:
   a. Name: Planetarium Graphic
   b. Width: 8 inches
   c. Height 8 inches
   d. Resolution: 300 pixels/inch
   e. Color Mode: RGB Color, 8 bit
   f. Background Contents: White
3. Click the Save As command on the File menu. Click the Format box arrow and then click PSD in the list. Browse to your USB flash drive storage device. Click the Save button. If Photoshop displays a Format Options dialog box, click the OK button.
4. Select the Gradient tool. On the Gradient options bar, click the Gradient Editor box arrow and then click the Chrome gradient.
5. On the options bar, click the Radial Gradient button, and then drag from the upper-left corner to the lower-right corner.
6. Select the Eyedropper tool and sample the darkest brown color in the Chrome gradient. In the Color palette, if a warning triangle displays, click the square next to it to select a gamut color.
7. Select the Brush tool. Display the Brushes palette and then click the palette menu button. On the palette menu, click Assorted Brushes and append the brushes.
8. Click the Brush Tip Shape button. Scroll as necessary and then click the Ornament 7 15 brush tip. Click the Shape Dynamics check box so it displays a check mark. Set the Diameter to 200 pixels, and the Spacing to 150%.
9. Drag with short strokes, randomly in the image. Your design does not have to match exactly the one in Figure 4-73.
10. Double-click the Set foreground color button in the toolbox. When Photoshop displays the Color Picker dialog box, click the Only Web Colors check box so it displays a check mark. Click green in the color slider and then click an appropriate green color in the color field. Click the OK button.
11. Select the Shape tool. On the shape options bar, click the Shape layers button. Click the Custom Shape Tool button. Click the Shape box arrow, and then click the shape menu button. On the menu, click Web. When Photoshop asks if you want to replace or append, click the Append button. Scroll as necessary and then select the World Wide Web Search Shape.
12. In the document window, SHIFT+drag to add the sphere and magnifying glass in the lower-right corner.
13. On the File menu, click Save.
14. On the Layer menu, click Flatten Image.
15. Press SHIFT+CTRL+S to access the Save As dialog box. In the File name box, type `Planetarium Graphic Complete` as the name. Save the file using the TIF format.
16. For extra credit, create a simple Web page and display your image. Send your instructor a copy of the image as an e-mail attachment or send the URL.
17. Quit Photoshop.

3 Creating a Wallpaper Border

Problem: A wallpaper company has hired you as a graphic designer to create a new wallpaper border for a kitchen. The border, which is 5 inches high, should repeat its pattern every 7.5 inches. The background should be a tan color with a custom shape running across the center and random flowers, as shown in Figure 4-74.

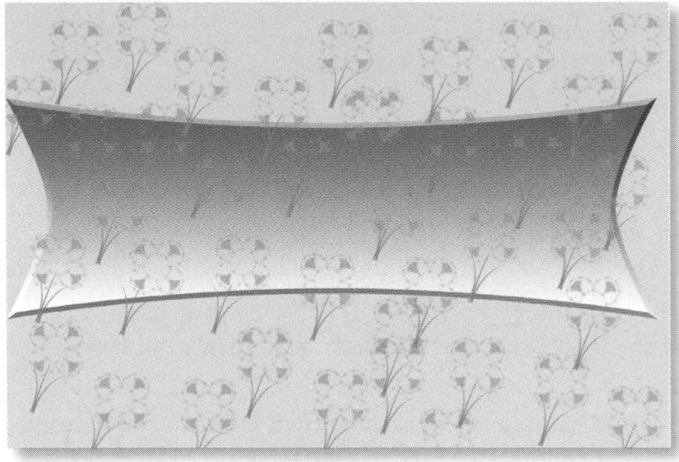

FIGURE 4-74

Instructions:

1. Start Photoshop. Set the Default Workspace and reset all tools.
2. Press CTRL+N to start a new file. When the New dialog box is displayed, type `Wallpaper Border` in the Name box. Set the width to 7.5 inches and the height to 5 inches. Set the resolution to 300 ppi. Choose the CMYK color mode with the white background color setting. Click the OK button.
3. Double-click the Set foreground color button in the toolbox to access the Color Picker and then enter `8`, `11`, `24`, and `0` respectively as the CMYK colors to create tan. Click the OK button. Choose the Paint Bucket tool and fill the document window with the tan color.
4. Click the Current Shape Tool button in the toolbox. On the shape options bar, click the Custom Shape Tool button and then click the menu button. Click Banners and then, when Photoshop displays a dialog box, click Append. Select the Banner 3 shape.
5. Click the Style button, click the menu button, and then append the Text Effects styles. Select the Chiseled Sky (Text) style.
6. Drag to draw a banner that fills the middle portion of the page.
7. On the Layer menu, click Flatten Image.
8. Use the Swatches palette to choose a dark pink magenta color. Press the B key to choose the current brush tool.
9. Press the B key to choose the current brush tool.
10. Use the Brushes palette menu to append the Special Effects Brushes. Select the second instance of the brush named, Sampled Tip 40. Create a brush tip with a diameter of 175 and spacing of 200. Single click to create the flowers. Your exact placement does not have to match Figure 4-74.
11. Use the Swatches palette to choose a medium green color.
12. Use the Brushes palette to select the brush named, Grass 134. Create a brush tip with a diameter of 175, a spacing of 200, and -20 degree angle. Click to create the stems.
13. Save the file with the name, Wallpaper Border. Use the TIF format and print a hard copy in landscape mode for your instructor
14. Quit Photoshop.

Cases and Places

The difficulty of these case studies varies:
■ are the least difficult and ■■ are the most difficult. The last exercise is a group exercise.

1 ■ Create a sign to place on the paper recycling box in your computer lab. Start with a blank page that is 8.5 inches by 11 inches. Choose a shape tool and then click the Custom Shape Tool button on the shapes options bar. Click the Shape box. When the shapes are displayed, click Shape Preset picker menu button and then click Symbols in the list. Click to Append the Symbols to the current set. Scroll to display the recycling logo and click it. Drag to create a recycling logo that fills the page, leaving a 1 inch margin on each side. Select a dark blue color from the Swatches palette and then use the Paint Bucket tool to color the logo. If you are asked to rasterize the layer, click the OK button. Find a graphic of a piece of paper with something printed on it. Drag a copy to the middle of the recycling logo. Print the sign on a color printer.

2 ■ Scan in a black and white photo and open it in Photoshop. Print a copy of the photo. Use the Magic Wand tool to select portions of clothing, buildings, sky, grass, or walls. Double-click the Set foreground color button in the toolbox, and then select a color using the Color Picker. Use the Paint Bucket tool to fill the selections with color. Save the colorized version of the photo with a different name. Print the colorized version. Turn in both the before and after printouts to your instructor.

3 ■■ Ask your instructor for a digital copy of your school's logo. Start a new document from scratch and create a background gradient using one of the Gradient buttons other than Linear. Open the logo file and drag a copy into the new document. Include at least four different strokes or shapes from the concepts presented in this project, such as a color change, brush strokes, shapes, or drawing with the Pen tool.

4 ■■ Create a new file that is 640 pixels by 480 pixels in size. Your image will be a collage of at least three other images. The other images can be from a digital camera, scanned photographs, available clip art, or some combination thereof. Use the Magic Eraser tool and selection tools to remove some of the background in each image. Do not leave any image rectangular. Create small selections in the collage and apply gradients to the selections. Use brush strokes to create short labels or graphics next to each of the images. Use the Line tool with a decorated brush tip to create a border around the collage.

5 ■■ **Working Together** Your team is in charge of special effects for a small movie production company. You need to plan a storyboard of special effects for an upcoming movie. Together, decide on a theme for your movie. Each member should bring a real digital or electronic image to use in the storyboard. As you did when adding motion lines to the Recital Graphic, use painting and drawing tools to add at least four of the following special effects to each of the real images: flames, lightning bolts, explosions, tattoos, a change of eye color, jet streams, rocket flares, spider webs, sun bursts, etc.

Enhancing and Repairing Photos

PROJECT 5

CASE PERSPECTIVE

Ethel Lykins is head of the Gentry County Historical Society, one of the oldest historical societies in the state of Missouri. This nonprofit organization, devoted to preserving the historical records of the area, collects and disseminates knowledge to residents and historians. The society also manages the renovation of local historical landmarks.

Ethel has accumulated many old photographs that the historical society would like to restore for an exhibit about the county's history. One photo is of the old bandstand from 1916 that needs enhancing. A picture of one of the founding fathers has several damaged areas. The historical society wants to publicize its renovation of an 1869 schoolhouse. They plan to take school groups through the Little Red Schoolhouse to show children what it was like to go to school more than 100 years ago, with inkwells, a potbelly stove, old textbooks, and a 36-star flag. The historical society's most important document, a letter from a wife to a husband during the Civil War, is difficult to read because of discoloration due to age. While they would like to display the original, it must be preserved from further damage caused by light and humidity. So a replica needs to be created.

Ethel has offered you a summer internship to help enhance and repair the damaged photos for use in exhibits and on the historical society Web site. Additionally, she wants a photo of local children turned into a postcard that she can mail to area schools. The photo has a red eye problem. The old schoolhouse photo needs some distortion repair and then should be superimposed in the background. The words, Play and Learn at the Little Red Schoolhouse, need to be added across the bottom of the image.

As you read through this project, you will learn how to repair damaged areas of documents and photos, correct red eye, edit lighting, fix distortion errors, and enhance images with text.

Enhancing and Repairing Photos

PROJECT 5

Objectives

You will have mastered the material in this project when you can:

- Discuss technical tips for digital cameras and scanners
- Repair documents with aging damage
- Make level corrections for contrast
- Sharpen images with the Unsharp Mask
- Correct small blemishes using the Spot Healing Brush tool
- Correct tears and scratches using the Healing Brush tool
- Retouch images using the Patch tool
- Use the Dodge and Burn tools
- Correct red eye
- Correct angle and perspective distortions
- Change the opacity to fade a layer
- Open a recently used file
- Use text elements
- Save a file in the EPS format

Introduction

Repairing and enhancing photos is an important skill for people such as graphic designers, restoration experts, and professional photographers. It is a good skill for the amateur photographer as well. Many families have old photographs that have been damaged, and most people have taken a red eye photo. Freelance photographers, genealogists, family historians, and proud parents all use Photoshop to restore, correct, and improve their photographs.

It is impossible to make every photo look perfect, however. Graphics-related professionals know that a camera lacks the flexibility to rival reality — the color tonal range is too small. The large number of colors visible to human eyes is a spectrum that cannot be matched by cameras or digital creations.

Therefore, enhancing and repairing photos is both an art and a science. Using the digital tools available in Photoshop, you can employ technology to make reparative and restorative changes. Artistically, you need a strong sense of color and design sensibility.

Because pictures are open to interpretation without explanatory text, designers and advertisers almost always use words or logos to force brand recognition and get their point across. Text is an element used in a majority of design and advertising graphics. Focus groups routinely are asked to remember what they saw in a commercial or advertisement. Ads with words, verbal or written, score higher than those without. The majority of designers feel that text elements are the most important visual communication component of their work.

Layout artists frequently use a combination of several software programs. If there will be more text than graphics in the finished product, a page-layout program may be the primary software of choice rather than Photoshop. Applications such as Microsoft Publisher and Adobe InDesign allow the ease of graphic placement along with advanced text capabilities that Photoshop does not possess. It is not uncommon to edit or create an image in Photoshop and then export it to a page-layout program. While Photoshop is the correct tool to use if text is embedded within the photo, a page-layout program is better for large amounts of related text. For example, if you are creating a newsletter or brochure that contains a lot of written data, you would want to create your graphics in Photoshop, then lay out the graphics and text in a page-layout application. On the other hand, if you are creating a poster, artwork for ads, or a Web graphic with fewer words, you most likely will want to incorporate text within your graphic — a natural role for Photoshop. You will discover the wide breadth of text editing techniques in Photoshop to be very useful.

Among the enhancing and repairing tools in Photoshop are the Healing Brush tool, the Spot Healing Brush tool, the Patch tool, and the Red Eye tool. The Dodge and Burn tools help you with light and dark areas. The Unsharp Mask brings images into focus and the Lens Correction dialog box allows you to fix several kinds of distortions. The type tools with their font, style, tracking, kerning, leading, orientation, anti-aliasing, and warping capabilities can be used to create an endless variety of embedded text elements. You will learn about each of these tools as you work through this project.

Project Five — Enhancing and Repairing Photos

Project 5 uses Photoshop to enhance and repair several photographs and documents. Specifically, an old letter needs to be restored for easier reading. An old photo of a man is damaged with age spots and defects. A photo of a bandstand needs to be enhanced by repairing some light damage. A photo of a schoolhouse needs a perspective correction. Finally, a picture of children needs to have the red eye removed. Photos and text are combined to make a postcard. The before and after photos are illustrated in Figure 5-1 on the next page.

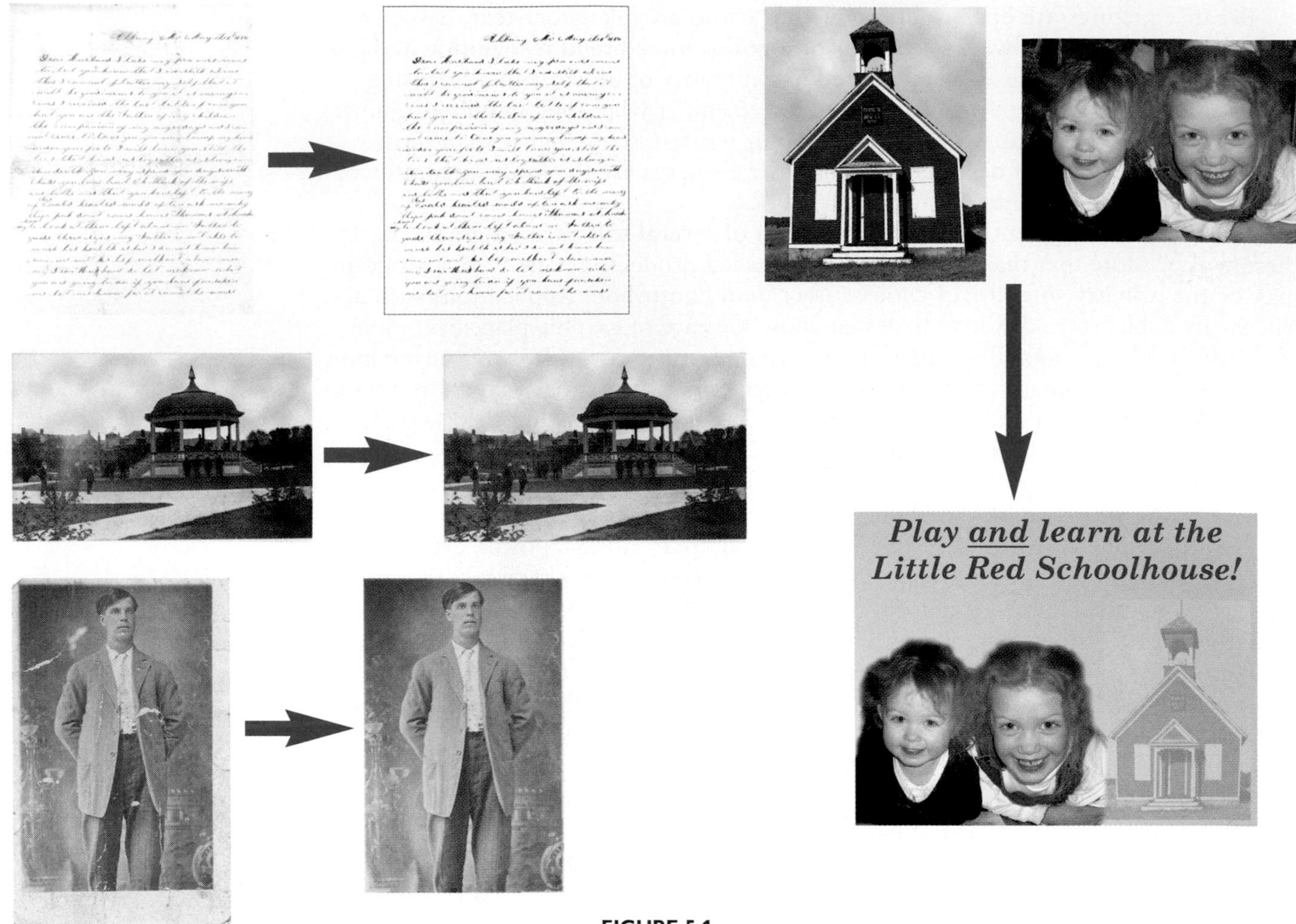

FIGURE 5-1

Gathering Images

Recall that there are a variety of ways that pictures and documents can be imported into Photoshop. Pictures taken using old photographic generating mechanisms, such as tintypes, daguerreotypes, and stereographic cameras, as well as those taken with film-producing and instant print cameras, must be scanned using a digital scanner. Many photo-processing services will digitize any type of film onto a photo CD. Modern digital cameras use simple software to transfer pictures directly into computer systems. Documents and personal papers can be scanned in as images; or, if they are typewritten and easily legible, some scanners can produce digital text files. But no matter how you generate the image, creating a high quality, high-resolution copy is the most important step in enhancing and repairing photos and documents.

Scanners

Considerations that affect the outcome of a scanned image include color, size, resolution, and file types, among others. When converting an original image to a digital copy some loss of resolution is inevitable. Table 5-1 displays some simple tips about digital scanners that will produce better results. In addition, you should review carefully your scanner documentation.

Table 5-1 Scanner Tips

ISSUE	TIP
File Type	Most scanners have a setting related to the type of file you are selecting. Scanners make automatic anti-aliasing adjustments and tonal changes based on the file type you choose. Use the closest possible settings to your original. For example, if you have a text only document, do not use a setting related to color photos; use the black and white, or grayscale, setting.
Multiple Scans	Do not assume that your first scan is the one you will use. Try scanning with various file types, settings, and at different sizes. Look at a black-and-white scan even if color was your first choice. Keep in mind your final use of the image.
Placement	Place the photo in the upper-left corner of the scanner bed. Align the long side of the original with the long side of the scanner. Use the scanner's preview capability so that the scanner will determine the size and location of the photograph. Use scanner settings to select the exact size rather than the entire scanner bed when possible. After a preview scan, if available, a scaling feature, such as Scale to Fit page, will produce a bigger copy.
Quality	Always choose the best resolution when scanning an image for use in Photoshop, keeping in mind that an image with higher resolution requires more disk space to store and may be slower to edit and print. Image resolution is a compromise between image quality and file size.
Resolution	The scanner's resolution is a measure of how many dots per inch are scanned. Higher-resolution images can reproduce greater detail and subtler color transitions than lower-resolution images because of the density of the pixels in the images. High-quality images often look good at any print size.
Shading	To maintain the background shading, especially in color, select a setting related to text with pictures rather than just text. A text only setting can create a picture area that appears as a solid black rectangle.
Size	Use the largest original you can. For instance, an 8 × 10-inch photo will make a higher quality 24-inch poster than a 4 × 6-inch photo. Only use a reduce or enlarge setting when absolutely necessary. Keep in mind that when you print a copy, most printers need at least ¼-inch margin. A printed copy produced from a scan may lose its edges if the original is the exact size as the paper.
Text	Most scanners have a text or drawing setting, which is appropriate only if your original contains just black and white areas, text only, or other solid areas, such as signatures, clip art, line drawings, maps, or blueprints. If you use this setting for a photograph or picture that also contains gray areas, the result may be unsatisfactory.
Tone	If the copy appears too light or too dark, or just appears as solid black, make sure that you have selected the correct file type for the original you are using. Look for darken and lighten settings that might be adjusted.

More About

Pixels versus Dots

Pixels per inch (ppi) refers to a measurement used in describing visual or monitor settings. The resolution of an image displayed on a monitor is determined by its ppi, or the number of pixels contained within one square inch of monitor space. Scanners and printers use dots per inch (dpi) to describe the image resolution. The more dots per inch, the higher the resolution. For example, a typical resolution for laser printers is 600 dots per inch. This means 600 dots across and 600 dots down, resulting in 360,000 dots per square inch.

Digital Cameras

The advent of digital cameras has reduced dramatically the need for the intermediate step of scanning. Images can be transferred directly from the camera's storage medium to a file or directly into Photoshop. A digital camera's resolution is measured in **megapixels**, or millions of dots per inch. It is not uncommon for a digital camera to create photos with 8 or more megapixels per image. Figure 5-2a displays a photo taken at 8 megapixels. Figure 5-2b displays the same image taken at 2 megapixels. Notice the finer details and brighter colors produced by more megapixels. Certain digital cameras import images using **Windows Image Acquisition** (**WIA**) support. When you use WIA, Photoshop works with Windows and your digital camera or scanner software to import images directly into Photoshop.

(a) 8 megapixels

(b) 2 megapixels

FIGURE 5-2

Professional cameras, as well as most point-and-shoot general consumer cameras, can save images in camera raw format. A **camera raw** file contains unprocessed picture data from a digital camera's image sensor. Camera raw image files contain the actual captured data without any in-camera processing; that way, photographers can interpret the image data rather than having the camera make the adjustments and conversions automatically. Working with camera raw files allows maximum control for settings such as white balance, tonal range, contrast, color saturation, and sharpening. It is similar to the way photo processors try to fix photos taken by traditional film, reprocessing the negative with different shades and tints. Photoshop displays a special dialog box when working with camera raw photos.

Table 5-2 displays some simple tips about digital cameras that will produce better results when working with Photoshop. Again, review carefully your camera's documentation.

Table 5-2 Digital Camera Tips

ISSUE	TIP
File Type	If possible, set the camera to save files in its own raw file format. The Adobe Web site, at www.adobe.com has a list of cameras supported by Photoshop.
Quality	Use memory cards with higher megapixel counts to take more images at a much higher resolution. Use the highest quality compression setting, as well.
Storage	Copy images from the camera to a storage device before editing them in Photoshop. Adobe Bridge can read from most media cards, or you can use the software that comes with your camera.

Table 5-2 Digital Camera Tips *(continued)*

ISSUE	TIP
Lighting and Speed	Experiment with the correlation between light and shutter speeds. Most of the newer digital cameras can take many pictures in a short amount of time, avoiding the shutter lag problem — the delay that occurs between pressing the shutter release button and the actual moment the picture is taken.
Balance	Consider changing your white balance setting from auto to cloudy when shooting outdoors. It creates a filtered, richer color increasing the reds and yellows.
Filters	If possible use a polarizing filter for landscapes and outdoor shooting. It reduces glare and unwanted reflections. Polarized shots have richer, more saturated colors, especially in the sky. You also can use sunglasses in front of the lens to reduce glare. When shooting through glass, use an infinity focus setting.
Flash	When shooting pictures of people or detailed subjects, use flash — even outdoors. If available, use the camera's fill flash or flash on mode. That way the camera exposes the background first and then adds just enough light to illuminate your subject. Keep in mind that most flash mechanisms only have a range of approximately 10 feet.
Settings	When possible use a plain background, look at your subject in a straight, level manner, and move in as close as possible. Consider the rule of thirds when taking photographs. For busy backgrounds, if your camera has a focus lock feature, center the subject and push the shutter button half way down to focus on the subject. Then move the camera horizontally or vertically away from the center before pressing the shutter button all the way down.
Motion	For moving objects use a fast shutter speed.

Web Graphics

A vast source of images and documents can be found on the Web. The advantage in using Web graphics is the fact that the pictures and documents already are digitized, so you do not have to manipulate or scan them; neither do you lose any resolution when transferring them to your computer system. The disadvantage of using Web graphics is in ownership. You must obtain permission to use images you download from the Web unless the image is free and unrestricted. You need to scrutinize carefully any Web sites that advertise free graphics. Some cannot be used for business purposes, for reproductions, or for resale. Some illegitimate sites that advertise free downloads also embed spyware on your system.

Starting and Customizing Photoshop

If you are stepping through this project on a computer and you want your screen to match the figures in this book, you should change your computer's resolution to 1024 × 768 and reset the tools and palettes. For more information about how to change the resolution on your computer, and other advanced Photoshop settings, read Appendix A.

The following steps describe how to start Photoshop and customize the Photoshop window. You may need to ask your instructor how to start Photoshop for your system.

To Start Photoshop and Reset the Palettes, Toolbox, and Options Bar

1. **Start Photoshop as described on pages PS 6 and PS 7.**
2. **Choose the Default Workspace as described on page PS 8.**
3. **Select the Rectangular Marquee tool and then reset all tools as described on pages PS 9 and PS 10.**

Photoshop starts and then resets the tools, palettes, and options.

Resetting the Layers Palette

The following steps show how to reset the Layers palette to make the thumbnails match the figures shown in this book.

To Reset the Layers Palette

1. **Click the Layers palette menu button and then click Palette Options on the list.**
2. **When Photoshop displays the Layers Palette Options dialog box, click the option button corresponding to the smallest of the thumbnail sizes, if necessary.**
3. **If necessary, click Layer Bounds.**
4. **Click the OK button.**

The Layers palette will display small thumbnails for each layer.

Resetting the Colors

The following step shows how to reset the default colors in the Photoshop window.

To Reset the Colors

1. **If black and white are not shown as the default colors in the toolbox, press the D key on the keyboard.**

Black is set as the foreground color; white is set as the background color.

Opening the First Image

The first image you will edit is the yellowed Civil War letter. The following steps open the scanned image from the CD that accompanies this book. Your instructor may designate a different location for the file.

To Open the Letter Image

1. **Insert the CD that accompanies this book into your CD drive. After a few seconds, if Windows displays a dialog box, click its Close button.**

2 **In Photoshop, press CTRL+O to open a file. Navigate to the Project05 folder, and then double-click the file named, Letter.**

3 **When Photoshop displays the image, if necessary, press CTRL+R to display the rulers.**

4 **If necessary, change the magnification to 16.67 percent.**

The image is displayed (Figure 5-3). Yellowed and brown aging areas can be seen in the letter. A damaged area displays half way down the letter, on the left.

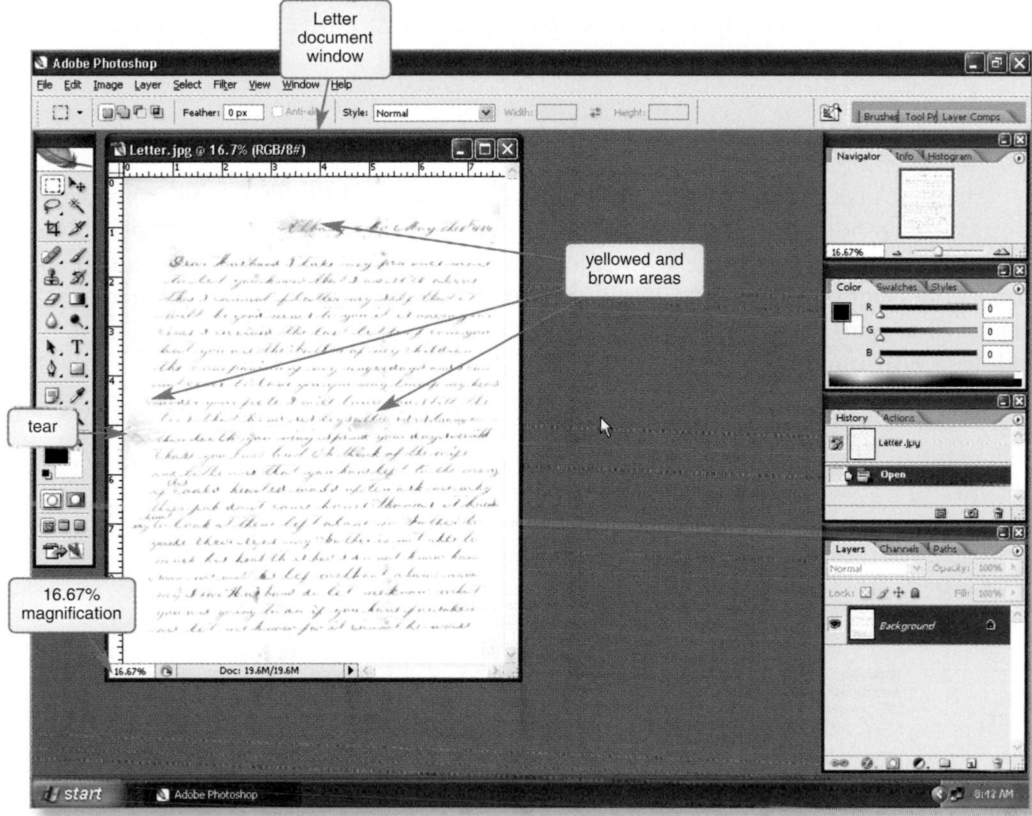

FIGURE 5-3

Repairing Documents

Restoring original documents is a highly skilled art. It takes education, research, and years of practice. When dealing with documents of great value, or when dealing with materials in advanced stages of deterioration, a professional conservator or restoration service should be consulted. Many restorers, however, choose to renovate or repair original documents using digital copies. If the document can be scanned or photographed, the original does not have to be disturbed. The repairs can be performed digitally. The old adage, "It is better to do nothing than to do the wrong thing," does not apply when you can manipulate a digital copy, over and over again. Photoshop has many tools to help refurbish and enhance documents.

Documents have some unique aging features that photos typically do not have. Common document paper is an organic substance composed of cellulose plant fibers that will deteriorate faster than professional photo paper. While some paper used before the year 1900 was very strong and durable, much of it was not. Rapid deterioration results from the use of production acids that break down the fibers, weakening the paper. Acid deterioration commonly is accompanied by yellow **discoloration**

> *More About*
>
> **Restorations**
>
> Many restoration companies have Web sites advertising cheap restorations. Be very careful when hiring a professional restorer — they may be using the same Photoshop techniques that you are learning in this project. Be sure to check a restoration company's references, and ask to see before and after samples. For severely damaged documents, professional restorers and researchers now are using dehumidification and freezing techniques for water damage, fiber-optic light to illuminate hidden text covered by paper binding or strong fungus, and ultraviolet fluorescence to recover faded, burned, or even erased text. For more information on restorations, visit the Shelly Cashman More About Web site.

due to the alum-resin, sizing agents. High temperatures and moisture compound the problem. Even now, unless the paper is designated as acid-free or permanent, its expected useful life is less than 50 years.

Other types of damage include dry and brittle creases caused by folding or rolling documents, brown spots due to water stains or fungus called **foxing**, brown edges due to airborne pollutants, the loss of strong colors due to light damage, mold, bacteria, improper storage, and animal or insect damage.

The Civil War letter has discoloration, foxing, crease damage, and fading. Handwritten portions of documents are particularly vulnerable. Ink and pencil exposed to significant amounts of sunlight dramatically fade. In order to create a copy for display at the historical society and on the Web, several restorative techniques will be employed.

Removing Discoloration

The first task is to remove all yellow and brown from the image by converting it to grayscale mode. **Grayscale mode** uses different shades of gray in an image. When Photoshop converts an image with color to grayscale, it discards all color information in the original image. The luminosity of the original pixels is represented by shades of gray in the converted pixels. The following steps show how to remove yellowed portions of the letter.

To Remove Yellowed Portions of the Letter

1

- **Click Image on the menu bar, then point to Mode.**

Photoshop displays the Mode submenu (Figure 5-4).

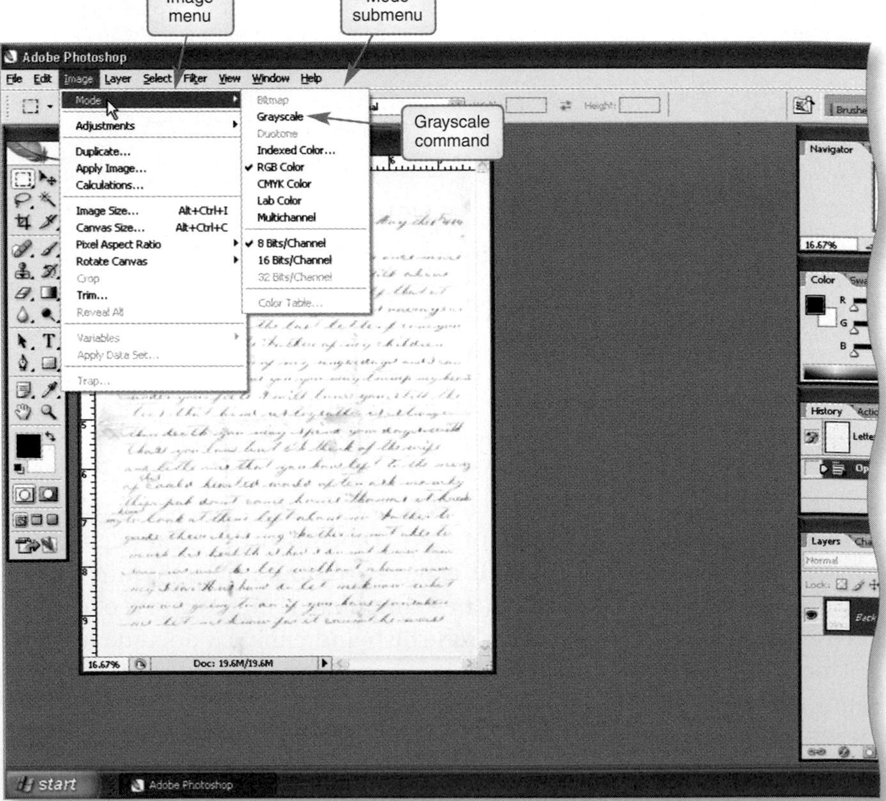

FIGURE 5-4

2

• **Click Grayscale. When Photoshop asks if you want to discard all color information, click the OK button.**

The letter displays in grayscale (Figure 5-5).

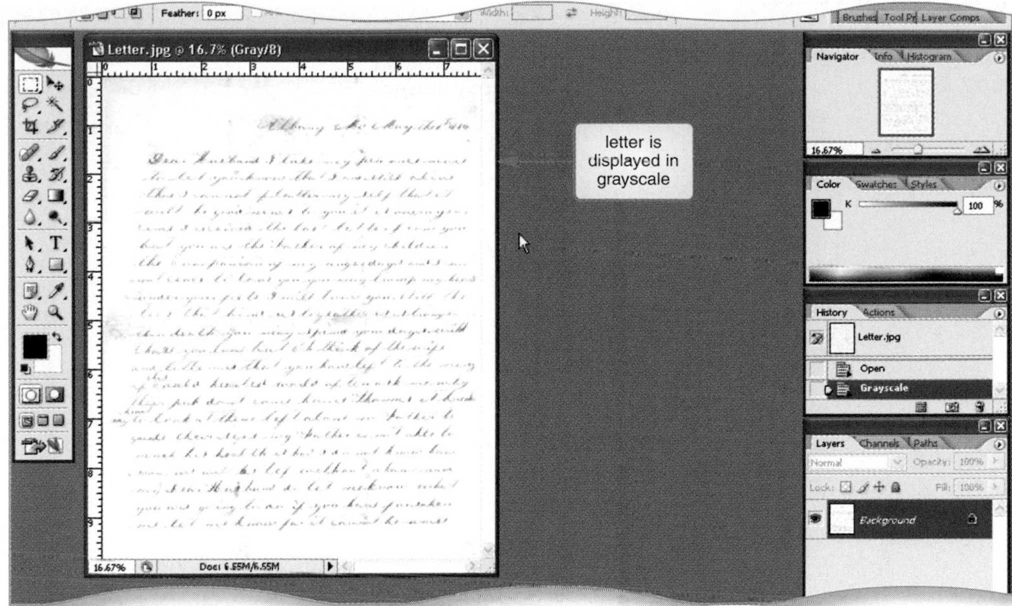

FIGURE 5-5

Setting Levels

After converting to grayscale, the next step is to adjust the levels to correct the tonal range and contrast. Recall from Project 3 that the Levels dialog box allows you to adjust the intensity levels of shadows, midtones, and highlights. The following steps show how to adjust black, gray, and white in the letter.

To Set Levels

1

• **Press CTRL+L to access the Levels dialog box.**

• **When Photoshop displays the Levels dialog box, type** 125 **in the first Input Levels box to adjust the black levels. Type** 1.5 **in the second Input Levels box to adjust the gray or midtones. Type** 240 **in the third box to adjust the white levels.**

Photoshop displays the Levels dialog box (Figure 5-6). Entering data or dragging the sliders adjusts the black, gray midtones, and white levels in the image.

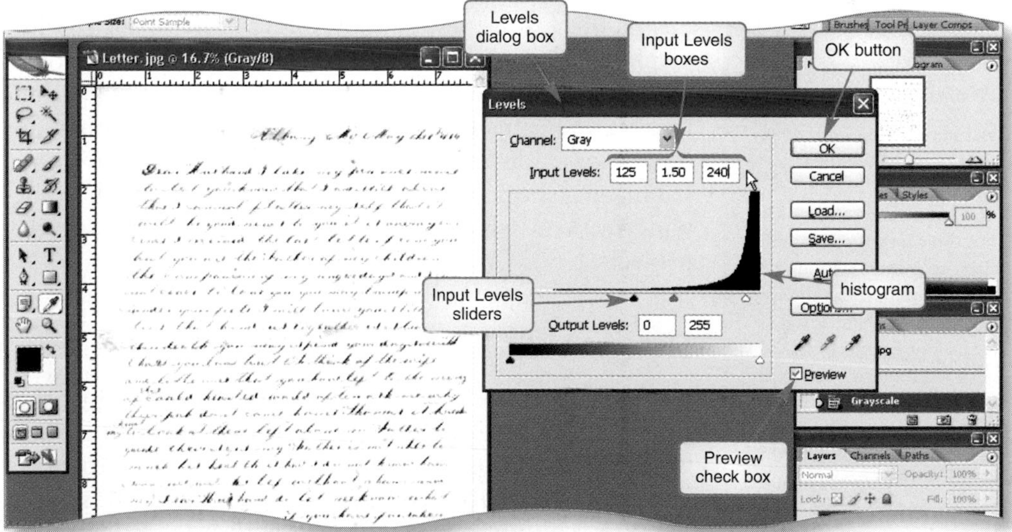

FIGURE 5-6

2

• **Click the OK button in the Levels dialog box.**

The contrast in the letter is changed (Figure 5-7).

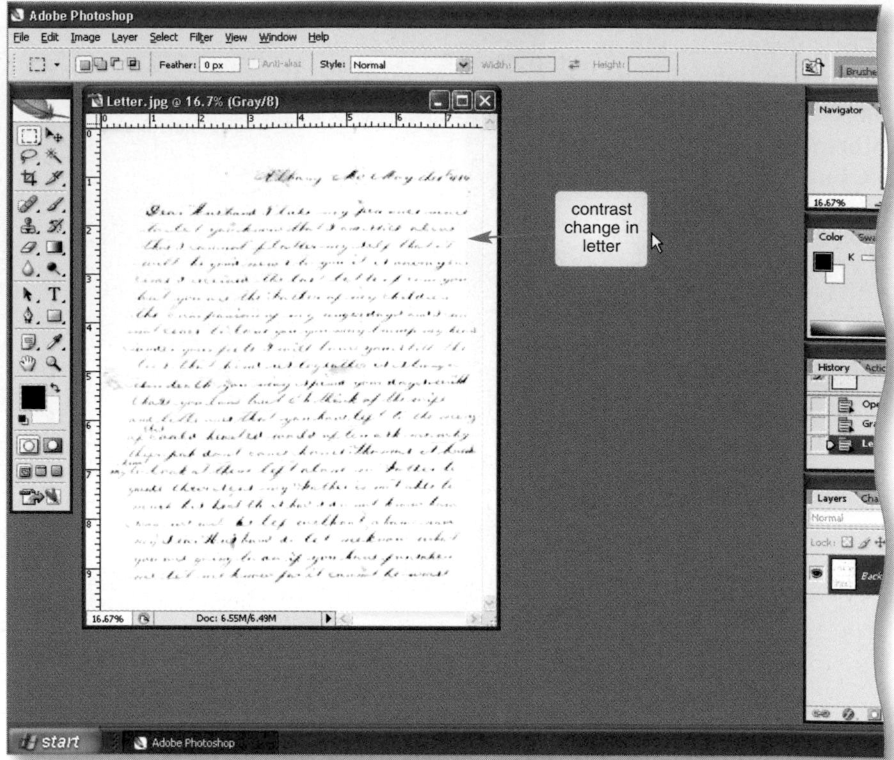

FIGURE 5-7

Other Ways

1. On Image menu, point to Adjustments, click Levels, drag sliders

More About

Levels

Most images look best when they utilize the full tonal range of dark to light that can be displayed on the screen or in print. This means that it often is best to make sure the histogram extends all the way from black to white. Images that do not extend to fill the entire tonal range often look washed out, lacking an impact. On the other hand, moving the sliders to the edge of the histogram can clip the subtle shadows and highlights, causing the image to lose its soft light or mood. Color photos are more prone to user levels errors than are black and white images.

The levels **histogram** in Figure 5-6 on the previous page, is a graph that charts the frequency of shades in the tonal range. It is a visual guide for adjusting the shadows, midtones, and highlights of the image. Much of the decision about where to set the input levels is aesthetic in nature; it is easy to overdo level changes and cause a loss of quality in the image. A few general strategies can be applied, however. The letter displayed a low frequency on the left side of the histogram which means there were few shadows, or totally black shades, in the image. If an image displays a low or nonexistent frequency of tone at one end of the scale, in general, that slider should be adjusted first. Drag it toward the center to a point where the frequency begins to increase. Then, adjust the other outer slider. Finally, adjust the middle or midtone slider by very small increments, to a point where the tones seem balanced. Check the Preview check box to watch your changes in the document window. You will learn more about histograms and the Histogram palette in later projects.

Sharpening Images

The **Unsharp Mask** command is a filter used to sharpen images. The Unsharp Mask works by evaluating the contrast between adjacent pixels, and increasing that contrast based on your settings. While Photoshop has a Sharpen command and a Sharpen More command, the Unsharp Mask command is more versatile because it allows you to sharpen with more precision. The Unsharp Mask dialog box (Figure 5-9 on page PS 282) has three settings: Amount, Radius, and Threshold. The way you adjust these settings depends primarily on the image content, and secondarily on the resolution and output purpose. Close subjects with soft details need adjusting in different ways from distant subjects with fine details.

While changing these settings is somewhat subjective and depends on your point of view, some general guidelines can be suggested.

The **Amount** value specifies how much of the sharpening effect to apply to the image. Dragging the slider, or entering an amount, you can preview the results. It is a good practice to keep the amount below 300. More than that tends to create a halo effect.

The **Radius** setting specifies the width of the sharpened edge, measured in pixels. Larger values will sharpen surrounding pixels. A good rule of thumb is to start with a radius value of 2 and then reduce the radius if the image has fine, crisp detail. Raise it if the image has soft details.

The **Threshold** setting specifies how different the sharpened pixels must be from the surrounding area before they are considered edge pixels and sharpened by the filter. For example, a threshold of 4 affects all pixels that have tonal values that differ by a value of 4 or more. A value of 0 sharpens all pixels in the image.

Many graphic artists set the radius first, the threshold second, and then the amount. That way, the width and edge are specified before the sharpening effect is applied, allowing the amount value to be more flexible. Additionally, sharpening at magnifications from 50 to 100 percent gives you a better feel for the final result. The following steps illustrate the use of the Unsharp Mask.

More About

Sharpening

Here are a few tips when sharpening.

Use an edits layer so that you can resharpen later. Set the layer's blending mode to Luminance to avoid color shifts along edges.

If you need to make other edits such as reducing image noise, do so before sharpening.

Sharpen your image multiple times in small amounts. Sharpen to correct capture blur then sharpen after colorization and resizing.

Adjust sharpening to fit the output media. Look at a final copy, print or Web, during sharpening.

To Use the Unsharp Mask

1

- **Zoom to 50 percent and then scroll to the beginning of the letter.**
- **Click Filter on the menu bar and then point to Sharpen.**

Photoshop displays the Sharpen submenu (Figure 5-8).

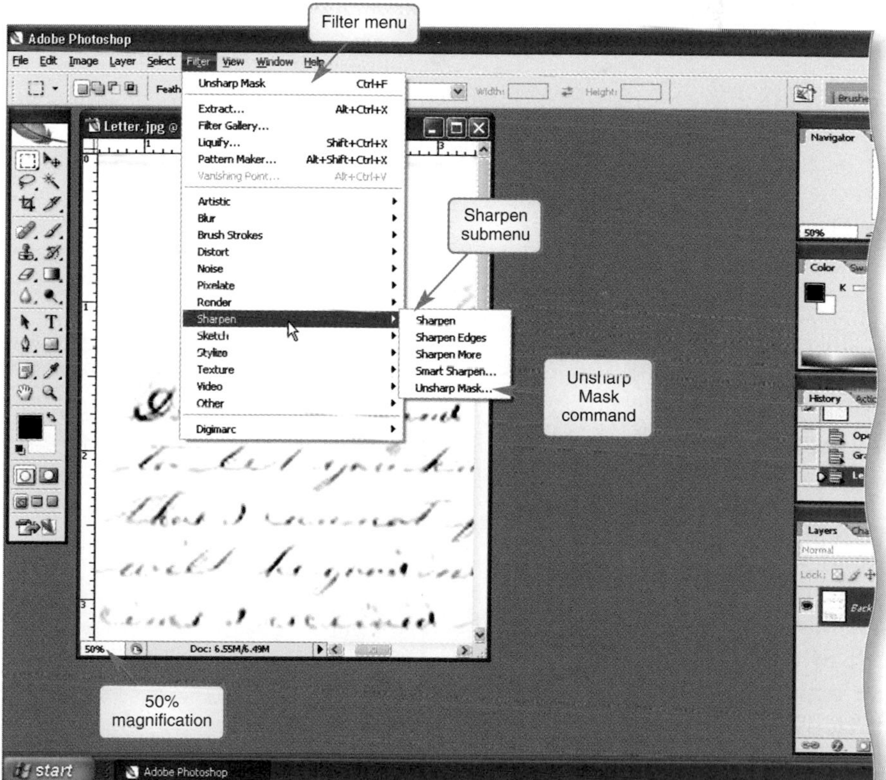

FIGURE 5-8

2

- **Click Unsharp Mask.**
- **When Photoshop displays the Unsharp Mask dialog box, type** 4 **in the Radius box. Type** 20 **in the Threshold box.**
- **Drag the Amount slider until the image is displayed more clearly.**

Photoshop sharpens the image (Figure 5-9).

3

- **Click the OK button in the Unsharp Mask dialog box.**

The Unsharp Mask dialog box closes.

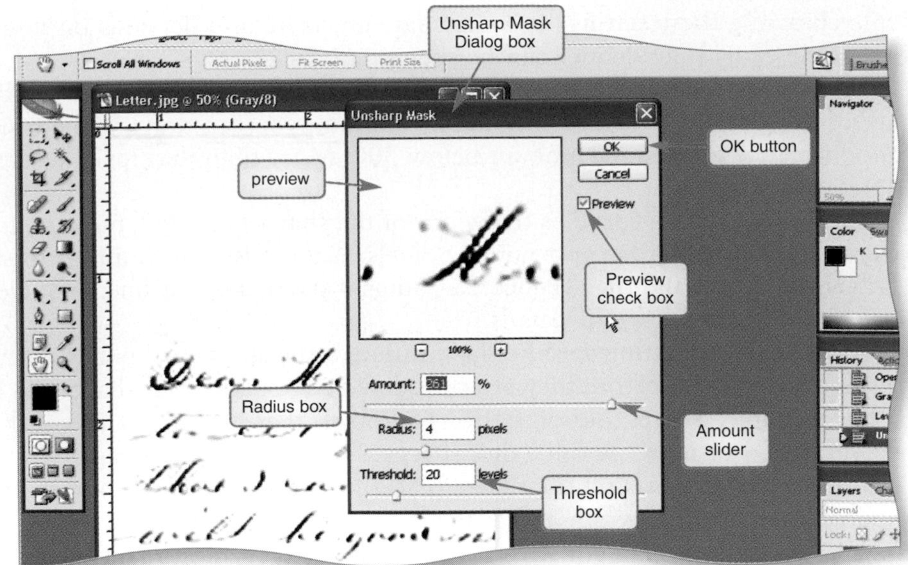

FIGURE 5-9

You will learn more about sharpening and other filters in a future project.

Cleaning Damaged Spots

Finally, the damaged spots in the letter will be cleaned using the Eraser tool as the following step illustrates.

To Use the Eraser Tool

1

- **Zoom out to display the entire letter.**
- **In the toolbox, click the Eraser Tool (E) button.**
- **Use the [or] keys to adjust the size of the eraser brush. With short strokes, drag through remaining gray areas that are not part of the handwriting itself. If you make a mistake, click the previous state in the History palette, or press CTRL+Z.**

Many of the dark and gray spots are removed (Figure 5-10).

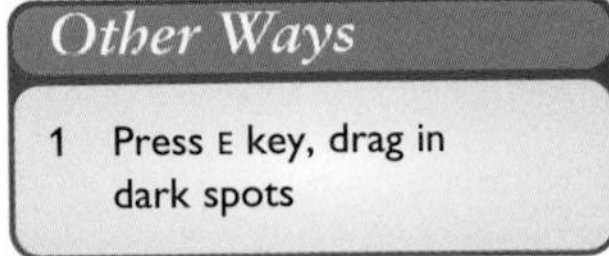

Other Ways

1. Press E key, drag in dark spots

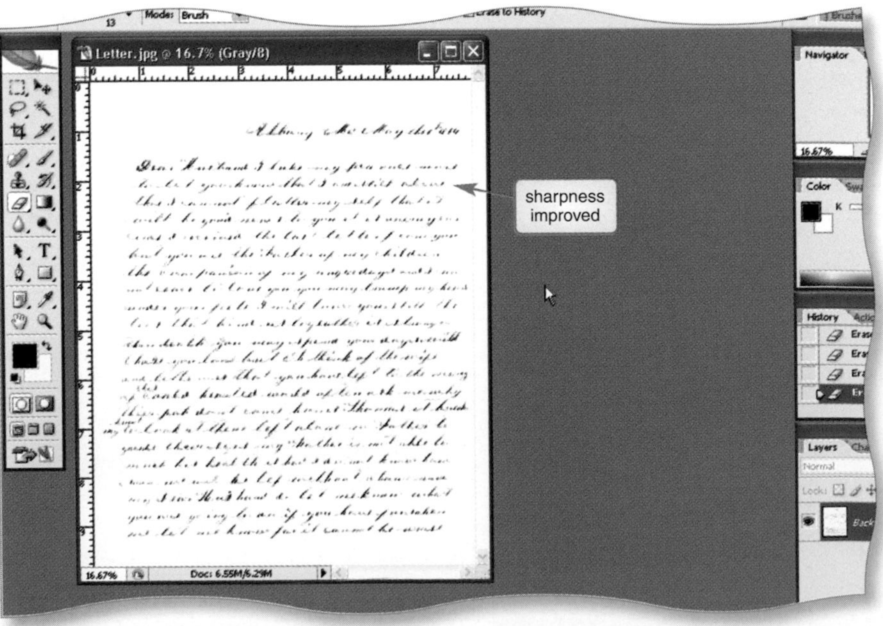

FIGURE 5-10

To prepare this image for display on the historical society's Web page, you will save the image as a Web graphic as shown in the following steps.

To Save for the Web

1. **With your USB flash drive connected to one of the computer's USB ports, click File on the menu bar and then Save for Web.**
2. **When the Save for Web dialog box is displayed, click the 4-Up tab if necessary. Click the preview other than the original, that looks the best for your system's connection speed. If necessary, use the Hand tool to display the text in the window.**
3. **Click the Save button.**
4. **When the Save Optimized As dialog box is displayed, type** `Letter Repaired` **in the File name text box. Do not press the ENTER key.**
5. **Click the Save in box arrow and then click USBDISK [G:], or the location associated with your USB flash drive, in the list.**
6. **Click the Save button.**

The letter is saved as a gif file appropriate for the Web.

Because the changes are saved as a Web file, you can close the original letter without saving as shown in the following step. If you want to save a copy of the edited image for print, do so before closing the file.

To Close the Letter File

1. **Click the Close button on the Letter document window title bar. If Photoshop asks if you want to save the changes, click the No button.**

Retouching Tools

Sometimes photos are damaged or worn from excessive use, age, physical damage, or improper storage. Photoshop has several tools that help you touch up spots, tears, wrinkles, and scratches in damaged photos. Table 5-3 on the next page lists some of the tools and their usage. Each of the retouching tools will be further explained as it is used.

Table 5-3 Retouching Tools

TOOL	BUTTON	USE
Burn tool		darkens areas in an image
Dodge tool		lightens areas in an image
Healing Brush tool		removes and repairs imperfections by first taking a sample from another place in the image and then painting to match the texture, lighting, transparency, and shading of the sampled pixels to the pixels being healed
Patch tool		repairs imperfections in a selected area of an image by copying a sample or pattern taken from another part of the image — commonly used for larger areas and does not allow brush size selection as with the Healing Brush tool
Red Eye tool		removes the red tint from all contiguous cells
Sponge tool		changes the color saturation of an area
Spot Healing Brush tool		removes blemishes and imperfections by sampling pixels around the spot and then paints with matching texture, lighting, transparency, and shading

The first photo you will edit will be a damaged picture of one of the early founders of the county. The following steps show how to open and crop the photo.

To Open and Crop the Founder Image

1. **Open the file named, Founder, from the Project05 folder on the CD that accompanies this book, or from a location specified by your instructor.**
2. **If necessary, change the magnification to 50 percent.**
3. **To remove the excess border, click the Crop Tool (C) button in the toolbox, and then, in the photo itself, drag from the top-left corner to the lower-right corner.**
4. **Press the ENTER key.**

The image is displayed (Figure 5-11). The Founder image has been cropped of its original border. Many tears and damaged areas are displayed.

FIGURE 5-11

The Healing Tools

Photoshop has four healing or restoration tools to correct imperfections in photos and images. The Spot Healing Brush tool, the Healing Brush tool, the Patch tool, and the Red Eye tool are used to make specific kinds of repairs to blemishes, tears, holes, and red eye problems.

The Spot Healing Brush Tool

The **Spot Healing Brush tool** removes blemishes and imperfections by sampling pixels around the spot. Photoshop then paints in the image with matching texture, lighting, transparency, and shading. Recall that sampling occurs when Photoshop stores the pixel values of a selected spot or area. The Spot Healing Brush options bar contains settings for the blending mode of the repair and the sampling methods.

In the Founder photo, many spots and tears need fixing. It is a good practice to create a layer for the corrections as shown in the following steps. The **Duplicate Layer** command creates an exact copy on which you can make changes, allowing you to review more easily the before and after images.

To Duplicate a Layer for Corrections

1

- **Right-click the Background layer in the Layers palette. When the shortcut menu is displayed, click Duplicate Layer.**

Photoshop displays the Duplicate Layer dialog box (Figure 5-12).

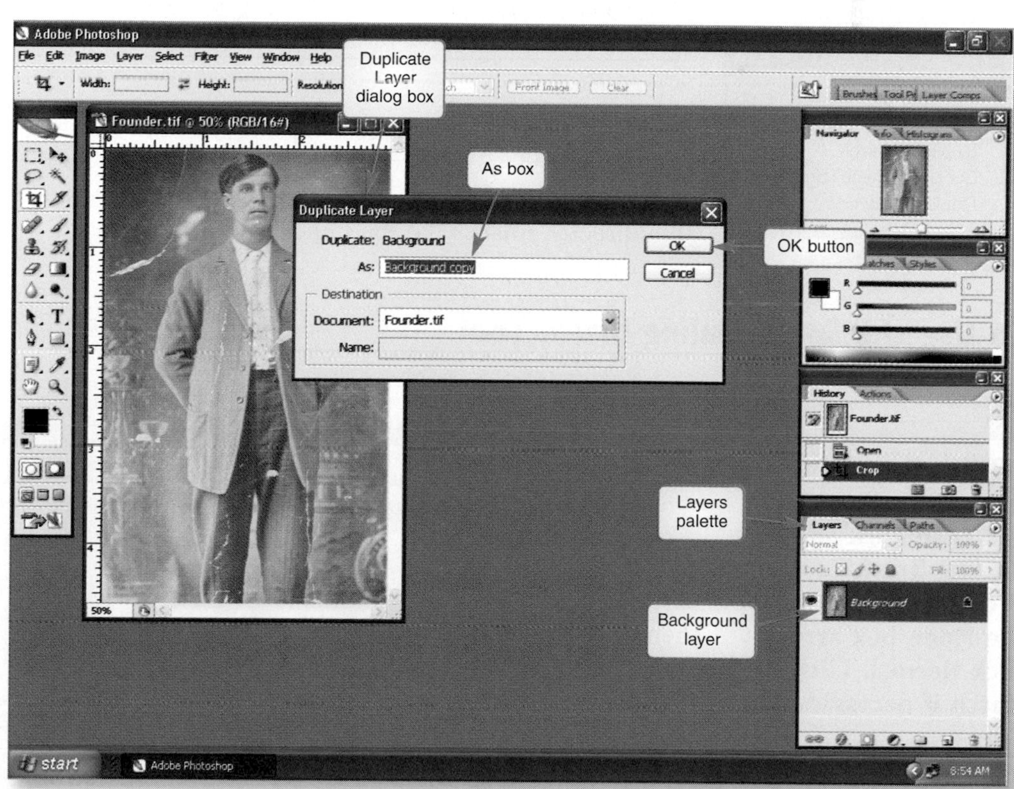

FIGURE 5-12

2

- **Type** `Corrections` **in the As box and then click the OK button.**
- **Zoom to 100 percent and scroll to display the man's face.**

The Layers palette displays the new layer (Figure 5-13). Several small areas on the face are damaged and display without color as white.

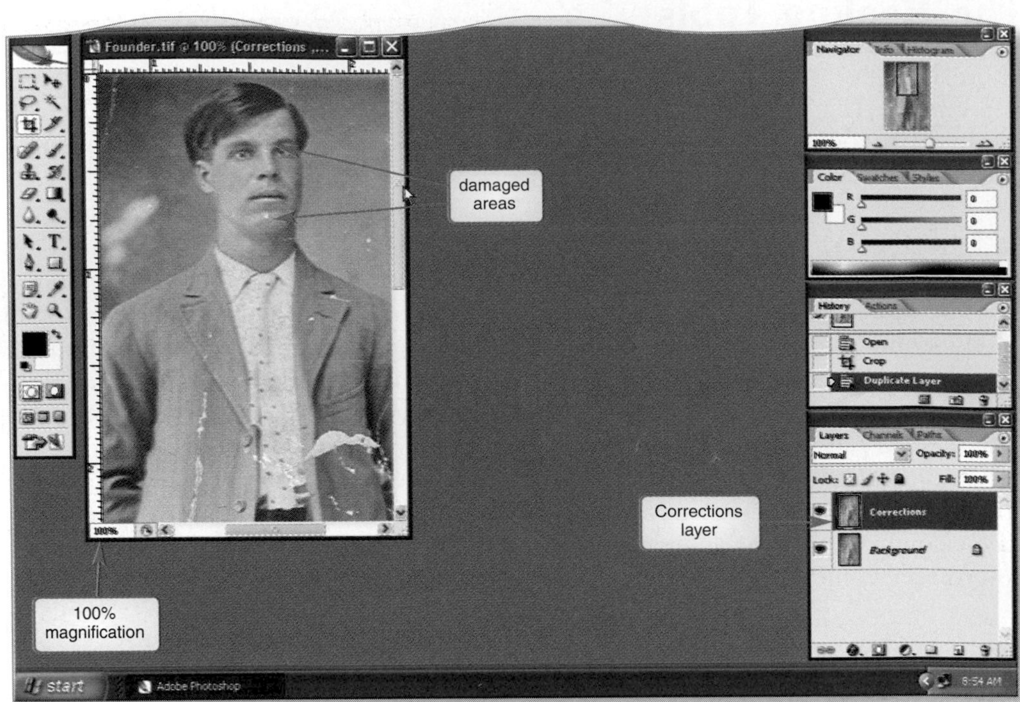

FIGURE 5-13

Other Ways

1. Click Layers palette menu button, click Duplicate Layer
2. On Layer menu, click Duplicate Layer

The following steps describe using the Spot Healing Brush tool to fix several small damaged spots on the face. When using the Spot Healing Brush tool, it is important to use the smallest possible brush tip so that the sample comes from the area directly adjacent to the imperfection.

To Use the Spot Healing Brush Tool

1

- **Right-click the current healing tool and then click Spot Healing Brush Tool in the list. If necessary on the options bar, click the Mode box arrow and then click Normal. Click Proximity Match if necessary.**
- **Move the mouse pointer into the document window and point to the white spot on the chin. Press the [key or the] key until the brush tip is just slightly larger than the spot.**

The brush tip displays as a circle around the imperfection (Figure 5-14).

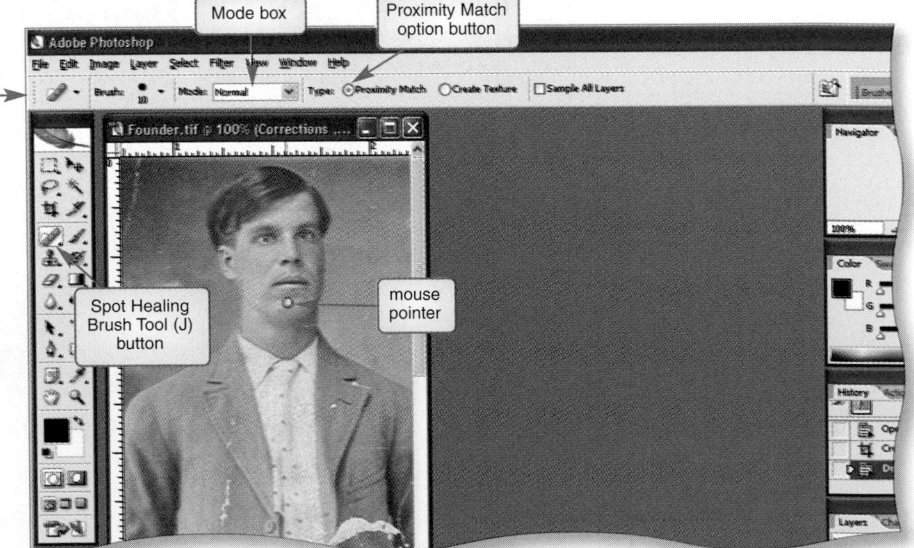

FIGURE 5-14

2

• **Click the spot and then move the mouse pointer away to view the results.**

The spot is repaired (Figure 5-15).

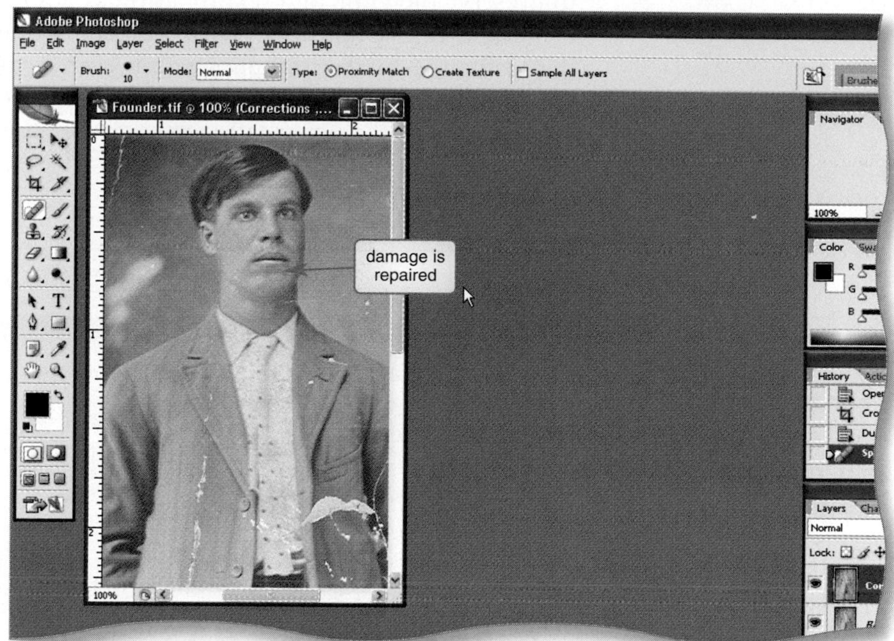

FIGURE 5-15

3

• **Move the mouse pointer to the spot between the eyes. Press the [key to reduce the size of the brush tip. Click the spot and then move the mouse pointer away to view the results.**

The second spot is repaired (Figure 5-16).

• **Repeat Step 3 for other spots on the face and neck. If you make a repair that does not look good, click the previous state in the History palette and try again.**

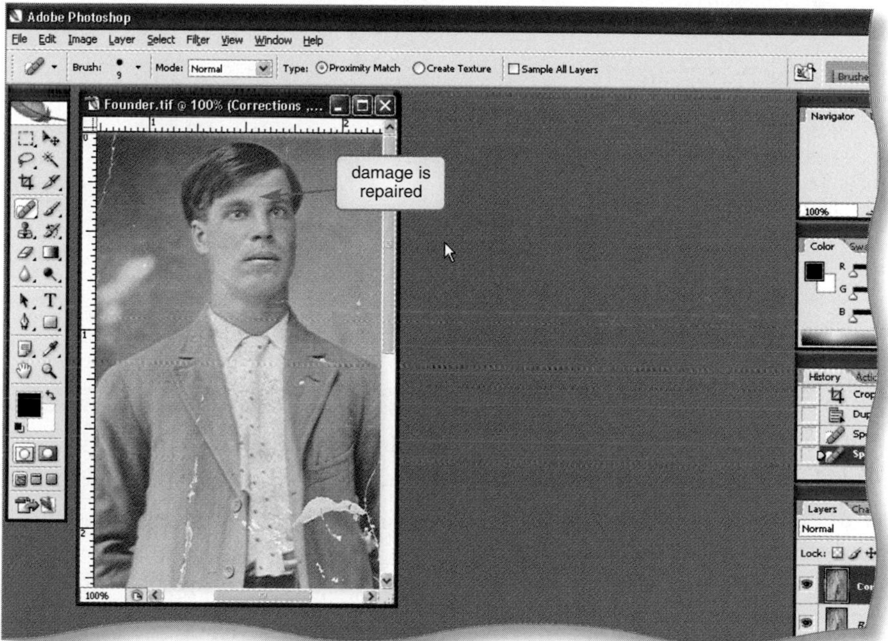

FIGURE 5-16

Other Ways

1. Press J key, adjust brush size, click imperfection

The Healing Brush Tool

The **Healing Brush tool** is better suited for larger areas such as tears or wrinkles. While the Spot Healing Brush tool samples the surrounding pixels automatically, the Healing Brush tool requires you to choose the sampled area, as you did with the Clone tool. When using the Healing Brush tool, the Brush picker allows you to set specific characteristics of the brush, including the use of a tablet pen. The Mode box allows you to choose one of several blending modes, or choose to replace the pixels to preserve the grain and texture at the edges of the brush stroke. Additionally, the Healing Brush options bar has an Aligned setting to sample pixels continuously, without losing the current sampling point, even if you release the mouse button.

The following steps describe how to use the Healing Brush tool to fix the tears and damage in the upper-left corner of the photo.

To Use the Healing Brush Tool

1

- **Scroll to display the upper-left corner of the photo.**
- **Right-click the Spot Healing Brush Tool (J) button.**

The context menu is displayed (Figure 5-17).

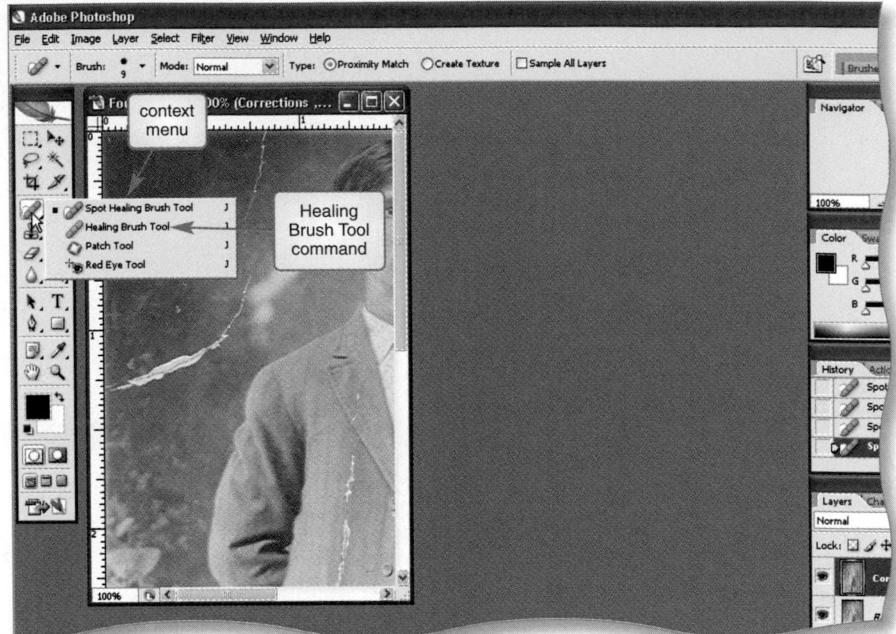

FIGURE 5-17

2

- **Click Healing Brush Tool in the list.**
- **If necessary, click Sampled on the options bar. Click the Aligned check box so it displays a check mark.**
- **Click the Brush picker button on the options bar.**
- **In the Diameter box, type** 19 **to set the brush size, if necessary. Click the Size box arrow, and then click Off in the list.**

The Healing Brush settings are displayed (Figure 5-18). The brush settings box will close automatically when you click anywhere else in the window.

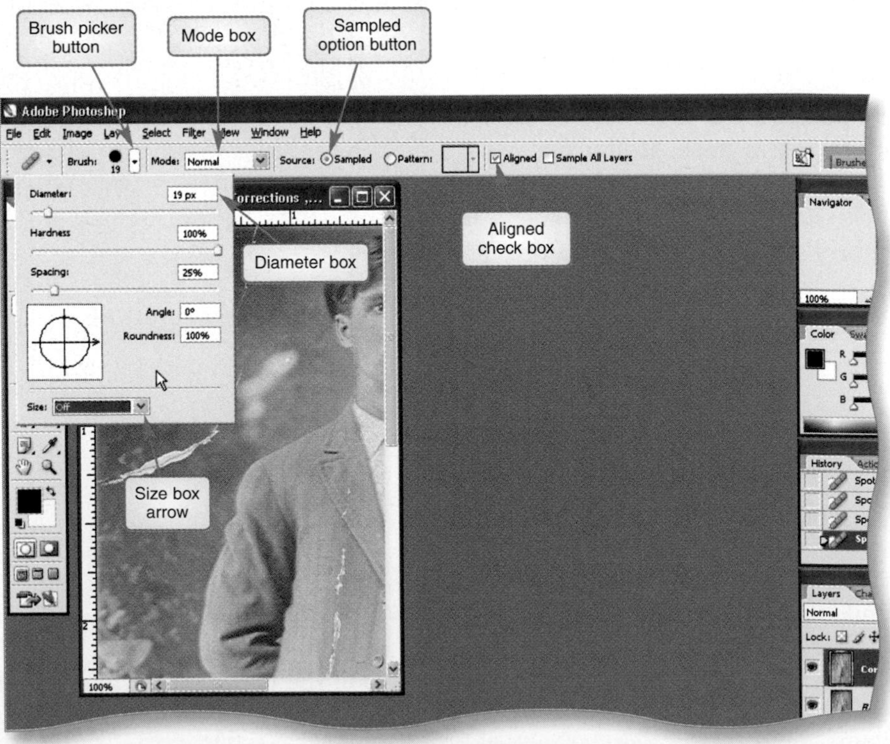

FIGURE 5-18

3

- **To sample the pixels, ALT+click to the right of the upper tear.**
- **Drag from the top of the tear, down, approximately .5 inches.**

Photoshop repairs the damage by applying the sampled pixels and matching the grain and texture (Figure 5-19).

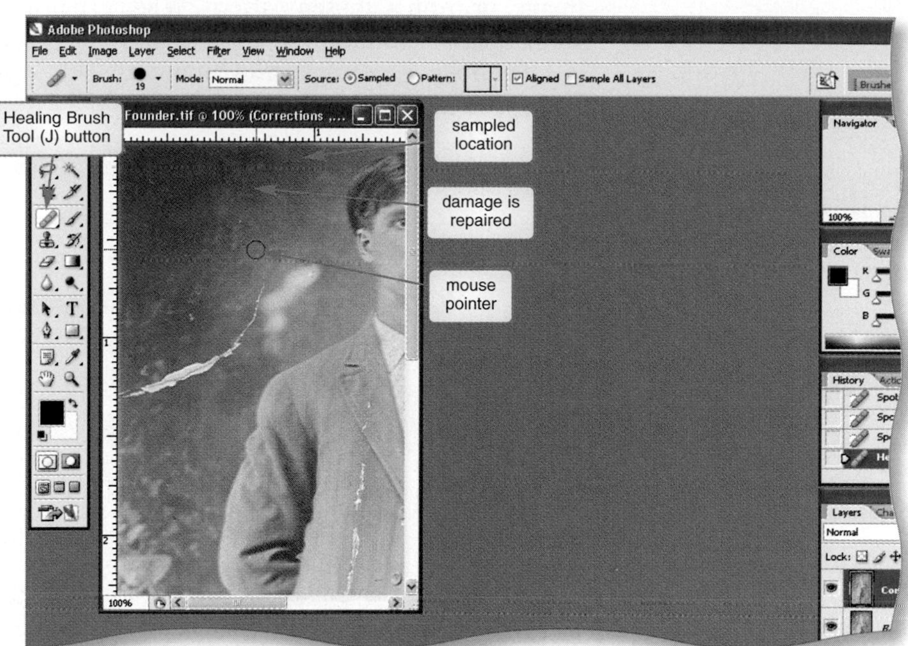

FIGURE 5-19

4

- **ALT+click below the tear at the left margin.**
- **On the options bar, click the Mode box arrow and then click Replace in the list.**
- **Drag from left to right, using short strokes to correct the tear. Resample as necessary to match color and grain.**

The tear is fixed (Figure 5-20).

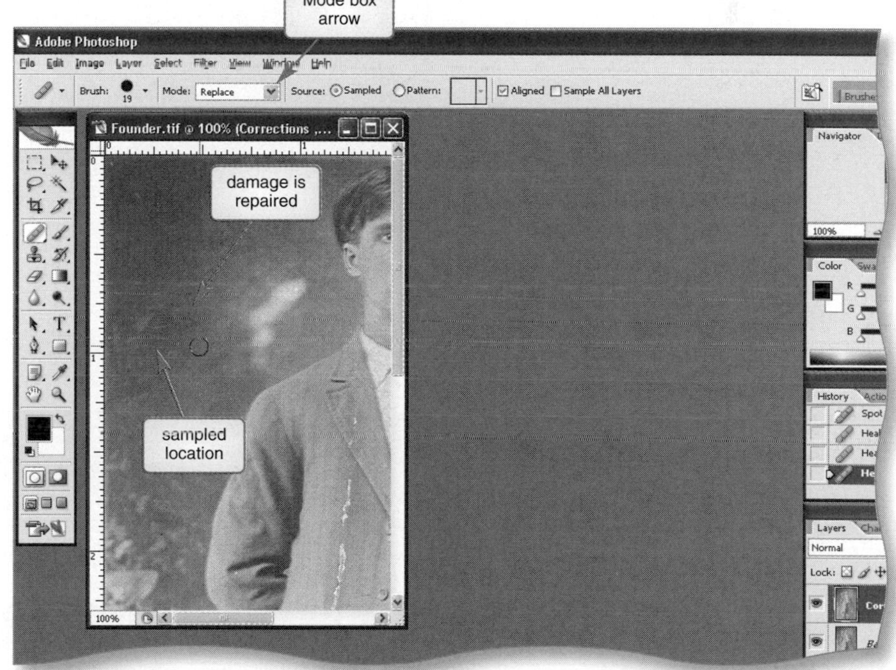

FIGURE 5-20

Other Ways

1. Press J key, ALT+click sample, drag flawed areas

The Patch Tool

The **Patch tool** lets you repair a selected area with pixels from another area or by using a pattern; however, the Patch tool is more than just a copy and paste mechanism. Like the Healing Brush tool, the Patch tool matches the texture, lighting, and shading of the pixels. The Patch tool can sample pixels from the same image, from a different image, or from a chosen pattern. When repairing with pixels from the image, select a small area to produce the best results.

The following steps show how to use the Patch tool to patch the light area to the left of the man's head.

To Use the Patch Tool

1

- **Right-click the Spot Healing Brush Tool (J) button, and then click Patch Tool in the list.**
- **If necessary, click Source on the Patch options bar.**
- **Move the mouser pointer to an area left of the light spot, near the man's head.**

The mouse pointer is displayed as the Patch tool (Figure 5-21).

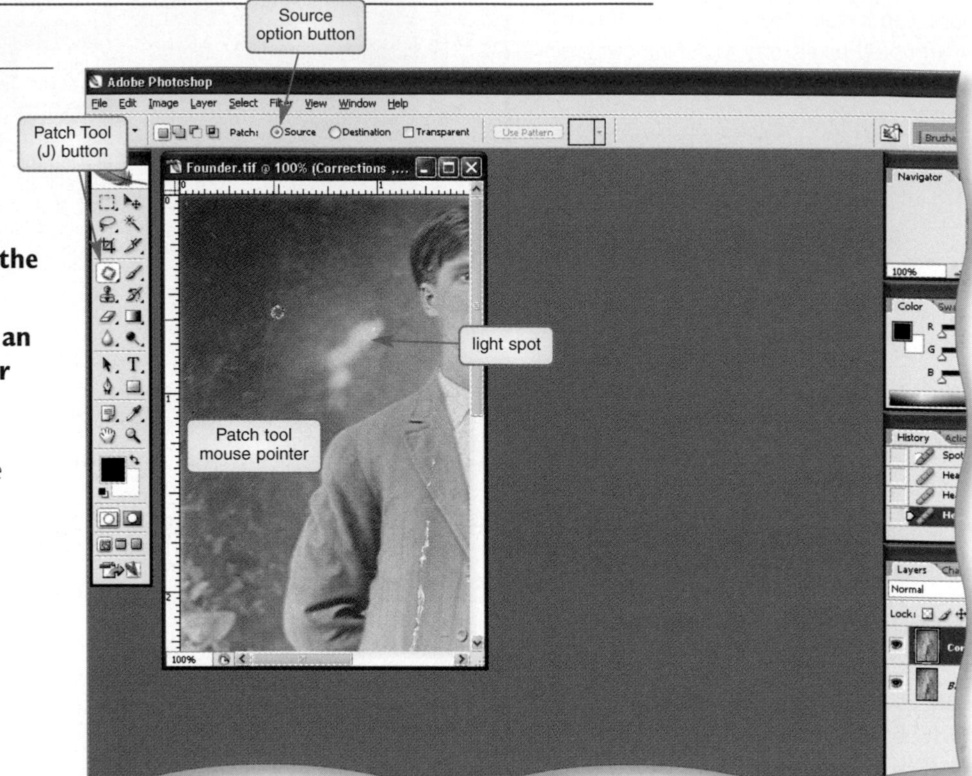

FIGURE 5-21

2

- **Drag an area approximately as big as the light spot, but do not include the light spot.**

The selection is displayed with a flashing marquee (Figure 5-22).

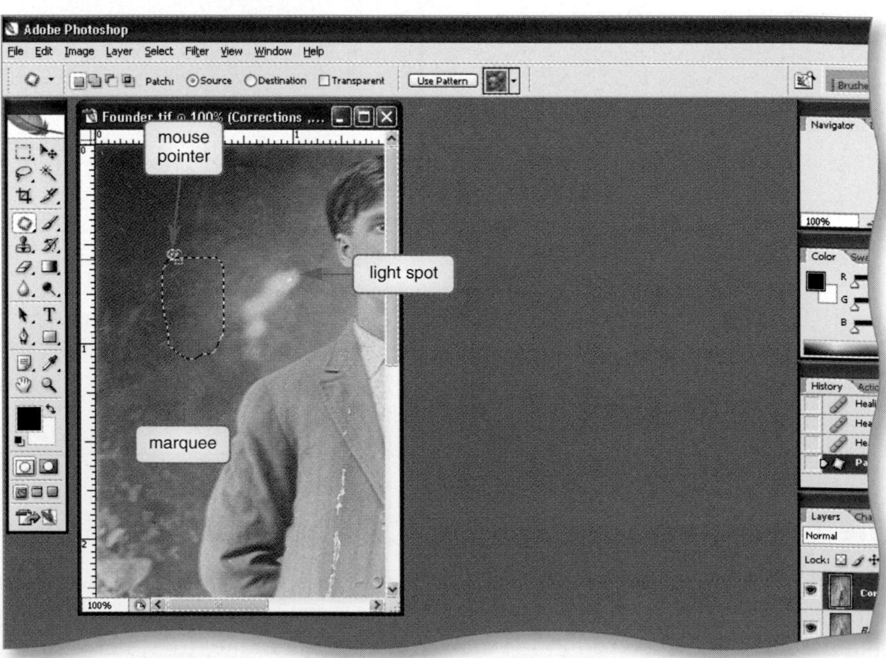

FIGURE 5-22

3

- **On the Patch options bar, click Destination.**
- **Drag the selection to cover the light spot.**
- **Press CTRL+D to remove the selection.**

The spot is patched (Figure 5-23).

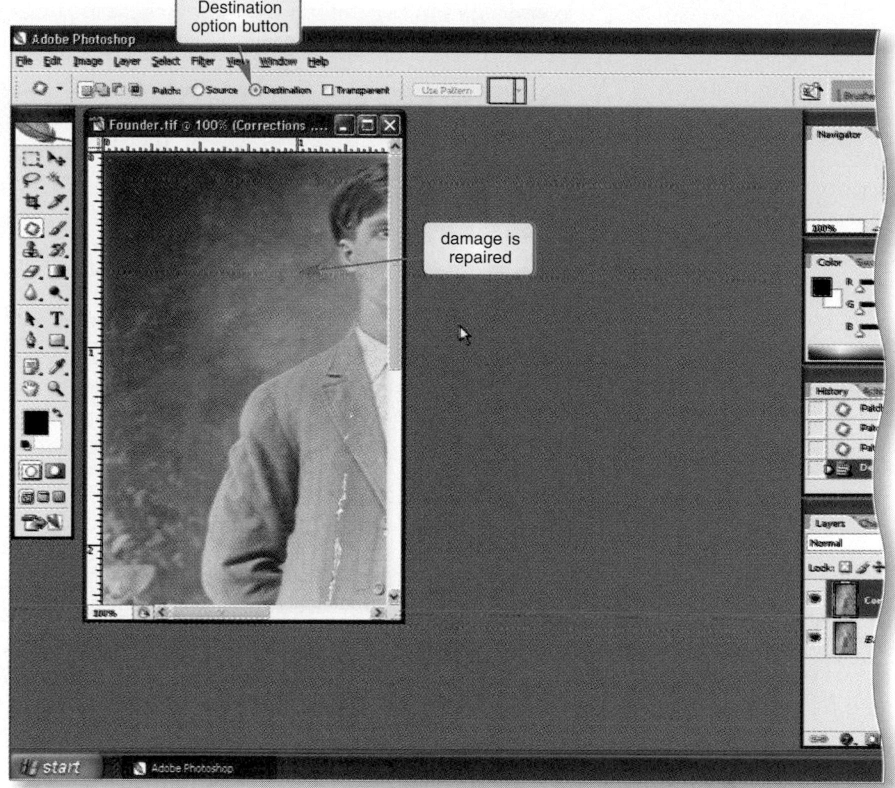

FIGURE 5-23

Other Ways

1. Press J key, on options bar click Source, drag area, click Destination, drag area

The final steps illustrate how to repair other damaged areas in the photo. If you make a repair that does not look good, click the previous state in the History palette or press CTRL+Z and then try again. Zoom and scroll as necessary.

To Repair Other Damage

1. **Right-click the Patch Tool (J) button and then click Spot Healing Brush Tool in the list.**
2. **Choose a very small damaged area in the photo. Adjust the brush size to be just larger than the damage. Click with the Spot Healing Brush tool to repair the damage.**
3. **Right-click the Spot Healing Tool (J) button and then click Healing Brush Tool in the list.**
4. **Choose a larger damaged area in the photo. ALT+click close to the damage. Drag with short strokes to repair the damage.**
5. **Repeat the steps as necessary to fix other damaged areas.**
6. **Zoom to 50 percent.**

The repaired photo is displayed (Figure 5-24 on the next page).

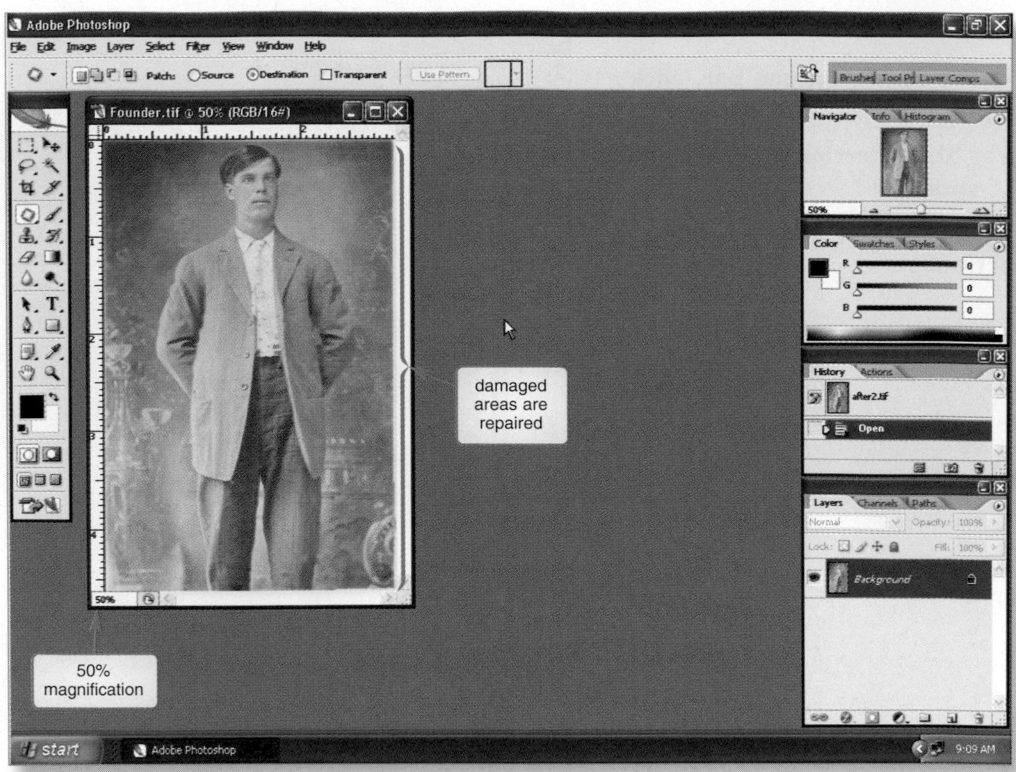

FIGURE 5-24

The final steps are to save and close the Founder file. During the process, Photoshop will ask if you want to save the layers. Clicking the OK button will increase the file size, but will retain your edit layers. If you wish to flatten the layers, click Flatten Image on the Layer menu and then save the file.

> *More About*
>
> **TIFs and JPGs**
>
> While most digital cameras create JPG files, some resolution is lost when saving JPG edits. Photoshop will compress the file to make it smaller. Many digital designers save their JPG files in the TIF format so they can exchange files between applications and across computer platforms. TIF is a flexible format supported by virtually all paint, image-editing, and page-layout applications. The disadvantage is that TIF files are larger in file size.

To Save and Close the Founder File

1. **With your USB flash drive connected to one of the computer's USB ports, click File on the menu bar and then Save As.**
2. **When the Save As dialog box is displayed, type** `Founder Repaired` **in the File name text box. Do not press the ENTER key.**
3. **Click the Save in box arrow and then click USBDISK [G:], or the location associated with your USB flash drive, in the list.**
4. **Click the Save button. When Photoshop displays the TIFF Options dialog box, click the OK button. When Photoshop asks to include layers, click the OK button.**
5. **Click the Close button on the Founder Repaired document window title bar.**

The file is saved and the document window is closed.

The next photo to enhance is the Children file that is opened as shown in the following steps.

To Open the Children Image

1 **Open the file named, Children, from the Project 05 folder on the CD that accompanies this book, or from a location specified by your instructor.**

2 **If necessary, change the magnification to 66.67 percent.**

The image is displayed (Figure 5-25). Notice the red eye problem in the Children image.

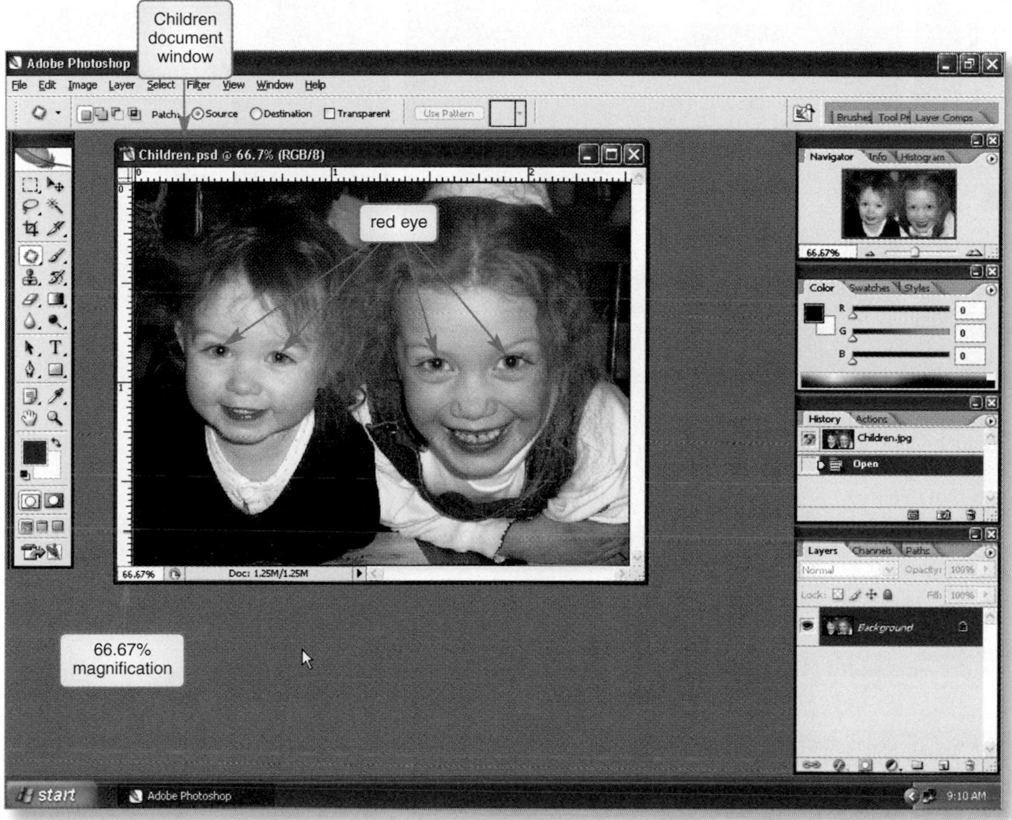

FIGURE 5-25

Using the Red Eye Tool

In photographs, **red eye** is when the pupils of the subject's eyes appear red. Red eye is caused in flash photography where the flash of a camera is bright enough to cause a reflection off the retina. The red color comes from the blood vessels in the eye. Red eye can be avoided by moving the flash farther away from the lens or by using a camera that has a red eye reduction feature. In those cameras, the flash goes off twice — once before the picture is taken and then again to take the picture. The first flash causes the pupils to contract, which significantly reduces the red eye.

Red eye can be corrected in Photoshop using a specialized tool designed specifically for this problem. The **Red Eye tool** removes red eye in flash photos by recoloring all contiguous red pixels. The Red Eye options bar has settings to change the pupil size and the darken amount. The Red Eye tool can be used only on photos in the RGB and Lab color formats. It does not work with CMYK color mode.

The steps on the next page show how to remove the red eye from the photo.

To Use the Red Eye Tool

1

- **Right-click the Healing Brush Tool (J) button and then click Red Eye Tool in the list.**
- **Move the mouse pointer to the child's eye on the left.**

The Red Eye tool mouse pointer displays as a crosshair (Figure 5-26).

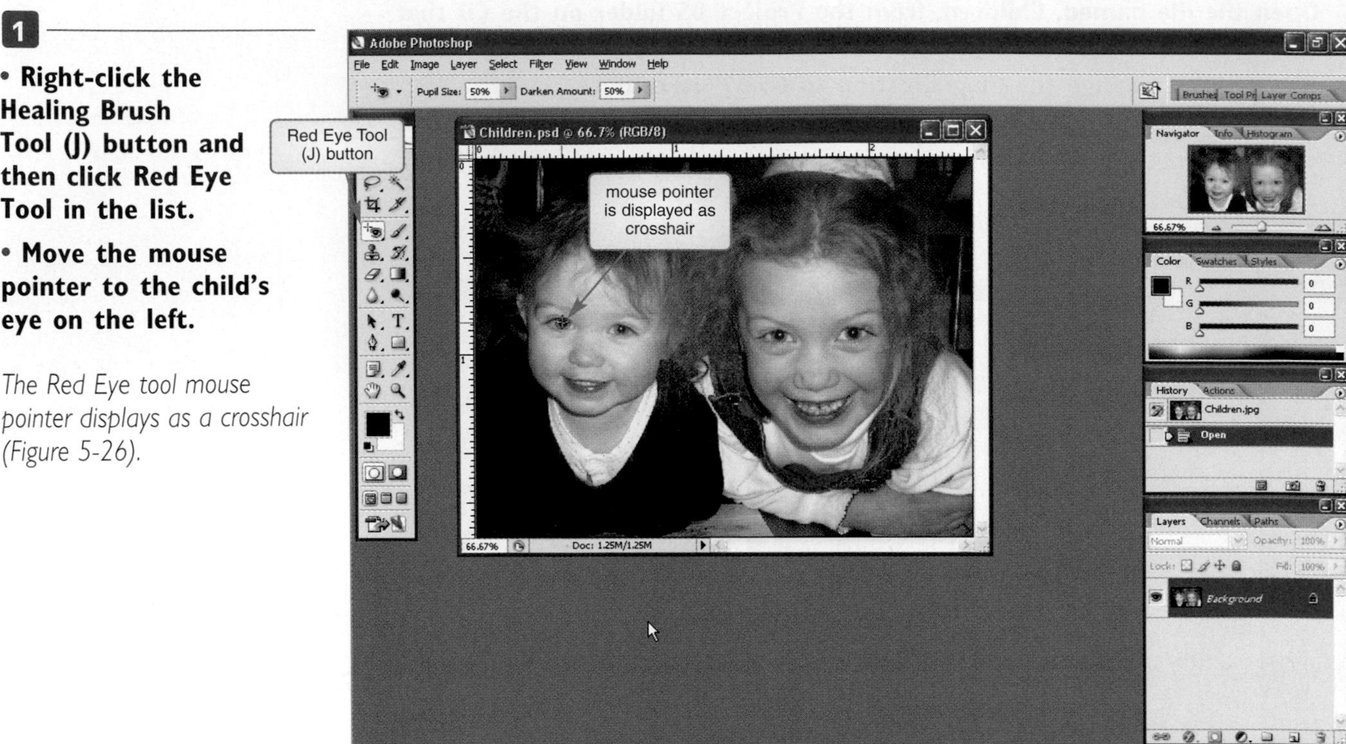

FIGURE 5-26

2

- **Click the red portion of the eye.**

The red eye is removed (Figure 5-27).

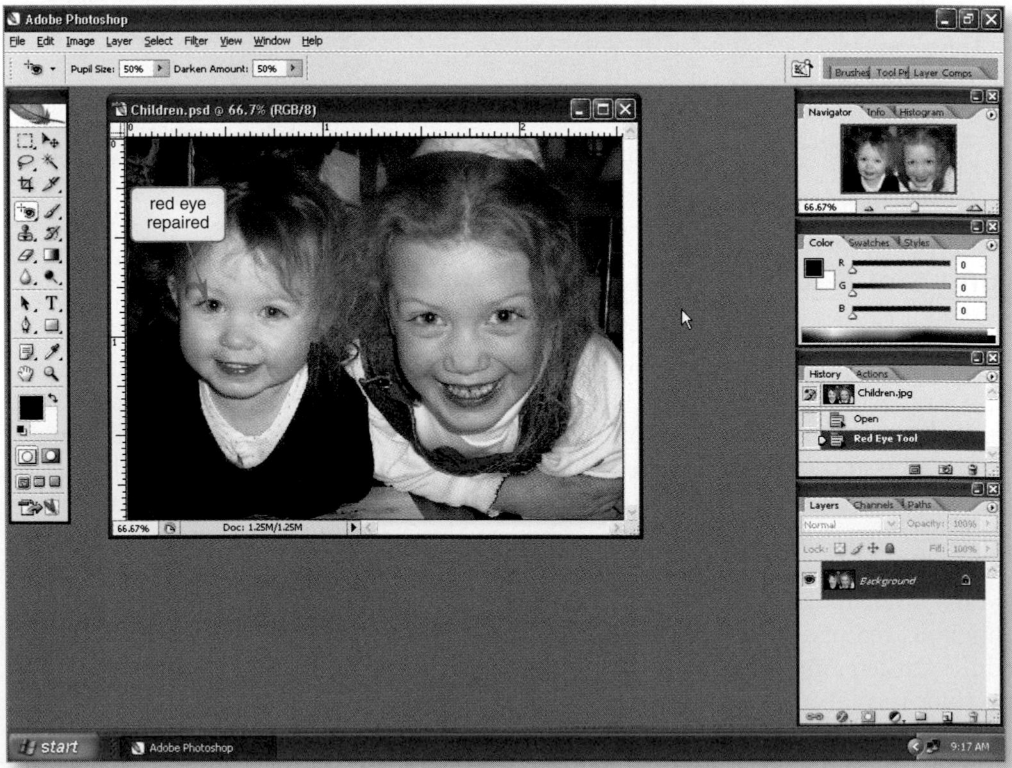

FIGURE 5-27

3

- **Click each of the other eyes.**

The red eye problems are fixed (Figure 5-28).

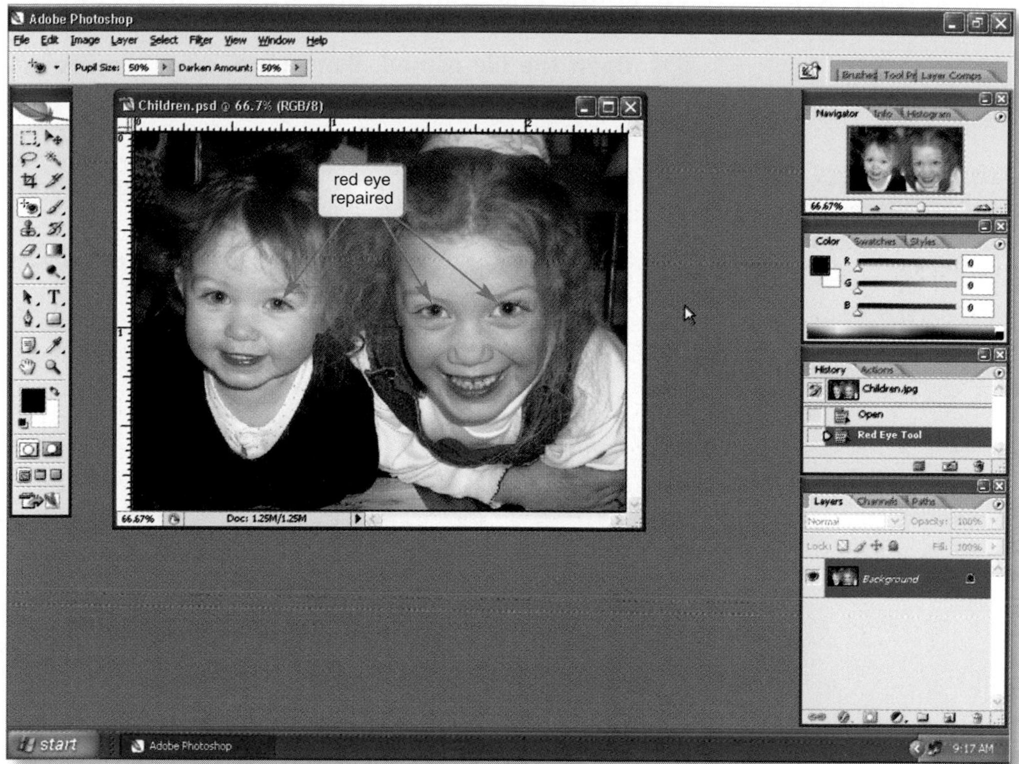

FIGURE 5-28

> **Other Ways**
>
> 1. Press J key, click red eye

Because you will use this picture in later steps to create a postcard, you will save the file in the TIF format and close the document window, opening it later to create a postcard.

To Save and Close the Children File

1. **With your USB flash drive connected to one of the computer's USB ports, click File on the menu bar and then Save As.**
2. **When the Save As dialog box is displayed, type** `Children Repaired` **in the File name text box. Do not press the ENTER key.**
3. **Click the Format box arrow and then click TIFF (*.TIF, *.TIFF) in the list.**
4. **Click the Save in box arrow and then click USBDISK [G:], or the location associated with your USB flash drive, in the list.**
5. **Click the Save button. When Photoshop displays the TIFF Options dialog box, click the OK button.**
6. **Click the Close button on the Children Repaired document window title bar.**

The file is saved and the window is closed.

The next photo to repair is the Bandstand file opened in the steps on the next page. A Corrections layer also is created.

> *More About*
>
> **Recipes**
>
> A recipe is a set of instructions that show how to prepare or make something. Many Photoshop users create and share recipes about common photo editing tasks. Adobe Photoshop Elements, a less-expensive, less powerful image editing software contains a help application called Recipes which provides the user with steps and instructions as well. On the Web you can find many step-by-step recipes for photo restoration and enhancement. Visit the Shelly Cashman More About Web site for a list of recipe Web sites.

To Open the Bandstand Image and Create a Corrections Layer

1. **Open the file named, Bandstand, from the Project 05 folder on the CD that accompanies this book, or from a location specified by your instructor.**
2. **If necessary, change the magnification to 66.67 percent.**
3. **In the Layers palette, right-click the Background layer, and then click Duplicate Layer in the shortcut menu.**
4. **When the Duplicate Layer dialog box is displayed, type** `Corrections` **in the As box, and then click the OK button.**

The image is displayed (Figure 5-29). Notice the light damage and dark area in the Bandstand photo. The Corrections layer is displayed in the Layers palette.

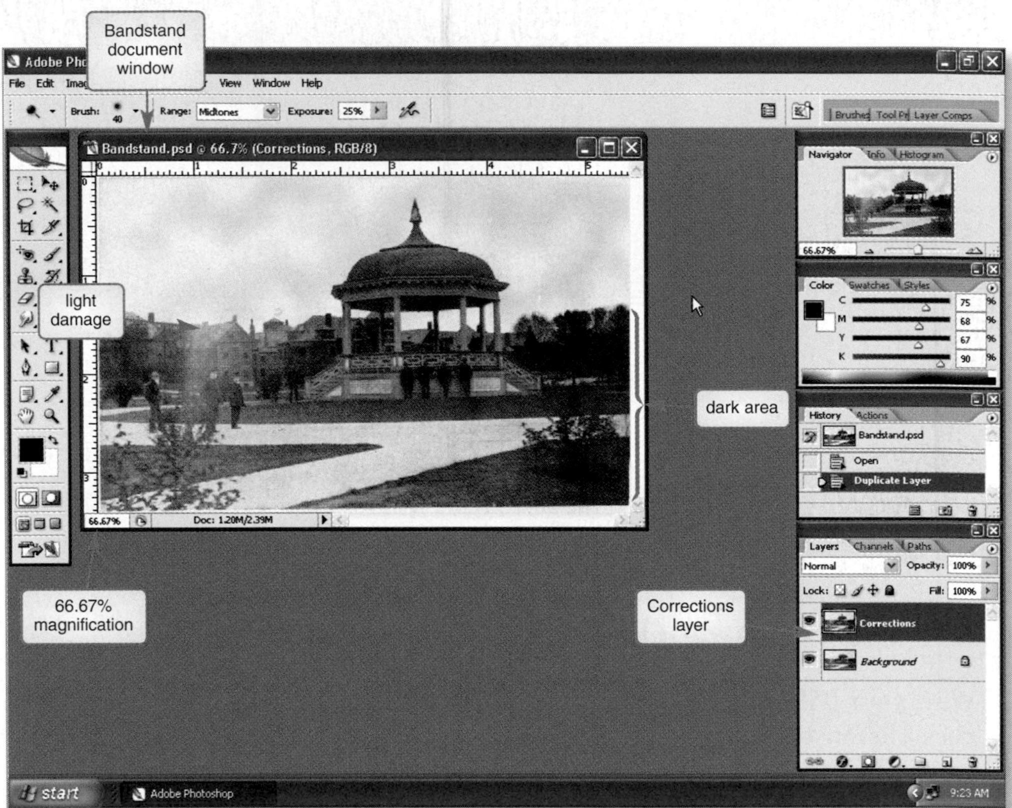

FIGURE 5-29

The Dodge, Burn, and Sponge Tools

The **Dodge tool** is used to lighten areas of an image. The **Burn tool** does just the opposite; it darkens areas of an image. Both tools are based on a technique of traditional photography, regulating exposure on specific areas of a print. Photographers reduce exposure to lighten an isolated area on the print, which is called **dodging**. Increasing the exposure to darken areas on a print is called **burning**. Another tool, the **Sponge tool** subtly changes the color saturation of an area. In Grayscale mode, the tool increases or decreases contrast by moving gray levels away from or toward the middle gray.

An Exposure box on the options bar allows you to specify a percentage of dodging or burning. The default value is 50 percent. A higher percentage in the Exposure box increases the effect, while a lower percentage reduces it.

More About

Colorization of Old Photos

Before color film, movies, portraits, and family groups were shot in black-and-white and sometimes printed as sepia-toned prints. These photos were often colorized by painting directly on the photographic prints with special paints or inks. Typical tinting included pink on the cheeks, red on the lips, and blue in the eyes — a time consuming, but profitable skill. The original photo of the bandstand was hand tinted with blue sky.

The following series of steps show how to fix some problem areas in the Bandstand photo. Part of the photo is too dark to be visible and another portion has light damage.

To Use the Dodge Tool

1

- **With the Corrections layer selected, click the Dodge Tool (O) button in the toolbox.**
- **Using short strokes and adjusting the brush size using the bracket keys, drag through the darker portions of the image on the right.**

The darker portions are lightened (Figure 5-30).

FIGURE 5-30

Other Ways

1. Press O key, drag darker portions of image

To Use the Burn Tool

1

- **Right-click the Dodge Tool (O) button and then click Burn Tool in the list.**
- **On the options bar, type** 25 **in the Exposure box.**
- **Using short strokes and adjusting the brush size, drag through the light damaged area in the image.**

The effects of the light damage are reduced (Figure 5-31).

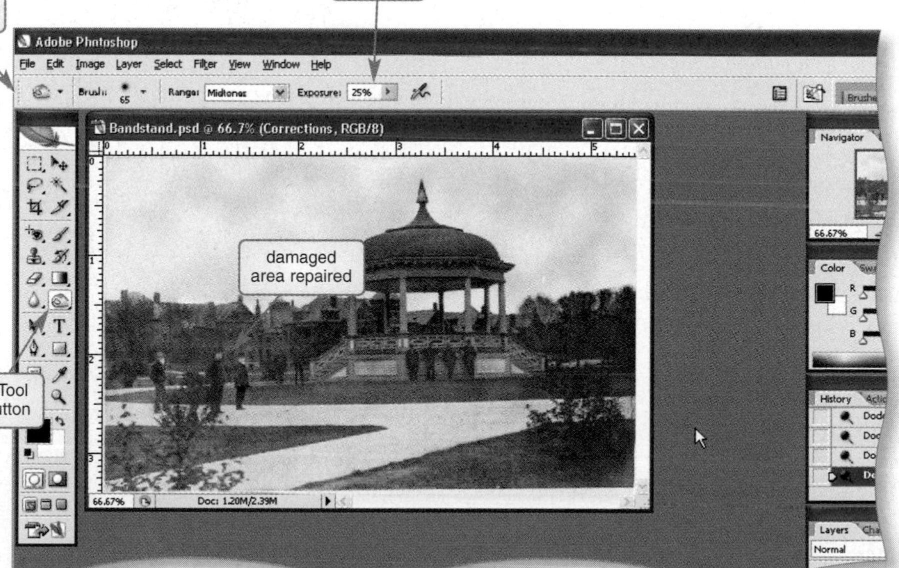

FIGURE 5-31

Other Ways

1. Press O key, drag areas with light damage

With the corrections complete, the steps below illustrate how to save the image in the TIF format and close the Bandstand file. If you wish to flatten the image, do so before converting it to the TIF format.

To Save and Close the Bandstand File

1. **With your USB flash drive connected to one of the computer's USB ports, click File on the menu bar and then Save As.**
2. **When the Save As dialog box is displayed, type** `Bandstand Repaired` **in the File name text box. Do not press the ENTER key.**
3. **Click the Format box arrow and then click TIFF (*.TIF, *.TIFF) in the list.**
4. **Click the Save in box arrow and then click USBDISK [G:], or the location associated with your USB flash drive, in the list.**
5. **Click the Save button. When Photoshop displays the TIFF Options dialog box, click the OK button. When Photoshop asks to include layers, click the OK button.**
6. **Click the Close button on the Bandstand Repaired document window title bar.**

The file is saved and the window is closed.

The following steps open the file named, Schoolhouse, used in the next discussion of lens correction.

To Open the Schoolhouse Image

1. **Open the file named, Schoolhouse, from the Project 05 folder on the CD that accompanies this book, or from a location specified by your instructor.**
2. **If necessary, change the magnification to 100 percent.**

The image is displayed (Figure 5-32). Notice the slight angle to the left and top in the Schoolhouse photo.

FIGURE 5-32

Lens Correction Tools

Many kinds of photographic errors can be corrected in Photoshop. The most common mistakes include lens flaws, focus errors, distortions, unintended angle errors, and perspective errors. Every photographer has made an error from time to time. The next series of steps uses the **Lens Correction filter** to fix some of the lens flaws, distortions, and errors in the Schoolhouse photo. You can try out different settings before committing them permanently to the image. Table 5-4 displays some typical errors, their description, and correction method using the Lens Correction filter.

Table 5-4 Kinds of Distortions

TYPE OF ERROR	DESCRIPTION	CORRECTION METHOD
Angle error	an image is crooked or tilted in the photograph	rotate image
Barrel distortion	a lens defect that causes straight lines to bow out toward the edges of the image	decrease the barrel effect by negatively removing distortion
Chromatic aberration	appears as a color fringe along the edges of objects caused by the lens focusing on different colors of light in different planes	increase or decrease the red/cyan fringe or blue/yellow fringe
Keystone distortion or perspective	occurs when an object is photographed from an angle	correct vertical and/or horizontal perspective error
Pincushion distortion	a lens defect that causes straight lines to bend inward	decrease the pincushion effect by positively removing distortion
Vignette distortion	a defect where the edges, especially the corners, of an image are darker than the center.	lighten or darken the amount of color at the four corners based on a midpoint in the image

Some lenses exhibit these defects because of the focal length or the f-stop used. You can set the Lens Correction filter with settings based on the camera, lens, and focal length used to make the image.

You also can use the filter to rotate an image, or fix image perspective caused by vertical or horizontal camera tilt. The filter's image grid makes these adjustments easier and more accurate than using the Transform command.

Angle and Perspective Errors

While the Crop tool and warp grids can be used to transform and correct the perspective in an image, the Lens Correction dialog box has the added advantages of very precise measurements and other ways to correct errors. This is useful particularly when working with photos that contain keystone distortion. **Keystone distortion** in perspective occurs when an object is photographed from an angle. For example, if you take a picture of a tall building from ground level, the edges of the building appear closer to each other at the top than they do at the bottom. Keystone distortions can be corrected by changing the vertical or horizontal perspective in the photo. **Angle errors** occur when the camera is tilted to the left or right making objects in the photo appear slanted.

After correcting keystone and angle errors, it is sometimes necessary to scale the image in order to regain any edges that were clipped by the correction. You also may need to fill in transparent edges created by changing the angle. The Lens Correction dialog box (Figure 5-34) has boxes, sliders, and buttons both to correct the distortions and repair collateral damage created by the correction.

Table 5-5 lists the corrections you will make to the Schoolhouse photo.

Table 5-5 Correction to the Schoolhouse Photo

DESCRIPTION OF PROBLEM	EDIT SETTING
Keystone distortion	adjust the vertical perspective to -38
Right-to-left distortion	adjust the horizontal perspective to -8
Angle distortion (straightening)	adjust the angle to 358.7
Scale after previous corrections in order to view the entire image	adjust the scale to 85 percent
Replace transparent pixels created by previous corrections	add edge extensions

To straighten the photo and correct the angle distortion, the following steps illustrate how to use the Lens Correction dialog box.

To Correct Angle and Perspective Errors

1

- **Click Filter on the menu bar and then point to Distort.**

The Distort submenu lists correction techniques as well as ways to distort purposefully (Figure 5-33).

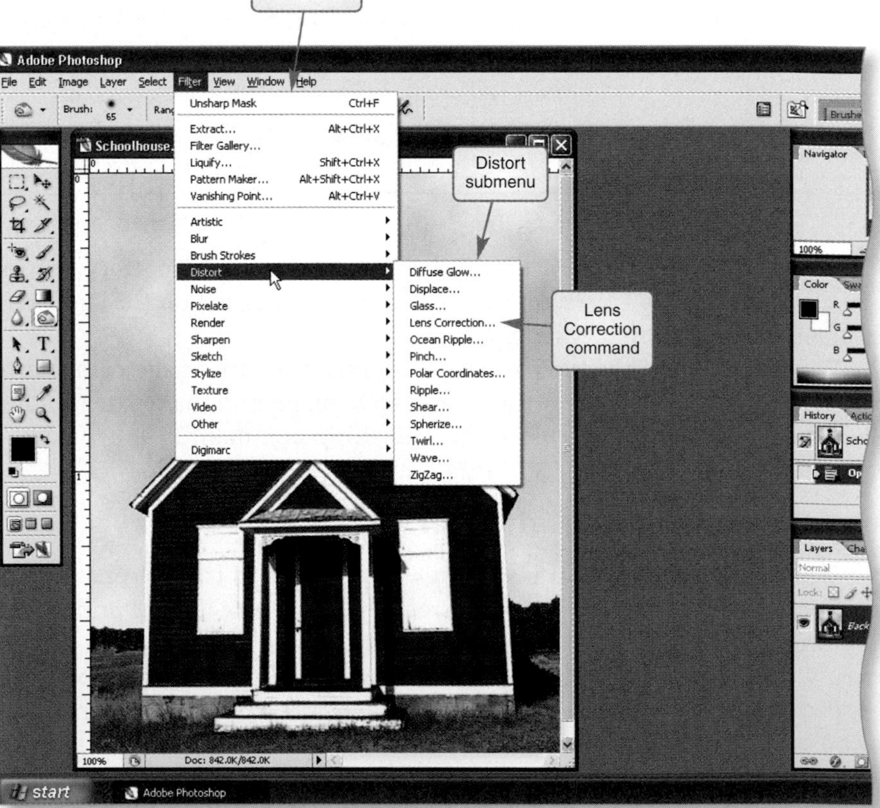

FIGURE 5-33

2

• Click Lens Correction on the Distort submenu.

Photoshop opens the Lens Correction dialog box (Figure 5-34). Grid lines that display in the image preview can be turned on and manipulated using the settings at the bottom of the dialog box.

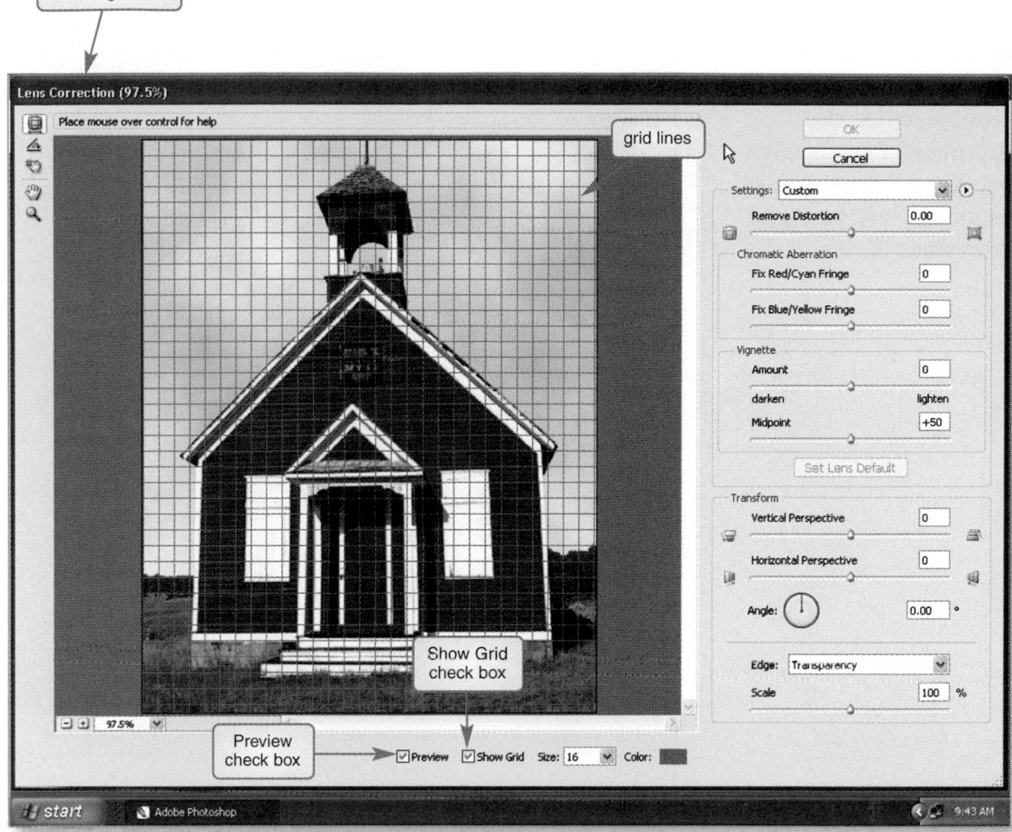

FIGURE 5-34

3

• Double-click the Vertical Perspective box. Type -38 to remove the keystone distortion.

The keystone distortion is repaired (Figure 5-35). A negative value in the Vertical Perspective box brings the top of the picture closer. Notice that some transparent areas are created when the vertical perspective is changed.

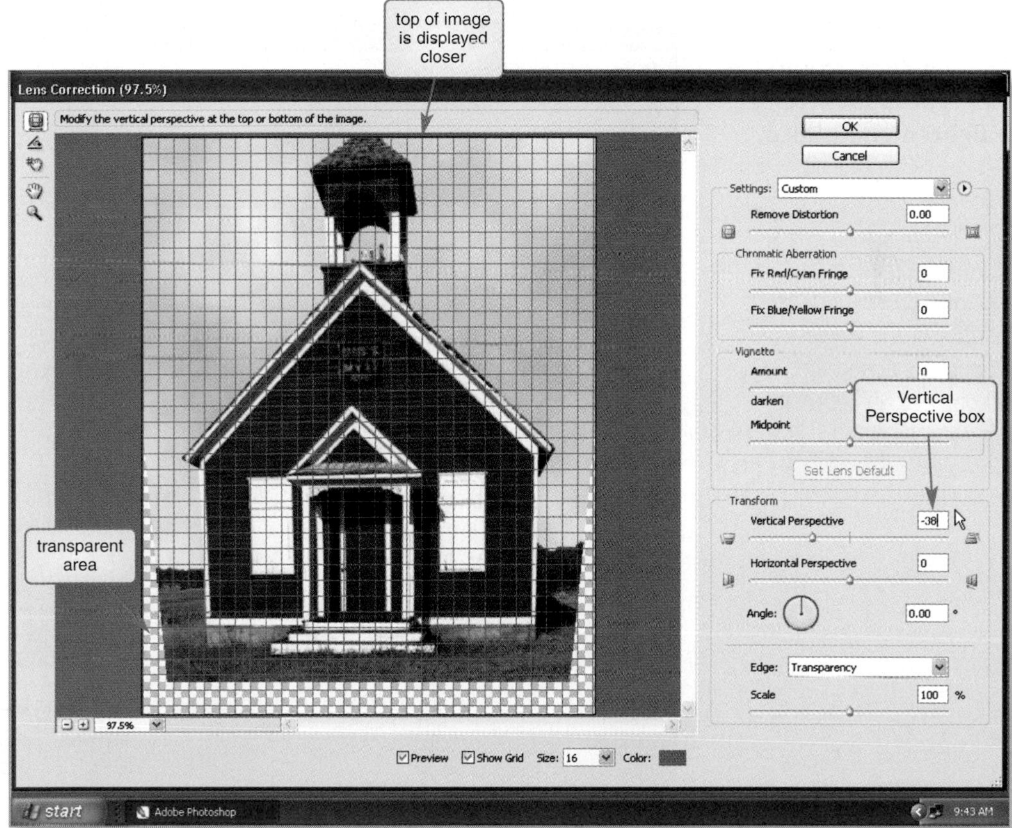

FIGURE 5-35

4

• **Double-click the Horizontal Perspective box. Type** -8 **to adjust the slight left-to-right distortion.**

A negative value in the Horizontal Perspective box brings the left side of the picture closer. (Figure 5-36).

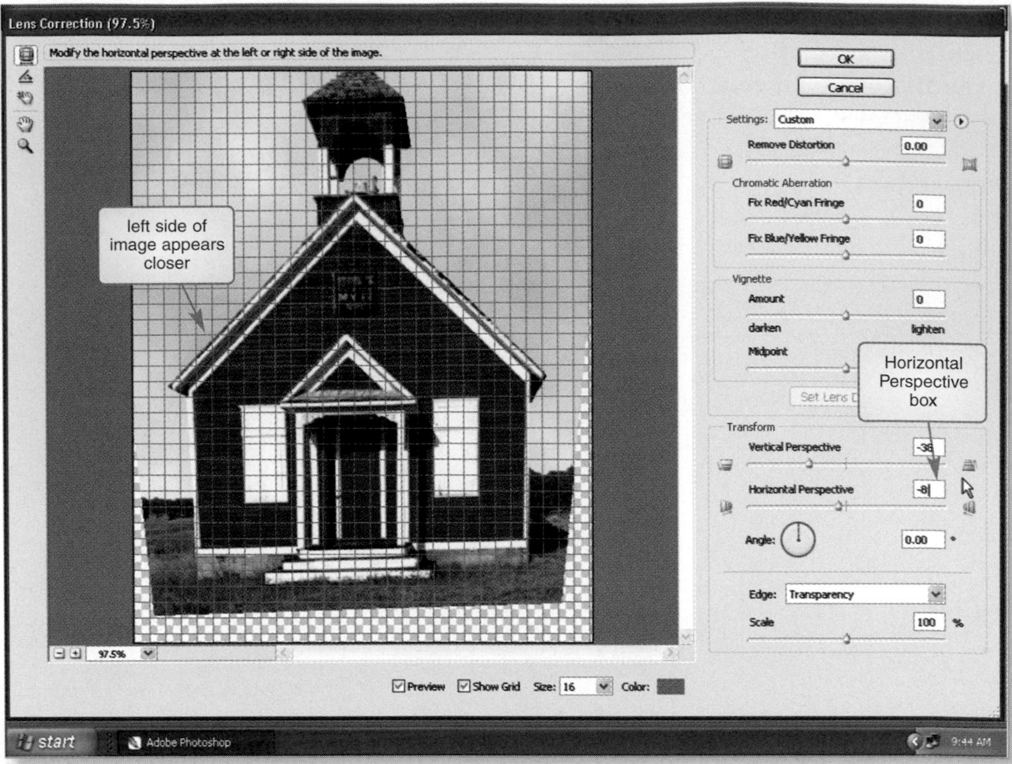

FIGURE 5-36

5

• **Double-click the Angle box. Type** 358.7 **to straighten the photo.**

Notice the grids now align more closely with the edges of the building (Figure 5-37). The angle also can be adjusted by dragging the Angle icon. The angle is based on 360 degrees. Acceptable values run from 1 to 359 with counterclockwise rotation.

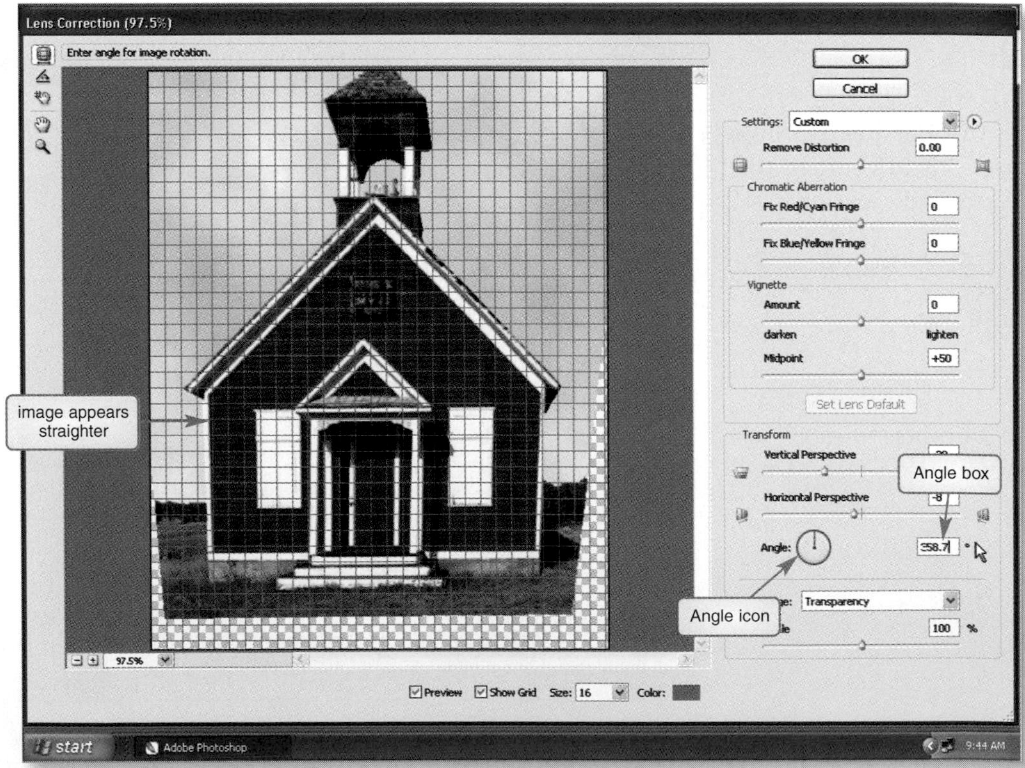

FIGURE 5-37

6

• **Double-click the Scale box and then type** 85 **as the percentage.**

The top of the Schoolhouse steeple is now displayed (Figure 5-38).

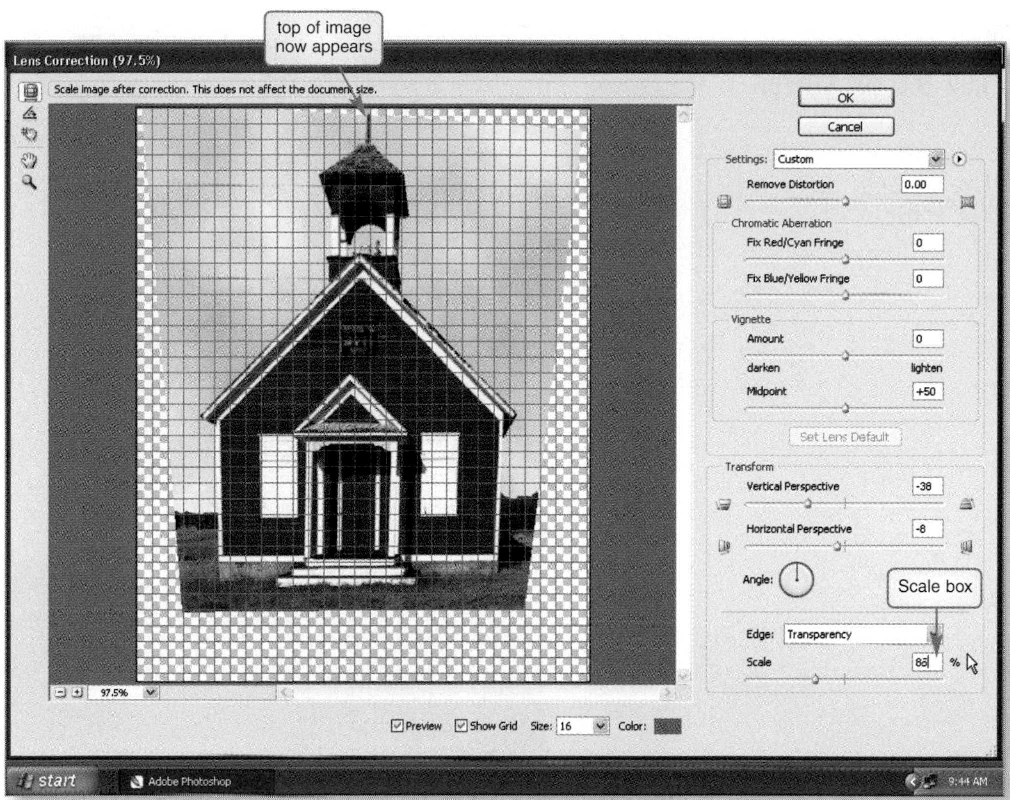

FIGURE 5-38

7

• **Click the Edge box arrow and then click Edge Extension in the list.**

The transparent pixels in the image are filled in with matching textures (Figure 5-39).

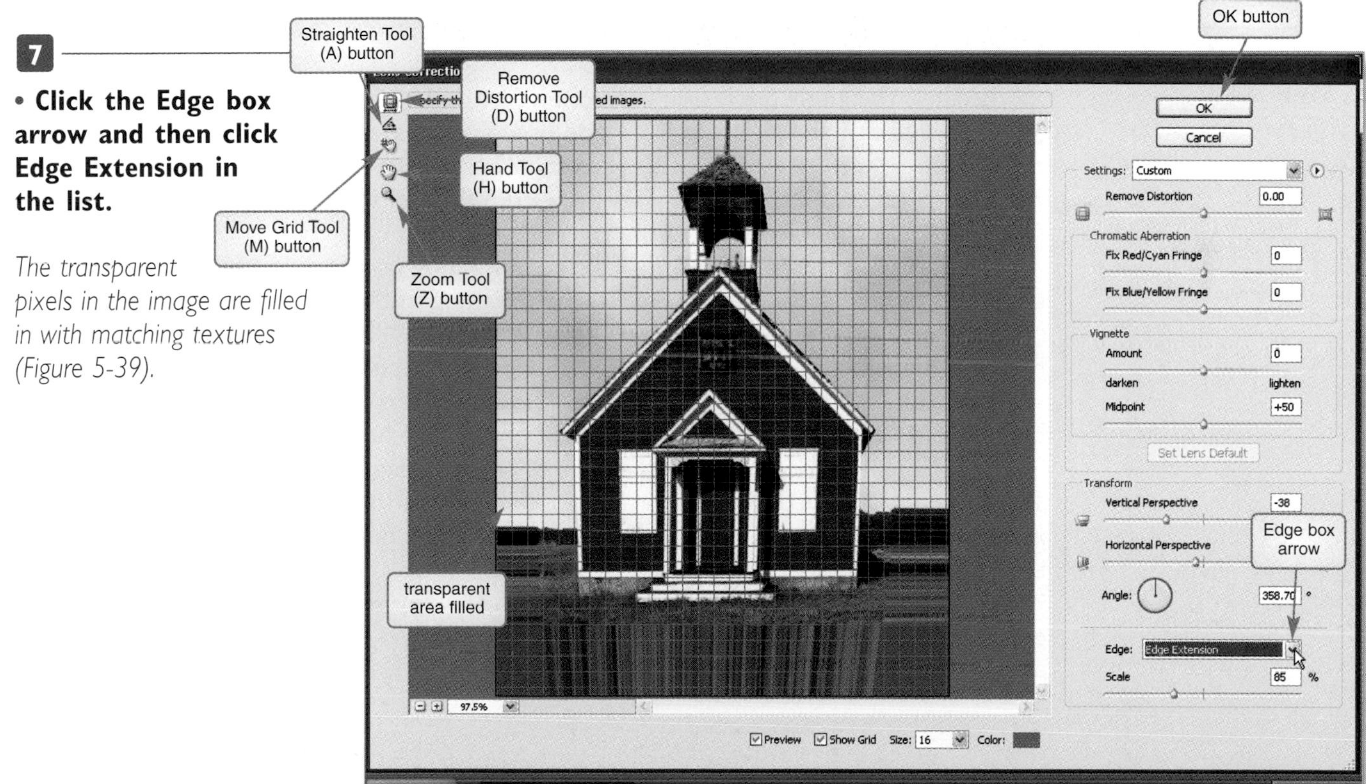

FIGURE 5-39

- **Click the OK button.**

The Lens Distortion dialog box closes and the edited image is displayed (Figure 5-40).

FIGURE 5-40

Because the angle distortion corrections created some blank or transparent areas along the edge of the photo, it is a good practice to extend the edges after a lens correction if you want an image with square corners. Even though the extension does not look good on all four sides (Figure 5-40), filling in the transparent areas allows you to crop to the maximum usable area.

Additional features of the Lens Correction dialog box are the buttons in the upper-left corner that make corrections by dragging in the image itself (Figure 5-39 on the previous page). The Remove Distortion Tool (D) button corrects barrel and pincushion distortions. The Straighten Tool (A) button allows you to draw a line to straighten the image to a new vertical or horizontal axis. The Move Grid Tool (M) button is used to drag the grid lines to any position to help align edges within the image. The Hand Tool (H) button moves or scrolls images that are more than 100 percent magnified. Finally, the Zoom Tool (Z) button allows you to zoom in and out. As you click or point to each button, a short description displays above the button.

With the image distortion corrected, the following steps show how to crop the edited image.

To Crop the Image

1

- **Click the Crop Tool (C) button in the toolbox.**
- **In the image, move the mouse to the lower-right portion of the grass that is still in focus.**

The Crop tool mouse pointer is displayed (Figure 5-41).

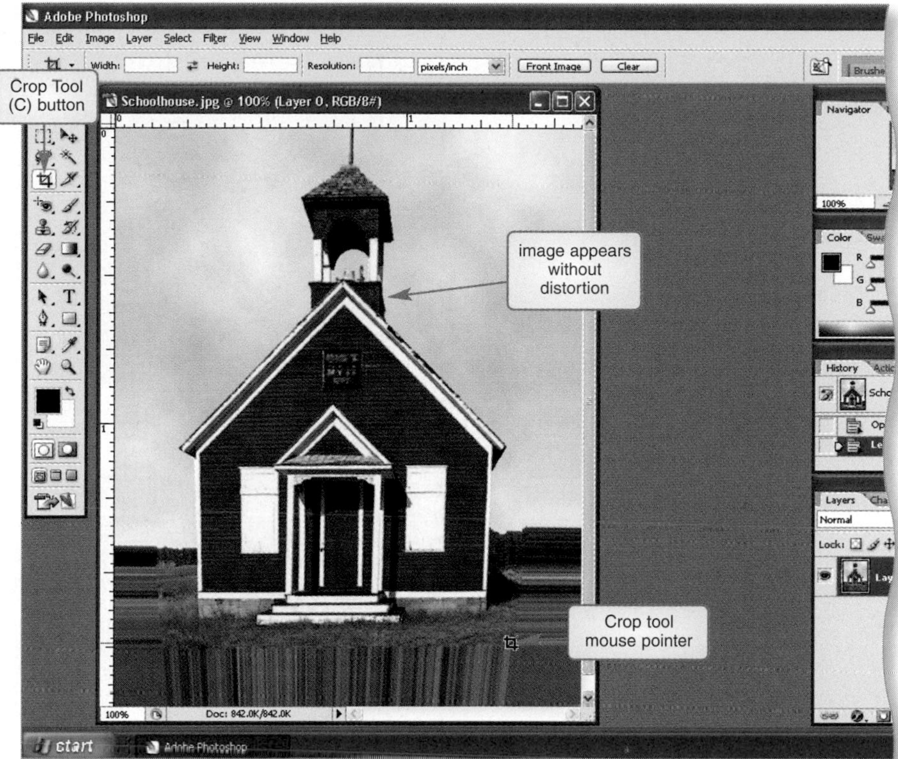

FIGURE 5-41

2

- **Drag to the upper-left corner of the image just far enough to include the grass that is still in focus to the left of the schoolhouse. If necessary, use the sizing handles to adjust the selected area.**

Photoshop displays the cropped area (Figure 5-42).

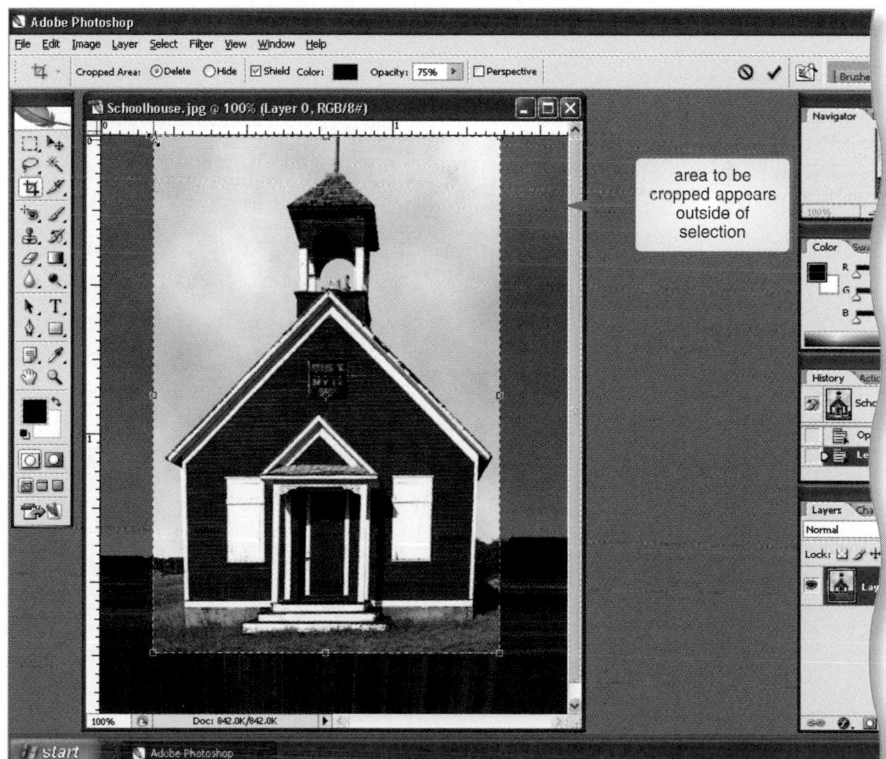

FIGURE 5-42

3

- **Press the ENTER key.**

The image is cropped (Figure 5-43).

FIGURE 5-43

Other Ways

1. Press C key, drag area

In the next steps, the image is saved and minimized for use in creating the postcard.

To Save and Minimize the Image

1. **With your USB flash drive connected to one of the computer's USB ports, click File on the menu bar and then Save As.**
2. **When the Save As dialog box is displayed, type** `Schoolhouse Repaired` **in the File name text box. Do not press the ENTER key.**
3. **Click the Save in box arrow and then click USBDISK [G:], or the location associated with your USB flash drive, in the list.**
4. **Click the Save button. When Photoshop displays an options dialog box, click the OK button.**
5. **Click the Minimize button on the Schoolhouse Repaired document window title bar.**

The file is saved and the document window is minimized.

Creating the Postcard

Marketing specialists know that a promotional postcard, or postcard marketing, has a high consumer impact. Letters enclosed in envelopes keep the message hidden and can be thrown away unopened. With a postcard, readers invariably glance at the message and turn it over. Furthermore, postcards are cheaper to produce and less costly to mail than are traditional newsletters or brochures, as there is nothing to assemble, fold, or seal. A four-color postcard allows you to present text and color pictures, which reemphasizes the message for the viewer. Postcards make sense for small businesses, special event advertising, and mass marketing.

The historical society wants to send postcards to teachers to invite classes to visit the Little Red Schoolhouse, a refurbished schoolhouse from the 1800s. As an educational field trip, the schoolhouse offers a look at a school day in the past, which children find fascinating. The historical society wants to emphasize fun, children, and the schoolhouse in its promotional postcard.

To achieve this, Photoshop will be used to put together an image of the schoolhouse, an image of happy children, and text.

Creating the Background Layer

The postcard will be created from scratch using standard postcard dimensions. The various settings for the new image are provided in Table 5-6.

A background emphasizing yellow and blue will be used to provide both visual contrast and overall unity between the three components — the schoolhouse, the children, and the text — as illustrated in the following steps. The radial gradient will provide a strong, colorful figure-ground relationship that emphasizes the photos.

Table 5-6 Postcard Settings

ATTRIBUTE	SETTING
Name	Postcard
Preset	Custom
Width	5.5 inches
Height	4.25 inches
Resolution	300 pixels/inch
Color Mode	CMYK Color 8 bit
Background Contents	White

To Create the Background

1

- **Click File on the menu bar and then click New.**
- **When Photoshop displays the New dialog box, in each text box, double-click and enter the settings from Table 5-6. For each list box, click the box arrow and then click the setting listed in Table 5-6.**

The new settings are displayed (Figure 5-44).

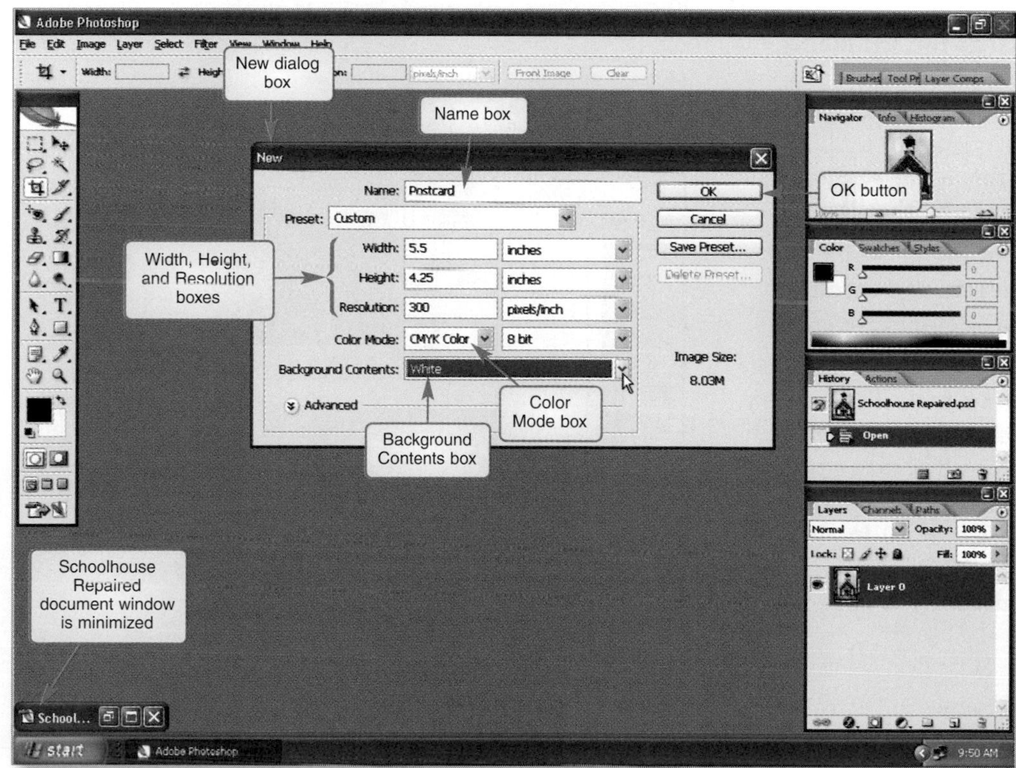

FIGURE 5-44

2

- **Click the OK button. If Rulers do not display, press CTRL+R.**
- **Click the Color palette menu button and then click CMYK sliders in the list.**
- **Press G to access the Gradient tool. If necessary, right-click the Paint Bucket Tool (G) button and then click Gradient Tool in the list.**
- **Click the Radial Gradient button on the options bar.**

The postcard is displayed (Figure 5-45). CMYK sliders display in the Color palette. The Gradient tool is selected.

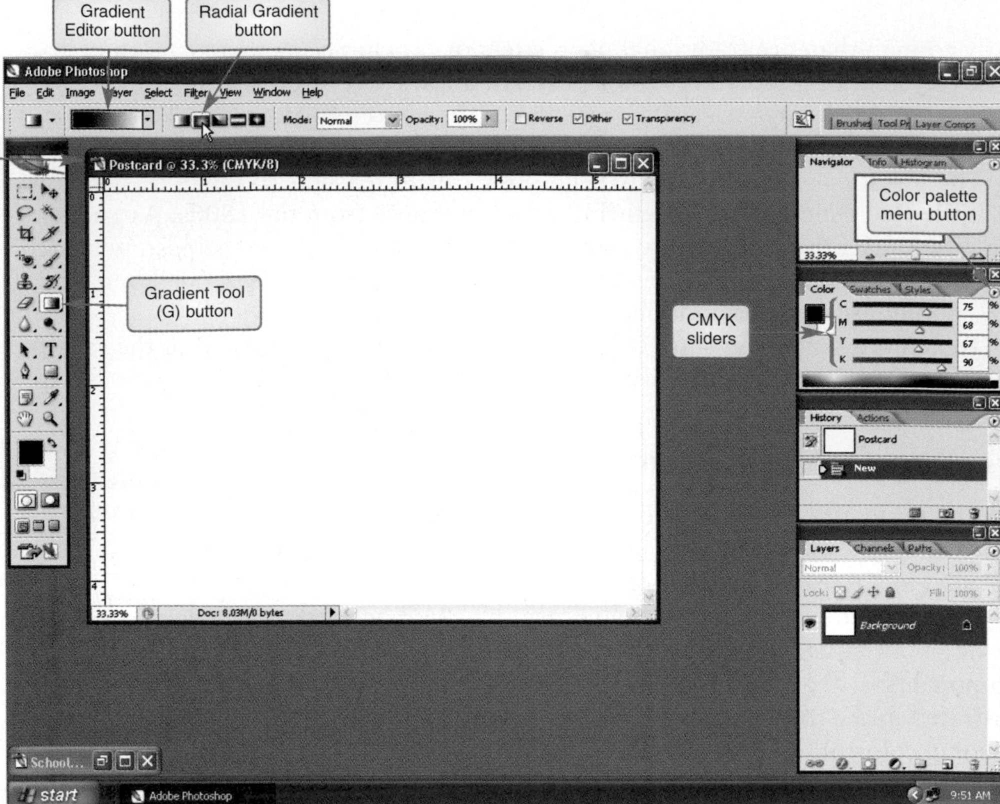

FIGURE 5-45

3

- **Click the Gradient Editor button. If necessary, click the Foreground to Background gradient preset in the list.**
- **Double-click the left Color Stop button.**
- **When Photoshop displays the Color Picker dialog box, if necessary, click the Only Web Colors box to remove its check mark. Enter** 0 **in the C box,** 0 **in the M box,** 80 **in the Y box, and** 0 **in the K box.**

The Color Picker dialog box displays the yellow color (Figure 5-46).

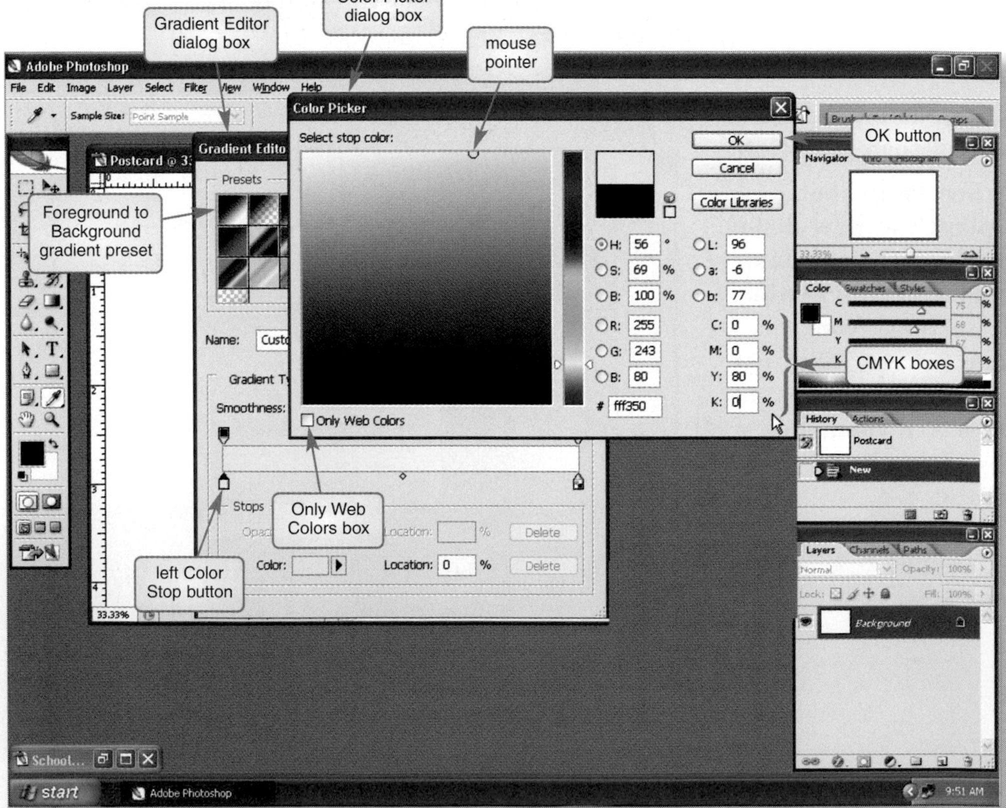

FIGURE 5-46

4

- **Click the OK button in the Color Picker dialog box.**
- **Double-click the right Color Stop button.**
- **When Photoshop displays the Color Picker dialog box, enter** 32 **in the C box,** 13 **in the M box,** 0 **in the Y box, and** 0 **in the K box.**

The Color Picker dialog box displays the light blue color (Figure 5-47).

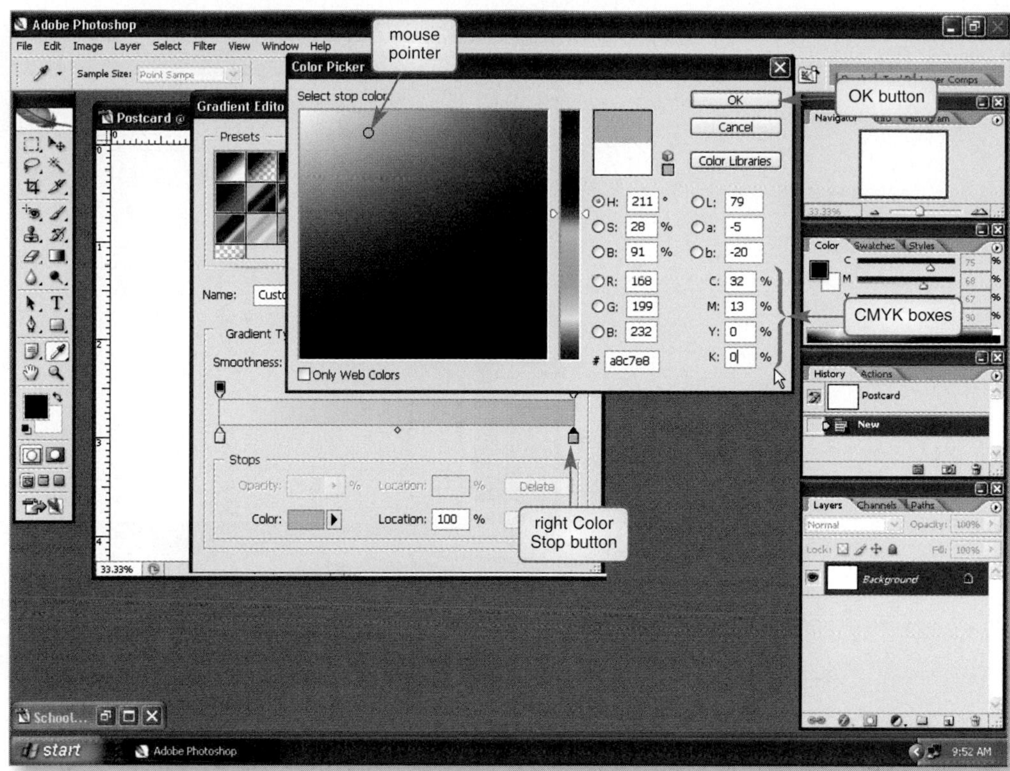

FIGURE 5-47

5

- **Click the OK button in the Color Picker dialog box. If the Gradient Editor displays a middle Color Stop button, click it, and then click the Delete button.**
- **Click the OK button in the Gradient Editor dialog box.**
- **Drag from the lower-left corner of the postcard toward the upper-right and stop approximately 1 inch from the corner. Do not release the mouse button.**

The angle and length of the gradient will be determined by the drag line (Figure 5-48).

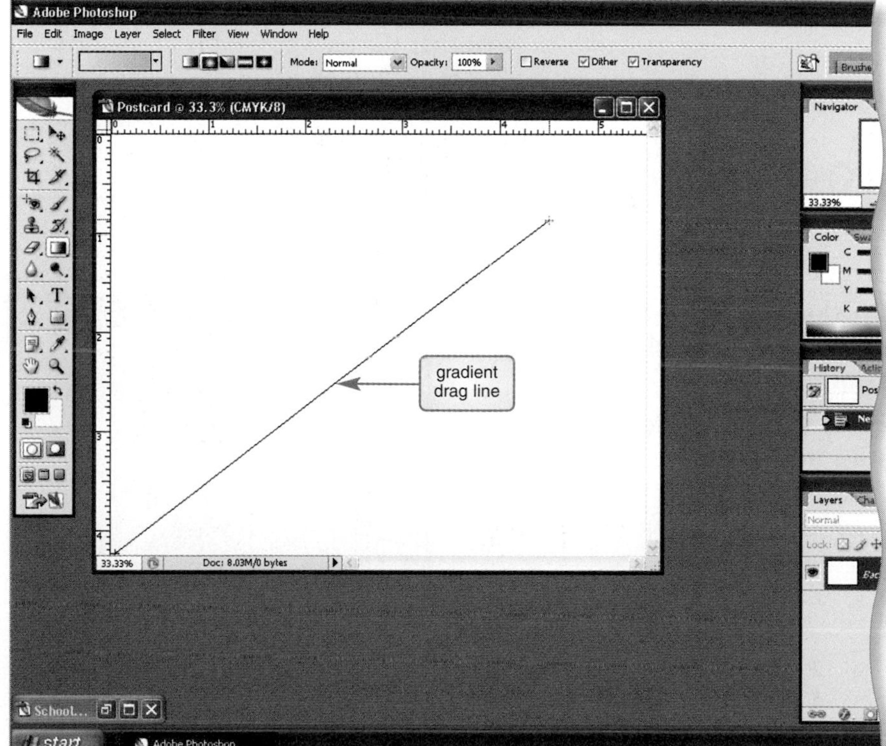

FIGURE 5-48

6

• **Release the mouse button.**

The radial gradient is created (Figure 5-49).

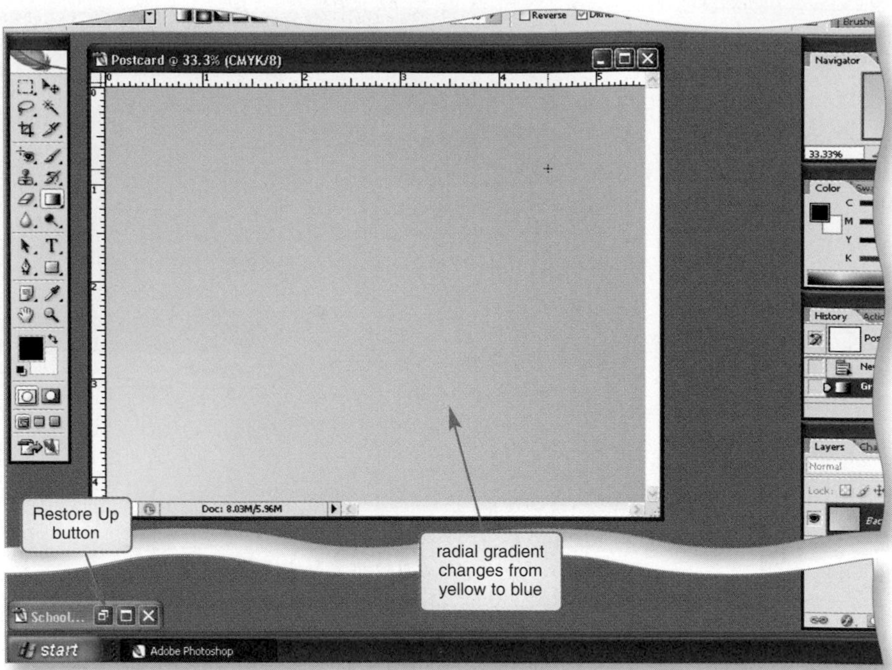

FIGURE 5-49

Creating the Schoolhouse Layer

Now that the background is developed, the following steps create a faded out image of the schoolhouse in the lower-right corner of the postcard.

To Create the Schoolhouse Layer

1

• **On the minimized Schoolhouse Repaired title bar, click the Restore Up button.**

• **Press CTRL+A to select the entire image.**

The entire Schoolhouse Repaired image is selected (Figure 5-50).

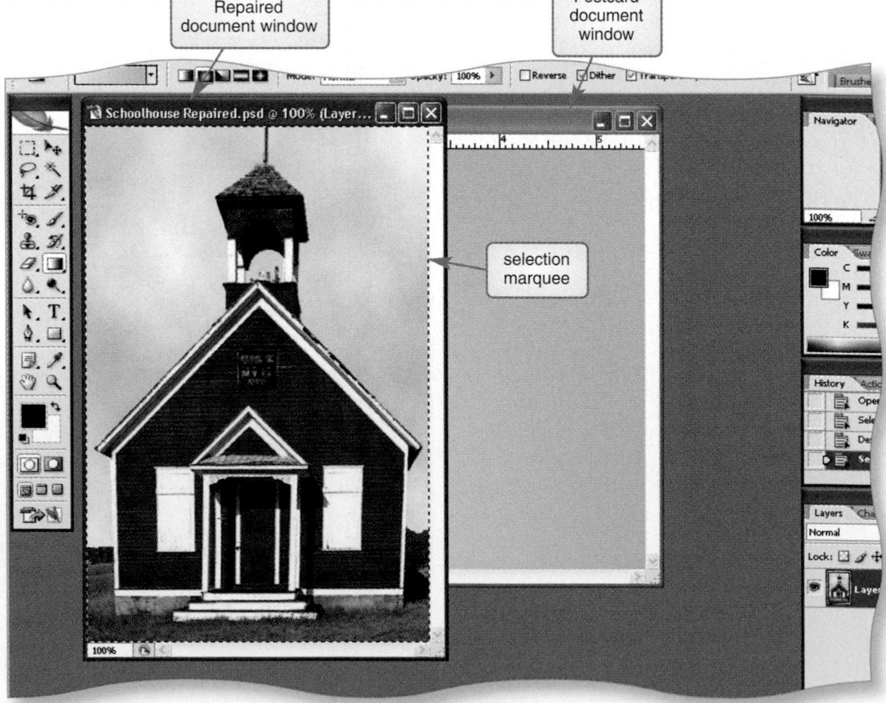

FIGURE 5-50

2

- **Click the Move Tool (V) button in the toolbox.**
- **Drag the selection to the lower-right corner of the Postcard document window.**
- **Press CTRL+T to display the bounding box.**

A new layer is created (Figure 5-51).

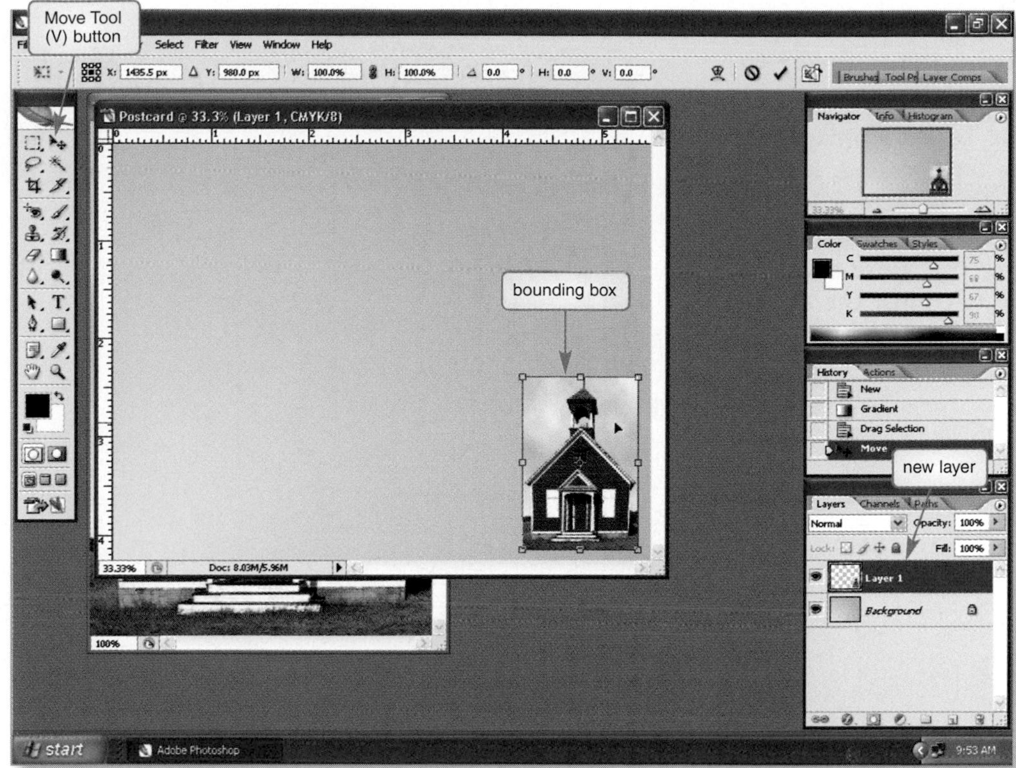

FIGURE 5-51

3

- **SHIFT+drag the upper-left sizing handle until the schoolhouse is approximately 3.25 inches tall.**

Recall that pressing SHIFT+drag maintains the width-to-height proportions of the image (Figure 5-52).

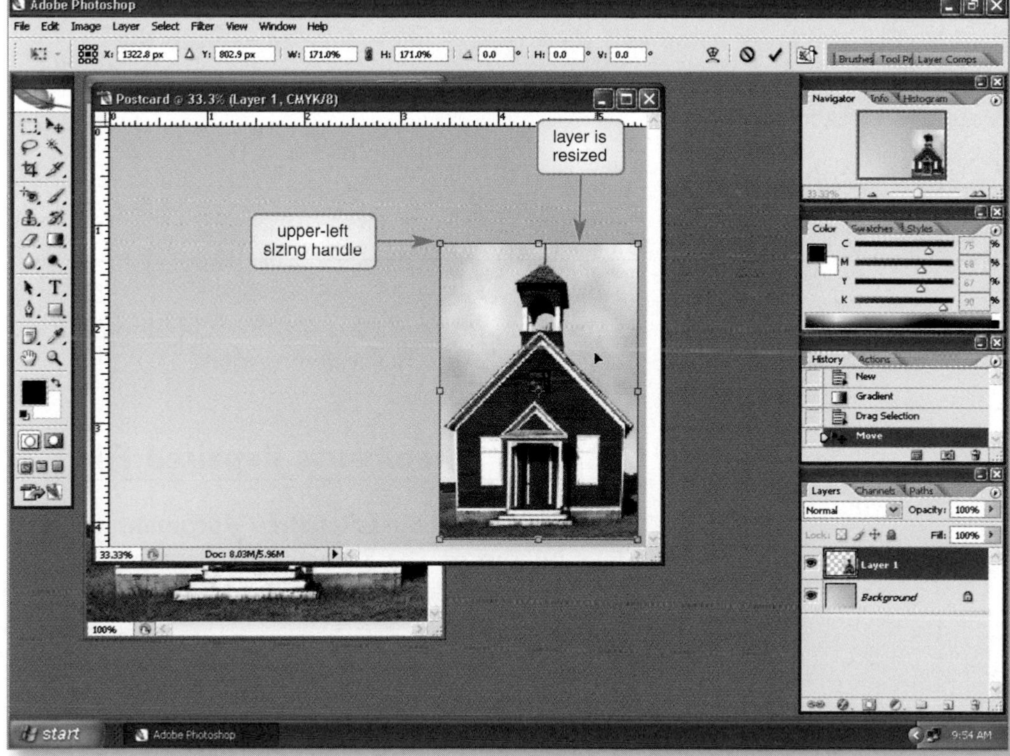

FIGURE 5-52

4

- **Press the ENTER key to commit the changes.**
- **To fade the image into the background, in the Layers palette, click the Fill box arrow and then drag the slider slowly to the left until the sky fades into the background.**

Photoshop displays the faded layer (Figure 5-53).

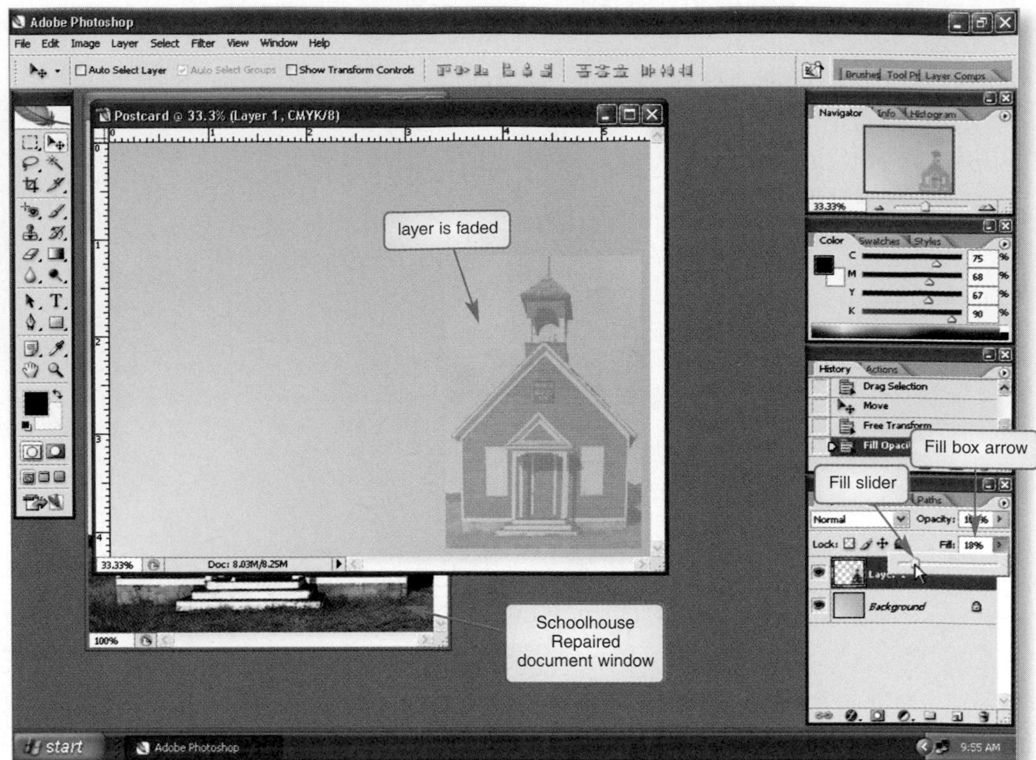

FIGURE 5-53

5

- **Double-click the layer name and then type** `Schoolhouse` **to replace the layer name.**
- **Press the ENTER key.**

The layer is renamed.

Because you are finished using the Schoolhouse Repaired file, you can close its document window to save system resources.

To Close the Schoolhouse Repaired File

1 **Click the Schoolhouse Repaired document window to select it. Click the Close button on the Schoolhouse Repaired document window title bar. If Photoshop asks if you want to save the file again, click the No button.**

The window is closed.

Opening a Recently Used File

The next step is to open the Children Repaired image as shown in the following steps. Because the Children Repaired image is a recently used file, the Open Recent submenu on the File menu will display the title, which saves time.

To Open a Recently Used File

1

• **On the File menu, point to Open Recent.**

Photoshop displays a list of recently used files (Figure 5-54).

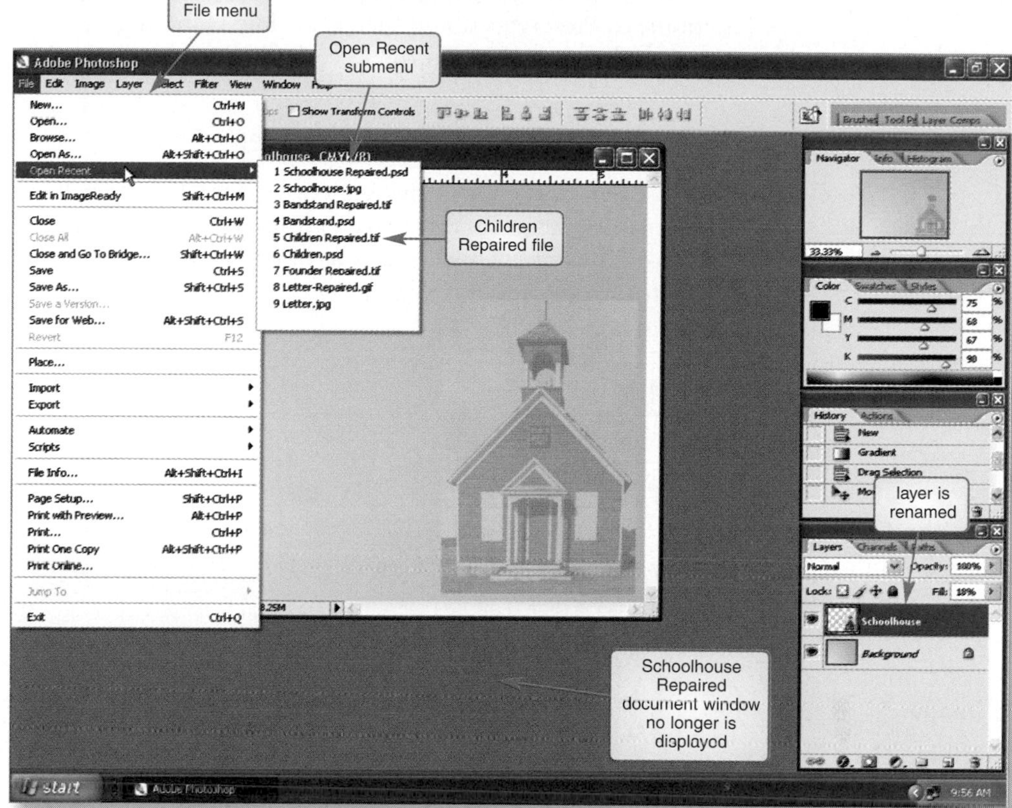

FIGURE 5-54

2

• **Click Children Repaired.tif. If Children Repaired is not on your list, press CTRL+O and then browse to your storage location and double-click the file.**

The Children Repaired document window is displayed (Figure 5-55).

FIGURE 5-55

If your list of recent files is shorter than the one shown in Figure 5-54, it may be that someone has changed a preference setting. In that case, click Edit on the menu bar, point to Preferences, and then click File Handling. In the dialog box that is displayed, type a larger number in the Recent file list contains box.

Creating the Children Layer

The next step is to move a copy of the Children Repaired photo into the postcard, add a layer mask and remove extraneous background, and then resize the layer. If you make a mistake while removing portions of the image, click the previous state in the History palette and try again.

To Create the Children Layer

1

- **With the Children Repaired window active, press CTRL+A to select the entire image.**
- **Press CTRL+C to copy the image.**
- **Minimize the Children Repaired window.**
- **With the Postcard document window selected, press CTRL+V to paste the image. Position it in the lower-left corner.**

Photoshop displays the new layer (Figure 5-56).

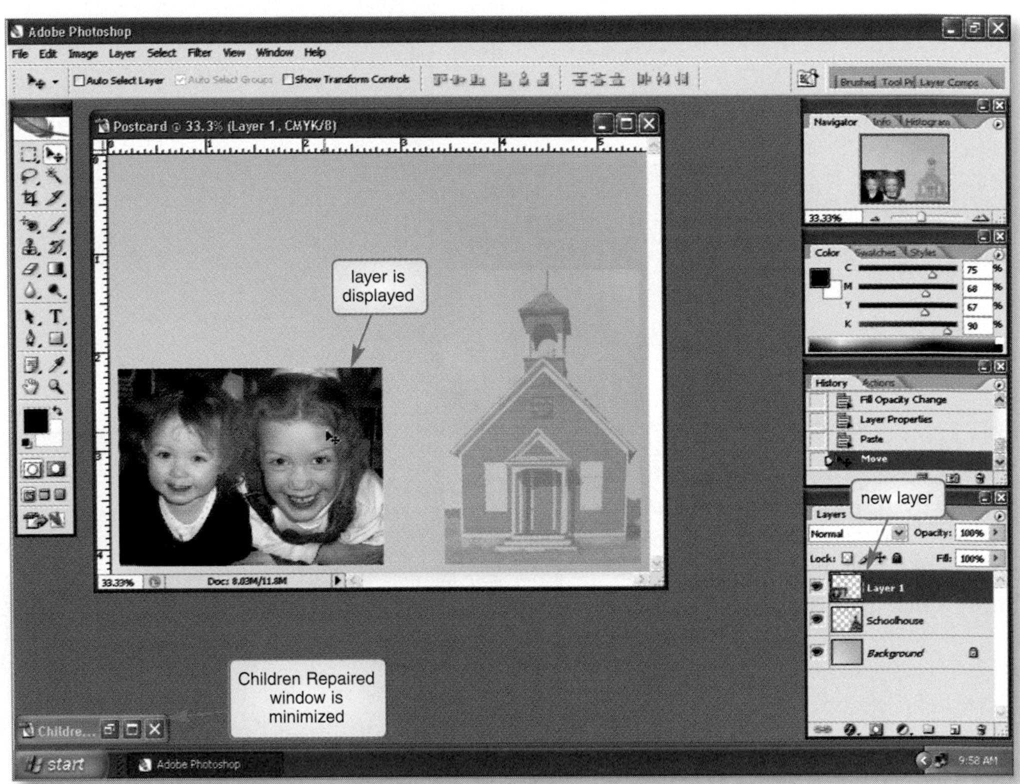

FIGURE 5-56

2

- **In the Layers palette, click the Add layer mask button.**
- **Press the B key to activate the Brush tool. If necessary, press the D key to access the default colors. If necessary, press the X key to make black the foreground color.**
- **Click the Set to enable airbrush capabilities button on the Brush options bar.**
- **Move the mouse pointer into the Postcard document window. Press the] key until the mouse pointer displays as a small circle.**

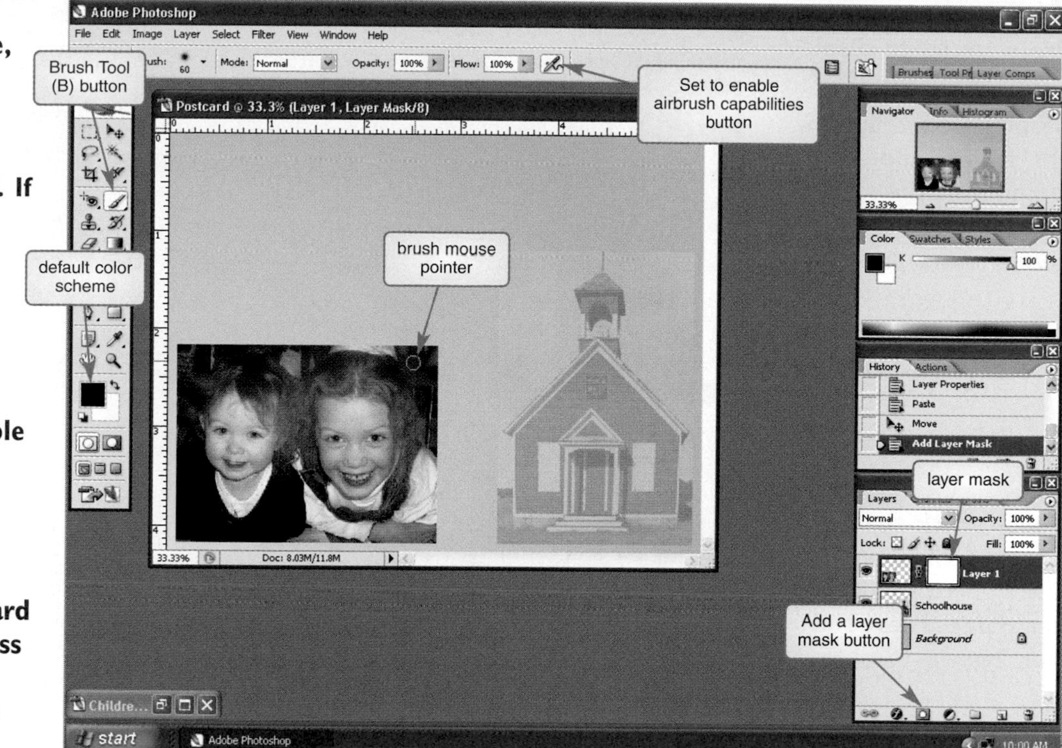

FIGURE 5-57

Photoshop displays the layer mask in the Layers palette and the brush mouse pointer in the document window (Figure 5-57).

3

- **Using short strokes, drag in the layer above the heads of the children to mask the images behind the children.**
- **Drag down the right side to outline the child.**
- **Reduce the size of the brush by pressing the [key and then drag the very edge of the child to soften the image.**
- **Click the lower-right corner to soften the corner.**

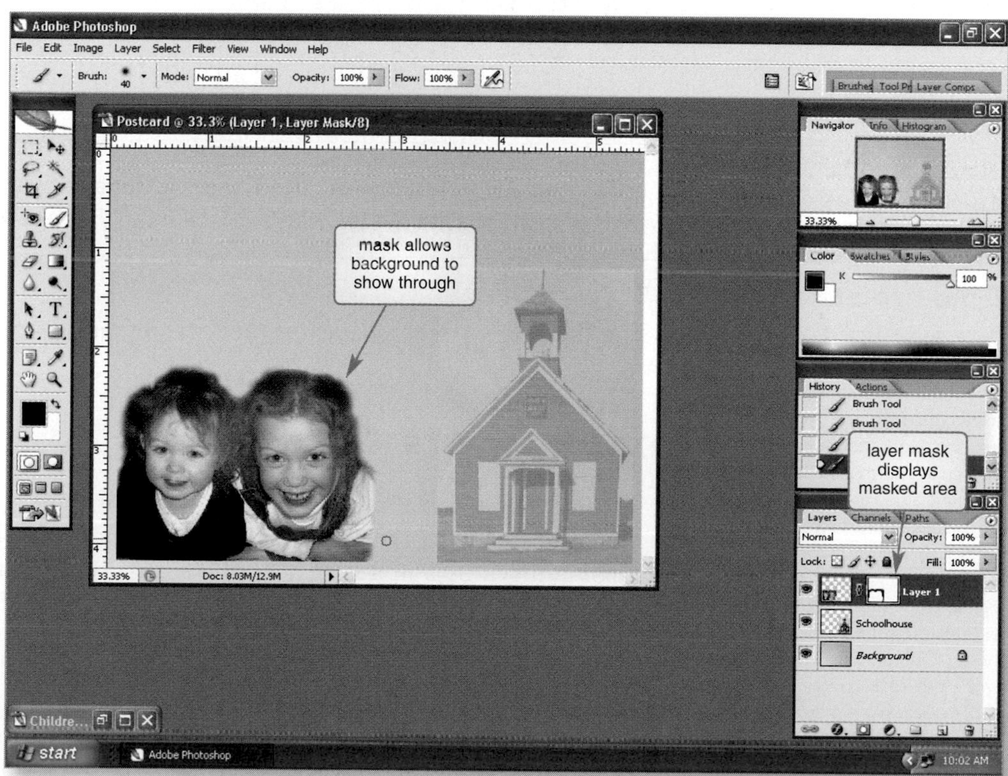

FIGURE 5-58

Recall that painting with black in a layer mask erases portions of the image to make the background show through (Figure 5-58).

4

• **Press CTRL+T to display the bounding box.**

• **SHIFT+drag the upper-right sizing handle until the child on the right touches the grass in the Schoolhouse layer.**

• **Press the ENTER key.**

The layer is resized (Figure 5-59).

5

• **Double-click the layer name and then type** `Children` **to replace the layer name. Press the enter key.**

The layer is renamed.

FIGURE 5-59

Because you are finished using the Children Repaired file, you can close its document window to save system resources as shown in the following steps.

To Close the Children Repaired File

1 **Click the Close button on the Children Repaired document window title bar. If Photoshop asks if you want to save the file again, click the No button.**

The window is closed.

The final series of steps creates the text for the postcard.

> *More About*
>
> **Type Professions**
>
> The art of designing typefaces is called type design, and the people who design them are called type designers. Type designers work for software companies and graphic design firms, and also freelance as calligraphers and artists. Typographers are responsible for designing the layout of the printed word and blocks of text on a page. Because the chosen font contributes significantly to an overall layout, typographers have in-depth knowledge and understanding about the intricacies in which typefaces are utilized to convey particular messages.

Text Elements

Text elements are special type layers in Photoshop that contain typed words. Graphic designers use the term, **type**, to refer to the mathematically defined shapes of letters, numbers, and symbols in a typeface. The terms, type, text, and copy have become interchangeable with the advent of desktop publishing; however, Photoshop uses the word, type, when referring to the various tools that manipulate text.

Many of the terms used when working with type tools come from the field of typesetting. **Typeface**, the design of the individual characters, now is commonly synonymous with the word, **font**. Typefaces are available in more than one format. The most common formats are TrueType, Type 1 or PostScript Type, OpenType, and New CID, a format developed to support non-English characters.

Photoshop uses four basic type tools: the **Horizontal Type tool**, the **Vertical Type tool**, the **Horizontal Type Mask tool**, and the **Vertical Type Mask tool**. As the names imply, the text is created either horizontally or vertically. The two masking tools create selections in the shape of individual letters rather than in a box, which is useful particularly for special effects.

The Type Tool options bar is displayed in Figure 5-60. It includes list boxes for the font family, font style, font size, and anti-aliasing. The list boxes are followed by three text alignment buttons, a Set the text color button, the Create warped text button, and the Toggle the Character and Paragraph palettes button. As you enter text, the Cancel and Commit buttons are added to the options bar.

More About

Warped Text

The Create warped text button allows you to distort type in a variety of shapes, such as waves and arcs. The warp style you select becomes an attribute of the type layer that you can change at any time. Several warping options are available in the Warp Text dialog box that displays when you click the Create warped text button on the Type Tool options bar. The buttons give you precise control over the orientation and perspective of the warp effect.

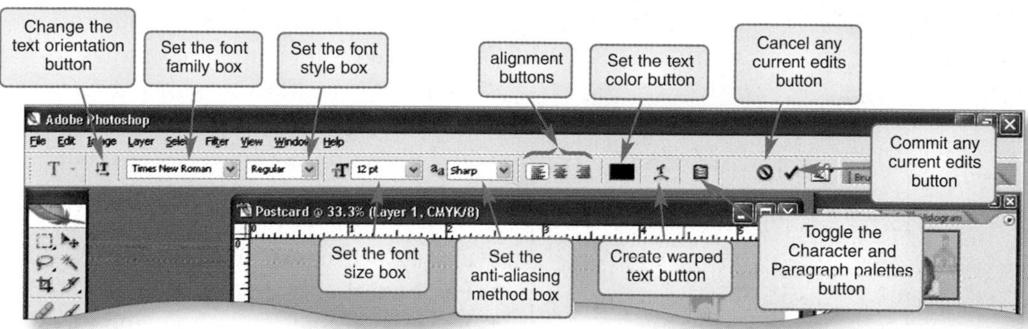

FIGURE 5-60 Type Tool Options Bar

Besides the basic text and style buttons and boxes shown on the options bar, Photoshop provides a set of extended type tools in the Character palette (Figure 5-61). Included are some of the same tools as are contained on the options bar with the addition of scaling, tracking, kerning, leading, baseline shift, special effects, and language.

Scaling, the process of shrinking or stretching text, changes the width of individual characters. **Tracking**, on the other hand, refers to the adjustment of the general spacing between characters. Tracking text compensates for the spacing irregularities caused when you make text much bigger or much smaller. For example, smaller type is easier to read when it has been tracked loosely. Tracking both maintains the original height and width of the characters and overrides adjustments made by justification or bounding box changes.

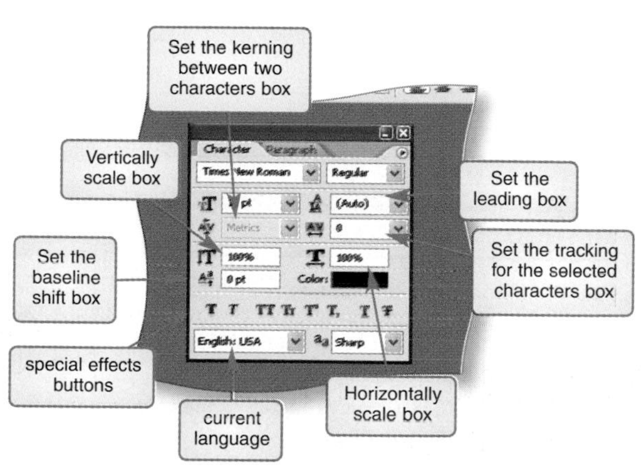

FIGURE 5-61 Character Palette

Kerning is a special form of tracking related to pairs of adjacent characters that can appear too far apart. For instance, certain letters such as T, V, W, and Y, often need kerning when they are preceded or followed by a, e, i, o, or u. The word, Tom, typed in a large font might create too much space between the letters T and o. Clicking between the letters and then adjusting the kerning would make the word more readable. The term, kerning, comes from the pre-computer era, when individual type characters were made from metals, including lead. Bits of lead were shaved off wider characters, thus allowing the smaller character to be moved underneath. The resulting overhang was called a kern.

Leading, also called line spacing, refers to the amount of vertical spacing between lines of type. This again refers to the pre-computer practice of adding lead to create space between lines of metal type characters.

Baseline shift controls the distance of type from its original baseline, either raising or lowering the selected type. Shifting the baseline is especially useful when using superscripts, subscripts, and fractions. Below the Color box are the **special effects buttons**, and below that is the **Language list box**. The Character palette menu button displays many of the same commands and provides the capability to reset all value boxes so fractional settings can be used.

The Paragraph palette (Figure 5-62) contains buttons to change the formatting of columns and paragraphs, also called **text blocks**. Unique to the Paragraph palette are settings to change the justification for paragraphs, indenting margins and first lines, and changing the spacing above and below paragraphs. The palette's menu button displays other commands to change settings including access to the **Hyphenation dialog box** where you can be very specific about how and when hyphenation occurs.

FIGURE 5-62 Paragraph Palette including Hyphenation Dialog Box

Creating Text

Table 5-7 describes the three ways to create type: at a point, inside a paragraph, or along a path.

Table 5-7 Ways to Create Type

METHOD	APPEARANCE	STEPS	USE
Point	text displays in a horizontal or vertical line	1. Select the type tool and settings. 2. Click the image. 3. Enter text.	used for limited amounts of words on a single line; text is aligned at the point of click
Paragraph	text displays in resizable bounding box	1. Select the type tool and settings. 2. Drag to create a bounding box. 3. Enter text.	used to create one or more paragraphs, such as for a brochure
Path	text flows along the edge of a designated path	1. Create a path. 2. Select the type tool and settings. 3. Click the path. 4. Enter text.	used to create limited amounts of text in freeform lines

While you are typing text, you are working in **edit mode**. In edit mode, you can enter and edit characters and perform limited menu commands; however, other operations require that you first commit changes on the options bar. When you commit changes, a new **type layer** is added to the Layers palette. In images that do not support layers, Photoshop converts text elements to bitmaps and embeds them in the image.

The following steps illustrate how to enter paragraph text on the postcard. First, the Horizontal Type Tool (T) button is clicked and the settings are selected. Then, the bounding box is drawn. Finally, the text is entered and committed.

To Enter Text

1

- **Right-click the current type tool.**

Photoshop displays the context menu (Figure 5-63).

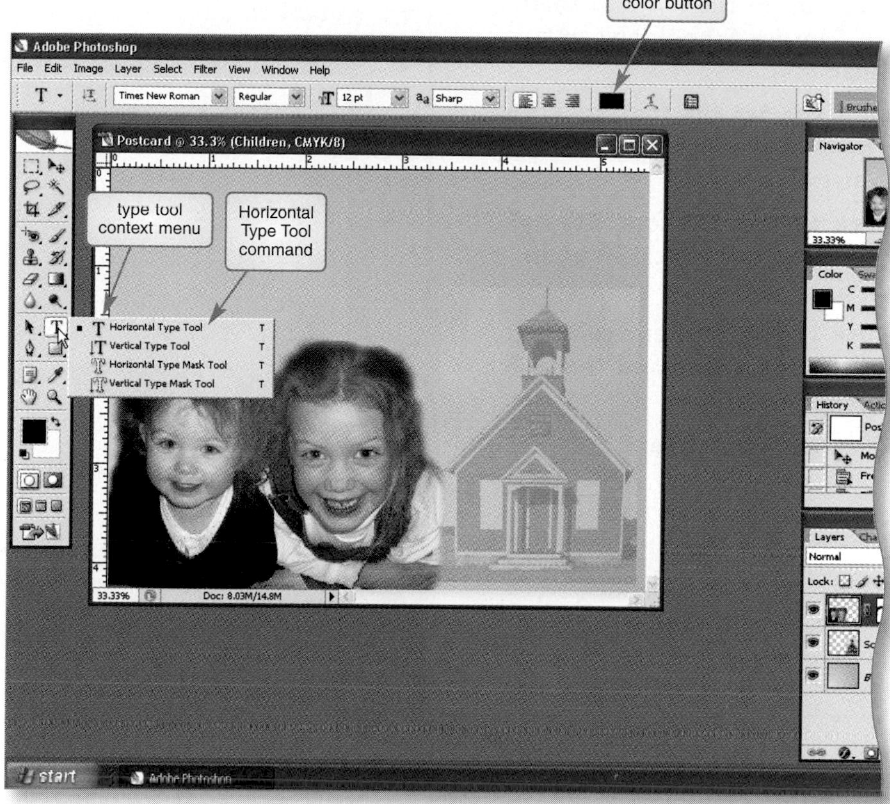

FIGURE 5-63

2

- **Click Horizontal Type Tool in the list.**
- **On the options bar, click the Set the font family box arrow.**

The current font displays a check mark (Figure 5-64). Notice that Photoshop displays a sample of each font family.

FIGURE 5-64

3

- **Scroll up in the list and then click Century Schoolbook or a similar font.**
- **Click the Set the font style box arrow and then click Bold Italic in the list.**
- **Click the Set the font size box arrow, and then click 30 pt in the list.**
- **Click the Set the anti-aliasing method box arrow and then click Smooth in the list.**
- **Click the Center text button.**

The new settings are displayed on the options bar (Figure 5-65).

FIGURE 5-65

4

- **Click the Set the text color button.**
- **When Photoshop displays the Color Picker dialog box, select a bright red color.**

Red is displayed as the new color (Figure 5-66).

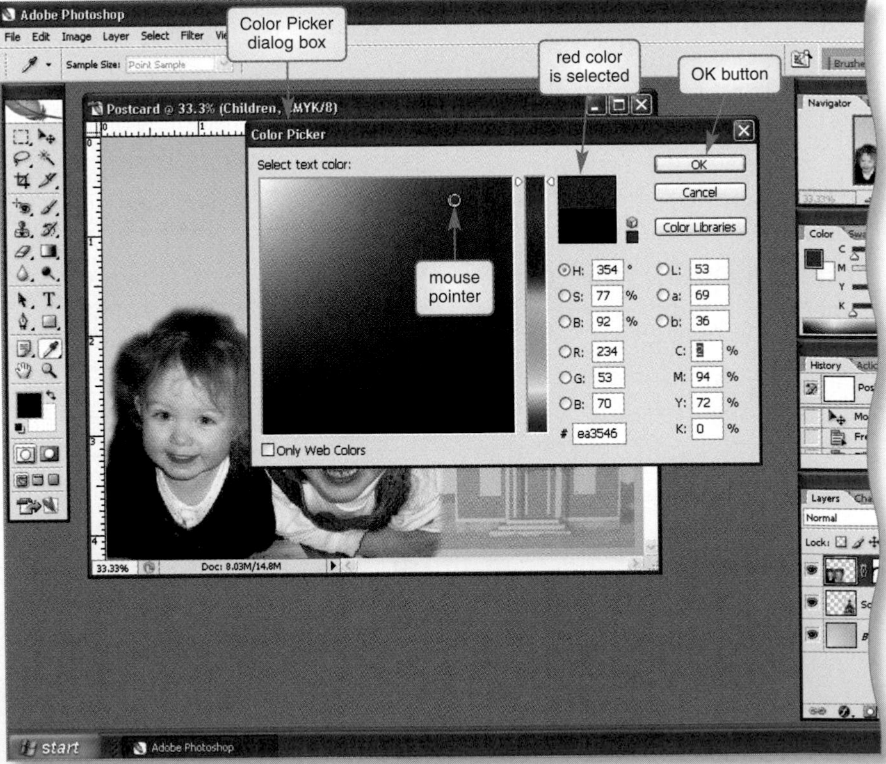

FIGURE 5-66

5

- **Click the OK button.**
- **In the image, drag a box starting at the upper-left margin. Drag down and to the right to fill the space above the images.**

The type bounding box is displayed (Figure 5-67). The red color has replaced black on the options bar. Because center text has been selected, Photoshop displays the insertion point in the middle of the bounding box.

FIGURE 5-67

6

- **Type** `Play and learn at the Little Red Schoolhouse!` **in the bounding box.**

The text is displayed (Figure 5-68).

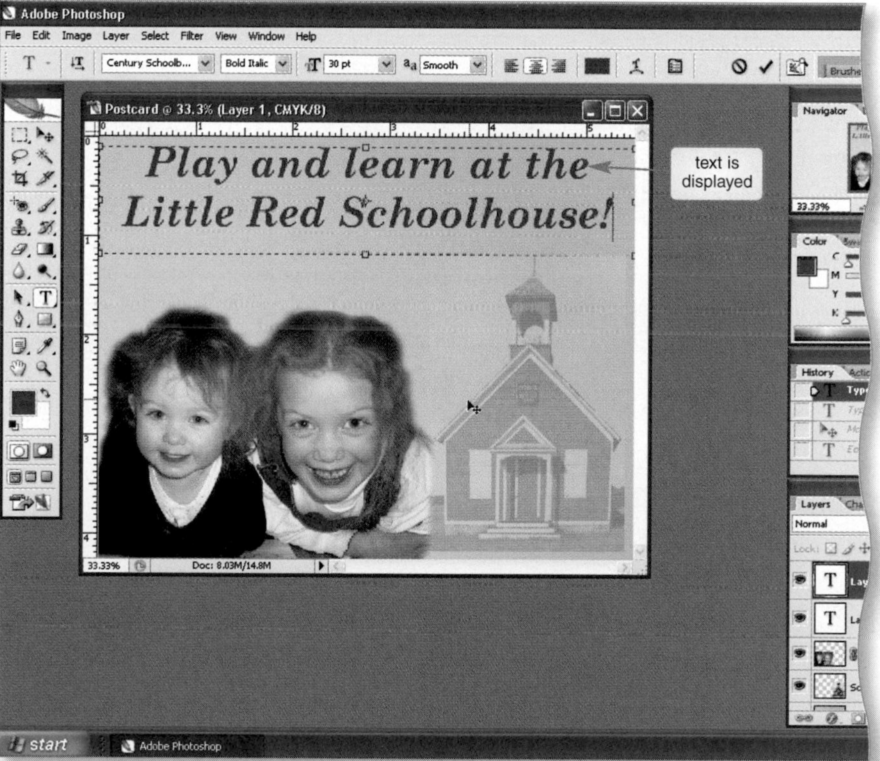

FIGURE 5-68

7

- **Drag to highlight the word, and, in the sentence.**
- **On the options bar, click the Toggle the Character and Paragraph palettes button.**
- **If necessary, click the Character tab when the palettes display.**
- **Click the Underline button.**

The word, and, is displayed with an underline (Figure 5-69).

FIGURE 5-69

8

- **Click the Commit any current edits button on the options bar.**

The text entry becomes a layer in the palette.

Other Ways

1. Press T key, set options, type text

In the previous steps, you used the paragraph method by drawing a bounding box to add text to the postcard. For added flexibility, Photoshop's type tools allow you to convert between methods. For example, you can convert point type to paragraph type to adjust the flow of characters within a bounding box. Alternately, you can convert paragraph type to point type to make each text line flow independently from the others. You will learn more about adding text elements using the paths method in a later project.

Many type commands are available on the Layer menu. For example, if you wanted an image rather than a color to fill the boundaries of each character, create a layer that contains the image directly above the type layer in the Layers palette. Then, with the image layer selected, click the Create Clipping Mask command on the Layer menu. The image will appear inside the text as shown in Figure 5-70. You can use the Move tool to adjust the placement of the image within the text.

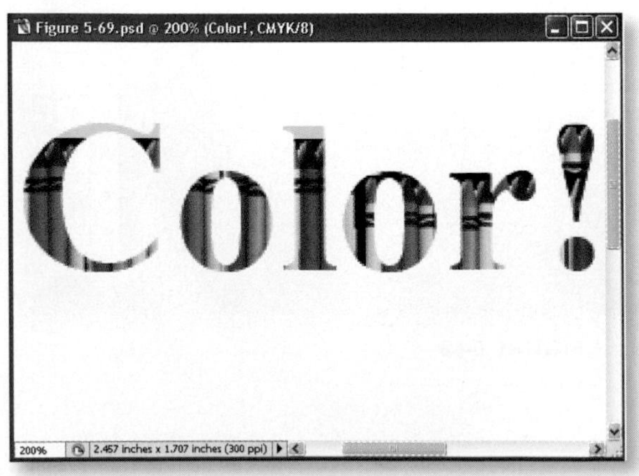

FIGURE 5-70

Some type settings, such as the default font size and the use of curly versus straight quotes have to be set in Photoshop's preferences. To do so, press CTRL+K and then proceed to the Units & Rulers or Type preference. For more information about setting preferences, see Appendix A.

Photoshop even has a find and replace feature and a dictionary to check the spelling in your text elements. With the type layer selected, click Find and Replace Text on the Edit menu to locate or change specific characters or words. If you click Check Spelling on the Edit menu, Photoshop will offer a suggestion if it finds a word that is not in its dictionary. The find, replace, and spelling features are similar to those in popular word processing programs.

The postcard is complete. Because the postcard is a composite of many layers, the following steps show how to save the postcard in PSD format, in case it needs to be edited at a later time.

To Save the Postcard with Layers

1. **With your USB flash drive connected to one of the computer's USB ports, click File on the menu bar and then Save As.**
2. **When the Save As dialog box is displayed, type** `Postcard With Layers` **in the File name text box. Do not press the ENTER key.**
3. **If necessary, click the Format box arrow and then click Photoshop (*.PSD;*PDD) in the list.**
4. **Click the Save in box arrow and then click USBDISK [G:], or the location associated with your USB flash drive, in the list.**
5. **Click the Save button. When Photoshop displays the Photoshop Format Options dialog box, click the OK button.**

The file is saved in the PSD format.

In order to maximize the portability of the postcard file and in preparation for sending the file to a print shop, the following steps flatten the layers and then save the file in the EPS format. **EPS** stands for encapsulated PostScript and is best used for print, because it is printer device independent and delivers the best output at any size or resolution. EPS was designed with color modes like CMYK in mind. While the saved file does not look as good on the screen because it uses a dithered preview, when it prints on a PostScript printer, the output is excellent. **PostScript printers** contain a built-in interpreter that executes PostScript instructions with the ability to handle the complex text and graphics typical in graphic design and desktop publishing. EPS is not, however, the best file type for ink-jet printers. Most desktop printers produce good quality with files saved in the TIFF format.

Remember that flattened images take less disk space, but the layers cannot be edited. If the need to edit will exist, always save a copy of your document with a different name before flattening as you did in the previous steps.

To Flatten the Postcard and Save It in the EPS Format

1. **Click Layer on the menu bar and then click Flatten Image.**
2. **With your USB flash drive connected to one of the computer's USB ports, click File on the menu bar and then Save As.**
3. **When the Save As dialog box is displayed, type** `Postcard For Print` **in the File name text box. Do not press the ENTER key.**
4. **Click the Format box arrow and then click Photoshop DCS 1.0 (*.EPS) in the list.**
5. **Click the Save in box arrow and then click USBDISK [G:], or the location associated with your USB flash drive, in the list.**
6. **Click the Save button. When Photoshop displays the DCS 1.0 Format dialog box, click the OK button.**

The image is saved.

The final step is to close the document window and quit Photoshop.

To Close the Document Window and Quit Photoshop

1. **Click the Close button on the Postcard For Print document window title bar.**
2. **Click the Close button on the right side of the Photoshop title bar.**

The Photoshop window closes.

Project Summary

To repair photos and enhance them with text, you used healing tools, tools that repaired damage, tools to straighten and align, and tools to create text. You first edited a yellowed letter and used the Unsharp Mask tool to bring it into better focus. You then repaired scratches and damage to a black and white photo. You removed the red eye from a color photo of children. Next, you repaired light damage to an old picture of a bandstand. You opened a schoolhouse photo that had keystone and angle distortion, which you corrected using the Lens Correction dialog box. Finally, you embedded the children's photo and the schoolhouse onto a postcard and used the Horizontal Type tool in paragraph mode to add text.

What You Should Know

Having completed this project, you should be able to perform the tasks below. The tasks are listed in the same order they were presented in this project. For a list of the buttons, menus, toolbars, and other commands introduced in this project, see the Quick Reference Summary at the back of this book and refer to the Page Number column.

1. Start Photoshop and Reset the Palettes, Toolbox, and Options Bar (PS 276)
2. Reset the Layers Palette (PS 276)
3. Reset the Colors (PS 276)
4. Open the Letter Image (PS 276)
5. Remove Yellowed Portions of the Letter (PS 278)
6. Set Levels (PS 279)
7. Use the Unsharp Mask (PS 281)
8. Use the Eraser Tool (PS 282)
9. Save for the Web (PS 283)
10. Close the Letter File (PS 283)
11. Open and Crop the Founder Image (PS 284)
12. Duplicate a Layer for Corrections (PS 285)
13. Use the Spot Healing Brush Tool (PS 286)
14. Use the Healing Brush Tool (PS 288)
15. Use the Patch Tool (PS 290)
16. Repair Other Damage (PS 291)
17. Save and Close the Founder File (PS 292)
18. Open the Children Image (PS 293)
19. Use the Red Eye Tool (PS 294)
20. Save and Close the Children File (PS 295)
21. Open the Bandstand Image and Create a Corrections Layer (PS 296)
22. Use the Dodge Tool (PS 297)
23. Use the Burn Tool (PS 297)
24. Save and Close the Bandstand File (PS 298)
25. Open the Schoolhouse Image (PS 298)
26. Correct Angle and Perspective Errors (PS 300)
27. Crop the Image (PS 305)
28. Save and Minimize the Image (PS 306)
29. Create the Background (PS 307)
30. Create the Schoolhouse Layer (PS 310)
31. Close the Schoolhouse Repaired File (PS 312)
32. Open a Recently Used File (PS 313)
33. Create the Children Layer (PS 314)
34. Close the Children Repaired File (PS 316)
35. Enter Text (PS 319)
36. Save the Postcard with Layers (PS 323)
37. Flatten the Postcard and Save it in the EPS Format (PS 323)
38. Close the Document Window and Quit Photoshop (PS 324)

Learn It Online

Instructions: To complete the Learn It Online exercises, start your browser, click the Address bar, and then enter the Web address `scsite.com/photoshop/learn`. When the Photoshop CS2 Learn It Online page is displayed, follow the instructions in the exercises below. Each exercise has instructions for printing your results, either for your own records or for submission to your instructor.

1 Project Reinforcement TF, MC, and SA

Below Photoshop Project 5, click the Project Reinforcement link. Print the quiz by clicking Print on the File menu for each page. Answer each question.

2 Flash Cards

Below Photoshop Project 5, click the Flash Cards link and read the instructions. Type 20 (or a number specified by your instructor) in the Number of playing cards text box, type your name in the Enter your Name text box, and then click the Flip Card button. When the flash card is displayed, read the question and then click the ANSWER box arrow to select an answer. Flip through Flash Cards. If your score is 15 (75%) correct or greater, click Print on the File menu to print your results. If your score is less than 15 (75%) correct, then redo this exercise by clicking the Replay button.

3 Practice Test

Below Photoshop Project 5, click the Practice Test link. Answer each question, enter your first and last name at the bottom of the page, and then click the Grade Test button. When the graded practice test is displayed on your screen, click Print on the File menu to print a hard copy. Continue to take practice tests until you score 80% or better.

4 Who Wants To Be a Computer Genius?

Below Photoshop Project 5, click the Computer Genius link. Read the instructions, enter your first and last name at the bottom of the page, and then click the PLAY button. When your score is displayed, click the PRINT RESULTS link to print a hard copy.

5 Wheel of Terms

Below Photoshop Project 5, click the Wheel of Terms link. Read the instructions, and then enter your first and last name and your school name. Click the PLAY button. When your score is displayed, right-click the score and then click Print on the shortcut menu to print a hard copy.

6 Crossword Puzzle Challenge

Below Photoshop Project 5, click the Crossword Puzzle Challenge link. Read the instructions, and then enter your first and last name. Click the SUBMIT button. Work the crossword puzzle. When you are finished, click the Submit button. When the crossword puzzle is redisplayed, click the Print Puzzle button to print a hard copy.

7 Tips and Tricks

Below Photoshop Project 5, click the Tips and Tricks link. Click a topic that pertains to Project 5. Right-click the information and then click Print on the shortcut menu. Construct a brief example of what the information relates to in Photoshop to confirm you understand how to use the tip or trick.

8 Expanding Your Horizons

Below Photoshop Project 5, click the Expanding Your Horizons link. Click a topic that pertains to Project 5. Print the information. Construct a brief example of what the information relates to in Photoshop to confirm you understand the contents of the article.

9 Search Sleuth

Below Photoshop Project 5, click the Search Sleuth link. To search for a term that pertains to this project, select a term below the Project 5 title and then use the Google search engine at google.com (or any major search engine) to display and print two Web pages that present information on the term.

10 Photoshop Online Training

Below Photoshop Project 5, click the Photoshop Online Training link. When your browser displays the Web page, click one of the Photoshop tutorials that covers one or more of the objectives listed at the beginning of the project on page PS 270. Print the first page of the tutorial before stepping through it.

Apply Your Knowledge

1 Enhancing a Photo for the Web

Instructions: Start Photoshop, and set the workspace and tools to default settings. Open the Antique file from the Project05 folder, located either on the CD that accompanies this book, or in a location specified by your instructor. The purpose of this exercise is to repair a photo of an antique typewriter and enhance it for use on an auction Web site. The edited photo is shown in Figure 5-71.

FIGURE 5-71

1. Use the Save As command to save the image on your USB flash drive as a PSD file, with the file name, Antique Enhanced.
2. In the Layers palette, right-click the Background layer and then click Duplicate Layer on the shortcut menu.
3. In the Duplicate Layer dialog box, type `Corrections` in the As box, and then click the OK button.
4. With the Corrections layer selected, click Filter on the menu bar, point to Distort, and then click Lens Correction.
5. When the Lens Correction dialog box is displayed, edit the following settings:
   a. To adjust the barrel distortion, type `15` in the Remove Distortion box.
   b. To straighten the photo, type `358` in the Angle box.
   c. To correct the keystone distortion, type `50` in the Vertical Perspective box.
   d. To adjust the scale and remove transparent areas in the photo, type `123` in the Scale box.
6. Click the OK button in the Lens Correction dialog box.
7. Click Filter on the menu bar, point to Sharpen, and then click Unsharp Mask. When the Unsharp Mask dialog box is displayed, edit the following settings:
   a. Type `4` in the Threshold box.
   b. Type `1` in the Radius box.
   c. Type `50` in the Amount box.
8. Click the OK button in the Unsharp Mask dialog box.
9. In the toolbox, right-click the current healing tool and then click Spot Healing Brush Tool in the list. Use the Spot Healing Brush tool to correct the damaged area that displays on the wall to the right of the typewriter. Remember to adjust the brush size to be only slightly larger than the damaged area.
10. Use the Spot Healing Brush tool to correct flaws in the white baseboard and remove the small red ball to the left of the table.
11. Right-click the Spot Healing Brush tool and then click Healing Brush Tool in the list. On the options bar, click the Mode box arrow and then click Replace.
12. ALT+click a light area in the floor and then, using short strokes, drag through the darker areas in the floor. Resample as necessary.

Apply Your Knowledge

13. To remove the electrical cord in the photo:
    a. Click the Clone Stamp tool.
    b. ALT+click the floor at the bottom of the photo just inside the left leg of the table. Drag from left to right-through the parts of the electrical cord that display on the floor.
    c. ALT+click below the table at the top of the baseboard, close to the left leg of the table. Drag from left to right through the parts of the electrical cord that display on the baseboard.
14. Press CTRL+S to save the file again. If Photoshop displays an options dialog box, click the OK button.
15. Click File on the menu bar and then click the Save for Web command. When the Save for Web dialog box is displayed, click the 4-Up tab and then click the best preview for your system. Click the Save button. When the Save As Optimized dialog box is displayed, save the image on your USB flash drive. Photoshop will fill in the name, Antique-Enhanced, and the file type for you.
16. Upload the picture to the Web or see your instructor for ways to submit this assignment.

1 Repairing Blemishes and Red Eye

Problem: You are very proud of your baby niece. You would like to fix one of the photos that you have taken of her and print several copies. The photo has several blemishes and a red eye problem. You also would like to remove the date that was embedded when the photo was taken with a digital camera. The repaired photo is shown in Figure 5-72.

Instructions:

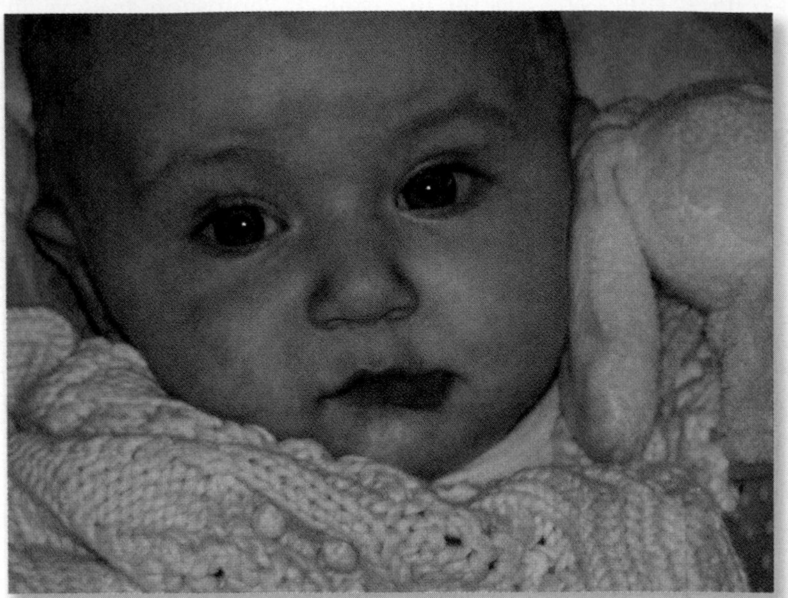

FIGURE 5-72

1. Start Photoshop. Set the Default Workspace and then reset all tools. Reset the previews in the Layers palette and then reset the default colors.
2. Open the file, Baby, from the Project05 folder on the CD that accompanies this book, or from a location specified by your instructor.
3. Click the Save As command on the File menu. Type `Baby Repaired` as the file name. If necessary, click the Format box arrow and then click PSD in the list. Browse to your USB flash drive storage device. Click the Save button. When the Photoshop Format Options dialog box is displayed, click the OK button.
4. Duplicate the Background layer and name it Corrections. Hide the Background layer.

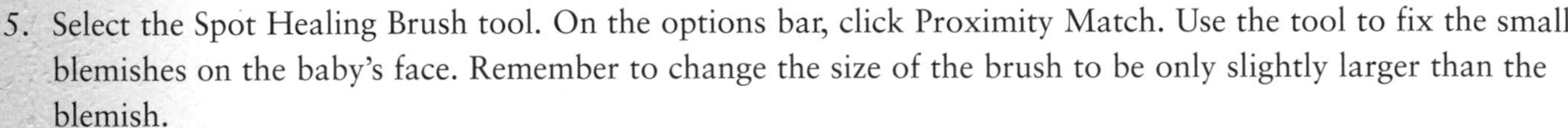

5. Select the Spot Healing Brush tool. On the options bar, click Proximity Match. Use the tool to fix the small blemishes on the baby's face. Remember to change the size of the brush to be only slightly larger than the blemish.
6. Use the Spot Healing Brush tool to fix reflections from the flash on the baby's nose, lips, and chin. If you make a bad correction, click the previous state in the History palette and decrease your brush size before trying again.
7. On the options bar, click Create Texture. Move the mouse pointer to the baby's chin. Increase the brush size to include the larger blemish. Click the blemish.
8. To remove the date from the lower-right corner, select the Healing Brush tool. In the options bar, click the Mode box arrow and then click Replace. Adjust the brush size to be just bigger than an individual number in the date. ALT+click below the left side of the date. Drag across the date.
9. Select the Red Eye tool. On the options bar, change the Pupil Size to 40 percent. Change the Darken Amount to 45 percent. In the image, click each eye.
10. Make any other adjustments you feel necessary.
11. Save the image again.
12. Flatten the layers. If Photoshop displays a dialog box asking to discard hidden layers, click the OK button.
13. Save the image with the file name, Baby Final, in the TIF format, and then print a copy for your instructor.

In the Lab

2 Repairing a Web Photo

Problem: Your friend is doing his dissertation on the lives of children during World War II. To accompany his dissertation, he is creating a Web site with childhood pictures of people that he has interviewed. During an interview, he was given a photo, but it has severe light damage. It is also in need of cropping and sharpening. He has asked you to repair the image. Using Photoshop's healing tools, sharpening tools, and lighting tools, you repair the image as displayed in Figure 5-73.

FIGURE 5-73

Instructions:

1. Start Photoshop. Set the Default Workspace and then reset all tools. Reset the previews in the Layers palette and then reset the default colors.
2. Open the file, Boys, from the Project05 folder on the CD that accompanies this book, or from a location specified by your instructor.
3. Click the Save As command on the File menu. Type `Boys Repaired` as the file name. If necessary, click the Format box arrow and then click PSD in the list. Browse to your USB flash drive storage device. Click the Save button. When Photoshop displays a Format Options dialog box, click the OK button.
4. Duplicate the Background layer and name it Corrections. Hide the Background layer.
5. Click Filter on the menu bar, point to Distort, and then click Lens Correction.
6. When the Lens Correction dialog box is displayed, set the angle to 9.
7. Set both the vertical and horizontal perspectives to -17.
8. Choose Edge Extension.
9. Click the OK button.
10. Crop the photo as shown in Figure 5-73.
11. Click Filter on the menu bar, point to Sharpen, and then click Unsharp Mask. When the Unsharp Mask dialog box is displayed, set the radius to 1. Set the threshold to 10. Drag the Amount slider until the image is sharpened to your satisfaction. Click the OK button.
12. Select the Clone Stamp tool. Using a small brush size, sample the grass in an area with no light damage. Drag to create grass on both sides of the boys. Resample as necessary. If you make a mistake, click the previous state in the History palette and sample again.
13. Select the Dodge tool. On the options bar, set the range to midtones and set the exposure to 50 percent. Increase the magnification and scroll to display the upper portion of the photo. Using short strokes, lighten the area around the heads of the boys and the surrounding trees.
14. Select the Burn tool. On the options bar, set the range to midtones and set the exposure to 50 percent.
15. Drag in the area that has the light damage. Use short strokes. You will not be able to remove all of the damage. As you darken the area, if small black dots appear use the Spot Healing Brush tool to remove them.
16. Make any other corrections you think necessary.
17. Use the Save for Web command and save the best of the 4-Up previews.
18. For extra credit, upload the file to a Web page and send your instructor the link.

In the Lab

3 Fixing Distortions

Problem: On your recent trip to Germany with the international exchange program, you took a picture of a famous cathedral in Berlin. When you got home, you realized that it was slightly out of perspective and slanted. It had been a cloudy day and the photo is dark. Before preparing a slide show for your fellow students and family, you want to fix the photo. The top-right side of the photo should be brought closer and the building's base should be leveled. The details of the cathedral also might be improved with sharpening and lightening. After your repairs, the photo should appear as shown in Figure 5-74.

FIGURE 5-74

Instructions:

1. Start Photoshop. Set the Default Workspace and then reset all tools. Reset the previews in the Layers palette and then reset the default colors.
2. Open the file, Cathedral, from the Project05 folder on the CD that accompanies this book, or from a location specified by your instructor.
3. Click the Save As command on the File menu. Type `Cathedral Repaired` as the file name. If necessary, click the Format box arrow and then click PSD in the list. Browse to your USB flash drive storage device. Click the Save button. When Photoshop displays a Format Options dialog box, click the OK button.
4. Duplicate the Background layer and name it, Corrections.
5. With the Corrections layer selected, open the Lens Correction dialog box.
   a. Change the vertical perspective to -43 to correct the keystone distortion.
   b. Change the horizontal perspective to 23 to bring the right side of the photo closer. (*Hint*: Because the picture was taken at a significant angle, the correction will not make the face of the building perfectly flat.)

c. Change the angle to 359 to correct the slant.
d. Change the edge to Edge Extension.
e. Change the scale to 90 percent to display the top of the cathedral.
f. Make any other changes that you feel would help the photo, and then click the OK button in the Lens Correction dialog box.

6. Crop the photo to include only the sidewalk and building.
7. Open the Unsharp Mask dialog box.
   a. Set Radius to 1.3.
   b. Set Threshold to 30.
   c. Slide the Amount slider until the image is sharpened to your satisfaction.
8. Select the Dodge tool. On the Dodge Tool options bar, select the following settings.
   a. Click the Brush Preset picker button and then type 900 in the Master Diameter box to increase the brush size to cover the entire image.
   b. Click the Range box arrow and then click Shadows in the list to adjust the darker portions of the photo.
   c. Type 30 in the Exposure box.
   d. Click the Set to enable airbrush capabilities button.
9. Move the mouse pointer into the image and click.
10. Make any other adjustments you feel necessary.
11. Save the image again.
12. Flatten the layers.
13. Use the Save As command to save a copy of the image named Cathedral for Print. Use the EPS format, selecting Photoshop DCS 1.0 (*.EPS) in the Format box. If Photoshop displays a dialog box about saving options, click the OK button.
14. If possible, print the image on a PostScript printer.

Cases and Places

The difficulty of these case studies varies:
■ are the least difficult and ■■ are the most difficult. The last exercise is a group exercise.

1 ■ You are tracing your family history back to the 1800s in England. You found a photo that has a crease across the bottom and some light areas. Start Photoshop and then reset all the defaults. Open the Family History photo that is located in the Project05 folder. Crop the border. Save the photo in the PSD format on your USB flash drive storage device as Family History Repaired. Create a layer named Corrections. Use the Healing Brush tool to repair the crease across the bottom. Use the Patch tool, or the Burn tool, to correct the light area. Save the photo again.

2 ■ Your grandmother's favorite photo of your mother has a tear on the edge. You decide to fix it for her. Start Photoshop and then reset all the defaults. Open the Girl With Carriage photo that is located in the Project05 folder. Use the Polygonal Lasso tool to outline the torn corner. On the Layer menu, point to New and then click Layer via cut. Select the new layer and hide the background. Use the Magic Wand tool to select all white areas and delete them, if necessary. Redisplay the background image and move the layer closer to the rest of the picture. When you have the best match, flatten the image. Use the Healing Brush tool to repair any remains of the tear. Crop the border. Save the photo in the PSD format on your USB flash drive storage device as Girl With Carriage Repaired.

3 ■■ Find a print photo in need of repair. With your system attached to a scanner, place the photo in the top-left corner of the scanner bed. Start Photoshop and reset all the defaults. On the File menu, point to the Import command, and then click your scanner in the list. When your scanner's dialog box is displayed, choose the highest resolution with the most colors. Save the scan. Scan the image again in black and white. Save the scan. Choose the better of the two scans and repair any damage. Print your best effort.

4 ■■ Find a color photo that has been taken with a digital camera that came out too dark. Open it in Photoshop. Convert it to the CMYK color mode. Use the Dodge tool to lighten it as much as you can. Use the Unsharp Mask command to sharpen the image. Use the Lens Correction dialog box to correct any distortion. Save the file in the TIF format and print it on a desktop printer. Save the file in the EPS format and, if possible, print it on a PostScript printer. Write a paragraph describing the differences between the two printouts. List specific changes in the photo that look better in EPS print. Turn in the paragraph and both photos to your instructor.

5 ■■ **Working Together** Your team is in charge of creating a postcard to remind new freshmen and their parents of the upcoming orientation. Gather photos of students having fun on campus and several campus buildings. As a group, choose the best photos. One at a time, open each of the images in Photoshop. Correct all damaged areas, distortions, and flaws. Save each of the repaired images. Create a CMYK formatted, 5.5 by 4.25 inch file. At a group meeting, decide on a background for your postcard. Import the best photos and superimpose and fade them as necessary. Create appropriate text using your school colors, or colors that are highly visible, for the type color.

ADOBE Photoshop CS2

Creating Color Channels and Actions

PROJECT 6

CASE PERSPECTIVE

Kid Central, a chain of toy stores, has contracted with your graphics design firm to create a series of advertising pieces. They are planning a spring campaign on outdoor play equipment with an emphasis on safe toys for children, ages five through nine. A photographer for Kid Central has submitted a photograph of a group of toys. You have been asked to create a floating image of the toys that could be placed in various sales flyers and catalogs, a black-and-white version for local newspaper inserts, and a stand-alone ad with attention-getting graphics and text.

You need to decide the most efficient way to remove the background and make decisions about color. The resulting floating image will be converted to black and white. You realize that you have done previous jobs where color was removed, so you decide to investigate automating that process. In the future you could use a shortcut to perform those kinds of conversions, complete with color and tonal adjustments.

Because Kid Central plans to print one advertisement using a four-color process, you check with the service bureau to determine the color matching system. For CMYK colors, they use either the PANTONE system or the Trumatch 4-color matching system that provides for accurate color matching on press and on printers or copiers.

The advertisement with text must be in a special format with regard to dimensions and resolution, so you may have to resize and resample. This project has multiple components and Kid Central wants them done quickly and professionally.

Creating Color Channels and Actions

PROJECT

Objectives

You will have mastered the material in this project when you can:

- Save a master copy and view channel color separations
- Use the Channels palette to create alpha channels
- Create a snapshot
- Open a new document window based on a state
- Create a new action set, and record, save, edit, and play back an action
- Describe different methods of converting to black and white
- Make adjustments with the Channel Mixer
- Create decorative graphics
- Align and distribute shape layers, and warp text
- Convert an RGB image to Lab color and then to CMYK
- List prepress activities, and print color separations
- Resize and resample images

Introduction

Photographers and graphic artists routinely create different versions of the same image. Think about the number of special effect photos that portrait studios produce and sell. Multiple versions of photos are common in advertising, photo cataloging, and on photo Web sites where more photos are sold when different colorizations, such as black and white or tints, are available.

With versions come inevitable color mode, tonal adjustments, and sizing issues. Having a version to return to in case you make errors is important. In Photoshop, the History palette permits you to take snapshots of states. A snapshot is a temporary copy of an image that can be accessed even after making a large number of edits. In a full installation of the Adobe Suite, you can save versions of files with metadata that tracks changes, and facilitates collaboration between members of a production team.

In addition to snapshots, another time-saving tool is the ability to record your steps as you edit and play them back when needed. The saved recording, a Photoshop action, is a powerful automation device. Tasks that you perform over and over again, such as converting images to black and white, can be recorded and then played back with a single keystroke.

The Channels palette also makes the creation of a different version much easier. You may edit an image's individual color tracks and create color separations in preparation for advanced printing techniques, such as four-color process printing.

You will learn about channels, color mixing, actions, resizing, and resampling as you work through this project.

Project Six — Creating Color Channels and Actions

Project 6 uses Photoshop to edit a photograph, to remove its background, and to create a floating image piece of artwork that can be dropped into other backgrounds and page layout applications. Second, a black-and-white version of the photo will be created for newspaper placement. The conversion to black and white will be recorded and saved for future use. Finally, an image with exact size and resolution requirements will be created for a flyer insert. The ad, complete with graphics and text, will be converted to the CMYK color model and printed with color separations. The images are illustrated in Figure 6-1.

Original Photograph

Floating Version

Black-and-white Version

Advertising Version

FIGURE 6-1

Starting and Customizing Photoshop

If you are stepping through this project on a computer and you want your screen to match the figures in this book, you should change your computer's resolution to 1024 × 768 and reset the tools and palettes. For more information about how to change the resolution on your computer, and other advanced Photoshop settings, read Appendix A.

The following steps describe how to start Photoshop and customize the Photoshop window. You may need to ask your instructor how to start Photoshop for your system.

To Start Photoshop and Reset the Palettes, Toolbox, and Options Bar

1. **Start Photoshop as described on pages PS 6 and PS 7.**
2. **Choose the Default Workspace as described on page PS 8.**
3. **Select the Rectangular Marquee tool and then reset all tools as described on pages PS 9 and PS 10.**

Photoshop starts and then resets the tools, palettes, and options.

The following steps show how to reset the colors.

To Reset the Colors

1. **Press D to access the default colors.**
2. **If black is not the foreground color in the toolbox, press X to exchange the foreground and background colors.**

The foreground color is black and the background color is white.

Opening a File

To open a file in Photoshop it must be stored as a digital file on your computer system. The photos and images used in this book are stored on a CD located in the back of the book. Your instructor may designate a different location for the photos.

The following steps illustrate how to open the file, Toys, from a CD located in drive E.

To Open a File

1. **Insert the CD that accompanies this book into your CD drive. After a few seconds, if Windows displays a dialog box, click the Close button.**
2. **Click File on the Photoshop menu bar and then click Open. Navigate to the Project06 folder and then double-click the file named, Toys.**
3. **When Photoshop displays the image in the document window, if the magnification is not 16.67 percent, double-click the magnification box on the document window status bar, type** `16.67` **as the entry, and then press the ENTER key.**
4. **Click the status bar menu button, point to Show, and then click Document Dimensions in the list.**

5 **If the rulers do not display, press CTRL+R.**

6 **If CMYK sliders are displayed in the Color palette, click the palette menu button, and then click RGB Sliders in the list.**

Photoshop opens the file, Toys, from the CD in drive E and displays it in the document window at 16.67 percent magnification (Figure 6-2).

FIGURE 6-2

Table 6-1 displays information about the Toys photo. Toys is a photo saved in the JPG file format.

The edited photo will appear in printed format as part of a series of advertisements. Therefore, the photo needs to be converted to the PSD format for maximum editing flexibility before resizing and printing.

Graphic professionals sometimes use print shops, labs, or service bureaus for their advanced printing needs. A **service bureau** is a business that offers data processing, color proofing, and online services, typically using imagesetters to create high quality prints. An **imagesetter** is a high-resolution output device that can transfer electronic files directly to photosensitive paper, plates, or film. While many service bureaus can resize and edit color at the time of printing, you save both time and money by performing these prepress tasks ahead of time in Photoshop. **Prepress** tasks are the various printing-related services performed before ink is actually put on the printed page.

Table 6-1 Toys Image Characteristics

CHARACTERISTIC	DESCRIPTION
File Name	Toys
File Type	JPG
Image Dimensions	17.067 by 12.8 inches
Color Mode	RGB
Resolution	180 pixels/inch
File Size	1.67 MB

Saving a Master Copy

When creating multiple versions of an image, you should create a master copy in PSD format. That way, new versions can be created from an original that remains unchanged. Recall that PSD is the only format that supports all Photoshop features.

The following steps show how to save the file in the PSD format using the Save As command.

To Save a Master Copy

1. **With your USB flash drive connected to one of the computer's USB ports, click File on the menu bar and then click Save As.**
2. **When the Save As dialog box is displayed, type** `Toys Master` **in the File name text box. Do not press the ENTER key after typing the file name.**
3. **Click the Format box arrow and then click Photoshop (*.PSD, *.PDD) in the list.**
4. **Click the Save in box arrow and then click USBDISK [G:], or the location associated with your USB flash drive, in the list.**

The Save As dialog box displays the file name, format, and location settings (Figure 6-3). Your system will display any currently saved PSD files.

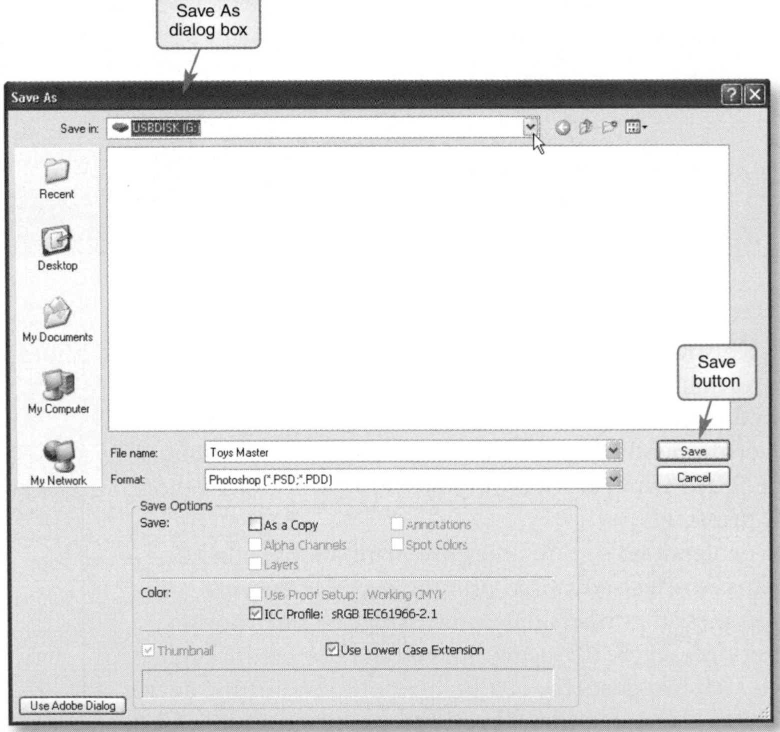

FIGURE 6-3

5. **Click the Save button in the Save As dialog box.**

Photoshop saves the file on the USB flash drive with the file name Toys Master, in the PSD format, and displays the new name on the document window title bar as shown in Figure 6-4.

Creating an Edits Layer

The following steps show how to create an Edits layer on top of the Background layer.

To Create an Edits Layer

1 **On the Layers palette, right-click the Background layer and then click Duplicate Layer on the shortcut menu.**

2 **When the Duplicate Layer dialog box is displayed, type** `Edits` **in the As box and then click the OK button.**

3 **Click the visibility icon of the Background layer to hide it.**

Photoshop displays the new layer (Figure 6-4).

FIGURE 6-4

The first version of the toys will be the floating image without a background. Many ways exist to remove a background including the ones you have used before, such as the Eraser tool, layer masks, or editing selections. Another way to isolate the background is to use Photoshop channels.

> *More About*
>
> **Version Cue**
>
> If you use the entire Adobe Creative Suite, you have access to **Version Cue**, a feature that saves versions of the same photo as snapshots for file sharing, tracking, workflow collaboration, alternates, or online PDF review and re-creation. Version Cue makes it easy to manage variations of a design. For example, you can create alternates based on different versions, or completely different photos for various editions of a publication.

Using Channels

Digital images are made of many pixels, or tiny dots, each of which represents an abstract sample of color. Pixels use combinations of primary colors. A **primary color** is one that cannot be created by mixing other colors in the gamut of a given color space. Traditionally, the colors red, yellow, and blue are considered to be primary colors, or pigments, in the art world. Those colors, however, are not the same hue as the red, yellow, and blue used on most computer monitors. Many modern computer applications and hardware devices use the primary additive colors of red, green, and blue, and the primary subtractive colors of magenta, yellow, and cyan. Recall that **additive colors** involve light emitted directly from a source. **Subtractive colors** absorb some wavelengths of light and reflect others. The two color modes, RGB and CMYK, are based respectively on the additive and subtractive primary colors.

More About

Color Channels

When you display one channel at a time, by default it displays in grayscale. If you want to make the channels display in color, however, click Edit on the menu bar, point to Preferences, and then click Display & Cursors. Click the Color Channels in Color check box to select it.

Each of the colors is considered a **channel** in Photoshop. An image from a digital camera will have a red, green, and blue channel, while a printed image will have a cyan, magenta, yellow, and black channel. Channels are used in Photoshop to separate and store information about the colors in an image so that users can manipulate them. Traditionally, **color separations** referred to the process of separating image colors into individual films or pattern plates of cyan, magenta, yellow, and black in preparation for printing. Photoshop takes that one step further by automatically creating the color separation anytime you convert to the CMYK Color mode. A CMYK image has four channels, one each for cyan, magenta, yellow, and black information, as well as a **composite** image showing all four colors. A grayscale image has just one channel. The number of default color channels in an image depends on its color mode.

In addition to the default color channels, extra channels, called **alpha channels**, are used for storing and editing selections as masks; spot color channels can be added to incorporate spot color plates for printing. A **spot color plate** is an extra part of the separation printing process that applies a single color to areas of the artwork.

Channels are created automatically when you open a new image. The color mode determines the number of color channels created. An image can have up to 56 channels. By default, bitmap, grayscale, duotone, and indexed-color images have one channel; RGB and Lab images have three, plus a composite; and CMYK images have four plus a composite. You can add specialized channels to all image types except Bitmap mode images.

More About

Saving Channels

As long as you save a file in a format supporting color modes, the normal color channels are preserved. Alpha channels are preserved only when you save a file in Photoshop, PDF, PICT, Pixar, TIF, or camera raw formats. Saving in other formats may cause channel information to be discarded.

The Channels Palette

The **Channels palette** (Figure 6-5) is used to create and manage channels. The palette lists all channels in the image — the composite channel first, then each individual color channel, followed by the spot colors, and finally the alpha channels. As in the Layers palette, the Channels palette displays a visibility icon followed by a thumbnail of each channel's contents. The visibility icon is useful for viewing specific colors in the document window, or to see how edits affect a specific color.

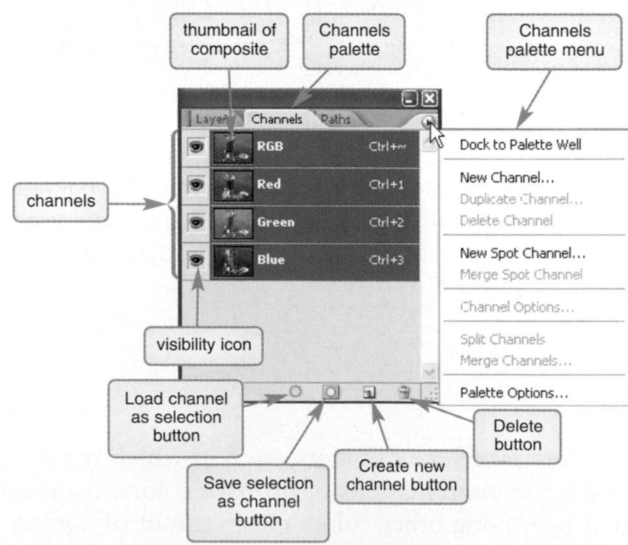

FIGURE 6-5

When you select one specific channel, it is displayed in grayscale in the document window by default. If more than one channel is selected, the channels appear in color combinations.

The Channels palette menu button displays commands to create new channels, change the color overlay, or set other channel options.

The first goal in editing the Toys Master image is to remove the background to create a floating image. Removing the background involves isolating it in a selection area and then deleting it. Channels can help you isolate certain colors, such as green in grass areas or blue in sky areas. The following steps demonstrate how to open the Channels palette and view individual channels.

As you view each channel, look for strong contrast between the lightest and darkest colors in the image. The channel with the most contrast will help you in the selection process described later in this project.

More About

Thumbnails

Viewing thumbnails is a convenient way of tracking channel contents; however, turning off the display of thumbnails can improve performance. To resize or hide channel thumbnails, choose Palette Options from the Channels palette menu. Click a thumbnail size, or click None, to turn off the display of thumbnails.

To View Channels

1

- **Click the Channels tab to access the Channels palette.**

Photoshop displays the Channels palette (Figure 6-6). The composite channel is displayed above the Red, Green, and Blue channels.

FIGURE 6-6

2

- **Click the Red channel. Do not click the thumbnail.**

The Red channel is displayed in grayscale (Figure 6-7). Pixels that display white are closest to the Red color.

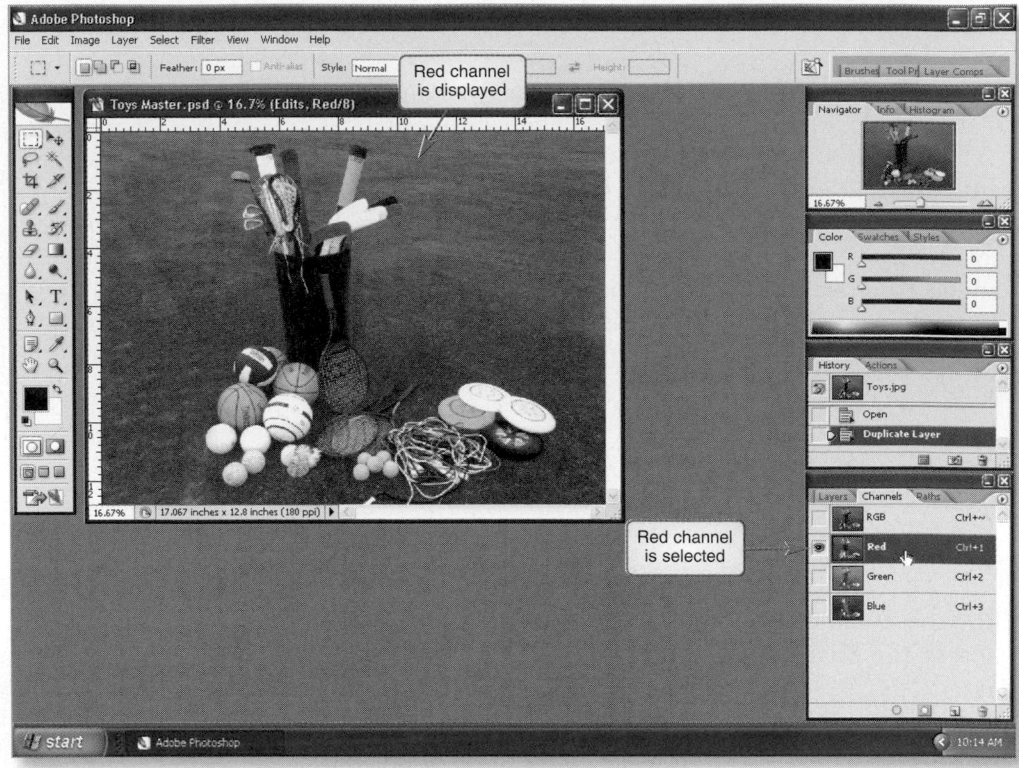

FIGURE 6-7

3

- **Click the Green channel. Do not click the thumbnail.**

The Green channel is displayed in grayscale (Figure 6-8).

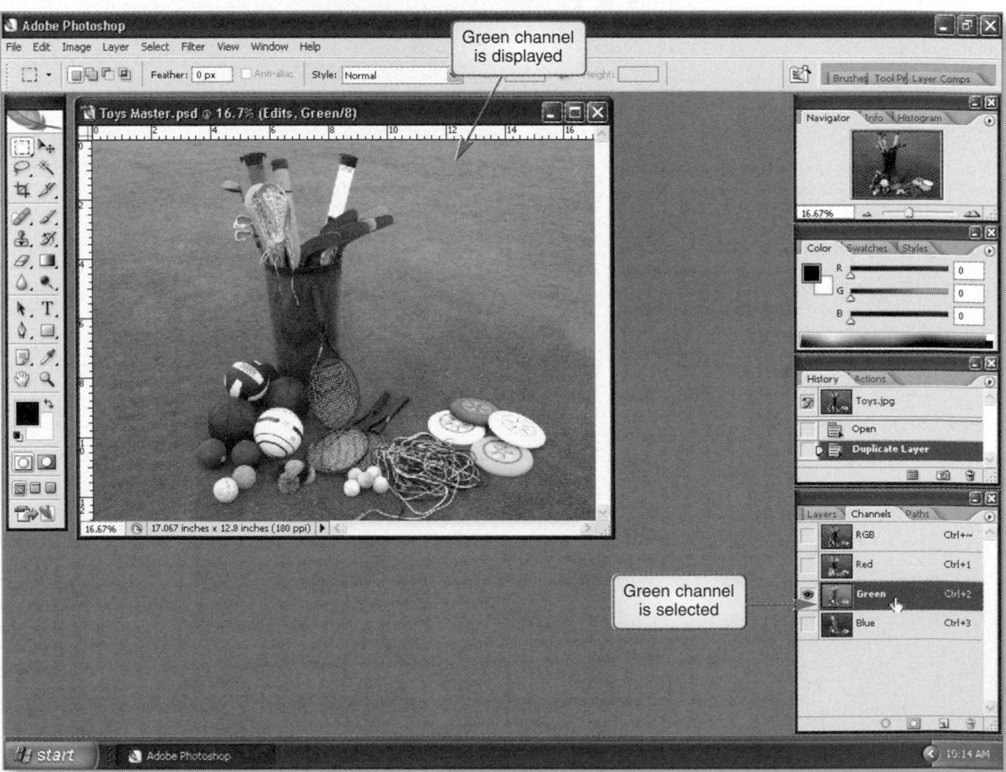

FIGURE 6-8

4

• **Click the Blue channel. Do not click the thumbnail.**

The Blue channel is displayed in grayscale (Figure 6-9).

5

• **Because the Green channel displayed the most contrast, click the Green channel. Do not click the thumbnail.**

The Green channel has the most contrast between the toys in the image and the background.

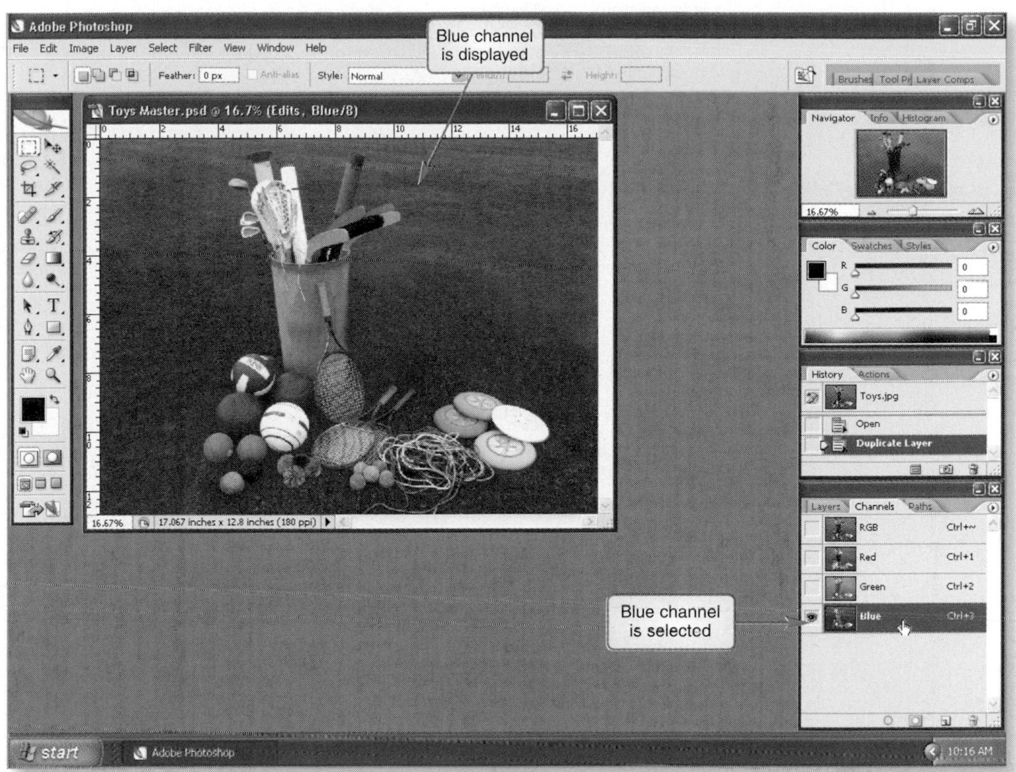

FIGURE 6-9

Other Ways

1. To display composite, press CTRL+~
2. To display first channel, press CTRL+1
3. To display second channel, press CTRL+2
4. To display third channel, press CTRL+3

If an image uses the CMYK Color mode, there will be four channels in addition to the composite.

When you have a solid background, it is easy to select and delete it. But often, the background is busy or shaded so that it is necessary to take some more creative steps to remove it. Before creating a special channel to mask the background, you will use the magic wand to select as much of the grass as possible, as shown in the following steps.

To Select with the Magic Wand

1 **With the Green channel selected, click the Magic Wand Tool (W) button in the toolbox.**

2 **On the options bar, click the Add to selection button. Type** 17 **in the Tolerance box. Make sure the Anti-alias and Contiguous check boxes are selected.**

3 **SHIFT+click the grass in all the areas around the toys. Small pieces of the grass may not be selected.**

The grass is selected (Figure 6-10 on the next page). Your selections may differ.

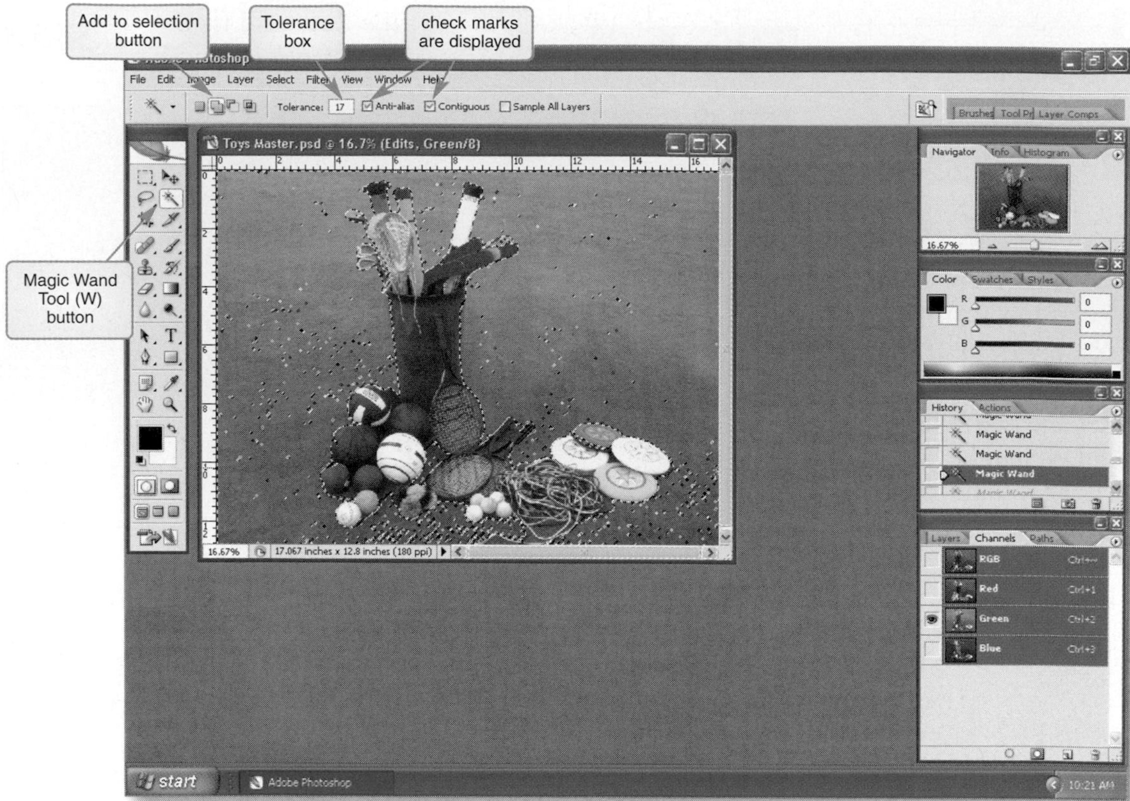

FIGURE 6-10

The next step is to create an alpha channel based on the selection.

Alpha Channels

When you create a new channel, by default it becomes an alpha channel. An **alpha channel** is similar to a new layer in that it is used to edit or mask parts of an image; however, alpha channels allow you to save and load selections. Alpha channel masks can be performed on the background layer, whereas masks created via the Layers palette cannot. Channel masks represent selections, and exist independently of any particular layer — for that reason, storing selections as alpha channels creates more permanent masks than layer masks. You can reuse stored selections or even load them into another image. The Channel Options command on the palette menu allows you to name the alpha channel and adjust settings related to editing.

Most commonly, alpha channels are used to isolate and protect areas of an image as you apply color changes, filters, or other effects to the rest of the image. Additionally, alpha channel masks are used for complex image editing, such as gradually applying color or filter effects to an image. For instance, viewing an alpha channel and the composite channel together allows you to see how changes made in the alpha channel relate to the entire image. When you display an alpha channel at the same time as a color channel, the alpha channel appears as a transparent color overlay in the document window.

When making an alpha channel, you can create the channel first and then paint the selected area, or you can select the area first and then create the channel. The following steps create an alpha channel where the background already has been selected.

To Create an Alpha Channel

1

- **With the Green channel still selected, in the Channels palette, ALT+click the Create new channel button.**
- **When the New Channel dialog box is displayed, type** `Grass Mask` **as the name of the new channel. If necessary, click the Selected Areas option button and then type** `50%` **in the Opacity box.**

Photoshop displays the New Channel dialog box (Figure 6-11). Your color may differ. Pressing the ALT key while clicking the Create new channel button creates an alpha channel. You also can create a new alpha channel by clicking the New Channel command on the palette menu.

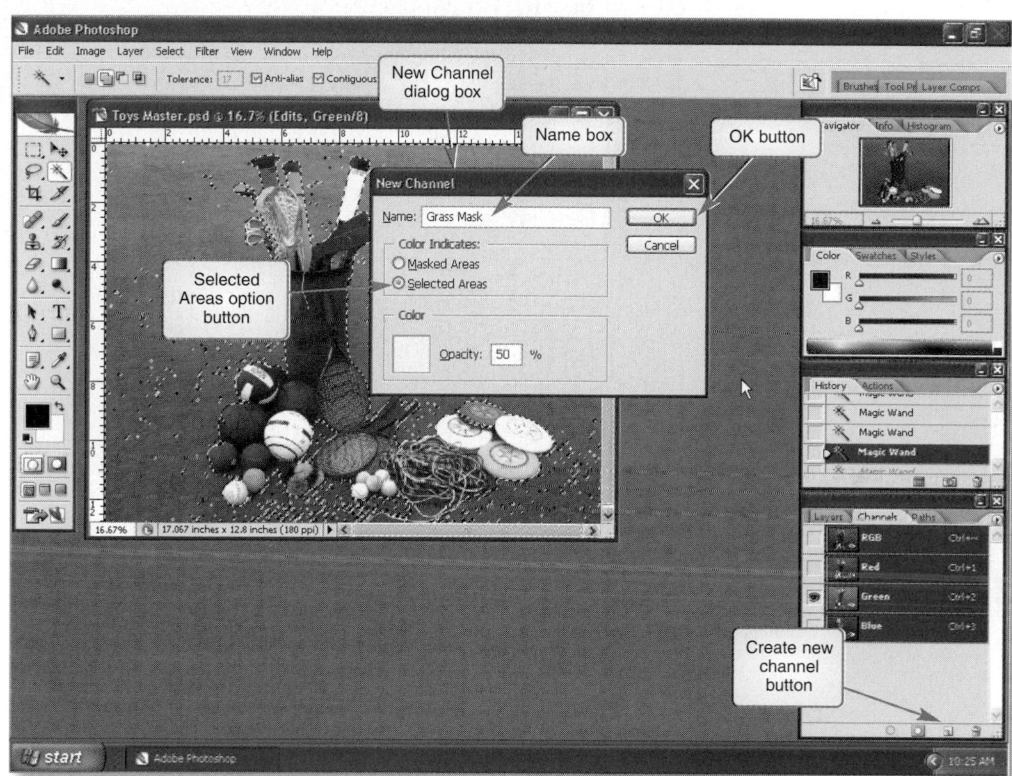

FIGURE 6-11

2

- **Click the OK button.**
- **In the Channels palette, click the Green visibility icon and also select the Green channel.**

Both the new Grass Mask alpha channel and the Green channel are visible (Figure 6-12).

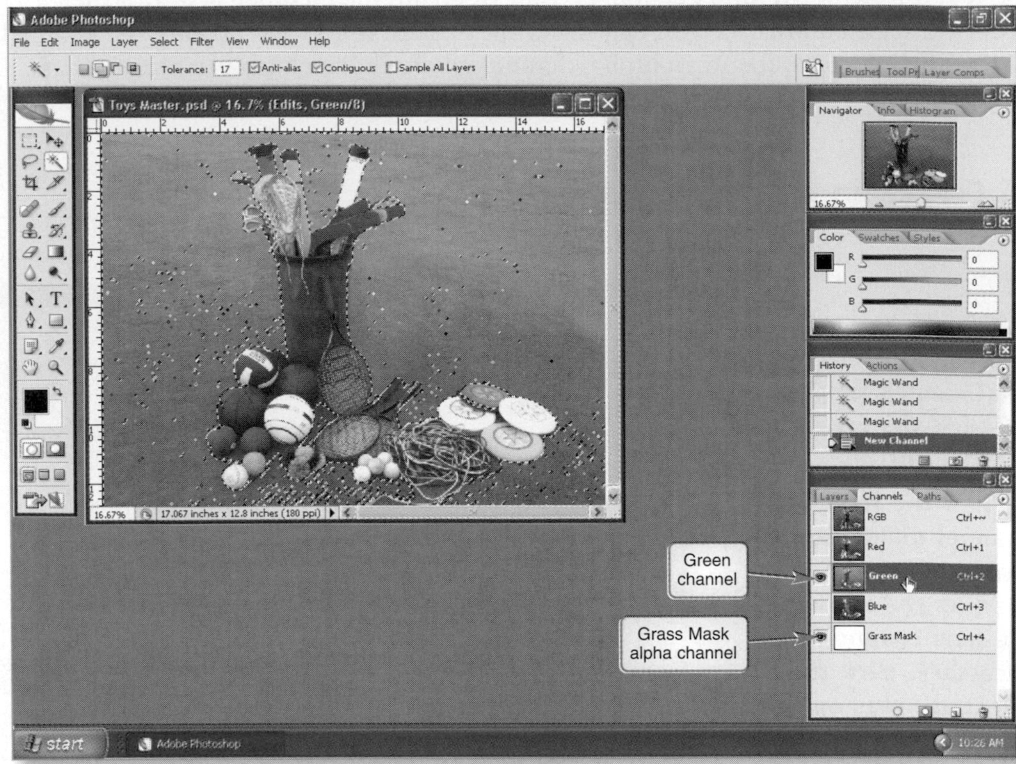

FIGURE 6-12

Other Ways

1. Click Create new channel button, double-click thumbnail, edit settings
2. On Channels palette menu, click New Channel, edit settings

In Figure 6-11 on page PS 345, neither the Color setting nor the Opacity setting has any effect on how the mask works. They only change the mask color that displays in the document window when another channel is selected. Some Photoshop users change the color and opacity to make the mask more easily visible against the other colors in the image.

Editing the Alpha Channel

Recall that masks use black-and-white painted areas to indicate the location of the mask versus the revealed areas. Alpha channels created from selected areas, however, use white paint to mask and black paint to reveal by default. In the next series of steps, the inverse of the selection in the alpha channel is selected and the areas are painted.

To Edit the Alpha Channel

1

- **Click the visibility icon beside the Green channel to remove it.**
- **If necessary, click the Green Mask alpha channel to select it.**
- **Click Select on the menu bar and then click Inverse.**

The area with the toys is selected in the alpha channel (Figure 6-13).

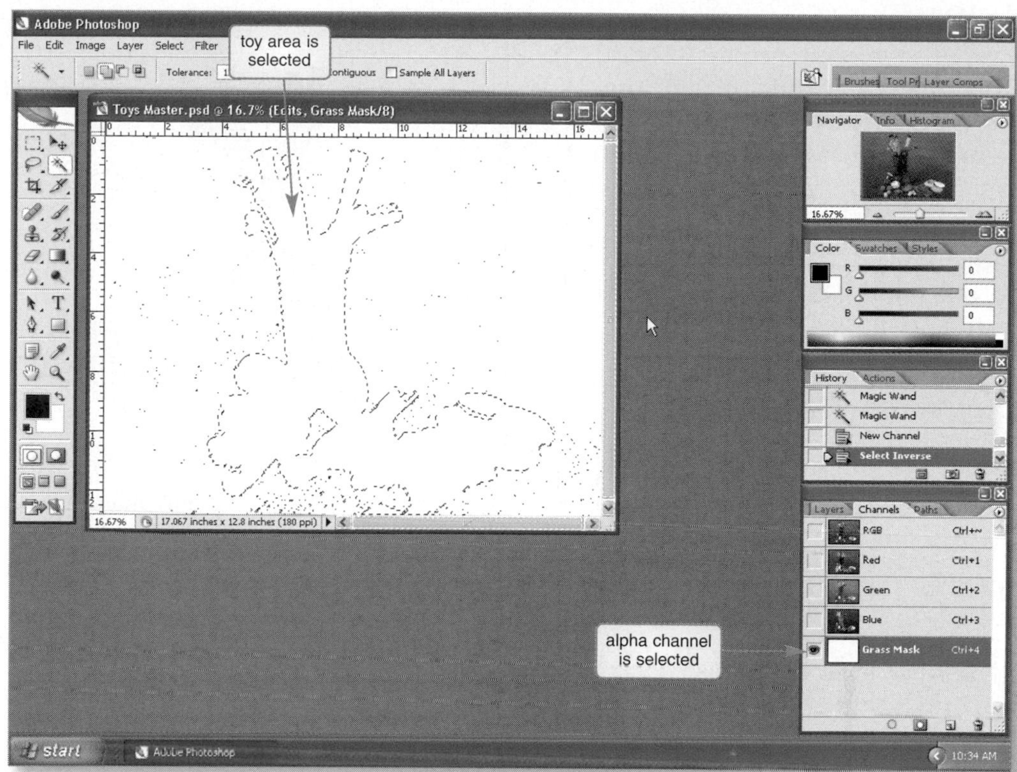

FIGURE 6-13

2

- **If necessary, press X to reverse the colors so that black is the foreground color.**
- **Right-click the Gradient Tool (G) button and then click Paint Bucket Tool.**
- **Click the toy area.**

The Paint Bucket tool fills the selection with the black foreground color (Figure 6-14). Recall that painting with black will reveal areas in an alpha channel.

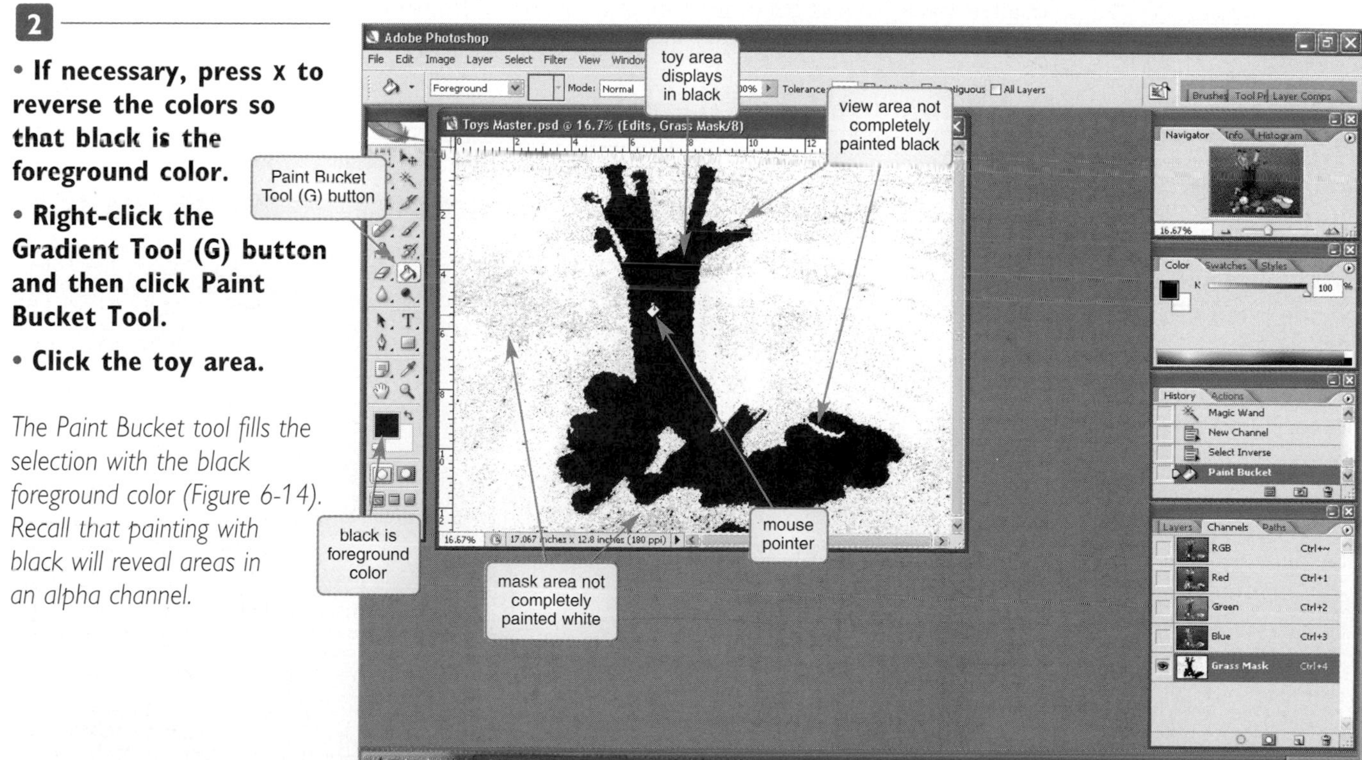

FIGURE 6-14

3

- **Press CTRL+D to remove the selection.**
- **Press the B key to access the Brush tool. Paint any areas of the toys that are not black. Change the brush size using the bracket keys, as necessary.**
- **Press the X key to change the brush to white and then paint any remaining grass. Scroll and zoom as necessary.**

The toys are black and the surrounding areas are white (Figure 6-15).

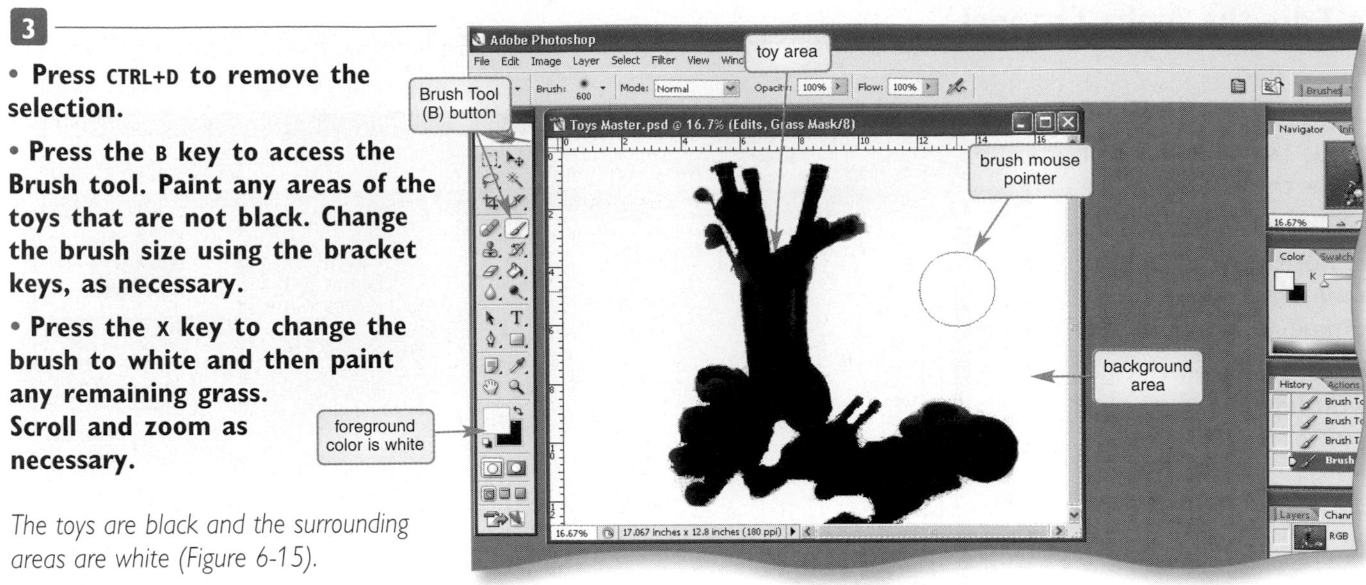

FIGURE 6-15

Deleting a Background Using an Alpha Channel

The final step in creating the floating image is to delete the background using the alpha channel. The background is represented by the white area in the alpha channel. Selecting the white area and then viewing the composite, creates a selection border in the image around all of the background, as shown in the following steps. The deleted background becomes transparent in the floating image.

To Delete a Background Using an Alpha Channel

1

- **Press the W key to access the Magic Wand tool and then click the White area.**
- **On the Channels palette, click the RGB composite channel.**

The background is selected (Figure 6-16).

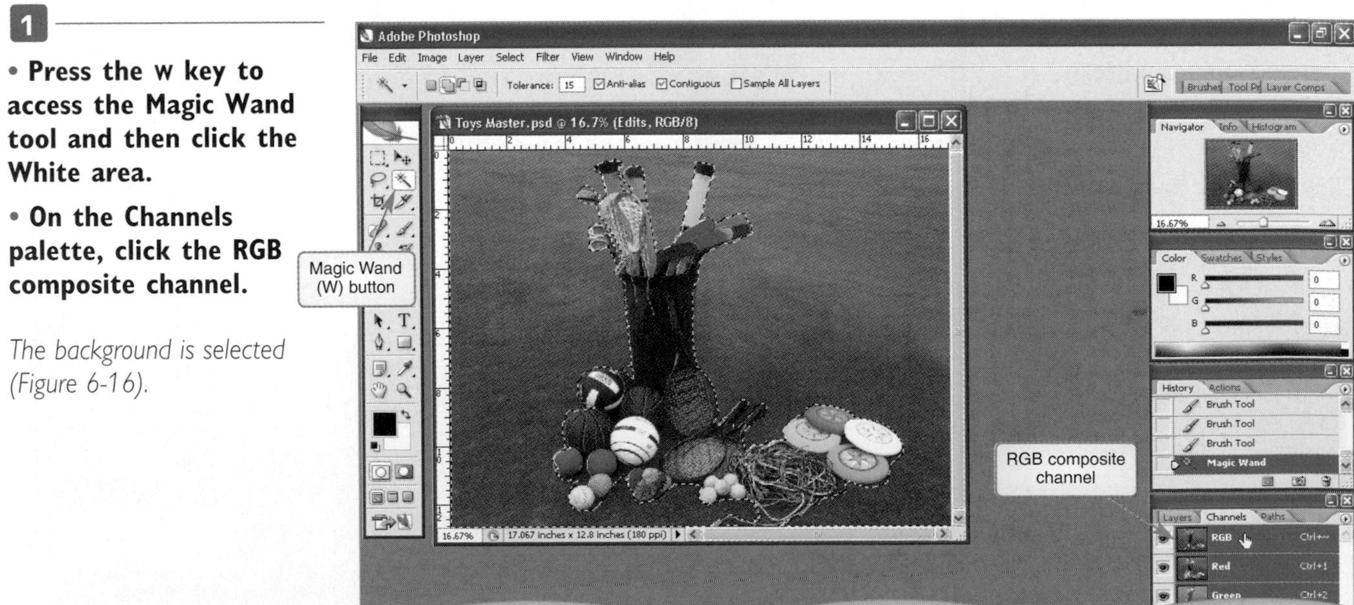

FIGURE 6-16

2

- **Press the DELETE key.**

After a few moments, the background is deleted (Figure 6-17).

3

- **Press CTRL+D to deselect.**

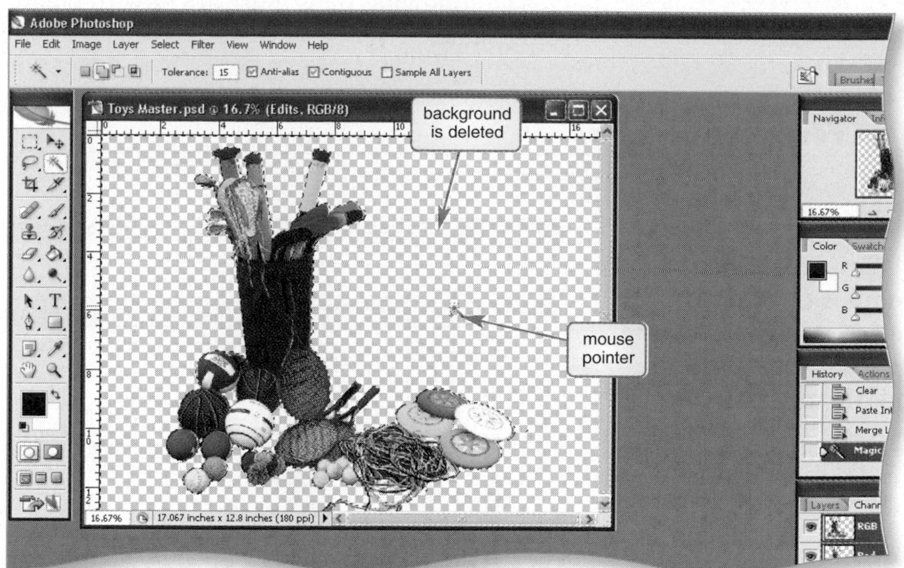

FIGURE 6-17

If some areas of grass still remain, select the Grass Mask alpha channel, click the Green channel visibility button, and then use the Brush tool to paint the remaining areas white.

Another special channel in Photoshop is the **spot color channel**, added to specify additional printing plates for printing with spot color inks. This option lets you simulate the density of the printed spot color. A value of 100 percent simulates an ink that completely covers the inks beneath; 0 percent simulates a transparent ink that completely reveals the inks beneath. To create a spot color channel, press CTRL and then click the Create new channel button.

Notice that the area around the toys is transparent, ready for anyone to drop in a new background or use the floating image in other artwork. This is the floating image that the toy company wants. The next section describes saving this version using a Photoshop snapshot.

Snapshots

A **snapshot** is a temporary copy of an image that can be accessed even after making a large number of edits. Available on the History palette menu, or from a state's shortcut menu, snapshots are useful when you want to make different versions of the same image, or for occasions where many edits need to be made. For instance, suppose you have an image perfectly cropped, masked, and layered. You then decide to make a series of restorative edits using the Healing Brush tools. After making numerous changes, you realize that, by mistake, you edited the Background instead of the Corrections layer. By default the History palette saves only the last 20 states, therefore, you cannot back up far enough to remove the erroneous edits. The only thing to do is to start over. If you had created a snapshot at the point where the image was cropped and masked, however, you could return to that saved state and avoid having to begin again.

Another snapshot tool that is useful particularly for versions is the History palette's New Document command. At any point in the editing process, you can create a new document from a state. The state is opened in a new document window, so you can save it with a new file name.

The following steps illustrate how to create a snapshot and a new document from a state.

To Create a Snapshot

1

• **With the RGB composite channel selected, right-click the last Deselect state on the History palette.**

The shortcut menu displays the New Snapshot command (Figure 6-18).

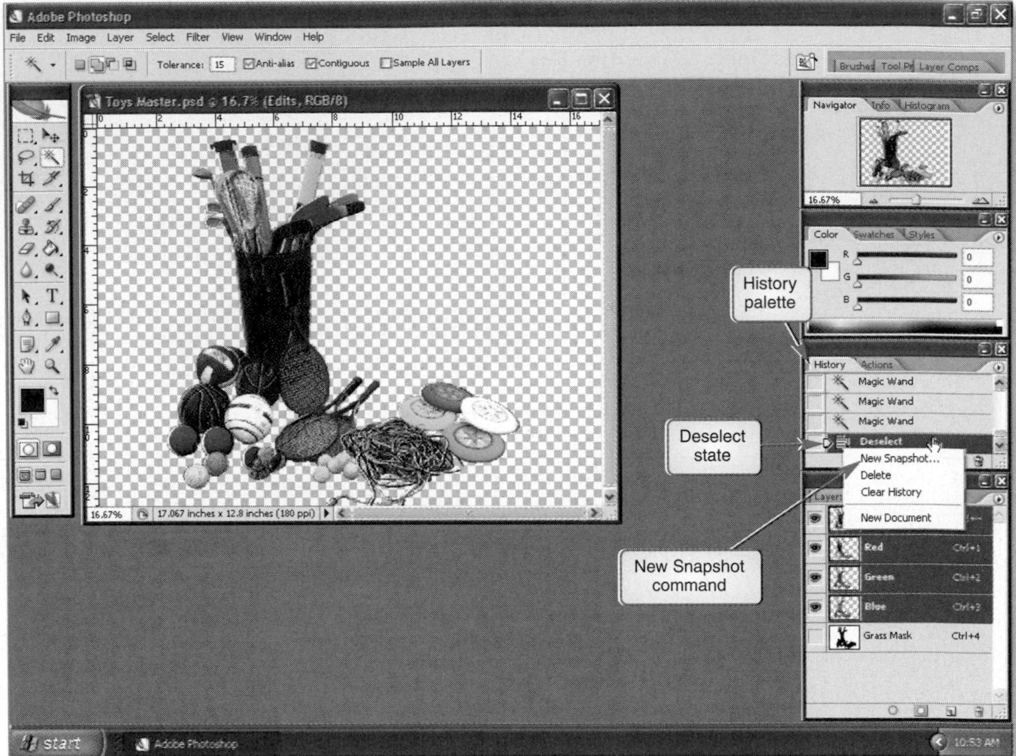

FIGURE 6-18

2

• **Click New Snapshot.**

• **When the New Snapshot dialog box is displayed, type** `floating image` **in the Name box.**

The New Snapshot dialog box lets you create a snapshot from the full document or specific layers (Figure 6-19).

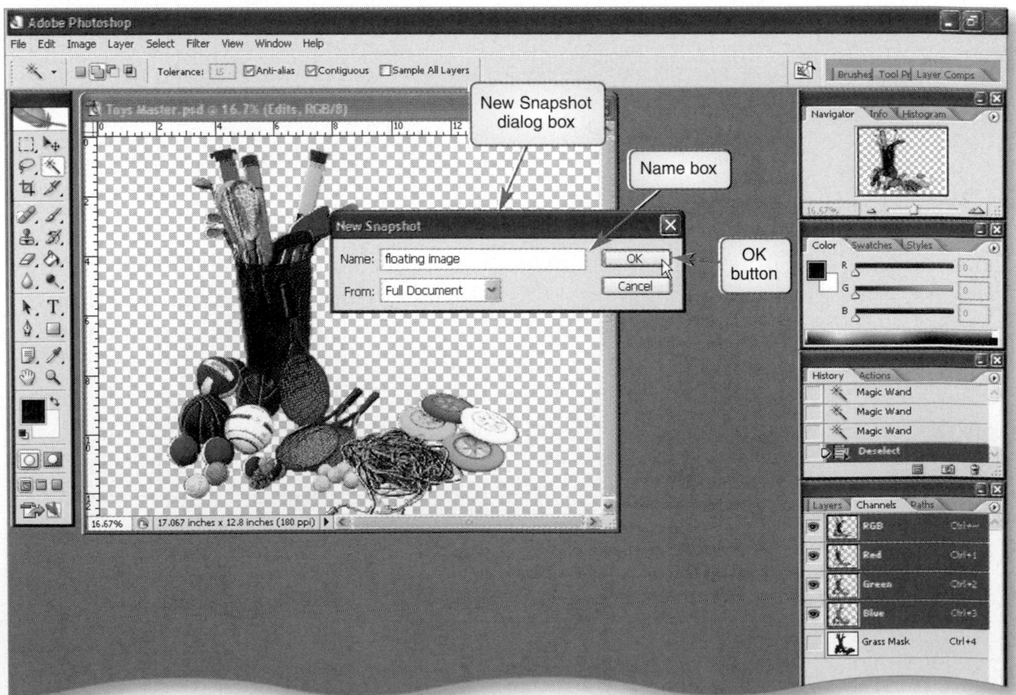

FIGURE 6-19

3

• **Click the OK button. Scroll up on the History palette to display the new snapshot.**

The floating image snapshot is displayed below the original file (Figure 6-20).

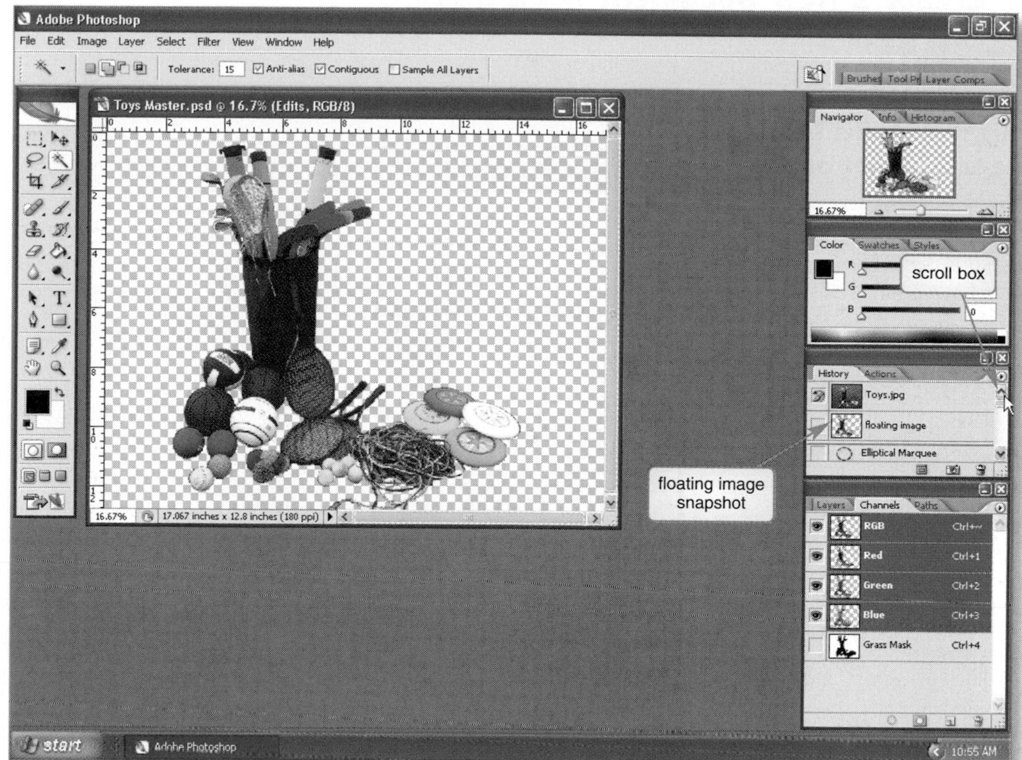

FIGURE 6-20

Other Ways

1. On History palette status bar, click Create new snapshot button
2. On History palette menu, click New Snapshot

If you click the snapshot and begin editing from that image, Photoshop begins a new branch of edits — the other edits are lost. Selecting a snapshot lets you work from that version of the image unless you have chosen the Allow Non-Linear History option in the History palette options. Another option on the History palette menu is to create a new snapshot automatically when saving, which is useful when you need to go back to edits prior to the previous save.

Snapshots are not saved when you close the file. They exist only during the editing session. Closing an image deletes its snapshots. Therefore, to save a snapshot you have to create a new document from the snapshot image, as shown in the steps on the next page.

To Create a New Document from a State

1

- **Right-click the floating image snapshot on the History palette.**

The shortcut menu is displayed (Figure 6-21).

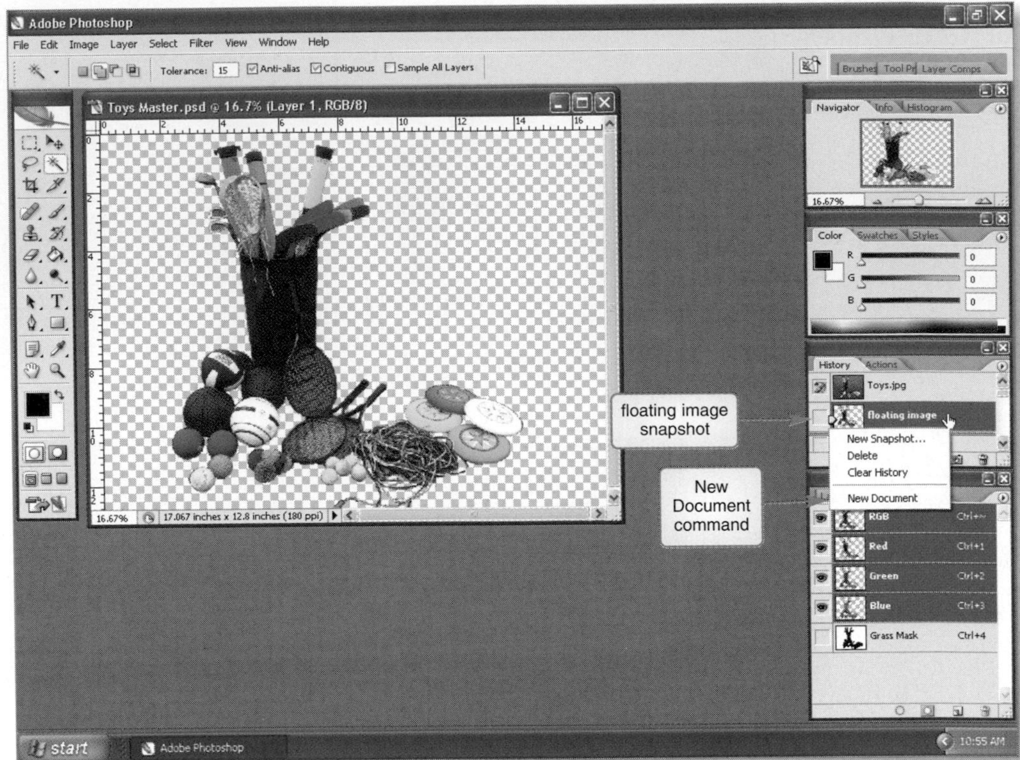

FIGURE 6-21

2

- **Click New Document. If necessary, change the magnification to 16.67 percent.**

Photoshop displays the new document, created from the snapshot, in its own window (Figure 6-22).

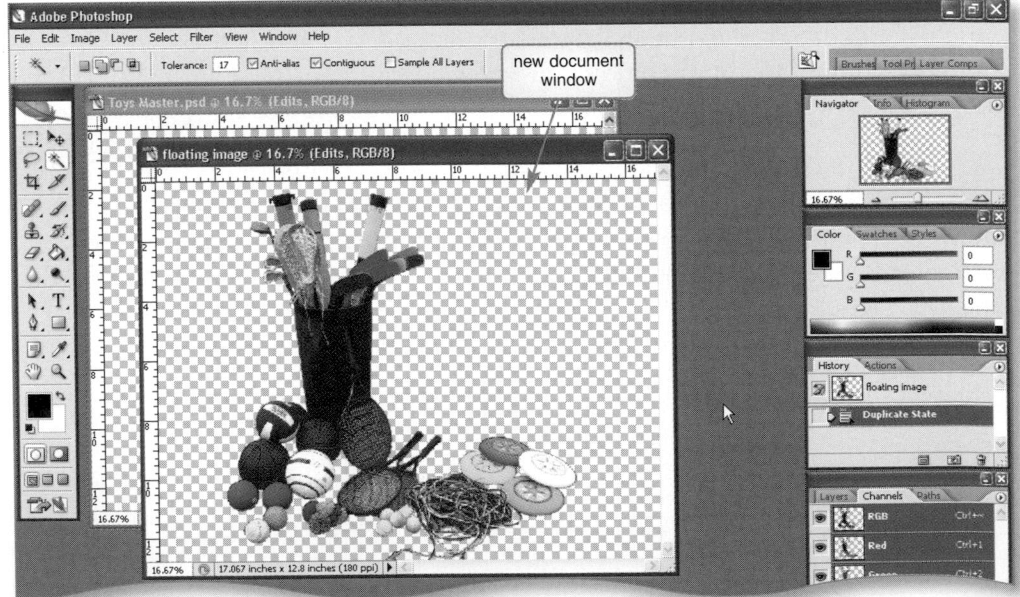

FIGURE 6-22

Other Ways

1. On History palette menu, click New Document

You can create a new document from any snapshot, or any state visible in the History palette, by using either the shortcut menu, the palette menu, or the buttons at the bottom of the History palette. The steps on the next page show how to save the new document.

To Save the New Document

1. **With your USB flash drive connected to one of the computer's USB ports, click File on the menu bar and then click Save As.**
2. **When the Save As dialog box is displayed, type** `Toys Float` **in the File name text box.**
3. **If necessary, click the Save in box arrow and then click USBDISK [G:], or the location associated with your USB flash drive, in the list.**
4. **Click the Save button in the Save As dialog box. When Photoshop displays the Photoshop Format Options dialog box, click the OK button.**
5. **Close the Toys Float document window.**
6. **Select the Toys Master document window if necessary.**
7. **Click the Layers palette tab and select the Edits Layer, if necessary.**

With that version complete, a new version of the Toys image can be created from the master copy. This new version will be used in black-and-white newspapers with a possible single spot color. Because converting to black and white may be a process needed for other photos, the next section records the steps as an action.

Actions

An **action** is a series of commands that you play back on a single file or a batch of files. For example, if your digital camera always takes pictures that turn out to be 32 by 24 inches when imported into Photoshop, you could save the resize process as an action. Then, each time you edit a photo from your camera, you could press a function key to perform the steps. You can create your own actions, download sample actions from the Web, or use predefined actions that come with Photoshop.

An action is created in a manner similar to that of a tape recorder. The steps are recorded as they happen and then saved in a location on your system. The next time you need it, the action can be loaded and played back. Action recording and playback steps are not recorded as states on the History palette.

Actions are comparable to macros or functions in other software applications. As an automation tool, they record complicated steps, and reduce them to a single command. Actions may include **stops**, or places in the series of steps that pause during playback, waiting for the user to perform a task such as choosing a brush size. Actions may include **modal controls** that stop to let you enter values in a dialog box while playing an action. If there are no modal controls in an action, you can choose not to display the various dialog boxes. When you toggle them off, the playback runs through the steps seamlessly without any visible dialog boxes.

More About

Droplets

The Droplet command is one of the new automation features of Photoshop CS2. It converts an action into a stand alone program with its own icon. Dragging a file on top of the icon will start Photoshop and perform the action on the image. Droplets are cross-platform and transferable. Most graphic intensive publications — from yearbooks to church directories — use droplets to standardize size and resolution of photos.

The Actions Palette

The **Actions palette**, usually located in the third set of palettes on the right in the Photoshop window, helps you manage actions you have created and those predefined actions that come with Photoshop (Figure 6-23 on the next page). Each time you create a new action, it is added to the palette. On most systems, the default display includes two sets of predefined actions, Commands and Frames. An **action set** is a folder that can be opened or expanded by clicking the triangle to the left of the set.

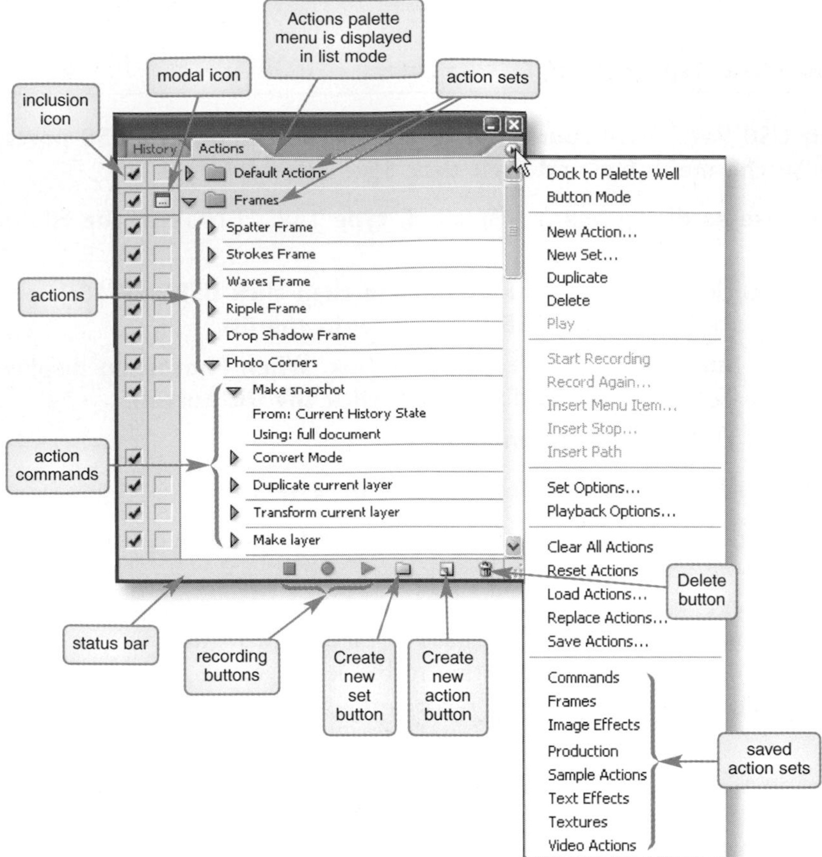

FIGURE 6-23

In Figure 6-23, the Frames set is expanded to display the predefined actions. The Photo Corners action is expanded to display the individual commands. On the left, a column of check marks indicates each command's inclusion in the action. Photoshop allows you to exclude specific commands during playback if you wish. The second column indicates whether or not the action is **modal**, meaning that it will stop at all dialog boxes. On the palette's status bar are tape recorder style buttons for stop, record, and play, as well as buttons to create sets and actions. The Actions palette menu displays commands to manage actions, set options, and load new sets of predefined actions.

The Actions palette can be displayed in two modes. The **list mode**, shown in Figure 6-23, allows you to make more choices about selecting, editing, playing, and managing your actions. The **button mode**, shown in Figure 6-24, is used for quick playbacks. To switch modes, choose the command from the Actions palette menu.

Action sets can be saved independently for use in other images. A saved action displays a file extension of **atn**. In the Save Action dialog box, Photoshop opens the folder where it stores other atn files by default. On most systems, the location is C:\Program Files\Adobe\Adobe Photoshop CS2\Presets\Photoshop Actions. If you are working in a lab setting, however, you should browse to your storage device in the Save Action dialog box and then save your action set.

FIGURE 6-24

When creating and saving an action, the general workflow is as follows:

1. Create a new action set, or select one you have previously created.
2. Create a new action, giving it a name and keyboard shortcut.
3. Click the Record button.
4. Carefully go through the steps of your task.
5. Click the Stop button.
6. Turn on dialog boxes and then edit stop points as necessary.
7. Save the set as an atn file for use in other documents.

This procedure will be used to create an action that converts the image of the playground toys to black and white.

Creating a New Action Set

The following steps create a new action set named, Personal Actions, in the Toys Master file.

To Create a New Action Set

1

- **Click the Actions tab to display the Actions palette.**
- **On the Actions palette status bar, click the Create new set button.**
- **When the New Set dialog box is displayed, type** `Personal Actions` **in the Name box.**

Photoshop displays the New Set dialog box (Figure 6-25). Your list of default action sets may differ.

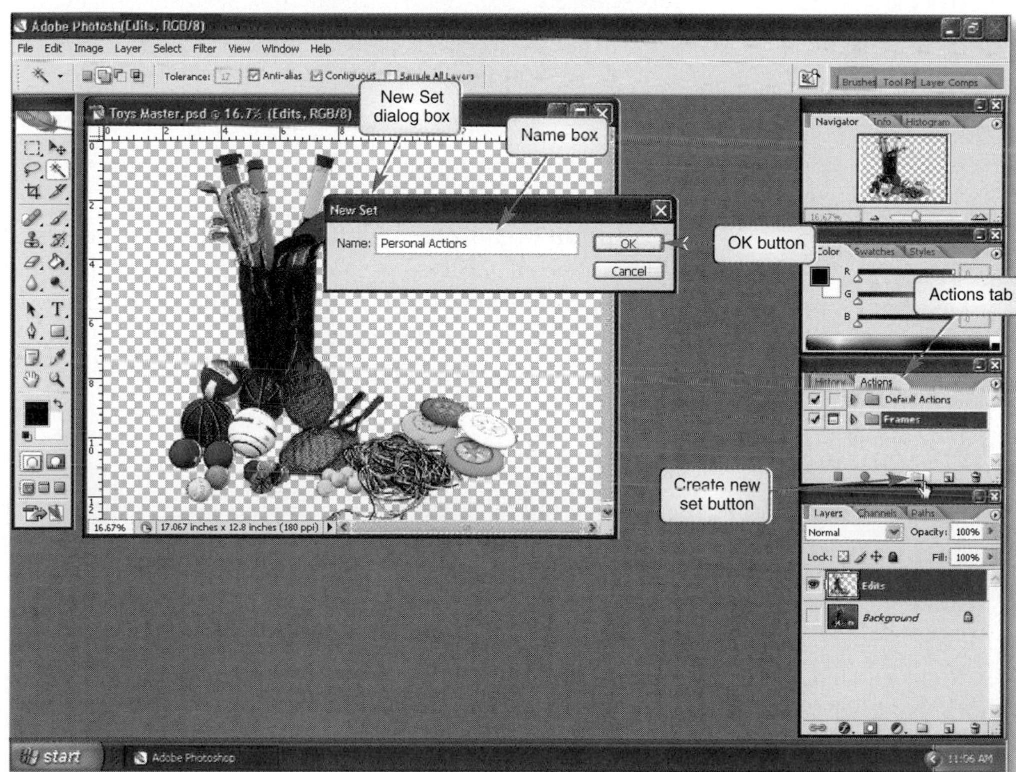

FIGURE 6-25

2

• **Click the OK button.**

The new action set is displayed on the Actions palette (Figure 6-26).

FIGURE 6-26

Other Ways

1. On Actions palette menu, click New Set

You can organize sets of actions for different types of work, such as online publishing or print publishing, and then transfer sets to other computers. Normally user-defined action sets are stored with the file in which they are created. You can save your sets and actions to a separate actions file, however, so you can recover them if the file is destroyed.

Creating a New Action

When you click the Create new action button, the New Action dialog box is displayed. The New Action dialog box allows you to name your action, position it within a set, assign a function key, and choose a display color for the action in the palette. After editing the settings, a Record button begins the process, as explained in the next series of steps.

More About

Creating Actions

You must be careful when you record actions that involve selecting a named layer. When you play back the action in a different file, Photoshop will look for that layer. If the named layer does not exist, the action will not function correctly.

To Create a New Action

1

- **On the Actions palette status bar, click the Create new action button.**
- **When the New Action dialog box is displayed, type** `Convert to Black & White` **in the Name box.**
- **If necessary, click the Set box arrow and then click Personal Actions in the list.**
- **Click the Function Key box arrow and then click F11 in the list.**
- **Click the Color box arrow and then click Gray in the list.**

Photoshop displays the New Action dialog box (Figure 6-27).

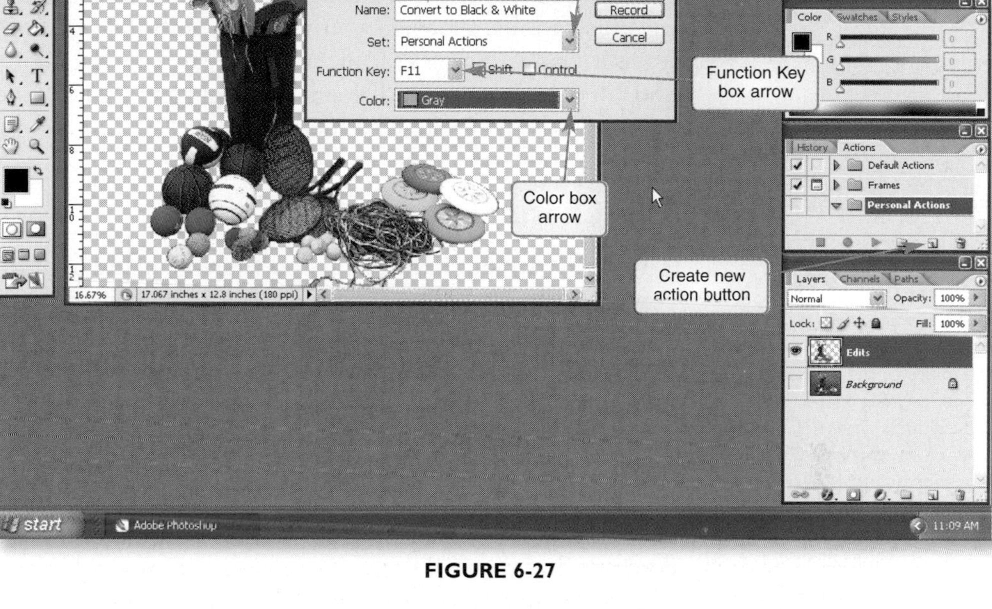

FIGURE 6-27

2

- **Click the Record button. Do not click anywhere else.**

The Begin recording button is highlighted (Figure 6-28). All keystrokes and mouse actions will be recorded.

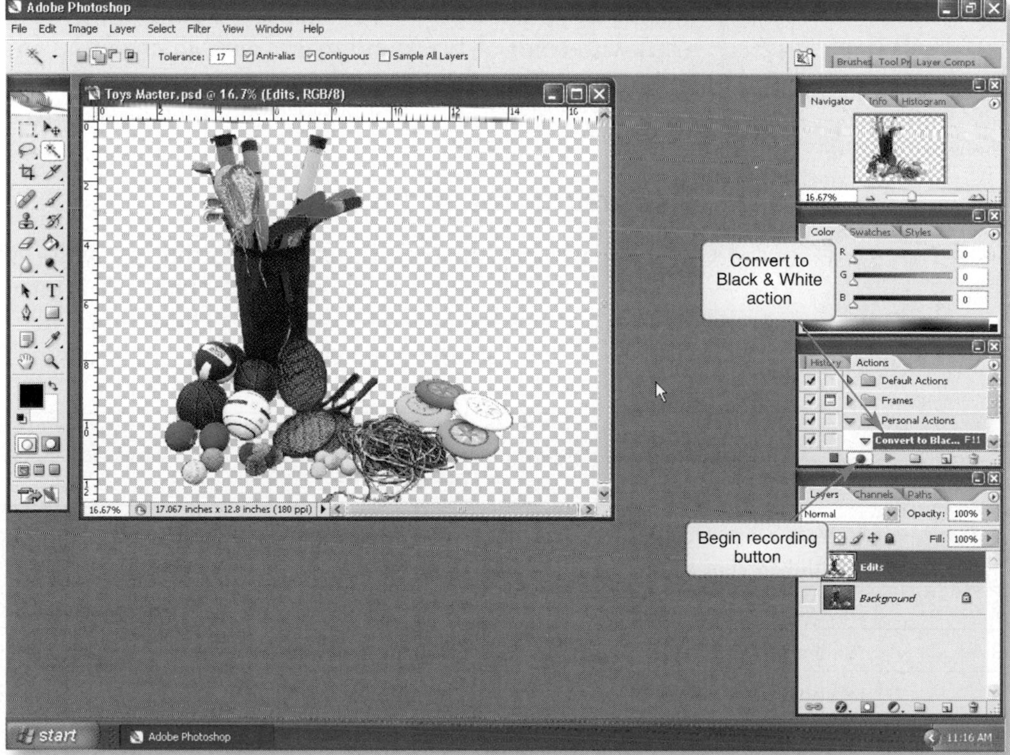

FIGURE 6-28

More About

Adobe Studio Exchange

Adobe Studio Exchange is an online community where users share free actions, plug-ins, and other content for Adobe products. With a registered version of Photoshop, the exchange is free. For more information, and a link to Adobe Studio Exchange, visit the Shelly Cashman More About web site.

More About

Converting to Black and White

Another way to change to black and white is by converting the image to the Lab Color mode, creating a layer from the Lightness channel. Creating layers from channels offers you more control over contrast than some other conversion methods. It also offers you the flexibility of being able to change aspects of the conversion at any time in the future. Many design professionals prefer to use channels when converting to black and white because it permits precise control of shades, levels, and the conversion process.

If you click inadvertently while creating an action, you can press CTRL+Z to cancel the recording and then start over.

Converting to Black and White

Recall that converting a color image to the grayscale mode on the Image Adjustment submenu is one way to discard color information from the pixels in the image. The **Desaturate command** on the Adjustments submenu, also produces a grayscale image, but leaves the image in the same color mode, usually rendering a flat, uninspiring version. The Desaturate command is appropriate, however, for many technical illustrations, or when you want to neutralize or de-emphasize a background but leave it visible. Some graphic artists create two adjustments layers to emulate the film and filter process of traditional photography. Yet another way to convert to black and white is using the Channel Mixer.

The Channel Mixer

The **Channel Mixer** command lets you create high-quality images by choosing the percentage contribution from each color channel, including black and white, grayscale, and other tints. The Channel Mixer works by modifying the document window using a fine-tuned mix of one or more color channels in the image. It lends itself more toward artistic expression than for tasks related to simple restoration or technical graphics. Artists use the Channel Mixer to create a variety of tints, pastels, infrareds, and **sepia** tones, which means a deep reddish-brown tone applied to the entire image.

The Channel Mixer will be used in an action to convert the toys image to monochrome and make adjustments. **Monochrome** literally means one color, but the term is common to images that use various shades of a color, such as gray, to create a black-and-white image. The Channel Mixer dialog box allows you to select a channel and then choose a monochrome setting. The sliders, which match the color system of your image, let you sharpen and bring out portions of the image. The Channel Mixer can be used with color or black and white, with all channels, one channel, or even a selection in the image for added versatility. If you select and then deselect the monochrome option, the blend of each channel is modified separately, creating a hand-tinted look.

Recording an Action

The next set of steps illustrates recording an action that creates a new document from a snapshot, converts the image to black and white using the Channel Mixer, and then issues the Save As command. The action will be stored in the F11 function key. Table 6-2 lists the basic steps.

Table 6-2 Action Steps

NUMBER	STEP	COMMANDS
1	Create a new document based on the current state	On History palette status bar, click Create new document from current state button
2	Access the Channel Mixer	On Image menu, point to Adjustments, click Channel Mixer
3	Select channel	Click Output Channel box arrow and then click Green
4	Choose Monochrome	Click Monochrome box
5	Make color adjustments	Drag color sliders
6	Close the Channel Mixer	Click the OK button
7	Save	Press SHIFT+CTRL+S

After recording the action, you will turn on the modal control; therefore, the action will be generic enough to work with any image, as it will pause at each dialog box, allowing the user to make adjustments. The following steps illustrate how to record an action.

To Record an Action

1

- **With the Begin recording button still highlighted on the Actions palette, click the History palette tab.**
- **Click the Create new document from current state button on the status bar.**

Photoshop opens a new document window, displaying the state as an image (Figure 6-29).

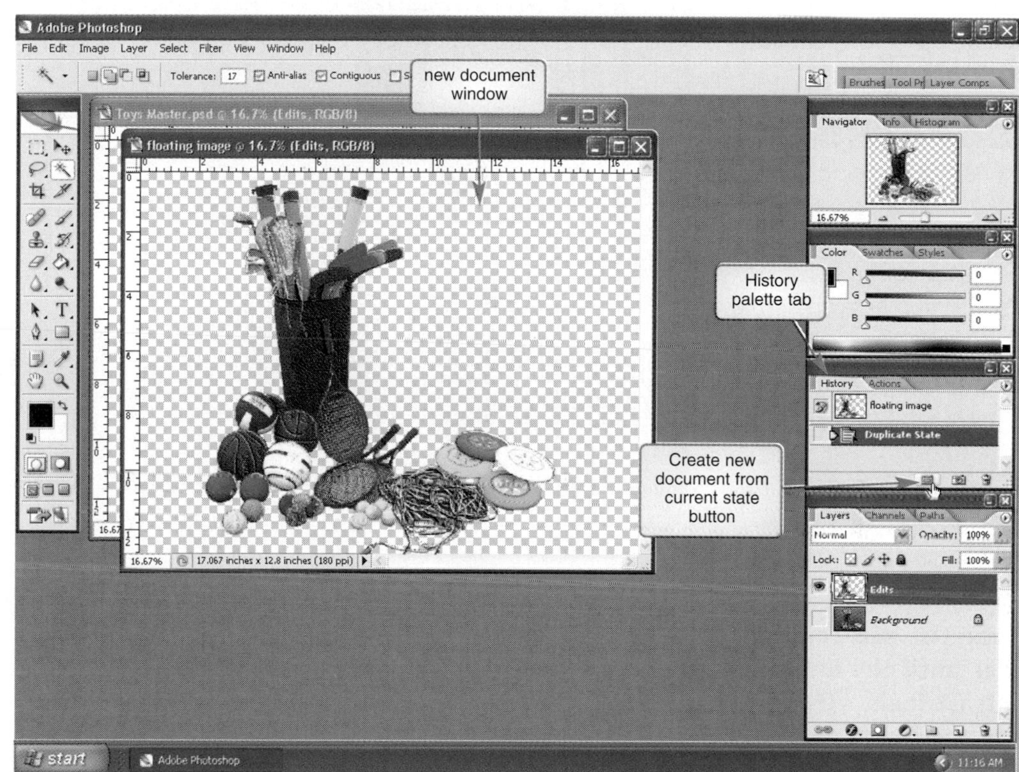

FIGURE 6-29

2

- **Click Image on the menu bar and then point to Adjustments.**

The Adjustments submenu shows the color adjustment commands (Figure 6-30).

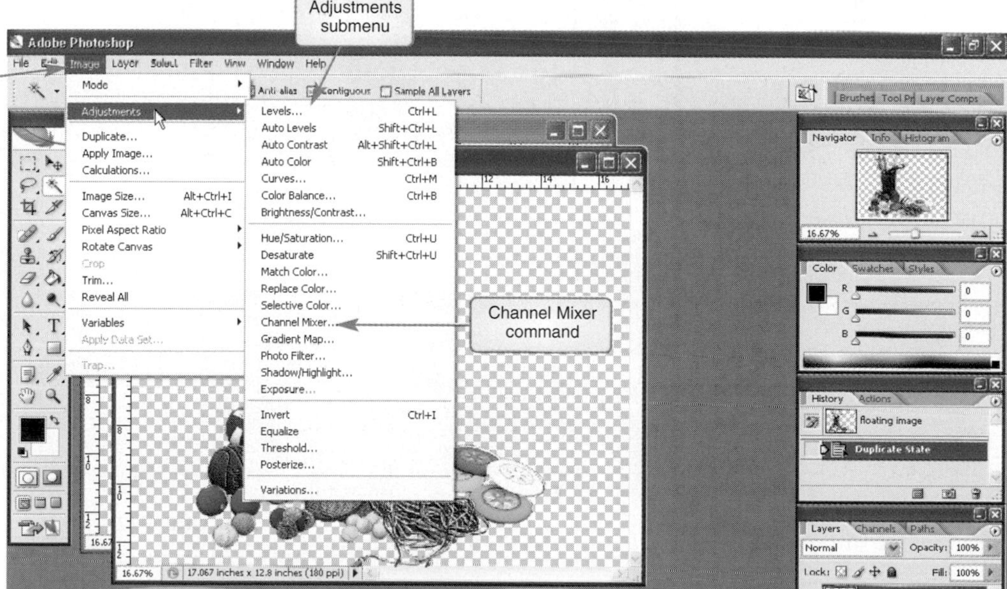

FIGURE 6-30

3

- **Click Channel Mixer.**
- **When the Channel Mixer dialog box is displayed, click the Output Channel box arrow and then click Green.**
- **Click the Monochrome check box.**

Photoshop displays the Channel Mixer dialog box (Figure 6-31). Recall that the Green channel contained the most contrast. The action will be set to stop here and allow adjustments unique to any given image.

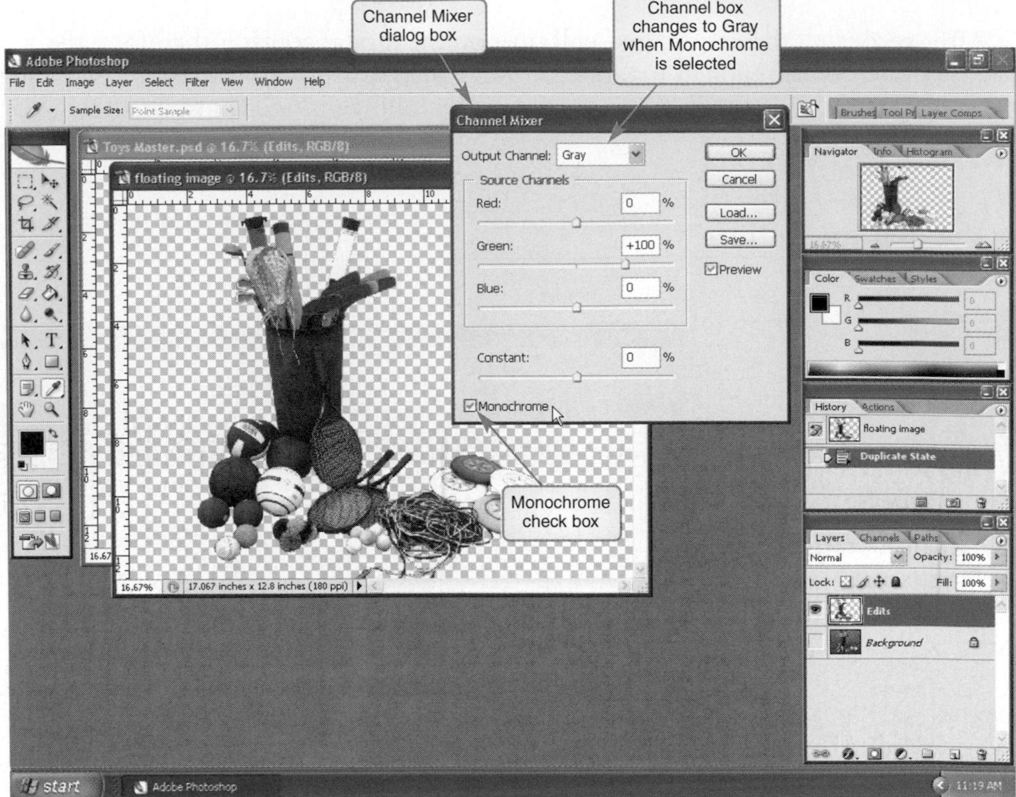

FIGURE 6-31

4

- **Drag the Red color slider until the image contrast looks strong. Drag the Blue color slider slightly in the other direction, until the image has good contrast and tonal value.**

The image is adjusted (Figure 6-32). A good rule of thumb is to add the slider values together. They should equal a number close to 100.

FIGURE 6-32

5

- **Click the OK button.**
- **Press SHIFT+CTRL+S.**
- **When the Save As dialog box is displayed, type** `temp file` **in the File name text box.**

The black-and-white version will be saved in the same location and in the same file format as the color version (Figure 6-33). Your list of files will vary.

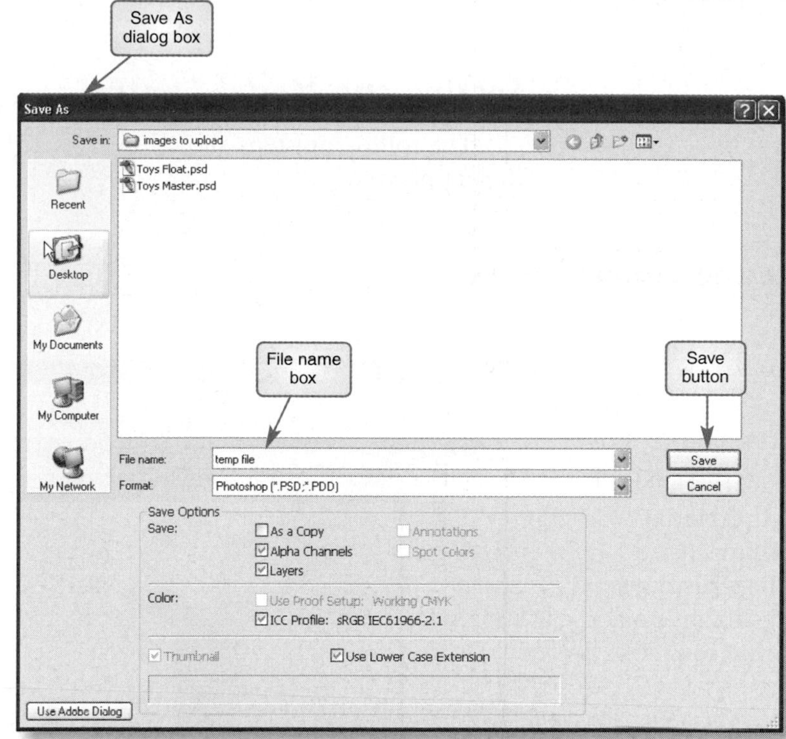

FIGURE 6-33

6

- **Click the Save button in the Save As dialog box. When Photoshop displays the Photoshop Format Options dialog box, click the OK button.**
- **Click the Actions palette tab and then click the Stop playing/recording button.**

The image is saved and the recording is stopped (Figure 6-34).

FIGURE 6-34

Other Ways

1. On Actions palette menu, click Start/Stop Recording

Remember, when played back, the action will stop at each dialog box, allowing you to make adjustments and create a file name when saving. By saving the image with the name, temp file, even if you press the ENTER key by mistake during the playback, you will not overwrite the current image.

Setting the Modal Control

The following steps show how to set the modal control to pause at dialog boxes during playback.

To Set the Modal Control

1

- **On the Actions palette, select the Convert to Black & White action.**
- **Click the Modal control box. If Photoshop displays a warning dialog box, click the OK button.**

Photoshop displays the Toggle dialog on/off icon in the Modal control box (Figure 6-35).

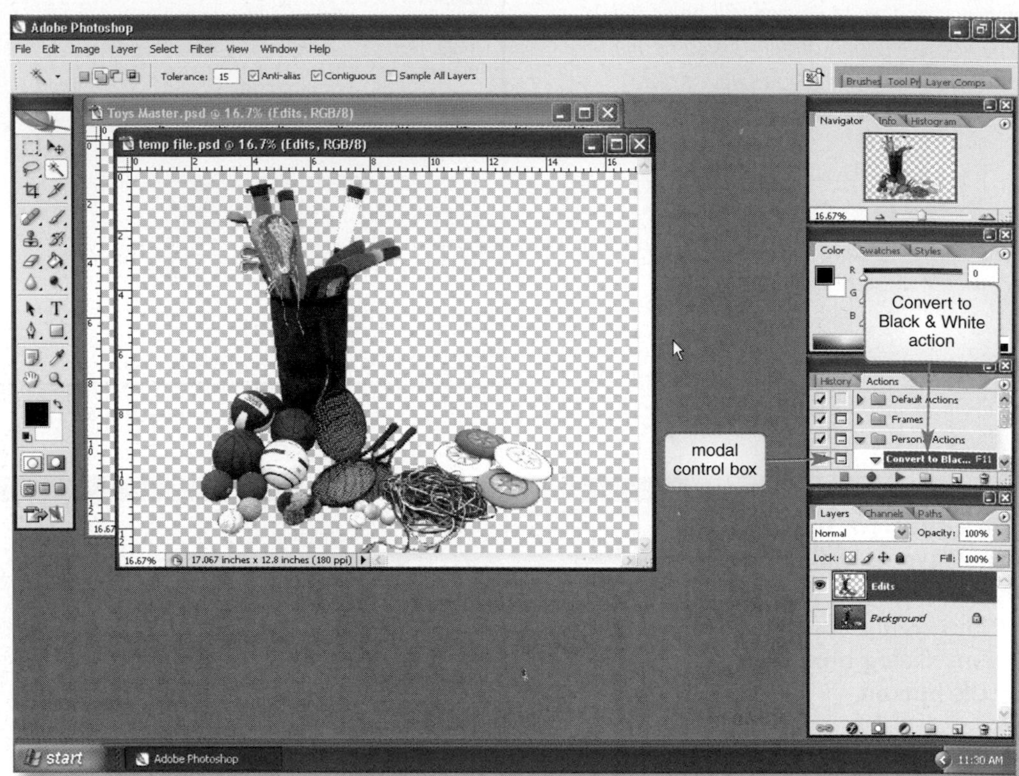

FIGURE 6-35

2

- **In the Actions palette, click the down arrow to scroll down and display the recorded commands.**

Notice the Toggle dialog on/off icon is displayed next to some of the commands (Figure 6-36). If you click a right-pointing triangle, Photoshop displays setting changes, if any, that are related to each command.

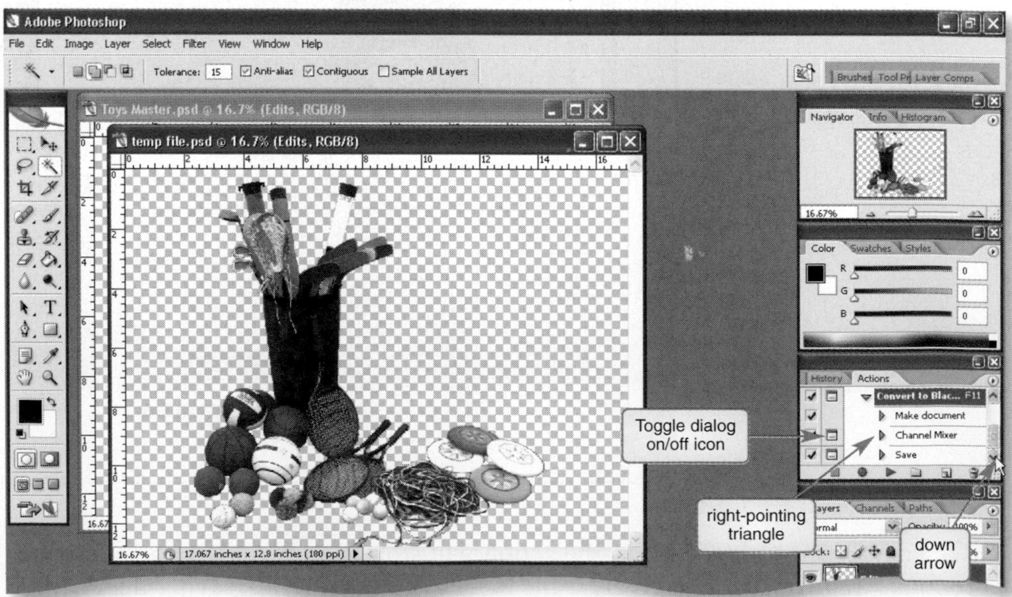

FIGURE 6-36

Other edits that you can perform on the recorded steps include deselecting some check boxes, dragging a command to the Delete button on the status bar to remove it permanently, and setting playback options on the Actions palette menu.

> *More About*
>
> **Stop Actions**
>
> After recording an action, you can delete image-specific steps and then insert an action stop using the palette menu. You can even include a reminder message. When the action is played back, it will pause so users can create their own brush stroke for example, and then continue with the action.

Saving Action Sets

Besides the Default Actions set that automatically displays on the Actions palette (Figure 6-35), Photoshop comes with eight other action sets — each with numerous individual actions. Your default actions may differ. Users are able to save new action sets as well via the Actions palette menu, as described in the following steps.

To Save an Action Set

1

- **On the Actions palette, scroll up and then click the Personal Actions set.**
- **Click the Actions palette menu button.**

Photoshop displays the palette menu (Figure 6-37). Other Photoshop saved action sets display on the menu.

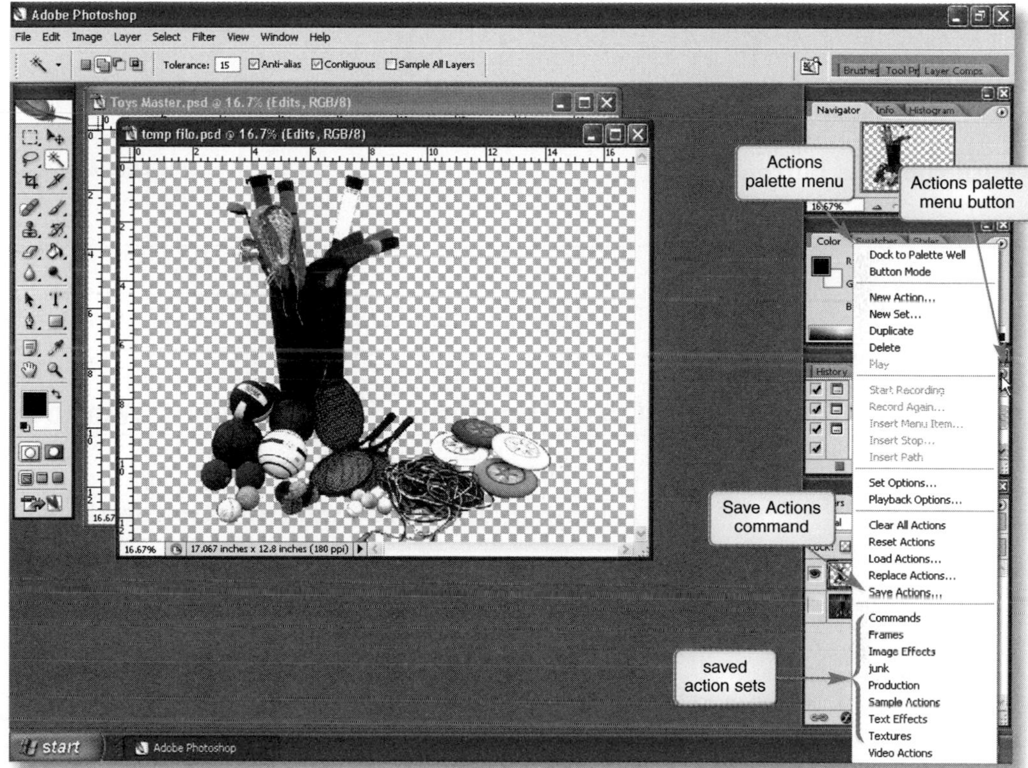

FIGURE 6-37

2

- **With your USB flash drive connected to one of the computer's USB ports, click Save Actions.**
- **When the Save dialog box is displayed, click the Save in box arrow and then click USBDISK [G:], or the location associated with your USB flash drive, in the list.**

Photoshop displays the Save dialog box with the atn format selected (Figure 6-38). Saving on a personal storage device keeps lab installation actions unchanged.

3

- **Click the Save button.**

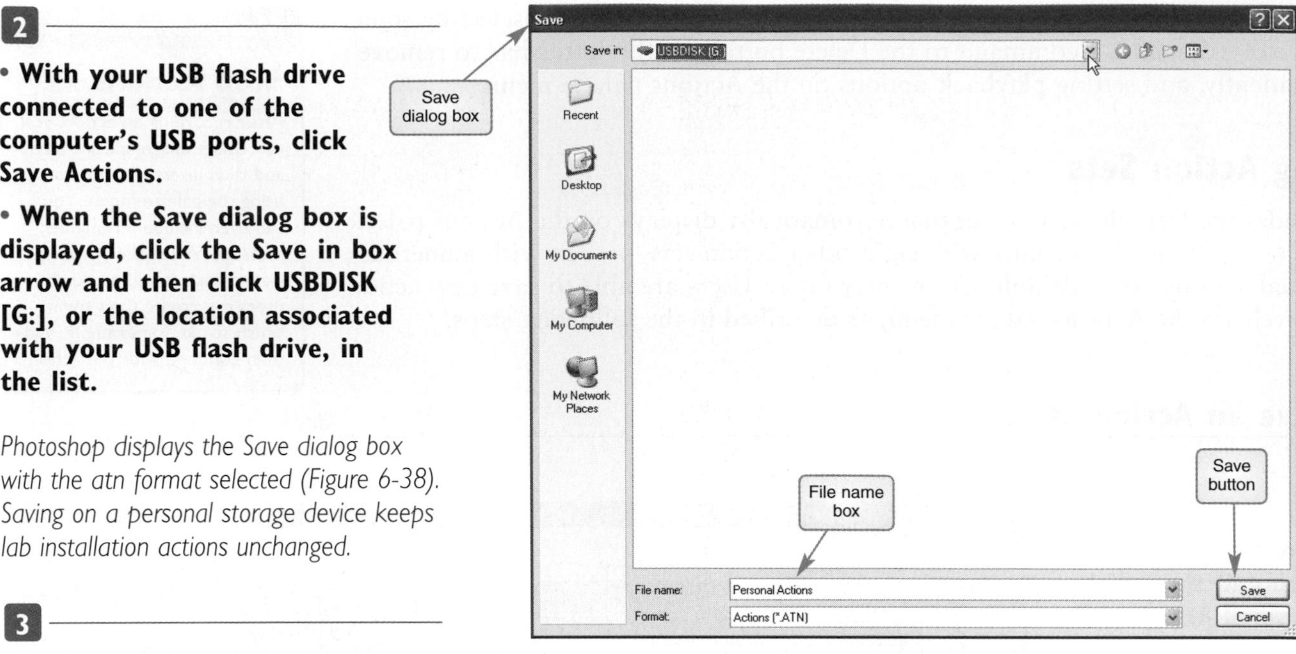

FIGURE 6-38

The following step shows how to close the temp file document window.

To Close the Temp File Document Window

1 **Click the Close button on the temp file document window title bar. If Photoshop asks if you want to save the changes, click the No button.**

The temp file image is closed and the Toys Master image again is displayed.

Playing an Action

To play back a recorded action, it must be saved with the image, or its action set must be loaded into the image. On the Actions palette menu, the Load Actions command opens a dialog box so you can navigate to the location of the desired action set. Then, you can play a loaded action by selecting it and clicking the play button. Alternately, you can press an associated function key.

In the steps that follow, the Convert to Black & White action is activated with the function key as you play back the steps to convert the Toys Master image to black and white, once again.

To Play an Action

1

- **If necessary, select the Toys Master document window. With your USB flash drive still connected to one of the computer's USB ports, press the F11 key.**

The action begins to play and stops at the Channel Mixer dialog box (Figure 6-39).

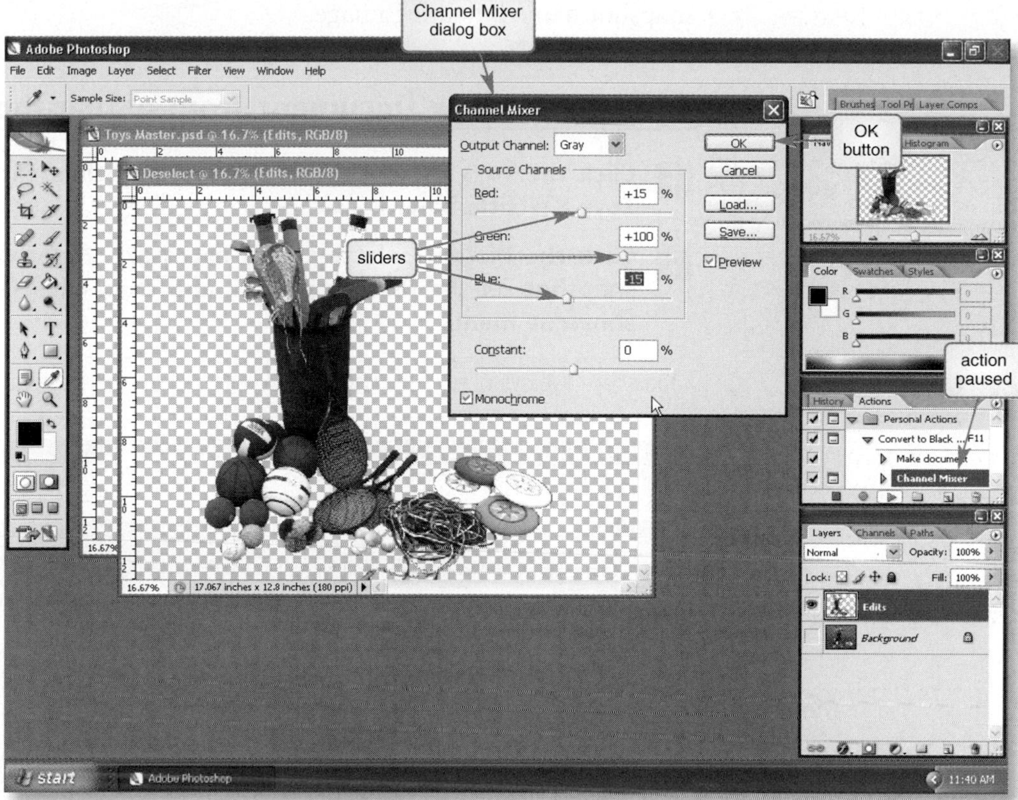

FIGURE 6-39

2

- **Drag the sliders to create an image with good contrast and tonal values.**
- **Click the OK button in the Channel Mixer dialog box.**
- **When Photoshop displays the Save As dialog box, type** `Toys BW` **in the Name box.**
- **If necessary, click the Save in box arrow and then click USBDISK [G:], or the location associated with your USB flash drive, in the list.**

The action continues and then stops at the Save As dialog box (Figure 6-40).

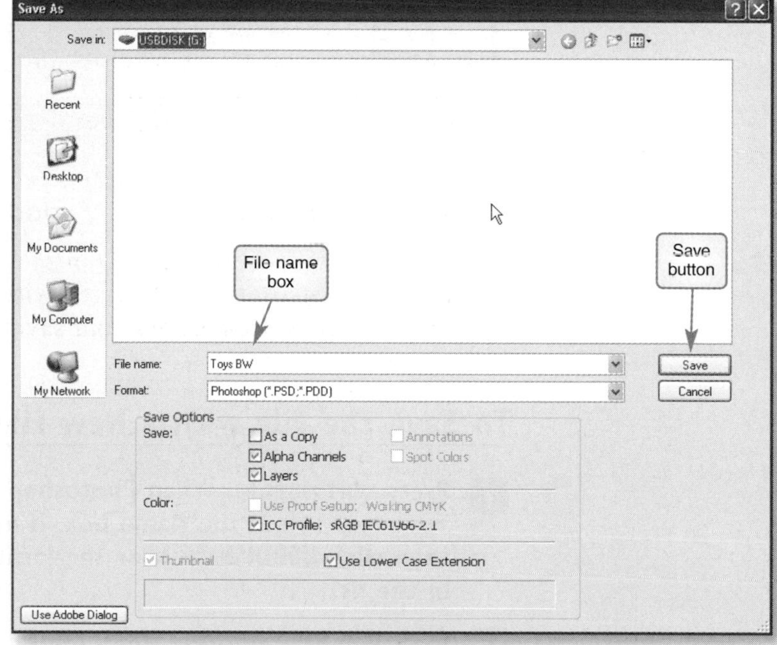

FIGURE 6-40

**3**

- **Click the Save button.**

The document is saved.

In preparation for the final version of the toys image, the following steps illustrate how to close the black-and-white version and then create a new document from the snapshot named, floating image.

To Create a New Document from a Snapshot

1. **Click the Toys BW document window and then click the Close button on the Toys BW title bar.**
2. **Click the History palette tab, if necessary. Right-click the floating image snapshot on the History palette and then click New Document on the shortcut menu.**

Photoshop displays a new document window based on the snapshot (Figure 6-41).

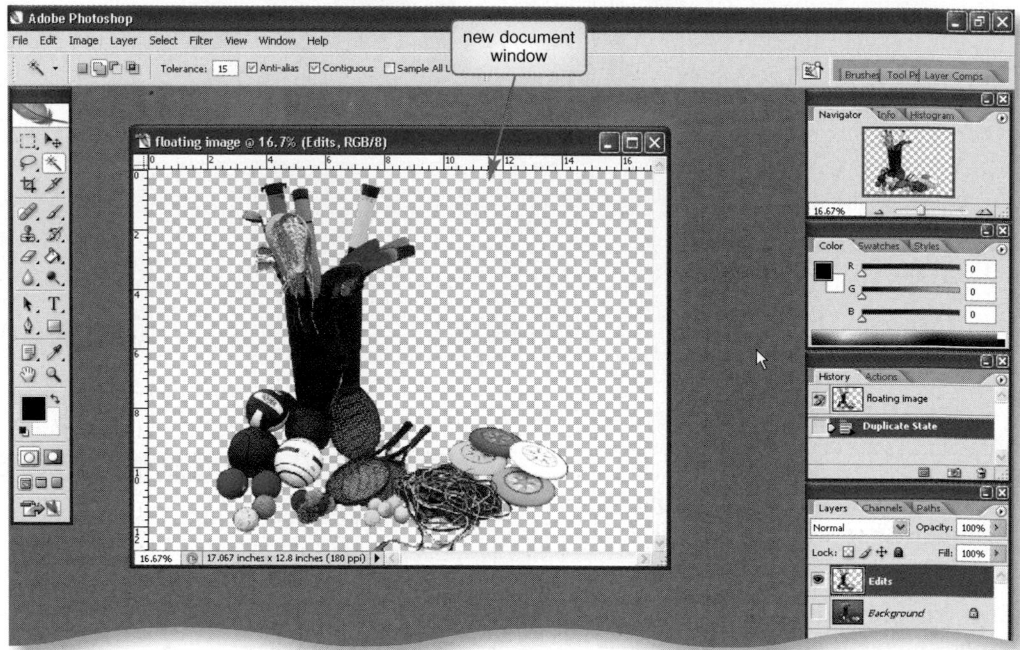

FIGURE 6-41

In the next steps, the file is saved with the name, Toys 4color. The Toys Master document window is closed without saving.

To Save the File with a New File Name

1. **Press SHIFT+CTRL+S. When Photoshop displays the Save As dialog box, type** `Toys 4color` **in the Name box. If necessary, click the Save in box arrow and then click USBDISK [G:], or the location associated with your USB flash drive, in the list.**
2. **Click the Save button. When Photoshop displays the Photoshop Format Options dialog box, click the OK button.**
3. **Click the Toys Master document window and then click the Close button on the document window title bar. When Photoshop displays a dialog box asking if you want to save the changes, click the No button.**

The Toys 4color document window is displayed.

This new version also will contain a border, shapes, and text for the toy company's color advertisement. Ultimately converted to the CMYK Color mode for four-color printing, the final version will require color adjustments.

Decorative Shapes and Text

Decorative shapes and borders are both eye-catching and delineating. From a design perspective, using shapes helps direct the viewer to important details. Sometimes called attention getters, shapes with text are used to highlight points of interest and make the user notice parts of an advertisement that they might otherwise skip over.

Recall that the Shape tool comes in various configurations, such as rectangle, rounded rectangle, ellipses, and custom shapes. Each shape comes with a wide array of styles as well, allowing you to create dimensional shapes through contour and 3D effects.

Creating a Border

Borders also add a decorative touch. Recall that creating a selection and modifying its border, is an easy way to create a custom-sized border around an image. The following steps show how to create a blue border, using a sample color selected from the toy bag.

To Create a Border

1

- **In the toolbox, click the Eyedropper Tool (I) button. Click the toy bag to sample a blue color.**

Dark blue becomes the foreground color (Figure 6-42).

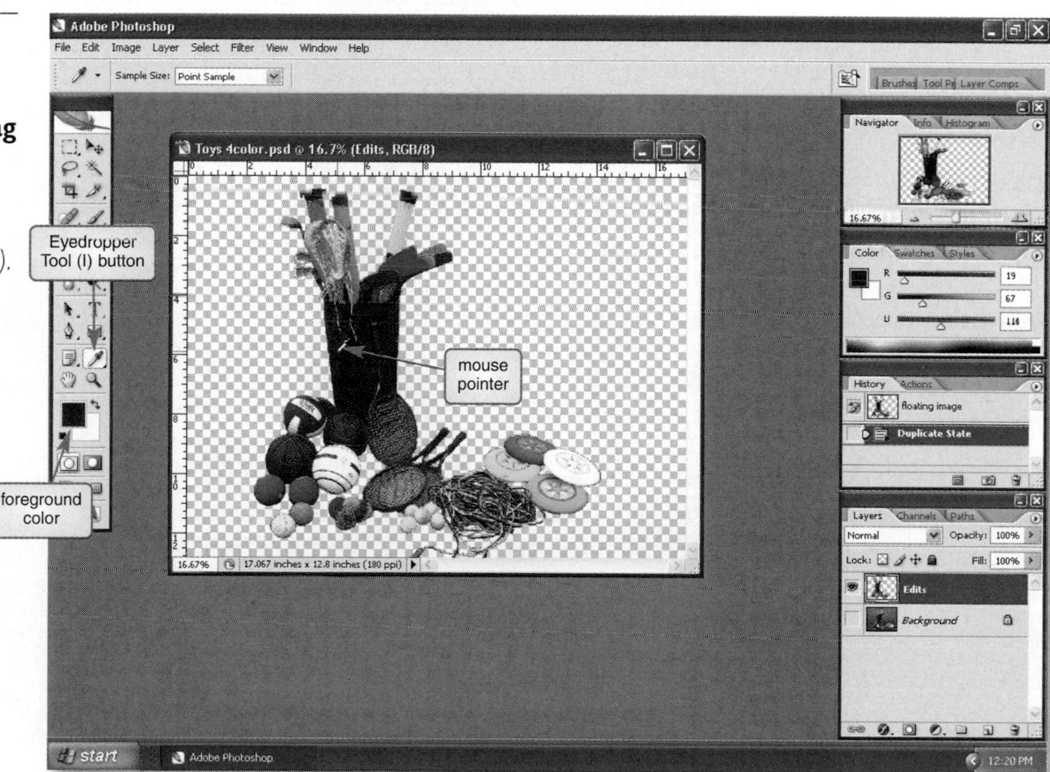

FIGURE 6-42

2

- **Press CTRL+A to select the entire image.**
- **Click Select on the menu bar, point to Modify, and then click Border.**
- **When the Border Selection dialog box is displayed, type** 100 **in the Width box.**

The value of 100 pixels may seem like a large number to enter in the Width box; however, it is a small percentage of the image size (Figure 6-43). You will resize the image later in the project.

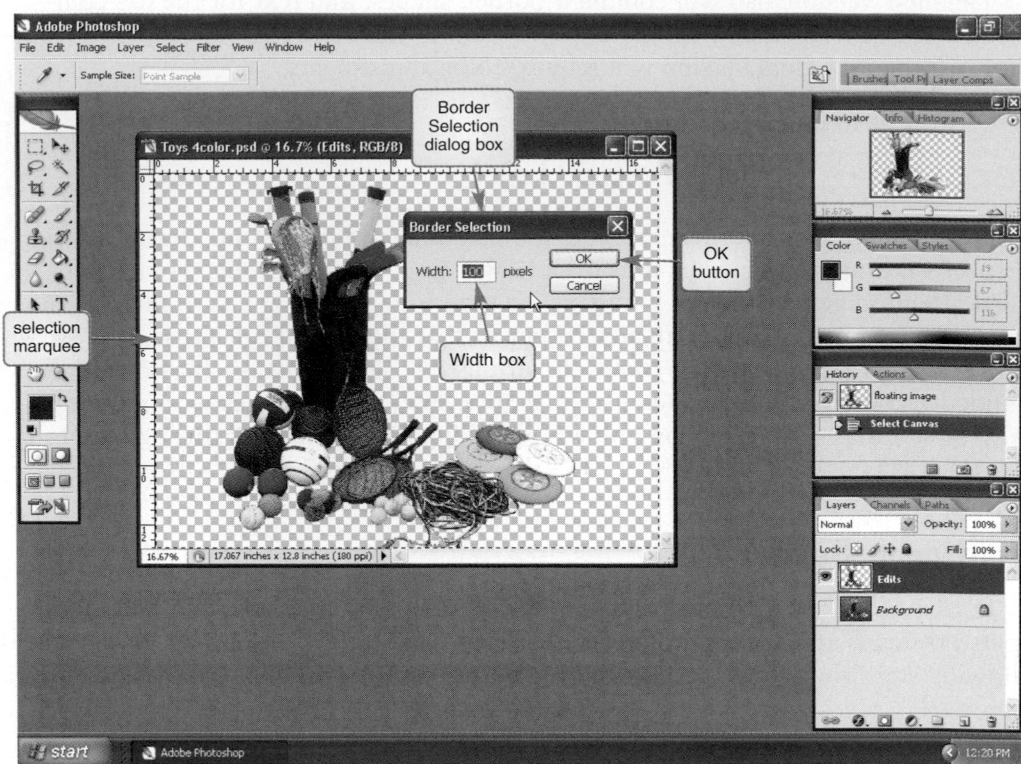

FIGURE 6-43

3

- **Click the OK button.**
- **Click the Paint Bucket Tool (G) button in the toolbox.**
- **Click the border selection. If necessary, at the bottom of the image, click the selected areas around the jump rope.**

After a few moments, the blue border is created (Figure 6-44).

4

- **Press CTRL+D to deselect.**

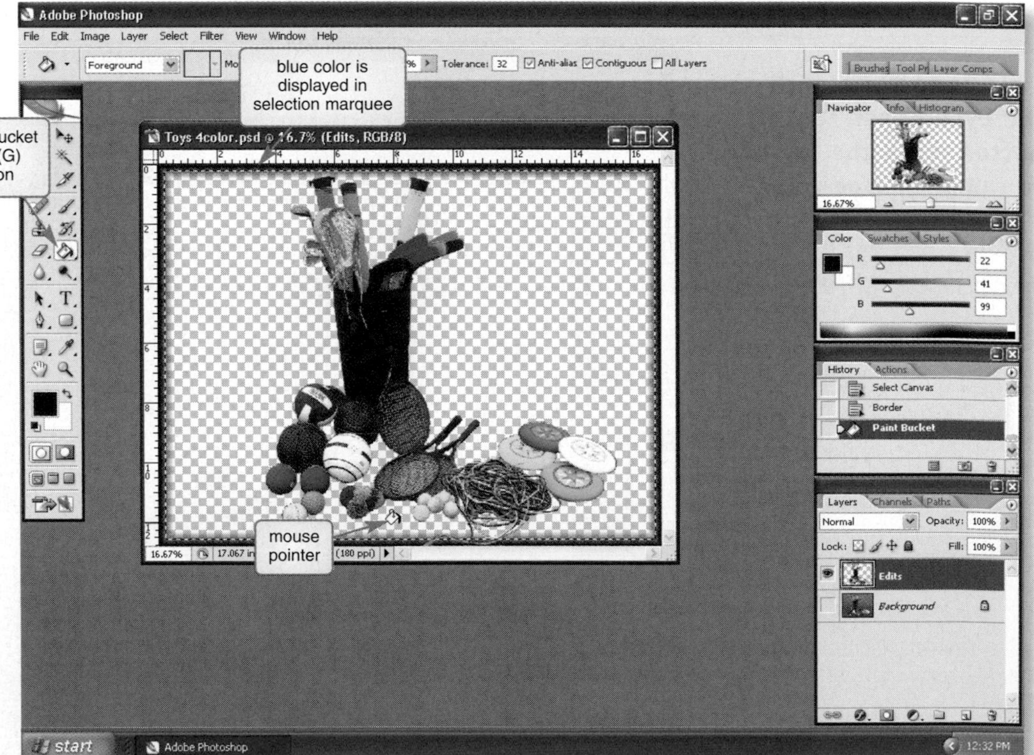

FIGURE 6-44

Creating Decorative Shapes

In the Toys 4color image, you will create seven rounded rectanglular shapes down the left side of the image. Each of the seven shapes will use a color from the floating image and each eventually will hold the name of a piece of game equipment.

The following steps illustrate how to create the shape.

To Create a Decorative Shape

1

- **Click the Eyedropper Tool (I) button in the toolbox.**
- **Click one of the basketballs to sample a dark orange color.**

Dark orange becomes the foreground color (Figure 6-45).

FIGURE 6-45

2

- **Right-click the current shape tool in the toolbox and then click Rounded Rectangle Tool in the list.**
- **On the options bar, click the Shape layers button, if necessary.**
- **Click the Geometry options button.**
- **When the Rounded Rectangle Options box is displayed, click Fixed Size. Type** 3 **in the W box and** 1.7 **in the H box. Click the From Center check box to select it. If necessary, click the Snap to Pixels check box to deselect it.**

The Rounded Rectangle Options box is displayed (Figure 6-46).

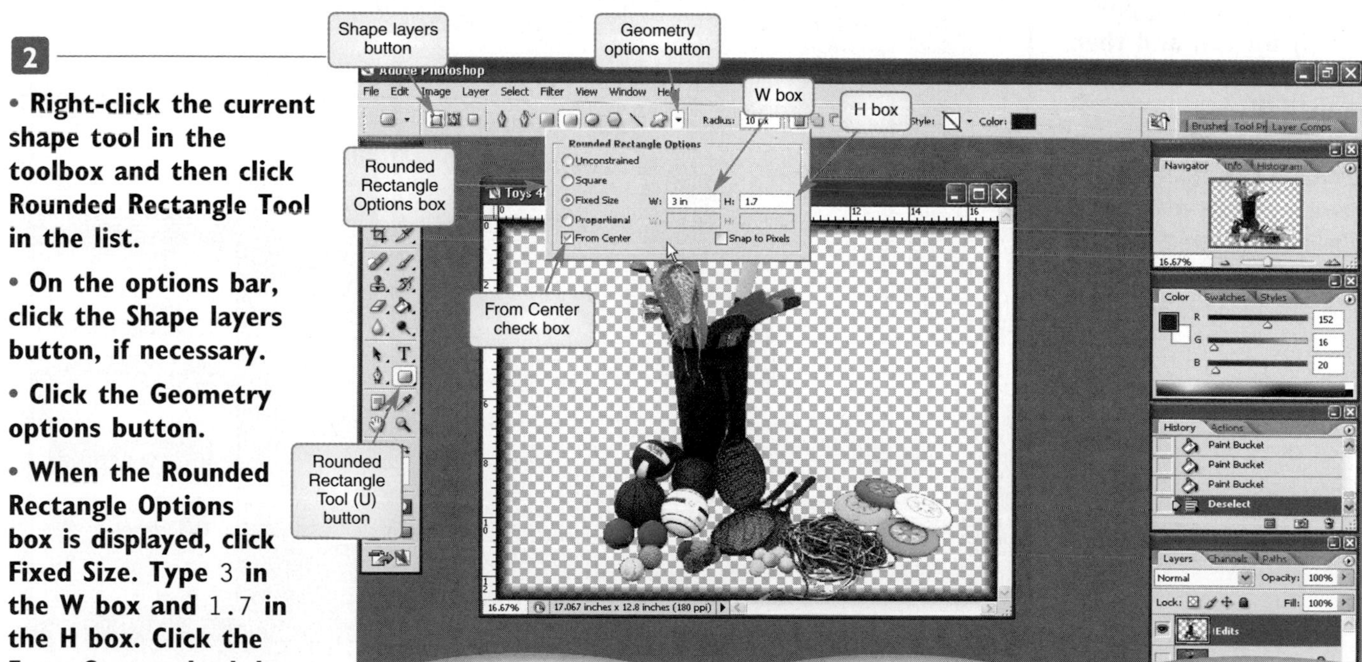

FIGURE 6-46

3

- **On the options bar, type** 60 px **in the Radius box.**
- **In the document window, click and hold down the mouse button in the upper-left corner of the image.**
- **Drag the rounded rectangle to a position as shown in Figure 6-47.**

A new shape layer is created.

FIGURE 6-47

4

- **Release the mouse button.**
- **Click the Eyedropper Tool (I) button and then click a yellow area of a tennis ball.**

The orange rounded rectangle displays in the upper-left corner of the image (Figure 6-48). The Eyedropper tool selects yellow as the foreground color.

FIGURE 6-48

5

- **Click the Rounded Rectangle Tool (U) button in the toolbox.**
- **On the options bar, click the Create new shape layer button.**
- **Click the image and drag to position a second rounded rectangle directly beneath the first one.**

Two rounded rectangles are displayed (Figure 6-49). Clicking the Create new shape layer button on the options bar resets the shape color to the current foreground color.

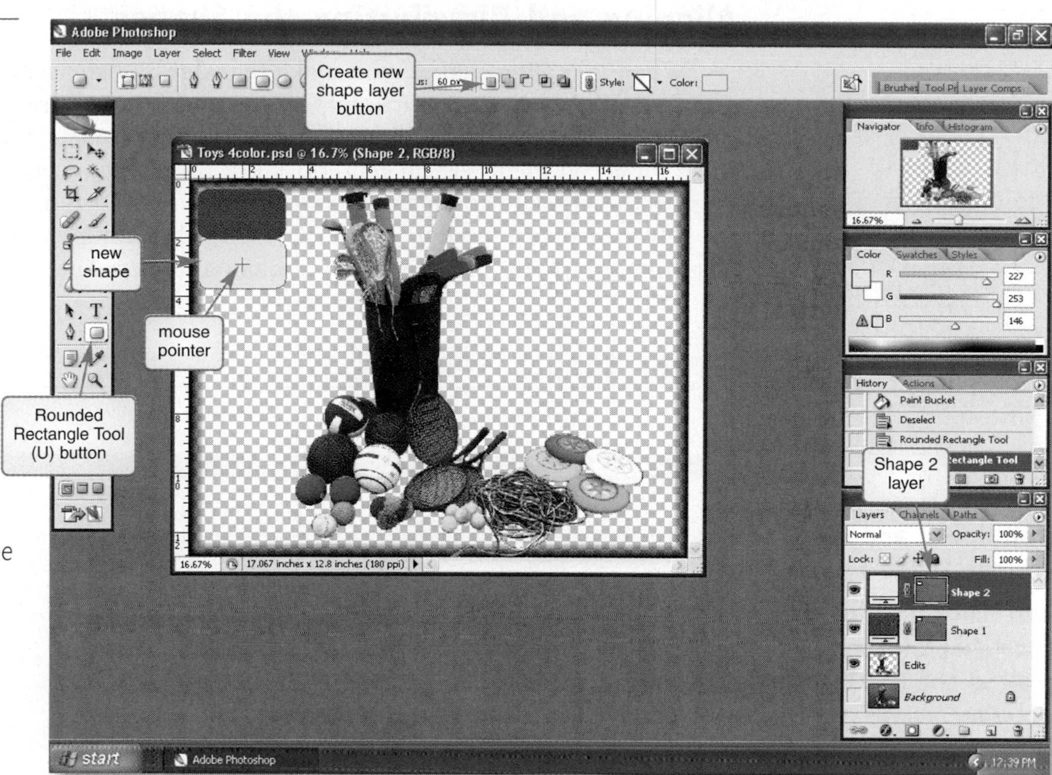

FIGURE 6-49

6

- **Repeat Steps 4 and 5, sampling the teal, pink, and green frisbees to create three more rounded rectangles. Your placement does not have to be exact.**
- **Sample the red hockey stick, and the light blue edge of the lacrosse stick, to create two more rounded rectangles. If you make a mistake, click the previous state on the History palette.**

The seven rounded rectangles display colors sampled from the floating image (Figure 6-50). Your placement may vary.

FIGURE 6-50

Aligning and Distributing the Shapes

When you **align** shapes, you make the edges, or the centers, line up with one another. When you **distribute** shapes, you create equal distances between the edges or centers. The next steps align the seven shapes on their left edge and distribute them based on their vertical centers. All of the shape layers must be selected for the align and distribute commands to work properly. Once selected, the commands on the Layer menu are used to make the rounded rectangles evenly spaced and lined up. The following steps illustrate how to align and distribute shapes.

To Align and Distribute the Shapes

1

- **On the Layers palette, scroll down, and then click the Shape 1 layer.**
- **CTRL+click each of the other shape layers. Scroll in the palette, as necessary.**

All seven shape layers are selected (Figure 6-51).

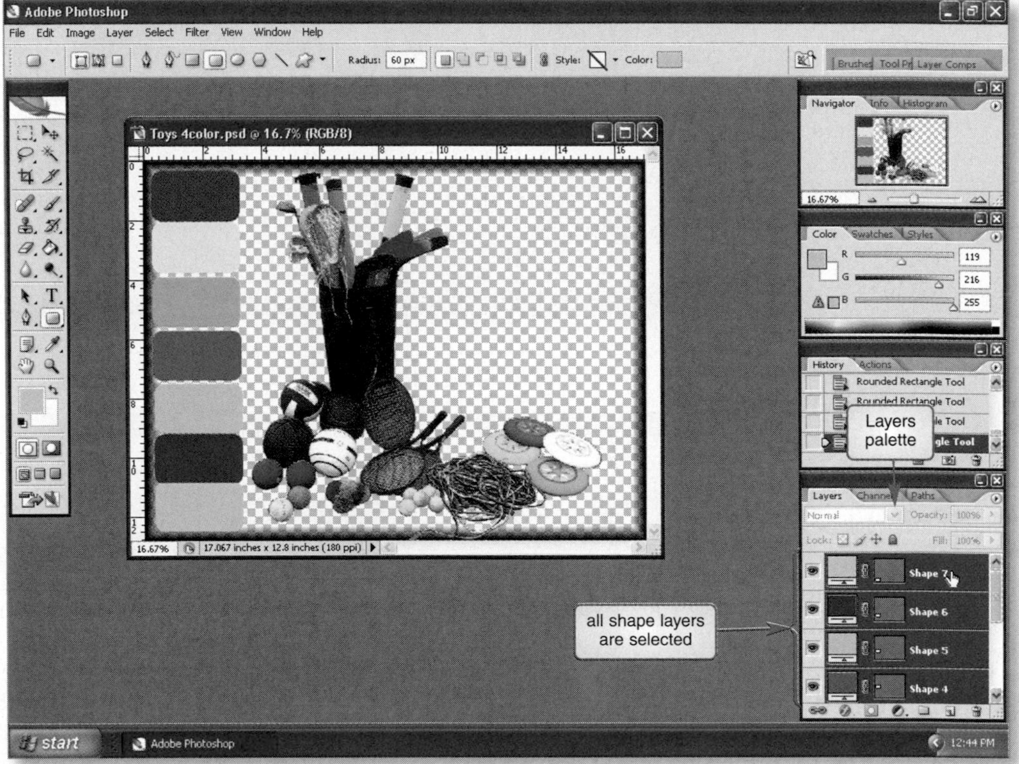

FIGURE 6-51

2

- **Click Layer on the menu bar and then point to Align.**

The various alignment possibilities display as commands on the Align submenu (Figure 6-52).

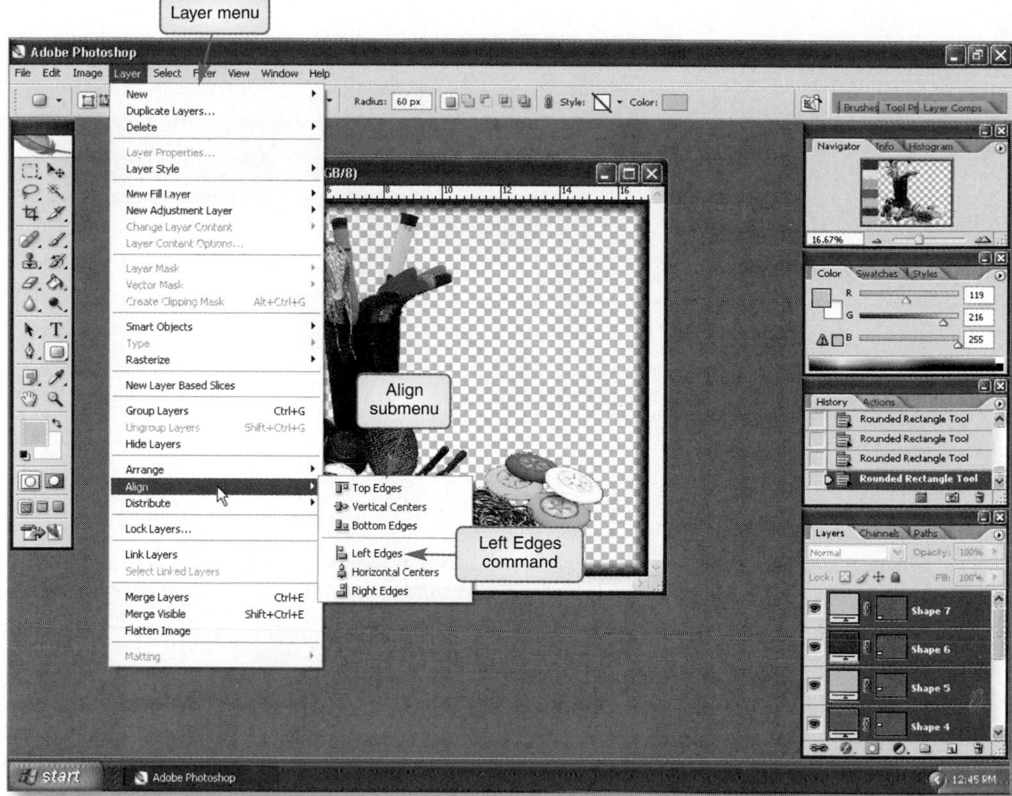

FIGURE 6-52

3

- **Click Left Edges.**
- **Click Layer on the menu bar and then point to Distribute.**

The distribute possibilities include distributing at any of the four edges, as well as vertical and horizontal centers (Figure 6-53).

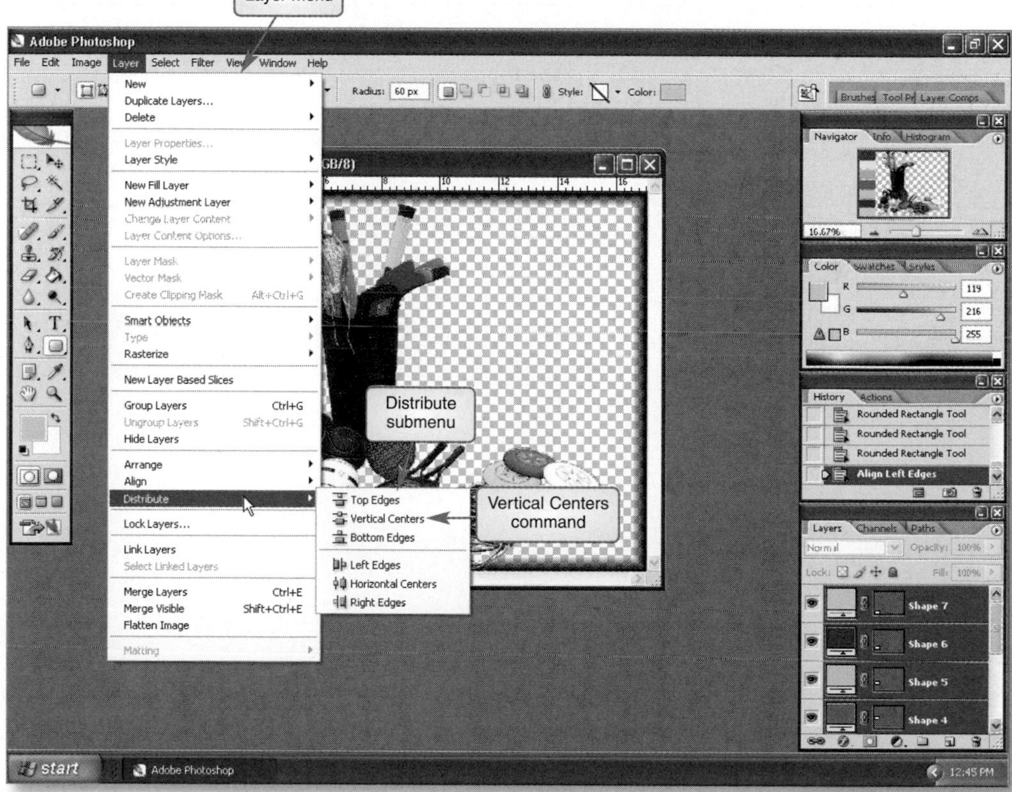

FIGURE 6-53

4

• **Click Vertical Centers.**

The shapes are distributed (Figure 6-54).

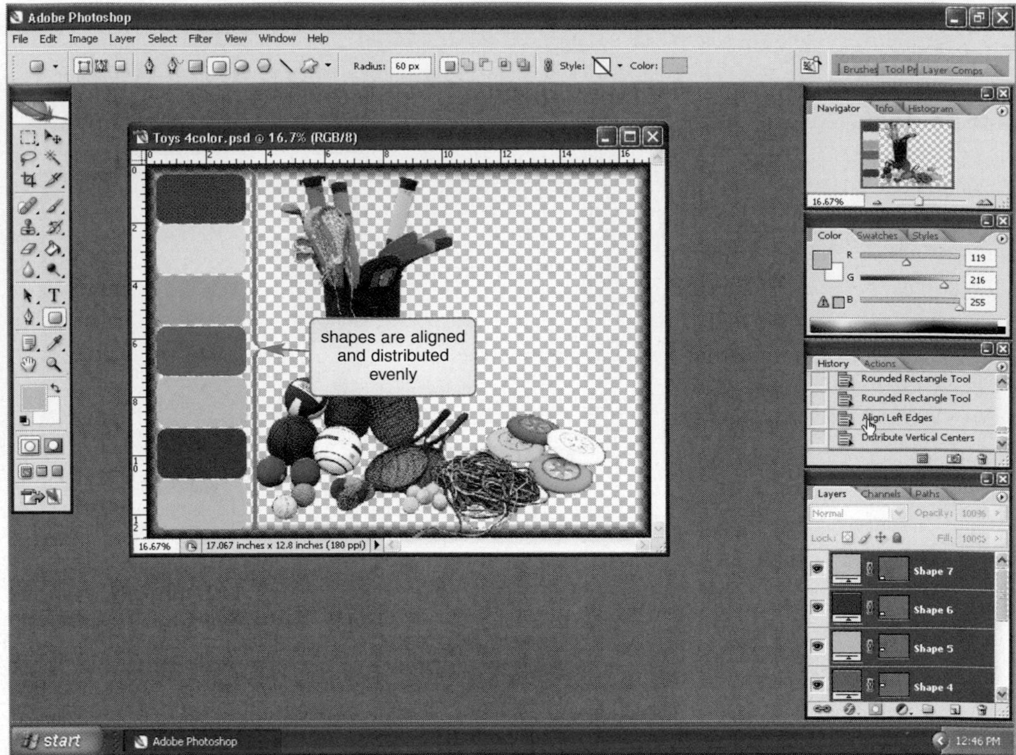

FIGURE 6-54

Inserting Text

The next steps use the Type tool to create text in each of the rectangles. First a layer is created, then the text is entered. The font color for the text will be sampled from the toy bag in the floating image.

To Insert Text

1

- **Click the Eyedropper Tool (I) button in the toolbox.**
- **Sample the blue toy bag.**
- **Press SHIFT+CTRL+N to create a new layer.**
- **When the New Layer dialog box is displayed, click the OK button.**

The new layer is displayed on the Layers palette (Figure 6-55). You do not need to name the new layer because the Type tool will provide a layer name. The foreground color is blue.

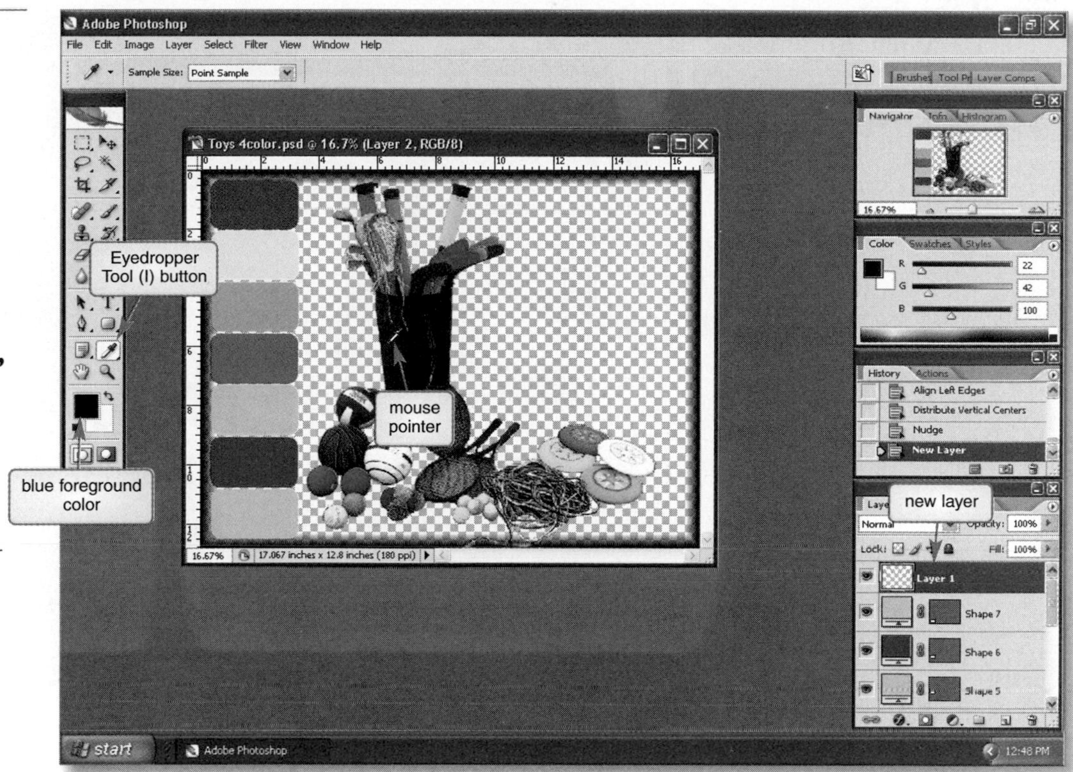

FIGURE 6-55

- **Click the Horizontal Type Tool (T) button in the toolbox.**
- **On the options bar, click the Set the font family box arrow and then click Arial Black in the list.**
- **Click the Set the font size box arrow and then click 36 in the list.**
- **Click the Set the anti-aliasing method box arrow and then click Smooth.**
- **Click the Center text button.**

The text settings are changed on the options bar (Figure 6-56).

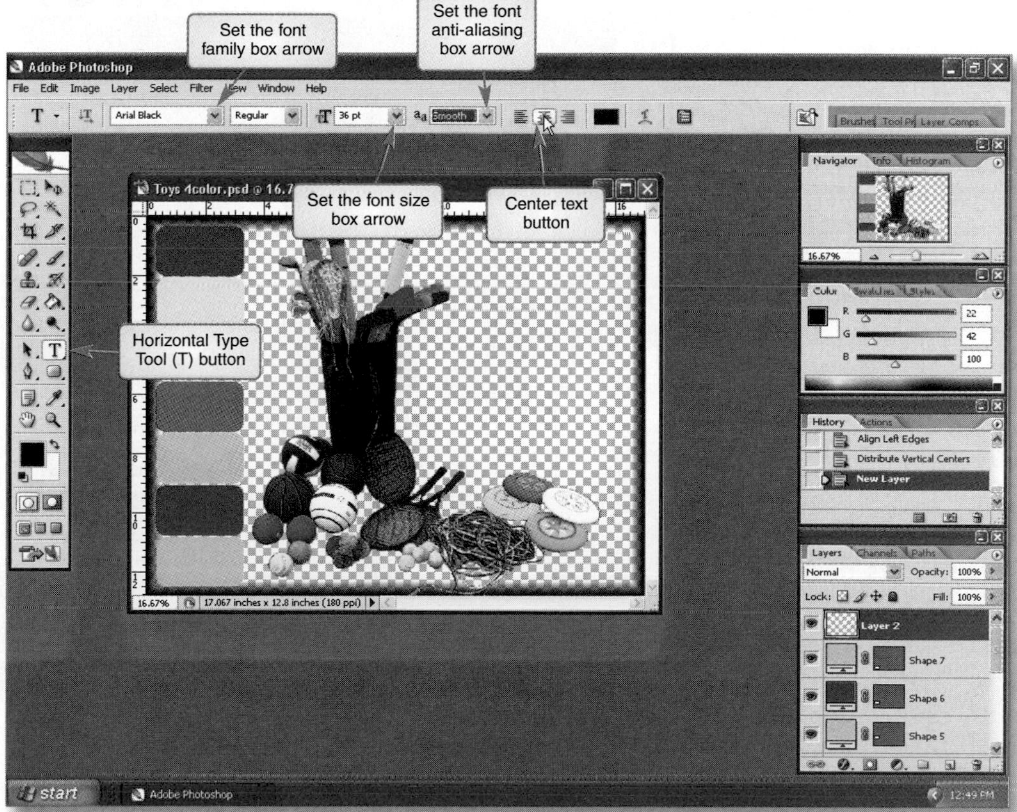

FIGURE 6-56

3

- **Point to the upper-left corner of the first rounded rectangle. Drag a text box that is slightly smaller than the rectangle.**
- **Type** `Lawn Toys` **in the text box.**

The text displays in front of the rounded rectangle (Figure 6-57).

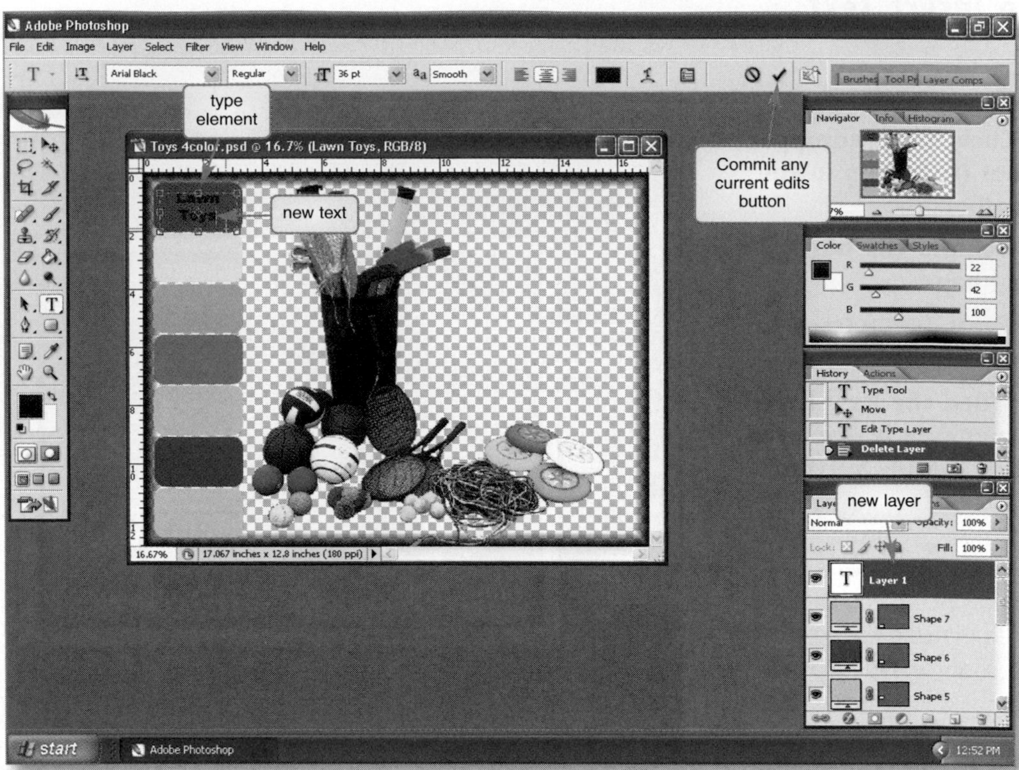

FIGURE 6-57

4

- **Click the Commit any current edits button on the options bar.**
- **Press SHIFT+CTRL+N to create a new layer.**
- **When Photoshop displays the New Layer dialog box, click the OK button.**
- **Drag a second text box that is slightly smaller than the second rounded rectangle.**
- **Type** `Soccer Balls` **in the text box.**
- **Click the Commit any current edits button on the options bar.**

The second type layer displays the text (Figure 6-58).

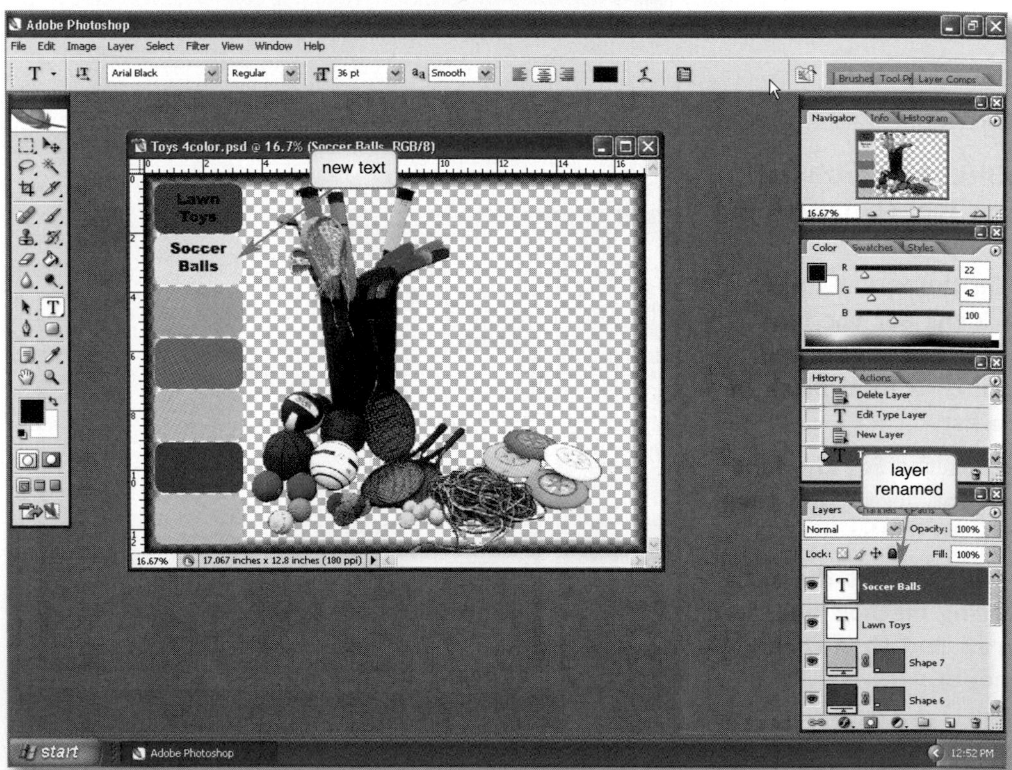

FIGURE 6-58

5

- **Repeat Step 4 for each of the rounded rectangles with the following text:** `Tennis Racquets, Frisbees, Jump Ropes, Golf Clubs, And more...` **as shown in Figure 6-59.**
- **If necessary, select all of the type layers on the Layers palette, and then align and distribute.**

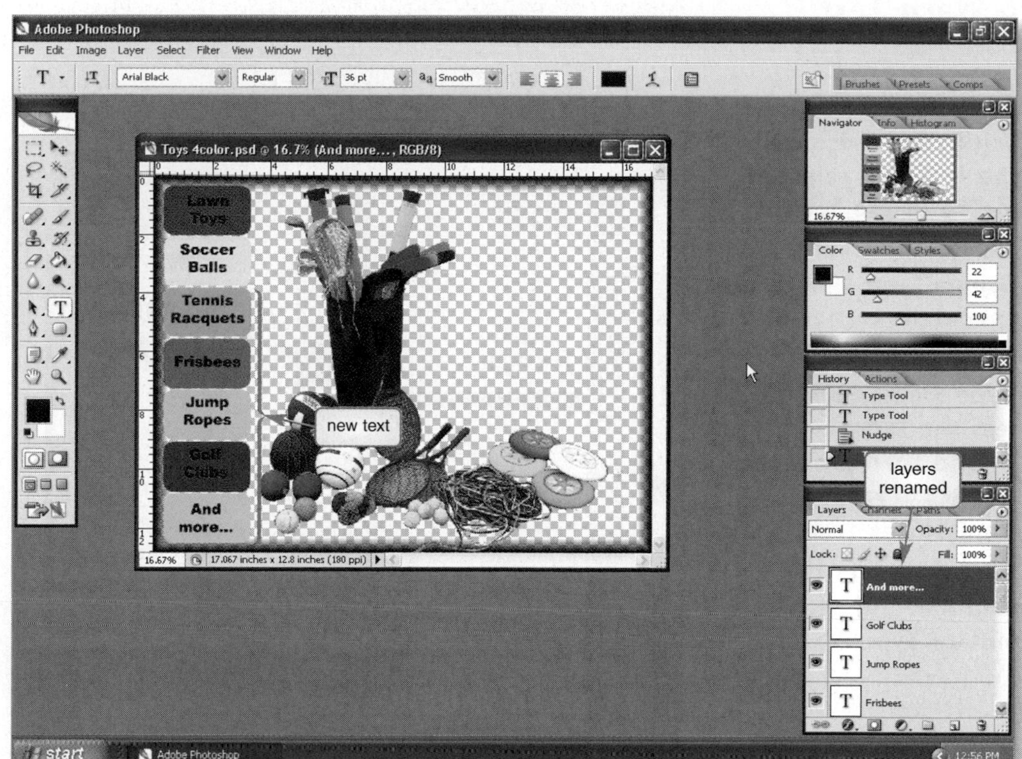

FIGURE 6-59

The final text will be converted into a graphic element using the Warp Text command.

Warping Text

One way to make your text eye catching is to use the Warp Text dialog box. Photoshop has 15 different warp styles, each with adjustable settings, to create an endless number of possibilities for warped text.

In the steps on the next page, the text, Summer FUN Sale, is warped using the Inflate warp style, adjusted for maximum bend or inflation in the middle.

More About

Nudging

If you need to move a shape or layer by just a little bit, you can select the Move tool and then press an arrow key on the keyboard to nudge the object by 1 pixel. Pressing SHIFT+ arrow nudges the object by 10 pixels.

To Warp Text

1

- **With the Horizontal Type tool still selected, type** 90 **in the Set the font size box.**
- **Drag a large box in the upper-right corner of the image.**
- **Type** Summer **and then press the ENTER key. Type** FUN **and then press the ENTER key. Type** Sale **to complete the text.**
- **Click Layer on the menu bar and then point to Type.**

The Layer menu displays commands related to converting text, alignment, placement, anti-alias methods, and warping (Figure 6-60).

FIGURE 6-60

2

- **Click Warp Text.**
- **When the Warp Text dialog box is displayed, click the Style box arrow.**

The 15 warp styles are displayed in the list (Figure 6-61).

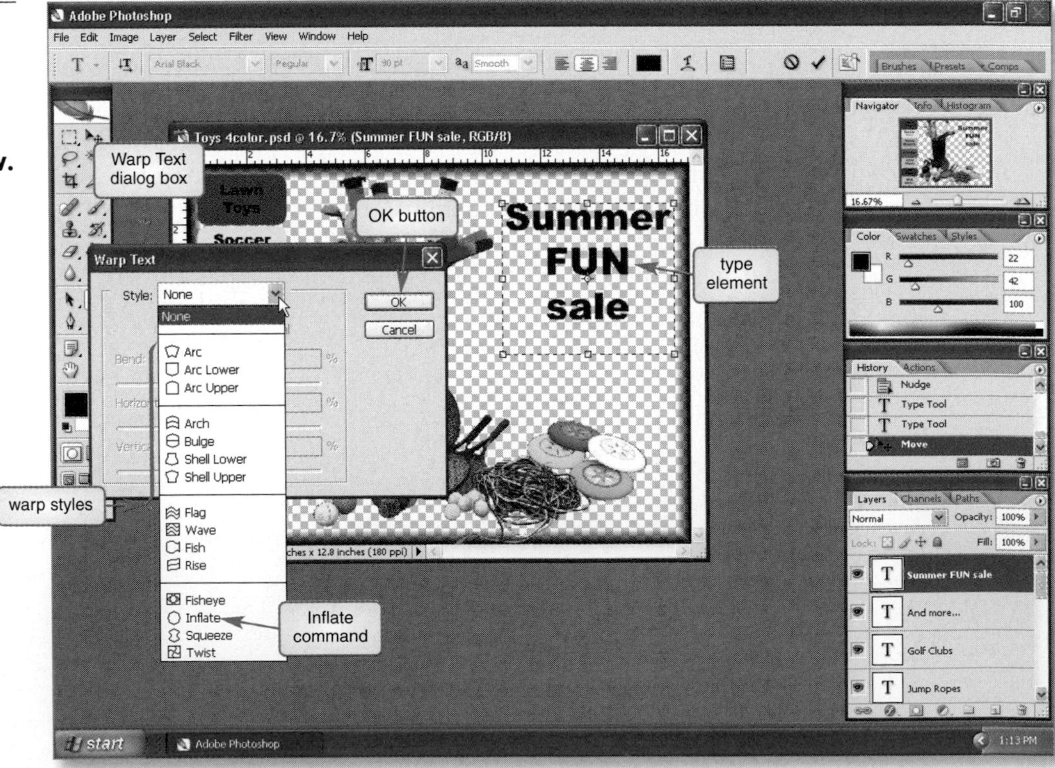

FIGURE 6-61

3

- **Click Inflate.**
- **Drag the Bend slider to 80%.**
- **If necessary, drag the Horizontal Distortion and Vertical Distortion sliders to 0.**

Notice that the document window displays a preview of the warp (Figure 6-62).

4

- **Click the OK button.**
- **Click the Commit any current edits button on the options bar.**
- **If necessary, in the toolbox, click the Move Tool (V) button and adjust the placement of the layer.**

The text element is complete.

FIGURE 6-62

Other Ways

1. On options bar, click Create warped text button

With the edits complete, it is time to convert the image to CMYK and make tonal adjustments in preparation for printing.

Preparing for Four-Color Processing

Most digital cameras create an RGB file. While that is fine for online viewing and Web graphics, many traditional full-color printing presses can print only four colors: cyan, magenta, yellow, and black (CMYK). Other colors in the spectrum are simulated using various combinations of those colors. When you plan to print a photo professionally, you may have to convert it from one color model to the other. The toys image was taken with a digital camera and uses the RGB color model. The toy company wants a professional print of the floating image, in color. The service bureau has specified the Trumatch 4-color matching system that uses the CMYK Color model.

Photoshop allows you to convert directly from RGB to CMYK; however, using the intermediary Lab color mode gives you more flexibility in color changes and contrast.

Using Lab Color

Lab color is an internationally accepted color mode that defines colors mathematically using a lightness or luminance setting, and two color or chromatic channels — an A-axis color for colors from magenta to green, and a B-axis color for colors from yellow to blue. The Lab color mode, which tries to emulate the colors viewable by the human eye, incorporates all the colors in the RGB and CMYK color spectrums and is often used as an intermediary when converting from one format to another.

In Figure 6-63, the Lab color space is represented by the color spectrum. The black outline represents RGB's color space. The white outline represents CMYK's color space. RGB and CMYK are subsets, but they also are slanted in the color spectrum. For example, when converting from RGB to CMYK, you loose some of the blue's intensity but gain yellow. Reds and greens are better in RGB, cyans and magentas are better in CMYK, as you would suspect. The **contrast**, a matter of how bright the white is and how dark the black is, is poorly represented in CMYK. The printer cannot make white any brighter than the paper on which it is printed. A solid black does not exist in CMYK on a display monitor. Therefore, when adjusting color and contrast during a conversion, it is appropriate to convert it to Lab color, make your adjustments, and then convert it to CMYK.

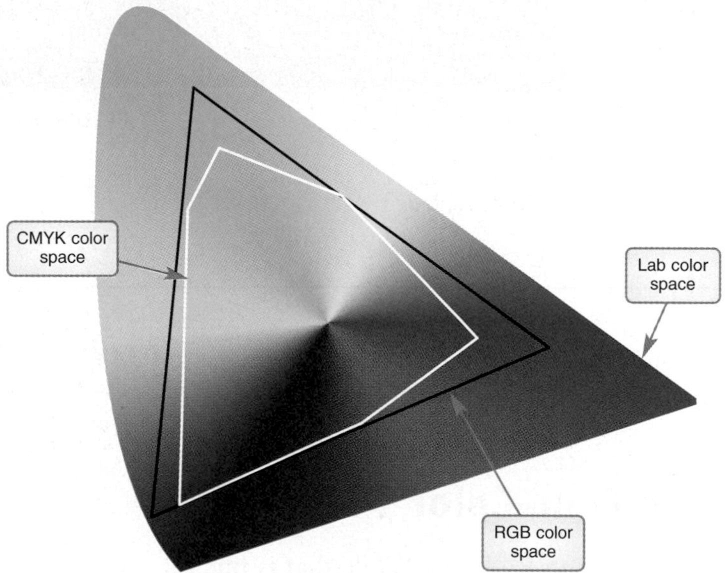

FIGURE 6-63

The Lab Color mode calculates each color description, rather than generating it from a combination, as is the case for RGB. Because RGB colors are combinations of colors, they may look different on different devices. For example, a row of televisions in a department store displaying the same program, will look different because different manufacturers combine RGB in slightly different ways. Working with Lab colors usually provides more consistent colors across platforms.

The Lab Color mode is independent of the type of device or media, and may be used for either display or printing. Many photo CD images use Lab colors where the luminance and color values are edited independently.

The Lab Color mode will be used in the conversion process for the advertisement. The layers will be merged, and the image will be converted to Lab color and sharpened. Finally, the image will be converted to CMYK, so color and tonal changes can be applied before printing. The following step shows how to convert to Lab color.

To Convert to Lab Color

1

- **Click Image on the menu bar, point to Mode, and then click Lab Color.**
- **When Photoshop displays a message about merging layers, click the Merge button.**

The layers are merged and the color mode is changed (Figure 6-64).

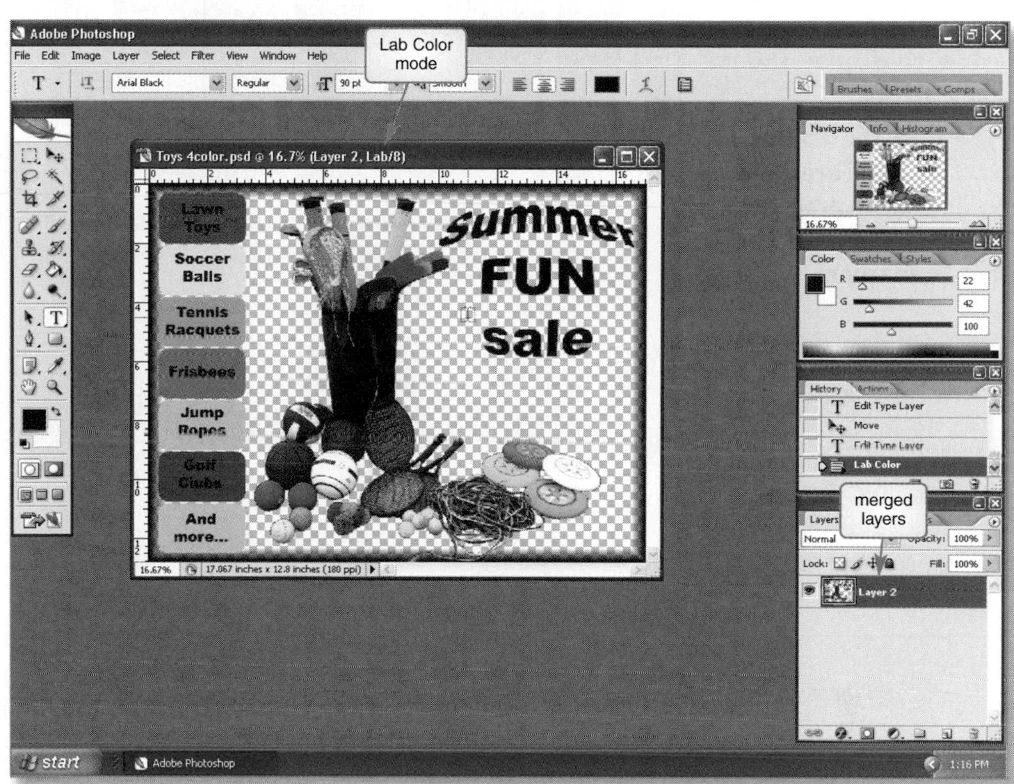

FIGURE 6-64

When converting to Lab Color, the Channels palette will display three channels: Lightness, a, and b. The Lab composite and any alpha channels also will display in the palette. The Lightness channel contains no color, so sharpening is easier as shown in the steps on the next page.

To Sharpen the Image

1

- **Click the Channels palette and select only the Lightness channel.**
- **Click Filter on the menu bar, point to Sharpen, and then click Unsharp Mask.**
- **In the Unsharp Mask dialog box, drag in the preview to display the hockey sticks.**
- **Type** 6 **in the Radius box,** 0 **in the Threshold box, and then drag the Amount slider until the detail is sharper.**

Your Amount value may differ (Figure 6-65).

FIGURE 6-65

2

- **Click the OK button.**

The image is sharpened.

Other adjustments that can be performed on the intermediary Lab color include filtering out noise or artifacts, applying spot color and alpha channels, or applying a varnish or tint to the image.

The final conversion will be to CMYK as illustrated in the following step.

To Convert to CMYK

1

- **In the Channels palette, click the Lab channel.**
- **Click Image on the menu bar, point to Mode, and then click CMYK Color.**

The color mode is changed (Figure 6-66). Photoshop displays a composite and individual CMYK color channels on the Channels palette, as well as the Grass Mask alpha channel.

FIGURE 6-66

Making Color Adjustments

When you used the Channel Mixer to create a monochrome version of the toys image, you were using just one of many color adjustment tools in Photoshop. Most of the tools work in the same way — they map or plot an existing range of pixel values to a new range of values. The main difference is in the amount of control each tool provides.

Recall that the Levels dialog box had sliders and a histogram to adjust the blacks, grays, and whites in an image. The Channel Mixer adjusted the reds, greens, and blues. Other color and tonal adjustments tools act upon different parts of an image, including highlights, midtones, shadows, among others.

The various color adjustment commands on the Image menu and its Adjustments submenu, alter the pixels in the active layer. Another way to adjust color is to use an adjustment layer via the Layer menu. This approach allows you to experiment with color and tonal adjustments first, before committing them to the image. Using an adjustment layer adds to the file size of the image and demands more random access memory (RAM) from your computer.

Table 6-3 on the next page displays some of the commands and their purpose. Each of the commands can be applied directly onto the active layer, and some can be applied via an adjustment layer.

Table 6-3 Color Adjustment Commands

COMMAND	PURPOSE	MENU ACCESS
Auto Color	fine tunes and corrects color balance and color casts in an image	Image | Adjustments
Auto Contrast	clips the shadow and highlight values by 5 percent and then assigns the black point to the darkest pixel and the white point to the lightest pixel in an image	Image | Adjustments
Auto Levels	automatically assigns the black point to the darkest pixel and the white point to the lightest pixel in an image, clipping shadows and highlights	Image | Adjustments
Brightness/Contrast	makes simple linear adjustments to the tonal range of an image and makes the same amount of adjustment to every pixel	Image | Adjustments Layer | New Adjustment Layer
Channel Mixer	modifies a color channel and makes color adjustments	Image | Adjustments Layer | New Adjustment Layer
Color Balance	changes the overall mixture of colors in an image	Image | Adjustments Layer | New Adjustment Layer
Curves	makes nonlinear adjustments via control points to make highlight, midtone, and shadow adjustments	Image | Adjustments Layer | New Adjustment Layer
Desaturate	produces a grayscale image but leaves the image in the same color mode	Image | Adjustments
Equalize	redistributes the brightness values of all pixels, so they represent the entire range of brightness levels more evenly	Image | Adjustments
Exposure	makes tonal adjustments to high dynamic range images by using a linear color space	Image | Adjustments
Gradient Map	maps the equivalent grayscale range in an image to the colors of a specified gradient fill	Image | Adjustments Layer | New Adjustment Layer
Hue/Saturation	adjusts the hue, saturation, and lightness values of the entire image or of individual color components	Image | Adjustments Layer | New Adjustment Layer
Invert	each pixel's brightness value is converted to the inverse value on the 256 color scale	Image | Adjustments Layer | New Adjustment Layer
Levels	adjusts color balance by setting the pixel distribution for individual color channels	Image | Adjustments Layer | New Adjustment Layer
Match Color	matches the color across selections, layers, or photos as well as adjusting luminance, color range, and color casts in an image	Image | Adjustments
Photo Filter	makes color adjustments by simulating the effects of a photographer's lens	Image | Adjustments Layer | New Adjustment Layer
Posterize	creates a specified number of tonal levels for each color in the color mode	Image | Adjustments Layer | New Adjustment Layer
Replace Color	replaces specified colors in an image with new color values	Image | Adjustments
Selective Color	adjusts the amount of process colors in individual color components	Image | Adjustments Layer | New Adjustment Layer

Table 6-3 Color Adjustment Commands (continued)

COMMAND	PURPOSE	ACCESSED VIA
Shadow/Highlight	lightens or darkens based on surrounding pixels to correct photos with strong backlighting or other lighting errors	Image | Adjustments
Threshold	identifies representative highlights and shadows	Image | Adjustments Layer | New Adjustment Layer
Variations	adjusts the color balance, contrast, and saturation of an image via thumbnail samples	Image | Adjustments

The toys image is brightly colored and eye-catching, but some minor color adjustments will make the yellows and greens stand out. At the end of the color adjustment steps below, the image is flattened and ready to resize. Remember, if you flatten the image, its layers can no longer be edited. If you expect to have further edits, save the image with a different file name before flattening.

To Make Color Adjustments

1

- **Click the Layers palette tab.**
- **Click Layer on the menu bar and then point to New Adjustment Layer.**

Photoshop displays the New Adjustment Layer submenu (Figure 6-67).

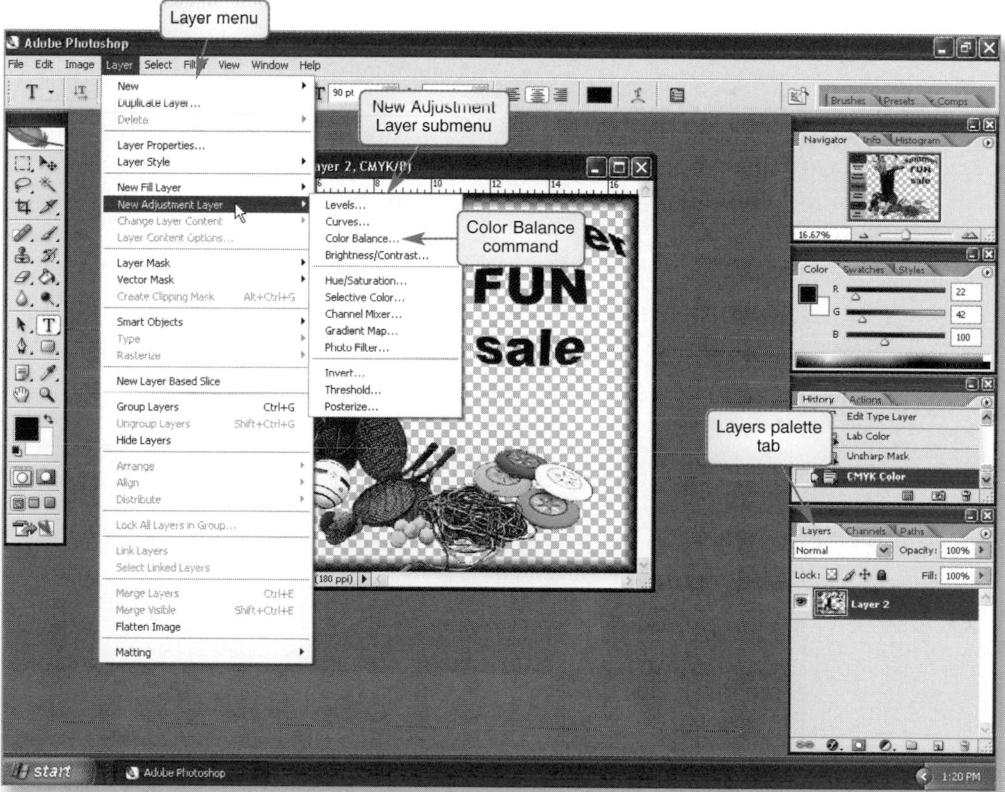

FIGURE 6-67

2

- **Click Color Balance.**
- **When Photoshop displays the New Layer dialog box, click the OK button.**

The Color Balance dialog box is displayed (Figure 6-68).

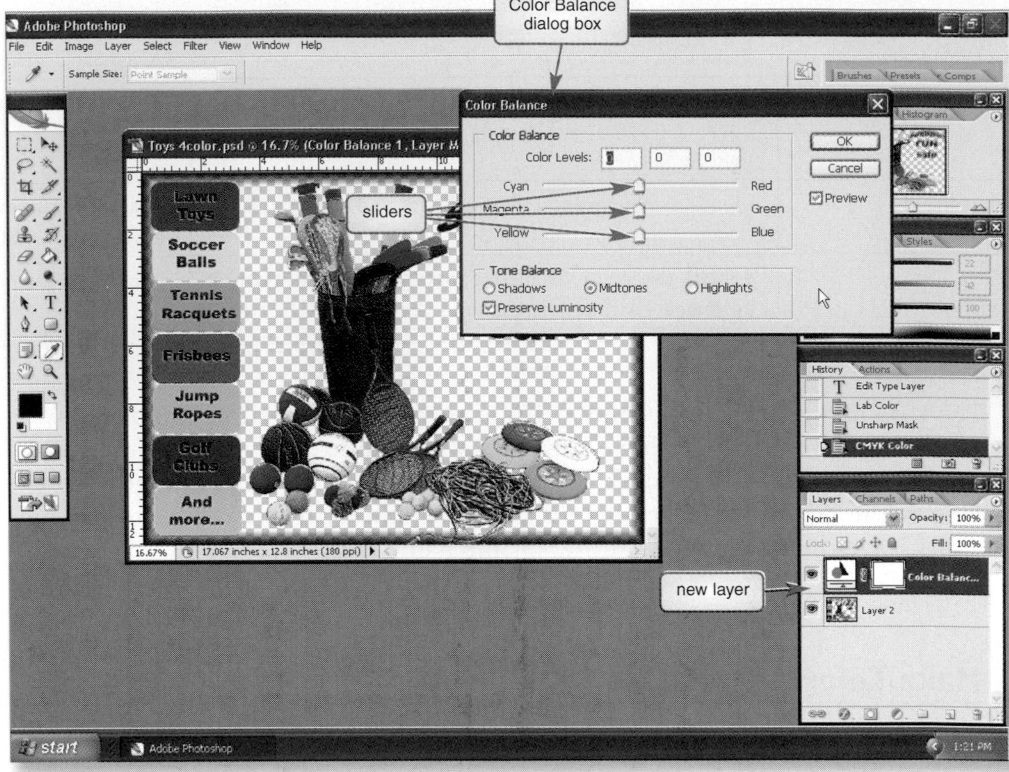

FIGURE 6-68

3

- **Drag the Magenta to Green slider to +48.**
- **Drag the Yellow to Blue slider to -77.**

The document window displays stronger yellows and greens (Figure 6-69).

4

- **Click the OK button.**
- **Click Layer on the menu bar and then click Flatten Image.**

The tonal adjustments are made and the image is flattened.

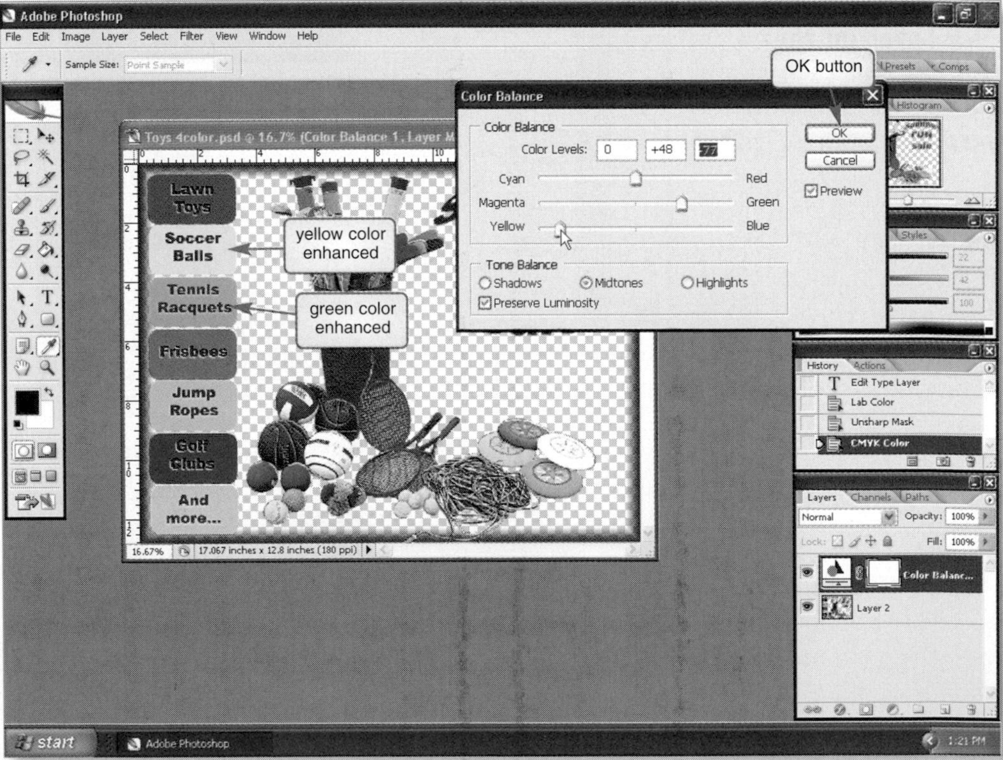

FIGURE 6-69

Now that you have completed the versions of the advertisement, it is time to resize them and set appropriate resolutions for each version's use.

Resizing, Resampling, and Interpolation

Many ways exist to resize an image. Recall that Photoshop offers a Resize Image Wizard that helps you change the size of images destined for print or the Web. Anytime that you resize an image, however, it can result in poorer image quality. For example, when you resize an image to larger dimensions, the image may lose some detail and sharpness because Photoshop has to add or stretch pixels. When you make an image smaller, some pixels must be reduced or discarded and cannot be recovered once the image is saved. That is why it always is suggested that you work with a copy of the original image, in case you do not like the changes.

Changing the **document size**, or physical size, of photos is one of the most common tasks in digital imagery. The Resize Image Wizard matches the image parameters to the way the image will be used. The wizard does a good job of estimating the kind of pixel manipulation needed to increase or decrease the size of the image, but it is not perfect. The wizard does not allow you to make decisions on all possible settings involved in the resizing process. Some adjustments usually are required after using the wizard. Also, the **file size**, or number of required bytes to store the image, is determined automatically by the wizard, allowing you few choices.

The alternative in resizing is to make the interpolation, resampling, and sizing changes, yourself. **Interpolation** is the mathematical process of adding or subtracting pixels in an image either to enlarge or reduce the size. Once the location of the interpolated pixels is determined, Photoshop uses a **resampling** method that assigns a new color value to pixels by taking a sample of the surrounding ones. Before you resample, however, it is important to check with your lab or service bureau, as some services automatically resample and resize at the time of printing. In those cases, retaining as much digital data as possible is the best choice. On the other hand, if a digital image must have a specific resolution and a specific size, then resampling may be warranted.

If you **downsample**, or decrease, the number of pixels, information is deleted from the image. Downsampling reduces image data by representing a group of pixels with a single pixel. For instance, if an image needs to be reduced by 50 percent, Photoshop will have to destroy half of the pixels. If during the destruction, black and white pixels come next to each other, both pixels are changed using a complex calculation to produce a smoother tonal gradation of gray. The disadvantage of downsampling is the loss of data, or **lossiness**.

If you **upsample**, or increase, the number of pixels, Photoshop assigns a new color to the pixel based on an average interpolation. For example, if an image needs to be enlarged, the interpolation notes where a new pixel should be added. If that new pixel falls at the edge of a yellow insignia on a red sweater, the new pixel would be orange. Photoshop samples the two colors and averages the color values. At the pixel level, it would be hard to notice orange in the finished product; but it is something to keep in mind when upsampling. Remember that Photoshop cannot insert detailed information that was not captured from the original image. Photos will start to look softer, with less detail, as they are enlarged.

Table 6-4 on the next page displays information about the five interpolation methods offered by Photoshop; however, other interpolation methods can be downloaded from the Web.

Table 6-4 Photoshop Interpolation Methods

INTERPOLATION METHOD	DESCRIPTION
Bicubic	a slow, but precise, interpolation method based on an examination of the values of surrounding pixels — applies more complex calculations, to produce smoother tonal gradations
Bicubic Sharper	a bicubic interpolation method that works well for reducing images with enhanced sharpening while maintaining details
Bicubic Smoother	an interpolation method that works well for enlarging images with smoother results than bicubic alone
Bilinear	an interpolation method that produces medium-quality results by averaging the color values to produce new pixels
Nearest Neighbor	a fast interpolation method that produces a smaller file size, but may become jagged when scaling as it tries to preserve hard edges

No matter what resampling method you choose, it may introduce **artifacts**, or changed pixels, that do not look good and were not in the original image. Blurs or halos may be introduced. Jagged edges may appear when upsampling, and moiré patterns may appear when downsampling. A **moiré pattern** is an alternating of blurred and clear areas, forming thin stripes or dots on the screen. Table 6-5 describes some of the problems.

Table 6-5 Resampling Problems

PROBLEM	DESCRIPTION	POSSIBLE SOLUTION	SAMPLE
Aliasing	jagged edges or moiré patterns (during down-scaling)	Set anti-aliasing options	
Blur	a loss of image sharpness, more visible at higher magnifications	Use the Unsharp Mask filter	
Halos	appears as a halo around edges — while a small amount may improve the perceived sharpness, a high amount does not look good	Use Defringe matting	

The Image Size Dialog Box

Photoshop shop uses the **Image Size dialog box** to make choices about the number of pixels, the document size, and the resampling method. Each setting in the Image Size dialog box makes a difference in the resulting type of file and document. Table 6-6 displays the settings and their effect. When resampling, pixels are added or subtracted during resizing. Without resampling, you are stretching or compressing the existing pixels by changing the resolution.

Table 6-6 Image Size Dialog Box Settings

SETTING	UNIT OF MEASUREMENT	EFFECT WITH RESAMPLING	EFFECT WITHOUT RESAMPLING
Pixel Dimensions	percent or pixels	The document size is adjusted in proportion to pixel dimensions, but the resolution does not change.	The pixel dimensions remain the same, but the resolution value changes to represent what the image can provide at that size.
Document Size	percent, inches, centimeters, millimeters, points, picas, or columns	The pixels are adjusted in proportion to document size, but the resolution does not change.	The pixel dimensions remain the same, but the resolution value changes to represent what the image can provide at that size.
Resolution	pixels per inch or pixels per centimeter	The pixel dimensions change and the document size remains the same.	The document size changes. The pixel dimensions remain the same.

If you make changes in the Image Size dialog box and wish to go back to the original dimensions or resolution, press and hold the ALT key before closing the dialog box. The Cancel button will change to a Reset button.

Resizing with Resampling

The current dimensions of the Toys 4color image are approximately 17 inches by 12 inches. The advertisement for the advertising flyer should be a half-page ad measuring approximately 5.5 inches wide. In addition, the printing service has specified 300 pixels per inch. The steps on the next page show how to resize the file with resampling, which means the pixels will be downsampled using the Bicubic Sharper method because it works well for reducing images while maintaining details.

More About

Scale Styles

If your image has layers with styles applied to them, select Scale Styles in the Image Size dialog box, to scale the effects in the resized image. This option is available only if you select the Constrain Proportions check box.

More About

Resampling

In the General Preferences dialog box, you can specify which default interpolation method to use whenever you resample images using the Image Size or transformation commands. The Image Size command also lets you specify an interpolation method other than the default.

To Resize the Toys 4color File with Resampling

1

- **Click Image on the menu bar and then click Image Size.**
- **When the Image Size dialog box is displayed, click the Resample Image check box to select it, if necessary.**
- **Click the Constrain Proportions check box to select it, if necessary.**
- **Click the Resample Image box arrow and then click Bicubic Sharper.**
- **If necessary, click the Width unit box arrow in the Document Size area and then click inches in the list.**
- **Type** 5.5 **in the Width box.**
- **Type** 300 **in the Resolution box.**

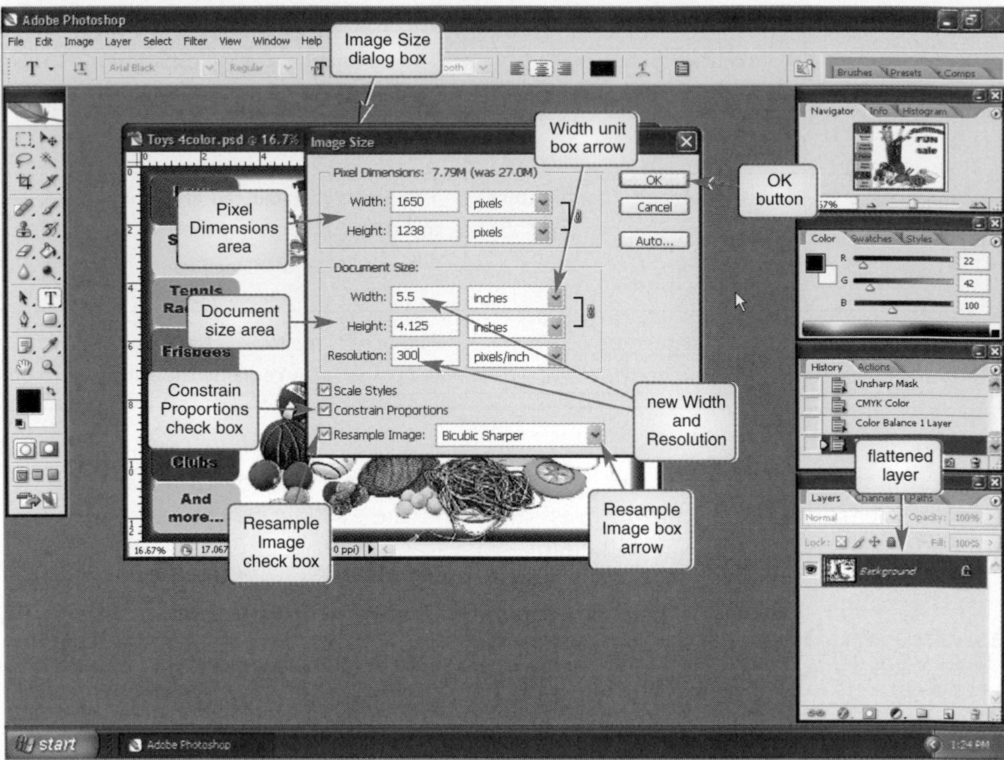

FIGURE 6-70

Notice that the Height value was completed automatically because Constrain Proportions was selected (Figure 6-70). The Pixel Dimensions settings also are adjusted.

2

- **Click the OK button.**
- **Increase the magnification to** 33.33 **percent and resize the document window to display the entire image.**

The resized image is displayed in the document window.

Printing Color Separations

When preparing your image for prepress, and working with CMYK images or images with spot color, you can print each color channel as a separate page. Photoshop also has a Split Channels command on the Channels palette menu that will split the channels into separate document windows for view and adjusting, if desired. Different service bureaus and labs require different kinds of submissions that are highly printer dependent. Even when supplying a composite, you may want to print color separations for proofing purposes. Separations help you see if your composite file will separate correctly, and help you catch other mistakes that might not be apparent by looking at the composite. The following steps illustrate how to print color separations.

To Print Color Separations

1

- **Ready the printer attached to your system.**
- **If necessary, click the document window to select it. Click File on the menu bar and then click Print with Preview.**
- **If a More options button is displayed below the Page Setup button, click it.**
- **Click the Color Handling box arrow and then click Separations in the list.**

The Print dialog box displays many choices for printing locations, scaled versions, and page setup (Figure 6-71). If you want to print the color separations in Landscape mode, click the Page Setup button and then click Landscape.

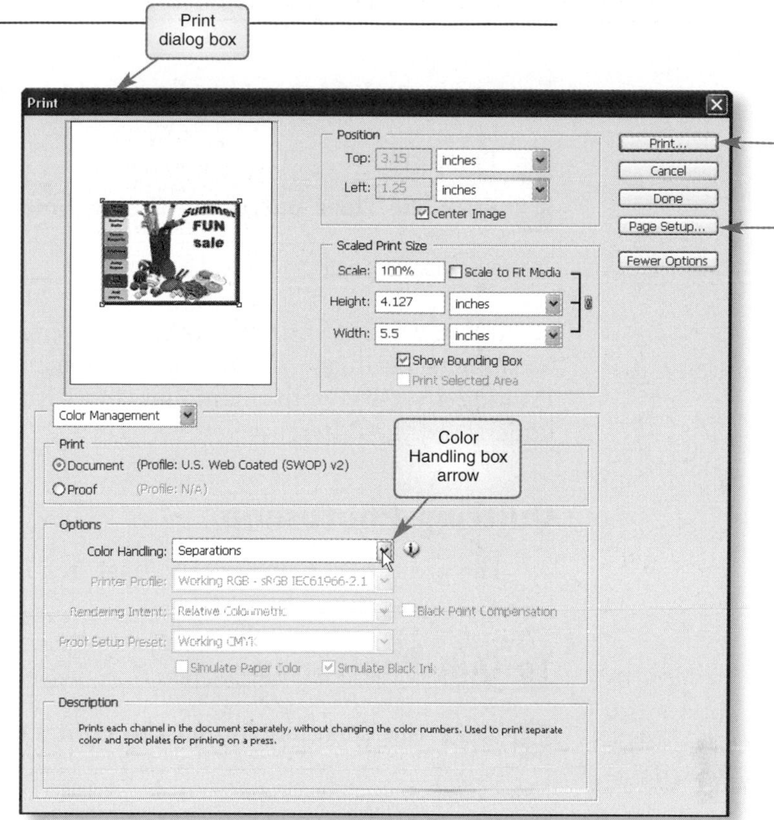

FIGURE 6-71

2

- **Click the Print button.**

The Print dialog box that Photoshop displays is printer dependent (Figure 6-72). Your dialog box may differ.

3

- **Click the OK button or the appropriate button for your printer.**

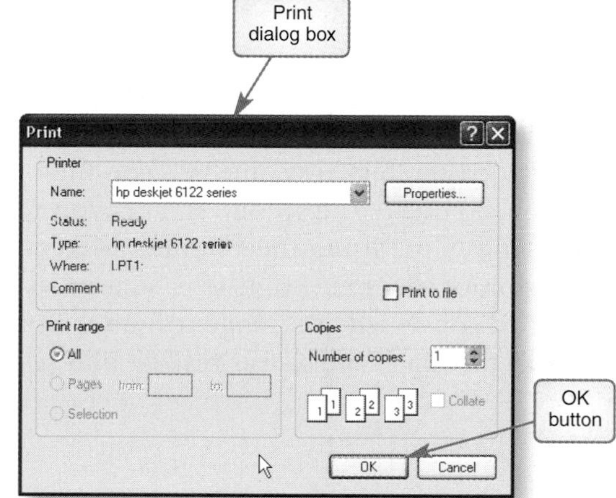

FIGURE 6-72

After a few moments, the four color separations print. Retrieve the pages from the printer.

The following steps show how to save and close the four-color version.

To Save and Close the Four-color Version

1. **Press CTRL+S.**
2. **Click the Close button on the document window title bar.**

The four-color version is saved and closed.

If you want to resize the other two versions of the toy image, one at a time, open each file, click Image Size on the Image menu, and then enter appropriate sizes. Printing a version with resampling and without resampling allows you to visually understand the difference.

Quitting Photoshop

The project is complete. The final step is to quit Photoshop.

To Quit Photoshop

1. **Click the Close button on the right side of the Photoshop title bar.**

The Photoshop window closes.

Project Summary

In this project, you used a master copy of an image as the basis for creating three new versions. First, you created a floating image with the background removed by using an alpha channel. You viewed the channels, noting the green channel contained the highest contrast. You then created a snapshot and new document based on the floating image. Then, to create the second image, you recorded an action in a new action set as you converted the image to black and white using the Channel Mixer. You learned about the different methods of conversion. Finally, for the version of the image that will be used as an advertisement, you added a colored border, shapes, and warped text. You converted the image to Lab Color mode, sharpened it, and then converted it to CMYK color. Among the prepress activities, you resized and resampled the image, and then printed color separations.

What You Should Know

Having completed this project, you should be able to perform the tasks below. The tasks are listed in the same order they were presented in this project. For a list of the buttons, menus, toolbars, and other commands introduced in this project, see the Quick Reference Summary at the back of this book and refer to the Page Number column.

Learn It Online

Instructions: To complete the Learn It Online exercises, start your browser, click the Address bar, and then enter the Web address `scsite.com/photoshop/learn`. When the Photoshop CS2 Learn It Online page is displayed, follow the instructions in the exercises below. Each exercise has instructions for printing your results, either for your own records or for submission to your instructor.

1 Project Reinforcement TF, MC, and SA

Below Photoshop Project 6, click the Project Reinforcement link. Print the quiz by clicking Print on the File menu for each page. Answer each question.

2 Flash Cards

Below Photoshop Project 6, click the Flash Cards link and read the instructions. Type 20 (or a number specified by your instructor) in the Number of playing cards text box, type your name in the Enter your Name text box, and then click the Flip Card button. When the flash card is displayed, read the question and then click the ANSWER box arrow to select an answer. Flip through Flash Cards. If your score is 15 (75%) correct or greater, click Print on the File menu to print your results. If your score is less than 15 (75%) correct, then redo this exercise by clicking the Replay button.

3 Practice Test

Below Photoshop Project 6, click the Practice Test link. Answer each question, enter your first and last name at the bottom of the page, and then click the Grade Test button. When the graded practice test is displayed on your screen, click Print on the File menu to print a hard copy. Continue to take practice tests until you score 80% or better.

4 Who Wants To Be a Computer Genius?

Below Photoshop Project 6, click the Computer Genius link. Read the instructions, enter your first and last name at the bottom of the page, and then click the PLAY button. When your score is displayed, click the PRINT RESULTS link to print a hard copy.

5 Wheel of Terms

Below Photoshop Project 6, click the Wheel of Terms link. Read the instructions, and then enter your first and last name and your school name. Click the PLAY button. When your score is displayed, right-click the score and then click Print on the shortcut menu to print a hard copy.

6 Crossword Puzzle Challenge

Below Photoshop Project 6, click the Crossword Puzzle Challenge link. Read the instructions, and then enter your first and last name. Click the SUBMIT button. Work the crossword puzzle. When you are finished, click the Submit button. When the crossword puzzle is redisplayed, click the Print Puzzle button to print a hard copy.

7 Tips and Tricks

Below Photoshop Project 6, click the Tips and Tricks link. Click a topic that pertains to Project 6. Right-click the information and then click Print on the shortcut menu. Construct a brief example of what the information relates to in Photoshop to confirm you understand how to use the tip or trick.

8 Expanding Your Horizons

Below Photoshop Project 6, click the Expanding Your Horizons link. Click a topic that pertains to Project 6. Print the information. Construct a brief example of what the information relates to in Photoshop to confirm you understand the contents of the article.

9 Search Sleuth

Below Photoshop Project 6, click the Search Sleuth link. To search for a term that pertains to this project, select a term below the Project 6 title and then use the Google search engine at google.com (or any major search engine) to display and print two Web pages that present information on the term.

10 Photoshop Online Training

Below Photoshop Project 6, click the Photoshop Online Training link. When your browser displays the Web page, click one of the Photoshop tutorials that covers one or more of the objectives listed at the beginning of the project on page PS 334. Print the first page of the tutorial before stepping through it.

Apply Your Knowledge

1 Creating an Alpha Channel

Instructions: The following steps start Photoshop and edit a file to create an alpha channel, removing a background. You will use the CD that accompanies this book, or see your instructor for information about accessing the files available with this book.

The photo you open is a picture of a fruit. You are to remove the background, make tonal adjustments, and then add the text to create the photo shown in Figure 6-73.

FIGURE 6-73

1. Start Photoshop. Perform the steps on pages PS 8 through PS 10 to customize the Workspace and set default values.
2. On the File menu, click Open. Open the file named, Fruit, from the Project06 folder.
3. On the File menu, click Save As. Save the image on your USB flash drive as a PSD file, with the file name, Fruit Edited.
4. On the Layers palette, right-click the Background layer and then click Duplicate Layer. Name the new layer, Edits. Select only the Edits layer, and hide the background by clicking its visibility icon.
5. Click the Channels palette and then, one at a time, view each channel independent of the others. Decide which channel has the most contrast to facilitate removing the background.

(continued)

Creating an Alpha Channel *(continued)*

6. First, to select the background so only it is visible:
   a. Use the Magic Wand tool with a Tolerance setting of 20. Click many times to select the different shades of color in the background. You will not be able to select everything.
   b. If some of the fruit or bowl becomes selected, select the Elliptical Marquee tool. On the options bar, click the Subtract from selection button. Carefully select the fruit or bowl, which will remove it from the background selection.
   c. Select the Rectangular Marquee tool. On the options bar, click the Add to selection button. Carefully draw large rectangles on the four edges of the photo to add the remaining pixels to the section. Do not include the fruit or bowls. If some of the plant becomes selected, you will remove it from the selection in the next step.
7. Next, to create the alpha channel:
   a. ALT+click the Create new channel button on the Channels palette status bar.
   b. When Photoshop displays the New Channel dialog box, name the channel, Background Mask. Click the Selected Areas option button. Click the OK button.
   c. When the alpha channel displays the image all in white, right-click the selection, and then click Select Inverse on the shortcut menu.
   d. Select the Paint Bucket tool and then fill the selection with black. Press CTRL+D to remove the selection.
   e. Use the Brush tool to paint with black any areas of the fruit, bowls, or plant that are not black. Use the bracket keys to change the size of the brush as necessary.
   f. Select the Eraser tool and erase any remaining background spots, so only the fruit, bowls, and plant are black.
8. To delete the background:
   a. Select the Magic Wand tool and then click the white area.
   b. In the Channels palette, click the RGB composite channel.
   c. Press the DELETE key.
   d. Press CTRL+D to deselect. If some areas of background still remain, select the alpha channel, make the channel with the highest contrast visible, and then paint them with white.
9. Click the RGB composite channel, if necessary. On the History palette, right-click the current state and then click New Snapshot. Name the snapshot, Fruit with Background.
10. Using the Layer menu, flatten the image. Discard any hidden layers. Convert the image to Lab color. On the Channels palette, access the Lightness channel. Press CTRL+L to access the Levels dialog box. Drag both the black and white sliders toward the middle until a strong contrast is displayed. Click the composite channel and verify your adjustments. If you do not like the changes, click the previous state on the History palette and try again.
11. Convert the image to CMYK. Click Image on the menu bar, point to Adjustments, and then click Channel Mixer. Select the Black channel and drag the Black slider to the left until the avocados are lighter. Make any other Channel Mixer changes that cause the colors to look more vivid.
12. To create the text:
   a. Click the Horizontal Type Tool (T) button in the toolbox.
   b. On the options bar, choose the Harlow Solid Italic font, or a similar font on your system, using Figure 6-73 as a guide. Choose a font size of 100. Choose Smooth in the list of anti-aliasing methods. Choose a gray font color. Your alignment may different if you use a different font.
   c. Drag a text box that covers the entire image.
   d. On the options bar, click the Right align text button. Type `Have you` and then press the ENTER key twice.

Apply Your Knowledge

   e. Click the Left align text button. Type `eaten` and then press the ENTER key three times.
   f. Click the Right align text button. Type `your five today?` to complete the text.
   g. Click the Commit any current edits button.
13. Save the image with the name, Fruit Complete.
14. To resize the image for printing on a desktop printer:
   a. On the Image menu, click Image Size.
   b. Click the Resample Image check box to deselect it.
   c. Type `9` in the Width box.
   d. Click the OK button.
15. Ready your printer. Print color separations in Landscape mode and turn them in to your instructor.
16. Quit Photoshop without saving the file.

1 Creating Versions

Problem: Your local art gallery is planning an exhibit of a collection of vases donated by the family of a local celebrity. In preparation for marketing the event, the gallery would like you to add a background to a photograph of the vases and then resize the image. You decide to try three different resampling methods and see which one prints the best image. The edited photo displays in Figure 6-74.

FIGURE 6-74

(continued)

Creating Versions *(continued)*

Instructions:

1. Start Photoshop. Perform the customization steps found on pages PS 8 through PS 10.
2. Open the file, Vases, from the Project06 folder on the CD that accompanies this book.
3. Click the Save As command on the File menu. Type `Vases Edited` as the file name. Browse to your USB flash drive storage device. Click the Save button. If Photoshop displays a dialog box, click the OK button.
4. Use the Navigator palette to zoom the photo to 16.67% magnification, if necessary.
5. To add a decorative background:
   a. Select the Paint Bucket tool. On the options bar, click the Set source for fill area box arrow, and then click Pattern to change from the foreground color.
   b. Click the Pattern Picker button. When the Pattern Picker is displayed, click its menu button and then click Color Paper in the list. Choose to append the patterns.
   c. When the new patterns are displayed, scroll down if necessary, and then click Blue Crepe.
   d. In the document window, click the transparent background area to apply the pattern.
6. Click Image on the menu bar, point to Mode, and then click CMYK Color. If Photoshop asks to merge layers, click the Merge button.
7. Press CTRL+S to save the image again.
8. Create a snapshot using the History palette menu. Name the snapshot, Before Resizing.
9. To resize the image using the Nearest Neighbor interpolation:
   a. Click Image on the menu bar and then click Image Size.
   b. When Photoshop displays the Image Size dialog box, click the Resample Image check box to select it. Click the Resample Image box arrow and then click Nearest Neighbor in the list. Type `10` in the Width box.
   c. Click the OK button.
   d. Ready the printer. Print a copy of the resized image. On the back of the printout, write the words, Nearest Neighbor.
10. On the History palette, scroll up and then click the Before Resizing snapshot.
11. To resize the image using the Bilinear interpolation method:
    a. Click Image on the menu bar and then click Image Size.
    b. When Photoshop displays the Image Size dialog box, click the Resample Image check box to select it. Click the Resample Image box arrow and then click Bilinear in the list. Type `10` in the Width box.
    c. Click the OK button.
    d. Ready the printer. Print a copy of the resized image. On the back of the printout, write the word, Bilinear.
12. On the History palette, scroll up if necessary, and then click the Before Resizing snapshot.
13. To resize the image using the Bicubic interpolation method:
    a. Click Image on the menu bar and then click Image Size.
    b. When Photoshop displays the Image Size dialog box, click the Resample Image check box to select it. Click the Resample Image box arrow and then click Bicubic in the list. Type `10` in the Width box.
    c. Click the OK button.
    d. Ready the printer. Print a copy of the resized image. On the back of the printout, write the word, Bicubic.
14. Examine the three printouts. Write a paragraph describing why you think one of the printouts is better than the others. Turn in all three printouts and the paragraph to your instructor.
15. Quit Photoshop without saving the resized image.

In the Lab

2 Using Predefined Actions

Problem: Your cousin wants you to use her senior picture to create an invitation to a graduation open house. You decide to investigate Photoshop's predefined actions to see if there is a specialized frame that you can apply to the photo. The finished product is displayed in Figure 6-75.

FIGURE 6-75

Instructions:

1. Start Photoshop. Perform the customization steps found on pages PS 8 through PS 10.
2. Open the file, Senior Picture, from the Project06 folder on the CD that accompanies this book.
3. Click the Save As command on the File menu. Type `Invitation` as the file name. Browse to your USB flash drive storage device. Click the Save button. If Photoshop displays a dialog box, click the OK button.
4. Select the Elliptical Marquee tool. Drag a large selection that encompasses the face and neck of the girl. Without clicking anywhere else, drag the selection to center it. Some of the selection may overlap the top and bottom edges.
5. Click the Actions palette tab. If the Frames action set is not listed, click the palette menu button, and then click Frames. If necessary, click the left pointing triangle of the Frames action set to display the actions stored in the set. Scroll down and click the Vignette (selection) action.
6. Click the Play selection button on the Actions palette status bar. When the action pauses to request a feather selection, type `5` in the Feather Radius box. Click the OK button.
7. When the action is complete, click the Layers palette tab. Select the layer of the vignette itself and then select the Move tool. Drag the layer to the right of the document window.

(continued)

Using Predefined Actions *(continued)*

8. Click the Magic Wand Tool (W) button in the toolbox and select the white areas around the vignette. Use the Color Palette to choose a beige color. Click the Paint Bucket Tool (G) button and fill the white areas with beige.
9. Click the Horizontal Type Tool (T) button in the toolbox.
10. To adjust the text settings:
    a. On the options bar, select the Lucida Handwriting font family or a similar font.
    b. Set the font style to Italic.
    c. Set the font size to 24.
    d. Set the anti-aliasing method to Smooth.
    e. Click the Center text button. Choose a black font color.
    f. Click the Toggle the Character and Paragraph palettes button. When the palettes are displayed, click the Paragraph tab, and then click the Hyphenate check box to deselect it.
11. Drag a text box that fills the left side of the image. In the text box, type `You are invited to a graduation open house, Saturday, June 7th, 2008` and then click the Commit any current edits button on the options bar.
12. When you are finished, use the Flatten Image command to flatten all of the layers into the background.
13. Save the flattened image on your storage device with the file name, Invitation.
14. E-mail your instructor with the Invitation file as an attachment, or see your instructor for another way to submit this assignment.

3 Creating an Attention Getter

Problem: Brookside Trophy and Awards is publishing a flier to attract new business. They have asked you to create a simple attention getter that they can use to advertise their group discounts. The attention getter is displayed in Figure 6-76.

Instructions:

1. Start Photoshop. Perform the customization steps found on pages PS 8 through PS 10.
2. Open the File menu, click New. When Photoshop displays the New dialog box, change the width and height to 2 inches. Set the resolution to 300 ppi. Change the color mode to CMYK and the background to white. Click the OK button.
3. Click the Save As command on the File menu. Type `Attention Getter` as the file name. If necessary, click the Format box arrow and choose PSD in the list. Browse to your USB flash drive storage device. Click the Save button. If Photoshop displays a Format Options dialog box, click the OK button.
4. To create a border, select the entire image. On the Select menu, point to Modify, and then click Border. Choose a 30 pixel border.

FIGURE 6-76

In the Lab

5. When the border selection is displayed, double-click the foreground color in the toolbox. Select a gold color. Click the Paint Bucket Tool (G) button in the toolbox and then click the selection. Press CTRL+D to deselect.
6. Click the current shape tool. On the options bar, click the Custom Shape Tool button. Click the Shape Picker button. When the Shape Picker is displayed, click its menu button and then click Shapes. When Photoshop displays a dialog box, choose to append the new shapes. Scroll down and select a starburst shape similar to that shown in Figure 6-76.
7. On the options bar, click the Set color for new layer button. When the Color Picker dialog box is displayed, select a red color.
8. Drag the shape to fill the area within the border.
9. In the toolbox, select the Horizontal Type tool. On the options bar, select the Times New Roman font family, the Bold Italic font style, a font size of 14, and the Sharp anti-aliasing method. Click the Center button. Click the Set the text color button. When the Color Picker dialog box is displayed, sample the gold border. Click the OK button.
10. In the document window, drag a text box that fills the shape. Type `Group` and then press the ENTER key. Type `Discounts` to complete the text.
11. Click the Create warped text button on the options bar. When the Warp Text dialog box is displayed, choose the Bulge style. Select a 74% bend. Click the OK button.
12. When you are finished, use the Flatten Image command to flatten all of the layers into the background.
13. Press CTRL+S to save the image again.
14. Print the image and turn it in to your instructor.
15. For extra credit, open an application such as Microsoft Publisher or Adobe InDesign and create a new file. Choose a flyer or announcement template. Use the application's Insert Picture command to insert a copy of the attention getter into the document. Print a copy for your instructor.

Cases and Places

The difficulty of these case studies varies:
■ are the least difficult and ■■ are the most difficult. The last exercise is a group exercise.

1 ■ A wedding planner wants to use a picture of a tulip on her business cards. The tulip is in full color, but her business cards are going to use brown spot color on ivory paper. Open the Tulip image that is located in the Project06 folder. Save the image on your storage device with the name, Tulip Edited. Use an alpha channel to remove the background. Flatten the image. Convert the image to grayscale and then convert the image to duotone. When the Duotone dialog box is displayed, double-click the Color Picker and choose a brown color. Type `brown` in the Name box. Click the OK button. Convert the image to CMYK color. Save the image again and then print a copy.

2 ■ Open any image in Photoshop. On the Actions palette, click the palette menu button. Choose one of the stored action sets, such as Image Effects. When the stored action set is displayed on the Actions palette, if necessary open the set to display the actions. On a piece of paper, write down the name of the first action. Click the Play recording button. On the paper, write a short description of what happened to the photo. If the action does not play, try to figure out why. For example, if the action has the word, selection, in parentheses, you first must make a selection before playing the action. After writing down your description, open the action itself by clicking the right-pointing triangle. Scroll through the steps in the palette and compare that to your description. On the History palette, click the original file thumbnail and then choose another action to play. Repeat the process until you have tried five different actions. Turn in your paper to your instructor.

3 ■■ Your school wants to use its name and address in many pieces of artwork, such as the banner at the top of their Web page, on stationery, on promotional pieces, and on a student resume template. If you did not create a Personal Actions set in the project, create one for this exercise. Record a new action named, School Address, which displays a text box with the school's name and address. Use an Arial font with a font size of 14. Choose a font color that matches one of your school colors. Open one of your previous Photoshop assignments, load the action set if necessary, and then play back the action.

4 ■■ Choose a digital photo that you have recently taken. Open it in Photoshop and then save it with the name, Master Copy. Create an Edits layer. Use the techniques learned in this project to create three versions of the photo: one in black and white, one with background images removed, and one in CMYK Color mode. Use snapshots to store each version in the Master Copy. Choose one of the three versions and then add a decorative shape with text. Print all three versions.

5 ■■ **Working Together** Graphic designers who have art skills, and those who can make tonal and color adjustments, are in demand in the marketplace. To practice these skills, your instructor has divided you into teams for a group project. Ask each member of your team to bring in a digital picture of their choice. As a group, examine the pictures and select the one that needs the most color management. Distribute a copy to each member, via e-mail or a class Web server. Then, individually have each member make color adjustments using the Channel Mixer and other tools on the Adjustments submenu. Choose the photo with the best tonal adjustments and submit it to your instructor.

ADOBE Photoshop CS2

Designing Basic Layouts Using Color and Typography

Objectives

You will have mastered the material in this special feature when you can:

- Collect graphic design layout samples for analysis
- Identify the components of a graphic design layout
- Understand the difference between a static and dynamic layout
- Explain the importance of visual hierarchy
- Identify a bleed
- Design a layout, with consideration to background, using multiple elements
- Differentiate between a one-, two-, and four-color job
- Understand the difference between a halftone and duotone
- Describe differences between CMYK, RGB, PANTONE, and Web color
- Select job appropriate colors and identify basic characteristics of letterforms
- Use the terminology related to type including font, point size, and line space
- Determine appropriate typographic choices for a graphic design

Developing Design and Layout Skills

Developing skills in graphic design layout takes research and practice. Research involves being aware of the designs that exist all around you, as well as collecting and documenting those designs. Practice involves understanding basic components and options for a layout, and applying variations to your layout designs.

Researching Design Layouts

Researching design layouts is easy and fun, if you know what you are looking for. Nearly all designers keep a collection of examples that includes both appealing and unappealing designs. A collection can include anything. You might collect: two-dimensional printed materials, such as brochures, magazines, and ads; and three-dimensional items, such as CD liners, cereal boxes, and clothing tags. Multimedia designs, such as your favorite Web sites, TV advertisements, or movie credits, can be documented by keeping a list of titles and topics. Because graphic design is everywhere, resources for good and bad designs are unlimited.

To analyze a layout, designers try to identify what part of the design formed the initial impression. Often it is the way the image, the topic, or the color is used. For example, the brochure cover in Figure SF 2-1a immediately is appealing because of the image of the dog. Bright colors and contrast also contribute to making the cover eye catching and effective. Figure SF 2-1b shows the inside of the brochure. Typographic elements align with images according to a grid, providing visual unity from panel to panel. Balance exists between the photos and text.

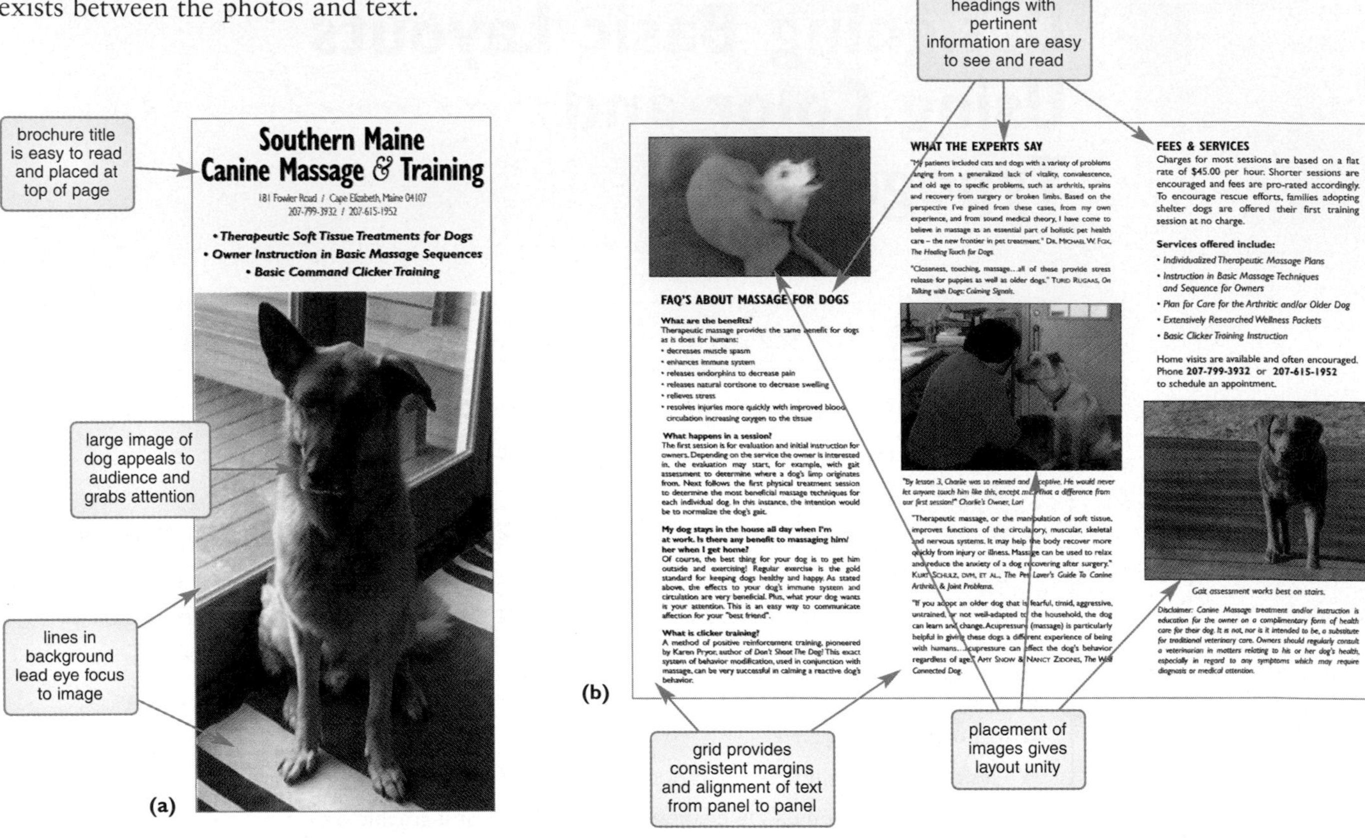

FIGURE SF 2-1

Developing Design Layout Techniques

All layouts evolve from arranging visual images on a surface or background. To begin, you will be most effective if you consider three essential components of a layout. The three components are the background, the image, and the message. The background, which is either paper or screen, displays the image. The image is referred to as the object, or element, on the background. The message is the overall meaning implied by the whole layout. Table SF 2-1 lists the three parts of a layout.

Table SF 2-1 Three Parts of a Layout

PART	DESCRIPTION
Background	color and texture of a plane, or surface, such as paper or computer screen display
Image	any object on the background including photographs, illustrations, graphics, and typographic elements
Message	overall, implied meaning of the layout perceived by the combination of image, color, and/or text

A background sets the overall tone — sometimes referred to as the **look and feel** of a design. The **figure-ground relationship** describes how an image is placed on a background, thereby creating a visual relationship between the image and its surroundings. The image, depending on its color, scale, contrast, and placement, either stands out or is absorbed by the background. For example, an object centered on a white or light colored solid background floats within the frame. The visual focus therefore is on the object itself, creating simple visual harmony as illustrated in Figure SF 2-2a. In Figure SF 2-2b, the same object, centered on a black or dark colored background, creates more visual contrast and a strong figure-ground relationship because the background then becomes a defined visual element, interacting with the object itself. When the background has texture, as in Figure SF 2-2c, even more visual tension or contrast is apparent. Designers determine whether the objective is to create visual contrast, or to create harmony between the figure and ground. It is important that the background supports the message and is not so busy as to distract from the communication.

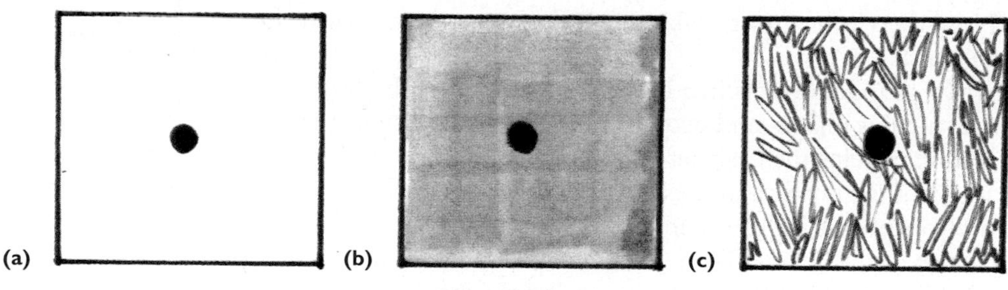

FIGURE SF 2-2

The position of an object on a surface is the next critical decision that designers must make in developing a layout. Figure SF 2-3 uses a basic grid to illustrate some of the many ways an object can be placed in a simple layout. You learned in Special Feature 1 that placing an object in the center of a page produces a static, stable, and symmetrical balance. Moving an object away from the center engages the viewer because the look and feel becomes asymmetrically balanced and visually dynamic. The placement variations are endless.

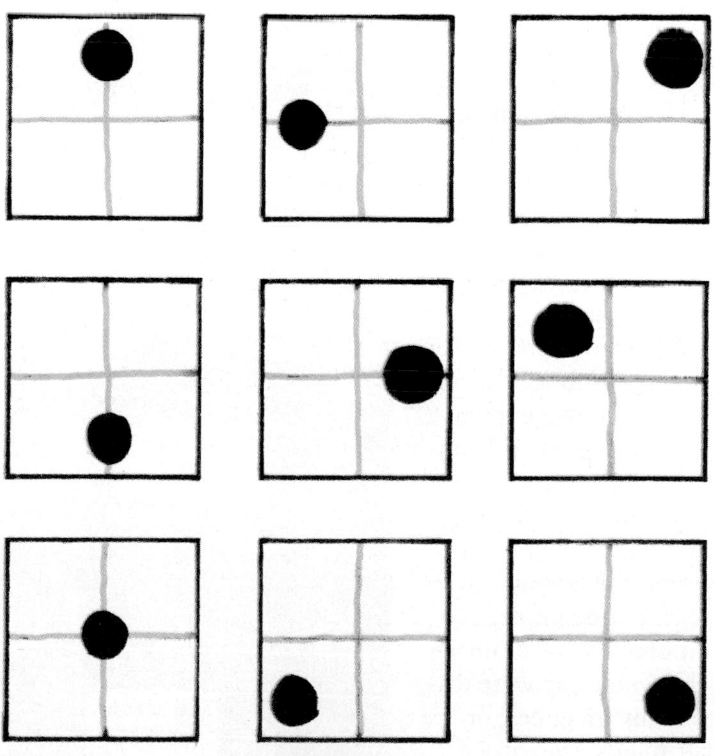

FIGURE SF 2-3

When you add an additional object to a layout, whether it is another image or text graphic, there is an automatic and inherent relationship created between these two objects. The relationship between the objects and the background then becomes secondary. Figure SF 2-4 illustrates how the visual focus shifts to a dynamic relationship between the two objects on the surface of the background. Two images on a page force the viewer or audience to engage thought and derive meaning from the layout.

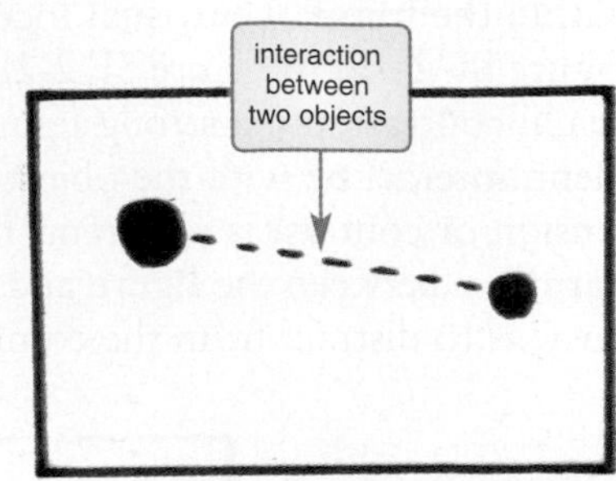

FIGURE SF 2-4

Adding a third object creates an even more dynamic relationship as shown in Figure SF 2-5. Now the viewer must make a visual connection between the three images on the surface.

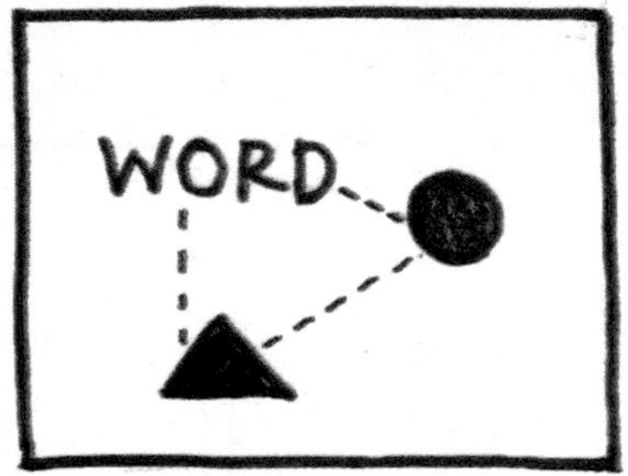

FIGURE SF 2-5 Interaction Between Three Objects

When there are two or more objects in a layout, hierarchy must be considered. **Hierarchy** refers to laying out images and text according to what is most and least important. Visual hierarchy helps the designer determine the placement, size, and color of images in a layout. Figure SF 2-6 uses abstract shapes to explain the importance of hierarchy. Automatically and immediately your eye first sees the large red circle at the top of the layout. Then, you notice the other shapes. The poster in Figure SF 2-7 is dominated by a large image and six smaller images. Because this poster is advertising a student art show, the designer wants to catch the viewer's attention with the art. The artwork dominates the page. The text at the top of the poster could be considered another image. While secondary to the images, it is still important. Placing the text at the top of the page ensures its visibility. The least important information is small and placed at the bottom.

large red image is noticed first

secondary, less important information is placed smaller and lower on background

FIGURE SF 2-6

When an image is placed to the very edge of the page, it is referred to as a **bleed** because the image is cropped off the page. Bleeding an image is a useful design layout technique because it encourages viewer interaction. The viewer must complete the whole image in their mind, suggested from the portion they can actually see. Bleeding an image also makes maximum use of the layout area, literally freeing space within the layout to position other images or text. For example, Figure SF 2-8 shows a portion of a car — an image that works just as well as if the whole car were displayed. The audience automatically imagines, or pictures, the whole car in their minds' eye. Space becomes available for placing text to complement or reinforce the overall message. In addition, bleeding an image portrays motion, giving the layout visual dynamics. If an image bleeds on the right side of the page, the viewer imagines it entering the

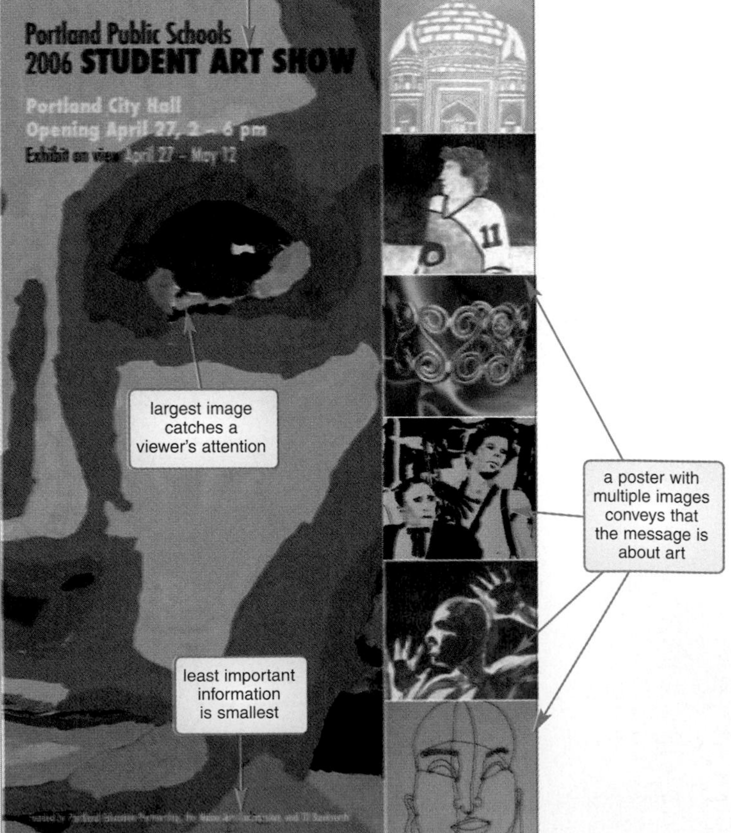

FIGURE SF 2-7

space; whereas if the image is placed on the left, it may be perceived to be leaving the page.

The mere act of bleeding a single image can convey a mood, or message. Compare the placement of the images in Figures SF 2-9a and SF 2-9b. The centered image layout in Figure SF 2-9a is static and complete. Bleeding the image, as shown in Figure SF 2-9b, conveys a sense of mystery — something hidden and incomplete. The audience is encouraged to participate by using their imagination to complete the image of a whole cat.

Creating an effective design layout takes practice. Repeated effort is required to gain experience. Most designers begin their design layouts with simple grids and arrangements that are proven to work. As projects become more complex, such as those with multiple images, different backgrounds, and text elements, you will be able to build your layouts on the foundation of information learned in this section.

FIGURE SF 2-8

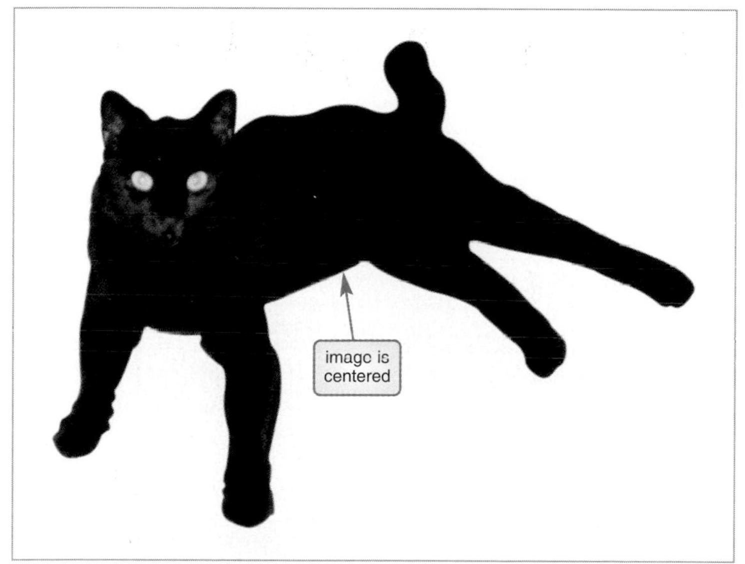

(a)

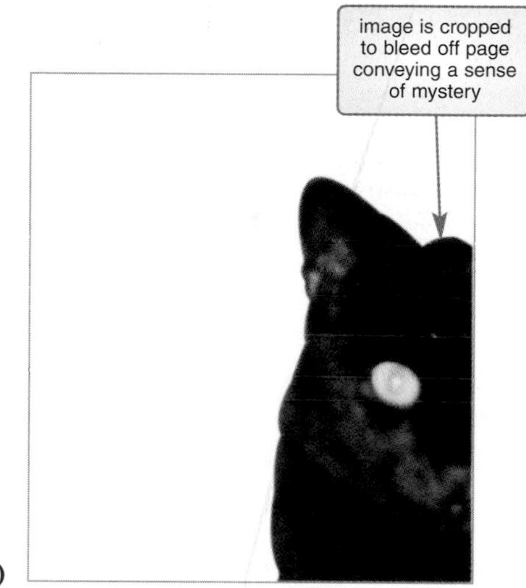

(b)

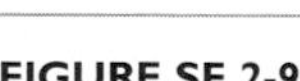

FIGURE SF 2-9

Designing Effectively with Color

Color as a design element has technical and aesthetic characteristics. When beginning to develop a design concept for a client, it is important to identify the final product from the start, because this determines how best to incorporate color. Many decisions must be made. Color choice is based on the needs of the client, the message you are trying to convey, the cost or project budget, and the available reproduction or printing processes. Color combinations ideally help reinforce the intended message. Designers must consider all technical aspects when selecting color for a project.

You will learn about the technical considerations of color for print and the Web, followed by the aesthetic considerations, such as selecting appropriate color for any given design project.

Technical Considerations of Color for Print

Nearly all printed design uses one color, two colors, or four colors of ink. A **one-color** job, often abbreviated as **1c**, means that a single, specified ink color is applied to the page. The color can be black or any other color. Figure SF 2-10 illustrates a one-color job.

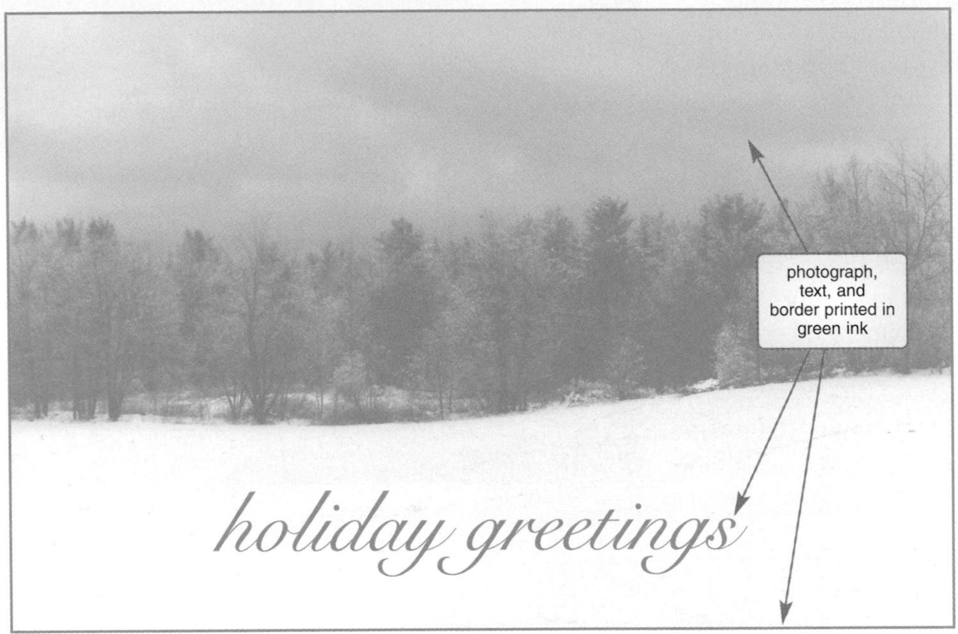

FIGURE SF 2-10

A **two-color** job, or **2c**, means that any two specified colors are used for printing, as illustrated in Figure SF-11.

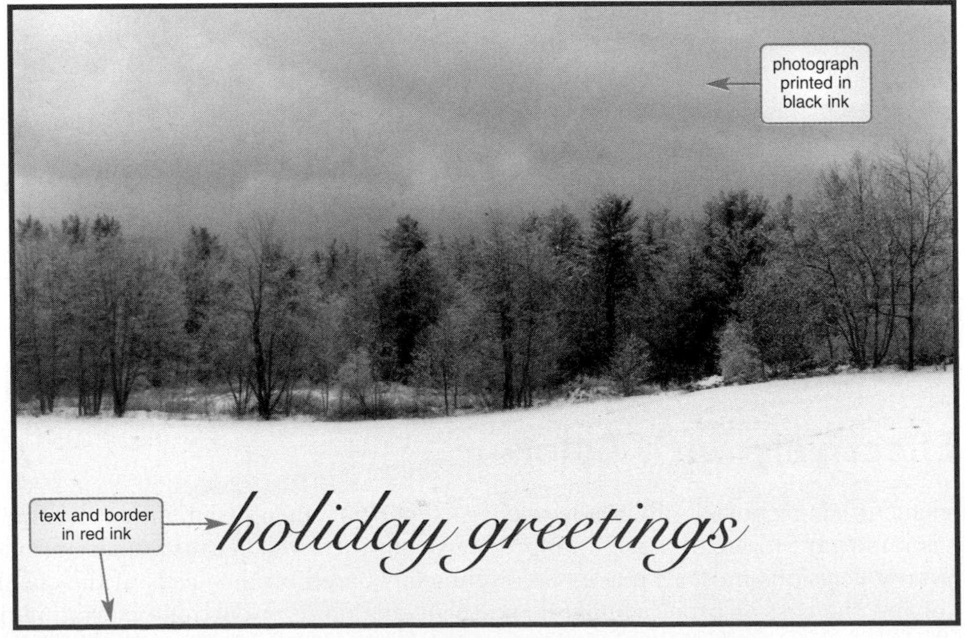

FIGURE SF 2-11

When printing one or two color jobs, ink typically is selected from a range of PANTONE® colors. **PANTONE** is the most widely used ink color system in the graphic design and printing industry. The PANTONE color system, sometimes referred to as the **PANTONE MATCHING SYSTEM®**, standardizes solid ink color, also known as **spot color** by ascribing a number which corresponds with each color. Printing companies and graphic designers use PANTONE Guides that show the range of selection of spot colors with their corresponding color number. Figure SF 2-12 shows a page from a PANTONE swatch book.

A job that is printed in **full color** uses the **four-color process**. The four process colors always are referred to as CMYK, which represents cyan, magenta, yellow, and black. **Four-color process** refers to the ink colors used in offset printing. In **offset printing**, a full color image is scanned and separated into dots of varied percentages of cyan, magenta, yellow, and black. The separations are referred to as **color separations**, or in design vernacular as color seps. During the printing process, the separate colors are printed on top of one another to create the illusion of full color. Figures SF 2-13a, SF 2-13b, SF 2-13c, and SF 2-13d display the four color separations used to reproduce the photograph in Figure SF 2-14. If you look closely at the photograph through a very strong magnifying glass, you should be able to discern the dots of process colors that make up the printed photo.

Halftones are used to print photographs in black or any other single color. When an original photograph is scanned, all the light and dark areas, and all the shades of gray in between, are translated into dots. The dots are printed close together, or far apart, to create the illusion of tonal value.

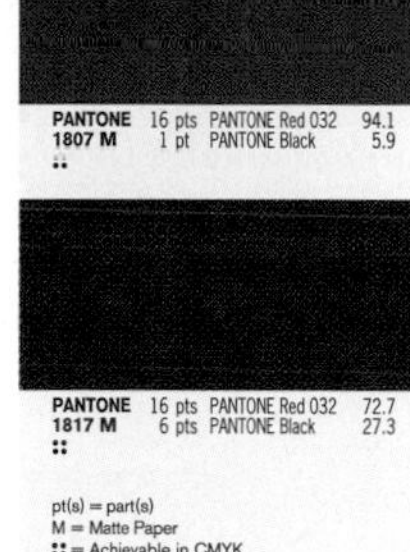

FIGURE SF 2-12

(a) Cyan Separation

(b) Magenta Separation

(c) Yellow Separation

(d) Black Separation

FIGURE SF 2-13

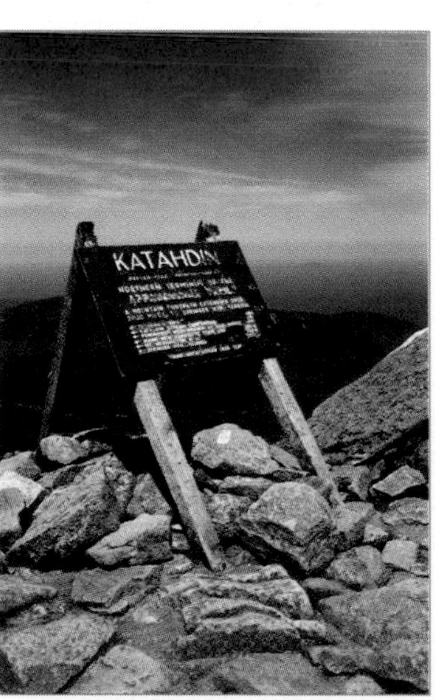

FIGURE SF 2-14

Figure SF 2-15 is a black and white photograph converted to a halftone. Figure SF 2-16 shows a **duotone** that works like a halftone, but uses two layers of dots to reproduce a black and white photo in two colors. Duotones add depth and dimension to an image and have the advantage of being less expensive to print than full color.

FIGURE SF 2-15 Halftone

FIGURE SF 2-16 Duotone using PANTONE 370 and PANTONE 458

Technical Considerations of Color for the Web

The 216 **Web safe color palette** used in Web design contains a standard selection of colors that should appear consistently on any display. These colors could be considered the screen equivalent of PANTONE colors, but with a much more limited choice of selections. Because computer monitors create color using the RGB color mode, the range is not as broad as colors that can be achieved by mixing actual ink. To see the selection of Web safe colors, search online for the phrase, Web safe color palette. After taking time to design your Web site carefully, you want to make sure it appears as you intended. Using Web safe colors especially is important when color accuracy is critical, for instance when displaying a logo or ensuring that contrast between background and foreground is discernable.

The perception of color varies according to individuals and the equipment used to achieve color output. Monitors, printers, and printing processes all affect the outcome of color. You never can assume that what you see on the screen will match the printed outcome, because a monitor translates color into the RGB mode; it then is converted to CMYK for print output. A computer printout also will vary in color depending on the printing device. Different devices, such as laser or ink-jet printers, will print the exact same color differently because they use different technical reproduction processes for printing the image on the page. Additionally, color can vary dramatically depending on the paper you choose. It is not a perfect world. Perception is different among equipment and people. You should design with this in mind.

Color Design Considerations

Color is one of the most effective, visual design elements because it catches the viewer's attention. For example, printing an office memo on bright yellow paper will ensure that it is highly visible among a stack of white pages. Color also has the ability to evoke an emotional response. A sign printed with the words, WATCH OUT, in red letters likely will make the viewer take the message more seriously than if the words were only in black.

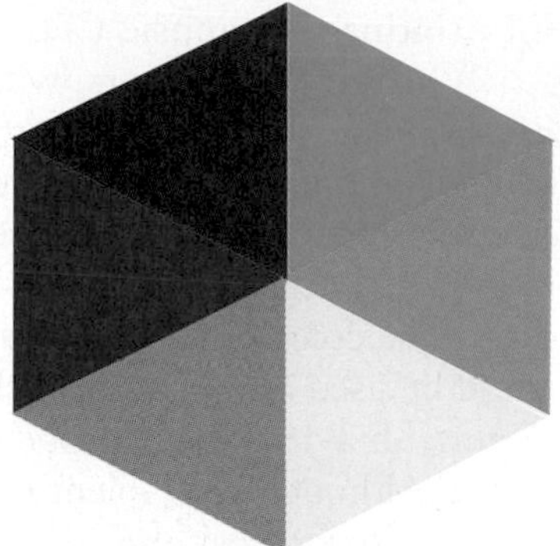

FIGURE SF 2-17

Designers must consider critical aspects of color such as contrast, visibility, readability, mood, and look and feel. When selecting color, you should research your intended audience. For example, some cultures consider certain colors to be lucky or unlucky. Adults tend to like earth tones, while children find primary colors visually more attractive. Marketing research has found that certain color combinations have a psychological effect on the viewer. For example, red and yellow prove to stimulate hunger. That is why many popular fast food franchises often use red and yellow in the design of their graphic identity. The color model is shown in Figure SF 2-17. **Complementary colors**, or colors that are opposite one another on the color model, tend to create good visual contrast.

A background sets the overall tone of a design. An object placed on a background creates a feeling between the image and its surroundings. The layouts in Figures SF 2-18b, and SF 2-18c place the same image in exactly the same place — only the background is changed. That change, however, affects the overall feeling of each layout.

(a)

(b)

(c)

FIGURE SF 2-18

Figure SF-18a would provide a good visual image for a rock concert poster. The guitar is on a dark blue background, which suggests an older audience. The dark background somewhat absorbs the image, the same way one might become absorbed in music at a concert. The contrast of the image against the solid dark background suggests drama and also evokes the idea of a stage. The background would provide good contrast for placing a minimum of light colored text, which could be readable at a distance.

Figure SF 2-18b shows the same image on a light background. This background would be good for an advertisement because the guitar stands out; dark colored, more detailed text would be very readable.

Figure SF 2-18c shows the same image again, but on a textured background. The image and background are equally busy visually, creating active visual tension. Any text on this background would be difficult to read.

Figure SF 2-18c only would be appropriate if no text were required. Sometimes more active visuals without text are appropriate for a particular project. For example, this image would be suitable as a graphic without words, for printing on a music CD.

When selecting colors, whether you are using two or four colors, you need to consider the cost and the message. For example, an annual report for an insurance company with a large budget would be reproduced in full color to impress and report to investors. A fundraising brochure might be printed in two colors to save money, so the budget goes to the actual cause. A newsletter for a preschool needs to be distributed frequently and produced inexpensively. Therefore, it would best be designed in black and white. The following example explains how you would determine color as it relates to cost. Figures SF 2-19a, SF 2-19b, and SF 2-19c show a photograph of radishes that could be used to advertise fresh produce for a farmer's market. The look and feel of the image in black and white (Figure SF 2-19a), in duotone (Figure SF 2-19b), or in four-color reproduction (Figure SF 2-19c) is dramatically different. Although your client may have a restricted budget, you would recommend using four colors because fresh produce looks most appealing when it is reproduced in full color. Although the client is spending more on advertising print cost, the product will be displayed more attractively and therefore will be more visible. The extra cost would be justified by the potential increase in sales.

(a) Black-and-white Image of Radishes

(b) Duotone of Radishes using black and PANTONE 1788C

(c) Four-color Radishes

FIGURE SF 2-19

The Art of Typography

Matthew Carter, a contemporary type designer and typographer, has said of type, "There is nothing so visible that is so invisible." Type is everywhere. People take for granted the letterforms that communicate everything from ingredients on labels and numerals on a clock face, to signage and newspapers. Type is the foundation of the way we communicate visually.

Type is more than words on a page; individually each character can be considered an image as well. Letterforms are essentially symbols. Each character has a meaning and associated sound that is understood by the reader. For example, an ampersand symbol, &, is generally understood to symbolize the word, and; the numeral 3 represents the quantity and number three.

Typography is the art of arranging letters and words. Graphic designers give thoughtful and practiced consideration to the use of letterforms and text. The best way to develop typography skills is through practice. It is essential that you have an understanding of the fundamentals of type, which includes physical and perceptual characteristics of letterforms.

Physical Characteristics of Letterforms

The physical characteristics of letterforms include the font, style, and classifications. The font is the name of a typeface, for example, Helvetica or Times New Roman. The text of this book is set in the font Sabon. Variations of a font are described as styles, such as italic, bold, or condensed. Nearly all typefaces fall into the category of serif, sans serif, script, or display. Table SF 2-2 defines the various classifications of fonts. **Serif** type is identified by the end strokes on each character. **Sans serif,** literally without serif, defines type without end strokes or flourishes. **Script** covers a broad range of fonts that look like handwriting. **Display** type is usually ornamental, and is a type that does not fall into any of the other categories. The different classifications are illustrated in Figure SF 2-20.

Table SF 2-2 General Classifications of Fonts

FONT	DESCRIPTION
Serif	type that has an end stroke
Sans serif	type without an end stroke
Script	slanted type that mimics handwriting
Display	decorative type that is not serif, sans-serif, or script

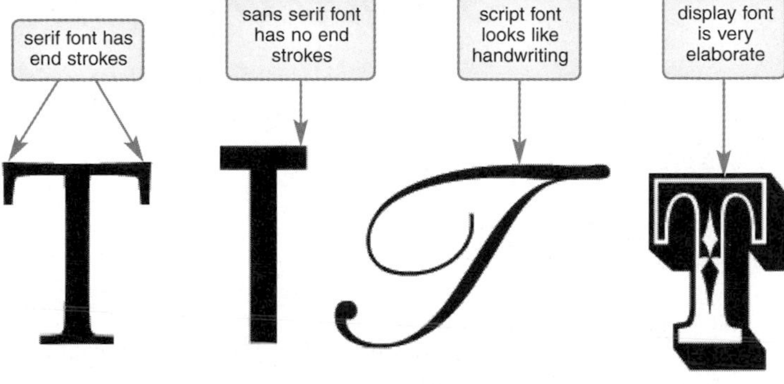

Figure SF 2-20

Type Measurement and Appearance

Fonts have physical characteristics that are determined by the graphic designer or typographer. These are listed in Table SF 2-3.

Table SF 2-3 Physical Characteristics of Type

CHARACTERISTIC	DESCRIPTION
Point size	size of the letter
Leading or line space	space between lines of type
Line length	length of a line of type
Kerning	space between two individual characters
Tracking	space adjustment between all the characters in the selected word, line, or paragraph
Placement	position of type in relationship to its surface — flush left or right, centered, or justified

Picas and points are units of measurement used by graphic designers, typographers, and printers. One pica is equal to one inch. A pica has 12 points. Type is measured in **point size**, which relates to the size of the letter. **Leading** (pronounced led-ing), or **line space**, is the measurement from the base of one line to the base of the next line, and is measured in points. Line space is as visually important as the lines of text. Line space either can unify or separate the information in a paragraph. **Line length,** the length of a paragraph or single line, or lines of type, is usually measured in inches. Line length is determined by extremes — the longest and shortest line of type that can fit within the grid.

Kerning and **tracking** describe the space between characters. Kerning usually refers to adjusting the space between individual characters, while tracking adjusts the space between all the characters in a word, line, or paragraph of text. Paragraphs of text are sometimes referred to as **body copy**, or a **text block**. The placement of type on a page or surface is either centered, justified, flush left, or flush right. Placement concerns individual lines of type such as a headline, or a text block such as a paragraph. Figure SF 2-21 shows type set within a border.

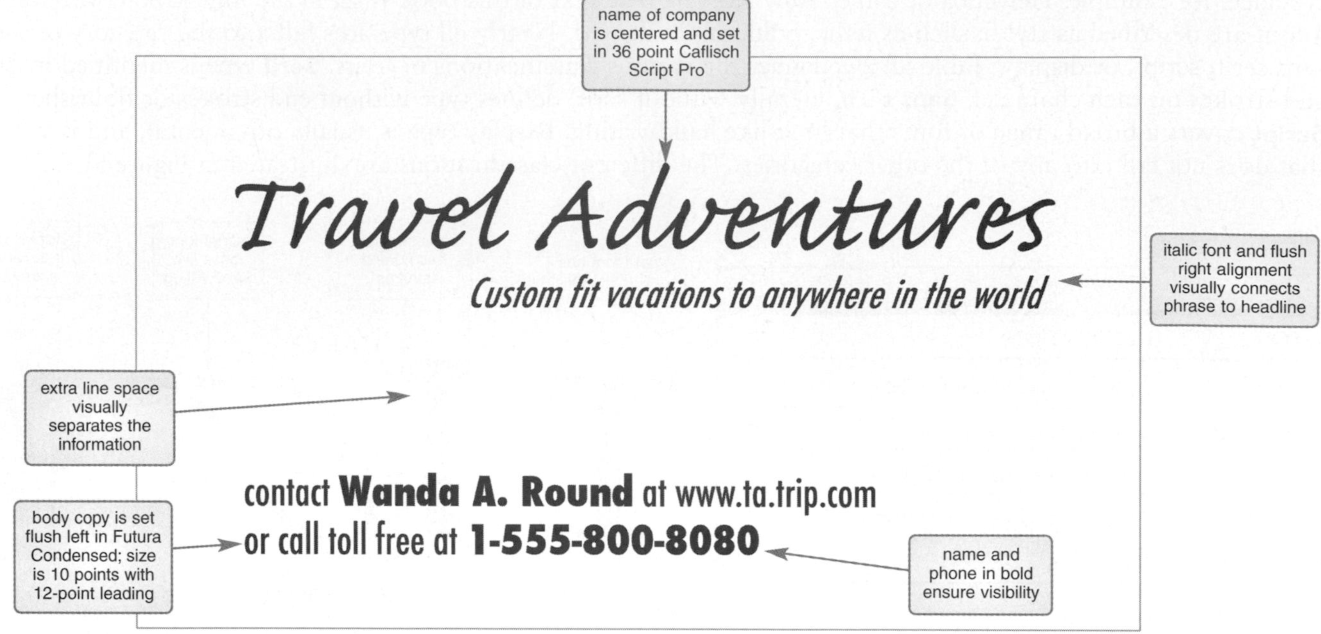

FIGURE SF 2-21

In the figure, the maximum line length for text, determined by the margins or grid, is three inches. The headline is centered at the top of the card and set in 36 point Caflisch Script Pro. Headlines are usually set in 18 points or larger. Body copy usually is set in 12 points or smaller. Software programs have automatic settings for leading — usually about two points more than the point size. If you choose 12-point type, the automatic setting would be 14 points of leading. You can override the automatic setting and determine your own line spacing to set lines closer together or further apart.

The choice of font, size, style, and color set the tone for a layout. Sometimes type should be very noticeable, for example, on a book jacket cover. Other times, type should be secondary to the actual words, like type used to set the pages of a novel. Table SF 2-4 lists some of the perceptual characteristics of type. The look and feel describes the appropriateness of the font choice, its size, leading, and other characteristics. Readability is determined by font, point size, line space, line length, and style, for example, italic or all caps.

Table SF 2-4 Perceptual Characteristics of Type

CHARACTERISTIC	DESCRIPTION
Look and feel	relates to the mood given by particular choice of font
Color	relates to how visible the type is in relationship to the color of the background
Readability	relates to how easy characters are to see and read

As you have learned, color also is an important consideration. The best contrast for type that is intended to be read is black letters on a white or light colored surface. Type that is used as a graphic image to catch the viewer's attention might be set in color, against a color background. Figure SF 2-22a illustrates a body of text that does not have good readability. All capital letters, also referred to as all caps, are difficult to read. A centered text block with small point size and tight leading also are poor choices for easy readability. Figure SF 2-22b illustrates how colored type against a colored background affects the visibility of a headline. Figure SF 2-22c is an example of type set with attention to look and feel. The different fonts each give a different feeling to the same words.

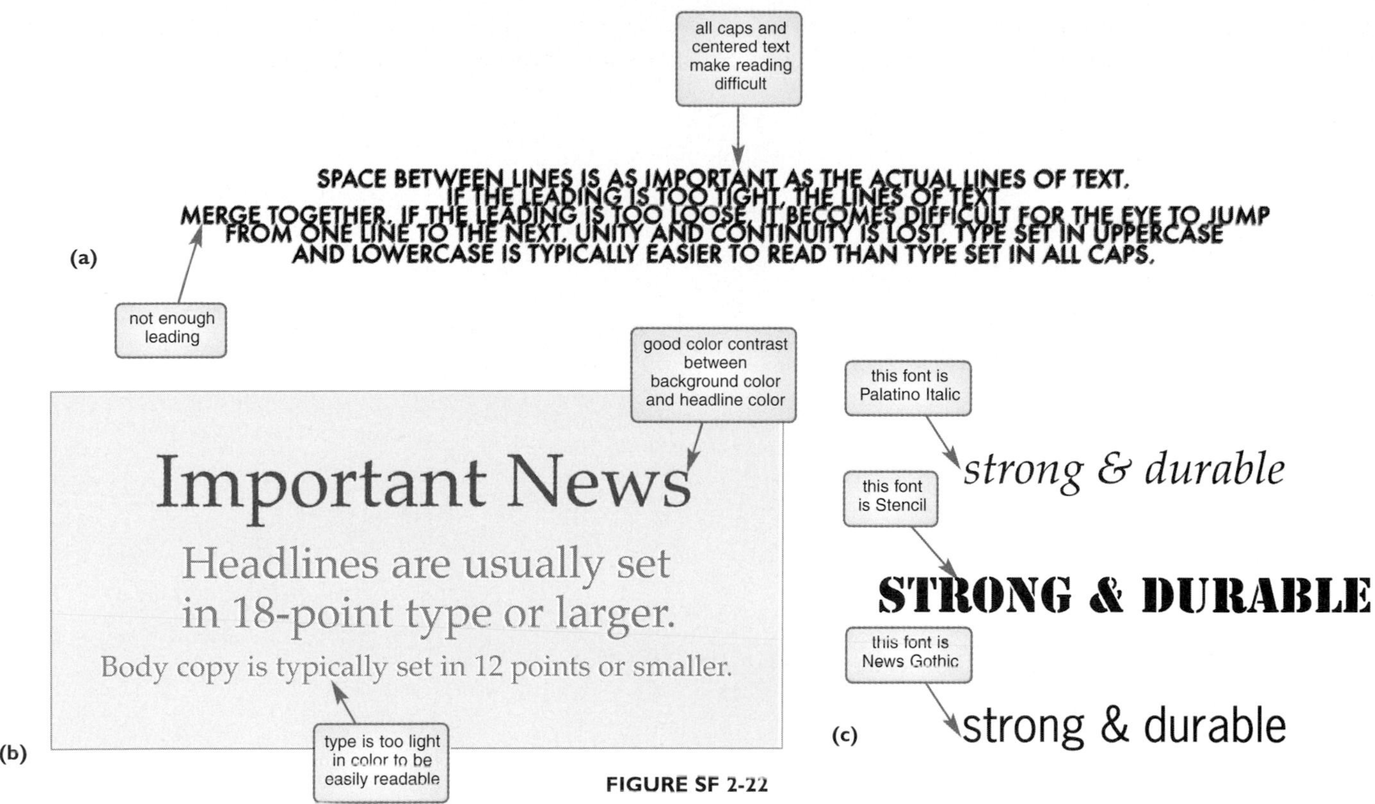

FIGURE SF 2-22

Summary

Developing skills in graphic design layout takes both research and practice. Research involves collecting samples of existing designs and analyzing their effectiveness. Practice involves trying and experimenting with different layout techniques. Three basic parts of any layout are the background, the image or object, which includes type or graphics, and the message, which is the overall meaning implied by the layout. The background, usually paper or a screen display, can be white or light colored, dark, or textured. Variations of a layout include placing one or more objects on a background. Hierarchy refers to applying images in a layout so that the viewer sees the most important information first.

Color, an important design element, has technical and aesthetic characteristics and considerations. To select appropriate color for a layout you need to determine whether to use one, two, or four colors for printing. The four-color printing is based on CMYK, or process colors, while 1c and 2c printing use PANTONE color inks. When designing for display screens and computer monitors, you should select your colors from the 216 Web safe color palette to ensure that your colors will be consistent on any type of display. Because color has the ability to evoke emotional response, graphic designers pay close attention to color choice in images and backgrounds.

Type is an important design element and is critical to the way we communicate visually. Type or fonts, are classified according to their general attributes: serif, sans serif, script, and display. Physical characteristics of type, such as point size, line length, and placement, are important factors to consider when designing a layout. Perceptual characteristics pertain to the aesthetic appearance of type: its look and feel, color, and readability.

ADOBE
Photoshop CS2

Applying Filters and Patterns

PROJECT

7

CASE PERSPECTIVE

The editor of *Fast Freddie's Racing Magazine*, Monty Strider, has seen some of the artistic products you have created in Photoshop. Monty wants you to design the magazine's front cover for an upcoming special issue about historic racing cars. Besides the text elements for the title and a special edition notation, the magazine's characteristic racing flag stripe should appear on the cover. The editor has provided several views of a 1954 Mercedes Formula One racer for you to use in your design. The magazine cover will measure 8.5 × 10.75 inches and ultimately will be reproduced using CMYK process colors.

Fast Freddie's Racing Magazine caters to racing fans and antique auto collectors. Monty wants you to attract readers with an eye-catching layout that portrays motion and uses sharp colors to feature a large photo of the Mercedes in the middle of the cover. By placing the front of the car on the right side of the cover, with angle perspective and motion blur, the reader will be led into the magazine. You are to leave room for some headlines, or teasers, about what is inside the issue — text that will be added later as the inside articles are identified.

As you read through this project, you will learn how to use the many Photoshop filters to create special effects on the magazine cover. You also will learn how to create patterns and use knockouts.

Applying Filters and Patterns

PROJECT 7

Objectives

You will have mastered the material in this project when you can:

- Create a file from scratch, and insert and enhance graphics
- Describe the categories of filters in Photoshop
- Use the Filter Gallery to create special effects
- Apply a Plastic Wrap, Glowing Edges, Emboss, and Motion Blur filter
- Stroke and fill a selection with color
- Create a circular mask
- Define, create, use, and delete a new pattern
- Discuss rendering filters such as Lighting Effects
- Explain the terms knockout, trapping, surprinting, and misregistration
- Create a line knockout
- Create dynamic headline text with effects
- Use cover overlays with text
- Print a hard proof

Introduction

Special effects or visual effects are commonplace and somewhat expected, as computers now are used to create nearly all commercial graphics and animation. What seemed rare and unusual 20 years ago, is now the norm. Special effects visually spice up static graphics with distortions, blurs, contour alterations, color manipulations, and applied overlays. Imaginative visual effects create a customized, attention grabbing appearance in everything from DVD liners to branding logos to billboards. Most people subconsciously expect to see fancy, stimulating graphics in every advertisement; indeed, when a special effect is not present, some may interpret the graphic as retro or even boring.

The entertainment industry has led the way with artistic rendering and advanced animation techniques. Specialized graphic manipulations are saved and sold as filters that can be downloaded into most popular graphic editing software packages. Filters are the most popular way to create special effects in Photoshop. In fact, entire books have been written about the vast number of filters included in the Photoshop installation along with the thousands of filters that can be added. Filters have the capability to mimic many traditional forms of art such as pastels, line drawings, or watercolors. You can blend, blur, or warp graphics in every way imaginable, allowing you to enliven commercial artwork in-house with relative ease.

In this project, as you learn about filters and patterns, you may discover the many options and settings to be overwhelming at first. It is easy to get carried away when applying filters. Your goal will be a subtle, judicious, and purposeful use of filters to enhance the meaning of the digital image.

Project Seven — Applying Filters and Patterns

Project 7 uses Photoshop to create a front cover for a racing magazine. The magazine cover incorporates graphics, color, shapes, lines, and patterns. Photoshop filters are applied to the multiple views of a racecar. The large image employs a motion filter. From left to right, the smaller images within the circles use a Plastic Wrap, Glowing Edges, and Emboss filter. In the upper-left portion of the magazine cover, a Spotlight filter highlights the special edition text. A pattern created from the classic racing flag is displayed horizontally across the upper portion of the cover. Space is provided for headlines and teasers on the side of the main graphic. The completed image is displayed in Figure 7-1.

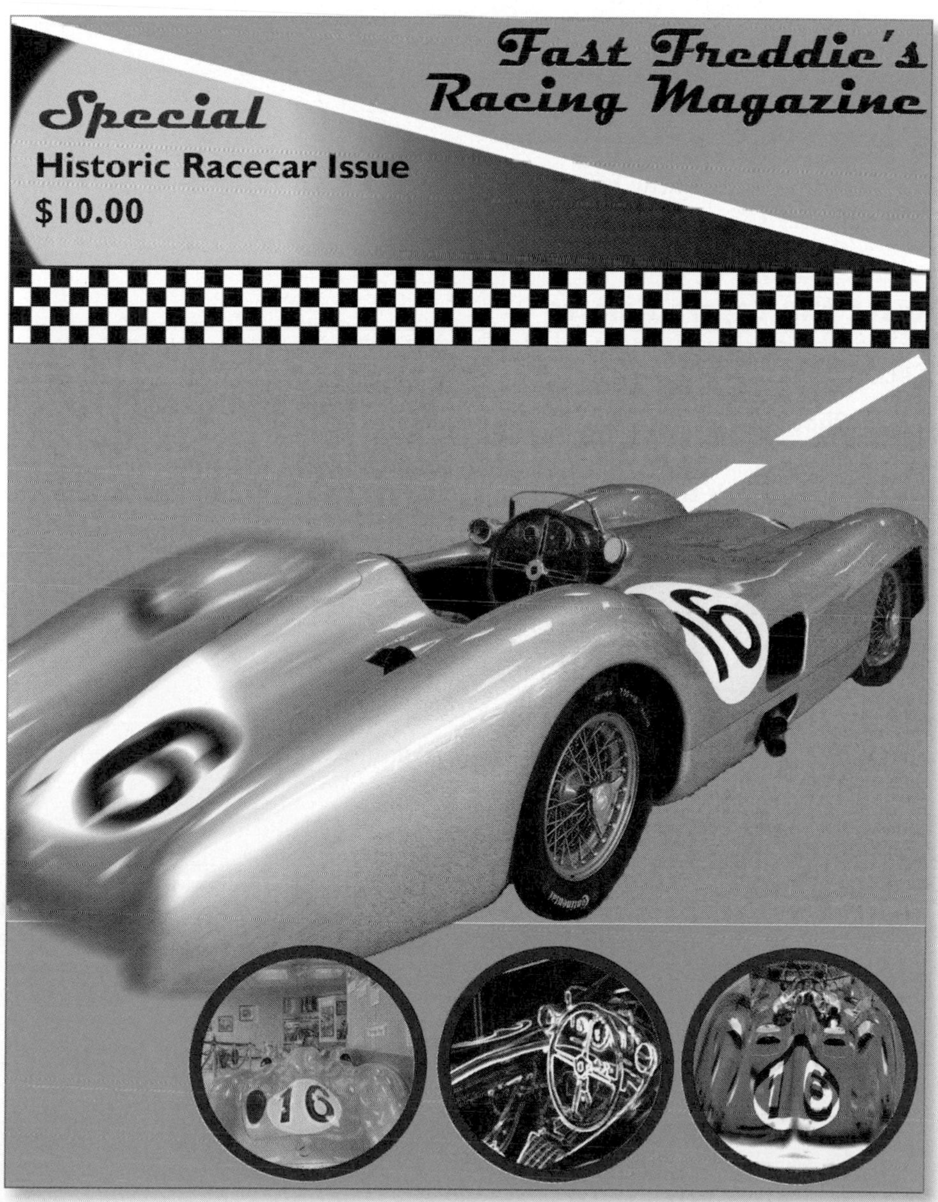

FIGURE 7-1

Starting and Customizing Photoshop

If you are stepping through this project on a computer and you want your screen to match the figures in this book, you should change your computer's resolution to 1024 × 768 and reset the tools and palettes. For more information about how to change the resolution on your computer, and other advanced Photoshop settings, read Appendix A.

The following steps describe how to start Photoshop and customize the Photoshop window. You may need to ask your instructor how to start Photoshop for your system.

To Start Photoshop and Reset the Palettes, Toolbox, and Options Bar

1. **Start Photoshop as described on pages PS 6 and PS 7.**
2. **Choose the Default Workspace as described on page PS 8.**
3. **Select the Rectangular Marquee Tool (M) in the toolbox and then reset all tools as described on pages PS 9 and PS 10.**

Photoshop starts and then resets the tools, palettes, and options.

Resetting the Layers palette

The following steps show how to reset the Layers palette to make the thumbnails match the figures shown in this book.

To Reset the Layers Palette

1. **Click the Layers palette menu button and then click Palette Options on the list.**
2. **When Photoshop displays the Layers Palette Options dialog box, click the option button corresponding to the smallest of the thumbnail sizes, if necessary.**
3. **If necessary, click the Layer Bounds option button.**
4. **Click the OK button.**

The Layers palette will display small thumbnails for each layer.

Resetting the Colors

The following step shows how to reset the default colors in the Photoshop window.

To Reset the Colors

1. **If black and white are not shown as the default colors in the toolbox, press the D key on the keyboard. If black is not the foreground color, press the X key on the keyboard.**

Black is set as the foreground color; white is set as the background color.

Creating a File from Scratch

Magazines come in a variety of sizes from digest size, which is 5.5 × 8.25 inches, to tabloid size, which typically is 11 × 17 inches. The magazine cover for *Fast Freddie's Racing Magazine* will be 8.5 × 10.75 inches — a common size for sporting and fan magazines. A resolution of 300 ppi is recommended to maintain a high quality printed image. The color mode will start as RGB to allow access to the complete inventory of filters, and then it will be converted to CMYK later in the project.

The following steps show how to use the New command on the File menu to set the attributes for a new document image.

To Create a File From Scratch

1. **Click File on the menu bar, and then click New. When the New dialog box is displayed, type** `Magazine Cover` **in the Name box.**
2. **Click the Preset box arrow, and then click Custom in the list.**
3. **Double-click the Width box and then type** `8.5` **as the entry. If necessary, click the Width unit box arrow, and then click inches in the list.**
4. **Double-click the Height box and then type** `10.75` **as the entry. If necessary, click the Height unit box arrow, and then click inches in the list.**
5. **If necessary, double-click the Resolution box and then type** `300` **as the entry. If necessary, click the Resolution unit box arrow, and then click pixels/inch in the list.**
6. **Click the Color Mode box arrow. Click RGB Color in the list. If necessary, click the Color Mode unit box arrow, and then click 8 bit in the list.**
7. **If necessary, click the Background Contents box arrow, and then click White in the list.**

The attributes for the new file are set (Figure 7-2).

8. **Click the OK button.**
9. **If necessary, change the magnification in the document window to 16.67 percent. Resize the window to display the entire page, with a small amount of workspace on each side of the page.**
10. **If the rulers do not display in the document window, press CTRL+R.**
11. **If the document dimensions are not displayed, on the document window status bar, click the menu button, point to Show, and then click Document Dimensions.**

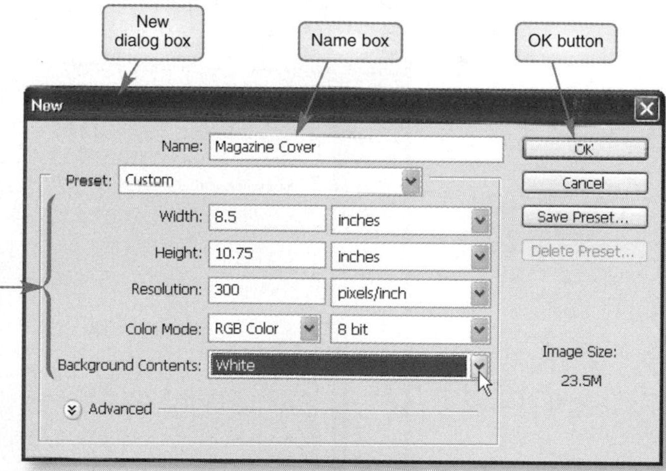

FIGURE 7-2

Because you are working with a magazine medium that prints to the edge of the paper, leaving a small amount of workspace on each side of the margins will make it easier to place objects and color. Photoshop will truncate, or cut off, part of the objects and colors that overlap the edge; but this way you easily can specify selections that touch the edge. Photoshop will snap selections to the edge.

With the settings complete, it is a good practice to save the new blank document on a storage device as described in the steps on the next page.

To Save the New Document

1. **With your USB flash drive connected to one of the computer's USB ports, click File on the menu bar and then click Save As.**
2. **When the Save As dialog box is displayed, if necessary, type** `Magazine Cover` **in the File name text box. Do not press the ENTER key.**
3. **Click the Save in box arrow and then click USBDISK [G:], or the location associated with your USB flash drive, in the list.**
4. **Click the Save button.**

The file is saved.

Changing the Background

The first step will be to edit the Background layer, changing it from white to light cyan as shown in the following steps. The color is chosen from the Swatches palette and then applied with the Paint Bucket tool.

To Change the Background

1. **Click the Swatches palette tab. Click the Light Cyan color.**
2. **Press the G key. If the Gradient tool is displayed in the toolbox, right-click the Gradient Tool (G) button and then click Paint Bucket Tool in the list.**
3. **Click the document page to color the background layer.**

The layer is filled with color (Figure 7-3).

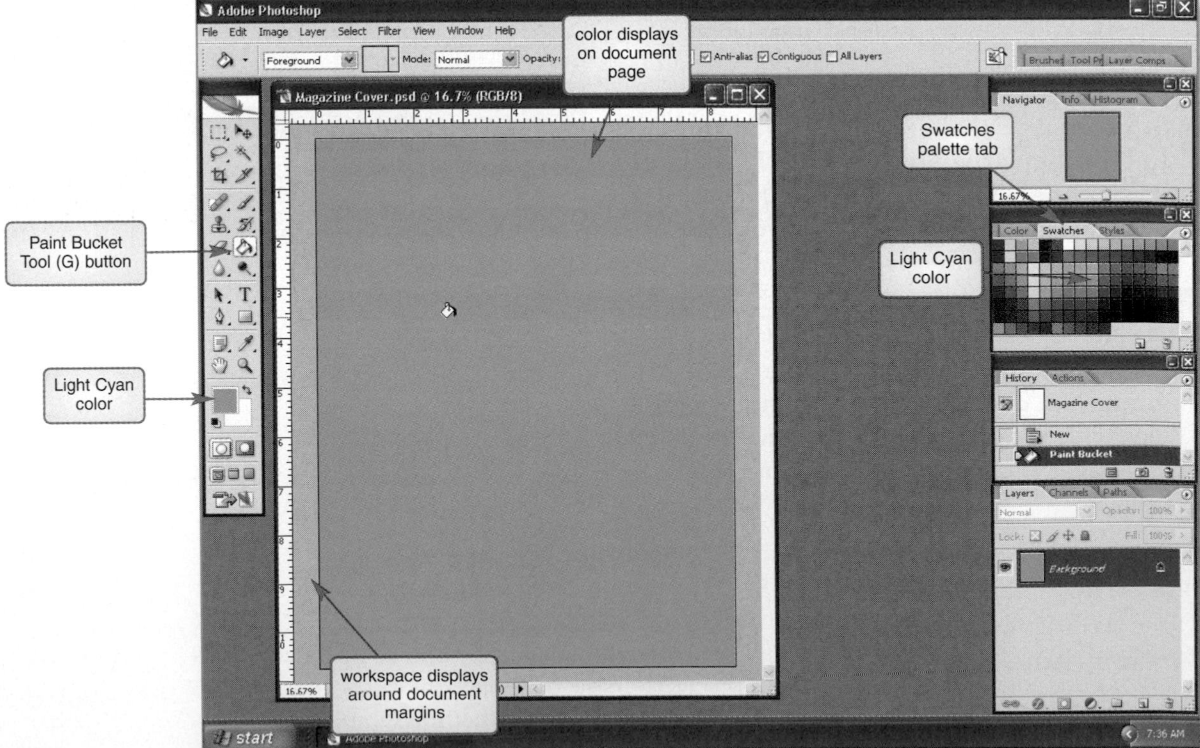

FIGURE 7-3

Using the Swatches palette is a good way to manage colors destined for professional printing, even if you start in the RGB color mode. The Swatches palette only displays RGB colors that also are used in the four-color printing process.

Creating the Road Layer

The next steps show how to draw a rectangular marquee, fill it with gray, and then use the Line and Brush tools to create a dotted white line to represent a road. The road will become a new layer in the magazine cover.

To Create the Road Layer

1

- **Press the M key. If the Rectangular Marquee tool is not displayed in the toolbox, right-click the current marquee tool button, and then click Rectangular Marquee Tool in the list.**
- **Draw a rectangle beginning at the left margin, approximately 3 inches from the top as measured on the vertical ruler. Drag down to approximately 8.25 inches and then across to the right margin.**

The marquee snaps to the margins (Figure 7-4).

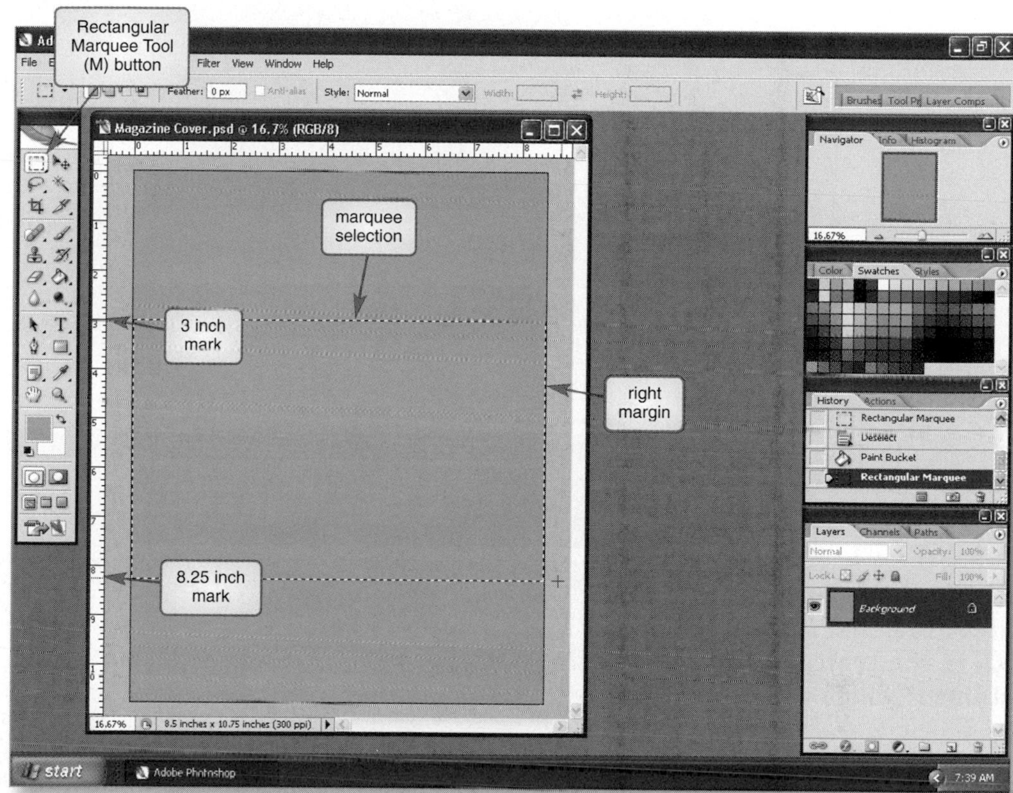

FIGURE 7-4

2

- **Press SHIFT+CTRL+J to create a new layer via cut.**
- **When Photoshop displays the new layer on the Layers palette, double-click the layer name, type** `road` **as the entry, and then press the ENTER key.**

The new layer is displayed on the Layers palette (Figure 7-5).

FIGURE 7-5

3

- **In the Swatches palette, click 45% Gray.**
- **Press the G key to activate the Paint Bucket tool and then click in the center of the document window.**

Photoshop fills the road layer with color (Figure 7-6).

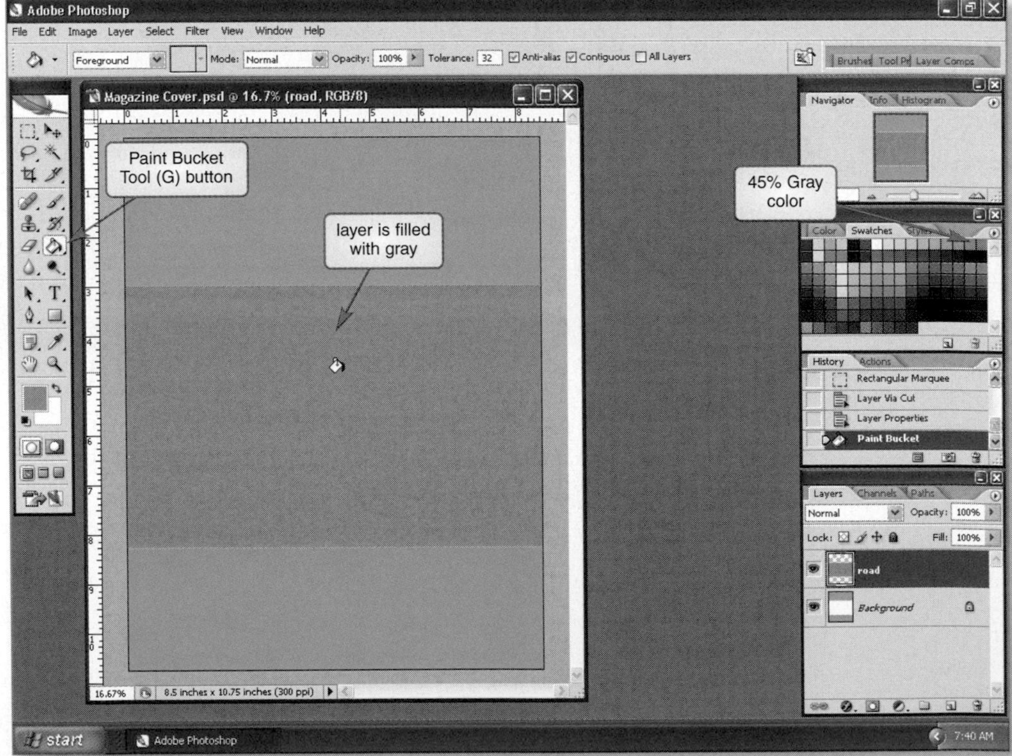

FIGURE 7-6

4

- **Press the** x **key to invert the colors so white is the foreground color.**
- **Press the** U **key to activate the Shape tool.**
- **On the options bar, click the Fill pixels button and the Line Tool button. Type** 50 px **in the Weight box.**
- **In the gray rectangle, drag a line from the lower-left corner to the upper-right corner.**

The white line is displayed (Figure 7-7). Your line does not have to match exactly.

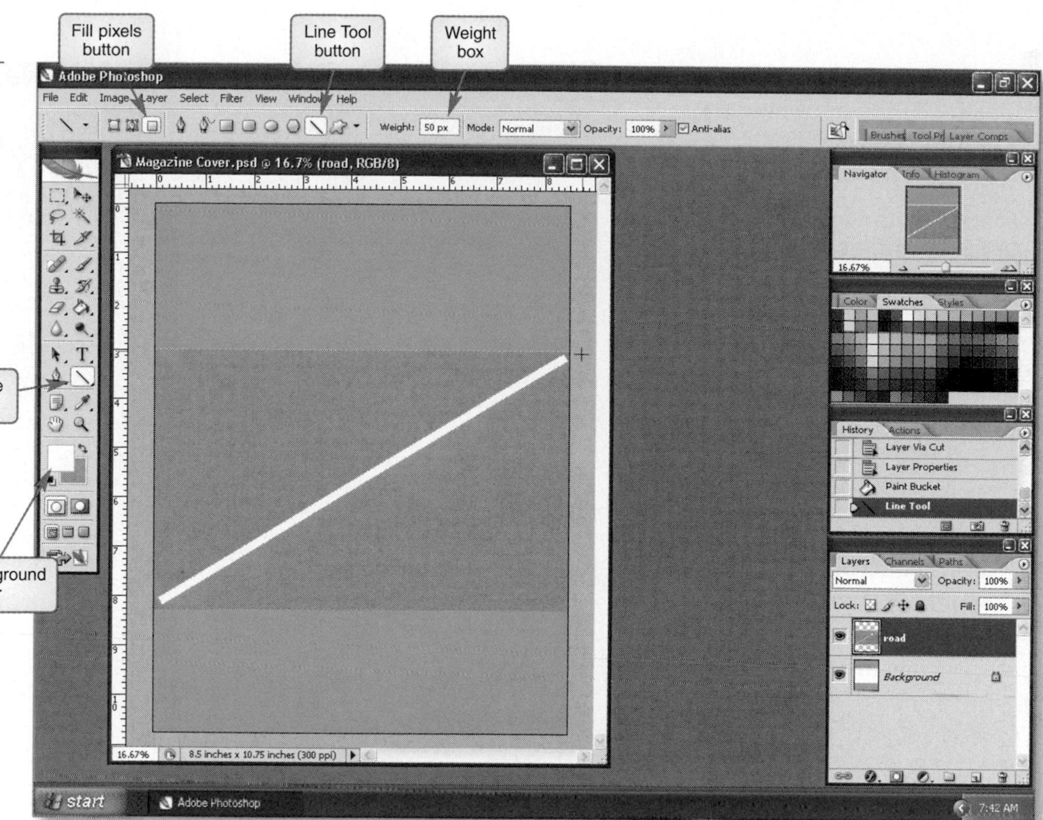

FIGURE 7-7

5

- **In the toolbox, right-click the current Brush tool button and then click Brush tool in the list.**
- **On the options bar, click the Brush Preset picker button.**
- **Type** 85 px **in the Master Diameter box. Type** 75 **in the Hardness box.**

Photoshop displays the Brush Preset picker box with the new settings (Figure 7-8). A hardness level of 75 will create straight, crisp edges on the brush.

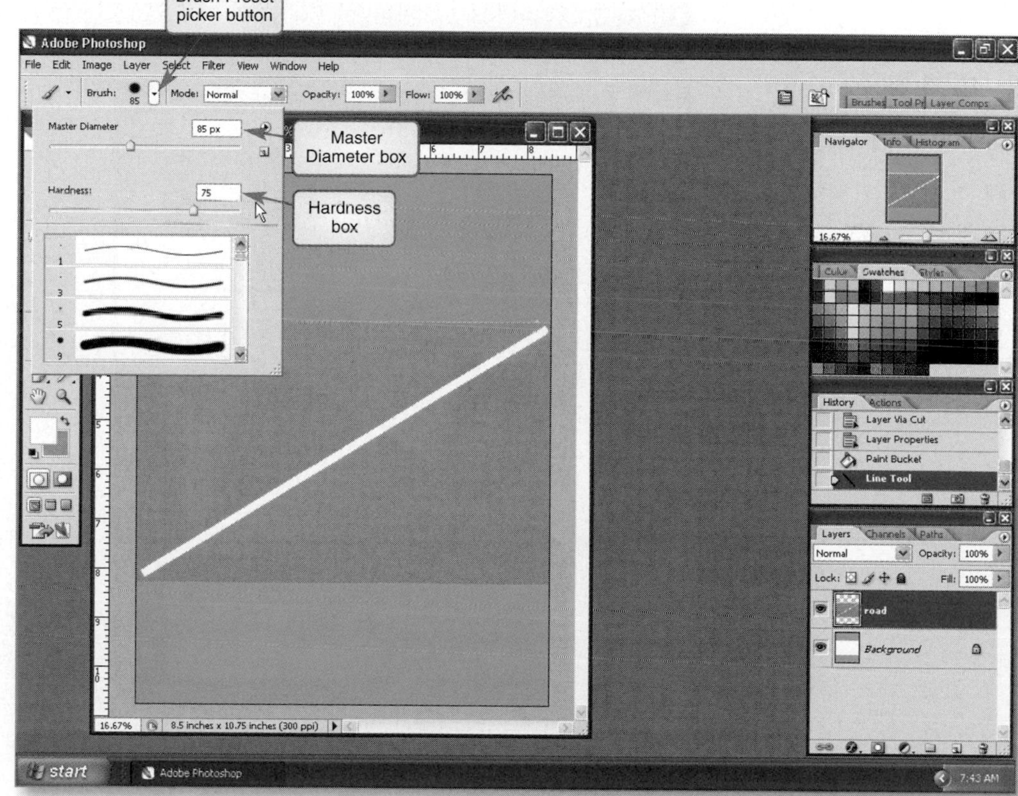

FIGURE 7-8

6

- **If necessary, press the ENTER key to close the Brush Preset picker box.**
- **Press the X key to invert the colors so gray is again the foreground color.**
- **In the document window, beginning approximately one inch from the left margin and one inch from the bottom of the gray rectangle, drag a short stroke from left to right horizontally, across the white line to create a gray break in the white line.**

A stripe of gray breaks the white line (Figure 7-9).

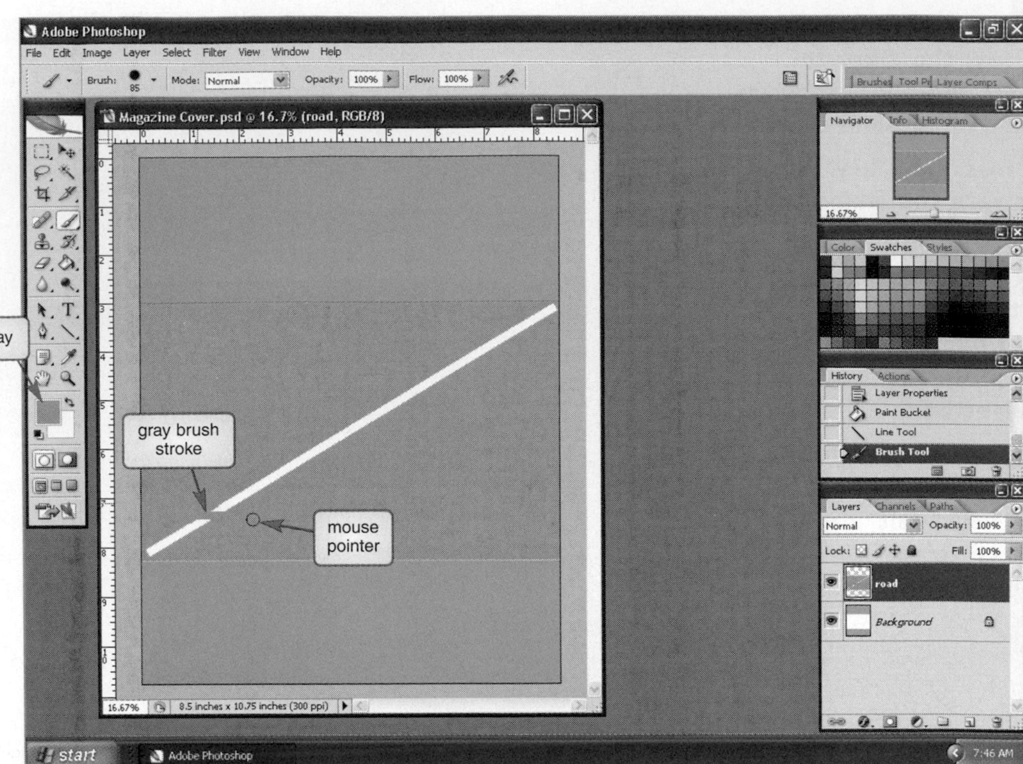

FIGURE 7-9

7

- **Repeat the horizontal stroke four more times at approximately one-inch intervals. Use the vertical ruler as a guide.**

The white line is broken, simulating a dotted line in the road (Figure 7-10).

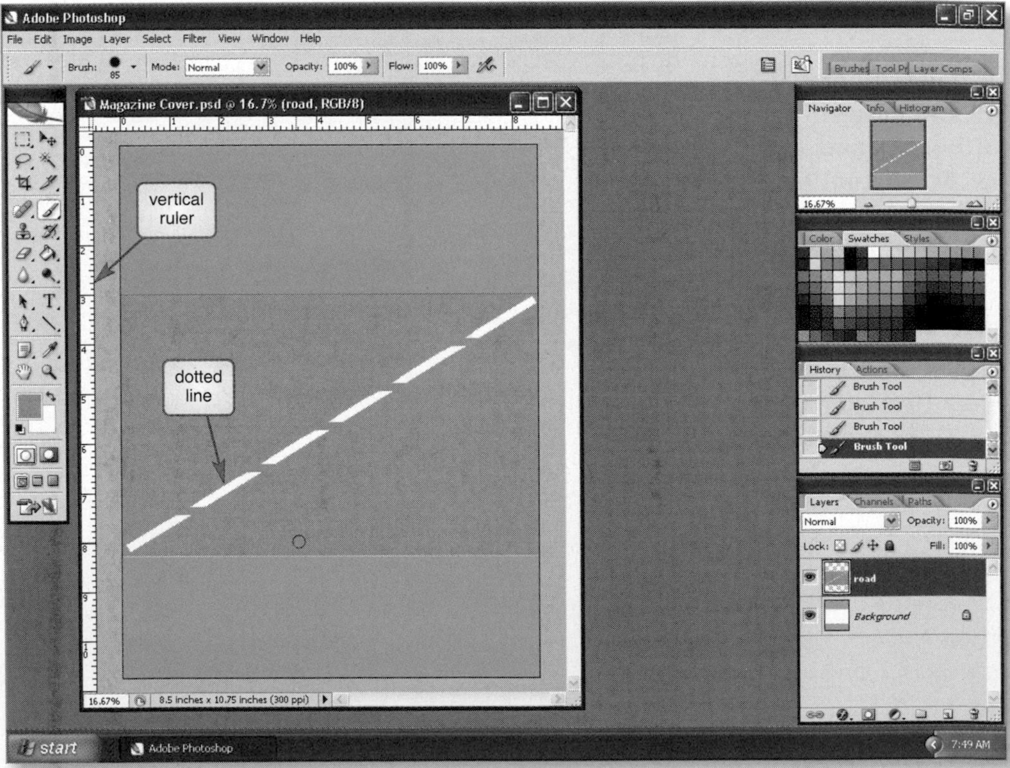

FIGURE 7-10

The road layer is complete. By using the Layer via cut command, the light cyan color is **knocked out** or removed. During printing, the gray color will be printed on the paper itself rather than over the top of the cyan.

Inserting the Graphics

The first graphic to insert is the main graphic of the racecar on the magazine cover. You then will insert three other views of the racecar to place in the lower-right corner of the magazine cover. The following steps open the Racecar file and move the image into the Magazine Cover document window, creating a new layer.

To Insert the Racecar Graphic

1. **Insert the CD that accompanies this book into your CD drive. After a few seconds, if Windows displays a dialog box, click the Close button.**
2. **Press CTRL+O to open a file. Navigate to the Project07 folder on the CD and then double-click the file named, Racecar.**
3. **When Photoshop displays the image in the document window, press the V key to activate the Move tool and then drag the racecar image into the Magazine Cover document window.**
4. **Drag the image to the lower-center portion of the window so that the left side of the car aligns with the left margin and the back wheel is on the road.**
5. **On the Layers palette, double-click the newly created layer name, and then type** `racecar` **as the new layer name.**
6. **Because you are finished with the Racecar file, click the Close button on the Racecar document window.**

The racecar is displayed in the Magazine Cover document window (Figure 7-11). The layer is renamed.

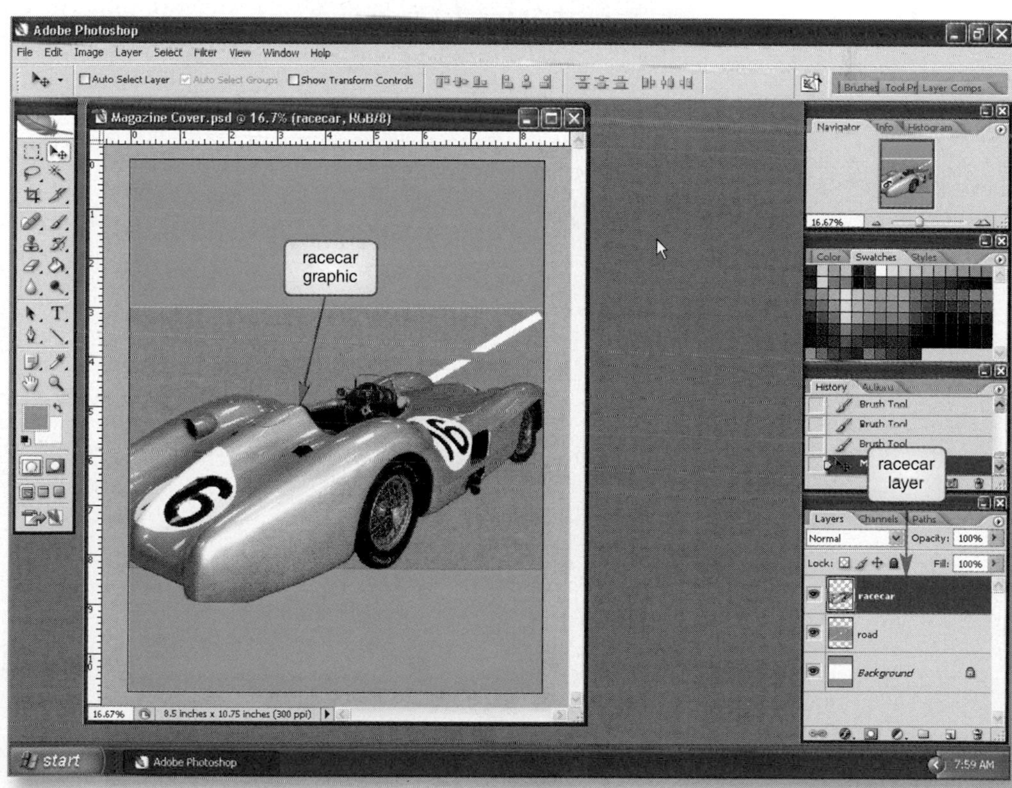

FIGURE 7-11

The steps on the next page demonstrate how to insert three other views of the racecar and resize them to fit in the lower-right corner of the magazine cover.

To Insert Additional Graphics

1. **Open the file named, Front View, from the Project07 folder on the CD that accompanies this book, or from a location specified by your instructor.**
2. **When Photoshop displays the image in the document window, press the V key to activate the Move tool and then drag the image into the Magazine Cover document window.**
3. **Press CTRL+T to display the bounding box. Drag the upper-left sizing handle until the image is approximately 2 × 2 inches. Press the ENTER key to commit the change.**
4. **Drag the image to the lower portion of the document window, approximately two inches from the left margin. Some of the image may overlap the racecar layer.**
5. **On the Layers palette, double-click the layer name, type** `front view` **as the name, and then press the ENTER key.**
6. **Close the Front View document window.**
7. **Repeat Steps 1 through 6 with the file named, Cockpit View. Position the resized graphic to the right of the front view layer. Name the new layer,** `cockpit view`.
8. **Repeat Steps 1 through 6 with the file named, Rear View. Position the resized graphic to the right of the cockpit view layer. Name the new layer,** `rear view`.

The three new layers are resized and positioned as shown in Figure 7-12.

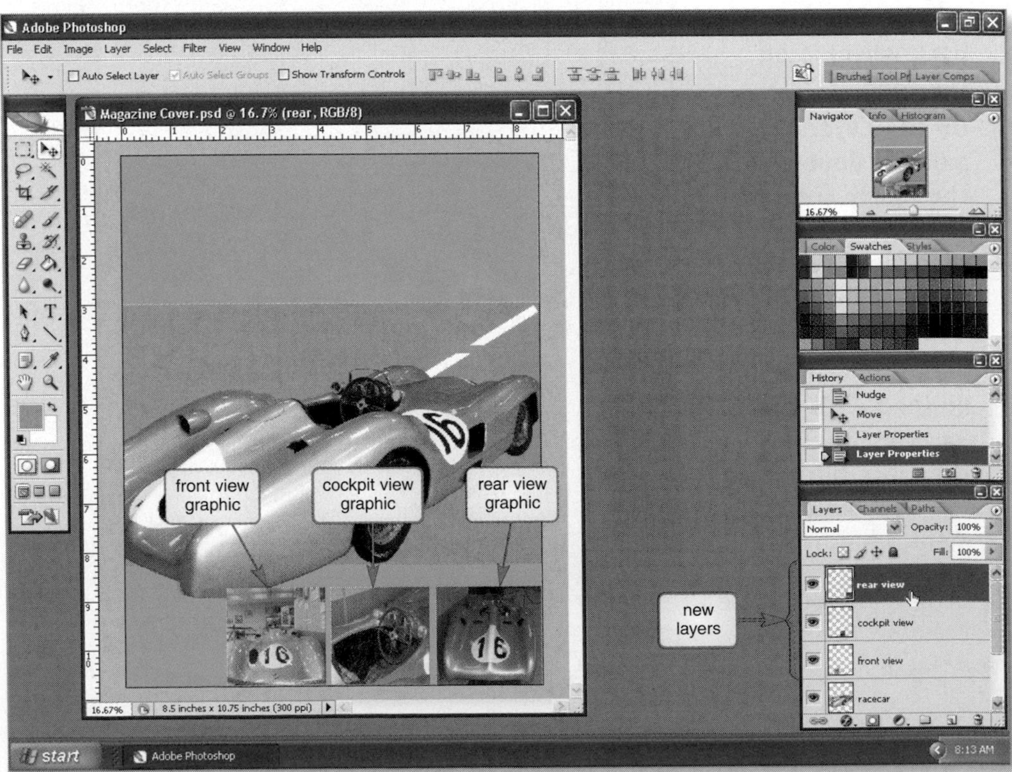

FIGURE 7-12

Filters

A **filter** is a special effect to change the look of your image or selection by altering the pixels either via their physical location or via a color change. Filters can mimic traditional photographic filters, which are pieces of colored glass or gelatin placed over the lens to change the photo's appearance, or they can be more complex creating advanced artistic effects. For example, you might use a filter to simulate the appearance of tiles or paintings. You might create unique distortions and lighting scenarios using pixel moving filters. Some filters in Photoshop help you perform restorations on your photos. Others alter color to create sophisticated color rendering. The possibilities are endless. You even can download new filters and load them into Photoshop. Most filters can be applied either to the entire image or to a specific layer, channel, or selection. In addition, many interesting effects can be created when combining filters as well as applying them more than once. The only restrictions are that filters cannot be applied to Bitmap or Index color images, and some filters will only work on 8-bit or RGB images, which is another good reason to work in the RGB color mode and then later convert the file to CMYK.

You already have used filters in previous projects, when you rendered clouds, corrected perspective, reduced noise, and used the Unsharp Mask command. In this project, you will use new filters to change the appearance of the graphics on the magazine cover.

More About

Add-on Filters

A large number of filter plug-ins are available to add to your installation of Photoshop. These after-market filters are specifically developed to add more power and features to Photoshop. Add-on filters can be purchased or downloaded as shareware from reputable Web sites. The large number of add-on filters, along with the many years of solid success dominating the image editing software market, indicates how important Photoshop is to the graphics industry. To install a filter, you simply copy it into the Filters subfolder usually located at C:\Program Files\Adobe\Adobe Photoshop CS2\Plug-Ins\Filters. For more information about filters on the Web, visit the Shelly Cashman Web site.

Types of Filters

Photoshop filters can be divided into eight basic categories: artistic, blur, brush stroke, distort, pixelate, sketch, stylize, and texture. Some of the filters alter color or texture, while others actually rearrange the pixels themselves or recreate the image with new brush strokes. Although you will not use all of the filter categories in the magazine cover for this project, the following sections provide a general description of each category and a table of specific filters and their adjustable settings.

Artistic Filters

The **Artistic filters** (Table 7-1) create painting and artistic effects, adding a certain amount of texture, dimension, and abstraction to an image. The Artistic filters replicate traditional media effects such as grain patterns, oils, watercolors, charcoals, pastels, line drawings, neon shading, and sponges. Artistic filters are used in typography, commercial art, and personal art expression.

Table 7-1 Artistic Filters

ARTISTIC FILTER	DESCRIPTION	ADJUSTABLE SETTINGS
Colored Pencil	redraws to simulate colored pencils on a solid background to create a crosshatched effect	Pencil Width Stroke Pressure Paper Brightness
Cutouts	redraws to simulate roughly cut pieces of colored paper, such as a collage or a silk screen print	Number of Levels Edge Simplicity Edge Fidelity
Dry Brush	uses a dry brush technique on all edges and reduces the range of color	Brush Size Brush Detail Texture

Table 7-1 Artistic Filters (continued)

ARTISTIC FILTER	DESCRIPTION	ADJUSTABLE SETTINGS
Film Grain	applies a film grain pattern to shadow tones and midtones with a smoother pattern to lighter areas; helps to unify diverse elements in an image	Grain Highlight Area Intensity
Fresco	repaints using coarse, short, and rounded daubs	Brush Size Brush Detail Texture
Neon Glow	inserts various types of glows to objects in the image; colorizes and softens based on the glow color	Glow Size Glow Brightness Glow Color
Paint Daubs	redraws to simulate an oil painting	Brush Size Sharpness Brush Type
Palette Knife	reduces detail to simulate a thinly painted canvas, revealing underlying textures	Stroke Size Stroke Detail Softness
Plastic Wrap	redraws the image as if it were coated in shiny plastic	Highlight Strength Detail Smoothness
Poster Edges	reduces the number of colors in an image and draws black lines on edges	Edge Thickness Edge Intensity Posterization
Rough Pastels	applies strokes of chalk, pastel-like color on a textured background; appears thicker in brighter colors	Stroke Length Stroke Detail Scaling Relief
Smudge Stick	uses short diagonal strokes to smudge or smear darker parts of the image; lighter areas become brighter with a spotty texture and less detail	Stroke Length Highlight Area Intensity
Sponge	creates textured areas of contrasting color that simulate the effect of sponge painting	Brush Size Definition Smoothness
Underpainting	creates a textured background, and then paints the image over the background to create a paler, softer version; commonly used in conjunction with other filters	Brush Texture Coverage Scaling Relief
Watercolor	creates a watercolor style that flattens yet brightens color; the greater the detail, the more realistic the image will appear	Brush Detail Shadow Intensity Texture

Blur Filters

The **Blur filters** (Table 7-2) soften or smooth an image by locating defined edges, lines, and shadows, adding together the color value, and then averaging the pixels to create a new value. Commonly used for retouching, most of the Blur filters allow you to specify the radius of affected pixels. You can blur the background to draw attention to foreground objects, create dreamlike scenes and portraits, or add visual movement to an image.

Table 7-2 Blur Filters

BLUR FILTER	DESCRIPTION	ADJUSTABLE SETTINGS
Average	creates a smooth look by averaging the pixels in the entire selection or image to create a new replacement color	None
Blur Blur More	eliminates extraneous noise in areas with strong color transitions by averaging pixels	None
Box Blur	averages the pixel color values of all neighboring pixels to create special effects; the larger the radius setting, the greater the blur	Radius
Gaussian Blur	blurs using a weighted average to add low-frequency detail that produces a hazy effect	Radius
Lens Blur	applies a blur with a narrower depth of field so that some objects in the image stay in focus and others are blurred	Blur Focal Distance Radius Blade Curvature Rotation Brightness Threshold Amount Distribution
Motion Blur	blurs in a specified direction and at a specified intensity or distance	Angle Distance
Radial Blur	simulates the blur of a zooming or rotating camera	Amount Blur Method Quality
Shape Blur	blurs in a specified pattern or shape	Radius Shape
Smart Blur	blurs with precise settings	Radius Threshold Quality Mode
Surface Blur	blurs an image while preserving edges	Radius Threshold

Brush Stroke Filters

The **Brush Stroke filters** (Table 7-3) paint with an artistic impression using different brush and ink stroke effects. Many of the filters allow you to set smoothness, sharpness, and intensity. Graphic artists use the Brush Stroke filters to achieve natural or traditional media effects.

Table 7-3 Brush Stroke Filters

BRUSH STROKE FILTER	DESCRIPTION	ADJUSTABLE SETTINGS
Accented Edges	accentuates edges based on a brightness control	Edge Width Edge Brightness Smoothness
Angled Strokes	creates brush strokes at opposite angles	Direction Balance Stroke Length Sharpness
Crosshatch	preserves details while adding pencil hatching texture	Stroke Length Sharpness Strength
Dark Strokes	paints dark areas with short, dark strokes, and light areas with long, white strokes	Balance Black Intensity White Intensity
Ink Outlines	redraws with fine narrow lines creating a strong edge effect similar to an ink outline	Stroke Length Dark Intensity Light Intensity
Spatter	simulates an airbrush, creating an exaggerated spatter and ripple effect	Spray Radius Smoothness
Sprayed Strokes	repaints using dominant colors, with angled, sprayed strokes in specific directions	Stroke Length Spray Radius Direction
Sumi-e	creates soft, blurred edges with full ink blacks and uses a saturated brush style similar to Japanese rice paper painting	Stroke Width Stroke Pressure Contrast

Distort Filters

The **Distort filters** (Table 7-4) reshape images not by color, but by moving pixels in a geometric fashion to create 3-D effects and reshaping effects. Some of the distort filters purposefully add noise or altering effects to the image, while others correct the same kinds of problems. Recall using the Lens Correction filter in a previous chapter to correct perspective, keystone, and barrel distortions. Distortion is used in advertising to give an emotional, comical, or exaggerated dimension for product recognition, or to express shape, size, and spatial relations.

Table 7-4 Distort Filters

DISTORT FILTER	DESCRIPTION	ADJUSTABLE SETTINGS
Diffuse Glow	a soft diffusion filter that adds see-through white noise; glow fades from the center	Graininess Glow Amount Clear Amount
Displace	distorts using a displacement map	Scale Displacement Map Undefined Areas
Glass	distorts as if viewed through glass	Distortion Smoothness Texture Scaling
Lens Correction	fixes common lens flaws such as keystone, barrel, and pincushion distortion; corrects chromatic aberration and vignetting	Chromatic Aberration Vignette Transform
Ocean Ripple	ripples the surface randomly as if underwater	Ripple Size Ripple Magnitude
Pinch	squeezes from the center	Amount
Polar Coordinates	toggles between rectangular and polar coordinates simulating a mirrored cylinder	Coordinate style
Ripple	redraws with ripples	Amount Size
Shear	distorts or warps along a line	Drag distortion line Undefined Areas
Spherize	creates a spherical distortion	Amount Mode
Twirl	rotates, creating a twirl pattern	Angle
Wave	precisely redraws with ripples	Number of Generators Wavelength Amplitude Scale Type
ZigZag	distorts radially, with reversals from center	Amount Ridges Style

Pixelate Filters

The **Pixelate filters** (Table 7-5) redraw an image or selection by joining, grouping, or clustering pixels of similar color values into cells defined by the tolerance settings. The cells become blocks, rectangles, circles, or dots of color, creating an impression of looking at an image through a powerful magnifying glass. Many of the Pixelate filters replicate artistic movement styles such as pointillism, divisionism, or stippling.

Table 7-5 Pixelate Filters

PIXELATE FILTER	DESCRIPTION	ADJUSTABLE SETTINGS
Color Halftone	replaces rectangular areas with circles of halftone screening on each color channel	Max. Radius Screen Angles (Degrees)
Crystallize	creates a solid color polygon shape by clustering pixels	Cell Size
Facet	creates solid color by clustering similarly colored pixels; commonly used to remove color noise and specks	None
Fragment	draws four copies of pixels and then averages the values and offsets them, creating a hazy blur	None
Mezzotint	randomizes black-and-white areas or color areas creating pixilation according to the chosen type	Type
Mosaic	creates solid-colored, square blocks based on original pixel colors	Cell Size
Pointillize	randomizes foreground colors and creates dots similar to pointillism; background simulates a canvas texture	Cell Size

Sketch Filters

The **Sketch filters** (Table 7-6) add texture and changes in color, creating artistic 3-D effects and hand-drawn looks. Many of the filters mimic sketch media used for loosely executed freehand drawing, not intended as a finished work. The Sketch filters use many techniques including overlapping lines, dry media imitation, pencil, pen, and watercolor simulations. Most of the Sketch filters convert the image to black and white, however, they can be applied to individual channels to create interesting color combinations in the composite.

Table 7-6 Sketch Filters

SKETCH FILTER	DESCRIPTION	ADJUSTABLE SETTINGS
Bas Relief	accents surface variations with carving-like strokes; dark areas use the foreground color, and light areas use the background color	Detail Smoothness Light
Chalk & Charcoal	simulates a coarse chalk sketch with black diagonal charcoal lines in the foreground	Charcoal Area Chalk Area Stroke Pressure
Charcoal	redraws with a smudged, posterized effect using diagonal strokes; a charcoal color is used on the foreground while the background simulates paper	Charcoal Thickness Detail Light/Dark Balance
Chrome	creates a polished chrome surface	Detail Smoothness

Table 7-6 Sketch Filters (continued)

SKETCH FILTER	DESCRIPTION	ADJUSTABLE SETTINGS
Conté Crayon	simulates the Conté style with textured crayon-like, chalk strokes	Foreground Level Background Level Texture Scaling Relief Light
Graphic Pen	redraws using thin, linear ink strokes for the foreground color, and uses background color to simulate paper	Stroke Length Light/Dark Balance Stroke Direction
Halftone Pattern	a halftone screen effect that maintains a continuous range of tones, consisting of dots that control how much ink is deposited at a specific location	Size Contrast Pattern Type
Note Paper	replicates handmade paper with dark areas masked out to reveal background colors	Image Balance Graininess Relief
Photocopy	creates a photocopy effect	Detail Darkness
Plaster	simulates molded plaster, with dark areas raised, and light areas recessed	Image Balance Smoothness Light
Reticulation	distorts similar to film emulsion patterns in negatives caused by extreme changes of temperature or acidity and alkalinity during processing	Density Foreground Level Background Level
Stamp	simulates a rubber or wooden stamp version	Light/Dark Balance Smoothness
Torn Edges	redraws to look like ragged, torn pieces of paper	Image Balance Smoothness Contrast
Water Paper	daubs with color imitating fibrous, damp paper	Fiber Length Brightness Contrast

Stylize Filters

The **Stylize filters** (Table 7-7) displace pixels and heighten contrast in an image or selection, producing an impressionistic, painting-like effect. Graphic artists use the Stylize filters to create unique and interesting effects and accents to artwork. Several of the Stylize filters accent edges of contrast in the image, which then can be inverted to highlight the image inside the outlines.

Table 7-7 Stylize Filters

STYLIZE FILTER	DESCRIPTION	ADJUSTABLE SETTINGS
Diffuse	softens focus by rearranging pixels randomly or by dark and light settings	Mode
Emboss	converts fill color to gray and traces the edges to create raised or stamped effects	Angle Height Amount
Extrude	adds a 3-D texture based on specific settings	Type Size Depth
Find Edges	outlines edges with dark lines against a white background for a high quality, outlined, coloring book effect	None
Glowing Edges	adds a neon glow to edges	Edge Width Edge Brightness Smoothness
Solarize	creates a photographic light exposure tint	None
Tiles	creates a series of offset blocks with tiled edges	Number Of Tiles Maximum Offset Fill Empty Areas With
Trace Contour	outlines transition areas in each channel, creating a contour map effect	Level Edge
Wind	redraws using small horizontal lines to create a windblown effect	Method Direction

Texture Filters

The **Texture filters** (Table 7-8) add substance or depth to an image by simulating a texture or organic representation. Graphic artists use the Texture filters to add a 3-D effect or to apply a segmented style to photos.

Table 7-8 Texture Filters

TEXTURE FILTER	DESCRIPTION	ADJUSTABLE SETTINGS
Craquelure	creates an embossing effect with a network of cracks on a plaster-like background	Crack Spacing Crack Depth Crack Brightness
Grain	simulates different types of graininess	Intensity Contrast Grain Type
Mosaic Tiles	creates small tiles with grout	Tile Size Grout Width Lighten Grout
Patchwork	redraws with randomly filled squares replicating highlights and shadows	Square Size Relief
Stained Glass	repaints using random, five-sided, polygonal shapes to emulate stained glass	Cell Size Border Thickness Light Intensity
Texturizer	applies selected texture with settings	Texture Scaling Relief Light

The Filter Gallery

Photoshop filters are accessible via the Filter menu. One command on that menu, in particular, provides access to many of the default filters. The **Filter Gallery command** lets you apply filters cumulatively and apply individual filters more than once. With thumbnail examples of what each filter does and preview displays of what the filter will do to your image, you can use the Filter Gallery to make appropriate choices, rearrange filters, and change individual settings to achieve the desired special effect.

Those filters with adjustable settings, which are not in the Filter Gallery, present their own preview when selected from the menu system. The Adobe Help Center also has many visual examples of the various filters.

Applying a Plastic Wrap Filter

Using the Filter Gallery, you will apply one of the Artistic filters named Plastic Wrap to the front view layer in the lower portion of the magazine cover as shown in the following steps. The Plastic Wrap filter redraws the image as if it were coated in shiny plastic wrap or shrink wrap. The Highlight Strength setting controls how close together the pockets of plastic wrap are displayed. The Detail setting adds white or nontransparency to the plastic wrap. Finally the Smoothness setting delineates the edges of the plastic wrap pockets.

To Apply a Plastic Wrap Filter

1

- **On the Layers palette, select the front view layer.**
- **Click Filter on the menu bar.**

The Filter menu is displayed with the many categories of filters as well as a command to access the Filter Gallery (Figure 7-13).

FIGURE 7-13

2

- **Click Filter Gallery.**
- **When Photoshop displays the Filter Gallery, click Artistic in the filter list, and then click the Plastic Wrap thumbnail.**
- **Type** 8 **in the Highlight Strength box.**
- **Type** 8 **in the Detail box.**
- **Type** 11 **in the Smoothness box.**

The Filter Gallery dialog box is displayed with thumbnails of many of the Photoshop filters, and a preview that is updated when settings are changed (Figure 7-14).

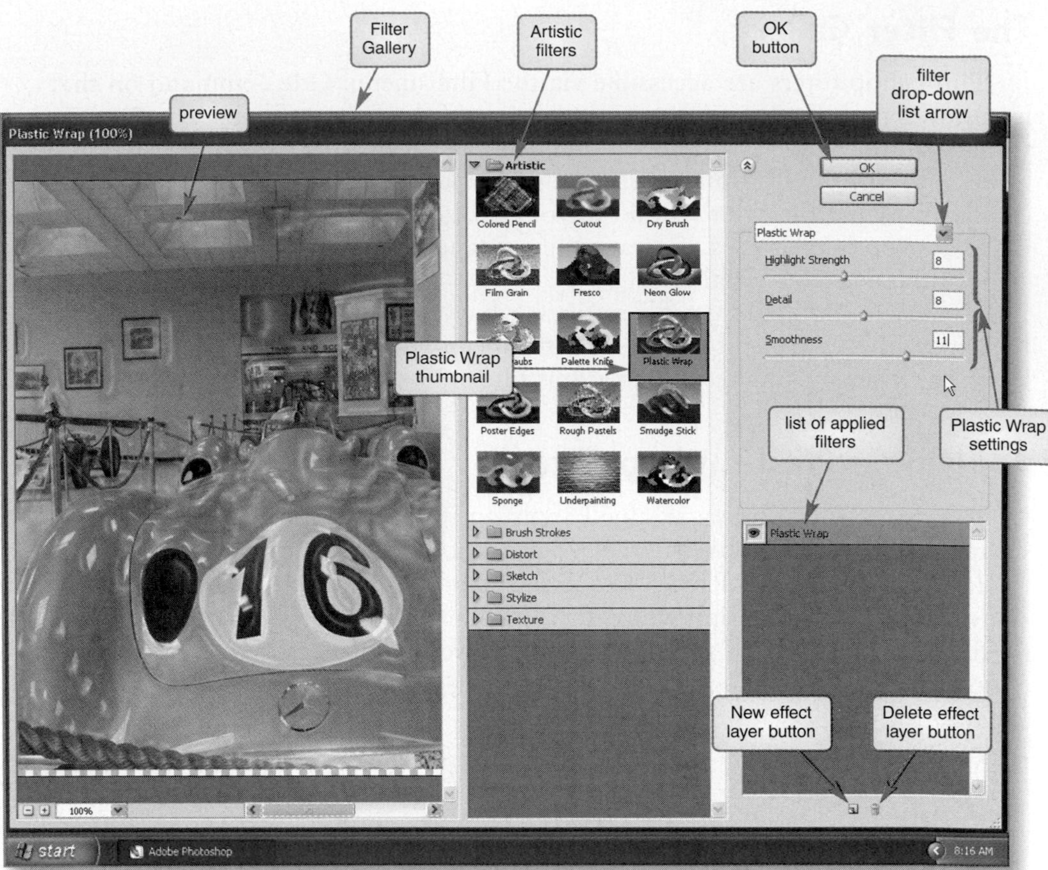

FIGURE 7-14

3

- **Click the OK button.**

Photoshop applies the Plastic Wrap filter to the front view layer (Figure 7-15).

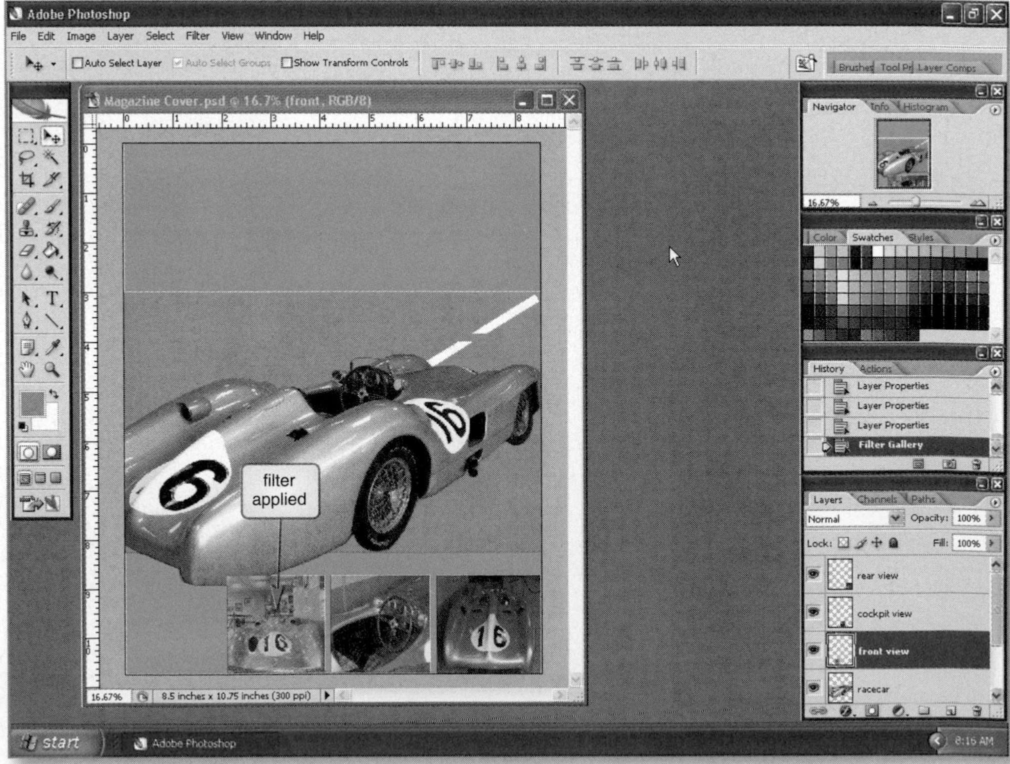

FIGURE 7-15

Other Ways

1. On Filter menu, point to Artistic, click Plastic Wrap

The drop down list in the Filter Gallery dialog box (Figure 7-14) lists all of the filters in the gallery in alphabetical order, which is useful if you cannot remember the category. In the lower-right portion of the Filter Gallery dialog box, the New effect layer button lets you apply multiple filters to the same image. Each layer is added to the list as it is created. To delete a filter, drag it to the Delete effect layer button. If you change your mind and do not wish to apply any filters, click the Cancel button. If the filter already has been applied, you can click Undo on the Edit menu or press CTRL+Z.

Applying a Glowing Edges Filter

You will apply one of the Stylize filters named Glowing Edges to the cockpit view layer in the lower portion of the magazine cover as illustrated in the following steps. The Glowing Edges filter adds a neon glow to obvious edges in the images. Photoshop looks for strong color change to define an edge. Three settings are adjusted when using the Glowing Edges filter. The Edge Width setting increases or decreases the thickness of the edge lines. The Edge Brightness setting adjusts the contrast between the edges and the background. Finally, the Smoothness setting softens the color change between the edges and the background.

To Apply a Glowing Edges Filter

1

- **On the Layers palette, select the cockpit view layer.**
- **Click Filter on the menu bar and then click Filter Gallery.**
- **When Photoshop displays the Filter Gallery, click Stylize in the Filter list, and then click the Glowing Edges thumbnail.**
- **Type** 5 **in the Edge Width box.**
- **Type** 9 **in the Edge Brightness box.**
- **If necessary, type** 5 **in the Smoothness box.**

The Filter Gallery preview is displayed with the result of adjusting the settings (Figure 7-16).

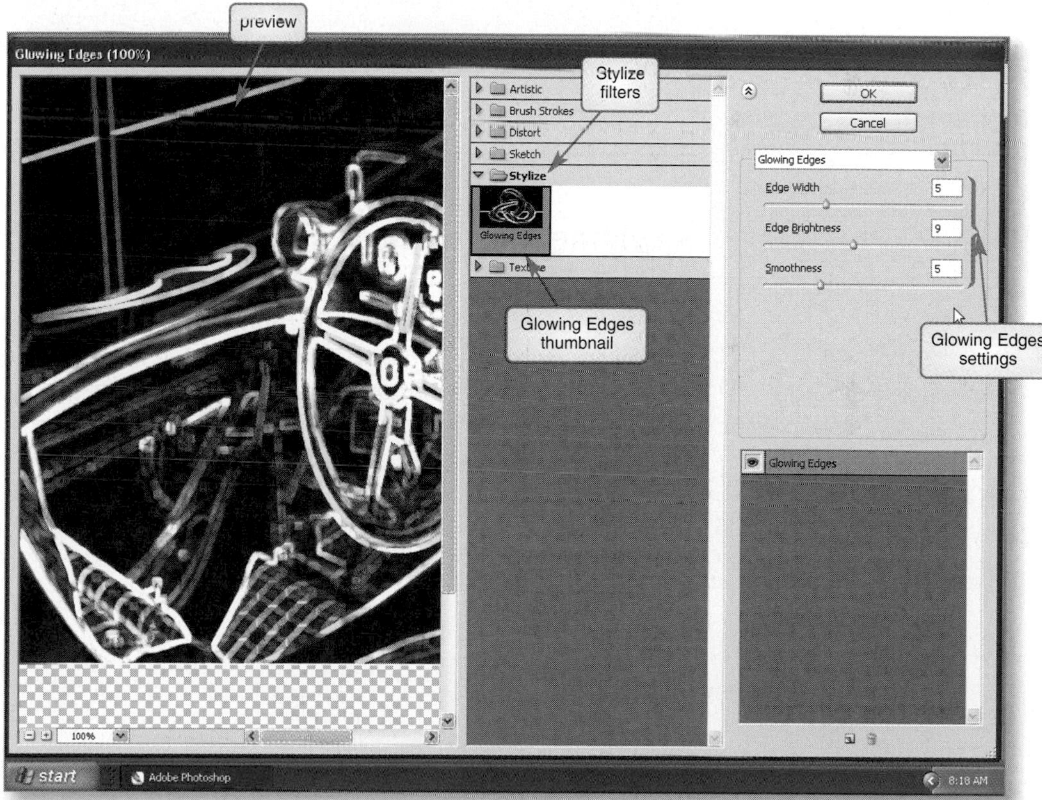

FIGURE 7-16

2

• **Click the OK button.**

Photoshop applies the Glowing Edges filter to the cockpit view layer (Figure 7-17).

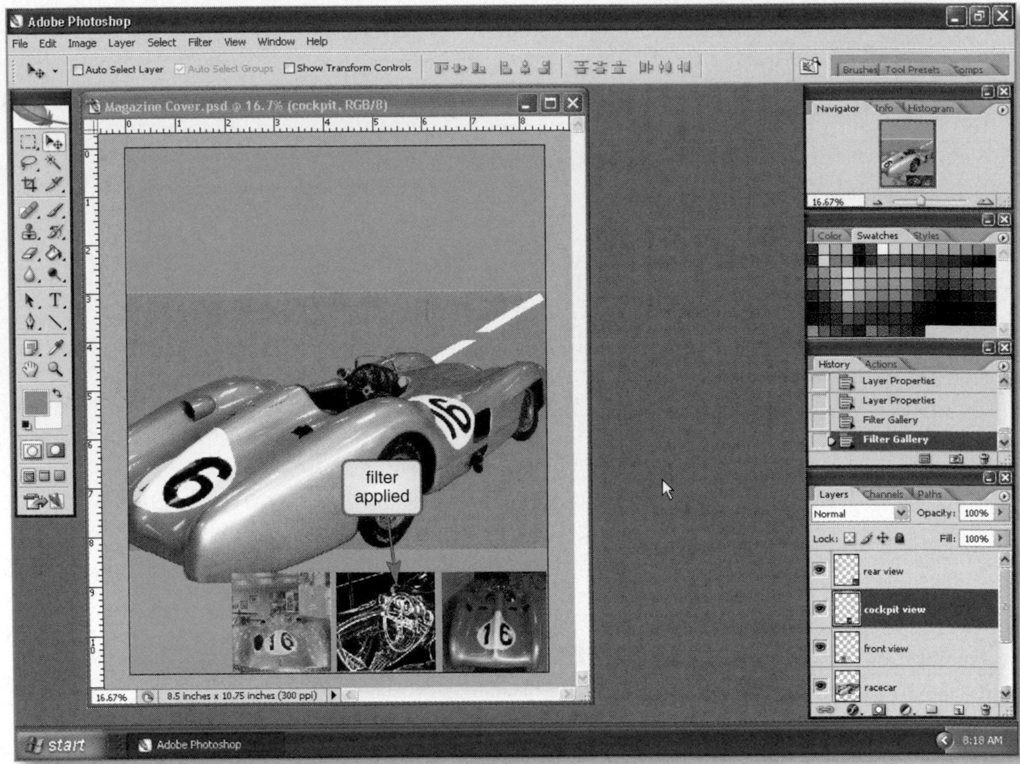

FIGURE 7-17

Other Ways

1. On Filter menu, point to Stylize, click Glowing Edges

Applying the Emboss Filter

You will apply the Emboss filter to the rear view layer at the bottom of the magazine cover, as shown in the following steps. This time you will use the menu system to access the filter because it is not in the Filter Gallery.

The Emboss filter in the Stylize category converts portions of the image to gray. It then traces the edges and offsets a copy of the image to create a raised or stamped effect. The Angle setting determines the direction of the offset. The Height setting is a pixel measurement of the distance between the original and the offset. Finally, the Amount setting is a percentage indicating the magnitude of the embossment.

To Apply an Emboss Filter

1

- **On the Layers palette, select the rear view layer.**
- **Click Filter on the menu bar and then point to Stylize.**

Photoshop displays the Stylize submenu (Figure 7-18).

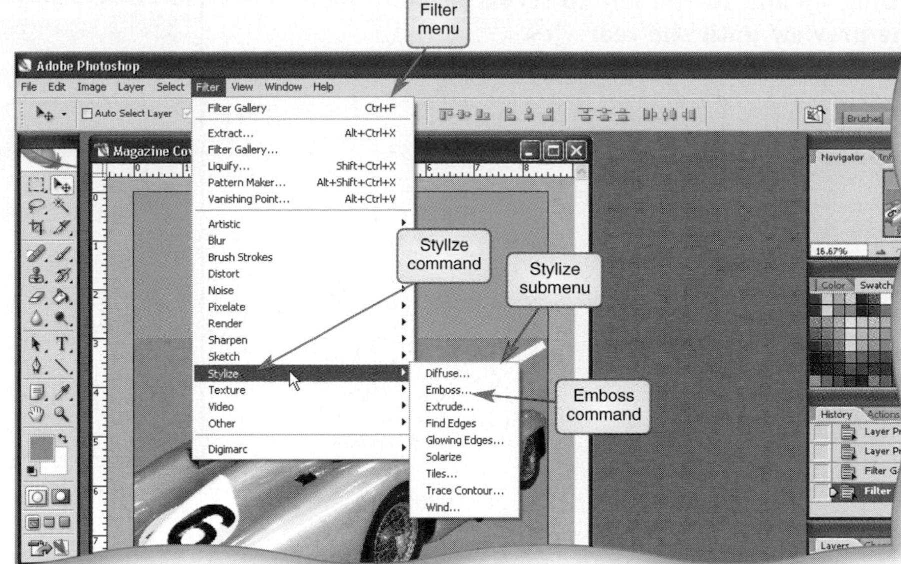

FIGURE 7-18

2

- **Click Emboss.**
- **When the Emboss dialog box is displayed, click the Zoom out (-) button until the magnification is set at 33%.**
- **Position the mouse pointer in the lower-right portion of the Preview box.**

The mouse pointer changes to a hand icon (Figure 7-19).

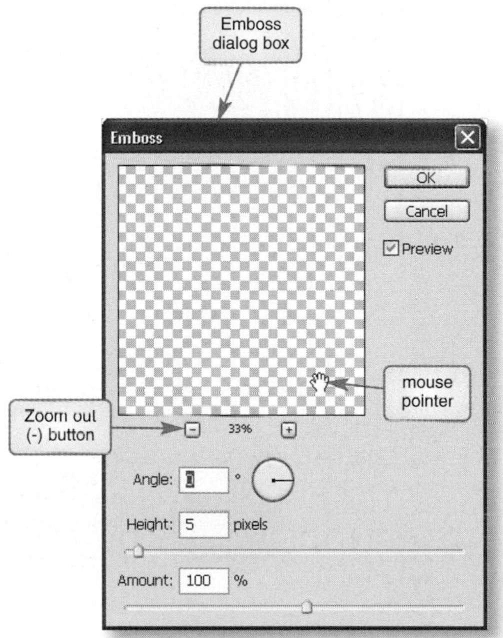

FIGURE 7-19

3

- **Drag up and to the left to scroll the preview until the rear view layer becomes visible.**
- **Type** 90 **in the Angle box.**
- **Type** 33 **in the Height box.**
- **Type** 175 **in the Amount box.**

The preview is displayed with the result of adjusting the settings (Figure 7-20).

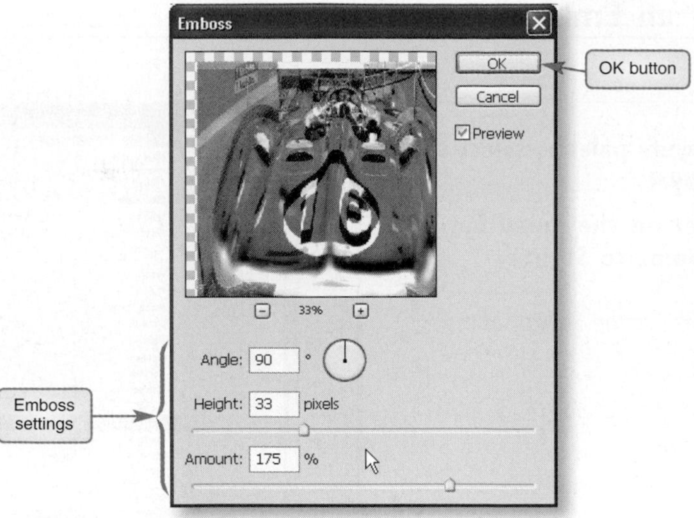

FIGURE 7-20

4

- **Click the OK button.**

Photoshop applies the Emboss filter to the rear view layer (Figure 7-21).

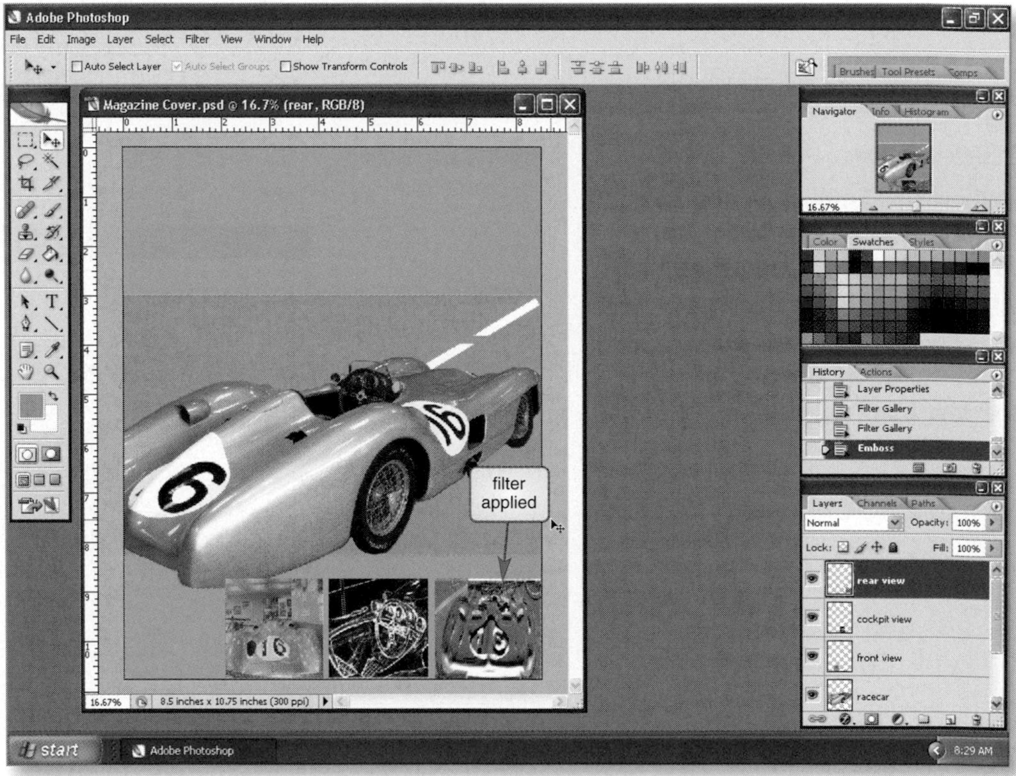

FIGURE 7-21

Applying a Motion Blur Filter

You will apply a Motion Blur filter to a portion of the large racecar layer in the center of the magazine cover to suggest movement as shown in the following steps. The Motion Blur filter blurs in a specified direction and at a specified intensity or distance. The Angle setting allows you to indicate the direction of the blur. The Distance setting specifies the pixel depth of the blur. Recall that you can apply filters to an entire image, layer, or just a selection. The Motion Blur filter does not display in the Filter Gallery, however, it does show a preview in its own dialog box.

To Apply a Motion Blur Filter

1

- **On the Layers palette, select the racecar layer.**
- **Press the M key. If the Rectangular Marquee tool does not display in the toolbox, right-click the current marquee tool button, and then click Rectangular Marquee Tool (M) in the list.**
- **Drag a rectangle over the left one-third of the racecar.**

Photoshop displays the marquee (Figure 7-22). Your selection does not have to match exactly.

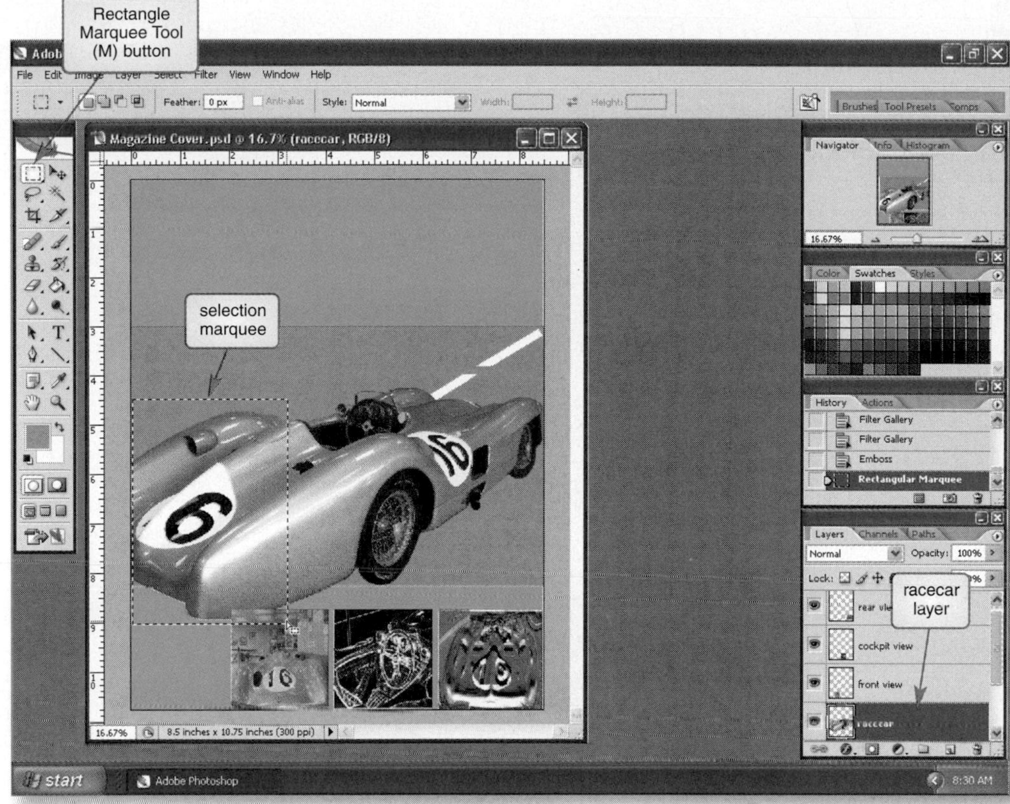

FIGURE 7-22

2

- **Click Filter on the menu bar and then point to Blur.**

The Blur submenu is displayed (Figure 7-23).

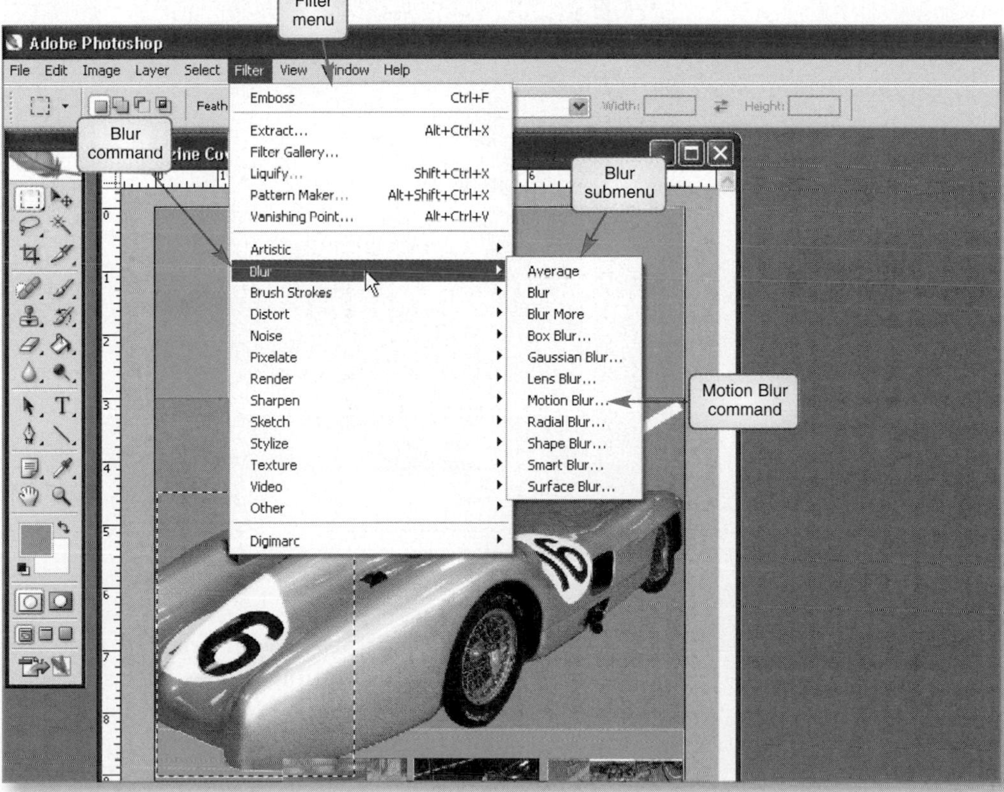

FIGURE 7-23

3

- **Click Motion Blur.**
- **When Photoshop displays the Motion Blur dialog box, click the Zoom out (-) button until the magnification is set at 13%.**
- **If necessary, drag in the preview until the left side of the racecar is displayed.**
- **Type** 35 **in the Angle box.**
- **Type** 75 **in the Distance box.**

The preview is displayed with the result of adjusting the settings (Figure 7-24).

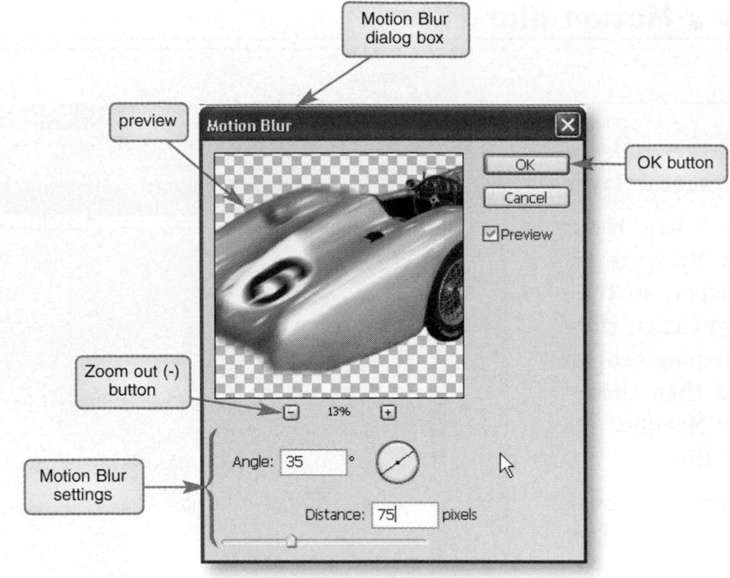

FIGURE 7-24

4

- **Click the OK button.**
- **Press CTRL+D to deselect.**

Photoshop applies the Motion Blur filter to the selection (Figure 7-25).

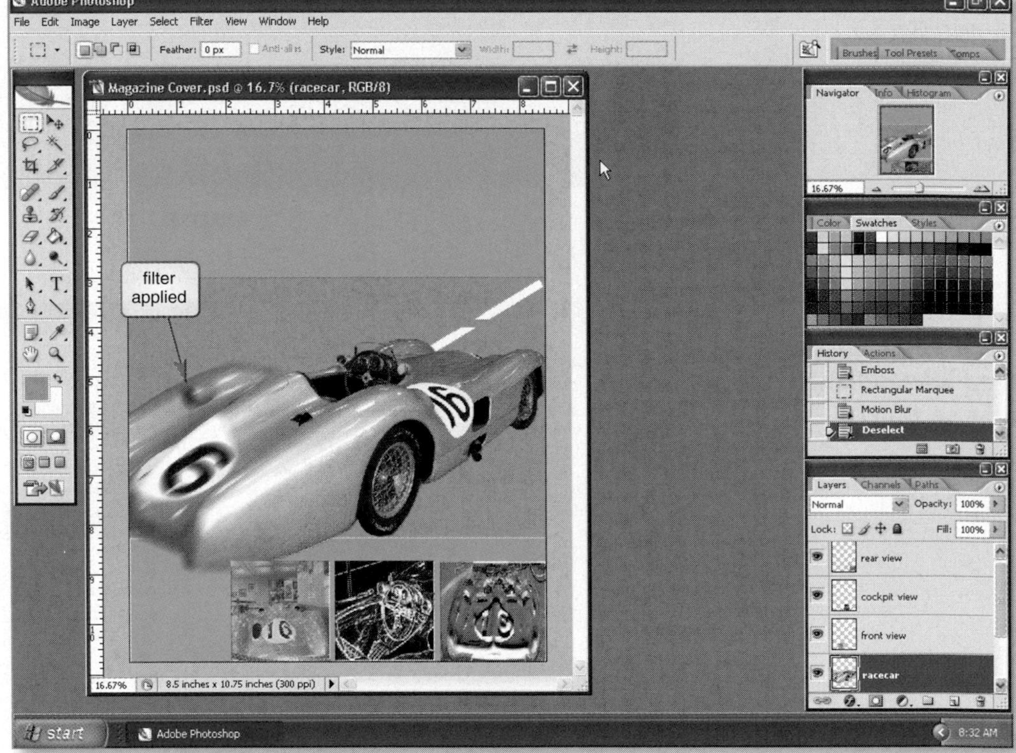

FIGURE 7-25

Some filters are created using your system's random access memory (RAM). When applied to a high-resolution image, your system may slow down. If several applications are running, you may get a low memory warning message. To reduce the strain on your system's memory, you can experiment with filters on small portions of an image, apply filters to individual channels instead of the entire image, or use the Purge command on the Edit menu to remove your previous history states. Closing other running applications also will increase available RAM.

After adding many layers and applied filters, it is a good time to save the file again as demonstrated in the following step.

To Save the File

1 Press CTRL+S. If Photoshop displays a dialog box, click the OK button.

The file is saved.

Strokes and Fills

In Photoshop, a **stroke** is a way to create a quick border around a selection. In the Stroke dialog box, you can choose the width and color of the stroke, and its placement — outside of the selection, just inside the selection, or centered on the selection border. Additionally, you can choose a blending mode and an opacity setting. Color strokes are used to outline, emphasize, or highlight. Adding a simple border helps to make a portion of an image stand out; or, in the case of a Web graphic, a stroke adds another design element sometimes used for brand identification or to indicate an active button. Multiple strokes of different widths, colors, positions, and opacity can be applied for a layering effect. Strokes do not have to be circles or squares; they can be created on any form of selection — rectangular, elliptical, or polygonal. For example, you might want a stroke around a starburst selection to create an attention getting image within a layout.

A stroke is also one of the layer style options. When you click the Add a layer style button on the Layers palette, you are presented with the same choices for width, color, opacity, and blending mode, as those displayed in the Stroke dialog box.

A special kind of stroke is used with paths. Recall that a path is a defined outline or shape that you can turn into a selection. Because paths are vector graphics, they are resolution-independent and maintain crisp edges when resized or printed. When you create a stroke along a path, you have the ability to edit its shape by changing the anchor points — the stroke does not have to fall automatically along the border of the selection.

In Photoshop, the opposite of stroke is fill. A **fill** creates color within the selection rather than on its edge or border. Fills commonly are used to blend backgrounds, to add tints or shades, or to change the color in selected areas of an image. Fills are similar to some of the color changing filters you learned about earlier, however, fills create no distortion or collage effect. For example, if you had a photo of people that had a very dark background, you could fill that background with 50% opacity of white to make the people in the photo stand out.

The Fill dialog box allows you to choose the fill color or to use a pattern. Opacity and color are important settings when using a fill. A setting of 100% obscures the entire selection. While a lower opacity permits the image to show through, when it is applied with a noncomplementary color, the fill can appear unnatural and awkward. If you are filling a layer that includes transparent areas, and want to fill only areas containing pixels, you can choose to preserve the transparency.

Both the Stroke and Fill commands are available on the Edit menu. It is a good practice to create a stroke or fill in its own layer, or via a layer mask, so adjustments can be made independent of the image, if necessary.

Creating a Circular Mask

Each of the small photos in the lower portion of the magazine cover will be stroked in a circular pattern with the color red. This will add a third color to the magazine cover and draw attention to the three views of the racecar. The following steps illustrate how to create a circular mask on each of the three layers in preparation for stroking the color.

To Create a Circular Mask

1

- **On the Layers palette, select the front view layer. Increase the magnification setting to 50% and scroll as necessary to view the layer.**
- **Press the M key. If the Elliptical Marquee tool does not display in the toolbox, right-click the current marquee tool button, and then click Elliptical Marquee Tool in the list.**
- **On the options bar, click the New selection button, if necessary.**

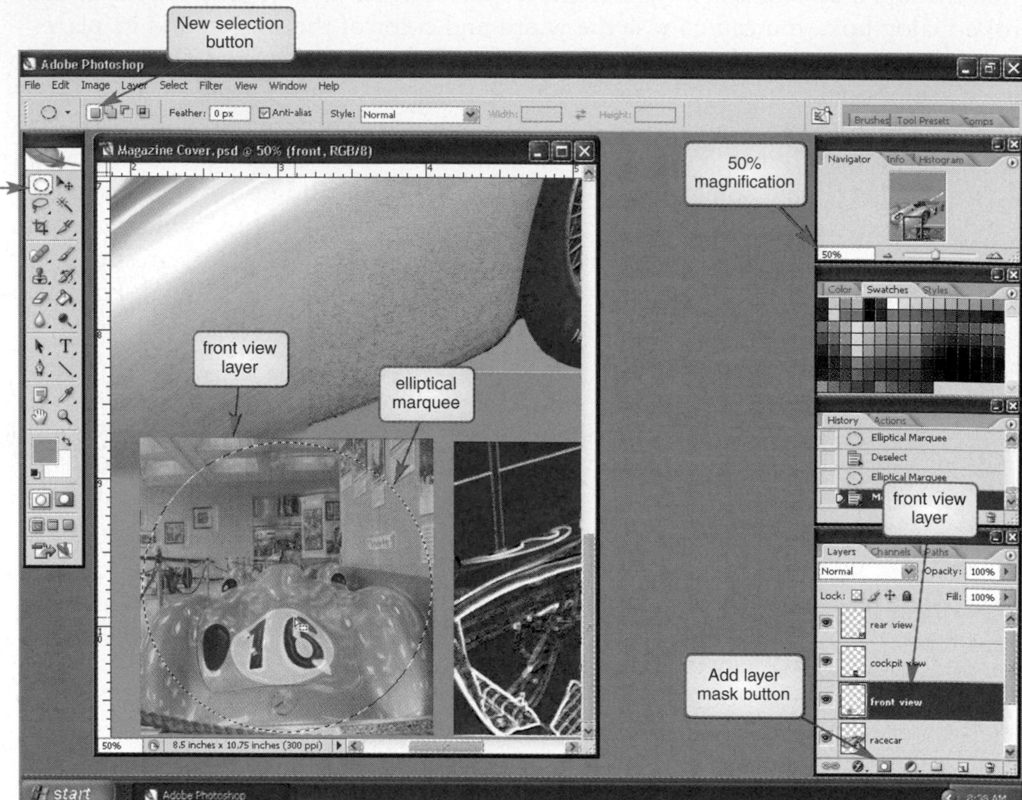

FIGURE 7-26

2

- **In the document window, SHIFT+drag a circle that encompasses most of the front view layer.**
- **After releasing the mouse, if the circle is not centered on the layer, drag it to the center. The selection should stay within the border of the image. If you make a mistake, drag a new circle.**

The elliptical marquee is displayed in the layer (Figure 7-26).

3

- **On the Layers palette, click the Add layer mask button.**
- **Click Select on the menu bar.**

The layer is masked in a circular shape (Figure 7-27). The Select menu also is displayed.

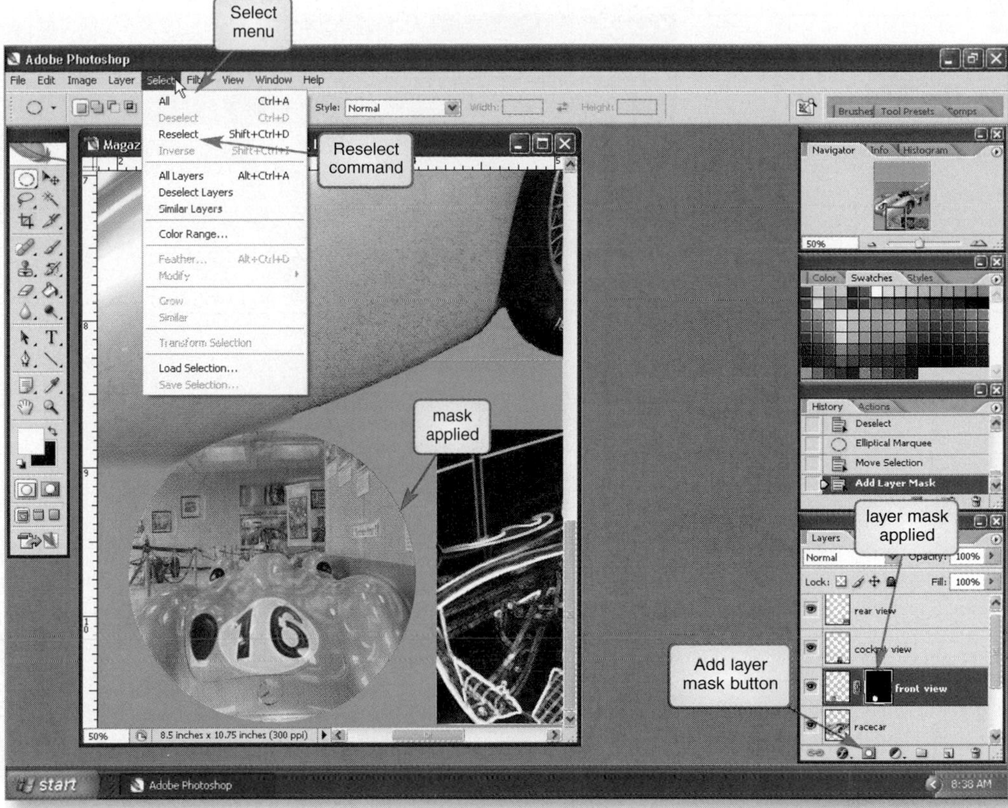

FIGURE 7-27

4

- **On the Select menu, click Reselect.**
- **In the document window, drag the circular selection to position it over the cockpit view image. Scroll as necessary. Make sure the selection does not overlap the edge of the image.**
- **On the Layers palette, click the cockpit view layer.**

A selection of the same size and shape now is placed over the cockpit view layer (Figure 7-28).

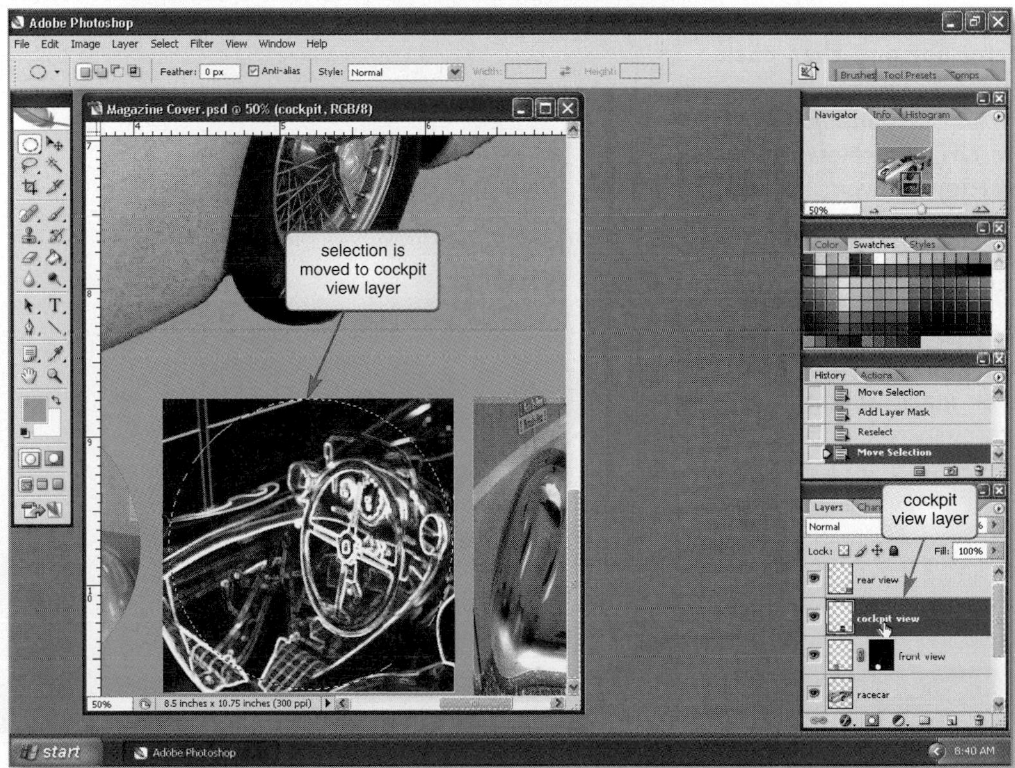

FIGURE 7-28

5

• **On the Layers palette, click the Add layer mask button.**

The second layer is masked in a circular shape (Figure 7-29).

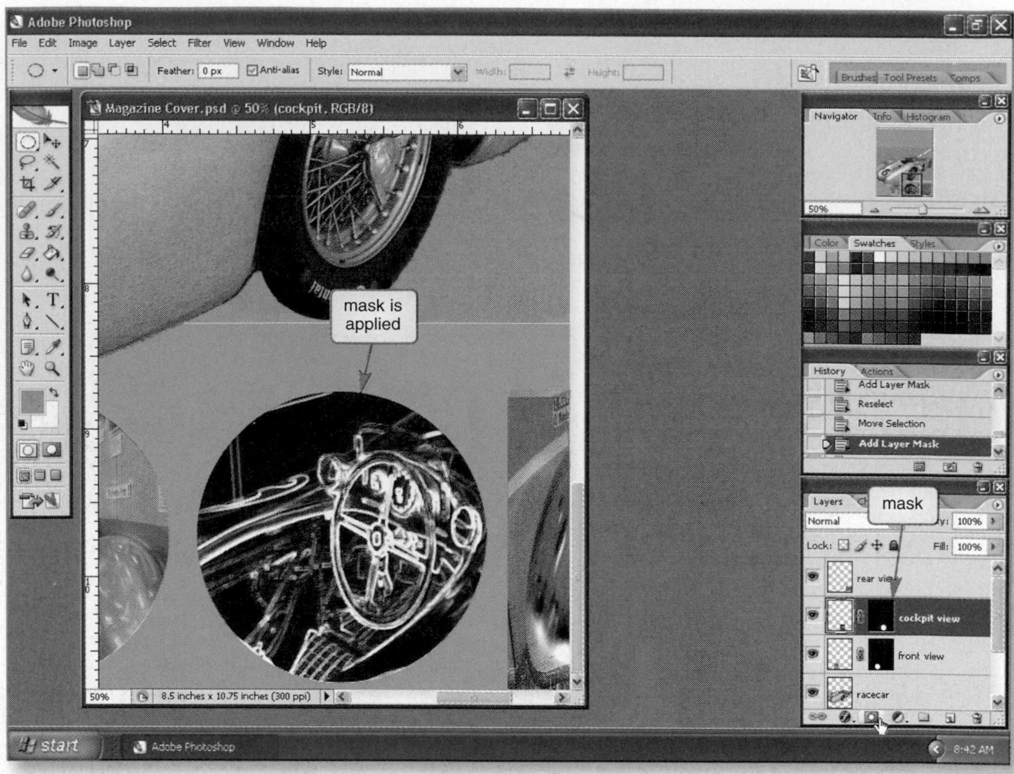

FIGURE 7-29

6

• **Click Select on the menu bar and then click Reselect. In the document window, drag the circular selection to position it over the rear view image. Scroll as necessary.**

• **On the Layers palette, click the rear view layer and then click the Add layer mask button.**

The third layer is masked in a circular shape (Figure 7-30).

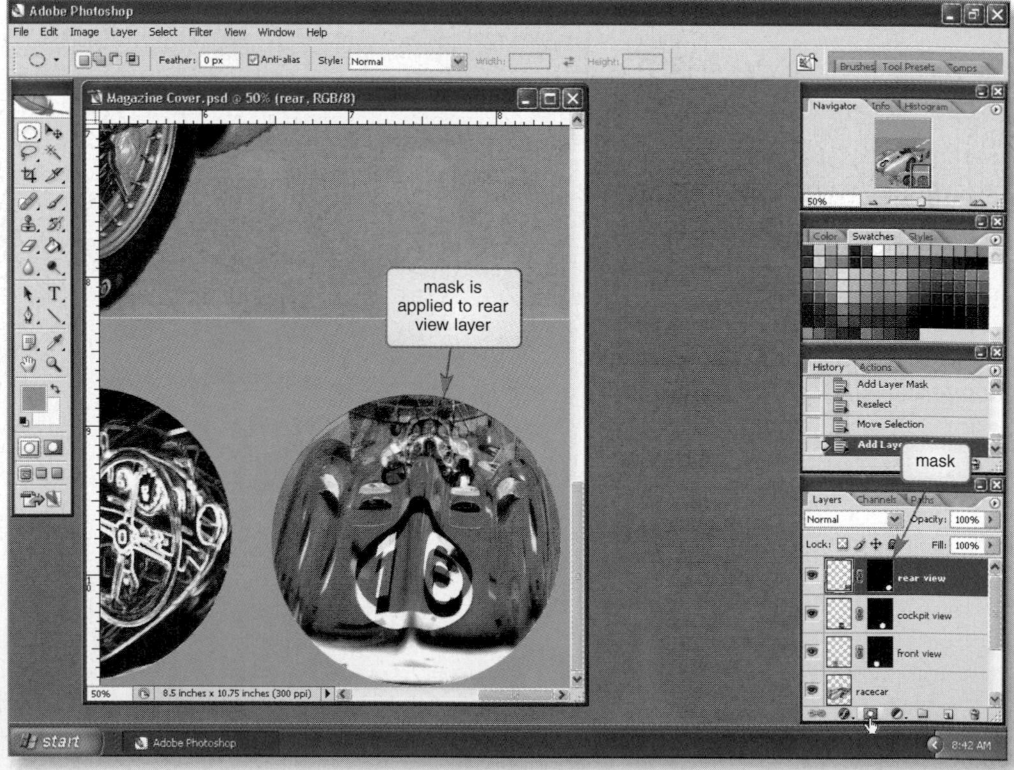

FIGURE 7-30

Other Ways

1. To create layer mask, on Layer menu, point to Layer Mask, click Reveal Selection
2. To reselect, press SHIFT+CTRL+D

The next steps create a stroke of color on the front view layer, and then copy the layer effect to the other two layers. Recall that you can create a stroke by using the Stroke command on the Edit menu, or by using the Add a layer style button on the Layers menu as shown in the following steps.

To Stroke Color and Copy the Effect

1

- **Zoom to 16.67 percent magnification.**
- **On the Layers palette, click the front view layer, and then click the Add a layer style button.**

The shortcut menu of layer styles is displayed (Figure 7-31).

FIGURE 7-31

2

- **Click Stroke.**
- **When the Layer Style dialog box is displayed, type** 35 **in the Size box.**
- **If necessary, set the Position to Outside, the Blend Mode to Normal, the Opacity to 100%, and the Fill Type to Color.**
- **Click the Color box. When the Color Picker is displayed, select a bright red color, and then close the Color Picker.**

The Layer Style settings will create a red stroke of 35 pixels (Figure 7-32).

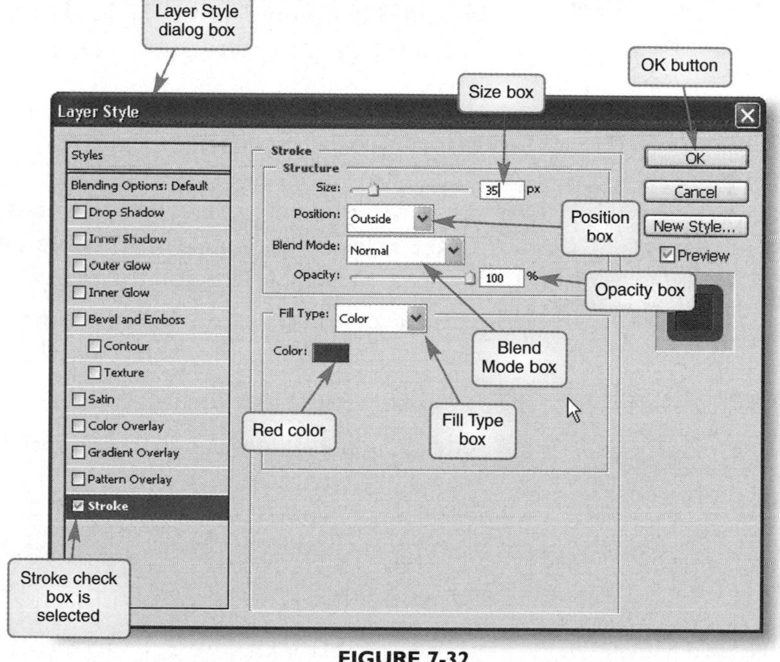

FIGURE 7-32

3

- **Click the OK button.**
- **On the Layers palette, ALT+drag the Indicates layer effects button from the front view layer to the cockpit view layer, and then again to the rear view layer.**

The three strokes display in the document window (Figure 7-33). Your display may differ.

FIGURE 7-33

Other Ways

1. On Edit menu, click Stroke

The final step in preparing the lower portion of the magazine cover is to align and distribute the three stroked layers.

To Align and Distribute Layers

1. **If necessary, use the Move tool to adjust each layer so it does not touch any other layer or the margins. Use the arrow keys to nudge the layers if it is necessary to make fine adjustments.**
2. **On the Layers palette, one at a time, SHIFT+click the front view, cockpit view, and rear view layers to select all three.**
3. **Click Layer on the menu bar, point to Align, and then click Bottom Edges.**
4. **Click Layer on the menu bar, point to Distribute, and then click Vertical Centers.**

The layers are aligned and distributed.

Patterns

A **pattern** is an image that is **tiled**, or repeated, to fill a selection or a layer. Photoshop has libraries of preset patterns that can be loaded and used in any document, but by default ten patterns are loaded into the Pattern Picker box, including bubbles, clouds, tie dye, and others. You can access the **Pattern Picker box** from the Layer Style dialog box or from the options bar associated with the Paint Bucket tool, the Pattern Stamp tool, the Healing Brush tool, and the Patch tool. Commands on the Pattern Picker box menu allow users to load, save, and manage pattern libraries. Recall that libraries associated with many kinds of presets including gradients, brushes, styles, and custom shapes also can be managed using the Preset Manager command on the Edit menu.

Creating Patterns

In Photoshop, you can use one of the preset patterns or you can create your own patterns and save them for use with different tools and commands. Photoshop gives you the ability to create a specific pattern, either from scratch or from another image, with the Define Pattern command on the Edit menu. Or, you can use the **Pattern Maker Filter** that generates a random pattern based on a selection or image.

You will use a racing flag image to make a pattern using the Define Pattern command as described in the following steps.

To Define a Pattern

1

- **Open the file named, Race Flag, from the Project07 folder on the CD that accompanies this book, or from a location specified by your instructor.**

Photoshop displays the racing flag image in a new document window (Figure 7-34).

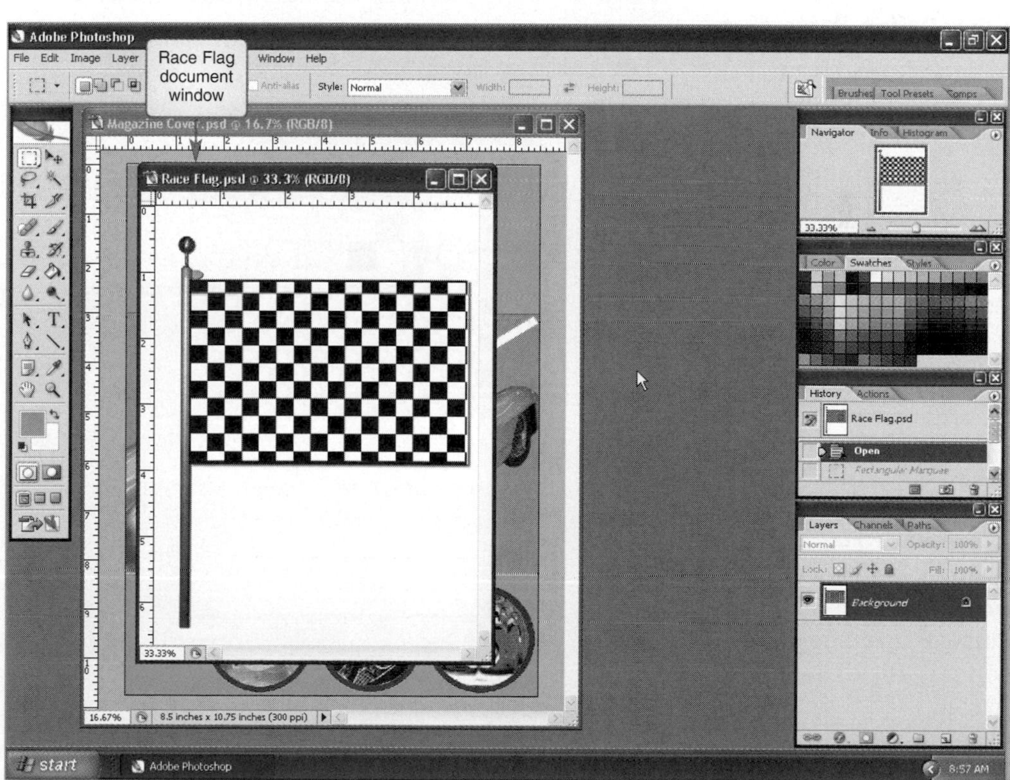

FIGURE 7-34

2

- **Press the** `M` **key. If the Rectangular Marquee tool is not displayed in the toolbox, right-click the current marquee tool button and then click Rectangular Marquee Tool in the list.**
- **Drag to form a selection rectangle around four contiguous squares in the flag.**
- **Click Edit on the menu bar.**

The selection is displayed including two black and two white squares on opposite corners (Figure 7-35).

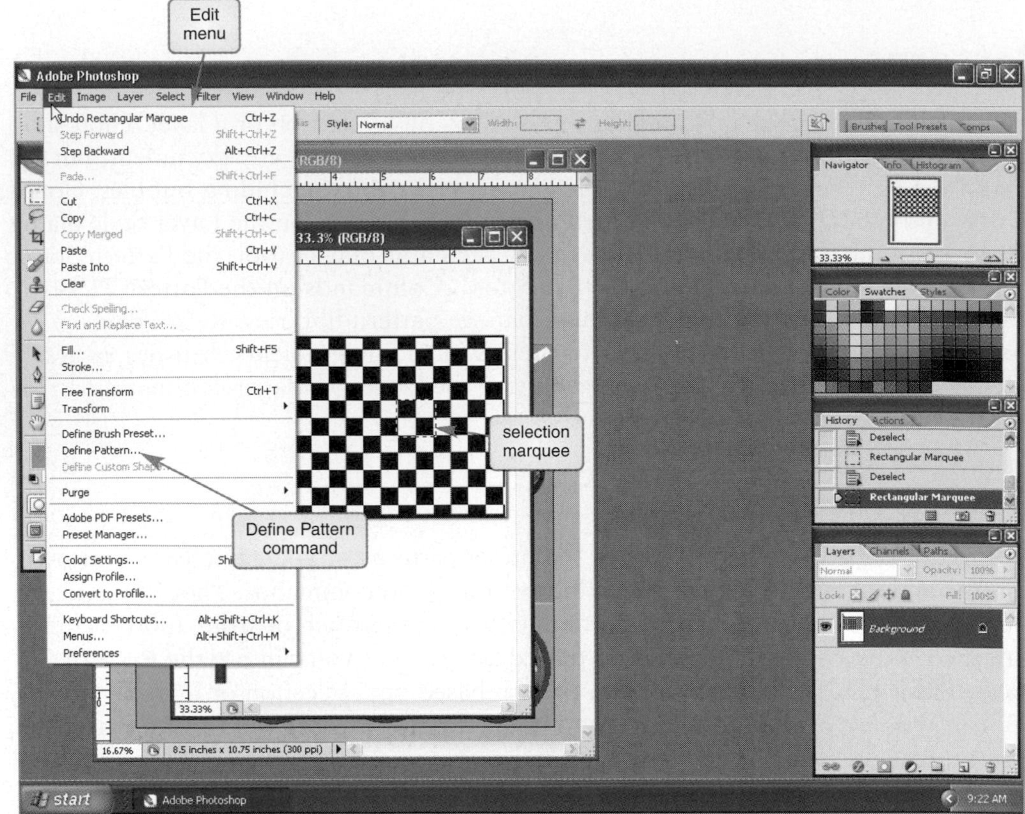

FIGURE 7-35

3

- **Click Define Pattern.**
- **When the Pattern Name dialog box is displayed, type** `racing flag` **in the Name box.**

Photoshop displays the Pattern Name dialog box with a preview of the pattern (Figure 7-36).

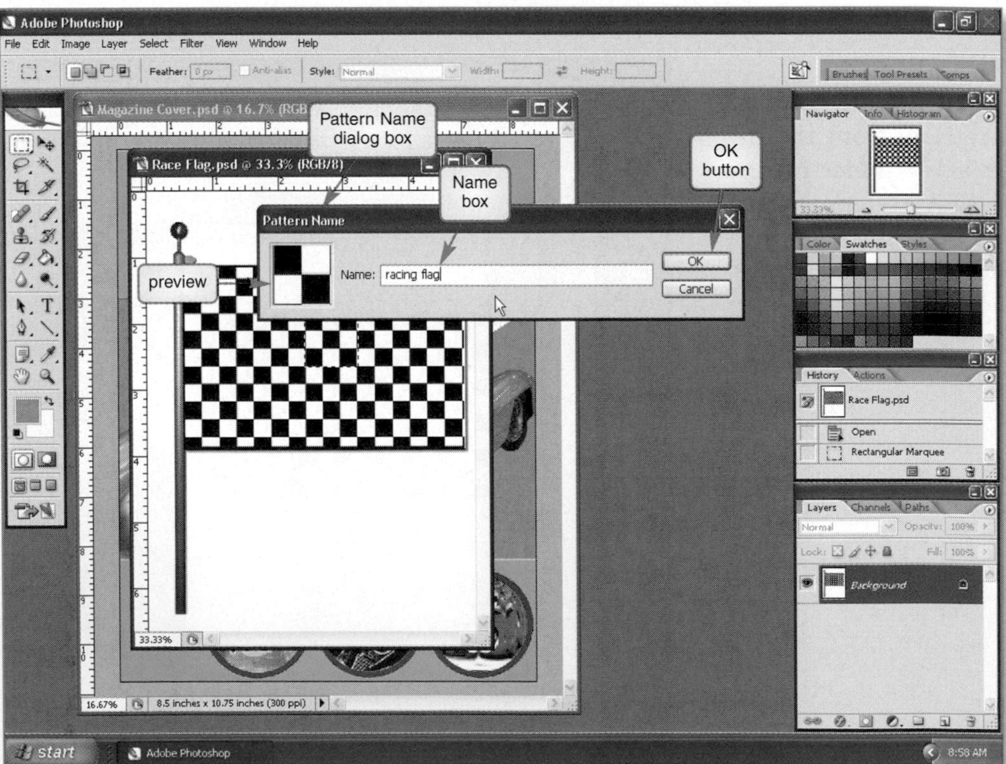

FIGURE 7-36

4

- **Click the OK button.**
- **Click the Close button on the Race Flag document window. If Photoshop asks if you want to save the changes, click the No button.**

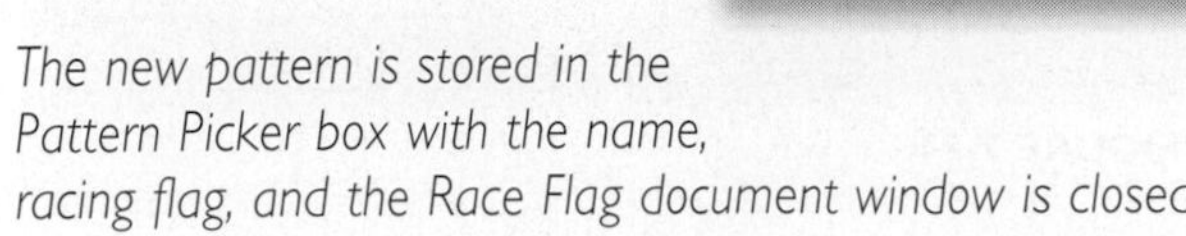

The new pattern is stored in the Pattern Picker box with the name, racing flag, and the Race Flag document window is closed.

In the next steps, the new pattern is used to create a stripe to further define the upper portion of the magazine cover. Rulers are used to precisely place the stripe.

To Use a Pattern

1

- **On the Layers palette, select the Background layer. From the horizontal ruler, drag a ruler guide into the Magazine Cover document window to just meet the upper edge of the gray road layer.**
- **Drag another ruler guide 3/4 of an inch above the previous one.**

Photoshop displays the green guide lines (Figure 7-37).

FIGURE 7-37

2

- **With the Rectangular Marquee tool still selected, drag a rectangle to fill the area between the two ruler guides.**

The selection snaps to the ruler guides (Figure 7-38).

FIGURE 7-38

3

- **Press the G key. If the Gradient tool displays in the toolbox, right-click the Gradient Tool (G) button and then click Paint Bucket Tool in the list.**
- **On the options bar, click the Set source for fill area box arrow, and then click Pattern in the list.**
- **Click the Pattern Picker box.**

The default patterns and the newly defined pattern are displayed (Figure 7-39). If you point to the newly defined pattern, Photoshop displays the name in a tool tip.

FIGURE 7-39

4

- **Click the racing flag pattern and then click in the selection rectangle.**
- **Press SHIFT+CTRL+J to create a new layer via cut. On the Layers palette, double-click the layer name, type** `stripe` **as the name, and then press the ENTER key.**
- **Press CTRL+; so the guides no longer display.**

Photoshop displays the defined pattern in the new layer (Figure 7-40).

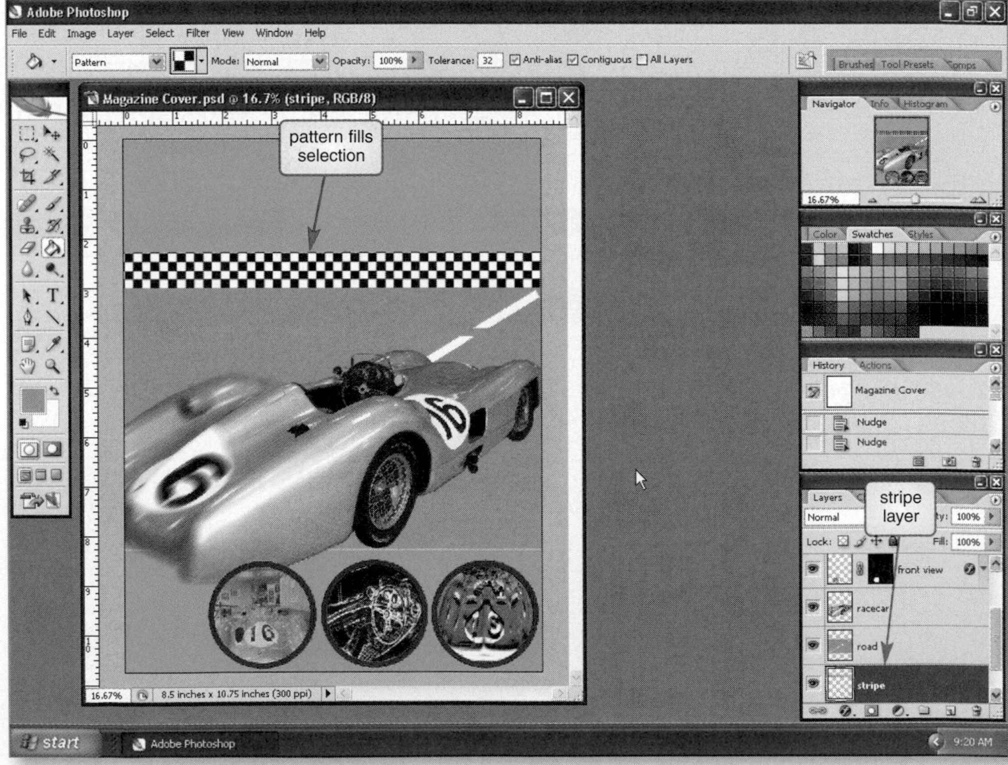

FIGURE 7-40

Unless you plan on using the new pattern in multiple documents, it is a good practice to delete your patterns — especially in lab situations. The next steps show how to delete a pattern.

To Delete a Pattern

- **Press the G key. On the options bar, click the Pattern Picker box.**
- **Right-click the racing flag pattern.**

The patterns again are displayed (Figure 7-41). The shortcut menu is displayed with commands to name, rename, and delete patterns.

2

- **Click Delete Pattern on the shortcut menu.**

The pattern is deleted.

FIGURE 7-41

The next step is to create a diagonal line to separate the information and graphics in the upper portion of the magazine cover.

To Create a Line

1. **On the Layers palette, click the Background layer.**
2. **Press the D key to access the default colors. Press the X key to exchange the colors so that white is the foreground color.**
3. **Press the U key to access the Shape tools. On the options bar, click the Fill pixels button and the Line Tool button, if necessary. Type** `40 px` **in the Weight box and then press the ENTER key.**
4. **Drag a line from the upper-left corner of the magazine cover to the right margin, just above the racing flag stripe. Make sure that the line touches the border of the page at both edges.**

Photoshop displays the white line (Figure 7-42 on the next page).

FIGURE 7-42

Rendering

In publishing, graphic design, and image editing, the term **render** simply means to create an artistic change. Photoshop's rendering effects or render filters (Table 7-9) transform images by creating 3-D shapes, cloud patterns, refraction patterns, and simulated light reflections. The Render effects are on the Filter menu. During rendering, image data on the active layer is replaced, so it is best to use the commands on layer copies rather than on the original. Recall that you used a rendered cloud effect in a previous project.

Table 7-9 Render Effects

RENDER EFFECT	DESCRIPTION	ADJUSTABLE SETTINGS
Clouds	randomly creates a cloud pattern using the foreground and background colors	None
Difference Clouds	randomly creates a cloud pattern using the existing pixels	None
Fibers	generates a woven fiber look using the foreground and background colors	Variance Strength Randomize
Lens Flare	simulates the flare of a bright light shining into a camera lens	Flare Center Brightness Lens Type
Lighting Effects	creates lighting effects on RGB images by varying a wide array of settings	Style Light type Properties Texture Channel

Creating a Lighting Effect

The left portion of the magazine cover, above the racing flag stripe, will employ a spotlight effect to highlight the text that will be placed in that area later in the project (see Figure 7-1 on page PS 419).

The **Lighting Effects** command on the Render submenu displays a dialog box that contains numerous settings to create an almost endless number of effects. First you will select a lighting style from those shown in Table 7-10. Styles have to do with the number of light sources in the lighting effect, and their color, intensity, direction, and focus.

Table 7-10 Lighting Effects Styles

LIGHTING EFFECTS STYLE	DESCRIPTION
2 O'clock Spotlight	a yellow spotlight of medium intensity with a wide focus
Blue Omni	a blue overhead omni-directional light of full intensity with no focus
Circle of Light	uses four spotlights: white, yellow, red, and blue
Crossing	a white spotlight of medium intensity with a wide focus
Crossing Down	two white spotlights of medium intensity with a wide focus
Default	a white spotlight of medium intensity with a wide focus
Five Lights Down/Five Lights Up	five white spotlights of full intensity with a wide focus
Flashlight	an omnidirectional yellow light of medium intensity
Flood Light	a white spotlight of medium intensity with a wide focus
Parallel Directional	a directional blue light of full intensity with no focus
RGB Lights	red, blue, and green lights of medium intensity with a wide focus
Soft Direct Lights	two unfocused white and blue directional lights
Soft Omni	a soft, omni-directional light of medium intensity
Soft Spotlight	a white spotlight of full intensity with a wide focus
Three Down	three white spotlights of soft intensity with a wide focus
Triple Spotlight	three spotlights of slight intensity with a wide focus

Three lighting types are available as described in Table 7-11. Types specify the distance of the perceived light in the lighting effect.

Table 7-11 Lighting Effects Types

LIGHTING EFFECTS TYPE	DESCRIPTION
Omni	shines in all directions directly above the image
Directional	shines as if from a distance
Spotlight	shines an elliptical beam of light

Table 7-12 on the next page displays the light properties which are set using sliders. Properties set the reflection and quantity of the perceived light source.

Table 7-12 Lighting Effects Properties

LIGHTING EFFECTS PROPERTY	DESCRIPTION
Gloss	simulates reflection of light off a surface
Material	sets the amount of reflection from either the light source or the object in the image
Exposure	increases or decreases light
Ambience	simulates light from another room or another source

The Lighting Effects dialog box has a preview where you can change the direction and angle of the light by dragging the handles that define the edges of an ellipse. To change the color of the light, you click the Color box that opens the Color Picker. A Texture channel setting allows you to specify which channel to render. If you choose none, the lighting effect is applied to all channels.

Because rendering replaces all pixels, you first should make a layer via copy of the selected area before it is rendered, as illustrated in the following steps.

To Create a Layer via Copy

1 **With the Background layer still selected, press the W key and then click in the area to the left of the diagonal line.**

2 **Press CTRL+J to create a layer via copy.**

3 **On the Layers palette, double-click the layer name, type `lighting` as the name, and then press the ENTER key.**

The new layer is created (Figure 7-43).

4 **If necessary, press CTRL+D to remove the selection marquee.**

FIGURE 7-43

The next steps render the lighting effect on the newly created layer. A Preview box in the Lighting Effects dialog box displays an ellipse with four handles and a center point positioned over a background rectangle. The ellipse allows you to set the direction of the light source graphically.

To Create a Lighting Effect

1

- **With the lighting layer still selected, click Filter on the menu bar, and then point to Render.**

The Render submenu is displayed with a choice of rendering effects (Figure 7-44).

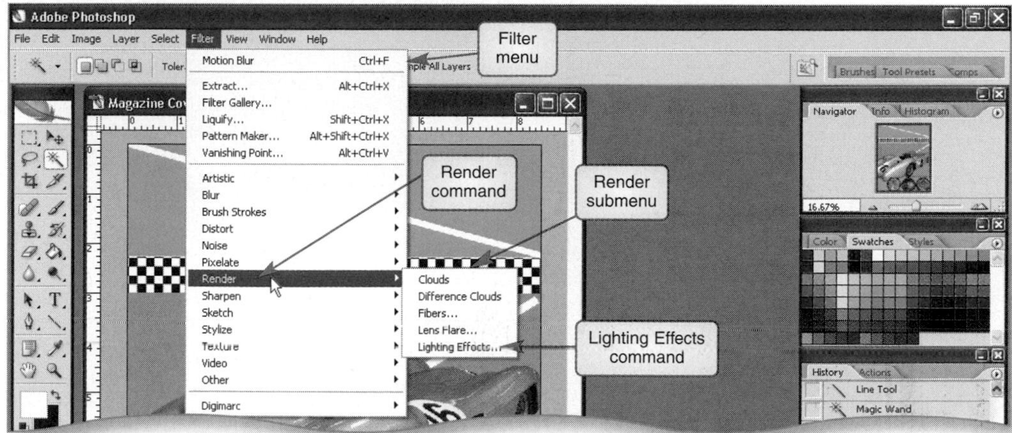

FIGURE 7-44

2

- **Click Lighting Effects.**
- **When the Lighting Effects dialog box is displayed, if necessary, click the Light type box arrow and then click Spotlight in the list.**
- **In the preview box, if necessary, use the handles to move and resize the ellipse so it completely fits inside the box to start.**
- **Locate the radial line handle and drag it to the left until the line is horizontal.**
- **Drag the center point of the ellipse to the right edge of the background rectangle.**
- **Drag the radial line handle to the left edge of the background rectangle, keeping the line straight.**
- **Drag the Intensity slider to 45. Drag the Focus slider to 68. All other sliders should be at zero.**

The settings are displayed (Figure 7-45).

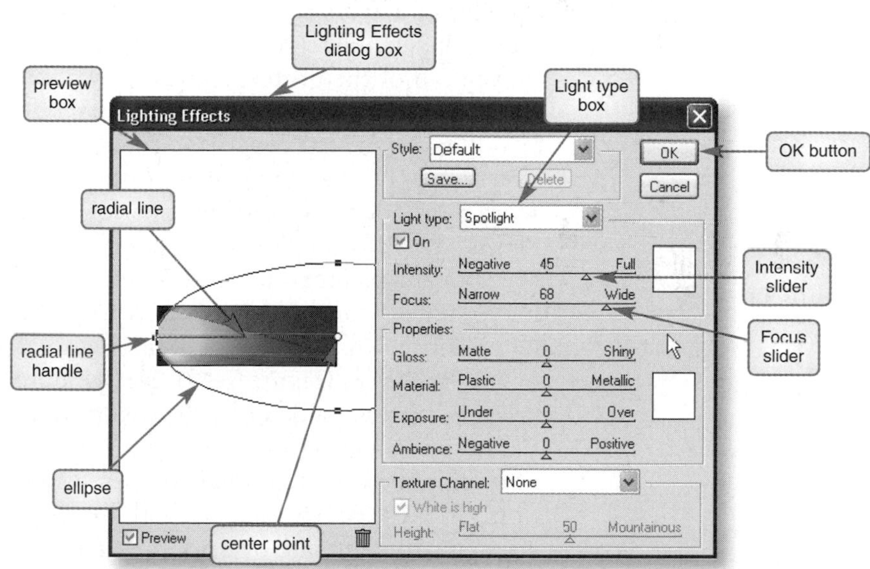

FIGURE 7-45

• **Click the OK button.**

The spotlight effect is rendered (Figure 7-46).

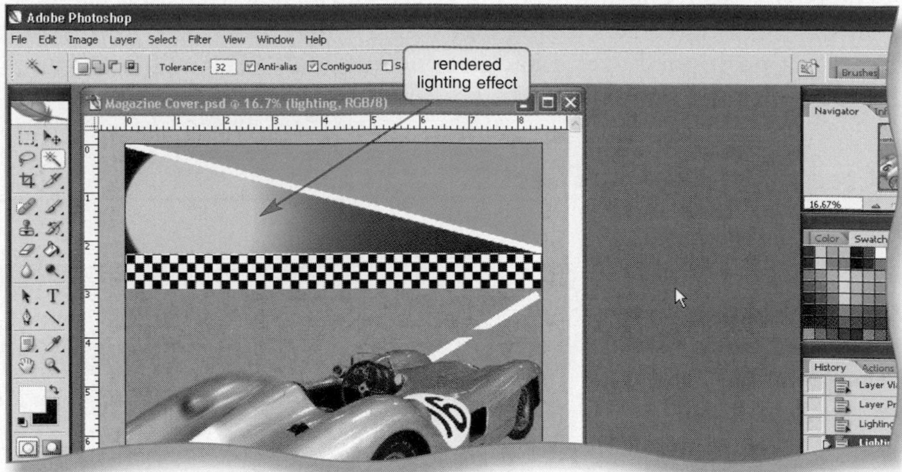

FIGURE 7-46

Knockouts and Trapping

In most printing media, when two objects of different colors overlap they create a **knockout** — the inks will not print on top of each other. At the point where the top layer overlaps the bottom one, the bottom one is not printed at all. In Photoshop, the Flatten Layers command automatically saves only the topmost color in overlapped layers, which creates the knockout for you. Sometimes that is not enough to prevent all of the problems caused by overlapping colors, however.

When you print a hard copy using a desktop printer, the color is applied all at once; each color normally is printed where you expect it to be. In commercial printing, the printing device makes more than one pass over the paper as you learned in the discussion of four-color printing and color separations. The speed of the printer and possible shifts in the paper may make some colors run together creating spreads of blended color; or, the printer may leave small missed areas between very close objects or layers (Figure 7-47). Service bureaus use the term **misregistration** to describe those gaps in printing that are out of the printer's register or alignment. **Trapping** is a prepress activity of calculating an intentional compensation for the misregistration. Chokes and spreads are both methods of trapping. **Chokes**, intentionally shrink an image to eliminate overprinting, and **spreads** intentionally overlap images to avoid gaps in the ink coverage where the base paper might show through.

gap

FIGURE 7-47

If you do not want to worry about trapping and misregistration, eliminating the possibility of gaps is the best way to avoid the problem. Table 7-13 lists some ways to avoid the problem as you plan your graphic designs.

Table 7-13 Ways to Avoid Misregistration

METHOD	DESCRIPTION
Avoid putting colored objects too close together	Leave some white space between objects in your design
Use common process colors when colors need to touch	Use colors within 20 percent of each other in the CMYK color spectrum
Use black trim	Stroke objects that overlap, or meet, with black outlines
Overprint black text	Use an overlay blending mode on type layers to cancel the knockout and force black ink to print on the background color

When you cannot avoid placing colors close together, intentionally printing one layer of ink on top of another is called **overprinting**, or **surprinting**. Most service bureaus determine if trapping is needed in the overprinting process and can perform that prepress activity for you. It is not recommended you do this yourself, but if you need or want to do it, you will have to enter values in the Trap dialog box. The Trap command is on the Image menu. The service bureau, who understands its printing process best, is the ideal source for correctly gauging these values.

Photoshop's automatic settings use industry standard rules when applying a trap:

- White is knocked out automatically.
- All colors spread under black.
- Lighter colors spread under darker colors.
- Yellow spreads under cyan, magenta, and black.
- Pure cyan and pure magenta spread under each other equally.

Therefore, in the magazine cover, a white line will not cause any problem because it will be knocked out to the paper color. Surprinting black text over the cyan — instead of having it automatically knockout — will prevent any white gaps.

If you want to knock out colors that normally are not trapped according to the above rules, the **Knockout layer effect** lets you specify which layers to knockout or punch through to reveal content from other layers or to reveal the paper. The layers must be in order from the top, which creates the shape of the knockout; to the bottom, which is the color or paper that should show through.

In the magazine cover you will head off any potential chokes, spreads, and trapping errors. The following steps create a black line around the racing flag stripe so that the gray road will not bleed into the white parts of the racing pattern. The line also will cover any potential misregistration gap between the road and the stripe pattern.

To Stroke the Racing Flag Stripe

1. **Press the D key to activate the default colors.**
2. **On the Layers palette, select the stripe layer.**
3. **Click Edit on the menu bar and then click Stroke.**
4. **Type** 20 px **in the Width box. If necessary, click Center in the Location area. If necessary, set the Mode to Normal and the Opacity to 100%. Click Preserve Transparency to select it.**

The edited settings in the Stroke dialog box will create a small black border centered along the edges of the layer, which will help to head off potential chokes or misregistration gaps (Figure 7-48 on the next page).

FIGURE 7-48

5 **Click the OK button in the Stroke dialog box.**

Headline Text

Two headlines appear on the magazine cover. The first is the title of the magazine, and the second is information about the special issue. Before publication, other text might be added that would lead the readers to certain articles or attract the attention of certain populations. Both headlines will use the Overlay blending mode to help avoid any misregistration problems.

Recall from Special Feature 2, that font family, font style, classification, and color, all play important roles in typography. The choice of font, size, style, and color also sets the tone for a layout. Readability is determined by font, point size, line space, line length, and style, such as italics or all caps.

In the magazine cover, you will use the Magneto font that emulates handwriting, yet is brassy enough for a sports magazine headline. The other settings are listed in Table 7-14.

Table 7-14 Font Settings for Headline Text

FONT SETTING	SETTING
Font Family	Magneto
Font Style	Bold
Font Size	36
Anti-Aliasing	Sharp
Alignment	Right align text
Color	Black

The following steps show how to insert headline text.

To Insert Headline Text

1

- **On the Layers palette, select the Background layer.**
- **Press the T key. If the Horizontal Type tool does not display in the toolbox, right-click the current type tool button, and then click Horizontal Type Tool in the list.**
- **On the options bar, enter the settings from Table 7-14. If you do not have the specific font on your system, choose a similar font.**
- **Drag a box in the upper-right corner of the magazine cover, approximately 5 inches wide and 1.5 inches tall.**
- **Type** `Fast Freddie's Racing Magazine` **in the bounding box.**

The new text is displayed (Figure 7-49).

FIGURE 7-49

2

- **Press CTRL+A to select all of the text.**
- **On the options bar, click the Toggle the Character and Paragraph palettes button.**
- **When the palettes are displayed, click the Character tab, if necessary.**
- **Click the Set the leading box arrow and then click 30 in the list.**

The lines of text are displayed closer together (Figure 7-50).

FIGURE 7-50

3

- **On the options bar, click the Commit any current edits button.**
- **Click the Close button on the Character and Paragraph palette title bar.**
- **If necessary, press the V key and then move the type layer to a position that neither overlaps the white diagonal line nor touches the magazine's edge.**

So you do not have to worry about trapping the red text, the following steps show how to overprint or create an overlay on the type layers. An overlay will guarantee a solid black color without any cyan showing through.

To Create the Overlay

1

- **With the type layer still selected on the Layers palette, click the Add a layer style button, and then click Color Overlay in the list.**
- **When the Layer Style dialog box is displayed, click the Blend Mode box arrow, and then click Overlay in the list.**
- **If the color is not black, click the Color box. When the Color Picker is displayed, select a black color, and then close the Color Picker.**
- **If necessary, drag the Opacity slider to 100%.**

Photoshop will overlay the cyan color with solid black text (Figure 7-51).

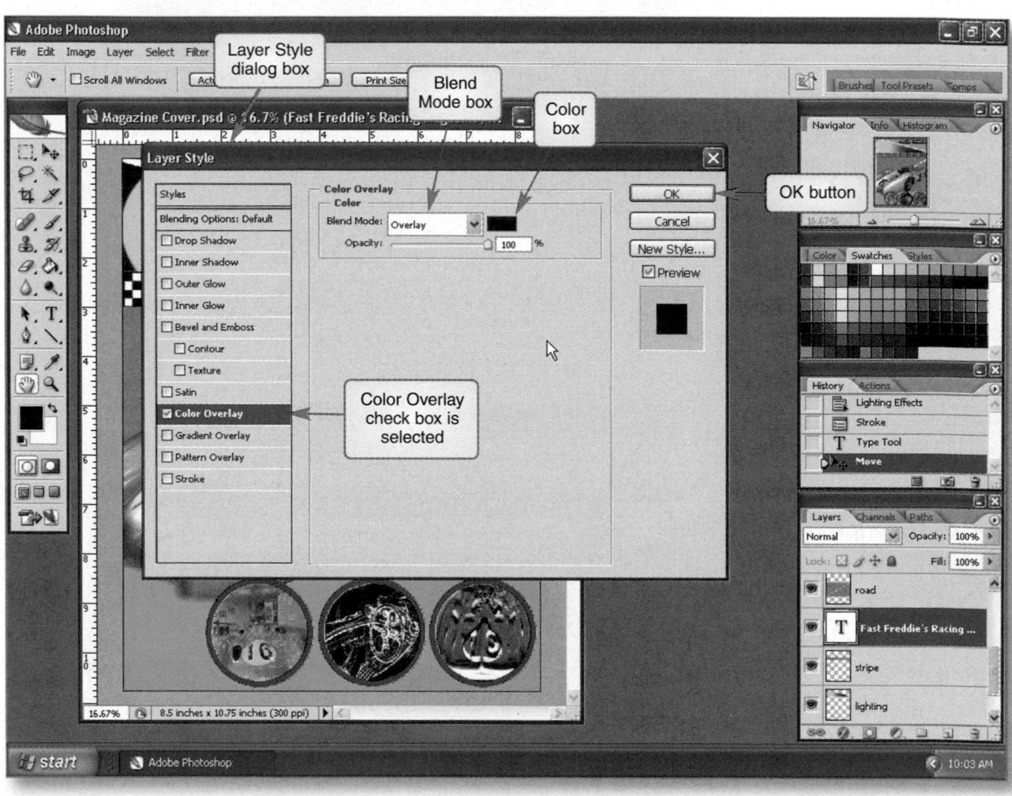

FIGURE 7-51

- **Click the OK button in the Layer Style dialog box.**

The Color Overlay state is displayed on the History palette. There is no change in the document window on the screen. The overlay will take place during the print process.

Creating the Secondary Headline

In the secondary headline, the first line of text will use the Magneto font from the magazine title text, along with the red color from the circle strokes in the lower part of the magazine cover. The second and third lines will use a sans serif font called Gill Sans MT. Recall that sans serif fonts define type without end strokes or flourishes. Fonts like Gill Sans MT work well with decorative fonts, because the sans serif fonts are less distracting visually. Gill Sans MT emphasizes and supports the decorative font, making it easier to read.

The following steps show how to insert the secondary text in two separate type bounding boxes so the color overlay for red and black will work properly.

To Insert Secondary Headline Text

1

- **On the Layers palette, select the lighting layer.**
- **Press the** T **key to activate the Type tool. Drag a box in the upper-left portion of the lighting layer, approximately 2.5 inches wide and .5 inches tall.**
- **Enter** `36 pt` **in the Set the font size box, if necessary.**
- **Click the Set the text color box. When the Color Picker is displayed, select the same bright red color that you used for the circles in the lower portion of the magazine cover, and then click the OK button to close the Color Picker.**
- **Click the Left align text button.**
- **Type** `Special` **in the type bounding box.**

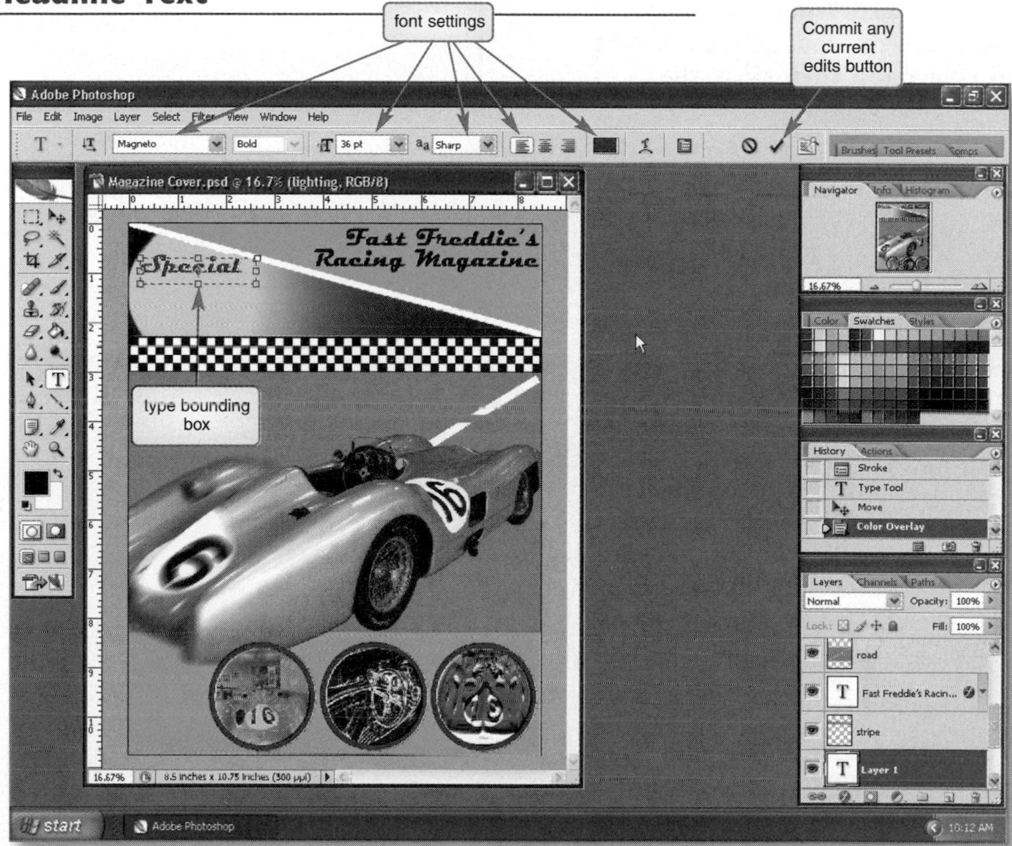

FIGURE 7-52

Photoshop applies the settings and displays the red text (Figure 7-52).

2

- **On the options bar, click the Commit any current edits button.**
- **With the type layer still selected on the Layers palette, click the Add a layer style button, and then click Color Overlay in the list.**
- **When the Layer Style dialog box is displayed, click the Blend Mode box arrow, and then click Overlay in the list.**
- **If the color is not red, click the Color box. When the Color Picker is displayed, select a bright red color, and then close the Color Picker.**
- **If necessary, drag the Opacity slider to 100%.**

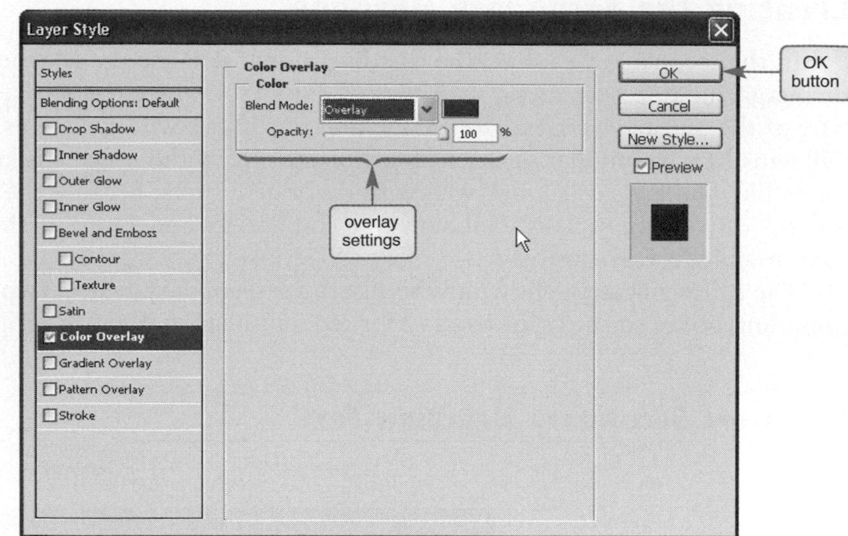

FIGURE 7-53

Photoshop displays the Color Overlay settings of the Layer Style dialog box (Figure 7-53). Again, an overlay, or surprinting, will guarantee that the red color will display strongly next to the cyan background.

3

- **Click the OK button in the Layer Style dialog box.**
- **Drag another type bounding box in the document window just below the word, Special, approximately 3.5 inches wide and 1 inch tall.**
- **On the options bar, click the Set the font family box arrow, and then click Gill Sans MT in the list. If you do not have the specific font on your system, choose a similar font.**
- **Click the Set the font style box arrow and then click Bold in the list.**
- **Click the Set the font size box arrow, and then click 24 in the list.**
- **Change the color to black.**
- **Type** `Historic Racecar Issue` **in the type bounding box.**
- **Press the ENTER key and then type** `$10.00` **to complete the entry.**

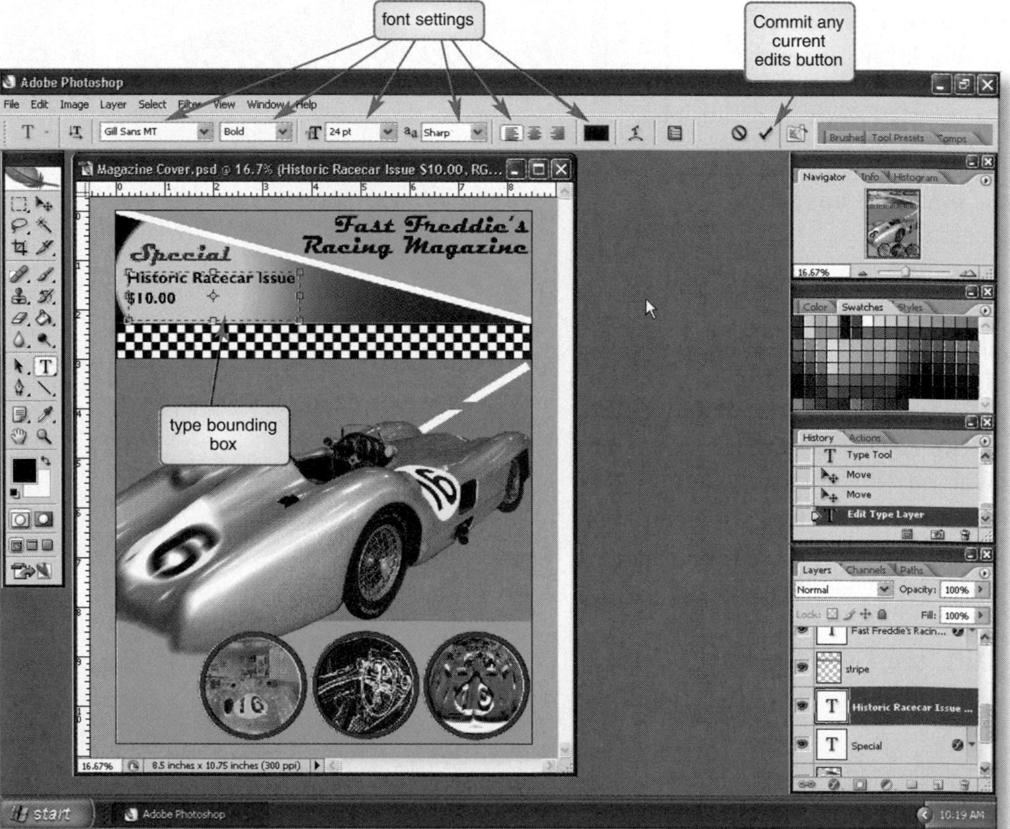

FIGURE 7-54

Photoshop displays the new text in black (Figure 7-54).

4

- **On the options bar, click the Commit any current edits button.**
- **With the type layer still selected on the Layers palette, click the Add a layer style button, and then click Color Overlay in the list.**
- **When the Layer Style dialog box is displayed, click the Blend Mode box arrow, and then click Overlay in the list. Choose black and 100% opacity.**
- **Click the OK button in the Layer Style dialog box.**
- **If necessary, press the V key and then move the type layer to a position that neither overlaps the white diagonal line nor touches the magazine's edge.**

The final Color Overlay is created.

Before converting the image to CMYK and flattening the layers, you should save the file again.

To Save the File with Layers

1. **With your USB flash drive connected to one of the computer's USB ports, press SHIFT+CTRL+S to open the Save As dialog box.**
2. **When the Save As dialog box is displayed, type** `Magazine Cover with Layers` **in the File name text box. Do not press the ENTER key.**
3. **Click the Save in box arrow and then click USBDISK [G:], or the location associated with your USB flash drive, in the list.**
4. **Click the Save button. If Photoshop displays a Photoshop Format Options warning message box, click the OK button.**

The file is saved.

Converting to CMYK Color Mode

The next step is to convert the image to CMYK and merge the layers. Recall that the color mode is changed using the Image menu. CMYK is the correct color mode for professional print jobs.

To Convert to the CMYK Color Mode

1

- **On the Image menu, point to Mode, and then click CMYK Color.**

Photoshop displays a warning message about merging layers (Figure 7-55).

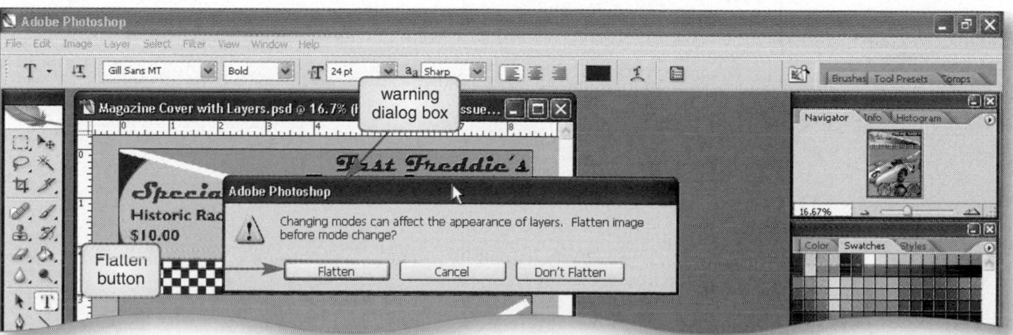

FIGURE 7-55

2

• **Click the Flatten button.**

After a few moments, the layers are merged in the Layers palette and the color mode is changed to CMYK as noted on the document window title bar.

With the magazine cover complete and flattened, the next section describes how to print a proof copy to check for errors.

Proofs

A **proof** is a copy of a document that you can look at to check color, layout, spelling, and other details before printing the final copy. A **hard proof** simulates what your final output will look like on a printing press. Sometimes called a proof print, or a match print, a hard proof is produced on an output device that is less expensive than a printing press. Some ink-jet printers have the resolution necessary to produce inexpensive prints that can be used as hard proofs. Hard proofs need to fit on the page of the proof printer, so it sometimes is necessary to scale the proof. Alternately, if you need to see a full-size proof, you may be able to **tile** or **poster print** the image, printing smaller portions of the image, each on its own sheet of paper, but at actual size. Be careful about judging color with a desktop printer. Some less expensive printers may produce output that does not represent the screen color accurately. For example, lower quality printers can produce a blue hue that appears slightly purple; red hues sometimes appear orange. Users should be aware that the use of inferior printers can result in somewhat false output. Ask your service bureau about color matching.

While a hard proof is a printed copy, a **soft proof** is a copy you look at on the screen. Soft proofs can be as simple as a preview, or more complex when color adjustments and monitor calibrations take place.

The next series of steps prints a hard proof that resembles what a final copy of the magazine cover should look like. Settings in the Print Preview dialog box are adjusted to match professional print settings. Your result will be printer dependent. Some printers handle color matching and overlays better than others. See your instructor for exact settings.

To Print a Hard Proof

1

- **On the View menu, point to Proof Setup. If the Working CMYK command does not display a check mark, click it.**
- **On the File menu, click Print with Preview.**
- **When Photoshop displays the Print dialog box, if a More Options button is present, click it.**
- **Click the Scale to Fit Media check box to select it.**
- **Below the preview, click the box arrow and then click Color Management, if necessary.**
- **In the Print area, click Proof.**
- **Click the Color Handling box arrow and then click Let Photoshop Determine Colors.**

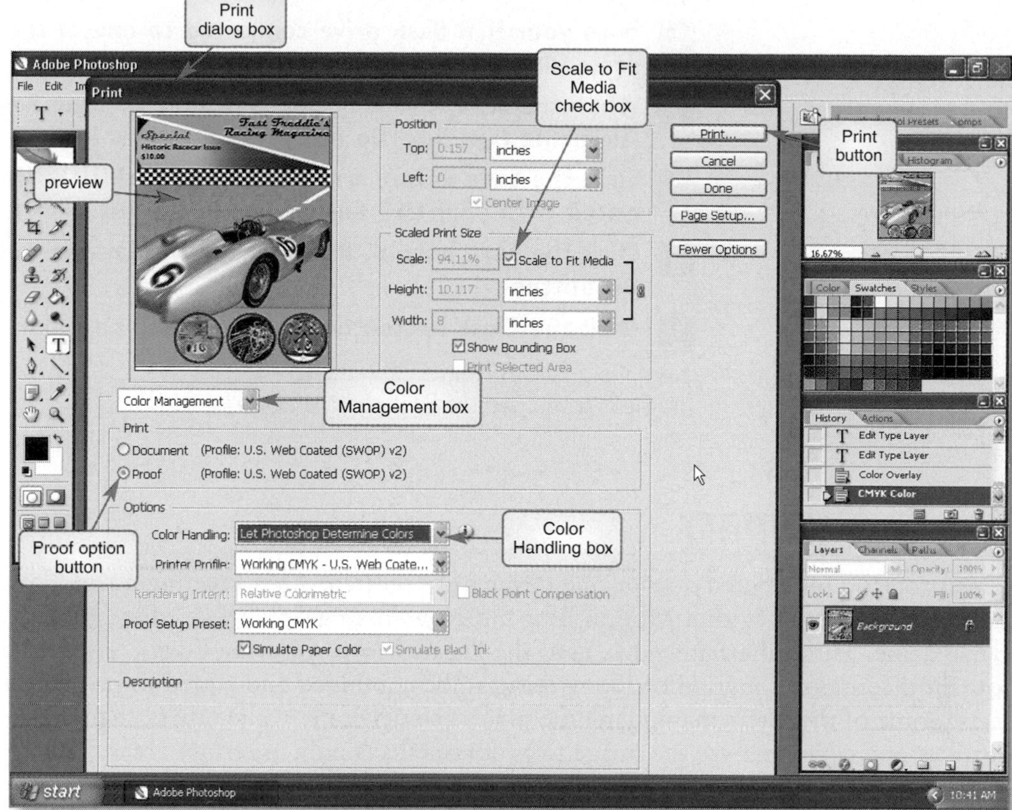

FIGURE 7-56

The Print dialog box is displayed with the settings related to color management and creating a hard proof (Figure 7-56).

2

- **Click the Print button. When your printer's Print dialog box is displayed, look through the tabs or settings for a Properties button. Turn off color management if possible, so the printer profile settings do not interfere with the CMYK process color printing.**
- **Click the OK or Print button in your printer's Print dialog box.**

After a few moments, the magazine cover prints on the printer. Retrieve the printout.

The magazine cover is complete. The final steps are to save the file and quit Photoshop as shown on the next page.

To Save the File and Quit Photoshop

1. **With your USB flash drive connected to one of the computer's USB ports, press SHIFT+CTRL+S to open the Save As dialog box.**
2. **When the Save As dialog box is displayed, type** `Magazine Cover CMYK` **in the File name text box. Do not press the ENTER key.**
3. **Click the Save in box arrow and then click USBDISK [G:], or the location associated with your USB flash drive, in the list.**
4. **Click the Save button. If Photoshop displays an options dialog box, click the OK button.**
5. **Click the Close button on the Photoshop title bar.**

The file is saved and the Photoshop window closes.

Project Summary

In this project, you created a magazine cover from scratch. After creating a road layer, you imported several graphics of a racecar. With a Motion Blur filter, the main graphic was edited to display as if it were moving into the magazine. Three alternate views used the Plastic Wrap, Glowing Edges, and Emboss filters. You learned that Photoshop contains a myriad of filters that can be combined and edited to produce an endless number of special effects. Some of the filters manipulate the pixels geometrically while others change the color. Filters that specialize in strokes and edges analyze the image to produce effects only in certain areas. You applied a Lighting Effects filter that simulated a spotlight.

After the filters were applied, you defined a new pattern to create a racing flag stripe across the magazine. You used the stroke feature to add decorative borders.

Finally, you learned about misregistration and the potential printing problems associated with objects being close to one another. You created headline text that will overprint the background rather than knock it out to avoid any printing gaps.

With the magazine cover complete, you flattened the image, converted it to CMYK, and printed a hard proof.

What You Should Know

Having completed this project, you should be able to perform the tasks below. The tasks are listed in the same order they were presented in this project. For a list of the buttons, menus, toolbars, and other commands introduced in this project, see the Quick Reference Summary at the back of this book and refer to the Page Number column.

1. Start Photoshop and Reset the Palettes, Toolbox, and Options Bar (PS 420)
2. Reset the Layers Palette (PS 420)
3. Reset the Colors (PS 420)
4. Create a File from Scratch (PS 421)
5. Save the New Document (PS 422)
6. Change the Background (PS 422)
7. Create the Road Layer (PS 423)
8. Insert the Racecar Graphic (PS 427)
9. Insert Additional Graphics (PS 428)
10. Apply a Plastic Wrap Filter (PS 437)
11. Apply a Glowing Edges Filter (PS 439)
12. Apply an Emboss Filter (PS 441)
13. Apply a Motion Blur Filter (PS 443)
14. Save the File (PS 445)
15. Create a Circular Mask (PS 446)
16. Stroke Color and Copy the Effect (PS 449)
17. Align and Distribute Layers (PS 450)
18. Define a Pattern (PS 451)
19. Use a Pattern (PS 453)
20. Delete a Pattern (PS 455)
21. Create a Line (PS 455)
22. Create a Layer via Copy (PS 458)
23. Create a Lighting Effect (PS 459)
24. Stroke the Racing Flag Stripe (PS 461)
25. Insert Headline Text (PS 463)
26. Create the Overlay (PS 464)
27. Insert Secondary Headline Text (PS 465)
28. Save the File with Layers (PS 467)
29. Convert to the CMYK Color Mode (PS 467)
30. Print a Hard Proof (PS 469)
31. Save the File and Quit Photoshop (PS 470)

Learn It Online

Instructions: To complete the Learn It Online exercises, start your browser, click the Address bar, and then enter the Web address `scsite.com/photoshop/learn`. When the Photoshop CS2 Learn It Online page is displayed, follow the instructions in the exercises below. Each exercise has instructions for printing your results, either for your own records or for submission to your instructor.

1 Project Reinforcement TF, MC, and SA

Below Photoshop Project 7, click the Project Reinforcement link. Print the quiz by clicking Print on the File menu for each page. Answer each question.

2 Flash Cards

Below Photoshop Project 7, click the Flash Cards link and read the instructions. Type 20 (or a number specified by your instructor) in the Number of playing cards text box, type your name in the Enter your Name text box, and then click the Flip Card button. When the flash card is displayed, read the question and then click the ANSWER box arrow to select an answer. Flip through Flash Cards. If your score is 15 (75%) correct or greater, click Print on the File menu to print your results. If your score is less than 15 (75%) correct, then redo this exercise by clicking the Replay button.

3 Practice Test

Below Photoshop Project 7, click the Practice Test link. Answer each question, enter your first and last name at the bottom of the page, and then click the Grade Test button. When the graded practice test is displayed on your screen, click Print on the File menu to print a hard copy. Continue to take practice tests until you score 80% or better.

4 Who Wants To Be a Computer Genius?

Below Photoshop Project 7, click the Computer Genius link. Read the instructions, enter your first and last name at the bottom of the page, and then click the PLAY button. When your score is displayed, click the PRINT RESULTS link to print a hard copy.

5 Wheel of Terms

Below Photoshop Project 7, click the Wheel of Terms link. Read the instructions, and then enter your first and last name and your school name. Click the PLAY button. When your score is displayed, right-click the score and then click Print on the shortcut menu to print a hard copy.

6 Crossword Puzzle Challenge

Below Photoshop Project 7, click the Crossword Puzzle Challenge link. Read the instructions, and then enter your first and last name. Click the SUBMIT button. Work the crossword puzzle. When you are finished, click the Submit button. When the crossword puzzle is redisplayed, click the Print Puzzle button to print a hard copy.

7 Tips and Tricks

Below Photoshop Project 7, click the Tips and Tricks link. Click a topic that pertains to Project 7. Right-click the information and then click Print on the shortcut menu. Construct a brief example of what the information relates to in Photoshop to confirm you understand how to use the tip or trick.

8 Expanding Your Horizons

Below Photoshop Project 7, click the Expanding Your Horizons link. Click a topic that pertains to Project 7. Print the information. Construct a brief example of what the information relates to in Photoshop to confirm you understand the contents of the article.

9 Search Sleuth

Below Photoshop Project 7, click the Search Sleuth link. To search for a term that pertains to this project, select a term below the Project 7 title and then use the Google search engine at google.com (or any major search engine) to display and print two Web pages that present information on the term.

10 Photoshop Online Training

Below Photoshop Project 7, click the Photoshop Online Training link. When your browser displays the Web page, click one of the Photoshop tutorials that covers one or more of the objectives listed at the beginning of the project on page PS 419. Print the first page of the tutorial before stepping through it.

Apply Your Knowledge

1 Creating a Digital Painting

Instructions: The following steps start Photoshop and edit a file to create a digital painting from a digital photograph. You will use the CD that accompanies this book, or see your instructor for information about accessing the files available with this book.

The photo you open is a picture of a garden. You are to increase the saturation of color, adjust the lighting, and then add filters to create the painting shown in Figure 7-57.

FIGURE 7-57

Apply Your Knowledge

1. Start Photoshop. Perform the steps on pages PS 8 through PS 10 to customize the Workspace and set default values.
2. On the File menu, click Open. Open the file named, Garden, from the Project07 folder.
3. On the File menu, click Save As. Save the image on your USB flash drive as a PSD file, with the file name, Garden Painting. If Photoshop displays a JPEG Options dialog box, click the OK button.
4. On the Layers palette, right-click the Background layer and then click Duplicate Layer. Name the new layer, Edits. Select only the Edits layer, and hide the Background layer by clicking its visibility icon.
5. To increase the saturation of the colors, click Layer on the menu bar, point to New Adjustment Layer, and then click Hue/Saturation. When Photoshop displays the New Layer dialog box, click the OK button. When Photoshop displays the Hue/Saturation dialog box, use the Edit box to set each of the following. Click the OK button when you are done setting the values.
   a. Select Reds. Enter a Saturation of 50.
   b. Select Yellows. Enter a Saturation of 60.
   c. Select Blues. Enter a Saturation of 73.
6. On the Layers palette, select the Edits layer. On the Filter menu, click Filter Gallery. In the lower-right portion of the Filter Gallery, locate the filter list. If more than one filter is displayed, click the Delete effect layer button until only one filter is displayed in the list.
7. Click the Zoom box arrow and then click Fit in View. If the Artistic filters are not displayed, click Artistic.
8. Click the Dry Brush thumbnail. Set the Brush Size to 7, the Brush Detail to 8, and the Texture to 2.
9. In the lower-right portion of the Filter Gallery, click the New effect layer button.
10. Click the Cutout thumbnail. Set the Number of Levels to 5, the Edge Simplicity to 2, and the Edge Fidelity to 1.
11. Click the New effect layer button to add another filter to the list.
12. Click the Rough Pastels thumbnail. Adjust the settings as shown in Table 7-15.
13. Click OK in the Filter Gallery dialog box.
14. On the Layers palette, select all three layers. On the Image menu, point to Mode, and then click CMYK Color. When Photoshop displays a dialog box, click the Merge button. On the View menu, point to Proof Setup. If the Working CMYK command does not display a check mark, click it.
15. On the File menu, click Print with Preview. When Photoshop displays the Print dialog box, if a More Options button is present, click it. Click the Scale to Fit Media check box so it is selected. Below the preview, click the box arrow, and then click Color Management, if necessary. In the Print area, click the Proof option button. Click the Color Handling box arrow and then click Let Photoshop Determine Colors.
16. Ready the Printer. Click the Print button and then when your printer's Print dialog box is displayed, click its Print button. Turn in the printout to your instructor.
17. Save the file again and then quit Photoshop.

Table 7-15 Rough Pastels Settings

SETTING	VALUE
Stroke Length	4
Stroke Detail	3
Texture	Canvas
Scaling	120
Relief	24
Light	Bottom
Invert	No

In the Lab

1 Using Filters and Strokes

Problem: As an intern with the state Department of Tourism, your job is to help create tourist pamphlets and posters. Your latest project is a promotional series advertising boating on Lake Michigan. Your supervisor has given you a photo of a sailboat. She wants you to turn it into a poster with a classy, 1930s feel, and a stroked border. The completed poster is displayed in Figure 7-58.

FIGURE 7-58

Instructions:

1. Start Photoshop. Perform the customization steps found on pages PS 8 through PS 10.
2. Open the file, Sailboat, from the Project07 folder on the CD that accompanies this book.
3. Click the Save As command on the File menu. Type `Sailboat Edited` as the file name. Browse to your USB flash drive storage device. Click the Save button. If Photoshop displays a dialog box, click the OK button.
4. Using the Layers palette menu, create a duplicate layer of the Background layer and name it Edits. Hide the Background layer.
5. On the Filter menu, click Filter Gallery. When the Filter Gallery is displayed, click the Zoom box arrow in the lower-left corner, and then click Fit in View.
6. Locate the list of filters in the lower-right portion of the Filter Gallery. If more than one filter is displayed, click the Delete effect layer button until only one filter is displayed in the list.
7. If the Artistic filters are not displayed, click Artistic in the category list. Click the Poster Edges thumbnail. Type `2` in the Edge Thickness box, type `1` in the Edge Intensity box, and type `3` in the Posterization box.
8. In the lower-right portion of the Filter Gallery, click the New effect layer button.

(continued)

Using Filters and Strokes *(continued)*

9. If the Brush Strokes filters are not displayed, click Brush Strokes in the category list. Click the Ink Outlines thumbnail. Type 4 in the Stroke Length box, type 2 in the Dark Intensity box, and type 33 in the Light Intensity box.
10. Click the OK button in the Filter Gallery.
11. In the toolbox, select the Elliptical Marquee tool. Drag an oval around the sailboat. Be sure to include the top of the sail and some water underneath the boat, but do not let the marquee go outside of the margin.
12. In the Layers palette, click the Add layer mask button.
13. When Photoshop displays the sailboat in the oval, click the Add a layer style button on the Layers palette. Click Stroke on the shortcut menu.
14. When the Layer Style dialog box is displayed, type 30 in the Size box. Click the Color box and then select a black color. Click the OK button in the Color Picker dialog box and then click the OK button in the Layer Style dialog box.
15. Save the file again.
16. Merge the layers, discarding hidden layers, and then save the file with the name, Sailboat Complete.
17. See your instructor for ways to print this poster-size image, if available at your school. Otherwise, use the Resize Image Wizard to reduce the photo to fit on available printer paper. Print a hard proof using the directions from the project.

2 Enhancing a Photo with Lighting and Text

Problem: You work for a small ad agency whose client is a cosmetics company named, Your Way. Your supervisor has given you a photo to enhance with lighting effects and text. The completed advertising piece is displayed in Figure 7-59.

Instructions:

1. Start Photoshop. Perform the customization steps found on pages PS 8 through PS 10.
2. Open the file, Cosmetics, from the Project07 folder on the CD that accompanies this book.
3. Click the Save As command on the File menu. Type `Cosmetics Edited` as the file name. Browse to your USB flash drive storage device. Click the Save button. When Photoshop displays a TIFF Options dialog box, click the OK button.
4. On the Filter menu, point to Render, and then click Lighting Effects. When the Lighting Effects dialog box is displayed, click the Light type box arrow, and, if necessary, click Spotlight in the list. Adjust the preview ellipse as shown in Figure 7-60. The position of each point on the ellipse, as well as the center point, is important.

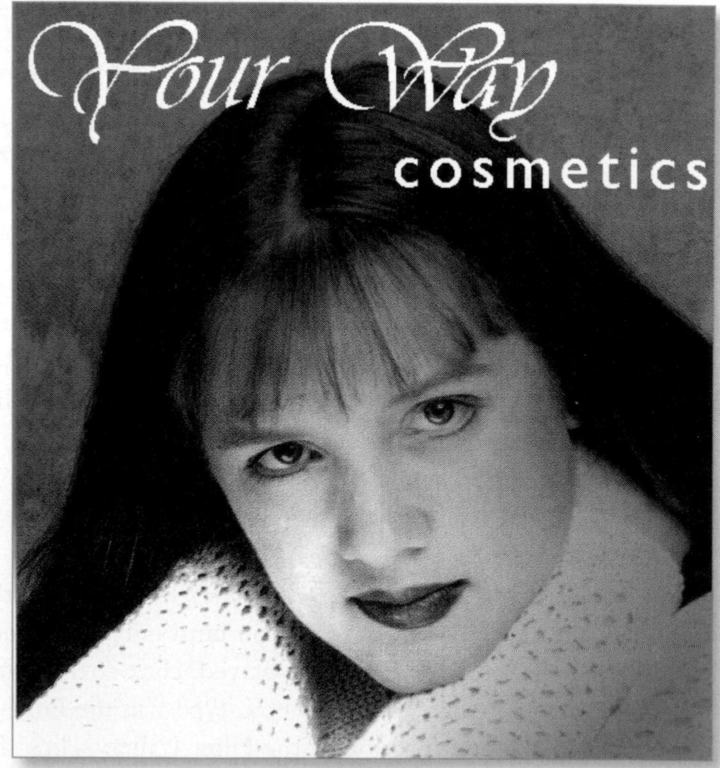

FIGURE 7-59

In the Lab

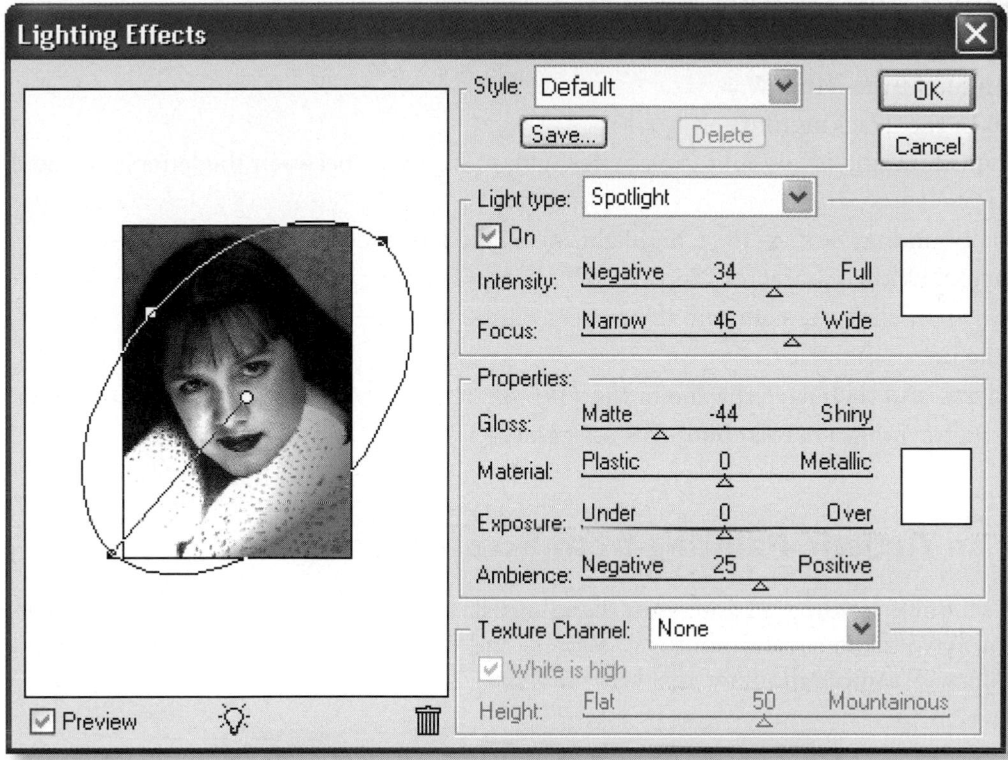

FIGURE 7-60

5. Drag the Intensity slider to 34. Drag the Focus slider to 46. Drag the Gloss slider to -44. Drag the Ambience slider to 25. Reset the other sliders to zero, if necessary.
6. Click the OK button in the Lighting Effects dialog box.
7. When the document window again is displayed, press the `T` key to activate the Type tool.
8. On the options bar, click the Set the font family box arrow and then click Vivaldi or a similar font. Type `48 pt` in the Set the font size box. Click the Set the anti-aliasing method box arrow and then click Strong in the list. Click the Left align text button.
9. On the options bar, click the Set the text color button. When Photoshop displays the Color Picker dialog box, select a white color, and then click the OK button.
10. In the document window, drag a type bounding box from the left margin to the right margin, approximately 1 inch tall near the top margin. In the box, type `Your Way` to complete the text.
11. Press the ENTER key. On the options bar, click the Set the font family box arrow and then click Gill Sans MT, or a similar font. If necessary, click the Set the font style box arrow and then click Regular in the list. Type `24 pt` in the Set the font size box. Click the Right align text button.
12. In the type bounding box, type `cosmetics` to complete the entry. Do not press the ENTER key.
13. Because there is too much space between the letters Y and o in the word, Your, and between the letters W and a in the word, Way, you will track those sets of letters with a negative value to move them closer together.
    a. Drag to highlight the letter Y.
    b. On the options bar, click the Toggle the Character and Paragraph palettes button.

(continued)

Enhancing a Photo with Lighting and Text *(continued)*

c. Click the Character tab, if necessary. Type -180 in the Tracking box.
d. Drag to highlight the letter W.
e. Type -240 in the Tracking box.

14. Because the word, cosmetics, would look better with more space between the letters, you will use a positive tracking value.
    a. In the type bounding box, drag to highlight the entire word, cosmetics.
    b. If necessary, click the Character tab. Type 120 in the Tracking box.
15. On the options bar, click the Commit any current edits button.
16. Save the file again.
17. Flatten the layers and then save the file in the TIFF file format, with the file name, Cosmetics Complete.
18. See your instructor for ways to submit this assignment.

3 Creating an Artistic Painting from Scratch

Problem: Your school is holding a contest for digital artists. There are categories for both original artwork and edited photos. You have taken several photos of flowers and decide to try your hand at combining them into one painting, using filters. A sample montage displays in Figure 7-61.

FIGURE 7-61

Instructions:

1. Start Photoshop. Perform the customization steps found on pages PS 8 through PS 10.
2. Click File on the menu bar, and then click New. When the New dialog box is displayed, type `Flower Montage` in the Name box. Choose a Custom preset with a size of 12 by 18 inches, which is appropriate for small posters. Use a Resolution of 300 and RGB Color, 8 bit as the Color Mode. Make the background white.
3. Open the file, Red Flower, from the Project07 folder on the CD that accompanies this book. Use the Move tool to move a copy of the flower into the Flower Montage document window. Close the Red Flower document window. Name the new layer, red.
4. Erase the background, or use a layer mask and paint with black, so only the flower is visible. You can use the Magic Wand tool to select large similarly colored pixels. Zoom and scroll as necessary. Because filters will be applied later, your erasures do not have to be perfect.
5. Open the file, Lilac Flower, from the same folder. Use the Move tool to move a copy of the flower into the Flower Montage document window. Close the Lilac Flower document window. Name the new layer, lilac, and erase the background as you did for the previous flower.
6. Open the file, Yellow Flower. Use the Move tool to move a copy of the flower into the Flower Montage document window. Close the Yellow Flower document window. Name the new layer, yellow, and erase the background as you did for the previous flower.
7. Finally, open the file, Magenta Flower. Use the Move tool to move a copy of the flower into the Flower Montage document window. Close the Magenta Flower document window. Name the new layer, magenta, and erase the background as you did for the previous flower.
8. With the Flower Montage document window selected, save the file with the name, Flower Montage before Filters, on your storage device.
9. Select a flower layer. Open the Filter Gallery. Click the Zoom box arrow and then click Fit in View in the list. If more than one applied filter is displayed, click the Delete effect layer button. Select the Paint Daubs filter in the Artistic category. Click the Brush Type box arrow and then click Sparkle in the list. Adjust the Brush Size and Sharpness settings as desired. Click the OK button to close the Filter Gallery.
10. Repeat Step 9 with each of the other flower layers. Use the Filter Gallery to apply filters, such as the Glass filter in the Distort category and the Grain filter in the Texture category. Use the menu system to apply a filter, such as the Extrude filter on the Stylize submenu. Experiment with the settings to achieve a look similar to Figure 7-61.
11. Click the Background layer. Use the Swatches palette and the Paint Bucket tool to fill it with light green. Use the Filter Gallery to apply the Craquelure filter in the Texture category.
12. Save the file with the name, Flower Montage after Filters, on your storage device.
13. For each flower, make three or four copies by ALT+dragging. Rotate or resize each copy. Experiment to achieve a look similar to Figure 7-61.
14. Flatten the layers and then apply a filter to the entire image, if desired.
15. Save the file with the name, Flower Montage Complete, on your storage device. Send an electronic copy to your instructor via e-mail or via your virtual classroom dropbox.

Cases and Places

The difficulty of these case studies varies:
■ are the least difficult and ■■ are the most difficult. The last exercise is a group exercise.

1 ■ You found an old picture of your grandparents when they were first married. The photo has a lot of background, irrelevant people, and things. You would like to blur those out to focus on just the central two people. Open the file named, Couple, from the Project07 folder on the CD provided with this book. Use the Elliptical Marquee tool to outline the couple and create a layer via cut. Hide the new layer. Use a Surface Blur filter in the Blur category to blur the background and then add the new layer back on. Experiment with different settings until the photo seems to blur into the background.

2 ■■ You decide to make a coloring book for your nephew. Take several digital pictures of animals, either pets or go to the local zoo. Open the first photo. Use the Find Edges filter in the Stylize category. Save the file with a name such as Dog Find Edges. Open the second photo and use the Trace Contour filter in the Stylize category. Adjust the level to 50 or a suitable value for your photo. Save the file with a name such as Cat Trace Contour 50. Open the third photo and convert it to grayscale. Use the Photocopy filter in the Sketch category and adjust the settings to 8 and 11, or suitable values for your photo. Save the file with a name such as Cat Photocopy 8 11. Open each of your other animal photos and experiment with different filters and settings to create areas that could be colored. Save each file with a name indicative of the filter and settings. Print a copy of each edited photo and staple them together in book form.

3 ■■ Choose a Photoshop project that you have completed in the past. Consider the audience and purpose of the graphic. Identify the parts of the image that might be improved or might better portray a meaning with an applied filter. Decide whether that filter should alter the pixels geometrically or via color — with or without distortion. Open the Adobe Help System and look through the samples. Choose a category and two or three filters that might enhance your photo for a specific purpose. Open the photo in Photoshop and apply one of the filters. Print a hard proof. Go back into the Filter Gallery, delete previous filters if necessary, and then apply a second filter. Print a hard proof. Compare the two different proofs, specify which proof you like better and why. Write a paragraph about your selection process.

4 ■■ **Working Together** Each member of the group should choose a different category of filters. Then, individually each member should create a short tutorial about the filters. The tutorial should include at least 10 steps with illustrations. Use the Print Screen button to capture screen shots of the various steps and then paste them into a word processing program along with stepwise instructions. Make sure to specify which filter, the order of filters, and filter setting values. Come back together as a group with copies of the tutorial for each member as well as a copy of the digital file to manipulate. Work through the tutorials submitted by your teammates. Make suggestions for improvements or corrections. When each member receives all the feedback, make the corrections and distribute the final copy to the class or your instructor.

ADOBE
Photoshop CS2

Working with Vector Graphics

PROJECT 8

CASE PERSPECTIVE

You recently accepted a position with the *Northmen's Log* — a student newspaper published at Northern University. The *Northmen's Log* runs articles of interest for the university community with a focus on student news. Because it is a small staff, your job will encompass a variety of tasks, including layout, graphics, prepress activities, and maybe even photography and reporting!

The editor is going to start a weekly column entitled, I.T. Aid Station, which addresses student questions about information technology on campus. Students can ask anything from "How do I connect wirelessly?" to "How do I get my stuck CD out of the drive?" The questions will come from a variety of places including a drop box on campus, telephone questions called in to the I.T. Center, and those submitted on the I.T. Web site. The editor would like you to create a clip art logo to accompany the weekly feature — something amusing, but still relative to the topic.

The newspaper runs a 5 column page with standard newspaper margins, on paper that is 11 × 17 inches. The logo is to display across 2 columns using 2 vertical inches, so its dimension will be approximately 3.88 inches wide × 2 inches tall.

As you think about possible graphics and captions for the logo, you remember seeing examples of clip art that portray computers in funny situations or with human characteristics. As most clip art is copyrighted, you decide to use a photo and convert it to a vector graphic that resembles clip art, using Photoshop. A further exploration of paths, along with pen and anchor tools, may be necessary to help create the drawing.

Reading through this project, you will learn how to use advanced features of layers and paths as you create special effect areas in a vector illustration. You also will learn how to manipulate anchor points with the Pen tool and the Freeform Pen tool to place the border of colors and layers. Finally, you will add annotation to the clip art using the Notes tool.

Working with Vector Graphics

PROJECT 8

Objectives

You will have mastered the material in this project when you can:

- Describe the characteristics of vector graphics, including clip art
- Create and manage layer groups using the Layers palette
- Explain the difference between vector and raster graphic images
- Create shape layers and paths with the Pen and Freeform Pen tools
- Draw line segments and curved paths
- Add, delete, and convert anchor points
- Move and reshape using the Path Selection and Direct Selection tools
- Use the Freeform Pen tool with the magnetic pen option
- Add detail to clip art images
- Use Note and Audio Annotation tools
- Select GIF formatting options
- Make choices to optimize clip art using the Export Transparent Image wizard

Introduction

With the advent of page layout and word processing software, images have become common in all kinds of documents. Web sites without graphics are passé. Business stationery now includes artwork and logos in addition to the standard address and communication data. Lectures and oral presentations are considered boring without graphics and multimedia effects. Now students routinely insert clip art into papers and presentations.

The term, **clip art**, refers to individual images or groups of graphics that can be transferred across computer applications. Clip art commonly is an illustrative, colorful drawing, rather than a photo, but the term is applied loosely to any image that accompanies or decorates text, including black and white images. Clip art also may include visual elements such as bullets, lines, shapes, and callouts. The term, **stock images**, refers to illustrations, typically with full-color backgrounds, or to photographs.

Clip art can be created from scratch, produced from a photo, copied and pasted from another source, or imported directly as a file into some applications. The use of clip art can save artists time, and make artwork both possible and economical for non-artists.

Clip art galleries that come with some page layout and word processing applications may contain hundreds of images. Clip art galleries also are available on the Web. Galleries typically are organized into categories, such as people, objects, or nature, among others, which is especially helpful when browsing through thousands of images.

Most clip art images have searchable keywords associated with them. For example, a clip art image of a tiger may have the keywords, tiger, animal, zoo, Africa, orange, or stripes associated with it. Appendix C describes how to use Adobe Bridge to add metadata keywords to images to aid image searches.

Clip art may come in a variety of file formats. Raster, or bitmap, images are ideal for the Web because they can be cropped, colorized, converted to black and white, and combined with other images. These images work best at the size and orientation at which they were created. The file format, GIF, is used for many clip art Web images including those with animation. For example, you may have tried to insert animated clip art into a presentation program. Imported in its own file type and size, it works fine. Once you rotate or scale the image, however, it may become distorted, or the animation may not play.

For print publications, vector images may be a better choice, because they can be resized, rotated, and stretched easily without specialized graphic-editing software. The disadvantage is that many vector images are specific to the creation software. For example, Windows Metafile is a format used with Microsoft products and associated clip art. It is saved with the extension, WMF. A graphic created with Macromedia Flash has the extension, SWF. While you can copy and import those types of vector images, you may not be able to edit them without the original software.

Clip art is not always free. Application software companies may provide a license for registered users to import and distribute the clip art provided with the package without charge. Some Web clip art galleries may specify royalty-free images for one-time use, but not for profit-making distribution. For other uses, you must purchase clip art packages on CD or for download. It is important to read carefully all licensing agreements. Some artwork requires written permission. Copyright laws apply to all images equally — the right of legal use depends on the intended use and conditions of the copyright owner. All images are copyrighted, whether or not they are marked.

Table 8-1 displays some of the categories, descriptions, and usages of clip art sources.

Table 8-1 Categories of Clip Art

CLIP ART CATEGORY	WARNINGS	USE
Free — An image that is given or provided free of charge	It is important to check the Web site owner's motive for giving away clip art. Some free graphics are really unlabeled, copyrighted images. Images may contain spyware or viruses.	Appropriate for personal use and sometimes for educational purposes, but because the original source may be obscure, free clip art is not recommended for business use.
Published clip art — images in print or online	Ask for written permission to use the image. Do not use the image unless you can track it to its original source.	Published clip art is appropriate for personal use, educational purposes, and one-time use on a Web site. With permission, it may be used commercially.

Table 8-1 Categories of Clip Art (*continued*)

CLIP ART CATEGORY	WARNINGS	USE
Copyrighted — trademarked images that have legal owners	Do not use unless you have a written agreement with the copyright holder.	Copyrighted clip art has limited legal use. Only fully licensed resellers may use copyrighted clip art. It is not appropriate for any personal or educational use.
Royalty-Free — images provided at little or no cost by the owner	Carefully read the rights and usages. Trading post Web sites require the permission of the artist or photographer. Even legitimate images may contain spyware or viruses.	With written permission from the owner, royalty-free clip art and stock images normally can be used by anyone — even for commercial use such as Web sites and business stationery, but without redistribution rights.
Rights-protected — images created and sold for a specific use	You must buy the right to use the image exclusively. You may not use the image for any use other than its intended purpose.	Written businesses contract with artists to design rights-protected logos and artwork. The seller promises not to sell that image to anyone else for that purpose.
Editorial-rights — photos used in public interest	Some editorial use images are also copyrighted. Read the agreement carefully.	Editorial-rights images are used with written permission for news, sports, entertainment, and other public purposes with appropriate citation. These images are usually less restrictive and less expensive than rights-protected images.

In this project, you will create your own clip art — clip art that has no legal restrictions because you are designing it yourself. Artists, graphic design professionals, typographers, and casual users all use Photoshop to create specialized graphics such as clip art to avoid possible copyright problems.

To create the clip art, you will learn some advanced layering techniques as you experiment with anchor points and paths. You will incorporate some new blending modes. You will investigate Photoshop's annotation tools to add visual and audio notes to the clip art as you work through this project.

Project 8 — Working with Vector Graphics

A photograph is converted to clip art in Project 8, creating a graphic for a newspaper help column about computer problems. The original photo, a bitmap image of a computer monitor and tower, is used as a kind of outline or tracing to create a vector graphic of the same image. Using opacity changes, layer styles, and blending modes, some portions of the images are recolored to reinforce the clip art cartoon. A band aid and thermometer are added to characterize a computer problem. A background color brings the image forward giving it depth, as well as giving it the look and feel of clip art. Finally, a sign is created to illustrate the name of the help column. The before and after images are displayed in Figure 8-1.

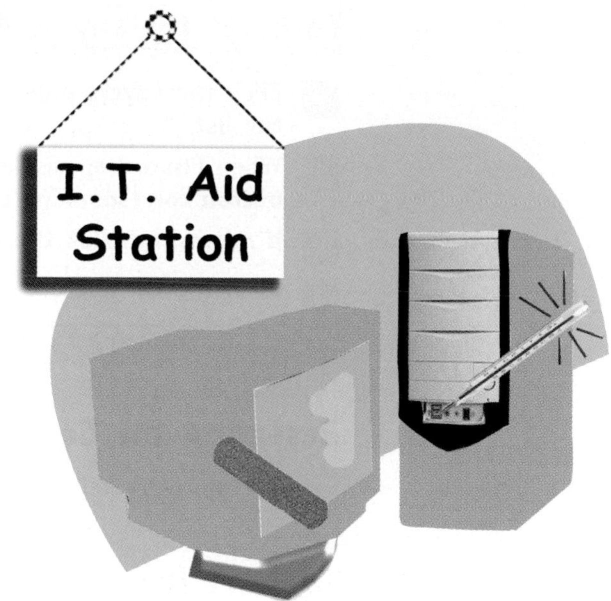

FIGURE 8-1

Starting and Customizing Photoshop

If you are stepping through this project on a computer and you want your screen to match the figures in this book, you should change your computer's resolution to 1024 × 768 and reset the tools and palettes. For more information about how to change the resolution on your computer, and other advanced Photoshop settings, read Appendix A.

The following steps describe how to start Photoshop and customize the Photoshop window. You may need to ask your instructor how to start Photoshop for your system.

To Start Photoshop and Reset the Palettes, Toolbox, and Options Bar

1. **Start Photoshop as described on pages PS 6 and PS 7.**
2. **Choose the Default Workspace as described on page PS 8.**
3. **Select the Rectangular Marquee Tool (M) button in the toolbox and then reset all tools as described on pages PS 9 and PS 10.**

Photoshop starts and then resets the tools, palettes, and options.

Resetting the Layers Palette

The steps on the next page show how to reset the Layers palette to make the thumbnails match the figures shown in this book.

To Reset the Layers Palette

1. **Click the Layers palette menu button and then click Palette Options on the list.**
2. **When Photoshop displays the Layers Palette Options dialog box, click the option button corresponding to the smallest of the thumbnail sizes, if necessary.**
3. **If necessary, click the Layer Bounds option button.**
4. **Click the OK button.**

The Layers palette will display small thumbnails for each layer.

Resetting the Colors

The following step shows how to reset the default colors in the Photoshop window.

To Reset the Colors

1. **If black and white are not shown as the default colors in the toolbox, press the D key on the keyboard. If black is not the foreground color, press the X key on the keyboard.**

Black is set as the foreground color; white is set as the background color.

Creating a New File with a Transparent Background

A desirable attribute of clip art is the **transparent background**. A clip art with transparency can be placed closer to text and other graphics when inserted into Web pages, slide presentations, and print publications. It will display without a white, cornered background obstructing the view. In Photoshop, when you create an image with transparent content, the image does not have a background layer. Each layer is neither drawn on, nor constrained by, the background; you can add layers anywhere in the document window.

The following steps show how to use a shortcut key to access the New dialog box and then set the attributes for an image with a transparent background.

To Create a File with a Transparent Background

1. **Press CTRL+N. When the New dialog box is displayed, type** `Computer Clip Art` **in the Name box.**
2. **Click the Preset box arrow, scroll up in the list if necessary, and then click Custom.**
3. **Double-click the Width box and then type** `5` **as the entry. Click the Width unit box arrow, and then click inches in the list, if necessary.**
4. **Double-click the Height box and then type** `5` **as the entry. If necessary, click the Height unit box arrow, and then click inches in the list.**
5. **If necessary, double-click the Resolution box and then type** `300` **as the entry. If necessary, click the Resolution unit box arrow, and then click pixels/inch in the list.**

6 **If necessary, click the Color Mode box arrow, and then click RGB Color in the list. If necessary, click the Color Mode unit box arrow, and then click 8 bit in the list.**

7 **Click the Background Contents box arrow, and then click Transparent in the list.**

The attributes for the new file are set (Figure 8-2).

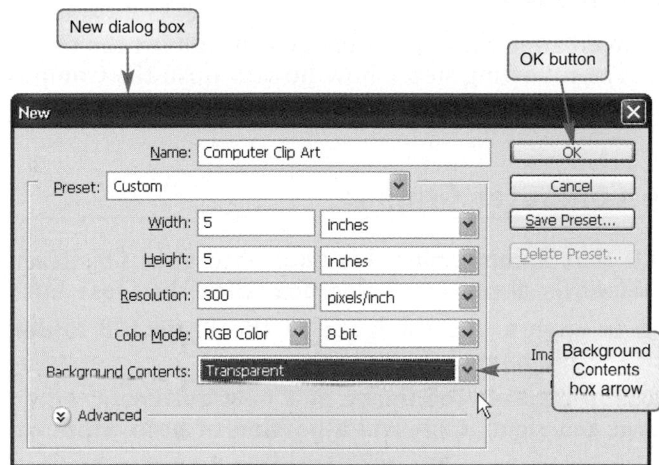

FIGURE 8-2

8 **Click the OK button.**

9 **When the document window is displayed, if necessary, change the magnification to 33.33 percent. If the rulers do not display in the document window, press CTRL+R.**

10 **On the document window status bar, click the menu button, point to Show and then click Document Sizes, if necessary.**

Notice that the new image, with transparent content, has no background layer. The bottommost layer is not constrained like the background layer; you can move it anywhere in the Layers palette, and change its opacity and blending mode.

Managing the Layers Palette

Converting a photo into clip art requires many steps with many layers. First, you must import the original photo into your transparent background to use as a basis for drawing the clip art. Locking, or partially locking, the original photo is a good way to keep you from accidentally deleting the image.

Each color you create in the clip art becomes a new path or shape, at least temporarily until the image is flattened and prepared for distribution. To manage the many layers, users find it easier to group multiple shapes and their special effects by style, category, or object.

The following sections rename the transparent layer, import the photo, create layer groups, and save the file.

Renaming the Transparent Layer

The first step is to rename the layer that was created by choosing a transparent background, as shown on the next page.

To Rename the Transparent Layer

1 On the Layers palette, double-click Layer 1. Type `transparent background` **and then press the ENTER key to rename the layer.**

The layer is renamed.

Importing the Photo

The next step in creating the clip art image is to import the original photo of a computer system. The following steps show how to open the Computer file and move the image into the Computer Clip Art document window, creating a new layer.

To Insert the Computer Graphic

1 Insert the CD that accompanies this book into your CD drive. After a few seconds, if Windows displays a dialog box, click the Close button.

2 Press CTRL+O to open a file. Navigate to the Project08 folder and then double-click the file named, Computer.

3 When Photoshop displays the image in a new document window, drag the title bar down and right, to reveal a portion of both windows.

4 Press the V key to activate the Move tool, and then drag the Computer image into the Computer Clip Art document window. Click the Close button on the Computer document window title bar.

5 Position the image in the lower portion of the Computer Clip Art document window, slightly right of the center.

6 On the Layers palette, double-click the newly created layer name. Type `computer system` **and then press the ENTER key to rename the layer.**

The computer system appears in the Computer Clip Art document window (Figure 8-3). The layer is renamed.

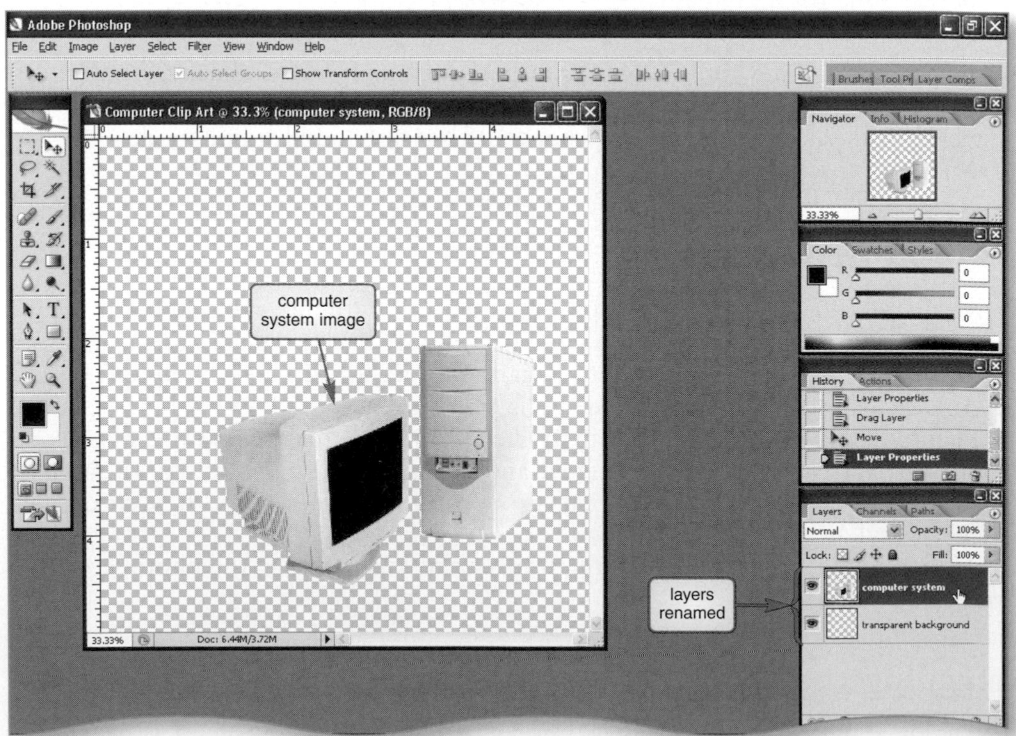

FIGURE 8-3

Some file formats, such as JPG, do not support transparent backgrounds. If you open a JPG image and want a transparent background, you must convert the image to GIF or PNG and then select everything except the background as a layer via cut. You then can unlock and delete the background layer. If you import a JPG image into a previously created PSD, GIF, or PNG file, it becomes a new layer. You then can select and delete the background.

Layer Groups

A **layer group** is a folder on the Layers palette with a unique name. Layers can be created within the folder or moved into the folder. Recall that a new image in Photoshop has a single layer. The number of additional layers, layer effects, and layer groups is limited only by the computer's memory capacity.

By helping organize and manage layers, layer groups reduce clutter on the Layers palette and logically order the various parts of an image. Layer groups also may be used to apply attributes and masks to multiple layers simultaneously, which saves time and effort. Other advantages of using groups include being able to create a new document from a layer group, moving layer groups from one image to another, nesting layer groups within one another, as well as aligning and merging groups.

When you create a new layer group you can specify its name, its color on the Layers palette, a blending mode, and an opacity setting. The settings apply to all layers created in, or moved to, the group. A layer group displays on the palette with a folder icon and with a triangle that points down to reveal the individual layers in the group, or points right to hide them (Figure 8-4). The triangle does not affect the document window, however. The visibility icon determines whether or not the layer group is hidden or displays in the document window. Just like layers, a hidden layer group does not print.

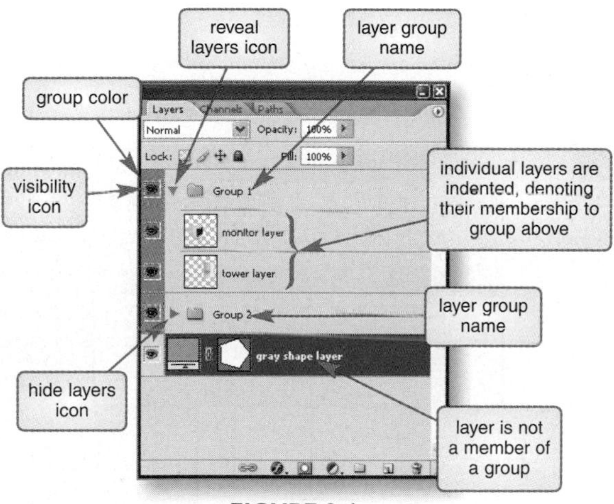

FIGURE 8-4

Three groups will be created for the Computer Clip Art image: one to hold color and shapes related to the monitor, one for the tower, and one for the sign that will be created above the computer system. The first folder is created as shown in the steps on the next page.

To Create Layer Groups

1

- **With the computer system layer selected on the Layers palette, click the palette menu button.**

The Layers palette menu is displayed (Figure 8-5).

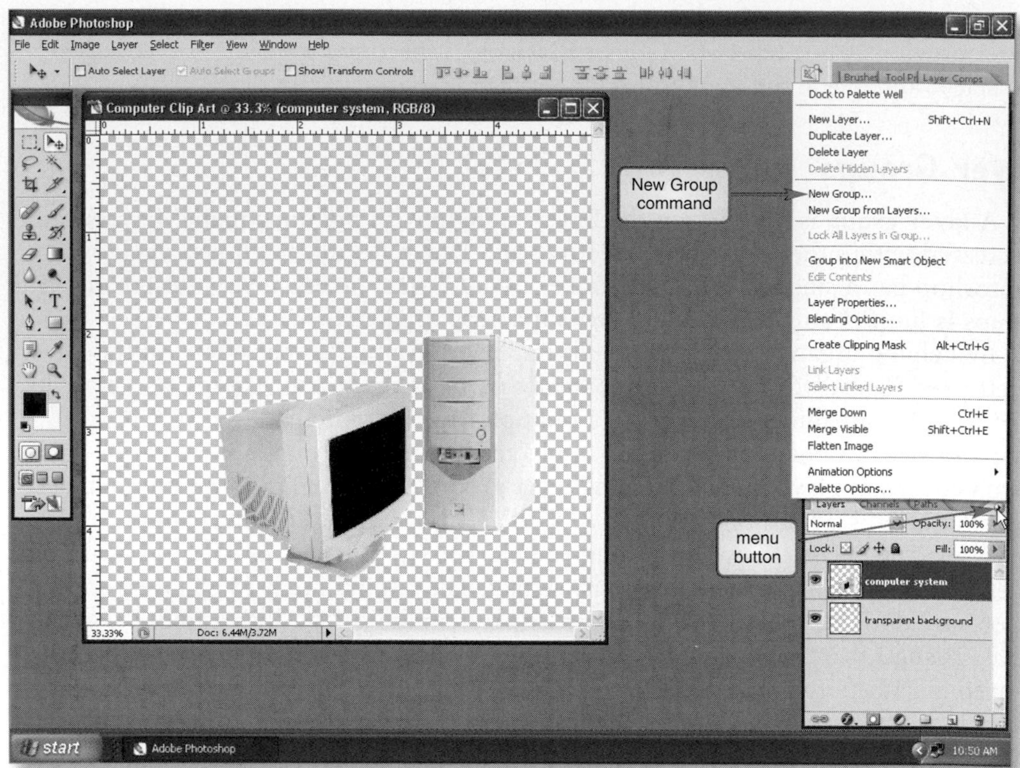

FIGURE 8-5

2

- **Click New Group.**
- **When the New Group dialog box is displayed, type** `Monitor` **in the Name box.**
- **Click the Color box arrow, and then click Blue in the list.**
- **Do not change any of the other settings.**

Photoshop displays the settings for the new group (Figure 8-6).

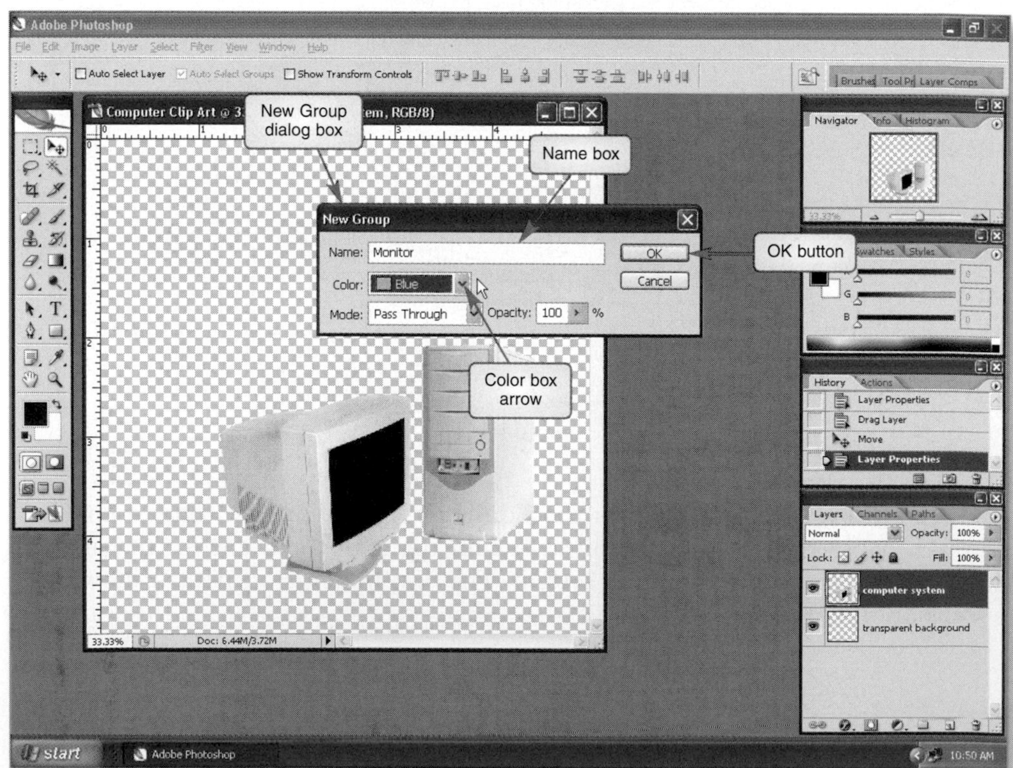

FIGURE 8-6

3

• **Click the OK button.**

The folder icon identifies the new layer group on the Layers palette and displays a reveal layers icon on the Layers palette (Figure 8-7). Photoshop displays the blue color around the visibility icon.

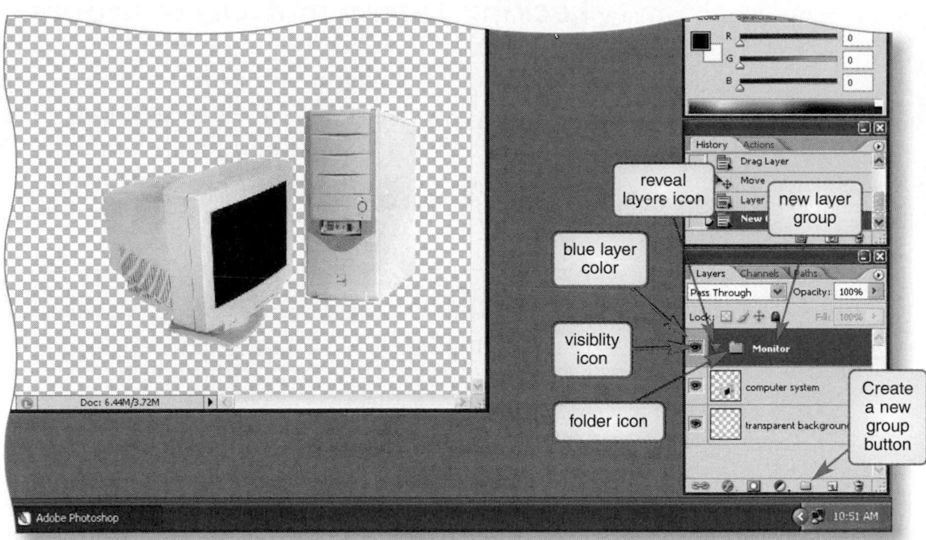

FIGURE 8-7

Other Ways

1. On Layer menu, point to New, click Group
2. Click Create a new group button

The following steps show how to create two more groups, one for the computer tower and the other for the sign that will display in the final version of the clip art.

To Create More Groups

1 **Click the palette menu button again and create a group named Tower with the color Gray.**

2 **Click the palette menu button again and create a group named Sign with the color Yellow.**

The Layers palette displays all three layer groups (Figure 8-8).

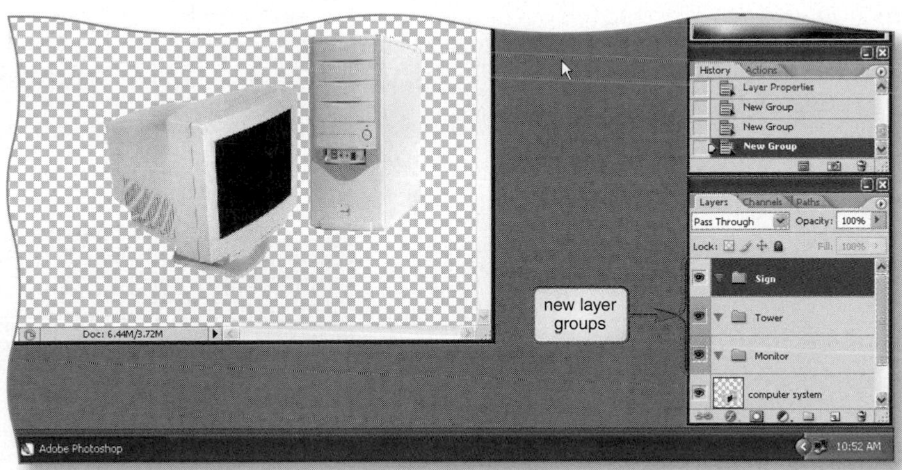

FIGURE 8-8

Locking Layers and Layer Groups

Layers and layer groups can be fully locked for no further editing, or partially locked to allow movement of the layer group without disturbing the effects and settings. For instance, you may want to lock a layer fully when you finish with it. You may want to lock a layer partially if it has the correct transparency and styles, but you still are deciding on the layer's position.

Table 8-2 displays information about the four locking buttons.

Table 8-2 Layers Palette Locking Buttons

TYPES OF LOCK	DESCRIPTION	BUTTON
Lock transparent pixels	confines editing to the opaque portions of the layer	
Lock image pixels	prevents painting tool modifications of the layer	
Lock position	prevents the layer's pixels from being moved	
Lock all	locks transparent pixels, image pixels, and position	

The following steps show how to lock the transparent background fully, and partially lock the computer system layer.

To Lock Layers

1

- **On the Layers palette, select the transparent background layer.**
- **Click the Lock all button.**

Photoshop locks the layer and displays the lock icon (Figure 8-9). Locking the layer keeps erroneous strokes and objects from affecting the transparency of the clip art.

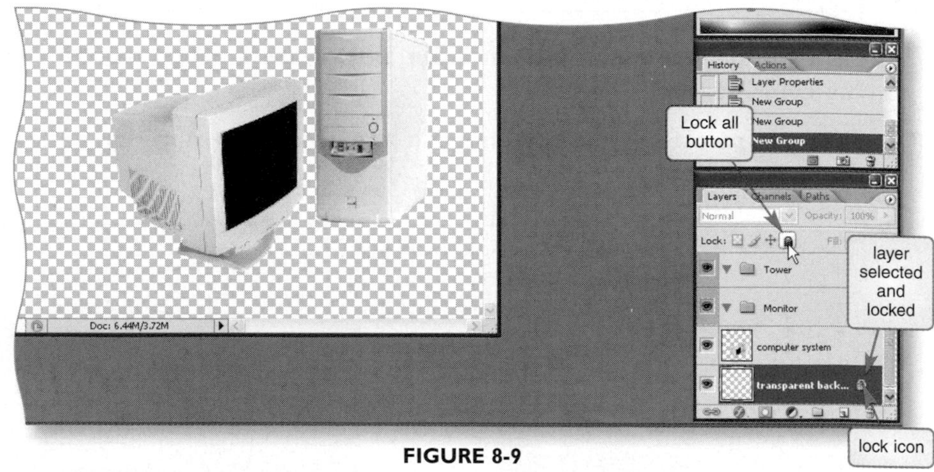

FIGURE 8-9

2

- **Click the computer system layer.**
- **Click the Lock transparent pixels button.**
- **Click the Lock position button.**

The layer is partially locked (Figure 8-10).

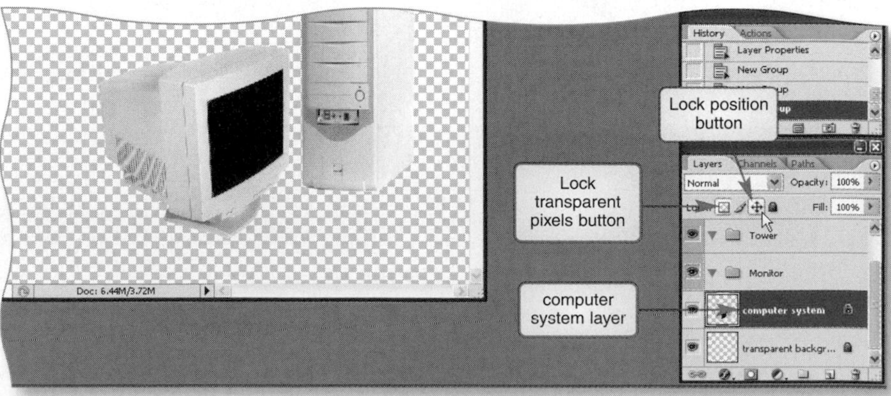

FIGURE 8-10

3

• **Click the Monitor layer group.**

Notice the lock icon for the transparent background is solid, indicating a full lock (Figure 8-11). The lock icon on the computer system layer is hollow, indicating a partial lock.

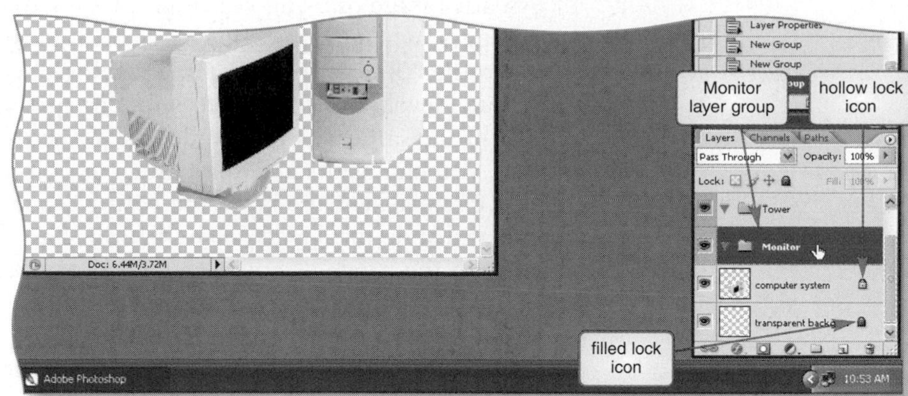

FIGURE 8-11

Saving the File

The edited photo will appear in printed format as a clip art logo for a newspaper column. Therefore, the photo will be saved in the PSD file format for maximum editing flexibility.

To Save the Computer Clip Art File

1. **With your USB flash drive connected to one of the computer's USB ports, click File on the menu bar and then click Save As.**
2. **When the Save As dialog box is displayed, if necessary, type** `Computer Clip Art` **in the File name text box. Do not press the ENTER key.**
3. **If necessary, click the Format box arrow and then choose Photoshop (*.PSD;*.PDD) in the list.**
4. **Click the Save in box arrow and then click USBDISK [G:], or the location associated with your USB flash drive, in the list.**
5. **Click the Save button. If Photoshop displays a Photoshop Format Options dialog box, click the OK button.**

The file is saved.

Vectors and Path Lines

Graphic images are of two types. As you have learned, vectors — also called vector graphics — are made up of shapes, lines, and curves that are defined by mathematical objects, or vectors. Vector graphics are high-quality graphics used in illustrations, typography, logos, and advertisements, which retain their crisp edges when resized, moved, or recolored. In a previous project, you used the Shape layers button on the Shape options bar to create a vector graphic automatically. You may have seen or used vector graphics as clip art in page layout and word processing programs.

The other type of graphic images are bitmap images, also called raster images. **Raster images** are made up of pixels of color and are resolution dependent; thus, they are appropriate for photographs and artwork with continuous color, such as paintings. Images from scanners and digital cameras are raster images because they need to use continuous color to form the image.

An advantage of using vector graphics is that they do not **pixilate**, or display jagged edges, when magnified. That is because they are made up of individual, scalable objects rather than bitmap pixels. Therefore, vector graphics are not directly editable at the pixel level, and changes are nondestructive. You can change a vector graphic, but not in the same way as you do a non-vector graphic. When you edit a vector graphic, you change its **attributes** such as color, fill, and outline. For example, if you create a circle as a shape layer, the vector graphic is generated using the current color scheme and style displayed on the options bar. The vector graphic can neither be edited with the brush or eraser tools, nor can it be filled with color using the Paint Bucket tool. If you change your mind about the color, for instance, you must select the shape layer and then change the color using the options bar. Changing the attributes of a vector object does not affect the object itself; it merely applies the change as it shapes and transforms the layer along a path.

Because vector graphics are drawn instead of compiled from pixels, they are more difficult to edit in Photoshop because you cannot change single pixels. If there is text, you cannot edit it directly in a vector graphic. Therefore, most of the time you have to convert vector graphics to bitmap images when you want to edit and print them. The process is called **rasterizing**. When you rasterize, you may be asked to include settings such as the pixel dimensions, color mode, anti-aliasing, dithering, and resolution. The disadvantage in rasterizing is that the converted raster image becomes resolution dependent; it is difficult to increase or decrease the size within photo editing software without sacrificing a degree of image quality. While raster images are scaled quite successfully in page layout programs, a permanent change in size is harder to interpolate.

In this project, in order to create a final product that can be used in the newspaper's page layout program, and one that has a transparent background and is scalable, you will convert a photo into a vector graphic. The conversion process will use the pen tools to create a path around various parts of the photo and then fill them with color. Details will be added with blends and special effects.

Path Lines and Anchors

While any of the shape tools can be used to create vector graphics, the most versatile are the Pen tool and the Freeform Pen tool that create paths. You have worked with simple paths in previous projects. Recall that a path is an outline that you can turn into a shape, selection, or fill and stroke with color. When you use one of the pen tools to create path lines, each click in the document window becomes an anchor point, or node. An **anchor point** is a single spot that has been clicked along a path line. An anchor point is displayed as a small square (Figure 8-12). The current or latest anchor point is always a solid square, indicating it is selected. Non-selected anchor points are used to alter the shape and angle of line segments at adjacent segments along the path. Photoshop displays non-selected anchor points as hollow squares as you add further anchor points.

To create a straight line path, you click the document window using one of the pen tools. The anchor point is displayed. When you click again, a new anchor point is displayed and a line connects the two anchor points in the document window.

When you want to create curved lines, you drag with the Pen tool. First, you set the beginning of the curved line by choosing a point and dragging. Photoshop will display an anchor point at that position and two **direction lines** with **direction points** (Figure 8-13). The direction lines move outward as you drag. The **direction** of the drag determines the eventual direction of the curve. For instance, if you drag to the right, the bump of the curve will be to the right. The **length** of the drag determines how much influence the anchor point will have over the curve — the longer the drag, the more exaggerated the curve. To create the other end of the curved line, simply click the desired end point and drag again. Dragging the end point in the opposite direction creates an arc; dragging in

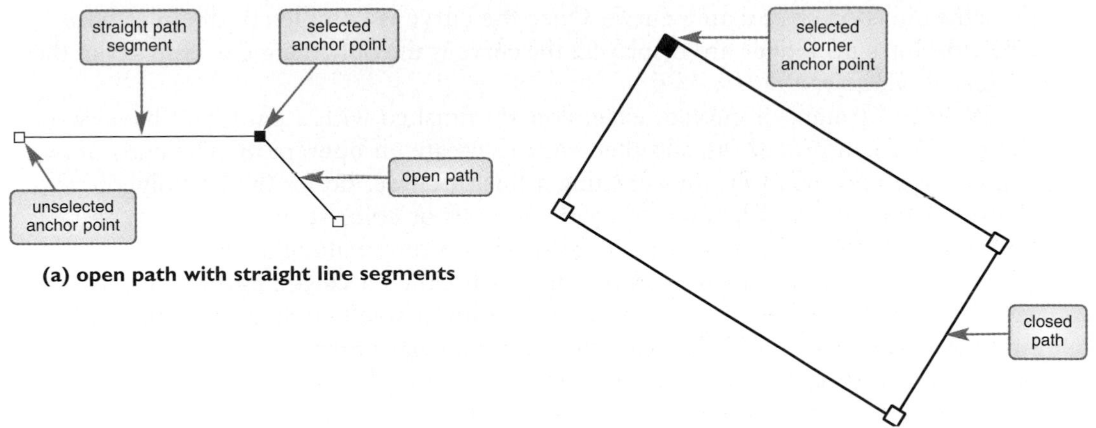

(a) open path with straight line segments

(b) closed path with straight line segments

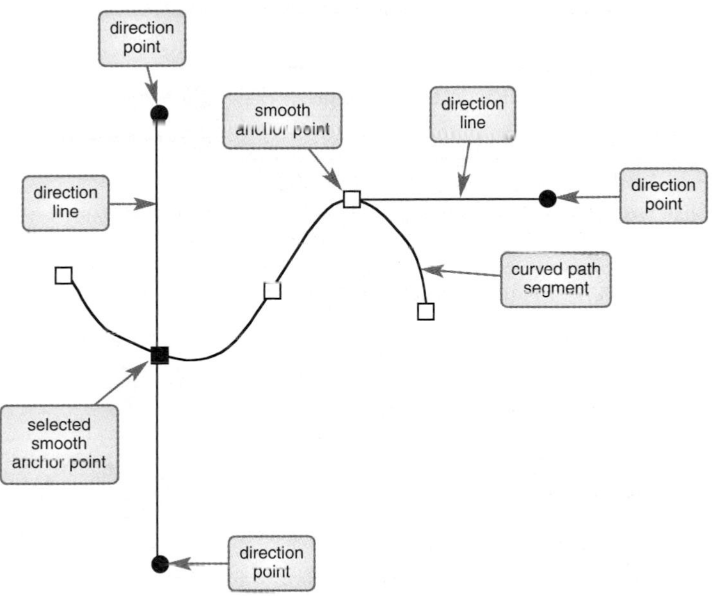

(c) curved path segment with smooth anchor points

FIGURE 8-12

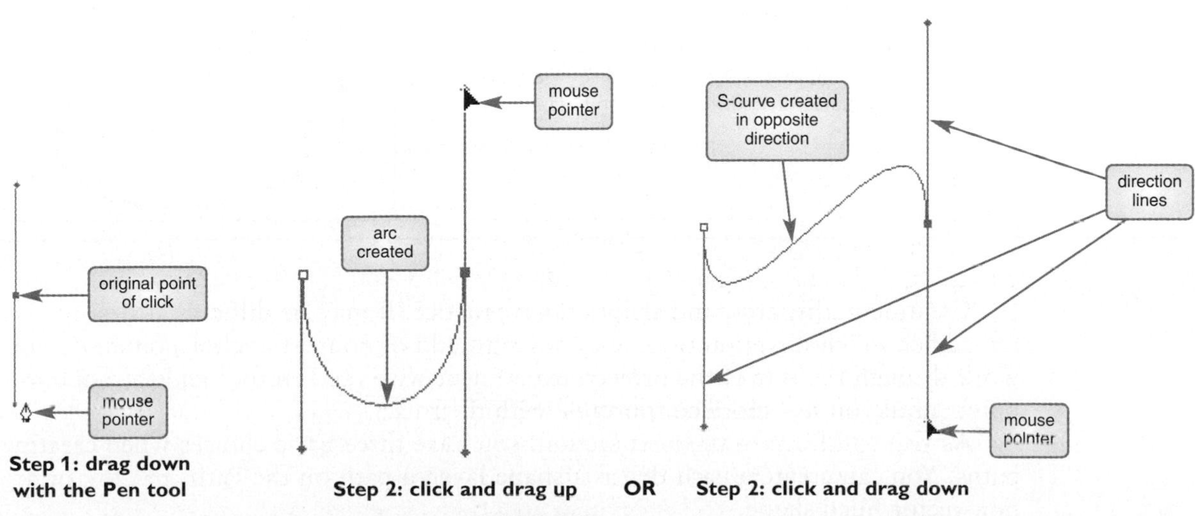

Step 1: drag down with the Pen tool **Step 2: click and drag up** **OR** **Step 2: click and drag down**

FIGURE 8-13

the same direction creates an S curve. Once the curve is completed, the lines with direction lines no longer are displayed; the curve is the only thing that displays in the document window.

Whether straight or curved, when you are finished with a path, you have two choices. You can press CTRL and then click to create an **open path**. The ends of an open path do not connect, thus creating a line or curve, rather than a polygon or ellipse. Open paths can be used to create outlines or color strokes, or they can be used to place text, such as words that display contoured along a curve.

If you finish a path by joining the ends, it is called a **closed path**. When your mouse pointer gets close to the first anchor point, a small circle displays next to the tip of the current pen tool. Clicking the mouse at that point connects the anchor points. A closed path creates a shape such as a rectangle, triangle, or oval.

Table 8-3 displays some of the possible tasks when creating path lines.

Table 8-3 Creating Path Lines

TASK	STEPS	RESULT
to create a straight line path	Click a beginning point. Click an ending point.	
to add an anchor point	Click along a path.	
to delete an existing anchor point	If the Auto Add/Delete option is selected on the options bar, you can click an existing point to delete it.	
to create an arc	Drag the first anchor point in the direction of the bump of the curve. Drag the second anchor point in the opposite direction.	
to create an S curve	Drag both anchor points in the same direction.	
to create a polygon	Click at least three times to create anchor points and then click the original anchor point again.	
to create an ellipse	Drag a beginning point. Drag an ending point in the opposite direction. Click the beginning point.	

Creating paths, arcs, and shapes takes practice. It may be difficult at first to remember which direction to drag or when to add or convert anchor points. As you work through the rest of the project, experiment with the Pen tool and the anchor points until you feel more comfortable with their use.

As you will learn in the next section, you have three basic choices when creating paths. You can create a path that is a shape layer, a path on the Paths palette, or a non-vector filled shape.

Shape Layers

As you create paths, if you select the **Shape layers button** on the options bar, Photoshop creates a shape on the Layers palette. Two clicks create a line path that is displayed in gray in the document window; a path with more than two points creates a fill with the current foreground color. A shape layer consists of a fill layer that defines the shape color and a linked vector mask that defines the path or shape outline. The outline of a shape appears as a path on the Paths palette as well, but the shape exists in its own layer on the Layers palette, making it easier to edit than other paths.

You can use either the shape tools or the pen tools to create shape layer paths. Because they are easily moved, aligned, resized, and distributed, shape layers are ideal for making graphics for clip art and for Web pages. Additionally, you can create multiple shapes on a single shape layer.

Creating a Shape Layer with the Pen Tool

The following steps illustrate how to create a closed path with the Pen tool to silhouette the computer image with a green color as shown in Figure 8-1 on page PS 485. The path will become a shape layer on the Layers palette. Photoshop displays new shape layers above single layers, or within layer groups in the Layers palette.

To Create a Shape Layer with the Pen Tool

1

- **If necessary, in the toolbox, right-click the current pen tool button and then click Pen Tool in the list.**
- **On the options bar, click the Shape layers button. Click the Set color for new layer box. When Photoshop displays the Color Picker, select a light green color and then click the OK button.**

The options bar displays the current settings of the Pen tool (Figure 8-14).

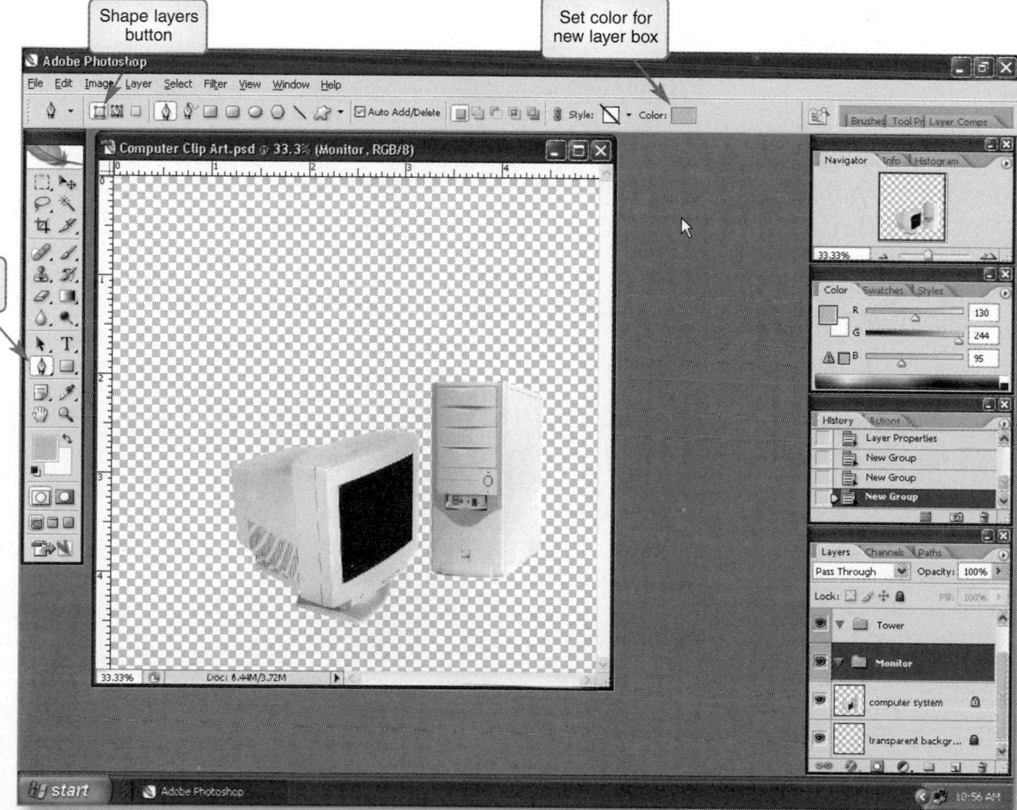

FIGURE 8-14

2

- **On the Layers palette, click the transparent background layer.**
- **In the document window, click to the left of the base of the computer monitor.**

Photoshop displays an anchor point (Figure 8-15). The small filled square indicates that the anchor point is selected or current. A new shape layer is displayed on the Layers palette.

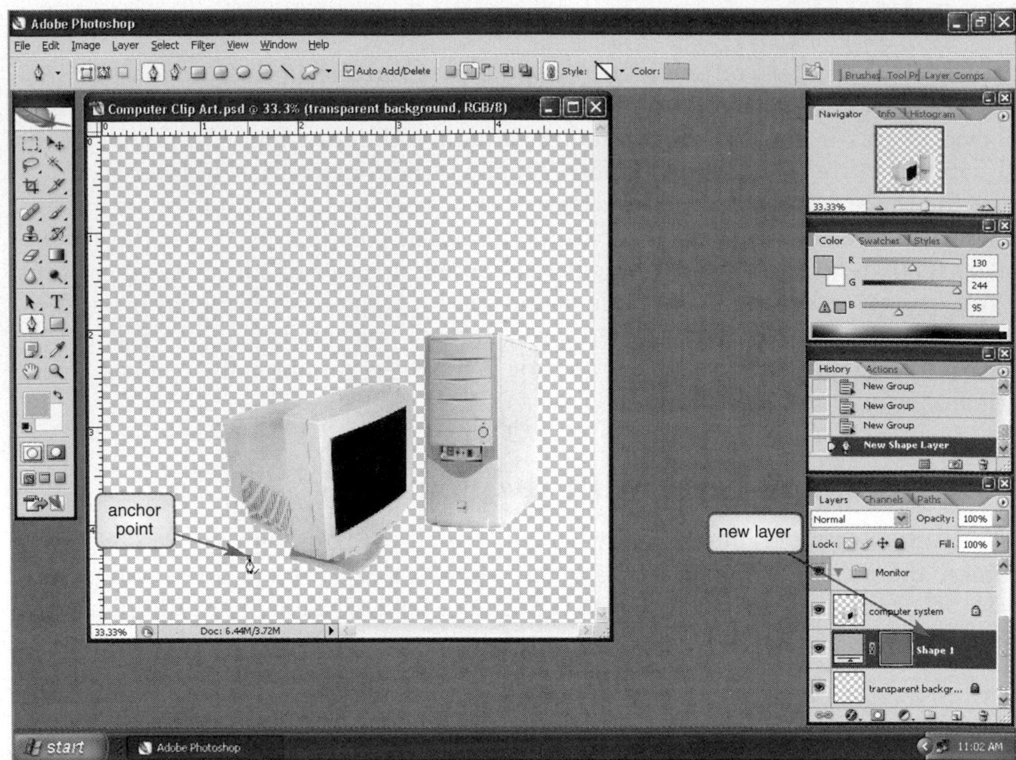

FIGURE 8-15

3

- **With the Pen tool still selected, click to the right of the computer tower, approximately halfway between the top and bottom of the tower.**

Photoshop displays a second anchor point (Figure 8-16). The first anchor is displayed hollow and the second one now is current.

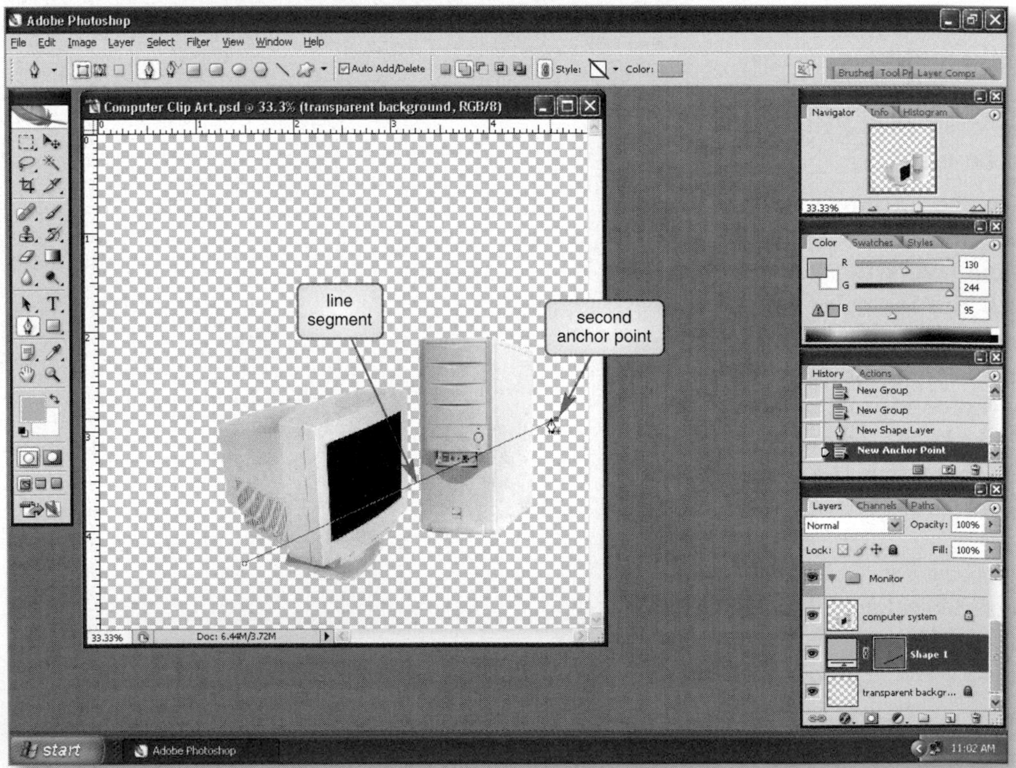

FIGURE 8-16

4

• **Click above the monitor and the tower, approximately equidistant from the other two anchor points, to form an equilateral triangle.**

Photoshop displays a third anchor point and fills the selection with green (Figure 8-17).

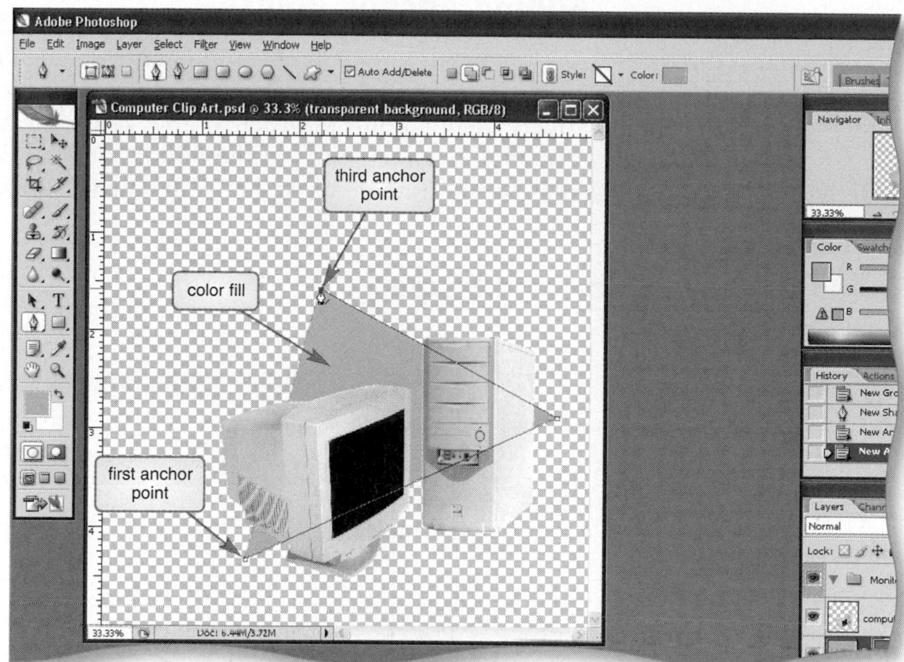

FIGURE 8-17

5

• **Click the first anchor point to close the path.**

The path is closed and the anchor points no longer are displayed along the shape's path (Figure 8-18).

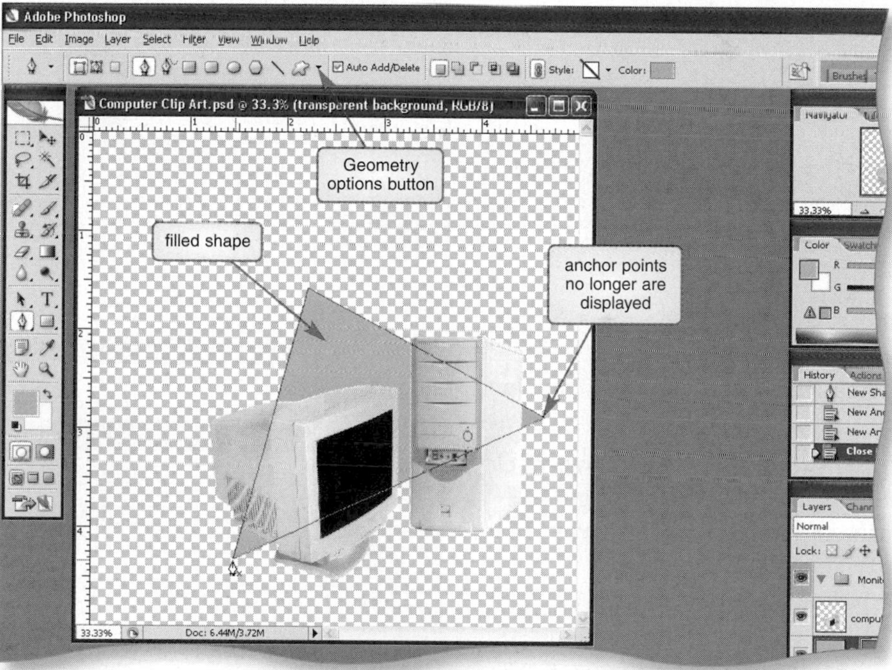

FIGURE 8-18

If you want to see a line while you create new anchor points, you can click the Geometry options button on the options bar (Figure 8-18). One of the geometry options for the Pen tool is a Rubber Band check box. The Rubber Band feature will help you guide your next anchor point by displaying a stretch line between anchor points, even before you click.

The next step is to adjust the new path shape from a triangle into a kind of semi-circle by creating curves within the shape's border, as shown on the next page.

Adding Anchor Points

For precise adjustments along path segments, you sometimes need to insert additional anchor points. Photoshop creates direction lines automatically with each added anchor point in order to give you more flexibility in editing. The following steps add anchor points in the middle of each line segment on the left and right sides of the triangle using the **Add Anchor Point tool**.

To Add Anchor Points to a Shape

1

- **In the toolbox, right-click the Pen Tool (P) button.**

Photoshop displays various pen tools (Figure 8-19).

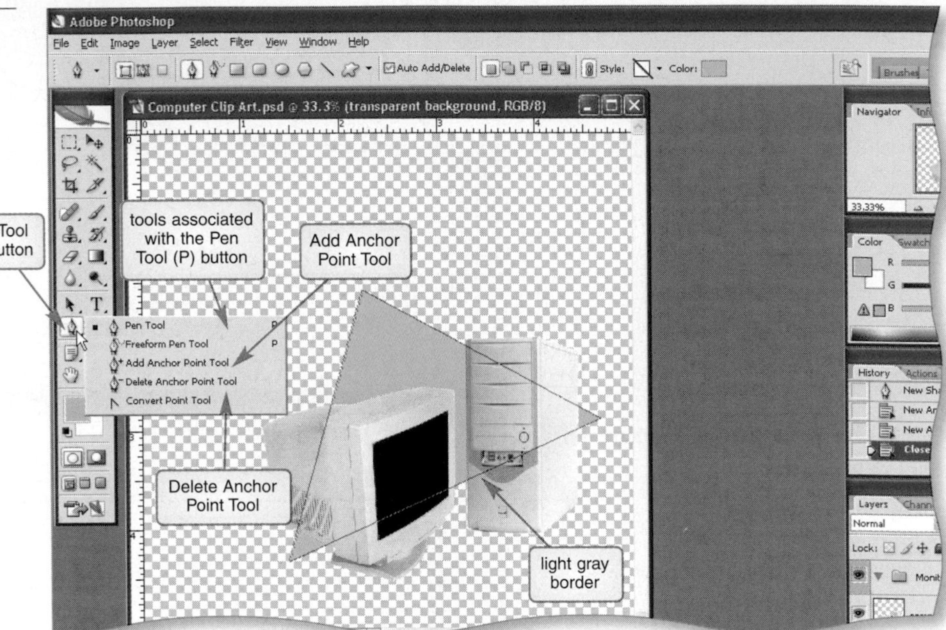

FIGURE 8-19

2

- **Click Add Anchor Point Tool in the list.**
- **In the document window, click the left side of the triangular path approximately halfway between the corners.**
- **Drag the newly created anchor point outward until the curve is smooth as shown in Figure 8-20.**

The new anchor point displays an extra line with arrowheads, because it is a curve. The mouse pointer displays a plus sign (+) next to the tip of the pen when you add anchor points.

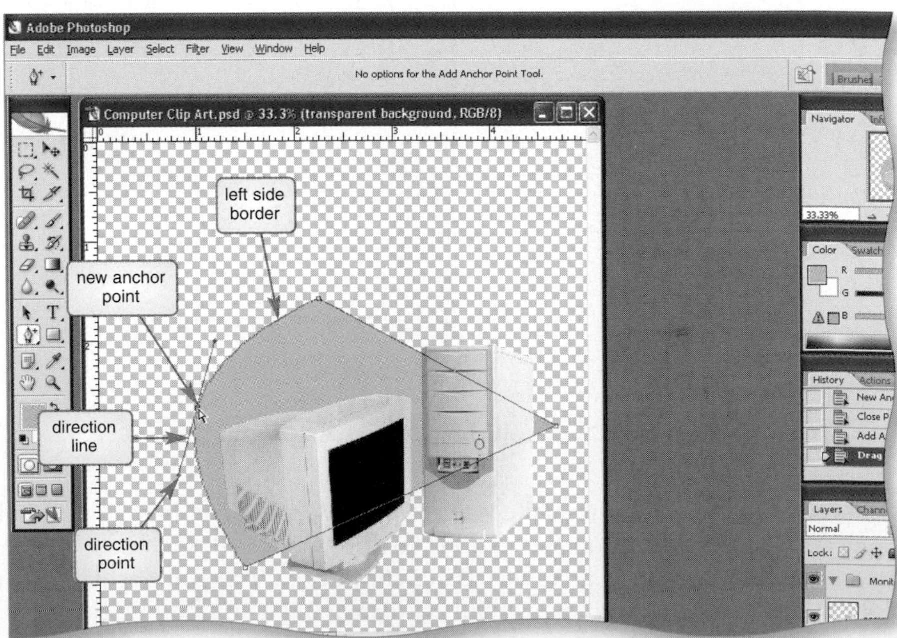

FIGURE 8-20

3

- **Click the right side of the triangular path approximately halfway between the corners to create a second anchor point.**
- **Drag the newly created anchor point outward until the curve is smooth.**

The half circle shape is complete (Figure 8-21).

4

- **Press SHIFT+CTRL+H.**

The non-printing light gray border that is displayed around the filled shape in Figure 8-21 is turned off to get a better representation of the final product (Figure 8-22).

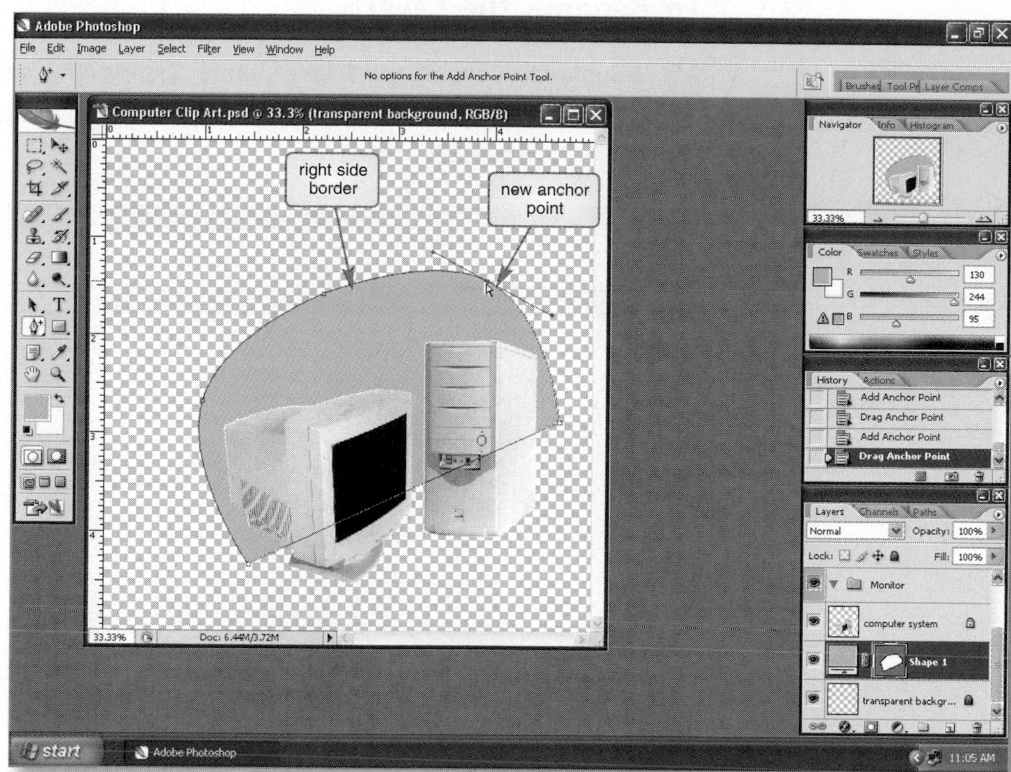

FIGURE 8-21

Sometimes deleting an anchor point will help you straighten path lines. To delete an anchor point, select the **Delete Anchor Point tool** (Figure 8-19), and then click the anchor point. A minus sign will appear next to the mouse pointer. The path then straightens between the two adjacent anchor points.

While various triangles and other shapes are available within the custom shapes on the options bar, drawing with the Pen tool adds the extra flexibility of size and shape. Once the path or shape is created, you can change the order of the layer's appearance by repositioning it on the Layers palette. The step on the next page renames the layer.

To Rename the Layer

1 Double-click the Shape 1 layer name. Type green **and then press the ENTER key.**

The layer is renamed (Figure 8-22).

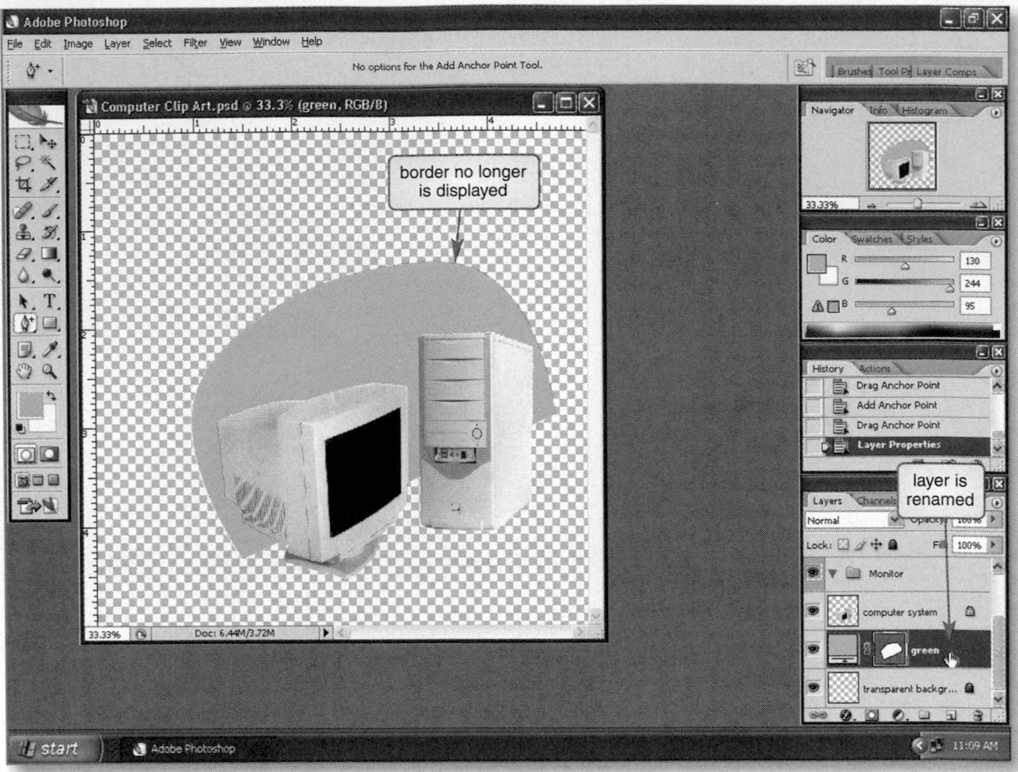

FIGURE 8-22

Paths

If you select the **Paths button** on the Shapes options bar, the path does not create a shape on the Layers palette; it becomes a path or work path on the Paths palette. Paths are outlines, created directly on the currently selected layer. Once created, you can use a path to make a selection, create a vector mask, or fill and stroke with color to create raster graphics. A work path is temporary unless you save or rename it.

More About

Work Paths

You can use work paths in several ways. Work paths can become vector masks to hide areas of a layer, or they can be converted to a selection to fill or stroke with color. A work path also can be designated as a clipping path to make part of an image transparent when exporting the image to a page-layout or vector-editing application.

Creating a Path with the Pen Tool

In the Computer Clip Art document window, you will use the Pen tool to create a path on the black screen of the computer monitor. After adjusting the path, you will fill it with a cyan color to simulate clip art. The following steps illustrate how to create a path with the Pen tool.

To Create a Path with the Pen Tool

1

- **On the Navigator palette, click the Zoom In button until the magnification is 66.67%. Scroll to display the monitor in the document window.**
- **On the Layers palette, select the computer system layer.**
- **In the toolbox, right-click the current pen tool button and then click Pen Tool in the list.**
- **On the options bar, click the Paths button. Click the Add to path area (+) button.**
- **One at a time, in a clockwise manner, click the four corners of the monitor's black screen.**
- **Click the original anchor point to create a closed path.**
- **Click the Paths palette tab.**

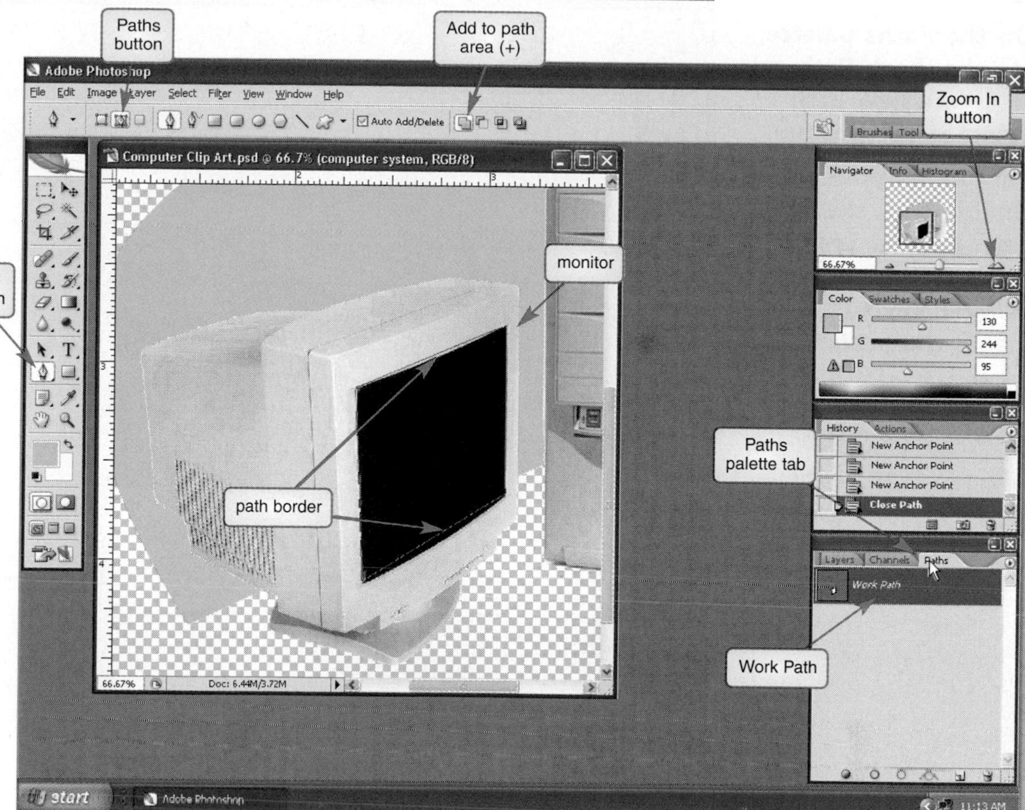

FIGURE 8-23

The path closes to form a rectangle around the monitor's screen (Figure 8-23). Your path will not match the edges of the monitor's screen perfectly. The Paths palette displays the Work Path.

2

- **On the Paths palette, drag the Work Path to the Create new path button at the bottom of the palette.**
- **Double-click the new name, Path 1. Type** `blue` **and then press the ENTER key to rename the path.**

Photoshop saves the temporary Work Path and changes its name to blue (Figure 8-24).

FIGURE 8-24

The next step adds anchor points at the top and bottom of the monitor's screen along the path using the Add Anchor Point tool.

To Add Anchor Points

1. **In the toolbox, right-click the current pen tool and then click Add Anchor Point Tool in the list.**
2. **In the document window, click in the middle of the top line segment.**
3. **Click in the middle of the bottom line segment.**

Two new anchor points are displayed (Figure 8-25).

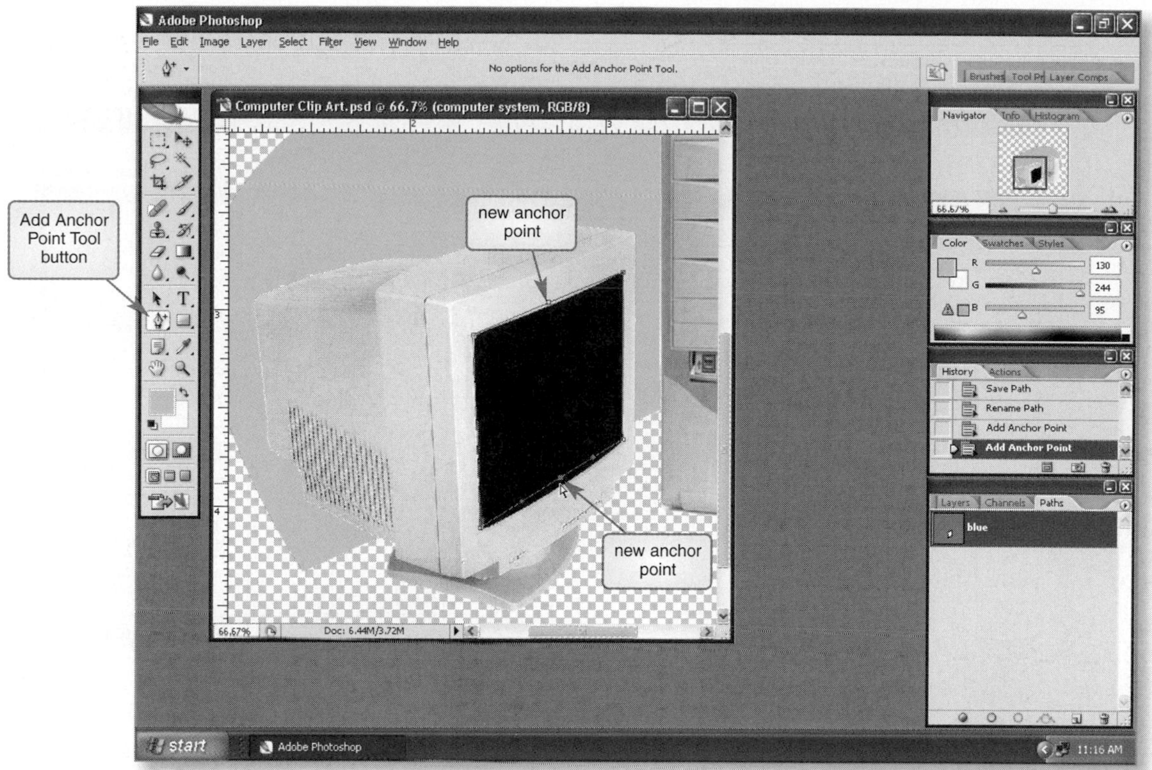

FIGURE 8-25

Another way to change the number of anchor points is to use the Auto Add/Delete box on the Pen tool's options bar (Figure 8-24). If the Auto Add/Delete box is checked, clicking a path segment creates a new anchor automatically, and clicking an existing anchor point automatically deletes it.

The Path Selection and Direct Selection Tools

Two tools are particularly useful to edit the shape and placement of paths by moving lines and anchor points. The **Path Selection tool** moves the entire path. The **Direct Selection tool** moves a path segment — the line between two anchor points — or individual anchor points.

In the step on the next page, the two new anchor points are dragged using the Direct Selection tool, to align better with the edge of the monitor's screen.

To Reshape a Path

1

- **Press the A key. Right-click the current selection tool button and then click Direct Selection Tool in the list.**
- **Drag the upper-center anchor point to align better with the upper edge of the monitor's screen.**
- **Drag the lower-center anchor point to align better with the bottom edge of the monitor's screen.**

The path now more closely follows the edge of the monitor's screen (Figure 8-26).

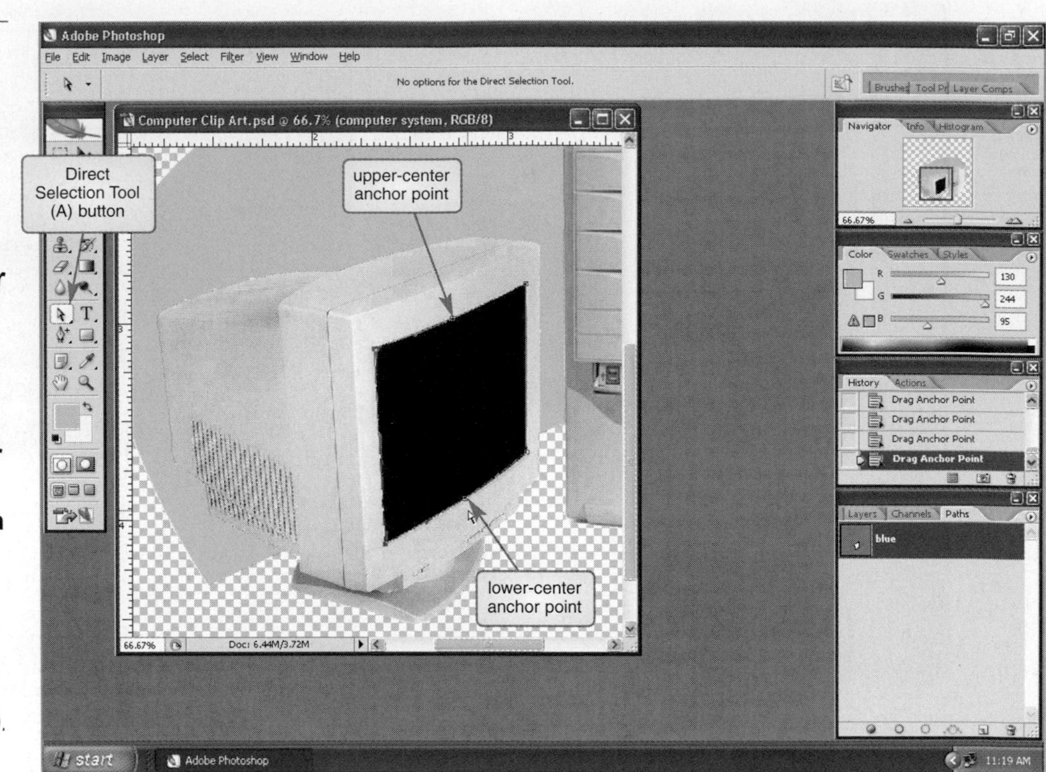

FIGURE 8-26

If at any time, you cannot see the anchor points on a path, select the appropriate path or shape layer, select the Path Selection Tool (A) button or the Direct Selection Tool (A) button, and then click the border of the path.

Fill a Path with Color

To fill a closed path with color, you first choose the color and then use the Fill path with foreground color button at the bottom of the Paths palette as shown in the following steps.

To Fill a Path with Color

1

- **Click the Swatches palette tab and then click the color, Pastel Cyan.**
- **On the Paths palette, click the Fill path with foreground color button.**

The path is filled with pastel cyan (Figure 8-27).

2

- **If some of the monitor's black screen is still displayed, drag to adjust the appropriate anchor point and then click the Fill path with foreground color button again.**

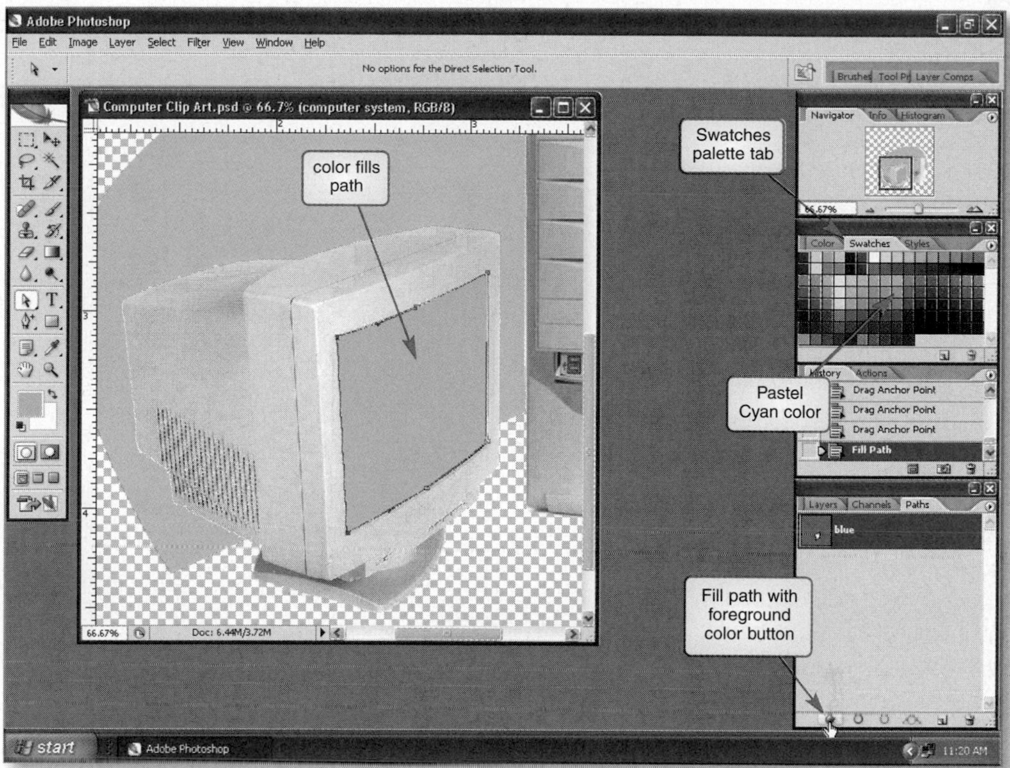

FIGURE 8-27

Other Ways

1. On Paths palette menu, click Fill Path
2. Right-click path, click Fill Path

Converting Anchor Points

An anchor point with direction lines that are straight sometimes is called a **smooth point**; when you drag the direction points, the resulting arc is curved smoothly. An anchor point without direction lines, or one with a direction line that creates an angle, sometimes is called a **corner point**; when you drag a corner point, the resulting line segments create a corner. When you add an anchor point, Photoshop automatically adds a smooth point. The **Convert Point tool** allows you to change from one kind of anchor point to the other.

In the steps on the next page, a gray shape layer is created around the computer monitor. Some of the anchor points then are converted to help define corners and curves.

To Create Another Shape Layer

1

- **On the Swatches palette, click 35% Gray.**
- **Click the Layers palette tab. Select the Monitor layer group.**
- **In the toolbox, select the Pen Tool (P) button.**
- **On the options bar, click the Shape layers button.**
- **In the document window, click the top-left corner of the monitor.**

The anchor point is displayed on the corner of the monitor (Figure 8-28). A new shape layer is defined within the Monitor layer group.

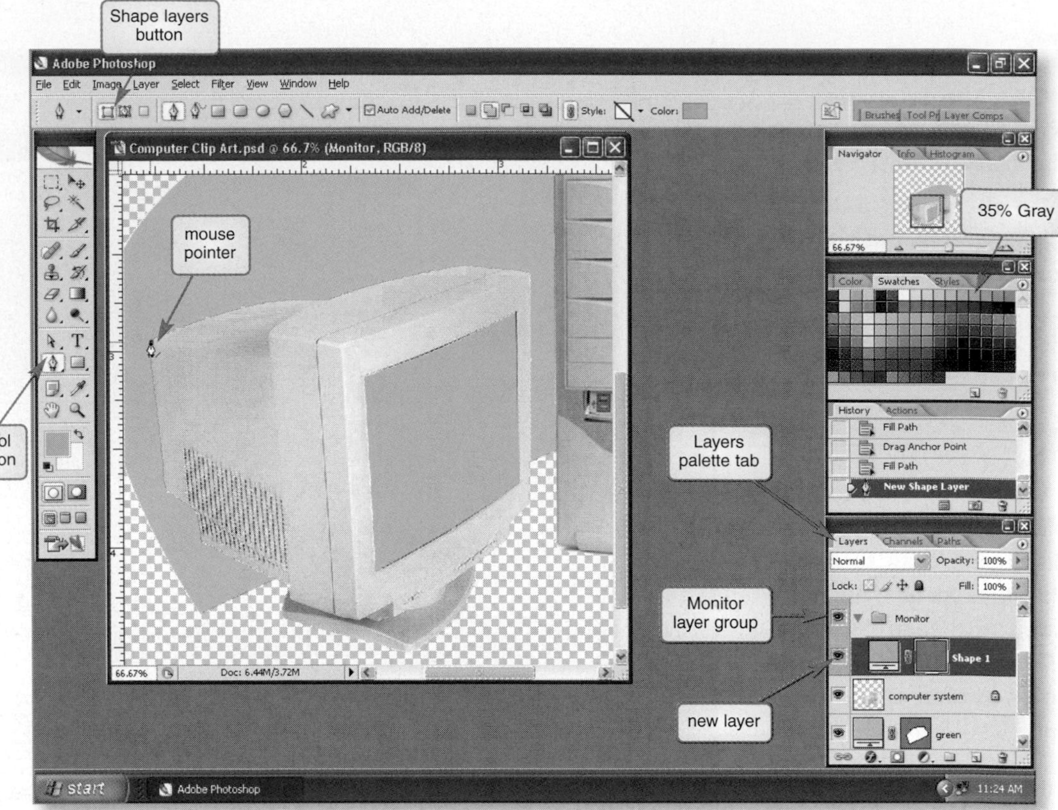

FIGURE 8-28

2

- **Proceed around the monitor in a clockwise fashion, clicking at each of the major corners. You do not have to be exact.**
- **When you get all the way around, click the beginning point.**
- **On the Layers palette, double-click the name, Shape 1. Type** `gray` **and then press the ENTER key to rename the layer.**

The selection is displayed in gray (Figure 8-29).

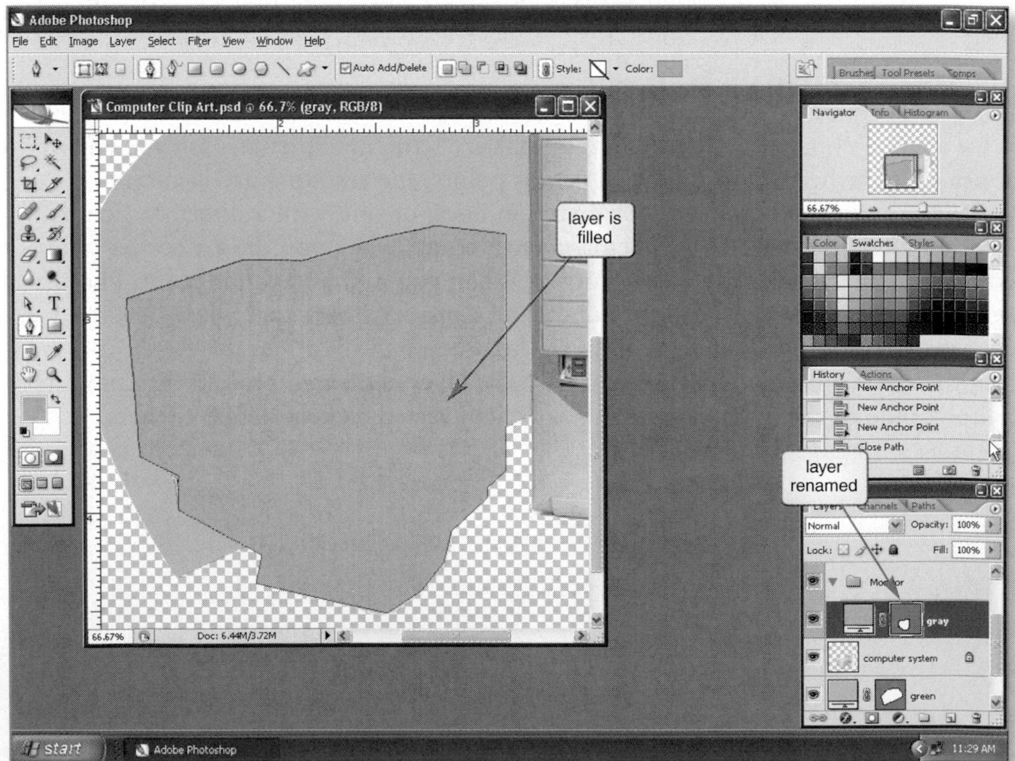

FIGURE 8-29

The next steps show how to display only the path border of the monitor shape and then convert some of the anchor points to help define corners and curves.

To Convert Anchor Points and Reshape

1

- **Click the visibility icon beside the Monitor layer so it no longer is displayed. If necessary, click the Vector mask thumbnail on the Monitor layer.**

The Vector mask thumbnail is selected and the border of the vector graphic is displayed around the monitor (Figure 8-30).

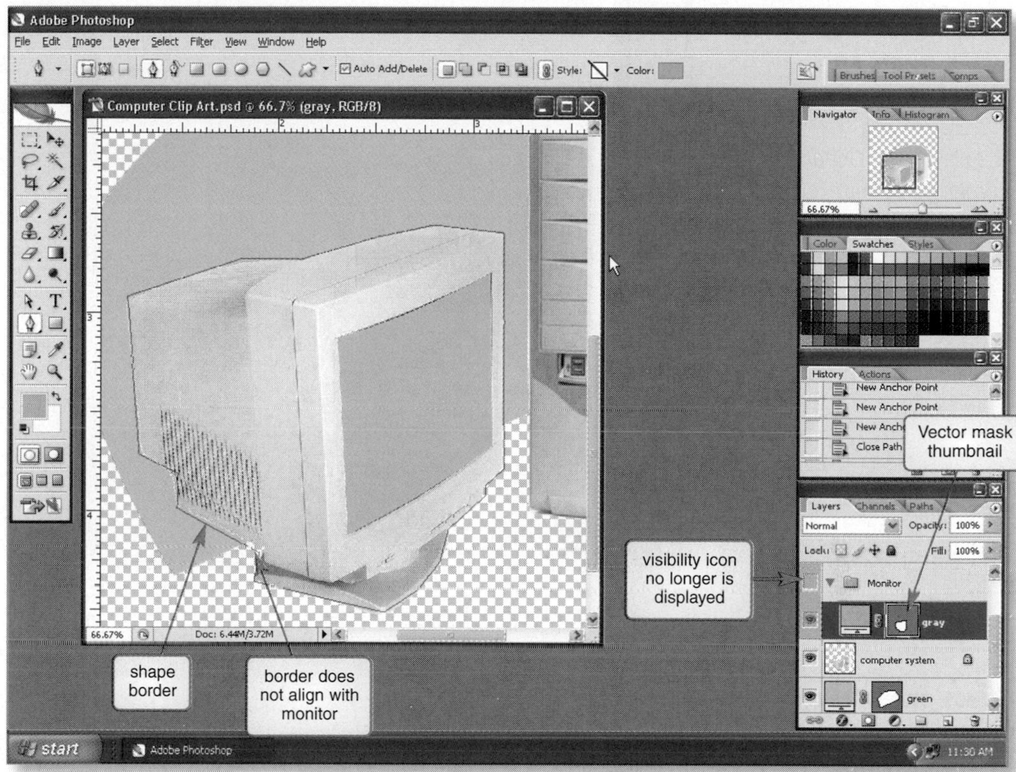

FIGURE 8-30

2

- **In the toolbox, right-click the current pen tool button and then click Add Anchor Point Tool in the list.**
- **In the document window, choose a point that does not match the edge of the monitor. Click the path at that point to add an anchor.**

Recall that all added anchor points first display as smooth points with straight direction lines and direction points (Figure 8-31).

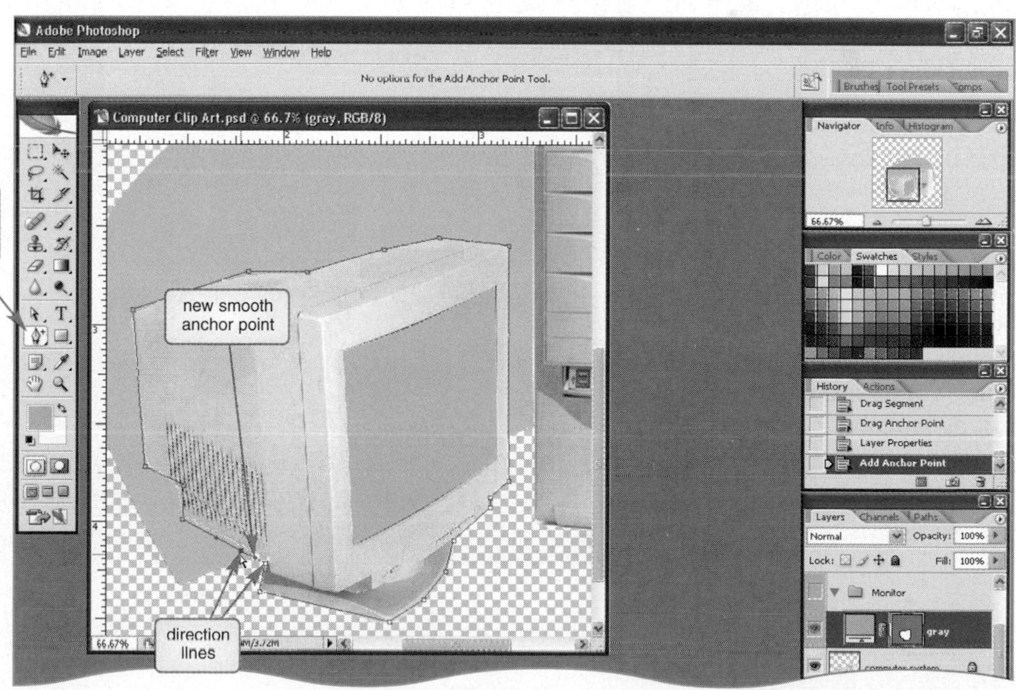

FIGURE 8-31

3

- **In the toolbox, right-click the current pen tool button and then click Convert Point Tool in the list.**
- **Click the new anchor point to convert it.**

The anchor point changes to a corner point with no direction lines (Figure 8-32).

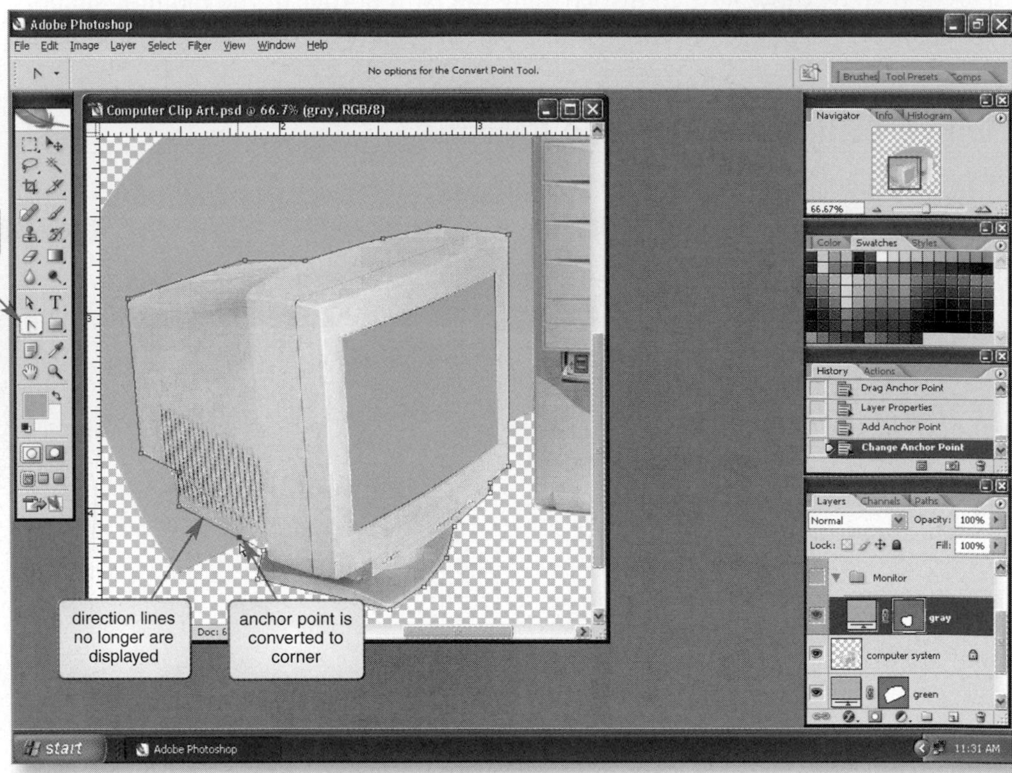

FIGURE 8-32

4

- **Press the A key. If the Direct Selection tool is not current, press SHIFT+A.**
- **Drag the added anchor point closer to the monitor graphic.**

The path is reshaped (Figure 8-33).

5

- **Repeat Steps 2 through 4 for any other points along the path that do not align along the edge of the monitor.**

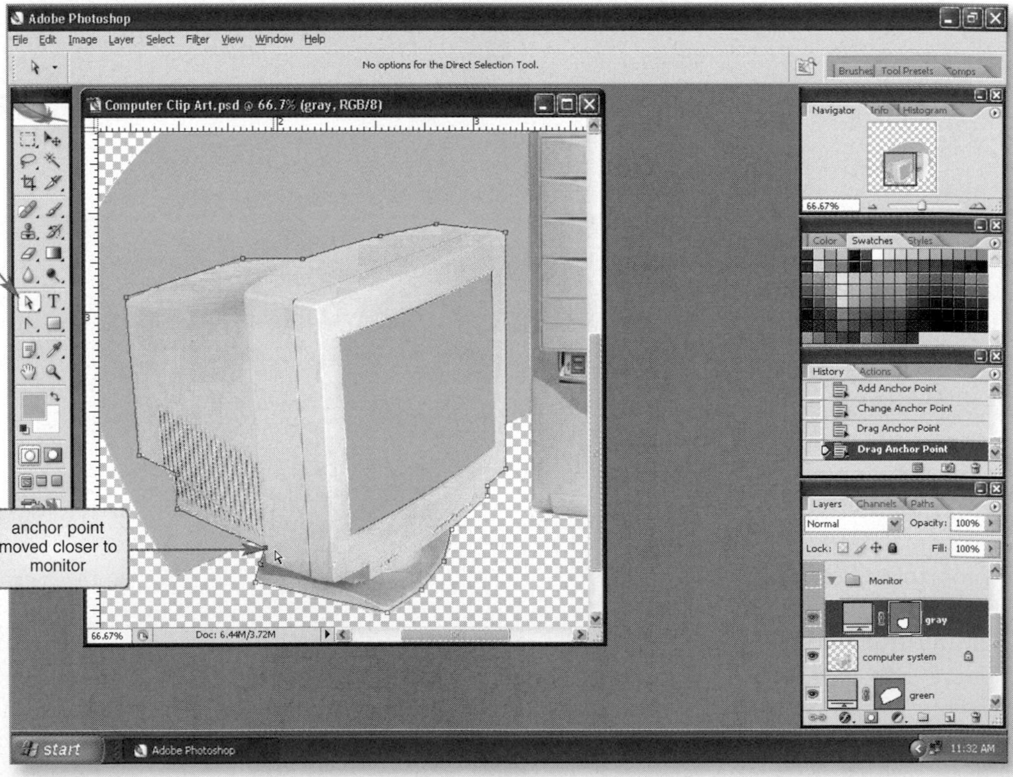

FIGURE 8-33

Other Ways

1. To use Convert Point tool, ALT+click anchor point

Finally, to reveal the blue filled path of the monitor's screen, the following steps show how to subtract from the gray shape layer.

To Subtract from a Shape Layer

1

- **Click the visibility icon beside the Monitor layer so it is displayed. If necessary, click the visibility icon beside the gray layer so it is not displayed. Click the Vector mask thumbnail on the gray layer.**

The Vector mask thumbnail is selected and the border of the vector graphic is displayed around the monitor (Figure 8-34).

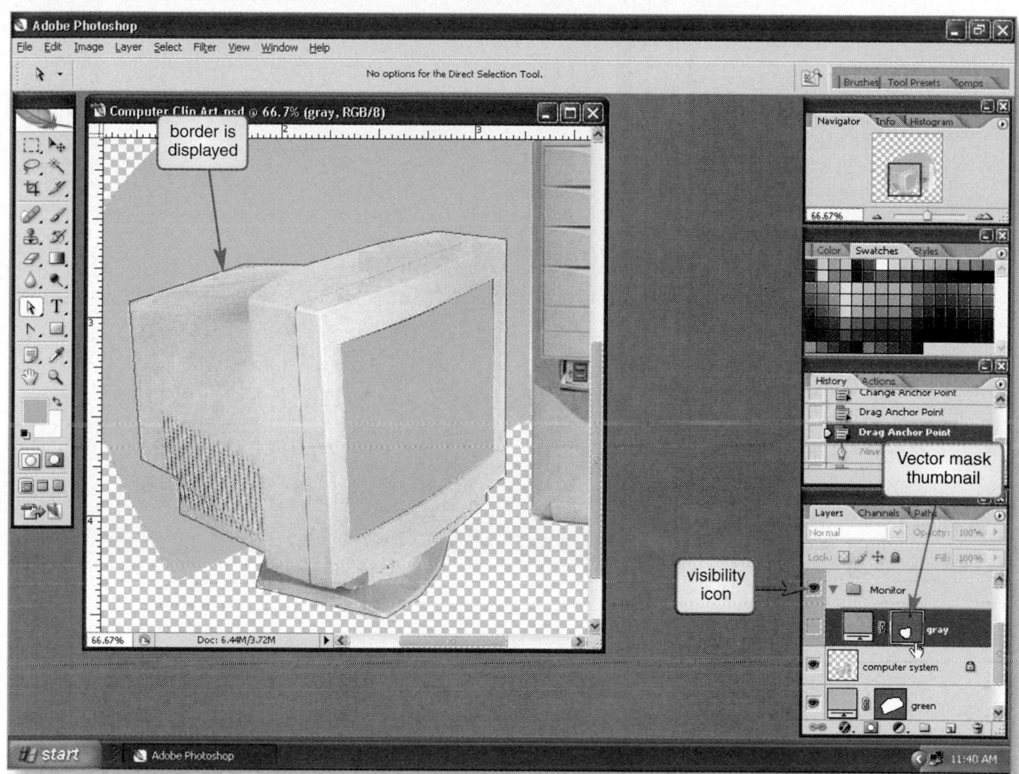

FIGURE 8-34

2

- **In the toolbox, right-click the current pen tool button and then click Pen Tool in the list.**
- **On the options bar, click the Subtract from shape area (-) button.**
- **Click around the monitor's screen again to form a path.**

The monitor's screen is included in a subtraction path (Figure 8-35).

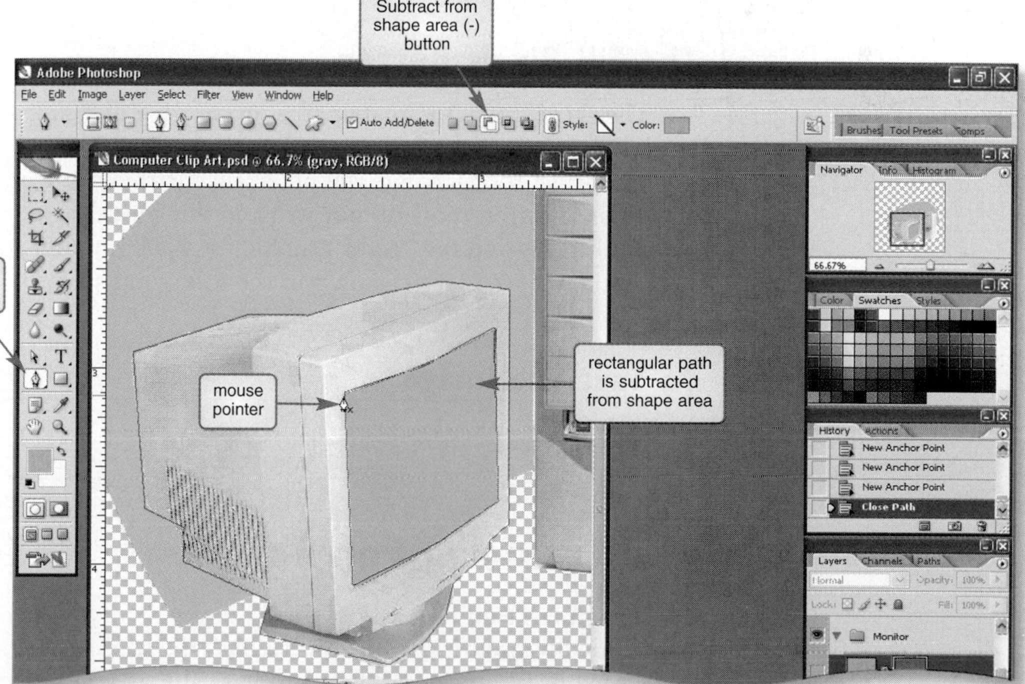

FIGURE 8-35

3

• Click the visibility icon on the gray layer.

The blue shows through the gray shape layer path (Figure 8-36).

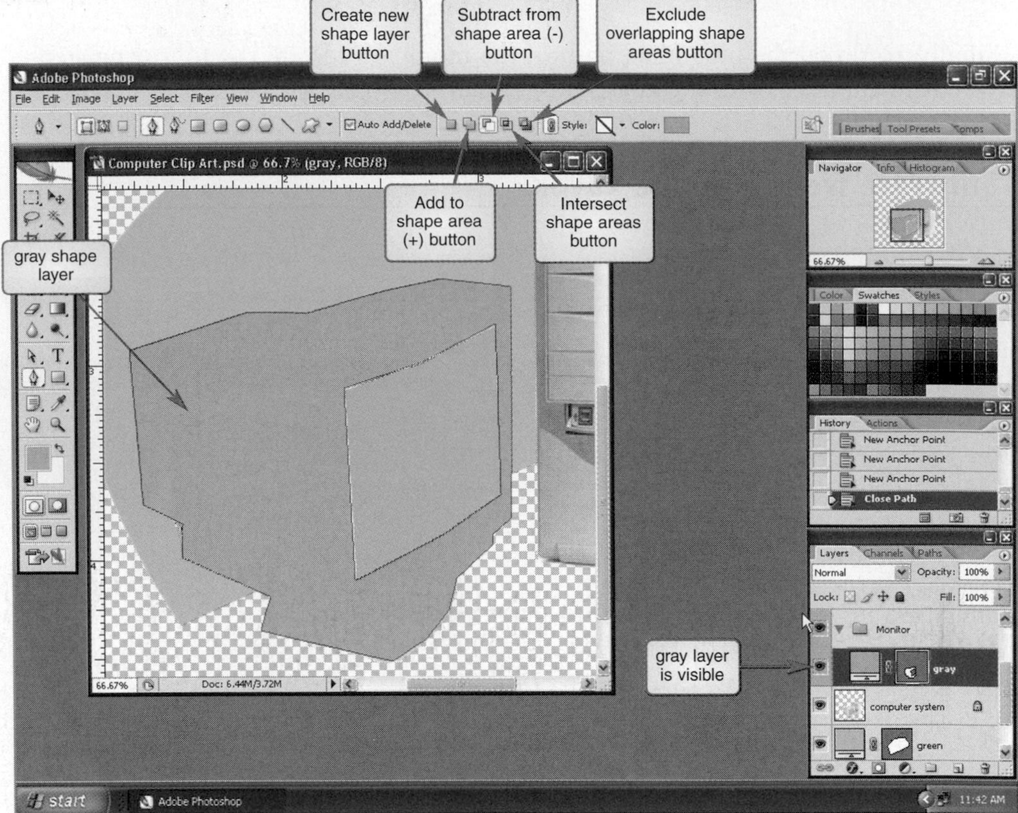

FIGURE 8-36

Five buttons are on the Shapes options bar that help you in creating paths: the Create new shape layer button, the Add to shape area (+) button, the Subtract from shape area (-) button, the Intersect shape areas button, and the Exclude overlapping shape areas button.

The Fill Pixels Button

The third mode to create paths, using the **Fill Pixels button**, paints directly on a layer. When you work in this mode, you are not creating vector graphics. The painting and brush tools change the pixels just as they do with any raster image. The pen and path selection tools do not work in this mode.

Before creating the vector graphic for the computer tower, it is a good idea to save your work so far as shown in the following step.

To Save the Image

1 Press 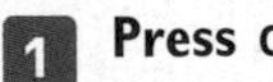 **CTRL+S.**

The Freeform Pen Tool

The **Freeform Pen tool** allows you to draw as if you were drawing with a pen on paper. Ideally used with a graphic tablet, the tool easily can be used with a mouse, as well. Anchor points are added automatically as you move the mouse. The frequency of the anchor points is based on a Curve Fit setting available via the Geometry options button on the options bar. The setting represents how far apart the anchor points are placed as your draw; a higher pixel value creates fewer anchor points. Other anchor points can be added or deleted when the path is complete, if necessary.

A unique feature of the Freeform Pen tool is the magnetic pen option. Similar to the Magnetic Lasso tool, the **magnetic pen** snaps the anchor points to existing color changes as you drag. While the Magnetic Lasso tool helps you create a selection, the magnetic pen creates a shape layer or path. To turn on the magnetic pen, you click the Magnetic check box on the Freeform Pen options bar.

Creating a Shape with the Magnetic Pen

In the Computer Clip Art document window, you will use the magnetic pen option of the Freeform Pen tool to draw around the darker portion on the front of the computer tower, creating a shape layer. Then, you will use the same color that you used on the monitor to create a shape layer around the lighter portion of the computer tower.

As you move the mouse with the magnetic pen, work slowly. If the line goes astray, move the mouse backward. If several anchor points become misaligned, press the ESC key and begin again.

To Create a Shape with the Magnetic Pen

1

- **Press the D key to activate the default colors. If black does not display as the foreground color, press the X key to exchange black and white.**
- **On the Layers palette, select the Tower group layer.**
- **Right-click the current pen tool and then click Freeform Pen Tool in the list.**
- **On the options bar, click the Magnetic check box to select it.**
- **Scroll in the document window to display the computer tower. Move the mouse pointer to a location near the top-left corner of the tower.**

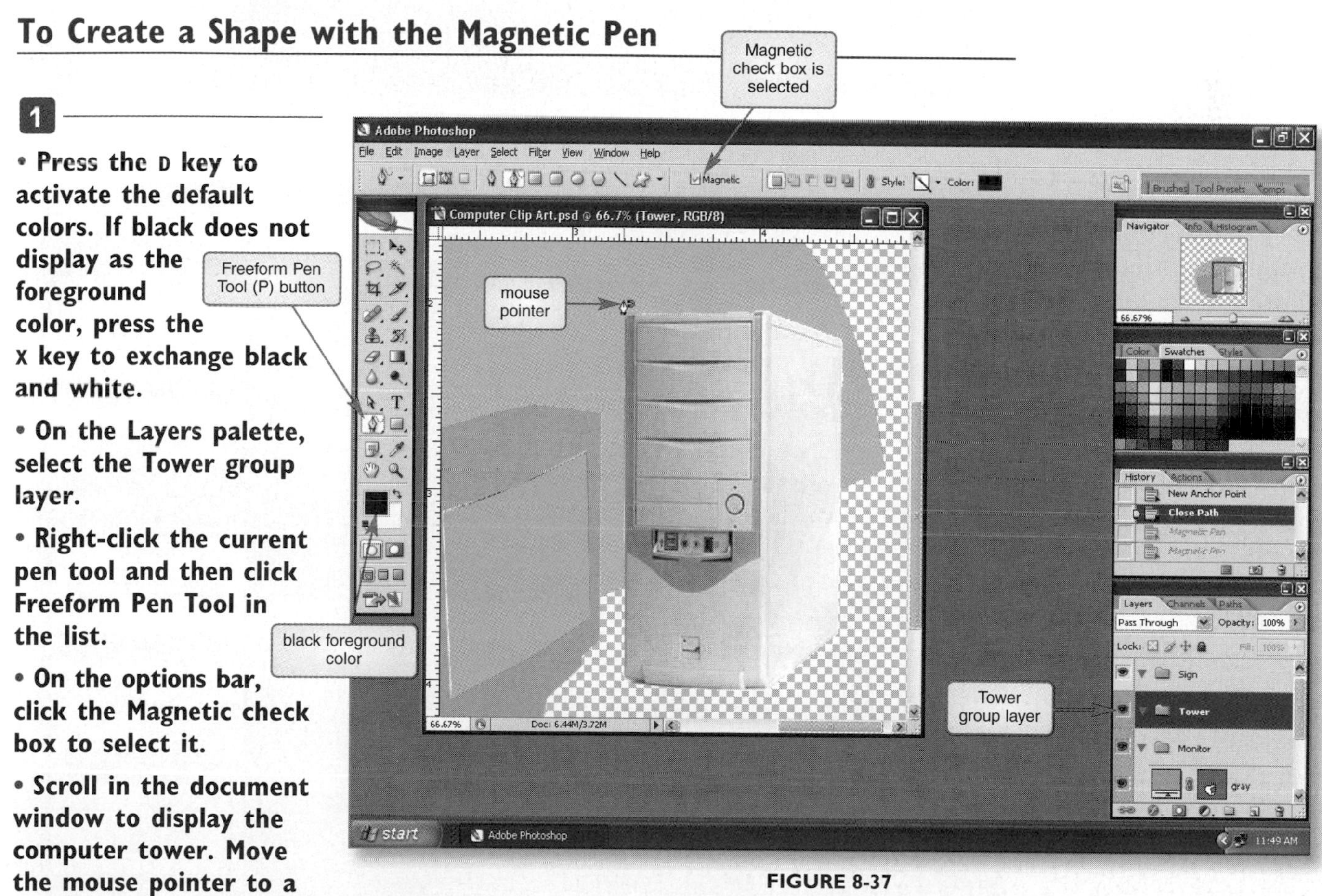

FIGURE 8-37

The Freeform Pen tool displays a horseshoe magnet when the Magnetic check box is selected (Figure 8-37).

2

- **To create a shape layer around the darker portions of the tower, click the top left corner of the tower and slowly move the mouse pointer straight down. Do not drag. Stop when you get to the lighter portion of the tower.**

The magnetic pen creates the path line based on the color change of the pixels (Figure 8-38).

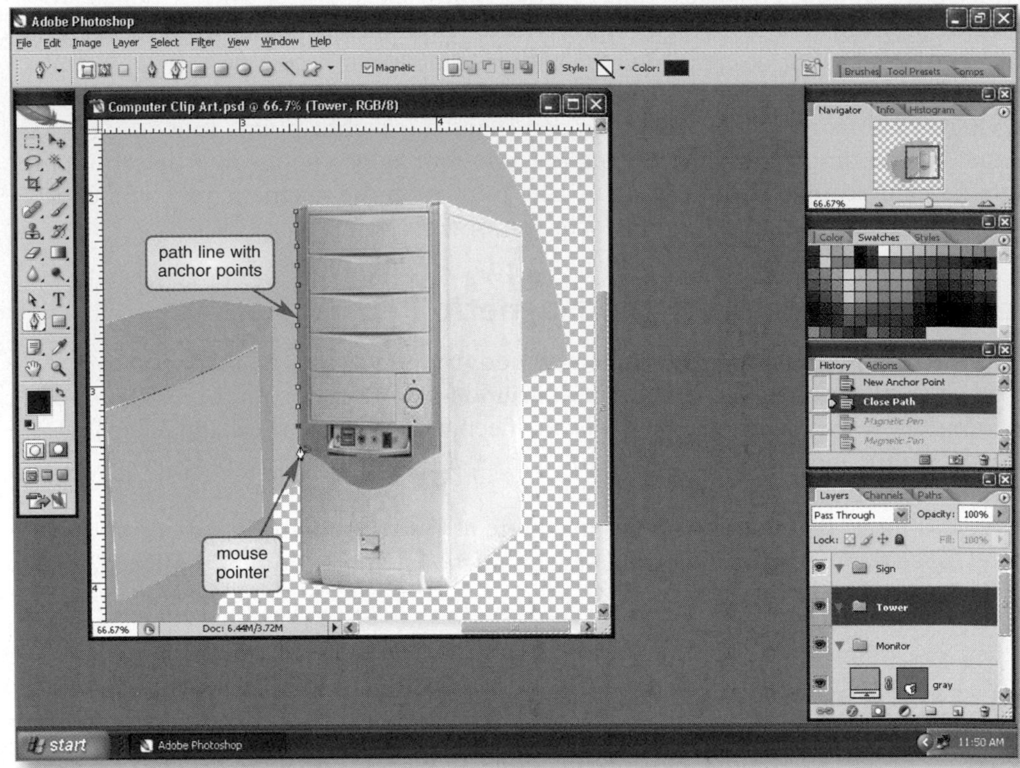

FIGURE 8-38

- **Click and then move the mouse to the right, following the contour of the curve.**
- **When you reach the right side of the tower, click and move upward to the top of the tower.**

The created path displays anchor points all along the path (Figure 8-39).

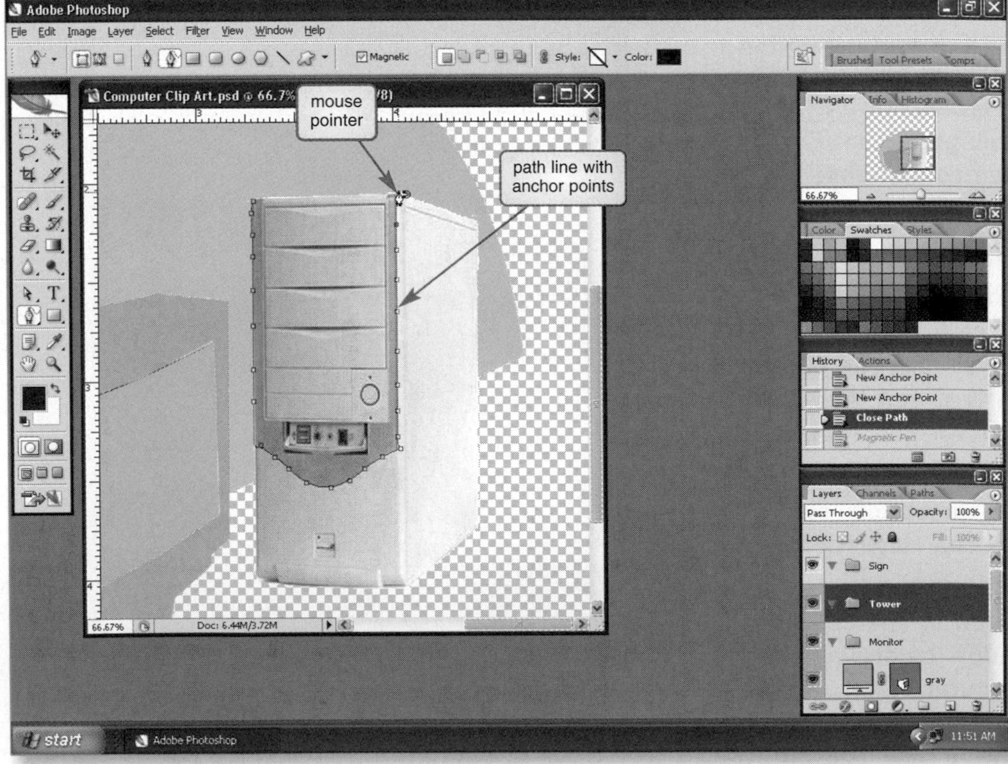

FIGURE 8-39

4

- **Continue clicking at corners and move the mouse around the darker portion of the tower as shown in Figure 8-40. Do not include the loading bays for the disk drives or the port panel. Stop when you get close to the upper-left corner again.**

The darker portion of the tower is outlined by the new path.

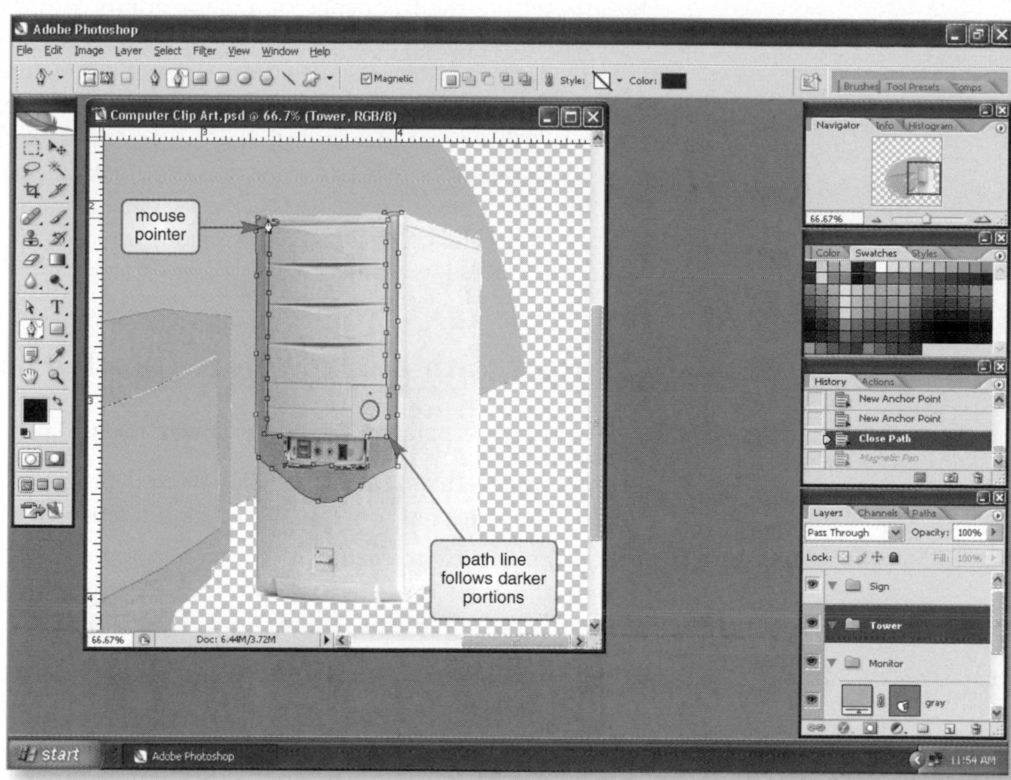

FIGURE 8-40

5

- **Move the mouse to the beginning point of the path and click the beginning anchor point to close the path. Zoom as necessary.**
- **On the Layers palette, double-click the new shape layer name. Type** `black` **and then press the ENTER key to rename the layer.**

Photoshop fills the shape layer with black and renames the layer (Figure 8-41). If some of the path lines need to be adjusted, drag the appropriate anchor point. If necessary, click the Fill path with foreground color button again.

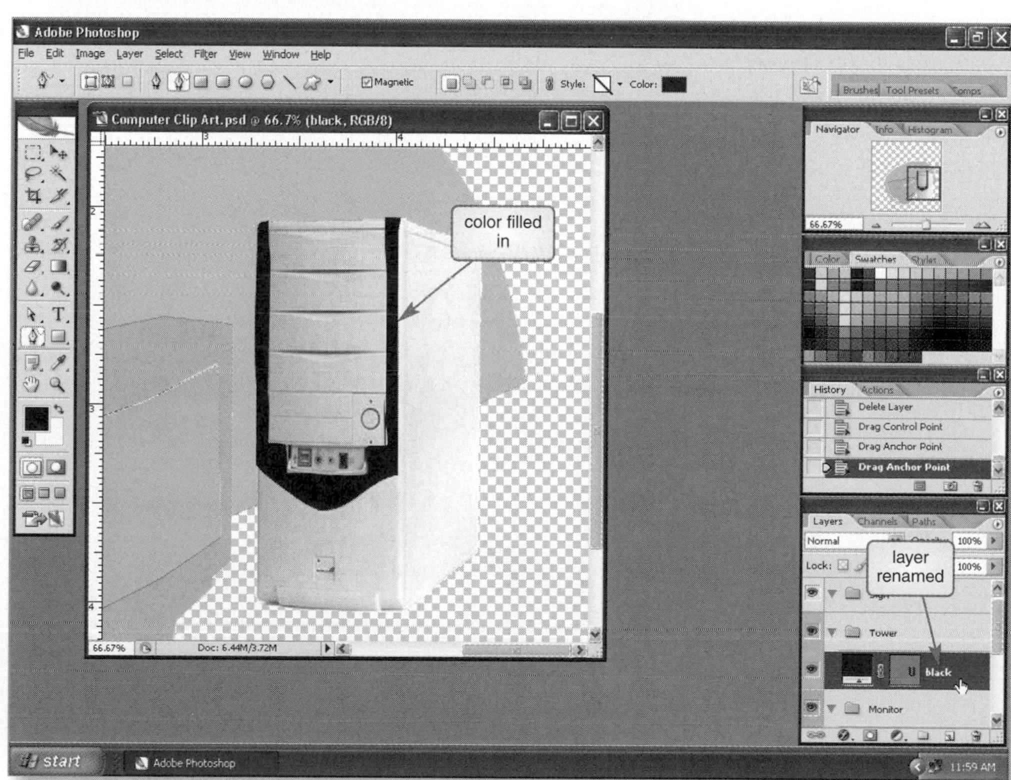

FIGURE 8-41

Besides setting the frequency of anchor points, other settings used with the magnetic pen are displayed when you click the Geometry options button on the options bar. Photoshop can detect edges within a specified distance from the mouse pointer. The contrast setting determines what percentage of contrast is considered an edge; for example, 10 percent means very light differentiation. If you are working with a stylus tablet, you can select pen pressure to adjust the width.

The following steps create another gray path around the lighter portion of the computer tower. The color is picked up from the monitor's shape layer color. The magnetic pen is used again.

To Create a Path around the Lighter Portions of the Tower

1. **On the Layers palette, click the Tower group layer.**
2. **With the Freeform Pen tool still selected in the toolbox, and the Magnetic check box selected, on the Swatches palette, click 35% Gray.**
3. **Click the top-right corner of the computer tower. Slowly move the mouse down and turn the corner left at the bottom of the tower. Continue following the contour of the lighter portions of the tower until you return close to the beginning point.**

The new path is displayed (Figure 8-42).

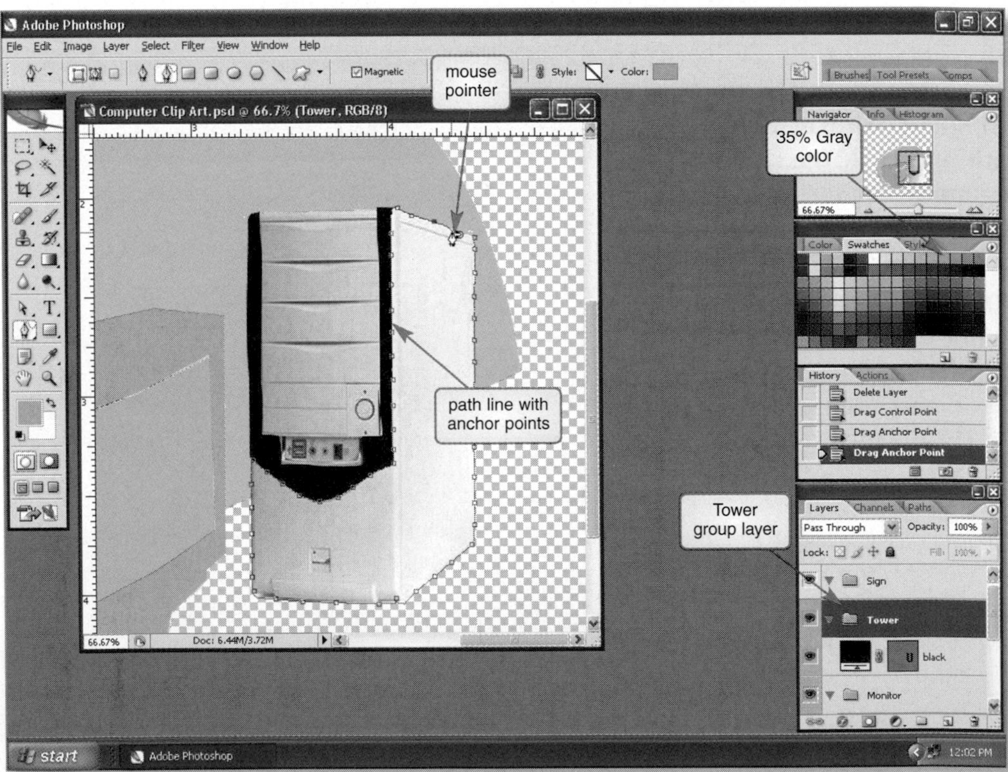

FIGURE 8-42

4. **Click the beginning anchor point to close the path.**
5. **On the Layers palette, double-click the new shape layer name. Type `gray` and then press the ENTER key to rename the layer.**

Now that the two colors of the computer tower contain shape layers, you may need to make adjustments to the paths so they better align. If so, follow these steps: 1) select the Convert Point tool; 2) click any anchor point that needs to be moved to convert each to a smooth point; 3) select the Direct Selection tool; and, 4) drag the anchor point to a new location.

Clip Art Detail

Clip art has some unique characteristics that you do not find in other kinds of images. Transparency is commonly used so clip art can be placed over, under, or through other graphics and text. Good clip art uses strong lines and colors with enough detail to highlight the purpose. A clip art's purpose may be as simple as object identification, which might require modest detail, or as complex as an idea within a context, which might require intensive detail to get the point across. Movement, depth, and light play an important role in clip art as well. **Iconization** is the process of turning something real into something simpler, but possibly more symbolic with implied meaning. Real objects and people are transformed into simple clip art or cartoon versions; but without purpose, context, and visual character, clip art is flat, static, and simplistic.

When adding a **color overlay** to give dimension and perspective to an image, use a contrast of tone to portray depth and complexity. Additionally, you can use color and blending modes to demonstrate lighting. **Chiaroscuro**, the art word for working with light and dark tonal values, describes the idea of imagining a light source, and using tints and shades to give an image perspective and dimension. For example, if you want to portray light and movement coming from the computer screen, you might change the color on part of the screen, scalloping some edges to help show direction. A background like the green half circle behind the computer components gives a sense of depth.

Another way to represent depth is by using shadows. A **shadow** is a small extension on one or two sides of a graphic with a different, non-obtrusive color, usually a shade of gray with no visible border. Shadows not only depict depth, but they also intimate a light source. A shadow is displayed opposite the perceived direction of light, or behind the object.

A **reflection** is a mirror image attached to a graphic, which is distorted both by color and shape. A reflection does not always mean mirrors or water. A subtle reflection can be used as a graphic device to not only give the appearance of a shiny surface, but also to glamorize and accessorize images, shapes, and even text. To create a reflection, you simply create a semi-transparent copy of the object, flip it horizontally or vertically, and crop as necessary. Positioned correctly, and attached or grouped, a reflection moves and resizes with the object.

Figure 8-43 displays examples of color overlays, shadows, and reflections.

FIGURE 8-43

Photoshop's many shapes, filters, and blending options can create a variety of other special effects to add detail to clip art. Surface and texture sometimes are used to differentiate parts of the clip art from one another. A group of short lines, positioned in a sunburst effect — also called impact lines — provide highlighting and draw the viewer's focus. Many advertising pieces also use overlap and broken borders to support depth and direction.

Adding a Color Overlay

You will use a color overlay to add motion to the monitor's screen. The following steps show how to add a color overlay.

To Add a Color Overlay

1

- **On the Layers palette, select the computer system layer.**
- **Press I to access the Eyedropper tool and then sample the color of the monitor's screen.**
- **In the toolbox, click the foreground color box.**
- **When the Color Picker dialog box is displayed, select a color slightly lighter than the monitor's screen.**

A lighter version of the same color will add depth to the screen without being too distracting (Figure 8-44).

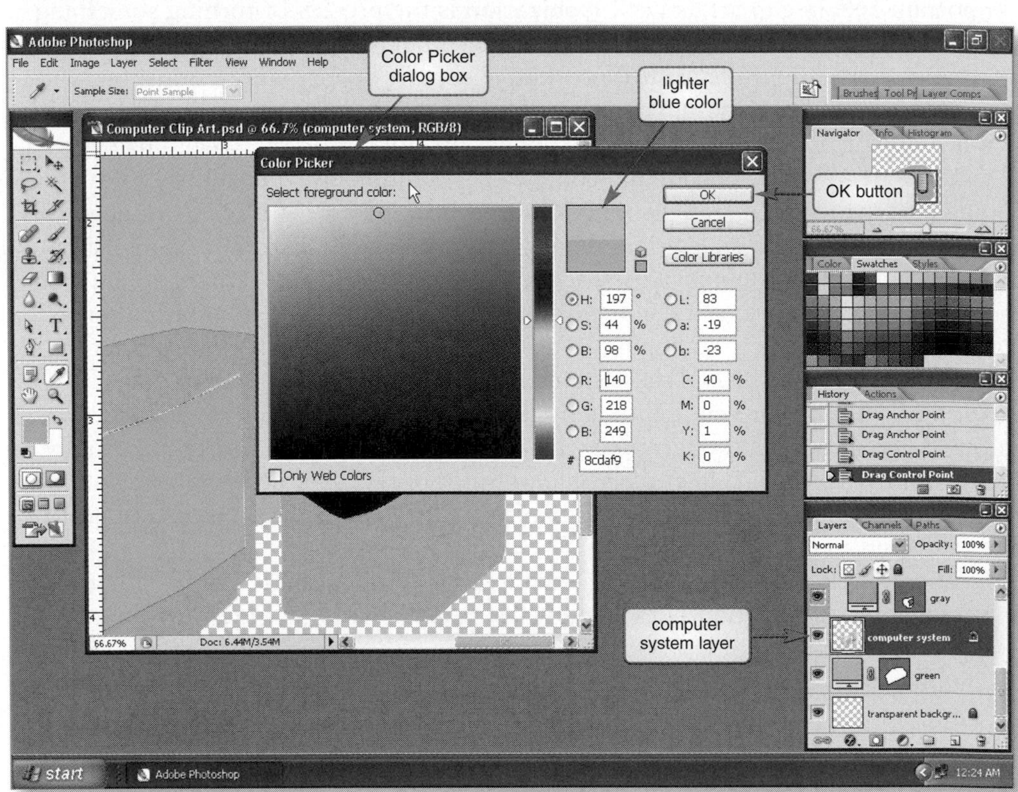

FIGURE 8-44

2

- **Click the OK button.**
- **Press the B key to access the Brush tool. Adjust the size of the brush with the bracket keys.**
- **Draw a shape on the right side of the screen, with a scalloped edge on one side and a fairly straight edge on the other.**

The color overlay displays on the monitor's screen (Figure 8-45). Your shape does not have to match the one in the figure.

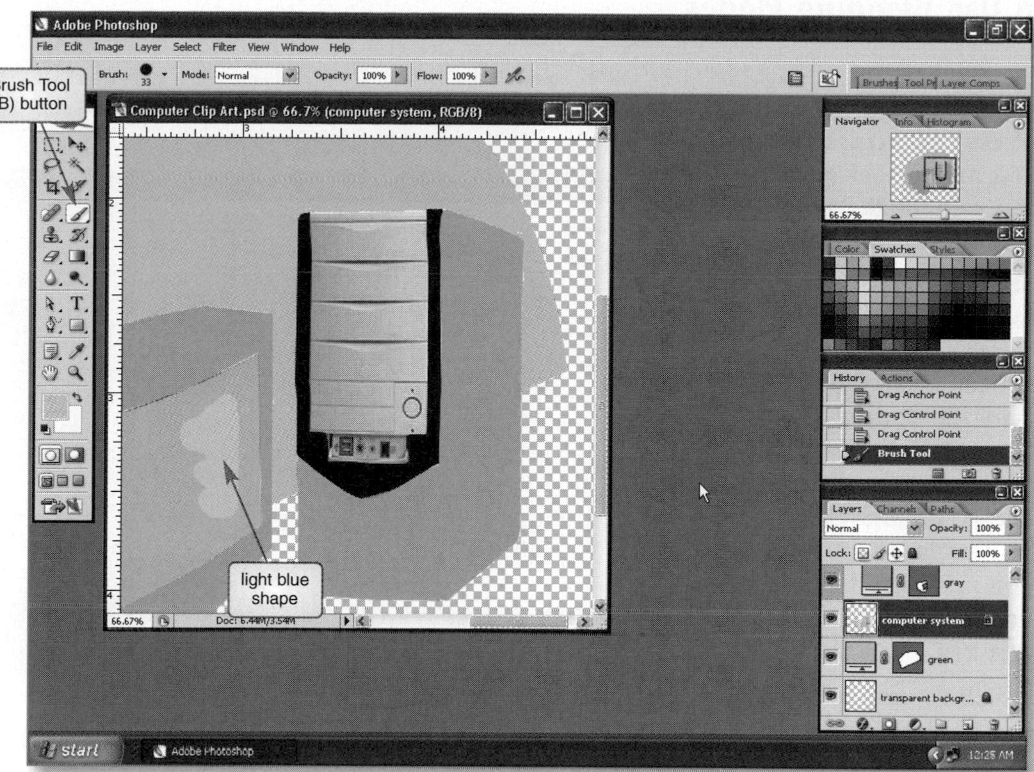

FIGURE 8-45

Using Blending Modes

You will use a blending mode to create a special effect for the base of the computer monitor. Table 8-4 displays the settings for the Bevel and Emboss layer style.

Table 8-4 Bevel and Emboss Settings for Monitor Base

BEVEL AND EMBOSS EFFECT	SETTING
Style	Inner Bevel
Technique	Smooth
Depth	171
Direction	Up
Size	21
Soften	2
Angle	-135
Use Global Light	not checked
Altitude	34
Highlight Mode	Normal
Opacity	99%

The steps on the next page illustrate how to create a new layer and then add the blending effect.

To Use Blending Modes

1

- **Press I to access the Eyedropper tool and then sample the gray color of the monitor.**
- **On the Layers palette, click the gray layer in the Monitor layer group. At the bottom of the Layers palette, click the Create a new layer button. Double-click the new layer name. Type** `monitor base` **and then press the ENTER key.**
- **Scroll to center the base of the monitor in the document window.**
- **Press P to select the Pen tool. If the Freeform Pen tool is selected, press SHIFT+P to toggle to the Pen tool. On the options bar, click the Shape layers button, if necessary.**

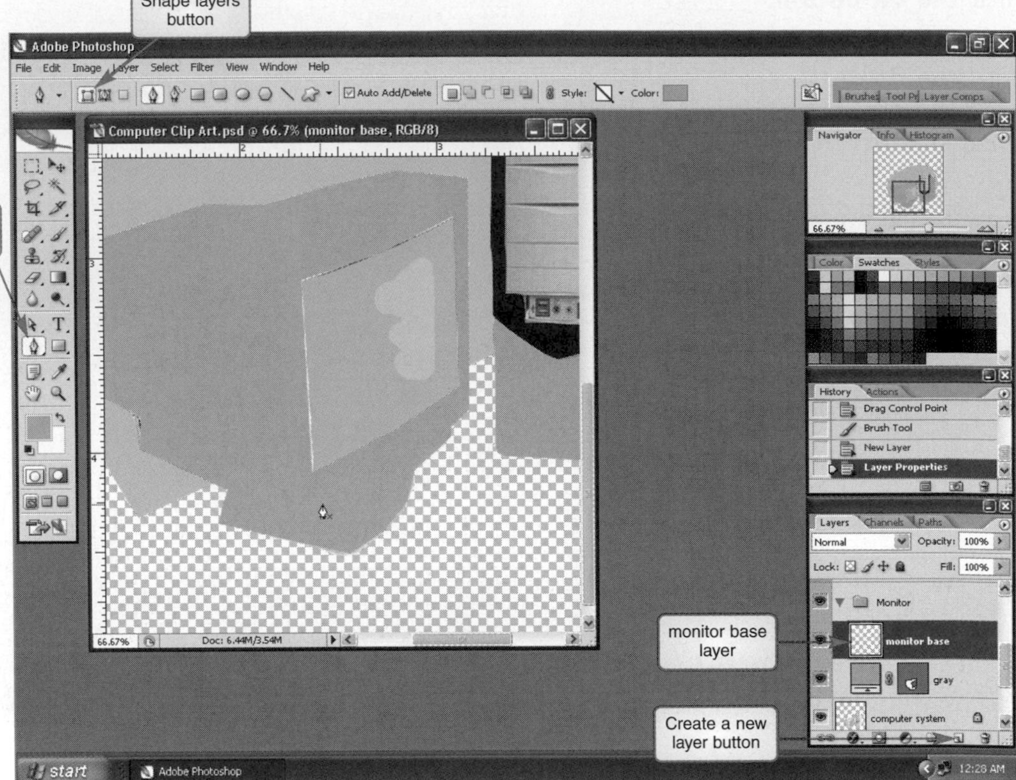

FIGURE 8-46

The new layer will be part of the Monitor layer group (Figure 8-46).

2

- **Click the lower-right corner of the base.**
- **Working counterclockwise, click at each corner of the base. Do not include the monitor itself.**
- **When you get all the way around, click the original corner.**

The new monitor base layer is outlined (Figure 8-47). Your outline does not have to match exactly.

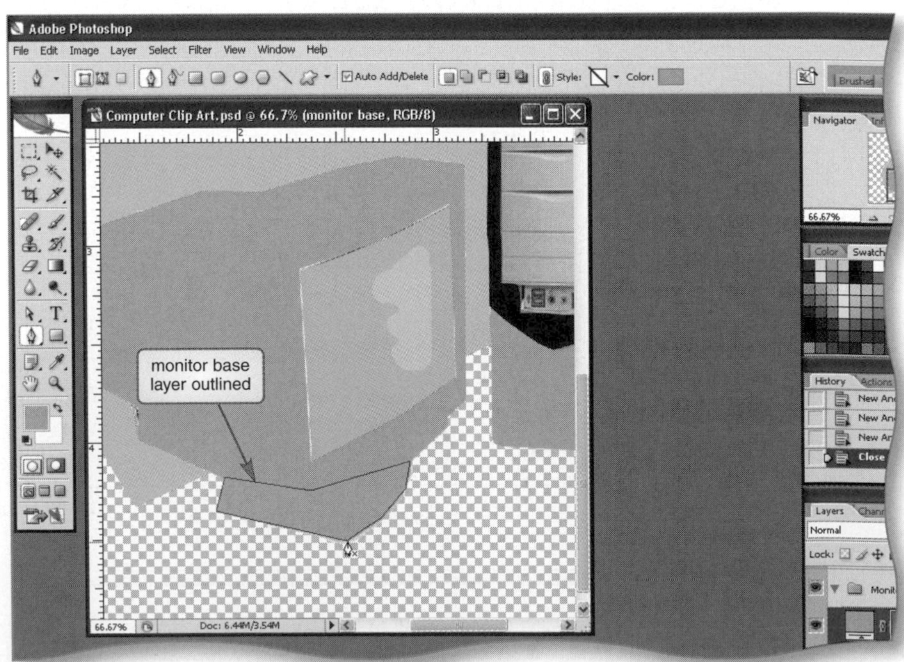

FIGURE 8-47

3

- **On the Layers palette, click the Add a layer style button and then click Bevel and Emboss.**
- **When the Layer Style dialog box is displayed, enter the settings from Table 8-4.**
- **Click the Gloss Contour box arrow. Point to the Cove - Deep preview.**

The Contour list displays several different patterns that Photoshop uses to shape the special effect (Figure 8-48).

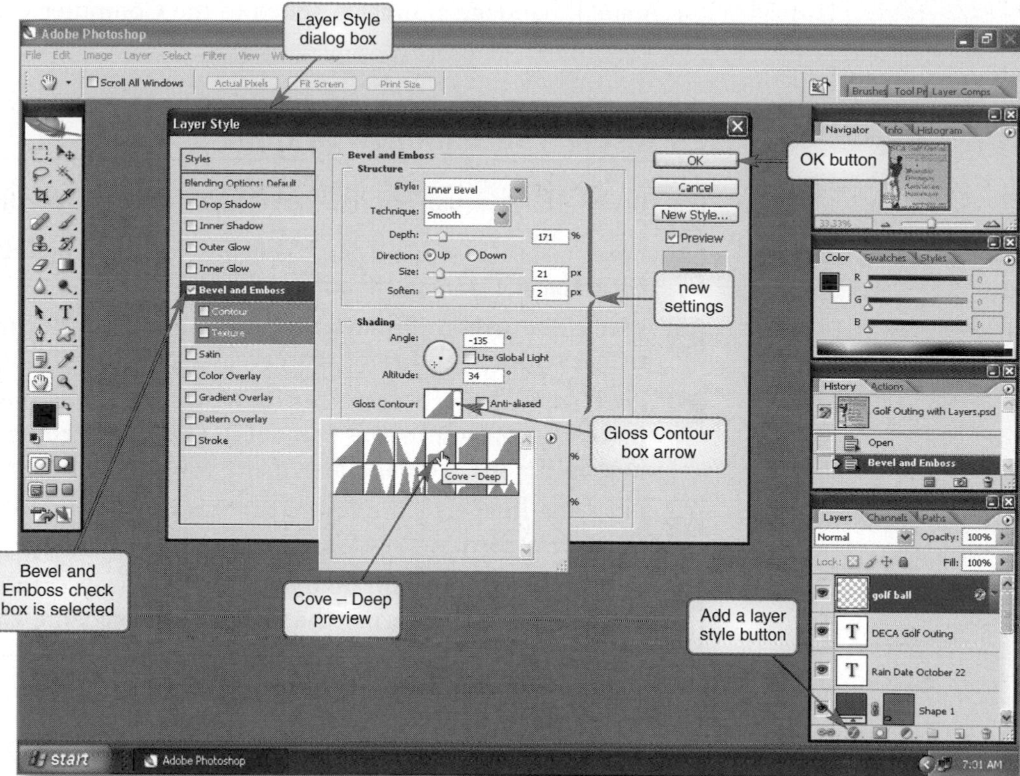

FIGURE 8-48

4

- **Click the Cove - Deep preview.**
- **Click the OK button.**
- **Press SHIFT+CTRL+H to turn off the layer border display.**
- **Zoom to 33.33% magnification.**

The new blending options are displayed on the base of the monitor (Figure 8-49).

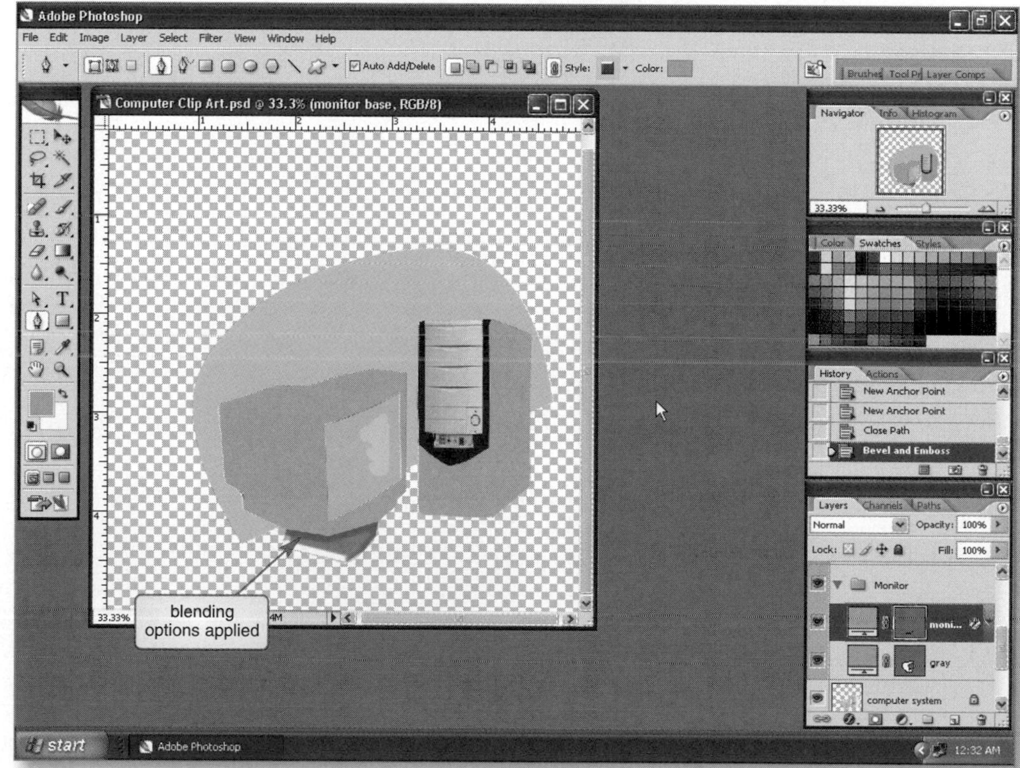

FIGURE 8-49

A small bandage graphic is added to the Computer Clip Art image, as shown in the following steps.

To Insert the Bandage Graphic

1. **On the Layers palette, click the layer named gray in the Monitor layer group.**
2. **Press CTRL+O to open a file. Navigate to the Project08 folder and then double-click the file named, Bandage.**
3. **When Photoshop displays the image in a new document window, drag the title bar down and right, to reveal a portion of both windows.**
4. **Press the V key to activate the Move tool, and then select and drag the Bandage image into the Computer Clip Art document window. Click the Close button on the Bandage document window title bar.**
5. **Drag the image to the lower portion of the monitor's screen, across the lower-left corner.**
6. **On the Layers palette, double-click the newly created layer name. Type** bandage **and then press the ENTER key to rename the layer.**

The bandage is displayed on the monitor (Figure 8-50).

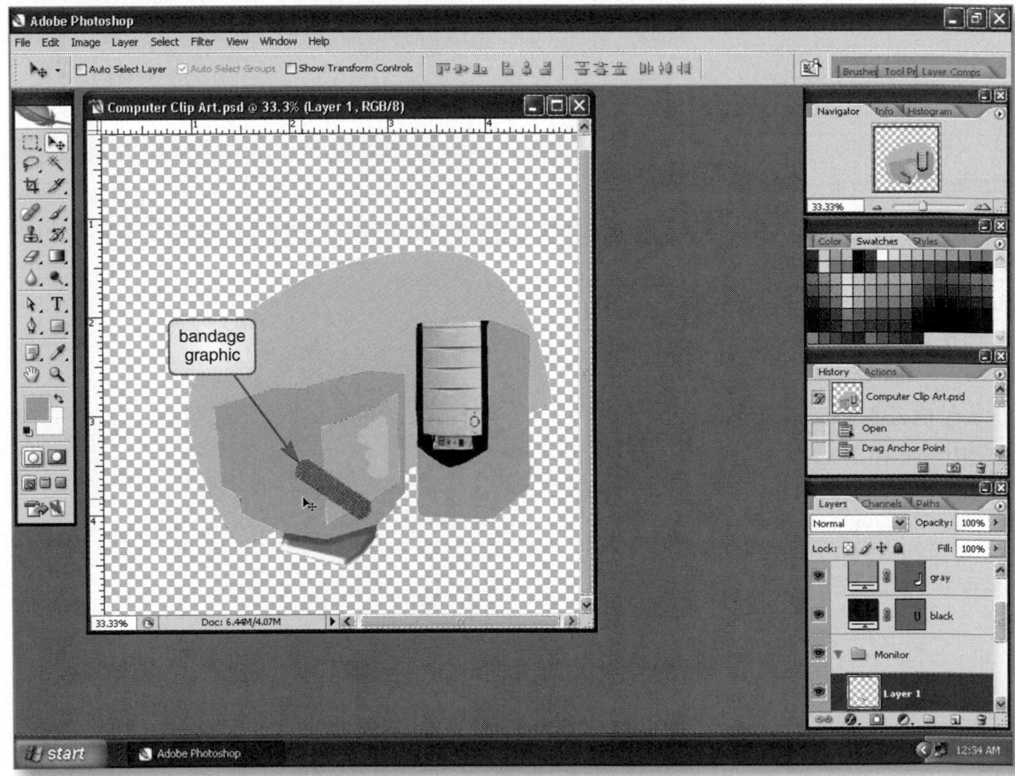

FIGURE 8-50

The following steps illustrate how to add a thermometer graphic to the Computer Clip Art image.

To Insert the Thermometer Graphic

1. **On the Layers palette, click the layer named gray in the Tower layer group.**
2. **Press CTRL+O to open a file. Navigate to the Project08 folder and then double-click the file named, Thermometer.**
3. **When Photoshop displays the image in a new document window, drag the title bar down and right, to reveal a portion of both windows.**
4. **Press the V key to activate the Move tool, and then select and drag the Thermometer image into the Computer Clip Art document window. Click the Close button on the Thermometer document window title bar.**
5. **Drag the image to the middle of the tower.**

The thermometer is displayed on the tower (Figure 8-51).

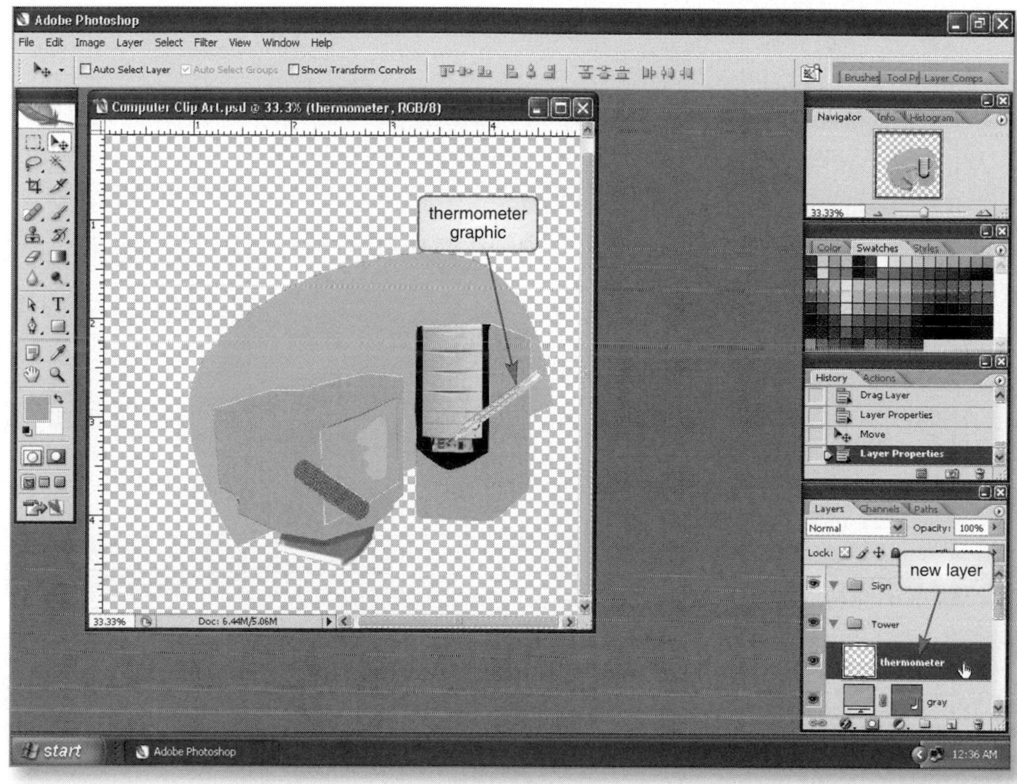

FIGURE 8-51

The steps on the next page add small red impact lines to indicate a temperature on the thermometer.

To Create Impact Lines

1. **On the Swatches palette, click RGB red.**
2. **Press the U key to access the shape tools. On the options bar, click the Line Tool button. Type** `5 px` **in the Weight box.**
3. **Drag a line from one end of the thermometer to the other, representing the mercury temperature display within the thermometer.**
4. **On the options bar, click the Add to shape area (+) button.**
5. **Drag six short lines in a starburst pattern around the end of the thermometer as shown in Figure 8-52.**
6. **In the Layers palette, double-click the shape layer name. Type** `impact lines` **and then press the ENTER key to rename the layer.**
7. **On the Layers palette, click the Sign layer group.**

The red impact lines represent the computer's temperature for the clip art.

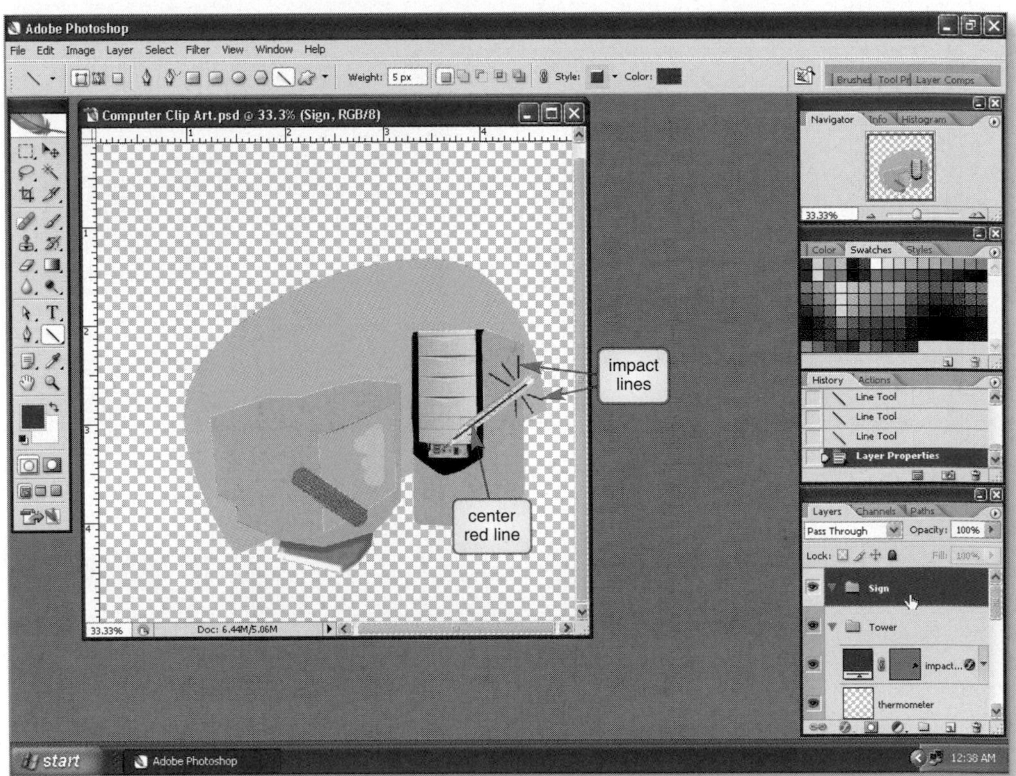

FIGURE 8-52

Creating the Sign

The sign that is displayed in Figure 8-1 on page PS 485, is comprised of a rectangle with a shadow, text, two patterned lines, and a circle. Each of the components will become a layer within the Sign layer group.

You will use a new layer style to create a rectangle with a drop shadow setting as shown in Table 8-5.

Table 8-5 Drop Shadow Settings

DROP SHADOW EFFECT	SETTING
Blend Mode	Multiply
Opacity	70%
Angle	38
Use Global Light	not checked
Distance	25
Spread	46
Size	24
Layer Knocks Out Drop Shadow	checked

Then, you will create a type element and enter text with the settings shown in Table 8-6.

Table 8-6 Type Tool Settings

TYPE OPTION	SETTING
Set the font family	Comic Sans or a similar font
Set the font style	Bold
Set the font size	24 pt
Set the anti-aliasing method	Smooth
Center text	selected
Set the text color	black

Finally, the two lines and small circle that create the hanging mechanism for the sign will be created as a shape layer with a Black 3pt No Fill style chosen from the options bar.

More About

Global Layer Effects

Some commands in the Layer Effects dialog box will effect more than the current layer. Commands such as the Use Global Light check box will change every layer that has a layer effect to provide a standardized shadow, inner bevel or lighting affect across the entire image. Turning off the check box allows you to individualize the shadows or lighting by layer.

To Create the Sign

1

- **With the Sign layer group still selected, press the D key to access the default colors. Press the X key to make white the foreground color.**
- **On the shape options bar, click the Rectangle Tool button. Click the Create new shape layer button. If necessary, click the Style box arrow and then click the Default Style (None) preview.**
- **In the document window, drag a rectangle above the monitor, approximately 1 inch tall and 1.5 inches wide.**

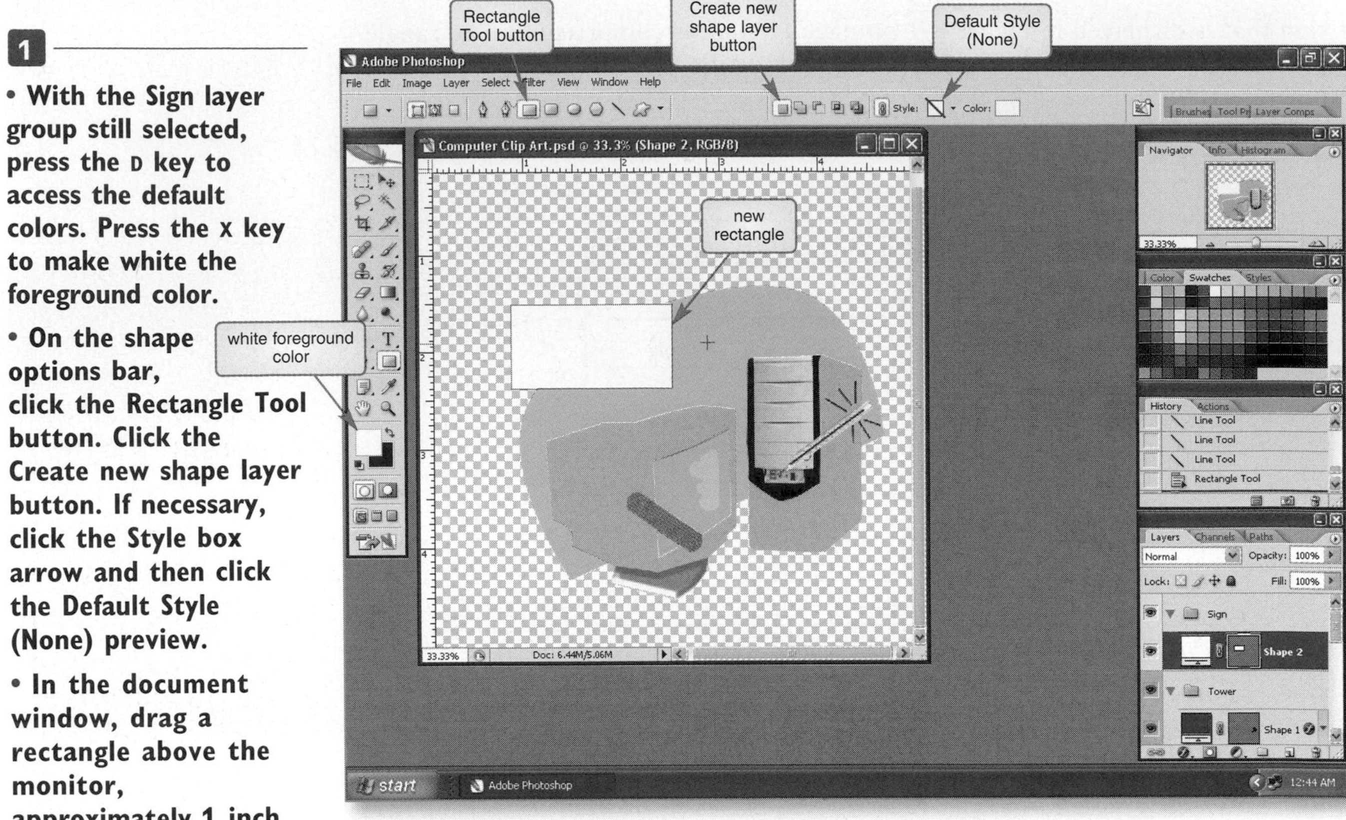

FIGURE 8-53

Photoshop displays the plain white rectangle (Figure 8-53).

2

- **With the new shape layer still selected, on the Layers palette, click the Add a layer style button, and then click Drop Shadow on the list.**
- **When the Layer Style dialog box is displayed, enter the settings from Table 8-5 on the previous page. Leave all other settings at their default value.**

The settings will produce a modest shadow on the left and bottom of the sign (Figure 8-54).

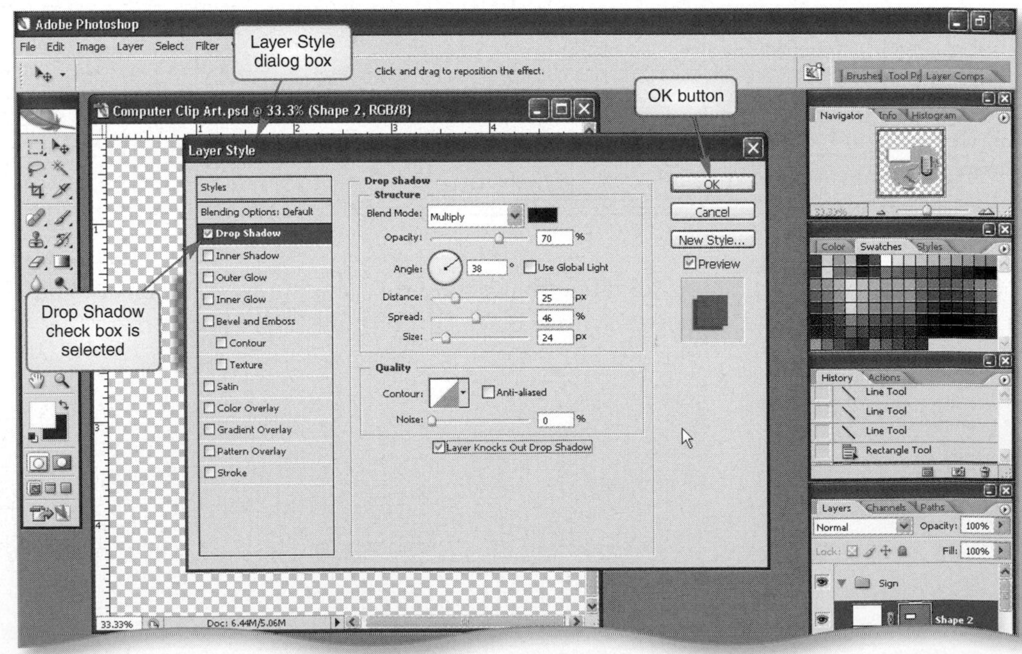

FIGURE 8-54

3

- **Click the OK button.**
- **Press the X key to exchange black and white as foreground color.**
- **Press the T key to access the Horizontal Type tool.**
- **On the options bar, enter the settings from Table 8-6.**

The settings are displayed on the options bar (Figure 8-55).

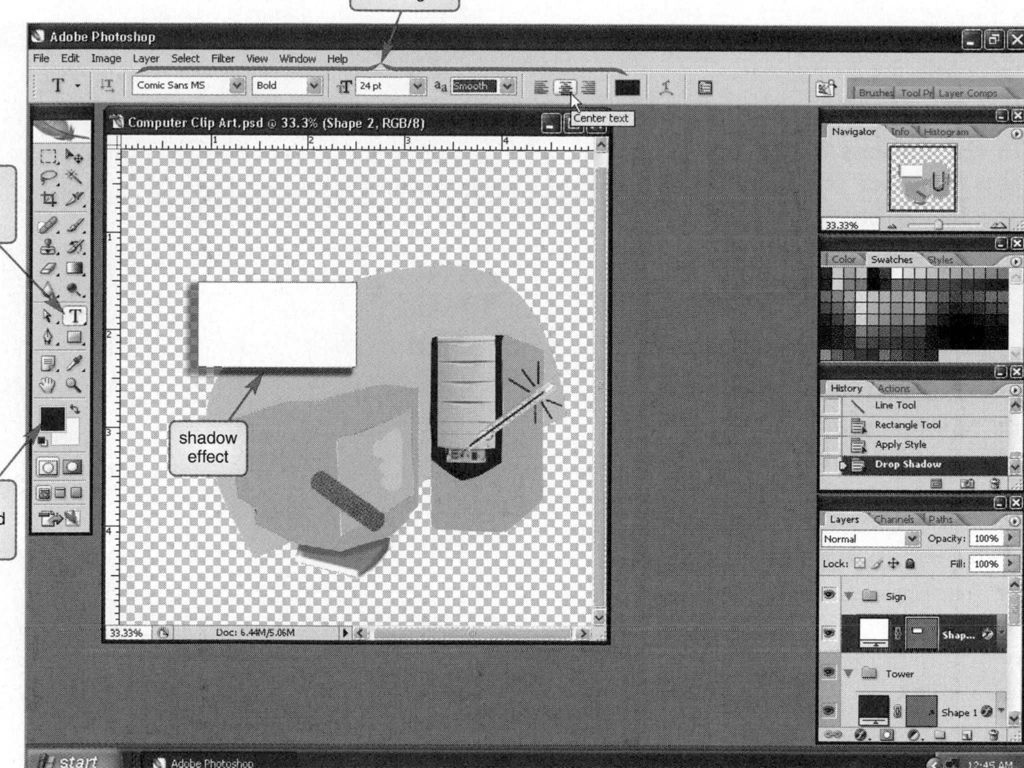

FIGURE 8-55

4

- **Click the center of the white rectangle.**
- **When the bounding box is displayed, type** `I.T. Aid Station` **and then adjust the sizing handles if necessary so the text is displayed as shown in Figure 8-56.**
- **Click the Commit any current edits button on the options bar.**
- **Press SHIFT+CRTL+H to turn off the border display.**

The text is displayed.

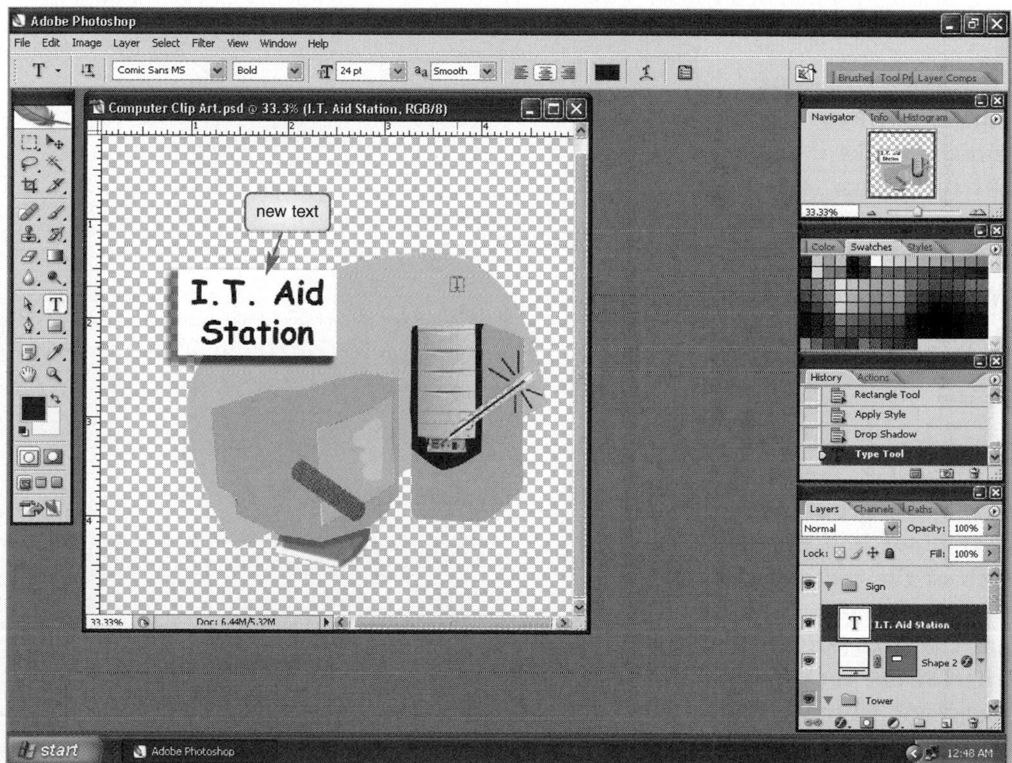

FIGURE 8-56

5

- **Press the U key to access the shape tools.**
- **On the options bar, if necessary, click the Shape layers button, the Line Tool button, and the Create a new shape layer button.**
- **Click the Style box arrow and then click the Style box menu button to display the Style box menu.**

Photoshop displays the Style box menu (Figure 8-57).

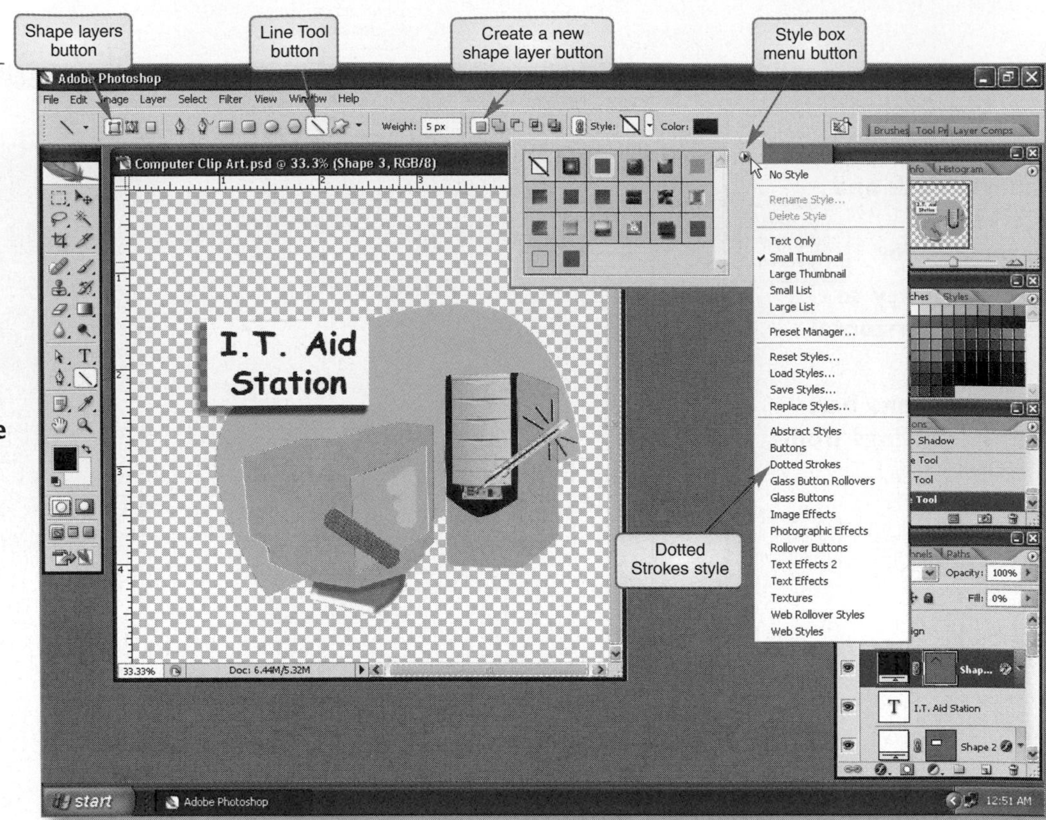

FIGURE 8-57

6

- **Click Dotted Strokes in the list. When Photoshop asks if you want to replace the current styles, click the Append button.**
- **When the new styles are displayed, click the Black 3pt No Fill preview.**
- **SHIFT+drag a line from the upper-left corner of the rectangle, up and right, about half the width of the rectangle. SHIFT+drag another line from the upper-right corner of the rectangle, up and left to meet the first line.**

Photoshop displays the lines in the selected style (Figure 8-58). Recall that pressing the SHIFT key while dragging creates a straight line at either 45 or 90 degree angles.

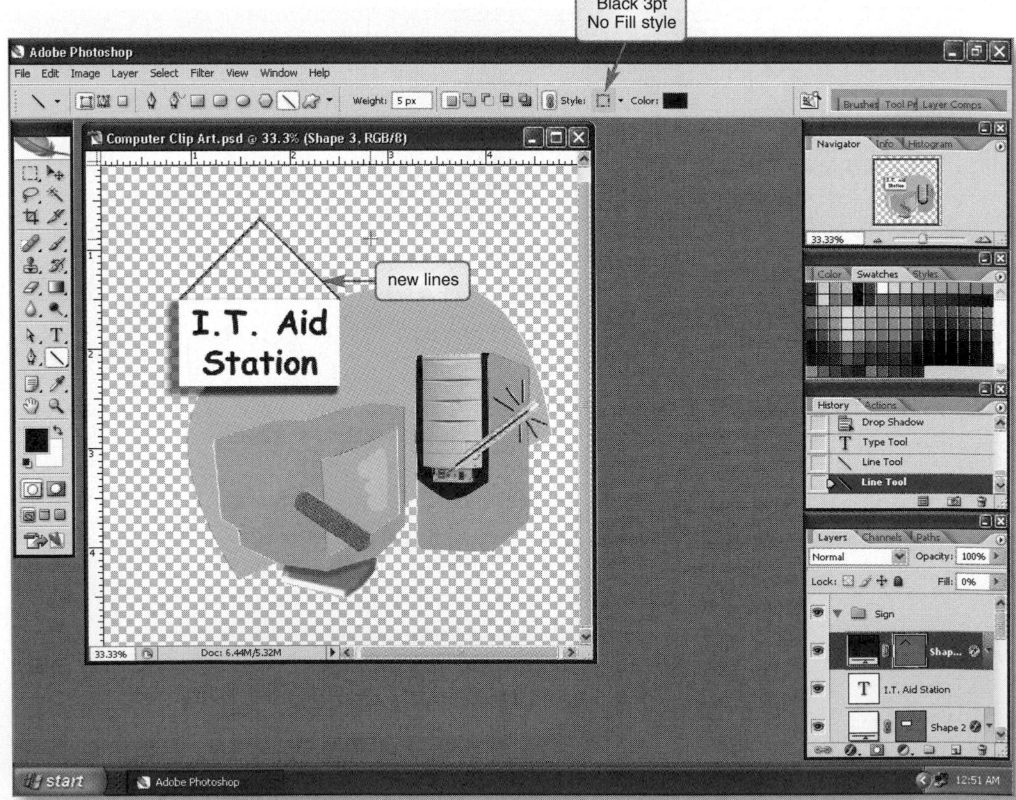

FIGURE 8-58

7

- **On the options bar, click the Ellipse Tool button. SHIFT+drag a small circle around the position where the two lines meet.**

Pressing the SHIFT key while dragging with the Ellipse tool constrains the shape to a circle (Figure 8-59).

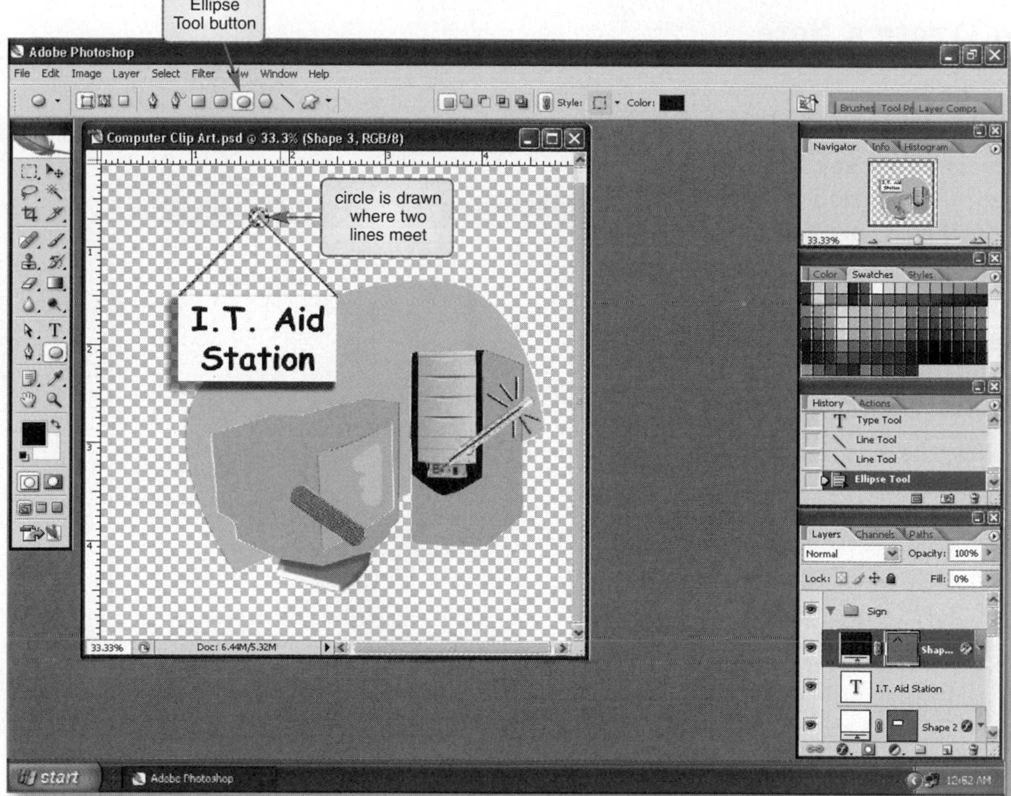

FIGURE 8-59

Note and Audio Annotation Tools

Photoshop gives you the opportunity to save notes with any image file. Sometimes you might want to write a note to another person on your team about the use of the graphic, or you might want to keep some notes for yourself about which filter you used, or which settings you changed on a blend mode. Still other times, you might want to record some special instructions.

These notes are different from the metadata and keywords stored by Adobe Bridge. The notes are more like the popular, small, yellow sticky notes that you might attach physically, a comment note inserted in many Office application programs, or a short phone message.

The **Notes tool** opens a small text-editing window, in which you can enter comments. Note windows have scrolling capabilities, standard editing functions, and a Close button in the corner. The Notes options bar contains choices for author, color, and font size. The name you enter in the Author box becomes the text for the note's title bar. **Audio Annotation Notes** are recorded with a microphone and can be played back when someone opens the file. Both kinds of notes can be edited, deleted, or repositioned anywhere on the image for greater emphasis. Notes stay with the file until they are deleted.

Creating a Note

The steps on the next page show how to create a note in the Computer Clip Art image. If you have a microphone, you can record an audio note as well. The note will remind a coworker to add keywords to the clip art in Adobe Bridge.

To Create a Note

1

- **Press the N key. If the Audio Annotation tool is displayed, press SHIFT+N.**
- **On the options bar, type your name in the Author box, if necessary.**
- **Click the upper-left corner of the document window.**

Photoshop displays an open note window (Figure 8-60).

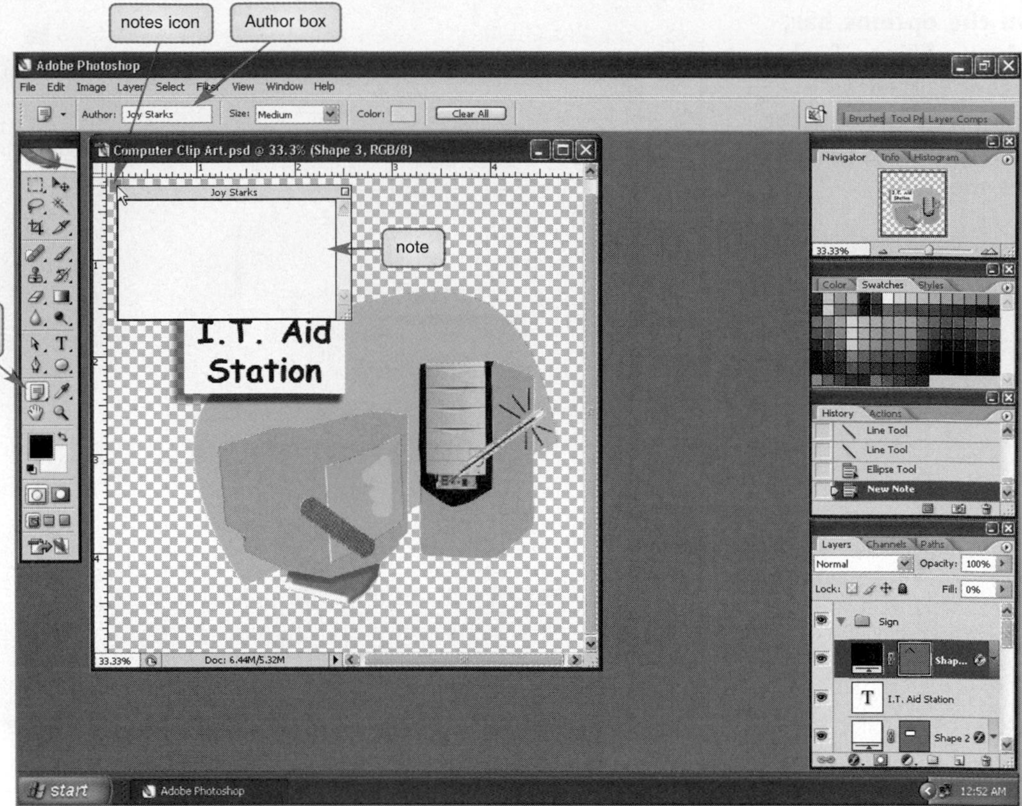

FIGURE 8-60

2

- **In the Note window, type** `Donna: Don't forget to add keywords to this image using Adobe Bridge, before you upload it to the server.`

The message displays in the Note window (Figure 8-61).

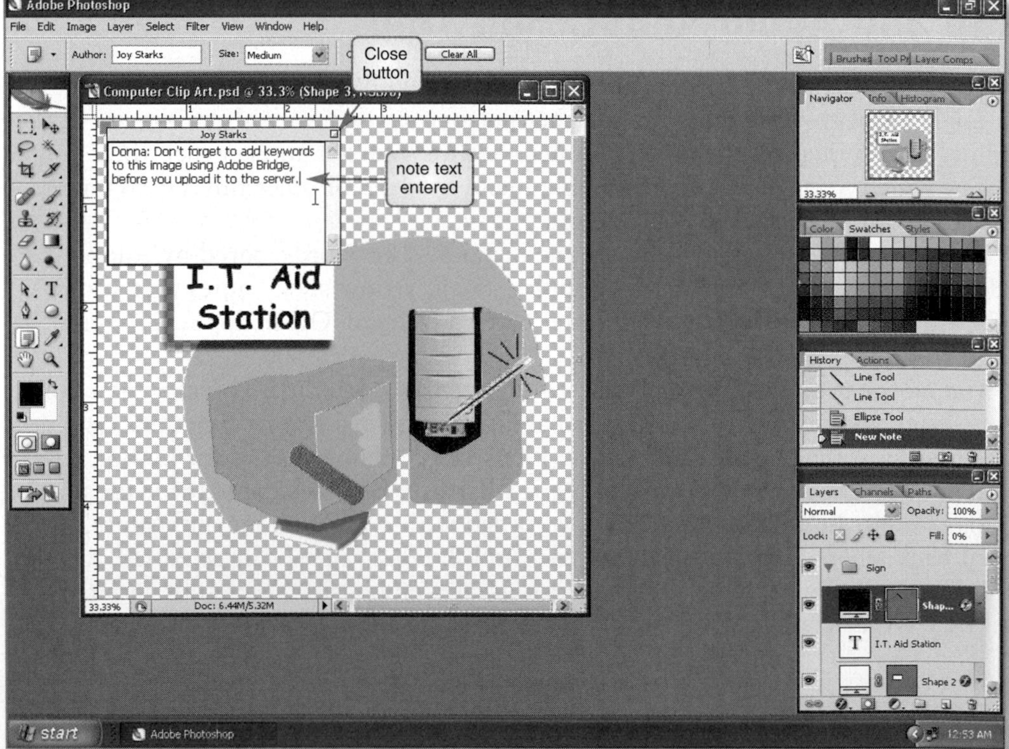

FIGURE 8-61

3

- **Click the Close button in the upper-right corner of the note.**

Photoshop closes the note and an icon is displayed (Figure 8-62).

FIGURE 8-62

To read notes, double-click them. You do not have to click the Notes tool to read notes. Notes do not print. Notes are unique to Photoshop and do not display in other graphic-editing software packages.

Saving the Layers

Before converting the image to a GIF, the following steps save the fully layered, PSD version of the image one last time. Then, after hiding the transparent background layer, the visible layers of the image are flattened. Flattening all the layers, except the transparent background, will reduce the file size dramatically while maintaining the characteristic transparency of clip art.

To Save and Flatten the Layers

1. **With your USB flash drive connected to one of the computer's USB ports, press CTRL+S.**
2. **On the Layers palette, scroll down and then click the visibility icon next to the transparent background layer so it does not display.**
3. **Right-click the green layer, and then click Merge Visible on the shortcut menu.**

All of the layers except the background are merged.

Other Ways

1. To Merge Visible, press SHIFT+CTRL+E

Graphics Interchange Format (GIF) images

Graphics Interchange Format (GIF) is the file format commonly used to create clip art. GIF is an indexed-color mode, which produces 8 bit files with at most 256 colors. When converting to indexed color, Photoshop builds a color lookup table, which stores and indexes the colors in the image. If a color in the original image does not appear in the table, the program chooses the closest one, or uses dithering to simulate the color using available colors. **Dithering** is a way to mix pixels of several colors to create the illusion of extra colors or shading. With just 256 colors, the indexed color mode can reduce file size yet maintain a fairly high, visual quality. GIF files are used in multimedia presentations and Web pages in addition to clip art. Because editing is limited in an indexed color mode, it is common to edit and work in RGB mode and then convert the image to indexed color before exporting to page layout applications. When converting an RGB image to indexed color, you can specify a number of conversion options. Table 8-7 displays some of the settings and their descriptions.

Table 8-7 Indexed Color Conversion Settings

SETTING	DESCRIPTION
Palette Type	Choosing a palette type sets the kind of Color palette used in the conversion process including Exact, System, Web, Uniform, Local, and Custom.
Number Of Colors	For the Uniform or Local palettes, you can specify the exact number of colors to be displayed up to 256.
Forced	This setting forces the inclusion of certain colors: Black and White, Primaries, Web, or Custom.
Transparency	This setting preserves transparent areas of the image during conversion. Otherwise, Photoshop fills transparent areas with the matte color, or with white.
Matte	If Transparency is selected, this setting fills anti-aliased edges with the specified color or Custom color. Otherwise, the matte is applied to transparent areas.
Dithering	In all Palette Types except Exact, dithering mixes the pixels to simulate missing colors. Options include Diffusion, Pattern, Noise, or None. When you enter a percentage value for the dither amount, a higher amount dithers more colors, but may increase file size.

The GIF format is an LZW (Lemple-Zif-Welch) compressed format designed to minimize file size and transfer time while maintaining as much of the original data in the image as possible. Photoshop can preserve transparency in the GIF format.

Optimizing Clip Art

Photoshop provides several ways to save images in the GIF format and optimize them for future use. **Optimize** means to choose a file format, color mode, compression method, and format that maximizes quality while reducing file size and download time. The Save As dialog box provides a way to save in the GIF format in its Format box, but offers few formatting options. The Save for Web dialog box gives you a great deal of flexibility in optimization settings, including dithering, transparency, and estimated download time. A third way is to use the Export Transparent Image wizard.

Using the Export Transparent Image Wizard

Like the Resize Image wizard, the **Export Transparent Image wizard** displays several windowed steps with choices about the desired purpose. When saving in the GIF format, the wizard formats images with transparent backgrounds. The following steps illustrate how to use the wizard to save the Computer Clip Art image in the GIF format.

To Use the Export Transparent Image Wizard

1

- **With your USB flash drive connected to one of the computer's USB ports, click Help on the menu bar.**

Photoshop displays the Help menu (Figure 8-63).

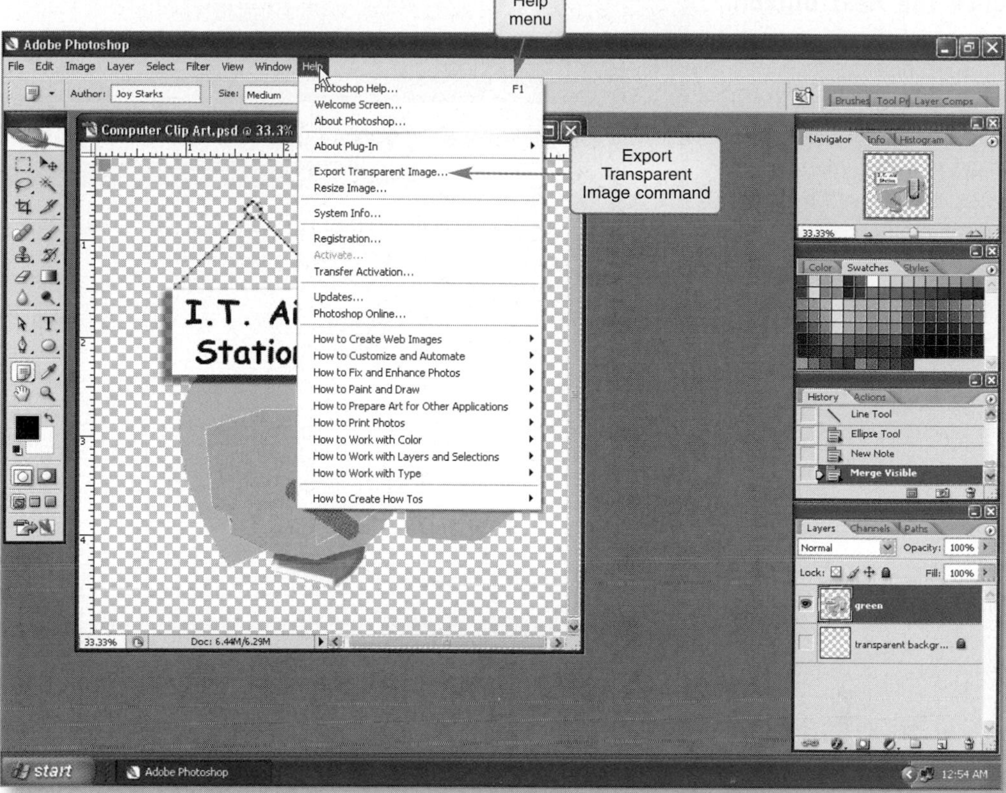

FIGURE 8-63

2

- **Click Export Transparent Image.**

The first window of the wizard is displayed (Figure 8-64). Because the background of the Computer Clip Art image is already transparent, no setting change is necessary.

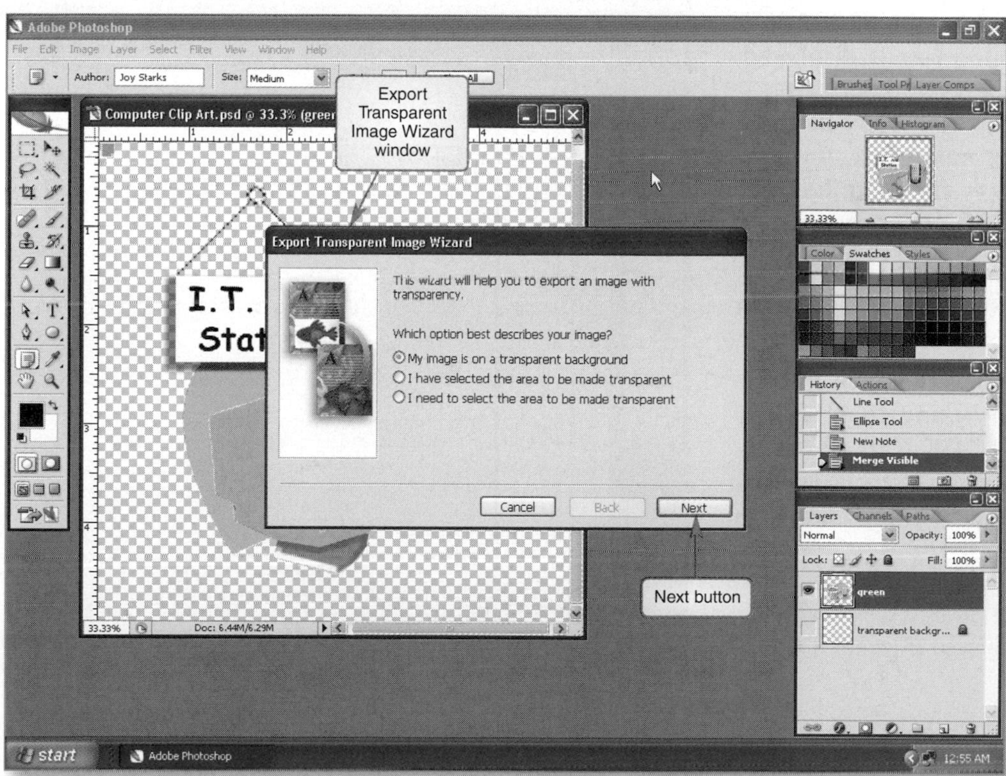

FIGURE 8-64

3

• **Click the Next button.**

Photoshop displays the second window (Figure 8-65). The clip art is destined for print. A new document window is displayed behind the wizard.

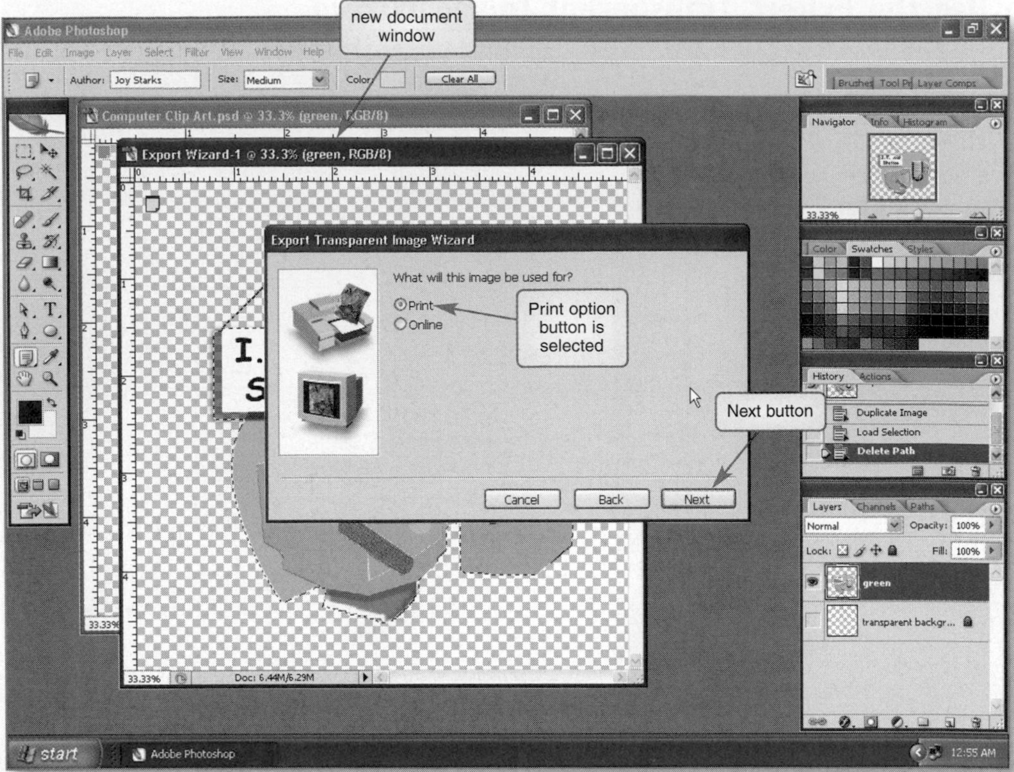

FIGURE 8-65

4

• **Click the Next button.**

• **When the Save As dialog box is displayed, type** `Computer Clip Art GIF Copy` **in the File name box. Do not press the ENTER key.**

• **Click the Format box arrow and then click CompuServe GIF (*.GIF) in the list.**

• **Click the Save in box arrow and then click USBDISK [G:], or the location associated with your USB flash drive, in the list.**

The Save As dialog box is displayed (Figure 8-66).

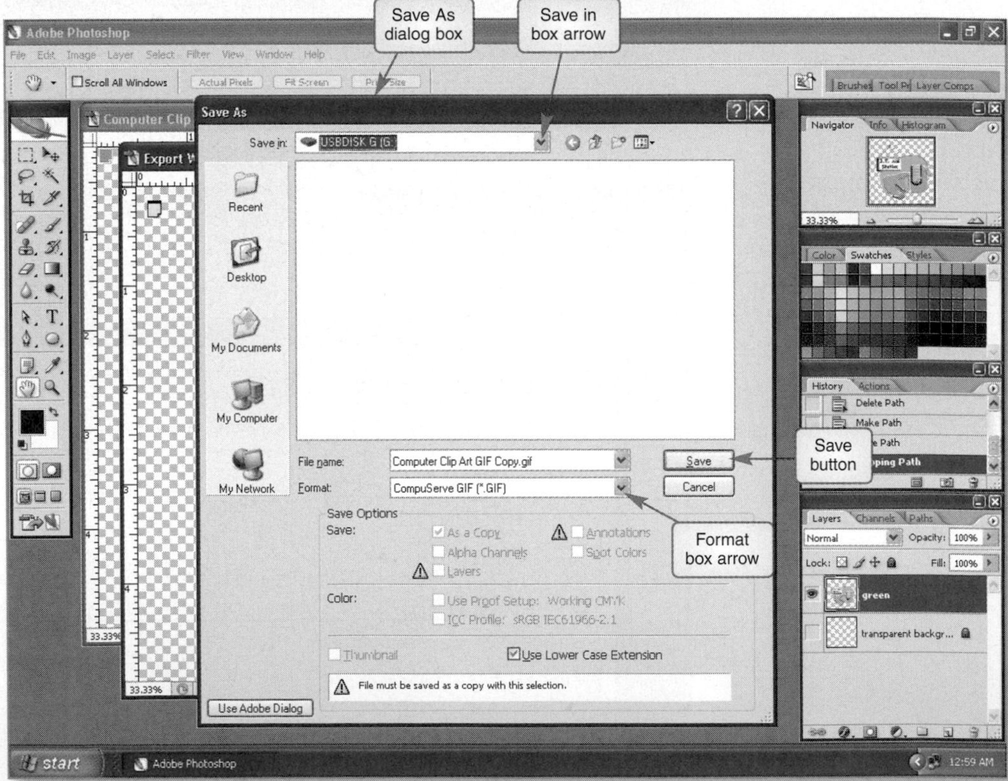

FIGURE 8-66

5

- **Click the Save button.**
- **When Photoshop displays the Indexed Color dialog box, if necessary, click the Palette box arrow and then click Web in the List. If necessary, click the Transparency box and the Preserve Exact Colors box to select them.**

The Indexed Color dialog box is displayed (Figure 8-67). Your number of colors may differ.

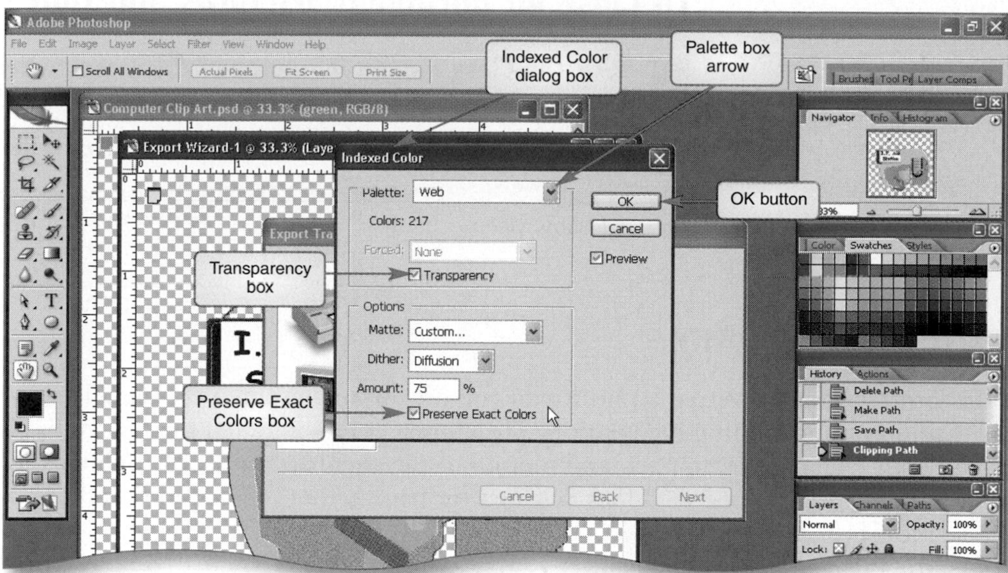

FIGURE 8-67

- **Click the OK button in the Indexed Color dialog box.**

Photoshop displays the GIF Options dialog box (Figure 8-68).

- **Click the OK button in the GIF Options dialog box.**
- **When the last step of the wizard is displayed, click the Finish button.**

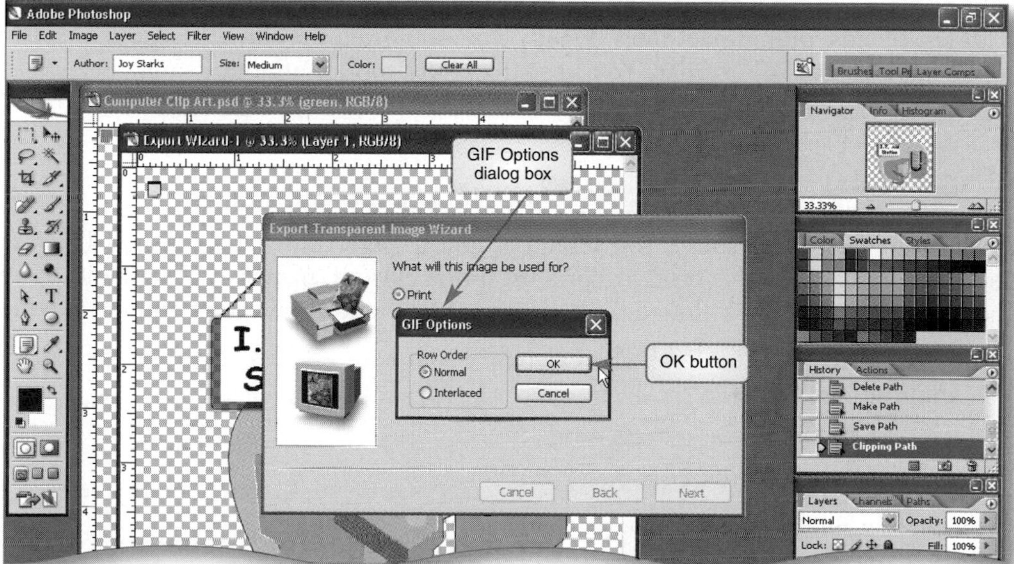

FIGURE 8-68

If this graphic were used on the Web, the Normal setting (Figure 8-68) would cause it to display after the rest of the page was loaded. An Interlaced setting would display a low resolution version of the image from the top down, as the Web page was loaded. Interlacing makes download time seem shorter, but it also increases file size.

The clip art is complete. The final steps are to close the document windows and quit Photoshop.

To Close All Document Windows and Quit Photoshop

1. **Click the Close button in any open document window. If Photoshop asks to save the file, click the No button.**
2. **Click the Close button on the Photoshop title bar.**

The Photoshop window closes.

Project Summary

In this project, you converted a photo into clip art for a newspaper column. The purpose of the clip art was to provide humor and column recognition. The chosen colors imitated the real colors of the objects. The details added depth, perspective, impact, and motion to the clip art. You learned about the general characteristics of clip art and transparency-based files destined for page layout applications and the difference between vector and raster graphics.

As you created layer groups and organized your objects, you created both paths and shape layers. You used the Pen and Freeform Pen tools to draw line segments and anchor points. You added, subtracted, and converted anchor points to create straight lines and curves. The Path Selection and Direct Selection tools helped position paths and shapes. You added detail to the clip art image including background shape and color, color overlays, shadows, blends, and impact lines. Finally, you optimized the clip art using the Export Transparent Image wizard, converting it to the GIF format. You used the Notes tool to annotate your file.

What You Should Know

Having completed this project, you should be able to perform the tasks below. The tasks are listed in the same order they were presented in this project. For a list of the buttons, menus, toolbars, and other commands introduced in this project, see the Quick Reference Summary at the back of this book and refer to the Page Number column.

1. Start Photoshop and Reset the Palettes, Toolbox, and Options Bar (PS 485)
2. Reset the Layers Palette (PS 486)
3. Reset the Colors (PS 486)
4. Create a File with a Transparent Background (PS 486)
5. Rename the Transparent Layer (PS 488)
6. Insert the Computer Graphic (PS 488)
7. Create Layer Groups (PS 490)
8. Create More Groups (PS 491)
9. Lock Layers (PS 492)
10. Save the Computer Clip Art File (PS 493)
11. Create a Shape Layer with the Pen Tool (PS 497)
12. Add Anchor Points to a Shape (PS 500)
13. Rename the Layer (PS 502)
14. Create a Path with the Pen Tool (PS 503)
15. Reshape a Path (PS 506)
16. Fill a Path with Color (PS 507)
17. Create Another Shape Layer (PS 508)
18. Convert Anchor Points and Reshape (PS 509)
19. Subtract from a Shape Layer (PS 511)
20. Save the Image (PS 512)
21. Create a Shape with the Magnetic Pen (PS 513)
22. Create a Path Around the Lighter Portions of the Tower (PS 516)
23. Add a Color Overlay (PS 518)
24. Use Blending Modes (PS 520)
25. Insert the Bandage Graphic (PS 522)
26. Insert the Thermometer Graphic (PS 523)
27. Create Impact Lines (PS 524)
28. Create the Sign (PS 526)
29. Create a Note (PS 530)
30. Save and Flatten the Layers (PS 531)
31. Use the Export Transparent Image Wizard (PS 533)
32. Close All Document Windows and Quit Photoshop (PS 536)

Learn It Online

Instructions: To complete the Learn It Online exercises, start your browser, click the Address bar, and then enter the Web address `scsite.com/photoshop/learn`. When the Photoshop CS2 Learn It Online page is displayed, follow the instructions in the exercises below. Each exercise has instructions for printing your results, either for your own records or for submission to your instructor.

1 Project Reinforcement TF, MC, and SA

Below Photoshop Project 8, click the Project Reinforcement link. Print the quiz by clicking Print on the File menu for each page. Answer each question.

2 Flash Cards

Below Photoshop Project 8, click the Flash Cards link and read the instructions. Type 20 (or a number specified by your instructor) in the Number of playing cards text box, type your name in the Enter your Name text box, and then click the Flip Card button. When the flash card is displayed, read the question and then click the ANSWER box arrow to select an answer. Flip through Flash Cards. If your score is 15 (75%) correct or greater, click Print on the File menu to print your results. If your score is less than 15 (75%) correct, then redo this exercise by clicking the Replay button.

3 Practice Test

Below Photoshop Project 8, click the Practice Test link. Answer each question, enter your first and last name at the bottom of the page, and then click the Grade Test button. When the graded practice test is displayed on your screen, click Print on the File menu to print a hard copy. Continue to take practice tests until you score 80% or better.

4 Who Wants To Be a Computer Genius?

Below Photoshop Project 8, click the Computer Genius link. Read the instructions, enter your first and last name at the bottom of the page, and then click the PLAY button. When your score is displayed, click the PRINT RESULTS link to print a hard copy.

5 Wheel of Terms

Below Photoshop Project 8, click the Wheel of Terms link. Read the instructions, and then enter your first and last name and your school name. Click the PLAY button. When your score is displayed, right-click the score and then click Print on the shortcut menu to print a hard copy.

6 Crossword Puzzle Challenge

Below Photoshop Project 8, click the Crossword Puzzle Challenge link. Read the instructions, and then enter your first and last name. Click the SUBMIT button. Work the crossword puzzle. When you are finished, click the Submit button. When the crossword puzzle is redisplayed, click the Print Puzzle button to print a hard copy.

7 Tips and Tricks

Below Photoshop Project 8, click the Tips and Tricks link. Click a topic that pertains to Project 8. Right-click the information and then click Print on the shortcut menu. Construct a brief example of what the information relates to in Photoshop to confirm you understand how to use the tip or trick.

8 Expanding Your Horizons

Below Photoshop Project 8, click the Expanding Your Horizons link. Click a topic that pertains to Project 8. Print the information. Construct a brief example of what the information relates to in Photoshop to confirm you understand the contents of the article.

9 Search Sleuth

Below Photoshop Project 8, click the Search Sleuth link. To search for a term that pertains to this project, select a term below the Project 8 title and then use the Google search engine at google.com (or any major search engine) to display and print two Web pages that present information on the term.

10 Photoshop Online Training

Below Photoshop Project 8, click the Photoshop Online Training link. When your browser displays the Web page, click one of the Photoshop tutorials that covers one or more of the objectives listed at the beginning of the project on page PS 482. Print the first page of the tutorial before stepping through it.

Apply Your Knowledge

1 Converting a Photo to Clip Art

Instructions: Start Photoshop, and set the workspace and tools to default values. Open the Rocker file from the Project08 folder, located either on the CD that accompanies this book, or in a location specified by your instructor. The purpose of this exercise is to create a clip art image from a digital photograph. The photo you open is a picture of a rocker, shown on the left in Figure 8-69. You will convert the image to a clip art image as shown on the right.

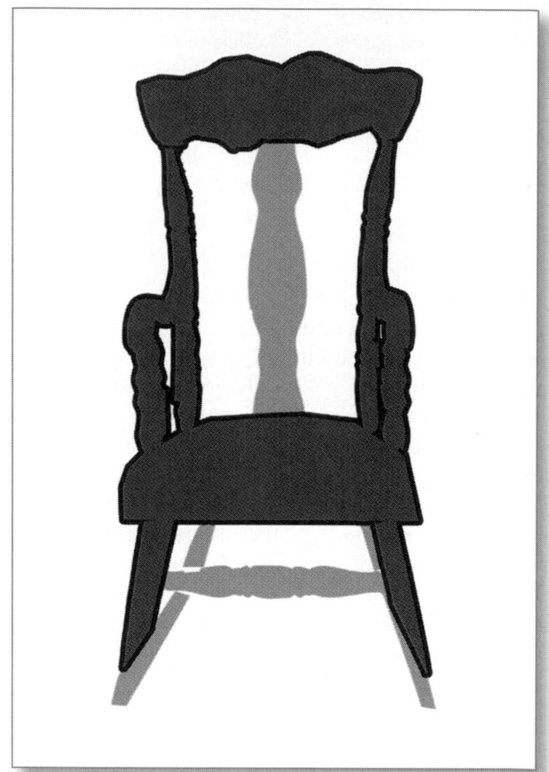

FIGURE 8-69

1. On the File menu, click Save As. Save the image on your USB flash drive as a PSD file, with the file name, Rocker Clip Art. If the Photoshop Format options dialog box is displayed, click the OK button.
2. On the Layers palette, click the Create a new group button. Name the group, Brown.
3. In the toolbox, click the Eyedropper Tool (I) button. Sample a medium brown color in the rocker.
4. With the Brown group still selected, select the Freeform Pen tool in the toolbox. On the options bar, click the Magnetic check box to select it. Click the top-left corner of the rocker and then move the mouse slowly around the headboard of the rocker. Do not drag. Do not include the rungs. When you get all the way around the headboard, click the beginning point to close the path.
5. Click the Add to shape area (+) button on the options bar. Repeat Step 4 to include the seat of the rocker. Repeat Step 4 to include the corner legs, arm rests, and back outer rungs.
6. On the Layers palette, select Layer 1 and then click the Create a new group button. Name the group, Tan.
7. Select the Swatches palette, click a tan color such as #CC9966.
8. With the Tan group still selected on the Layers palette, click the Freeform Pen Tool (P) button if necessary. On the options bar, click the Create new shape layer button.

Apply Your Knowledge

9. Click the top-left corner of the center rung on the back of the rocker. Move the mouse slowly around the rung. Do not drag. When you get all the way around the rung, click the beginning point to close the path.
10. Click the Add to shape area (+) button on the options bar. Repeat Step 9 to include the rockers at the bottom of the image and the cross rung.
11. Save the image again.
12. Unlock the background layer, if necessary, and delete it.
13. On the Layers palette, select the shape layer in the Brown layer group. Click the Add a layer style button. When the shortcut menu is displayed, click Stroke.
14. In the Layer Style dialog box, type `16` in the Size box. Click the Position box arrow and then click Outside in the list, if necessary. Click the Blend Mode box arrow and then click Normal in the list, if necessary. Type `100%` in the Opacity box. Click the Fill Type box arrow and then click Color in the list, if necessary. Click the Color box. When the Color Picker dialog box is displayed, select a black color and then click the OK button.
15. Close the Layer Style dialog box.
16. To display the shape layer's bounding box, press CTRL+T. On the options bar, click the Switch between free transform and warp modes button.
17. When the side control handles are displayed, drag each of them slightly toward the center of the image to create a cartoon-like effect as shown in Figure 8-69.
18. Press the ENTER key to commit the changes.
19. On the Layer menu, click Flatten image.
20. Save the image again. Print a copy for your instructor.
21. For extra credit, open a page layout program such as Microsoft Publisher, Microsoft Word, or Adobe InDesign. Insert the Rocker Clip Art file as a picture. Experiment with inline versus square graphic placement and scaling.

1 Creating a Sign

Problem: Your summer job is working at the public library. Your supervisor has asked you to make a sign for the Bookworm Corner — a section of the children's library with carpeting and bean bag chairs. He would like the same image in a scalable format for use in the desktop publishing products of the library. You have taken a picture of some books and decide to add a clip art of a worm as shown in Figure 8-70. You will save it in both the PSD and GIF formats to preserve the transparency.

FIGURE 8-70

(continued)

Creating a Sign *(continued)*

Instructions:

1. Start Photoshop. Perform the customization steps found on pages PS 8 through PS 10.
2. Open the file, Books, from the Project08 folder on the CD that accompanies this book.
3. Click the Save As command on the File menu. Type `Books Clip Art` as the file name. Browse to your USB flash drive storage device. Click the Save button. If Photoshop displays a dialog box, click the OK button.
4. Use the Navigator palette to zoom the photo to 16.67% magnification, if necessary.
5. To create a transparent background:
   a. Press the w key to access the Magic Wand tool. On the options bar, click the Add to selection button.
   b. Select all of the white areas.
   c. On the Select menu, click Inverse.
   d. On the Layer menu, point to New, and then click Layer via Cut. Name the new layer, Books.
   e. Delete the background layer.
6. To create a color shape layer of an individual book:
   a. Select the Swatches palette. Choose a bright color in the red family.
   b. In the toolbox, click the Pen Tool (P) button. On the options bar, click the Create new shape layer button.
   c. Choose a book in the document window and then click each corner to create a red shape layer.
   d. Add and subtract anchor points as necessary to match the edges. Convert any anchor points that need moving. Use the Path Selection tool to adjust anchor points along the path.
7. Repeat Step 6 choosing a different color from the Swatches palette for each book.
8. To add a special effect:
   a. Select the Shape 1 layer.
   b. Click the Add a layer style button and then click Bevel and Emboss on the shortcut menu.
   c. When the Layer Style dialog box is displayed, choose the settings displayed in Table 8-8.

Table 8-8 Layer Style Settings for the Books Clip Art

NAME	SETTING
Style	Inner Bevel
Technique	Smooth
Depth	100
Direction	Down
Size	24
Soften	3
Angle	-138
Altitude	21
Gloss Contour	Linear
Highlight Mode	Screen
Highlight Mode Opacity	75
Shadow Mode	Multiply
Color	Black
Shadow Mode Opacity	75

9. To copy the layer style to the other shape layers:
   a. Right-click the Shape 1 layer. When the shortcut menu is displayed, click Copy Layer Style.
   b. SHIFT+click each of the other shape layers.
   c. Right-click the selected layers and then click Paste Layer Style on the shortcut menu.
10. To add the worm graphic:
    a. Click the Books layer.
    b. Press CTRL+O and then open the file named, Worm, from the Project08 folder. When the Worm document window is displayed, drag the title bar so parts of both windows can be seen.
    c. Select the Rectangular Marquee Tool (M) button in the toolbox. Drag a rectangle around the right half of the worm. Press the V key to access the Move tool. Drag the selection and drop it in the Books Clip Art window. Place it on the right side of the books as shown in Figure 8-70 on page PS 539. Press CTRL+T and resize the layer as necessary.
    d. Click the Worm window again. Select the Rectangular Marquee Tool (M) button in the toolbox. Drag a rectangle around the left half of the worm. Press the V key to access the Move tool. Drag the selection and drop it in the Books Clip Art window. Place it on the left side of the books as shown in Figure 8-70. Press CTRL+T and resize the layer as necessary.
11. Save the file again.
12. On the Layers palette, right-click the Books layer and then click Merge Visible.
13. Use the Save As command to save the file in the GIF format with the same name. Accept the default settings in the GIF dialog boxes.
14. Print a copy and turn it in to your instructor.

2 Creating a Cartoon from Scratch

Problem: Cartoons are a popular and legitimate use of graphics in many areas of the media. In preparation for a back to school feature, you have been asked to create a cartoon of a hamburger thinking about students, or other food, in the school cafeteria. You decide to use shape layers and layer groups to create a clip art hamburger with a thought bubble. The cartoon is displayed in Figure 8-71.

FIGURE 8-71

(continued)

Creating a Cartoon from Scratch *(continued)*

1. Press CTRL+N to start a new file. When the New dialog box is displayed, use the settings from Table 8-9.

Table 8-9 New Settings for Hamburger Graphic

NAME	HAMBURGER
Preset	Custom
Width	5 inches
Height	5 inches
Resolution	300 pixels/inch
Color Mode	RGB Color 8 bit
Background Contents	Transparent

2. Click the Save As command on the File menu. Type `Hamburger` as the file name. Browse to your USB flash drive storage device. Select the PSD file format, if necessary. Click the Save button. If Photoshop displays a dialog box, click the OK button.
3. To create the bottom portion of the hamburger bun:
   a. Choose a light brown color on the Swatches palette.
   b. Press the U key to access the Shape tool. On the options bar, click the Shape layers button, the Rounded Rectangle Tool button, and the Create new shape layer button.
   c. In the lower-center portion of the document window, drag a shape, approximately 1 inch tall × 3.5 inches wide.
   d. Press CTRL+T to display the bounding box. On the options bar, click the Switch between free transform and warp modes button. When the warp handles are displayed, drag the top-left and top-right handles to round off the upper corners.
   e. Press the ENTER key to commit the changes.
   f. On the Layers palette, name the layer, bottom.
4. To create the top portion of the hamburger bun:
   a. In the toolbox, select the Pen Tool (P) button.
   b. In the document window, create a triangle as follows. Click approximately .5 inches above the upper-left corner of the previous layer. Move the mouse to the right in a straight line. Click above the upper-right corner. Move the mouse up about an inch and toward the center, and then click to form a triangle. Click the beginning point to close the path.
   c. In the toolbox, right-click the Pen Tool (P) button and then click Add Anchor Point Tool in the list.
   d. Add an anchor point on either side of the triangle. Drag the new anchor points to create a curved shape.
   e. On the Layers palette, name the layer, top.
5. To create the burger:
   a. On the Swatches palette, choose a medium brown color.
   b. Press the U key to access the Shape tool. On the options bar, click the Create new shape layer button and the Custom Shape Tool button. Click the Shape Picker button. When the shapes are displayed, click the Shape Picker menu button and then click All. Click Append if necessary. When all the shapes are displayed, click the Cloud 1 shape.
   c. Drag a shape just above the bottom portion of the hamburger bun. The shape should fill approximately half of the blank space between the two halves of the bun, but be slightly wider.

d. Press the V key and drag the shape to overlap the bottom portion of the hamburger bun slightly.
e. On the Layers palette, name the layer, burger.
f. Click the Add a layer style button at the bottom of the Layers palette, and then click Inner Shadow in the list. When the Layer Style dialog box is displayed, change the settings to those shown in Table 8-10.

Table 8-10 Layer Style Settings for Burger Layer

BLEND MODE	MULTIPLY
Opacity	30
Angle	–87
Use Global Light	selected
Distance	55
Choke	34
Size	79
Contour	Cone – Inverted
Anti-aliased	not selected
Noise	0

6. To create the cheese:
   a. On the Swatches palette, choose a medium yellow color.
   b. Press the U key to access the Shape tool. On the options bar, click the Create new shape layer button. Click the Custom Shape Tool button, if necessary. Click the Shape Picker button. When the shapes are displayed, click the Crescent Moon shape.
   c. In a blank portion of the document window, drag a shape 1 inch tall and .5 inches wide. Press CTRL+T to display the bounding box. On the options bar, enter 45 in the Rotate box. Press the ENTER key to commit the changes.
   d. On the Layers palette, name the layer, cheese.
   e. Click the Add a layer style button at the bottom of the Layers palette, and then click Inner Shadow in the list. When the Layer Style dialog box is displayed, change the settings to those shown in Table 8-11.

Table 8-11 Layer Style Settings for Burger Layer

BLEND MODE	COLOR BURN
Opacity	29
Angle	–87
Use Global Light	selected
Distance	31
Choke	21
Size	6
Contour	Half Round
Anti-aliased	not selected
Noise	0

(continued)

Creating a Cartoon from Scratch *(continued)*

f. Press the V key and move the shape to position on top of the burger layer.
g. ALT+drag the cheese layer to create another copy and move it to a second location on the burger.

7. To create the tomato:
   a. Choose a red color on the Swatches palette.
   b. Use the Rounded Rectangle Tool to create a thin red shape.
   c. Position it above the hamburger and cheese layers.
   d. Press CTRL+T to display the bounding box. On the options bar, click the Switch between free transform and warp modes button. When the warp handles are displayed, experiment with dragging the handles to create a slightly uneven shape resembling a slice of tomato.
   e. Press the ENTER key to commit the changes and name the layer, tomato.
8. To create the lettuce:
   a. On the Swatches palette, choose a medium green color.
   b. Select the Custom Shape tool. On the options bar, click the Create a new shape layer button. Choose the Cloud 1 shape from the Custom Picker.
   c. Drag a thin shape to fill the space between the top bun and the tomato.
   d. Name the layer, lettuce.
9. If the layers need to be closer together or overlapped, select the layer on the Layers palette and then select the Move tool. Drag the layers and reorder them as necessary.
10. To create the eyes:
    a. On the Layers palette, click the Create a new group button. Name the new group, Left Eye.
    b. In a blank portion of the document window, use the Ellipse Tool button to create a new shape layer with the color white, approximately 1 inch wide and .75 inches tall. Name the layer, eye. Click the Add a layer style button and then click Stroke. When Photoshop displays the Layer Style dialog box, set the Size to 8 px. Change the color to black, if necessary. If any other layer styles display a check mark, click to deselect them.
    c. Click the Left Eye layer group. Choose a blue color on the Swatches palette. On the options bar, click the Create new shape layer button. Click the Style picker button and then click Default Style (None) in the list. Drag an ellipse to create the iris as shown in Figure 8-71 on page PS 541. Name the layer, iris.
    d. Click the Left Eye layer group. Choose a black color on the Swatches palette. On the options bar, click the Create a new shape layer button and then drag a circle to create the pupil as shown in Figure 8-71. Name the layer, pupil.
    e. Right-click the Left Eye layer group and then click Duplicate Group. Name the new layer group, Right Eye.
    f. Drag the group layers to position the eyes on top of the hamburger.
11. To create the thought bubble:
    a. On the Swatches palette, choose a light cyan color.
    b. Press the U key to access the Shape tool. On the options bar, click the Create new shape layer button. Click the Custom Shape tool, if necessary. Click the Shape Picker button. When the shapes are displayed, click the Thought 1 shape.
    c. In a blank portion of the document window, drag a shape approximately 2 × 2 inches. Name the shape, Thought Bubble.
    d. Press the V key and move the bubble to a position as shown in Figure 8-71.
    e. On the Layers palette, drag the Thought Bubble layer to a position above the other layers and layer groups.

12. Use the Horizontal Type Tool (T) button to create text inside the thought bubble. Choose an appropriate funny phrase.
13. Save the image again. Merge the visible layers. Rename the resulting single layer, Hamburger Complete. Save the image in the GIF format. Accept the default settings in the GIF dialog boxes.
14. Drop both versions in your instructor's virtual drop box, or see your instructor for ways to submit this assignment.

3 Using Annotation Tools

Problem: As a teaching assistant (TA), your job is to help one of the professors with grading and lab assistance. You have just received a set of assignments where the students were required to convert a photo into clip art. The professor has asked you to include written and audio notes about each of the submissions.

As directed by your instructor, exchange files with three other people in your class. The files should be images created from this project — either the previous Apply Your Knowledge exercise, previous In the Lab exercises, or one from the Cases and Places on the next page.

Instructions:

1. Start Photoshop. Perform the customization steps found on pages PS 8 through PS 10.
2. Open one of the files submitted to you.
3. Click the Save As command on the File menu. In the Name box, click at the end of the previous file name, but before any displayed period and extension. Type `Edited by` and then type your initials as the new file name. For example, if the file were named Hamburger, you would save it as Hamburger Edited by xxx, where xxx represents your initials. Browse to your USB flash drive storage device. Use the PSD format. Click the Save button. If Photoshop displays a dialog box, click the OK button.
4. Carefully look at the clip art assignment. Look for the details and characteristics mentioned in this project. Choose a portion of the image that you like the best — one that contains no errors and represents good practices and thoughtful conversion.
5. In the toolbox, click the Notes Tool (N) button. On the options bar, insert your name as the author. Click the image close to the location chosen in Step 4. In the displayed note, type a sentence or two describing why you like that portion of the image and why you think it adds to the purpose of the clip art.
6. Look at the clip art again, this time for minor errors. Look for lines, contours, and borders that may not perfectly meet. Look for colors that are not characteristic of the theme of the clip art. Look for layering errors or problems with transparency.
7. With the Notes tool still selected, click the image close to a location chosen in Step 6. In the displayed note, type a sentence or two describing the perceived problem. Close the Notes tool.
8. Finally, look at the clip art and find places where extra detail could be added. Look for a spot that might need a shadow, reflection, impact lines, blend, or filter to improve its appearance. Think about the overall perception and placement of the clip art.
9. With a microphone attached to your computer system, right-click the Notes tool and then click Audio Annotation Tool in the list. Click the document window. When the Audio Annotation dialog box is displayed, click the Start button. Suggest places where it might be appropriate to add details. Reinforce another positive aspect of the submitted assignment. When you are finished, click the Stop button. (If you do not have a microphone available, use the Notes tool for the previous suggestions.)
10. Press CTRL+S to save the file again. Return the file to its owner or your instructor as directed.

Cases and Places

The difficulty of these case studies varies:
■ are the least difficult and ■■ are the most difficult. The last exercise is a group exercise.

1 ■ You recently took a job with a company that produces graphical adventure games for computers. Your assignment is to convert a historical ruin into a clip art type of graphic to display on the CD liner. The photo, Archway, is located in the Project08 folder on the CD that accompanies this book. Open the photo and create a layer group named, Columns. Use the Pen tool to create shape layers with the group for each column. Fill the area with a dark tan color. Use the Shape layer button along with the pen tools and anchor point tools to draw around other parts of the archway with darker and lighter shades. Do not recolor the blue sky. Save the file as a GIF format and submit a copy to your teacher.

2 ■ Your political science professor has given you the assignment of creating an electoral map for your state from the last presidential election. Find a free graphic of your state map with county outlines. Research county election data using your state government's Web site. With the Freeform Pen tool and the Shape layers button, draw around each county, filling it with either red for Republican or blue for Democrat. Save and print the file.

3 ■■ You have decided to run for student council and need a photo to use in posters around campus. Create a new document in Photoshop with a solid, bright background. Have a friend take a digital picture of you. Copy the photo into your new document and then convert everything from the neck down into vector graphics, maintaining size and proportion. Use subtle colors that complement the background. Create other shadows, reflections, and blends that enhance the poster. Use the type tool to insert your name, slogan, or office above your picture.

4 ■■ A friend would like you to create a logo for his new veterinary business. You decide to use a picture of your own pet or a friend's pet, and turn it into clip art to include in the logo. Take a digital photo of a pet and open it in Photoshop. Remove the background. Choose several colors that match the colors of the pet. Use the Pen tool to create shapes around each part of the pet. Create different shapes for the pet's head, body, and other distinctive parts. Add at least three blending modes to the shapes. Create a background or border for the clip art. Convert the image to a GIF file and save it on your storage device.

5 ■■ **Working Together** As a group, pick a subject that commonly is portrayed in clip art, such as animals, people, attention getters, vehicles, or holidays. Each individual in the group should bring to the group five examples of clip art related to the chosen subject. Use sources such as clip art galleries, Web pages, magazines, or software applications. As a group, decide what message the clip art is trying to send and then rate the clip art on clarity, purpose, and graphic techniques. Write your responses and turn them in to your instructor, along with copies of the clip art graphics.

Using Web Tools

PROJECT

CASE PERSPECTIVE

You soon will graduate with a degree from the Computer Graphics department. As you think about entering the job market, you notice that many employers are requesting e-portfolios — a Web site that contains a resume, samples of created products, references, and contact information.

To show off your skills, you decide to create a Web page complete with animation and rollover hyperlinks. You also plan to explore Photoshop's automation technique of creating a Web photo gallery and link it to your Web page.

Because Web pages and Web sites need to reside on a computer with constant Internet connection, you are going to investigate free server space at your school, or purchase space from your Internet Service Provider (ISP). When you upload the Web page and the accompanying Web folders that contain your examples, your service will provide you with the URL or Web address that you can distribute.

With employment posting Web sites and the Department of Labor predicting dramatic growth in the I.T. and desktop publishing fields, it is a perfect time to post your e-portfolio!

As you read through this project, you will learn how to create a Web photo gallery and use Web-safe colors and slices to create an optimized Web page. You will create a navigation bar with links that change when visitors to your page point at the link with a mouse. In addition, you will learn about animation frames and how to manipulate the frames in Adobe ImageReady.

Using Web Tools

PROJECT

Objectives

You will have mastered the material in this project when you can:

- Describe the purpose and content of an e-portfolio
- Draw a home page storyboard
- Explain why planning is the most important step in Web design
- Generate a Web photo gallery
- Differentiate between a Web page and a Web site
- Choose Web-safe colors
- Insert hyperlinks and a navigation bar
- Create a rollover and apply hyperlink settings
- Slice an image
- Jump to ImageReady
- Describe the process of creating an animation and optimization

Introduction

An electronic portfolio, or **e-portfolio**, is a collection of artifacts and supporting information presented electronically, which documents an individual's efforts, progress, and achievements over time. E-portfolios typically are performance-based and provide a way to present your knowledge, skills, and attitudes for assessment.

For those entering the job market in graphic design, e-portfolios typically are presented to prospective employers via a Web site with links to sample products and a resume, references, or contact information. Alternately, graphic design job seekers create an interactive CD with samples of their work. Employment Web sites commonly ask for e-portfolios.

Photoshop has several tools to help you create e-portfolios. While Photoshop is not a Web page creation or layout program, it can be used to mock up or create the design for a Web page. Photoshop allows you to use Web-safe colors and pixel measurements to plan your Web page. An exciting feature of Photoshop is the Web photo gallery, which is a Web page with thumbnail links to documents, images, and photos. Using ImageReady — a software application that comes with Photoshop — you can create optimized Web pages complete with rollover buttons and other links or hot spots. Photoshop also uses ImageReady to animate graphics and then optimize them for display on the Web. Each of these features helps you display high-quality products on the Web for worldwide distribution. In this project, as you learn about hyperlinks, slices, and rollovers, you will create an interactive Web site complete with animation and a working photo gallery.

Project Nine — Using Web Tools

Project 9 examines some of Photoshop's Web tools as you create a home page for an e-portfolio. A **home page** is a Web page designated as the first page and point of entry into a Web site. Also called the main page or index page, a home page typically welcomes the viewer by introducing the purpose of the site, the sponsor of the page, and links to the lower-level pages of the site. In the My E-Portfolio home page a two-color background area is created using Web-safe colors. Next, a heading is added. A set of links to future Web pages displays in a bar below the heading. Each link will be highlighted when the mouse is moved over it. One of the links will take visitors to a Web photo gallery generated with a Photoshop automation command. Finally, when the Web page first displays, the graphic in the upper-right corner will be created via a series of animations. The Web page is illustrated in Figure 9-1a. The Web photo gallery, opened via a link from the Web page, is illustrated in Figure 9-1b.

(a) E-Portfolio Web Page

(b) Web Photo Gallery

FIGURE 9-1

Web Photo Galleries

Anyone who creates graphics, or digital photos, appreciates the opportunity to show them off. In today's technology-oriented world, distribution of your personal artwork and photographs commonly is done via the Web. Photoshop, and its complements Adobe Bridge and Adobe Image Ready, provide a particularly functional set of tools to create a display of artwork on the Web. A **Web photo gallery** is a Web site that features a home page with thumbnail images of your photos. Each thumbnail is linked to a gallery page that displays a full-size image. The home page and each gallery page contain links that allow visitors to navigate your site.

On the File menu, the Automate submenu contains several commands including the Web Photo Gallery command to help display your artwork and automate your processes. Table 9-1 displays the Automate commands, a description, and an example.

Table 9-1 Commands on the Automate Submenu

COMMAND	DESCRIPTION	EXAMPLE
Batch	runs a saved action on a folder of files	photos from a digital camera can be processed and resized as a group
PDF Presentation	converts Photoshop images into PDF format, a cross-platform page layout file format	files attached to e-mail or posted on servers can be opened and viewed with a free downloadable reader
Create Droplet	a small, independent application that applies a saved action to one or more images that you drag onto the Droplet icon	apply an action to multiple files without having to open each one in Photoshop
Conditional Mode Change	a command that is added to an action to assist the action to perform correctly across image modes	an action created originally on an image in RGB mode can be run on an image in CMYK mode without generating an error
Contact Sheet II	a command to preview and catalog groups of images by displaying a series of thumbnails on a single page	generating a printable sheet of sample photos for proofs or for final selection
Crop and Straighten Photos	creates separate image files from multiple images in a single scan	separate photos from a catalog or other printed page easily, dividing them into separate, editable files
Fit Image	resamples an image to fit within the specified pixel height and width dimensions you specify	convert an image from portrait to landscape because the command resamples without changing the aspect ratio
Picture Package	places multiple copies of a source image on a single page, choosing from a variety of size and placement options	typically used for school or other photo packages as the command customizes the layout similar to portrait studios
Web Photo Gallery	creates a Web site that features a home page with thumbnail images and links to gallery pages with full-size images	presenting artwork via the Web with a complete navigation system for a gallery of products and photos
Photomerge	combines several photographs into one continuous image either vertically or horizontally	photos of a mountain range or skyline that cannot fit into one camera frame
Merge to HDR	provides the ability to merge photos of the same image shot at different exposures, capturing the high dynamic range of lighting in a single image	HDR images used in motion pictures, special effects, 3D work, and some high-end photography

Organizing Photos for Automation

The photos that you use for any of the automation options should be organized into a folder for more efficient manipulation. The eight files included in the following steps come from each of the chapter examples in this book. Table 9-2 displays the names of the eight files. Your instructor may designate a different set of photos.

Table 9-2 Files to be Included for Automation

PROJECT #	FILE NAME
1	Parasailing Edited
2	Candles Edited
3	House Complete
4	Recital Graphic Complete
5	Postcard with Layers
6	Toys 4Color
7	Magazine Cover CMYK
8	Computer Clip Art GIF Copy

The following steps illustrate how to create a folder and copy the eight files into the new folder.

To Create a Folder of Images

1

- **Click the Start button on your system taskbar and then click My Computer on the Start menu.**
- **Double-click the icon for your storage device.**
- **If the File and Folder Tasks do not display, click the display button next to File and Folder Tasks.**

A window is displayed showing the files from a USB storage device on drive G (Figure 9-2). Your storage device, drive letter, and list of files may differ.

FIGURE 9-2

2

- **Click Make a new folder.**
- **When the new folder is displayed in the window, type** `Project files` **and then press the ENTER key.**

The new folder is displayed in the window (Figure 9-3).

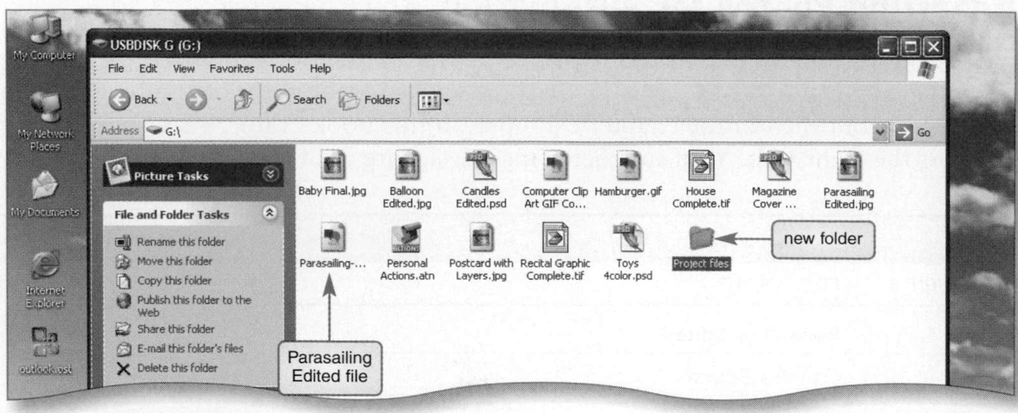

FIGURE 9-3

- **Right-drag the Parasailing Edited file icon and drop it on the new Project files folder. Your instructor may designate a different photo.**

Windows displays a shortcut menu with folder tasks (Figure 9-4).

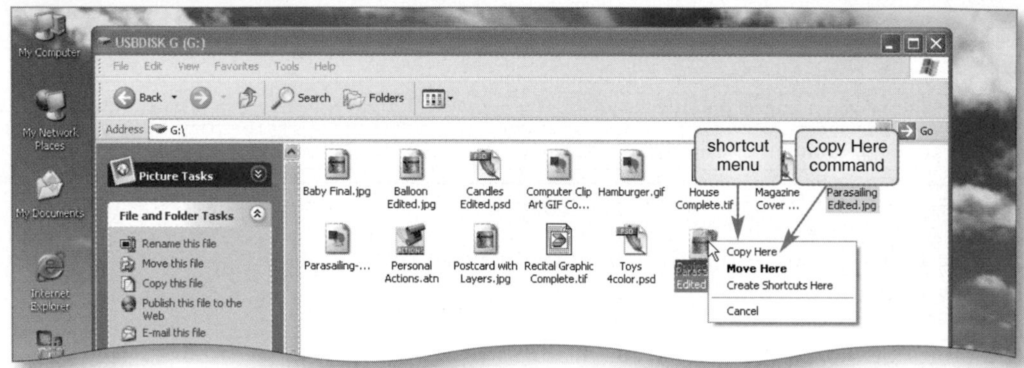

FIGURE 9-4

- **Click Copy Here. Repeat the process for the rest of the files listed in Table 9-2.**
- **Click the Close button in the My Computer window.**

Copies of all eight files now exist in the Project files folder on the USB drive.

Other Ways

1. To create a folder, right-click window, point to New, click Folder
2. To copy into folder, right-click file icon, click Copy, right-click folder icon, click Paste

Now that a folder contains the desired images, the next steps open Photoshop and reset the Workspace in preparation for creating the Web photo gallery.

Starting and Customizing Photoshop

If you are stepping through this project on a computer and you want your screen to match the figures in this book, you should change your computer's resolution to 1024 × 768 and reset the tools and palettes. For more information about how to change the resolution on your computer, and other advanced Photoshop settings, read Appendix A.

The steps on the next page describe how to start Photoshop and customize the Photoshop window. You may need to ask your instructor how to start Photoshop for your system.

To Start Photoshop and Reset the Palettes, Toolbox, and Options Bar

1. **Start Photoshop as described on pages PS 6 and PS 7.**
2. **Choose the Default Workspace as described on page PS 8.**
3. **Select the Rectangular Marquee Tool (M) in the toolbox and then reset all tools as described on pages PS 9 and PS 10.**

Photoshop starts and then resets the tools, palettes, and options.

Resetting the Layers palette

The following steps show how to reset the Layers palette to make the thumbnails match the figures shown in this book.

To Reset the Layers Palette

1. **Click the Layers palette menu button and then click Palette Options on the list.**
2. **When Photoshop displays the Layers Palette Options dialog box, click the option button corresponding to the smallest of the thumbnail sizes, if necessary.**
3. **If necessary, click the Layer Bounds option button.**
4. **Click the OK button.**

The Layers palette will display small thumbnails for each layer.

Resetting the Colors

The following step shows how to reset the default colors in the Photoshop window.

To Reset the Colors

1. **If black and white are not shown as the default colors in the toolbox, press the D key on the keyboard. If black is not the foreground color, press the X key on the keyboard.**

Black is set as the foreground color; white is set as the background color.

Creating a Web Photo Gallery

You use the Web Photo Gallery command to generate automatically a Web site displaying your photos and graphic creations. It is easiest when all the desired files are stored in a single folder. When you create a Web photo gallery, you can choose from a variety of display styles with many options. Additionally, those who know HTML can edit the style template to create custom styles.

The steps on the next page create a Web photo gallery from the folder of project files created previously.

To Create a Web Photo Gallery

1

- **Click File on the menu bar, point to Automate.**

Photoshop displays the Automate submenu (Figure 9-5).

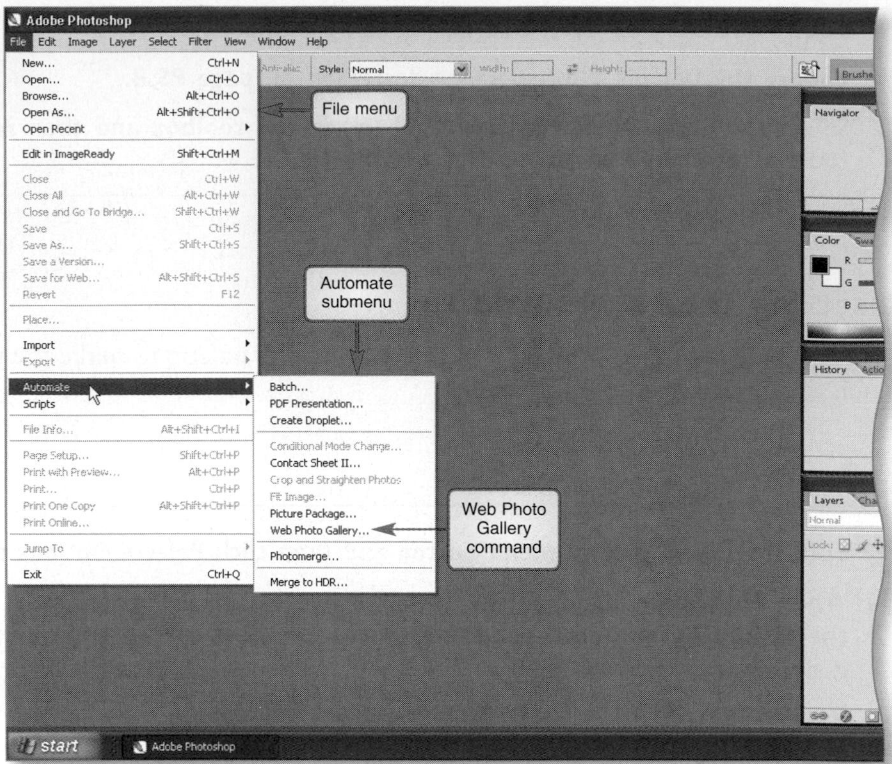

FIGURE 9-5

- **Click Web Photo Gallery.**
- **When the Web Photo Gallery dialog box is displayed, click the Styles box arrow and then click Gray Thumbnails in the list.**

A preview of the home page for the chosen style is displayed in the dialog box (Figure 9-6).

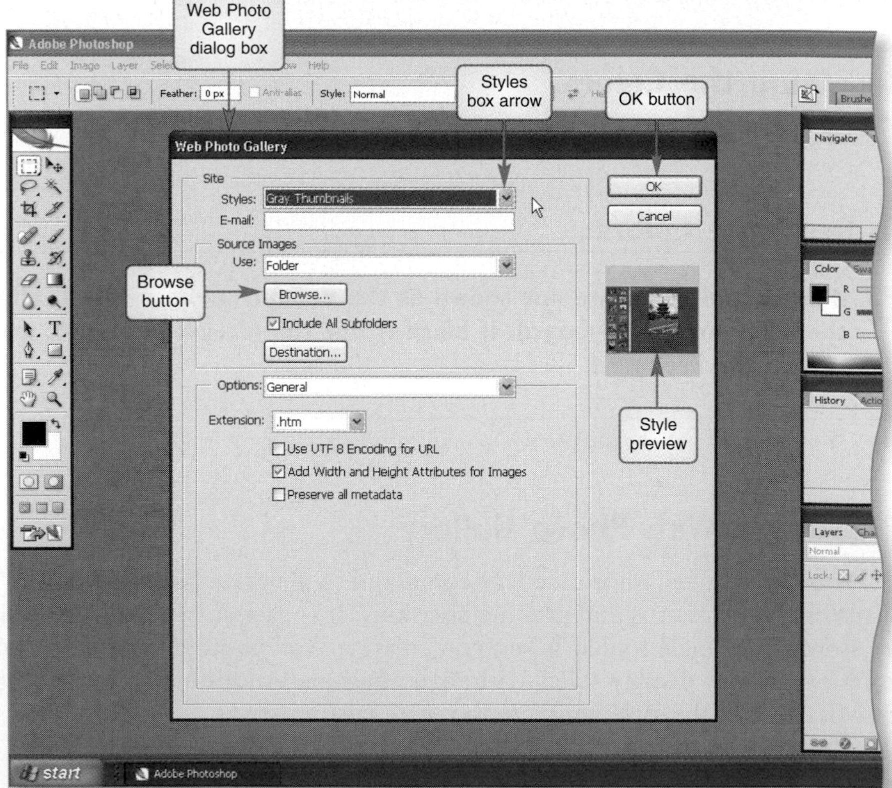

FIGURE 9-6

3

- **Click the Browse button.**
- **When Photoshop displays the Browse For Folder dialog box, click the plus sign left of the My Computer location.**
- **Click the plus sign left of the USBDISK G (G:) location, or navigate to your storage device.**
- **Click the Project files folder.**

The Project files folder is selected (Figure 9-7).

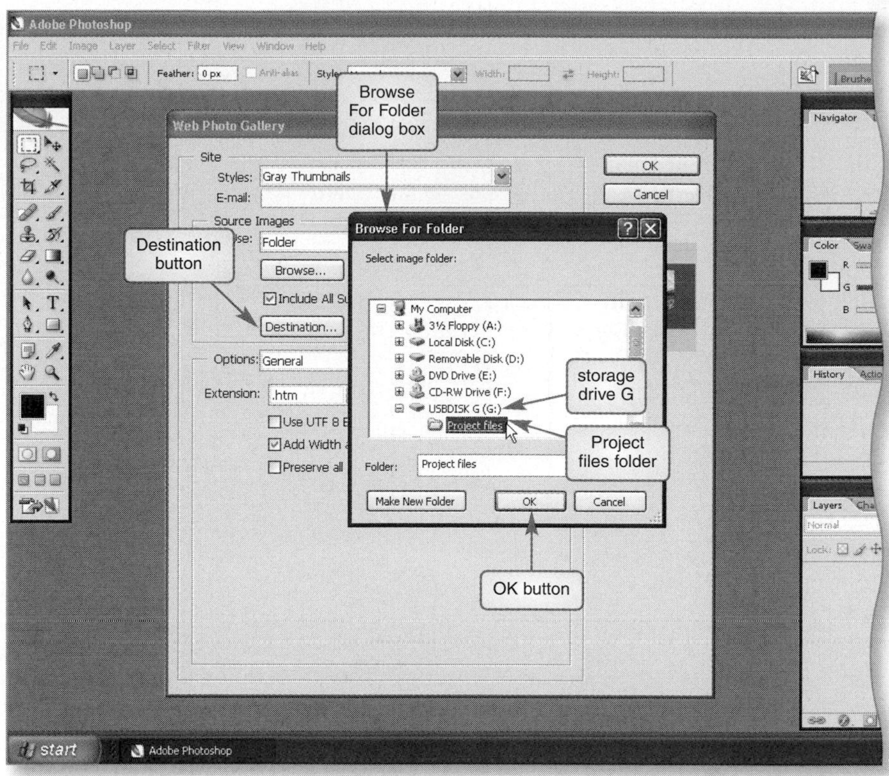

FIGURE 9-7

4

- **Click the OK button in the Browse For Folder dialog box.**
- **When the Web Photo Gallery dialog box again is displayed, click the Destination Button.**
- **Again, click the plus signs to navigate to the USBDISK G (G:) location, or navigate to your storage location. Click the name of the storage device to select it.**
- **Click the Make New Folder button.**

A new folder is displayed below the storage location (Figure 9-8).

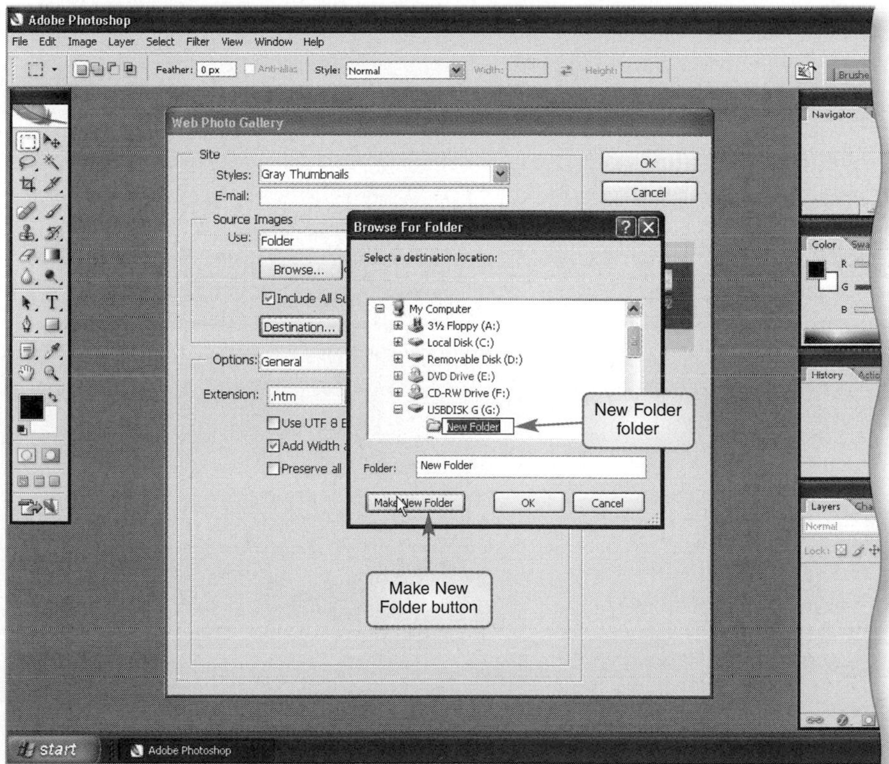

FIGURE 9-8

5

- **Type** My Web Site **and press the ENTER key to name the folder.**
- **Click the OK button in the Browse For Folder dialog box.**
- **When the Web Photo Gallery dialog box again is displayed, if necessary, click the Options box arrow and then click General in the list.**

The settings for the Web photo gallery are complete (Figure 9-9). Optionally, in the E-mail box, you can enter an e-mail address that Photoshop will place on each page of the gallery for visitor reference.

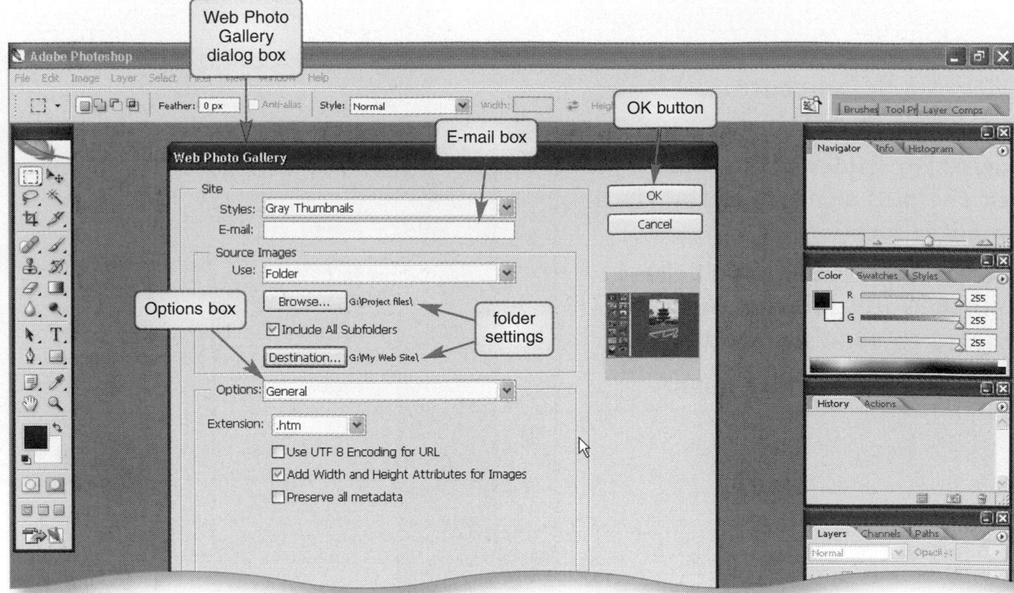

FIGURE 9-9

6

- **Click the OK button in the Web Photo Gallery dialog box.**
- **After a wait, the browser window opens. If a yellow bar displays below the toolbars, click the yellow bar, click Allow Blocked Content, and then, if necessary, click the Yes button in the Security Warning dialog box.**

The home page of the gallery is displayed in a browser window (Figure 9-10).

7

- **Click any of the links and experiment with navigating the site.**
- **When you are finished, click the Close button in the browser window.**

The browser window closes.

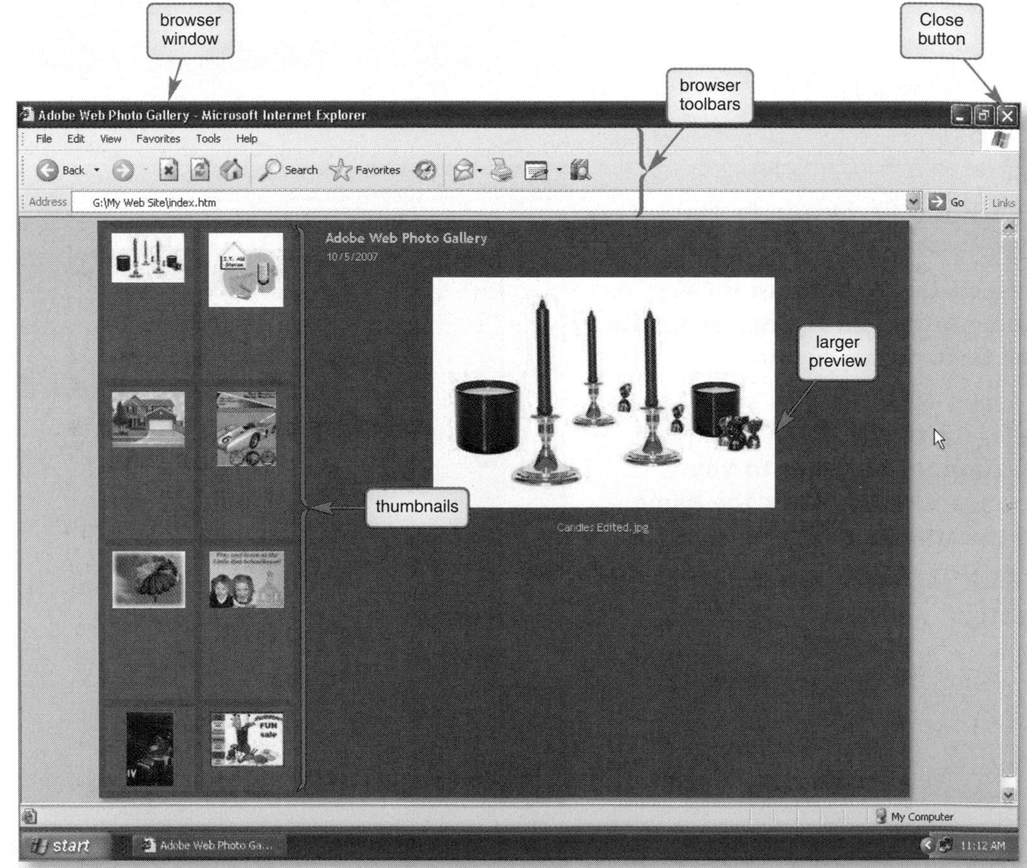

FIGURE 9-10

Other Ways

1. In Adobe Bridge, on Tools menu, point to Photoshop, click Web Photo Gallery

Your images will be presented in the order in which they display in the Project files folder. If you prefer a different order, change the order of the files using Adobe Bridge or a My Computer window. By default, Photoshop creates a home page for the gallery with the name index.htm, in the destination folder. It also creates a set of accompanying files and folders in the destination folder, similar to those shown in Figure 9-11.

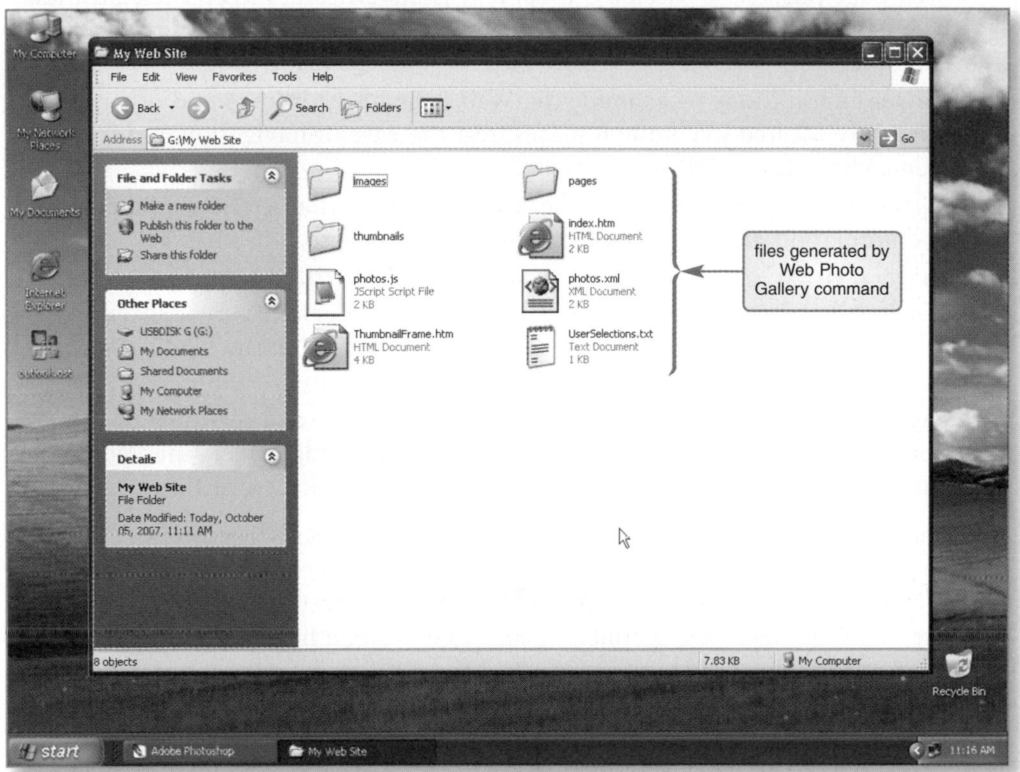

FIGURE 9-11

Each style and option in the Web Photo Gallery dialog box has its own set of parameters. Experiment using different styles and options for your gallery. Use the Adobe Help system and search for the phrase, Web photo gallery options, if you need help with setting values.

Because you will use the My Web Site folder and its index.htm page later in the project, it is a good idea to write down the exact drive and location of your folder for future reference. In the previous steps, the location was G://My Web Site.

With your Web photo gallery complete, the next section describes how to make a home page to access the gallery as well as your future resume and contact information. Figure 9-1a on page PS 549 shows what the Web page will look like.

Designing a Web Page

Planning is the most important step when designing Web pages and Web sites. A **Web page** is a single page of graphics and information, accessible via a browser. A **browser** is an application program used to view and interact with various types of Web pages. A **Web site** is a group of Web pages, logically linked, and positioned together on a hosting computer. A Web site usually is traversed, or browsed, using some kind of navigation system. To be an effective Web designer, you need to do an in-depth study of Web design, protocols, and styles, and become proficient with many planning and design tools including Web programming languages and scripting tools. As a graphic designer, however, you may use Photoshop to prepare graphics for the Web page, or to plan the site with galleries, graphics, color, links, and animation. Without the visual impact of color, shapes, and contrast, Web pages are neither interesting nor motivating.

When planning Web pages, several important issues must be considered:

- Web page purpose — decide if the intent is advertising, direct sales, business-to-business tasks, prospect generation, customer support, or education, for example.
- viewer expectations — examine the Web page to see if links and other elements are located in common places, test the ease of navigation and form fields, check for usability issues, etc.
- nature of planned elements — check to make sure that text, images, color and animation are used judiciously and with purpose.
- viewer's visual impact — research shows that Web users form first impressions of Web pages in as little as 50 milliseconds, making nearly instantaneous judgments of a Web site's visual appeal, including the loading speed, perceived credibility, usability, and customer attraction.
- page's placement within the Web site structure — careful planning of the home page, secondary pages, links, and accompanying folders involves standard naming conventions, file hierarchy issues, and structure.

For more information on designing Web pages, read Special Feature 3.

The purpose of the Web page designed in this project is to be a home page or starting place to access several other pages including a resume, the Web gallery created in the previous steps, and a contact page. Therefore, a heading and links are important elements. For visual impact, each of the links will brighten and highlight when the user's mouse rolls over them. Additionally, an animation when the page is loaded will attract attention.

Selecting a Web-Safe Background Color

The first step in creating the Web page for this project will be to select a color scheme. Because your file will be used on the Web, Web-safe colors are recommended. Recall that Web-safe colors are the 216 colors used by browsers regardless of the platform. By working only with these colors, you can be sure your artwork will not dither on a system set to display 256 colors. Recall that dithering combines colors to approximate exact shades and tints not found on particular monitors or available in certain browsers. Viewed from a distance, a dither gives the effect of the desired color, but viewed closely, the pixels are visible.

The steps on the next page show how to choose Web-safe colors on the Swatches palette, and then select a burgundy color for the background of the Web page.

To Select a Web-Safe Background Color Using the Swatches Palette

1

- **Click the Adobe Photoshop button on your system's taskbar if necessary to display the Photoshop Workspace.**
- **Click the Swatches palette tab and then click the Swatches palette menu button.**

Photoshop displays the Swatches palette menu that includes many different color palettes (Figure 9-12).

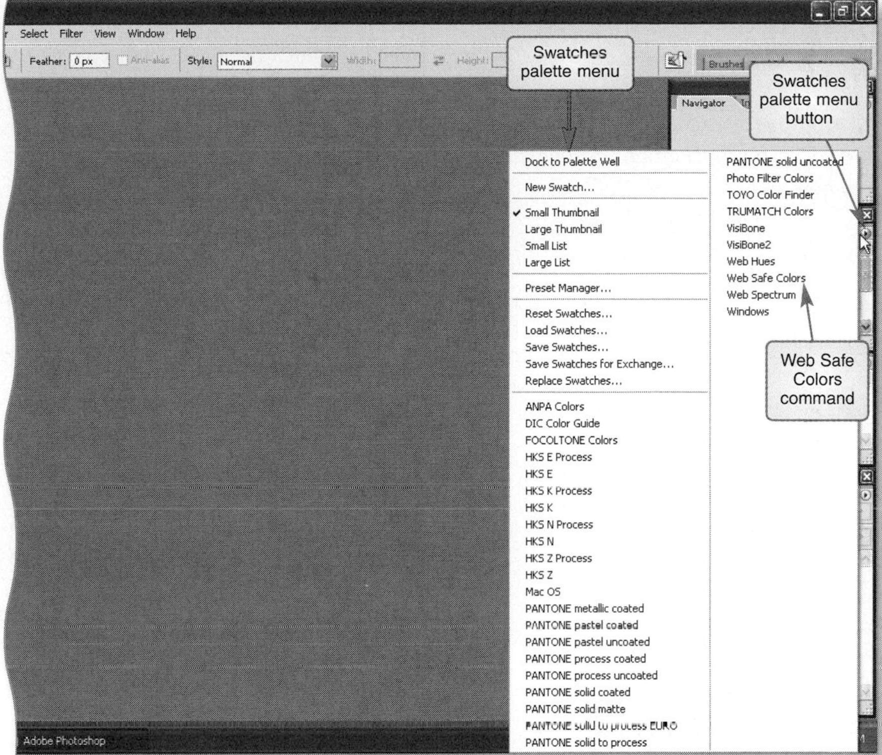

FIGURE 9-12

2

- **Click Web Safe Colors. When Photoshop displays a dialog box asking if you want to replace the colors, click the OK button.**
- **Point to the burgundy color, #990033.**

Web-safe colors are displayed on the Swatches palette (Figure 9-13). Each color's hexadecimal color value displays for a few seconds when you point to it.

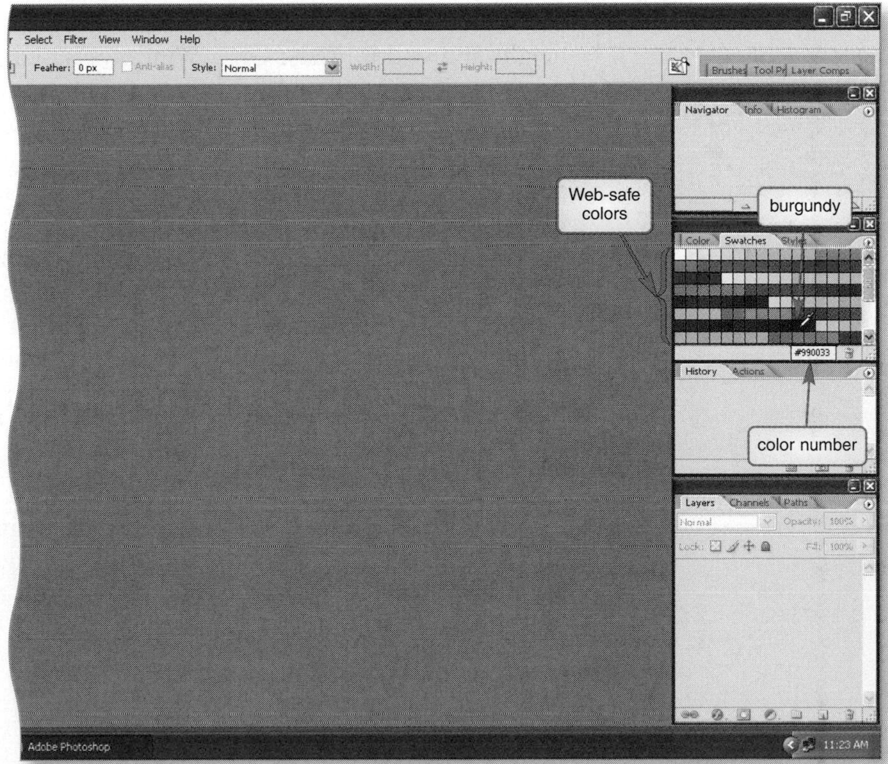

FIGURE 9-13

3

• **CTRL+click the burgundy color, #990033.**

The burgundy color is displayed as the background color in the toolbox (Figure 9-14). Pressing CTRL while clicking a color on the Swatches palette places that color in the background rather than the foreground.

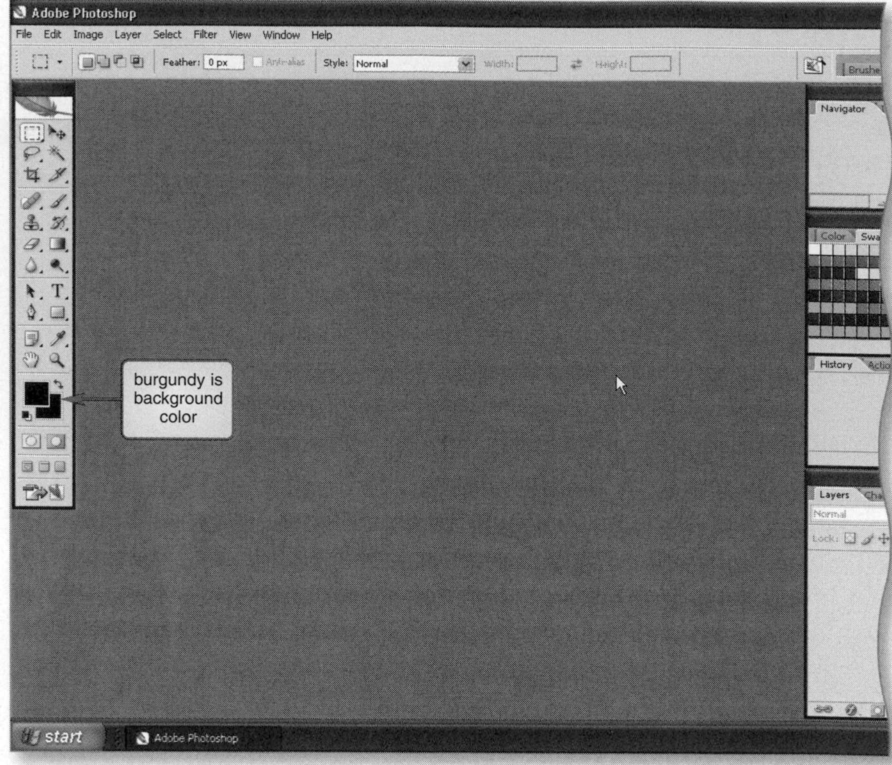

FIGURE 9-14

Other Ways

1. On Color palette menu, click Make Ramp Web Safe
2. In Color Picker dialog box, click Only Web Colors check box

Setting Web Page Dimensions

While Web pages come in a variety of sizes, most usually fall within certain height and width limits. On a Windows based system, the Web browser window will make use of the full width of the screen by default. On a Macintosh system, however, the browser usually will be narrower, allowing the user to view the icons commonly placed on the right side of the screen. It is important to choose a size for your Web page that will accommodate the majority of user monitors and screen size settings. Oversized Web pages, designed on larger screens with resolutions of 1024 × 768, become unreadable on smaller monitors with narrower browser widths. The graphics may be too wide to fit the browser window, and unwrapped text may create long, unreadable lines. Most Web users do not want to scroll from side to side; they also prefer limited vertical scrolling. Therefore, when designing Web pages, you should choose a page size used by a majority of users, while allowing for the occasional small monitor. Web designers constantly analyze and compare existing Web sites for do's and don'ts related to screen colors, screen size, scrolling, graphics, and readability of text.

Another concern is the possibility of printing the Web page. A setting of 800 × 600 will accommodate most users visually, but for Web pages destined for print on 8.5 × 11-inch paper, you should try to keep text and graphics within 760 pixels wide and 410 pixels high (Figure 9-15 on the next page).

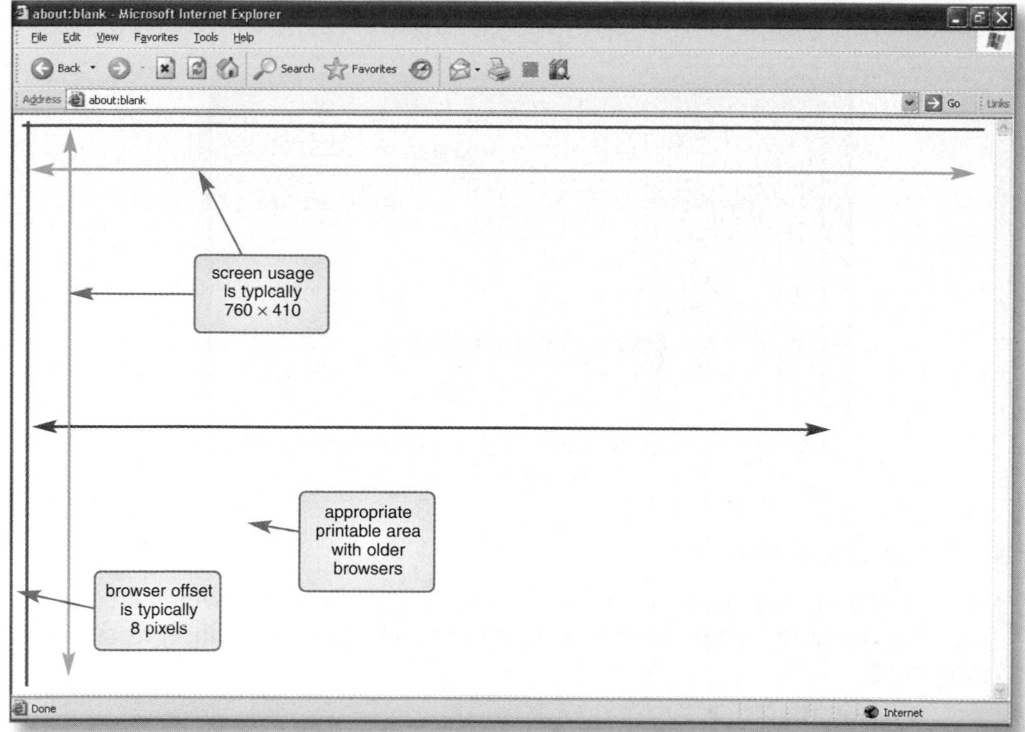

FIGURE 9-15

The following steps show how to use the New command on the File menu to set the attributes for a new document, destined for the Web. Recall that a common resolution for Web products is 72 pixels per inch.

To Set Attributes for a New Web Document

1. **Click File on the menu bar, and then click New. When the New dialog box is displayed, type** `E-Portfolio` **in the Name box.**
2. **Click the Preset box arrow, scroll up in the list if necessary, and then click Custom.**
3. **Double-click the Width box and then type** `800` **as the entry. Click the Width unit box arrow, and then click pixels in the list.**
4. **Double-click the Height box and then type** `600` **as the entry. If necessary, click the Height unit box arrow, and then click pixels in the list.**
5. **Double-click the Resolution box and then type** `72` **as the entry. If necessary, click the Resolution unit box arrow, and then click pixels/inch in the list.**
6. **Click the Color Mode box arrow. If necessary, click RGB Color in the list. If necessary, click the Color Mode unit box arrow and then click 8 bit in the list.**
7. **Click the Background Contents box arrow, and then click Background Color in the list.**

The attributes for the new file are set (Figure 9-16).

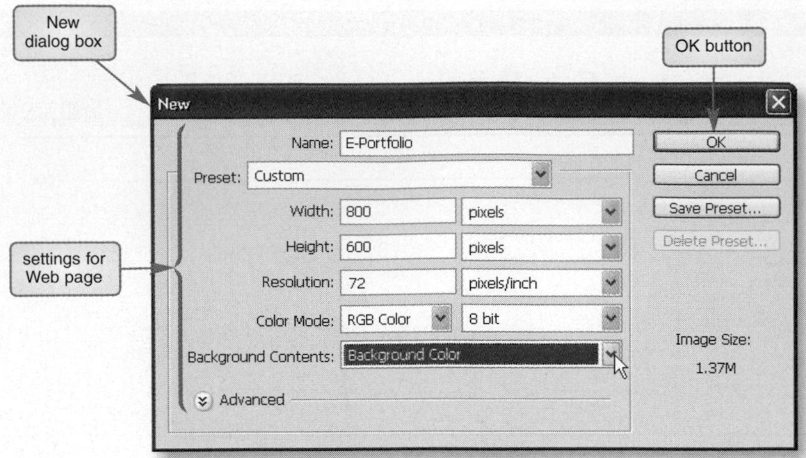

FIGURE 9-16

8 **Click the OK button.**

9 **Adjust the magnification as necessary. Resize the document window to display the entire page, with a small amount of Workspace on each side of the page.**

10 **If the rulers do not display in the document window, press CTRL+R.**

11 **Right-click either of the rulers, and then click Pixels in the list.**

Using pixels as the unit of measurement in the rulers allows you to keep in mind the page layout, both for browsers and printing of graphics and text. By using 800 × 600 pixels, most visitors to the Web page will not have to scroll to see your information. Later, as part of a complete Web site solution, HTML code could be added to create more flexibility and to adjust screen size further.

With the settings complete, it is a good practice to save the new blank document on a storage device as described in the following steps. You will save it in the PSD format for now; later in the project, it will be saved in the HTML Web format.

To Save the New Document

1 **With your USB flash drive connected to one of the computer's USB ports, click File on the menu bar and then click Save As.**

2 **When the Save As dialog box is displayed, if necessary, type** `E-Portfolio` **in the File name text box. Do not press the ENTER key.**

3 **Click the Format box arrow, and then click Photoshop (*.PSD,*.PDD) in the list, if necessary.**

4 **Click the Save in box arrow and then click USBDISK [G:], or the location associated with your USB flash drive, in the list. Double-click the My Web Site folder.**

5 **Click the Save button.**

The file is saved in the My Web Site folder on drive G.

1. Press SHIFT+CTRL+S

Adding Contrast with a Secondary Color

The next steps show how to draw a curved line, dividing the Web page into two areas. The upper-left portion will be filled with a gold color. The lower-right portion will remain burgundy.

To Add Contrast with a Secondary Color

1

- **On the Swatches palette, click the gold color, #FFCC66.**
- **Press the P key. If the Pen tool is not displayed in the toolbox, right-click the current Pen tool button and then click Pen Tool in the list.**
- **On the options bar, click the Shape layers button, if necessary.**
- **In the document window, click the upper-left corner of the burgundy area. Move the mouse down and click the left edge at approximately 225 pixels. Move the mouse up and to the right. Click the upper edge at approximately 700 pixels. Click the upper-left corner to close the path.**

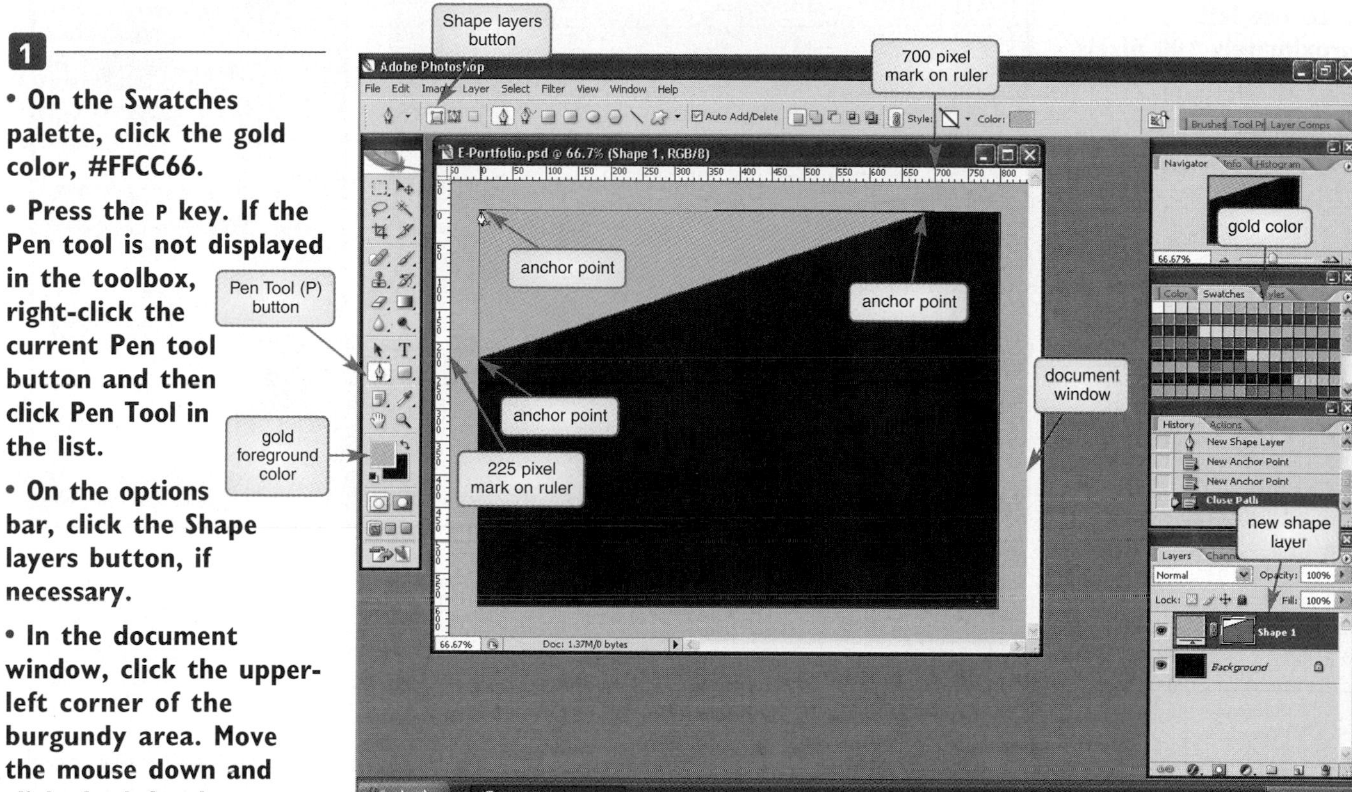

FIGURE 9-17

The clicks create a triangular, color-filled shape layer (Figure 9-17). The new layer is displayed on the Layers palette.

2

- **Right-click the Pen Tool (P) button and then click Add Anchor Point Tool in the list.**
- **Click two points spaced equally along the diagonal edge of the rectangle.**

The two new anchor points are displayed (Figure 9-18).

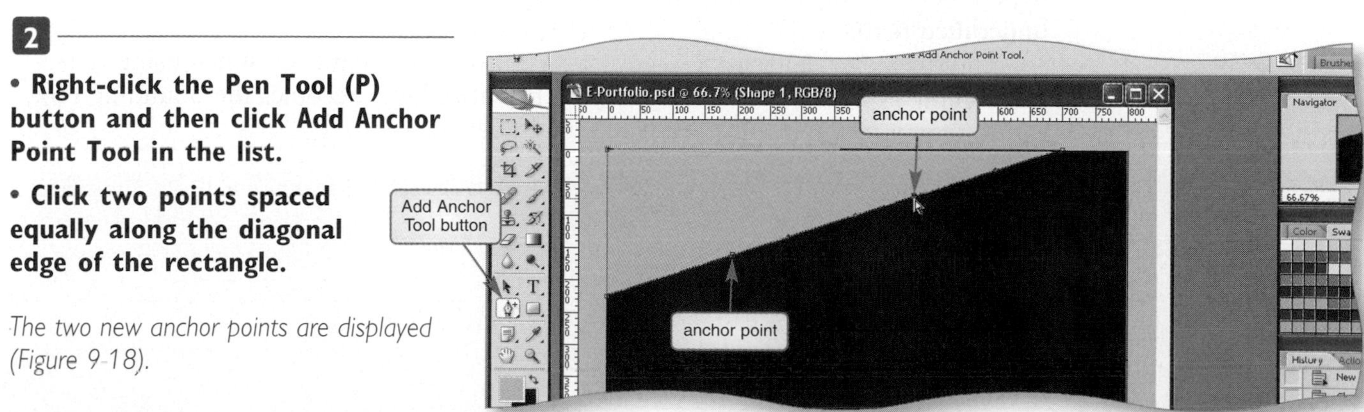

FIGURE 9-18

3

• **Right-click the current Selection tool button and then click Direct Selection Tool in the list.**

• **Drag the right new anchor point, down and to the left approximately 100 pixels.**

• **Drag the left new anchor point, up and slightly left as shown in Figure 9-19.**

Dragging each anchor point creates curved line segments.

4

• **On the Layers palette, double-click the Shape 1 layer name, type** `gold area` **and then press the ENTER key.**

The layer is renamed.

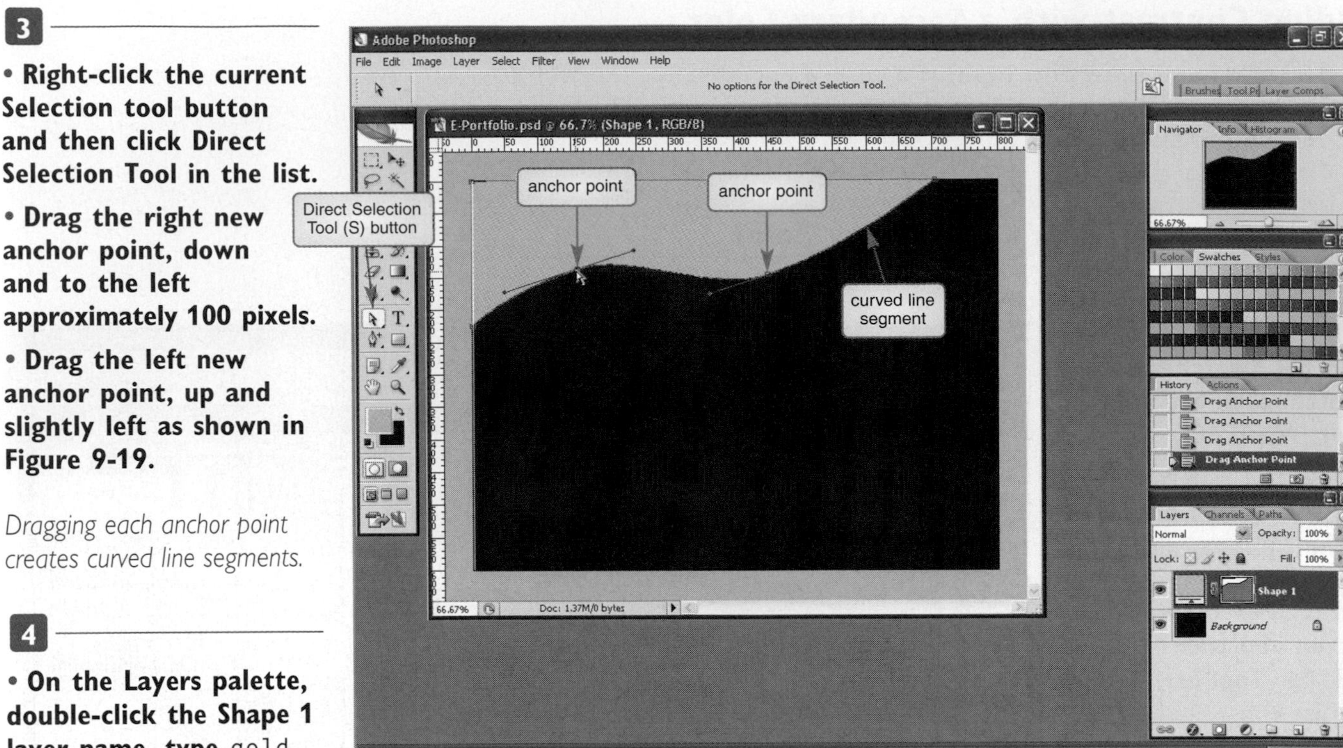

FIGURE 9-19

The background is complete. Using contrasting Web-safe colors and 800 × 600 pixels, the Web page will look good to all viewers.

Inserting the Heading

The heading, or headline text, is the first place that users will look. It is important to use both placement, font size, and font style to emphasis the text. Color is a secondary consideration for headings, because not all users will be able to distinguish colors. Contrast is the best choice for accessibility and readability. Also, because hyperlinks typically are underlined and blue, most Web designers avoid blue and underlined text.

The steps on the next page show how to insert heading text. When using the Horizontal Type tool with a shape layer, the entire layer becomes the bounding box, rather than a rectangular area created by dragging.

To Insert Heading Text

1

- **Press the X key to invert the colors.**
- **Press the T key. If the Horizontal Type tool is not active, right-click the current type tool button and then click Horizontal Type Tool in the list.**
- **In the document window, click the gold area.**
- **When the sizing handles are displayed, drag the upper-left sizing handle down and right so the box will begin approximately 25 pixels from the upper-left corner of the page.**

The resized type bounding box is ready for data entry (Figure 9-20). A new text layer is displayed on the Layers palette.

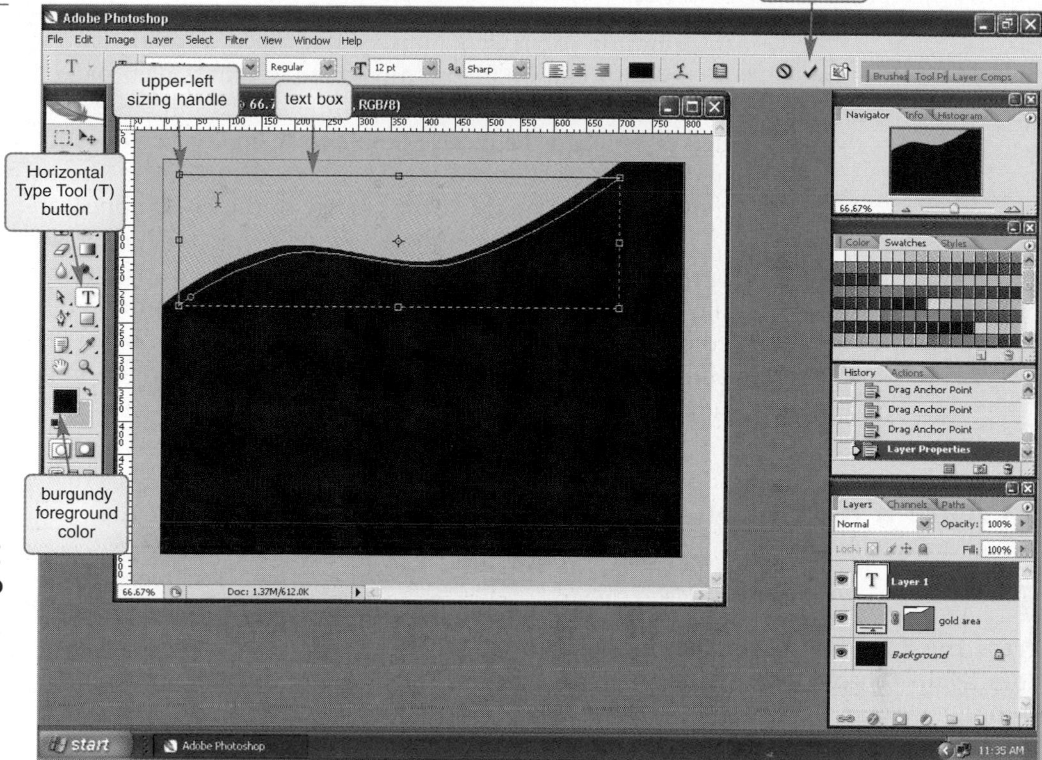

FIGURE 9-20

2

- **Using the box arrows on the options bar, select Arial, Bold, 72 pt, and Crisp.**
- **Click inside the type bounding box and then type** `My E-Portfolio` **to enter the heading text.**
- **On the options bar, click the Commit any current edits button.**

The heading text is displayed (Figure 9-21).

FIGURE 9-21

Creating Navigational Bars and Hyperlinks

A **hyperlink** is text or a graphic that, when clicked, opens a new Web page or jumps to a new location within the current page. Hyperlinks are useful to present information to viewers in accessible pieces rather than crowded on a home page. Hyperlinks can be placed anywhere within a Web page. Hyperlinks used to be identified by color and underline. While that is still common, many links now are identified only when the mouse points to them — they become highlighted, delineated, underlined, or changed graphically to denote their interactivity. When a mouse moves over a hyperlink, the change in the link's appearance is called a **rollover**.

Hyperlinks grouped horizontally or vertically that point to locations within the current Web site are called a **navigation bar**. Navigation bars typically are placed at the top, left, or bottom of a Web page. Many times a border, line, or background color change identifies the grouped links. In the E-Portfolio Web page, three text entries grouped by their placement within a navigation bar rectangle create hyperlinks as shown in the following steps.

To Create a Navigation Bar Rectangle

1

- **Press the x key to invert the colors again to gold and burgundy.**
- **Click the current shape tool in the toolbox.**
- **On the options bar, click the Shape layers button. If necessary, click the Rounded Rectangle Tool button, and the Create new shape layer button.**
- **Click the Style picker button and then point to the 1 Px Stroke 0% Fill Opacity style.**

Photoshop displays the default styles (Figure 9-22). Your list of styles may differ.

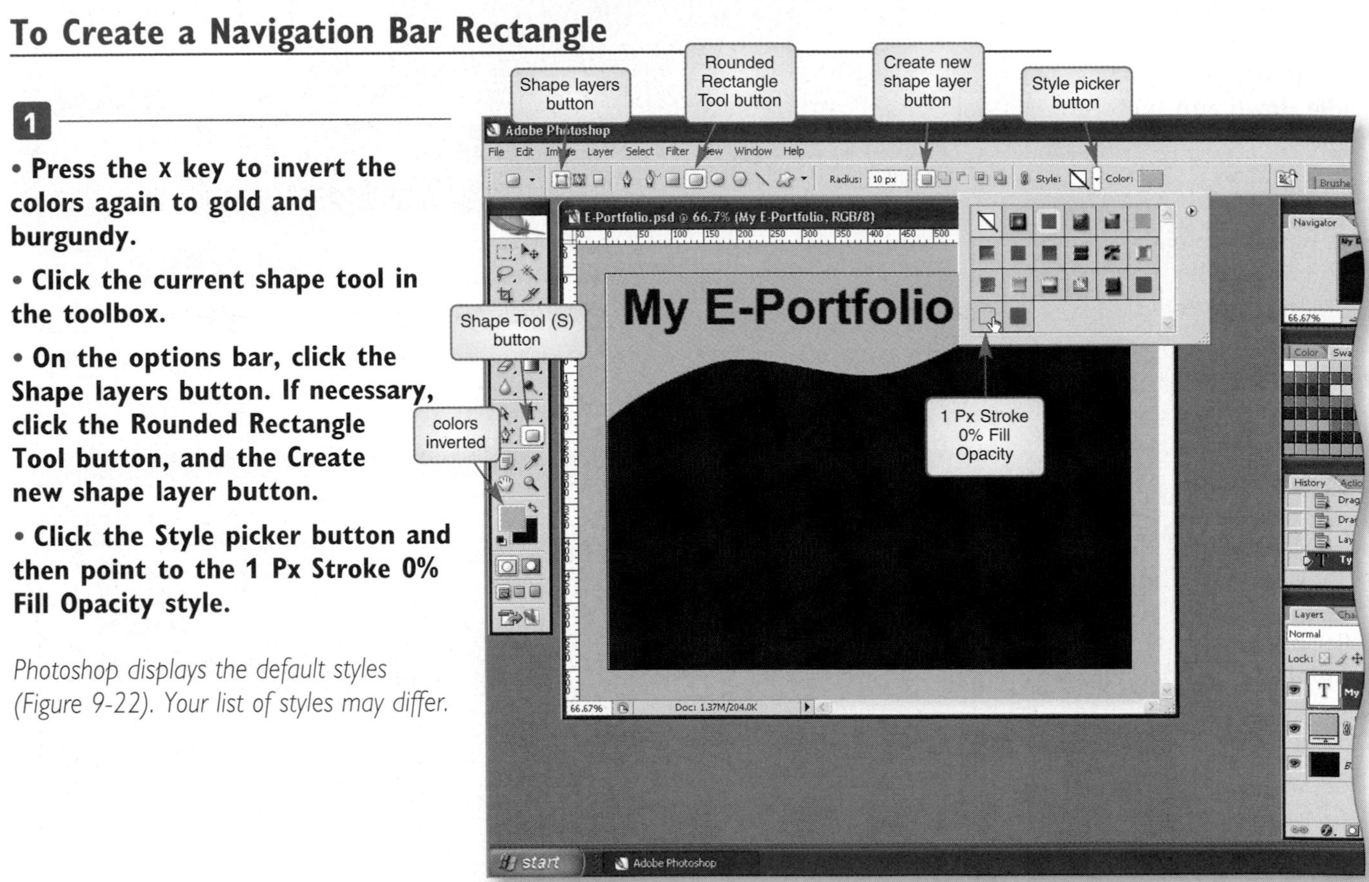

FIGURE 9-22

2

- **Click the 1 Px Stroke 0% Fill Opacity style.**
- **In the document window, beginning at the lower-left corner of the gold area, drag right and down to create a rectangle shape the full width of the page, approximately 115 pixels tall.**
- **On the Layers palette, double-click the Shape1 layer name. Type** `navigation bar` **and then press the ENTER key.**

Photoshop displays the shape in the document window (Figure 9-23). The layer is renamed.

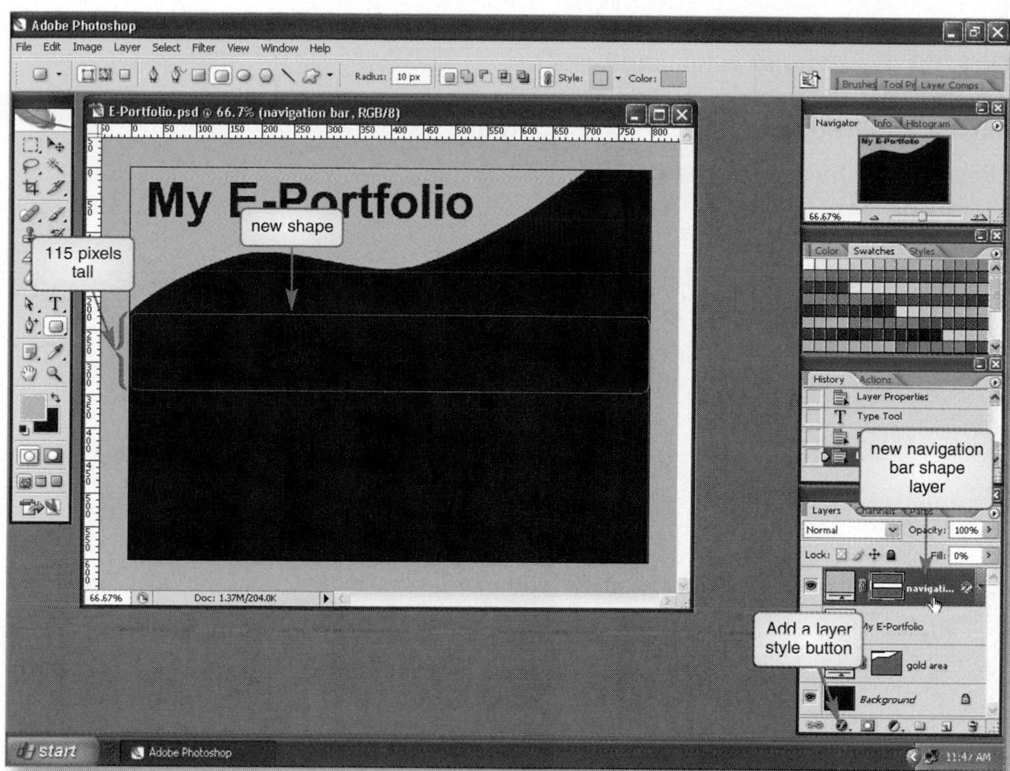

FIGURE 9-23

3

- **On the Layers palette, click the Add a layer style button. When the list is displayed, click Stroke, if necessary.**
- **When Photoshop displays the Layer Style dialog box, type** 6 **in the Size box.**
- **Click the Color box.**
- **Point to the foreground color in the toolbox.**

Photoshop displays the eyedropper, allowing you to pick up a color from anywhere on the screen (Figure 9-24).

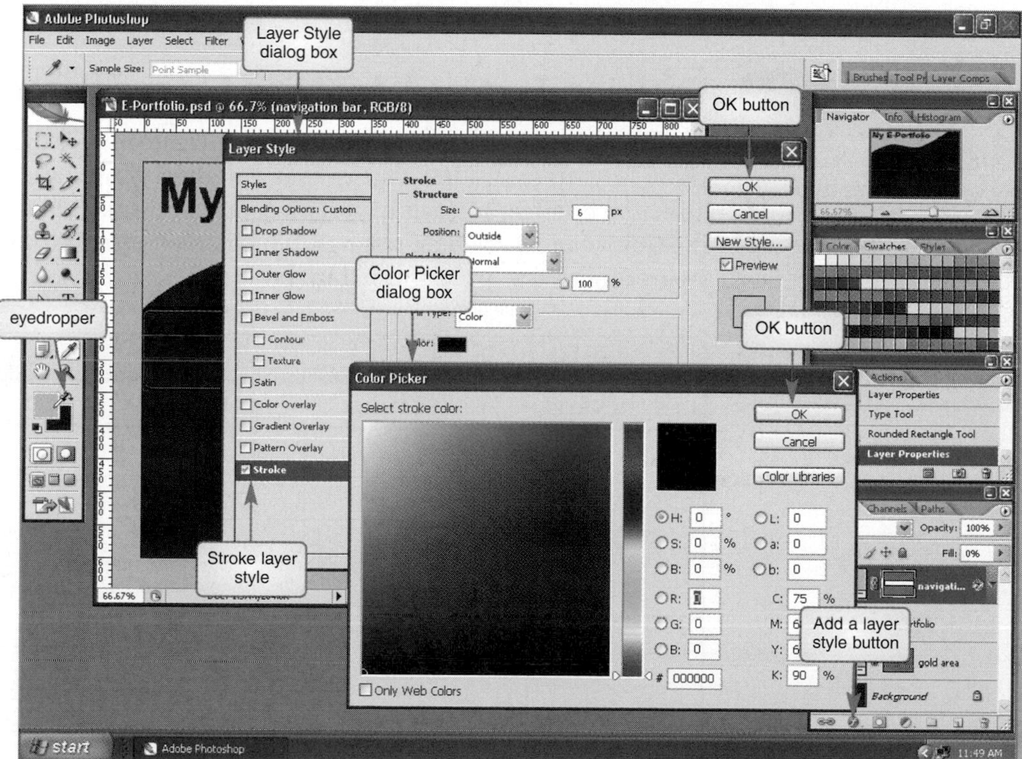

FIGURE 9-24

4

- **Click the Foreground color and then click the OK button in the Color Picker dialog box.**
- **Click the OK button in the Layer Style dialog box.**

The border of the rectangle shape is displayed six pixels wide and gold colored (Figure 9-25).

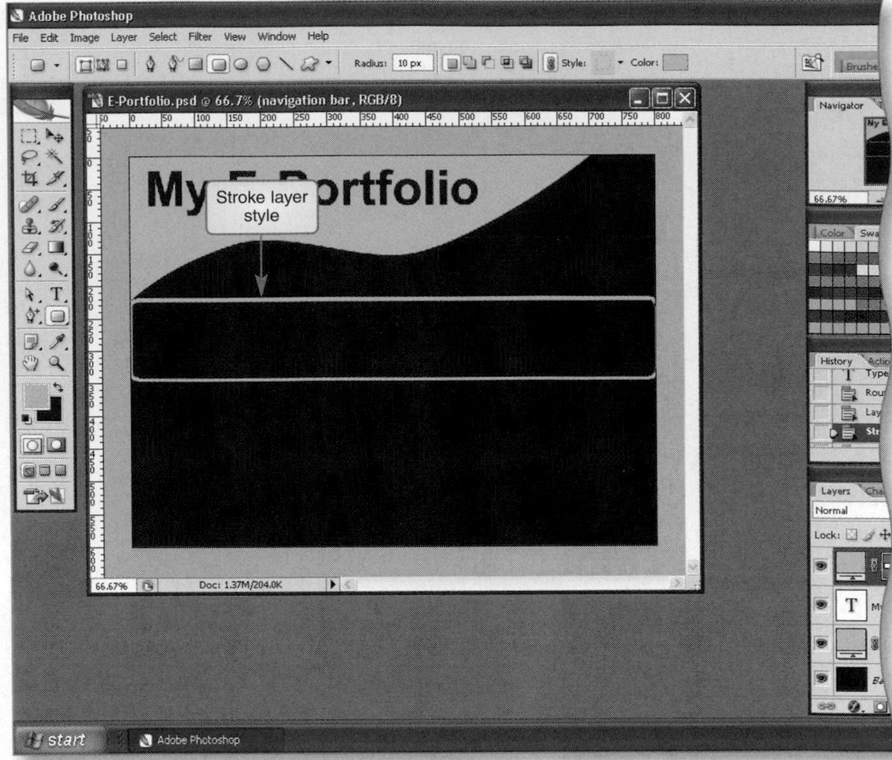

FIGURE 9-25

More About

Styles

In a lab situation, someone may have loaded different styles into the Styles picker box. If you want to reset the styles back to the defaults, click the Style picker box arrow, click its menu button, and then click Reset Styles.

Entering Text and Applying Layer Effects

With the rectangle in place for the navigation bar, the steps on the next page show how to create text entries that will display as static hyperlinks. You then will add a layer effect to each hyperlink that will display when the mouse is rolled over the link. The layer effect settings, which create brighter, enlarged lettering with a spattering effect, are displayed in Table 9-3.

Table 9-3 Layer Effect Settings

LAYER STYLE	SETTING	VALUE
Outer Glow	Blend Mode	Screen
	Opacity	62
	Noise	1
	Gradient	Foreground to Background
	Technique	Softer
	Spread	34
	Size	10
Bevel and Emboss	Style	Outer Bevel
	Technique	Smooth

To Enter Text and Apply Layer Effects

1

- **In the Layers palette, scroll as necessary and then click the Background Layer.**
- **Press the T key to access the Horizontal Type tool.**
- **In the document window, drag a box in the left portion of the navigation bar rectangle, approximately 200 pixels wide and 100 pixels tall.**

The new type bounding box is displayed in the navigation bar (Figure 9-26).

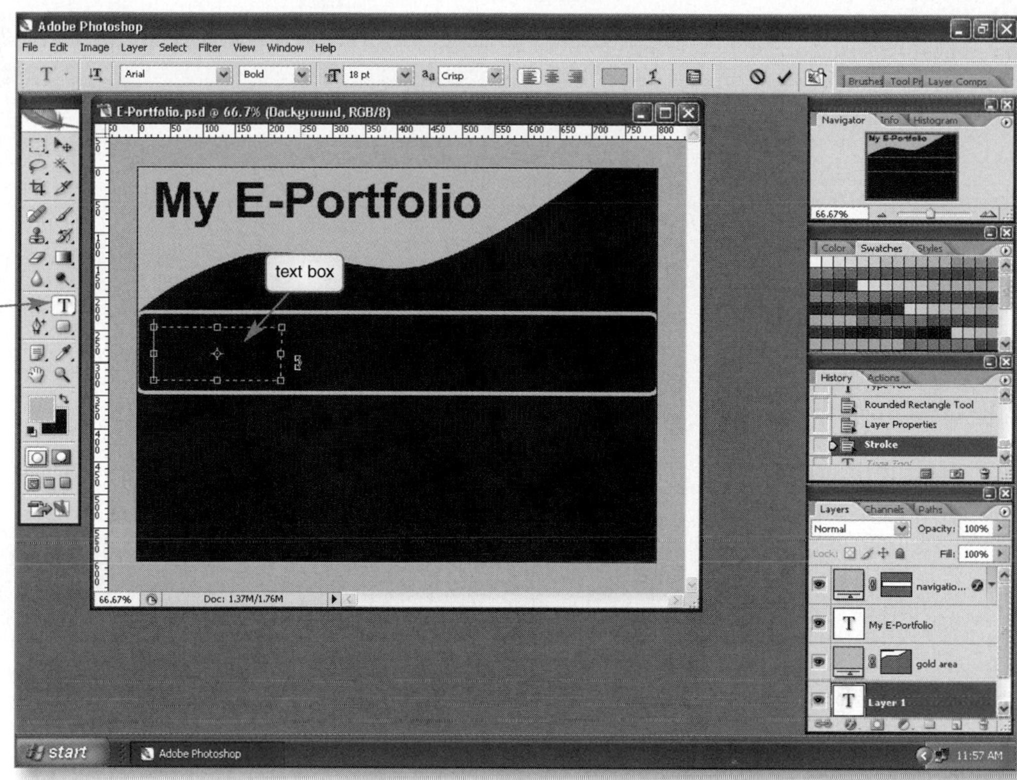

FIGURE 9-26

2

- **Using the box arrows on the options bar, select Georgia, Bold, 48 pt, and Crisp.**
- **Type `Gallery` in the type bounding box as shown in Figure 9-27.**

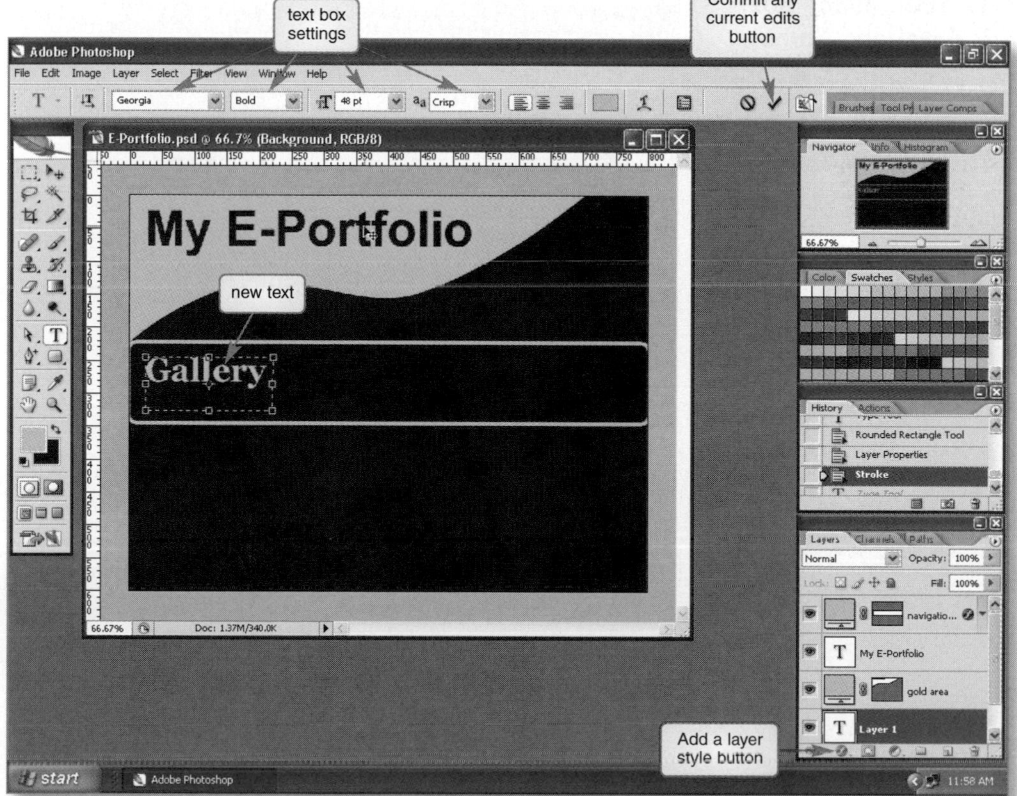

FIGURE 9-27

3

- **On the options bar, click the Commit any current edits button.**
- **On the Layers palette, click the Add a layer style button, and then click Outer Glow on the shortcut menu.**
- **When the Layer Style dialog box is displayed, enter the Outer Glow settings from Table 9-3 on page PS 568. Leave all other settings at their default values.**

The Outer Glow settings are displayed in Figure 9-28.

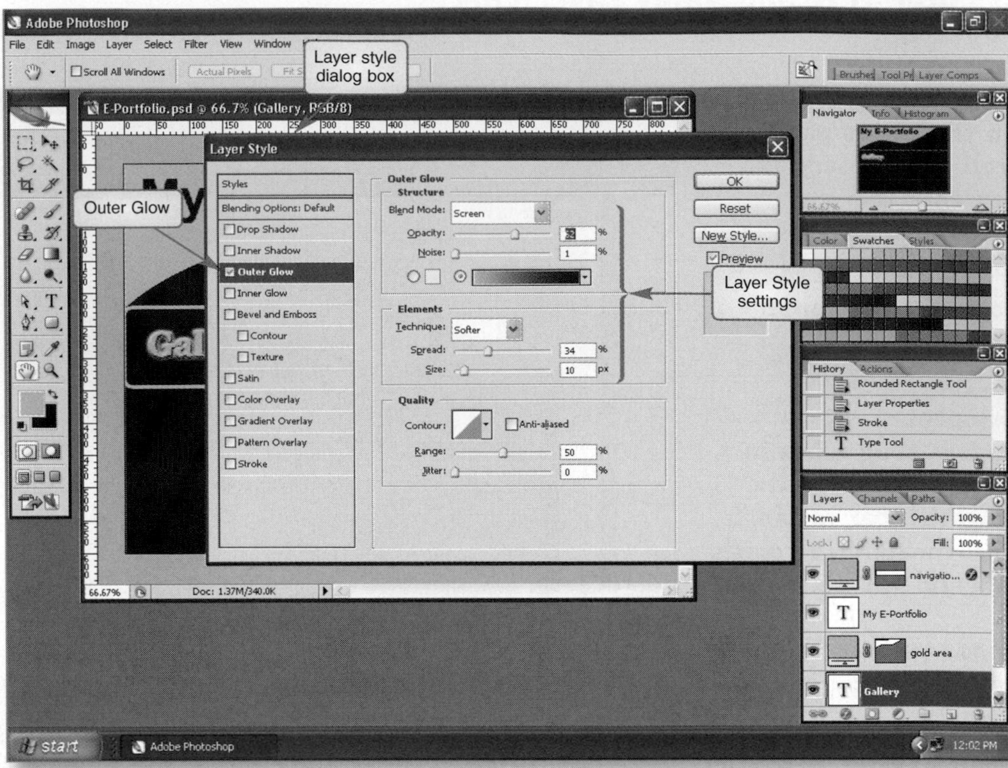

FIGURE 9-28

- **On the left side of the Layer Style dialog box, click Bevel and Emboss.**
- **Enter the Bevel and Emboss settings from Table 9-3. Leave all other settings at their default values.**

The Bevel and Emboss settings currently are displayed in Figure 9-29.

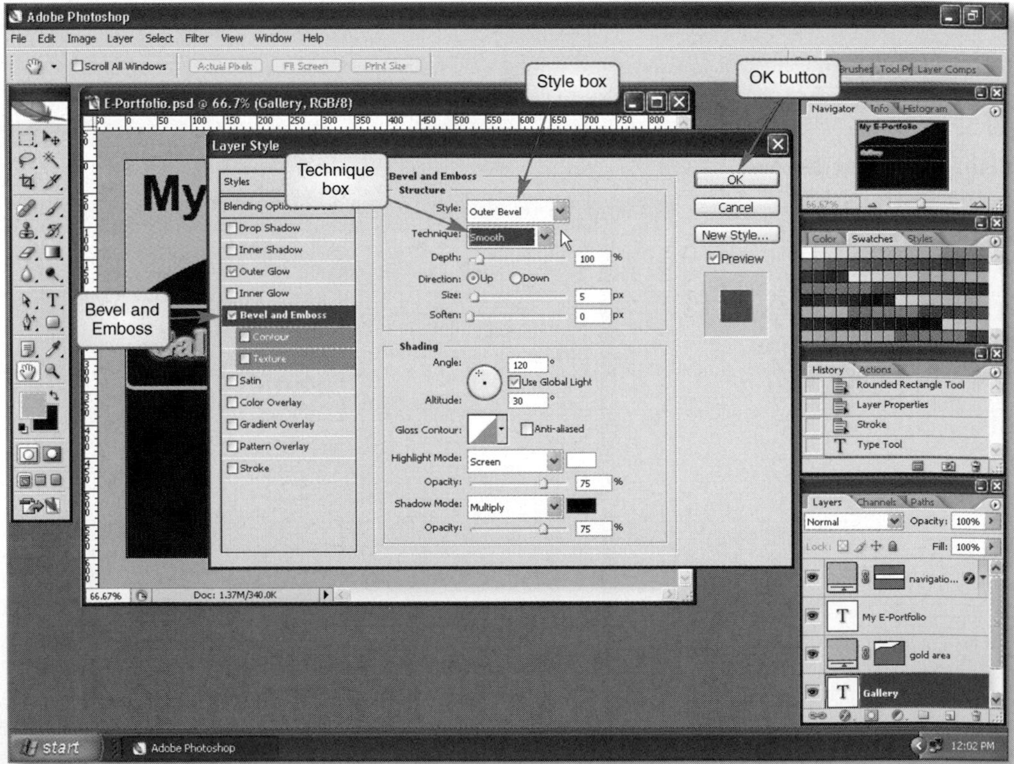

FIGURE 9-29

5

• **Click the OK button in the Layer Style dialog box.**

The layer is displayed with special effects (Figure 9-30).

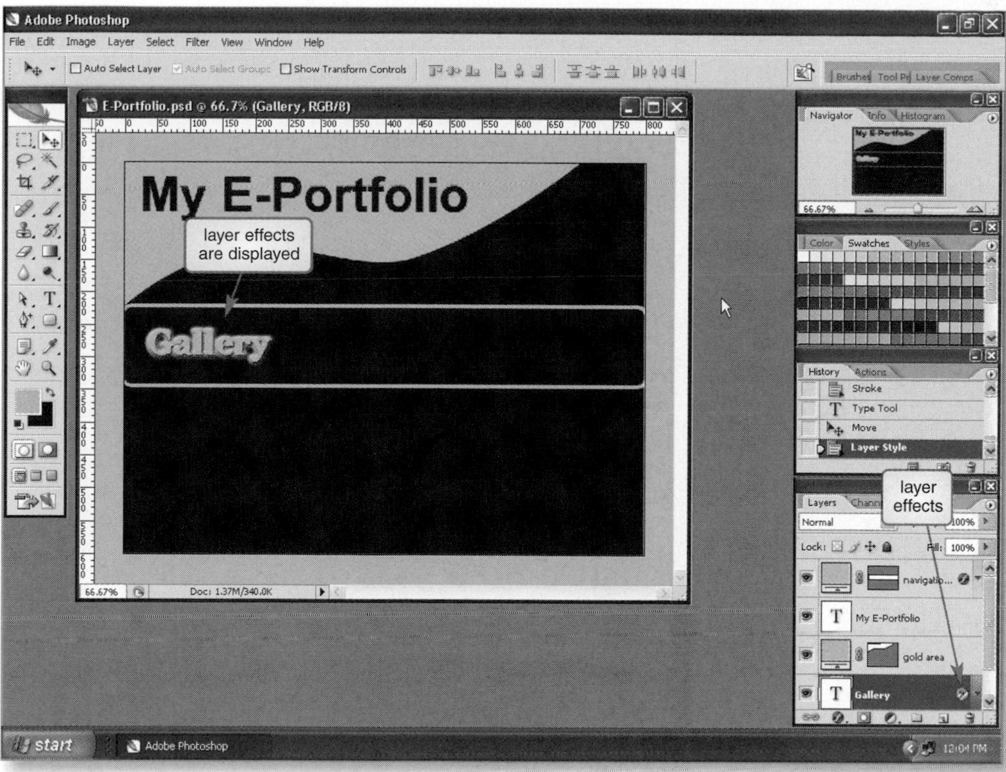

FIGURE 9-30

6

• **Press the** V **key and** ALT**+drag the text to the right, to create a new copy.**

• **Press the** T **key. Double-click the text in the new copy to select it, and then type** Resume **in the type bounding box. Resize the box, if necessary.**

• **Click the Commit any current edits button on the options bar.**

The duplicated layer is displayed with its new text (Figure 9-31). A new layer is created on the Layers palette

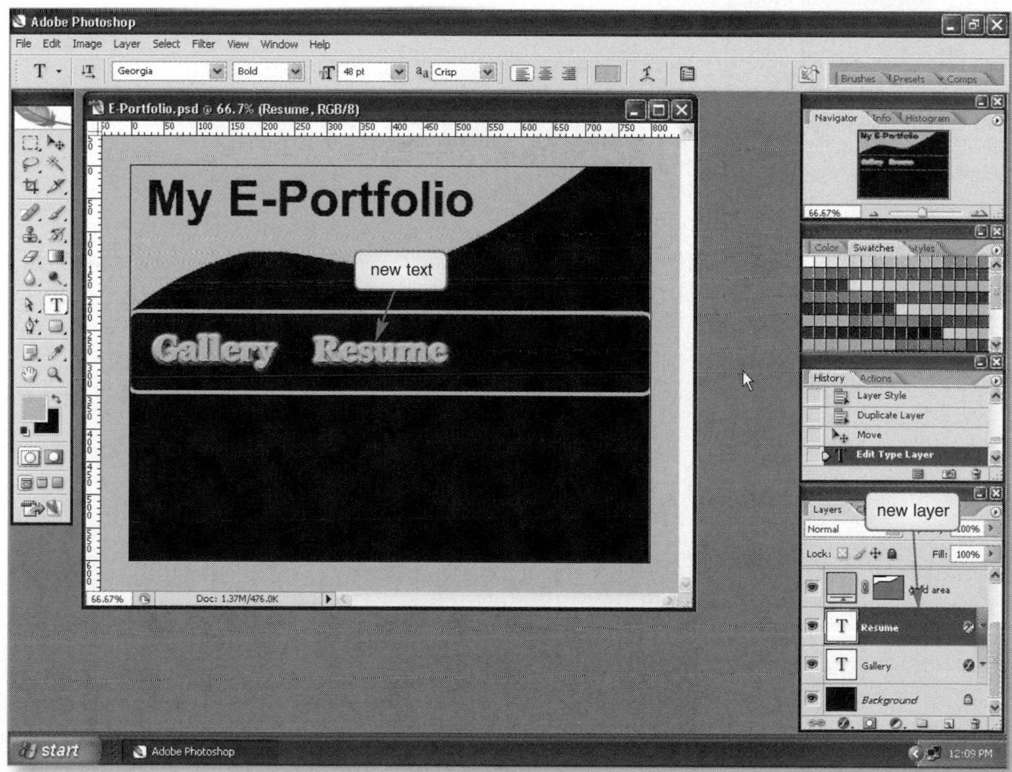

FIGURE 9-31

7

- **Repeat Step 6 to create another layer with the text, Contact. Position the layer on the right side in the navigation bar.**

The layer is displayed with its new position, text, and name (Figure 9-32).

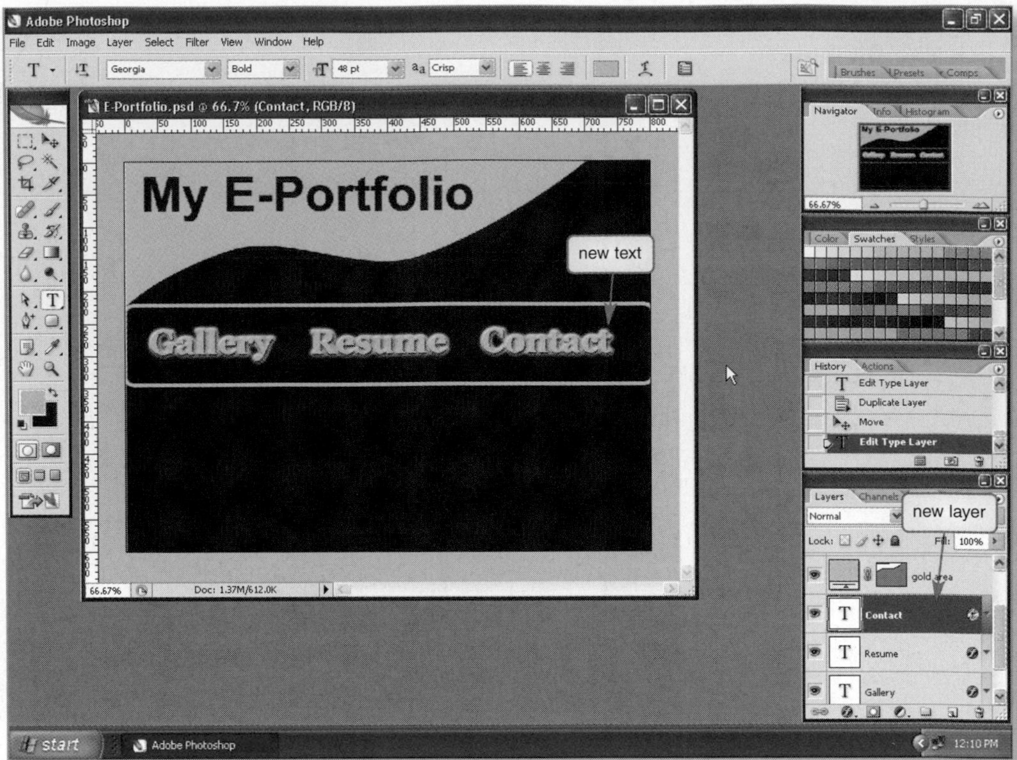

FIGURE 9-32

> ***More About***
>
> **Rollovers**
>
> Photoshop's many layer effects and filters provide an endless number of special effects that can be used for rollovers. The goal of a rollover is to draw attention while still making any text legible. It is a good idea to look at examples on the Web and get ideas for rollovers that help the user find hyperlinks and invite user interaction. For some rollover examples, visit the Shelly Cashman Photoshop Web site.

Creating Rollovers

Recall that a change in a link's appearance when the mouse pointer moves over it is called a rollover. Creating a rollover is a three-step process. First, you must create both a version of what the link will look like in its static state as well as a version of the rolled over state. The text entry that you created in the previous steps is the static version; the layer effects will become the rollover version. Second, you must identify the hyperlink by creating a slice. Finally, you will use ImageReady to specify the two states and the destination of the hyperlink.

Hyperlink Slices

A **slice** is a defined rectangular area of an image that becomes functional as a hyperlink. Slices also can be used for animation. Slices give you better control over the function and file size of your image, because slices can be optimized individually. When you save a sliced image for the Web, each slice is saved as an independent file with its own settings and color palette, and the proper links, rollover effects, and animation effects are preserved.

You can create a slice by using the Slice tool or by creating layer-based slices. Once created, a slice can be selected, moved, resized, or aligned. Each slice can be assigned an individual hyperlink and linked with animation or layer style changes for a rollover effect.

The steps on the next page illustrate how to make slices.

To Make Hyperlink Slices

1

- **On the Layers palette, select the Gallery layer.**
- **In the toolbox, click the Slice Tool (K) button.**
- **In the document window, drag a rectangle around the word, Gallery.**

Photoshop slices the page into five, numbered pieces, a slice around the word, Gallery, and slices on each of the four sides (Figure 9-33). The slice badge indicates that the slice contains colored pixels or images. The mouse pointer displays a Slice icon.

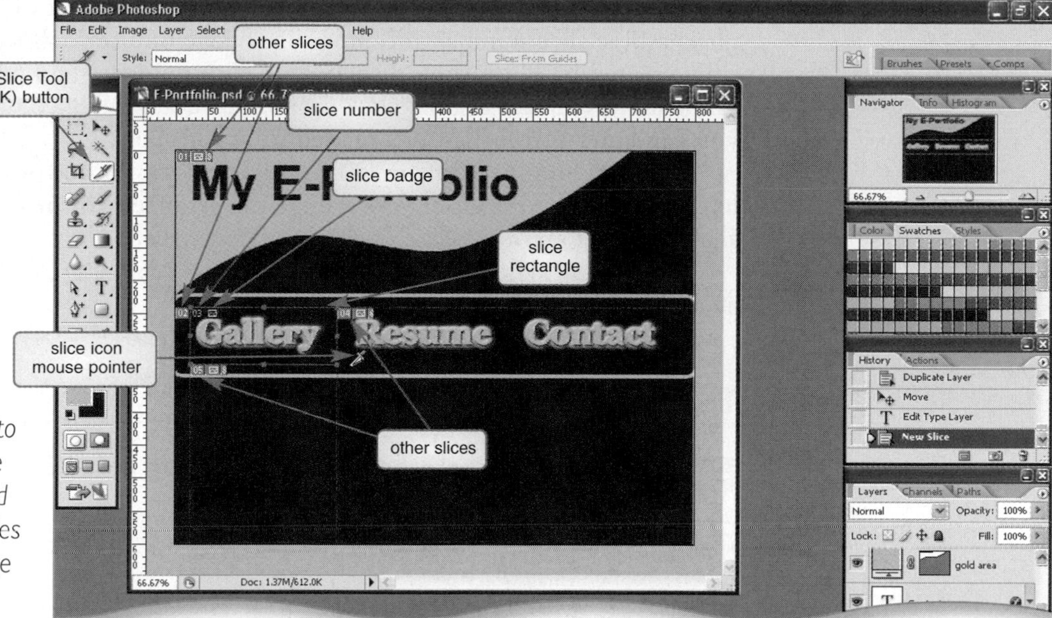

FIGURE 9-33

2

- **On the Layers palette, select the Resume layer.**
- **In the document window, drag a rectangle around the word, Resume.**
- **On the Layers palette, select the Contact layer.**
- **In the document window, drag a rectangle around the word, Contact.**

Photoshop slices the page into more pieces. As new slices are created, Photoshop renumbers the slices. In Figure 9-34, slices 3, 4, and 5 are user-created slices. Slices 1, 2, 6, and 7 were automatically generated by Photoshop. Your slices and numbers may differ.

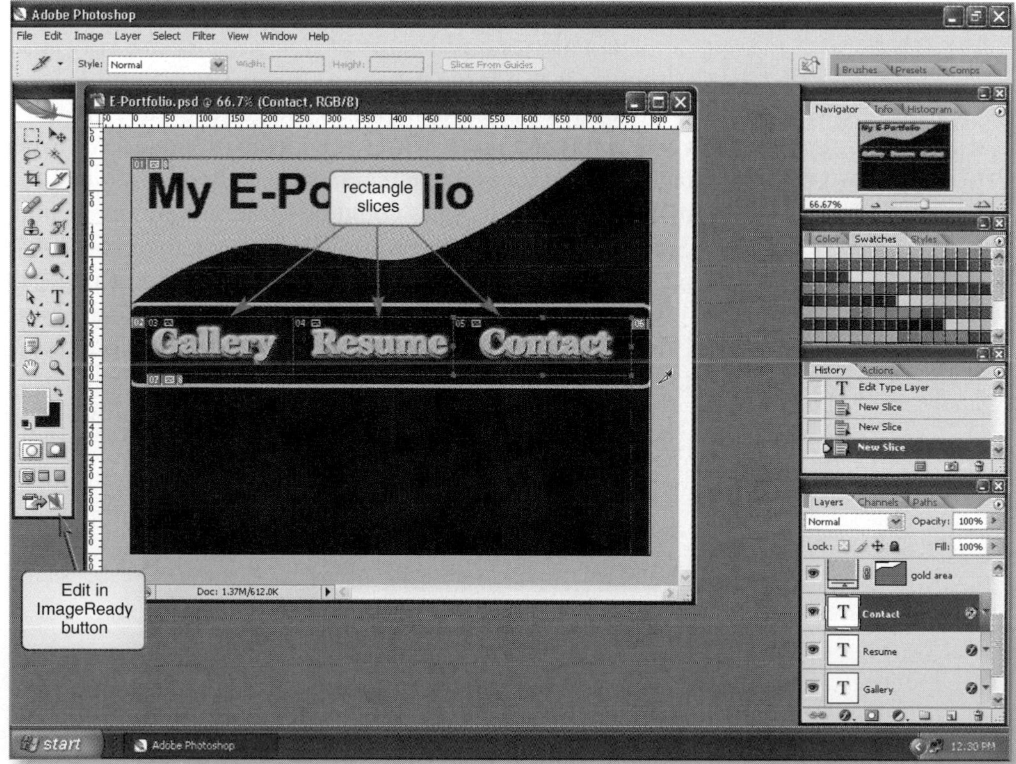

FIGURE 9-34

Other Ways

1. On Layer menu, click New Layer Based Slice

When a slice is created, Photoshop displays a number and a badge (Figure 9-33). A **slice badge** is an icon that displays next to the slice number, indicating certain information about the slice. A slice badge might indicate whether or not the slice is linked, is layer based, includes a rollover effect, or is part of a table. Photoshop displays a blue slice number and blue slice badge on user-defined slices; slices automatically created by Photoshop display gray slice numbers and gray slice badges. In Photoshop, you can double-click a badge to open the Slice Options dialog box where you can enter certain settings related to hyperlinks.

Slices are numbered from left to right and top to bottom, beginning in the upper-left corner of the image. If you change the arrangement or total number of slices, slice numbers are updated to reflect the new order.

With many slices, layers, and layer styles, it is a good time to save the file again as demonstrated in the following step.

To Save the File Again

1 Press CTRL+S. If Photoshop displays a dialog box, click the OK button.

The file is saved.

Using ImageReady

> *More About*
>
> **Optimization**
>
> Optimization is the act of balancing the quality of an image with its file size. Because large graphic files can make a Web page load slowly, achieving the smallest file size possible without compromising picture quality is critical. The Web preview dialog boxes in both Photoshop and ImageReady allow you to compare results and settings for up to four versions and make the best choice for your Web page.

Adobe **ImageReady** is a Web production software program included with Photoshop. It allows you to optimize, choose layouts, preview Web pages in a browser, and animate images. Because ImageReady is fully integrated with Photoshop, you can jump seamlessly between the two programs just as you do with Adobe Bridge.

The palettes and menus in ImageReady are very similar to those in Photoshop. Although it is a large program, ImageReady can be used easily if you know how Photoshop works. Some things ImageReady does better than Photoshop and vice versa. ImageReady is better for image mapping. An **image map** is a graphic containing one or more invisible regions, called hotspots, which are hyperlinked. For example, a map of the United States could be sliced into an image map by assigning hotspots to each state. Clicking the state would cause the browser to display a different Web page or move to another location on the current page. In addition, ImageReady has advanced features as animated GIF creation, image compression optimization, and HTML code generation, including table definition and the ability to include JavaScript code to implement Web sites.

ImageReady can be launched from Photoshop by using the Edit in ImageReady button as shown in the step on the next page.

To Launch ImageReady

1

- **Click the Edit in ImageReady button at the bottom of the Photoshop toolbox.**
- **After a wait, when the E-Portfolio image displays in ImageReady, click Window on the ImageReady menu bar. Point to Workspace and then click Default Palette Locations.**

The Edit in ImageReady button causes Photoshop to launch ImageReady and load the image there (Figure 9-35). The time that it takes varies from system to system. Notice that both the Photoshop and ImageReady applications are open and display buttons on the Windows taskbar.

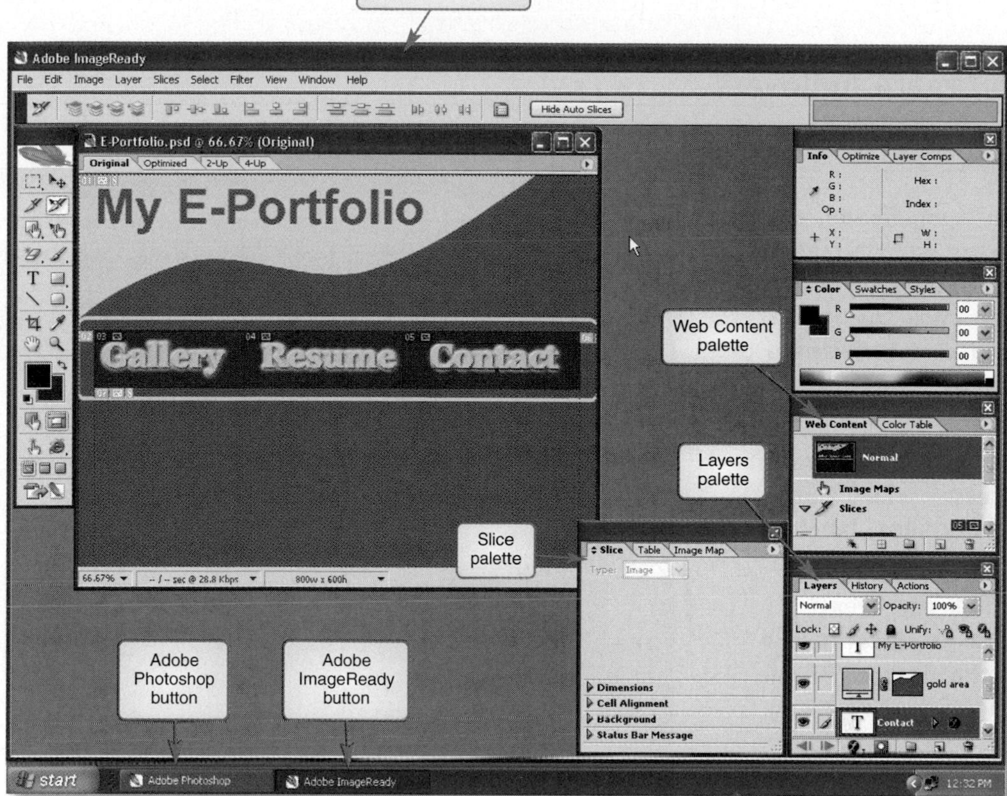

FIGURE 9-35

Other Ways

1. To launch ImageReady, click Windows Start button, point to All programs, click Adobe ImageReady CS2
2. To open a file in ImageReady, press CTRL+O, browse to file

Using ImageReady to Create Rollovers

While Photoshop has a Slice tool that effectively cuts apart pieces of a Web page for optimization purposes or for hyperlinks, the ability to create rollovers exists exclusively in ImageReady. Rollovers are created by using the Web Content palette, which is displayed in Figure 9-36. First, you create a rollover state by clicking the Create rollover state button at the bottom of the palette. Then, you set the visibility for both the static slice and its rollover. The slice, as the static state, will have no visible special effects. The rollover will display the previously created layer effects.

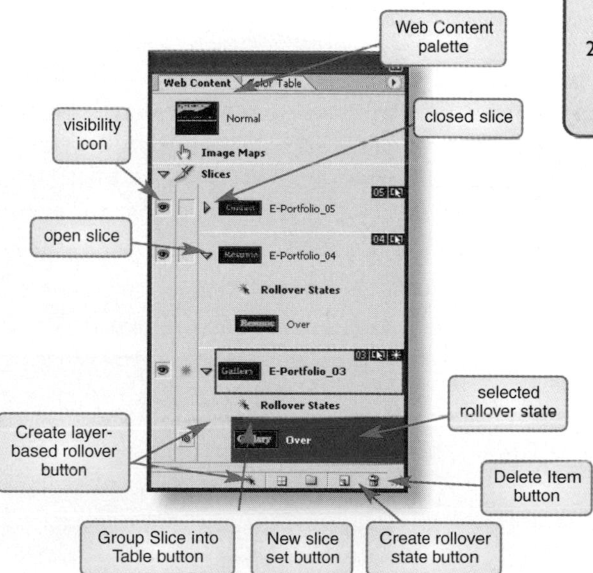

FIGURE 9-36

The following steps create the rollovers using the Web Content palette and the Layers palette.

To Create Rollovers

1

- **In ImageReady, on the Layers palette, select the Gallery layer and then click the Indicates layer effects triangle to display its attached layer effects.**
- **On the Web Content palette, select the Gallery slice, labeled E-Portfolio_03.**
- **Click the Create rollover state button at the bottom of the palette.**

The Outer Glow and Bevel and Emboss effects are displayed below the word, Effects, on the Layers palette (Figure 9-37). The Web Content palette displays a rollover state below the E-Portfolio_03 slice.

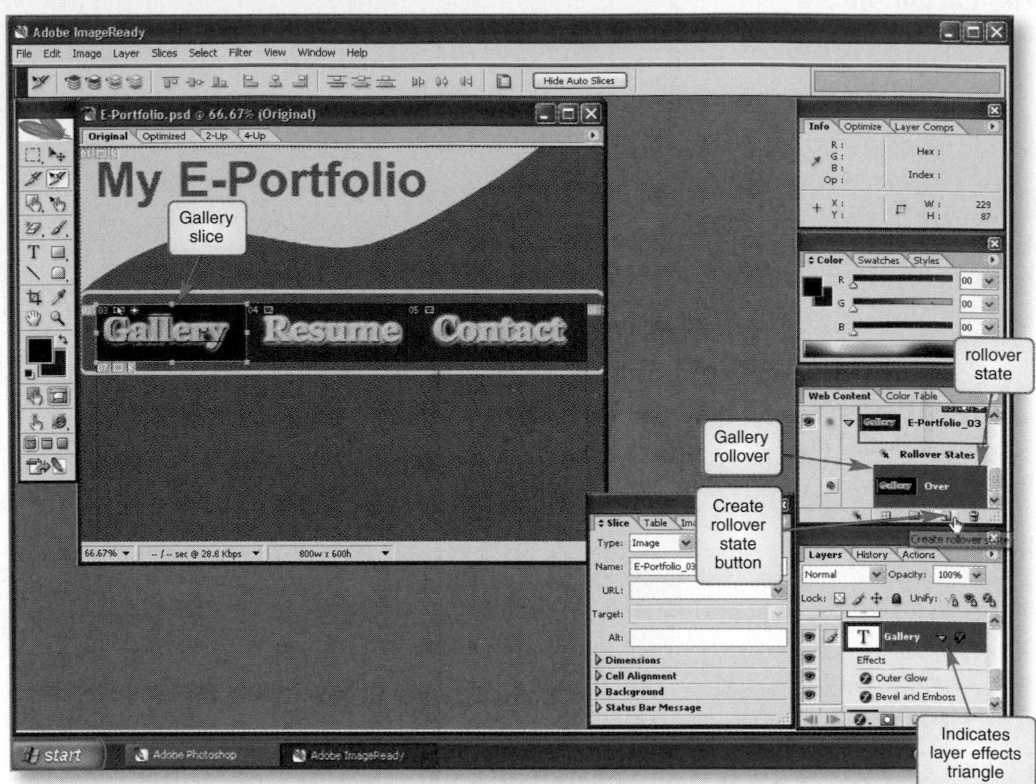

FIGURE 9-37

2

- **On the Web Content palette, click the Gallery slice to select it.**
- **On the Layers palette, click to remove the visibility icon beside the word, Effects.**

The layer effect is turned off for the Gallery slice (Figure 9-38).

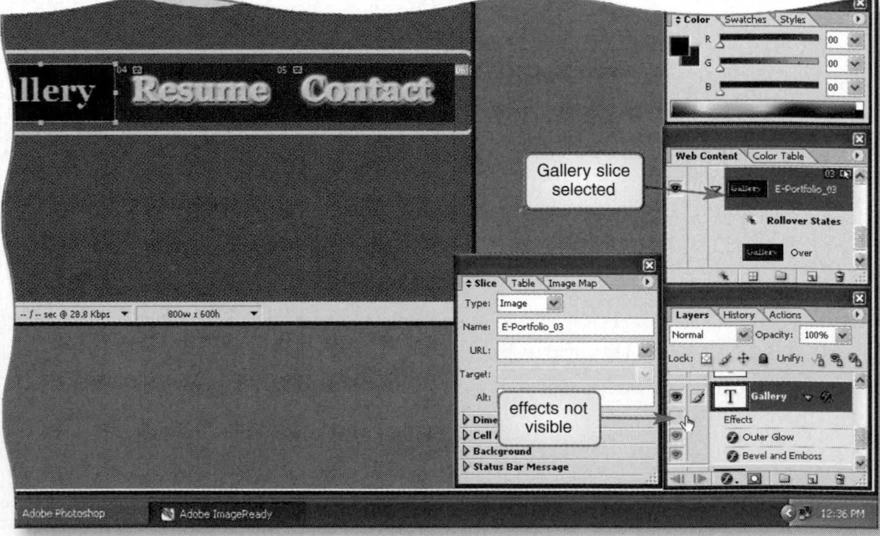

FIGURE 9-38

3

- **On the Web Content palette, click the Gallery slice rollover state, labeled Over.**
- **On the Layers palette, click to display the visibility icon beside the word, Effects.**

The layer effect is turned on for the Rollover state (Figure 9-39).

4

- **Repeat Steps 1 through 4 for the Resume and Contact layers.**

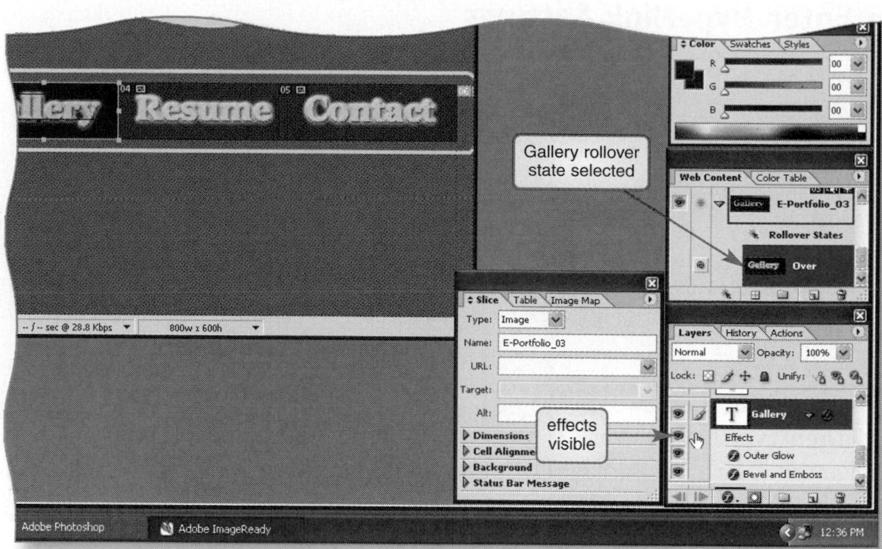

FIGURE 9-39

It is important to remember that any change made with the slice selected, creates the static state. Changes made while the rollover is selected, creates the rollover state.

Hyperlink Settings

The Slice palette (Figure 9-40) allows you to set values associated with the hyperlink. The Type setting allows you to choose between image slices, an empty portion of the image with perhaps only color, or table slices that act as containers for a subset of slices, also called a nested table.

Recall that each slice becomes a small image when converted to HTML. The name of that image is supplied automatically by ImageReady, although it can be changed. The **URL** box holds the desired Web page address or a relative location. The **Target** box allows you to specify how the link will open — in a new page or in the current page. For example, a target setting of _blank will cause the hyperlink to open the Web page in a new browser window. The **Alt** box is used to create alternate text used by aural screen readers. The text also is displayed as a tool tip in most browsers and as place-holder text when a user chooses not to download graphics. At the bottom of the Slice palette are other settings related to Web pages.

In the E-Portfolio image, you will enter hyperlink settings for only the Gallery slice. The link will take Web page visitors to the index.htm page of the Web photo gallery, as shown in the steps on the next page.

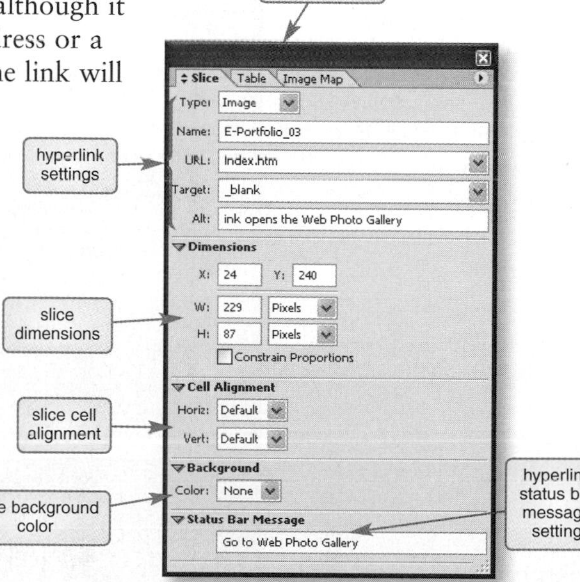

FIGURE 9-40

To Enter Hyperlink Settings

1

- **On the Web Content palette, select the Gallery slice.**
- **On the Slice palette, click the URL box and then type** `index.htm` **as the entry.**
- **Click the Target box and then type** `_blank` **as the entry.**
- **Click the Alt box and then type** `This link opens the Web photo gallery` **as the entry.**

The hyperlink settings are displayed on the Slice palette (Figure 9-41). The file, index.htm, is the name of the Web photo gallery page created earlier in this project.

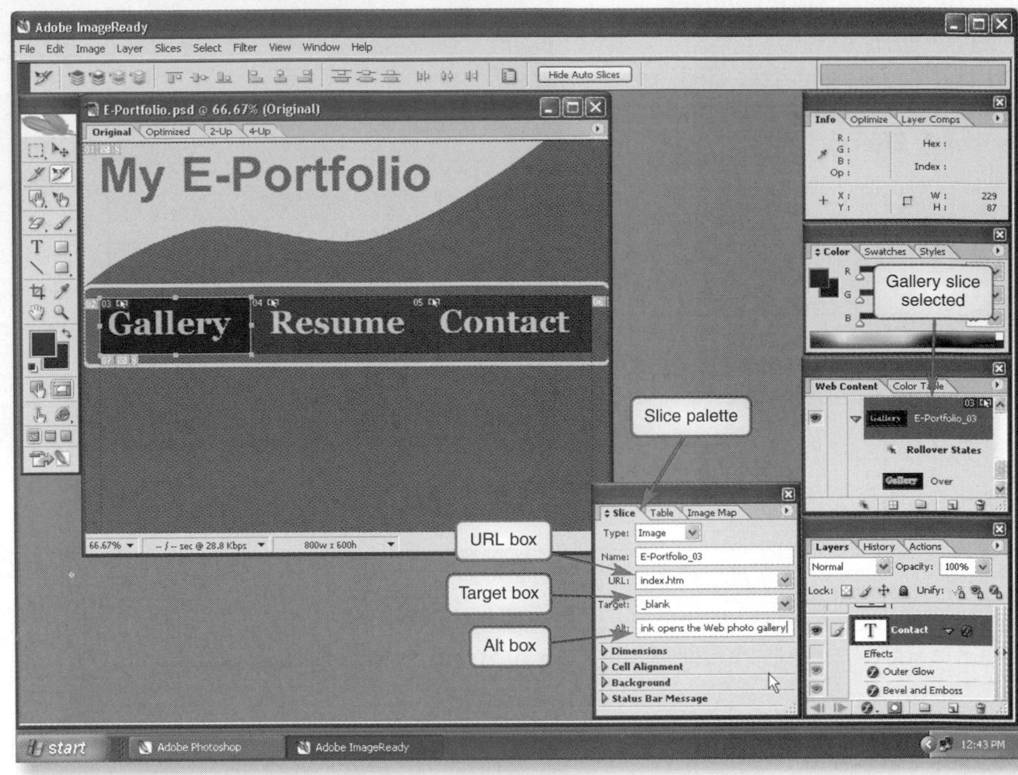

FIGURE 9-41

2

- **Click the triangle beside Status Bar Message in the lower portion of the Slice palette.**
- **When the Status Bar Message box is displayed, type** `Go to Web photo gallery` **as the entry.**

The message will be displayed on the browser's status bar during a rollover of the slice (Figure 9-42).

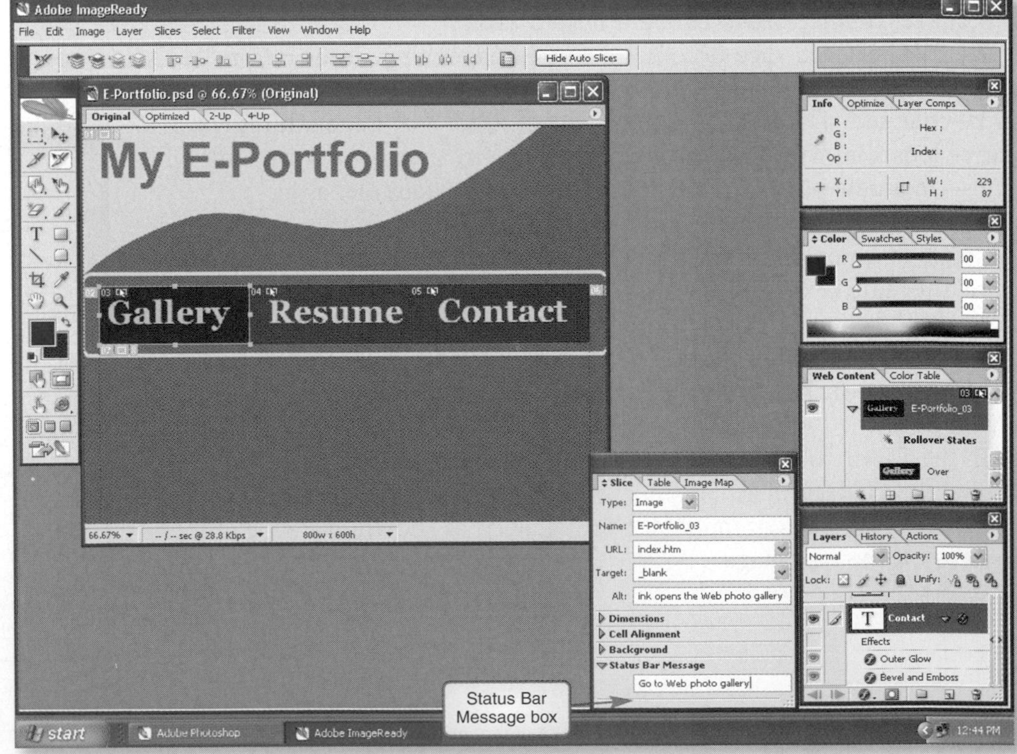

FIGURE 9-42

1. In Photoshop, double-click slice icon, enter settings

A URL without a full Web address, such as index.htm, creates a **relative reference** and links to a page within the site (Figure 9-41). An **absolute reference** has a full notation such as C:/Documents and Settings/index.htm, or http://www.scsite.com. The target designation, _blank, will force either kind of reference to open in a new window when the hyperlink is clicked.

More About

Target Tags

HTML target tags can be used in the Target box on the Slice palette. The _blank tag displays the linked file in a new window, leaving the original browser window open. The _self tag displays the linked file in the same frame as the original file. The _parent tag displays the linked file in its own original parent frameset. The _top tag replaces the entire browser window with the linked file, removing all current frames.

Previewing the Web Page

ImageReady has a button in its toolbox to preview the image or Web page within a browser. While that is fine for viewing the page and its rollover effects, it will not connect to hyperlinks unless you are connected to the Web. Because the preview is created in a temporary location, also known as a temp file on your system, the preview will not connect to relative links at all.

The steps on the following page illustrate how to preview the rollover effect.

To Preview the Rollover Effect

1

- **In the ImageReady toolbox, click the Preview In (browser) button.**
- **After a wait, when the browser window opens, if a yellow security bar displays across the top of the window, click it and then click Allow Blocked Content on the shortcut menu.**
- **If Windows displays a security warning dialog box, click the Yes button.**

The browser window opens and the Web page is displayed (Figure 9-43). The Preview In (browser) button will display the name of the default Web browser.

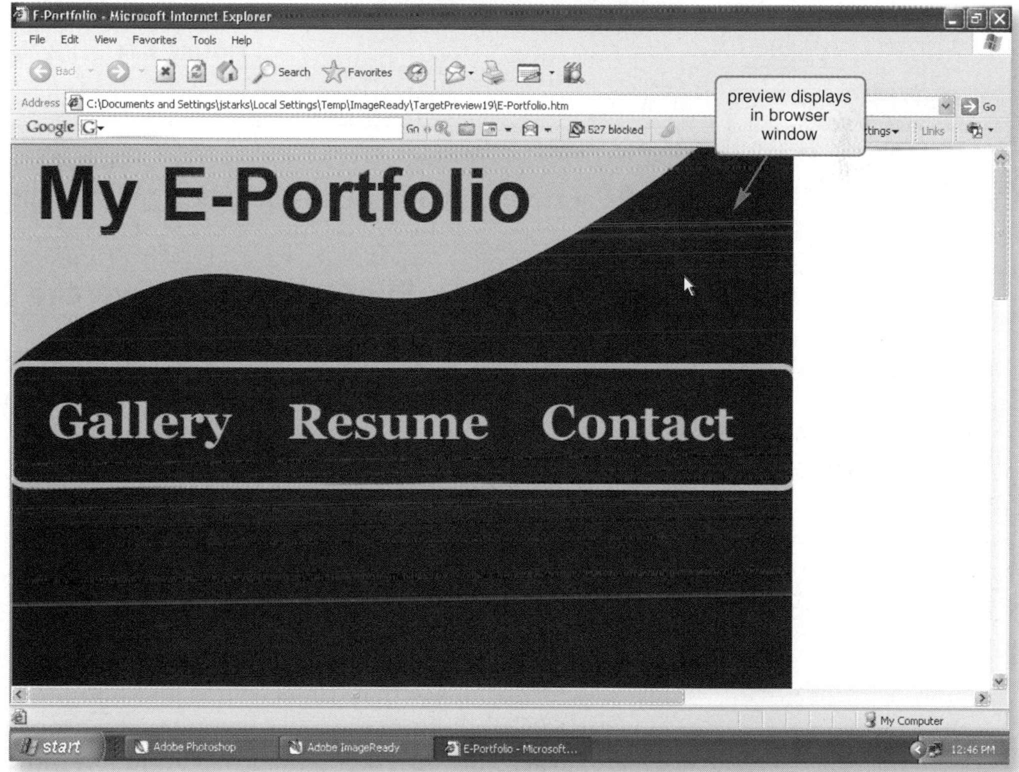

FIGURE 9-43

• **Move the mouse pointer over the Gallery link.**

The rollover is displayed with the special effects and the status bar message (Figure 9-44). The alternate text briefly displays in a tool tip window.

3

• **Click the Close button on the browser title bar.**

The browser window is closed and the ImageReady Workspace again is displayed.

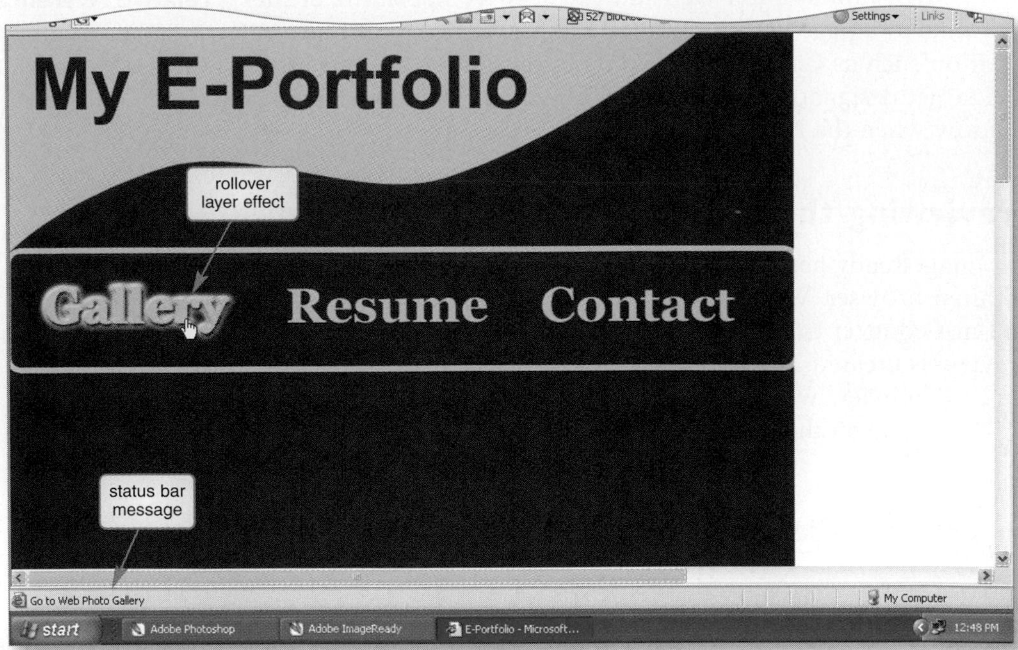

FIGURE 9-44

Other Ways

1. In Photoshop, on File menu, click Save for Web, click Preview in Default Browser button

The next steps jump back to Photoshop and save the file.

To Jump Back to Photoshop and Save the File

1. **Click the Edit in Photoshop button in the ImageReady toolbox.**
2. **When Photoshop again displays the image, press CTRL+S.**

The file is saved.

Using Animation

An **animation** is a sequence of frames or images, displayed over time. A **frame** is a single view of the image that can be edited and optimized. Each frame in an animation is varied slightly from the preceding frame by changing effects, filters, or repositioning objects. This variation creates the illusion of movement when the frames are viewed or played in quick succession. Professional animators create hundreds or thousands of frames, each with a tiny change from the one before it, to emulate smooth movement. In small animations, also called animated GIFs, which are used on the Web, the number of frames varies, but commonly includes from 5 to 50 frames.

Animation can be created using a wide variety of application software. While Photoshop and ImageReady are high-end graphic editing tools, they are not designed to create more advanced animations with film or movie quality. You can create basic animations in both software packages, however. In ImageReady, you even can import a folder of images as an animation; ImageReady will create a frame from each image, automatically.

To learn all of the animation and optimization features in Photoshop and ImageReady takes a lot of time and practice. In this project, you will create a simple animation with approximately 30 frames. Building this animation presents you with an introduction to the basic techniques and tools used in animation and optimization. Further study will be required to master these tools and techniques.

Creating the Animation Graphic for the E-Portfolio Web Page

The animation in the E-Portfolio Web page generates a graphic for the upper-right corner (see Figure 9-1 on page PS 549). The graphic will start as a small dot in the lower-left corner, and then will twist and expand until it becomes a line in the final graphic. One at a time, each line will be created using the same process.

It will be easier to create the graphic independently and then export the animation frames into the E-Portfolio Web page. That way, you will work with a smaller file size as you edit, and you will not be distracted by other layers. Also, it will be easier to work on a white background which you can delete later when the animation is combined with the Web page.

The following steps show how to close the E-Portfolio document window and open a new file for the animation. Table 9-4 displays the settings for the new document window.

Table 9-4 Settings for the New Document Window

OPTION	SETTING
Name	Animation Graphic
Preset	Custom
Width	800 pixels
Height	600 pixels
Resolution	72 pixels/inch
Color Mode	RGB Color 8 bit
Background Contents	White

To Close the E-Portfolio file and Open a New Document Window

1. **Click the Close button on the E-Portfolio document window. If Photoshop asks you save the file again, click the NO button.**
2. **Press CTRL+N to open a new file.**
3. **When the New dialog box is displayed, enter the settings from Table 9-4.**
4. **Click the OK button.**

The first line's animation will be created as six layers. To keep the lines and layers organized you will use a layer group created in the following step.

To Create a Layer Group

1 **On the Layers palette, click the Create a new group button.**

Photoshop creates a layer group named, Group 1, on the Layers palette.

Drawing the Shapes

Each of the lines in the final product will begin as a dot in the lower-left corner and then slowly elongate and twist to its final position in the upper-right corner of the window. You will create six layers to represent each stage of the line's animation. As you create the shapes, you do not have to match the position and placement exactly, except for the final shape that is positioned precisely using the Transform options bar in Step 6 of the following steps.

To Draw the Six Shapes

1

- **On the Swatches palette, select the color #CC9900, which is medium, orange-tan, located in Row 4 of the Swatches palette.**
- **Press the U key to activate the shape tool.**
- **On the options bar, click the Shape layers button and the Ellipse Tool button. If necessary, click the Style Picker button and then click Default Style (None) in the list.**
- **In the document window, drag a small circle in the lower-left corner.**

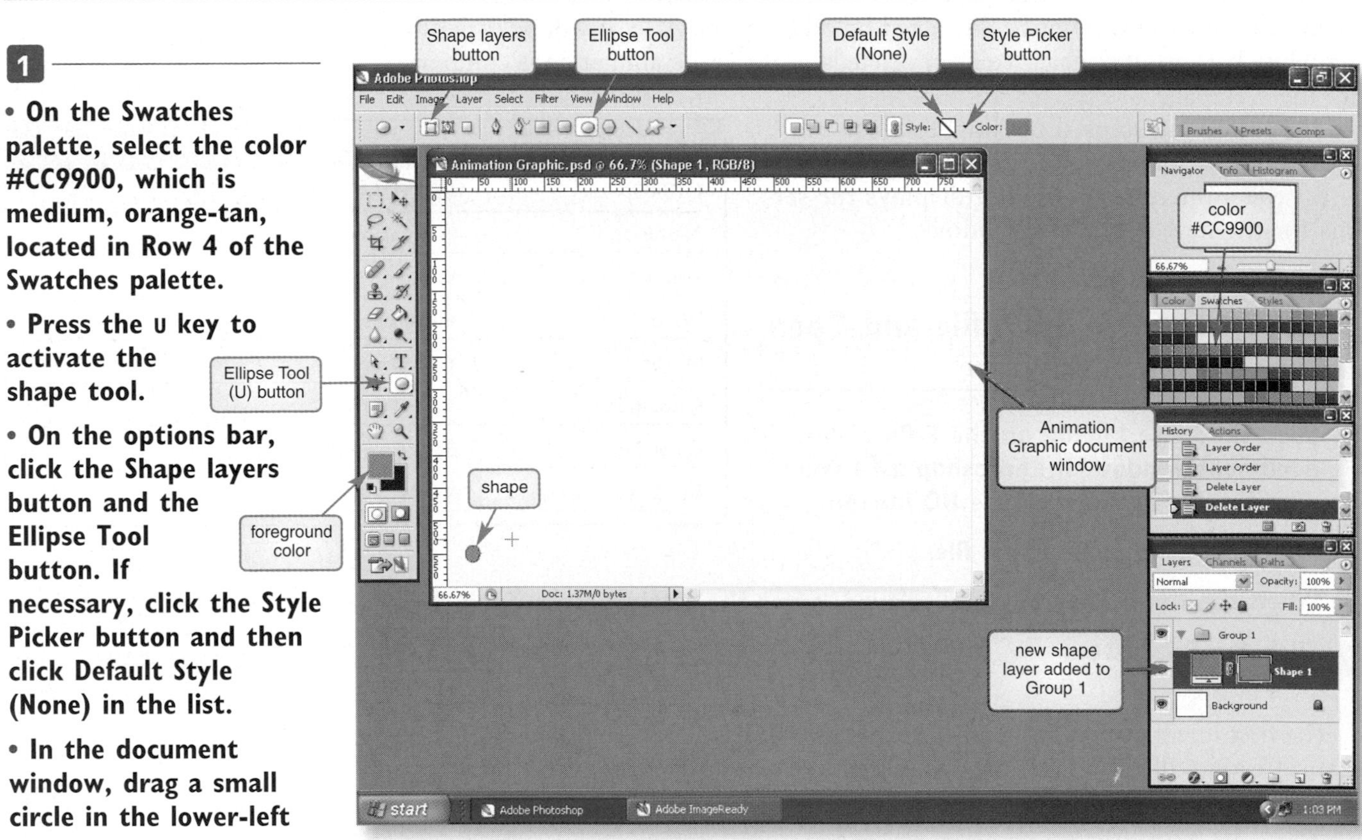

FIGURE 9-45

The first shape, an ellipse, is displayed and a new shape layer is added to the Group 1 layer (Figure 9-45).

2

- **On the options bar, click the Line Tool button. Type** 8 px **in the Weight box.**
- **Drag a short line at a slight angle to create a shape similar in size and location to Figure 9-46.**

The second shape is displayed.

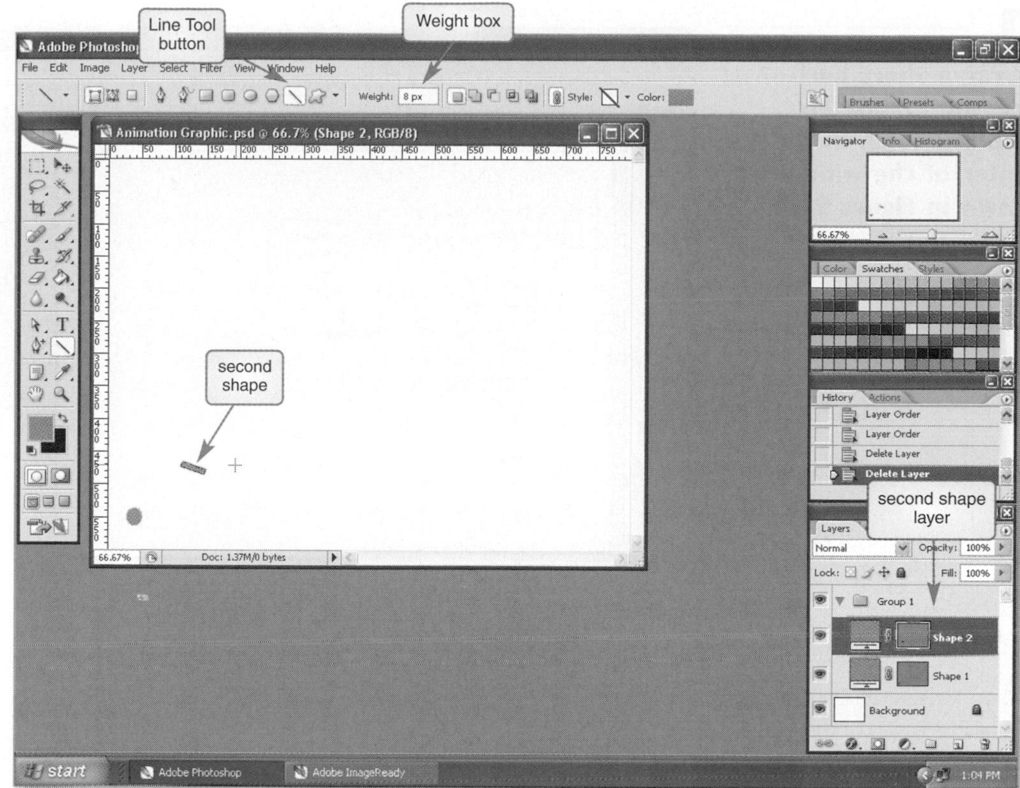

FIGURE 9-46

3

- **On the options bar, click the Line Tool button, if necessary. Type** 10 px **in the Weight box.**
- **Drag a short line at approximately a 45-degree angle to create a shape similar in size and location to Figure 9-47.**

A third shape is displayed in the document window. Notice that each shape creates a new layer inside the Group 1 layer group.

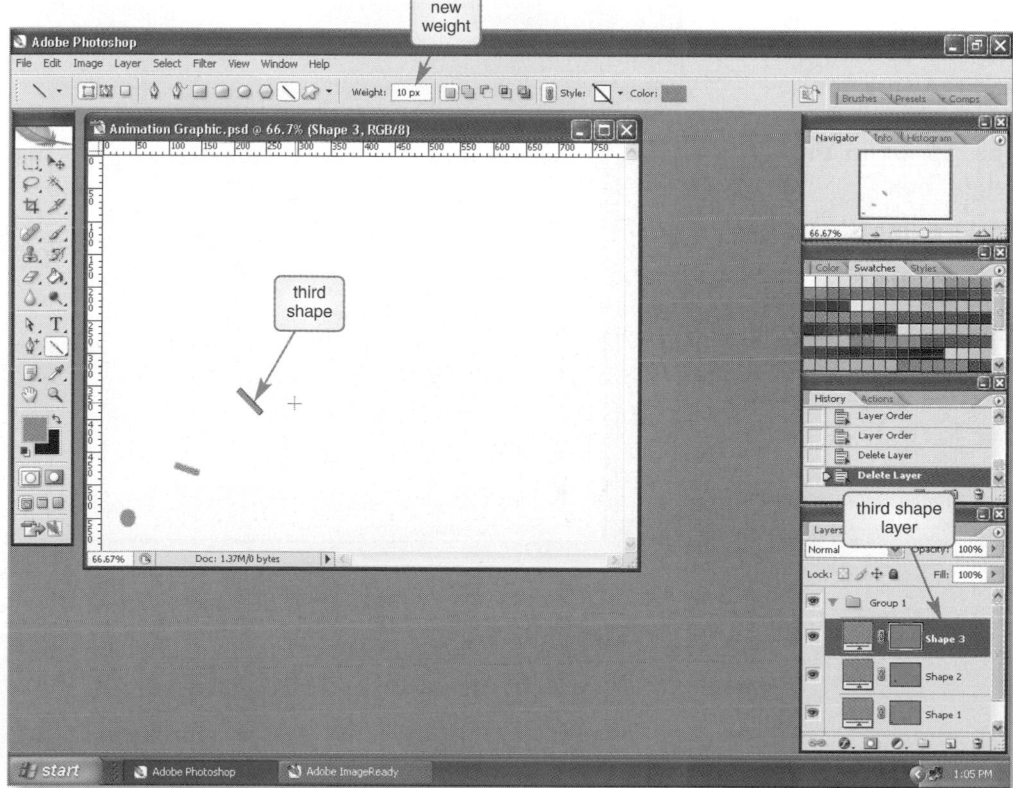

FIGURE 9-47

4

• **Drag a short horizontal line, approximately 70 pixels long, in the center of the window, as shown in Figure 9-48.**

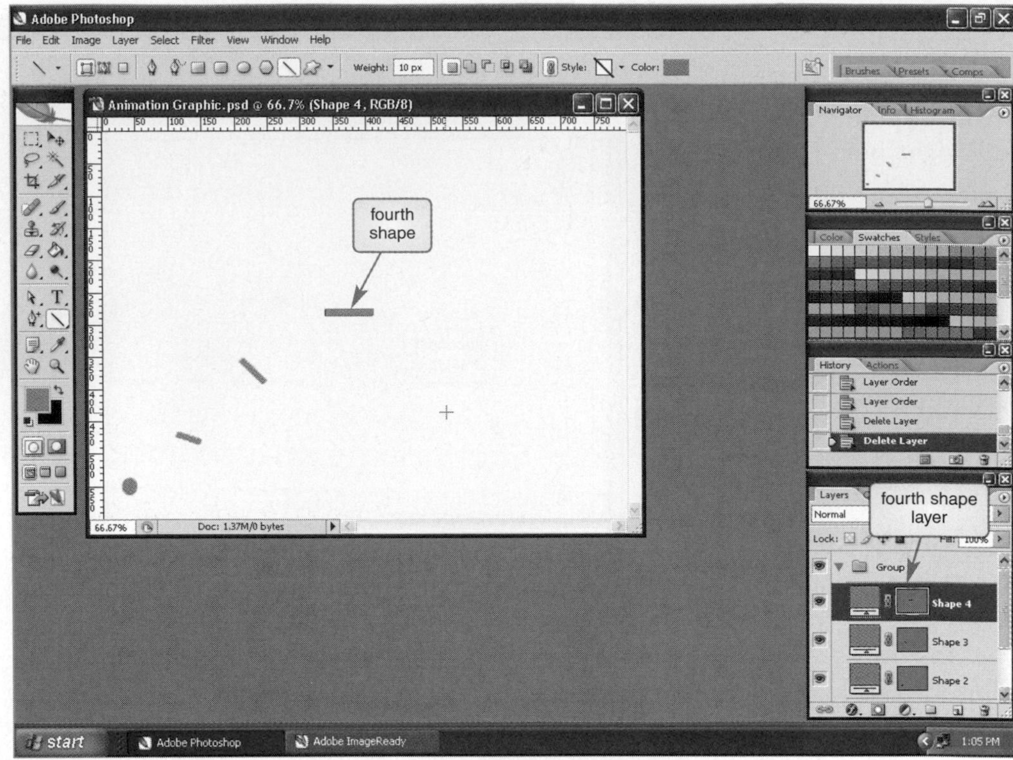

FIGURE 9-48

5

• **On the options bar, click the Line tool button, if necessary. Type** `15 px` **in the Weight box.**

• **Drag a line above the previous one and to the right. The line should display at a 45-degree angle in the opposite direction as the line in Step 3.**

The fifth line is longer and thicker than the previous shapes (Figure 9-49).

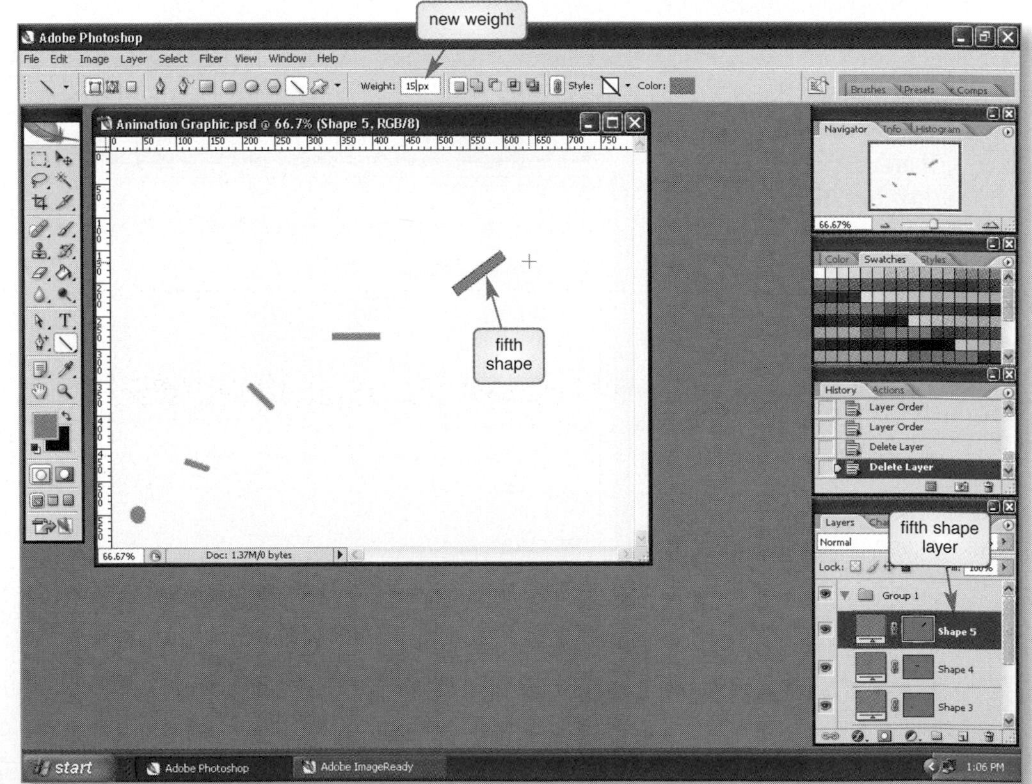

FIGURE 9-49

6

- **Finally, in the document window, drag a vertical line, approximately 100 pixels tall.**
- **Press CTRL+T to transform the shape. On the Transform options bar, type** 720 **in the Set horizontal position of reference point box. Type** 132 **in the Set vertical position of reference point box.**
- **Press the ENTER key to commit the change.**
- **Reposition any of the other shape layers as necessary, by selecting the layer on the Layers palette and moving it using the Move tool.**

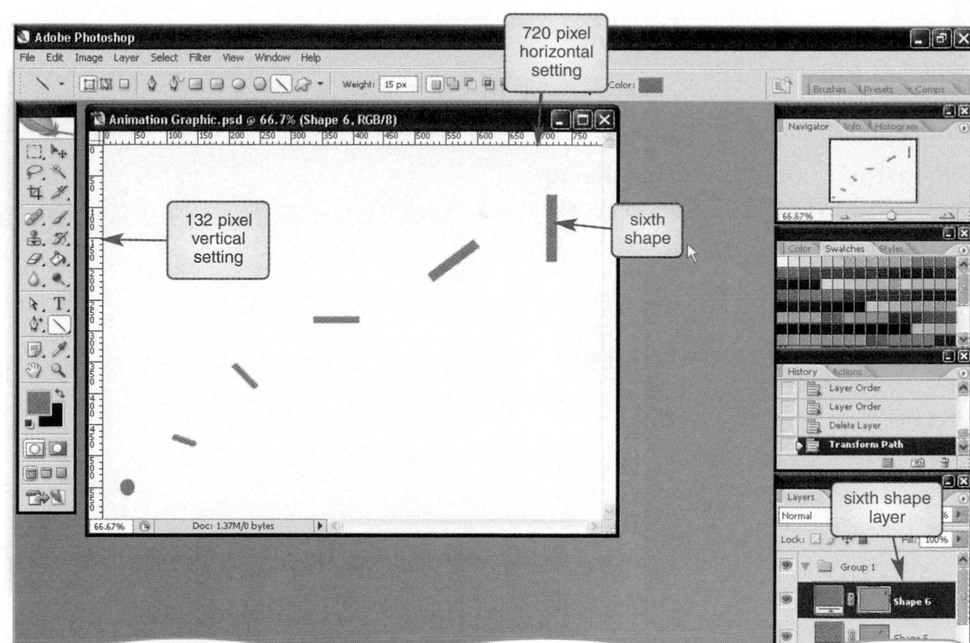

FIGURE 9-50

The sixth line is displayed in its final position for the graphic (Figure 9-50). Recall that the reference point is the center of a bounding box; therefore, the transformation settings center the shape at the specified pixel locations.

Drawing More Shapes

Now that the shapes are created, it is time to make copies of the group for the other four lines. First, you will turn off their visibility in preparation for animation. Then, you will copy the group and rename it. Finally, you will edit the color of the new shape layers.

To Draw More Shapes

1

- **Click the visibility icon beside each layer and then the layer group, so they no longer display.**
- **Click the triangle in the Group 1 layer group to close its contents.**

Only the background layer is visible (Figure 9-51).

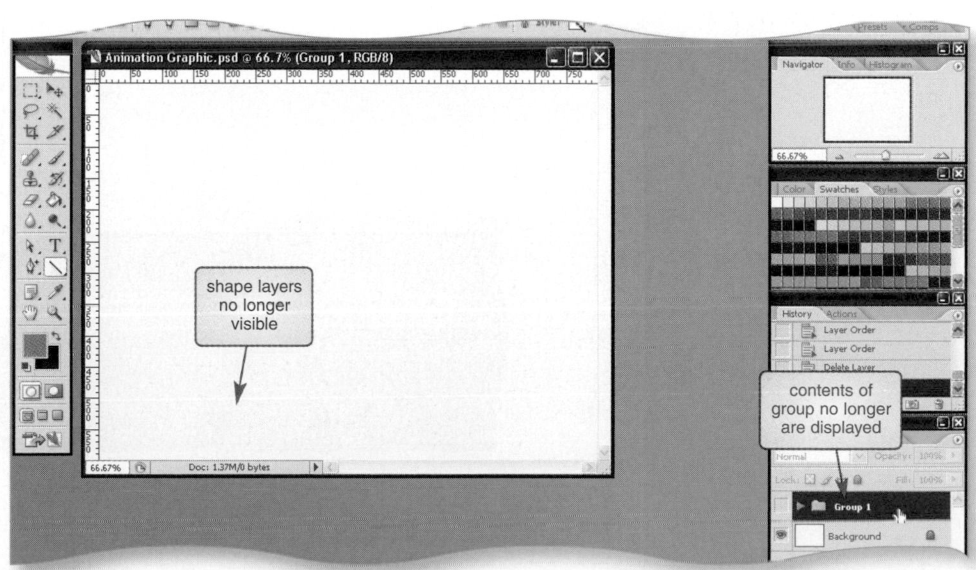

FIGURE 9-51

2

- **Right-click the Group 1 layer group and then click Duplicate Group on the shortcut menu.**
- **When the Duplicate Group dialog box is displayed, type** `Group 2` **as the new name.**
- **Click the OK button.**
- **Duplicating the top layer group on the palette each time, create three more copies, named Group 3, Group 4, and Group 5.**

The new duplicated layers are displayed on the Layers palette (Figure 9-52). Duplicating the top layer group orders the group layer numbers correctly.

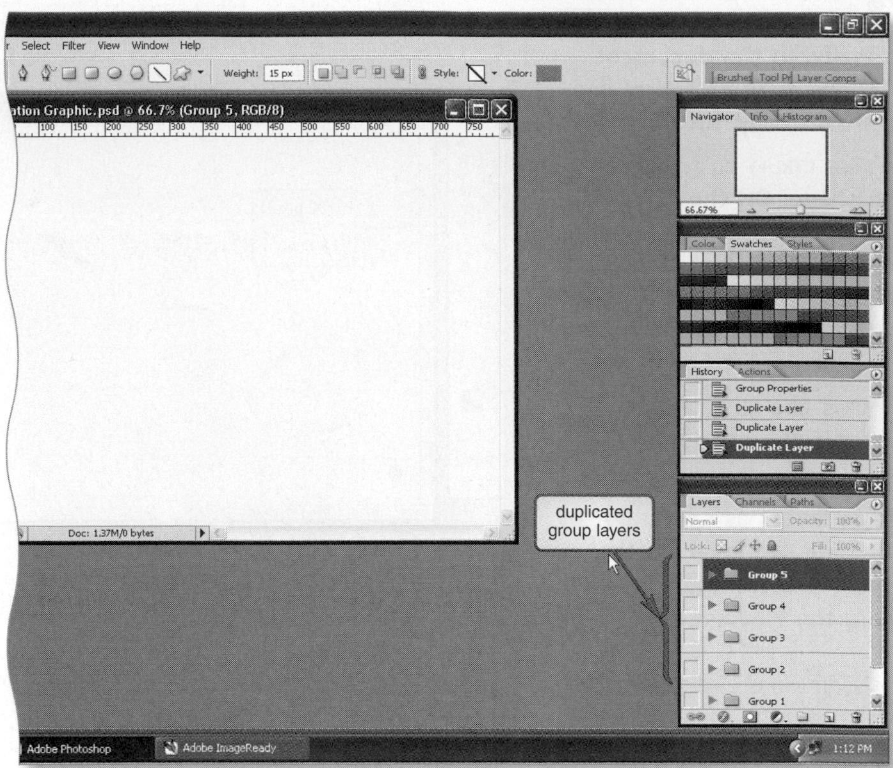

FIGURE 9-52

3

- **Click the triangle in the Group 2 layer to display its contents. Move and resize the palette so all of the layers within the group can be seen.**

The contents of Group 2 are displayed (Figure 9-53).

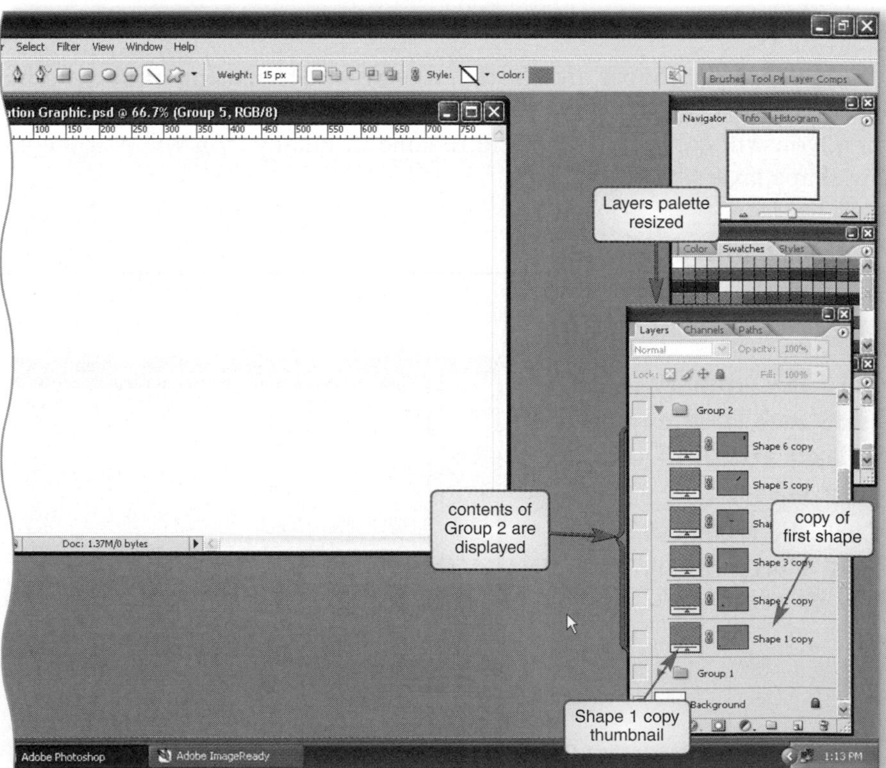

FIGURE 9-53

4

- **In the Layers palette, double-click the Shape 1 copy thumbnail.**
- **When the Color Picker dialog box is displayed, double-click the # box and then type** 999900 **to choose a new color.**
- **To facilitate repetition, double-click the value, 999900 in the # box to select it, and then press CTRL+C to copy.**

The medium, yellow-green color, 999900, is a Web-safe color (Figure 9-54).

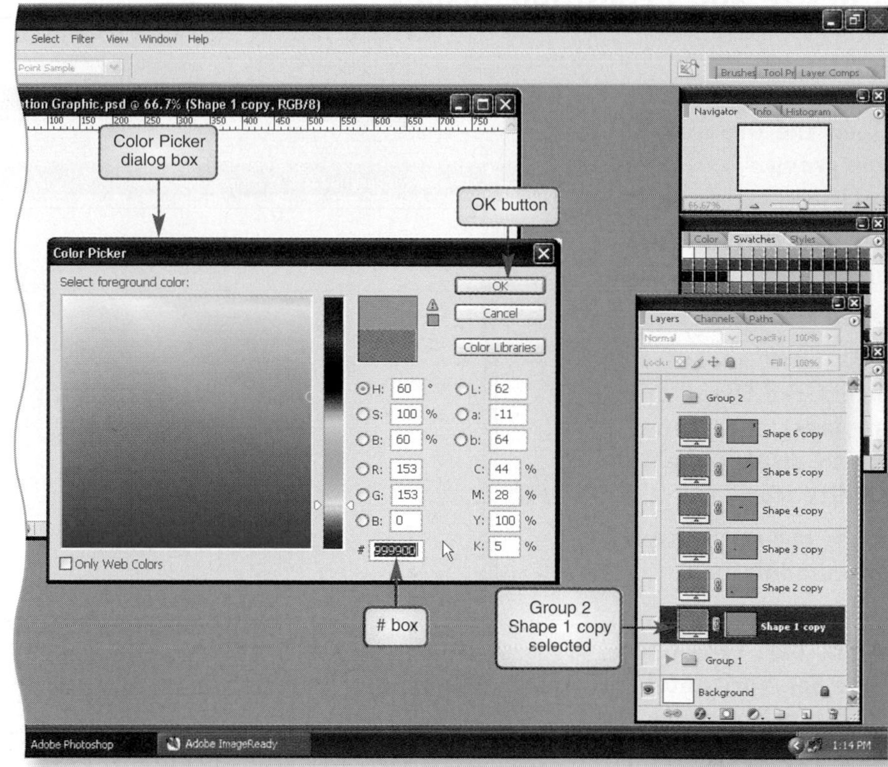

FIGURE 9-54

5

- **Click the OK button.**
- **Repeat Step 4 for each of the other layer copies in the Group 2 layer group, using CTRL+V to paste the color value in the # box when needed. Click the OK button in the Color Picker dialog box each time.**

Each of the layers now are displayed with the yellow-green color (Figure 9-55).

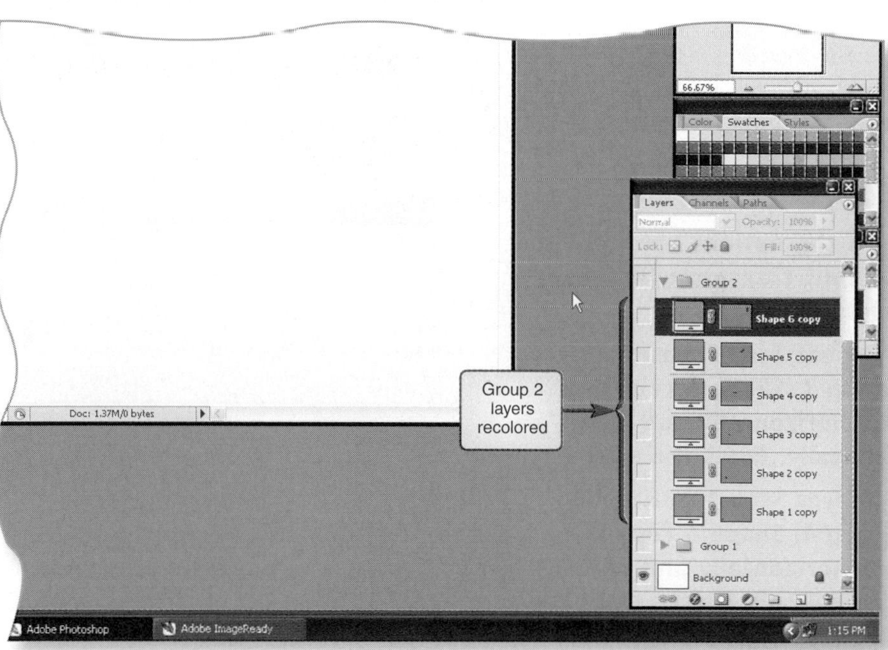

FIGURE 9-55

6

- **Repeat the process of opening the group and changing the layer colors for Groups 3, 4, and 5. Use the colors, FF9900, 996600, and FFCC66, respectively.**
- **When you are finished, close each group.**

The five layer groups are complete — each with its own set of colored shapes.

The final step before creating the animation is to resize and reposition Shape 6 in Groups 2 through 5, as shown in the steps on the following page.

To Resize and Reposition Shapes

1

- **Open the Group 1 layer group.**
- **Select the Shape 6 layer and then click to display its visibility icon.**
- **Open Group 2 layer group.**
- **Select the Shape 6 copy layer and then click to display the visibility icon.**
- **Press CTRL+T to display the bounding box.**
- **On the Transform options bar, type** 690 **in the Set horizontal position of reference point box. Type** 80% **in the Set vertical scale box.**

The yellow-green shape is repositioned and resized so it will be displayed beside the Group 1 line and slightly shorter (Figure 9-56).

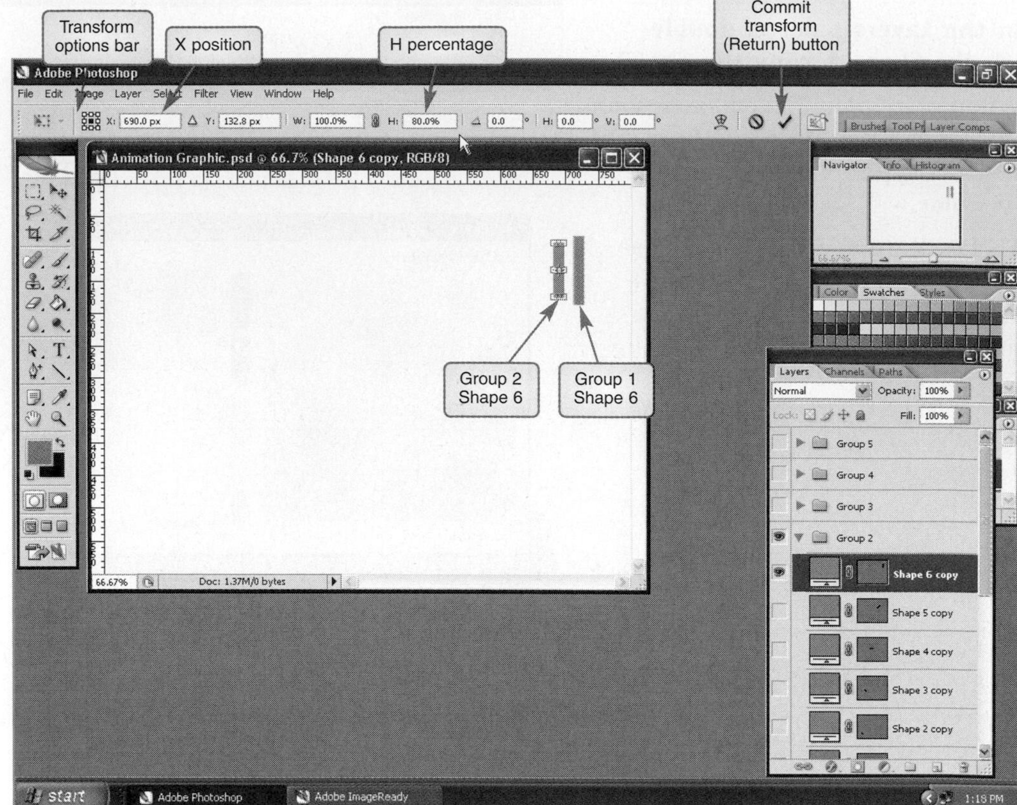

FIGURE 9-56

2

- **On the options bar, click the Commit transform (Return) button.**
- **Repeat Step 1 positioning Group 3, Shape 6 copy at 750 horizontally and 80% vertically. Press the ENTER key**
- **Repeat Step 1 positioning Group 4, Shape 6 copy at 660 horizontally and 60% vertically. Press the ENTER key**
- **Repeat Step 1 positioning Group 5, Shape 6 copy at 780 horizontally and 60% vertically. Press the ENTER key**

The five Shape 6 layers are displayed in the document window (Figure 9-57).

FIGURE 9-57

3

• Turn off the visibility of all the layers and then all the groups, including the Background layer.

With the shapes complete, it is a good time to save the file with the name, Animation Graphic, as shown in the following steps.

To Save the Animation Graphic File

1 With your USB flash drive connected to one of the computer's USB ports, click File on the menu bar and then Save As.

2 When the Save As dialog box is displayed, if necessary, type `Animation Graphic` **in the File name text box. Do not press the ENTER key.**

3 If necessary, click the Format box arrow and then click Photoshop (*.PSD,*.PDD) in the list. Click the Save in box arrow and then click USBDISK [G:], or the location associated with your USB flash drive, in the list. Double-click the folder named, My Web Site.

4 Click the Save button. If Photoshop displays a dialog box, click the OK button.

The file is saved.

The Animation Palette

The **Animation palette** is used in conjunction with the Layers palette to create animation frames (Figure 9-58). To display the Animation palette, click Animation on the Window menu. The palette usually is displayed at the bottom of the Photoshop or ImageReady window. The current visible view of your image layers becomes the first frame, so it is a good idea to edit the layers appropriately before opening the palette. To create an animation, you insert a new frame from the palette menu, and then edit the layers. As you create them, frames are added sequentially from left to right in the center of the palette.

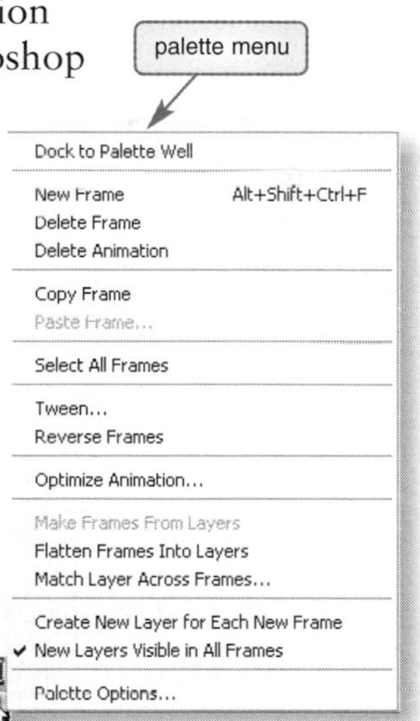

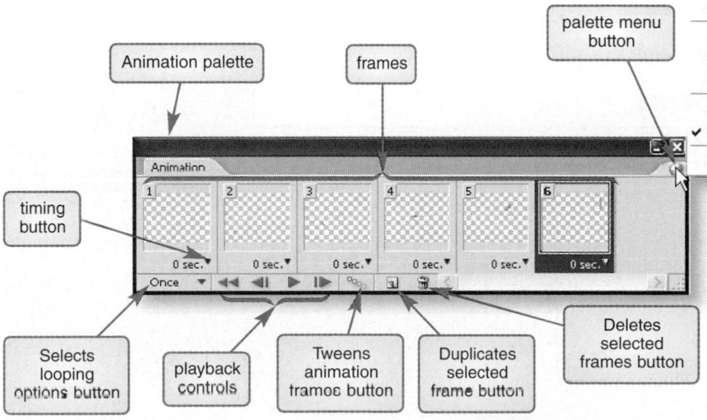

FIGURE 9-58

The palette menu displays commands to create, manipulate, and optimize the frames. Below each frame is a button used to set the timing or delay between the current frame and the next frame.

The Animation palette displays buttons along the bottom that are used to manipulate the frames. You can edit how the animation loops; play, rewind, and fast-forward the animation; and tween, duplicate, and delete frames. **Tweening**, a corruption of the phrase in-between, is a way to allow Photoshop to create new frames automatically between two existing frames. When you tween between two frames, Photoshop parses the data equally in the frames creating graduated changes; the opacity of the layer is reduced evenly across the new frames. For example, if two frames contain an opacity change from 50 percent to 100 percent, Photoshop would create a tween frame with 75 percent opacity. Similarly, if two frames display an object that has been moved, the tween frame will display the object placed halfway between the two. Tweening significantly reduces the time required to create animation effects. Tweened frames are fully editable. You can choose whether the tween should affect the opacity, the position, or the special effect.

The following steps demonstrate how to create frames and build the animation using the Animation palette.

To Use the Animation Palette

1

- **On the Window menu, click Animation.**
- **On the Layers palette, open Group 1 if necessary and click the visibility icon next to Shape 1.**

The animation palette creates an initial frame by default (Figure 9-59). The Shape 1 layer is added to the frame.

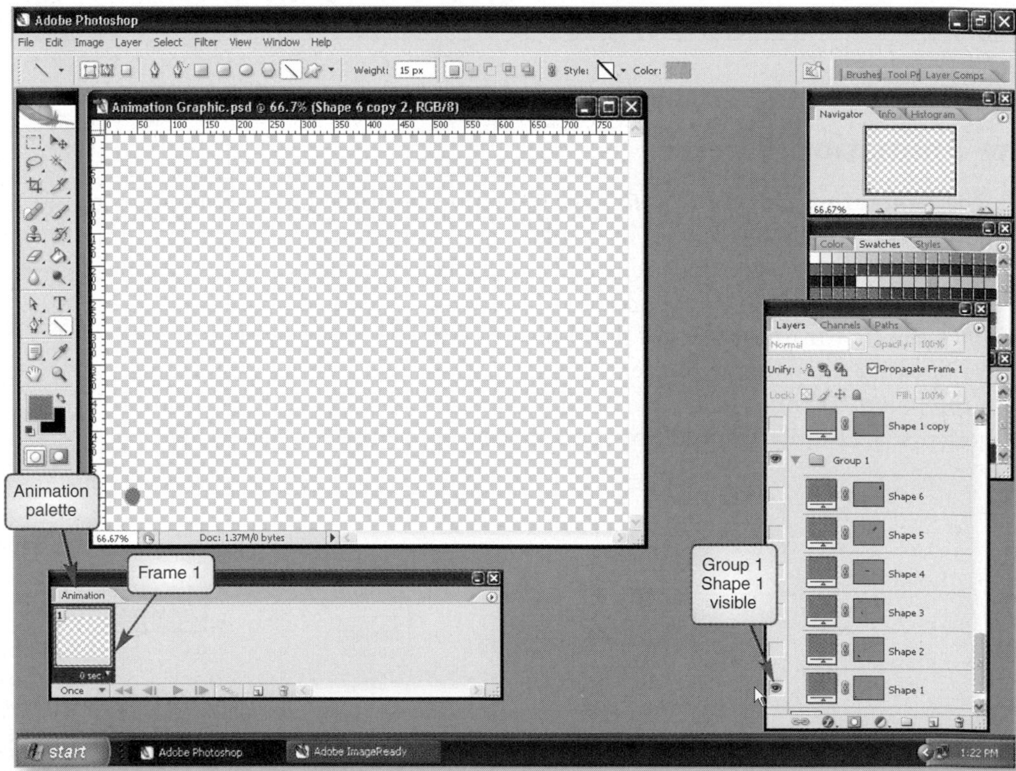

FIGURE 9-59

2

- **In the lower portion of the Animation palette, click the Duplicates selected frames button.**
- **Hide the visibility of Shape 1 and turn on the visibility of Shape 2.**

A second frame is created (Figure 9-60).

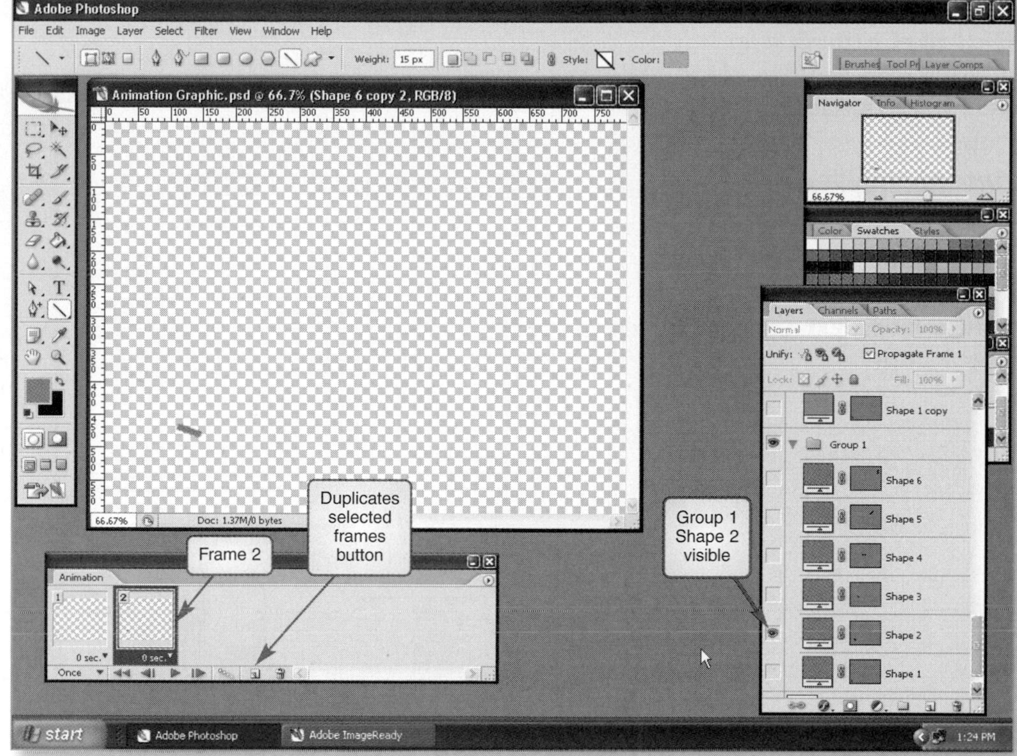

FIGURE 9-60

3

- **Repeat Step 2 hiding and viewing each subsequent Shape layer with each new frame.**

The six frames, each with their own shape, are created on the Animation palette (Figure 9-61).

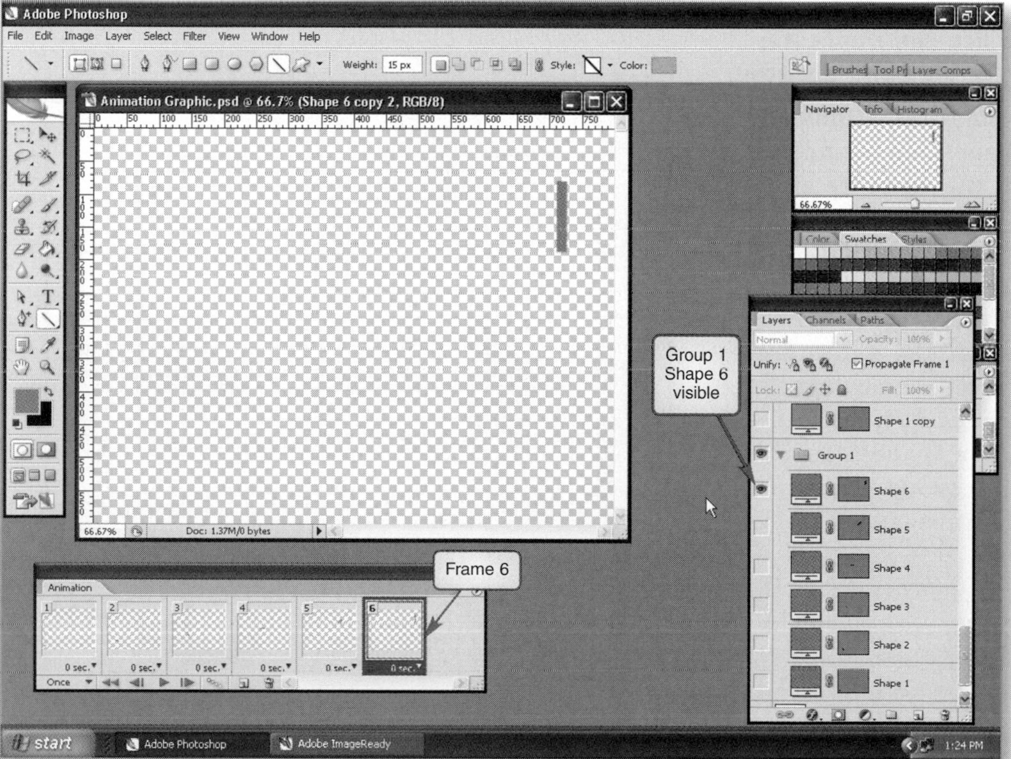

FIGURE 9-61

4

- **With the Shape 6 layer still visible on the Layers palette, close Group 1.**
- **Click the Duplicates selected frames button.**
- **Open Group 2, if necessary, and click the visibility icon next to Shape 1 copy.**

The Animation palette creates a new frame by default (Figure 9-62). The Shape 1 copy layer is added to the frame.

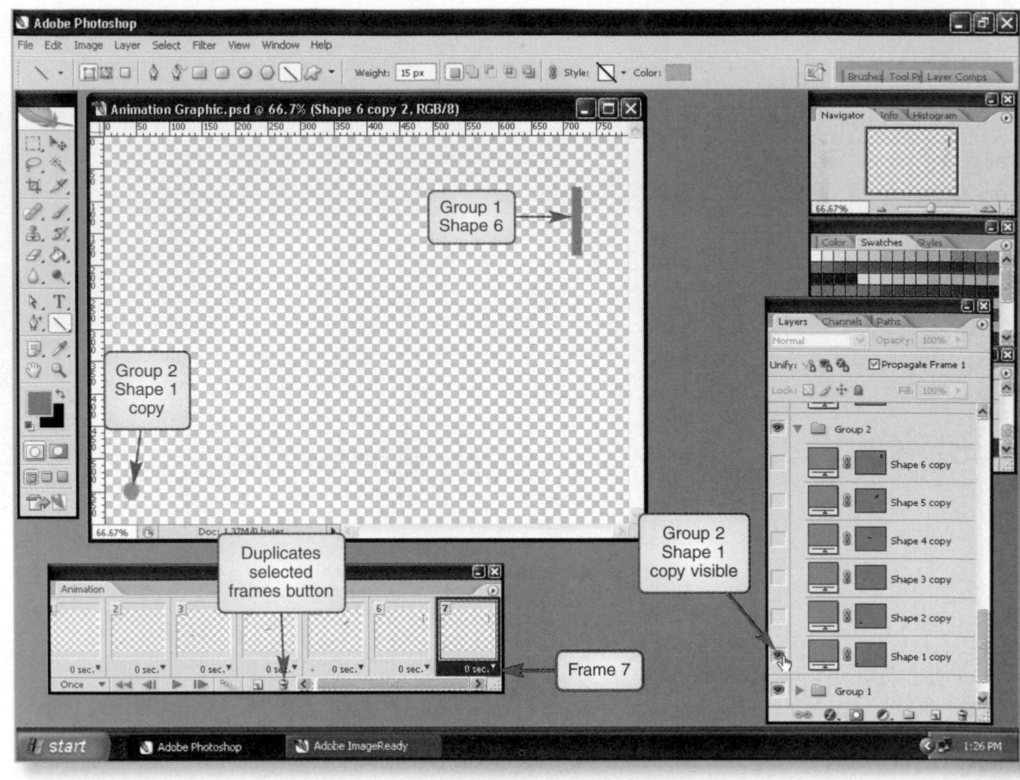

FIGURE 9-62

5

- **Click the Duplicates selected frames button.**
- **Hide the visibility of Shape 1 copy and turn on the visibility of Shape 2 copy as you did in Step 2. Repeat the process for each shape in the group. Then repeat the entire process in steps 1 through 5 for Groups 3, 4, and 5. Leave Shape 6 copy in each group visible for the subsequent frames.**

The 30 frames are displayed on the Animation palette (Figure 9-63).

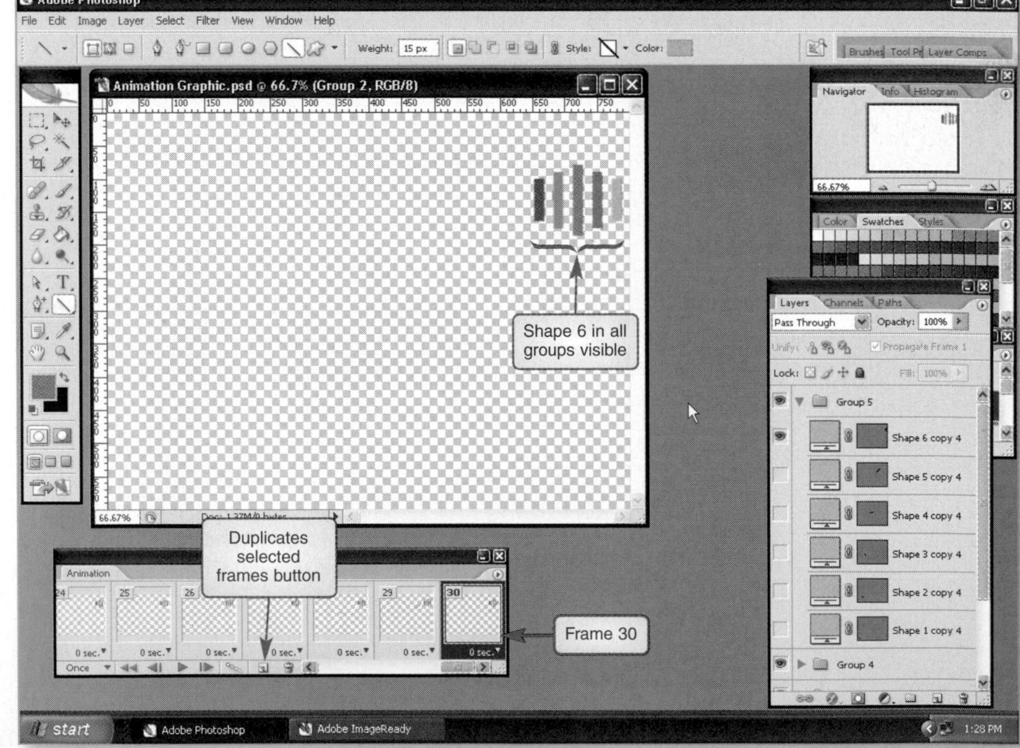

FIGURE 9-63

Other Ways

1. In ImageReady, on Window menu, click Animation, create frames

Previewing the Animation Graphic

The following steps preview the animation by clicking the Plays animation button at the bottom of the Animation palette.

To Preview the Animation Graphic

• **On the Animation palette, click the Plays animation button.**

The animation begins playing over and over.

• **If necessary, click the Stops animation button.**

The animation stops.

Other Ways

1. In ImageReady, click Preview in (browser) button

Before saving the file and exporting it to the Web page, you will make animation setting changes as shown in the next section.

Animation Settings

You can choose to have an animation display just once, a specified number of times, or continuously, which is called **looping.** The three choices are offered when you click the Selects looping options button at the bottom of the Animation palette.

Additionally, you can optimize the animation with two settings. The **Bounding Box** setting crops each frame to only the area that has changed from the preceding frame. The Bounding Box setting creates much smaller files. The **Redundant Pixel Removal** setting makes all pixels in a frame that are unchanged from the preceding frame, transparent. Later, when the file is saved as a GIF or HTML file, you must select the Transparency option on the Optimize palette for the setting to work properly.

After changing the animation settings as shown in the steps on the next page, you will delete the white background in preparation for copying the animation into the E-Portfolio Web page.

More About

Offsetting for Animation

If you want to create an animation that moves an object without any rotation, you can use a special filter in Photoshop. First, duplicate the layer that contains the object. On the Filter menu, point to Other and then click Offset. In the resulting dialog box, you may specify exactly how many pixels to move the object. On the Animation palette, when you create the first frame, make only the original layer visible. When you create the second frame, make only the filtered frame visible.

To Change Animation Settings

1

- **Click the Selects looping options button and then click Once, if necessary.**
- **Click the Animation palette menu button.**

The palette menu is displayed (Figure 9-64).

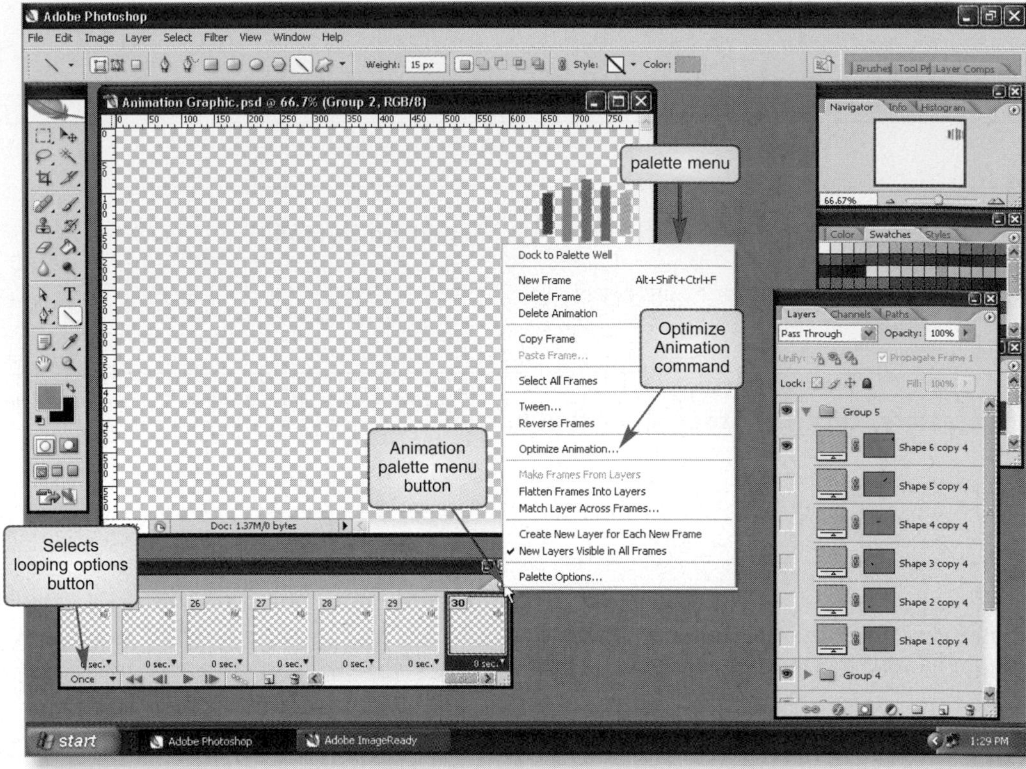

FIGURE 9-64

2

- **Click Optimize Animation.**
- **When the Optimize Animation dialog box is displayed, if necessary, click both Bounding Box and Redundant Pixel Removal to select them.**

The animation will be optimized with the selected settings (Figure 9-65).

3

- **Click the OK button.**
- **On the Layers palette, select the Background layer. Right-click the Background layer and then click Delete Layer on the shortcut menu. When the Delete Layer dialog box is displayed, click the Yes button.**
- **Press CTRL+S to save the file again.**

The settings are complete and the file is saved.

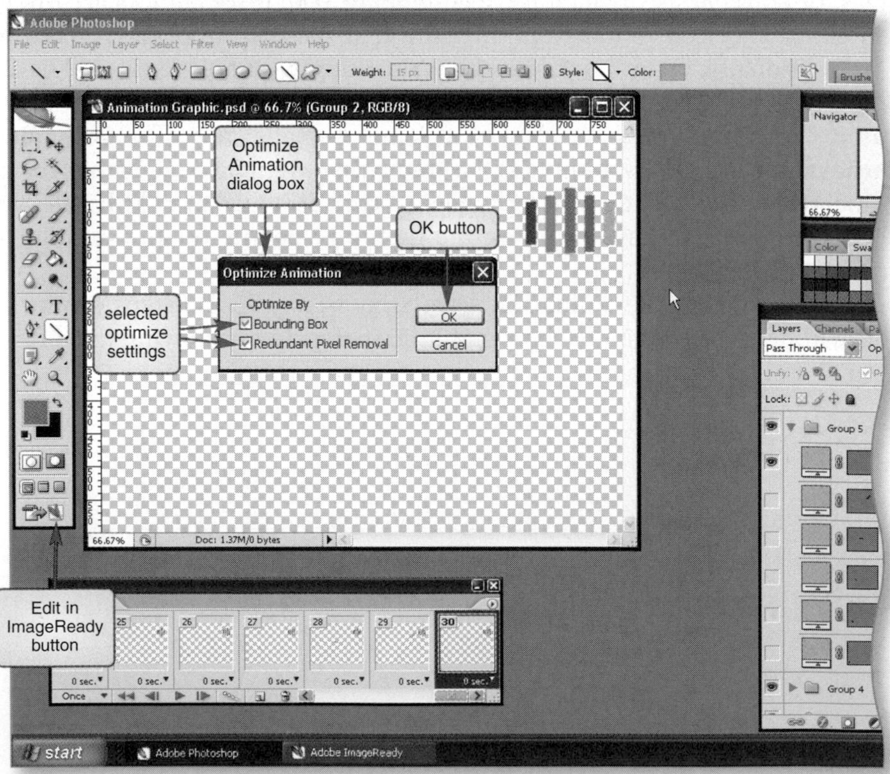

FIGURE 9-65

Adding the Animation Graphic to the Web Page

ImageReady, with its Web and optimization tools, is an easier place to combine the Animation Graphic and E-Portfolio files. In the following steps, you will jump back to ImageReady, open the E-Portfolio file, and then copy the animation from one file to another. The **Match command** in ImageReady will apply the E-Portfolio layers across the animations frames.

To Add Animation to a Web Page

1

- **Click the Edit in ImageReady button.**
- **When the Animation Graphic file displays in ImageReady, press CTRL+O and then open the E-Portfolio file.**
- **Drag the windows, so parts of both windows display in the workspace.**
- **Click the Animation Graphic document window to select it.**

The Animation Graphic and E-Portfolio document window are displayed in ImageReady (Figure 9-66). Your display may differ depending on what frame, layer, or layer group, is selected.

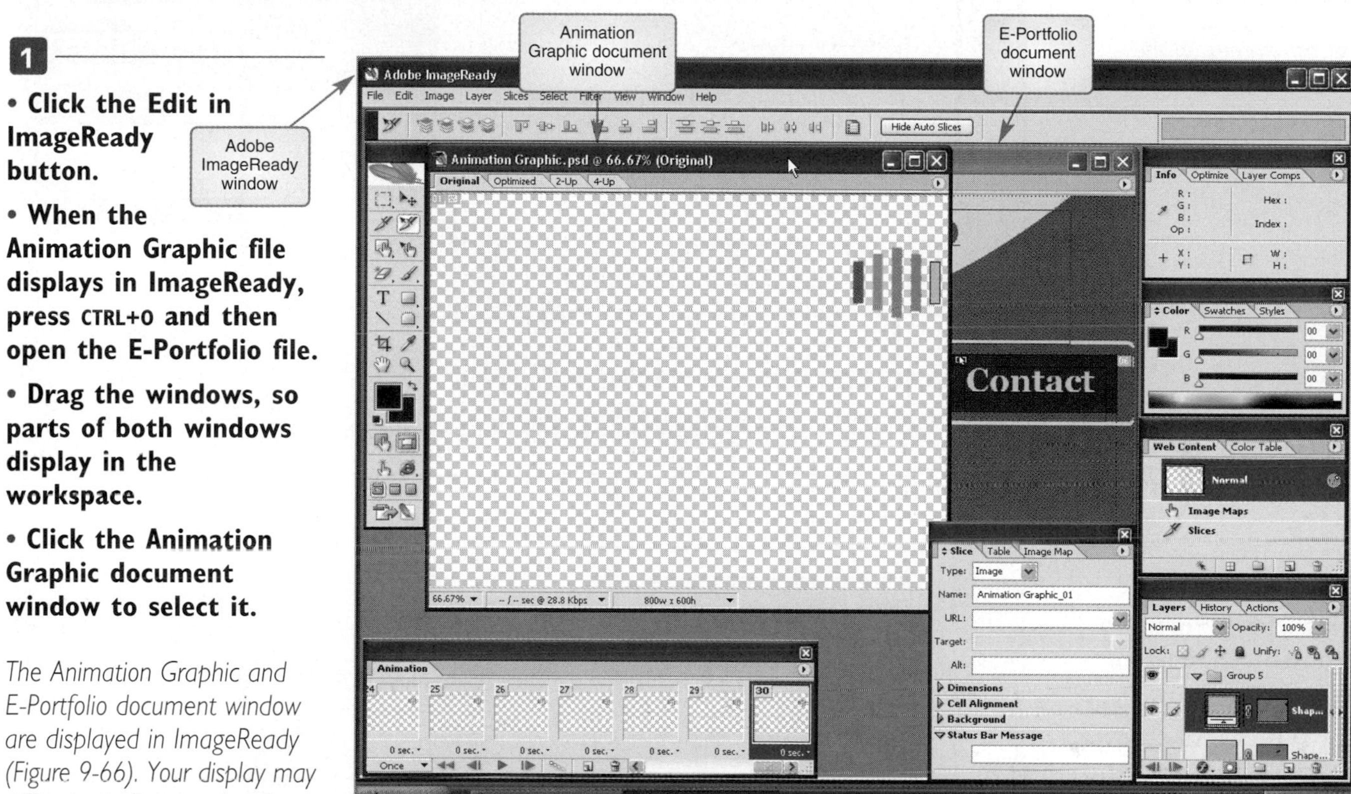

FIGURE 9-66

2

- **Click the Animation palette menu button, and then click Select All Frames in the list.**
- **Click the Animation palette menu button again, and then click Copy Frames.**

All of the frames on the Animation palette are selected and copied (Figure 9-67).

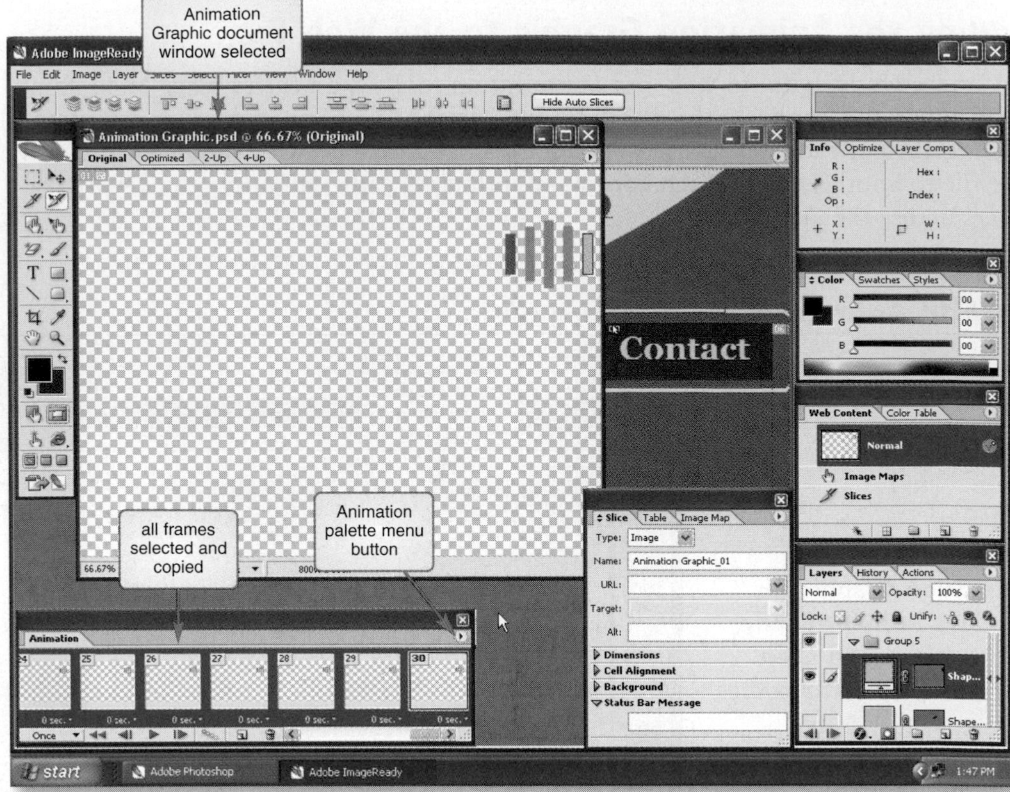

FIGURE 9-67

3

- **Click the E-Portfolio document window to select it.**
- **On the Layers palette, SHIFT+click the first and last layers, so all layers will be included in the final animation.**
- **Click the Animation palette menu button and then click Paste Frames. When ImageReady displays the Paste Frames dialog box, click Paste After Selection.**

The Paste Frames dialog box is displayed (Figure 9-68).

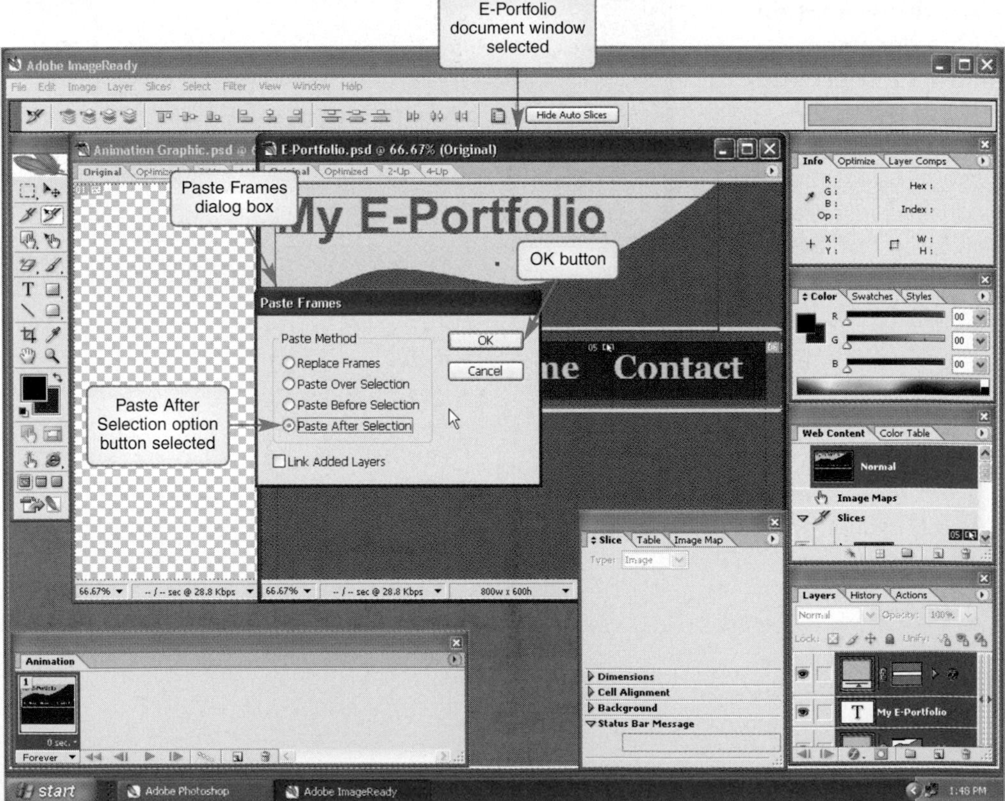

FIGURE 9-68

4

- **Click the OK button.**
- **Click Frame 1 on the Animation palette.**
- **Click the Layers palette menu button and then click Match on the shortcut menu.**
- **When ImageReady displays the Match Layer dialog box, click Current Animation and select all three What to Match options, if necessary.**

The Match Layer dialog box allows you to apply layers across the current animation, across the current slice or image map, or across all rollovers (Figure 9-69).

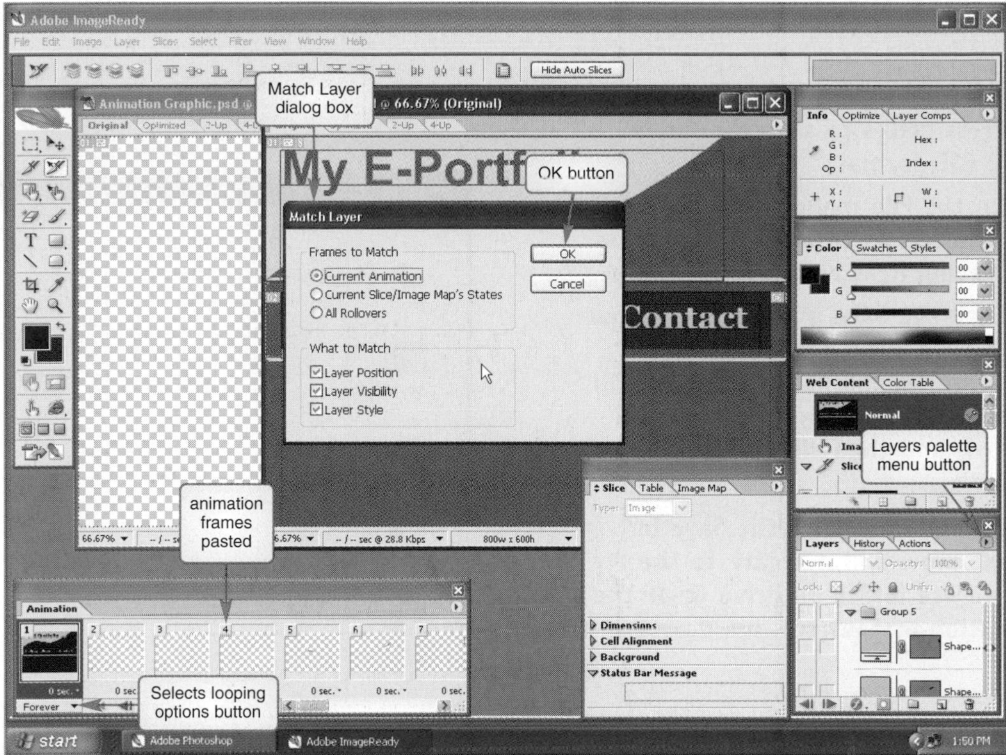

FIGURE 9-69

5

- **Click the OK button.**
- **Click the Selects looping options button and then click Once.**

The layers of Frame 1 are applied across the animation. The animation will play once on the Web page.

You may preview the animation by clicking the Plays animation button on the Animation palette.

Because you are finished with the Animation Graphic file, and in order to save system resources, the following step closes the Animation Graphic document window.

To Close the Animation Graphic Document Window

1 **Select the Animation Graphic document window and then click its Close button. If ImageReady displays a dialog box asking you to save changes, click the No button.**

The Animation Graphic file is closed.

Saving the Web Page

Saving the file in ImageReady preserves the rollovers and animation. Because you have used Web-safe colors and appropriate sizes and slices, no further optimization is necessary.

First, you will save the file in the PSD format for future edits. Then, you will save the file in the HTML format that can be uploaded to a Web server.

To Save the Web Page

- **Press CTRL+S to save the file in the PSD format.**
- **On the File menu, click Save Optimized As to begin the process of saving it as an HTML file.**
- **Click the Save as type box arrow and then click HTML and Images (*.html) in the list, if necessary. If necessary, click the Slices box arrow and then click All Slices in the list.**
- **If necessary, click the Save in box arrow and navigate to the My Web Site folder on drive G, or the location of your storage device.**

ImageReady displays the Save Optimized As dialog box (Figure 9-70).

2

- **Click the Save button.**

ImageReady saves the file and a folder of images on the storage device.

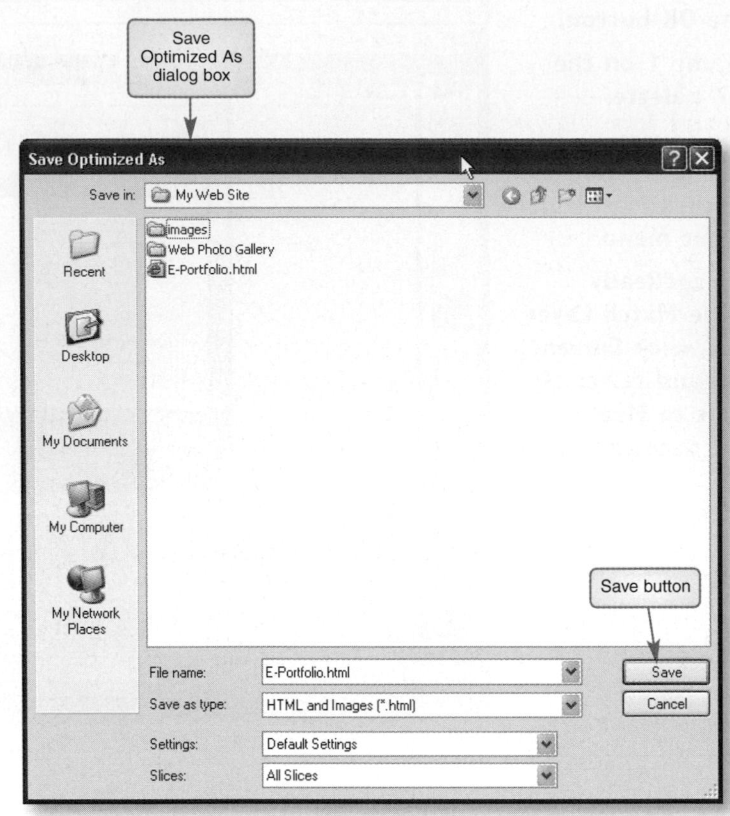

FIGURE 9-70

The Web page is complete. The final steps are to close the file and quit ImageReady and Photoshop.

To Close the File and Quit the Applications

1. **Click the Close button in the E-Portfolio document window. If ImageReady displays a message about the file not existing in the Photoshop window, click the Yes button.**
2. **Click the Close button on the ImageReady title bar.**
3. **Select the Adobe Photoshop window and then click the Close button on the Photoshop title bar.**

The file is closed and the windows close.

Viewing the Web Page Interactively

To make a final check of the interactivity of the Web page, the next steps show how to open the E-Portfolio HTML file with a browser and watch the animation. After clicking the Gallery link, the Web photo gallery will open.

To View the Web Page Interactively

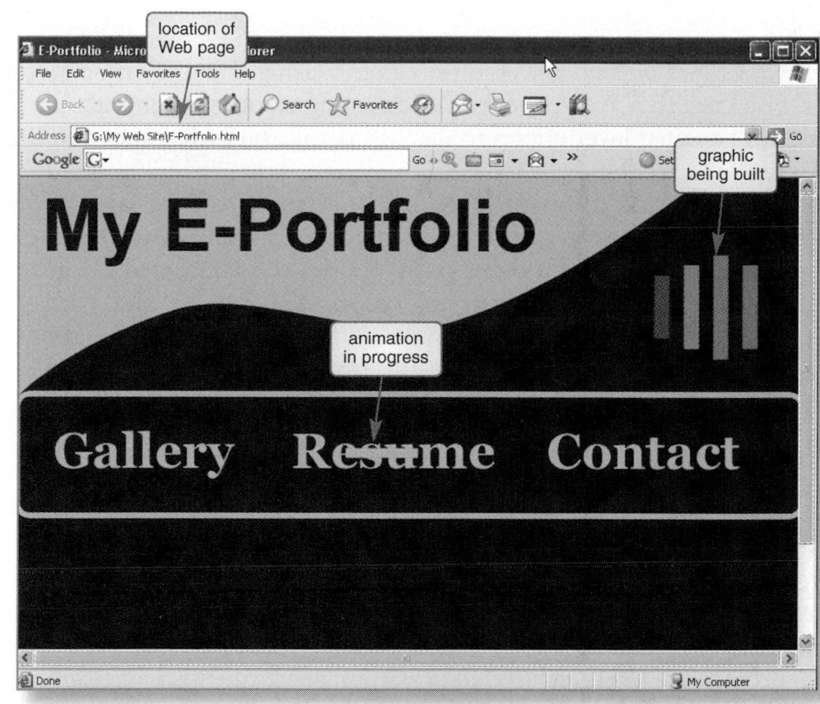

FIGURE 9-71

1

- **Click the Start button on the Windows desktop and then click My Computer on the Start menu.**
- **When the My Computer window opens, navigate to your USB storage drive and open the folder named, My Web Site.**
- **Double-click the HTML file, E-Portfolio.**
- **If a yellow bar displays below the browser toolbars, click the yellow bar, click Allow Blocked Content, and then click Yes in the Security Warning dialog box.**

The Web page opens and the animation begins (Figure 9-71). If your animation does not play, your browser may not accept ActiveX controls. See your instructor for ways to play the animation in your browser.

2

- **When the animation is finished, click the Gallery link.**
- **When the second window opens, if a yellow bar displays below the browser toolbars, click the yellow bar, click Allow Blocked Content, and then click Yes in the Security Warning dialog box.**
- **Click any of the thumbnails to display a larger view.**

The Web photo gallery is displayed in a new window (Figure 9-72).

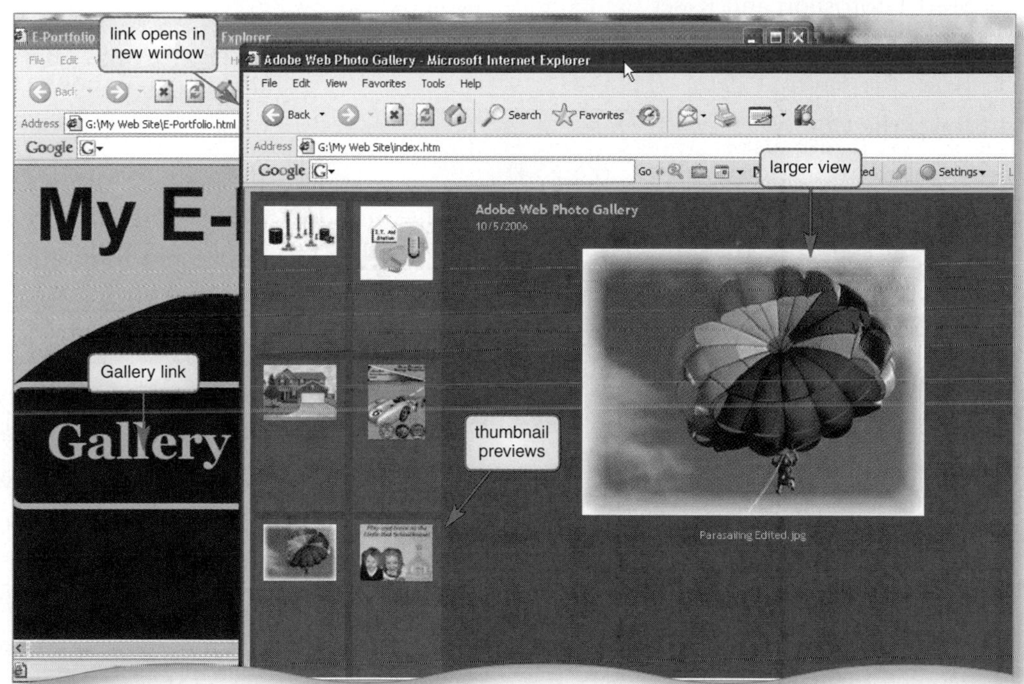

FIGURE 9-72

3

- **Click the Close button on the Web Photo Gallery window title bar.**
- **Click the Close button on the E-Portfolio window title bar.**

The browser windows close.

Project Summary

In this project, you created a Web site to display an e-portfolio. First, you organized your photos and other products in a folder and created a Web photo gallery using an automation feature in Photoshop. After choosing Web-safe colors, you created a Web page with contrasting color sections and a navigation bar. You entered text to serve as hyperlinks and created layer effects to display as rollovers when the Web page is viewed in a browser. You sliced the image into multiple sections, one for each hyperlink. You used ImageReady to set the static state of each slice to display only the layer. You then set the rollover state to include the layer effects. You used the Slice palette to enter specific settings for the hyperlink, such as destination URL and status bar message.

Finally you created a series of 30 frames that animated the generation of a graphic for the Web site. Small dots became longer lines in varying colors. You created each part of the animation as a separate layer and then displayed each layer in its own animation frame. You learned about the Animation palette and animation techniques such as looping, tweening, and optimizing. The completed animation was added to the home page of the Web site and the Match command was used to make sure the background displayed throughout the animation.

With the Web site complete, you tested the animation and the hyperlinks in a Web browser.

What You Should Know

Having completed this project, you should be able to perform the tasks below. The tasks are listed in the same order they were presented in this project. For a list of the buttons, menus, toolbars, and other commands introduced in this project, see the Quick Reference Summary at the back of this book and refer to the Page Number column.

1. Create a Folder of Images (PS 551)
2. Start Photoshop and Reset the Palettes, Toolbox, and Options Bar (PS 553)
3. Reset the Layers Palette (PS 553)
4. Reset the Colors (PS 553)
5. Create a Web Photo Gallery (PS 554)
6. Select a Web-Safe Background Color Using the Swatches Palette (PS 559)
7. Set Attributes for a New Web Document (PS 561)
8. Save the New Document (PS 562)
9. Add Contrast with a Secondary Color (PS 563)
10. Insert Heading Text (PS 565)
11. Create a Navigation Bar Rectangle (PS 566)
12. Enter Text and Apply Layer Effects (PS 569)
13. Make Hyperlink Slices (PS 573)
14. Save the File Again (PS 574)
15. Launch ImageReady (PS 575)
16. Create Rollovers (PS 576)
17. Enter Hyperlink Settings (PS 578)
18. Preview the Rollover Effect (PS 579)
19. Close the E-Portfolio File and Open a New Document Window (PS 580)
20. Create a Layer group (PS 581)
21. Draw the Six Shapes (PS 582)
22. Draw More Shapes (PS 585)
23. Resize and Reposition Shapes (PS 588)
24. Save the Animation Graphic File (PS 589)
25. Use the Animation Palette (PS 590)
26. Preview the Animation Graphic (PS 593)
27. Change Animation Settings (PS 594)
28. Add Animation to a Web Page (PS 595)
29. Close the Animation Graphic Document Window (PS 597)
30. Save the Web Page (PS 598)
31. Close the File and Quit the Applications (PS 598)
32. View the Web Page Interactively (PS 599)

Learn It Online

Instructions: To complete the Learn It Online exercises, start your browser, click the Address bar, and then enter the Web address `scsite.com/photoshop/learn`. When the Photoshop CS2 Learn It Online page is displayed, follow the instructions in the exercises below. Each exercise has instructions for printing your results, either for your own records or for submission to your instructor.

1 Project Reinforcement TF, MC, and SA

Below Photoshop Project 9, click the Project Reinforcement link. Print the quiz by clicking Print on the File menu for each page. Answer each question.

2 Flash Cards

Below Photoshop Project 9, click the Flash Cards link and read the instructions. Type 20 (or a number specified by your instructor) in the Number of playing cards text box, type your name in the Enter your Name text box, and then click the Flip Card button. When the flash card is displayed, read the question and then click the ANSWER box arrow to select an answer. Flip through Flash Cards. If your score is 15 (75%) correct or greater, click Print on the File menu to print your results. If your score is less than 15 (75%) correct, then redo this exercise by clicking the Replay button.

3 Practice Test

Below Photoshop Project 9, click the Practice Test link. Answer each question, enter your first and last name at the bottom of the page, and then click the Grade Test button. When the graded practice test is displayed on your screen, click Print on the File menu to print a hard copy. Continue to take practice tests until you score 80% or better.

4 Who Wants To Be a Computer Genius?

Below Photoshop Project 9, click the Computer Genius link. Read the instructions, enter your first and last name at the bottom of the page, and then click the PLAY button. When your score is displayed, click the PRINT RESULTS link to print a hard copy.

5 Wheel of Terms

Below Photoshop Project 9, click the Wheel of Terms link. Read the instructions, and then enter your first and last name and your school name. Click the PLAY button. When your score is displayed, right-click the score and then click Print on the shortcut menu to print a hard copy.

6 Crossword Puzzle Challenge

Below Photoshop Project 9, click the Crossword Puzzle Challenge link. Read the instructions, and then enter your first and last name. Click the SUBMIT button. Work the crossword puzzle. When you are finished, click the Submit button. When the crossword puzzle is redisplayed, click the Print Puzzle button to print a hard copy.

7 Tips and Tricks

Below Photoshop Project 9, click the Tips and Tricks link. Click a topic that pertains to Project 9. Right-click the information and then click Print on the shortcut menu. Construct a brief example of what the information relates to in Photoshop to confirm you understand how to use the tip or trick.

8 Expanding Your Horizons

Below Photoshop Project 9, click the Expanding Your Horizons link. Click a topic that pertains to Project 9. Print the information. Construct a brief example of what the information relates to in Photoshop to confirm you understand the contents of the article.

9 Search Sleuth

Below Photoshop Project 9, click the Search Sleuth link. To search for a term that pertains to this project, select a term below the Project 9 title and then use the Google search engine at google.com (or any major search engine) to display and print two Web pages that present information on the term.

10 Photoshop Online Training

Below Photoshop Project 9, click the Photoshop Online Training link. When your browser displays the Web page, click one of the Photoshop tutorials that covers one or more of the objectives listed at the beginning of the project on page PS 548. Print the first page of the tutorial before stepping through it.

Apply Your Knowledge

1 Creating a Web Banner

Instructions: The following steps start Photoshop and edit a file to create a Web banner for a company that specializes in printing campaign materials. You will use the CD that accompanies this book, or see your instructor for information about accessing the files available with this book.

The file you open is a banner with the name of the company, a logo, and a motto. You are to create a folder to hold all of the associated files, convert the colors to Web-safe colors, animate the company's logo, and add text slices with rollover effects in preparation for hyperlink entries. The final product is shown in Figure 9-73.

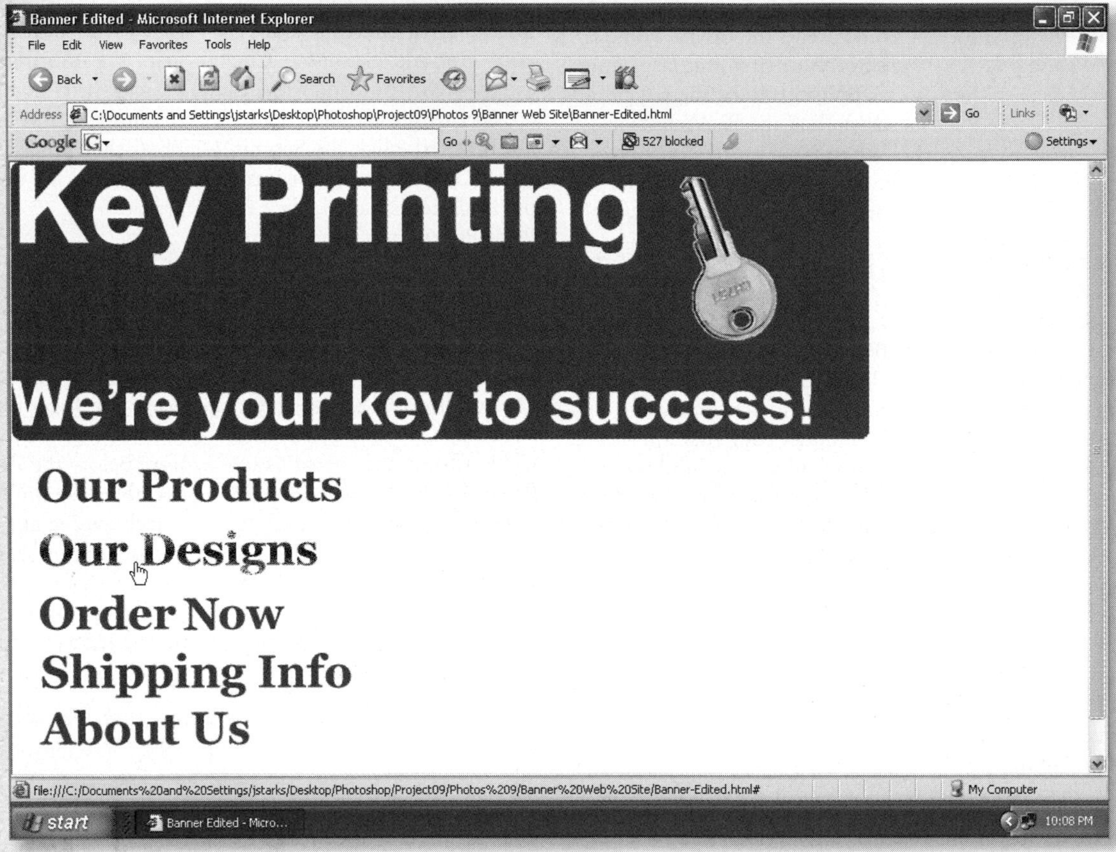

FIGURE 9-73

1. Start Photoshop. Perform the steps on pages PS 8 through PS 10 to customize the Workspace and set default values.
2. On the File menu, click Open. Open the file named, Banner, from the Project09 folder.
3. On the File menu, click Save As. When the Save As dialog box is displayed, navigate to your storage device and then click the Create New Folder button on the toolbar. When the new folder is displayed, type `Banner Web Site` as the entry, and then press the ENTER key to rename the folder. Double-click the Banner Web Site folder. In the File name text box, type `Banner Edited` to name the file. If necessary, click the Save as type box arrow and then click Photoshop (*.PSD;*.PDD) in the list. Click the Save button. If Photoshop displays an options dialog box, click the OK button.

Apply Your Knowledge

4. To select Web-safe colors:
   a. Select the Swatches palette tab. Click the Swatches palette menu button and then click Web Safe Colors. Click the OK button in the dialog box.
   b. On the Layers palette, select the Shape 1 layer. Double-click the blue thumbnail. Choose a color in the Swatches palette that is similar to the blue color in the image. Click the OK button.
5. To create new layers for the animation:
   a. On the Layers palette, right-click the key layer and then click Duplicate Layer. Repeat the process until you have the key layer and four copies. Rename the copies 45 degrees, 90 degrees, 135 degrees, and 180 degrees, respectively.
   b. Click the 45 degrees layer and press CTRL+T to display the Transform options bar. In the Set Rotation box, type `45` to rotate the layer. Press the ENTER key to commit the change.
   c. Repeat Step b for each of the other key copy layers rotating them to the degree mentioned in their layer names.
   d. On the Layers palette, turn off the visibility of all the key layers, except the original.
6. To create animation frames:
   a. On the Window menu, click Animation. When the Animation palette is displayed, press SHIFT+CTRL+ALT+F to create a new frame.
   b. On the Layers palette, turn off the visibility of the original key layer and turn on the visibility of the 45 degrees layer.
   c. Press SHIFT+CTRL+ALT+F to create a third frame. On the Layers palette, turn off the visibility of the 45 degrees layer and turn on the visibility of the 90 degrees layer.
   d. Press SHIFT+CTRL+ALT+F to create a fourth frame. On the Layers palette, turn off the visibility of the 90 degrees layer and turn on the visibility of the 135 degrees layer.
   e Press SHIFT+CTRL+ALT+F to create a fifth frame. On the Layers palette, turn off the visibility of the 135 degrees layer and turn on the visibility of the 180 degrees layer.
   f. On the Animation palette, click Frame 1. SHIFT+click Frame 4. Click the palette menu button and then click Copy Frames. Click Frame 5, click the palette menu button, and then click Paste Frames. When Photoshop asks, choose to Paste After Selection. With the four new frames still selected, click the palette menu button and then click Reverse frames.
7. Plan the animation and make any changes you feel necessary. When you are done, click Frame 1 to select it.
8. To create the text hyperlinks:
   a. In the toolbox, click the Horizontal Type Tool (T) button. On the options bar, set the font to Georgia, set the size to 14, and set the color to match the blue in the shape.
   b. Drag a box on the left side of the document window, just below the blue shape. Type `Our Products` in the type bounding box and then click the Commit any current edits button on the options bar.
   c. On the Layers palette, click the Add a layer style button and then click Gradient Overlay in the list. In the Layer Style dialog box, set Blend Mode to Dissolve. Set Opacity to 70. Choose the default, Foreground to Background Gradient. Set Style to Reflected. Set Angle to 90 and Scale to 100. The Reverse box should not be selected. The Align with Layer box should be selected. Click OK button.
   d. Press the V key to access the Move tool. ALT+drag four copies of the type bounding box and position them along the left edge, below each other. One at a time, select each new layer and type the words as shown in Figure 9-73.

(continued)

Creating a Web Banner *(continued)*

9. To slice the text:
   a. On the Layers palette, select the Our Products text layer.
   b. In the toolbox, click the Slice Tool (K) button.
   c. Draw a slice around the Our Products text element.
   d. Repeat the process for the remaining four new layers.
10. To save the file before launching ImageReady, press CTRL+S.
11. To create the rollovers:
    a. In the Photoshop toolbox, click the Edit in ImageReady button.
    b. When ImageReady displays the file, resize the Layers palette and the Web Content palette so you easily can see the five text elements and slices.
    c. To turn off the special effect for the static state of the slice, on the Web Content palette, select the slice associated with the Our Products layer. On the Layers palette, select the Our Products layer. Click the Indicates layer effects button, if necessary, to view the effects on the palette. Click the Visibility icon beside the word, Effects, so it no longer displays.
    d. To turn on the special effect for the rollover, on the Web Content palette, click the Create rollover state button. On the Layers palette, click the Visibility icon beside the word, Effects, to display it.
12. Repeat Steps 11c and 11d for each of the other text elements.
13. In the toolbox, click the Preview in (browser) button. After a wait, when the browser window opens, if a yellow bar displays across the top of the window below the browser toolbars, click the yellow bar, click Allow Blocked Content, and then click Yes in the Security Warning dialog box. Watch the animation. Rollover each of the hyperlinks. Close the browser window.
14. Click File on the ImageReady menu bar and then click Save Optimized As. When the Save Optimized As dialog box is displayed, if necessary, navigate to the Banner Web Site folder. If necessary, type `Banner` in the File name box. If necessary, click the Save as type box and then select HTML and Images (*.html) in the list. Click the Save button.
15. Close the Banner Edited document window. If ImageReady asks if you want to save the file again, click the No button. Quit ImageReady. Quit Photoshop.
16. Drop the Banner Web Site folder into your instructor's virtual dropbox or see your instructor for other ways to submit this assignment.

In the Lab

1 Creating an Image Map

Problem: As an assignment for your geography class, you decide to make an image map of the Midwest portion of the United States, with links to each state's Web site. When users view the image map, clicking any state in the graphic will hyperlink them to the state's Web site. Table 9-5 shows the URL of each state's Web site.

Table 9-5 Midwest State Web Sites

STATE	URL
Illinois	http://www.illinois.gov
Indiana	http://www.in.gov
Iowa	http://www.iowa.gov
Kansas	http://www.accesskansas.org
Michigan	http://www.michigan.gov
Minnesota	http://www.state.mn.us
Missouri	http://www.state.mo.us
Nebraska	http://www.nebraska.gov
Ohio	http://ohio.gov
Wisconsin	http://www.wisconsin.gov

The image map displays in a browser in Figure 9-74.

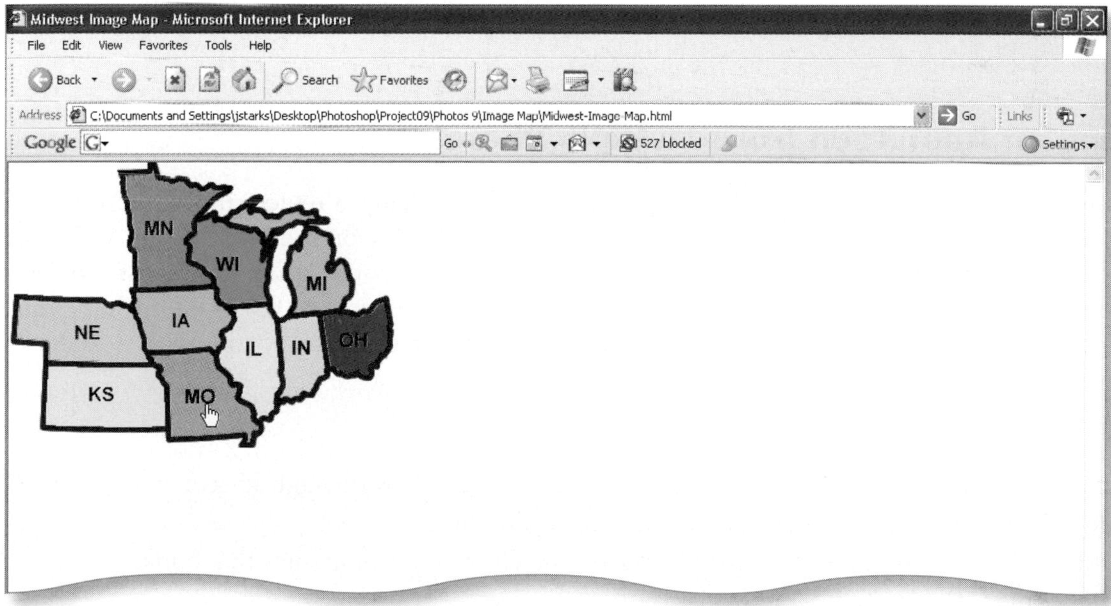

FIGURE 9-74

(continued)

Creating an Image Map *(continued)*

Instructions:

1. Open the My Computer window, navigate to your storage device, and create a new folder named, Image Map.
2. Start Photoshop. Perform the customization steps found on pages PS 8 through PS 10.
3. Open the file, Midwest, from the Project09 folder on the CD that accompanies this book.
4. Click the Save As command on the File menu. Type `Midwest Image Map` as the file name. Select the PSD format. Browse to your USB flash drive storage device and the Image Map folder. Click the Save button. When Photoshop displays an options dialog box, click the OK button.
5. To create a slice for each state:
   a. In the toolbox, click the Slice Tool (K) button.
   b. Drag a rectangle around the outline of the state of Nebraska. Stay as close to the border as possible.
   c. Double-click the slice badge next to the slice number. When Photoshop displays the Slice Options dialog box, enter information about the state. Type the name of the state in the Name box. Enter the URL from Table 9-5. Leave the Target box blank. In the Message Text box, type `State of Nebraska` as the entry. In the Alt Tag box, type `Click here to go to the official Web site of Nebraska`. Click the OK button.
   d. Repeat Steps b and c for each state. In state outlines that are not rectangular, draw as large a slice as possible that does not overlap any other state. You can create two slices that point to the same Web site for the two parts of Michigan, if desired.
6. When all the states are complete, click the Save for Web command on the Photoshop File menu. Choose the best optimization and save the file with the name, Midwest-Image-Map using the HTML and Images (*.html) format, in the Image Map folder.
7. Save the PSD file again and then quit Photoshop. Preview the Web site using a browser.
8. See your instructor for ways to submit this assignment.

2 Tweening an Animation from Multiple Photos

Problem: Your friend has recently opened the Terpsichore Dance Academy, a dance studio for children. She has a Web site, but would like to create an animation of a dancer to display on the home page. A photographer has submitted four photographs of a young dancer taken at various stages of a dance movement; however, the photographs have a rugged background and contain dark, non-contrasting colors. Using Photoshop, you will need to eliminate the background. You decide to investigate ImageReady's capability to import a folder of files as frames for animation.

Instructions:

1. Start Photoshop. Perform the customization steps found on pages PS 8 through PS 10.
2. On your storage device, create a folder named, Dancer Animation.
3. Open the folder, Dancer, from the Project09 folder on the CD that accompanies this book.
4. Open the file named, Dancer1.
5. To facilitate transparency and keep the file size small for the Web site, resize the image to three inches wide using the Image Size command on the Image menu. The height command will adjust automatically.

6. Remove the background using a combination of the following techniques. Zoom in and scroll in the image as necessary.
   a. Select large portions of the background and then press the DELETE key.
   b. Use the Magnetic Lasso tool as necessary, to draw around the dancer. Invert the selection and then delete.
   c. Use the Magic Wand tool to select remaining contiguous color portions and delete them.
   d. Use the Eraser tools, resizing the mouse pointer as necessary, to erase finer portions of the background that remain.
   e. Save the edited image on your storage device, in the Dancer Animation folder created in Step 2. Use the GIF format and name the file, Dancer1. When Photoshop displays an Indexed Color dialog box, click the OK button. When Photoshop displays the GIF Options dialog box, click the OK button.
7. Repeat Steps 3 through 6 for the files, Dancer2, Dancer3, and Dancer4.
8. Quit Photoshop. Start ImageReady. On the ImageReady Window menu, point to Workspace, and then click Default Palette Locations.
9. Click File on the menu bar, point to Import, and then click Folder as Frames. When ImageReady displays the Browse For Folder dialog box, click the plus sign beside your storage device and then click the folder named, Dancer Animation. Click the OK button.
10. When the four photos display as frames on the Animation palette, select Frame 2. Click the palette menu button and copy the frame. Click Frame 4. Use the Paste frame command on the palette menu to paste the frame at the end of the animation sequence. Copy and paste Frame 1 to the end, in the same manner.
11. Click Frame 1 and CTRL+click Frame 2 to select them.
12. On the palette menu, click Tween. When the Tween dialog box is displayed, type 5 in the Frames to add box. If necessary, select All Layers. If necessary, select all three Parameter check boxes. Click the OK button.
13. When the Animation palette displays the new Frames 2 through 6, click Frame 7 and CTRL+click Frame 8 to select them. Repeat Step 12.
14. When the Animation palette displays the new Frames 8 though 12, click Frame 13 and CTRL+click Frame 14 to select them. Repeat Step 12.
15. When the Animation palette displays the new Frames 14 through 18, click Frame 19 and CTRL+click Frame 20 to select them. Repeat Step 12.
16. When the Animation palette displays the new Frames 20 through 24, click Frame 25 and CTRL+click Frame 26 to select them. Repeat Step 12.
17. Adjust the animation to play once. Play the animation.
18. On the File menu, click Save Optimized As. Save the file in the Dancer Animation folder using the HTML format. Name the file, Animation Complete.
19. Quit ImageReady. Open the folder named, Dance Animation. Right-click the file named, Animation Complete, point to Open With, and then choose your browser. Watch the animation play.
20. Close the window. Send the Animation Complete HTML file and the folder of images to your instructor as directed. Compress or zip the file and folders if necessary.

3 Exploring ImageReady

Problem: Your instructor has asked you to explore the features of ImageReady — especially those that are different than Photoshop. You decide to look at the different palettes and create a report showing what the palettes look like and what they do.

Instructions:

1. Open a word processing or page layout application program on your system. Create a blank page. Type your name, course number, and date. Create a heading with the words, ImageReady Palettes.
2. Start ImageReady for your system. On the Window menu, point to Workspace, and then click Default Palette locations.
3. In ImageReady, open the file created in this project or another project that contains layers, slices, or rollovers, saved in the PSD format. When the image is displayed, minimize the document window.
4. Use the Window menu to open each of the following ImageReady palettes: Animation, Image Map, Slice, Web Content, Table, and Optimize, as necessary.
5. Do the following for each palette:
   a. Drag the palette title bar to move the palette to the middle of the Workspace.
   b. Resize the palette to demonstrate its features. For example, if you were using the Layers palette, you would want to enlarge the palette to show at least two layers with displayed effects, or an open layer group.
   c. Select a layer, frame, or visibility icon if necessary, so buttons at the bottom of the palette are enabled.
   d. Point to each button and make a note of its name listed in the tool tip.
   e. Click the palette menu button. Then, with the menu still open, press the PRINT SCRN key on your keyboard.
6. On the Windows taskbar, click the button associated with your page layout program. When the document page opens, do the following:
   a. Type the name of the ImageReady palette. Press the ENTER key several times to create blank lines.
   b. Press CTRL+V to paste the screen capture, and then press the ENTER key several times.
   c. Make a list of all buttons on the palette, underneath the screen shot.
7. Open the Adobe Help Center. In the Search box, type the name of the palette and then click the Search button. When the list of links is displayed on the left, search for a link that has words such as About, or Using. Click the link.
8. Read the information about the palette. Look for the palette's purpose and typical uses. Click links that may explain the function of each of the buttons.
9. After researching the palette, click the button on the Windows taskbar for your page layout program. Below the screen shot, type a paragraph describing the palette's purpose and use. Beside each listed button, type its purpose. After the last button, press CTRL+ENTER to create a new page, or issue the command for your program that creates a new page.
10. Repeat Steps 5 through 9 for each of the palettes listed in Step 4.
11. Save the research document and print a copy for your instructor.
12. Close ImageReady, the Adobe Help Center, and your research document.

Cases and Places

The difficulty of these case studies varies:
■ are the least difficult and ■■ are the most difficult. The last exercise is a group exercise.

1 ■ Create a My Favorite Sites Web page. Use Web-safe colors and draw a large shape for the background. Use the Vertical Type tool to create a text element down the left edge of the page. Use a contrasting color for the text. Type your name in the type bounding box. Using the same color, create a horizontal text element heading that says, My Favorite Sites. Below the heading and to the right of your name, create five more horizontal text elements in a complementary font, but use a smaller font size. Type the names of a favorite Web site in each element. Use the name of the page rather than the Web address. Use pages that represent genres, such as musical artists, sports teams, search engines, or videos. Include your school or work as one of the text elements. Slice each text element and then click the Edit in ImageReady button. Use the Slice palette to insert a URL, a _blank target specification, an Alt tag, and a status bar message for each slice. Preview the Web page and make any necessary changes. Save the page as HTML with the name My_Favorite_Sites.

2 ■ You need to make buttons for an upcoming slide show presentation and want something more than the traditional clip art buttons that come with your presentation software. Open a blank Web document in ImageReady. Press the `U` key to access the Rectangle tool. Draw four rectangles approximately 200 pixels square. The layers will display on the Layers palette. Open the Styles palette and choose a different style for each rectangle. Press the `T` key to access the Type tool. One at a time, click each button. On the options bar choose a contrasting color for the text that complements the button. On the buttons, type `Home`, `Back`, `Forward`, and `End`, respectively. On the Layers palette, add a shadow effect on each text layer. For each button, point the shadow a different direction. Order the layers, so each text layer displays just above its button. One set at a time, click the button layer and then SHIFT+click the button's text layer. On the palette menu, click Link Layers to link the button and its text together. Have your instructor choose the best of the four buttons and then copy and paste it into a presentation.

3 ■■ You have decided to put your name up in lights! Create a Web banner with a bold, Web-safe color background. Create a type bounding box using a large font in a contrasting color. Type your name. On the Layers palette, make sure the opacity is set to 100 percent. Duplicate the layer and set the opacity of the copy to 10 percent. Turn the visibility off on both text layers. Open the Animation palette. In the first frame, turn on the visibility of the 10 percent layer. Create a second frame in which you turn off the 10 percent layer and turn on the 100 percent layer. Set the time delay on each frame to .5 seconds. Set the animation to play only once. Tween the two frames with 10 frames in between with opacity changes only. Save the file optimized for the Web in HTML format. View your name up in lights via a browser window.

Cases and Places

4 ■■ As an intern for a Web design company, you have been assigned to create an animated GIF for an ice cream shop. The client has provided several photos of an ice cream cone melting, which are included with the CD that accompanies this book. In the Project 09 folder, the photos are stored in a folder named, Ice Cream Photos. You need to remove the background in each of the photos and then save each one in the GIF format in a new folder you create named, Ice Cream Animation. To create a clip art feeling, use the Pen tool to draw around the cone itself, and use the techniques you have learned about creating a shape layer for a cartoon-like effect. Use an appropriate color and filter on the ice cream cone. Copy the shape layer to the other photos. Use ImageReady's Import command on the File menu to import the folder of ice cream photos into frames. Tween each set of two frames and adjust the animation settings as necessary. Save the file in the HTML format and view it in a browser to watch the ice cream melt.

5 ■■ **Working Together** Each member of the group should surf the Web to look for dramatic rollover effects. Each member should bring five examples of Web sites that have unusual or fancy rollover buttons or effects. As a group, look at the rollover effects on the Web. Choose three of the best ones. Discuss how each effect was probably created. Decide if the rollover effect is a completely different image, a different layer, a layer effect, a filter, or something else. Write down five characteristics of the static version and five characteristics of the rollover. Then individually, each member should try to recreate one of the effects using Photoshop and ImageReady. Save the file, optimized in the HTML format. Come back together as a group with copies of the rollover, and again view them together on the Web. Make suggestions to each other for improvements or corrections. When each member receives all the feedback, make the corrections and distribute the final copy to the class or your instructor.

Graphic Design From Concept to Finished Product

Objectives

You will have mastered the materials in this special feature when you can:

- Discuss the development of a graphic design project from concept to finished product
- State the similarities and differences between designing for print and for the Web
- Explain the function of a navigation map
- Define the terms die-cutting and scoring
- Describe the basic characteristics of paper
- Determine why computer monitors vary
- Illustrate the significance of working with Web-safe colors
- Demonstrate the iterative design process
- Describe the importance of contracts, budgets, and schedules
- List the information necessary to provide to the print company
- Apply methods of critiquing to improve the quality of your design work
- Identify methods for gaining experience and continuing formal design education

An Overview of the Graphic Design Process

Graphic design is the act of arranging words and images to communicate a specific message to an intended audience. Graphic designers develop ideas or concepts into products, by manipulating elements such as images, text, and color using techniques such as contrast, juxtaposition, and perspective.

Although the specific expertise provided by a professional graphic designer is concept development, an idea is only a thought until it becomes something tangible, such as a sketch, a storyboard, or a product. Many designers agree that developing the idea is only a fraction of their job. The majority of the work that defines a graphic designer's ability includes how to access the available, necessary resources, and execute the many different stages required to produce a finished piece.

Each graphic design assignment is different, yet most graphic design jobs follow a similar path of development and production. Figure SF 3-1 lists the basic concerns for a graphic designer. Directing a project through to completion requires problem solving skills, creativity, and knowledge of technical procedures to ensure successful results. A practiced understanding of the developmental process of a design project is essential to being a graphic design professional.

The Development of an Idea

Designers are typically creating a product for someone else, as indicated in Figure SF 3-1. A design problem, presented to the graphic designer by the client, is usually referred to as a project, a piece, an assignment, or a product. The client's intent usually is to sell, to inform, or to educate. The goal of both the designer and the client is to communicate a message or present a product to an audience or consumer. A consumer is sometimes referred to as a **user**, **user group**, or **target audience**. To solve any specific design problem, the designer's job is to understand both the needs of the client and the target audience. To ensure that the design functions as intended, satisfying both the client and audience, the designer tests the idea by showing comps to the client and a sampling of the target audience. You may recall that a comp is an abbreviation of the word, comprehensive. Comps are developed from the best ideas taken from your rough sketches. Comps are renderings, which look as close as possible to how you imagine the finished product.

Graphic designers often rely on inspiration to come up with an idea. But truly great ideas rarely develop in isolation. Researching and documenting, listening to and brainstorming with other people, and making sketches and prototypes are some of the methods designers use to transform great concepts into workable solutions for their design projects.

GRAPHIC DESIGNER'S CONCERNS

1. CLIENT/AUDIENCE/CONSUMER
You are usually making it for someone else.

2. DESIGN OF AN IDEA
Defined by its purpose, it must function as intended.

3. PROCESS
Technical & creative methods are combined to achieve results.

FIGURE SF 3-1

Anatomy of a Design

Graphic design takes all forms and shapes. Although most people do not take time to deeply analyze the objects they use every day, graphic design professionals appreciate the creative challenge of each project no matter how mundane or practical. An in-depth breakdown of any project becomes a fascinating and involved process when viewed through the eyes of a designer. Figure SF 3-2 displays an unfolded butter box. Each facet of making this box involved the integration of design decisions, technical processes, and subsequently, many different people.

The client and designer work together to identify what is special about the product, who it is for, and how and what ideas should be conveyed. The content and graphics, such as the required nutritional and legal information and logo, are determined and provided by the client. The designer has liberty to make decisions about type size, style, color, placement, and layout of all text and images. The designer also must ensure that essential details, such as ink color, type of paper, and fold marks are communicated to the printer.

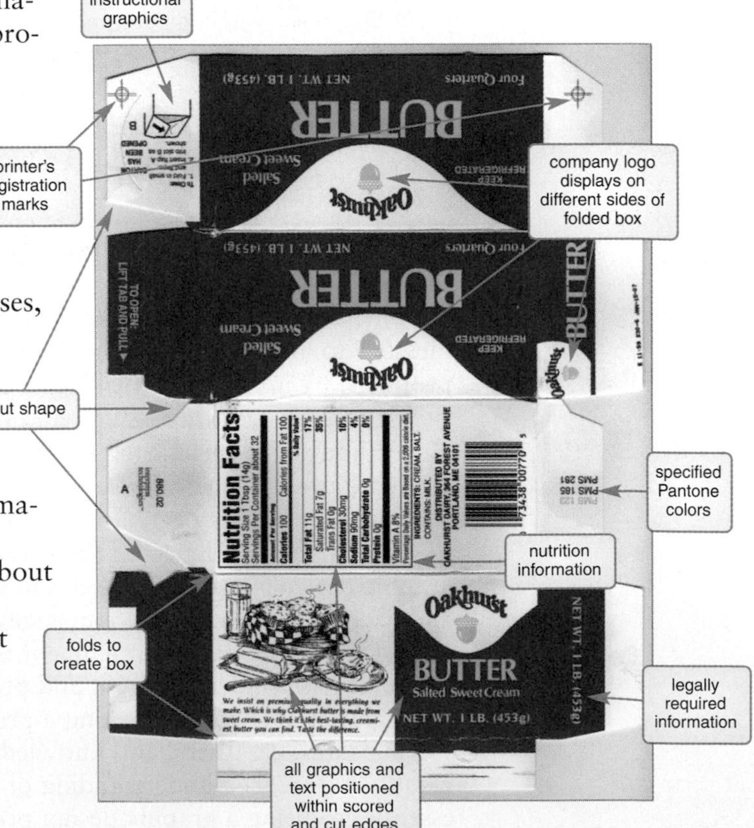

FIGURE SF 3-2

Folding is integral to this particular design, therefore the designer must consider how each side of the box relates to the other. The designer commonly makes several preliminary mock-ups of the box in order to imagine the end product, before completing the design. Although in the figure the box appears flat, the printed sheet ultimately will be cut and folded, creating the finished product. The print production process is called die-cutting. **Die-cutting** refers to cutting a printed sheet to a specific shape or shapes. In the die-cutting process, paper also is scored. Folded paper will have a rough, cracked edge if folded against its grain. **Scoring** paper means making indents in the paper so it folds smoothly without cracking. When a design involves die-cutting or scoring, it is important to consider the layout of individual elements. The text and images should be placed clear of any folds and cuts. Notice in Figure SF 3-2 that all graphics and text are placed within the layout area, away from edges created by folds and cuts.

From Idea to Finished Product

When designing for the Web or for print, the stages of planning and development are essentially the same. The production stages differ because the medium of the final product is different. For a Web site the outcome is screen graphics, while for print it is paper or a printable material. Because many people are involved in producing any kind of design, good communication between all involved parties is essential for both Web and print design.

Figure SF 3-3 shows the basic progression of a graphic design project. Stages 1 through 4 deal predominantly with planning and development. Stages 5 through 7 involve production. In Stage 1, the client identifies a need and contracts a graphic designer. In Stage 2, the designer guides the client in identifying the necessary essentials for the project to proceed, such as defining the project goals, schedule, and budget.

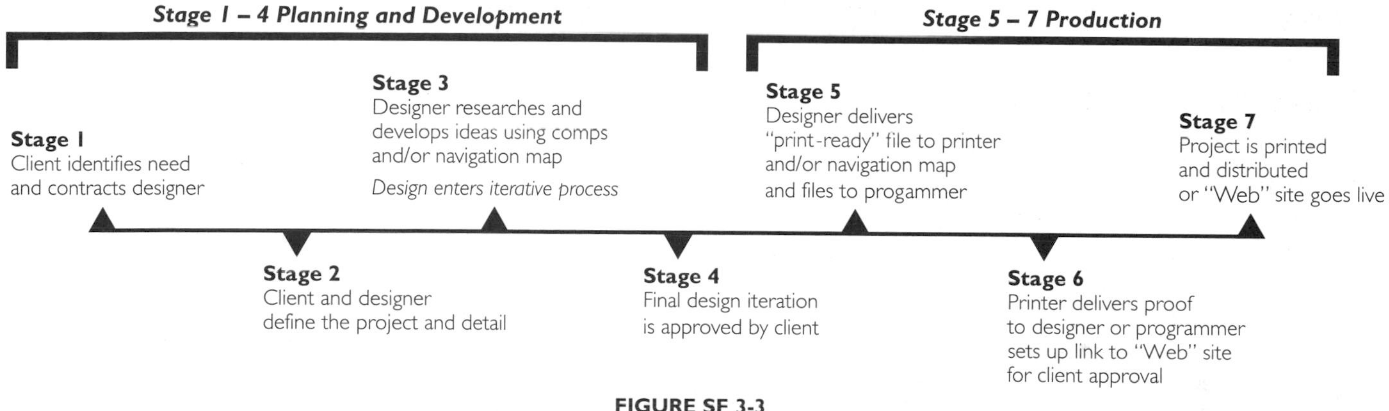

FIGURE SF 3-3

In Stage 3, the designer begins research by analyzing existing pieces and learning as much as possible about the project. Ideas are made into preliminary roughs or sketches. The best sketches are developed into comps. For print, the designer may be required to produce a **dummy**, which is a layout that shows multiple pages or panels such as for a newsletter or magazine. Dummies can be very simple, such as the dummy in Figure SF 3-4 for an advertising brochure that illustrates both sides of the brochure and labels the order of the panels.

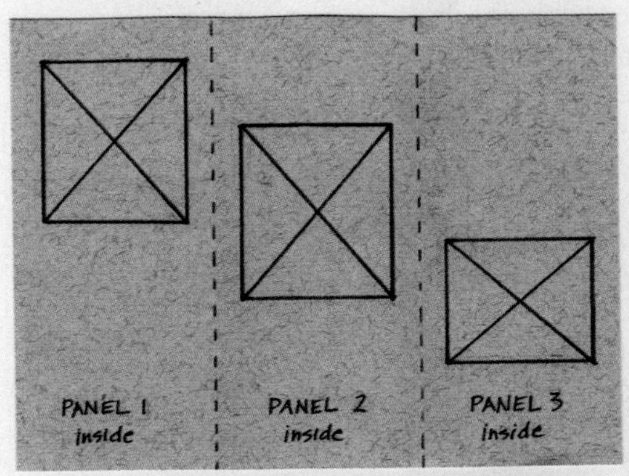

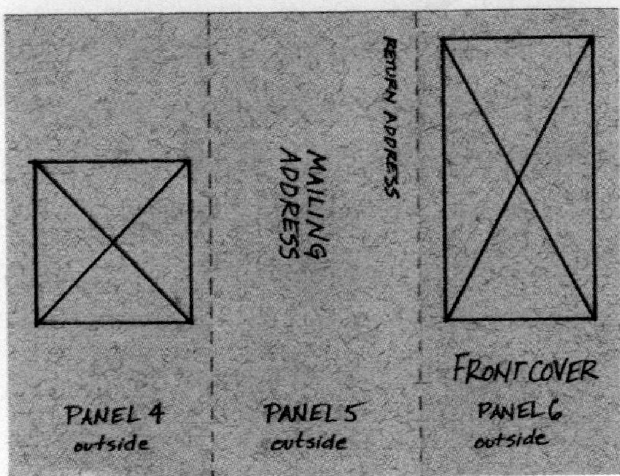

FIGURE SF 3-4

For a Web site, the designer usually begins with a **navigation map**. A navigation map is a simplified version of a storyboard used to illustrate how a user might move or navigate through a series of pages. Figure SF 3-5 shows an example of a navigation map. Navigation maps also are used to identify the number of pages needed for a particular Web site.

Between Stages 3 and 4, the design undergoes changes and improvements, also known as **iterations**, until the client approves the final design in Stage 4. A more detailed discussion of design iteration will be covered later in this special feature.

During Stage 5, the design enters its production phase. For a Web site, the designer usually works closely with an experienced programmer to ensure that the Web site's interactivity functions properly. The designer provides the navigation map and any necessary graphic files to produce the Web site. For a print project, the designer communicates with the print company representative. The designer provides the printing service with print-ready files that contain all the necessary graphics to complete the project. Table SF 3-1 includes essential information for the designer to provide to the printing service.

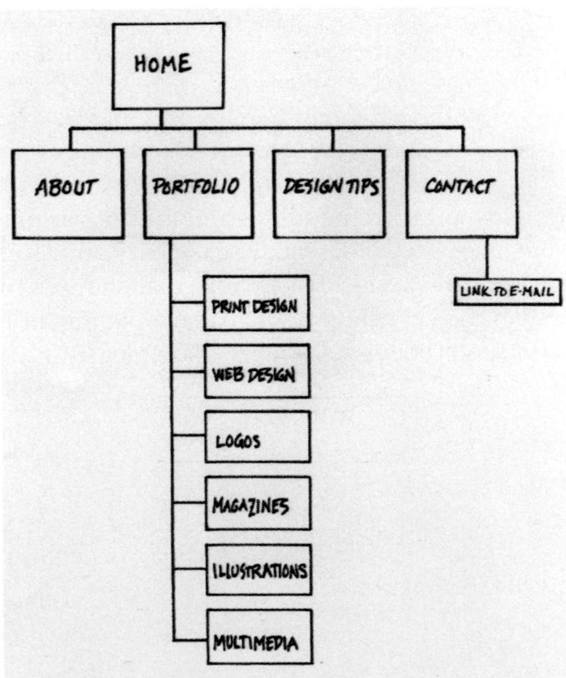

FIGURE SF 3-5

When designing for print, the designer commonly determines the choice of paper. Paper typically is packaged in a **ream**, which is a package of 500 sheets. The label on a ream of paper, illustrated in Figure SF 3-6, displays information about the paper contained in the package.

Although we often think of paper as flat, it is dimensional and tactile. Paper has front and back sides, and edges. Holding a piece of paper we may notice if it feels flimsy, like newsprint, or strong, like cardboard. The first sensation to affect our senses, consciously or subconsciously, when we touch a printed piece is the paper. **Paper stock** is the term used to encompass the different characteristics of paper. Paper comes in a variety of colors, including very subtle differences between whites and off whites. **Finish** refers to the surface of paper and can be smooth, textured, glossy, or matte. Paper comes in two basic categories of weight, cover and text. **Cover** describes thick, heavyweight paper; **text** describes lighter weight paper. Paper weight is measured in **pounds** and abbreviated as **lb.** or the symbol **#.** For example, a magazine cover might be printed on 60# glossy cover, while the inside pages might be printed on a 24 lb. matte text. The inside pages of this book are printed on 50 lb. Schooner, matte. The cover is printed on 100 lb. cover stock, coated one side. To choose the most appropriate paper stock for a job, it is useful to talk with a printer about the variety of papers available, including recycled and specialty papers. You also can research paper companies online to request samples of their paper selections.

Table SF 3-1 Project Specifications for Printing Services

PROJECT SPECIFICATIONS FOR THE PRINTER	EXAMPLE
Job description	Advertising brochure
Deadline due dates	March 9
Paper stock	80 lb. white glossy text
Quantity of printed pieces	500
Color (1, 2, or 4-color)	2c black and Pantone 185
Size of finished piece	8½ x 11
Special instructions for printing, folding, binding, or cutting	Printed 2 sides 2 folds to 3 panels
List of fonts used	Helvetica Narrow and Times Roman
Software and versions used	Photoshop CS2 version 9
Delivery of print-ready file	Designer will send PDF
Hard copy printout of the project	Included

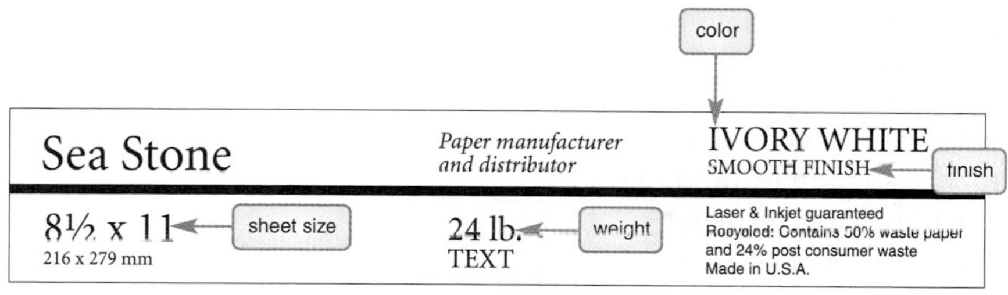

FIGURE SF 3-6

In Stage 6 of Figure SF 3-3, the printing service or programmer delivers a proof of the finished project for client and designer approval. A **proof** is a general term used to describe a version of the finished project before it enters final production to ensure that all text and graphics are correct and accurate. For print, there are various methods for producing proofs, such as ink-jet or laser print. For the Web programmer, this means setting up an access link so that the design can be viewed on screen.

The completion of a project is Stage 7 in Figure SF 3-3. In Web design, the site now is live and accessible to the viewer. For print, the product is printed, delivered to the client, and appropriately distributed.

The similarities between creating a design for Web and print include paying attention to the hierarchy of information, use of color, use of layout space, and understanding the ultimate medium for presentation. The major difference in the end product is that a Web site always can be adjusted to accommodate any changes, even after the project is complete. A printed piece is final and can only be changed by reprinting.

Color Considerations for Web Sites

In Special Feature 2, you learned about the 216 colors in the Web-safe color palette. Computer monitors are designed with a built-in capacity for interpreting colors. Depending on the age, brand, and model of computer monitor, some are able to render a broader range of colors, while others render a more limited selection of colors.

The Web-safe color palette was developed by programmers as a standard selection of colors that ideally would look the same to each viewer regardless of the computer's capacity for color rendering. Although selecting your colors from this palette ensures a level of consistency, the colors may still appear differently to individual viewers because the conditions for viewing vary widely. It is very important to remember that no two monitors will render color exactly the same because no two computer systems are precisely alike. Both hardware and software affect how the colors used in a Web site will appear to a viewer. Additionally, images on a monitor will appear lighter, or more vibrant, depending on the physical location of the monitor in relation to light sources. It generally is easier to view a monitor in a slightly darkened room rather than near a bright window. Macintosh computers initially were designed to accommodate colors for print; they generally display more brightly than PCs. Also, each computer system has preference settings that allow the user to select conditions for page size and color viewing — conditions that change the way a site appears.

The particular browser that a user chooses is another factor contributing to the difference in color appearance. A **browser** is the software application that allows a computer user to view a Web site. Web browsers, such as Safari and Internet Explorer, interpret Web sites differently from each other.

Table SF 3-2 lists some of the conditions that affect how the viewer sees a Web site.

With the listed conditions that contribute to inconsistent viewing, there exists dispute among designers whether using the Web-safe palette is useful in ensuring accurate viewing. The fact is, there is no guarantee that colors will appear accurately. But it is generally believed that because the palette is optimized for cross-platform viewing, selecting from the Web-safe palette reduces the possibility of drastic color variation.

Table SF 3-2 Conditions that Affect Web Site Viewing

CONDITIONS AFFECTING WEB SITE VIEWING	SPECIFIC EXAMPLES
Brand, model, age of monitor	NEC Multisync, Sony Trinitron, etc.
Location of computer	Ambient light
Computer systems	Macintosh or PC
System preference settings	Color and viewing size
Web browser software	Netscape, Safari, Firefox, Internet Explorer, etc.
Type of display	LCD, Plasma, CRT

Design Iterations

The **iterative design process** refers to making changes during the early stages of a project, until the client, user, and designer are satisfied with the results. Figure SF 3-7 is a basic diagram of the iterative cycle. The initial design begins the iterative process when the designer makes a prototype or comp, and tests it on a user group. The **user group** should be a sampling of the audience who ultimately will be using the product. The client and designer identify changes for improvement. The designer makes the revisions, creates another prototype, and the cycle begins again. As many iterations are performed as necessary, until the client and designer agree that the project development is complete. The design then continues to the next stage of production.

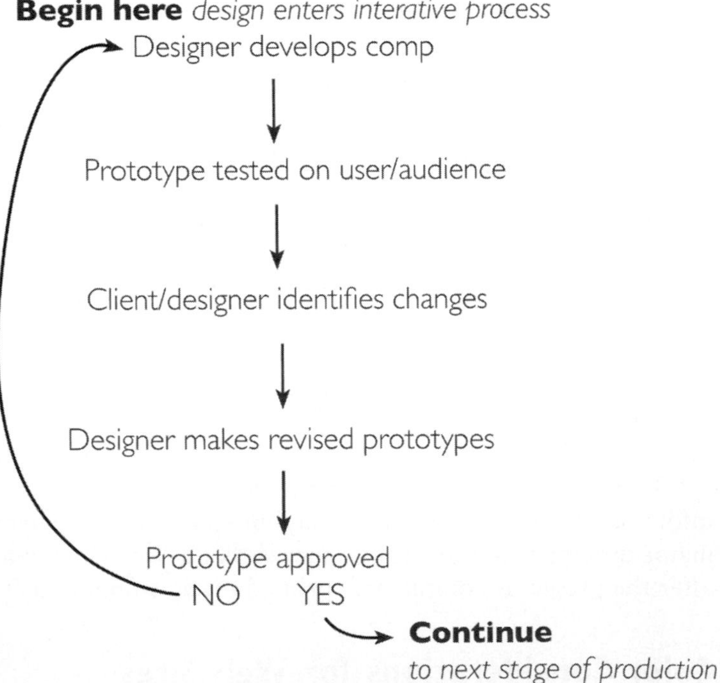

FIGURE SF 3-7

Figures SF 3-7 through SF 3-11 illustrate examples of the stages in the iterative process. Figure SF 3-8 shows a company's order form designed for print. A user test uncovered several issues. User testing of the initial prototype proved that there was not enough space for the user to fill in the required information. Information hierarchy and content appeared confusing. The tracking number used by the company's business office was difficult to locate and read. The company logo was positioned poorly. Overall, the layout was unbalanced with too much white space at the top and too much crowding at the bottom of the page. The designer identified the problems to the client and suggested changes.

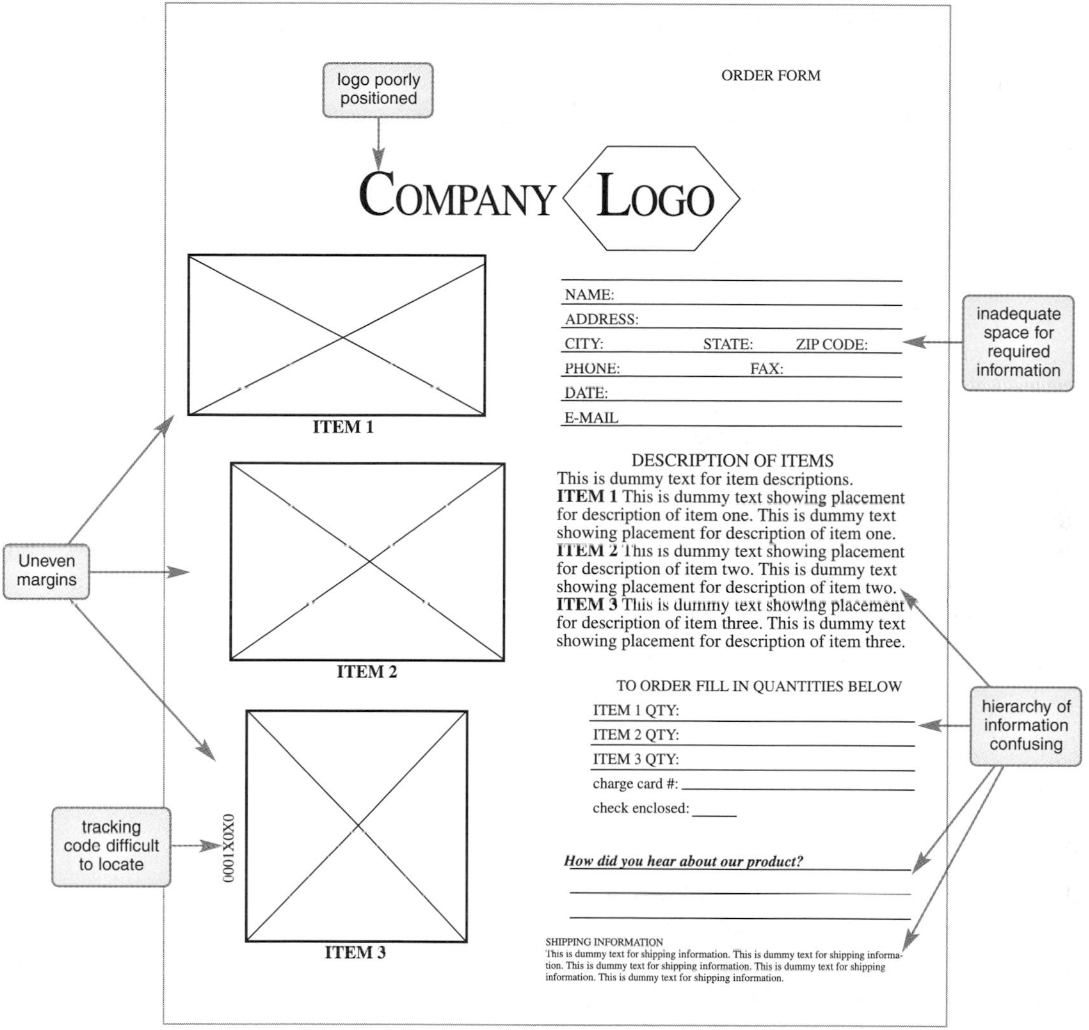

FIGURE SF 3-8

Figure SF 3-9 shows revisions made to the design. Repositioning and reducing the logo size allows more space for required information below. By increasing the right margin, changing the type size, leading, and format to upper- and lowercase, the form appears easier for the user to fill out. Repositioning the tracking number makes organization easier for the business office.

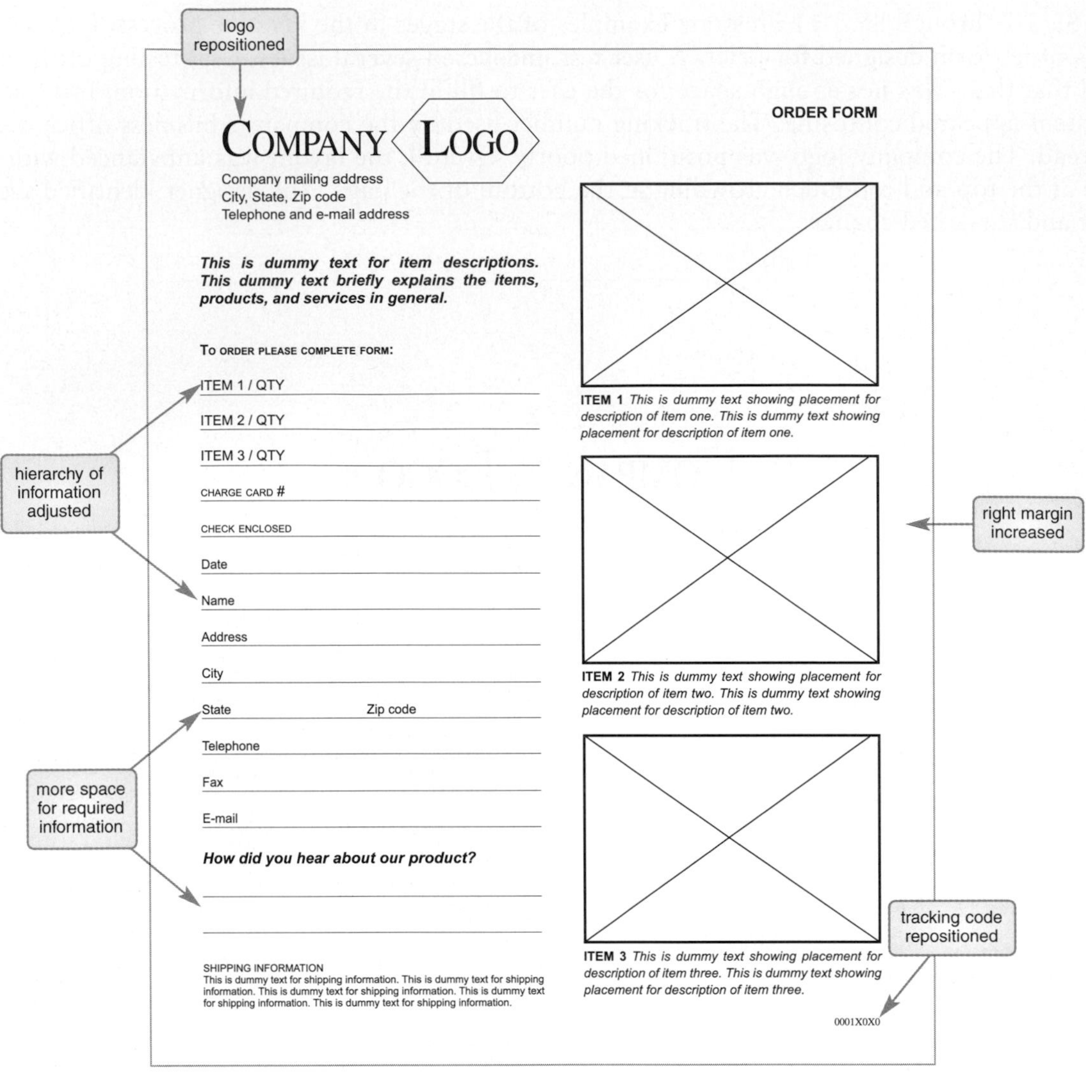

FIGURE SF 3-9

The company also intended to use the order form on their Web site. Figure SF 3-10 shows the form adapted for a horizontal format, with color indicating the active field. In Web design, adding more color does not add additional cost to the project. The designer used color to alert the user to input fields. **Input fields**, also called **active fields** are data entry areas in a Web site that the user completes and sends directly to the company.

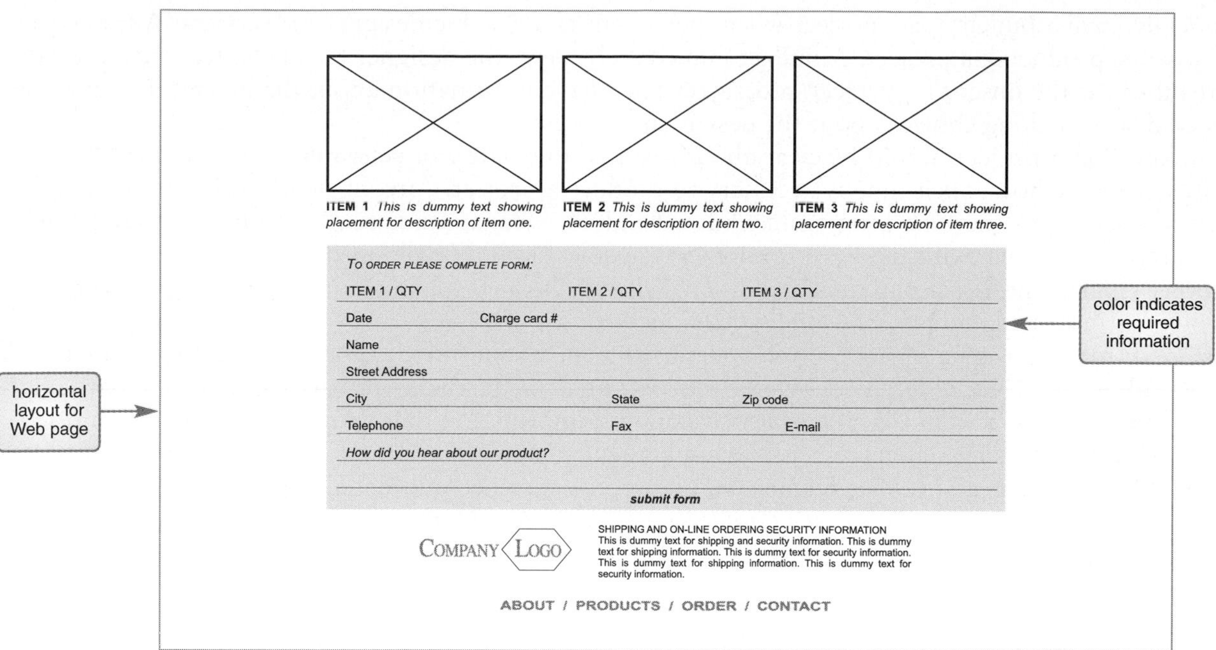

ITEM 1 *This is dummy text showing placement for description of item one.*
ITEM 2 *This is dummy text showing placement for description of item two.*
ITEM 3 *This is dummy text showing placement for description of item three.*

To order please complete form:
ITEM 1 / QTY
ITEM 2 / QTY
ITEM 3 / QTY
Date
Charge card #
Name
Street Address
City
State
Zip code
Telephone
Fax
E-mail
How did you hear about our product?
submit form

COMPANY LOGO

SHIPPING AND ON-LINE ORDERING SECURITY INFORMATION
This is dummy text for shipping and security information. This is dummy text for shipping information. This is dummy text for security information. This is dummy text for shipping information. This is dummy text for security information.

ABOUT / PRODUCTS / ORDER / CONTACT

FIGURE SF 3-10

In this example, once the client saw how well color was used to indicate active fields in the Web site, they requested that the designer make one more iteration to the printed version of the form — the client wanted to add a second color to the print version in order to emphasize customer and order information visually. The designer instead recommended using a single color with a screen tint, to give the illusion of a second color while saving on printing costs. Figure SF 3-11 displays the final iteration of the form for print. The design then proceeded to the next stage of production, as illustrated in the iterative design diagram.

Budgets, Schedules, and Contracts

Budgets, schedules, and contracts are important regardless of whether you work within a company or work for yourself. When you work within a company, there often are other people designated to manage business-related details. As a freelance designer, you likely will have to manage every detail yourself.

10 % screen indicates area to be filled in

COMPANY LOGO

ORDER FORM

Company mailing address
City, State, Zip code
Telephone and e-mail address

This is dummy text for item descriptions. This dummy text briefly explains the items, products, and services in general.

To order please complete form:
ITEM 1 / QTY
ITEM 2 / QTY
ITEM 3 / QTY
CHARGE CARD #
CHECK ENCLOSED
Date
Name
Address
City
State
Zip code
Telephone
Fax
E-mail
How did you hear about our product?

SHIPPING INFORMATION
This is dummy text for shipping information. This is dummy text for shipping information. This is dummy text for shipping information. This is dummy text for shipping information. This is dummy text for shipping information.

ITEM 1 *This is dummy text showing placement for description of item one. This is dummy text showing placement for description of item one.*

ITEM 2 *This is dummy text showing placement for description of item two. This is dummy text showing placement for description of item two.*

ITEM 3 *This is dummy text showing placement for description of item three. This is dummy text showing placement for description of item three.*

0001X0X0

FIGURE SF 3-11

Clients typically have a budget for a project when they contract a graphic designer for services. A **budget** is the monetary cost for producing a project. A budget immediately alerts the designer to certain technical considerations and realities. At the onset of a project, a designer must have information about the budget, because cost directly is involved with making choices about the design and process.

Everyone involved in a project should be clear about required due dates, or **schedules**. The client and designer usually determine how much time is necessary to produce a project. Anyone involved in production, such as the printing service or the Web programmer, must be given adequate time to accomplish the designated task. A design rarely is complete with the first prototype. Schedules should be planned to accommodate design iterations, as every change and revision requires additional time. Schedules may be adjusted as long as every individual involved is informed and agrees to the scheduling change.

Contracts are written agreements between the designer and client, and the designer and printing company. A sample contract is shown in Figure SF 3-12, however the look of a contract will vary according to the particular job and company format. Table SF 3-3 is a checklist of standard information that should be included in most contracts. Because a contract is a legal agreement, it should include the date and signatures of anyone named in the contract. Each person involved in the agreement should receive a signed and dated copy of the contract. Many graphic designers use the *Graphic Artist's Guild Pricing & Ethical Guidelines Handbook* as a resource for industry standards related to pricing and contracts.

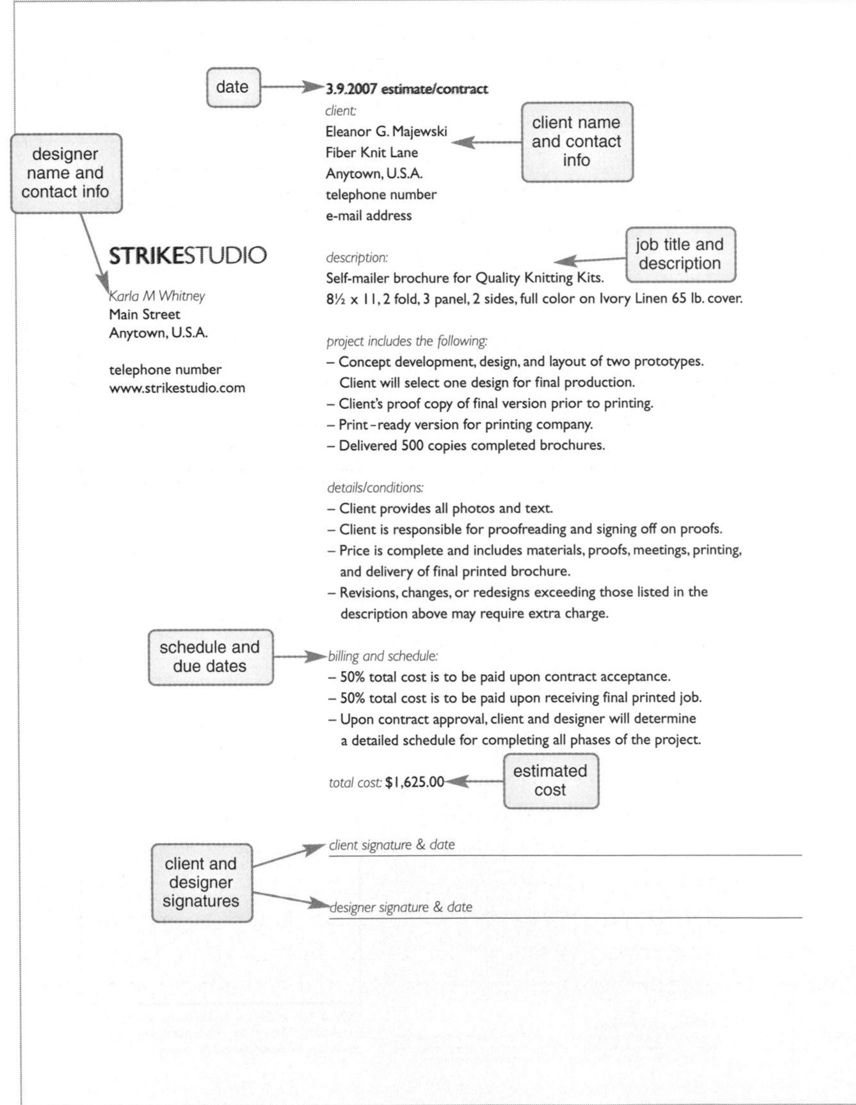

3.9.2007 estimate/contract

client:
Eleanor G. Majewski
Fiber Knit Lane
Anytown, U.S.A.
telephone number
e-mail address

STRIKESTUDIO

Karla M Whitney
Main Street
Anytown, U.S.A.

telephone number
www.strikestudio.com

description:
Self-mailer brochure for Quality Knitting Kits.
8½ x 11, 2 fold, 3 panel, 2 sides, full color on Ivory Linen 65 lb. cover.

project includes the following:
– Concept development, design, and layout of two prototypes. Client will select one design for final production.
– Client's proof copy of final version prior to printing.
– Print-ready version for printing company.
– Delivered 500 copies completed brochures.

details/conditions:
– Client provides all photos and text.
– Client is responsible for proofreading and signing off on proofs.
– Price is complete and includes materials, proofs, meetings, printing, and delivery of final printed brochure.
– Revisions, changes, or redesigns exceeding those listed in the description above may require extra charge.

billing and schedule:
– 50% total cost is to be paid upon contract acceptance.
– 50% total cost is to be paid upon receiving final printed job.
– Upon contract approval, client and designer will determine a detailed schedule for completing all phases of the project.

total cost: $1,625.00

client signature & date

designer signature & date

FIGURE SF 3-12

Table SF 3-3 Contract Checklist

STANDARD CONTRACT INFORMATION
Client's name, location, e-mail address, and telephone number
Designer's name, location, e-mail address, and telephone number
Job title
Job description
Estimated cost
Schedule and due dates
Signatures of client and designer

Improving The Quality of Your Graphic Design

Your instinct, which can be described as your initial, immediate reaction to a design, is often a good gauge in determining the effectiveness of a layout. Yet, no matter how objective you perceive yourself to be, you likely are affected by deep-rooted influences, such as cultural attitudes and personal taste that may prejudice your design perception and aesthetic judgment. Graphic designers continually strive to produce the best results possible.

Critiquing Design Work

Critiquing is a method of analyzing how successfully a design piece does and does not accomplish what it sets out to do. Critiquing improves your visual perception and design objectivity.

The questions in Table SF 3-4 are guidelines for critiquing work. The answers to these questions help determine which particular portion of a piece solves the design problem and why. For example, when asking, "Why was the particular color(s) selected?", the answer may be that the color provides good contrast and visibility. The answers also identify which particular areas need to be developed further or changed. For example, when asking, "Does the design solve the communication problem?", the answer may be that the overall message is unclear.

Table SF 3-4 Critiquing Questions

SUGGESTED QUESTIONS FOR DESIGN CRITIQUING
What is your initial reaction and impression?
What is the message being conveyed?
What is the overall look and feel?
Who is the intended audience?
How is color used? Why was the particular color(s) selected?
Are format and layout appropriate?
How is type used? Are type, style, size, and placement appropriate?
Does the image reinforce the message?
Is the information accurate?
Is information hierarchy clear?
For Web design, is the navigation and interaction of the site easy to use?
Does the design solve the communication problem?
Should the designer continue to develop the concept or begin again?

Figure SF 3-13 is a screen shot from a graphic designer's Web site. Analyzing this page using some of the questions for critiquing in Table SF 3-4 helps to determine both the success of the design and potential areas for improvement.

What is the look and feel? Who is the intended audience? How is color used? A first reaction might be that there is motion and energy, the colors are vivid, and the layout and images are unique. Because the intended audience is someone who needs to hire a designer, uniqueness and energy are excellent qualities to convey. What is the message being conveyed? How is type used? Are style, size, and placement appropriate? The type works because it is readable and bold. The text block is placed towards the right of the screen and partially obscures the eye in the background image. This is somewhat distracting, causing the viewer's vision to trail off to the right of the screen, away from the button menu. Placing the text box a little to the left would lead the viewer to connect the text box more easily with the menu bar at the far left of the screen. The message contained in the text block is interesting and entertaining, but might be read by more viewers if edited to fewer words.

A design piece is rarely complete with the first attempt. It is sometimes difficult, yet very important, to remember that critiquing is about the work, not about you personally. It is useful and necessary to ask others for their opinions and objective feedback. You have seen how the iterative process contributes to an overall, better end result. The same can be said for critiquing. You do not have to make every suggested change during the iterative process. Nor do you have to include other's opinions about post-design critiquing. But, as you become more discerning, you will learn to value all opinions, and apply recommendations that will actually improve the quality of your work.

Tips for Improving Design Work

Graphic designers strive to produce the best designs possible. Difficulty sometimes occurs when the designer can no longer objectively see his or her own work. This often happens when there is no opportunity for outside feedback, or when the designer works on the same design problem for an extended period of time. Stepping back from your work, literally and figuratively, often is the key to improving your designs. In addition to asking yourself the critique questions in Table SF 3-4, the tips for improving designs in Table SF 3-5 provide suggestions and solutions to common graphic design layout and visualization problems.

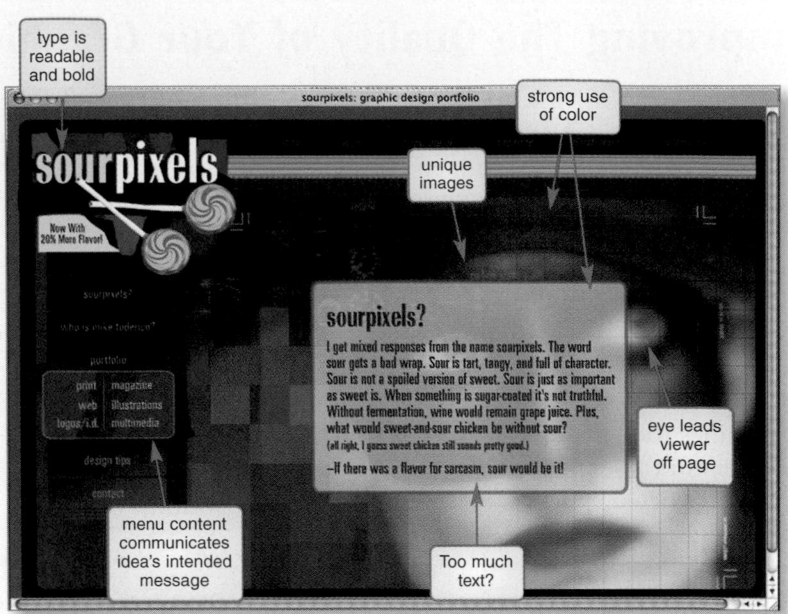

FIGURE SF 3-13

Table SF 3-5 Tips for Improving Designs

DESIGNS	TIPS FOR IMPROVEMENT
For all layouts	Use bigger margins because white space frames the message and focuses the viewer's attention.
	Convey the message with as little copy as possible — when in doubt, throw it out.
	Turn the layout upside down.
	Enlarge or reduce the image and/or text.
	Move the image and/or text off vertical and horizontal center.
	Bleed the image.
	Try reversing colors.
	When appropriate, use humor.
For multiple page layouts	Consider page-to-page continuity.
	Remember viewers see titles, captions, and images first. Grab their attention.
	Remember right-hand pages use odd page numbers, left-hand pages use odd numbers.
For posters	Simplify the text and graphics.
	Look at the design from a distance.
For logos	Make sure the design is decipherable — very small and very big.

Careers in Graphic Design

If you are interested in pursuing a career in any area related to graphic design, you will want to research the available career paths, and options for continued education.

Two-year and certificate programs usually provide the foundation necessary for you to obtain employment. Most two-year and certificate programs emphasize the technical aspects of graphic design, such as printing and computer technologies, although some certificate programs stress the creative side, such as layout and portfolio development. Four-year programs focus on technology, creativity, or a combination of both. Many students opt to begin in a two-year program to discover their interests and aptitude and then continue their education in an appropriate four-year program. To find the best program for your particular interests, research the school and talk with students who have participated in the program.

The best education is actual experience. Once you have learned the basics of graphic design, you can apply at local businesses — such as newspaper publishers, print companies, or advertising agencies to gain confidence and expand your skills.

Graphic design is constantly changing. Whether through courses, workshops, or self-directed study, keeping up with design trends and technology is important if you want to be a competitive, competent professional.

Summary

Each graphic design project, from idea to finished product, involves a series of stages which include both creative and technical processes. Each graphic design assignment is different, yet most graphic design jobs follow a similar path of development and production. Directing a project through to completion requires problem-solving skills, creativity, and knowledge of technical procedures to ensure successful results.

Similarities and differences exist in creating a design for Web and print. The major difference is in the end product; a Web site can be adjusted to adapt any changes, even after the project is complete, whereas a printed piece is final and can only be changed by reprinting.

It is rare that a design project is complete with the first attempt. The iterative design process involves making changes and revisions to the design, based on feedback, to ensure successful results. Another method of producing successful results is to critique work by objectively analyzing its effectiveness.

To pursue a career in graphic design it is important to keep up with design trends and technology. Formal education and actual experience are means to gaining confidence and exploring your potential as a graphic designer.

Appendix A

Changing Screen Resolution and Editing Preferences

This appendix shows you how to change the screen resolution on your system and set preferences in Photoshop.

Screen Resolution

Screen resolution determines the amount of information that appears on your screen, measured in pixels. A low resolution, such as 640 by 480 pixels, makes the overall screen area small, but items on the screen, such as windows, text, and icons, appear larger on the screen. A high resolution, such as 1024 by 768 pixels, makes the overall screen area large, but items appear smaller on the screen.

Changing Screen Resolution

The following steps show how to change your screen's resolution from 800 by 600 pixels to 1024 by 768 pixels, which is the screen resolution used in this book.

To Change Screen Resolution

1

- **Click the Start button on the Windows taskbar, and then point to Control Panel on the Start menu.**

The Start menu is displayed, and Control Panel is highlighted on the Start menu (Figure A-1). Your menu options may differ.

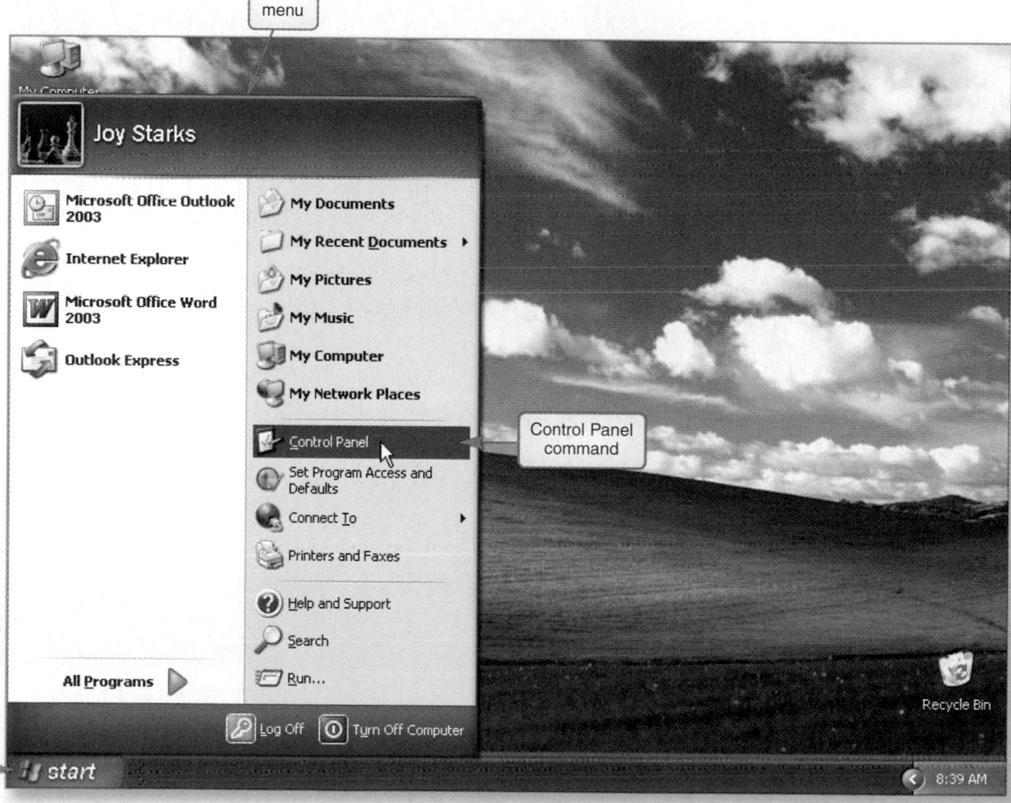

FIGURE A-1

2

- **Click Control Panel.**
- **If necessary, click Switch to Category View in the Control Panel area.**
- **If the window is maximized, double-click the Control Panel title bar.**

The Control Panel window opens (Figure A-2).

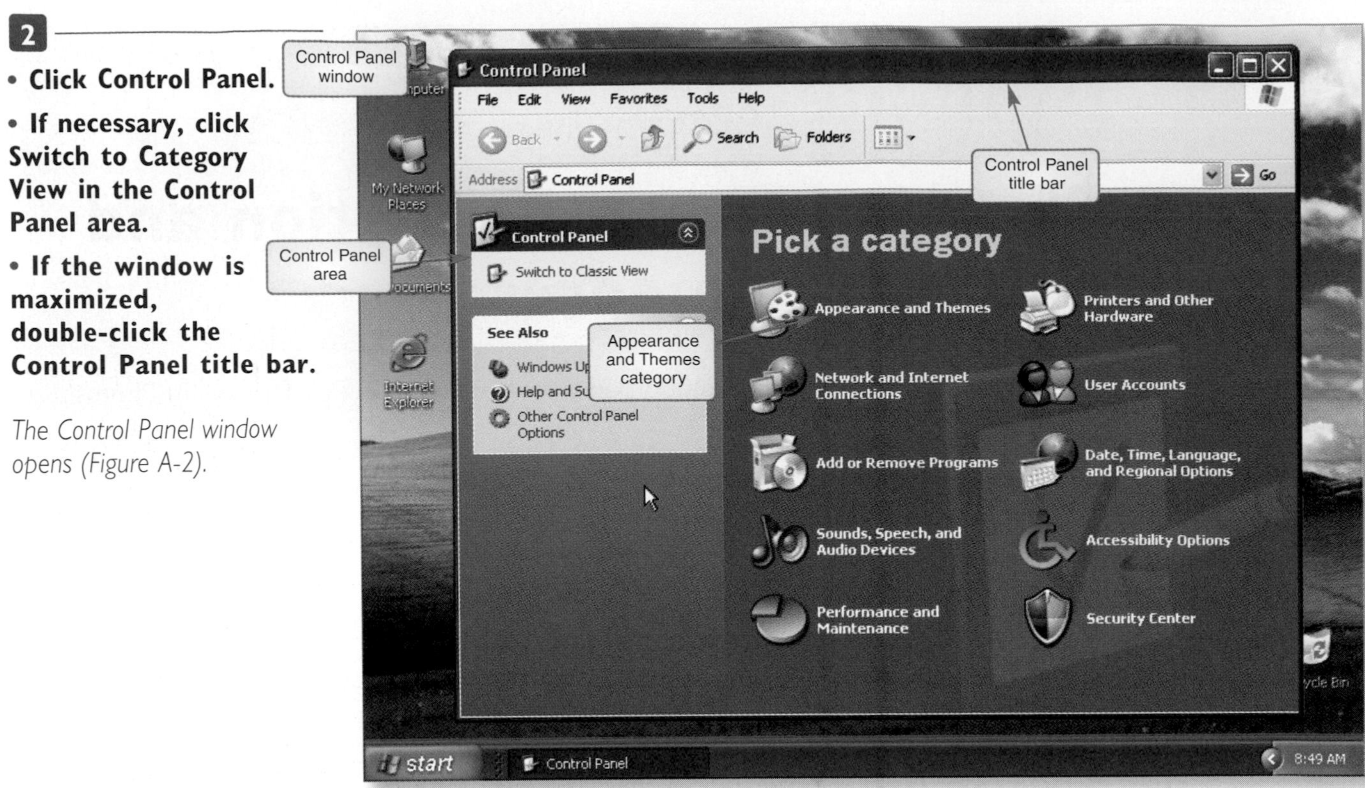

FIGURE A-2

3

- **Click the Appearance and Themes category.**

The Appearance and Themes window opens (Figure A-3).

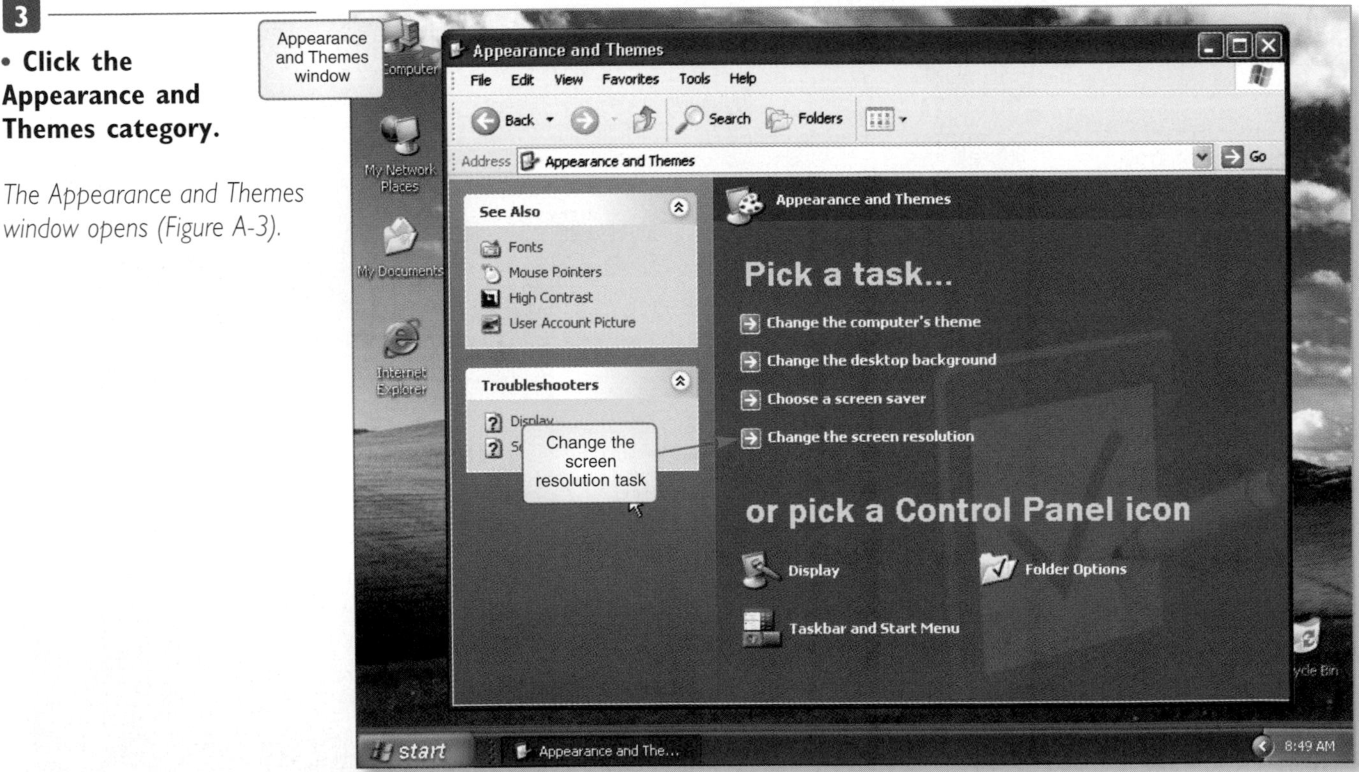

FIGURE A-3

4

- **Click the Change the screen resolution task.**

The Display Properties dialog box is displayed with the Settings tab selected (Figure A-4). The current screen resolution is displayed in the Screen resolution area.

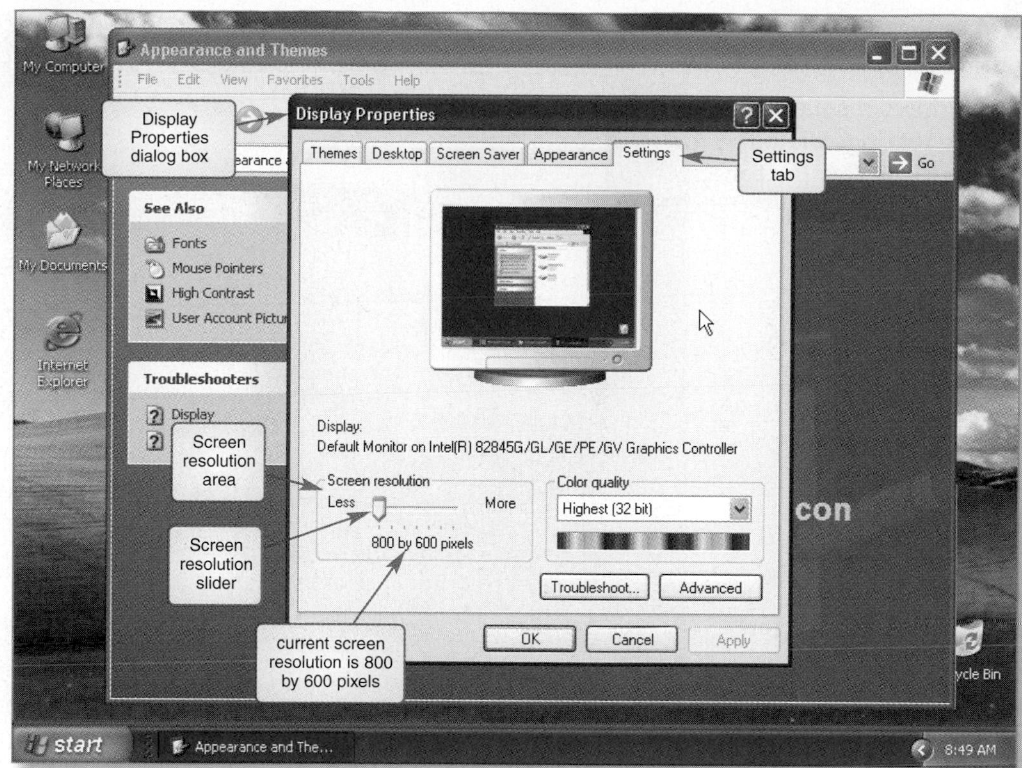

FIGURE A-4

5

- **Drag the Screen resolution slider one tick mark to the right or until the screen resolution below the slider reads 1024 by 768 pixels.**

As the slider is moved one mark to the right, the screen resolution displayed below the slider changes to 1024 by 768 pixels (Figure A-5).

FIGURE A-5

6

- **Click the OK button.**
- **If Windows displays a Monitor Settings dialog box, click the Yes button to keep the new settings.**

The Display Properties dialog box closes. The screen is displayed at a resolution of 1024 by 768 pixels (Figure A-6). Your screen may flicker while the resolution change takes place.

- **Click the Close button on the Appearance and Themes window title bar.**

The new screen resolution is set.

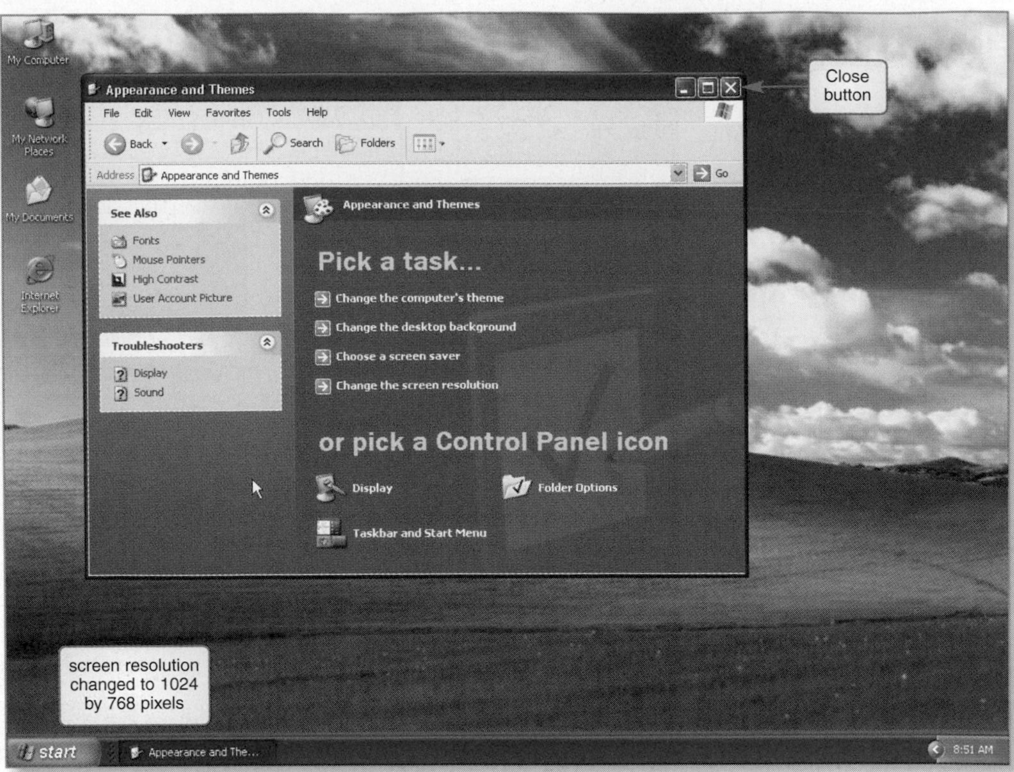

FIGURE A-6

Compare Figure A-6 with Figure A-3 on page APP 2 to see the difference in the display when screen resolution is set to 800 by 600 pixels or 1024 by 768 pixels. As shown in these figures, using a higher resolution allows more items, such as windows, text, and icons, to fit on the screen, but the items display at a smaller size.

You can experiment with various screen resolutions. Depending on your monitor and the video adapter installed in your computer, the screen resolutions available on your computer will vary.

Editing Photoshop Preferences

In Project 1, you learned how to start Photoshop and reset the default workspace, select the default tool, and reset all tools to their default settings. There are other preferences and settings you can edit to customize the Photoshop workspace and maximize your efficiency.

Editing General Preferences

General preferences include how Photoshop displays and stores your work. For example, you can change how many states are saved in the History palette, change the number of files shown on the Open Recent menu, or reset the display and cursors. As shown in the following steps, Photoshop allows you to traverse through several Preferences dialog boxes to reset values and change preferences. You can access this set of dialog boxes from the Edit menu or by pressing CTRL+K.

To Edit General Preferences

1

- **Start Photoshop.**
- **Click Edit on the Photoshop menu bar, and then point to Preferences.**

The Edit menu and Preferences submenu are displayed (Figure A-7).

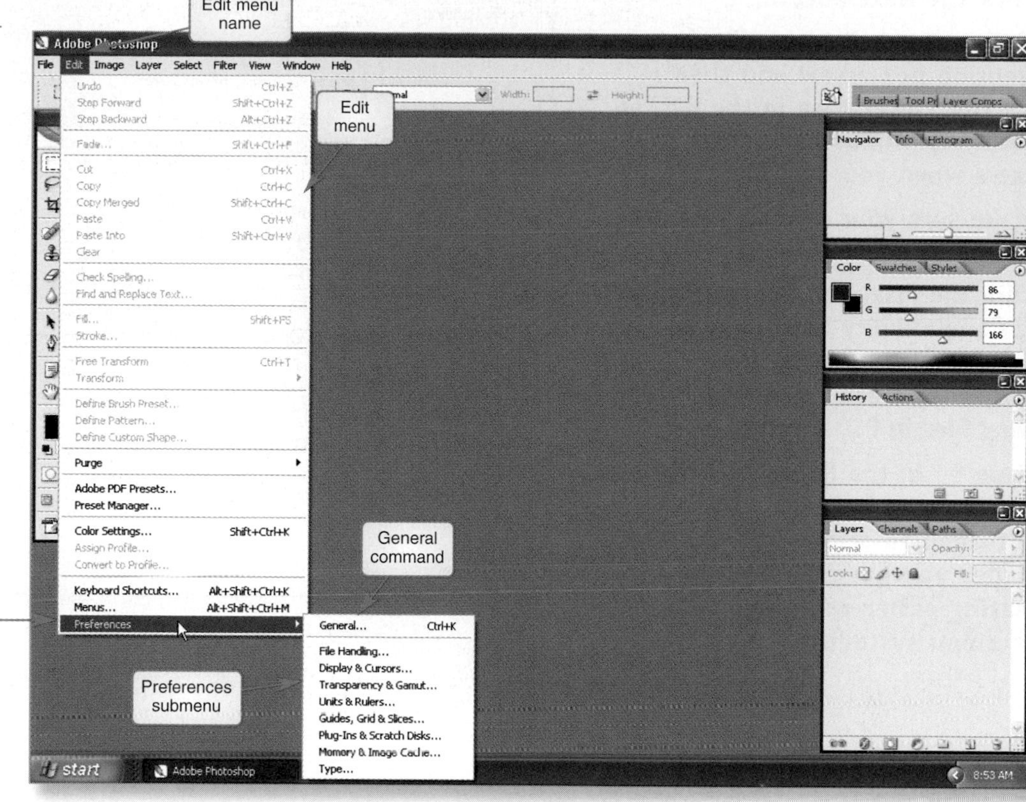

FIGURE A-7

2

- **Click General on the Preferences submenu.**
- **When the Preferences dialog box is displayed, if necessary, type** 20 **in the History States box, so Photoshop will allow you to back up through the last 20 steps of any editing session.**
- **Make sure your Options check boxes are selected as shown in Figure A-8.**
- **Click the Reset All Warning Dialogs button, so your dialog boxes will match the ones in this book.**
- **When Photoshop displays a dialog box, click the OK button.**

The General preferences are displayed (Figure A-8). Photoshop will save 20 states in the History palette and show all warning dialog boxes.

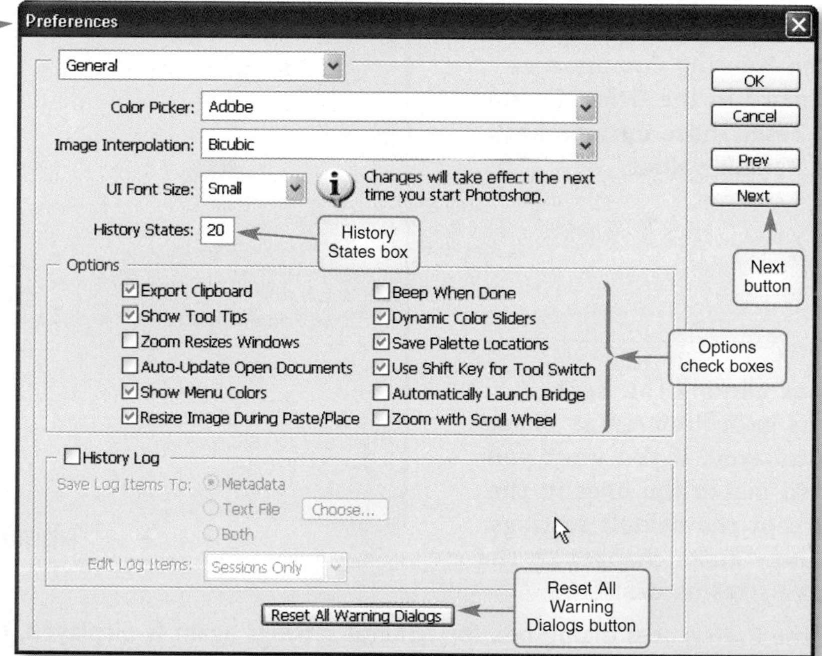

FIGURE A-8

3

- **Click the Next button.**
- **If necessary, click the File Extension box arrow and then click Use Lower Case in the list, so Photoshop will use lowercase letters when you save files.**
- **Make sure your check boxes are selected as shown in Figure A-9.**
- **Click the Maximize PSD and PSB File Compatibility box arrow and then click Ask, in order for Photoshop to ask you about saving files in PSD format.**
- **Type** 10 **in the Recent file list contains box, in order for Photoshop to display the last 10 files you have worked on, creating easier access through the menu system.**

The File Handling preferences are displayed (Figure A-9).

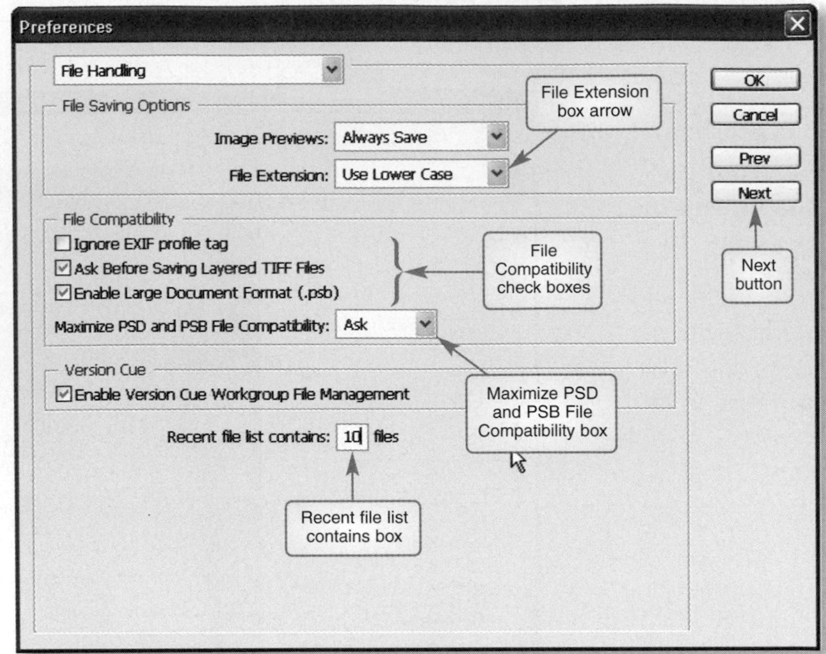

FIGURE A-9

4

- **Click the Next button.**
- **If necessary, select Normal Brush Tip in the Painting Cursors area and Standard in the Other Cursors area, to reset those options back to their default values.**

The Display and Cursors preferences are displayed (Figure A-10).

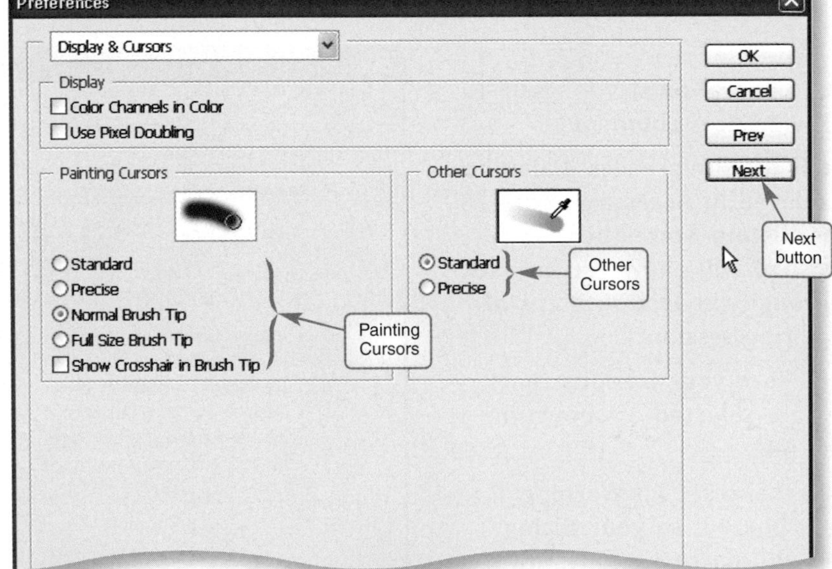

FIGURE A-10

5

- **Continue clicking the Next button as each Preferences dialog box is displayed. If you want your screens to match the ones in the book, accept the default settings. Or, you may make changes to the colors and sizes as desired.**
- **When the Preferences dialog box for General settings again is displayed, click the OK button.**

The preferences are changed.

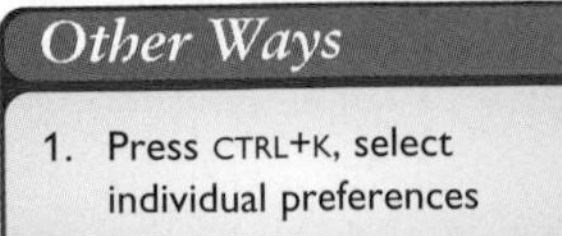
Other Ways

1. Press CTRL+K, select individual preferences

The Preferences dialog boxes contain a variety of settings that can be changed to suit individual needs and styles. The Reset All Warning Dialogs button in Figure A-8 is especially useful to display the dialog boxes if someone has turned them off by clicking the Don't show again check box.

In Figure A-10, the **Normal Brush Tip** causes the mouse pointer outline to correspond to approximately 50 percent of the area that the tool will affect. This option shows the pixels that would be most visibly affected. It is easier to work with the Normal Brush Tip than **Full Size Brush Tip**, especially when using larger brushes. A **Standard painting cursor** displays mouse pointers as tool icons; a **Precise painting cursor** displays the mouse pointer as a crosshair.

If there is one particular setting you wish to change, you can open that specific Preferences dialog box. For example, if you want to change the color of a ruler guide, you can click Guides, Grid & Slices on the Preferences submenu (Figure A-7) to go directly to those settings and make your edits. To restore all preferences to their default settings, you can press and hold ALT+CONTROL+SHIFT as you start Photoshop, which causes the system to prompt that you are about to delete the current settings.

Menu Command Preferences

Photoshop allows users to customize both the application menus and the palette menus in several ways. You can hide commands that you seldom use. You can set colors on the menu structure to highlight or organize your favorite commands. Or, you can let Photoshop organize your menus with color based on functionality. If changes have been made to the menu structure, you can reset the menus back to their default states.

Hiding and Showing Menu Commands

If there are menu commands that you seldom use, you can hide them in order to access other commands more quickly. A **hidden command** is a menu command that does not display currently on a menu. If menu commands have been hidden, a Show All Menu Items command will display at the bottom of the menu list. When you click the Show All Menu Items command or press and hold the CTRL key as you click the menu name, Photoshop displays all menu commands including hidden ones.

The steps on the next page illustrate how to hide a menu command and then show it. The last step turns the hidden menu command back on so it always displays.

To Hide and Show Menu Commands

1

- **Click Edit on the menu bar, and then click Menus.**

The Keyboard Shortcuts and Menus dialog box is displayed (Figure A-11).

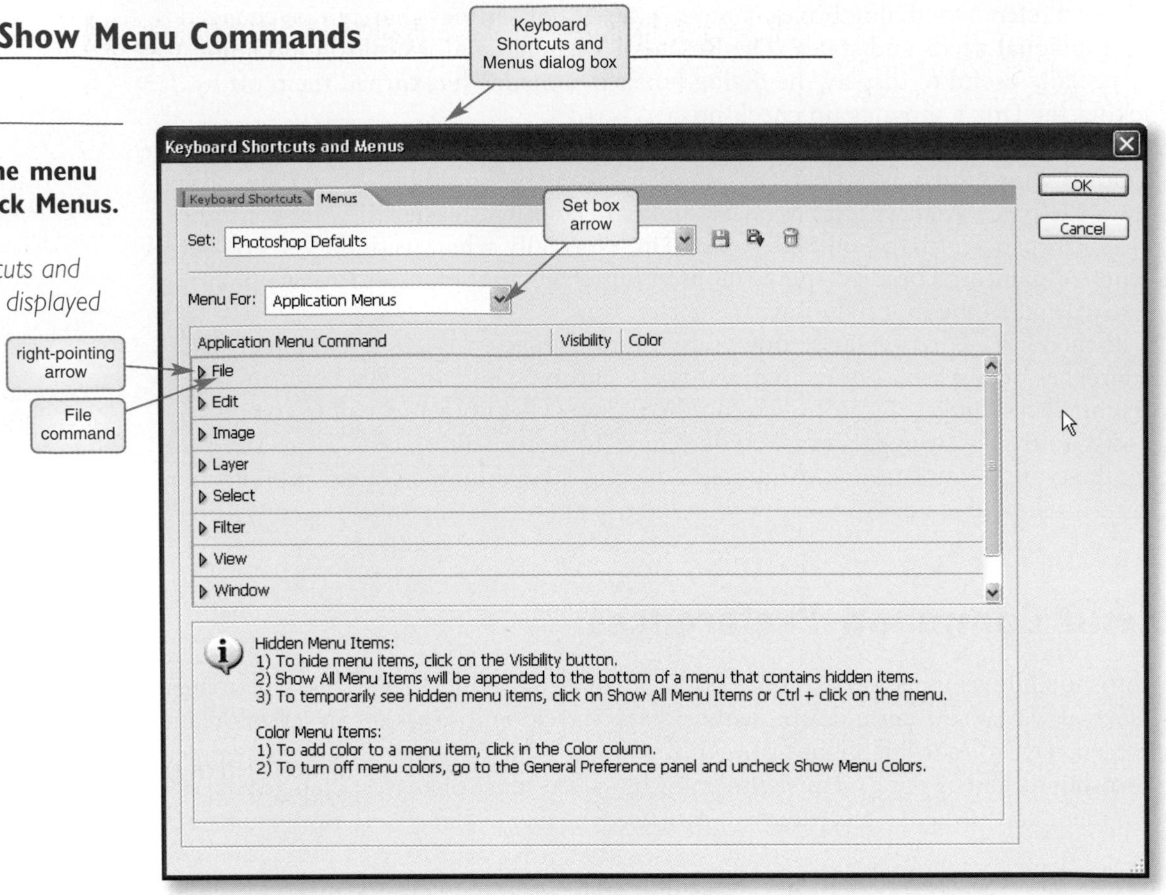

FIGURE A-11

2

- **If necessary, click the Set box arrow and then click Photoshop Defaults.**
- **Click the right-pointing arrow next to the word, File.**

The File commands are displayed (Figure A-12). The right-pointing arrow changes to a down-pointing arrow.

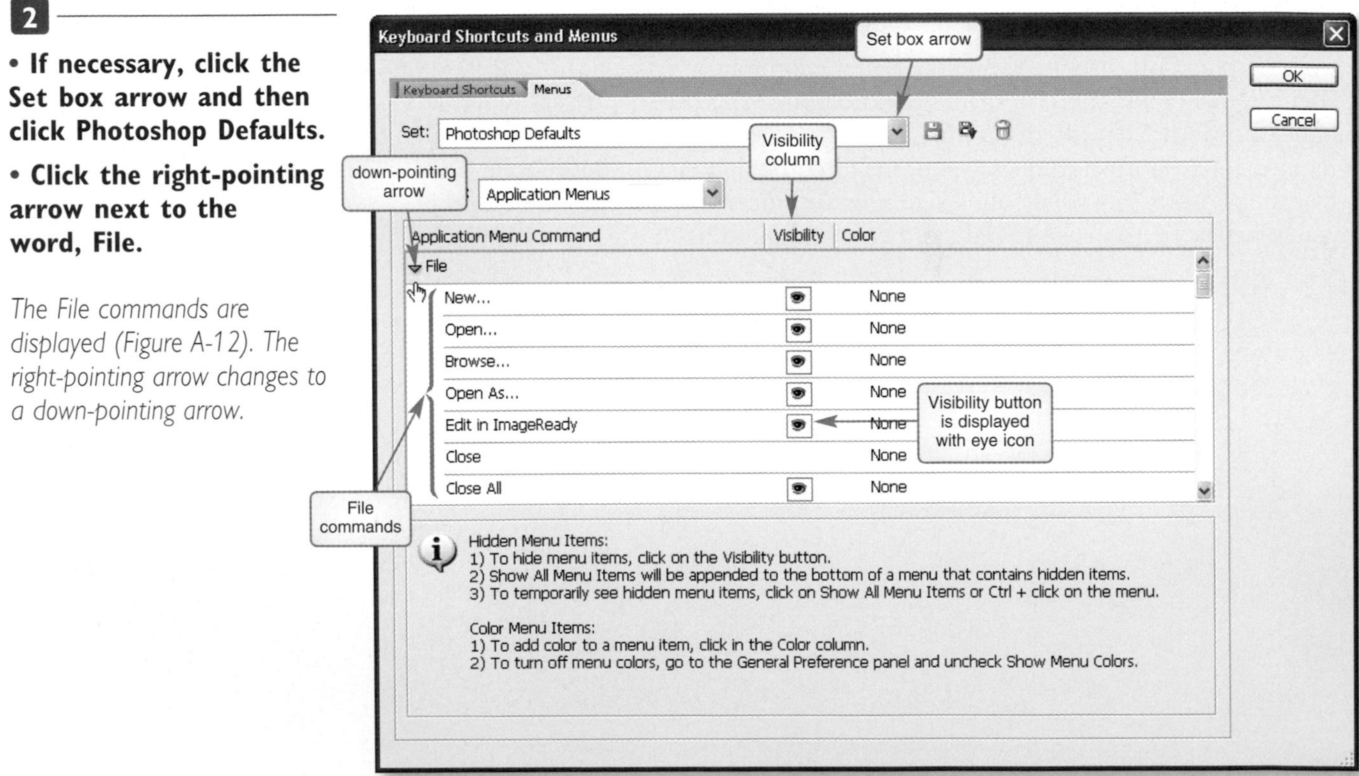

FIGURE A-12

3

• In the Visibility column, click the Visibility button next to Edit in ImageReady.

The eye on the Visibility button no longer is displayed (Figure A-13). Photoshop notes that the default settings have been modified.

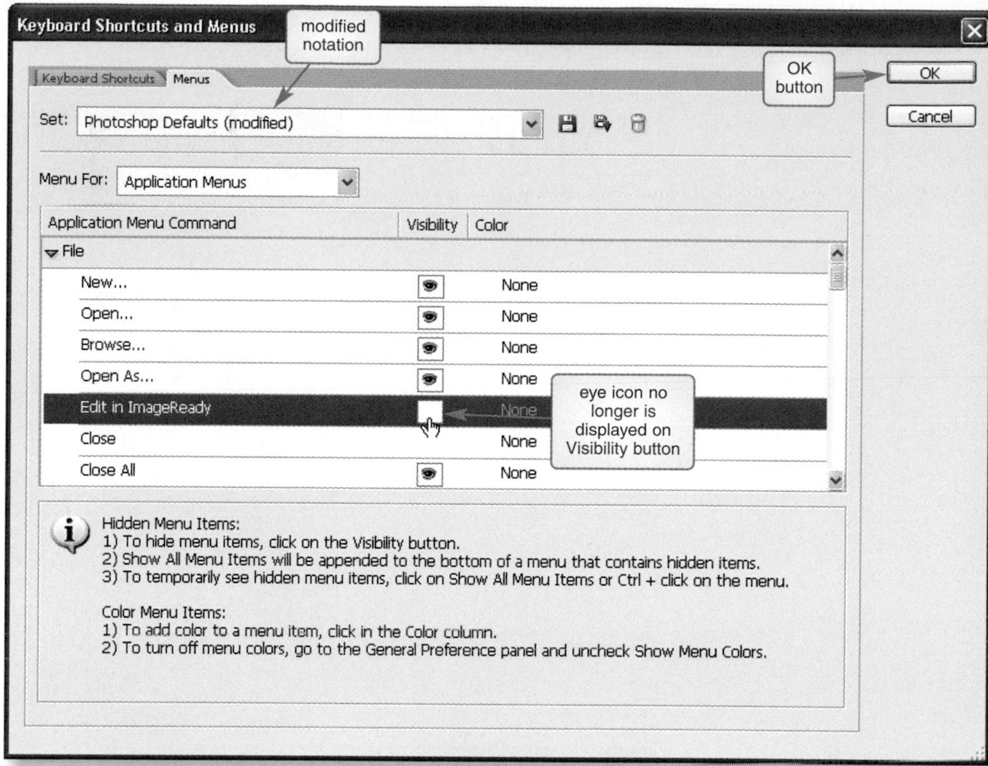

FIGURE A-13

4

• Click the OK button in the Keyboard Shortcuts and Menus dialog box.

• Click File on the menu bar.

The Keyboard Shortcuts and Menus dialog box closes and Photoshop displays the File menu (Figure A-14). The Show All Menu Items command is added to the bottom of the menu. The Edit in ImageReady command is not displayed.

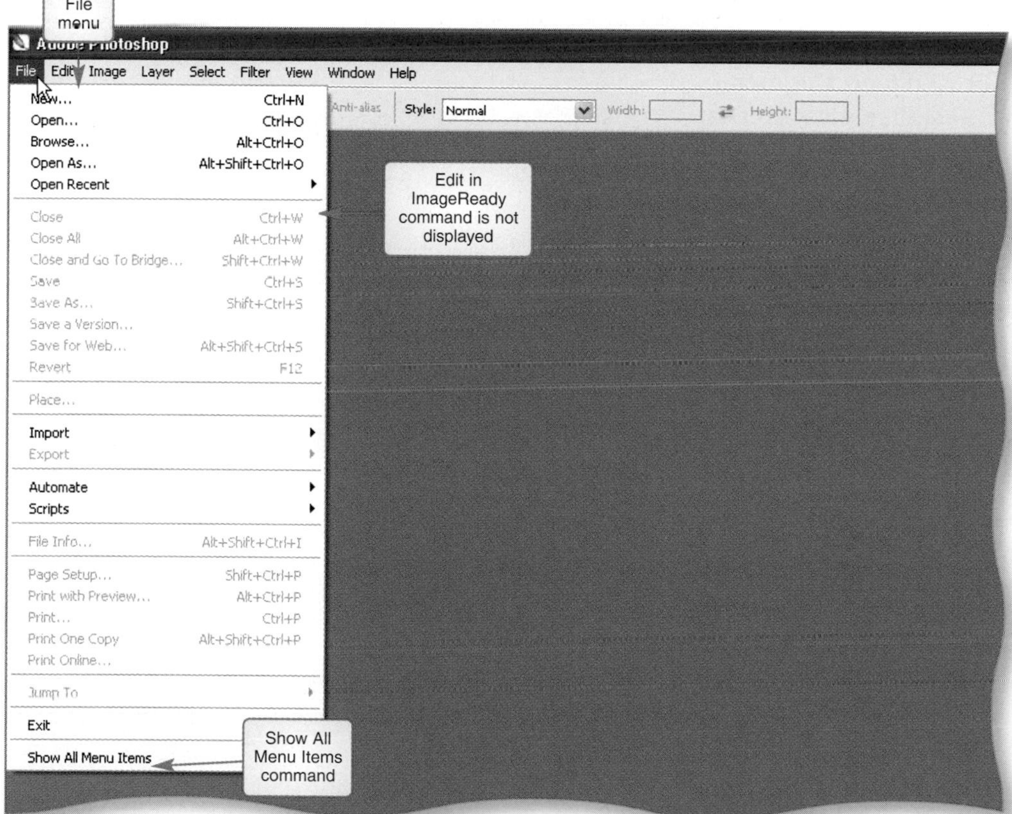

FIGURE A-14

5

• **Click Show All Menu Items.**

The File menu displays the Edit in ImageReady command (Figure A-15).

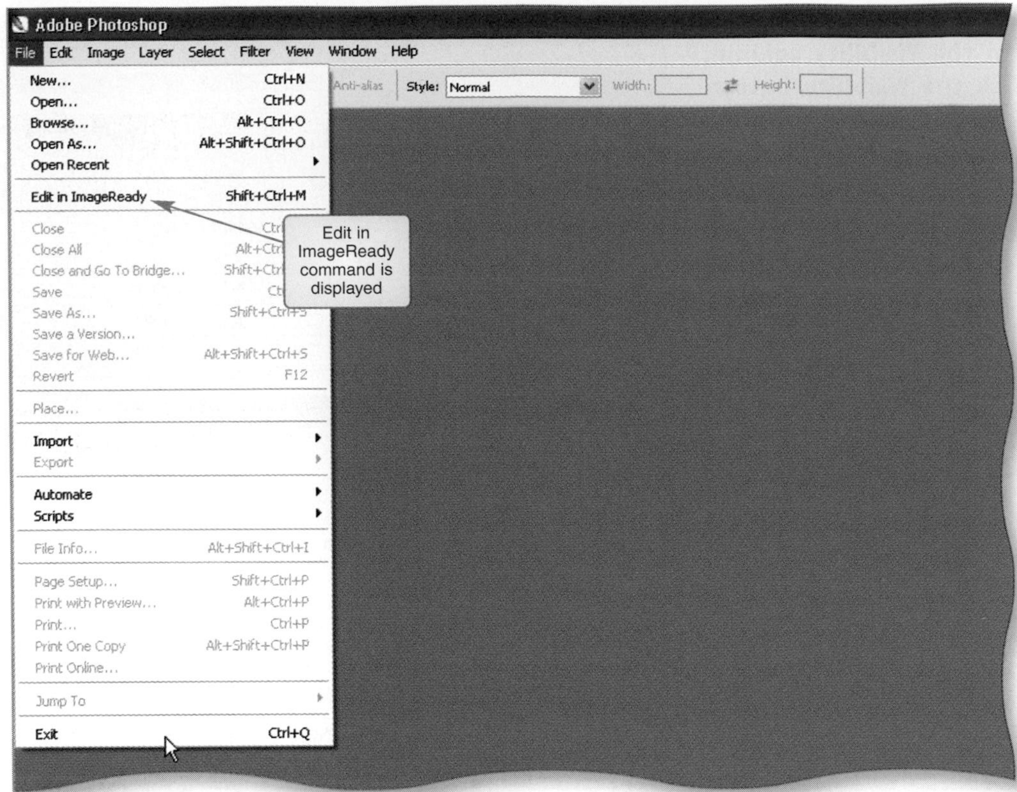

FIGURE A-15

6

• **Click Edit on the menu bar and then click Menus.**

• **When the Keyboard Shortcuts and Menus dialog box is displayed, if necessary, click the right-pointing arrow next to the word, File. Click the Visibility button next to the Edit in ImageReady command.**

The eye icon again is displayed (Figure A-16). The next time the File menu is accessed, Photoshop will display the Edit in ImageReady command.

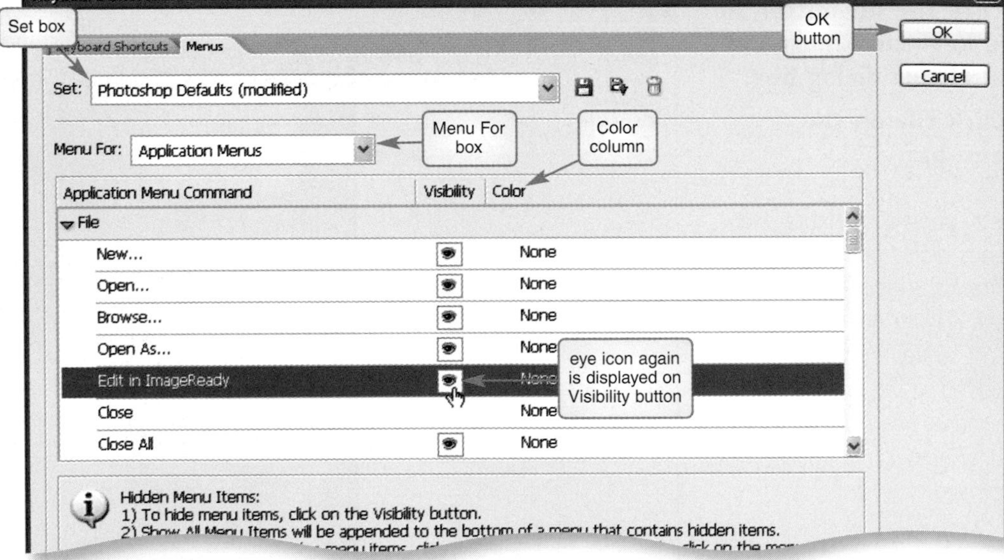

FIGURE A-16

Other Ways

1. On menu bar, click Window, point to Workspace, click Keyboard Shortcuts and Menus
2. Press ALT+SHIFT+CTRL+M

You can add color to your menu commands to help you find them easily or to organize them into groups based on personal preferences, as shown in the following steps.

To Add Color to Menu Commands

1

- **With the Keyboard Shortcuts and Menus dialog box still displayed, click the word, None, in the row associated with the Open command.**

Photoshop displays a list of possible colors (Figure A-17).

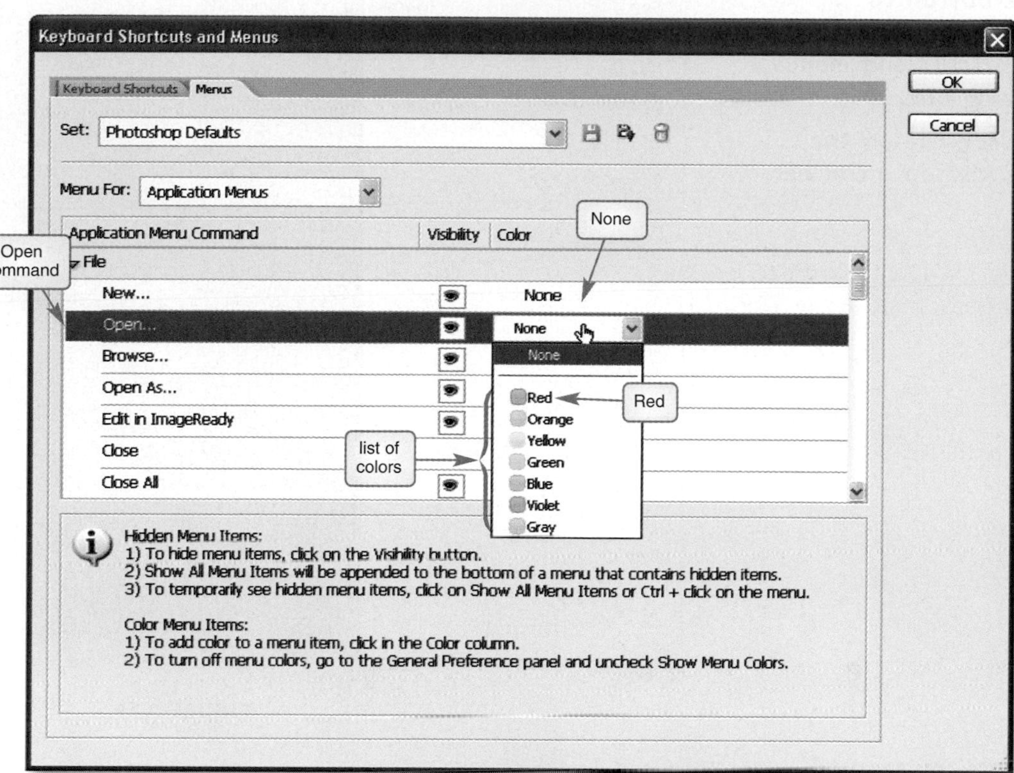

FIGURE A-17

2

- **Click Red in the list.**
- **Click the word, None, in the row associated with the Open As command, and then click Red in the list.**

The changes are displayed (Figure A-18).

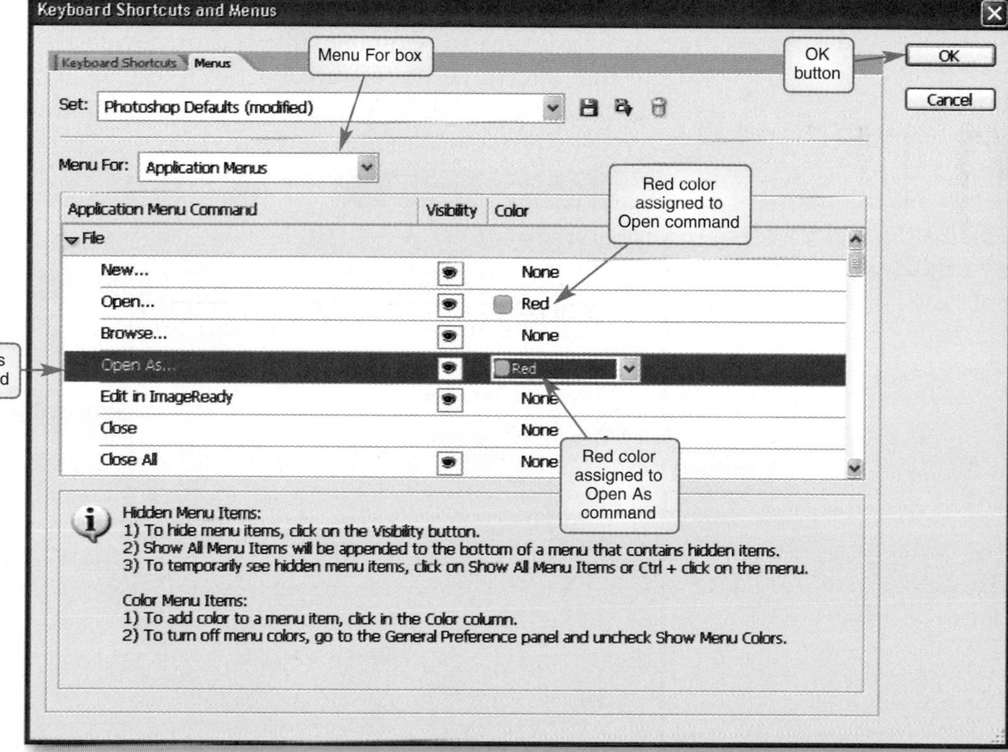

FIGURE A-18

3

• Click the OK button to close the Keyboard Shortcuts and Menus dialog box.

• Click File on the Photoshop menu bar.

The menu is displayed with the Open and Open As commands highlighted in red (Figure A-19).

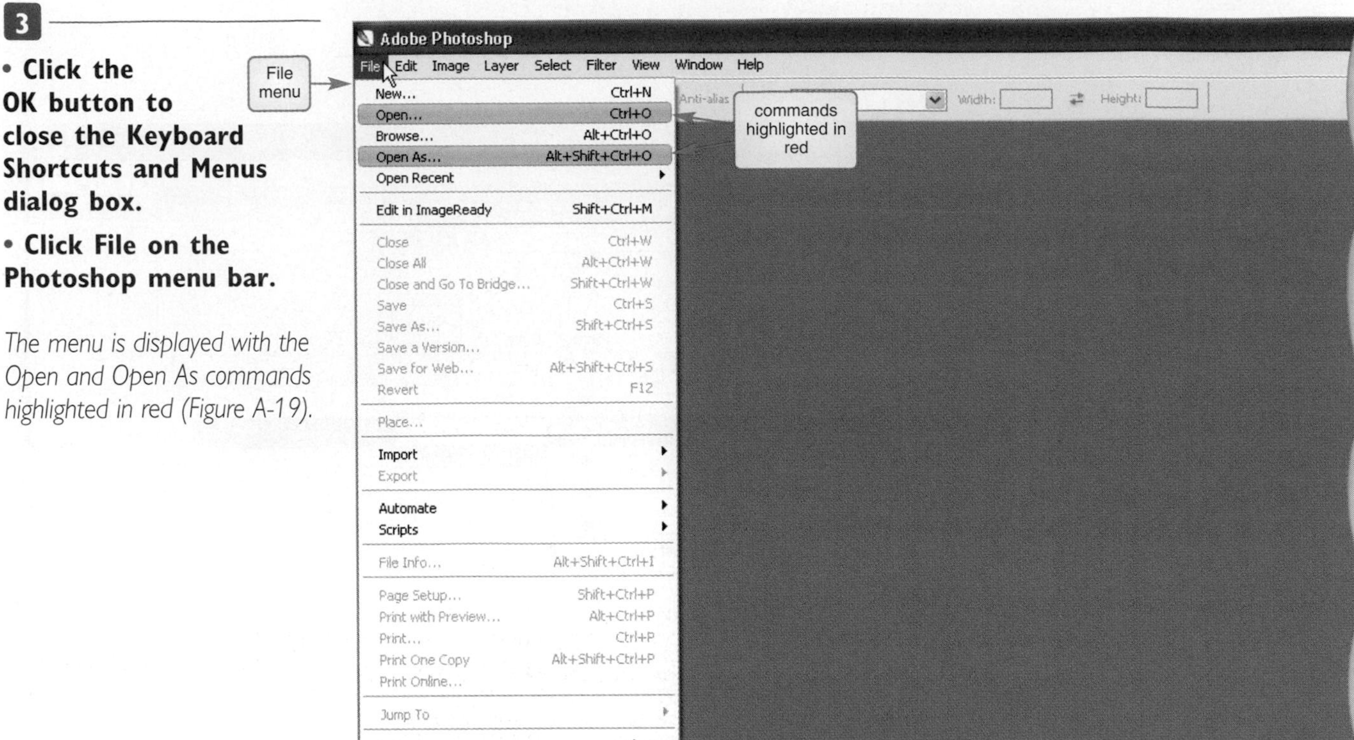

FIGURE A-19

The Set box (Figure A-20) lists several different categories of menu commands related to common tasks. Choosing a set causes Photoshop to display related commands with color. For example, if you choose Web Design, the commands on all menus that directly relate to Web design will display in purple. This category list also is displayed when you click Window on the menu bar and then point to Workspace.

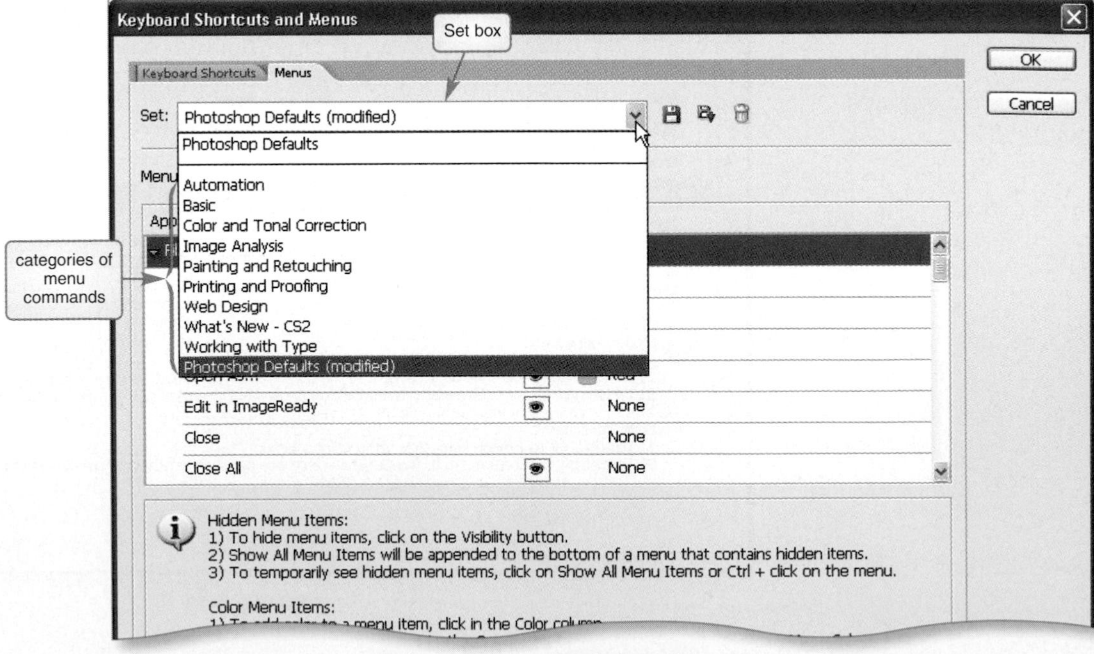

FIGURE A-20

The Menu For box (Figure A-18 on page APP 11) allows you to set options for Applications Menus or Palette Menus.

Resetting User Changes

If you are working in a lab situation and you notice that Photoshop does not display the workspace, menus, and brushes the way you are used to, someone may have changed the settings. The next sections describe how to reset those changes.

Resetting the Palettes, Keyboard Shortcuts, and Menus

The following steps show how to reset the location of the palettes, reset the keyboard shortcuts to their default settings, and remove any changes to the menus.

To Reset the Palettes, Keyboard Shortcuts, and Menus

1

- **Click Window on the menu bar, and then point to Workspace.**

The Workspace submenu is displayed (Figure A-21).

2

- **Click Reset Palette Locations.**
- **Click Window on the menu bar, point to Workspace, and then click Reset Keyboard Shortcuts.**
- **Click Window on the menu bar, point to Workspace, and then click Reset Menus.**
- **If Photoshop displays a dialog box asking you to save the current settings, click the No button.**

Each of the options is reset.

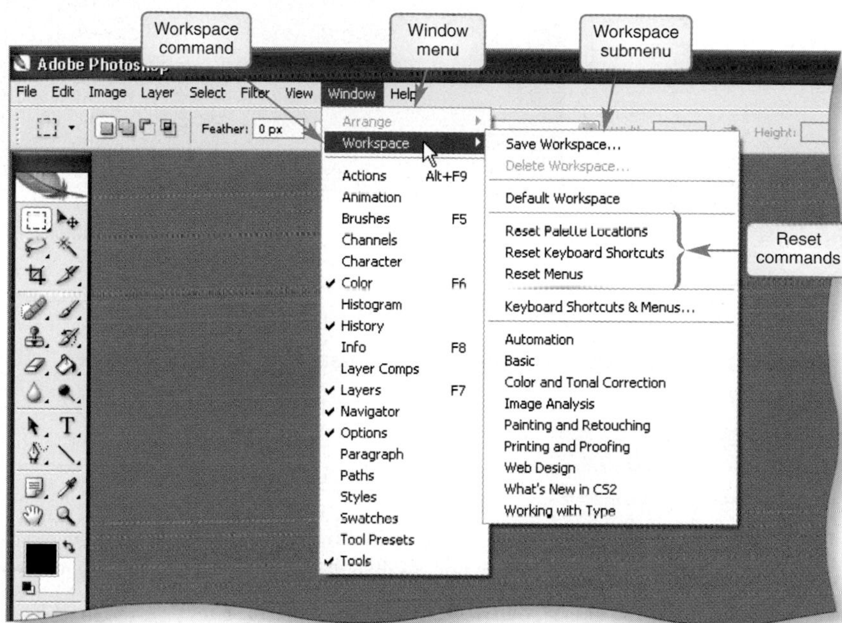

FIGURE A-21

Other Ways

1. To reset all three, on menu bar, click Window, point to Workspace, click Default Workspace

Resetting the Brushes

One of the most used tools in Photoshop is the Brush tool. Users make many choices in the Brushes palette and options bar that carry over from one session to another. In order to begin with a clean set of brushes in the default settings, the steps on the next page illustrate how to clear the brush controls and reset the brush tips.

To Reset the Brushes

1

- **In the toolbox, click the Brush Tool (B) button.**
- **In the palette well, click the Brushes tab.**
- **When the expanded view of the palette is displayed, click the Brushes palette menu button.**

Photoshop displays the Brushes palette menu (Figure A-22).

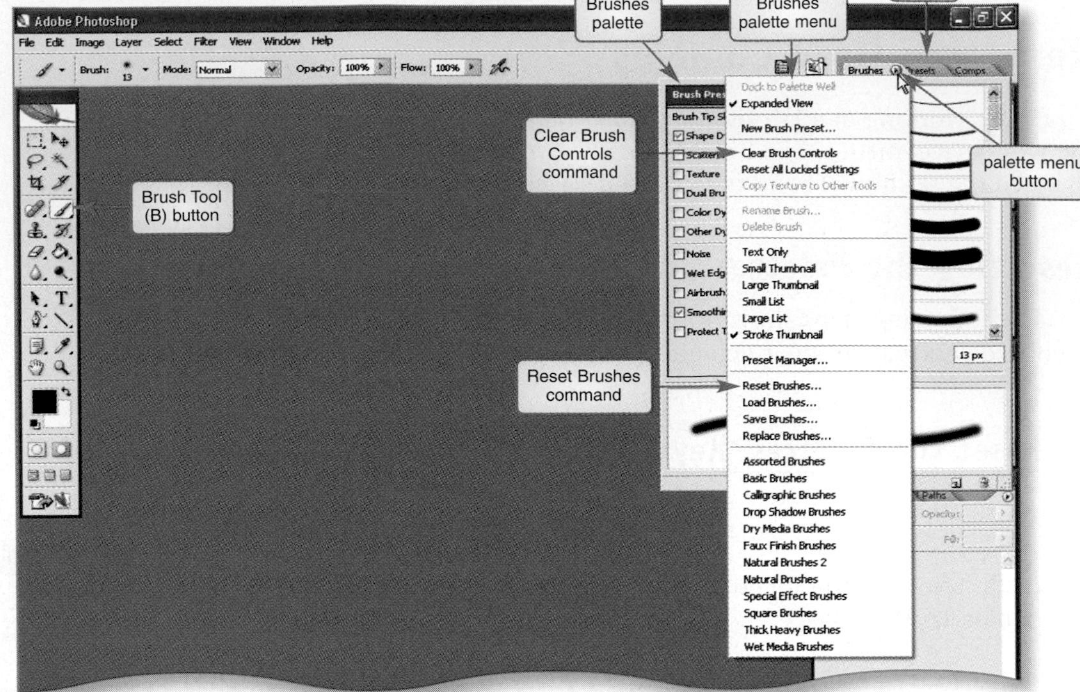

FIGURE A-22

2

- **Click Clear Brush Controls.**
- **Click the Brushes palette menu button again, and then click Reset Brushes.**
- **When Photoshop asks if you want to use the default brushes, click the OK button.**

Other Ways

1. On Brush options bar, click Brush Preset Picker, click menu button, click Reset Brushes
2. In Preset Manager, click menu button, click Reset Brushes

Users may have changed the color settings related to your brushes as well. As you learned in Project 3, pressing the D key restores the Color palette to its default setting of black and white.

Changing the Screen Mode

Photoshop offers three screen modes from which users may choose. The buttons are located in the lower part of the toolbox. The **standard screen mode** is the default setting where the menu bar, options bar, toolbox, palettes, and document window display. The **full screen mode with menu bar** removes the title bars from the Photoshop window and document window while maximizing the screen. The **full screen mode** removes the title bars and the Windows task bar, and changes the background to black. Using the Hand tool, full screen mode also allows you to move a maximized document window around on the black background. In full screen mode, the menu system is available via a toolbox menu button.

To Change Screen Modes

1

- **Open any image file in Photoshop.**
- **In the toolbox, click the Full Screen Mode with Menu Bar (F) button.**

Photoshop displays the workspace in full screen mode with a menu bar (Figure A-23).

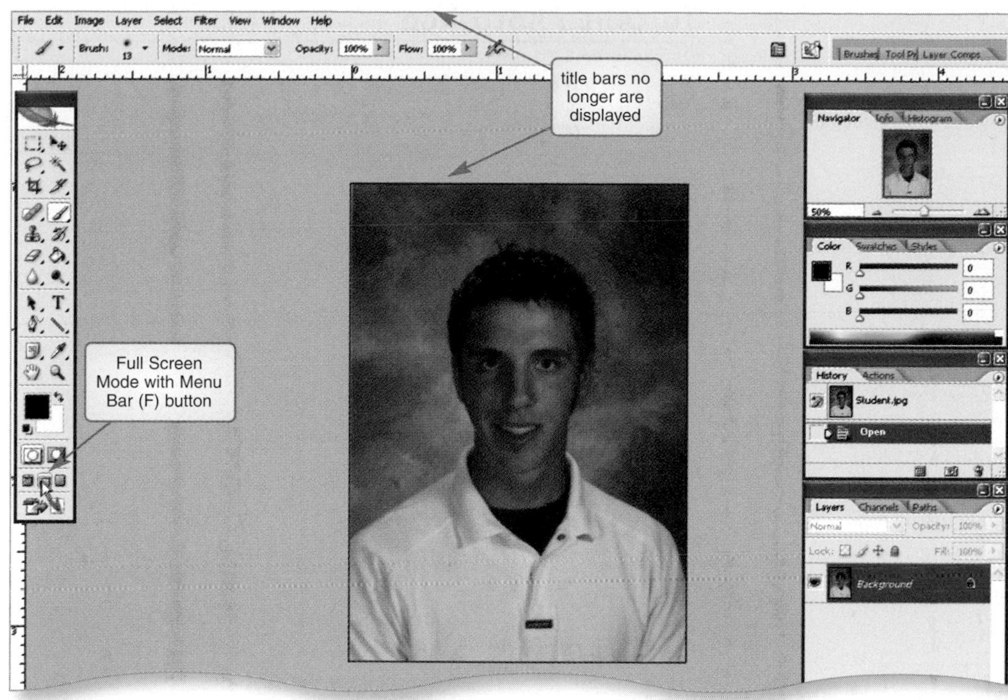

FIGURE A-23

2

- **Click the Full Screen Mode (F) button.**

Photoshop displays the workspace in full screen mode (Figure A-24). The toolbox displays a menu button to allow access to the Photoshop menus. Notice that the workspace background changes to black.

- **Click the Standard Screen Mode (F) button.**

Photoshop returns the display to standard screen mode.

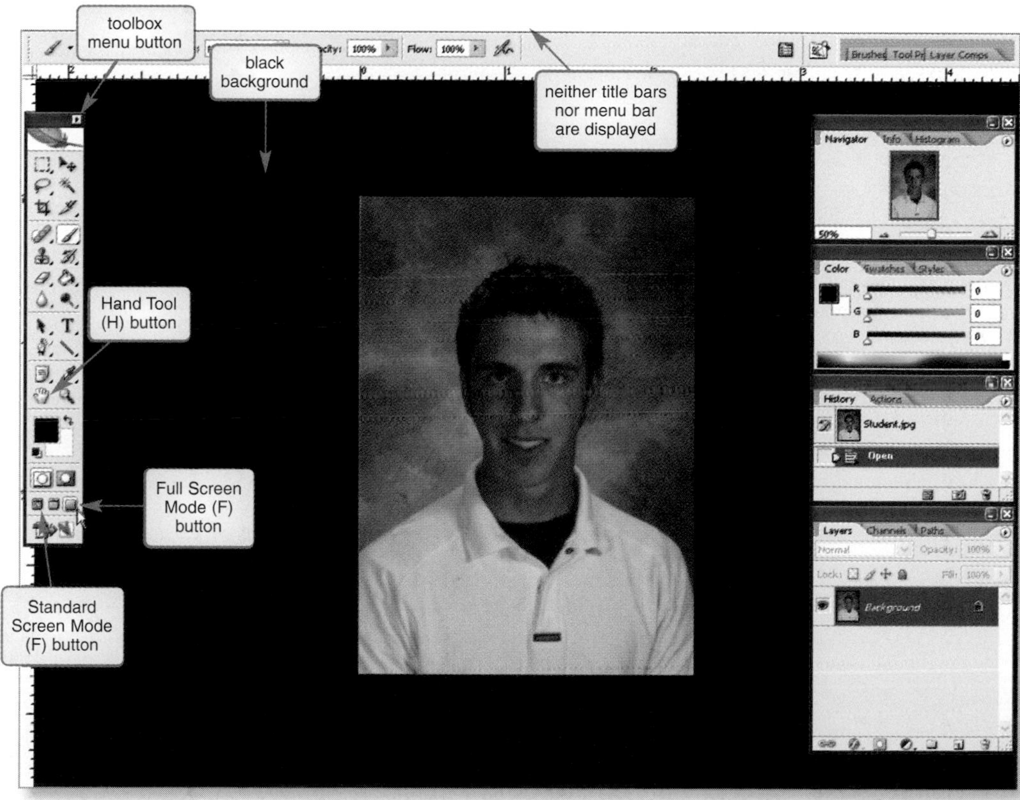

FIGURE A-24

Other Ways

1. Press F key to cycle through screen modes

The final step is to quit Photoshop.

To Quit Photoshop

1 Click the Close button on the Photoshop title bar. If Photoshop displays a dialog box, click the No button.

The Photoshop window closes.

Changing Preferences

1 Changing the Color and Style of Guides, Grid & Slices

Instructions: You would like to use some different colors and styles for grids and guides because the current colors are too close to the colors in your image, making them hard to see. You decide to change the color and style preferences on your system as described in the following steps.

1. Start Adobe Photoshop CS2 on your system.
2. On the Edit menu, point to Preferences, and then click Guides, Grid, and Slices.
3. When the Preferences dialog box is displayed, change the color and Style settings as shown in Figure A-25.

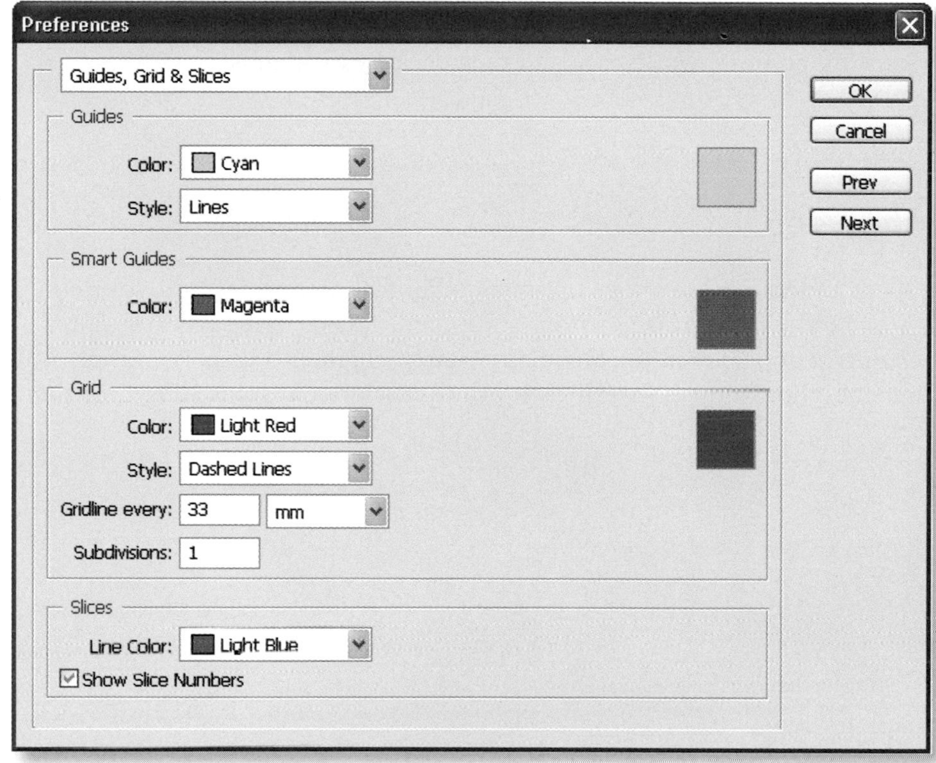

FIGURE A-25

4. Click the OK button.
5. Open any image file you have saved on your system and drag a guide from the horizontal ruler. Note the Cyan colored line.
6. On the View menu, point to Show, and then click Grid. Note the 3 by 3 grid with dashed Light Red lines.
7. To clear the guides, on the View menu, click Clear Guides.
8. To clear the gird, on the View menu, point to Show and then click Grid.
9. To reset the colors and styles, either change them back in the Preferences dialog box, or quit Photoshop and then restart Photoshop while pressing ALT+CTRL+SHIFT.

Changing Preferences

2 Changing Menu Command Preferences

Instructions: You plan on creating Web graphics over the next few Photoshop sessions, so you would like to highlight Web commands on the menu system as described in the following steps.

1. Start Adobe Photoshop CS2 on your system.
2. On the Window menu, point to Workspace, and then click Web Design.
3. When Photoshop displays a dialog box, click the Yes button.
4. One at a time, click each menu command on the menu bar. Make a list of each highlighted command. Next to each listed command, make a notation on how that command affects Web design and Web graphics. Turn the list in to your instructor.
5. On the Window menu, point to Workspace and then click Reset Menus.
6. Quit Photoshop.

3 Searching the Web

Instructions: You want to learn more about optimizing Photoshop settings and your computer system's memory by setting preferences for file size, history states, and cached views. Perform a Web search by using the Google search engine at google.com (or any major search engine) to display and print three Web pages that pertain to optimizing Photoshop CS2. On each printout, highlight something new that you learned by reading the Web page.

Appendix B

Using the Adobe Help Center

The Adobe Help Center

This appendix shows you how to use the Adobe Help Center. At any time, whether you are currently accessing Photoshop or not, you can interact with the Adobe Help Center and display information on any Photoshop topic. It is a complete reference manual at your fingertips. The Figures in this appendix use the educational version of Adobe Help Center 1.0.0. If you have a different version, your screens may differ slightly.

As shown in Figure B-1, three methods for accessing the Adobe Help Center are available:

1. Photoshop Help command on the Help menu
2. Function key F1 on the keyboard
3. Adobe Help Center command on the All Programs submenu

The complete help documentation for using Photoshop is a browser-based system with buttons to navigate back and forth, as well as a table of contents, index, bookmarks, and hyperlinks.

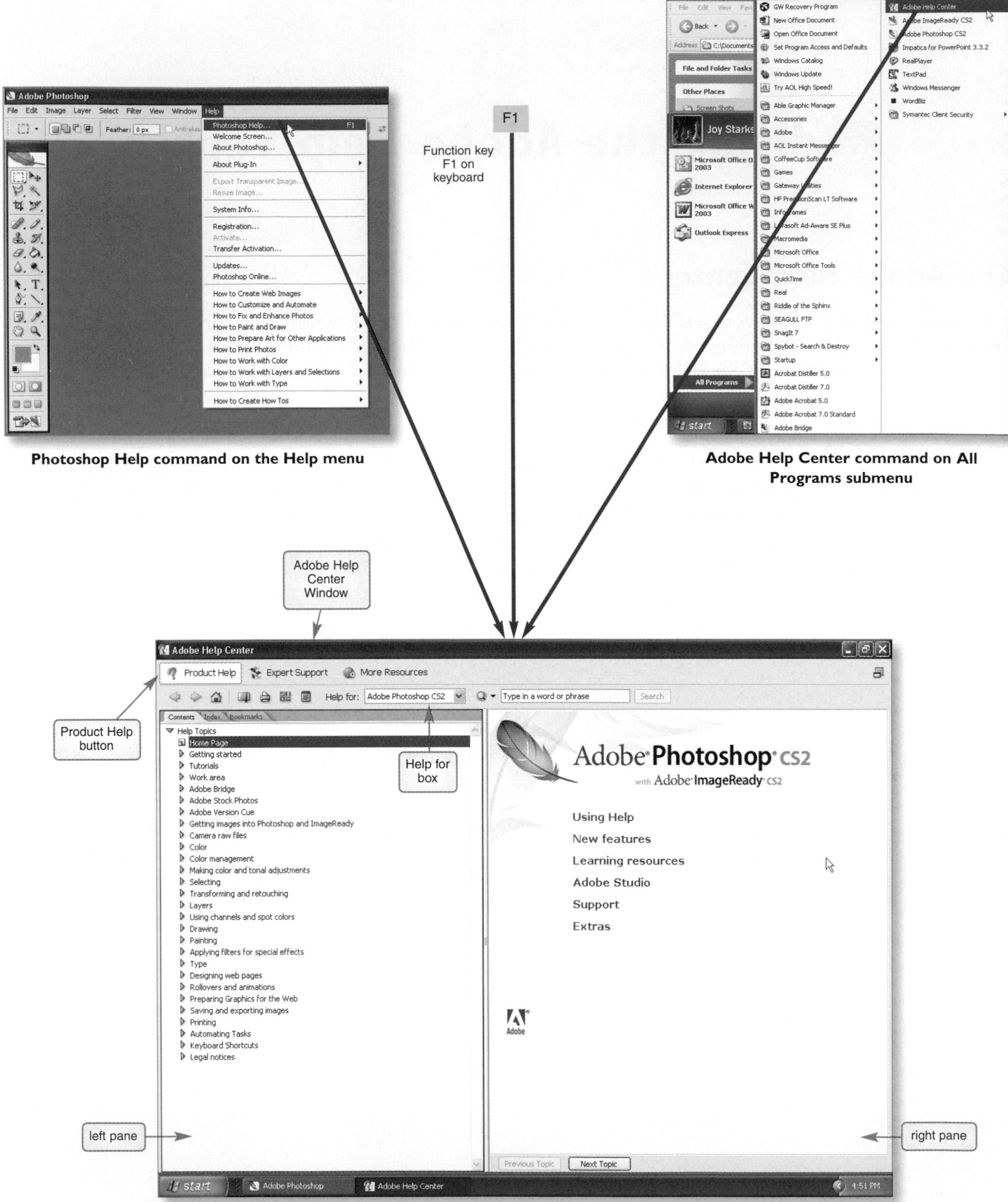
F1
Function key F1 on keyboard
Photoshop Help command on the Help menu
Adobe Help Center command on All Programs submenu
Adobe Help Center Window
Product Help button
Help for box
left pane
right pane
Adobe Help Center
Product Help
Expert Support
More Resources
Help for:
Adobe Photoshop CS2
Type in a word or phrase
Search
Help Topics
Home Page
Getting started
Tutorials
Work area
Adobe Bridge
Adobe Stock Photos
Adobe Version Cue
Getting images into Photoshop and ImageReady
Camera raw files
Color
Color management
Making color and tonal adjustments
Selecting
Transforming and retouching
Layers
Using channels and spot colors
Drawing
Painting
Applying filters for special effects
Type
Designing web pages
Rollovers and animations
Preparing Graphics for the Web
Saving and exporting images
Printing
Automating Tasks
Keyboard Shortcuts
Legal notices
Adobe Photoshop CS2
with Adobe ImageReady CS2
Using Help
New features
Learning resources
Adobe Studio
Support
Extras
Previous Topic
Next Topic

FIGURE B-1

All three methods described in Figure B-1 result in the Adobe Help Center displaying a new window. If you access the stand-alone application from the All Programs submenu, you may have to click the Product Help button and then select Photoshop CS2 from the Help for list box. If you use the Help menu or the function key, the Adobe Help Center displays help for Photoshop CS2 automatically.

The Adobe Help Center displays two main panes. The left pane displays a navigation system. The right pane displays help information on the selected topic.

Above the panes are buttons and boxes to assist you in making help selections as described in the following sections of this appendix.

Searching for Help Using Words and Phrases

The quickest way to navigate the Adobe Help Center is through the **Type in a word or phrase box**, or the Search box in some versions of Adobe Help, on the right side of the toolbar at the top of the screen. Here you can type words, such as layer mask, hue, or file formats; or you can type phrases, such as preview a Web graphic, or create master palette. The Adobe Help Center responds by displaying the Search Results for pane, with a list of topics you can click.

Here are some tips regarding the words or phrases you enter to initiate a search: (1) check the spelling of the word or phrase; (2) keep your search specific, with fewer than seven words, to return the most accurate results; (3) if you search using a specific phrase, such as shape tool, put quotation marks around the phrase — the search returns only those topics containing all words in the phrase; and, (4) if a search term does not yield the desired results, try using a synonym, such as Web instead of Internet.

For the following example, assume that you want to learn more about isolating objects with the Extract filter. The likely keyword is extract. The following steps show how to open the Adobe Help Center and use the Type in a word or phrase box to obtain useful information by entering the keyword, extract.

To Obtain Help Using the Type in a Word or Phrase Box

1

- **With Photoshop running on your system, press the F1 function key.**
- **When the Adobe Help Center window is displayed, double-click the title bar to maximize the window, if necessary.**
- **If the window does not display two panes and a toolbar, click the Full View button in the upper-right corner of the window.**

The Adobe Help Center is launched and opens in a new window (Figure B-2).

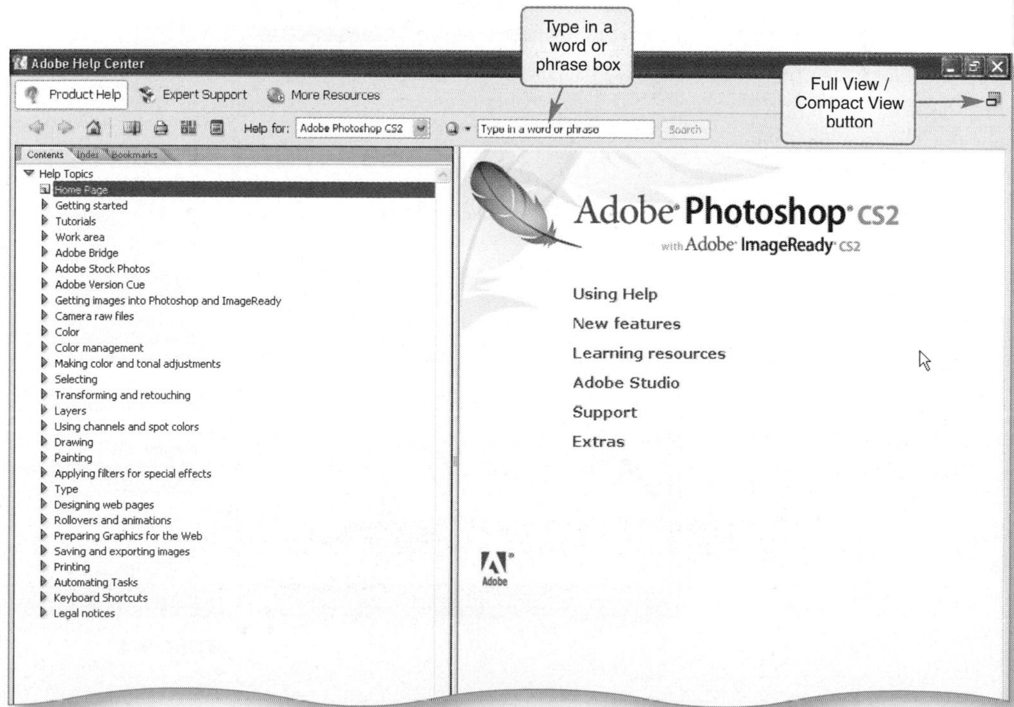

FIGURE B-2

2

- **Click the Type in a word or phrase box on the right side of the toolbar, type** `extract` **as the entry, and then press the ENTER key.**

The Adobe Help Center displays the Search Results for pane on the left side of the window. The Search Results for pane includes several resulting topics (Figure B-3). Depending on your version of the Adobe Help Center, your display may differ.

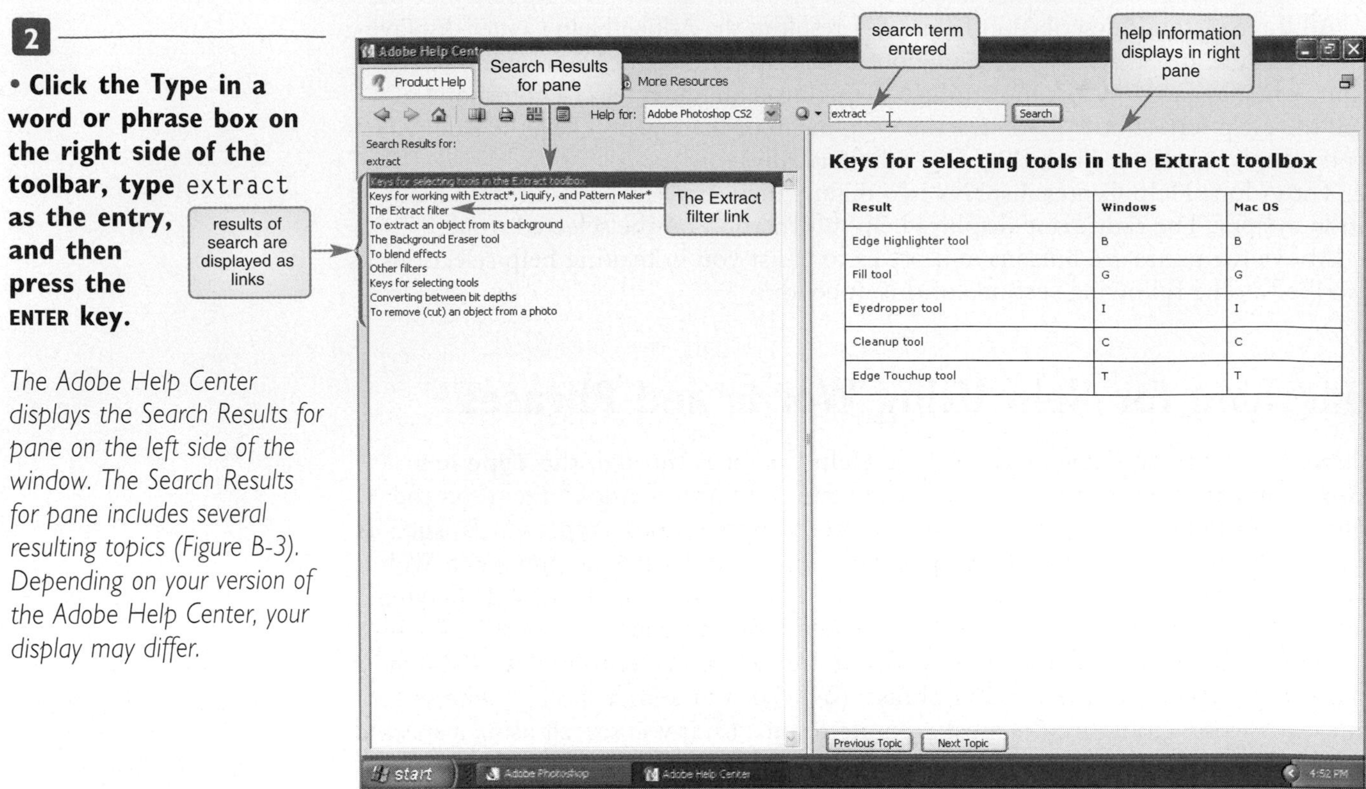

FIGURE B-3

3

- **In the Search Results for pane, click The Extract filter topic.**

The Adobe Help Center displays information about the topic in the right pane (Figure B-4).

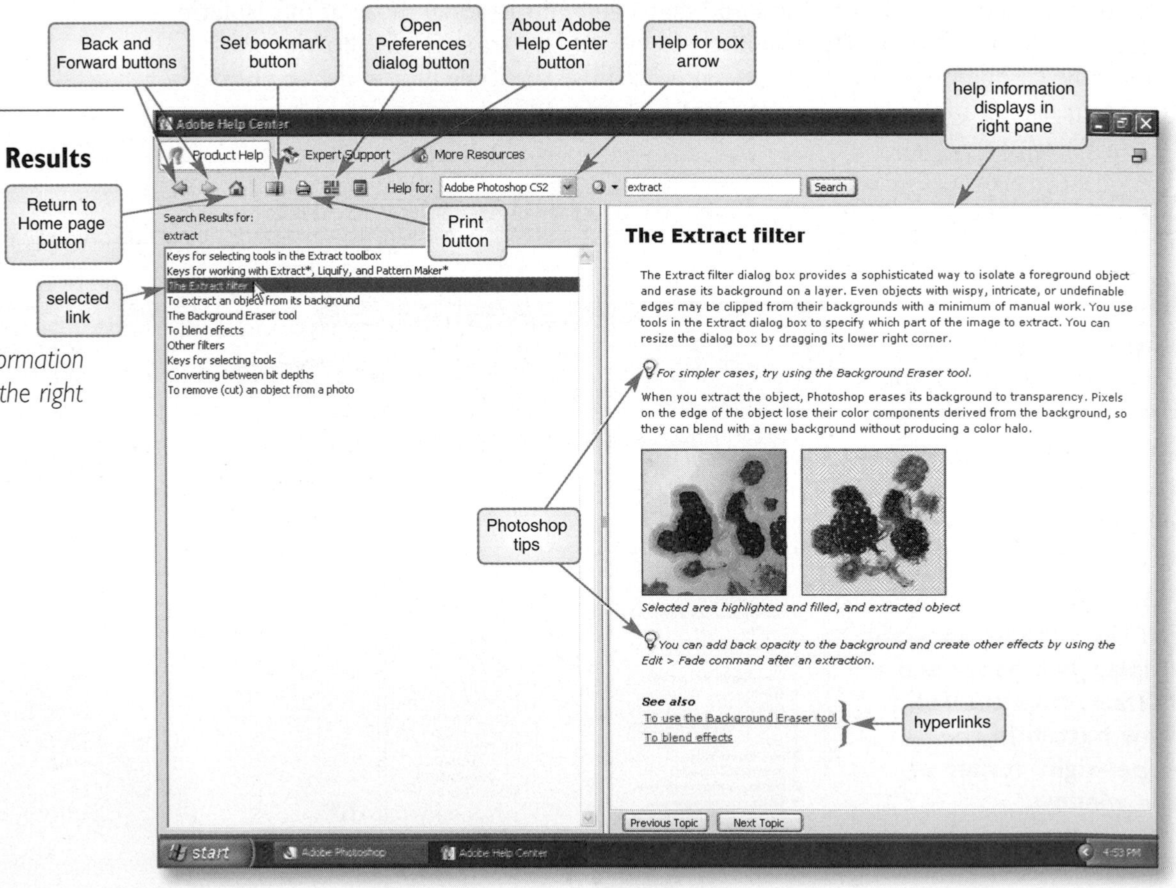

FIGURE B-4

In the right pane, the Adobe Help Center displays hyperlinks in red, which you can click to seek additional information. A light bulb icon indicates a Photoshop tip.

If none of the topics presents the information you want, you can refine the search by entering another word or phrase in the Type in a word or phrase box.

Use the buttons on the toolbar of the Adobe Help Center window (Figure B-4) to navigate through the Adobe Help Center, return to the Home page, or print the contents of the window. Additionally, buttons are provided to set bookmarks, set preferences, and display an About box. If other Adobe products are installed on your system, the Help for box arrow will display a list. Click another product in the list to access its help system.

As you click topics in the Search Results for pane, the Adobe Help Center displays new pages of information. The Adobe Help Center remembers the topics you visited and allows you to redisplay the pages visited during a session by clicking the Back and Forward buttons.

Using the Adobe Help Center Tabs

From the Home page of the Adobe Help Center, tabs display in the left pane. These tabs are Contents, Index, and Bookmarks. Your version may display a Search tab, as well.

Using the Contents Tab

The **Contents tab** is similar to a table of contents in a book. To use the Contents tab, click the tab from the Home page in the Adobe Help Center. Then click any topic on the Contents tab to display subtopics as shown in the following steps.

To Use the Contents Tab

1

- **Click the Return to Home page button on the toolbar.**
- **When the tabs are displayed, if necessary, click the Contents tab.**

The Adobe Help Center displays the table of contents (Figure B-5).

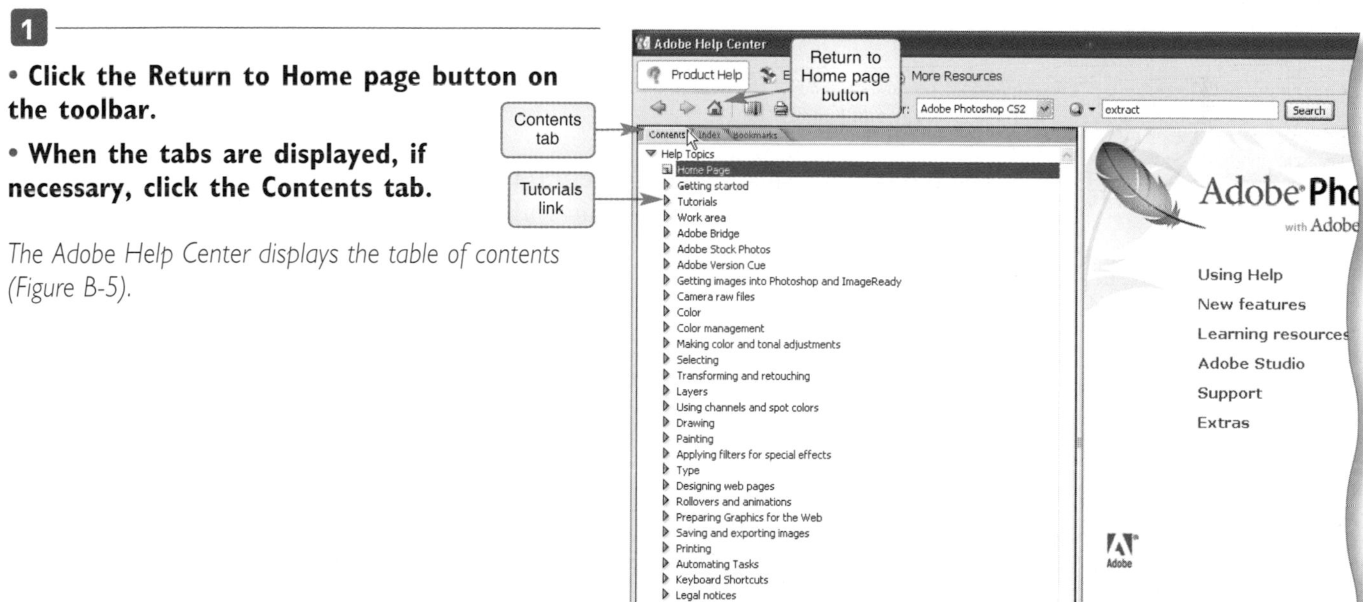

FIGURE B-5

2

• Click Tutorials in the list. When the subtopic displays, click Tutorials, and then click the Tutorials in that list.

Information displays about tutorials (Figure B-6).

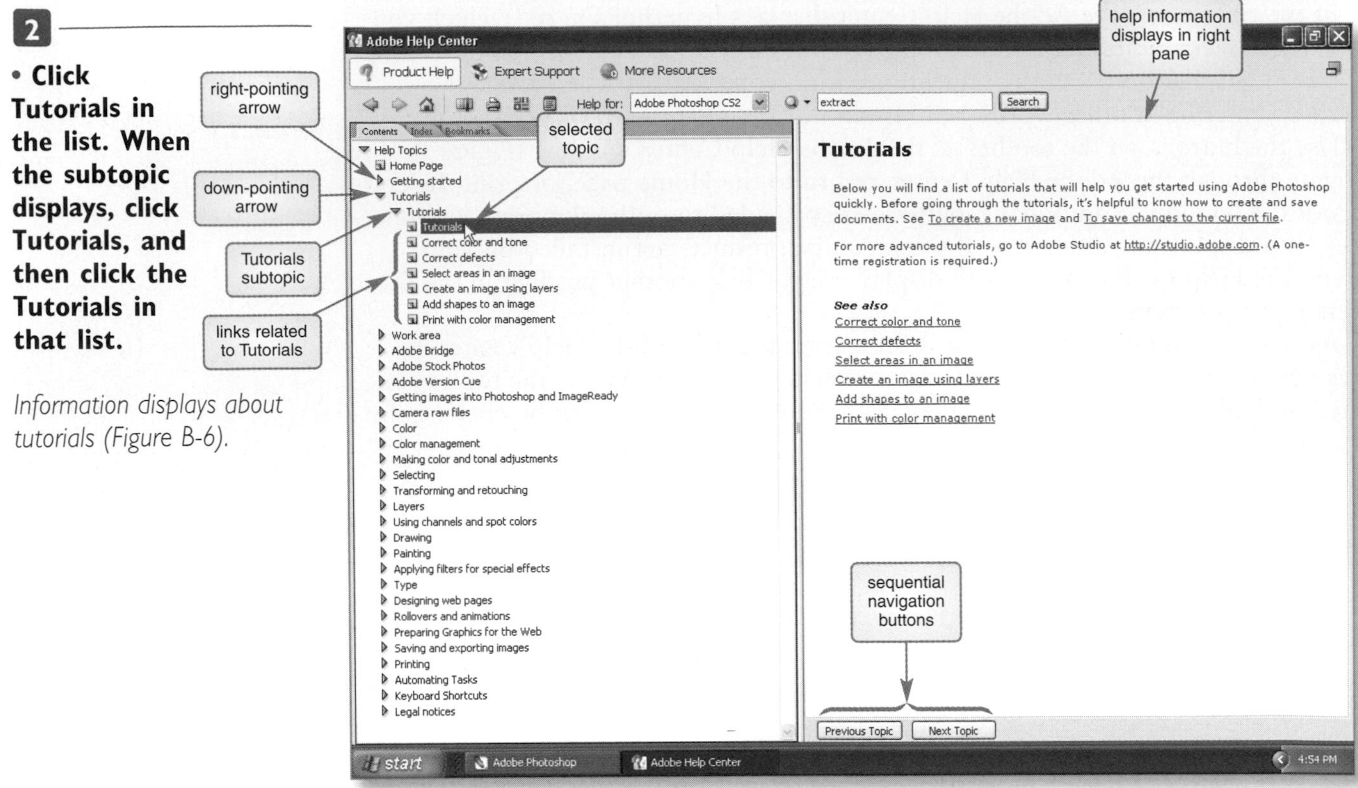

FIGURE B-6

When using any of the help tabs, Previous Topic and Next Topic buttons display at the bottom of the right pane (Figure B-6). Clicking one of those buttons moves to the next sequential topic.

To expand any topic in the left pane, click a right-pointing arrow. To collapse a topic, click a down-pointing arrow.

Using the Index Tab

The **Index tab** displays an alphabetical listing of topics. Click the letter of the alphabet to display subtopics beginning with the selected letter as the following steps illustrate.

To Use the Index Tab

1

- **Click the Index tab.**

The Adobe Help Center displays the alphabetical listing (Figure B-7).

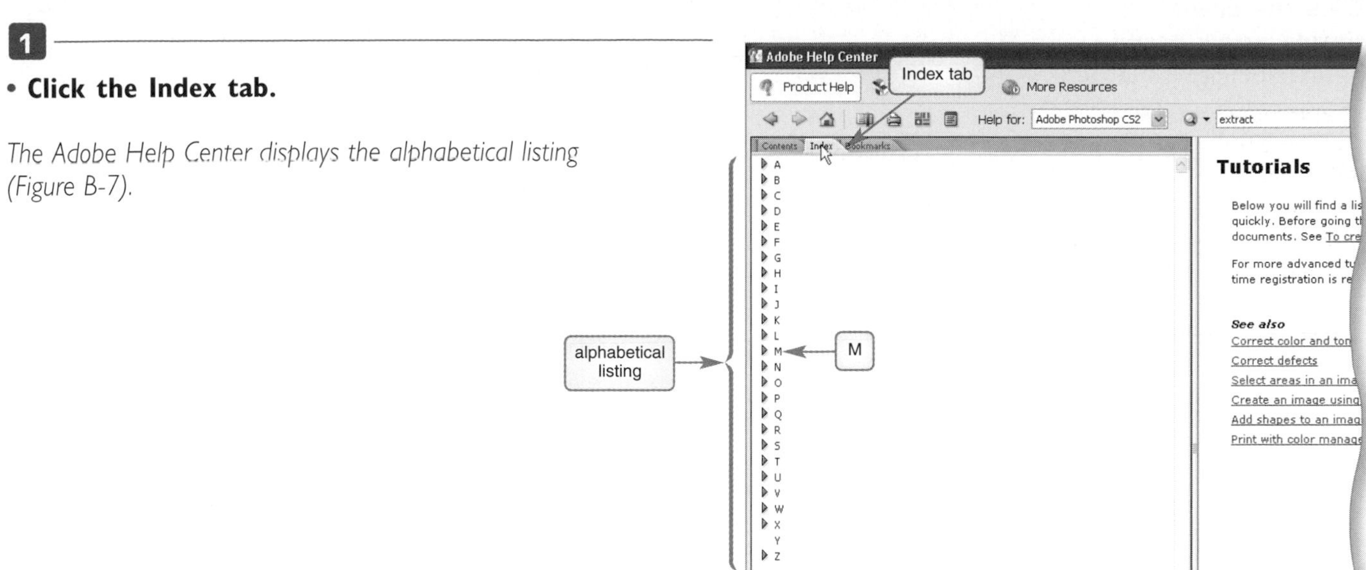

FIGURE B-7

2

- **Click M. When the subtopics are displayed, click magnifying images, and then click the To magnify by dragging topic.**

Information is displayed about magnifying a selection by dragging (Figure B-8).

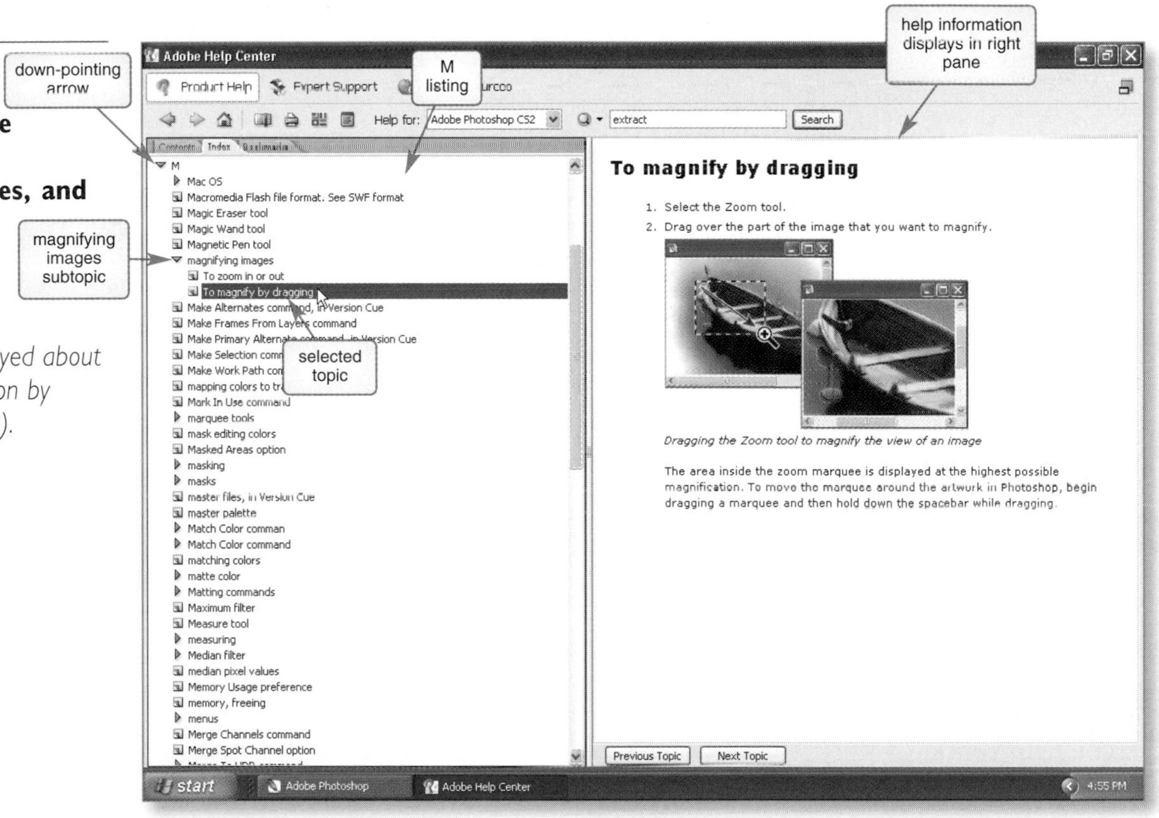

FIGURE B-8

3

• **Click the down-pointing arrow next to the letter M, to collapse the topics (Figure B-9).**

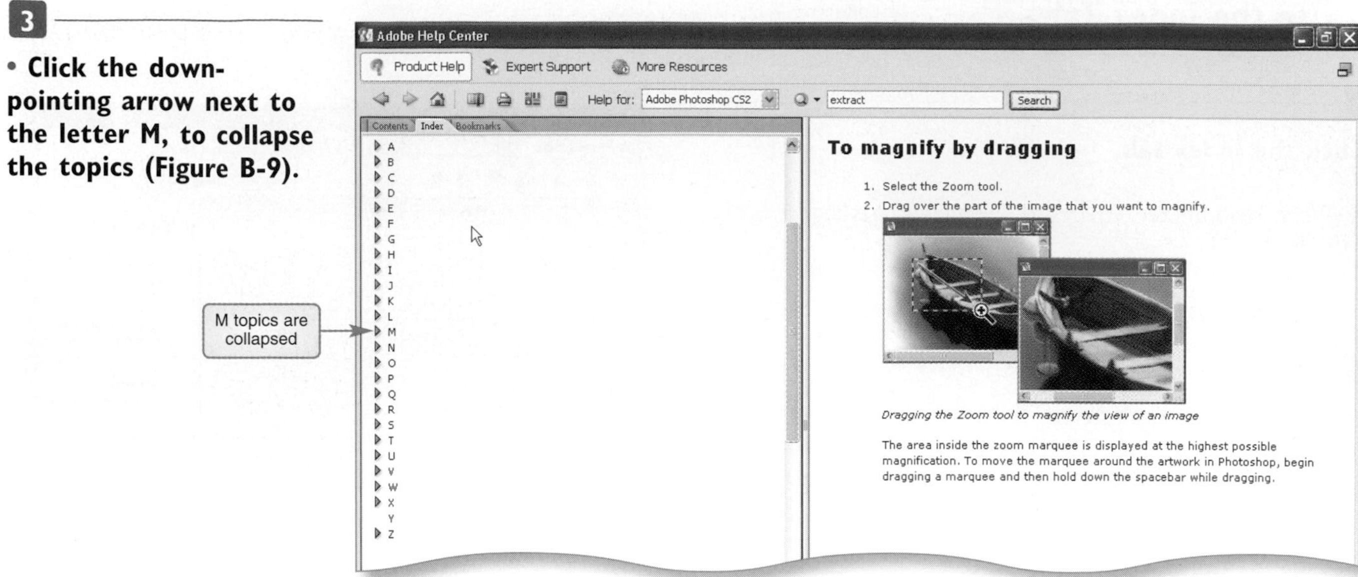

FIGURE B-9

From any of the tabs in the Adobe Help Center, you can create bookmarks as discussed in the next section.

Using Bookmarks

The **Bookmarks tab** shows links previously bookmarked on your system. In many computer applications, a **bookmark** is an electronic marker or link, identifying a topic for later reference or retrieval. To create a bookmark in the Adobe Help Center, click the Add a bookmark for the current help topics button on the toolbar. To display all bookmarks, click the Bookmarks tab. To access a specific bookmark, click the link on the Bookmarks tab.

To Create and Access a Bookmark

1

• **With the To magnify by dragging topic still displayed in the right pane, click the Add a bookmark for the current help contents button.**

The Adobe Help Center displays a New Bookmark dialog box (Figure B-10).

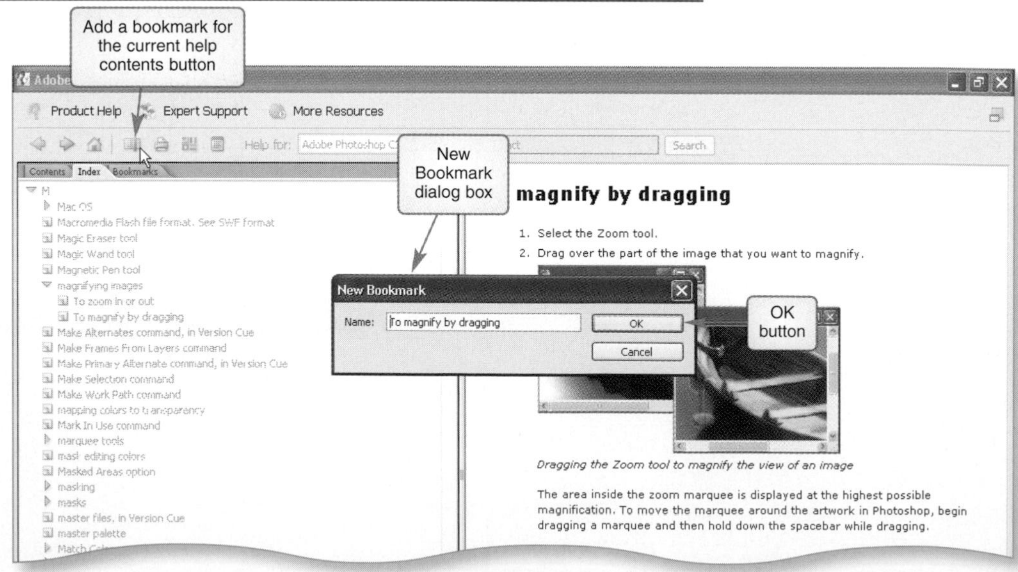

FIGURE B-10

2

- **When the New Bookmark dialog box is displayed, click the OK button.**
- **Click the Bookmarks tab.**

The new bookmark is displayed as a link on the Bookmarks tab as shown in Figure B-11. Your list of bookmarks may differ.

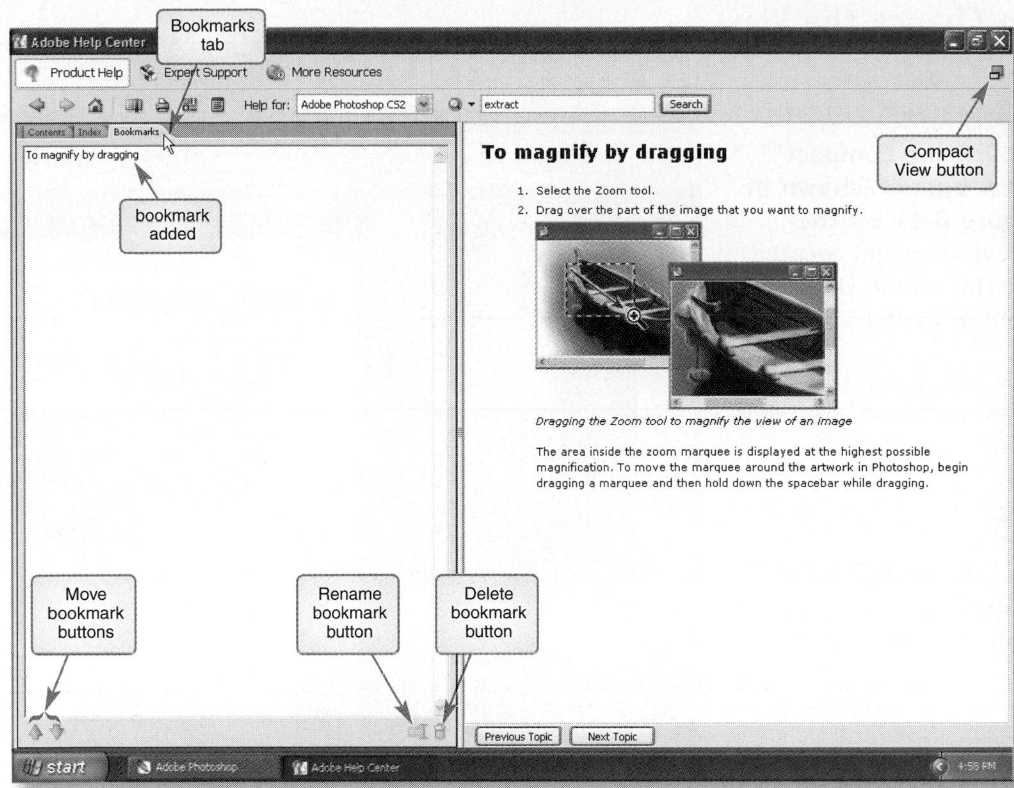

FIGURE B-11

If you have multiple bookmarks, the Move bookmark up in the list and Move bookmark down in the list buttons assist you in managing your bookmarks. You also can rename or delete bookmarks by selecting a bookmark and using the buttons in the lower part of the Bookmarks tab (Figure B-11).

Changing the View

In an initial installation, the Adobe Help Center opens in Full view. **Full view** gives you access to the Product Help and More Resources sections. It also may give you access to Expert Support. Full view opens in a new window that is maximized. If you click the Compact View button, the view changes. **Compact view** displays only the selected Help topic and keeps the Help window open on top of, or floating over, the Adobe Photoshop window. Clicking the button again toggles back to Full view.

To Change the View

1

• **Click the Compact View button (shown in Figure B-11 on the previous page) located on the Adobe Help Center toolbar.**

The right pane information floats over the Photoshop window (Figure B-12).

2

• **Click the Full View button on the Adobe Help Center toolbar.**

The window maximizes and both panes of the Adobe Help Center again are displayed.

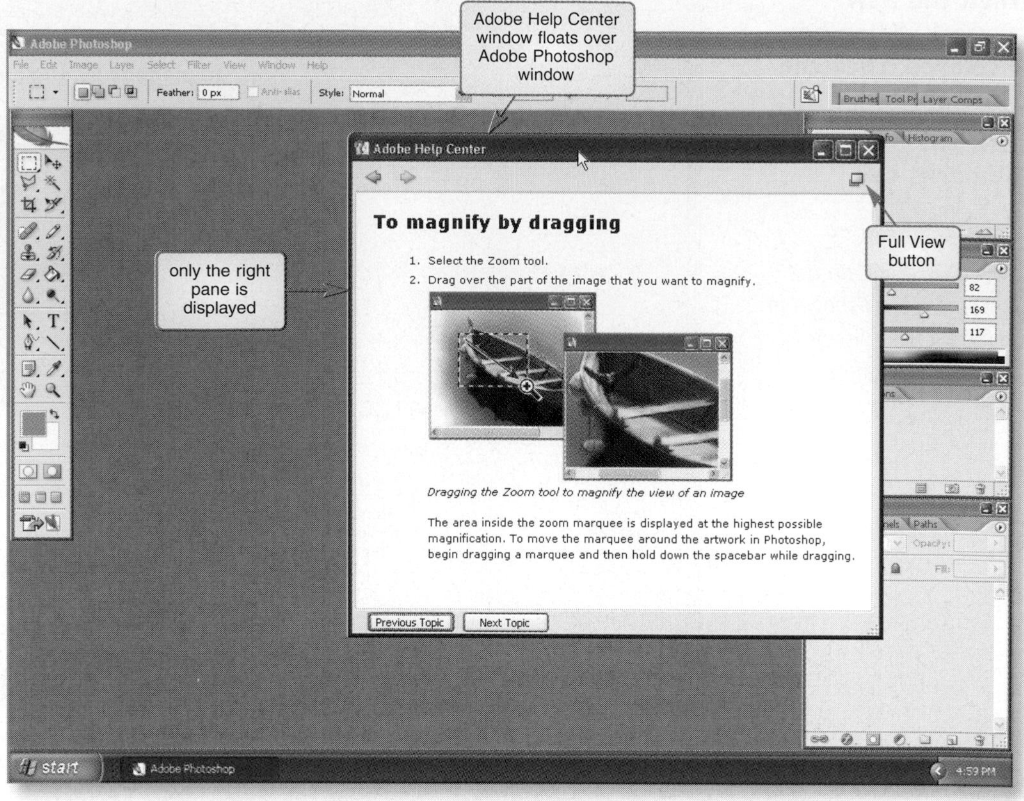

FIGURE B-12

Other Help Sources in the Adobe Help Center

If your system displays an **Expert Support button**, you can click it to display topics with information about support plans. When clicked, the topics Expert Support Details and Support Plan Details, display panes describing plans purchased for your system. The Supported Products topic displays a list of Adobe products. If you are connected to the Web, clicking the fourth topic, Complimentary Support, displays a pane offering three free hyperlinks to Web pages maintained by Adobe as shown in Figure B-13. The Resource Center hyperlink connects you to the Adobe Design Center, which contains online tips, tutorials, and resources. The Forums hyperlink connects you to the User to User forums, which allow users to share questions, suggestions, and information about all of the Adobe products. The Downloads hyperlink connects you to the Downloads page, which offers online product updates and plug-ins.

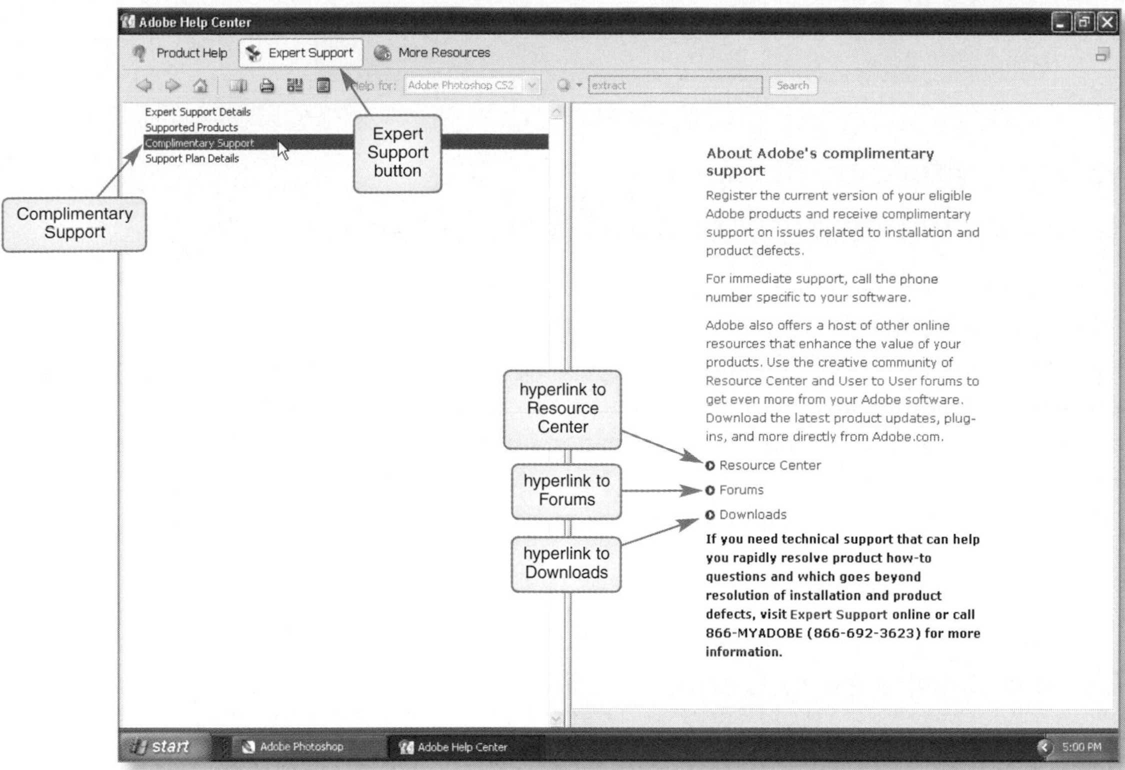

FIGURE B-13

The **More Resources button** in Adobe Help Center version 1.0.0 displays two topics (Figure B-14). When clicked, the Online Resources topic displays a pane to access online support. The Personal Contacts topic displays a pane where you can keep a file of people you know, or work with, who have Photoshop knowledge. In other versions of the Adobe Help Center, the More Resources button may take you to the Adobe Support home page on the Web.

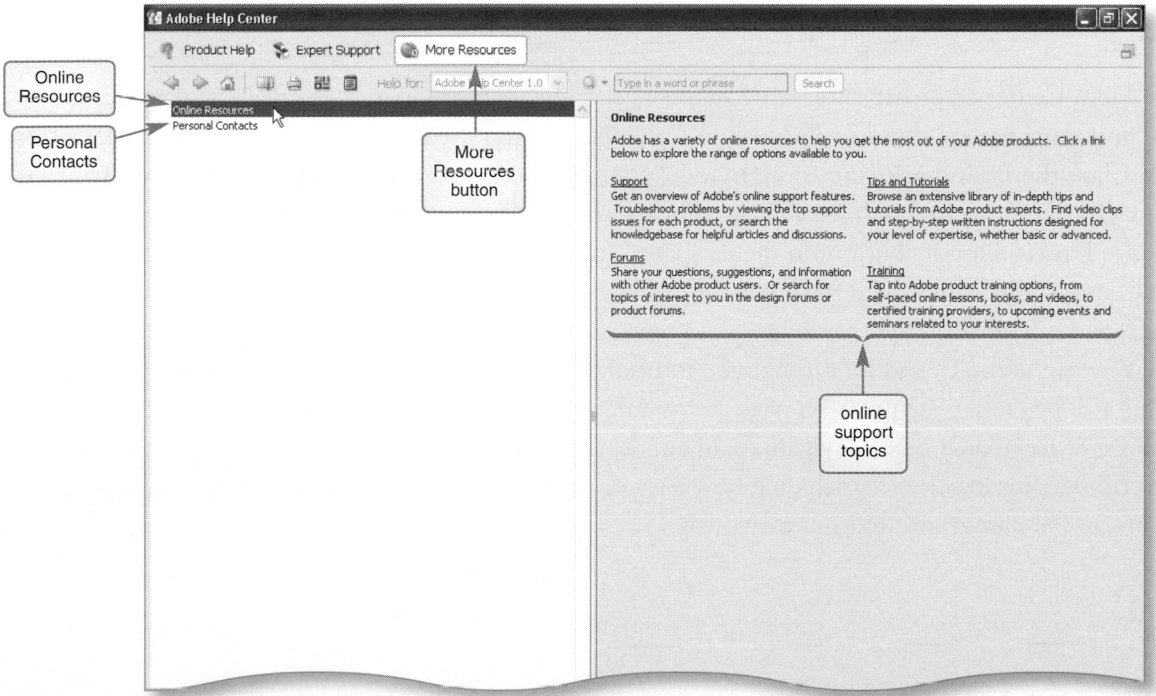

FIGURE B-14

1 Using the Type in a Word or Phrase Box

Instructions: Perform the following tasks using the Adobe Help Center.

1. Type `Pencil tool` in the Type in a word or phrase box to obtain help on using the Pencil tool.
2. When the topics display in the Search Results for pane, click To use the Brush Tool or Pencil tool.
3. One at a time, click two additional hyperlinks in the right pane and print the information. Hand in the printouts to your instructor. Use the Back and Forward buttons to return to the original page.
4. Use the Type in a word or phrase box to search for information on alignment. Click the To align selections and layers within an image topic in the Search Results for pane. Read and print the information. One at a time, click the hyperlinks on the page and print the information for any new page that displays.
5. Close the Adobe Help Center window.

2 Expanding On the Adobe Help Center Basics

Instructions: Use the Adobe Help Center to understand the topics better and answer the questions listed below. Answer the questions on your own paper, or hand in the printed Help information to your instructor.

1. Use the Adobe Help Center to find help on snapping. Use the Type in a word or phrase box, and enter `snapping` as the word. One at a time, click each hyperlink and print the page. Hand in the printouts to your instructor.
2. Use the Adobe Help Center to find help on using Photoshop images in other applications. Using the Contents tab, click the Saving and Exporting Images topic. Choose two appropriate hyperlinks and print the information. Hand in the printouts to your instructor.
3. Use the Adobe Help Center to find help on creating knockouts. Using the Index tab, click K. Then click the knockouts subtopic. One at a time, click each hyperlink and print the page. Hand in the printouts to your instructor.
4. Use the Adobe Help Center to create three bookmarks. Look through the Contents tab to find topics of interest to you and your personal use of Photoshop CS2. As you find a page, click the Set bookmark button on the toolbar. Click the Bookmarks tab to verify that your system has saved the bookmarks.
5. Use the Adobe Help Center to find online tutorials about gradients. With your system connected to the Web, if available, click the Expert Support button. In the left pane, click Complimentary Support. In the right pane, click Resource Center. When the Adobe Resource Center Web page is displayed, click Tips & Tutorials. Click the Search tab, type `gradients` in the search box, and then press the ENTER key. When the list of tutorials is displayed, click one of the topics and go through the tutorial. If your system does not display an Expert Support button, go to the Adobe Design Center Web page at www.adobe.com/designcenter/tutorials/ and then enter gradients in the Enter Keywords box. Navigate to an appropriate tutorial and follow the directions. Write three paragraphs describing your experience including how easy or difficult it was to follow the tutorial and what you learned. Turn in the paragraphs to your instructor.

Appendix C

Using Adobe Bridge

This appendix shows you how to use Adobe Bridge. Adobe Bridge is a file exploration tool similar to Windows Explorer, but with added functionality related to images. New to Photoshop CS2, Bridge replaces previous file browsing techniques, and now is the control center for the Adobe Creative Suite. Bridge is used to organize, browse, and locate the assets you need to create content for print, the Web, and mobile devices with drag and drop functionality.

Adobe Bridge

You can access Adobe Bridge from Photoshop or from the Start menu. Both Adobe Bridge and the Adobe Help Center can run independently from Photoshop as stand-alone programs.

Starting Adobe Bridge

The following steps show how to start Adobe Bridge from the Windows Start menu.

To Start Bridge Using Windows

1

- **Click the Start button. Point to All Programs on the Start menu.**

The All Programs submenu is displayed (Figure C-1).

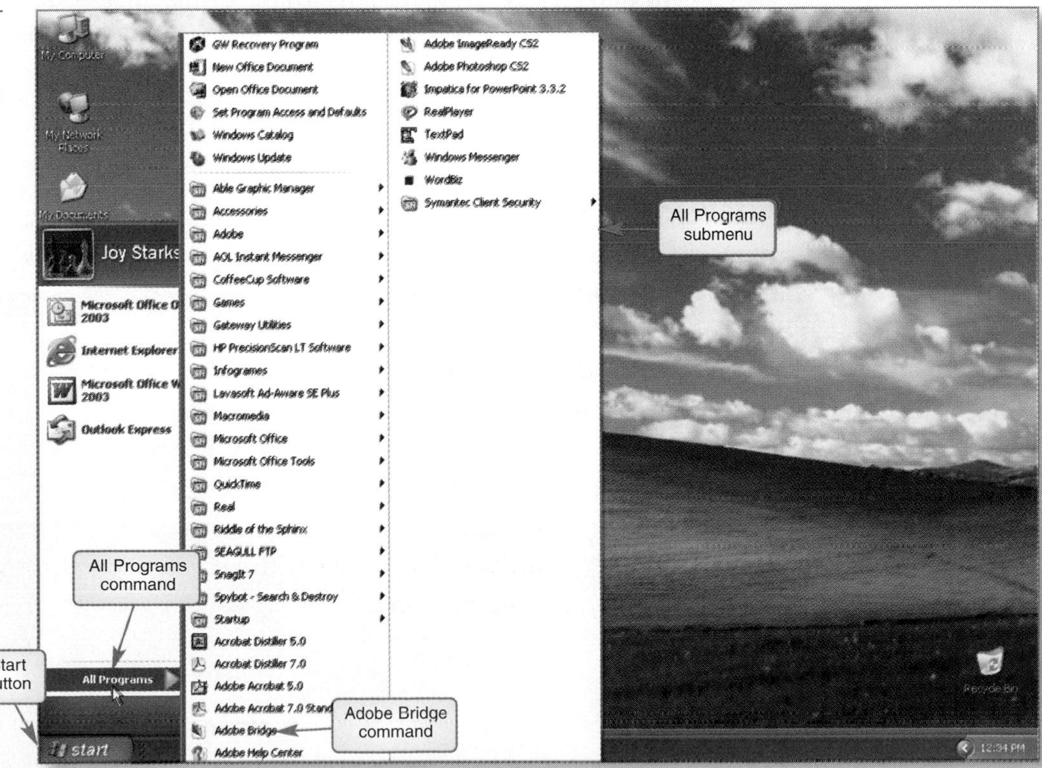

FIGURE C-1

2

• **Click Adobe Bridge in the list. When the Adobe Bridge window is displayed, double-click its title bar to maximize the window, if necessary.**

The Adobe Bridge window is displayed (Figure C-2). Your list of files and folders may differ.

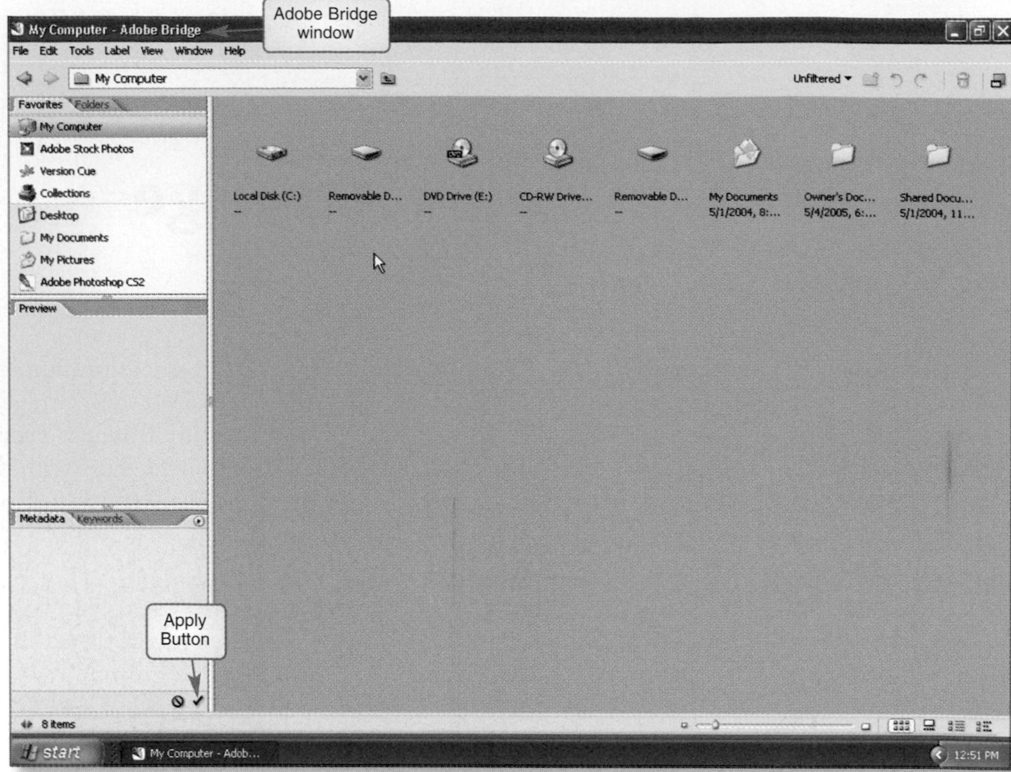

FIGURE C-2

Other Ways

1. In Photoshop, click File on menu bar, click Browse
2. In Photoshop, click Go To Bridge button on options bar

Setting the Default Workspace

To make your installation of Adobe Bridge match the figures in this book, you will need to rest the workspace to its default settings as the following steps illustrate.

To Set the Default Workspace

1

• **Click Window on the menu bar, and then point to Workspace.**

Bridge displays the Workspace submenu (Figure C-3).

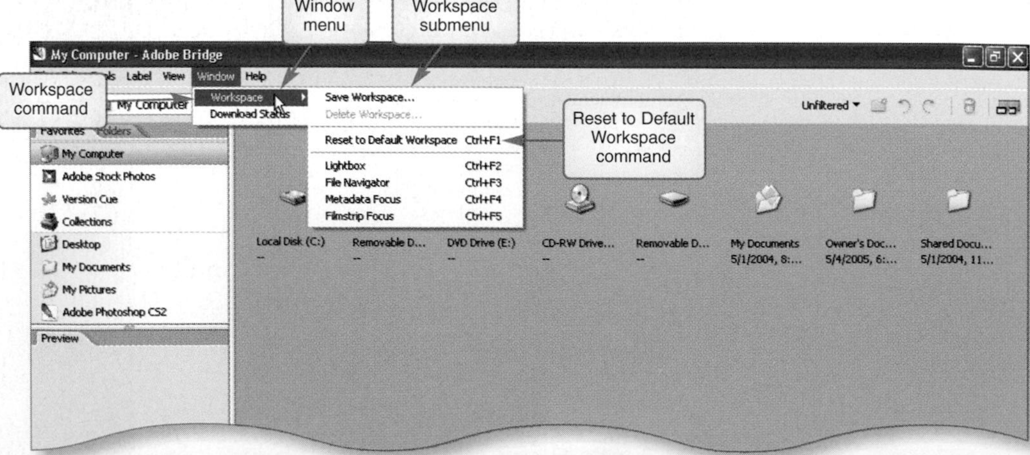

FIGURE C-3

2

- **Click Reset to Default Workspace on the Workspace submenu.**
- **In the Favorites panel, click My Computer.**

Bridge displays panels on the left, and the files and folders in Thumbnails view on the right (Figure C-4).

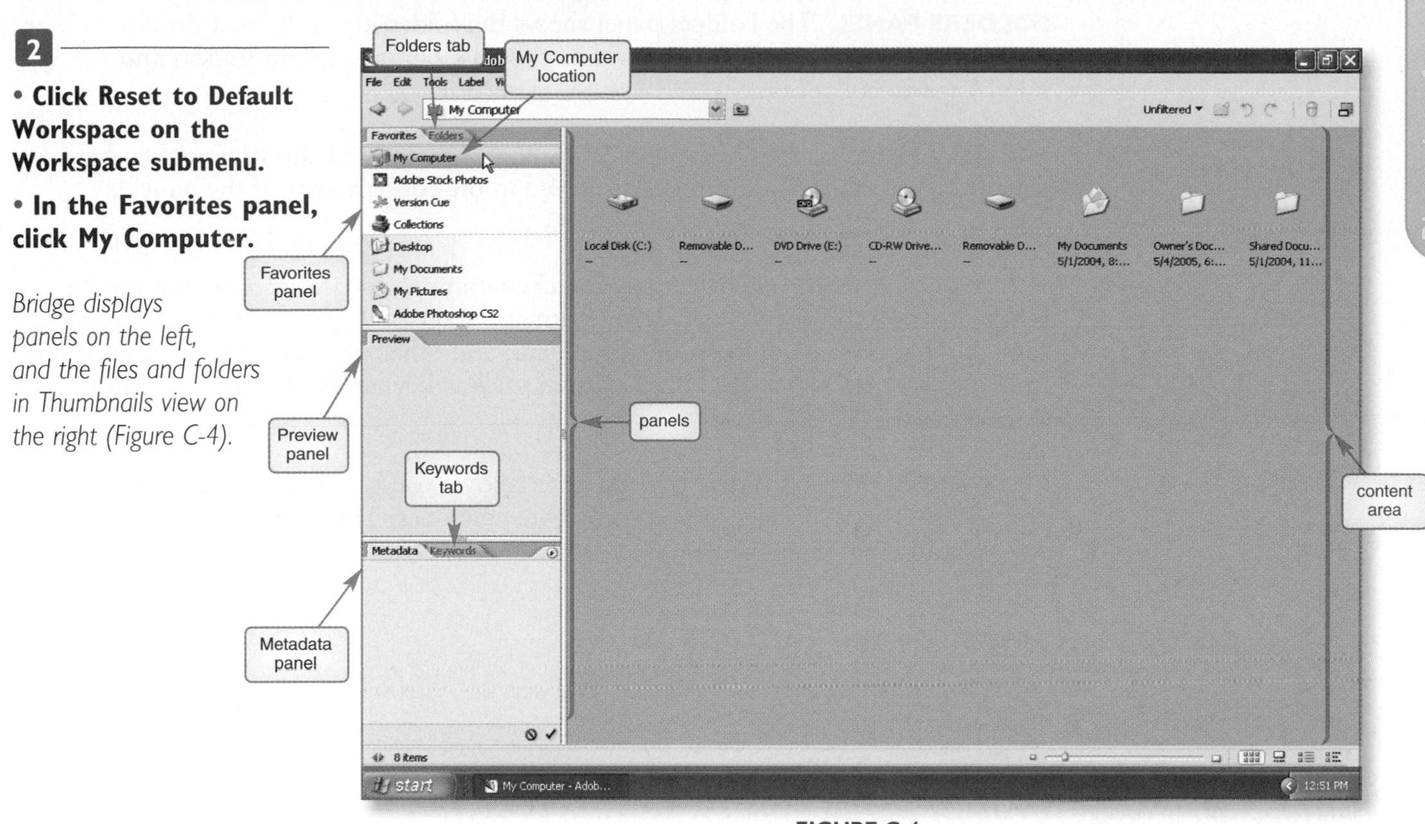

FIGURE C-4

Other Ways

1. Press CTRL+F1

The Adobe Bridge Window

The parts of the Adobe bridge Window are displayed in Figure C-4. They can be divided into three basic parts: the content area, the panels, and the toolbars and buttons. The following sections discuss these components.

The Content Area

The **content area** is displayed in a large pane on the right side of the Adobe Bridge window. The content area includes a view of each file and folder, its name, the creation date, and other information about each item. The content area is used to select files and open folders. To select a file, click it. To open a folder, double-click it. You can change how the content area is displayed on the status bar.

The Panels

Several panels display on the left side of the Bridge workspace in default view. To select a panel, click its tab. You can rearrange the panels by dragging their tabs. You can enlarge or reduce the size of the panels by dragging their borders.

FAVORITES PANEL The Favorites panel allows quick access to common locations and folders, as well as access to other Adobe applications. Click a location to display its contents in the content area. If you click an application name, Windows will launch or open the application.

FOLDERS PANEL The Folders panel shows the folder hierarchy in a display similar to that of Windows Explorer. Users click the plus sign to expand folders and the minus sign to collapse them.

PREVIEW PANEL The Preview panel displays a preview of the selected file that is usually larger than the thumbnail displayed in the content area. If the panel is resized, the preview also is resized.

METADATA PANEL The Metadata panel contains metadata information for the selected file. Recall that metadata is information about the file including properties, camera data, creation and modification data, and other pieces of information. If multiple files are selected, shared data is listed such as keywords, date created, and exposure settings.

KEYWORDS PANEL The Keywords panel allows you to assign keywords using categories designed by Bridge, or you can create new ones. The keywords help you organize and search your images.

Toolbars and Buttons

Bridge displays several toolbars and sets of buttons to help you work more efficiently (Figure C-5).

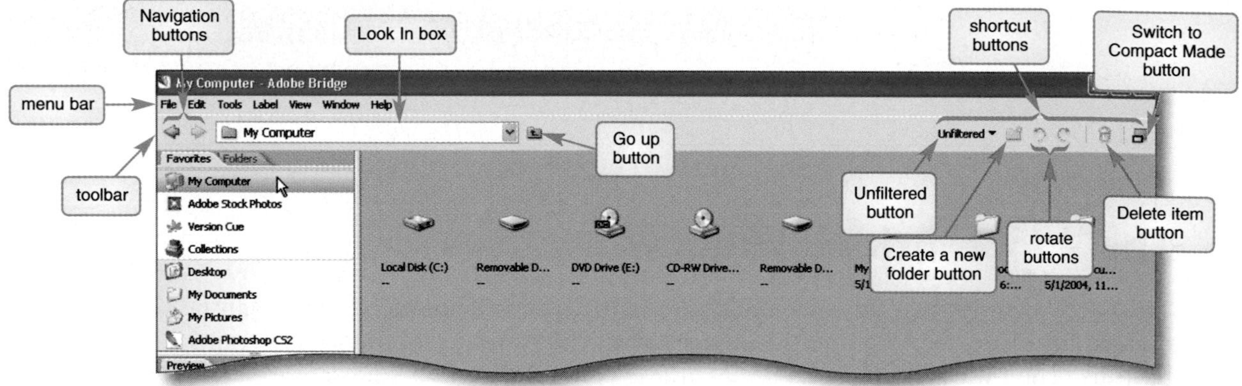

FIGURE C-5

MENU BAR The menu bar is displayed at the top of the Bridge window and contains commands specific to Bridge.

NAVIGATION BUTTONS Below the menu bar are navigation buttons that allow you to move back to previous locations and then forward again.

LOOK IN BOX To the right of the Navigation buttons is the Look In box. When you click the box arrow, Bridge displays the current folder's hierarchy, as well as favorite and recent folders. To the right of the Look In box is a Go up button to move up in the file hierarchy.

SHORTCUT BUTTONS On the right side of the toolbar are shortcut buttons to help you work with your files. When you click the Unfiltered button, Bridge displays ways to group your files based on a star rating or color-coding system. The Create a new folder button inserts a new folder in the current location. The rotate buttons are active when an image file is selected in the content area. The Delete item button deletes the selected item. The final shortcut button switches to compact view, which removes the panels and menus, and reduces the size of the window.

STATUS BAR At the bottom of the Bridge window, the status bar displays information and contains buttons (Figure C-6). On the left side of the status bar is a Show/Hide Panels button followed by information regarding the number of items in the current location and how many files are selected, if any. On the right side of the status bar, a slider sets the size of the thumbnails. On the ends of the slider are buttons to choose the smallest and largest thumbnails. Four buttons change the display of the content area, including Thumbnails view, Filmstrip view, Details view, and Versions and alternates view. The four views also are available via commands on the View menu.

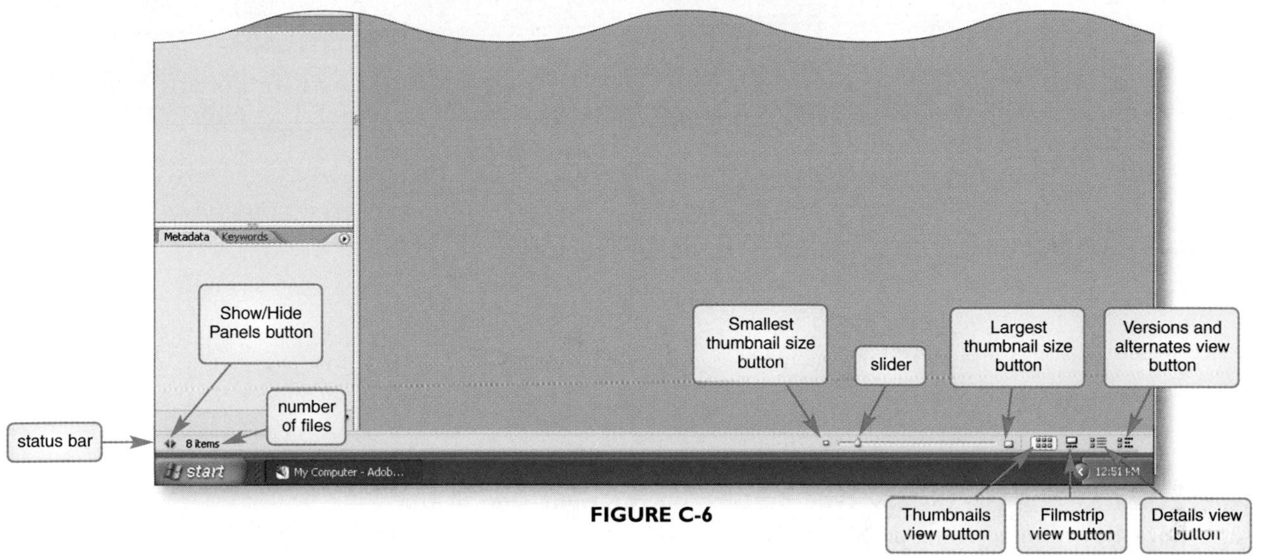

FIGURE C-6

Bridge Navigation and File Viewing

The advantages of using Bridge to navigate through the files and folders on your computer system include an interface that looks the same in all folders, the ability to see the images quickly, and the ease with which you can open the files in Photoshop or other image editing software. Besides the four kinds of display represented by the buttons on the right side of the status bar, Bridge offers four other configurations or layouts of the work area accessible via the Window menu. The **Lightbox workspace** displays just the content area for viewing files. The **File Navigator workspace** displays the content area in Thumbnails view, along with the Favorites panel and Folder panel. The **Metadata Focus workspace** displays the content area in Thumbnails view, along with an enlarged Metadata panel. The **Filmstrip Focus workspace** displays just the content area, in Filmstrip view.

The steps on the next page show how to navigate to a CD and view files. Your instructor may specify a different location for these files.

To Navigate and View Files Using Bridge

• Insert the CD that accompanies this book into your CD drive.

• After a few seconds, if Windows displays a dialog box, click its Close button.

• In the content area, double-click the CD icon associated with your CD drive.

• When the folders and files of the CD are displayed, double-click the Project01 folder.

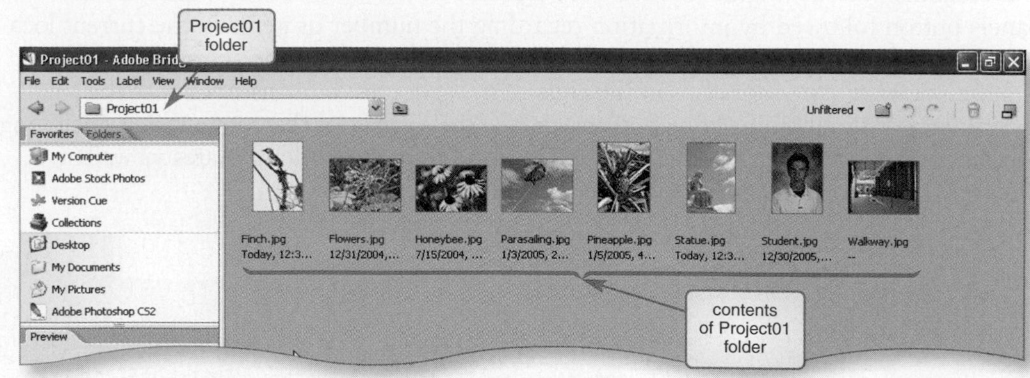

FIGURE C-7

The photos in the Project01 folder are displayed (Figure C-7).

2

• One at a time, click each of the display type buttons on the right side of the status bar and note how the content area changes.

• One at a time, click Window on the menu bar, point to Workspace, and then click a workspace choice and note how the content area changes.

• Click Window on the menu bar, point to Workspace, and then click Reset to Default Workspace to reset the content area and panels.

Bridge is reset back to its default.

Other Ways

1. To view Lightbox workspace, press CTRL+F2
2. To view File Navigator workspace, press CTRL+F3
3. To view Metadata Focus workspace, press CTRL+F4
4. To view Filmstrip Focus workspace, press CTRL+F5

Managing Files

If you want to move a file to a folder that is currently displayed in the content area, you can drag and drop the file. The right-drag option is not available. If you want to copy a file, you can choose Copy on the Edit menu, navigate to the new folder and then choose Paste on the Edit menu. At any time you can press the **delete** key to delete a file or folder, or right-click and then click Send to Recycle Bin on the shortcut menu. To rename a photo in Bridge, click the File icon, and then click the file name. Type the new name.

The next steps illustrate copying a file from a CD to a USB flash drive using Bridge.

To Copy a File

1

- **With the Project01 folder contents still displaying in the content area, click the Flowers thumbnail.**
- **Click Edit on the menu bar.**

Bridge displays the Edit menu (Figure C-8).

FIGURE C-8

2

- **Click Copy on the Edit menu.**
- **In the Favorites panel, click My Computer.**
- **When the My Computer locations display in the content area, double-click drive G or the drive associated with your USB flash drive.**

The contents of the USB flash drive are displayed (Figure C-9). Your list will vary.

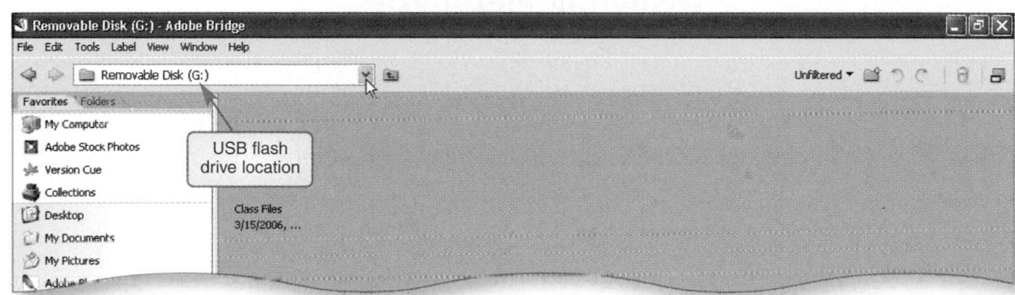

FIGURE C-9

3

- **Click Edit on the menu bar, and then click Paste.**

Bridge displays the copy in its new location (Figure C-10).

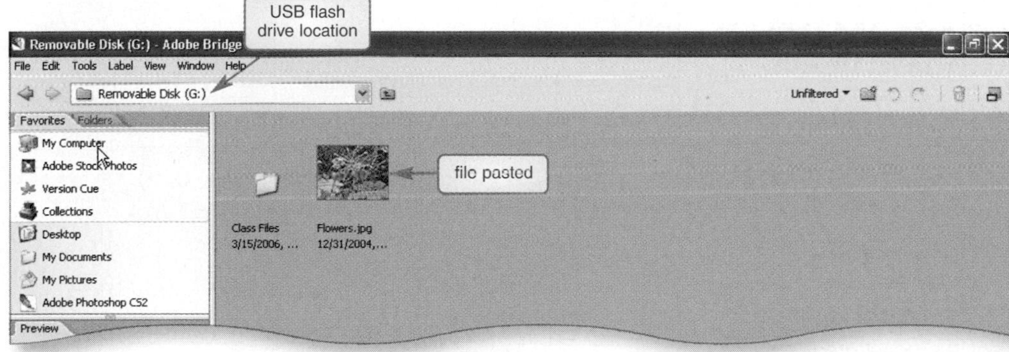

FIGURE C-10

Other Ways

1. To copy, press CTRL+C
2. To paste, press CTRL+V

Bridge also offers a Duplicate command on the Edit menu (Figure C-8) that makes a copy in the same folder. Bridge renames the second file with the word, Copy, appended to the file name.

Metadata

A popular use for Bridge allows you to assign metadata. Metadata, such as information about the file, author, resolution, color space, and copyright is used for searching and categorizing photos. You can utilize metadata to streamline your workflow and organize your files.

Metadata is divided into three categories: File Properties, IPTC Core, and Camera Data (Exif). **File Properties** include things like file type, creation date, dimensions, and color mode. **IPTC Core** stands for International Press Telecommunications Council, which is data used to identify transmitted text and images, such as data describing the image or the location of a photo. **Camera Data (Exif)** refers to the Exchangeable Image File Format, a standard for storing interchange information in image files, especially those using JPEG compression. Most digital cameras now use the EXIF format. The standardization of ITPC and EXIF encourages interoperability between imaging devices.

Assigning Metadata

The Metadata Focus workspace makes it easier to assign or enter metadata for photos, as shown in the following steps where a description and location are entered. In the Metadata panel, you can click the pencil icon to select fields of metadata, or you can move through the fields by pressing the TAB key.

To Assign Metadata

1

- **Click the Flowers thumbnail to select it.**
- **Click Window on the menu bar, point to Workspace, and then click Metadata Focus.**
- **In the Metadata panel, scroll down to the Description field.**

The Metadata Focus workspace widens the panel area (Figure C-11). Depending on your system's installed Adobe applications, your Metadata panel may display different fields.

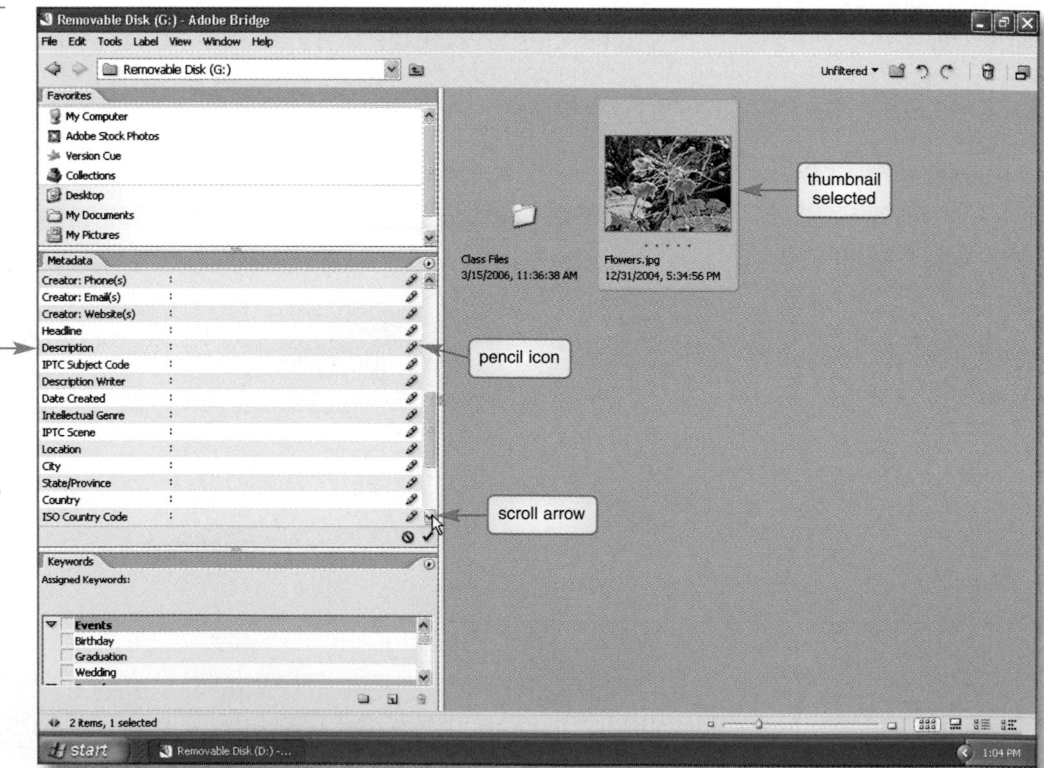

FIGURE C-11

2

- **Click the pencil icon to the right of the Description field. Type** `Hawaiian Flowers` **as the description.**
- **Click the pencil icon to the right of the Location field. Type** `Kauai` **as the location.**
- **Press the TAB key, Type** `Kilauea` **as the city.**
- **Press the TAB key. Type** `Hawaii` **as the state.**

The metadata is entered (Figure C-12).

FIGURE C-12

3

- **Click the Apply button at the bottom of the Metadata panel.**
- **Click File on the menu bar and then click File Info (Figure C-13).**
- **Click the OK button.**

The metadata is applied, or stored, with the picture.

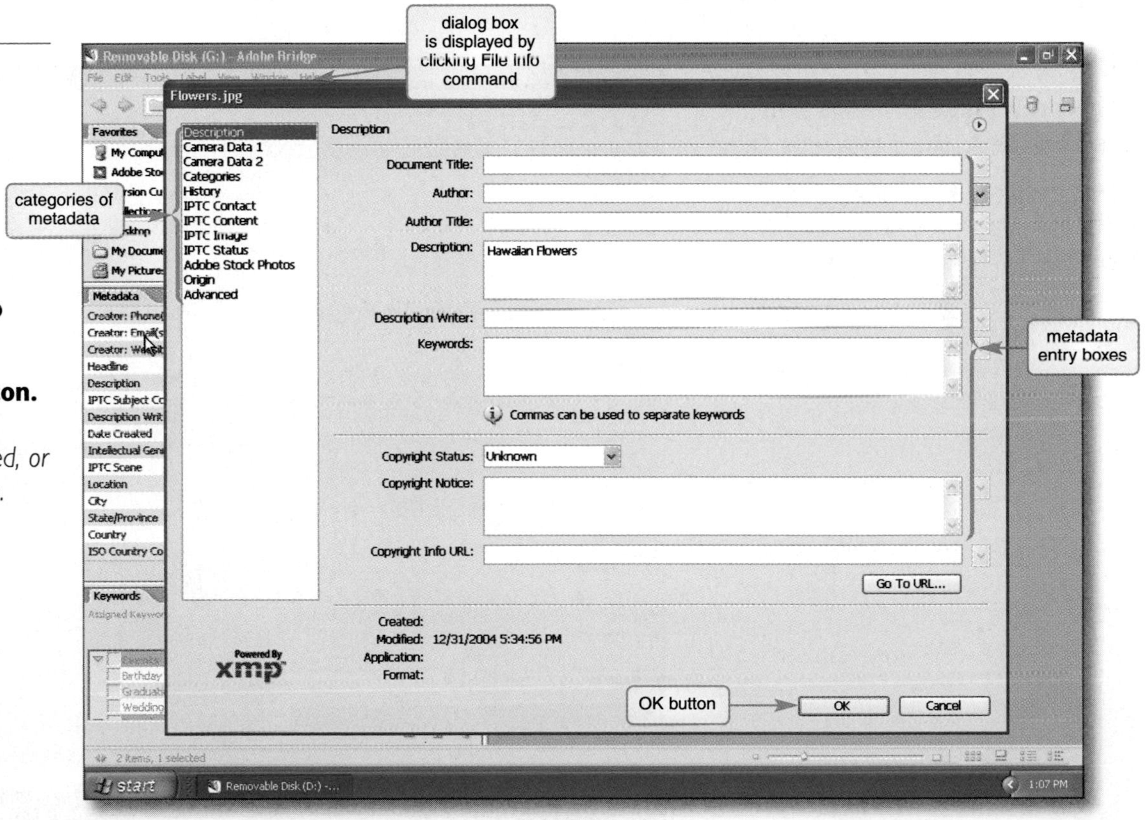

FIGURE C-13

Other Ways

1. Press CTRL+F4, enter data

The Metadata panel menu button (Figure C-12 on the previous page) displays options to increase or decrease the font size of the fields in the panel. Additionally, the menu displays options to set Metadata preferences as well as finding and adding new fields. For example, if your digital camera records global positioning system (GPS) navigational information, you can use the menu to append that data to the file.

A second way to enter Metadata information is to use the File info command on Bridge's File menu. Figure C-13 on the previous page displays a dialog box to enter information about the Flowers image. As you click each category of metadata on the left, text boxes in the main window allow you to enter extensive metadata. This extended set of metadata is particularly useful for large businesses, such as the newspaper industry, which contracts with many photographers and must maintain photo history.

Keywords

The Keywords panel lets you create and apply Bridge keywords to files. Keywords can be organized into categories called keyword sets. Using keywords and sets, you identify files based on their content. Later, you can view all files with shared keywords as a group. To assign a keyword, you click the box to the left of the keyword in the Keywords panel. Buttons at the bottom of the Keywords panel allow you to create new sets and new words.

The following steps describe how to enter keywords associated with the Flowers image.

To Enter a New Keyword

1

- **With the Flowers image still selected, click the Keywords tab.**
- **Scroll down to display the keyword set named, Places, and then click Places.**

The Places keyword set is selected (Figure C-14).

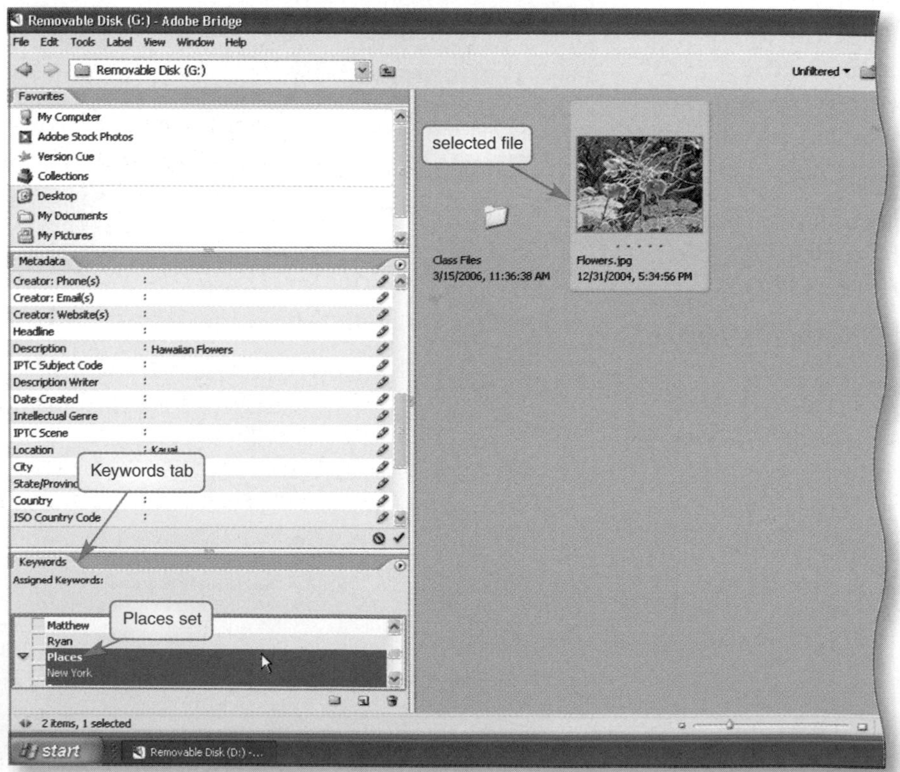

FIGURE C-14

2

- **Click the New Keyword button at the bottom of the panel.**
- **When the new field is displayed, type** `Hawaii` **and then press the ENTER key.**
- **Click the check box to the left of Hawaii.**

Bridge displays the new keyword and selects it (Figure C-15).

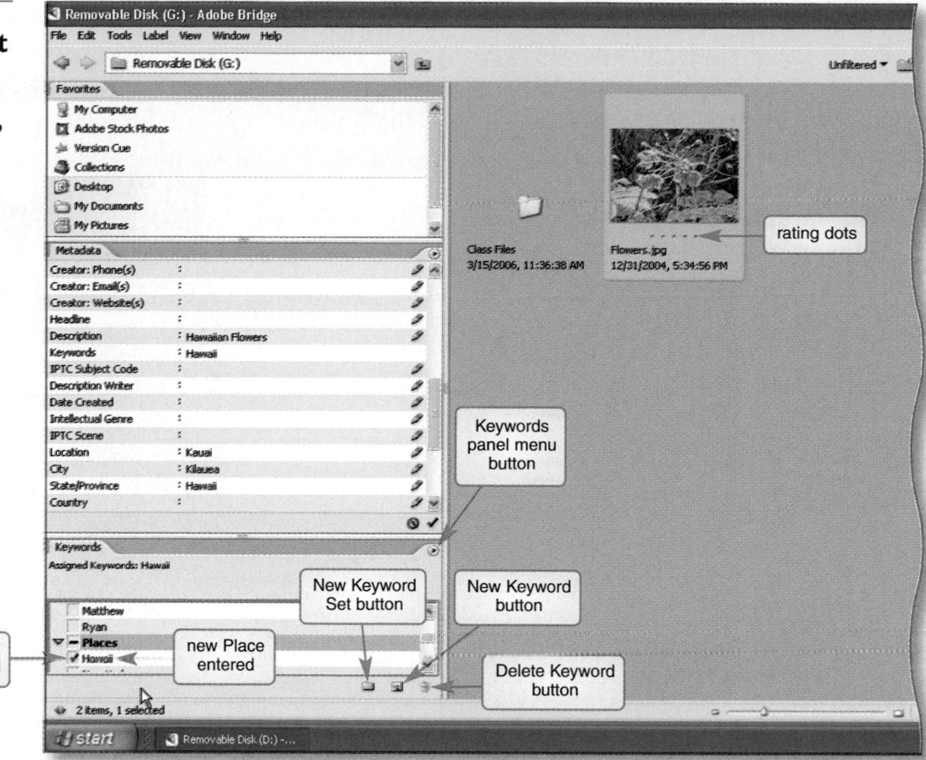

FIGURE C-15

To create a new keyword set, click the New Keyword Set button at the bottom of the panel. To remove a keyword assignment, click the box to the left of the keyword to remove its check mark. To delete a keyword permanently, remove its check mark assignment, select the keyword, and then click the Delete Keyword button at the bottom of the Keywords panel.

The Keywords panel menu button also displays options for new keywords, new sets, deleting, renaming, and finding keywords.

Rating Photos

A rating system from zero stars to five stars is available in Bridge to rate your images and photos. A rating system helps you organize and flag your favorite, or best, files. Many photographers transfer their digital photos from a camera into Bridge and then look back through them, rating and grouping the photos. The step on the next page shows how to rate a photo.

To Rate a Photo

1

• With the Flowers image still selected in the content area, click the middle dot below the thumbnail.

Bridge assigns a three-star rating (Figure C-16).

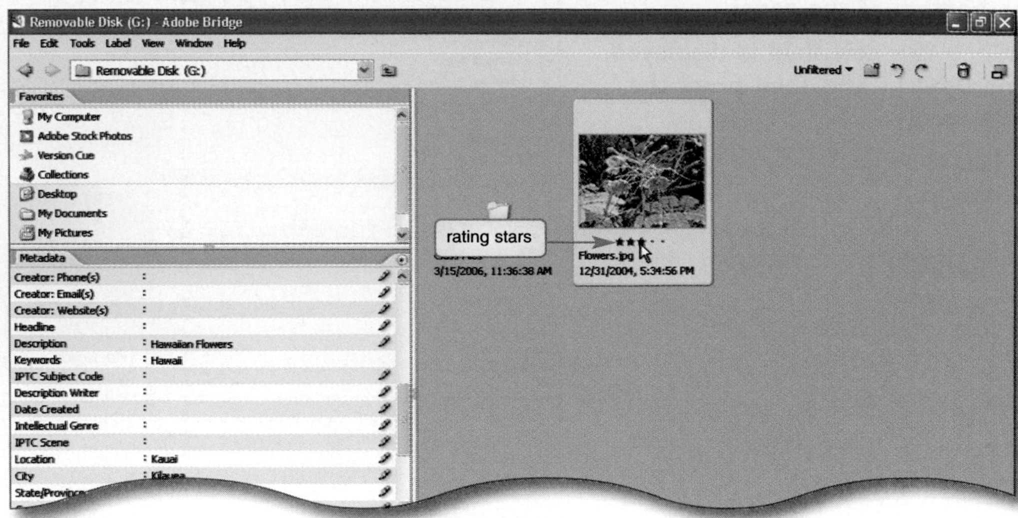

FIGURE C-16

Other Ways

1. On Label menu, click ***
2. Press CTRL+3

To change a rating, either click a different dot below the thumbnail, or click Label on the menu bar and then either increase or decrease the rating. To remove all stars, below the thumbnail, click to the left of the stars; or, click Label on the menu bar and then click No Rating.

Color-Coding Photos

Another way to group photos in Bridge is to use a color-coding system. Bridge provides five colors for users to group in any way they see fit. The following steps describe how to add a green color to the Flowers image.

To Color-Code a Photo

1

• With the Flowers image still selected in the content area, click Label on the menu bar.

Bridge displays the Label menu (Figure C-17).

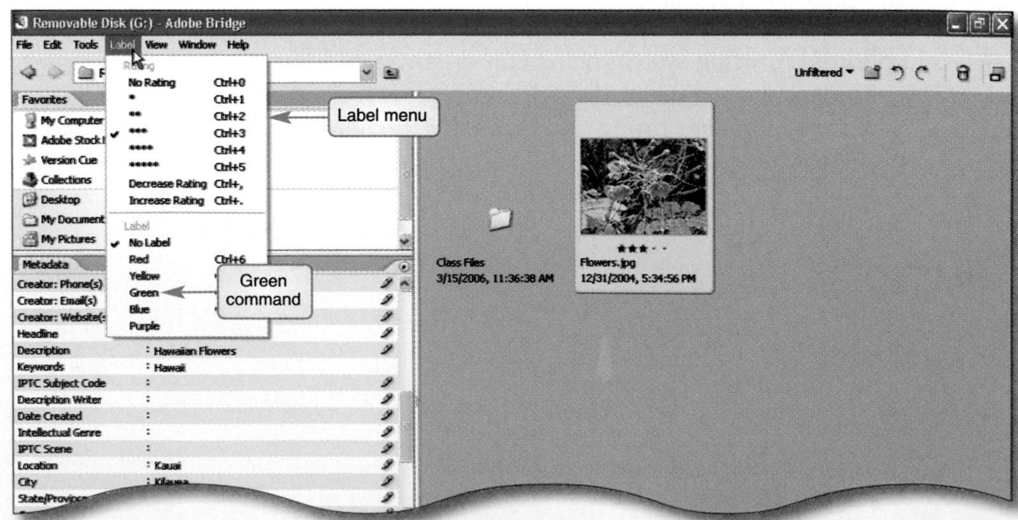

FIGURE C-17

2

- **Click Green.**
- **If Bridge displays a dialog box, click its OK button.**

The color green is applied around the star rating in the content area (Figure C-18).

FIGURE C-18

Other Ways

1. Press CTRL+8

Color coding and ratings are permanent only when photos have embedded extensible markup platform (XMP) storage space. Otherwise, the colors and ratings are stored in your system's cached memory.

Searching Bridge

Searching is a powerful tool in Adobe Bridge, especially as the number of stored image files increases on your computer system. It is a good idea to enter keywords, or metadata, for every image file you store, so searching is more efficient. Without Adobe Bridge and the search tool, you would have to view all files as filmstrips in Windows, and then look at them a screen at a time until you found what you wanted.

Using the Find Command

In Bridge, you can enter the kind of data or field that you want to search, parameters for that field, and the text you are looking for using the Find command. For example, you could search for all files with a rating of three stars or better, for files less than one megabyte in size, or files that begin with the letter m.

The Find dialog box displays many boxes and buttons to help you search effectively as shown in the steps on the next page. You will look for all files with metadata that includes the word, Hawaii.

To Use the Find Command

1

- **Click Edit on the menu bar, and then click Find.**

Bridge displays the Find dialog box (Figure C-19).

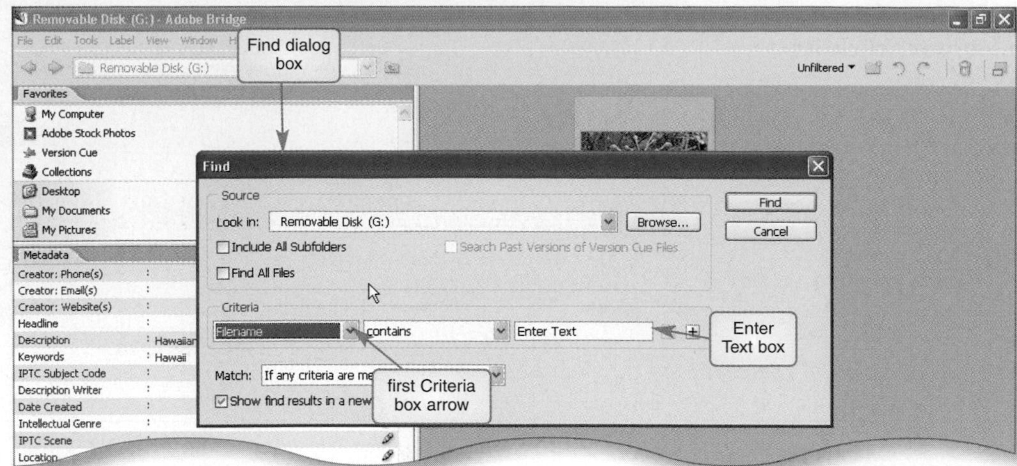

FIGURE C-19

2

- **Click the first Criteria box arrow, and then click All Metadata in the list.**
- **Press the TAB key twice, and then type** Hawaii **in the Enter Text box.**

The criteria are entered (Figure C-20).

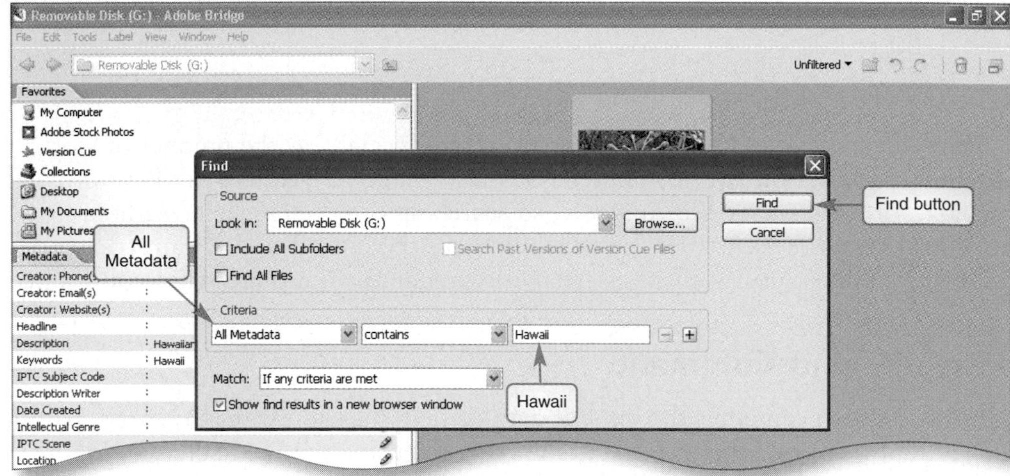

FIGURE C-20

3

- **Click the Find button.**

Bridge opens a second window displaying all files that have the word, Hawaii, in any part of the metadata (Figure C-21).

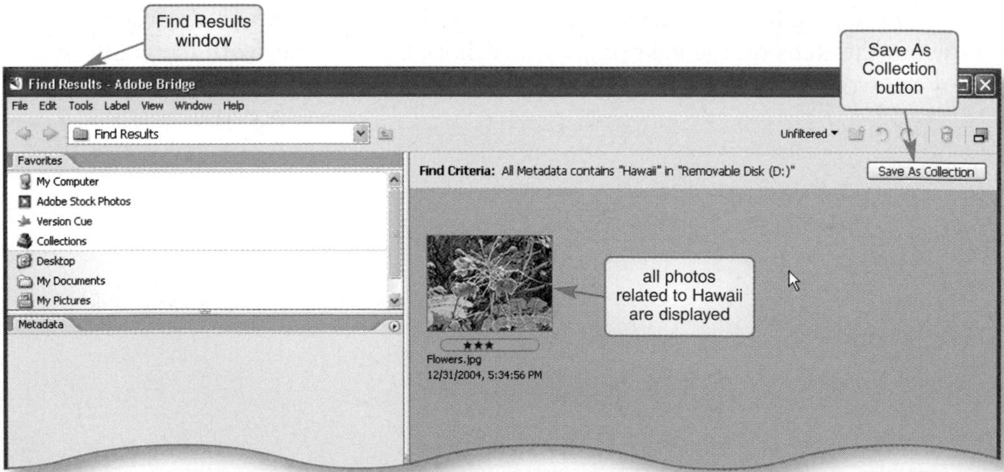

FIGURE C-21

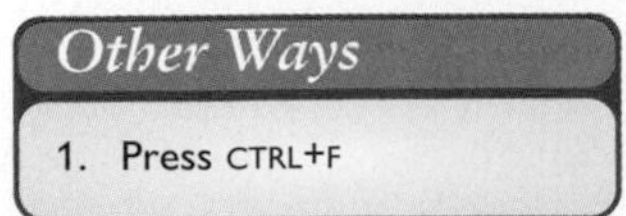

Other Ways

1. Press CTRL+F

The plus button to the right of the search boxes in the Find dialog box allows you to search multiple fields. When you click the button, a second line of search boxes is displayed. For example, if you needed to find photos that were created last winter from your vacation in the Rockies, you could search for the date in the first line of boxes, click the plus button, and then enter the keyword to narrow your search even further in the second line of boxes (Figure C-22). When clicked, the Match box arrow allows you to match any or all criteria.

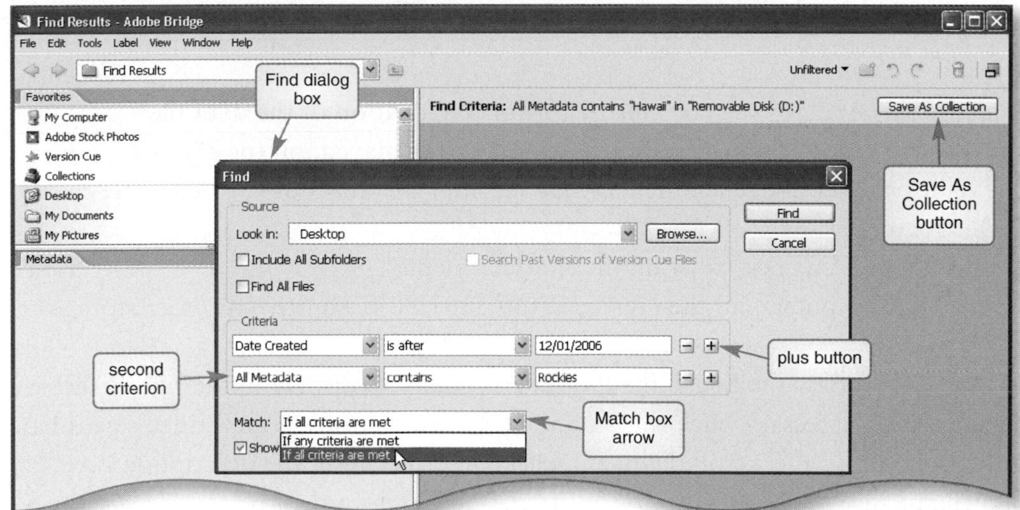

FIGURE C-22

Bridge offers you a way to save common searches as a **collection** for use later. For example, if you were working for a grocery wholesaler who stores many files for artwork in advertising, searching for pictures related to dairy products would be a common search. Looking through folders of images for pictures of milk or eggs or cheese would be very time consuming. Once you establish your search criteria, click the Save As Collection button (Figure C-22). Bridge then offers to name the search and store it. To display stored collections, click Collections in the Favorites panel. Then to perform the search again, double-click the collection. With metadata and collection searches, Bridge saves a lot of time.

The final steps show how to close the Find Results window and quit Adobe Bridge.

To Close the Find Results Window and Quit Bridge

1. **Click the Close button in the Find Results window.**
2. **Click the Close button in the Adobe Bridge window.**

1 Assigning Metadata

Instructions: You would like to assign metadata to some of the photos you worked on in previous projects in this book. The photos can be found on the CD that accompanies this book, or your instructor may direct to you to a different location. You will copy the photos from the CD to a local storage device and then assign metadata using Adobe Bridge.

1. Insert the CD that accompanies this book or see your instructor for the location of the data files.
2. Start Adobe Bridge on your system. When the Adobe Bridge window is displayed, on the Favorites tab, click My Computer. In the right pane, double-click the CD that accompanies this book, or navigate to the location specified by your instructor.
3. Right-click the Project01 folder, and then click Copy on the shortcut menu.
4. Using the Favorites tab, click My Computer, and then navigate to your USB flash drive or other storage location.
5. On the Edit menu, click Paste. After a few moments, the Project01 folder will display in the right pane. Double-click the folder to open it. If necessary, click the Thumbnails View button on the Bridge status bar.
7. Click the first photo. In the Metadata pane, scroll down and click Description. In the description box, enter a short description of the picture. Click Description Writer. Enter your name.
8. With the first photo still selected, click the Keywords tab. When the Adobe Bridge dialog box appears, click Apply to apply the changes you just made in the Metadata pane. On the Keywords tab, click to place a check mark next to any keywords that apply to the photo.
9. Scroll to the bottom of the keywords list. If there is not an Other Keywords category, create one by right-clicking on the empty space below the last keyword, clicking New Keyword Set on the shortcut menu, and typing in Other Keywords when the words Untitled Set are displayed. Right-click the Other Keywords category and then click New Keyword on the shortcut menu. When the words, Untitled Keyword are displayed, type a new keyword relating to the selected photo.
10. Repeat steps 7 through 9 for each photo in the right pane of the Adobe Bridge window.

2 Rating and Categorizing Photos

Instructions: You would like to rate and categorize some of the photos you worked on in previous projects in this book. The photos can be found on the CD that accompanies this book, or your instructor may direct to you to a different location.

1. If you did not perform exercise 1 Assigning Metadata, perform steps 1 through 6 from exercise 1 to copy images to your storage location.
2. With the photos from the Project01 folder displayed in the right pane of the Adobe Bridge window, click the first photo. Rate the photo on a scale from 1 to 5 with 1 being the worst photo in the group and 5 being the best photo in the group. Click the dot underneath the image, which corresponds to your rating. Repeat the process for each of the photos in the folder.
3. Click the first photo again to select it. Click Label on the menu bar. Choose a color that is present in the photo, or a color that has meaning for the photo – such as green for living plants, blue for photos with sky, etc. If a dialog box appears, click OK to apply the label color. Repeat the process for each of the photos in the folder.

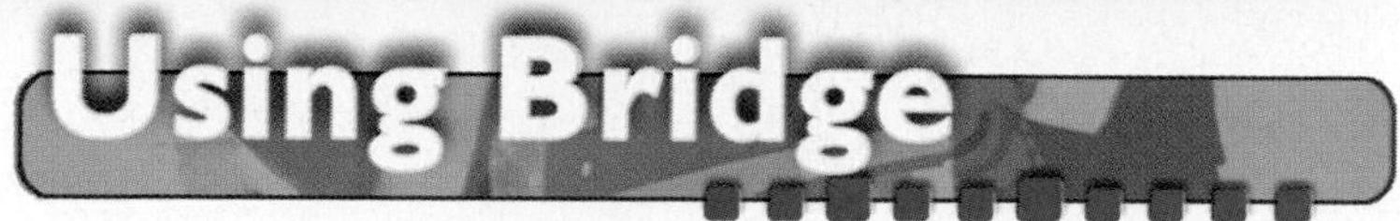

4. Choose your favorite photo in the folder and right-click the image. Click Add to Favorites on the shortcut menu.
5. Consult with at least three other members of your class to compare your ratings and color choices.

3 Copyrighting Photos

Instructions: You want to store title and copyright information about a photo you have created in preparation for using it on the Web. Title information appears in the web browser's title bar when the image is exported with an HTML file. Copyright information is not displayed in a browser; however, it is added to the HTML file as a comment and to the image file as metadata.

Using Adobe Bridge you decide to enter author and copyright information and save it in a metadata template that you can use with future image files that you create. The following steps show how to add the copyright.

1. Start Adobe Bridge on your system. When the Adobe Bridge window is displayed, navigate to a photo that you have created from one of the projects in this book, or a photo you took with a digital camera. Click the photo to select it.
2. On the File menu, click File Info. When Bridge opens the dialog box, enter a document title. Type your name in the Author box.
3. Click the Copyright Status box arrow and then click Copyright in the list.
4. In the Copyright Notice box, type `All rights reserved`. Type your name and then `Personal Copyright` and then type the year.
5. Click the Menu button in the upper right corner of the dialog box and then click Save Metadata Template in the list. When Bridge displays the Save Metadata Template dialog box, type Personal Copyright in the Template Name box. Click the Save button.
6. Click the OK button in the dialog box.
7. Navigate to a second photo that you have created or taken. Click the photo to select it.
8. On the Bridge menu bar, click Tools, point to Append Metadata, and then click Personal Copyright.
9. Close Adobe Bridge.

Index

Photo Credits

Project 1
Fig 1-1, Figure 1-75, Figure 1-77 Courtesy of Katie Starks; Fig 1-74 Courtesy of Kevin Marshall; Fig 1-76 U.S. Fish and Wildlife Service;

Project 2
Fig 2-1, Figure 2-66 Courtesy of Kevin Marshall; Fig 2-67 Courtesy of Katie Starks, Fig 2-68 Joy Starks

Project 3
Fig 3-1 Joy Starks and Jill Valle; Fig 3-72 Property of Morguefile.com; Fig 3-73 Used by permission of the State of Connecticut; Fig 3-75 Joy Starks

Special Feature
SF 1-4abc, SF 1-5acd, SF 1-9, SF 1-10, SF 1-11 Courtesy of Karla Whitney; SF 1-5b Courtesy of Michael Llanos

Project 4
Fig 4-1, Figure 4-71, Figure 4-72 Joy Starks

Project 5
Fig 5-1 Joy Starks and Mali Jones; Fig 5-2 Courtesy of Katie Starks; Fig 5-71 Julie Malone; Fig 5-72 Courtesy of Chip Emmons; Fig 5-73 Jill Valle; Fig 5-74 Courtesy of Katie Starks

Project 6
Fig 6-1, Fig 6-73, Fig 6-74 Jill Valle; Fig 6-75 Courtesy of Katie Starks

Special Feature 2
SF 2-1ab Courtesy of Gayle Hickok; SF 2-7 Courtesy of Susan Steele; SF 2-8, SF 2-10, SF 2-11, SF 2-19 Courtesy of Karla Whitney; SF 2-9ab, SF 2-15, SF 2-16 Courtesy of Stephanie M. Putland; SF 2-13abcd, SF 2-14 Courtesy of Jeremy Majewski; SF 2-18abc Courtesy of Heather Gendron

Project 7
Fig 7-1 Courtesy of Frederick Starks; Fig 7-57, Fig 7-59, Joy Starks; Fig 7-58, Fig 7-61 Jill Valle

Project 8
Fig 8-69 Joy Starks

Special Feature 3
SF 3-2 Courtesy of Stanley Bennett II; SF 3-2 Courtesy of Mike Toderico

Adobe Photoshop CS2 Quick Reference *(continued)*

TOOL OR TASK	PAGE #	MENU	MOUSE	KEYBOARD SHORTCUT
Export Transparent Image Wizard	PS 532	Help | Export Transparent Image		
Eyedropper Tool	PS 231		Eyedropper Tool button	I
Fade	PS 312		Fill Box slider	
Fill	PS 36	Edit | Fill		SHIFT+F5
Fill Path	PS 249		Fill path with foreground color button	
Fill Pixels	PS 425		Fill Pixels button	
Filter Gallery	PS 437	Filter | Filter Gallery		
Flatten Image	PS 177	Layer | Flatten Image		
Flip Horizontal	PS 76	Edit | Transform | Flip Horizontal		
Flip Vertical	PS 76	Edit | Transform | Flip Vertical		
Free Transform	PS 76	Edit | Free Transform		CTRL+T
Freeform Pen Tool	PS 512		Freeform Pen Tool button	P
Gradient	PS 212		Gradient Tool button	G
Group Layers	PS 582			CTRL+G
Guides	PS 95		Drag from ruler	
Healing Brush Tool	PS 288		Healing Brush Tool button	J
Hide Layer	PS 135	Layer | Hide Layer	Indicates layer visibility button	
Horizontal Type Tool	PS 319		Horizontal Type Tool button	T
Hyperlink	PS 566		slice badge	
Hyperlink (ImageReady)	PS 577		Slice palette	
ImageReady	PS 574	File| Edit in ImageReady	Edit in ImageReady button	SHIFT+CTRL+M
Insert Text	PS 374		Type tool button	T
Keyboard Shortcuts	PS 106	Edit | Keyboard Shortcuts		ALT+SHIFT+CTRL+K
Keystone Distortion	PS 301	Filter | Distort | Lens Correction	Drag perspective slider	
Lasso Tool	PS 83		Lasso Tool button	L
Layer Group	PS 489	Layer | New | Group	Layers Palette menu button | New Group or Create a new group button	
Layer Mask	PS 155		Add layer mask button	
Layer Mask Reveal All	PS 158	Layer | Layer Mask | Reveal All		
Layer Palette Options	PS 130	Layer palette menu button | Palette Options		
Layer Properties	PS 134	Layer | Layer Properties		
Layer Style	PS 168		Add layer style button	
Layer via Cut	PS 127	Layer | New | Layer via Cut		SHIFT+CTRL+J
Levels	PS 165	Image | Adjustments | Levels		CTRL+L
Line Tool	PS 4		Line Tool button	U
Load Actions	PS 364	On palette menu, Load Actions		
Lock Layers	PS 492		Lock All button	

Adobe Photoshop CS2 Quick Reference *(continued)*

TOOL OR TASK	PAGE #	MENU	MOUSE	KEYBOARD SHORTCUT
Lock Transparent Pixels	PS 492		Lock Transparent pixels button	/
Loop Animation	PS 588		Selects looping options button	
Magic Eraser Tool	PS 145		Magic Eraser Tool button	E
Magic Wand Tool	PS 101		Magic Wand Tool button	W
Magnetic Lasso Tool	PS 83		Magnetic Lasso Tool button	L
Magnetic Pen	PS 513		Magnetic Pen button	
Match (ImageReady)	PS 595	Layer | Match	Layers Palette menu button | Match	CTRL+M
Modal Control	PS 362		Modal Control box	
Modify Border	PS 33	Select | Modify | Border		
Modify Smooth	PS 35	Select | Modify | Smooth		
Move Tool	PS 74		Move Tool button	V
Name Layer	PS 133		Double-click layer name	
Navigator Palette Options	PS 26	Navigator palette menu button | Palette Options		
New Document from State	PS 352	On palette menu, New Document	Right-click snapshot, click New Document	
New File	PS 207	File | New		CTRL+N
New Frame	PS 588		Animation palette menu button | New Frame	ALT+SHIFT+CTRL+F
New Guide	PS 97	View | New Guide		
Notes Tool	PS 529		Notes Tool button	N
Open File	PS 11	File | Open	Right-click file, click Open With	CTRL+O
Open Recent	PS 313	File | Open Recent		
Optimize Animation	PS 593		Animation palette menu button | Optimize Animation	
Overlay	PS 464		Add a layer style button | Color Overlay	
Paint Bucket Tool	PS 4.43		Paint Bucket Tool button	G
Paste	PS 76	Edit | Paste		CTRL+V or F4
Paste Frames	PS 596		Animation palette menu button | Paste Frames	
Patch Tool	PS 290		Patch Tool button	J
Path Selection Tool	PS 505		Path Selection Tool button	A
Paths	PS 508		Paths button	
Pattern	PS 451	Edit | Define Pattern		
Pattern Stamp Tool	PS 179		Pattern Stamp Tool button	S
Pen Tool	PS 2		Pen Tool button	P
Perspective	PS 76	Edit | Transform | Perspective		
Photoshop Help	PS 53	Help | Photoshop Help		F1
Play Action	PS 364	On palette menu, Play	Play selection button	
Play Animation	PS 593		Plays animation button	
Polygonal Lasso Tool	PS 83		Polygonal Lasso Tool button	L

Adobe Photoshop CS2 Quick Reference (continued)

TOOL OR TASK	PAGE #	MENU	MOUSE	KEYBOARD SHORTCUT
Preview (ImageReady)	PS 593		Preview (in browser) button	CTRL+ALT+P
Print	PS 44	File | Print		CTRL+P
Print Color Separations	PS 390	File | Print with Preview		
Print One Copy	PS 44	File | Print One Copy		ALT+SHIFT+CTRL+P
Print with Preview	PS 469	File | Print with Preview		ALT+CTRL+P
Proof Setup	PS 469	View | Proof Setup		
Quit Photoshop	PS 55	File | Exit	Close button	CTRL+Q
Record Action	PS 356	On palette menu, Start Recording	Begin recording button	
Rectangular Marquee Tool	PS 71		Rectangular Marquee Tool button	M
Red Eye Tool	PS 294		Red Eye Tool button	J
Remove Border Displays	PS 521			SHIFT+CTRL+H
Render Effects	PS 456	Filter | Render		
Resample	PS 389	Image | Image Size		
Reselect	PS 447	Select | Reselect		SHIFT+CTRL+D
Reset All Tools	PS 10	Tool Presets palette menu button | Reset All Tools	Right-click tool button on options bar, click Reset All Tools	
Reset Colors	PS 278		Default Foreground and Background Colors button	D
Reset Layers Palette	PS 204	On palette menu, Palette Options		
Resize Document Window	PS 84		document window sizing handle	
Resize Image	PS 40	Help | Resize Image		
Rollover (ImageReady)	PS 575		Create Rollover State button	
Rotate	PS 76	Edit | Transform | Rotate		
Rotate 180°	PS 76	Edit | Transform | Rotate 180°		
Rotate 90° CCW	PS 76	Edit | Transform | Rotate 90° CCW		
Rotate 90° CW	PS 76	Edit | Transform | Rotate 90° CW		
Rulers	PS 28	View | Rulers		CTRL+R
Save a File	PS 39	File | Save		CTRL+S
Save a File with a New Name	PS 21	File | Save As		SHIFT+CTRL+S or ALT+CTRL+S
Save an Action Set	PS 363	On palette menu, Save Actions		
Save for Web	PS 46	File | Save for Web		ALT+SHIFT+CTRL+S
Scale	PS 76	Edit | Transform | Scale		
Scale Distortion	PS 303	Filter | Distort | Lens Correction	Scale slider	
Screen Mode	APP 14	View | Screen Mode	Screen Mode button	F
Select All	PS 32	Select | All		CTRL+A
Select All Frames	PS 596		Animation palette menu button | Select All Frames	

Adobe Photoshop CS2 Quick Reference (continued)

TOOL OR TASK	PAGE #	MENU	MOUSE	KEYBOARD SHORTCUT
Select Bottom Layer	PS 131			ALT+,
Select Color in Swatches Palette	PS 240		color squares in Swatches palette	
Select Layer	PS 131		layer in Layers palette	
Select Next Layer	PS 131			ALT+]
Select Previous Layer	PS 131			ALT+[
Select Top Layer	PS 131			ALT+.
Shape Layers	PS 497		Shape Layers button	
Shape Tool	PS 243		Shape Tool button	U
Show Guides	PS 97	View | Show | Guides		CTRL
Show Layers	PS 137	Layer | Show Layers		
Single Column Marquee Tool	PS 71		Single Column Marquee Tool button	
Single Row Marquee Tool	PS 71		Single Row Marquee Tool button	
Skew	PS 76	Edit | Transform | Skew	Enter width and height	Drag sizing handle
Slice	PS 572	Layer | New Layer Based Slice	Slice Tool button	K
Slice Select	PS 578		Slice Selection Tool button	K
Spot Healing Brush Tool	PS 286		Spot Healing Brush Tool button	J
Stop Recording Action	PS 361	On palette menu, Stop Recording	Stop playing/recording button	
Stroke	PS 449	Edit | Stroke	Add a layer style button | Stroke	
Subtract from Selection	PS 90		Subtract from selection button	ALT+drag
Thumbnail, change size	PS 131		Layers palette menu button | Palette Options or right-click thumbnail, select size	
Transform Again	PS 76	Edit | Transform | Again		SHIFT+CTRL+T
Tween	PS 589		Tweens animation frames button	
Undo/Redo	PS 31	Edit | Undo/Redo		CTRL+Z
Unsharp Mask	PS 281	Filter | Sharpen | Unsharp Mask		
View Channels	PS 341	Window | Channels	Indicates channel visibility button	
View Layer	PS 135		Indicates layer visibility button	
Warp	PS 76	Edit | Transform | Warp		
Warp Text	PS 377	Layer | Type | Warp Text		
Web Photo Gallery	PS 583	File | Automate | Web Photo Gallery		
Web-Safe Colors	PS 558		Swatches palette menu button | Web Safe Colors	
Zoom In	PS 24	View | Zoom In		CTRL++ CTRL+=
Zoom Tool	PS 24		Zoom Tool button	Z